PSYCHOLOGICAL TESTING: AN INTRODUCTION
Second Edition

This book is an introductory text to the field of psychological testing primarily suitable for undergraduate students in psychology, education, business, and related fields. This book will also be of interest to graduate students who have not had prior exposure to psychological testing and to professionals such as lawyers who need to consult a useful source. *Psychological Testing* is clearly written, well organized, comprehensive, and replete with illustrative materials. In addition to the basic topics, the text covers in detail topics that are often neglected by other texts such as cross-cultural testing, the issue of faking tests, the impact of computers, and the use of tests to assess positive behaviors such as creativity.

George Domino is the former Director of Clinical Psychology and Professor of Psychology at the University of Arizona. He was also the former director of the Counseling Center and Professor of Psychology at Fordham University.

Marla L. Domino has a BA in Psychology, an MA in Criminal Law, and a PhD in Clinical Psychology specializing in Psychology and Law. She also completed a postdoctoral fellowship in Clinical-Forensic Psychology at the University of Massachusetts Medical School, Law and Psychiatry Program. She is currently the Chief Psychologist in the South Carolina Department of Mental Health's Forensic Evaluation Service and an assistant professor in the Department of Neuropsychiatry and Behavioral Sciences at the University of South Carolina. She was recently awarded by the South Carolina Department of Mental Health as Outstanding Employee of the Year in Forensics (2004).

SECOND EDITION

Psychological Testing

An Introduction

George Domino

University of Arizona

Marla L. Domino

Department of Mental Health, State of South Carolina

CAMBRIDGE
UNIVERSITY PRESS

CAMBRIDGE UNIVERSITY PRESS
Cambridge, New York, Melbourne, Madrid, Cape Town, Singapore, São Paulo

Cambridge University Press
40 West 20th Street, New York, NY 10011-4211, USA

www.cambridge.org
Information on this title: www.cambridge.org/9780521861816

First published 2006

Printed in the United States of America

A catalog record for this publication is available from the British Library.

Library of Congress Cataloging in Publication Data

Domino, George, 1938–
Psychological testing : an introduction/George Domino, Marla L. Domino. – 2nd ed.
    p. cm.
Includes bibliographical references and index.
ISBN-13: 978-0-521-86181-6 (hardback)
ISBN-10: 0-521-86181-0 (hardback)
1. Psychological tests – Textbooks   I. Domino, Marla L., 1970–   II. Title.
BF176.D65   2006
150.28′.7 – dc22   2006001006

ISBN-13   978-0-521-86181-6 hardback
ISBN-10   0-521-86181-0 hardback

Contents

Preface

My first professional publication in 1963 was as a graduate student (with Harrison Gough) on a validational study of a culture-fair test. Since then, I have taught a course on psychological testing with fair regularity. At the same time, I have steadfastly refused to specialize and have had the opportunity to publish in several different areas, to work in management consulting, to be director of a counseling center and of a clinical psychology program, to establish an undergraduate honors program, and to be involved in a wide variety of projects with students in nursing, rehabilitation, education, social work, and other fields. In all of these activities, I have found psychological testing to be central and to be very challenging and exciting.

In this book, we have tried to convey the excitement associated with psychological testing and to teach basic principles through the use of concrete examples. When specific tests are mentioned, they are mentioned because they are used as an example to teach important basic principles, or in some instances, because they occupy a central/historical position. No attempt has been made to be exhaustive.

Much of what is contained in many testing textbooks is rather esoteric information, of use only to very few readers. For example, most textbooks include several formulas to compute interitem consistency. It has been our experience, however, that 99% of the students who take a course on testing will never have occasion to use such formulas, even if they enter a career in psychology or allied fields. The very few who might need to do such calculations will do them by computer or will know where to find the relevant formulas. It is the principle that is important, and that is what we have tried to emphasize.

Because of my varied experience in industry, in a counseling center, and other service-oriented settings, and also because as a clinically trained academic psychologist I have done a considerable amount of research, I have tried to cover both sides of the coin – the basic research-oriented issues and the application of tests in service-oriented settings. Thus Parts One and Two, the first eight chapters, serve as an introduction to basic concepts, issues, and approaches. Parts Three and Four, Chapters 9 through 15, have a much more applied focus. Finally, we have attempted to integrate both classical approaches and newer thinking about psychological testing.

The area of psychological testing is fairly well defined. I cannot imagine a textbook that does not discuss such topics as reliability, validity, and norms. Thus, what distinguishes one textbook from another is not so much its content but more a question of balance. For example, most textbooks continue to devote one or more chapters to projective techniques, even though their use and importance has decreased substantially. Projective techniques are important, not only from a historical perspective, but also for what they can teach us about basic issues in testing. In this text, they are discussed and illustrated, but as part of a chapter (see Chapter 15) within the broader context of testing in clinical settings. Most textbooks also have several chapters on intelligence testing, often devoting considerable space to such topics as the heritability of intelligence, theories of trait organization, longitudinal studies of intelligence, and similar topics. Such topics are of course important and fascinating, but do they really belong in a textbook on psychological testing? If they do, then that means that some other topics more directly relevant to testing are omitted or given short shrift. In this textbook, we have chosen to focus on testing and to minimize the theoretical issues associated with intelligence, personality, etc., except where they may be needed to have a better understanding of testing approaches.

It is no surprise that computers have had (and continue to have) a major impact on psychological testing, and so an entire chapter of this book (Chapter 17) is devoted to this topic. There is also a vast body of literature and great student interest on the topic of faking, and here too an entire chapter (Chapter 16) has been devoted to

this topic. Most textbooks begin with a historical chapter. We have chosen to place this chapter last, so the reader can better appreciate the historical background from a more knowledgeable point of view.

Finally, rather than writing a textbook about testing, we have attempted to write a textbook about testing the individual. We believe that most testing applications involve an attempt to use tests as a tool to better understand an individual, whether that person is a client in therapy, a college student seeking career or academic guidance, a business executive wishing to capitalize on strengths and improve on weaknesses, or a volunteer in a scientific experiment.

Acknowledgments

In my career as a psychologist, I have had the excellent fortune to be mentored, directly and indirectly, by three giants in the psychological testing field. The first is Harrison Gough, my mentor in graduate school at Berkeley, who showed me how useful and exciting psychological tests can be when applied to real-life problems. More importantly, Gough has continued to be not only a mentor but also a genuine model to be emulated both as a psychologist and as a human being. Much of my thinking and approach to testing, as well as my major interest in students at all levels, is a direct reflection of Gough's influence.

The second was Anne Anastasi, a treasured colleague at Fordham University, a generous friend, and the best chairperson I have ever worked with. Her textbook has been truly a model of scholarship and concise writing, the product of an extremely keen mind who advanced the field of psychological testing in many ways.

The third person was Lee J. Cronbach of Stanford University. My first undergraduate exposure to testing was through his textbook. In 1975, Cronbach wrote what is now a classic paper titled, "Beyond the two disciplines of scientific psychology" (*American Psychologist*, 1975, vol. 30, pp. 116–127), in which he argued that experimental psychology and the study of individual differences should be integrated. In that paper, Cronbach was kind enough to cite at some length two of my studies on college success as examples of this integration. Subsequently I was able to invite him to give a colloquium at the University of Arizona. My contacts with him were regrettably brief, but his writings greatly influenced my own thinking.

On a personal note, I thank Valerie, my wife of 40 years, for her love and support, and for being the best companion one could hope for in this voyage we call life. Our three children have been an enormous source of love and pride: Brian, currently a professor of philosophy at Miami University of Ohio; Marisa, a professor of health economics at the University of North Carolina, Chapel Hill; and Marla, chief forensic psychologist in the Department of Mental Health of South Carolina, and co-author of this edition. Zeno and Paolo, our two grandchildren, are unbelievably smart, handsome, and adorable and make grandparenting a joy. I have also been truly blessed with exceptional friends whose love and caring have enriched my life enormously.

George Domino
Tucson, AZ

An abundance of gratitude to my father for giving me the opportunity to collaborate with one of the greatest psychologists ever known. And an immeasurable amount of love and respect to my heroes – my Dad and Mom. I would also like to thank my mentor and friend, Stan Brodsky, whose professional accomplishments are only surpassed by his warmth, kindness, and generous soul.

Marla Domino
Columbia, SC

1 The Nature of Tests

AIM In this chapter we cover four basic issues. First, we focus on what is a test, not just a formal definition, but on ways of thinking about tests. Second, we try to develop a "taxonomy" of tests, that is we look at various ways in which tests can be categorized. Third, we look at the ethical aspects of psychological testing. Finally, we explore how we can obtain information about a specific test.

INTRODUCTION

Most likely you would have no difficulty identifying a psychological test, even if you met one in a dark alley. So the intent here is not to give you one more definition to memorize and repeat but rather to spark your thinking.

What is a test? Anastasi (1988), one of the best known psychologists in the field of testing, defined a test as an "objective" and "standardized" measure of a sample of behavior. This is an excellent definition that focuses our attention on three elements: (1) *objectivity*: that is, at least theoretically, most aspects of a test, such as how the test is scored and how the score is interpreted, are not a function of the subjective decision of a particular examiner but are based on objective criteria; (2) *standardization*: that is, no matter who administers, scores, and interprets the test, there is uniformity of procedure; and (3) *a sample of behavior*: a test is not a psychological X-ray, nor does it necessarily reveal hidden conflicts and forbidden wishes; it is a sample of a person's behavior, hopefully a representative sample from which we can draw some inferences and hypotheses.

There are three other ways to consider psychological tests that we find useful and we hope you will also. One way is to consider the administration of a test as an experiment. In the classical type of experiment, the experimenter studies a phenomenon and observes the results, while at the same time keeping in check all extraneous variables so that the results can be ascribed to a particular antecedent cause. In psychological testing, however, it is usually not possible to control all the extraneous variables, but the metaphor here is a useful one that forces us to focus on the standardized procedures, on the elimination of conflicting causes, on experimental control, and on the generation of hypotheses that can be further investigated. So if I administer a test of achievement to little Sandra, I want to make sure that her score reflects what she has achieved, rather than her ability to follow instructions, her degree of hunger before lunch, her uneasiness at being tested, or some other influence.

A second way to consider a test is to think of a test as an interview. When you are administered an examination in your class, you are essentially being interviewed by the instructor to determine how well you know the material. We discuss interviews in Chapter 18, but for now consider the following: in most situations we need to "talk" to each other. If I am the instructor, I need to know how much you have learned. If I am hiring an architect to design a house or a contractor to build one, I need to evaluate their competency, and so on. Thus "interviews" are necessary, but a test offers many advantages over the standard interview. With a test I can "interview" 50 or 5,000 persons at one sitting. With a test I can be much more objective in my evaluation because for example, multiple-choice answer sheets do not discriminate on the basis of gender, ethnicity, or religion.

A third way to consider tests is as tools. Many fields of endeavor have specific tools – for example, physicians have scalpels and X-rays, chemists have Bunsen burners and retorts. Just because someone can wield a scalpel or light up a Bunsen burner does not make him or her an "expert" in that field. The best use of a tool is in the hands of a trained professional when it is simply an aid to achieve a particular goal. Tests, however, are not just psychological tools; they also have political and social repercussions. For example, the well-publicized decline in SAT scores (Wirtz & Howe, 1977) has been used as an indicator of the terrible shape our educational system is in (National Commission, 1983).

A test by any other name. . . . In this book, we use the term *psychological test* (or more briefly *test*) to cover those measuring devices, techniques, procedures, examinations, etc., that in some way assess variables relevant to psychological functioning. Some of these variables, such as intelligence, introversion-extraversion, and self-esteem are clearly "psychological" in nature. Others, such as heart rate or the amount of palmar perspiration (the galvanic skin response), are more physiological but are related to psychological functioning. Still other variables, such as socialization, delinquency, or leadership, may be somewhat more "sociological" in nature, but are of substantial interest to most social and behavioral scientists. Other variables, such as academic achievement, might be more relevant to educators or professionals working in educational settings. The point here is that we use the term *psychological* in a rather broad sense.

Psychological tests can take a variety of forms. Some are true-false *inventories*, others are *rating scales*, some are actual *tests*, whereas others are *questionnaires*. Some tests consist of materials such as inkblots or pictures to which the subject responds verbally; still others consist of items such as blocks or pieces of a puzzle that the subject manipulates. A large number of tests are simply a set of printed items requiring some type of written response.

Testing vs. assessment. *Psychological assessment* is basically a judgmental process whereby a broad range of information, often including the results of psychological tests, is integrated into a meaningful understanding of a particular person. If that person is a client or patient in a psychotherapeutic setting, we call the process *clinical assessment*. Psychological testing is thus a narrower concept referring to the psychometric aspects of a test (the technical information about the test), the actual administration and scoring of the test, and the interpretation made of the scores. We could of course assess a client simply by administering a test or *battery* (group) of tests. Usually the assessing psychologist also interviews the client, obtains background information, and where appropriate and feasible, information from others about the client [see Korchin, 1976, for an excellent discussion of clinical assessment, and G. J. Meyer, Finn, Eyde, et al. (2001) for a brief overview of assessment].

Purposes of tests. Tests are used for a wide variety of purposes that can be subsumed under more general categories. Many authors identify four categories typically labeled as: *classification, self-understanding, program evaluation*, and *scientific inquiry*.

Classification involves a decision that a particular person belongs in a certain category. For example, based on test results we may assign a diagnosis to a patient, place a student in the introductory Spanish course rather than the intermediate or advanced course, or certify that a person has met the minimal qualifications to practice medicine.

Self-understanding involves using test information as a source of information about oneself. Such information may already be available to the individual, but not in a formal way. Marlene, for example, is applying to graduate studies in electrical engineering; her high GRE scores confirm what she already knows, that she has the potential abilities required for graduate work.

Program evaluation involves the use of tests to assess the effectiveness of a particular program or course of action. You have probably seen in the newspaper, tables indicating the average achievement test scores for various schools in your geographical area, with the scores often taken, perhaps incorrectly, as evidence of the competency level of a particular school. Program evaluation may involve the assessment of the campus climate at a particular college, or the value of a drug abuse program offered by a mental health clinic, or the effectiveness of a new medication.

Tests are also used in scientific inquiry. If you glance through most professional journals in the social and behavioral sciences, you will find that a large majority of studies use psychological tests to operationally define relevant variables and to translate hypotheses into numerical statements that can be assessed statistically. Some argue that development of a field of science is, in large part, a function of the available measurement techniques (Cone & Foster, 1991; Meehl, 1978).

Tests as experimental procedure. If we accept the analogy that administering a test is very much like an experiment, then we need to make sure that the experimental procedure is followed carefully and that extraneous variables are not allowed to influence the results. This means, for example, that instructions and time limits need to be adhered to strictly. The greater the control that can be exercised on all aspects of a test situation, the lesser the influence of extraneous variables. Thus the scoring of a multiple-choice exam is less influenced by such variables as clarity of handwriting than the scoring of an essay exam; a true-false personality inventory with simple instructions is probably less influenced than an intelligence test with detailed instructions.

Masling (1960) reviewed a variety of studies of variables that can influence a testing situation, in this case "projective" testing (see Chapter 15); Sattler and Theye (1967) did the same for intelligence tests. We can identify, as Masling (1960) did, four categories of such variables:

1. *The method of administration.* Standard administration can be altered by disregarding or changing instructions, by explicitly or implicitly giving the subject a set to answer in a certain way, or by not following standard procedures. For example, Coffin (1941) had subjects read fictitious magazine articles indicating what were more socially acceptable responses to the Rorschach Inkblot test. Subsequently they were tested with the Rorschach and the responses clearly showed a suggestive influence because of the prior readings. Ironson and Davis (1979) administered a test of creativity three times, with instructions to "fake creative," "fake uncreative," or "be honest"; the obtained scores reflected the influence of the instructions. On the other hand, Sattler and Theye (1967) indicated that of twelve studies reviewed, which departed from standard administrative procedures, only five reported significant differences between standard and nonstandard administration.

2. *Situational variables.* These include a variety of aspects that presumably can alter the test situation significantly, such as a subject feeling frustrated, discouraged, hungry, being under the influence of drugs, and so on. Some of these variables can have significant effects on test scores, but the effects are not necessarily the same for all subjects. For example, Sattler and Theye (1967) report that discouragement affects the performance of children but not of college students on some intelligence tests.

3. *Experimenter variables.* The testing situation is a social situation, and even when the test is administered by computer, there is clearly an experimenter, a person in charge. That person may exhibit characteristics (such as age, gender, and skin color) that differ from those of the subject. The person may appear more or less sympathetic, warm or cold, more or less authoritarian, aloof, more adept at establishing rapport, etc. These aspects may or may not affect the subject's test performance; the results of the available experimental evidence are quite complex and not easily summarized. We can agree with Sattler and Theye (1967), who concluded that the experimenter-subject relationship is important and that (perhaps) less qualified experimenters do not obtain appreciably different results than more qualified experimenters. Whether the race, ethnicity, physical characteristics, etc., of the experimenter significantly affect the testing situation seems to depend on a lot of other variables and, in general, do not seem to be as powerful an influence as many might think.

4. *Subject variables.* Do aspects of the subject, such as level of anxiety, physical attractiveness, etc., affect the testing situation? Masling (1960)

used attractive female accomplices who, as test subjects, acted "warm" or "cold" toward the examiners (graduate students). The test results were interpreted by the graduate students more favorably when the subject acted warm than when she acted cold.

In general what can we conclude? Aside from the fact that most studies in this area seem to have major design flaws and that many specific variables have not been explored consistently, Masling (1960) concluded that there is strong evidence of situational and interpersonal influences in projective testing, while Sattler and Theye (1967) concluded that:

1. Departures from standard procedures are more likely to affect "specialized" groups, such as children, schizophrenics, and juvenile delinquents than "normal" groups such as college students;

2. Children seem to be more susceptible to situational factors, especially discouragement, than are college-aged adults;

3. Rapport seems to be a crucial variable, while degree of experience of the examiner is not;

4. Racial differences, specifically a white examiner and a black subject, may be important, but the evidence is not definitive.

Tests in decision making. In the real world, decisions need to be made. To allow every person who applies to medical school to be admitted would not only create huge logistical problems, but would result in chaos and in a situation that would be unfair to the candidates themselves, some of whom would not have the intellectual and other competencies required to be physicians, to the medical school faculty whose teaching efforts would be diluted by the presence of unqualified candidates, and eventually to the public who might be faced with incompetent physicians.

Given that decisions need to be made, we must ask what role psychological tests can play in such decision making. Most psychologists agree that major decisions should not be based on the results of a single test administration, that whether or not state university admits Sandra should not be based solely on her SAT scores. In fact, despite a stereotype to the contrary, it is rare for such decisions to be based solely on test data. Yet in many situations, test data represent the only source of objective data standard for all candidates; other sources of data such as interviews, grades, and letters of recommendation are all "variable" – grades from different schools or different instructors are not comparable, nor are letters written by different evaluators. Finally, as scientists, we should ask what is the empirical evidence for the accuracy of predicting future behavior. That is, if we are admitting college students to a particular institution, which sources of data, singly or in combination, such as interviewers' opinions, test scores, high school GPA, etc., would be most accurate in making relevant predictions, such as, "Let's admit Marlene because she will do quite well academically." We will return to this issue, but for now let me indicate a general psychological principle that past behavior is the best predictor of future behavior, and a corollary that the results of psychological tests can provide very useful information on which to make more accurate future predictions.

Relation of test content to predicted behavior. Rebecca is enrolled in an introductory Spanish course and is given a Spanish vocabulary test by the instructor. Is the instructor interested in whether Rebecca knows the meaning of the specific words on the test? Yes indeed, because the test is designed to assess Rebecca's mastery of the vocabulary covered in class and in homework assignments. Consider now a test such as the SAT, given for college admission purposes. The test may contain a vocabulary section, but the concern is not whether an individual knows the particular words; knowledge of this sample of words is related to something else, namely doing well academically in college. Finally, consider a third test, the XYZ scale of depression. Although the scale contains no items about suicide ideation, it has been discovered empirically that high scorers on this scale are likely to attempt suicide. These three examples illustrate an important point: In psychological tests, the content of the test items may or may not cover the behavior that is of interest – there may be a lack of correspondence between test items and the predicted behavior. But a test can be quite useful if an empirical correspondence between test scores and real-life behavior can be shown.

CATEGORIES OF TESTS

Because there are thousands of tests, it would be helpful to be able to classify tests into categories, just as a bookstore might list its books under different headings. Because tests differ from each other in a variety of ways, there is no uniformly accepted system of classification. Therefore, we will invent our own based on a series of questions that can be asked of any test. I should point out that despite a variety of advances in both theory and technique, standardized tests have changed relatively little over the years (Linn, 1986), so while new tests are continually published, a classificatory system should be fairly stable, i.e., applicable today as well as 20 years from now.

Commercially published? The first question is whether a test is commercially published (sometimes called a proprietary test) or not. Major tests like the Stanford-Binet and the Minnesota Multiphasic Personality Inventory are available for purchase by qualified users through commercial companies. The commercial publisher advertises primarily through its catalog, and for many tests makes available, for a fee, a *specimen set*, usually the test booklet and answer sheet, a scoring key to score the test, and a test manual that contains information about the test. If a test is not commercially published, then a copy is ordinarily available from the test author, and there may be some accompanying information, or perhaps just the journal article where the test was first introduced. Sometimes journal articles include the original test, particularly if it is quite short, but often they will not. (Examples of articles that contain test items are R. L. Baker, Mednick & Hocevar, 1991; L. R. Good & K. C. Good, 1974; McLain, 1993; Rehfisch, 1958a; Snell, 1989; Vodanovich & Kass, 1990). Keep in mind that the contents of journal articles are copyright and permission to use a test must be obtained from both the author and the publisher.

If you are interested in learning more about a specific test, first you must determine if the test is commercially published. If it is, then you will want to consult the *Mental Measurements Yearbook* (MMY), available in most university libraries. Despite its name, the MMY is published at irregular intervals rather than yearly. However, it is an invaluable guide. For many commercially

published tests, the MMY will provide a brief description of the test (its purpose, applicable age range, type of score generated, price, administration time, and name and address of publisher), a bibliography of citations relevant to the test, and one or more reviews of the test by test experts. Tests that are reviewed in one edition of the MMY may or may not be reviewed in subsequent editions, so locating information about a specific test may involve browsing through a number of editions. MMY reviews of specific tests are also available through a computer service called the Bibliographic Retrieval Services.

If the test you are interested in learning about is not commercially published, it will probably have an author(s) who published an article about the test in a professional journal. The journal article will most likely give the author's address at the time of publication. If you are a "legitimate" test user, for example a graduate student doing a doctoral dissertation or a psychologist engaged in research work, a letter to the author will usually result in a reply with a copy of the test and permission to use it. If the author has moved from the original address, you may locate the current address through various directories and "Who's Who" type of books, or through computer generated literature searches.

Administrative aspects. Tests can also be distinguished by various aspects of their administration. For example, there are *group* vs. *individual* tests; group tests can be administered to a group of subjects at the same time and individual tests to one person only at one time. The Stanford-Binet test of intelligence is an individual test, whereas the SAT is a group test. Clinicians who deal with one client at a time generally prefer individual tests because these often yield observational data in addition to a test score; researchers often need to test large groups of subjects in minimum time and may prefer group tests (there are of course, many exceptions to this statement). A group test can be administered to one individual; sometimes, an individual test can be modified so it can be administered to a group.

Tests can also be classified as *speed* vs. *power* tests. Speed tests have a time limit that affects performance; for example, you might be given a page of printed text and asked to cross out all the "e's" in 25 seconds. How many you cross out will be a function of how fast you respond. A power test, on the other hand, is designed to measure how well you can do and so either may have no time limit or a time limit of convenience (a 50-minute hour) that ordinarily does not affect performance. The time limits on speed tests are usually set so that only 50% of the applicants are able to attempt every item. Time limits on power tests are set so that about 90% of the applicants can attempt all items.

Another administrative distinction is whether a test is a *secure* test or not. For example, the SAT is commercially published but is ordinarily not made available even to researchers. Many tests that are used in industry for personnel selection are secure tests whose utility could be compromised if they were made public. Sometimes only the scoring key is confidential, rather than the items themselves.

A final distinction from an administrative point of view is how *invasive* a test is. A questionnaire that asks about one's sexual behaviors is ordinarily more invasive than a test of arithmetic; a test completed by the subject is usually more invasive than a report of an observer, who may report the observations without even the subject's awareness.

The medium. Tests differ widely in the materials used, and so we can distinguish tests on this basis. Probably, the majority of tests are *paper-and-pencil* tests that involve some set of printed questions and require a written response, such as marking a multiple answer sheet. Other tests are *performance* tests that perhaps require the manipulation of wooden blocks or the placement of puzzle pieces in correct juxtaposition. Still other tests involve *physiological* measures such as the galvanic skin response, the basis of the polygraph (lie detector) machine. Increasing numbers of tests are now available for computer administration and this may become a popular category.

Item structure. Another way to classify tests, which overlaps with the approaches already mentioned, is through their item structure. Test items can be placed on a continuum from objective to subjective. At the objective end, we have multiple-choice items; at the subjective end, we have the type of open-ended questions that clinical psychologists and psychiatrists ask, such as "tell me

more," "how do you feel about that?" and "tell me about yourself." In between, we have countless variations such as matching items (closer to the objective pole) and essay questions (closer to the subjective pole). Objective items are easy to score and to manipulate statistically, but individually reveal little other than that the person answered correctly or incorrectly. Subjective items are difficult and sometimes impossible to quantify, but can be quite a revealing and rich source of information.

Another possible distinction in item structure is whether the items are *verbal* in nature or require *performance*. Vocabulary and math items are labeled verbal because they are composed of verbal elements; building a block tower is a performance item.

Area of assessment. Tests can also be classified according to the area of assessment. For example, there are intelligence tests, personality questionnaires, tests of achievement, career-interest tests, tests of reading, tests of neuropsychological functioning, and so on. The MMY uses 16 such categories. These are not necessarily mutually exclusive categories, and many of them can be further subdivided. For example, tests of personality could be further categorized into introversion-extraversion, leadership, masculinity-femininity, and so on.

In this textbook, we look at five major categories of tests:

1. Personality tests, which have played a major role in the development of psychological testing, both in its acceptance and criticism. Personality represents a major area of human functioning for social-behavioral scientists and lay persons alike;

2. Tests of cognitive abilities, not only traditional intelligence tests, but other dimensions of cognitive or intellectual functioning. In some ways, cognitive psychology represents a major new emphasis in psychology which has had a significant impact on all aspects of psychology both as a science and as an applied field;

3. Tests of attitudes, values, and interests, three areas that psychometrically overlap, and also offer lots of basic testing lessons;

4. Tests of psychopathology, primarily those used by clinicians and researchers to study the field of mental illness; and

5. Tests that assess normal and positive functioning, such as creativity, competence, and self-esteem.

Test function. Tests can also be categorized depending upon their function. Some tests are used to *diagnose* present conditions. (Does the client have a character disorder? Is the client depressed?) Other tests are used to make *predictions.* (Will this person do well in college? Is this client likely to attempt suicide?) Other tests are used in *selection* procedures, which basically involve accepting or not accepting a candidate, as in admission to graduate school. Some tests are used for *placement* purposes – candidates who have been accepted are placed in a particular "treatment." For example, entering students at a university may be placed in different level writing courses depending upon their performance in a writing exam. A battery of tests may be used to make such a placement decision or to assess which of several alternatives is most appropriate for the particular client – here the term typically used is *classification* (note that this term has both a broader meaning and a narrower meaning). Some tests are used for *screening* purposes; the term screening implies a rapid and rough procedure. Some tests are used for *certification,* usually related to some legal standard; thus passing a driving test certifies that the person has, at the very least, a minimum proficiency and is allowed to drive an automobile.

Score interpretation. Yet another classification can be developed on the basis of how scores on a test are interpreted. We can compare the score that an individual obtains with the scores of a group of individuals who also took the same test. This is called a *norm-reference* because we refer to norms to give a particular score meaning; for most tests, scores are interpreted in this manner. We can also give meaning to a score by comparing that score to a decision rule called a *criterion,* so this would be a *criterion-reference.* For example, when you took a driving test (either written and/or road), the examiner did not say, "Congratulations your score is two standard deviations above the mean." You either passed or failed based upon some predetermined criterion that may or may not have been explicitly stated. Note that norm-reference and criterion-reference refer

not to the test but to how the score or performance is interpreted. The same test could yield either or both score interpretations.

Another distinction that can be made is whether the measurement provided by the test is *normative* or *ipsative,* that is, whether the standard of comparison reflects the behavior of others or of the client. Consider a 100-item vocabulary test that we administer to Marisa, and she obtains a score of 82. To make sense of that score, we compare her score with some normative data – for example, the average score of similar-aged college students. Now consider a questionnaire that asks Marisa to decide which of two values is more important to her: "Is it more important for you to have (1) a good paying job, or (2) freedom to do what you wish." We could compare her choice with that of others, but in effect we have simply asked her to rank two items in terms of her own preferences or her own behavior; in most cases it would not be legitimate to compare her ranking with those of others. She may prefer choice number 2, but not by much, whereas for me choice number 2 is a very strong preference.

One way of defining ipsative is that the scores on the scale must sum to a constant. For example, if you are presented with a set of six ice cream flavors to rank order as to preference, no matter whether your first preference is "crunchy caramel" or "Bohemian tutti-frutti," the sum of your six preferences will be 21 $(1+2+3+4+5+6)$. On the other hand, if you were asked to rate each flavor independently on a 6-point scale, you could rate all of them high or all of them low; this would be a normative scale. Another way to define ipsative is to focus on the idea that in ipsative measurement, the mean is that of the individual, whereas in normative measurement the mean is that of the group. Ipsative measurement is found in personality assessment; we look at a technique called Q sort in Chapter 18. Block (1957) found that ipsative and normative ratings of personality were quite equivalent.

Another classificatory approach involves whether the responses made to the test are interpreted *psychometrically* or *impressionistically.* If the responses are scored and the scores interpreted on the basis of available norms and/or research data, then the process is a psychometric one. If instead the tester looks at the responses carefully on the basis of his/her expertise and creates a psychological portrait of the client, that process is called impressionistic. Sometimes the two are combined; for example, clinicians who use the Minnesota Multiphasic Personality Inventory (MMPI), score the test and plot the scores on a profile, and then use the profile to translate their impressions into diagnostic and characterological statements. Impressionistic testing is more prevalent in clinical diagnosis and the assessment of psychodynamic functioning than, say, in assessing academic achievement or mechanical aptitude.

Self-report versus observer. Many tests are *self-report* tests where the client answers questions about his/her own behavior, preferences, values, etc. However, some tests require judging someone else; for example, a manager might rate each of several subordinates on promptness, independence, good working habits, and so on.

Maximal vs. typical performance. Yet another distinction is whether a test assesses *maximal performance* (how well a person can do) or *typical performance* (how well the person typically does) (Cronbach, 1970). Tests of maximal performance usually include achievement and aptitude tests and typically based on items that have a correct answer. Typical performance tests include personality inventories, attitude scales, and opinion questionnaires, for which there are no correct answers.

Age range. We can classify tests according to the age range for which they are most appropriate. The Stanford-Binet, for example, is appropriate for children but less so for adults; the SAT is appropriate for adolescents and young adults but not for children. Tests are used with a wide variety of clients and we focus particularly on children (Chapter 9), the elderly (Chapter 10), minorities and individuals in different cultures (Chapter 11), and the handicapped (Chapter 12).

Type of setting. Finally, we can classify tests according to the setting in which they are primarily used. Tests are used in a wide variety of settings, but the most prevalent are school settings (Chapter 13), occupational and military settings (Chapter 14), and "mental health" settings such as clinics, courts of law, and prisons (Chapter 15).

The NOIR system. One classificatory schema that has found wide acceptance is to classify tests according to their measurement properties. All measuring instruments, whether a psychological test, an automobile speedometer, a yardstick, or a bathroom scale, can be classified into one of four types based on the numerical properties of the instrument:

1. *Nominal scales.* Here the numbers are used merely as labels, without any inherent numerical property. For example, the numbers on the uniforms of football players represent such a use, with the numbers useful to distinguish one player from another, but not indicative of any numerical property – number 26 is not necessarily twice as good as number 13, and number 92 is not necessarily better or worse than number 91. In psychological testing, we sometimes code such variables as religious preference by assigning numbers to preferences, such as 1 to Protestant, 2 to Catholic, 3 to Jewish, and so on. This does not imply that being a Protestant is twice as good as being a Catholic, or that a Protestant plus a Catholic equal a Jew. Clearly, nominal scales represent a rather low level of measurement, and we should not apply to these scales statistical procedures such as computing a mean.

2. *Ordinal scales.* These are the result of ranking. Thus if you are presented with a list of ten cities and asked to rank them as to favorite vacation site, you have an ordinal scale. Note that the results of an ordinal scale indicate rankings but not differences in such rankings. Mazatlan in Mexico may be your first choice, with Palm Springs a close second; but Toledo, your third choice, may be a "distant" third choice.

3. *Interval scales.* These use numbers in such a way that the distance among different scores are based on equal units, but the zero point is arbitrary. Let's translate that into English by considering the measurement of temperature. The difference between 70 and 75 degrees is five units, which is the same difference as between 48 and 53 degrees. Each degree on our thermometer is equal in size. Note however that the zero point, although very meaningful, is in fact arbitrary; zero refers to the freezing of water at sea level – we could have chosen the freezing point of soda on top of Mount McKinley or some other standard. Because the zero point is arbitrary we

cannot make ratios, and we cannot say that a temperature of 100 degrees is twice as hot as a temperature of 50 degrees.

Let's consider a more psychological example. We have a 100-item multiple-choice vocabulary test composed of items such as:

cat = (a) feline, (b) canine, (c) aquiline, (d) asinine

Each item is worth 1 point and we find that Susan obtains a score of 80 and Barbara, a score of 40. Clearly, Susan's performance on the test is better than Barbara's, but is it twice as good? What if the vocabulary test had contained ten additional easy items that both Susan and Barbara had answered correctly; now Susan's score would have been 90 and Barbara's score 50, and clearly 90 is not twice 50. A zero score on this test does not mean that the person has zero vocabulary, but simply that they did not answer any of the items correctly – thus the zero is arbitrary and we cannot arrive at any conclusions that are based on ratios.

In this connection, I should point out that we might question whether our vocabulary test is in fact an interval scale. We score it as if it were, by assigning equal weights to each item, but are the items really equal? Most likely no, since some of the vocabulary items might be easier and some might be more difficult. I could, of course, empirically determine their difficulty level (we discuss this in Chapter 2) and score them appropriately (a real difficult item might receive 9 points, a medium difficulty item 5, and so on), or I could use only items that are of approximately equal difficulty or, as is often done, I can assume (typically incorrectly) that I have an interval scale.

4. *Ratio scales.* Finally, we have ratio scales that not only have equal intervals but also have a true zero. The Kelvin scale of temperature, which chemists use, is a ratio scale and on that scale a temperature of 200 is indeed twice as hot as a temperature of 100. There are probably no psychological tests that are true ratio scales, but most approximate interval scales; that is, they really are ordinal scales but we treat them as if they were interval scales. However, newer theoretical models known as item-response theory (e.g., Lord, 1980; Lord & Novick, 1968; Rasch, 1966; D. J. Weiss & Davison, 1981) have resulted in ways of developing tests said to be ratio scales.

ETHICAL STANDARDS

Tests are tools used by professionals to make what may possibly be some serious decisions about a client; thus both tests and the decision process involve a variety of ethical considerations to make sure that the decisions made are in the best interest of all concerned and that the process is carried out in a professional manner. There are serious concerns, on the part of both psychologists and lay people, about the nature of psychological testing and its potential misuse, as well as demands for increased use of tests.

APA ethics code. The American Psychological Association has since 1953 published and revised ethical standards, with the most recent publication of *Ethical Principles of Psychologists and Code of Conduct* in 1992. This code of ethics also governs, both implicitly and explicitly, a psychologist's use of psychological tests.

The Ethics Code contains six general principles:

1. Competence: Psychologists maintain high standards of competence, including knowing their own limits of expertise. Applied to testing, this might suggest that it is unethical for the psychologist to use a test with which he or she is not familiar to make decisions about clients.

2. Integrity: Psychologists seek to act with integrity in all aspects of their professional roles. As a test author for example, a psychologist should not make unwarranted claims about a particular test.

3. Professional and scientific responsibility: Psychologists uphold professional standards of conduct. In psychological testing this might require knowing when test data can be useful and when it cannot. This means, in effect, that a practitioner using a test needs to be familiar with the research literature on that test.

4. Respect for people's rights and dignity: Psychologists respect the privacy and confidentiality of clients and have an awareness of cultural, religious, and other sources of individual differences. In psychological testing, this might include an awareness of when a test is appropriate for use with individuals who are from different cultures.

5. Concern for others' welfare: Psychologists are aware of situations where specific tests (for

example, ordered by the courts) may be detrimental to a particular client. How can these situations be resolved so that both the needs of society and the welfare of the individual are protected?

6. Social responsibility: Psychologists have professional and scientific responsibilities to community and society. With regard to psychological testing, this might cover counseling against the misuse of tests by the local school.

In addition to these six principles, there are specific ethical standards that cover eight categories, ranging from "General standards" to "Resolving ethical issues." The second category is titled, "Evaluation, assessment, or intervention" and is thus the area most explicitly related to testing; this category covers 10 specific standards:

1. Psychological procedures such as testing, evaluation, diagnosis, etc., should occur only within the context of a defined professional relationship.

2. Psychologists only use tests in appropriate ways.

3. Tests are to be developed using acceptable scientific procedures.

4. When tests are used, there should be familiarity with and awareness of the limitations imposed by psychometric issues, such as those discussed in this textbook.

5. Assessment results are to be interpreted in light of the limitations inherent in such procedures.

6. Unqualified persons should not use psychological assessment techniques.

7. Tests that are obsolete and outdated should not be used.

8. The purpose, norms, and other aspects of a test should be described accurately.

9. Appropriate explanations of test results should be given.

10. The integrity and security of tests should be maintained.

Standards for educational and psychological tests. In addition to the more general ethical standards discussed above, there are also specific standards for educational and psychological tests (American Educational Research Association, 1999), first published in 1954, and subsequently revised a number of times.

These standards are quite comprehensive and cover (1) technical issues of validity, reliability, norms, etc.; (2) professional standards for test use, such as in clinical and educational settings; (3) standards for particular applications such as testing linguistic minorities; and (4) standards that cover aspects of test administration, the rights of the test taker and so on.

In considering the ethical issues involved in psychological testing, three areas seem to be of paramount importance: informed consent, confidentiality, and privacy.

Informed consent means that the subject has been given the relevant information about the testing situation and, based on that information, consents to being tested. Obviously this is a theoretical standard that in practice requires careful and thoughtful application. Clearly, to inform a subject that the test to be taken is a measure of "interpersonal leadership" may result in a set to respond in a way that can distort and perhaps invalidate the test results. Similarly, most subjects would not understand the kind of technical information needed to scientifically evaluate a particular test. So typically, informed consent means that the subject has been told in general terms what the purpose of the test is, how the results will be used, and who will have access to the test protocol.

The issue of *confidentiality* is perhaps even more complex. Test results are typically considered *privileged communication* and are shared only with appropriate parties. But what is appropriate? Should the client have access to the actual test results elucidated in a test report? If the client is a minor, should parents or legal guardians have access to the information? What about the school principal? What if the client was tested unwillingly, when a court orders such testing for determination of psychological sanity, pathology that may pose a threat to others, or the risk of suicide, etc. When clients seek psychological testing on their own, for example a college student requesting career counseling at the college counseling center, the guidelines are fairly clear. Only the client and the professional have access to the test results, and any transmission of test results to a third party requires written consent on the part of the client. But real-life issues often have a way of becoming more complex.

The right to *privacy* basically concerns the willingness of a person to share with others personal information, whether that information be factual or involve feelings and attitudes. In many tests, especially personality tests, the subject is asked to share what may be very personal information, occasionally without realizing that such sharing is taking place. At the same time, the subject cannot be instructed that, "if you answer true to item #17, I will take that as evidence that you are introverted."

What is or is not invasion of privacy may be a function of a number of aspects. A person seeking the help of a sex therapist may well expect and understand the need for some very personal questions about his or her sex life, while a student seeking career counseling would not expect to be questioned about such behavior (for a detailed analysis of privacy as it relates to psychological testing see Ruebhausen & Brim, 1966; for some interesting views on privacy, including Congressional hearings, see the November 1965 and May 1966 issues of the *American Psychologist*).

Mention might also be made of *feedback*, providing and explaining test results to the client. Pope (1992) suggests that feedback may be the most neglected aspect of assessment, and describes feedback as a dynamic, interactive process, rather than a passive, information-giving process.

The concern for ethical behavior is a pervasive aspect of the psychological profession, but one that lay people often are not aware of. Students, for example, at times do not realize that their requests ("can I have a copy of the XYZ intelligence test to assess my little brother") could involve unethical behavior.

In addition to the two major sets of ethical standards discussed above, there are other pertinent documents. For example, there are guidelines for providers of psychological services to members of populations whose ethnic, linguistic, or cultural background are diverse (APA, 1993), which include at least one explicit statement about the application of tests to such individuals, and there are guidelines for the disclosure of test data (APA, 1996). All of these documents are the result of hard and continuing work on the part of many professional organizations.

Test levels. If one considers tests as tools to be used by professionals trained in their use, then it becomes quite understandable why tests should not be readily available to unqualified users. In fact, the APA proposed many years ago a rating system of three categories of tests: level A tests require minimal training, level B tests require some advanced training, and level C tests require substantial professional expertise. These guidelines are followed by many test publishers who often require that prospective customers fill out a registration form indicating their level of expertise to purchase specific tests.

There is an additional reason why the availability of tests needs to be controlled and that is for *security*. A test score should reflect the dimension being measured, for example, knowledge of elementary geography, rather than some other process such as knowledge of the right answers. As indicated earlier, some tests are highly secured and their use is tightly controlled; for example tests like the SAT or the GRE are available only to those involved in their administration, and a strict accounting of each test booklet is required. Other tests are readily available, and their item content can sometimes be found in professional journals or other library documents.

INFORMATION ABOUT TESTS

It would be nice if there were one central source, one section of the library, that would give us all the information we needed about a particular test – but there isn't. You should realize that libraries do not ordinarily carry specimen copies of tests. Not only are there too many of them and they easily get out of date, but such a depository would raise some serious ethical questions. There may be offices on a college campus, such as the Counseling Center or the Clinical Psychology program, that have a collection of tests with scoring keys, manuals, etc., but these are not meant for public use. Information about specific tests is scattered quite widely, and often such a search is time consuming and requires patience as well as knowledge about available resources. The following steps can be of assistance:

1. The first step in obtaining information about a specific test is to consult the MMY. If the test is commercially published and has been reviewed

in the MMY, then our job will be infinitely easier; the MMY will give us the publishers' address and we can write for a catalog or information. It may also list references that we can consult, typically journal articles that are relevant. But what if the test is not listed in the MMY?

2. A second step is to check the original citation where mention of the particular test is made. For example, we may be reading a study by Jones which used the Smith Anxiety Scale; typically Jones will provide a reference for the Smith Anxiety Scale. We can locate that reference and then write to Smith for information about that scale. Smith's address will hopefully be listed in Smith's article, or we can look up Smith's address in directories such as the American Psychological Association Directory or a "Who's Who."

3. A third step is to conduct a computer literature search. If the test is well known we might obtain quite a few citations. If the test is somewhat more obscure, we might miss the available information. Keep in mind that currently most computer literature searches only go back a limited number of years.

4. If steps 2 and 3 give us some citations, we might locate these citations in the *Social Sciences Citation Index*; for example, if we locate the citation to the Smith Anxiety Scale, the Science Citation Index will tell us which articles use the Smith citation in their list of references. Presumably these articles might be of interest to us.

5. Suppose instead of a specific test we are interested in locating a scale of anxiety that we might use in our own study, or we want to see some of the various ways in which anxiety is assessed. In such a case, we would again first check the MMY to see what is available and take some or all of the following steps.

6. Search the literature for articles/studies on anxiety to see what instruments have been used. We will quickly observe that there are several instruments that seem to be quite popularly used and many others that are not.

7. We might repeat steps 2 and 3 above.

8. If the test is a major one, whether commercially published or not, we can consult the library to see what books have been written about that particular test. There are many books available on such tests as the Rorschach, the Minnesota Multiphasic Personality Inventory, and the Stanford-Binet (e.g., J. R. Graham, 1990; Knapp, 1976; Megargee, 1972; Snider & Osgood, 1969).

9. Another source of information is *Educational Testing Service* (ETS), the publisher of most of the college and professional school entrance exams. ETS has an extensive test library of more than 18,000 tests and, for a fee, can provide information. Also, ETS has published annually since 1975 *Tests in Microfiche*, sets of indices and abstracts to various research instruments; some libraries subscribe to these.

10. A number of journals such as the *Journal of Counseling and Development* and the *Journal of Psychoeducational Assessment*, routinely publish test reviews.

11. Finally, many books are collections of test reviews, test descriptions, etc., and provide useful information on a variety of tests. Some of these are listed in Table 1.1.

SUMMARY

A test can be defined as an objective and standardized measure of a sample of behavior. We can also consider a test as an experiment, an interview, or a tool. Tests can be used as part of psychological assessment, and are used for classification, self-understanding, program evaluation, and scientific inquiry. From the viewpoint of tests as an experiment, we need to pay attention to four categories of variables that can influence the outcome: the method of administration, situational variables, experimenter variables, and subject variables. Tests are used for decision making, although the content of a test need not coincide with the area of behavior that is assessed, other than to be empirically related.

Tests can be categorized according to whether they are commercially published or not administrative aspects such as group versus individual tests, the type of item, the area of assessment, the function of the test, how scores are interpreted, whether the test is a self-report or not, the age range and type of client, and the measurement properties.

Ethical standards relate to testing and the issues of informed consent, confidentiality, and privacy. There are many sources of information about tests available through libraries, associations, and other avenues of research.

Table 1–1. Sources for test information

Andrulis, R. S. (1977). *Adult assessment.* Springfield, IL: Charles C Thomas.

Six major categories of tests are listed, including aptitude and achievement, personality, attitudes, and personal performance.

Beere, C. A. (1979). *Women and women's issues: A handbook of tests and measures.* San Francisco: Jossey-Bass.

This handbook covers such topics as sex roles, gender knowledge, and attitudes toward women's issues, and gives detailed information on a variety of scales.

Chun, K. T. et al. (1975). *Measures for psychological assessment: A guide to 3000 original sources and their applications.* Ann Arbor: University of Michigan.

An old but still useful source for measures of mental health.

Compton, C. (1980). *A guide to 65 tests for special education.* Belmont, California: Fearon Education.

A review of tests relevant to special education.

Comrey, A. L., Backer, T. F., & Glaser, E. M. (1973). *A sourcebook for mental health measures.* Los Angeles: Human Interaction Research Institute.

A series of abstracts on about 1,100 lesser known measures in areas ranging from alcoholism through mental health, all the way to vocational tests.

Corcoran, K., & Fischer, J. (1987). *Measures for clinical practice: A sourcebook.* New York: Free Press.

A review of a wide variety of measures to assess various clinical problems.

Fredman, N., & Sherman, R. (1987). *Handbook of measurements for marriage and family therapy.* New York: Bruner Mazel.

A review of 31 of the more widely used paper-and-pencil instruments in the area of marriage and family therapy.

Goldman, B. A., & Saunders, J. L. (1974). *Directory of unpublished experimental mental measures, Vol. 1–4.* New York: Behavioral Publications.

The first volume contains a listing of 339 unpublished tests that were cited in the 1970 issues of a group of journals. Limited information is given on each one.

Hogan, J., & Hogan, R. (Eds.) (1990). *Business and industry testing.* Austin, TX: Pro-ed.

A review of tests especially pertinent to the world of work, such as intelligence, personality, biodata, and integrity tests.

Johnson, O. G. (1970; 1976). *Tests and measurements in child development.* San Francisco: Jossey-Bass.

The two volumes cover unpublished tests for use with children.

Keyser, D. J., & Sweetland, R. C. (Eds.) (1984). *Test critiques.* Kansas City: Test Corporation of America.

This is a continuing series that reviews the most frequently used tests, with reviews written by test experts, and quite detailed in their coverage. The publisher, Test Corporation of America, publishes a variety of books on testing.

Lake, D. G., Miles, M. B., & Earle, R. B., Jr. (1973). *Measuring human behavior.* New York: Teachers College Press.

A review of 84 different instruments and 20 compendia of instruments; outdated but still useful.

Mangen, D. J., & Peterson, W. A. (Eds.) (1982). *Research instruments in social gerontology; 2 volumes.* Minneapolis: University of Minnesota Press.

If you are interested in measurement of the elderly this is an excellent source. For each topic, for example death and dying, there is a brief overall discussion, some brief commentary on the various instruments, a table of the cited instruments, a detailed description of each instrument, and a copy of each instrument.

McReynolds, P. (Ed.) (1968). *Advances in psychological assessment.* Palo Alto: Science and Behavior Books.

This is an excellent series of books, the first one published in 1968, each book consisting of a series of chapters on assessment topics, ranging from reviews of specific tests like the Rorschach and the California Psychological Inventory (CPI), to topic areas like the assessment of anxiety, panic disorder, and adolescent suicide.

Newmark, C. S. (Ed.) (1985; 1989), *Major psychological assessment instruments,* volumes I and II. Boston: Allyn & Bacon.

A nice review of the most widely used tests in current psychological assessment, the volumes give detailed information about the construction, administration, interpretation, and status of these tests.

Reeder, L. G., Ramacher, L., & Gorelnik, S. (1976). *Handbook of scales and indices of health behavior.* Pacific Palisades, CA.: Goodyear Publishing.

A somewhat outdated but still useful source.

Reichelt, P. A. (1983). Location and utilization of available behavioral measurement instruments. *Professional Psychology, 14,* 341–356.

Includes an annotated bibliography of various compendia of tests.

Robinson, J. P., Shaver, P. R., & Wrightsman, L. S. (Eds.) (1990). *Measures of personality and social psychological attitudes.* San Diego, CA.: Academic Press.

Robinson and his colleagues at the Institute for Social Research (University of Michigan) have published a number of volumes summarizing measures of political attitudes (1968), occupational attitudes and characteristics (1969), and social-psychological attitudes (1969, 1973, & 1991).

Schutte, N. S., & Malouff, J. M. (1995). *Sourcebook of adult assessment strategies.* New York: Plenum Press.

A collection of scales, their description and evaluation, to assess psychopathology, following the diagnostic categories of the Diagnostic and Statistical Manual of Mental Disorders.

Table 1–1. (continued)

Shaw, M. E., & Wright, J. M. (1967). *Scales for the measurement of attitudes.* New York: McGraw-Hill.

An old but still useful reference for attitude scales. Each scale is reviewed in some detail, with the actual scale items given.

Southworth, L. E., Burr, R. L., & Cox, A. E. (1981). *Screening and evaluating the young child: A handbook of instruments to use from infancy to six years.* Springfield, IL: Charles C Thomas.

A compendium of preschool screening instruments, but without any evaluation of these instruments.

Straus, M. A. (1969). *Family measurement techniques.* Minneapolis: University of Minnesota Press.

A review of instruments reported in the psychological and sociological literature from 1935 to 1965.

Sweetland, R. C., & Keyser, D. J. (Eds.) (1983). *Tests: A comprehensive reference for assessments in psychology, education, and business.* Kansas City: Test Corporation of America.

This is the first edition of what has become a continuing series. In this particular volume, over 3,000 tests, both commercially available and unpublished, are given a brief thumbnail sketches.

Walker, D. K. (1973). *Socioemotional measures for preschool and kindergarten children.* San Francisco: Jossey-Bass.

A review of 143 measures covering such areas as personality, self-concept, attitudes, and social skills.

Woody, R. H. (Ed.) (1980). *Encyclopedia of clinical assessment. 2 vols.* San Francisco: Jossey-Bass.

This is an excellent, though now outdated, overview of clinical assessment; The 91 chapters cover a wide variety of tests ranging from measures of normality to moral reasoning, anxiety, and pain.

SUGGESTED READINGS

Dailey, C. A. (1953). The practical utility of the clinical report. *Journal of Consulting Psychology, 17,* 297–302.

An interesting study that tried to quantify how clinical procedures, based on tests, contribute to the decisions made about patients.

Fremer, J., Diamond, E. E., & Camara, W. J. (1989). Developing a code of fair testing practices in education. *American Psychologist, 44,* 1062–1067.

A brief historical introduction to a series of conferences that eventuated into a code of fair testing practices, and the code itself.

Lorge, I. (1951). The fundamental nature of measurement. In. E. F. Lindquist (Ed.), *Educational Measurement,* pp. 533–559. Washington, D.C.: American Council on Education.

An excellent overview of measurement, including the NOIR system.

Willingham, W. W. (Ed.). (1967). Invasion of privacy in research and testing. *Journal of Educational Measurement, 4,* No. 1 supplement.

An interesting series of papers reflecting the long standing ethical concerns involved in testing.

Wolfle, D. (1960). Diversity of Talent. *American Psychologist, 15,* 535–545.

An old but still interesting article that illustrates the need for broader use of tests.

DISCUSSION QUESTIONS

1. What has been your experience with tests?

2. How would you design a study to assess whether a situational variable can alter test performance?

3. Why not admit everyone who wants to enter medical school, graduate programs in business, law school, etc.?

4. After you have looked at the MMY in the library, discuss ways in which it could be improved.

5. If you were to go to the University's Counseling Center to take a career interest test, how would you expect the results to be handled? (e.g., should your parents receive a copy?).

2 Test Construction, Administration, and Interpretation

AIM This chapter looks at three basic questions: (1) How are tests constructed? (2) What are the basic principles involved in administering a test? and (3) How can we make sense of a test score?

CONSTRUCTING A TEST

How does one go about constructing a test? Because there are all sorts of tests, there are also all sorts of ways to construct such tests, and there is no one approved or sure-fire method of doing this. In general, however, test construction involves a sequence of 8 steps, with lots of exceptions to this sequence.

1. Identify a need. The first step is the identification of a need that a test may be able to fulfill. A school system may require an intelligence test that can be administered to children of various ethnic backgrounds in a group setting; a literature search may indicate that what is available doesn't fit the particular situation. A doctoral student may need a scale to measure "depth of emotion" and may not find such a scale. A researcher may want to translate some of Freud's insights about "ego defense" mechanisms into a scale that measures their use. A psychologist may want to improve current measures of leadership by incorporating new theoretical insights, and therefore develops a new scale. Another psychologist likes a currently available scale of depression, but thinks it is too long and decides to develop a shorter version. A test company decides to come out with a new career interest test to compete with what is already available on the market. So the need may be a very practical one (we need a scale to evaluate patients' improvement in psychother-

apy), or it may be very theoretical (a scale to assess "anomie" or "ego-strength"). Often, the need may be simply a desire to improve what is already available or to come up with one's own creation.

2. The role of theory. Every test that is developed is implicitly or explicitly influenced or guided by the theory or theories held by the test constructor. The theory may be very explicit and formal. Sigmund Freud, Carl Rogers, Emile Durkheim, Erik Erikson, and others have all developed detailed theories about human behavior or some aspect of it, and a practitioner of one of these theories would be heavily and knowingly influenced by that theory in constructing a test. For example, most probably only a Freudian would construct a scale to measure "id, ego, and superego functioning" and only a "Durkheimite" would develop a scale to measure "anomie." These concepts are embedded in their respective theories and their meaning as measurement variables derives from the theoretical framework in which they are embedded.

A theory might also yield some very specific guidelines. For example, a theory of depression might suggest that depression is a disturbance in four areas of functioning: self-esteem, social support, disturbances in sleep, and negative affect. Such a schema would then dictate that the measure of depression assess each of these areas.

The theory may also be less explicit and not well formalized. The test constructor may, for example, view depression as a troublesome state composed of negative feelings toward oneself, a reduction in such activities as eating and talking with friends, and an increase in negative thoughts and suicide ideation. The point is that a test is not created in a vacuum, nor is it produced by a machine as a yardstick might be. The creation of a test is intrinsically related to the person doing the creating and, more specifically, to that person's theoretical views. Even a test that is said to be "empirically" developed, that is, developed on the basis of observation or real-life behavior (how do depressed people answer a questionnaire about depression), is still influenced by theory.

Not all psychologists agree. R. B. Cattell (1986), for example, argues that most tests lack a true theoretical basis, that their validity is due to work done *after* their construction rather than before, and that they lack good initial theoretical construction. Embretson (1985b) similarly argues that although current efforts have produced tests that do well at predicting behavior, the link between these tests and psychological theory is weak and often nonexistent.

3. Practical choices. Let's assume that I have identified as a need the development of a scale designed to assess the eight stages of life that Erik Erikson discusses (Erikson, 1963; 1982; see G. Domino & Affonso, 1990, for the actual scale). There are a number of practical choices that now need to be made. For example, what format will the items have? Will they be true-false, multiple choice, 7-point rating scales, etc.? Will there be a time limit or not? Will the responses be given on a separate answer sheet? Will the response sheet be machine scored? Will my instrument be a quick "screening" instrument or will it give comprehensive coverage for each life stage? Will I need to incorporate some mechanism to assess honesty of response? Will my instrument be designed for group administration?

4. Pool of items. The next step is to develop a *table of specifications*, much like the blueprint needed to construct a house. This table of specifications would indicate the subtopics to be covered by the proposed test (in our example, the

eight life stages), perhaps their relative importance (are they all of equal importance?), and how many items each subtopic will contribute to the overall test (I might decide, for example, that each of the eight stages should be assessed by 15 items, thus yielding a total test of 120 items). This table of specifications may reflect not only my own thinking, but the theoretical notions present in the literature, other tests that are available on this topic, and the thinking of colleagues and experts. Test companies that develop educational tests such as achievement batteries often go to great lengths in developing such a table of specifications by consulting experts, either individually or in group conferences; the construction of these tests often represent major efforts of many individuals, at a high cost beyond the reach of any one person.

The table of specifications may be very formal or very informal, or sometimes absent, but leads to the writing or assembling of potential items. These items may be the result of the test constructor's own creativity, they may be obtained from experts, from other measures already available, from a reading of the pertinent literature, from observations and interviews with clients, and many other sources. Writing good test items is both an art and a science and is not easily achieved. I suspect you have taken many instructor made tests where the items were not clear, the correct answers were quite obvious, or the items focused on some insignificant aspects of your coursework. Usually, the classroom instructor writes items and uses most of them. The professional test constructor knows that the initial pool of items needs to be at a minimum four or five times as large as the number of items actually needed.

5. Tryouts and refinement. The initial pool of items will probably be large and rather unrefined. Items may be near duplications of each other, perhaps not clearly written or understood. The intent of this step is to refine the pool of items to a smaller but usable pool. To do this, we might ask colleagues (and/or enemies) to criticize, the items, or we might administer them to a captive class of psychology majors to review and identify items that may not be clearly written. Sometimes, *pilot testing* is used where a preliminary form is administered to a sample of subjects to determine whether there are any glitches, etc. Such pilot testing might involve asking the subjects to think aloud as they answer each item or to provide feedback as to whether the instructions are clear, the items interesting, and so on. We may also do some preliminary statistical work and assemble the test for a trial run called a *pretest*. For example, if I were developing a scale to measure depression, I might administer my pool of items (say 250) to groups of depressed and nondepressed people and then carry out *item analyses* to see which items in fact differentiate the two groups. For example, to the item "I am feeling blue" I might expect significantly more depressed people to answer "true" than nondepressed people. I might then retain the 100 items that seem to work best statistically, write each item on a 3 × 5 card, and sort these cards into categories according to their content; such as all the items dealing with sleep disturbances in one pile, all the items dealing with feelings in a separate pile, and so on. This sorting might indicate that we have too many items of one kind and not enough of another, so I might remove some of the excess items and write some new ones for the underrepresented category. Incidentally, this process is known as *content analysis* (see Gottschalk & Gleser, 1969). This step then, consists of a series of procedures, some requiring logical analysis, others statistical analysis, that are often repeated several times, until the initial pool of items has been reduced to manageable size, and all the evidence indicates that our test is working the way we wish it to.

6. Reliability and validity. Once we have refined our pool of items to manageable size, and have done the preliminary work of the above steps, we need to establish that our measuring instrument is *reliable*, that is, consistent, and measures what we set out to measure, that is, the test is *valid*. These two concepts are so basic and important that we devote an entire chapter to them (see Chapter 3). If we do not have reliability and validity, then our pool of items is not a measuring instrument, and it is precisely this that distinguishes the instruments psychologists use from those "questionnaires" that are published in popular magazines to determine whether a person is a "good lover," "financially responsible," or a "born leader."

7. Standardization and norms. Once we have established that our instrument is both reliable and valid, we need to standardize the instrument and develop norms. To *standardize* means that the administration, time limits, scoring procedures, and so on are all carefully spelled out so that no matter who administers the test, the procedure is the same. Obviously, if I administer an intelligence test and use a 30-minute time limit, and you administer the same test with a 2-hour time limit, the results will not be comparable. It might surprise you to know that there are some tests both commercially published and not that are not well standardized and may even lack instructions for administration.

Let's assume that you answer my vocabulary test, and you obtain a score of 86. What does that 86 mean? You might be tempted to conclude that 86 out of 100 is fairly good, until I tell you that second graders average 95 out of 100. You'll recall that 86 and 95 are called *raw scores*, which in psychology are often meaningless. We need to give meaning to raw scores by changing them into *derived* scores; but that may not be enough. We also need to be able to compare an individual's performance on a test with the performance of a group of individuals; that information is what we mean by *norms*. The information may be limited to the mean and standard deviation for a particular group or for many different groups, or it may be sufficiently detailed to allow the translation of a specific raw score into a derived score such as percentiles, T scores, z scores, IQ units, and so on.

The test constructor then administers the test to one or more groups, and computes some basic descriptive statistics to be used as norms, or normative information. Obviously, whether the normative group consists of 10 students from a community college, 600 psychiatric patients, or 8,000 sixth graders, will make quite a difference; test norms are not absolute but simply represent the performance of a particular sample at a particular point in time. The sample should be large enough that we feel comfortable with its size, although "large enough" cannot be answered by a specific number; simply because a sample is large, does not guarantee that it is representative. The sample should be representative of the population to which we generalize, so that an achievement test for use by fifth graders should have norms based on fifth graders. It is not unusual for achievement tests used in school systems to have normative samples in the tens of thousands, chosen to be representative on the basis of census data or other guiding principles, but for most tests the sample size is often in the hundreds or smaller. The sample should be clearly defined also so that the test user can assess its adequacy – was the sample a captive group of introductory psychology students, or a "random" sample representative of many majors? Was the sample selected on specific characteristics such as income and age, to be representative of the national population? How were the subjects selected?

8. Further refinements. Once a test is made available, either commercially or to other researchers, it often undergoes refinements and revisions. Well-known tests such as the Stanford-Binet have undergone several revisions, sometimes quite major and sometimes minor. Sometimes the changes reflect additional scientific knowledge, and sometimes societal changes, as in our greater awareness of gender bias in language.

One type of revision that often occurs is the development of a *short form* of the original test. Typically, a different author takes the original test, administers it to a group of subjects, and shows by various statistical procedures that the test can be shortened without any substantial loss in reliability and validity. Psychologists and others are always on the lookout for brief instruments, and so short forms often become popular, although as a general rule, the shorter the test the less reliable and valid it is. (For some examples of short forms see Burger, 1975; Fischer & Fick, 1993; Kaufman, 1972; Silverstein, 1967.)

Still another type of revision that occurs fairly frequently comes about by *factor analysis*. Let's say I develop a questionnaire on depression that assesses what I consider are four aspects of depression. A factor analysis might indeed indicate that there are four basic dimensions to my test, and so perhaps each should be scored separately, in effect, yielding four scales. Or perhaps, the results of the factor analysis indicate that there is only one factor and that the four subscales I thought were separate are not. Therefore, only one score should be generated. Or the factor analysis might indicate that of the 31 items on the test,

28 are working appropriately, but 3 should be thrown out since their contribution is minimal. (For some examples of factor analysis applied to tests, see Arthur & Woehr, 1993; Carraher, 1993; Casey, Kingery, Bowden & Corbett, 1993; Cornwell, Manfredo, & Dunlap, 1991; W. L. Johnson & A. M. Johnson, 1993).

Finally, there are a number of tests that are *multivariate*, that is the test is composed of many scales, such as in the MMPI and the CPI. The pool of items that comprises the entire test is considered to be an "open system" and additional scales are developed based upon arising needs. For example, when the MMPI was first developed it contained nine different clinical scales; subsequently hundreds of scales have been developed by different authors. (For some examples, see Barron, 1953; Beaver, 1953; Giedt & Downing, 1961; J. C. Gowan & M. S. Gowan, 1955; Kleinmuntz, 1961; MacAndrew, 1965; Panton, 1958.)

TEST ITEMS

Writing test items. Because the total test is no better than its components, we need to take a closer look at test *items*. In general, items should be clear and unambiguous, so that responses do not reflect a misunderstanding of the item. Items should not be double-barreled. For example, "I enjoy swimming and tennis" is a poor item because you would not know whether the response of "true" really means that the person enjoys both of them, only one of them, or outdoor activities in general. Items should not use words such as "sometimes" or "frequently" because these words might mean different things to different people. An item such as, "Do you have headaches frequently?" is better written as, "Do you have a headache at least once a week?" (For more detailed advice on writing test items see Gronlund, 1993; Kline, 1986; Osterlind, 1989; Thorndike & Hagen, 1977; for a bibliography of citations on test construction, see O'Brien, 1988).

Categories of items. There are two basic categories of items: (1) *constructed*-response items where the subject is presented with a stimulus and produces a response – essay exams and sentence-completion tests are two examples; (2) *selected*-response items where the subject selects the correct or best response from a list of options – the typical multiple-choice question is a good example.

There is a rather extensive body of literature on which approach is better under what circumstances, with different authors taking different sides of the argument (see Arrasmith, Sheehan, & Applebaum, 1984, for a representative study).

Types of items. There are many types of items (see Jensen, 1980; Wesman, 1971). Some of the more common ones:

1. Multiple-choice items. These are a common type, composed of a *stem* that has the question and the *response options* or choices, usually four or five, which are the possible answers. Multiple-choice items should assess the particular content area, rather than vocabulary or general intelligence. The incorrect options, called *distractors*, should be equally attractive to the test taker, and should differentiate between those who know the correct answer and those who don't. The correct response is called the *keyed* response. Sometimes, multiple-choice items are used in tests that assess psychological functioning such as depression or personality aspects, in which case there are no incorrect answers, but the keyed response is the one that reflects what the test assesses. When properly written, multiple-choice items are excellent. There are available guidelines to write good multiple-choice items. Haladyna and Downing (1989a; 1989b) surveyed some 46 textbooks and came up with 43 rules on how to write multiple-choice items; they found that some rules had been extensively researched but others had not. Properly constructed multiple-choice items can measure not only factual knowledge, but also theoretical understanding and problem-solving skills. At the same time, it is not easy to write good multiple-choice items with no extraneous cues that might point to the correct answer (such as the phrase "all of the above") and with content that assesses complex thinking skills rather than just recognition of rote memory material.

Although most multiple-choice items are written with four or five options, a number of writers have presented evidence that three option items may be better (Ebel, 1969; Haladyna & Downing, 1994; Lord, 1944; Sidick, Barrett, & Doverspike, 1994).

Multiple-choice items have a number of advantages. They can be answered quickly, so a particular test can include more items and therefore a broader coverage. They can also be scored quickly and inexpensively, so that results are obtained rapidly and feedback provided without much delay. There is also available computerized statistical technology that allows the rapid computation of item difficulty and other useful indices.

At the same time, multiple-choice items have been severely criticized. One area of criticism is that multiple-choice items are much easier to create for isolated facts than for conceptual understanding, and thus they promote rote learning rather than problem-solving skills. Currently, there seems to be substantial pressure to focus on constructed-response tasks; however, such an approach has multiple problems and may in fact turn out to be even more problematic (Bennet & Ward, 1993).

2. True-false items. Usually, these consist of a statement that the subject identifies as true or false, correct or incorrect, and so on. For example:

Los Angeles is the capital of California.

I enjoy social gatherings.

Note that in the first example, a factual statement, there is a correct answer. In the second example there is not, but the keyed response would be determined theoretically or empirically; if the item were part of a scale of introversion-extraversion, a true answer might be scored for extraversion.

From a psychometric point of view, factual true-false statements are not very useful. Guessing is a major factor because there is a 50% probability of answering correctly by guessing, and it may be difficult to write meaningful items that indeed are true or false under all circumstances. Los Angeles is not the capital of California but there was a period when it was. Often the item writer needs to include words like *usually*, *never*, and *always* that can give away the correct answer. Personality- or opinion-type true-false items, on the other hand, are used quite frequently and found in many major instruments.

Most textbooks argue that true-false items, as used in achievement tests, are the least satisfactory item format. Other textbooks argue that the limitations are more the fault of the item writer than with the item format itself. Frisbie and Becker (1991) reviewed the literature and formulated some 21 rules to writing true-false items.

3. Analogies. These are commonly found in tests of intelligence, although they can be used with almost any subject matter. Analogies can be quite easy or difficult and can use words, numbers, designs, and other formats. An example is:

46 is to 24 as 19 is to

(a) 9, (b) 13, (c) 38, (d) 106

(in this case, the answer is 9, because $4 \times 6 = 24$, $1 \times 9 = 9$).

Analogies may or may not be in a multiple-choice format, although providing the choices is a better strategy psychometrically. Like any good multiple choice item, an analogy item has only one correct answer.

4. Odd-man-out. These items are composed of words, numbers, etc., in which one component does *not* belong. For example:

donkey, camel, llama, ostrich

(Here ostrich does not belong because all the other animals have four legs, whereas ostriches have two.)

These items can also be quite varied in their difficulty level and are not limited to words. The danger here is that the dimension underlying the item (leggedness in the above example) may not be the only dimension, may not be necessarily meaningful, and may not be related to the variable being measured.

5. Sequences. This consists of a series of components, related to each other, with the last missing item to be generated by the subject or to be identified from a multiple-choice set. For example:

6, 13, 17, 24, 28,___

(a) 32, (b) 35, (c) 39, (d) 46

(Here the answer is 35 because the series of numbers increases alternately by 7 points and 4 points: $6 + 7 = 13$; $13 + 4 = 17$; $17 + 7 = 24$; etc.)

6. Matching items. These typically consists of two lists of items to be matched, usually of unequal length to counteract guessing. For example:

Cities	States
A. Toledo	1. California
B. Sacramento	2. Michigan
C. Phoenix	3. North Carolina
D. Ann Arbor	4. Ohio
E. Helena	5. Montana
	6. Arizona
	7. South Dakota
	8. Idaho

Matching items can be useful in assessing specific *factual* knowledge such as names of authors and their novels, dates and historical events, and so on. One problem with matching items is that mismatching one component can result in mismatching other components; thus the components are not independent.

7. Completion items. These provide a *stem* and require the subject to supply an answer. If potential answers are given, this becomes a multiple-choice item. Examples of completion items are:

Wundt established his laboratory in the year __.

I am always _____.

Note that the response possibilities in the first example are quite limited; the respondent gives either a correct or an incorrect answer. In the second example, different respondents can supply quite different responses. Sentence completion items are used in some tests of personality and psychological functioning.

8. Fill in the blank. This can be considered a variant of the completion item, with the required response coming in a variety of positions. For example:

_____ established the first psychological laboratory.

Wundt established a laboratory at the University of _____ in the year _____.

9. Forced choice items. Forced choice items consist of two or more options, equated as to attractiveness or other qualities, where the subject must choose one. This type of item is used in some personality tests. For example:

Which item best characterizes you:

(a) I would rather go fishing by myself.

(b) I would rather go fishing with friends.

Presumably, choice (a) would reflect introversion, while choice (b) would reflect extraversion; whether the item works as intended would need to be determined empirically.

10. Vignettes. A vignette is a brief scenario, like the synopsis of a play or novel. The subject is asked to react in some way to the vignette, perhaps by providing a story completion, choosing from a set of alternatives, or making some type of judgment. Examples of studies that have used vignettes are those of G. Domino and Hannah (1987), who asked American and Chinese children to complete brief stories; of DeLuty (1988–1989), who had students assess the acceptability of suicide; of Wagner and Sternberg (1986), who used vignettes to assess what they called "tacit" knowledge; and of Iwao and Triandis (1993), who assessed Japanese and American stereotypes.

11. Rearrangement or continuity items. This is one type of item that is relatively rare but has potential. These items measure a person's knowledge about the order of a series of items. For example, we might list a set of names, such as Wilhelm Wundt, Lewis Terman, Arthur Jensen, etc., and ask the test taker to rank these in chronological order. The difficulty with this type of item is the scoring, but Cureton (1960) has provided a table that can be used in a relatively easy scoring procedure that reflects the difference between the person's answers and the scoring key.

Objective-subjective continuum. Different kinds of test items can be thought of as occupying a continuum along a dimension of objective-subjective:

objective ———————————— subjective

From a psychometric point of view objective items, such as multiple-choice items are the best. They are easily scored, contain only one correct answer, and can be handled statistically with relative ease. The shortcoming of such items is that they only yield the information of whether the subject answered correctly or incorrectly, or whether the subject chose "true" rather than "false" or "option A" rather than "option B." They do not tell us whether the choice reflects lucky guessing, test "wiseness," or actual knowledge.

Subjective items, such as essay questions, on the other hand, allow the respondent to respond in what can be a unique and revealing way. Guessing is somewhat more difficult, and the information produced is often more personal and revealing. From a clinical point of view, open-ended items such as, "Tell me more about it?" "What brings you here?" or "How can I be of help?" are much more meaningful in assessing a client. Psychometrically, such responses are difficult to quantify and treat statistically.

Which item format to use? The choice of a particular item format is usually determined by the test constructor's preferences and biases, as well as by the test content. For example, in the area of personality assessment, many inventories have used a "true-false" format rather than a multiple-choice format. There is relatively little data that can serve as guidance to the prospective test author – only some general principles and some unresolved controversies.

One general principle is that statistical analyses require variation in the raw scores. The item, "are you alive at this moment" is not a good item because, presumably, most people would answer yes. We can build in variation by using item formats with several choices, such as multiple-choice items or items that require answering "strongly agree, agree, undecided, disagree, or strongly disagree," rather than simply true-false; we can also increase variation by using more items – a 10-item test can yield scores that range from 0 to 10, while a 20-item test can yield scores that range from 0 to 20. If the items use the "strongly agree . . . strongly disagree" response format, we can score each item from 1 to 5, and the 10-item test now can yield raw scores from 10 to 50.

One unresolved controversy is whether item response formats such as "strongly agree . . . strongly disagree" should have an "undecided" option or should force respondents to choose sides; also should the responses be an odd number so a person can select the middle "neutral" option, or should the responses be an even number, so the subject is forced to choose?

An example of the data available comes from a study by Bendig (1959) who administered a personality inventory to two samples, one receiving the standard form with a trichotomous response (true, ?, false), the other a form that omitted the ? response. The results were pretty equivalent, and Bendig (1959) concluded that using a dichotomous response was more economical in terms of scoring cost (now, it probably does not make any difference). For another example, see Tzeng, Ware, and Bharadwaj (1991).

Sequencing of items. Items in a test are usually listed according to some plan or rationale rather than just randomly. In tests of achievement or intelligence, a common strategy is to have easy items at the beginning and progressively difficult items toward the end. Another plan is to use a *spiral omnibus* format, which involves a series of items from easy to difficult, followed by another series of items from easy to difficult, and so on. In tests of personality where the test is composed of many scales, items from the same scale should not be grouped together, otherwise the intent of each scale becomes obvious and can alter the responses given. Similarly, some scales contain *filler* items that are not scored but are designed to "hide" the real intent of the scale. The general rule to be followed is that we want test performance to reflect whatever it is that the test is measuring, rather than some other aspect such as fatigue, boredom, speed of response, second-guessing, and so on; so where possible, items need to be placed in a sequence that will offset any such potential *confounding* variables.

Direct assessment. Over the years, great dissatisfaction has been expressed about these various types of items, especially multiple-choice items. Beginning about 1990, a number of investigators have begun to call for "authentic" measurement (Wiggins, 1990). Thus, more emphasis is being given to what might be called direct or performance assessment, that is, assessment providing for direct measurement of the product or performance generated. Thus, if we wanted to test the competence of a football player we would not administer a multiple-choice exam, but would observe that person's ability to throw a ball, run 50 yards, pass, and so on. If we wanted to assess Johnny's arithmetic knowledge we would give him arithmetic problems to solve. Note that in the latter case, we could easily test Johnny's performance by traditional test items, although a purist might argue that we need to take Johnny to the grocery store and see if he can compute how much six oranges and three apples cost, and how much change he will receive from a $5 bill. This is of course, not a new idea. Automobile driving tests, Red Cross swimming certification, and cardiopulmonary resuscitation are all examples of such performance testing. Advocates of direct assessment argue that such assessment should more closely resemble the actual learning tasks and should allow the candidate to show higher-order cognitive skills such as logical reasoning, innovative problem solving, and critical thinking. Thus, the multiple-choice format is being de-emphasized and more focus is being placed on portfolios, writing samples, observations, oral reports, projects, and other "authentic" procedures [see the special issue of *Applied Psychological Measurement*, 2000 (Vol. 24, No. 4)].

The concepts of reliability and validity apply equally well to standard assessment as to authentic measurement, and the difficulties associated with authentic testing are rather challenging (Hambleton & Murphy, 1992; M. D. Miller & Linn, 2000). In addition to individual scholars, researchers affiliated with Educational Testing Service and other companies are researching these issues, although it is too early to tell whether their efforts will have a major future impact.

PHILOSOPHICAL ISSUES

In addition to practical questions, such as what type of item format to use, there are a number of philosophical issues that guide test construction. One such question is, "How do we know when an item is working the way it is supposed to?" Three basic answers can be given: by fiat, by criterion keying, and by internal consistency.

By fiat. Suppose you put together a set of items to measure depression. How would you know that they measure depression? One way, is to simply state that they do, that because you are an expert on depression, that because the items reflect our best thinking about depression, and that because the content of all the items is clearly related to depression, therefore your set of items must be measuring depression. Most psychologists would not accept this as a final answer, but this method of *fiat* (a decree on the basis of authority), can be acceptable as a first step. The Beck Depression Inventory, which is probably one of the most commonly used measures of depression, was initially developed this way (A. T. Beck, 1967), although subsequent research has supported its utility. The same can be said of the Stanford-Binet test of intelligence.

Criterion-keyed tests. Many of the best known tests such as the MMPI, CPI, and Strong Vocational Interest Blank, were constructed using this method. Basically, a pool of items is administered to a sample of subjects, for whom we also obtain some information on a relevant *criterion*, for example, scores on another test, GPA, ratings by supervisors, etc. For each test item we perform a statistical analysis (often using correlation) that shows whether the item is empirically related to the criterion. If it does, the item is retained for our final test. This procedure may be done several times with different samples, perhaps using different operational definitions for the criterion. The decision to retain or reject a test item is based solely on its statistical power, on its relationship to the criterion we have selected.

The major problem with this approach is the choice of criterion. Let's assume I have developed a pool of items that presumably assess intelligence. I will administer this pool of items to a sample of subjects and also obtain some data for these subjects on some criterion of intelligence. What criterion will I use? Grade point average? Yearly income? Self-rated intelligence? Teacher ratings? Number of inventions? Listing in a "Who's Who?" Each of these has some serious limitations, and I am sure you appreciate the fact that in the real world criteria are complex and far from perfect. Each of these criteria might also relate to a different set of items, so the items that are retained reflect the criterion chosen.

Some psychologists have difficulties with the criterion-keyed methodology in that the retained set of items may work quite well, but the theoretical reason may not be obvious. A scale may

identify those who have leadership capabilities to different degrees, but it may not necessarily measure leadership in a theoretical sense because the items were chosen for their statistical relationship rather than their theoretical cogency.

Criterion-keyed scales are typically *heterogeneous* or *multivariate*. That is, a single scale designed to measure a single variable is typically composed of items that, theoretically and/or in content, can be quite different from each other, and thus, it can be argued, represent different variables. In fact, a content analysis or a factor analysis of the scale items might indicate that the items fall in separate clusters. This is because the criterion used is typically complex; GPA does not just reflect academic achievement, but also interest, motivation, grading policies of different teachers, and so on. Retained items may then be retained because they reflect one or more of these aspects.

A related criticism sometimes made about such scales is that the results are a function of the particular criterion used. If in a different situation a different criterion is used, then presumably the scale may not work. For example, if in selecting items for a depression scale the criterion is "psychiatric diagnosis," then the scale may not work in a college setting where we may be more concerned about dropping out or suicide ideation. This of course, is a matter of empirical validity and cannot be answered by speculation. In fact, scales from tests such as the CPI have worked remarkably well in a wide variety of situations.

A good example of empirical scale construction is the study by Rehfisch (1958), who set about to develop a scale for "personal rigidity." He first reviewed the literature to define the rigidity-flexibility dimension and concluded that the dimension was composed of six aspects: (1) constriction and inhibition, (2) conservatism, (3) intolerance of disorder and ambiguity, (4) obsessional and perseverative tendencies, (5) social introversion, and (6) anxiety and guilt. At this point, he could have chosen to write a pool of items to reflect these six dimensions and publish his scale on the basis of its theoretical underpinnings and his status as an "expert" – this would have been the fiat method we discussed above. Or he could have chosen to administer the pool of items to a large group of subjects and through factor analysis determine whether the results indicated one main factor, presumably rigidity, or six factors, presumably the above dimensions. We discuss this method next.

Instead he chose to use data that was already collected by researchers at the Institute of Personality Assessment and Research of the University of California at Berkeley. At this institute, a number of different samples, ranging from graduate students to Air Force captains, had been administered – batteries of tests, including the CPI and the MMPI, had been rated by IPAR staff on a number of dimensions, including "rigidity." Rehfisch simply analyzed statistically the responses to the combined CPI-MMPI item pool (some 957 true-false statements) of the subjects rated highest and lowest 25% on rigidity. He *cross-validated*, that is replicated the analysis, on additional samples. The result was a 39-item scale that correlated significantly with a variety of ratings, and which was substantially congruent with the theoretical framework. High scorers on this scale tend to be seen as anxious, overcontrolled, inflexible in their social roles, orderly, and uncomfortable with uncertainty. Low scorers tend to be seen as fluent in their thinking and in their speech, outgoing in social situations, impulsive, and original. Interestingly enough, scores on the scale correlated only .19 with ratings of rigidity in a sample of medical school applicants. It is clear that the resulting scale is a "complex" rather than a "pure" measure of rigidity. In fact, a content analysis of the 39 items suggested that they can be sorted into eight categories ranging from "anxiety and constriction in social situations" to "conservatism and conventionality." A subsequent study by Rehfisch (1959) presented some additional evidence for the validity of this scale.

Factor-analysis as a way of test construction. This approach assumes that scales should be *univariate* and *independent*. That is, scales should measure only one variable and should not correlate with scales that measure a different variable. Thus, all the items retained for a scale should be *homogeneous*, they should all be interrelated.

As in the criterion-keying method, we begin with a pool of items that are administered to a sample of subjects. The sample may be one of convenience (e.g., college sophomores) or one of theoretical interest (patients with the diagnosis of anxiety) related to our pool of items. The responses are translated numerically (e.g., true = 1, false = 2), and the numbers are subjected to factor analysis. There are a number of techniques and a number of complex issues involved in factor analysis, but for our purposes we can think of factor analysis as a correlational analysis with items being correlated with a mythical dimension called a *factor*. Each item then has a *factor loading*, which is like a correlation coefficient between responses on that item and the theoretical dimension of the factor. Items that load significantly on a particular factor are assumed to measure the same variable and are retained for the final scale. Factor analysis does not tell us what the psychological meaning of the factor is, and it is up to the test constructor to study the individual items that load on the factor, and name the factor accordingly. A pool of items may yield several factors that appear to be statistically "robust" and psychologically meaningful, or our interest may lie only in the first, main factor and in the one scale.

As with criterion-keying, there have been a number of criticisms made of the factor-analytic approach to test construction. One is that factor analysis consists of a variety of procedures, each with a variety of assumptions and arbitrary decisions; there is argument in the literature about which of the assumptions and decisions are reasonable and which are not (e.g., Gorsuch, 1983; Guilford, 1967b; Harman, 1960; Heim, 1975).

Another criticism is that the results of a factor analysis reflect only what was included in the pool of items. To the extent that the pool of items is restricted in content, then the results of the factor analysis will be restricted. Perhaps I should indicate here that this criticism is true of any pool of items, regardless of what is done to the items, but that usually those of the criterion-keying persuasion begin with pool items that are much more heterogeneous. In fact, they will often include items that on the surface have no relationship to the criterion, but the constructor has a "hunch" that the item might work.

Still another criticism is that the factor analytic dimensions are theoretical dimensions, useful for understanding psychological phenomena, but less useful as predictive devices. Real-life behavior is typically complex; grades in college reflect not just mastery of specific topic areas, but general intelligence, motivation, aspiration level, the pressures of an outside job, personal relationships such as being "in love," parental support, sleep habits, and so on. A factor analytic scale of intelligence will only measure "pure intelligence" (whatever that may be) and thus not correlate highly with GPA, which is a complex and heterogeneous variable. (To see how a factor analytic proponent answers these criticisms, see P. Kline, 1986.)

ADMINISTERING A TEST

If we consider a test as either an interview or an experiment, then how the test is administered becomes very important. If there is a manual available for the particular test, then the manual may (or may not) have explicit directions on how to administer the test, what specific instructions to read, how to answer subjects' questions, what time limits if any to keep, and so on.

Rapport. One of the major aspects of test administration involves *rapport*, the "bond" that is created between examiner and examinee, so that the subject is cooperative, interested in the task, and motivated to pay attention and put forth a best effort. Sometimes such motivation is strongly affected by outside factors. A premedical student eager to be accepted into medical school will typically be quite cooperative and engaged in the task of taking a medical college admissions test; a juvenile delinquent being assessed at the request of a judge, may not be so motivated.

In the American culture, tests and questionnaires are fairly common, and a typical high school or college student will find little difficulty in following test directions and doing what is being asked in the time limit allotted. Individuals such as young children, prisoners, emotionally disturbed persons, or individuals whose educational background has not given them substantial exposure to testing, may react quite differently.

Rapport then is very much like establishing a special bond with another person, such as occurs in friendships, in marriage, and in other human relationships. There are no easy steps to do so, and no pat answers. Certainly, if the examiner appears to be a warm and caring person, sensitive to the needs of the subject, rapport might be easier to establish. On the other hand, we expect a professional to be friendly but businesslike, so if the warmth becomes "gushiness," rapport might decrease. Rapport is typically enhanced if the subject understands why she or he is being tested, what the tests will consist of, and how the resulting scores will be used. Thus, part of establishing rapport might involve allaying any fears or suspicions the subject may have. Rapport is also enhanced if the subject perceives that the test is an important tool to be used by a competent professional for the welfare of the client.

INTERPRETING TEST SCORES

A test usually yields a raw score, perhaps the number of items answered correctly. Raw scores in themselves are usually meaningless, and they need to be changed in some way to give them meaning. One way is to compare the raw score to a group average – that is what the word "norm" means, normal or average. Thus, you obtained a raw score of 72 on a vocabulary test, and upon finding that the average raw score of a sample of college students is 48, you might be quite pleased with your performance. Knowing the average is, of course, quite limited information. When we have a raw score we need to locate that raw score in more precise terms than simply above or below average. Normative data then typically consist not just of one score or average, but the actual scores of a representative and sizable sample that allow you to take any raw score and translate it into a precise location in that normative group. To do this, raw scores need to be changed into *derived* scores.

Percentiles. Let's suppose that our normative group contained 100 individuals and, by sheer luck, each person obtained a different score on our vocabulary test. These scores could be ranked, giving a 1 to the lowest score and a 100 to the highest score. If John now comes along and takes the vocabulary test, his raw score can be changed into the equivalent rank – his score of 76 might be equivalent to the 85th rank. In effect, that is what percentile scores are. When we have a distribution of raw scores, even if they are not all different, and regardless of how many scores we have, we can change raw scores into percentiles. Percentiles are a rank, but they represent the upper limit of the rank. For example, a score at the 86th percentile is a score that is higher than 86 out of 100, and conversely lower than 14 out of 100; a score at the 57th percentile is a score that is higher than 57 out of 100, and lower than 43 out of 100. Note that the highest possible percentile is 99 (no score can be above all 100), and the lowest possible percentile is 1 (no one can obtain a score that has no rank).

Percentiles are intrinsically meaningful in that it doesn't matter what the original scale of measurement was, the percentile conveys a concrete position (see any introductory statistical text for the procedure to calculate percentiles). Percentiles have one serious limitation; they are an ordinal scale rather than an interval scale. Although ranks would seem to differ by only one "point," in fact different ranks may differ by different points depending on the underlying raw score distribution. In addition, if you have a small sample, not all percentile ranks will be represented, so a raw score of 72 might equal the 80th percentile, and a raw score of 73, the 87th percentile.

Standard scores. We said that just knowing the average is not sufficient information to precisely locate a raw score. An average will allow us to determine whether the raw score is above or below the average, but we need to be more precise. If the average is 50 and the raw score is 60, we could obviously say that the raw score is "10 points above the mean." That would be a useful procedure, except that each test has its own measurement scale – on one test the highest score might be 6 points above the mean, while on another test it might be 27 points above the mean, and how far away a score is from the mean is in part a function of how variable the scores are. For example, height measured in inches is typically less variable than body weight measured in ounces. To equalize for these sources of variation we need to use a scale of measurement that transcends the numbers used, and that is precisely what the *standard deviation* gives us. If we equate a standard deviation to one, regardless of the scale of measurement, we can express a raw score as being x number of standard deviations above or below the mean. To do so we change our raw scores into what are called *standard* or z scores, which represent a scale of measurement with mean equal to zero and SD equal to 1.

Consider a test where the mean is 62 and the SD is 10. John obtained a raw score of 60, Barbara, a raw score of 72, and Consuelo, a raw score of 78. We can change these raw scores into z scores through the following formula:

$$z = \frac{X - M}{SD}$$

where X is the raw score

   M is the mean and

   SD is the standard deviation

For John, his raw score of 60 equals:

$$z = \frac{60 - 62}{10} = -0.2$$

For Barbara, her raw score of 72 equals:

$$z = \frac{72 - 62}{10} = +1.0$$

and for Consuelo, her raw score of 78 equals:

$$z = \frac{78 - 62}{10} = +1.60$$

We can plot these 3 z scores on a normal curve graph and obtain a nice visual representation of their relative positions (see Figure 2.1).

Note that changing raw scores into z scores does not alter the relative position of the three individuals. John is still the lowest scoring person, Consuelo the highest, and Barbara is in the middle. Why then change raw scores into z scores? Aside from the fact that z scores represent a scale of measurement that has immediate meaning (a z score of +3 is a very high score no matter what the test, whereas a raw score of 72 may or may not be a high score), z scores also allow us to compare across tests. For example, on the test above with mean of 62 and SD of 10, Consuelo obtained a raw score of 78. On a second test, with mean of 106 and SD of 9, she obtained a raw score of 117. On which test did she do better? By changing the raw scores to z scores the answer becomes clear. On test A, Consuelo's raw score of 78 equals:

$$z = \frac{78 - 62}{10} = +1.60$$

On test B, Consuelo's raw score of 117 equals:

$$z = \frac{177 - 106}{9} = +1.22$$

Plotting these on a normal curve graph, as in Figure 2.2, we see that Consuelo did better on test A.

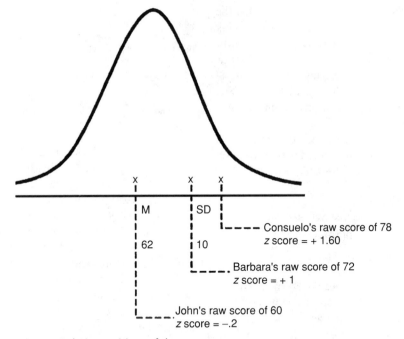

FIGURE 2-1. Relative positions of three z scores.

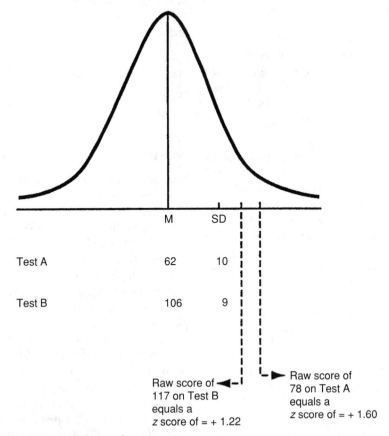

FIGURE 2-2. Equivalency of raw scores to z scores.

T scores. The problem with z scores is that they can involve both positive and negative numbers as well as decimal numbers, and so are somewhat difficult to work with. This is a problem that can be easily resolved by changing the mean and SD of z scores to numbers that we might prefer. Suppose we wanted a scale of measurement with a mean of 50 and a SD of 10. All we need to do is multiply the z score we wish to change by the desired SD and add the desired mean. For example, to change a z score of $+1.50$ we would use this formula:

$$\text{new score} = z(\text{desired SD}) + \text{desired mean}$$
$$= +1.50(10) + 50$$
$$= 65$$

This new scale, with a mean of 50 and SD of 10 is used so often in testing, especially for personality tests, that it is given a name: *T scores*; when you see T scores reported, you automatically know that the mean is 50 and the SD is 10, and that therefore a score of 70 is two standard deviations above the mean.

Educational Testing Service (ETS) uses a scale of measurement with mean of 500 and SD of 100 for its professional tests such as the SAT and the GRE. These are really T scores with an added zero. Note that an individual would not obtain a score of 586 – only 580, 590, and so on.

Stanines. Another type of transformation of raw scores is to a scale called *stanine* (a contraction of standard nine) that has been used widely in both the armed forces and educational testing. Stanines involve changing raw scores into a normally shaped distribution using nine scores that range from 1 (low) to 9 (high), with a mean of 5 and SD of 2. The scores are assigned on the basis of the following percentages:

stanine:	1	2	3	4	5	6	7	8	9
percentage:	4	7	12	17	20	17	12	7	4

Thus, in a distribution of raw scores, we would take the lowest 4% of the scores and call all of them ones, then the next 7% we would call two's, and so on (all identical raw scores would however be assigned the same stanine).

Stanines can also be classified into a fivefold classification as follows:

stanine:	1	2&3	4,5,6	7&8	9
defined as:	poor	below average	average	above average	superior
percentage:	4	19	54	19	4

or a tripartite classification:

stanine:	1,2,3	4,5,6	7,8,9
defined as:	low	average	high
percentage:	23	54	23

Sometimes stanines actually have 11 steps, where the stanine of 1 is divided into 0 and 1 (with 1% and 3% of the cases), and the stanine of 9 is divided into 9 and 10 (with 3% and 1% of the cases). Other variations of stanines have been prepared, but none have become popular (Canfield, 1951; Guilford & Fruchter, 1978). Note that unlike z scores and T scores, stanines force the raw score distribution into a normal distribution, whereas changing raw scores into z scores or T scores using the above procedures does not change the shape of the distribution. Don't lose sight of the fact that all of these different scales of measurement are really equivalent to each other. Figure 2.3 gives a graphic representation of these scales.

ITEM CHARACTERISTICS

We now need to take a closer look at two aspects of test items: *item difficulty* and *item discrimination*.

Item Difficulty

The difficulty of an item is simply the percentage of persons who answer the item correctly. Note that the higher the percentage the easier the item; an item that is answered correctly by 60% of the respondents has a p (for percentage) value of .60. A difficult item that is answered correctly by only 10% has a $p = .10$ and an easy item answered correctly by 90% has a $p = .90$. Not all test items have correct answers. For example, tests of attitudes, of personality, of political opinions, etc., may present the subject with items that require agreement-disagreement, but for which there is no correct answer. Most items however, have a keyed response, a response that if endorsed is given points. On a scale of anxiety, a "yes" response to the item, "are you nervous most of the time?" might be counted as reflecting anxiety and would be the keyed response.

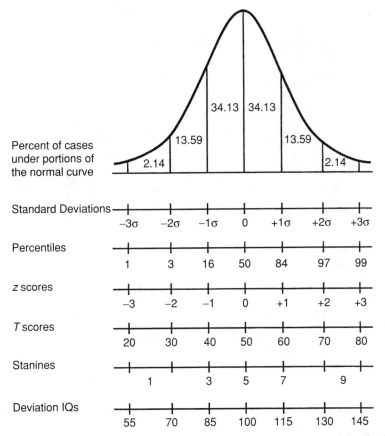

FIGURE 2–3. Relationships of different types of scores, based on the normal distribution.

If the test were measuring "calmness," then a "no" response to that item might be the keyed response. Thus item difficulty can simply represent the percentage who endorsed the keyed response.

What level difficulty? One reason we may wish to know the difficulty level of items is so we can create tests of different difficulty levels, by judicious selection of items. In general, from a psychometric point of view, tests should be of average difficulty, average being defined as $p = .50$. Note that this results in a mean score near 50%, which may seem quite a demanding standard. The reason for this is that a $p = .50$ yields the most discriminating items, items that reflect individual differences. Consider items that are either very difficult ($p = .00$) or very easy ($p = 1.00$). Psychometrically, such items are not useful because they do not reflect any differences between individuals. To the degree that different individuals give different answers, and the answers are related to some behavior, to that degree are the items useful, and thus generally the most useful items are those with p near .50.

The issue is, however, somewhat more complicated. Assume we have a test of arithmetic, with all items of $p = .50$. Children taking the test would presumably not answer randomly, so if Johnny gets item 1 correct, he is likely to get item 2 correct, and so on. If Mark misses item 1, he is likely to miss item 2, and so on. This means, at least theoretically, that one half of the children would get all the items correct and one half would get all of them incorrect, so that there would be only two raw scores, either zero or 100 – a very unsatisfactory state of affairs. One way to get around this is to choose items whose *average* value of difficulty is .50, but may in fact range widely, perhaps from .30 to .70, or similar values.

Another complicating factor concerns the target "audience" for which the test will be used.

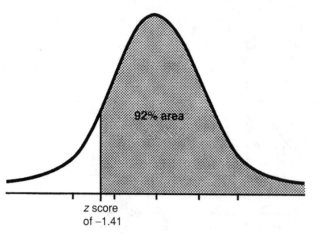

FIGURE 2–4. Example of an easy test item passed by 92% of the sample.

Let's say I develop a test to identify the brightest 10% of entering college freshmen for possible placement in an honors program. In that case, the test items should have an average $p = .10$, that is, the test should be quite difficult with the average p value reflecting the percentage of scores to be selected – in this example, 10%. Tests such as the SAT or GRE are quite demanding because their difficulty level is quite high.

Measurement of item difficulty. Item difficulty then represents a scale of measurement identical with percentage, where the average is 50% and the range goes from zero to 100%. This is of course an ordinal scale and is of limited value because statistically not much can be done with ordinal measurement. There is a way however, to change this scale to an interval scale, by changing the percent to z scores. All we need to do is have a table of normal curve frequencies (see appendix) and we can read the z scores directly from the corresponding percentage. Consider for example, a very easy item with $p = .92$, represented by Figure 2.4. Note that by convention, higher scores are placed on the right, and we assume that the 92% who got this item correct were higher scoring individuals (at least on this item). We need then to translate the percentage of the area of the curve that lies to the right (92%) into the appropriate z score, which our table tells us is equal to -1.41.

A very difficult item of $p = .21$ would yield a z score of $+0.81$ as indicated in Figure 2.5. Note that items that are easy have negative z scores, and items that are difficult have positive z scores. Again, we can change z scores to a more manageable scale of measurement that eliminates nega-

tive values and decimals. For example, ETS uses a *delta* scale with a mean of 13 and a SD = 4. Thus delta scores = $z (4) + 13$. An item with $p = .58$ would yield a z score of $-.20$ which would equal a delta score of:

$$(-.20)(4) + 13 = 12.2 \text{ (rounding off} = 12)$$

The bandwidth-fidelity dilemma. In developing a test, the test constructor chooses a set of items from a larger pool, with the choice based on rational and/or statistical reasons. Classical test theory suggests that the best test items are those with a .50 difficulty level – for example, a multiple choice item where half select the correct answer, and half the distractors. If we select all or most of the items at that one level of difficulty, we will have a very good instrument for measuring those individuals who indeed fall at that level on the trait being measured. However, for individuals who are apart from the difficulty level, the test will not be very good. For example, a person who is low on the trait will receive a low score based on the few correctly answered items; a person who is high will score high, but the test will be "easy" and again won't provide much information. In this approach, using a "peaked" conventional test (peaked because the items peak at a particular difficulty level), we will be able to measure some of the people very well and some very poorly.

We can try to get around this by using a rectangular distribution of items, that is, selecting a few items at a .10 level of difficulty, a few at .20, a few at .30 and so on to cover the whole range of difficulty, even though the average range of difficulty will still be .50. There will be items here that are appropriate for any individual no matter

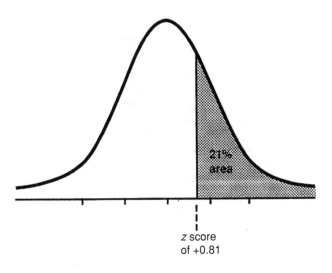

FIGURE 2–5. Example of a difficult test item passed by 21% of the sample.

where they are on the trait, but because a test cannot be too long, the appropriate items for any one person will be few. This means that the test will be able to differentiate between individuals at various levels of a trait, but the precision of these differentiations will not be very great.

A peaked conventional test can provide high fidelity (i.e., precision) where it is peaked, but little bandwidth (i.e., it does not differentiate very well individuals at other positions on the scale). Conversely, a rectangular conventional test has good bandwidth but low overall fidelity (Weiss, 1985).

Guessing. Still another complicating factor in item difficulty is that of guessing. Although individuals taking a test do not usually answer randomly, just as typically there is a fair amount of guessing going on, especially with multiple-choice items where there is a correct answer. This inflates the p value because a p value of .60 really means that among the 60% who answered the item correctly, a certain percentage answered it correctly by lucky guessing, although some will have answered it incorrectly by bad guessing (see Lord, 1952).

A number of item forms, such as multiple-choice items, can be affected by guessing. On a multiple-choice examination, with each item composed of five choices, anyone guessing blindly would, by chance alone, answer about one fifth of the items correctly. If all subjects guessed to the same degree, guessing would not be much of a problem. But subjects don't do that, so guessing can be problematic. A number of formulas or

corrections of the total score have been developed to take guessing into account, such as:

$$score = right - \frac{wrong}{k - 1}$$

where $k =$ the number of alternatives per item.

The rationale here is that the probability of a correct guess is $1/k$ and the probability of an incorrect guess is $k - 1/k$. So we expect, on the average, for a person to be correct once for every $k - 1$ times that they are incorrect. The problem is that correction formulas such as the above assume that item choices are equally plausible, and that items are of two types – those that the subject knows and answers correctly and those that the subject doesn't know, and guesses blindly.

Note that the more choices there are for each item, the less significant guessing becomes. In true-false items, guessing can result in 50% correct responses. In five-choice multiple-choice items, guessing can result in 20% correct answers, but if each item had 20 choices (an awkward state of affairs), guessing would only result in 5% correct responses.

A simpler, but not perfect, solution, is to include instructions on a test telling all candidates to do the same thing – that is, guess when unsure, leave doubtful items blank, etc. (Diamond & Evans, 1973).

Item Discrimination

If we have a test of arithmetic, each item on that test should ideally differentiate between those who know the subject matter and those who don't know. If we have a test of depression, each item should ideally differentiate between those who are depressed and those who are not. *Item discrimination* refers to the ability of an item to correctly "discriminate" between those who are higher on the variable in question and those who are lower. Note that for most variables we don't ordinarily assume a dichotomy but rather a continuous variable – that is, we don't believe that the world is populated by two types of people, depressed and nondepressed, but rather that different people can show different degrees of depression.

There are a number of ways of computing item-discrimination indices, but most are quite similar (Oosterhof, 1976) and basically involve comparing the performance of high scorers with that of low scorers, for each item. Suppose for example, we have an arithmetic test that we have administered to 100 children. For each child, we have a total raw score on the test, and a record of their performance on each item. To compute item discrimination indices for each item, we first need to decide how we will define "high scorer" vs. "low scorer."

Obviously, we could take all 100 children, compute the median of their total test scores, and label those who scored above the median as high scorers, and those below the median as low scorers. The advantage of this procedure is that we use all the data we have, all 100 protocols. The disadvantage is that at the center of the distribution there is a fair amount of "noise." Consider Sarah, who scored slightly above the median and is thus identified as a high scorer. If she were to retake the test, she might well score below the median and now be identified as a low scorer.

At the other extreme, we could take the five children who really scored high and label them high scorers and the five children who scored lowest and label them low scorers. The advantage here is that these extreme scores are not likely to change substantially on a retest; they most likely are not the result of guessing and probably represent "real-life" correspondence. The disadvantage is that now we have rather small samples, and we can't be sure that any calculations we perform are really stable. Is there a happy medium that on the one hand keeps the "noise" to a minimum and on the other maximizes the size of the sample? Years ago, Kelley (1939) showed that

Table 2–1

Test item	Upper 27	Lower 27	Index of discrimination
1	23 (85%)	6 (22%)	63%
2	24 (89%)	22 (81%)	8%
3	6 (22%)	4 (15%)	7%
4	9 (33%)	19 (70%)	−37%

the best strategy is to select the upper 27% and the lower 27%, although slight deviations from this, such as 25% or 30%, don't matter much. (Note that in the example of the rigidity scale developed by Rehfisch, he analyzed the top and bottom 25% of those rated on rigidity.)

For our sample of 100 children we would then select the top 27 scorers and call them "high scorers" and the bottom 27 and call these "low scorers." We would look at their answers for each test item and compute the difficulty level of each item, separately for each group, using percentages. The difference between difficulty levels for a particular item is the *index of discrimination* (abbreviated as D) for that item. Table 2.1 gives an example of such calculations.

Note that the index of discrimination is expressed as a percentage and is computed from two percentages. We could do the same calculations on the raw scores, in this cases the number of correct responses out of 27, but the results might differ from test to test, if the size of the sample changes.

The information obtained from such an analysis can be used to make changes in the items and improve the test. Note, for example, that item 1 seems to discriminate quite well. Most of the high scorers (85%) answered the item correctly, while far fewer of the low scorers (22%) answered the item correctly. Theoretically, a perfectly discriminating item would have a D value of 100%. Items 2 and 3 don't discriminate very well, item 2 is too easy and item 3 is too difficult. Item 4 works but in reverse! Fewer of the higher scorers got the item correctly. If this is an item where there is a correct answer, a negative D would alert us that there is something wrong with the item, that it needs to be rewritten. If this were an item from a personality test where there is no correct answer, the negative D would in fact tell us that we need to reverse the scoring.

We have chosen to define high scorer and low scorer on the basis of the total test score itself.

This may seem a bit circular, but it is in fact quite legitimate. If the test measures arithmetic knowledge, then a high scorer on arithmetic knowledge is indeed someone who scores high on the test. There is a second way, however, to define high and low scorers, or more technically to identify *extreme groups*, and that is to use a criterion that is not part of the test we are calibrating. For example, we could use teacher evaluations of the 100 children as to which ones are good in math and which ones are not. For a test of depression, we could use psychiatric diagnosis. For a personality scale of leadership, we could use peer evaluation, self-ratings, or data obtained from observations.

Does it matter whether we compute item discrimination indices based on total test scores or based on an external criterion? If we realize that such computations are not simply an exercise to fill time, but are done so we can retain those items with the highest D values, those items that work best, then which procedure we use becomes very important because different procedures result in the retention of different items. If we use the total test score as our criterion, an approach called *internal consistency*, then we will be retaining items that tend to be homogeneous, that is items that tend to correlate highly with each other. If we use an external criterion, that criterion will most likely be more complex psychologically than the total test score. For example, teachers' evaluations of being "good at math" may reflect not only math knowledge, but how likeable the child is, how physically attractive, outgoing, all-around intelligent, and so on. If we now retain those items that discriminate against such a complex criterion, we will most likely retain heterogeneous items, items that cover a wide variety of the components of our criterion. If we are committed to measuring arithmetic knowledge in as pure a fashion as possible, then we will use the total test score as our criterion. If we are interested in developing a test that will predict to the maximum degree some real-world behavior, such as teachers' recognition of a child's ability, then we will use the external criterion. Both are desirable practices and sometimes they are combined, but we should recognize that the two practices represent different philosophies of testing. Allen and Yen (1979) argue that both practices cannot be used simultaneously, that a test constructor must choose one or the other. Anastasi (1988), on the other hand, argues that both are important.

Philosophies of testing. And so once again we are faced with the notion that we have alternatives, and although the proponents of each alternative argue that theirs is *the* way, the choice comes down to personal preference and to compatible philosophy of testing. With regard to test construction, there seem to be two basic camps. One approach, that of factor analysis, believes that tests should be pure measures of the dimension being assessed. To develop such a pure measure, items are selected that statistically correlate as high as possible with each other and/or with the total test score. The result is a scale that is homogeneous, composed of items all of which presumably assess the same variable. To obtain such homogeneity, factor analysis is often used, so that the test items that are retained all center on the same dimension or factor. Tests developed this way must not correlate with other dimensions. For example, scores on a test of anxiety must not correlate with scores on a test of depression, if the two dimensions are to be measured separately. Tests developed this way are often useful for understanding a particular psychological phenomenon, but scores on the test may in fact not be highly related to behavior in the real world.

A second philosophy, that of *empiricism*, assumes that scales are developed because their primary function is to predict real-life behavior, and items are retained or eliminated depending on how well they correlate with such real-life behavior. The result is a test that is typically composed of heterogeneous items all of which share a correlation with a non test criterion, but which may not be highly correlated with each other. Such scales often correlate significantly with other scales that measure different variables, but the argument here is that, "that's the way the world is." As a group, people who are intellectually bright also tend to be competent, sociable, etc., so scales of competence may most likely correlate with measures of sociability, and so on. Such scales are often good predictors of real-life behaviors, but may sometimes leave us wondering why the items work as they do. For an interesting example of how these two philosophies can lead their proponents to entirely different views, see the reviews of the CPI in the seventh MMY (Goldberg, 1972; Walsh, 1972), and in the ninth MMY (Baucom, 1985; Eysenck, 1985).

Item response theory (IRT). The "classical" theory of testing goes back to the early 1900s when Charles Spearman developed a theoretical framework based on the simple notion that a test score was the sum of a "true" score plus random "error." Thus a person may obtain different IQs on two intelligence tests because of differing amounts of random error; the true score presumably does not vary. Reliability is in fact a way of assessing how accurately obtained scores covary with true scores.

A rather different approach known as item response theory (IRT) began in the 1950s primarily through the work of Frederic Lord and George Rasch. IRT also has a basic assumption and that is that performance on a test is a function of an unobservable proficiency variable. IRT has become an important topic, especially in educational measurement. Although it is a difficult topic that involves some rather sophisticated statistical techniques beyond the scope of this book (see Hambleton & Swaminathan, 1985; Lord, 1980), the basic idea is understandable.

The characteristics of a test item, such as item difficulty, are a function of the particular sample to whom the item was administered. A vocabulary item may, for example, be quite difficult for second graders but quite easy for college students. Thus in classical test theory, item difficulty, item discrimination, normative scores, and other aspects are all a function of the particular samples used in developing the test and generating norms; typically, a raw score is interpreted in terms of relative position within a sample, such as percentile rank or other transformation. IRT, on the other hand, focuses on a theoretical mathematical model that unites the characteristics of an item, such as item difficulty, to an underlying hypothesized dimension. Although the parameters of the theoretical model are estimated from a specific set of data, the computed item characteristics are not restricted to a specific sample. This means, in effect, that item pools can be created and then subsets of items selected to meet specific criteria – for example, a medium level of difficulty. Or subset of items can be selected for specific examinees (for a readable review of IRT see Loyd, 1988).

Basically, then, IRT is concerned with the interplay of four aspects: (1) the ability of the individual on the variable being assessed, (2) the extent to which a test item discriminates between high- and low-scoring groups, (3) the difficulty of the item, and (4) the probability that a person of low ability on that variable makes the correct response.

NORMS

No matter what philosophical preferences we have, ultimately we are faced with a raw score obtained from a test, and we need to make sense of that score. As we have seen, we can change that raw score in a number of ways, but eventually we must be able to compare that score with those obtained for a normative sample, and so we need to take a closer look at norms.

How are norms selected? Commercial companies that publish tests (for a listing of these consult the MMY) may have the financial and technical means to administer a test to large and representative groups of subjects in a variety of geographical settings. Depending on the purpose of the test, a test manual may present the scores of subjects listed separately for such variables as gender (males vs. females), school grade (e.g., fifth graders, sixth graders, etc.), time of testing (e.g., high-school seniors at the beginning of their senior year vs. high-school seniors near the end of the school year), educational level (high-school graduates, college graduates, etc.), geographical region (Northeast, Southwest, etc.) and other relevant variables or combination of variables.

Sometimes the normative groups are formed on the basis of *random sampling*, and sometimes they are formed on the basis of certain criteria, for example U.S. Census data. Thus if the census data indicate that the population is composed of different economic levels, we might wish to test a normative sample that reflects those specific percentages; this is called a *stratified sample*. More typically, especially with tests that are not commercially published, norms are made up of *samples of convenience*. An investigator developing a scale of leadership ability might get a sample of local business leaders to take the test, perhaps in return for a free lecture on "how to improve one's leadership competence," or might have a friend teaching at a graduate college of business agree to administer the test to entering students. Neither of these samples would be random, and one might argue neither would be representative. As the test finds continued use, a variety of samples would be tested by different investigators and norms would be accumulated, so that we could learn what average scores are to be expected from particular samples, and how different from each other specific samples might be. Often, despite the nonrandomness, we might find that groups do not differ all that much – that the leadership level exhibited by business people in Lincoln, Nebraska, is not all that different from that exhibited by their counterparts in San Francisco, Atlanta, or New York City.

Age norms. Often we wish to compare a person's test score with the scores obtained by a normative group of the same age. This makes sense if the variable being assessed changes with age. When we are testing children, such age norms become very important because we expect, for example, the arithmetic knowledge of a 5-year-old to be different from that of a 9-year-old. With some variables, there may be changes occurring well within a short time span, so we might need age norms based on a difference of a few months or less. With adults, age norms are typically less important because we would not expect, for example, the average 50-year-old person to know more (or less) arithmetic than the average 40-year-old. On the other hand, if we are testing college students on a measure of "social support" we would want to compare their raw scores with norms based on college students rather than on retired senior citizens.

School grade norms. At least in our culture, most children are found in school and schooling is a major activity of their lives. So tests that assess school achievement in various fields, such as reading, social studies, etc., often have norms based on school grades. If we accept the theoretical model that a school year covers 10 months, and if we accept the fiction that learning occurs evenly during those 10 months, we can develop a test where each item is assigned a score based on these assumptions. For example, if our fifth-grade reading test is composed of 20 items, each item answered correctly could be given one-half month-credit, so a child answering all items correctly would be given one school-year credit, a child answering 16 items correctly would be given eight months' credit, and so on.

Unfortunately, this practice leads to some strange interpretations of test results. Consider Maria, a fourth grader, who took a reading comprehension test. She answered correctly all of the items at the fourth grade and below, so she receives a score of 4 years. In addition however, she also answered correctly several items at the fifth-grade level, several items at the sixth-grade level, a few at the seventh-grade level, and a couple at the eighth-grade level. For all of these items, she receives an additional 2 years credit, so her final score is sixth school year. Most likely when her parents and her teacher see this score they will conclude incorrectly that Maria has the reading comprehension of a sixth grader, and that therefore she should be placed in the sixth grade, or at the very least in an accelerated reading group. In fact, Maria's performance is typical. Despite our best efforts at identifying test items that are appropriate for a specific grade level, children will exhibit *scatter*, and rarely will their performance conform to our theoretical preconceptions. The test can still be very useful in identifying Maria's strengths or weaknesses, and in providing an objective benchmark, but we need to be careful of our conclusions.

A related approach to developing grade-equivalent scores is to compute the median score for pupils tested at a particular point in time. Let's say, for example, we assess eight graders in their fourth month of school and find that their median score on the XYZ test of reading is 93. If a child is then administered the test and obtains a score of 93, that child is said to have a grade equivalent of 8.4. There is another problem with grade-equivalent scores and that is that school grades do not form an interval scale, even though the school year is approximately equal in length for any pupil. Simply consider the fact that a second grader who is one year behind his classmates in reading is substantially more "retarded" than an eighth grader who is one year behind.

Expectancy tables. Norms can be presented in a variety of ways. We can simply list the mean and SD for a normative group, or we can place the data in a table showing the raw scores and their equivalent percentiles, T scores, etc. For example,

Table 2–2

| Raw score | Equivalent percentiles | |
	Male	Female
47	99	97
46	98	95
45	98	93
44	97	90
43	96	86
42	94	81
etc.		

Table 2.2 gives some normative information, such as you might find in a test manual.

If we are using test scores to predict a particular outcome, we can incorporate that relationship into our table, and the table then becomes an *expectancy table*, showing what can be expected of a person with a particular score. Suppose, for example, we administer a test of mechanical aptitude to 500 factory workers. After 6 months we obtain for each worker supervisors' ratings indicating the quality of work. This situation is illustrated in Table 2.3. Note that there were 106 individuals who scored between 150 and 159. Of these 106.51 received ratings of excellent and 38 of above average. Assuming these are the type of workers we wish to hire, we would expect a new applicant to the company who scores between 150 and 159 to have a 89/106 or 84% chance to do well in that company. Note, on the other hand, that of the 62 individuals who scored between 60 and 69, only 1 achieved a rating of excellent, so that we would expect any new applicant with a score of 60–69 not to do well. In fact, we could calculate

what score a person would need to obtain to be hired; such a score is called the *cutoff* score.

A few additional points follow about expectancy tables. Because we need to change the frequencies into percentages, a more useful expectancy table is one where the author has already done this for us. Second, decisions based on expectancy tables will not be foolproof. After all, one of the lowest scoring persons in our example turned out to be an excellent worker. An expectancy table is based on a sample that may have been representative at the time the data was collected, but may no longer be so. For example, our fictitious company might have gotten a reputation for providing excellent benefits, and so the applicant pool may be larger and more heterogeneous. Or the economy might have changed for the worse, so that candidates who never would have thought of doing manual labor are now applying for positions. To compute an expectancy table, we need to have the scores for both variables for a normative sample, and the two sets of scores must show some degree of correlation. Once the data are obtained for any new candidate, only the test score is needed to predict what the expected performance will be. Expectancy tables need not be restricted to two variables, but may incorporate more than one variable that is related to the predicted outcome.

Relativity of norms. John, a high-school student, takes a test of mechanical aptitude and obtains a score of 107. When we compare his score with available norms, we might find that his score is at the 85th percentile when compared

Table 2–3

| Mechanical aptitude scores | Supervisors' ratings | | | | |
	Excellent	Above average	Average	Below average	Poor
150–159	51	38	16	0	1
140–149	42	23	8	3	0
130–139	20	14	7	2	1
120–129	16	9	3	0	0
110–119	0	2	4	7	8
100–109	1	0	3	12	16
90–99	1	0	0	14	19
80–89	2	1	2	23	23
70–79	0	1	0	19	26
60–69	1	0	0	30	31
Totals:	134	88	43	110	125

with the high-school sample reported in the test manual, that his score is at the 72nd percentile when compared with students at his own high school, and that his score is at the 29th percentile when compared with those applicants who have been admitted to the prestigious General Dynamics School of Automobile Training. Thus different normative groups give different meaning to a particular score, and we need to ask, "Which norm group is most meaningful?" Of course, that depends. If John is indeed aspiring to be admitted to the General Dynamics school, then that normative group is more meaningful than the more representative but "generic" sample cited in the test manual.

Local norms. There are many situations where local norms, data obtained from a local group of individuals, are more meaningful than any national norms that attempt to be representative. If decisions are to be made about an individual applicant to a particular college or a specific job, it might be better to have local norms; if career counseling is taking place, then national norms might be more useful. Local norms are desirable if we wish to compare a child's relative standing with other children in the same school or school district, and they can be especially useful when a particular district differs in language and culture from the national normative sample. How to develop local norms is described in some detail by Kamphaus and Lozano (1984), who give both general principles and a specific example.

Criterion-referenced testing. You might recall being examined for your driving license, either through a multiple choice test and/or a driving test, and being told, "Congratulations, you've passed." That decision did not involve comparing your score or performance against some norms, but rather comparing your performance against a *criterion*, a decision rule that was either explicit (you must miss less than 6 items to pass) or implicit (the examiner's judgment that you were skillful enough to obtain a driver's license).

Glaser (1963) first introduced the term *criterion-referenced* testing and since then the procedure has been widely applied, particularly in educational testing. The intent is to judge a person's performance on a test not on the basis of what others can do, but on the basis of some criterion. For example, we may define mental retardation not on the basis of a normative IQ, but whether a child of age 5 can show mastery of specific tasks such as buttoning her shirt, or following specific directions. Or we may admit a child to preschool on the basis of whether the child is toilet trained. Or we may administer a test of Spanish vocabulary and require 80% correct to register testees for Advanced Spanish.

Clearly, we must first of all be able to specify the criterion. Toilet training, mastery of elementary arithmetic, and automobile driving can all be defined fairly objectively, and generally agreed upon criteria can be more or less specified. But there are many variables, many areas of competency, where such criteria cannot be clearly specified.

Second, criteria are not usually arbitrary, but are based on real-life observation. Thus, we would not label a 5-year-old as mentally retarded if the child did not master calculus because few if any children of that age show such mastery. We would, however, expect a 5-year-old to be able to button his shirt. But that observation is in fact based upon norms; so criterion-referenced decisions can be normative decisions, often with the norms not clearly specified.

Finally, we should point out that criterion-referenced and norm-referenced refer to how the scores or test results are interpreted, rather than to the tests themselves. So Rebecca's score of 19 can be interpreted through norms or by reference to a criterion.

Criterion-referenced testing has made a substantial impact, particularly in the field of educational testing. To a certain degree, it has forced test constructors to become more sensitive to the domain being assessed, to more clearly and concretely specify the components of that domain, and to focus more on the concept of mastery of a particular domain (Carver, 1974; Shaycoft, 1979).

The term mastery is often closely associated with criterion-referenced testing, although other terms are used. Carver (1974) used the terms *psychometric* to refer to norm referenced and *edumetric* to refer to criterion referenced. He argued that the psychometric approach focuses on individual differences, and that item selection and the assessment of reliability and validity are determined by statistical procedures. The edumetric approach, on the other hand, focuses on the measurement of gain or growth of individuals, and item selection, reliability and validity, all center on the notion of gain or growth.

COMBINING TEST SCORES

Typically, a score that is obtained on a test is the result of the scoring of a set of items, with items contributing equal weight, for example 1 point each, or different weights (item #6 may be worth one point, but item #18 may be worth 3 points). Sometimes, scores from various subtests are combined into a composite score. For example, a test of intelligence such as the Wechsler Adult Intelligence Scale is composed of eleven subtests. Each of these subtests yields a score, and six of these scores are combined into a Verbal IQ, while the other five scores are combined into a Performance IQ. In addition, the Verbal IQ and the Performance IQ are combined into a Full Scale IQ. Finally, scores from different tests or sources of information may be combined into a single index. A college admissions officer may, for example, combine an applicant's GPA, scores on an entrance examination, and interview information, into a single index to decide whether the applicant should be admitted. There are thus at least three basic ways of combining scores, and the procedures by which this is accomplished are highly similar (F. G. Brown, 1976).

Combining scores using statistics. Suppose we had administered ten different tests of "knowledge of Spanish" to Sharon. One test measured vocabulary, another, knowledge of verbs, still a third, familiarity with Spanish idioms, and so on. We are not only interested in each of these ten components, but we would like to combine Sharon's ten different scores into one index that reflects "knowledge of Spanish." If the ten tests were made up of one item each, we could of course simply sum up how many of the ten items were answered correctly by Sharon. With tests that are made up of differing number of items, we cannot calculate such a sum, since each test may have a different mean and standard deviation, that is represent different scales of measurement. This would be very much like adding a person's weight in pounds to their height in inches and their blood pressure in millimeters to obtain an index of "physical functioning." Statistically, we must equate each separate measurement before we add them up. One easy way to do this, is to change the raw scores into z scores or T scores. This would make all of Sharon's ten scores equivalent psychometrically, with each z score reflecting her performance on that variable (e.g., higher on vocabulary but lower on idioms). The ten z scores could then be added together, and perhaps divided by ten.

Note that we might well wish to argue, either on theoretical or empirical grounds, that each of the ten tests should not be given equal weight, that for example, the vocabulary test is most important and should therefore be weighted twice as much. Or if we were dealing with a scale of depression, we might argue that an item dealing with suicide ideation reflects more depression than an item dealing with feeling sad, and therefore should be counted more heavily in the total score. There are a number of techniques, both statistical and logical, by which *differential weighting* can be used, as opposed to *unit weighting*, where every component is given the same scoring weight (see Wang & Stanley, 1970). Under most conditions, unit weighting seems to be as valid as methods that attempt differential weighting (F. G. Brown, 1976).

Combining scores using clinical intuition. In many applied situations, scores are combined not in a formal, statistical manner, but in an informal, intuitive, judgmental manner. A college admissions officer for example, may consider an applicant's grades, letters of recommendation, test scores, autobiographical sketch, background variables such as high school attended, and so on, and combine all of these into a decision of "admit" or "reject." A personnel manager may review an applicant's file and decide on the basis of a global evaluation, to hire the candidate. This process of "clinical intuition" and whether it is more or less valid than a statistical approach has been studied extensively (e.g., Goldberg, 1968; Holt, 1958; Meehl, 1954; 1956; 1957). Proponents of the intuitive method argue that because each person is unique, only clinical judgment can encompass that uniqueness; that clinical judgment can take into account both complex and atypical patterns (the brilliant student who flunks high school but does extremely well in medical school). Proponents of the statistical approach argue that in the long run, better predictive accuracy is obtained through statistical procedures, and that "intuition" operates inefficiently, if at all.

Multiple cutoff scores. One way to statistically combine test scores to arrive at a decision, is to use a *multiple cutoff* procedure. Let us assume we are an admissions officer at a particular college, looking at applications from prospective applicants. For each test or source of information we determine, either empirically or theoretically, a cutoff score that separates the range of scores into two categories, for example "accept" and "reject." Thus if we required our applicants to take an IQ test, we might consider an IQ of 120 as the minimum required for acceptance. If we also looked at high school GPA, we might require a minimum 86% overall for acceptance. These cutoff scores may be based on clinical judgment – "It is my opinion that students with an IQ less than 120 and high school GPA less than 86% do not do well here" – or on statistical evidence – a study of 200 incoming freshmen indicated that the flunk rate of those below the cutoff scores was 71% vs. 6% for those above the cutoff scores.

Note that using this system of multiple cutoffs, a candidate with an IQ of 200 but a GPA of 82% would not be admitted. Thus we need to ask whether superior performance on one variable can compensate for poor performance on another variable. The multiple cutoff procedure is a noncompensatory one and should be used only in such situations. For example, if we were selecting candidates for pilot training where both intelligence and visual acuity are necessary, we would not accept a very bright but blind individual.

There are a number of variations to the basic multiple cutoff procedure. For example, the decision need not be a dichotomy. We could classify our applicants as accept, reject, accept on probation, and hold for personal interview. We can also obtain the information sequentially. We might, for example, first require a college entrance admission test. Those that score above the cutoff score on that test may be required to take a second test or other procedure and may then be admitted on the basis of the second cutoff score.

Multiple regression. Another way of combining scores statistically is through the use of a multiple regression, which essentially expresses the relationship between a set of variables and a particular outcome that is being predicted. If we had only one variable, for example IQ, and are predicting GPA, we could express the relationship with a correlation coefficient, or with the equation of a straight line, namely:

$$Y = a + bX$$

where Y is the variable being predicted, in this case GPA

X is the variable we have measured, in this case IQ

b is the slope of the regression line (which tells us as X increases, by how much Y increases)

a is the intercept (that is, it reflects the difference in scores between the two scales of measurement; in this case GPA is measured on a 4-point scale while IQ has a mean of 100)

When we have a number of variables, all related statistically to the outcome, then the equation expands to:

$$Y = a + b_1 x_1 + b_2 x_2 + bx \ldots \text{etc.}$$

A nice example of a regression equation can be found in the work of Gough (1968) on a widely used personality test called the California Psychological Inventory (CPI). Gough administered the CPI to 60 airline stewardesses who had undergone flight training and had received ratings of in-flight performance (something like a final-exam grade). None of the 18 CPI scales individually correlated highly with such a rating, but a four-variable multiple regression not only correlated +.40 with the ratings of in-flight performance, but also yielded an interesting psychological portrait of the stewardesses. The equation was:

$$\text{In-flight rating} = 64.293 + .227(So) \\ -1.903(Cm) + 1.226(Ac) - .398(Ai)$$

where 64.293 is a weight that allows the two sides of the equation to be equated numerically,

So is the person's score on the Socialization scale

Cm   is the person's score on the Com-
        munality scale
Ac   is the person's score on the
        Achievement by Conformance
        scale
and *Ai*   is the person's score on the
        Achievement by Independence
        scale

Notice that each of the four variables has a number and a sign (+ or −) associated with it. To predict a person's rating of in-flight performance we would plug in the scores on the four variables, multiply each score by the appropriate weight, and sum to solve the equation. Note that in this equation, Communality is given the greatest weight, and Socialization the least, and that two scales are given positive weights (the higher the scores on the *So* and *Ac* scales, the higher the predicted in-flight ratings), and two scales are given negative weights (the higher the scores the lower the predicted in-flight rating). By its very nature, a regression equation gives differential weighting to each of the variables.

The statistics of multiple regression is a complex topic and will not be discussed here (see J. Cohen & P. Cohen, 1983; Kerlinger & Pedhazur, 1973; Pedhazur, 1982; Schroeder, Sjoquist, & Stephan, 1986), but there are a number of points that need to be mentioned.

First of all, multiple regression is a compensatory model, that is, high scores on one variable can compensate for low scores on another variable. Second, it is a *linear* model, that is, it assumes that as scores increase on one variable (for example IQ), scores will increase on the predicted variable (for example, GPA). Third, the variables that become part of the regression equation are those that have the highest correlations with the criterion *and* low correlations with the other variables in the equation. Note that in the CPI example above, there were 18 potential variables, but only 4 became part of the regression equation. Thus, additional variables will not become part of the equation even if they correlate with the criterion but do not add something unique, that is, have low or zero correlations with the other variables. In most practical cases, regression equations are made up of about two to six variables. The variables that are selected for the equation are selected on the basis of statistical

criteria, although their original inclusion in the study might have reflected clinical judgment.

Discriminant analysis. Another technique that is somewhat similar to multiple regression is that of *discriminant analysis.* In multiple regression, we place a person's scores in the equation, do the appropriate calculations, and out pops the person's predicted score on the variable of interest, such as GPA. In discriminant analysis we also use a set of variables, but this time we wish to predict group membership rather than a continuous score. Suppose for example, that there are distinct personality differences between college students whose life centers on academic pursuits (the "geeks") vs. students whose life centers on social and extracurricular activities (the "greeks"). John has applied to our university and we wish to determine whether he is more likely to be a geek or a greek. That is the aim of discriminant analysis. Once we know that two or more groups differ significantly from each other on a set of variables, we can assess an individual to determine which group that person most closely resembles. Despite the frivolous nature of the example, discriminant analysis has the potential to be a powerful tool in psychiatric diagnosis, career counseling, suicide prevention, and other areas (Tatsuoka, 1970).

SUMMARY

In this chapter we have looked at three basic issues: the construction, the administration, and the interpretation of tests. Test construction involves a wide variety of procedures, but for our purposes we can use a nine-step model to understand the process. Test items come in all shapes and forms, though some, like multiple choice, seem to be more common. Test construction is not a mere mechanical procedure, but in part involves some basic philosophical issues. A primary issue in test administration is that of establishing rapport. Once the test is administered and scored, the raw scores need to be changed into derived scores, including percentiles, standard scores, *T* scores, or stanines. Two aspects of test items are of particular interest to test constructors: item difficulty and item discrimination. Finally, we need to interpret a raw score in terms of available norms or a criterion. Scores can also be combined in a number of ways.

SUGGESTED READINGS

Dawis, R. V. (1987). Scale construction. *Journal of Counseling Psychology, 34*, 481–489.

This article discusses the design, development, and evaluation of scales for use in counseling psychology research. Most of the methods discussed in this article will be covered in later chapters, but some of the basic issues are quite relevant to this chapter.

Hase, H. D., & Goldberg, L. R. (1967). Comparative validity of different strategies of constructing personality inventory scales. *Psychological Bulletin, 67*, 231–248.

This is an old but still fascinating report. The authors identify six strategies by which personality inventory scales can be developed. From the same item pool, they constructed sets of 11 scales by each of the 6 strategies. They then compared these 66 scales with 13 criteria. Which set of scales, which type of strategy, was the best? To find the answer, check the report out!

Henderson, M., & Freeman, C. P. L. (1987). A self-rating scale for bulimia. The "BITE." *British Journal of Psychiatry, 150*, 18–24.

There is a lot of interest in eating disorders, and these authors report on the development of a 36-item scale composed of two subscales – the Symptom Subscale and the Severity scale, designed to measure binge eating. Like the study by Zimmerman and Coryell (1987) listed next, this study uses fairly typical procedures, and reflects at least some of the steps mentioned in this chapter.

Nield, A. F. (1986). Multiple-choice questions with an option to comment: Student attitudes and use. *Teaching of Psychology, 13*, 196–199.

The author reports on a study where introductory psychology students were administered multiple-choice questions with an option to explain their answers. Such items were preferred by the students and found to be less frustrating and anxiety producing.

Zimmerman, M., & Coryell, W. (1987). The Inventory to Diagnose Depression (IDD): A self-report scale to diagnose major depressive disorder. *Journal of Consulting and Clinical Psychology, 55*, 55–59.

The authors report on the development of a 22-item self-report scale to diagnose depression. The procedures and methodologies used are fairly typical and most of the article is readable, even if the reader does not have a sophisticated statistical background.

DISCUSSION QUESTIONS

1. Locate a journal article that presents the development of a new scale (e.g., Leichsenring, 1999). How does the procedure compare and contrast with that discussed in the text?

2. Select a psychological variable that is of interest to you (e.g., intelligence, depression, computer anxiety, altruism, etc.). How might you develop a direct assessment of such a variable?

3. When your instructor administers an examination in this class, the results will most likely be reported as raw scores. Would derived scores be better?

4. What are the practical implications of changing item difficulty?

5. What kind of norms would be useful for a classroom test? For a test of intelligence? For a college entrance exam?

3 Reliability and Validity

AIM This chapter introduces the concepts of reliability and of validity as the two basic properties that every measuring instrument must have. These two properties are defined and the various subtypes of each discussed. The major focus is on a logical understanding of the concepts, as well as an applied understanding through the use of various statistical approaches.

INTRODUCTION

Every measuring instrument, whether it is a yardstick or an inventory of depression, must have two properties: the instrument must yield consistent measurement, i.e., must be reliable, and the instrument must in fact measure the variable it is said to measure, i.e., must be valid. These two properties, reliability and validity, are the focus of this chapter.

RELIABILITY

Imagine that you have a rich uncle who has just returned from a cruise to an exotic country, and he has brought you as a souvenir a small ruler – not a pygmy king, but a piece of wood with markings on it. Before you decide that your imaginary uncle is a tightwad, I should tell you that the ruler is made of an extremely rare wood with an interesting property – the wood shrinks and expands randomly – not according to humidity or temperature or day of the week, but randomly. If such a ruler existed it would be an interesting conversation piece, but as a measuring instrument it would be a miserable failure. Any measuring instrument must first of all yield *consistent* measurement; the actual measurement should not change unless what we are measuring changes. Consistency or reliability does not

necessarily mean sameness. A radar gun that always indicates 80 miles per hour even when it is pointed at a stationary tree does not have reliability. Similarly, a bathroom scale that works accurately except for Wednesday mornings when the weight recorded is arbitrarily increased by three pounds, does have reliability.

Note that reliability is not a property of a test, even though we speak of the results as if it were (for example, "the test-retest reliability of the Jones Depression Inventory is .83"). Reliability really refers to the consistency of the data or the results obtained. These results can and do vary from situation to situation. Perhaps an analogy might be useful. When you buy a new automobile, you are told that you will get 28 miles per gallon. But the actual mileage will be a function of how you drive, whether you are pulling a trailer or not, how many passengers there are, whether the engine is well tuned, etc. Thus the actual mileage will be a "result" that can change as aspects of the situation change (even though we would ordinarily not expect extreme changes – even the most careful driver will not be able to decrease gas consumption to 100 miles per gallon) (see Thompson & Vacha-Haase, 2000).

True vs. error variation. What then is reliability? Consider 100 individuals of different heights.

When we measure these heights we will find variation, statistically measured by *variance* (the square of the standard deviation). Most of the variation will be "true" variation – that is, people really differ from each other in their heights. Part of the variation however, will be "error" variation, perhaps due to the carelessness of the person doing the measuring, or a momentary slouching of the person being measured, or how long the person has been standing up as opposed to lying down, and so on. Note that some of the error variation can be eliminated, and what is considered error variation in one circumstance may be a legitimate focus of study in another. For example, we may be very interested in the amount of "shrinkage" of the human body that occurs as a function of standing up for hours.

How is reliability determined? There are basically four ways: *test-retest* reliability, *alternate (or equivalent) forms* reliability, *split-half* reliability, and *interitem consistency*.

TYPES OF RELIABILITY

Test-retest reliability. You have probably experienced something like this: you take out your purse or wallet, count your money, and place the wallet back. Then you realize that something is not quite right, take the wallet out again and recount your money to see if you obtain the same result. In fact, you were determining test-retest reliability. Essentially then, *test-retest* reliability involves administering a test to a group of individuals and retesting them after a suitable interval. We now have two sets of scores for the same persons, and we compare the consistency of these two sets typically by computing a correlation coefficient. You will recall that the most common type of correlation coefficient is the Pearson product moment correlation coefficient, typically abbreviated as *r*, used when the two sets of scores are continuous and normally distributed (at least theoretically). There are other correlation coefficients used with different kinds of data, and these are briefly defined and illustrated in most introductory statistics books.

You will also recall that correlation coefficients can vary from zero, meaning that there is no relationship between one set of scores and the second set, to a plus or minus 1.00, meaning that there is a perfect relationship between one set of

scores and the second. By convention, a correlation coefficient that reflects reliability should reach the value of .70 or above for the test to be considered reliable.

The determination of test-retest reliability appears quite simple and straightforward, but there are many problems associated with it. The first has to do with the "suitable" interval before retesting. If the interval is too short, for example a couple of hours, we may obtain substantial consistency of scores, but that may be more reflective of the relative consistency of people's memories over a short interval than of the actual measurement device. If the interval is quite long, for example a couple of years, then people may have actually changed from the first testing to the second testing. If everyone in our sample had changed by the same amount, for example had grown 3 inches, that would be no problem since the consistency (John is still taller than Bill) would remain. But of course, people don't change in just about anything by the same amount, so there would be inconsistency between the first and second set of scores, and our instrument would appear to be unreliable whereas in fact it might be keeping track of such changes. Typically, changes over a relatively longer period of time are not considered in the context of reliability, but are seen as "true" changes.

Usually then, test-retest reliability is assessed over a short period of time (a few days to a few weeks or a few months), and the obtained correlation coefficient is accompanied by a description of what the time period was. In effect, test-retest reliability can be considered a measure of the stability of scores over time. Different periods of time may yield different estimates of stability. Note also that some variables, by their very nature, are more stable than others. We would not expect the heights of college students to change over a two-week period, but we would expect changes in mood, even within an hour!

Another problem is related to motivation. Taking a personality inventory might be interesting to most people, but taking it later a second time might not be so exciting. Some people in fact might become so bored or resentful as to perhaps answer randomly or carelessly the second time around. Again, since not everyone would become careless to the same degree, retest scores would change differently for different people, and therefore the proportion of error variation to true variation would become larger; hence the size of the correlation coefficient would be smaller.

There are a number of other problems with test-retest reliability. If the test measures some skill, the first administration may be perceived as a "practice" run for the second administration, but again not everyone will improve to the same degree on the second administration. If the test involves factual knowledge, such as vocabulary, some individuals might look up some words in the dictionary after the first administration and thus change their scores on the second administration, even if they didn't expect a retesting.

Alternate form reliability. A second way to measure reliability is to develop two forms of the same test, and to administer the two forms either at different times or in succession: Good experimental practice requires that to eliminate any practice or transfer effects, half of the subjects take form A followed by form B, and half take form B followed by form A. The two forms should be equivalent in all aspects – instructions, number of items, etc. – except that the items are different. This approach would do away with some of the problems mentioned above with test-retest reliability, but would not eliminate all of them.

If the two forms of the test are administered in rapid succession, any score differences from the first to the second form for a particular individual would be due to the item content, and thus reliability could be lowered due to *item sampling*, that is the fact that our measurement involves two different samples of items, even though they are supposed to be equivalent. If the two forms are administered with some time interval between them, then our reliability coefficient will reflect the variation due to both item sampling and temporal aspects.

Although it is desirable to have alternate forms of the same test to reduce cheating, to assess the effectiveness of some experimental treatment, or to maintain the security of a test (as in the case of the GRE), the major problem with alternate form reliability is that the development of an alternate form can be extremely time consuming and sometimes simply impossible to do, particularly for tests that are not commercially published. If we are developing a test to measure knowledge of arithmetic in children, there is almost an infinite number of items we can generate for an alternate form, but if we are developing a test to assess depression, the number of available items related to depression is substantially smaller.

Let's assume you have developed a 100-item, multiple-choice vocabulary test composed of items such as:

donkey = (a) feline, (b) canine, (c) aquiline, (d) asinine

You have worked for five years on the project, tried out many items, and eliminated those that were too easy or too difficult, those that showed gender differences, those that reflected a person's college major, and so on. You now have 100 items that do not show such undue influences and are told that you must show that your vocabulary test is indeed reliable. Test-retest reliability does not seem appropriate for the reasons discussed above. In effect, you must go back and spend another 5 years developing an alternate form. Even if you were willing to do so, you might find that there just are not another 100 items that are equivalent. Is there a way out? Yes, indeed there is; that is the third method of assessing reliability, known as split-half reliability.

Split-half reliability. We can administer the 100-item vocabulary test to a group of subjects, and then for each person obtain two scores, the number correct on even-numbered items and the number correct on odd-numbered items. We can then correlate the two sets of scores. In effect, we have done something that is not very different from alternate-form reliability; we are making believe that the 100-item test is really two, 50-item tests. The reliability estimate we compute will be affected by item sampling – the odd-numbered items are different from the even-numbered items, but will not be affected by temporal stability because only one administration is involved.

There is however, an important yet subtle difference between split-half reliability and test-retest. In test-retest, reliability was really a reflection of temporal stability; if what was being measured did not appreciably change over time, then our measurement was deemed consistent or reliable. In split-half reliability the focus of consistency has changed. We are no longer concerned about temporal stability, but are now concerned with *internal consistency*. Split-half reliability makes sense to the degree that each item in our vocabulary test measures the same variable, that is to the degree that a test is composed of *homogeneous* items. Consider a test to measure arithmetic where the odd-numbered items are multiplication items and the even-numbered items deal with algebraic functions. There may not be a substantial relationship between these two areas of arithmetic knowledge, and a computed correlation coefficient between scores on the two halves might be low. This case should not necessarily be taken as evidence that our test is unreliable, but rather that the split-half procedure is applicable only to homogeneous tests. A number of psychologists argue that indeed most tests should be homogeneous, but other psychologists prefer to judge tests on the basis of how well they work rather than on whether they are homogeneous or heterogeneous in composition. In psychological measurement, it is often difficult to assess whether the items that make up a scale of depression, or anxiety, or self-esteem are psychometrically consistent with each other or reflect different facets of what are rather complex and multidimensional phenomena.

There are of course many ways to split a test in half to generate two scores per subject. For our 100-item vocabulary test, we could score the first 50 items and the second 50 items. Such a split would ordinarily not be a good procedure because people tend to get more tired toward the end of a test and thus would be likely to make more errors on the second half. Also, items are often presented within a test in order of difficulty, with easy items first and difficult items later; this might result in almost everyone getting higher scores on the first half of the test and differing on the second half – a state of affairs that would result in a rather low correlation coefficient. You can probably think of more complicated ways to split a test in half, but the odd vs. even method usually works well. In fact, split-half reliability is often referred to as odd-even reliability.

Each half score represents a sample, but the computed reliability is based only on half of the items in the test, because we are in effect comparing 50 items vs. 50 items, rather than 100 items. Yet from the viewpoint of item sampling (not temporal stability), the longer the test the higher will its reliability be (Cureton, 1965; Cureton, et al., 1973). All other things being equal, a 100-item test will be more reliable than a 50-item test – going to a restaurant 10 different times will

give you a more "stable" idea of what the chef can do than only two visits. There is a formula that allows us to estimate the reliability of the entire test from a split-half administration, and it is called the *Spearman-Brown* formula:

$$\text{estimated } r = \frac{k \, (\text{obtained } r)}{1 + (k - 1)(\text{obtained } r)}$$

In the formula, k is the number of times the test is lengthened or shortened. Thus, in split-half reliability, k becomes 2 because we want to know the reliability of the entire test, a test that is twice as long as one of its halves. But the Spearman-Brown formula can be used to answer other questions as these examples indicate:

EXAMPLE 1 I have a 100-item test whose split-half reliability is .68. What is the reliability of the total test?

$$\text{estimated } r = \frac{2(.68)}{1 + (1)(.68)} = \frac{1.36}{1.68} = \boxed{.81}$$

EXAMPLE 2 I have a 60-item test whose reliability is .61; how long must the test be for its reliability to be .70? (Notice we need to solve for k.)

$$.70 = \frac{k(.61)}{1 + (k - 1)(.61)}$$

cross-multiplying we obtain:

$$k(.61) = .70 + .70(k - 1)(.61)$$
$$k(.61) = .70 + (.427)(k - 1)$$
$$k(.61) = .70 + .427k - .427$$
$$k(.183) = .273$$
$$k = \boxed{1.49}$$

the test needs to be about 1.5 times as long or about 90 items (60 × 1.5).

EXAMPLE 3 Given a 300-item test whose reliability is .96, how short can the test be to have its reliability be at least .70? (Again, we are solving for k.)

$$.70 = \frac{k(.96)}{1 + (k - 1)(.96)}$$
$$k(.96) = .70 + .70(.96)(k - 1)$$
$$k(.96) = .70 + .672(k - 1)$$
$$k(.96) = .70 + .672k - .672$$
$$k(.96) = .028 = .672k$$
$$k(.288) = 0.28$$
$$k = \boxed{.097}$$

The test can be about one tenth of this length, or 30 items long (300 × .097).

The calculations with the Spearman-Brown formula assume that when a test is shortened or lengthened, the items that are eliminated or added are all equal in reliability. In fact such is not the case, and it is quite possible to increase the reliability of a test by eliminating the least reliable items. In this context, note that reliability can be applied to an entire test or to each item.

The Rulon formula. Although the Spearman-Brown formula is probably the most often cited and used method to compute the reliability of the entire test, other equivalent methods have been devised (e.g., Guttman, 1945; Mosier, 1941; Rulon, 1939). The Rulon formula is:

$$\text{estimated } r = 1 - \frac{\text{variance of differences}}{\text{variance of total scores}}$$

For each person who has taken our test, we generate four scores: the score on the odd items; the score on the even items, a difference score (score on the odd items minus score on the even items), and a total score (odd plus even). We then compute the variance of the difference scores and the variance of the total scores to plug into the formula. Note that if the scores on the two halves were perfectly consistent, there would be no variation between the odd item score and the even item score, and so the variance of the difference scores would be zero, and therefore the estimated r would equal 1. The ratio of the two variances in fact reflects the proportion of error variance that when subtracted from 1 leaves the proportion of "true" variance, that is, the reliability.

Variability. As discussed in Chapter 2, variability of scores among individuals, that is, *individual differences,* makes statistical calculations such as the correlation coefficient possible. The item, "Are you alive as you read this?" is not a good test item because it would yield no variability – everyone presumably would give the same answer. Similarly, gender as defined by "male" or "female" yields relatively little variability, and from a psychometric point of view, gender thus defined is not a very useful measure. All other things being equal, the greater the variability in test scores the better off we are. One way to obtain such variability is to increase the range of responses.

For example, instead of just asking do you agree or disagree, we could use a five-point response scale of strongly agree, agree, undecided, disagree, strongly disagree. Another way to increase variability is to increase the number of items – a 10-item true-false scale can theoretically yield scores from 0 to 10, but a 25-item scale can yield scores from 0 to 25, and that of course is precisely the message of the Spearman-Brown formula. Still another way to increase variability is to develop test items that are neither too easy nor too difficult for the intended consumer, as we also discussed in Chapter 2. A test that is too easy would result in too many identical high scores, and a test that is too difficult would result in too many identical low scores. In either case, variability, and therefore reliability, would suffer.

Two halves = four quarters. If you followed the discussion up to now, you probably saw no logical fallacy in taking a 100-item vocabulary test and generating two, scores for each person, as if in fact you had two, 50-item tests. And indeed there is none. Could we not argue however, that in fact we have 4 tests of 25 items each, and thus we could generate four scores for each subject? After all, if we can cut a pie in two, why not in four? Indeed, why not argue that we have 10 tests of 10 items each, or 25 tests of 4 items each, or 100 tests of 1 item each! This leads us to the fourth way of determining reliability, known as *interitem consistency.*

Interitem consistency. This approach assumes that each item in a test is in fact a measure of the same variable, whatever that may be, and that we can assess the reliability of the test by assessing the consistency among items. This approach rests on two assumptions that are often not recognized even by test "experts." The first is that interitem reliability, like split-half reliability, is applicable and meaningful only to the extent that a test is made up of *homogeneous* items, items that all assess the same domain. The key word of course is "same." What constitutes the same domain? You have or will be taking an examination in this course, most likely made up of multiple-choice items. All of the items focus on your knowledge of psychological testing, but some of the items may require rote memory, others, recognition of key words, still others, the ability to reason logically, and others, perhaps the application of formulas. Do these items represent the same or different domains? We can partially answer this statistically, through *factor analysis*. But if we compute an interitem consistency reliability correlation coefficient, and the resulting r is below .70, we should not necessarily conclude that the test is unreliable.

A second assumption that lurks beneath interitem consistency is the notion that if each item were perfectly reliable, we would only obtain two test scores. For example, in our 100-item vocabulary test, you would either know the meaning of a word or you would not. If all the items are perfectly consistent, they would be perfectly related to each other, so that people taking the test would either get a perfect score or a zero. If that is the case, we would then only need 1 item rather than 100 items. In fact, in the real world items are not perfectly reliable or consistent with each other, and the result is individual differences and variability in scores. In the real world also, people do not have perfect vocabulary or no vocabulary, but differing amounts of vocabulary.

Measuring interitem consistency. How is interitem consistency measured? There are two formulas commonly used. The first is the Kuder-Richardson formula 20, sometimes abbreviated as K-R 20 (Kuder & Richardson, 1937), which is applicable to tests whose items can be scored on a dichotomous (e.g., right-wrong; true-false; yes-no) basis. The second formula is the coefficient alpha, also known as Cronbach's alpha (Cronbach, 1951), for tests whose items have responses that may be given different weights – for example, an attitude scale where the response "never" might be given 5 points, "occasionally" 4 points, etc. Both of these formulas require the data from only one administration of the test and both yield a correlation coefficient. It is sometimes recommended that Cronbach's alpha be at least .80 for a measure to be considered reliable (Carmines & Zeller, 1979). However alpha increases as the number of items increases (and also increases as the correlations among items increase), so that .80 may be too harsh of a criterion for shorter scales. (For an in-depth discussion of coefficient alpha, see Cortina, 1993).

Sources of error. The four types of reliability just discussed all stem from the notion that a test score is composed of a "true" score plus an "error" component, and that reliability reflects the relative ratio of true score variance to total or observed score variance; if reliability were perfect, the error component would be zero.

A second approach to reliability is based on *generalizability* theory, which does not assume that a person has a "true" score on intelligence, or that error is basically of one kind, but argues that different conditions may result in different scores, and that error may reflect a variety of sources (Brennan, 1983; Cronbach, Gleser, Rajaratnam, & Nanda, 1972; see Lane, Ankenmann, & Stone, 1996, for an example of generalizability theory as applied to a Mathematics test). The interest here is not only in obtaining information about the sources of error, but in systematically varying those sources and studying error experimentally. Lyman (1978) suggested five major sources of error for test scores:

1. The individual taking the test. Some individuals are more motivated than others, some are less attentive, some are more anxious, etc.

2. The influence of the examiner, especially on tests that are administered to one individual at a time. Some of these aspects might be whether the examiner is of the same race, gender, etc., as the client, whether the examiner is (or is seen as) caring, authoritarian, etc.

3. The test items themselves. Different items elicit different responses.

4. Temporal consistency. For example, intelligence is fairly stable over time, but mood may not be.

5. Situational aspects. For example, noise in the hallway might distract a person taking a test.

We can experimentally study these sources of variation and statistically measure their impact, through such procedures as analysis of variance, to determine which variables and conditions create lessen reliability. For example, whether the retest is 2 weeks later or 2 months later might result in substantial score differences on test X, but whether the administrator is male or female might result in significant variation in test scores for male subjects but not for female subjects. (See Brennan, 1983, or Shavelson, Webb, & Rowley,

1989, for a very readable overview of generalizability theory.)

Scorer reliability. Many tests can be scored in a straightforward manner: The answer is either correct or not, or specific weights are associated with specific responses, so that scoring is primarily a clerical matter. Some tests however, are fairly subjective in their scoring and require considerable judgment on the part of the scorer. Consider for example, essay tests that you might have taken in college courses. What constitutes an "A" response vs. a "B" or a "C" can be fairly arbitrary. Such tests require that they be reliable not only from one or more of the standpoints we have considered above, but also from the viewpoint of scorer reliability – would two different scorers arrive at the same score when scoring the same test protocol? The question is answered empirically; a set of test protocols is independently given to two or more scorers and the resulting two or more sets of scores are compared, usually with a correlation coefficient, or sometimes by indicating the percentage of agreement (e.g., Fleiss, 1975).

Quite often, the scorers need to be trained to score the protocols, especially with scoring sophisticated psychological techniques such as the Rorschach inkblot test, and the resulting correlation coefficient can be in part reflective of the effectiveness of the training. Note that, at least theoretically, an objectively scored test could have a very high reliability, but a subjectively scored version of the same test would be limited by the scorer reliability (for example, our 100-item vocabulary test could be changed so that subjects are asked to define each word and their definitions would be judged as correct or not). Thus, one way to improve reliability is to use test items that can be objectively scored, and that is one of several reasons why psychometricians prefer multiple-choice items to formats such as essays.

Rater reliability. Scorer reliability is also referred to as rater reliability, when we are dealing with ratings. For example, suppose that two faculty members independently read 80 applications to their graduate program and rate each application as "accept," "deny," or "get more information." Would the two faculty members agree with each other to any degree?

Chance. One of the considerations associated with scorer or rater reliability is chance. Imagine two raters observing a videotape of a therapy session, and rating the occurrence of every behavior that is reflective of anxiety. By chance alone, the observers could agree 50% of the time, so our reliability coefficient needs to take this into account: What is the actual degree of agreement over and above that due to chance? Several statistical measures have been proposed, but the one that is used most often is the *Kappa coefficient* developed by Cohen (1960; see also Hartmann, 1977). We could of course have more than two raters. For example, each application to a graduate program might be independently rated by three faculty members, but not all applications would be rated by the same three faculty. Procedures to measure rater reliability under these conditions are available (e.g., Fleiss, 1971).

Interobserver reliability. At the simplest level, we have two observers independently observing an event – e.g., did Brian hit Marla? Schematically, we can describe this situation as:

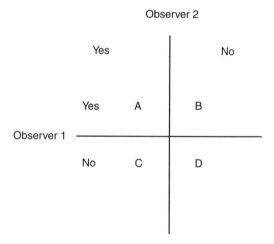

Cells A and D represent agreements, and cells B and C represent disagreements. From this simple schema some 17 different ways of measuring observer reliability have been developed, although most are fairly equivalent (A. E. House, B. J. House, & Campbell, 1981). For example, we can compute percentage agreement as:

$$\text{Percentage agreement} = \frac{A + D}{A + B + C + D} \times 100$$

From the same schema we can also compute coefficient Kappa, which is defined as:

$$\frac{Po - Pe}{1 - Pe}$$

where *Po* is the observer proportion of agreement and *Pe* is the expected or chance agreement.

To calculate Kappa, see Fleiss (1971) or Shrout, Spitzer, and Fleiss (1987).

Correction for attenuation. Reliability that is less than perfect, as it typically is, means that there is "noise in the system," much like static on a telephone line. But just as there are electronic means to remove that static, there are statistical means by which we can estimate what would happen if we had a perfectly reliable test. That procedure is called correction for attenuation and the formula is:

$$r_{\text{estimated}} = \frac{r_{12}}{\sqrt{r_{11}r_{22}}}$$

where $r_{\text{estimated}}$ is the "true" correlation between two measures if both the test and the second measure were perfectly reliable;

r_{12} is the observed correlation between the test and the second measure;

r_{11} is the reliability of the test; and

r_{22} is the reliability of the second measure.

For example, assume there is a correlation between the Smith scholastic aptitude test and grades of .40; the reliability of the Smith is .90 and that of grades is .80. The estimated true correlation between the Smith test and GPA is:

$$= \frac{.40}{(.90)(.80)} = \frac{.40}{.85} = \boxed{.47}$$

You might wonder how the reliability of GPA might be established? Ordinarily of course, we would have to assume that grades are measured without error because we cannot give grades twice or compare grades in the first three courses one takes vs. the last three courses in a semester. In that case, we would assign a 1 to r_{22} and so the formula would simplify to:

$$r_{\text{estimated}} = \frac{r_{12}}{\sqrt{r_{11}}}$$

The standard error of measurement. Knowing the reliability coefficients for a particular test gives us a picture of the stability of that test. Knowing for example, that the test-retest reliability of our 100-item vocabulary test is .92 over a 6-month period tells us that our measure is fairly stable over a medium period of time; knowing that in a sample of adults, the test-retest reliability is .89 over a 6-year period, would also tell us that vocabulary is not easily altered by differing circumstances over a rather long period of time. Notice however, that to a certain degree this approach does not focus on the individual subject. To compute reliability the test constructor simply administers the test to a group of subjects, chosen because of their appropriateness (e.g., depressed patients) or quite often because of their availability (e.g., college sophomores). Although the obtained correlation coefficient does reflect the sample upon which it is based, the psychometrician is more interested in the test than in the subjects who took the test. The professional who uses a test, however, a clinical psychologist, a personnel manager, or a teacher, is very interested in the individual, and needs therefore to assess reliability from the individual point of view. This is done by computing the *standard error of measurement (SEM)*.

Imagine the following situation. I give Susan, a 10-year-old, an intelligence test and I calculate her IQ, which turns out to be 110. I then give her a magic pill that causes amnesia for the testing, and I retest her. Because the test is not perfectly reliable, because Susan's attention might wander a bit more this second time, and because she might make one more lucky guess this time, and so on, her IQ this second time turns out to be 112. I again give her the magic pill and test her a third time, and continue doing this about 5,000 times. The distribution of 5,000 IQs that belong to Susan will differ, not by very much, but perhaps they can go from a low of 106 to a high of 118. I can compute the mean of all of these IQs and it will turn out that the mean will in fact be her "true" IQ because error deviations are assumed to cancel each other out – for every lucky guess there will be an unlucky guess. I can also calculate the variation of these 5,000 IQs by computing the standard deviation. Because this is a very special standard deviation (for one thing, it is a theoretical notion based on an impossible

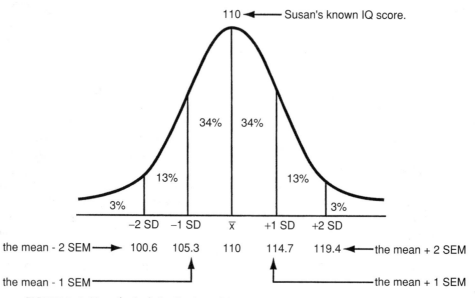

FIGURE 3–1. Hypothetical distribution of Susan's IQ scores.

example), it is given a special name: the standard error of measurement or SEM (remember that the word standard really means average). This SEM is really a standard deviation: it tells us how variable Susan's scores are.

In real life of course, I can only test Susan once or twice, and I don't know whether the obtained IQ is near her "true" IQ or is one of the extreme values. I can however, compute an estimate of the SEM by using the formula:

$$SEM = SD\sqrt{1 - r_{11}}$$

where SD   is the standard deviation of scores on the test, and

   r_{11} is the reliability coefficient.

Let's say that for the test I am using with Susan, the test manual indicates that the SD = 15 and the reliability coefficient is .90. The SEM is therefore equal to:

$$15\sqrt{(1-.90)} \text{ or } 4.7$$

How do we use this information? Remember that a basic assumption of statistics is that scores, at least theoretically, take on a normal curve distribution. We can then imagine Susan's score distribution (the 5,000 IQs if we had them) to look like the graph in Figure 3.1.

We only have one score, her IQ of 110, and we calculated that her scores would on the average deviate by 4.7 (the size of the SEM). There-

fore, we can assume that the probability of Susan's "true" IQ being between 105.3 and 114.7 is 68%, and that the probability of her "true" IQ being between 100.6 and 119.4 is 94%. Note that as the SD of scores is smaller and the reliability coefficient is higher, the SEM is smaller. For example, with an SD of 5, the

$$SEM = 5\sqrt{(1-.90)} = 1.58$$

with an SD of 5 and a reliability coefficient of .96 the

$$SEM = 5\sqrt{(1-.96)} = 1.$$

Don't let the statistical calculations make you lose sight of the logic. When we administer a test there is "noise in the system" that we call error or lack of perfect reliability. Because of this, an obtained score of 120 could actually be a 119 or a 122, or a 116 or a 125. Ordinarily we don't expect that much noise in the system (to say that Susan's IQ could be anywhere between 10 and 300 is not very useful) but in fact, most of the time, the limits of a particular score are relatively close together and are estimated by the SEM, which reflects the reliability of a test as applied to a particular individual.

The SE of differences. Suppose we gave Alicia a test of arithmetic and a test of spelling. Let's assume that both tests yield scores on the same

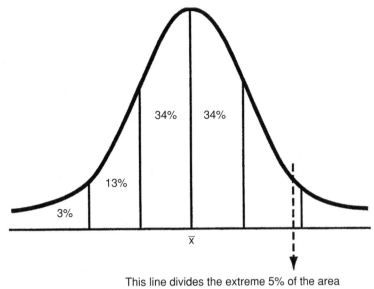

This line divides the extreme 5% of the area
from the other 95%. If our results is "extreme,"
that is, falls in that 5% area, we decide that
the two scores do indeed differ from each other.

FIGURE 3–2. Normal curve distribution.

numerical scale – for example, an average of 100 and a SD of 10 – and that Alicia obtains a score of 108 on arithmetic and 112 on spelling. Can we conclude that she did better on the spelling test? Because there is "noise" (that is, unreliability) on both tests, that 108 on arithmetic could be 110, and that 112 on spelling could be 109, in which case we would not conclude that she did better on spelling. How can we compare her two scores from a reliability framework? The answer again lies in the standard error, this time called the *standard error of differences, SED.* Don't lose sight of the fact that the SE is really a SD telling us by how much the scores deviate on the average.

The formula for the SED is:

$$SED = \sqrt{(SEM)_1^2 + (SEM)_2^2}$$

which turns out to be equal to

$$SED = SD\sqrt{2 - r_{11} - r_{22}}$$

where   the first SEM and the first r refer to the
first test
and the second SEM and the second r
refer to the second test
and SD = the standard deviation (which
is the same for both tests).

Suppose for example, that the two tests Alicia took both have a SD of 10, and the reliability of the arithmetic test is .95 and that of the spelling test is .88. The SED would equal:

$$10\sqrt{2 - .95 - .88} \text{ or } 4.1.$$

We would accept Alicia's two scores as being different, if the probability of getting such a difference by chance alone is 5 or fewer times out of 100, i.e., $p < .05$. You will recall that such a probability can be mapped out on the normal curve to yield a z score of +1.96. We would therefore take the SED of 4.1 and multiply it by 1.96 to yield approximately 8, and would conclude that Alicia's two scores are different only if they differ by at least 8 points; in the example above they do not, and therefore we cannot conclude that she did better on one test than the other (see Figure 3.2).

Reliability of difference scores. Note that in the above section we focused on the difference between two scores. Quite often the clinical psychologist, the school or educational psychologist, or even a researcher, might be more interested in the relationship of pairs of scores rather than individual single scores; we might for example be interested in relating discrepancies between verbal and nonverbal intelligence to evidence of possible brain damage, and so we must inquire into the reliability of difference scores. Such reliability is not the sum of the reliability of the two scores taken separately because the difference score is not only affected by the errors of measurement of each test, but is also distinguished by the fact that whatever is common to both measures is canceled out in the difference score – after all, we are looking at the difference. Thus the formula for the reliability of difference scores is:

$$r_{\text{difference}} = \frac{\frac{1}{2}(r_{11} + r_{22}) - r_{12}}{1 - r_{12}}$$

For example, if the reliability of test A is .75 and that of test B is .90, and the correlation between the two tests is .50 then

$$r_{\text{difference}} = \frac{\frac{1}{2}(.75 + .90) - .50}{1 - .50} = \frac{.325}{.50} = \boxed{.65}$$

In general, when the correlation between two tests begins to approach the average of their separate reliability coefficients, the reliability of the difference score lowers rapidly. For example, if the reliability of test A is .70, that of test B is also .70, and the correlation between the two tests is .65, then

$$r_{\text{difference}} = \frac{\frac{1}{2}(.70 + .70) - .65}{1 - .65} = \frac{.05}{.35} = \boxed{.14}$$

The point here is that we need to be very careful when we make decisions based on difference scores. We should also reiterate that to compare the difference between two scores from two different tests, we need to make sure that the two scores are on the same scale of measurement; if they are not, we can of course change them to z scores, T scores, or some other scale.

Special circumstances. There are at least two categories of tests where the determination of reliability requires somewhat more careful thinking. The first of these are speeded tests where different scores reflect different rates of responding. Consider for example a page of text where the task is to cross out all the letters "e" with a time limit of 40 seconds. A person's score will simply reflect how fast that person responded to the task. Both test-retest and equivalent forms reliability are applicable to speeded tests, but split-half and internal consistency are not, unless the split is based on time rather than number of items.

A second category of tests, requiring special techniques, are criterion-referenced tests, where performance is interpreted not in terms of norms but in terms of a pass-fail type of decision (think of an automobile driving test where you are either awarded a license or not). Special techniques have been developed for such tests (e.g., Berk, 1984).

VALIDITY

Consider the following: Using a tape measure, measure the circumference of your head and multiple the resulting number by 6.93. To this, add three times the number of fingers on your left hand, and six times the number of eyeballs that you have. The resulting number will be your IQ. When I ask students in my class to do this, most stare at me in disbelief, either wondering what the point of this silly exercise is, or whether I have finally reached full senility! The point, of course, is that such a procedure is extremely reliable, assuming your head doesn't shrink or expand, and that you don't lose any body parts between test and retest. But reliability is not sufficient.

Once we have established that a test is reliable, we must show that it is also *valid*, that it measures what it is intended to measure. Does a test of knowledge of arithmetic really measure that knowledge, or does it measure the ability to follow directions, to read, to be a good guesser, or general intelligence? Whether a test is or is not valid depends in part on the specific purpose for which it is used. A test of knowledge of arithmetic may measure such knowledge in fifth graders, but not in college students. Thus validity is not a matter of "is this test valid or not" but is the test valid for this particular purpose, in this particular situation, with these particular subjects. A test of academic aptitude may be predictive of performance at a large state university but not at a community college. From a classical point of view, there are three major categories of validity, and these are called content validity, criterion validity, and construct validity. The division of validity into various parts has been objected to by many (e.g., Cronbach, 1980; Guion, 1980; Messick, 1975; Tenopyr, 1977). As Tenopyr and Oeltjen (1982) stated, it is difficult to imagine a measurement situation that does not involve all aspects of validity. Although these will be presented as separate categories, they really are not; validity is best thought of as a unitary process with somewhat different but related facets (Cronbach, 1988). Messick (1989) defines validity as an integrated evaluative judgment of the adequacy and appropriateness of interpretations and actions based on the assessment measure.

Content Validity

Content validity refers to the question of whether the test adequately covers the dimension to be measured and is particularly relevant to achievement tests. The answer to this question lies less in statistical analyses and more in logical and rational analyses of the test content and in fact is not considered "true" validity by some (e.g., Guion, 1977; Messick, 1989). Messick (1989) considers content validity to have two aspects: content representativeness and content relevance. Thus items from a domain not only have to represent that domain but also have to be relevant to that domain.

When a test is constructed, content validity is often built in by a concentrated effort to make sure that the sample of behavior, that is the test, is truly representative of the domain being assessed. Such an effort requires first of all a thorough knowledge of the domain. If you are developing a test of depression, you must be very familiar with depression and know whether depression includes affect, sleep disturbances, loss of appetite, restricted interest in various activities, lowered self-esteem, and so on. Often teams of experts participate in the construction of a test, by generating and/or judging test items so that the end result is the product of many individuals. How many such experts should be used and how is their agreement quantified are issues for which no uniformly accepted guidelines exist. For some suggestions on quantifying content validity, see Lynn (1986); for a thorough analysis of content validity, see Hayes, Richard, and Kubany (1995).

Evaluating content validity is carried out by either subjective or empirical methods. Subjective methods typically involve asking experts to judge the relevance and representativeness of the test items with regard to the domain being assessed (e.g., Hambleton, 1984). Empirical methods involve factor analysis or other advanced statistical procedures designed to show that the obtained factors or dimensions correspond to the content domain (e.g., Davison, 1985).

Not only should the test adequately cover the contents of the domain being measured, but decisions must also be made about the relative representation of specific aspects. Consider a test in this class that will cover the first five chapters. Should there be an equal number of questions from each chapter, or should certain chapters be given greater preeminence? Certainly, some aspects are easier to test, particularly in a multiple-choice format. But would such an emphasis reflect "laziness" on the part of the instructor, rather than a well thought out plan designed to help build a valid test? As you see, the issue of content validity is one whose answer lies partly in expert skill and partly in individual preference. Messick (1989) suggests that content validity be discussed in terms of content relevance and content coverage rather than as a category of validity, but his suggestion has not been widely accepted as yet.

Taxonomies. Achieving content validity can be helped by having a careful plan of test construction, much like a blueprint is necessary to construct a house. Such plans take many forms, and one popular in education is based on a taxonomy of educational objectives (B. Bloom, 1956). Bloom and his colleagues have categorized and defined various educational objectives – for example, recognizing vocabulary, identifying concepts, and applying general principles to new situations. A test constructor would first develop a twofold table, listing such objectives on the left-hand side, and topics across the top – for example, for an arithmetic test such topics might be multiplication, division, etc. For each cell formed by the intersection of any two categories the test constructor decides how many test items will be written. If the total test items is to be 100, the test constructor might decide to have 5 multiplication items that assess rote memory, and two items that assess applying multiplicative strategies to new situations. Such decisions might be based on the relative importance of each cell, might reflect the judgment of experts, or might be a fairly subjective decision.

Such taxonomies or blueprints are used widely in educational tests, sometimes quite explicitly, and sometimes rather informally. They are rarely used to construct tests in other domains, such as personality, although I would strongly argue that such planning would be quite useful and appropriate.

Criterion Validity

If a test is said to measure intelligence, we must show that scores on the test parallel or are highly correlated to intelligence as measured in some other way – that is, a *criterion* of intelligence. That of course is easier said than done. Think about intelligence. What would be an acceptable measure of intelligence? GPA? Extent of one's vocabulary? Amount of yearly income? Reputation among one's peers? Self-perception? Each of these could be argued for and certainly argued against. What if we were trying to develop a test of ego-strength? Where would we find a criterion measure of ego-strength in the real world? In essence, a test can never be better than the criterion it is matched against, and the world simply does not provide us with clear, unambiguous criteria. (If it did, it would probably be a very dull place!)

Criteria. The assessment of criterion validity is in fact quite common, and the literature is replete with studies that attempt to match test scores with independent criteria. There are all sorts of criteria just as there are all sorts of tests, but some types of criteria seem to be used more frequently. One such criteria is that of *contrasted groups,* groups that differ significantly on the particular domain.

For example, in validating an academic achievement test we could administer the test to two groups of college students, matched on relevant variables such as age and gender, but differing on grade point average, such as honors students vs. those on academic probation.

Another common class of criteria are those reflecting academic achievement, such as GPA, being on a Dean's Honors List, and so on. Still other criteria involve psychiatric diagnosis, personnel ratings, and quite commonly, other previously developed tests.

Predictive and concurrent validity. In establishing criterion validity, we administer the test to a group of individuals and we compare their test scores to a criterion measure, to a standard, that reflects the particular variable we are interested in. Let's assume we have a scholastic aptitude test (such as the SAT) that we wish to validate to then predict grade point average. Ideally, we would administer the test to an unselected sample, let them all enter college, wait for 5 years, measure what each student's cumulative GPA is, and correlate the test scores with the GPA. This would be *predictive* validity. In real life we would have a difficult time finding an unselected sample, convincing school officials to admit all of them, and waiting 4 or 5 years. Typically, we would have a more homogeneous group of candidates, some of whom would not be accepted into college, and we might not wish or be able to wait any longer than a semester to collect GPA information.

Under other circumstances, it might make sense to collect both the test scores and the criterion data at the same time. For example, we might obtain the cooperation of a mechanics' institute, where all the students can be administered a mechanical aptitude test and have instructors independently rate each student on their mechanical aptitude. This would be *concurrent* validity because both the test scores and the criterion scores are collected concurrently. The main purpose of such concurrent validation would be to develop a test as a substitute for a more time-consuming or expensive assessment procedure, such as the use of instructors' ratings based on several months' observation.

We would need to be very careful with both predictive and concurrent validity that the criterion, such as the instructors' ratings is independent of the test results. For example, we would not want the faculty to know the test results of students before grades are assigned because such knowledge might influence the grade; this is called *criterion contamination* and can affect the validity of results.

Construct Validity

Most if not all of the variables that are of interest to psychologists do not exist in the same sense that a pound of coffee exists. After all, you cannot buy a pound of intelligence, nor does the superego have an anatomical location like a kidney. These variables are "constructs," theoretical fictions that encapsulate a number of specific behaviors, which are useful in our thinking about those behaviors. In studying these constructs, we typically translate them into specific operations, namely tests. Thus the theoretical construct of intelligence is translated or operationalized into a specific test of intelligence. When we validate a test, we are in effect validating the construct, and in fact quite often our professional interest is not so much on the test but on the construct itself. Tests are tools, and a psychologist or other professional is like a cabinetmaker, typically more interested in the eventual product that the tools can help create. He or she knows that poor tools will not result in a fine piece of furniture.

Construct validity is an umbrella term that encompasses any information about a particular test; both content and criterion validity can be subsumed under this broad term. What makes construct validity different is that the validity information obtained must occur within a theoretical framework. If we wish to validate a test of intelligence, we must be able to specify in a theoretical manner what intelligence is, and we must be able to hypothesize specific outcomes. For example, our theory of intelligence might include the notion that any gender differences reflect only cultural "artifacts" of child rearing; we would then experiment to see whether gender differences on our test do in fact occur, and whether they "disappear" when child rearing is somehow controlled. Note that construct validation becomes a rather complex and never-ending process, and one that requires asking whether the test is, in fact, an accurate reflection of the underlying construct. If it is not, then showing that the test is not valid does not necessarily invalidate the theory. Although construct validity subsumes criterion validity, it is not simply the sum of a bunch of criterion studies. Construct validity of a test must be assessed "holistically" in relation to the theoretical framework that gave birth to the test. Some argue that only construct validity will yield meaningful instruments (Loevinger, 1957; for a rather different point of view see Bechtoldt, 1959). In assessing construct validity, we then look for the correspondence between the theory and the observed data. Such correspondence is sometimes called *pattern matching* (Trochim, 1985; for an example see Marquart, 1989).

Messick (1995) argues that validity is not a property of the test but rather of the meaning of the test scores. Test scores are a function of at least three aspects: the test items, the person responding, and the context in which the testing takes place. The focus is on the meaning or interpretation of the score, and ultimately on construct validity that involves both score meaning and social consequences. (For an interesting commentary on construct validity see Zimiles, 1996.) Thus, although we speak of validity as a property of a test, validity actually refers to the inference that is made from the test scores (Lawshe, 1985). When a person is administered a test, the result is a sample of that person's behavior. From that sample we infer something – for example, we infer how well the person will perform on a future task (predictive or criterion validity), on whether the person possesses certain knowledge (content validity), or a psychological construct or characteristic related to an outcome, such as spatial intelligence related to being an engineer (construct validity).

Both content validity and criterion validity can be conceptualized as special cases of construct validity. Given this, these different approaches should lead to consistent conclusions. Note however, that the two approaches of content and criterion validity ask different questions. Content validity involves the extent to which items represent the content domain. Thus we might agree that the item "how much is $5 + 3$" represents basic arithmetical knowledge that a fifth grader ought to have. Criterion validity, on the other hand, essentially focuses on the difference between contrasted groups such as high and low performers. Thus, under content validity, an item need not show variation of response (i.e., variance) among the testees, but under criterion validity it must. It is then not surprising that the two approaches do not correlate significantly in some instances (e.g., Carrier, DaLessio, & Brown, 1990).

Methods for assessing construct validity. Cronbach and Meehl (1955) suggested five major methods for assessing construct validity, although many more are used. One such method is the study of *group differences.* Depending upon our particular theoretical framework we might hypothesize gender differences, differences between psychiatric patients and "normals," between members of different political parties, between Christians and agnostics, and so on.

A second method involves the statistical notion of *correlation* and its derivative of *factor analysis*, a statistical procedure designed to elucidate the basic dimensions of a data set. (For an overview of the relationship between construct validity and factor analysis see B. Thompson & Daniel, 1996.) Again, depending on our theory, we might expect a particular test to show significant correlations with some measures and not with others (see below on convergent and discriminant validity).

A third method is the study of the *internal consistency* of the test. Here we typically try to determine whether all of the items in a test are indeed assessing the particular variable, or whether performance on a test might be affected by some other variable. For example, a test of arithmetic would involve reading the directions as well as the problems themselves, so we would want to be sure that performance on the test reflects arithmetic knowledge rather than reading skills.

A fourth method, as strange as it may sound, involves test-retest reliability, or more generally, *studies of change over occasions*. For example, is there change in test scores over time, say 2 days vs. 4 weeks? Or is there change in test scores if the examiner changes, say a white examiner vs. a black examiner? The focus here is on discovering systematic changes through experimentation, changes that again are related to the theoretical framework (note the high degree of similarity to our discussion of generalizability theory).

Finally, there are *studies of process*. Often when we give tests we are concerned about the outcome, about the score, and we forget that the process – how the person went about solving each item – is also quite important. This last method, then, focuses on looking at the process, observing *how* subjects perform on a test, rather than just *what*.

Convergent and discriminant validity. D. P. Campbell and Fiske (1959) and D. P. Campbell (1960) proposed that to show construct validity, one must show that a particular test correlates highly with variables, which on the basis of theory, it ought to correlate with; they called this *convergent validity*. They also argued that a test should not correlate significantly with variables that it ought not to correlate with, and called this *discriminant validity*. They then proposed

an experimental design called the *multitrait-multimethod matrix* to assess both convergent and discriminant validity. Despite what may seem confusing terminology, the experimental design is quite simple, its intent being to measure the variation due to the trait of interest, compared with the variation due to the method of testing used.

Suppose we have a true-false inventory of depression that we wish to validate. We need first of all to find a second measure of depression that does not use a true-false or similar format – perhaps a physiological measure or a 10-point psychiatric diagnostic scale. Next, we need to find a different dimension than depression, which our theory suggests should not correlate but might be confused with depression, for example, anxiety. We now locate two measures of anxiety that use the same format as our two measures of depression. We administer all four tests to a group of subjects and correlate every measure with every other measure. To show convergent validity, we would expect our two measures of depression to correlate highly with each other (same trait but different methods). To show discriminant validity we would expect our true-false measure of depression not to correlate significantly with the true-false measure of anxiety (different traits but same method). Thus the relationship within a trait, regardless of method, should be higher than the relationship across traits. If it is not, it may well be that test scores reflect the method more than anything else. (For a more recent discussion of the multitrait-multimethod approach, see Ferketich, Figueredo, & Knapp, 1991; and Lowe & Ryan-Wenger, 1992; for examples of multitrait-multimethod research studies, see Morey & LeVine, 1988; Saylor et al., 1984.) Other more sophisticated procedures have now been proposed, such as the use of confirmatory factor analysis (D. A. Cole, 1987).

Other Aspects

Face validity. Sometimes we speak of *face validity*, which is not validity in the technical sense, but refers to whether a test "looks like" it is measuring the pertinent variable. We expect, for example, a test of intelligence to have us define words and solve problems, rather than to ask us questions about our musical and food preferences. A test may have a great deal of face validity yet may not in fact be valid. Conversely, a test may lack face validity but in reality be a valid measure of a particular variable. Clearly, face validity is related to client rapport and cooperation, because ordinarily, a test that looks valid will be considered by the client more appropriate and therefore taken more seriously than one that does not. There are occasions, however, where face validity may not be desirable, for example, in a test to detect "honesty" (see Nevo, 1985, for a review).

Differential validity. Lesser (1959) argued that we should not consider a test as valid or invalid in a general sense, that studies sometimes obtain different results with the same test not necessarily because the test is invalid, but because there is *differential* validity in different populations, and that such differential validity is in fact a predictable phenomenon.

Meta-analysis. Meta-analysis consists of a number of statistical analyses designed to empirically assess the findings from various studies on the same topic. In the past, this was done by a narrative literature review where the reviewer attempted to logically assess the state of a particular question or area of research.

For an example of a meta-analysis on the Beck Depression Inventory, see Yin and Fan (2000).

Validity generalization. Another approach is that of validity generalization, where correlation coefficients across studies are combined and statistically corrected for such aspects as unreliability, sampling error, and restriction in range (Schmidt & Hunter, 1977).

ASPECTS OF VALIDITY

Bandwidth fidelity. Cronbach and Gleser (1965) used the term *bandwidth* to refer to the range of applicability of a test – tests that cover a wide area of functioning such as the MMPI are broad-band tests; tests that cover a narrower area, such as a measure of depression, are narrow-band tests. These authors also used the term *fidelity* to refer to the thoroughness of the test. These two aspects interact with each other, so that given a specific amount (such as test items) as bandwidth increases, fidelity decreases.

Thus, with the 500+ items of the MMPI, we can assess a broad array of psychopathology, but none in any depth. If we had 500+ items all focused on depression, we would have a more precise instrument, i.e., greater fidelity, but we would only be covering one area.

Group homogeneity. If we look at various measures designed to predict academic achievement, such as achievement tests used in the primary grades, those used in high school, the SAT used for college admissions, and the GRE (Graduate Record Examination) used for graduate school admissions, we find that the validity coefficients are generally greater at the younger ages; there is a greater correlation between test scores and high-school grades than there is between test scores and graduate-school grades. Why? Again, lots of reasons of course, but many of these reasons are related to the notion that variability is lessened. For example, grades in graduate school show much less variability than those in high school because often only As and Bs are awarded in graduate seminars. Similarly, those who apply and are admitted to graduate school are more homogeneous (similar in intelligence, motivation to complete their degrees, intellectual interests, etc.) as a group than high-school students. All other things being equal, homogeneity results in a lowered correlation between test scores and criterion.

One practical implication of this is that when we validate a test, we should validate it on unselected samples, but in fact they may be difficult or impossible to obtain. This means that a test that shows a significant correlation with college grades in a sample of college students may work even better in a sample of high-school students applying to college.

Cross-validation. In validating a test, we collect information on how the test works in a particular sample or situation. If we have data on several samples that are similar, we would typically call this "validity generalization." However, if we make some decision based on our findings – for example, we will accept into our university any students whose combined SAT scores are above 1200 – and we test this decision out on a second sample, that is called *cross-validation*. Thus cross-validation is not simply collecting data on a second sample, but involves taking a second look at a particular decision rule.

Are reliability and validity related? We have discussed reliability and validity separately because logically they are. They are however also related. In the multitrait-multimethod approach, for example, our two measures of depression differ in their method, and so this is considered to be validity. What if the two forms did not differ in method? They would of course be parallel forms and their relationship would be considered reliability. We have also seen that both internal consistency and test-retest reliability can be seen from both a reliability framework or from a validity framework.

Another way that reliability and validity are related is that a test cannot be valid if it is not reliable. In fact, the maximum validity coefficient between two variables is equal to:

$$\sqrt{r_{11}r_{22}},$$

where r_{11} again represents the reliability coefficient of the first variable (for example, a test) and r_{22} the reliability coefficient of the second variable (for example, a criterion). If a test we are trying to validate has, for example, a reliability of .70 and the criterion has a reliability of .50, then the maximum validity coefficient we can obtain is .59. (Note, of course, that this is the same formula we used for the correction for attenuation.)

Interpreting a validity coefficient. Much of the evidence for the validity of a test will take the form of correlation coefficients, although of course other statistical procedures are used. When we discussed reliability, we said that it is generally agreed that for a test to be considered reliable, its reliability correlation coefficient should be at least .70. In validity, there is no such accepted standard. In general, validity coefficients are significantly lower because we do not expect substantial correlations between tests and complex real-life criteria. For example, academic grades are in part a function of intelligence or academic achievement, but they can also reflect motivation, interest in a topic, physical health, whether a person is in love or out of love, etc.

Whether a particular validity correlation coefficient is statistically significant, of sufficient magnitude to indicate that most likely there is a relationship between the two variables, depends in part upon the size of the sample on which it is based. But statistical significance may not be equivalent to practical significance. A test may correlate significantly with a criterion, but the significance may reflect a very large sample, rather than practical validity. On the other hand, a test of low validity may be useful if the alternative ways of reaching a decision are less valid or not available.

One useful way to interpret a validity coefficient is to square its value and take the resulting number as an index of the overlap between the test and the criterion. Let's assume for example, that there is a correlation of about .40 between SAT (a test designed to measure "scholastic aptitude") scores and college GPA. Why do different people obtain different scores on the SAT? Lots of reasons, of course – differences in motivation, interest, test sophistication, lack of sleep, anxiety, and so on – but presumably the major source of variation is "scholastic aptitude." Why do different people obtain different grades? Again, lots of different reasons, but if there is an r of .40 between SAT and GPA, then .40 squared equals .16; that is, 16% of the variation in grades will be due to (or explained by) differences in scholastic aptitude. In this case, that leaves 84% of the variation in grades to be "explained" by other variables. Even though an r of .40 looks rather large, and is indeed quite acceptable as a validity coefficient, its explanatory power (16%) is rather low – but this is a reflection of the complexity of the world, rather than a limitation of our tests.

Prediction. A second way to interpret a validity correlation coefficient is to recall that where there is a correlation the implication is that scores on the criterion can be predicted, to some degree, by scores on the test. The purpose of administering a test such as the SAT is to make an informed judgment about whether a high-school senior can do college work, and to predict what that person's GPA will be. Such a prediction can be made by realizing that a correlation coefficient is simply an index of the relationship between two variables, a relationship that can be expressed by the equation $Y = bX + a$, where Y might be the GPA we wish to predict, X is the person's SAT score and b and a reflect other aspects of our data (we discussed the use of such equations in Chapter 2).

Cumulative GPA

Combined SAT Score	3.5 and above	2.5 to 3.49	2.49 and below	Total
1400 and above	18	4	3	= (25)
1000 to 1399	6	28	11	= (45)
999 and below	2	16	12	= (30)

FIGURE 3–3. Example of an expectancy table.

Expectancy table. Still, a third way to interpret a validity correlation is through the use of an *expectancy* table (see Chapter 2). Suppose we have administered the SAT to a group of 100 students entering a university, and after 4 years of college work we compute their cumulative GPA. We table the data as shown in Figure 3.3.

What this table shows is that 18 of the 25 students (or 72%) who obtained combined SAT scores of 1,400 and above obtained a cumulative GPA of 3.5 or above, whereas only 6 of the 45 students (13%) who scored between 1,000 to 1,399 did such superior work, and only 2 of the 12 (16%) who scored 999 and below. If a new student with SAT scores of 1,600 applied for admission, our expectancy table would suggest that indeed the new student should be admitted.

This example is of course fictitious but illustrative. Ordinarily our expectancy table would have more categories, both for the test and the criterion. Note that although the correlation is based on the entire sample, our decision about a new individual would be based on just those cases that fall in a particular cell. If the number of cases in a cell is rather small (for example, the two individuals who scored below 999 but had a GPA of 3.5 and above), then we need to be careful about how confident we can be in our decision. Expectancy tables can be more complex and include more than two variables – for example, if gender or type of high school attended were related to SAT scores and GPA, we could include these variables into our table, or create separate tables.

Standard error of estimate. Still another way to interpret a validity coefficient is by recourse to the standard error. In talking about reliability, we talked about "noise in the system," that is lack of perfect reliability. Similarly with validity we

ordinarily have a test that has less than perfect validity, and so when we use that test score to predict a criterion score, our predicted score will have a margin of error. That margin of error can be defined as the SE of estimate which equals:

$$SD\sqrt{1 - r_{12}^2}$$

where SD is the standard deviation of the criterion scores and r_{12} is the validity coefficient. Note that if the test had perfect validity, that is $r_{12} = 1.00$, then the SE of estimate is zero; there would be no error, and what we predicted as a criterion score would indeed be correct. At the other extreme, if the test were not valid, that is $r_{12} = $ zero, then the SE of estimate would equal the SD, that is, what we predicted as a criterion score could vary by plus or minus a SD 68% of the time. This would be akin to simply guessing what somebody's criterion score might be.

Decision theory. From the above discussion of validity, it becomes evident that often the usefulness of a test can be measured by how well the test predicts the criterion. Does the SAT predict academic achievement? Can a test of depression predict potential suicide attempts? Can a measure of leadership identify executives who will exercise that leadership? Note that in validating a test we both administer the test and collect information on the criterion. Once we have shown that the test is valid for a particular purpose, we can then use the test to predict the criterion. Because no test has perfect validity, our predictions will have errors.

Consider the following example. Students entering a particular college are given a medical test (an injection) to determine whether or not they have tuberculosis. If they have TB, the test results will be positive (a red welt will form);

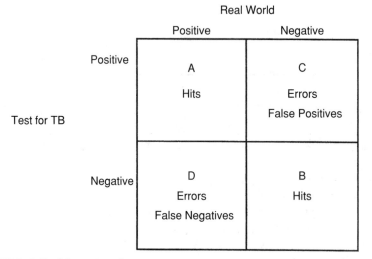

FIGURE 3–4. Decision categories.

if they don't, the test results will be negative (no welt). The test, however, does not have perfect validity, and the test results do not fully correspond to the real world. Just as there are two possible outcomes with the test (positive or negative), there are two possibilities in the real world: either the person has or does not have TB. Looking at the test and at the world simultaneously yields four categories, as shown in Figure 3.4.

Category A consists of individuals who on the test are positive for TB and indeed do have TB. These individuals, from a psychometric point of view, are considered "hits" – the decision based on the test matches the real world. Similarly, category B consists of individuals for whom the test results indicate that the person does not have (is negative for) TB, and indeed they do not have TB – another category that represents "hits." There are, however, two types of errors. Category C consists of individuals for whom the test results suggest that they are positive for TB, but they do not have TB; these are called *false positives.* Category D consists of individuals for whom the test results are negative. They do not appear to have TB but in fact they do; thus they are *false negatives.*

We have used a medical example because the terminology comes from medicine, and it is important to recognize that medically to be "positive" on a test is not a good state of affairs. Let's turn now to a more psychological example and use the SAT to predict whether a student will pass or fail in college. Let's assume that for sev-

eral years we have collected information at our particular college on SAT scores and subsequent passing or failing. Assuming that we find a correlation between these two variables, we can set up a decision table like the one in Figure 3.5.

Again we have four categories. Students in cell A are those for whom we predict failure based on their low SAT scores, and if they were admitted, they would fail. Category B consists of students for whom we predict success, are admitted, and do well academically. Both categories A and B are hits. Again, we have two types of errors: the false positives of category C for whom we predicted failure, but would have passed had they been admitted, and the false negatives of category D for whom we predicted success, but indeed once admitted, they failed.

Sensitivity, specificity, and predictive value. The relative frequencies of the four categories lead to three terms that are sometimes used in the literature in connection with tests (Galen & Gambino, 1975). The *sensitivity* of a test is the proportion of correctly identified positives (i.e., how accurately does a test classify a person who has a particular disorder?), that is, true positives, and is defined as:

Sensitivity
$$= \frac{\text{true positives}}{\text{true positives} + \text{false negatives}} \times 100$$

In the diagram of Figure 3.4, this ratio equals A/A + D.

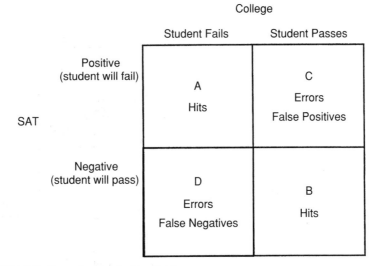

FIGURE 3–5. Example of a decision table.

The *specificity* of a test is the proportion of correctly identified negatives, (i.e., how accurately does a test classify those who do NOT have the particular condition?), that is, true negatives, and is defined as:

Specificity

$$= \frac{\text{true negatives}}{\text{true negatives} + \text{false positives}} \times 100$$

or B/C + B.

The *predictive value* (also called efficiency) of a test is the ratio of true positives to all positives, and is defined as:

Predictive value

$$= \frac{\text{true positives}}{\text{true positives} + \text{false positives}} \times 100$$

or A/A + C.

An ideal test would have a high degree of sensitivity and specificity, as well as high predictive value, with a low number of false positives and false negative decisions. (See Klee & Garfinkel [1983] for an example of a study that uses the concepts of sensitivity and specificity; see also Baldessarini, Finkelstein, & Arana, 1983; Gerardi, Keane, & Penk, 1989.)

An example from suicide. Maris (1992) gives an interesting example of the application of decision theory to some data of a study by Pokorny of 4,704 psychiatric patients who were tested and followed up for 5 years. In this group of patients, 63 committed suicide. Using a number of tests to make predictions about subsequent suicide, Pokorny obtained the results shown in Figure 3.6.

The sensitivity of Pokorny's procedure is thus:

$$\text{Sensitivity} = \frac{35}{35 + 28} = \frac{35}{63} = \boxed{55\%}$$

The specificity of Pokorny's procedure is:

$$\text{Specificity} = \frac{3435}{3435 + 1206} = \frac{3435}{4641} = \boxed{74\%}$$

and the predictive value is:

$$\text{Predictive value} = \frac{35}{35 + 1206} = \frac{35}{1241} = \boxed{2.8\%}$$

Note that although the sensitivity and specificity are respectable, the predictive value is extremely low.

Reducing errors. In probably every situation where a series of decisions is made, such as which 2,000 students to admit to a particular university, there will be errors made regardless of whether those decisions are made on the basis of test scores, interview information, flipping of a coin, or other method. Can these errors be reduced? Yes, they can. First of all, the more valid the measure or procedure on which decisions are based, the fewer the errors. Second, the more comprehensive the database available on which to make decisions, the fewer the errors; for example, if we made decisions based only on one source of

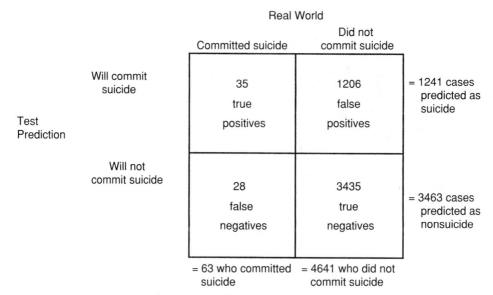

FIGURE 3–6. Example of a decision table as applied to suicide.

information, the SAT for example – vs. using multiple data sources, the SAT plus high-school grades, plus autobiographical statement, plus letters of recommendation, etc. – we would make greater errors where we used only one source of information. Of course, adding poor measures to our one source of information might in fact increase our errors. We can also use *sequential strategies.* In the example of TB screening, the initial test is relatively easy and inexpensive to administer, but produces a fair number of errors. We could follow up those individuals who show signs of being positive on the test by more sophisticated and expensive tests to identify more of the false positives.

We can also change the decision rule. For example, instead of deciding that any student whose combined SAT score is below 800 is at risk to fail, we could lower our standards and use a combined score of 400. Figure 3.7 shows what would happen.

Our rate of false positives, students for whom we are predicting failure but indeed would pass, is lowered. However, the number of false negatives, students for whom we predict success but in fact will fail, is now substantially increased. If we increase our standards, for example, we require a combined SAT score of 1,400 for admission, then we will have the opposite result: The number of false positives will increase and the number of false negatives will decrease. The standard we

use, the score that we define as acceptable or not acceptable, is called the *cutoff score* (see Meehl & Rosen, 1955, for a discussion of the problems in setting cutoff scores).

Which type of error? Which type of error are we willing to tolerate more? That of course depends upon the situation and upon philosophical, ethical, political, economic, and other issues. Some people, for example, might argue that for a state university it is better to be liberal in admission standards and allow almost everyone in, even if a substantial number of students will never graduate. In some situations, for example selecting individuals to be trained as astronauts, it might be better to be extremely strict in the selection standards and choose individuals who will be successful at the task, even if it means keeping out many volunteers who might have been just as successful.

Selection ratio. One of the issues that impinges on our decision and the kind of errors we tolerate is the *selection ratio,* which refers to the number of individuals we need to select from the pool of applicants. If there are only 100 students applying to my college and we need at least 100 paying students, then I will admit everyone who applies and won't care what their SAT scores are. On the other hand, if I am selecting scholarship recipients and I have two scholarships to award and

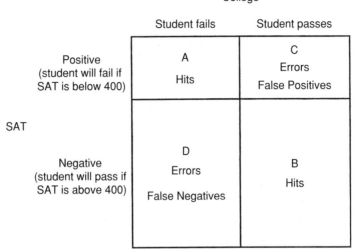

FIGURE 3–7. Decision table for college admissions.

100 candidates, I can be extremely demanding in my decision, which will probably result in a high number of false positives.

The base rate. Another aspect we must take into consideration is the *base rate,* that is the naturally occurring frequency of a particular behavior. Assume, for example, that I am a psychologist working at the local jail and over the years have observed that about one out of 100 prisoners attempts suicide (the actual suicide rate seems to be about 1 in 2,500 inmates, a rather low base rate from a statistical point of view; see Salive, Smith, & Brewer, 1989). As prisoners come into the jail, I am interested in identifying those who will attempt suicide to provide them with the necessary psychological assistance and/or take the necessary preventive action such as removal of belts and bed sheet and 24-hour surveillance. If I were to institute an entrance interview or testing of new inmates, what would happen? Let's say that I would identify 10 inmates out of 100 as probable suicide attempters; those 10 might not include the one individual who really will commit suicide. Notice then that I would be correct 89 out of 100 times (the 89 for whom I would predict no suicide attempt and who would behave accordingly). I would be incorrect 11 out of 100 times, for the 10 false positive individuals whom I would identify as potential suicides, and the I false negative whom I would not detect as a potential suicide. But if I were to do nothing and simply declare that "no one commits suicide in jail," I would be correct 99% of the time. When base rates are extreme, either high or low, our accuracy rate goes down. In fact, as Meehl and Rosen (1955) argued years ago, when the base rate of the criterion deviates significantly from a 50% split, the use of a test or procedure that has slight or moderate validity could result in increased errors. Base rates are often neglected by practitioners; for a more recent plea to consider base rates in the clinical application of tests see Elwood (1993).

Obviously, what might be correct from a statistical point of view (do nothing) might not be consonant with ethical, professional, or humanitarian principles. In addition, of course, an important consideration would be whether one individual who will attempt suicide can be identified, even if it means having a high false positive rate. Still another concern would be the availability of the information needed to assess base rates – quite often such information is lacking. Perhaps it might be appropriate to state the obvious: The use of psychological tests is not simply a function of their psychometric properties, but involves a variety of other concerns; in fact, the very issue of whether validity means utility, whether a particular test should be used simply because it is valid, is a source of controversy (see Gottfredson & Crouse, 1986).

Sample size. Another aspect that influences validity is the size of the sample that is studied when a test is validated, an issue that we have already mentioned (Dahlstrom, 1993). Suppose I administer a new test of intelligence to a sample of college students and correlate their scores on the test with their GPA. You will recall whether or not a correlation coefficient is statistically significant or is different from zero, is a function of the sample size. For example, here are correlation coefficients needed for samples of various size, using the .05 level of significance:

Sample size	Correlation coefficient
10	.63
15	.51
20	.44
80	.22
150	.16

Note that with a small sample of $N = 10$, we would need to get a correlation of at least .63 to conclude that the two variables are significantly correlated, but with a large sample of $N = 150$, the correlation would need to be only .16 or larger to reach the same conclusion. Schmidt and Hunter (1980) have in fact argued that the available evidence underestimates the validity of tests because samples, particularly those of working adults in specific occupations, are quite small.

Validity as a changing concept. What we have discussed above about validity might be termed the "classical" view. But our understanding of validity is not etched in stone and is evolving just as psychology evolves. In a historical overview of the concept of validity, Geisinger (1992) suggests that the concept has and is undergoing a metamorphosis and has changed in several ways. Currently, validity is focused on validating a test for a specific application with a specific sample and in a specific setting; it is largely based on theory, and construct validity seems to be rapidly gaining ground as the method.

In a recent revision of the *Standards for Educational and Psychological Testing* (1999), the committee who authored these standards argue persuasively that validity needs to be considered in the broad context of generalizability. That is, simply because one research study shows a correlation coefficient of +.40 between SAT scores and 1st-year college GPA at a particular institution, doesn't necessarily mean that the same result will be obtained at another institution. On the one hand, we expect a certain amount of stability of results across studies, but on the other, when we don't obtain such stability, we need to be aware and identify the various sources for obtaining different results. Changes occur from one setting to another and even within a particular setting. Perhaps a study conducted in the 1970s consisted primarily of white male middle-class students, whereas now any representative sample would be much more heterogeneous. Perhaps at one university we may have grade inflation while, at another, the grading standards may be more rigorous.

Taylor and Russell Tables. The selection ratio, the base rate, and the validity of a test are all related to the predictive efficiency of that test. In fact, H. C. Taylor and Russell (1939) computed tables that allow one to predict how useful a particular test can be in a situation where we know the selection ratio, the base rate, and the validity coefficient.

Validity from an Individual Point of View

Most, if not all, of our discussion of validity stems from what can be called a *nomothetic* point of view, a scientific approach based on general laws and relations. Thus with the SAT we are interested in whether SAT scores are related to college grades, whether SAT scores predict college achievement in minority groups to the same extent as in the majority, whether there may be gender differences, and whether scores can be maximized through calculated guessing. Note that these and other questions focus on the SAT as a test, the answers involve psychometric considerations, and we really don't care who the specific subjects are, beyond the requirements that they be representative, an so on.

The typical practitioner, however, whether clinical psychologist, school counselor, or psychiatric nurse, is usually interested not so much in the test as in the client who has taken the test. As Gough (1965) indicated, the practitioner uses tests to obtain a psychological description of the client, to predict what the client will say or do, and to understand how others react to this client.

Gough (1965) then developed a conceptual model of validity, not aimed at just a psychometric understanding of the test, but at a clinical understanding of the client. Gough (1965) proposed that if a practitioner wishes to use a particular test to understand a client, there are three questions or types of validity he or she must be concerned with. (For a slightly different tripartite conceptualization of validity, especially as applied to sociological measurement, see Bailey, 1988.)

Primary validity. The first question concerns the *primary validity* of the test; primary validity is basically similar to criterion validity. If someone publishes a new academic achievement test, we would want to see how well the test correlates with GPA, whether the test can in fact separate honors students from nonhonors students, and so on. This is called primary because if a test does not have this kind of basic validity, we must look elsewhere for a useful measure.

Secondary validity. If the evidence indicates that a test has primary validity, then we move on to *secondary validity* that addresses the psychological basis of measurement of the scale. If the new "academic achievement" test does correlate well with GPA, then we can say, "fine, but what does the test measure?" Just because the author named it an "academic achievement" test does not necessarily mean it is so. To obtain information on secondary validity, on the underlying psychological dimension that is being measured, Gough (1965) suggested four steps: (1) reviewing the theory behind the test and the procedures and samples used to develop the test; (2) analyzing from a logical-clinical point of view the item content (Is a measure of depression made up primarily of items that reflect low self-esteem?); (3) relating scores on the measure being considered to variables that are considered to be important, such as gender, intelligence, and socioeconomic status; (4) obtaining information about what high scorers and low scorers on the scale are like psychologically.

Tertiary validity. *Tertiary validity* is concerned with the justification for developing and/or using a particular test. Suppose for example, the new "academic achievement" test we are considering predicts GPA about as well as the SAT. Suppose also a secondary validity analysis suggests that the new test, like the SAT, is basically a measure of scholastic aptitude, and uses the kind of items that are relevant to school work. Because the SAT is so well established, why bother with a new measure? Suppose however, that an analysis of the evidence suggests that the new measure also identifies students who are highly creative, and the measure takes only 10 minutes to administer. I may not necessarily be interested in whether my client, say a business executive unhappy with her position, has high academic achievement potential, but I may be very interested in identifying her level of creativity. (For specific examples of how the three levels of validity are conceptualized with individual tests see Arizmendi, Paulsen, & G. Domino, 1981; G. Domino & Blumberg, 1987; and Gough, 1965.)

A Final Word about Validity

When we ask questions about the validity of a test we must ask "validity for what?" and "under what circumstances?" A specific test is not valid in a general sense. A test of depression for example, may be quite valid for psychiatric patients but not for college students. On the other hand, we can ask the question of "in general, how valid are psychological tests?" Meyer and his colleagues (2001) analyzed data from the available literature and concluded that not only is test validity "strong and compelling" but that the validity of psychological tests is comparable to the validity of medical procedures.

SUMMARY

Reliability can be considered from a variety of points of view, including stability over time and equivalence of items, sources of variation, and "noise in the system." Four ways to assess reliability have been discussed: test-retest reliability, alternate forms reliability, split-half reliability, and interitem consistency. For some tests, we need also to be concerned about scorer or rater reliability. Although reliability is most often measured by a correlation coefficient, the standard error of measurement can also be useful. A related measure, the standard error of differences is useful when we consider whether the difference between two scores obtained by an individual is indeed meaningful.

Validity, whether a test measures what it is said to measure, was discussed in terms of content validity, criterion validity, and construct validity. Content validity is a logical type of validity, particularly relevant to educational tests, and is the result of careful planning, of having a blueprint to how the test will be constructed. Criterion validity concerns the relationship of a test to specified criteria and is composed of predictive and concurrent validity. Construct validity is an umbrella term that can subsume all other types of validity and is principally related to theory construction. A method to show construct validity is the multitrait-multimethod matrix which gets at convergent and discriminant validity. There are various ways to interpret validity coefficients, including squaring the coefficient, using a predictive equation, an expectancy table, and the standard error of estimate. Because errors of prediction will most likely occur, we considered validity from the point of view of false positives and false negatives. In considering validity we also need to be mindful of the selection ratio and the base rate. Finally we considered validity from an "individual" point of view.

SUGGESTED READINGS

Cronbach, L. J., & Meehl, P. E. (1955). Construct validity in psychological tests. *Psychological Bulletin, 52,* 281–302.

A basic and classic paper that focused on construct validity.

Dahlstrom, W. G. (1993). Tests. Small samples, large consequences. *American Psychologist, 48,* 393–399.

The author argues that tests, if soundly constructed and responsibly applied, can offset the errors or judgment often found in daily decision making. A highly readable article.

Domino, G., & Blumberg, E. (1987). An application of Gough's conceptual model to a measure of adolescent self-esteem. *Journal of Youth and Adolescence, 16,* 179–190.

An illustration of Gough's conceptual model as applied to a paper-and-pencil measure of self-esteem.

Hadorn, D. C., & Hays, R. D. (1991). Multitrait-multimethod analysis of health-related quality-of-life measures. *Medical Care, 29,* 829–840.

An example of the multitrait-multimethod approach as applied to the measurement of quality of life.

Messick, S. (1995) Validity of psychological assessment. *American Psychologist, 50,* 741–49.

Messick argues that the three major categories of validity – content, criterion, and construct validity – present an incomplete and fragmented view. He argues that these are but a part of a comprehensive theory of construct validity that looks not only at the meaning of scores, but the social values inherent in test interpretation and use.

DISCUSSION QUESTIONS

1. I have developed a test designed to assess creativity in adults. The test consists of 50 true-false questions such as, "Do you consider yourself creative?" and "As a child were you extremely curious?" How might the reliability and validity of such a test be determined?

2. For the above test, assume that it is based on psychoanalytic theory that sees creativity as the result of displaced sexual and aggressive drives. How might the construct validity of such a test be determined?

3. Why is reliability so important?

4. Locate a meta-analytical study of a psychological test. What are the conclusions arrived at by the author(s)? Is the evidence compelling?

5. In your own words, define the concepts of sensitivity and specificity.

4 Personality

AIM This chapter focuses on the assessment of "normal" personality. The question of how many basic personality dimensions exist, and other basic issues are discussed. Nine instruments illustrative of personality assessment are considered; some are well known and commercially available, while others are not. Finally, the Big-Five model, currently a popular one in the field of personality assessment, is discussed.

INTRODUCTION

Personality

Personality occupies a central role both in the field of psychology and in psychological testing. Although the first tests developed were not of personality but of aptitude (by the Chinese) and of intelligence (by the French psychologist, Binet), the assessment of personality has been a major endeavor.

If this were a textbook on personality, we would probably begin with a definition of personality and, at the very least, an entire chapter would illustrate the diversity of definitions and the variety of viewpoints and arguments embedded in such definitions. Since this is not such a textbook, we defer such endeavors to the experts (e.g., Allport, 1937; 1961; Guilford, 1959b; Hall & Lindzey, 1970; McClelland, 1951; Mischel, 1981; Wiggins, 1973).

In general, when we talk about personality we are talking about a variety of characteristics whose unique organization define an individual, and to a certain degree, determine that person's interactions with himself/herself, with others, and with the environment. A number of authors consider attitudes, values, and interests under the rubric of personality; these are discussed in Chapter 6. Still others, quite correctly, include the assessment of psychopathology such as depression, and psychopathological states such as schizophrenia; we discuss these in Chapter 7 and in Chapter 15. Finally, most textbooks also include the assessment of positive functioning, such as creativity, under the rubric of personality. Because we believe that the measurement of positive functioning has in many ways been neglected, we discuss the topic in Chapter 8.

Internal or External?

When you do something, why do you do it? Are the determinants of your behavior due to inner causes, such as needs, or are they due to external causes such as the situation you are in? Scientists who focus on the internal aspects emphasize such concepts as personality traits. Those who focus on the external aspects, emphasize more situational variables. For many years, the trait approach was the dominant one, until about 1968 when Mischel published a textbook titled, *Personality and Assessment*, and strongly argued that situations had been neglected, and that to fully understand personality one needed to pay attention to the reciprocal interactions between person and situation. This message was not new; many other psychologists such as Henry Murray, had made the same argument much earlier. The message is also quite logical; if nothing else, we know that behavior is multiply determined, that typically a particular action is the result of many aspects.

Endler and Magnusson (1976) suggested that there are five major theoretical models that address the above question:

1. The *trait* model. This model assumes that there is a basic personality core, and that traits are the main source of individual differences. Traits are seen as quite stable.

2. The *psychodynamic* model. This model also assumes the presence of a basic personality core and traits as components. But much of the focus is on developmental aspects and, in particular, how early experiences affect later development.

3. The *situational* model. This model assumes that situations are the main source of behavioral differences. Change the situation and you change the behavior. Thus, instead of seeing some people as honest, and some less than honest, honesty is a function of the situation, of how much gain is at stake, of whether the person might get away with something, and so on.

4. The *interaction* model. This model assumes that actual behavior is the result of an interaction between the person and the situation. Thus, a person can be influenced by a situation (a shy person speaking up forcefully when a matter of principle is at stake), but a person also chooses situations (preferring to stay home rather than going to a party) and influences situations (being the "hit of the party").

5. The *phenomenological* model. This model focuses on the individual's introspection (looking inward) and on internal, subjective experiences. Here the construct of "self-concept" is an important one.

SOME BASIC ISSUES

Self-rating scales. Assume we wanted to measure a person's degree of responsibility. We could do this in a number of ways, but one way would be to administer the person a personality test designed to measure responsibility; another way would be simply to ask the person, "How responsible are you?" and have them rate themselves on a simple 5-point scale, ranging from "highly

responsible" to "not at all responsible." Two interesting questions can now be asked: (1) how do these two methods relate to each other – does the person who scores high on the scale of responsibility also score high on the self-rating of responsibility? and (2) which of these two methods is more valid – which scores, the personality inventory or the self-ratings, will correlate more highly with an external, objective criterion? (Note that basically we are asking the question: Given two methods of eliciting information, which is better?)

There seems to be some evidence that suggests, that at least in some situations, self-ratings tend to be the better method, that self-ratings turn out to be slightly more valid than corresponding questionnaire scales. The difference between the two methods is not particularly large, but has been found in a number of studies (e.g., M. D. Beck & C. K. Beck, 1980; Burisch, 1984; Carroll, 1952; Shrauger & Osberg, 1981). Why then use a test? In part, because the test parallels a hypothesized dimension, and allows us to locate individuals on that dimension. In essence, it's like asking people how tall they are. The actual measurement (5 feet 8 inches) is more informative than the rating "above average."

Self-report measures. One of the most common ways of assessing personality is to have the individual provide a report of their own behavior. The report may be a response to an open-ended question (tell me about yourself), may require selecting self-descriptive adjectives from a list, or answering true-false to a series of items. Such self-report measures assume, on the one hand, that individuals are probably in the best position to report on their own behavior. On the other hand, most personality assessors do not blindly assume that if the individual answers true to the item "I am a sociable person," the person is in fact sociable. It is the pattern of responses related to empirical criteria that is important. In fact, some psychologists (e.g., Berg, 1955; 1959) have argued that the content of the self-report is irrelevant; what is important is whether the response deviates from the norm.

Whether such reporting is biased or unbiased is a key issue that in part involves a philosophical issue: Are most people basically honest and objective when it comes to describing themselves?

Obviously, it depends. At the very least, it depends on the person and on the situation; some people are more insightful than others about their own behavior, and in some situations, some people might be more candid than others in admitting their shortcomings. Many self-report techniques, especially personality inventories, have incorporated within them some means of identifying the extent to which the respondent presents a biased picture; these are called *validity scales* because they are designed to tell us whether the measurement is valid or distorted. Some of these techniques are discussed in Chapter 16.

Projective measures. One common type of self-report is the *personality inventory* that consists of a number of scales with the items printed together, typically in a random sequence. These are often called *objective* personality tests because the scoring of the items and the meaning assigned to specific scores are not arbitrary. In contrast, there are a number of techniques called *projective* techniques that involve the presentation of an ambiguous set of stimuli, such as inkblots, sentence stems, or pictures, to which the respondents must impose some structure that presumably reflects their own personality and psychological functioning. Because these techniques are used more extensively in the clinic, we discuss them in Chapter 15.

Rating scales. Rating scales typically consist of a variable to be rated, for example, "leadership potential," and a set of *anchor points* from which the rater selects the most appropriate (e.g., low, average, or high). Rating scales can be used to assess a wide variety of variables, not just personality dimensions. Because ratings are quite often used in occupational settings, for example a manager rating employees, we discuss ratings in Chapter 14.

Situational methods. Sometimes, the personality of an individual can be assessed through direct observation of the person in a specific situation. In self-report, the person has presumably observed his or her behavior in a large variety of situations. In ratings, the observer rates the person based again on a range of situations, although the range is somewhat more restricted. In *situational methods*, the observation is based on a specific situation, which may extend over a time period, and may be natural (observing children on a playground), or contrived (bringing several managers together in a leaderless discussion). Interviews might be considered an example of situational methods, and these are discussed in Chapter 18.

Behavioral assessment. Most of the categories listed above depend on the assumption that what is being reported on or rated is a trait, a theoretical construct that allows us to explain behavior. Some psychologists argue that such explanatory concepts are not needed, that we can focus directly on the behavior. Thus behavioral assessment involves direct measures of behavior, rather than such constructs as anxiety, responsibility, or flexibility. We discuss this concept and its applications in Chapter 18.

Other approaches There are, of course, many ways of studying personality other than through the administration of a personality inventory. A wide variety of procedures have been used, some with moderate success, ranging from the study of eye pupil dilation and constriction (E. H. Hess, 1965; E. H. Hess & Polt, 1960), the study of head and body cues (Ekman, 1965), hand movement (Krout, 1954), voice characteristics (Mallory & Miller, 1958), and of course handwriting or graphology (Fluckiger, Tripp, & Weinberg, 1961).

Traits and Types

Two terms are often used in discussing personality, particularly in psychological testing. When we assess an individual with a personality test, that test will presumably measure some variable or combination of variables – perhaps sociability, introversion-extraversion, self-control, assertiveness, nurturance, responsibility, and so on. Ordinarily, we assume that individuals occupy different positions on the variable, that some people are more responsible than others, and that our measurement procedure is intended to identify with some degree of accuracy a person's position on that variable. The variable, assumed to be a continuum, is usually called a *trait*. (For an excellent discussion of trait see Buss, 1989.)

As you might expect, there is a lot of argument about whether such traits do or do not exist, whether they reside in the person's biochemistry or are simply explanatory constructs, whether they are enduring or transitory, whether the concept of trait is even useful, and to what degree traits are found in the person or in the interaction between person and environment (e.g., R. B. Cattell, 1950; Hogan, DeSoto, & Solano, 1977; Holt, 1971; Mischel, 1968; 1977). In the 1960s and 1970s, the notion of personality traits came under severe attack (e.g., D'Andrade, 1965; Mischel, 1968; Mulaik, 1964; Ullman & Krasner, 1975), but it seems to have reemerged recently (e.g., Block, Weiss, & Thorne, 1979; Goldberg, 1981; Hogan, 1983; McCrae & Costa, 1985). McCrae and Costa (1986) point out that the trait approach, attacked so vigorously, has survived because it is based on the following set of assumptions that are basically valid:

1. Personality is generally marked by stability and regularity (Epstein, 1979).

2. Personality is relatively stable across the age span; people do change, but rarely are changes dramatic (Block, 1981).

3. Personality traits do predict behavior (Small, Zeldin & Savin-Williams, 1983).

4. These traits can be assessed with a fair degree of accuracy both by self-reports and by ratings (McCrae & Costa, 1987).

A *type* is a category of individuals all of whom presumably share a combination of traits. Most psychologists prefer to think of traits as distributed along a normal curve model, rather than in dichotomous or multi types. Thus, we think of people as differing in the degree of honesty, rather than there being two types of people, honest and dishonest. However, from a theoretical point of view, a typology may be a useful device to summarize and categorize behavior. Thus, most typologies stem from theoretical frameworks that divide people into various categories, with the full understanding that "pure" types probably do not exist, and that the typology is simply a convenient device to help us understand the complexity of behavior. One of the earliest typologies was developed by the Greeks, specifically Hippocrates and Galen, and was based on an excess of body "humors" or fluids: Thus, there were individuals who were melancholic (depressed) due to too much dark bile, sanguine (buoyant) due to too much blood, choleric (irritable) due to too much yellow bile, and phlegmatic (apathetic) due to too much phlegm.

TYPES OF PERSONALITY TESTS

The internal consistency approach. As dicussed in Chapter 2, there are a number of ways of constructing tests, and this is particularly true of personality tests. One way to develop tests, sometimes called the method of *internal consistency* or the *inductive* method, is to use statistical procedures such as factor analysis. Basically, the method is to administer a pool of items to a sample or samples of individuals, and to statistically analyze the relationship of responses to the items to determine which items go together. The resulting set of variables presumably identifies basic factors. One of the pioneers of this approach was J. P. Guilford who developed the Guilford-Martin Inventory of Factors and the Guilford-Zimmerman Temperament Survey (Guilford, 1959b). In this approach, the role of theory is minimal. While the author's theory may play a role in the formation of the initial pool of items, and perhaps in the actual naming of the factors, and in what evidence is sought to determine the validity of the test, the items are assigned to specific scales (factors) on the basis of statistical properties. A good example of this approach is the *16 Personality Factors Inventory* (16PF), described later in this chapter.

The theoretical approach. A second method of test construction is called the *theoretical* or *deductive* method. Here the theory plays a paramount role, not just in the generation of an item pool, but in the actual assignment of items to scales, and indeed in the entire enterprise. We look at three examples of this approach: the *Myers-Briggs Type Indicator* (MBTI), the *Edwards Personal Preference Schedule* (EPPS), and the *Personality Research Form* (PRF).

Criterion-keying. A third approach is that of empirical *criterion-keying*, sometimes called the method of *contrasted groups*, the method of *criterion groups*, or the *external* method (Goldberg, 1974). Here the pool of items is administered to one or more samples of individuals, and criterion information is collected. Items that correlate significantly with the criterion are retained. Often the criterion is a dichotomy (e.g., depressed vs. nondepressed; student leader vs. not-a-leader), and so the contrasted groups label is used. But the criterion may also be continuous (e.g., GPA, ratings of competence, etc.). Presumably the process could be atheoretical because whether an item is retained or not is purely an empirical matter, based on observation rather than predilection. The basic emphasis of this empirical approach is validity-in-use. The aim is to develop scales and inventories that can forecast behavior and that will identify people who are described by others in specific ways. Empiricists are not tied to any one particular method or approach, but rather seek what is most appropriate in a particular situation. The outstanding example of a criterion-keyed inventory is the *California Psychological Inventory* (CPI) discussed in this chapter.

The fiat method. Finally, a fourth approach that we identified as the *fiat method*, is also referred to as the *rational* or *logical* approach, or the *content validity* approach. Here the test author decides which items are to be incorporated in the test. The first psychologists who attempted to develop personality tests assumed that such tests could be constructed simply by putting together a bunch of questions relevant to the topic and that whatever the respondent endorsed was in direct correspondence to what they did in real life. Thus a measure of leadership could be constructed simply by generating items such as, "I am a leader," "I like to be in charge of things," "People look to me for decisions," etc. Few such tests now exist because psychology has become much more empirical and demanding of evidence, and because many of the early personality tests built using this strategy were severely criticized (Landis, 1936; Landis, Zubin, & Katz, 1935). Quite often, "tests" published in popular magazines are of this type. There is, of course, nothing inherently wrong with a rational approach. It makes sense to begin rationally and to be guided by theory, and a number of investigators have made this approach their central focus (e.g., Loevinger, 1957). Perhaps it should be pointed out that many tests are the result of combined approaches, although often the author's "bias" will be evident.

Importance of language. Why select a particular variable to measure? Although, as we said, measurement typically arises out of need, one may well argue that some variables are more important than others, and that there is a greater argument for scaling them. At least two psychologists, Raymond Cattell and Harrison Gough, well known for their personality inventories, have argued that important variables that reflect significant individual differences become encoded in daily language. If for example, responsibility is of importance, then we ought to hear lay people describe themselves and others in terms of responsibility, dependability, punctuality, and related aspects. To understand what the basic dimensions of importance are, we need to pay attention to language because language encodes important experiences.

Psychopathology. Many theories of personality and ways of measuring personality were originally developed in clinical work with patients. For example, individuals such as Freud, Jung, and Adler contributed to much of our understanding about basic aspects of personality, but their focus was primarily on psychopathology or psychological disturbances. Thus, there is a substantial area of personality assessment that focuses on the negative or disturbed aspects of personality; the MMPI is the most evident example of a personality inventory that focuses on psychopathology. These instruments are discussed in Chapter 15.

Self-actualization. Other theorists have focused on individuals who are unusually effective, who perhaps exhibit a great deal of inventiveness and originality, who are self-fulfilled or self-actualized. One example of such a theorist is Abraham Maslow (1954; 1962). We look at tests that might fall under this rubric in Chapter 8.

Focus on motivation. One of the legacies of Freud is the focus on motivation – on what motivates people, and on how can these motives be assessed. Henry A. Murray (1938) was one individual who both theoretically and empirically focused on *needs*, those aspects of motivation that result in one action rather than another (skipping lunch to study for an exam). Murray realized that the physical environment also impinges on

Factor	Factor name	Brief explanation
Table 4–1. The dimensions of the 16PF		
A	Schizothymia-affectothymia	Reserved vs. outgoing
B	Intelligence	
C	Ego strength	Emotional stability
E	Submissiveness-dominance	
F	Desurgency-surgency	Sober-enthusiastic
G	Superego strength	Expedient-conscientious
H	Threctia-Parmia	Shy-uninhibited
I	Harria-Premsia	Tough minded vs. tender minded
L	Alaxia-protension	Trusting-suspicious
M	Praxernia-Autia	Practical-imaginative
N	Artlessness-shrewdness	Unpretentious-astute
O	Untroubled adequacy-guilt proneness	Self-assured vs. worrying
Q1	Conservative-radical	
Q2	Group adherence	Joiner-self sufficient
Q3	Self-sentiment integration	Undisciplined-controlled
Q4	Ergic tension	Relaxed-tense

Each factor was initially given a letter name and descriptive names were not assigned for a number of years, in part because R. B. Cattell felt that these descriptive labels are quite limited and often people assign them meanings that were not necessarily there to begin with. In fact, as you will see, when R. B. Cattell named the factors he typically used descriptive labels that are not popular.

Description. The 16PF is designed for ages 16 and older, and yields scores for the 16 dimensions listed in Table 4.1.

As shown in Table 4.1, each of the factors is identified by a letter, and then by a factor name. These names may seem quite strange, but they are the words that R. B. Cattell chose. For those names that are not self-evident, there is also a brief explanation in more familiar terms.

Six forms of the test are available, two of which are designed for individuals with limited education. The forms of the 16PF contain 187 items and require about 45 to 60 minutes for administration (25–35 minutes for the shorter forms of 105 items). Since its original publication, the 16PF has undergone five revisions. Some forms of the 16PF contain validity scales, scales that are designed to assess whether the respondent is producing a valid protocol, i.e., not faking. These scales include a "fake-bad" scale, a "fake-good" scale, and a random-responses scale.

The 16 dimensions are said to be independent, and each item contributes to the score of only one scale. Each of the scales is made up from 6 to 13 items, depending on the scale and the test form. The items are 3-choice multiple-choice items, or perhaps more correctly, *forced-choice* options. An example of such an item might be: If I had some free time I would probably (a) read a good book, (b) go visit some friends, (c) not sure. R. B. Cattell, Eber, and Tatsuoka (1972) recommend that at least two forms of the test be administered to a person to get a more valid measurement, but in practice, this is seldom done.

behavior, and therefore we need to focus on the environmental pressures or *press* that are exerted on the person. Both the EPPS and the PRF were developed based on Murray's theory.

EXAMPLES OF SPECIFIC TESTS

The Cattell 16PF

Introduction. How many words are there in the English language that describe personality? As you might imagine, there are quite a few such words. Allport and Odbert (1936) concluded that these words could actually be reduced to 4,504 traits. R. B. Cattell (1943) took these traits and through a series of procedures, primarily factor analysis, reduced them to 16 basic dimensions or *source traits*. The result was the *Sixteen Personality Factor Questionnaire*, better known as the 16PF (R. B. Cattell, A. K. Cattell, & H. E. Cattell, 1993).

Development. The 16PF was developed over a number of years with a variety of procedures. The guiding theory was the notion that there were 16 basic dimensions to personality, and that these dimensions could be assessed through scales developed basically by factor analysis. A great deal of work went into selecting items that not only reflected the basic dimensions, but that would be interesting for the subject and not offensive.

Administration. The 16PF is basically a self-administered test, and requires minimal skills on the part of the examiner to administer; interpretation of the results is of course a different matter.

Scoring. Scoring of the 16PF can be done by hand or by machine, and is quite straightforward – each endorsed keyed response counts 1 point. As with most other tests that are hand-scored, templates are available that are placed on top of the answer sheet to facilitate such scoring. Raw scores on the 16PF are then converted to *stens*, a contraction of standard ten, where scores can range from 1 to 10, and the mean is fixed at 5.5; such conversions are done by using tables provided in the test manual, rather than by doing the actual calculations. Despite the strange names given to the 16 factors, for each of the scales, the test manual gives a good description of what a low scorer or a high scorer might be like as a person. A number of computer scoring services are available. These can provide not only a scoring of the scales and a profile of results, but also a narrative report, with some geared for specific purposes (for example, selection of law enforcement candidates).

Reliability. An almost overwhelming amount of information on the 16PF can be found in the *Handbook for the 16PF* (R. B. Cattell, Eber, & Tatsuoka, 1970), in the test manual, in the professional literature, and in a variety of publications from the test publisher. Internal consistency of the scales is on the low side, despite the focus on factor analysis, and scales are not very reliable across different forms of the test – i.e., alternate form reliability (Zuckerman, 1985). Information about test-retest reliability, both with short intervals (2 to 7 days) and longer intervals (2 to 48 months) is available and appears adequate. The correlation coefficients range from the .70s and .80s for the brief interval, to the .40s and .50s for a 4-year interval. This is to be expected because test-retest reliability becomes lower as the interval increases, and in fact, a 4-year interval may be inappropriate to assess test stability, but more appropriate to assess amount of change.

Validity. The test manual gives only what may be called *factorial validity*, the correlation of scores on each scale with the pure factor the scale was designed to measure. These coefficients range from a low of .35 to a high of .94, with the majority of coefficients in the .60 to .80 range. The literature however, contains a multitude of studies, many that support the construct validity of the 16PF.

Norms. Three sets of norms are available, for high-school seniors, college students, and adults. These norms are further broken down into separate gender norms, and age-specific norms. These norms are based on more than 15,000 cases stratified according to U.S. census data. Thus, these were not simply samples of convenience; the data was gathered according to a game plan. R. B. Cattell, Eber, and Tatsuoka (1970) present norms for a very large number of occupational samples ranging from accountants to writers. For example, they tested a sample of 41 Olympic champion athletes. As a group, these individuals showed high ego strength (Factor C), high dominance (Factor E); low superego (Factor G), and an adventurous temperament (Factor H). Football players are described as having lower intelligence (Factor B), scoring lower on factor I (harria), factor M (praxernia), and factor Q2 (group adherence). In English, these players are described as alert, practical, dominant, action-oriented, and group-dependent.

Interesting aspects. Despite the fact that the 16PF scales were developed using factor analysis and related techniques designed to result in independent measures, the 16 scales do correlate with each other, some rather substantially. For example, Factors O and Q4 correlate +.75; factors G and Q3 + .56; and factors A and H + .44, just to cite some examples (R. B. Cattell, Eber, & Tatsuoka, 1970, p. 113). Thus, there seems to be some question whether the 16 scales are indeed independent (Levonian, 1961).

In addition to the 16 primary traits, other primary traits have been developed (at least 7) but have not been incorporated into the 16PF. In addition, factor analysis of the original 16 primary traits yields a set of 8 broader *secondary traits*. The 16PF can be scored for these secondary traits, although hand scoring is somewhat cumbersome.

The 16PF has also resulted in a whole family of related questionnaires designed for use with children, adolescents, and clinical populations (e.g., Delhees & R. B. Cattell, 1971).

A number of investigators have applied the 16PF to cross-cultural settings, although more such studies are needed (M. D. Gynther & R. A. Gynther, 1976).

A substantial amount of research with the 16PF has been carried out, primarily by R. B. Cattell, his colleagues, and students. One of the intriguing areas has been the development of a number of regression equations designed to predict a variety of criteria, such as academic achievement and creativity.

Criticisms. The 16PF has been available for quite some time and has found extensive applications in a wide variety of areas. Sometimes however, there has been little by way of replication of results. For example, the 16PF Handbook presents a number of regression equations designed to predict specific behaviors, but most of these regression equations have not been tested to see if they hold up in different samples.

The short forms are of concern because each scale is made up of few items, and short scales tend to be less reliable and less valid. In fact, the data presented by the test authors substantiate this concern, but a new test user may not perceive the difference between short forms and long forms in reliability and validity.

The Myers-Briggs Type Indicator (MBTI)

Introduction. Jung's theory and writings have had a profound influence on psychology, but not as much in the area of psychological testing. With some minor exceptions, most efforts in psychological testing stemming from Jungian theory have focused on only one concept, that of extraversion-introversion. The MBTI is unique in that it attempts to scale some important concepts derived from Jungian theory. The MBTI is a self-report inventory designed to assess Jung's theory of types. Jung believed that what seems to be random variation in human behavior is in fact orderly and consistent and can be explained on the basis of how people use perception and judgment. *Perception* is defined as the processes of becoming aware – aware of objects, people, or ideas. *Judgment* is defined as the processes

of coming to conclusions about what has been perceived.

One basic question then, is whether an individual tends to use perception or judgment in dealing with the world. Perception is composed of *sensing*, becoming aware directly through the senses of the immediate and real experiences of life, and of *intuition*, which is indirect perception by way of unconscious rather than conscious processes, becoming aware of possibilities and relationships. Judgment is composed of *thinking*, which focuses on what is true and what is false, on the objective and impersonal, and of *feeling*, which focuses on what is valued or not valued, what is subjective and personal. Finally, there is the dimension of *extraversion* or *introversion*; the extraverted person is oriented primarily to the outer world and therefore focuses perception and judgment upon people and objects. The introverted person focuses instead on the inner world, the world of ideas and concepts.

The manner in which a person develops is a function of both heredity and environment, as they interact with each other in complex ways, although Jung seemed to favor the notion of a predisposition to develop in a certain way (Jung, 1923). Once developed, types are assumed to be fairly stable.

Type is conceived to be categorical, even though the extent to which a person has developed in a particular way is continuous; a person is seen, in this schema, as being either sensing or intuitive, either thinking or feeling (Stricker & Ross, 1964a; 1964b).

Development. The MBTI was developed by Katharine Cook Briggs and her daughter, Isabel Briggs Myers. Myers in 1942 began to develop specific items for possible use in an inventory. From 1942 to about 1957, she developed a number of scales, did major pilot testing, and eventually released MBTI. In 1962, Educational Testing Service published form F for research use only. In 1975, Consulting Psychologists Press took over the publication of form F and in 1977 published form G, both for professional use. In 1975 also, a center for the MBTI was opened at the University of Florida in Gainesville.

Description The MBTI is geared for high-school students, college students, and adults. Form G of the MBTI consists of some 126 forced-choice items of this type: Are you (a) a gregarious person; (b) a reserved and quiet person, as well as a number of items that ask the respondent to pick one of two words on the basis of appeal – for example: (a) rational or (b) intuitive.

Form F consists of 166 items, and there is an abbreviated form of 50 items (form H). There is also a self-scorable short form composed of 94 items from form G. This form comes with a two-part answer sheet that allows the respondent to score the inventory. Finally, there is a form designed for children, as well as a Spanish version.

There are thus four scales on the MBTI:

Extraversion-introversion	abbreviated as E-I
Sensation-intuition	abbreviated as S-N
Thinking-feeling	abbreviated as T-F
Judging-perceiving	abbreviated as J-P

Administration. Like the 16PF, the MBTI can be easily administered, and simply requires the subject to follow the directions. There is no time limit, but the MBTI can be easily completed in about 20 to 30 minutes. The MBTI requires a seventh-grade reading level.

Scoring. Although continuous scores are obtained by summing the endorsed keyed responses for each scale, individuals are characterized as to whether they are extraverted or introverted, sensation type or intuition type, etc., by assigning the person to the highest score in each pair of scales. Preferences are designated by a letter and a number to indicate the strength of the preference – for example, if a person scores 26 on E and 18 on I, that person's score will be "8E"; however, typically the letter is considered more important than the number, which is often disregarded. The MBTI does not try to measure individuals or traits, but rather attempts to sort people into types. There are thus 16 possible types, each characterized by a four-letter acronym, such as INTJ or ISTP.

Reliability. Alpha coefficients and split-half reliabilities are given in the test manual (I. B. Myers & McCaulley, 1985), while test-retest reliability studies have been reported in the literature (e.g., Carlyn, 1977; Stricker & Ross, 1964a; 1964b). In general, the results suggest adequate reliability,

and the obtained coefficients are of the same magnitude as those found with most multivariate instruments.

Validity. Considerable validity data is presented in the test manual (I. B. Myers & McCaulley, 1985), especially correlations of the MBTI scales with those on a variety of other personality tests, career-interest inventories, self-ratings, as well as behavioral indices. In general, all of the evidence is broadly supportive of the construct validity of the MBTI, but there are exceptions. For example, Stricker and Ross (1964a; 1964b) compared the MBTI with a large battery of tests administered to an entering class of male students at Wesleyan University. The construct validity of each MBTI scale was assessed by comparing the scores with measures of personality, ability, and career interest. The findings are interpreted by the authors to somewhat support the validity of the Sensation-Intuition and Thinking-Feeling scales, but not for the Extraversion-Introversion and Judging-Perceiving scales. (Extensive reviews of the reliability and validity of the MBTI can be found in J. G. Carlson, 1985 and in Carlyn, 1977.)

Norms. In one sense, norms are not relevant to this test. Note first of all, that these are ipsative scales – the higher your score on E the lower on I. Thus basically, the subject is ranking his/her own preferences on each pair of scales. To complicate matters, however, the scales are not fully ipsative, in part because some items have more than two response choices, and in part because responses represent opposing rather than competing choices (DeVito, 1985). In addition, as was mentioned above, the focus is on the types rather than the scores. We could of course ask how frequent is each type in specific samples, such as architects, lawyers, art majors, and so on, and both the manual and the literature provide such information.

Interesting aspects. Jungian theory has always had wide appeal to clinicians, and so the MBTI has found quite a following with counselors, therapists, motivational consultants, and others who work directly with clients. In fact, it has become somewhat of a "cult" instrument, with a small but enthusiastic following, its own center to continue the work of Isabel Myers Briggs, and its own journal named *Research in Psychological Type*.

The MBTI manual (I. B. Myers & McCaulley, 1985) gives considerable information for the psychometrically oriented user, but it is clear that the focus of the Manual is on the applied use of the MBTI with individual clients in situations such as personal and/or career counseling. Thus, there are detailed descriptions of the 16 pure types in terms of what each type is like, and there are presumed "employment aspects" for each type; for example, introverts are said to be more careful with details, to have trouble remembering names and faces, and like to think before they act, as opposed to extroverts who are faster, good at greeting people, and usually act quickly.

Nevertheless, we can still ask some "psychometric" questions, and one of these is: How independent are the four sets of scales? Intercorrelations of the four scales indicate that three of the scales are virtually independent, but that JP correlates significantly with SN, with typical correlation coefficients ranging from about .26 to .47; one way to interpret this is that intuitive types are more common among perceptive types – the two tend to go together.

Criticisms. One basic issue is how well the test captures the essence of the theory. Jungian theory is complex and convoluted, the work of a genius whose insights into human behavior were not expressed as easily understood theorems. The MBTI has been criticized because it does not mirror Jungian theory faithfully; it has also been criticized because it does, and therefore is of interest only if one accepts the underlying theory (see McCaulley, 1981, and J. B. Murray, 1990, for reviews).

The Edwards Personal Preference Schedule (EPPS)

Introduction. There are two theoretical influences that resulted in the creation of the EPPS. The first is the theory proposed by Henry Murray (1938) which, among other aspects, catalogued a set of needs as primary dimensions of behavior – for example, need achievement, need affiliation, need heterosexuality. These sets of needs have been scaled in a number of instruments such as the EPPS, the Adjective Check List (Gough &

Heilbrun, 1965) and the Thematic Apperception Test (H. A. Murray, 1943). A second theoretical focus is the issue of *social desirability*. A. L. Edwards (1957b) argued that a person's response to a typical personality inventory item may be more reflective of how desirable that response is than the actual behavior of the person. Thus a true response to the item, "I am loyal to my friends" may be given not because the person *is* loyal, but because the person perceives that saying "true" is socially desirable.

Development. A. L. Edwards developed a pool of items designed to assess 15 needs taken from H. A. Murray's system. Each of the items was rated by a group of judges as to how socially desirable endorsing the item would be. Edwards then placed together pairs of items that were judged to be equivalent in social desirability, and the task for the subject was to choose one item from each pair.

Description. Each of the scales on the EPPS is then composed of 28 forced-choice items, where an item to measure need Achievement for example, is paired off with items representative of each of the other 14 needs, and this done twice per comparison. Subjects choose from each pair the one statement that is more characteristic of them, and the chosen underlying need is given one point. Let's assume for example, that these two statements are judged to be equal in social desirability:

Which of these is most characteristic? (a) I find it reassuring when friends help me out; (b) It is easy for me to do what is expected.

If you chose statement (a) you would receive one point for need Succorance; if you chose statement (b) you would receive a point for need Deference.

Note again, that this procedure of having to choose (a) vs. (b) results in ipsative measurement; the resulting score does not reflect the strength of a need in any "absolute" manner, but rather whether that need was selected over the other needs. Why is this point important? Suppose you and a friend enter a restaurant and find five choices on the menu: hamburger, salad, fishsticks, taco, and club sandwich. You may not care very much for any of those, but you select a hamburger because it seems the most palatable.

Table 4–2. The EPPS Scales	
Need	**Brief definition**
1. Achievement	To achieve, to be successful
2. Deference	To follow, to do what is expected
3. Order	To be orderly and organized
4. Exhibition	To be at the center of attention
5. Autonomy	To be independent
6. Affiliation	To have friends
7. Intraception	To analyze one's self and others
8. Succorance	To be helped by others
9. Dominance	To be a leader
10. Abasement	To accept blame
11. Nurturance	To show affection and support
12. Change	To need variety and novelty
13. Endurance	To have persistence
14. Heterosexuality	To seek out members of the opposite sex
15. Aggression	To be aggressive, verbally and/or physically

Your friend however, simply loves hamburgers and his selection reflects this. Both of you chose hamburgers but for rather different reasons. We should not assume that both of you are "hamburger lovers," even although your behavior might suggest that. Similarly, two people might score equally high on need aggression, but only one of them might be an aggressive individual.

In terms of the classificatory schema we developed in Chapter 1, the EPPS, like most other personality inventories, is commercially available, a group test, a self-report paper-and-pencil inventory, with no time limit, designed to assess what the subject typically does, rather than maximal performance.

The EPPS is designed primarily for research and counseling purposes, and the 15 needs that are scaled are presumed to be relatively independent normal personality variables. Table 4.2 gives a list of the 15 needs assessed by the EPPS.

Administration. The EPPS is easy to administer and is designed to be administered within the typical 50-minute class hour. There are two answer sheets available, one for hand scoring and one for machine scoring.

Reliability. The test manual gives both internal consistency (corrected split-half coefficients based on a sample of 1,509 subjects), and test-retest coefficients (1-week interval, $n = 89$); the corrected split-half coefficients range from $+.60$ for the need Deference scale to $+.87$ for the need Heterosexuality scale. The test-retest coefficients range from $+.74$ for need Achievement and need Exhibition, to $+.88$ for need Abasement.

Validity. The test manual presents little data on validity, and many subsequent studies that have used the EPPS have assumed that the scales were valid. The results do seem to support that assumption, although there is little direct evidence of the validity of the EPPS.

Norms. Because the EPPS consists of ipsative measurement, norms are not appropriate. Nevertheless, they are available and used widely, although many would argue, incorrectly. The initial normative sample consisted of 749 college women and 760 college men enrolled in various universities. The subjects were selected to yield approximately equal representation of gender and as wide an age spread as possible, as well as different majors. Basically then, the sample was one of convenience and not random or stratified. The manual also gives a table that allows raw scores to be changed into percentiles. Subsequently, the revised manual also gives norms for 4,031 adult males and 4,932 adult females who were members of a consumer purchase panel participating in a market survey. These norms are significantly different from those presented for college students; part of the difference may be that the adult sample seems to be somewhat more representative of the general population.

Interesting aspects. The EPPS contains two validity indices designed to assess whether a particular protocol is valid or not. The first index is based on the fact that 15 items are repeated; the responses to these items are compared and a *consistency score* is determined. If the subject answers at least 11 of the 15 sets consistently, then it is assumed that the subject is not responding randomly. Interestingly, in the normative sample of 1,509 college students, 383 (or 25%) obtained scores of 10 or below.

The second validity index, an index of *profile stability*, is obtained by correlating partial scores for each scale (based on 14 items) with the other 14 items. A correlation coefficient of at least +.44 across scales is assumed to indicate profile stability, and in fact 93% of the normative sample scored at or above this point. The calculation of this coefficient, if done by hand, is somewhat involved, and few if any test users do this.

What about the equating of the items on social desirability? Note first, that the equating was done on the basis of group ratings. This does not guarantee that the items are equated for the individual person taking the test (Heilbrun & Goodstein, 1961). Secondly, placing two "equal" items together may in fact cause a shift in social desirability, so that one of the items may still be seen as more socially desirable (McKee, 1972).

The 15 need scales are designed to be independent. A. L. Edwards (1959) gives a matrix of correlations based on the normative sample of 1,509 college students. Most of the correlation coefficients are low and negative, but this is due to the nature of the test – the higher a person scores on one need, the lower they must score on the other needs (if you select butter pecan ice cream as your favorite flavor, other flavors must be ranked lower). The largest coefficient reported is between need Affiliation and need Nurturance ($r = .46$). The generally low values do support A. L. Edwards' claim that the scales are relatively independent.

Criticisms. The criticisms of the EPPS are many; some are minor and can be easily overlooked, but some are quite major (e.g., Heilbrun, 1972; McKee, 1972). The use of ipsative scores in a normative fashion is not only confusing but incorrect. The relative lack of direct validity evidence can be changed but it hasn't, even although the EPPS has been around for some time. In general, the EPPS seems to be fading away from the testing scene, although at one time it occupied a fairly central position.

The Personality Research Form (PRF)

Introduction. The PRF (Jackson, 1967) is another example of the theoretical approach and shares with the EPPS its basis on the need theory of H. A. Murray (1938) and in the fact that it assesses needs.

Development. The development of the PRF shows an unusual degree of technical sophistication and encompasses a number of steps implemented only because of the availability of high-speed computers. D. N. Jackson (1967) indicates that there were four basic principles that guided the construction of the PRF:

1. Explicit and theoretically based definitions of each of the traits;
2. Selection of items from a large item pool, with more than 100 items per scale, with selection based on homogeneity of items;
3. The use of procedures designed to eliminate or control for such response biases as social desirability;
4. Both convergent and discriminant validity were considered at every stage of scale development, rather than after the scale was developed.

In constructing the PRF, D. N. Jackson (1967) used a series of steps quite similar to the ones outlined in Chapter 2:

1. Each of the traits (needs) was carefully studied in terms of available theory, research, etc.;
2. A large pool of items was developed, with each item theoretically related to the trait;
3. These items were critically reviewed by two or more professionals;
4. Items were administered to more than a thousand subjects, primarily college students;
5. A series of computer programs were written and used in conducting a series of item analyses;
6. Biserial correlations were computed between each item, the scale on which the item presumably belonged, scales on which the item did not belong, and a set of items that comprised a tentative social desirability scale;
7. Items were retained only if they showed a higher correlation with the scale they belonged to than any of the other scales;
8. Finally, items were retained for the final scales that showed minimal relation to social desirability, and also items were balanced for true or false as the keyed response.

The result of these steps is a set of scales that have high internal consistency and minimal overlap and are relatively free from response biases of acquiescence and social desirability.

Description. When first published in 1967, the PRF consisted of two parallel 440-item forms (forms AA and BB) and two parallel 300-item forms (forms A and B). In 1974, a revised and simplified 352-item version (form E) was published, and in 1984, form G was published for use in business and industry.

The PRF is designed to focus on normal functioning, but its primary focus was personality research and, secondly, applied work in various settings such as educational and business settings. Its scales, 15 or 22 depending on the form, of which 12 are identical in name with those on the EPPS, basically focus on seven areas of normal functioning: (1) impulse expression and control, (2) orientation toward work and play, (3) degree of autonomy, (4) intellectual and aesthetic style, (5) dominance, (6) interpersonal orientation, and (7) test-taking validity.

The last area, test-taking validity, is composed of two scales, *Desirability* and *Infrequency*; the Desirability scale assesses social desirability, or the tendency to respond on the test desirably or undesirably. The Infrequency scale is designed to identify carelessness or other "nonpurposeful" responding, and consists of items for which there is a clear modal answer, such as "I am unable to breathe."

Administration. The PRF can be easily administered to large groups and has clear instructions. There are no time limits, and the short form can be easily completed in about an hour.

Scoring. Both hand scoring and machine scoring are available.

Reliability. Because the development of the PRF consisted of some steps designed to select items that correlated highly with total scale scores, one would expect the reliability of the PRF, at least as measured by internal consistency methods, to be high. D. N. Jackson (1967) does list the Kuder-Richardson coefficients for the 22 scales, but the coefficients are inflated because they are based on the best 40 items for each scale, but each scale is made up of 20 items. To be really correct, the reliability coefficients should have either been computed on 20-item scales, or should have been corrected by the Spearman-Brown formula. Despite this, the coefficients are quite acceptable, with the exception of the Infrequency scale.

Test-retest reliabilities are also presented for a sample of 135 individuals retested with a 1-week interval. Coefficients range from a low of +.46 (again for the Infrequency scale) to a high of .90, with more than half of the coefficients in the .80s range. Odd-even reliabilities are also presented, with slightly lower coefficients.

Validity. D. N. Jackson (1967; 1984) presents considerable convergent validity data for the PRF. One set of studies consists of comparisons between PRF scores and ratings both by observers and by the subjects themselves on the same scales; correlation coefficients range from a low of +.10 to a high of +.80, with many of the coefficients in the .30 to .60 range. Correlations are also presented for PRF scales with scales of the Strong Vocational Interest Blank (SVIB) (most coefficients are quite low as one would expect because the SVIB measures career interests), and with the California Psychological Inventory (CPI), where high correlations are obtained where expected; for example, the PRF need Dominance scale and the CPI Dominance scale correlate +.78.

Norms. D. N. Jackson (1967) presents norms based on 1,029 males and 1,002 females, presumably college students.

Interesting aspects. The PRF has been hailed as a personality inventory that is very sophisticated in its development. Although it has been available for some time, it is not really a popular test, especially among practitioners. For example, Piotrowski and Keller (1984) inquired of all graduate programs that train doctoral students in clinical psychology as to which tests should a clinical PhD candidate be familiar with. The PRF was mentioned by only 8% of those responding.

The test manual does not make it clear why both short forms and long forms of the PRF were developed. Strictly speaking, these are not short forms but abbreviated forms that assess only 15 of the 22 scales. The parallel forms represent a potential plus, although in personality assessment there are probably few occasions where alternate forms might be useful. In addition, the revised version (form E) apparently does not have a parallel form. As with most multivariate instruments, the PRF has been subjected to factor analysis (see P. C. Fowler, 1985; D. N. Jackson, 1970).

Criticisms. Hogan (1989a) and Wiggins (1989) reviewed the PRF and they, like other reviewers, cited a number of problems. Perhaps the major criticisms concern the lack of validity studies and of noncollege normative data. Both of these can be remedied, but it is somewhat surprising that they have not, given that the PRF has now been available to researchers for some 30 years.

Another issue is the choice of Murray's needs as the variables that were scaled. Hogan (1989a) suggests that these variables were chosen because "they were there," rather than intrinsic utility or theoretical preference. In short, as Hogan (1989a) suggests, despite the technical excellence of the PRF, the CPI or the MBTI may be more useful to the practitioner.

The California Psychological Inventory (CPI)

Introduction. In the survey of clinical psychology programs (Piotrowski & Keller, 1984) mentioned before, the most popular personality inventory mentioned was the MMPI, which was listed by 94% of the respondents. The second most popular was the CPI which was mentioned by 49%. Thus, despite its focus on normality, the CPI is considered an important instrument by clinicians, and indeed it is. Surveys done with other professional groups similarly place the CPI in a very high rank of usefulness, typically second after the MMPI.

The author of the CPI, Harrison Gough, indicates (personal communication, August 3, 1993) that to understand the CPI there are five "axioms" or basic notions that need attention:

1. The first is the question, "what should be measured?" We have seen that for Edwards and for Jackson the answer lies in Murray's list of needs. For Gough the answer is *folk concepts*. Gough argues that across the ages, in all cultures, the important dimensions of behavior have become encapsulated in the language that people use to describe themselves, others, and behavior. These dimensions have survived the test of time, and do not reflect fads or ephemeral theories, but important dimensions of personality functioning that we, as social scientists, should pay attention to. These dimensions are labeled by Gough as folk concepts.

2. How many scales are needed in an inventory? In one sense, this is the question of how many basic dimensions of psychological functioning there are. Rather than provide a specific number, as many others do, Gough prefers the use of an *open system* that allows the development of new scales; or as Gough succinctly states, there should be "enough scales to do the job the inventory is intended to do." Some new scales for or on the CPI have been developed (e.g., Hakstian & Farrell, 2001), although nowhere near the large number of new MMPI scales.

3. How should the scales be conceptualized? Rather than take a factor analytic approach, Gough uses primarily the empirical method of criterion-keying and argues that the CPI scales are "instrumental" – that is, they have only two purposes: (a) to predict what people will say and do in specific contexts, and (b) to identify people who are described by others in specified ways (e.g., competent, friendly, leaders, etc.). There is nothing claimed here about the assessment of traits, or internal item homogeneity, or other traditional ways of thinking about personality assessment.

4. How should the scales relate to each other? Most psychologists would reply that the scales be uncorrelated, even although the empirical evidence suggests that most "uncorrelated" scales do correlate. Gough argues that independence is a preference and not a law of nature, and he argues that the scales should correlate to the same degree as the underlying concepts do in everyday usage. If we tend to perceive leaders as more sociable, and indeed leaders are more sociable, then scores on a scale of leadership and on one of sociability should in fact correlate.

5. Should a domain of functioning be assessed by a single scale or by a set of scales? If we wanted to measure and/or understand the concept of "social class membership," would simply knowing a

person's income be sufficient, or would knowing their educational level, their occupation, their address, their involvement in community activities, and so on, enrich our understanding? Gough argues for the latter approach.

Development. The CPI, first published in 1956, originally contained 480 true-false items and 18 personality scales. It was revised in 1987 to 462 items with 20 scales. Another revision that contains 434 items was completed in 1995; items that were out of date or medically related were eliminated, but the same 20 scales were retained. The CPI is usually presented as an example of a strictly empirical inventory, but that is not quite correct. First of all, of the 18 original scales, 5 were constructed rationally, and 4 of these 5 were constructed using the method of internal consistency analysis (see Megargee, 1972, for details). Second, although 13 of the scales were constructed empirically, for many of them there was an explicit theoretical framework that guided the development; for example, the Socialization scale came out of a role theory framework. Finally, with the 1987 revision, there is now a very explicit theory of human functioning incorporated in the inventory.

Description. Table 4.3 lists the names of the current CPI scales, with a brief description of each.

The 20 scales are arranged in four groups; these groupings are the result of logical analyses and are intended to aid in the interpretation of the profile, although the groupings are also supported by the results of factor analyses. Group I scales measure interpersonal style and orientation, and relate to such aspects as self-confidence, poise, and interpersonal skills. Group II scales relate to normative values and orientation, to such aspects as responsibility and rule-respecting behavior. Group III scales are related to cognitive-intellectual functioning. Finally, Group IV scales measure personal style.

The basic goal of the CPI is to assess those everyday variables that ordinary people use to understand and predict their own behavior and that of others – what Gough calls folk concepts. These folk concepts are presumed to be universal, found in all cultures, and therefore relevant to both personal and interpersonal behavior.

Table 4–3. The 20 Folk-Concept Scales of the CPI

Class I scales: Measures of interpersonal style	
Do	Dominance
Cs	Capacity for status
Sy.	Sociability
Sp	Social presence
Sa	Self-acceptance
In	Independence
Em	Empathy

Class II scales: Measures of normative orientation	
Re	Responsibility
So	Socialization
Sc	Self-control
Gi	Good impression
Cm	Communality
Wb	Well-being
To	Tolerance

Class III scales: Measures of cognitive functioning	
Ac	Achievement via conformance
Ai	Achievement via independence
Ie	Intellectual efficiency

Class IV scales: Measures of personal style	
Py	Psychological mindedness
Fx	Flexibility
F/M	Femininity/Masculinity

The CPI then is a personality inventory designed to be taken by a "normal" adolescent or adult person, with no time limit, but usually taking 45 to 60 minutes.

In addition to the 20 standard scales, there are currently some 13 "special purpose scales" such as, for example, a "work orientation" scale (Gough, 1985) and a "creative temperament" scale (Gough, 1992). Because the CPI pool of items represents an "open system," items can be eliminated or added, and new scales developed as the need arises (some examples are Hogan, 1969; Leventhal, 1966; Nichols & Schnell, 1963). Because the CPI scales were developed independently, but using the same item pool, there is some overlap of items; 42% of the items (192 out of 462) load on more than one scale, with most (127 of the 192) used in scoring on two scales, and 44 of the 192 items used on three scales.

The 1987 revision of the CPI also included three "vector" or structural scales, which taken together generate a theoretical model of

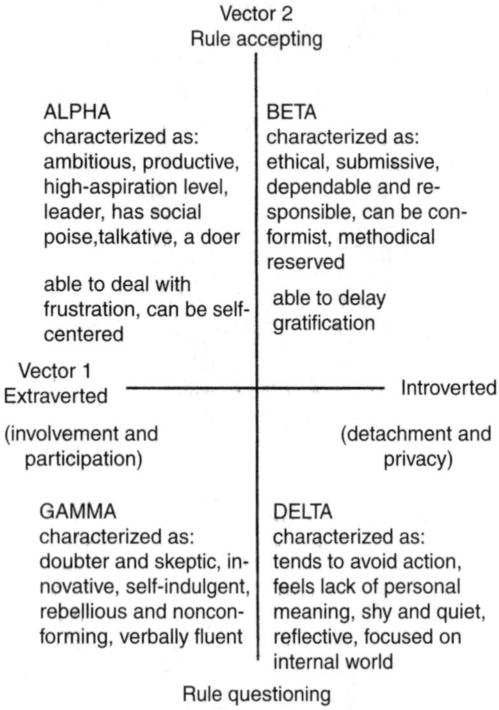

Vector 2
Rule accepting

ALPHA	BETA
characterized as:	characterized as:
ambitious, productive,	ethical, submissive,
high-aspiration level,	dependable and re-
leader, has social	sponsible, can be con-
poise, talkative, a doer	formist, methodical
	reserved
able to deal with	
frustration, can be self-	able to delay
centered	gratification

Vector 1
Extraverted ———————————————— Introverted

| (involvement and | (detachment and |
| participation) | privacy) |

GAMMA	DELTA
characterized as:	characterized as:
doubter and skeptic, in-	tends to avoid action,
novative, self-indulgent,	feels lack of personal
rebellious and noncon-	meaning, shy and quiet,
forming, verbally fluent	reflective, focused on
	internal world

Rule questioning

FIGURE 4–1. The CPI vectors 1 and 2.

personality. The first vector scale called "v1" relates to introversion-extraversion, while the second vector scale, "v2," relates to norm-accepting vs. norm-questioning behavior. A classification of individuals according to these two vectors yields a fourfold typology, as indicated in Figure 4.1.

According to this typology, people can be broadly classified into one of four types: the alphas who are typically leaders and doers, who are action oriented, and rule respecting; the betas who are also rule respecting, but are more reserved and benevolent; the gammas, who are the skeptics and innovators; and finally, the deltas who focus more on their own private world and may be visionary or maladapted.

Finally, a third vector scale, "v3," was developed with higher scores on this scale relating to a stronger sense of self-realization and fulfillment. These three vector scales, which are relatively uncorrelated with each other, lead to what Gough (1987) calls the cuboid model.

The raw scores on "v3" can be changed into one of seven different levels, from door to superior each level defined in terms of the degree of self-realization and fulfillment achieved. Thus the

actual behavior of each of the four basic types is also a function of the level reached on "v3"; a delta at the lower levels may be quite mal-adapted and enmeshed in conflicts while a delta at the higher levels may be highly imaginative and creative.

Administration. As with other personality inventories described so far, the CPI requires little by way of administrative skills. It can be administered to one individual or to hundreds of subjects at a sitting. The directions are clear and the inventory can be typically completed in 45 to 60 minutes. The CPI has been translated into a number of different languages, including Italian, French, German, Japanese, and Mandarin Chinese.

Scoring. The CPI can be scored manually through the use of templates or by machine. A number of computer services are available, including scoring of the standard scales, the vector scales, and a number of special purpose scales, as well as detailed computer-generated reports, describing with almost uncanny accuracy what the client is like.

The scores are plotted on a profile sheet so that raw scores are transformed into T scores. Unlike most other inventories where the listing of the scales on the profile sheet is done alphabetically, the CPI profile lists the scales in order of their psychological relationship with each other, so that profile interpretation of the single case is facilitated. Also each scale is keyed and graphed so that higher functioning scores all fall in the upper portion of the profile.

Reliability. Both the CPI manual (Gough, 1987) and the CPI Handbook (Megargee, 1972) present considerable reliability information, too much to be easily summarized here. But as examples, let us look at the Well-Being scale, one of the more reliable scales, and at the Self-Acceptance scale, one of the less reliable scales. For the Well-being scale test-retest reliability coefficients of .73 and .76 are reported, as well as internal consistency coefficients ranging from .76 to .81, and corrected split-half coefficient of .86. In contrast, for the Self-Acceptance scale, the test-retest reliability coefficients are .60 and .74, the internal consistency coefficients range from .51 to .58, and the corrected split-half coefficient is .70.

Validity. There are a very large number of studies that have used the CPI and thus are relevant to the question of its validity. Megargee (1972) attempted to summarize most of the studies that appeared before 1972, but an even larger number of studies have appeared since then. Although Gough and his students have been quite prolific in their contributions to the literature, the CPI has found wide usage, as well as a few vociferous critics.

Because of space limitations, we cannot even begin to address the issue of validity, but perhaps one small example will suffice. Over the years, the CPI has been applied with outstanding success to a wide variety of questions of psychological import, including that of college entrance. Nationwide, only about 50% of high-school graduates enter college. Can we predict who will enter college? Intellectual aptitude is certainly one variable and indeed it correlates significantly with college entrance, but not overwhelmingly so; typical correlations between scores on tests of intellectual aptitude and entering-not entering college are in the range of .30 to .40. Socioeconomic status is another obvious variable, but here the correlations are even lower.

In the CPI test manual, Gough (1987) reports on a nationwide normative study in which 2,620 students took the CPI while in high school and were surveyed 5 to 10 years later as to their college-going. Overall, 40% of the sample attended college, but the rates were different for each of the four types, as defined by vectors 1 and 2. Alphas had the highest rate (62%), while deltas had the lowest rate (23%); both betas and gammas had rates of 37%. High potential alphas (those scoring at levels 5, 6, or 7 on the "v3" scale) tended to major in business, engineering, medicine, and education, while high potential deltas tended to major in art, literature, and music; note that because fewer deltas were entering college, there are fewer such talented persons in a college environment. Within each type, going to college was also significantly related to level of self-realization. For example, for the alphas only 28% of those in level 1 went to college, but a full 78% of those in levels 5, 6, and 7 did. As Gough (1989) points out, the CPI has been applied to an incredibly wide range of topics, from studies of academic achievement in various settings and with various populations, to studies of criminal and delinquent behavior, studies of persons in varied occupations, creativity, intelligence, leadership, life span development, and so on. Recent studies that have looked at the revised CPI scales have found that such scales are as valid as the earlier versions and sometimes more so (e.g., DeFrancesco & Taylor, 1993; Gough & Bradley, 1992; Haemmerlie & Merz, 1991; Zebb & Meyers, 1993).

Norms. The CPI manual (Gough, 1987) contains very complete norms for a wide variety of samples, including a basic normative sample of 1,000 individuals, high school samples, college samples, graduate and professional school samples, occupational samples, and miscellaneous samples such as Catholic priests and prison inmates.

Interesting aspects. Gough (1987) argues that because all the CPI scales assess interpersonal functioning, positive correlations among the scales should be the rule rather than the exception, and indeed are proof that the CPI is working the way it was intended to. On the other hand, those of a factor analytic persuasion see such correlations as evidence that the scales are not pure measures. The data presented in the manual (Gough, 1987) do indeed show that the 20 folk-concept scales intercorrelate, some quite substantially and some to an insignificant degree. For example, at the high end, Tolerance and Achievement by Independence correlate +.81, while Dominance and Self-Acceptance correlate +.72. At the low end, Flexibility and Reliability correlate +.05 and Femininity-Masculinity and Good Impression correlate +.02 (these coefficients are based on a sample of 1,000 males).

Given the 20 folk-concept scales and the fact that they intercorrelate, we can ask whether there are fewer dimensions on the CPI than the 20 represented by the scales, and indeed there are. Gough (1987) presents the results of a factor analysis based on 1,000 males and 1,000 females, that indicates four factors:

1. The first factor is named *extraversion* and involves scales that assess poise, self-assurance, initiative, and resourcefulness.

2. The second factor is one of *control*, and is defined by scales that relate to social values and the acceptance of rules.

3. Factor 3 is called *flexibility*, and is defined by scales that assess individuality, ingenuity, and personal complexity.

4. Finally, the fourth factor is called *consensuality*, and is defined by scales that assess the degree to which a person sees the world as others do and behaves in accord with generally accepted principles, with what is accepted by consensus.

A more recent factor analysis of the CPI-R (Wallbrown & Jones, 1992), gives support both to the notion that there is one general factor of personal adjustment measured by the CPI, as well as three additional factors that coincide well with Gough's clinical analysis of the three vectors.

Much more can be said about the CPI. Its manual contains much information aimed at the practitioner, including case reports. The CPI has found wide usage not just as a research instrument, but for career counseling (e.g., McAllister, 1986) and organizational planning (e.g., P. Meyer & Davis, 1992). We should also mention that three of the CPI scales are designed to detect invalid protocols, in addition to having personological implications. Perhaps more than any other personality inventory, the CPI has been used in a wide variety of cross-cultural studies.

We now look at some personality scales that are not well known or commercially available, such as the inventories discussed so far. They are, however, illustrative of what is currently available in the literature and of various approaches.

The Inventory of Psychosocial Balance (IPB)

Introduction. The IPB is based upon the developmental theory of Erik Erikson (1963; 1980; 1982) who postulated that life is composed of eight stages, each stage having a central challenge to be met. The eight stages and their respective challenges are presented in Table 4.4.

Development. G. Domino and Affonso (1990) developed the IPB to assess these eight stages. They began by analyzing Erikson's writings and the related literature, and writing an initial pool

Table 4–4. The world according to erikson	
Life stage	Challenge to be met
Early infancy	trust vs. mistrust
Later infancy	autonomy vs. shame and doubt
Early childhood	initiative vs. guilt
Middle childhood	industry vs. inferiority
Adolescence	identity vs. role confusion
Early adulthood	intimacy vs. isolation
Middle adulthood	generativity vs. stagnation
Late adulthood	ego integrity vs. despair

of 346 items reflecting both positive and negative aspects of each stage. Unlike most other personality inventories that use a true-false format, the response format chosen was a 5-point scale, more formally known as a Likert scale (see Chapter 6), which gives the respondent five response choices: strongly agree, agree, uncertain, disagree, and strongly disagree. Each of the items was first presented to five psychologists familiar with Erikson's theory, who were asked to review the item for clarity of meaning, and were asked to identify which life stage did the item address. Items that were judged not to be clear or were not identified correctly as to stage were eliminated. Those procedures left 208 items. These items were then administered to various samples, ranging from high-school students to adults living in a retirement community – a total of 528 subjects. Each person was also asked to complete a questionnaire that asked the respondent to rate on a scale of 0 to 100% how successfully he or she had met each of 19 life challenges, such as trusting others, having sufficient food, and being independent. Eight of these 19 challenges represented those in Erikson's life stages.

The 528 protocols were submitted to a factor analysis, and each item was correlated with each of the eight self-ratings of life challenges. The factor analysis indicated eight meaningful factors corresponding to the eight stages. Items for each of the eight scales were retained if they met three criteria:

1. The item should correlate the highest with its appropriate dimension – for example, a trust item should correlate the most with the trust dimension.

Table 4–5. IPB factors and representative items

Factor	Representative item
Trust	I can usually depend on others
Autonomy	I am quite self-sufficient
Initiative	When faced with a problem, I am very good at developing various solutions
Industry	I genuinely enjoy work
Identity	Sometimes I wonder who I really am
Intimacy	I often feel lonely even when there are others around me
Generativity	Planning for future generations is very important
Ego integrity	Life has been good to me

2. The item should correlate the most with corresponding self-ratings. A trust item should correlate the most with the self-rating of trusting others.

3. The obtained correlation coefficients in each case must be statistically significant.

Finally, for each scale, the best 15 items were selected, with both positively and negatively worded items to control for any response bias.

Description. The IPB is brief, with 120 items, and consists of a question sheet and a separate answer sheet. It is designed for adults, although it may be appropriate for adolescents as well. Table 4.5 gives the eight scales with some representative items for each scale.

Administration. The IPB can be easily administered to an individual or a group, with most subjects completing the instrument in less than 30 minutes.

Scoring. The eight scales can be easily scored by hand.

Reliability. The authors assessed three samples for reliability purposes: 102 college students; 68 community adults who were administered the IPB twice with a test-retest period from 28 to 35 days, and a third sample of 73 adults living in a retirement community. The alpha coefficients for the first and third samples ranged from .48 to .79, acceptable but low. The authors interpreted these results as reflecting heterogeneity of item content. The test-retest coefficients for the second sample ranged from .79 to .90, quite high and indicative of substantial temporal stability, at least over a 1-month period.

Validity. The validity of a multivariate instrument is a complex endeavor, but there is some available evidence in a set of four studies by G. Domino and Affonso (1990). In the first study, IPB scores for a sample of 57 adults were correlated with an index of social maturity derived from the CPI (Gough, 1966). Six of the eight IPB scales correlated significantly and positively with the CPI social maturity index. Individuals who are more mature socially tend to have achieved the Eriksonian developmental goals to a greater degree. The two scales that showed nonsignificant correlation coefficients were the Autonomy scale and the Intimacy scale.

In a second study, 166 female college students were administered the IPB, their scores summed across the eight scales, and the 18 highest scoring and 18 lowest scoring students were then assessed by interviewers, who were blind as to the selection procedure. The high IPB scorers were seen as independent, productive, socially at ease, warm, calm and relaxed, genuinely dependable and responsible. The low IPB scorers were seen as self-defensive, anxious, irritable, keeping people at a distance, and self-dramatizing. In sum, the high scorers were seen as psychologically healthy people, while the low scorers were not. Incidentally, this study nicely illustrates part of secondary validity, we discussed in Chapter 3.

You will recall also from Chapter 3, that to establish construct validity, both convergent and discriminant validity must be shown. The first two studies summarized above, speak to the convergent validity of the IPB; a third study was carried out to focus on discriminant validity. For a sample of 83 adults, the IPB was administered together with a set of scales to measure variables such as social desirability and intelligence. A high correlation between an IPB scale and one of these scales might suggest that there is a nuisance component, that the scale in fact does not assess the relevant stage but is heavily influenced by, for example, intelligence. In fact, of the 48 correlations computed, only one achieved statistical significance even although quite low (.29), and thus quite easily due to chance.

Finally, a fourth study is presented by the authors to show that within the IPB there are developmental trends in accord with Erikson's theory. For example, adolescents should score lower than the elderly, and the results partially support this.

Norms. Formal norms are not presently available on the IPB other than summary statistics for the above samples.

Interesting aspects. In a separate study (G. Domino & Hannah, 1989), the IPB was administered to 143 elderly persons who were participating in a college program. They were also assessed with the CPI self-realization scale (vector 3) as a global self-report of perceived effective functioning. For men, higher effective functioning was related to a greater sense of trust and industry and lower scores on generativity and intimacy. For women, higher effective functioning was related most to a sense of identity and to lower scores on trust and industry. These results suggest that for people who grew up in the 1920s and 1930s, there were different pathways to success – for men success was facilitated by having basic trust, working hard, and not getting very close to others. For women, it meant developing a strong sense of identity, not trusting others, and not being as concerned with actual work output (see also Hannah, G. Domino, Figueredo, & Hendrickson, 1996).

Note that in developing the IPB the authors attempted to develop scales on the basis of both internal consistency and external validity.

Criticisms. The IPB is a new instrument, and like hundreds of other instruments that are published each year, may not survive rigorous analysis, or may simply languish on the library shelves.

The Self-Consciousness Inventory (SCI)

Introduction. "Getting in touch with oneself" or self-insight would seem to be an important variable, not just from the viewpoint of the psychologist interested in the arena of psychotherapy, for example, but also for the lay person involved in everyday transactions with the world. We all know individuals who almost seem obsessed with analyzing their own thoughts and those of others, as well as individuals who seem to be blessedly ignorant of their own motivation and the impact, or lack of it, they have on others.

Development. Fenigstein, Scheier, and Buss (1975) set about to develop a scale to measure such *self-consciousness*, which they defined as the consistent tendency of a person to direct his or her attention inwardly or outwardly. They first identified the behaviors that constitute the domain of self-consciousness, and decided that this domain was defined by seven aspects: (1) preoccupation with past, present, and future behavior; (2) sensitivity to inner feelings; (3) recognition of one's personal attributes, both positive and negative; (4) the ability to "introspect" or look inwardly; (5) a tendency to imagine oneself; (6) awareness of one's physical appearance; and (7) concern about the appraisal of others.

This theoretical structure guided the writing of 38 items, with responses ranging from extremely uncharacteristic (scored zero) to extremely characteristic (scored 4 points). These items were administered to undergraduate college students, 130 women and 82 men, whose responses were then factor analyzed. The results indicated three factors. This set of items was then revised a number of times, each time followed by a factor analysis, and each time a three-factor structure was obtained.

Description. The final version of the SCI consists of 23 items, with 10 items for factor 1 labeled *private self-consciousness*, 7 items for factor 2 labeled *public self-consciousness*, and 6 items for factor 3 labeled *social anxiety*. The actual items and their factor loadings are presented in the article by Fenigstein, Scheier, and Buss (1975). Examples of similar items are, for *factor 1*: "I am very aware of my mood swings"; for *factor 2*: "I like to impress others"; for *factor 3*: "I am uneasy in large groups."

Administration. This is a brief instrument easily self-administered, and probably taking no longer than 15 minutes for the average person.

Scoring. Four scores are obtained, one for each of the three factors, and a total score which is the sum of the three factor scores.

Reliability. The test-retest reliability for a sample of 84 subjects over a two-week interval ranges from +.73 for Social Anxiety (the shortest scale) to +.84 for Public Self-consciousness. The reliability of the total score is +.80. Note here, that the total scale, which is longer than any of its subscales, is not necessarily the most reliable.

Validity. No direct validity evidence was presented in the original paper, but subsequent research supports its construct validity (e.g., Buss & Scheier, 1976; L. C. Miller, Murphy, & Buss, 1981).

Norms. The authors present means and SDs separately for college men ($n = 179$) and for college women ($n = 253$), both for the total scale and for the three subscales. The results seem to indicate no gender differences.

Interesting aspects. Interscale correlations are presented by the authors. The coefficients are small (from −.06 to +.26), but some are statistically significant. Thus public self-consciousness correlates moderately with both private self-consciousness and social anxiety, while private self-consciousness does not correlate significantly with social anxiety.

Note that the three factors do not match the seven dimensions originally postulated, and the authors do not indicate the relationship between obtained factors and hypothesized dimensions.

Note also that the three subscales are scored by unitary weights; that is, each item is scored 0 to 4 depending on the keyed response that is endorsed. This is not only legitimate, but a quite common procedure. There is however, at least one alternative scoring procedure and that is to assign scoring weights on the basis of the factor loadings of the items, so that items that have a greater factor loading, and presumably measure "more" of that dimension, receive greater weight. For example, item 1 has a factor loading of .65 for factor 1, and could be scored .65 times 0 to 4, depending on the response choice selected. Item 5 has a loading of .73 for factor 1, and so could be scored .73 times 0 to 4, giving it a greater weight than item 1 in the subscale score. Clearly, this scoring procedure would be time consuming if the scoring were done by hand, but could be easily carried out by computer. Logically, this procedure makes sense. If an item measures more of a particular dimension, as shown by its larger factor loading, shouldn't that item be given greater weight? Empirically, however, this procedure of *differential weighting* does not seem to improve the validity of a scale. Various attempts have been made in the literature to compare various ways of scoring the same instrument, to determine whether one method is better. For an example of a study that compared linear vs. nonlinear methods of combining data see C. E. Lunneborg and P. W. Lunneborg (1967).

Criticisms. The initial pool of items was surprisingly small, especially in relation to the number of items that were retained, and so it is natural to wonder about the content validity of this test.

Boredom Proneness Scale (BP)

Introduction. The authors of this scale (Farmer & Sundberg, 1986), argue that boredom is a common emotion and one that is important not only in the overall field of psychology but also in more specialized fields such as industrial psychology, education, and drug abuse, yet few scales exist to measure this important variable.

Development. The authors began with a review of the relevant literature, as well as with interviews with various persons; this led to a pool of 200 true-false items, similar to, "I am always busy with different projects." Items that were duplicates and items for which three out of four judges could not agree on the direction of scoring were eliminated. Preliminary scales were then assessed in various pilot studies and items revised a number of times.

Description. The current version of the scale contains 28 items (listed in Farmer & Sundberg, 1986), retained on the basis of the following criteria: (1) responses on the item correlated with the total score at least +.20; (2) at least 10% of the sample answered an item in the "bored" direction; (3) a minimal test-retest correlation of +.20 (no time interval specified); and (4) a larger correlation with the total score than with either of two depression scales; depression was chosen because the variables of boredom and depression overlap but are seen as distinct.

Administration. This scale is easily self-administered and has no time limit; most subjects should be able to finish in less than 15 minutes.

Scoring. The scale is hand-scored; the score represents the number of items endorsed in the keyed direction.

Reliability. Kuder-Richardson 20 reliability for a sample of 233 undergraduates was +.79. Test-retest reliability for 28 males and 34 females, over a 1-week period, was +.83. Thus, this scale appears to be both internally consistent and stable over a 1-week period.

Validity. In a sample of 222 college undergraduates, scores on the BPS correlated +.67 with two boredom self-rating items scored on a 5-point scale, from never to most of the time. Essentially, this represents the correlation between one T-F scale of 28 items and one 5-point scale of 2 items.

In a second study, BPS scores were correlated with students' ratings of whether a lecture and its topic were boring. Most of the correlations were low but significant (in the .20s). BPS scores also correlated significantly ($r = +.49$) with another scale of boredom susceptibility, and a scale of job boredom ($r = +.25$). At the same time, BPS scores correlated substantially with measures of depression (.44 and .54), with a measure of hopelessness (.41), and a measure of loneliness (.53). These findings are in line with the observation that the bored individual experiences varying degrees of depression, of hopelessness, and of loneliness.

Norms. Formal norms on this scale are not available in the literature.

Interesting aspects. Note that the development of this scale follows the steps we outlined earlier. The scale is intended to be internally homogeneous, but a factor analysis has not been carried out. The significant correlations with depression, hopelessness, and loneliness could be seen as a "nuisance" or as a reflection of the real world, depending on one's philosophy of testing.

Criticisms. This seems like a useful measure that was developed in a careful and standard manner.

THE BIG FIVE

We must now return to the basic question we asked at the beginning of the chapter – how many dimensions of personality are there? We have seen that different investigators give different answers. The Greeks postulated four basic dimensions. Sir Francis Galton (1884) estimated that the English language contained a "thousand words" reflective of character. McDougall (1932) wrote that personality could be broadly analyzed into five separate factors, that he named *intellect, character, temperament, disposition,* and *temper.* Thurstone (1934), another pioneer psychologist especially in the field of factor analysis, used a list of 60 adjectives and had 1,300 raters describe someone they knew well using the list. A factor analysis of the ratings indicated five basic factors. Allport and Odbert (1936) instead found that the English language contained some 18,000 descriptive terms related to personality. Studies conducted at the University of Minnesota in the 1940s yielded an item pool of 84 categories (Gough, 1991). Meehl, Lykken, Schofield, and Tellegen (1971) in a study of therapists ratings of their psychiatric patients found 40 factors. Cattell considers his 16 dimensions primary traits, although there are other primary traits in the background, as well as secondary traits that seem just as important. Edwards considered 15 needs to be important, while Jackson using the same theory scaled 15 or 22 needs depending upon the test form. Gough on the other hand, prefers the idea of an open system that allows the number to be flexible and to be tied to the needs of applied settings. Many other examples could be listed here. In one sense we can dismiss the question as basically an ivory tower exercise – whether the continental United States has 48 states, six regional areas, 250 major census tracts, or other geopolitical divisions, does not make much difference, and depends upon one's purposes. But the search for *the* number of basic dimensions, like the search for Bigfoot, goes on.

One answer that has found substantial favor and support in the literature is that there are five basic dimensions, collectively known as the

Table 4–6. The five-factor model

Factor (alternative names)	Definition
1. Neuroticism (emotional stability; adjustment)	Maladjustment, worrying and insecure, depressed vs. adjustment, calm and secure
2. Extraversion-Introversion (surgency)	Sociable and affectionate vs. retiring and reserved
3. Openness to experience (intellect; culture)	Imaginative and independent vs. practical and conforming
4. Agreeableness (likability; friendliness)	Trusting and helpful, good natured, cooperative vs. suspicious and uncooperative
5. Conscientiousness (dependability; conformity)	Well organized and careful vs. disorganized and careless

"Big Five." One of the first to point to five basic dimensions were Tupes and Christal (1961) and Norman (1963), although the popularity of this model is mostly due to the work of Costa and McRae who have pursued a vigorous program of research to test the validity and utility of this five-factor model (e.g., McCrae & Costa, 1983b; 1987; 1989b; McCrae, Costa & Busch, 1986).

There seems to be general agreement as to the nature of the first three dimensions, but less so with the last two. Table 4.6 gives a description of these dimensions.

A number of researchers have reported results consonant with a five-factor model that attest to its theoretical "robustness," degree of generalizability, and cross-cultural applicability (e.g., Barrick & Mount, 1991; Borgatta, 1964; Digman, 1989; 1990; Digman & Inouye, 1986; Digman & Takemoto-Chock, 1981; Goldberg, 1990; Ostendorf, 1990 [cited by Wiggins & Pincus, 1992]; Watson, 1989); but some studies do not support the validity of the five factor model (e.g., H. Livneh & C. Livneh, 1989).

Note that the five-factor model is a descriptive model. The five dimensions need not occur in any particular order, so that no structure is implied. It is a model rather than a theory, and to that extent it is limited. In fact, McCrae and Costa (1989b) indicate that the five-factor model is not to be considered a replacement for other personality systems, but as a framework for interpreting them. Similarly, they write that measuring the big five factors should be only the first step in undertaking personality assessment. In line with their model, Costa and McCrae (1980; 1985) have presented an inventory to measure these five basic dimensions, and we now turn to this inventory as a final example.

The NEO Personality Inventory-Revised (NEO-PI-R)

Introduction. As the name indicates, this inventory originally was designed to measure three personality dimensions: neuroticism, extraversion, and openness to experience (Costa & McCrae, 1980). Eventually two additional scales, *agreeableness* and *conscientiousness*, were added to bring the inventory into line with the Big-Five model (Costa & McCrae, 1985). Finally, in 1990 the current revised edition was published (Costa & McCrae, 1992).

Development. The original NEO inventory, published in 1978, was made up of 144 items developed through factor analysis to fit a three-dimensional model of personality. The test was developed primarily by the rational approach, with the use of factor analysis and related techniques to maximize the internal structure of the scales. Despite the use of such techniques, the emphasis of the authors has been on convergent and discriminant validity coefficients, that is, external criteria rather than internal homogeneity.

The measures of agreeableness and conscientiousness were developed by first creating two 24-item scales, based on a rational approach. Then the scales were factor analyzed, along with the NEO inventory. This resulted in 10 items to measure the two dimensions, although it is not clear whether there were 10 items per dimension or 10 total (McCrae & Costa, 1987). A revised test was then constructed that included the 10 items, plus an additional 50 items intended to measure agreeableness and conscientiousness. An item analysis yielded two 18-item scales to measure the two dimensions, but inexplicably the two final scales consisted of 10 items to measure agreeableness and 14 items to measure conscientiousness. If the above seems confusing to you, you're in good company! In the current version of the NEO-PI-R each of the five domain scales is made up of six "facets" or subscales, with each facet made up of eight items, so the inventory is composed of a total of 240 items. The keyed response is balanced to control for acquiescence. There are then five major scales, called domain scales, and 30 subscales, called facet scales.

Description. There are two versions of the NEO-PI-R. Form S is the self-report form with items answered on a 5-point Likert scale from "strongly disagree" to "strongly agree." Form R is a companion instrument for *observer* ratings, with items written in the third person, for use by spouse, peer, or expert ratings (McCrae, 1982). An abbreviated version of the NEO-PI-R is also available consisting of 60 items, and yielding scores for the five domains only (Costa & McCrae, 1989). Like most commercially published personality inventories, the NEO-PI-R uses a reusable test booklet, and separate answer sheet that may be machine or hand scored. The NEO-PI-R is intended for use throughout the adult age range (see Costa & McCrae, 1992 for a discussion of the applicability of the NEO-PI-R to clinical clients).

Administration. As with all other personality inventories, the NEO-PI-R is easy to administer, has no time limit, and can be administered to one person or to many. It can be computer administered, scored, and interpreted, hand scored or machine scored, and professional scoring and interpretation services are available from the publisher.

Scoring. Because of the subscales, hand scoring can be tedious. Raw scores are first calculated for all 30 facet scales and 5 domain scales. These scores are then plotted on profile sheets that are separately normed for men and women. Plotting converts the raw scores into T scores. However, the T scores are then used to calculate domain factor scores. Each factor score involves adding (or subtracting) some 30 components (the facet scores), a horrendous procedure if done by hand. In fact, the manual (Costa & McCrae, 1992) indicates that domain scores give a good approximation of the factor scores, and so it is not worth calculating factor scores by hand for individual cases.

Reliability. Internal consistency and 6-month test-retest reliability coefficients for the first three (NEO) scales are reported to be from +.85 to +.93 (McCrae & Costa, 1987). The test manual (Costa & McCrae, 1992) reports both alpha coefficients and test-retest reliability coefficients, and these seem quite satisfactory. Caruso (2000) reported a metaanalysis of 51 studies dealing with the reliability of the NEO personality scales, and found that reliability was dependent on the specific NEO dimension-specifically Agreeableness scores were the weakest, particularly in clinical samples, for male only samples, and with test-retest reliability.

Validity. Much of the research using the NEO-PI and leading to the development of the NEO-PI-R is based on two major longitudinal studies of large samples, one of over 2,000 white male veterans, and the other based on a variable number sample of volunteers participating in a study of aging. Both the test manual and the literature are replete with studies that in one way or another address the validity of the NEO-PI and the NEO-PI-R, including content, criterion, and construct validity. Because we are considering 35 scales, it is impossible to meaningfully summarize such results, but in general the results support the validity of the NEO-PI-R, especially its domain scales.

Norms. The test manual (Costa & McCrae, 1992) gives a table of means and SDs for men and women separately, based on samples of 500 men and 500 women. There is a similar table for college-aged individuals, based on a sample of 148 men and 241 women aged 17 through 20 years. Tables are also available to change raw scores into percentiles.

Interesting aspects. The literature seems to confuse the Big-Five model with the NEO-PI. Although all the evidence points to the usefulness of the five-factor model, whether the NEO-PI-R is the best measure of the five factors is at present an open question.

We can once again ask whether the five dimensions, as assessed by the NEO-PI-R are independent. The test manual gives a table of intercorrelations among the 35 scales that indicates the five domain scales not to be all that independent; for example, scores on the Neuroticism scale correlate −.53 with scores on the Conscientiousness scale, and scores on the Extraversion scale correlate +.40 with scores on the Openness scale. In addition, the facet scales under each domain scale intercorrelate substantially. For example, Anxiety and Depression, which are facets of the Neuroticism scale, correlate +.64 with each other. Although one would expect the components of a scale to intercorrelate significantly, a substantial correlation brings into question whether the components are really different from each other.

Criticisms. Hogan (1989b) in reviewing the NEO-PI commends it highly because it was developed and validated on adult subjects rather than college students or mentally ill patients, because it represents an attempt to measure the Big-Five dimensions, and because there is good discriminant and convergent validity. Clearly, the NEO-PI has made an impact on the research literature and is beginning to be used in a cross-cultural context (e.g., Yank et al., 1999). Whether it can be useful in understanding the individual client in counseling and therapeutic settings remains to be seen.

SUMMARY

In this chapter, we have looked at a variety of measures of personality. Most have been personality inventories, made up of a number of scales, that are widely used and commercially available. A few are not widely known but still are useful teaching devices, and they illustrate the wide range of instruments available and the variables that have been scaled.

SUGGESTED READINGS

Broughton, R. (1984). A prototype strategy for construction of personality scales. *Journal of Personality and Social Psychology, 47*, 1334–1346.

In this study, Broughton examines six strategies by which personality scales can be constructed, including a "prototype" strategy not commonly used.

Burisch, M. (1984). Approaches to personality inventory construction. *American Psychologist, 39*, 214–227.

A very readable article in which the author discusses three major approaches to personality scale construction, which he labels as *external, inductive,* and *deductive*. The author argues that although one method does not appear to be better, the deductive approach is recommended.

Jung, C. G. (1910). The association method. *American Journal of Psychology, 21*, 219–235.

Jung is of course a well-known name, an early student of Freud who became an internationally known psychiatrist. Here he presents the word association method, including its use to solve a minor crime. Although this method is considered a projective technique rather than an objective test, the historical nature of this paper makes it appropriate reading for this chapter.

Kelly, E. J. (1985). The personality of chessplayers. *Journal of Personality Assessment, 49*, 282–284.

A brief but interesting study of the MBTI responses of chessplayers. As you might predict, chessplayers are more introverted, intuitive, and thinking types than the general population.

McCrae, R. R. & John, O. P. (1992). An introduction to the five-factor model and its applications. *Journal of Personality, 60*, 175–215.

A very readable article on the Big-Five model, its nature and history.

DISCUSSION QUESTIONS

1. Do you think that most people answer honestly when they take a personality test?

2. Compare and contrast the Cattell 16 PF and the California Psychological Inventory.

3. The EPPS covers 15 needs that are listed in Table 4.2. Are there any other needs important enough that should be included in this inventory?

4. How might you go about generating some evidence for the validity of the Self-Consciousness Inventory?

5. How can the criterion validity of a personality measure of "ego strength" (or other dimension) be established?

5 Cognition

AIM In this chapter we focus on the assessment of cognitive abilities, primarily intelligence. We take a brief look at various basic issues, some theories, and some representative instruments. We see that the assessment of intelligence is in a state of flux, partly because of and partly parallel to the changes that are taking place in the field of cognitive psychology.

INTRODUCTION

If you thought personality was difficult to define and a topic filled with questions for which there are no agreed-upon answers, then cognition, and more specifically intelligence, is an even more convoluted topic.

Not only is there no agreed-upon definition of intelligence, but the discoveries and findings of cognitive psychology are coming so fast that any snapshot of the field would be outdated even before it is developed. Fortunately for textbook writers, the field of testing is in many ways slow-moving, and practitioners do not readily embrace new instruments, so much of what is covered in this chapter will not be readily outdated.

In the field of intelligence, a multitude of theoretical systems compete with each other, great debate exists about the limits that heredity and environment impose upon intelligence as well as substantial argument as to whether intelligence is unitary or composed of multiple processes (A. S. Kaufman, 1990; Sternberg, 1985; 1988a; Wolman, 1985). It is somewhat of a paradox that despite all the turbulent arguments and differing viewpoints, the testing of intelligence is currently dominated basically by two tests: the Stanford-Binet and the Wechsler series. Very clearly, however, there is a revolution brewing,

and one concrete sign of it is the current shift from a more product orientation to a more process orientation. In the past, prediction of academic success was a major criterion both in the construction of intelligence tests by, for example, retaining items that correlated significantly with some index of academic achievement such as grades and in the interpretation of those test results, which emphasized the child's IQ as a predictor of subsequent school performance. Currently, the emphasis seems to be more on theory, and in the development and utilization of cognitive tests that are more closely related to a theoretical model, both in their development and in their utilization (Das, Naglieri, & Kirby, 1994). This should not be surprising, given our earlier discussion of the current importance of construct validity.

Some basic thoughts. Most individuals think of intelligence as an ability or set of abilities, thus implying that intelligence is composed of stable characteristics, very much like the idea of traits that we discussed in defining personality. Most likely, these abilities would include the ability to reason, to solve problems, to cope with new situations, to learn, to remember and apply what one has learned, and perhaps the ability to solve new challenges quickly.

Probably most people would also agree that intelligence, or at least intelligent behavior, can be observed and perhaps assessed or measured. Some psychologists would likely add that intelligence refers to the behavior rather than to the person – otherwise we would be forced to agree with circular statements such as, "Johnny is good at solving problems because he is intelligent," rather than the more circumscribed observation that "Johnny is solving this problem in an intelligent manner." Perhaps as a basic starting point we can consider intelligence tests as measures of achievement, of what a person has learned over his or her lifetime within a specific culture; this is in contradistinction to the more typical test of achievement that assesses what the individual has learned in a specific time frame – a semester course in introductory algebra, or basic math learned in primary grades.

Some basic questions. One basic question concerns the nature of intelligence. To what extent is intelligence genetically encoded? Are geniuses born that way? Or can intelligence be increased or decreased through educational opportunities, good parental models, nutrition, and so on. Or are there complex interactions between the *nature* and the *nurture* sides of this question, so that intellectual behavior is a reflection of the two aspects? Another basic question concerns the stability over time of cognitive abilities. Do intelligent children grow up to be intelligent adults? Do cognitive abilities decline with age? Another basic issue is how cognitive abilities interact with other aspects of functioning such as motivation, curiosity, initiative, work habits, personality aspects, and other variables. Still another basic question is whether there are gender differences. For example, do females perform better on verbal tasks and males, better on quantitative, mathematical tasks? (Maccoby & Jacklin, 1974).

There are indeed lots of intriguing questions that can be asked, and lots of different answers. Way back in 1921, the editors of the *Journal of Educational Psychology* asked a number of prominent psychologists to address the issue of what is intelligence. Recently, Sternberg and Detterman (1986) repeated the request of some 24 experts in the field of intelligence. In both cases, there was a diversity of viewpoints. Some psychologists

spoke of intelligence as within the individual, others within the environment, and still others as an interaction between the individual and the environment. Even among those who defined the locus of intelligence as the individual, there were those who were more concerned with biological aspects, others with processes such as cognition and motivation, and still others with observable behavior. Although we have made tremendous leaps since 1921 in our understanding of intelligence and in the technical sophistication with which we measure cognitive functioning, we are still hotly debating some of the very same basic issues. (See Neisser et al., 1996, for an overview of these issues.)

Intelligence: global or multiple. One of the basic questions directly related to the testing of intelligence, is whether intelligence is a global capacity, similar to "good health," or whether intelligence can be differentiated into various dimensions that might be called factors or aptitudes, or whether there are a number of different intelligences (Detterman, 1992; H. Gardner, 1983). One type of answer is that intelligence is what we make of it, that our definition may be appropriate for some purposes and not for others. After all, the concept of "good health" is quite appropriate for everyday conversation, but will not do for the internist who must look at the patient in terms both of overlapping systems (respiratory, cardiovascular, etc.), and specific syndromes (asthma, diabetes, etc.).

The early intelligence tests, especially the Binet-Simon, were designed to yield a single, global measure representing the person's general cognitive developmental level. Subsequent tests, such as the Wechsler series, while providing such a global measure, also began to separate cognitive development into verbal and performance areas, and each of these areas was further subdivided. A number of multiple aptitude batteries were developed to assess various components that were either part of intelligence tests but were represented by too few items, or that were relatively neglected, such as mechanical abilities. Finally, a number of tests designed to assess specific cognitive aptitudes were developed.

The progression from global intelligence test to a specification and assessment of individual components was the result of many trends. For one, the development of factor analysis led to the assessment of intelligence tests and the identification of specific components of such tests. Practical needs in career counseling, the placement of military personnel into various service branches, and the application of tests in industrial settings led to the realization that a global measure was highly limited in usefulness, and that better success could be attained by the use of tests and batteries that were more focused on various specialized dimensions such as form perception, numerical aptitude, manual dexterity, paragraph comprehension, and so on. (For an excellent review of the measurement of intelligence see Carroll, 1982.)

THEORIES OF INTELLIGENCE

The six metaphors. Because intelligence is such a fascinating, and in many ways, central topic for psychology, there are all sorts of theories and speculations about the nature of intelligence, and many disagreements about basic definitional issues. Sternberg (1990) suggests that one way to understand theories of intelligence is to categorize them according to the metaphor they use – that is, the model of intelligence that is used to build the theory. He suggests that there are six such metaphors or models:

1. *The geographic metaphor.* These theories, those of individuals including Spearman, Thurstone, and Guilford, attempt to provide a map of the mind. They typically attempt to identify the major features of intelligence, namely factors, and try to assess individual differences on these factors. They may also be interested in determining how the mental map changes with age, and how features of the mental map are related to real life criteria. The focus of these theories is primarily on structure rather than process; like the blueprint of a house, they help us understand how the structure is constructed but not necessarily what takes place in it. Currently, most tests of intelligence are related to, or come from, these geographic theories.

2. *The computational metaphor.* These theories see the intellect or the mind as a computer. The focus here is on the process, on the "software," and on the commonalities across people and processing rather than on the individual differences.

So the focus here is on how people go about solving problems, on processing information, rather than on why Johnny does better than Billy. Representative theories are those of Baron (1985), A. L. Brown (1978), and Sternberg (1985). Many of the tests that have evolved from this approach assess very specific processes such as "letter matching." Although some of these tests are components of typical intelligence tests, most are used for research purposes rather than for individual assessment.

3. *The biological metaphor.* Here intelligence is defined in terms of brain functions. Sternberg (1990) suggests that these theories are based or supported by three types of data: (1) studies of the localization of specific abilities in specific brain sites, often with patients who have sustained some type of brain injury; (2) electrophysiological studies where the electrical activity of the brain is assessed and related to various intellectual activities such as test scores on an intelligence test; and (3) the measurement of blood flow in the brain during cognitive processing, especially to localize in what part of the brain different processes take place. Representative theories here are those of Das, Kirby, and Jarman (1979) and Luria (1973). This approach is reflected in some tests of intelligence, specifically the Kaufman Assessment Battery for Children, and in neuropsychological batteries designed to assess brain functioning (see Chapter 15).

4. *The epistemological metaphor.* The word "epistemology" refers to the philosophical study of knowledge, so this model is one that looks primarily at philosophical conceptions for its underpinnings. This model is best represented by the work of the Swiss psychologist, Jean Piaget (1952). His theory is that intellectual development proceeds through four discrete periods: (1) a *sensorimotor* period, from birth to 2 years, whose focus is on direct perception; (2) a *preoperational* period, ages 2 to 7, where the child begins to represent the world through symbols and images; (3) a *concrete* operations period, ages 7 to 11, where the child can now perform operations on objects that are physically present and therefore "concrete"; and (4) *formal* operations, which begins at around age 11, where the child can think abstractly. A number of tests have been developed to assess these intellectual stages, such

as the Concept Assessment Kit – Conservation by Goldschmidt and Bentler, (1968).

5. *The anthropological metaphor.* Intelligence is viewed in the context of culture, and must be considered in relation to the external world. What is adaptive in one culture may not be adaptive in another. Representative theories based on this model are those of J. W. Berry (1974) and Cole (Laboratory of Comparative Human Cognition, 1982). These theories often take a strong negative view of intelligence tests because such tests are typically developed within the context of a particular culture and hence, it is argued, are not generalizable. Those who follow this model tend not to use tests in a traditional sense, but rather develop tasks that are culturally relevant. We return to this issue in Chapter 11.

6. *The sociological metaphor.* These theories, especially the work of Vygotsky (1978), emphasize the role of socialization processes in the development of intelligence. In one sense, this model of intelligence focuses on the notion that a child observes others in the social environment and internalizes their actions; what happens inside the person (intelligence) first happens between people. This is not mere mimicry but a process that continues over time, and involves continued interactions between child and others. This method is almost by definition an observational method. For example, Feuerstein (1979) has developed a test called the Learning Potential Assessment Device (LPAD). The LPAD consists of difficult tasks that the child tries to solve. Then the child receives a sequence of hints and the examiner observes how the child profits from these hints.

Other theories. Not all theories can be subsumed under the six metaphors, and it might be argued that Sternberg's schema, although quite useful, is both simplistic and arbitrary; theories are much more complex and are often categorized because they emphasize one feature, but do not necessarily neglect other aspects. Two theories that have particular relevance to psychological testing and perhaps require special mention are those of Guilford (1959a; 1959b) and of H. Gardner (1983).

Guilford has presented a theoretical model called the *structure of intellect*, sometimes called the *three faces of intellect*, which sees intellectual functions as composed of *processes* that are applied to *contents* and result in *products*. In this model, there are five types of processes: memory, cognition, divergent thinking, convergent production, and evaluation. These processes are applied to materials that can have one of four types of contents: figural, symbolic, semantic, or behavioral. The result of a process applied to a content is a product, which can involve units, classes, relations, systems, transformations, and implications.

These three facets, processes, contents, and products can interact to produce 120 separate abilities ($5 \times 4 \times 6$), and for many years Guilford and his colleagues sought to develop factor pure tests for each of these 120 cells. Although the tests themselves have not had that great an impact, the theoretical structure has become embedded in mainstream psychology, particularly educational psychology. We look at one test that emanates directly from Guilford's model (The Structure of Intellect Learning Abilities Test) and at some other tests based on this model when we discuss creativity in Chapter 8.

A second theory is that of H. Gardner (1983) who postulates multiple intelligences, each distinct from each other. Note that this is unlike the approach of factor analysts who view intelligence as composed of multiple abilities. H. Gardner believes that there are seven intelligences that he labels as linguistic, logical-mathematical, spatial (having to do with orientation), musical, bodily kinesthetic (the ability to use one's body as in athletics or dancing), interpersonal intelligence (understanding others), and intrapersonal intelligence (understanding oneself). For now, this theoretical model has had little influence on psychological testing, although it seems to have the potential for such an impact in the future.

Cognitive approaches. Cognitive psychology has had a tremendous impact on how we perceive brain functioning and how we think in theoretical terms about intelligence, although for now it has had less of an impact on actual assessment. Sternberg's (1985; 1988b) theory of intelligence is a good example of the cognitive approach. Sternberg focuses on information processing and distinguishes three kinds of information processing components. There are the *metacomponents* that are higher order processes – such as recognizing the existence of a problem, defining what the problem is, and selecting strategies to solve the problem. There are also *performance* components that are used in various problem solving strategies – for example, inferring that A and B are similar in some ways but different in others. Finally, there are *knowledge acquisition components* that are processes involved in learning new information and storing that information in memory. Sternberg's theory has resulted in an intelligence test – the Sternberg Triarchic Abilities Test – but it is too new to evaluate.

Much of the criticisms of standard intelligence tests such as the Stanford-Binet, can be summarized by saying that these efforts focus on the test rather than the theory behind the test. In many ways, these tests were practical measures devised in applied contexts, with a focus on criterion rather than construct validity. Primarily as part of the "revolution" of cognitive psychology, there has been a strong emphasis on different approaches to the study of intelligence, approaches that are more theoretical, that focus more on process (how the child thinks) rather than product (what the right answer is), and that attempt to define intelligence in terms of basic and essential capacities (Horn, 1986; Keating & MacLean, 1987; K. Richardson, 1991).

The basic model for cognitive theories of intelligence has been the computer, which represents a model of how the brain works. It is thus no surprise that the focus has been on information processing and specifically on two major aspects of such processing: the knowledge base and the processing routines that operate on this knowledge base (K. Richardson, 1991).

From a psychometric perspective. The various theories of intelligence can also be classified into three categories (with a great deal of oversimplification): (1) those that see intelligence as a global, unitary ability; (2) those that see intelligence as composed of multiple abilities; and (3) those that attempt to unite the two views into a hierarchical (i.e., composed of several levels) approach.

The first approach is well exemplified by the work of Spearman (1904; 1927), who developed the *two-factor* theory. This theory hypothesizes that intellectual activities share a common basis, called the *general* factor, or *g*. Thus if we administer several tests of intelligence to a group of people, we will find that those individuals who tend to score high on test A also tend to score high on the other tests, and those who score low tend to score low on all tests. If we correlate the data and do a factor analysis, we would obtain high correlations between test scores that would indicate the presence of a single, global factor. But the world isn't perfect, and thus we find variation. Marla may obtain the highest score on test A, but may be number 11 on test B. For Spearman, the variation could be accounted by *specific* factors, called *s*, which were specific to particular tests or intellectual functions. There may also be group factors that occupy an intermediate position between *g* and *s*, but clearly what is important is *g*, which is typically interpreted as general ability to perform mental processing, or a mental complexity factor, or agility of symbol manipulation. A number of tests such as the Raven's Progressive Matrices and the D-48 were designed as measures of *g*, and are discussed in Chapter 11 because they are considered "culture fair" tests. Spearman was British, and this single factor approach has remained popular in Great Britain, and to some extent in Europe. It is less accepted in the United States, despite the fact that there is substantial evidence to support this view; for example, A. R. Jensen (1987) analyzed 20 different data sets that contained more than 70 cognitive subtests and found a general factor in each of the correlation matrices. The disagreement then, seems to be not so much a function of empirical data, but of usefulness – how useful is a particular conceptualization?

The second approach, that of multiple factors, is a popular one in the United States, promulgated quite strongly by early investigators such as T. L. Kelley (1928) and Thurstone (1938). This approach sees intelligence as composed of broad multiple factors, such as a verbal factor, memory, facility with numbers, spatial ability, perceptual speed, and so on. How many such multiple factors are there? This is the same question we asked in the area of personality and just as in personality, there is no generally agreed-upon number. Thurstone originally proposed 12 primary mental abilities while more current investigators such as Guilford have proposed as many as 120. In fact, there is no generally agreed naming of such

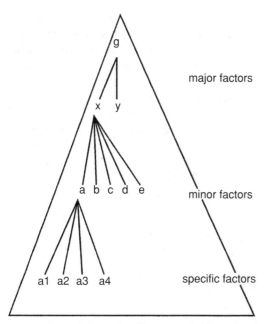

major factors

minor factors

specific factors

FIGURE 5-1. Schematic diagram of hierarchical theories.

factors, and what one investigator may label as a "perceptual speed" factor, another investigator may label quite differently (Ekstrom, French, & Harman, 1979).

As always, there are "middle of the road" approaches that attempt to incorporate the two opposing views. Several scientists have developed *hierarchical* theories that generally take a "pyramid" approach (e.g., Gustafsson, 1984; Humphreys, 1962; Vernon, 1960). At the top of the pyramid there is Spearman's g. Below that there are two or three major group factors. Each of these is subdivided into minor group factors, and these may be further subdivided into specific factors. Figure 5.1 illustrates a "generic" hierarchical theory.

OTHER ASPECTS

Intelligence and job performance. Correlations between general intelligence and job proficiency are typically in the .20s range (Ghiselli, 1966; 1973). It's been argued, however, that the typical study in this area involves a sample that is preselected and homogeneous. For example, workers at a particular factory who were hired on the basis of an application form and an interview probably survived a probationary period and continue to

be hired because they met some minimal criteria of performance. Because each of these conditions places restrictions on the variability of the sample and because of restrictions on the ratings of job performance, the "true" correlation between general intelligence and job proficiency is substantially higher, particularly as a job requires greater complexity (J. E. Hunter, 1986; J. E. Hunter & R. F. Hunter, 1984). J. E. Hunter (1986) pointed out that in well-executed studies where job proficiency is defined by objective criteria rather than supervisors' ratings, the relationship between intelligence and job performance could correlate as high as the mid .70s. Yet, we should not expect a very high correlation between any type of test and the amazing variety of skills, accomplishments, etc., to be found in different occupational activities (Baird, 1985).

Intelligence and academic achievement. Most psychologists would agree that standard intelligence tests are good measures or predictors of academic achievement. The literature confirms that there is a relationship between intelligence test scores and academic achievement of about .50 (Matarazzo, 1972). Such a relationship is somewhat higher in primary grades and somewhat lower in college (Brody, 1985). Keep in mind that in college the grading scale is severely restricted; in theory it is a 5-point scale (A to F), but in practice it may be even more restricted. In addition, college grades are a function of many more nonintellectual variables such as degree of motivation, good study habits, outside interests, than is true of primary grades. Intellectual abilities are also more homogeneous among college students than children in primary grades, and faculty are not particularly highly reliable in their grading habits.

Academic vs. practical intelligence. Neisser (1976) and others have argued that typical intelligence tests measure *academic* intelligence, which is different from *practical* intelligence. Neisser (1976) suggests that the assessment of academic intelligence involves solving tasks that are not particularly interesting, that are presented by others, and that are disconnected from everyday experience. Practical intelligence involves solving tasks as they occur in natural settings, and are "interesting" because they involve the well-being of the individual involved. Various other terms are used for practical intelligence, such as social competence or social-behavioral intelligence.

Wagner and Sternberg (1986) indicate that a good argument can be made for the need of practical intelligence as related to successful performance in the real world, and they indicate that typical intelligence tests only correlate about .20 with criteria of occupational performance, as we indicated above. They proceeded to assess what they call *tacit* knowledge, knowledge that is practical yet usually not directly taught, such as how to advance in one's career. To assess such tacit knowledge, they constructed a series of vignettes with a number of alternative responses to be ranked. For example, a vignette might indicate that you are a young assistant manager who aspires to be vice president of the company. The response alternatives list a number of actions you might undertake to reach your career goal, and you are to rank order these alternatives as to importance. What Wagner and Sternberg (1986) found is the same result as in studies of chessplayers, computer programmers and others – that experts and novices, or in this case seasoned executives vs. beginners, differ from each other primarily in the amount and organization of their knowledge regarding the domain involved, rather than the underlying cognitive abilities as measured by a traditional test of intelligence.

Still others (e.g., Frederiksen, 1962) have argued that traditional academic tests of intelligence do not capture the complexity and immediacy of real life, and that activities that simulate such real life endeavors are more useful (see Sternberg, Wagner, Williams, & Horvath, 1995).

Criticisms. Probably more than any other type of test, intelligence tests have generated a great deal of controversy and criticism, often quite acrimonious (e.g., Hardy, Welcher, Mellits, & Kagan, 1976; Hilliard, 1975; Lezak, 1988; Mercer, 1973; R. L. Williams, 1972; 1974). A. S. Kaufman (1979a) suggests that many of the criticisms of intelligence tests are more emotional than empirically defensible, especially criticisms related to supposed racial bias. But intelligence tests are certainly not perfect, and there seem to be a number of valid criticisms. One criticism is that these tests have not changed since the work of Binet at the beginning of the 1900s. They have been revised, and new ones have been introduced, but the basic strategy and structure remains the same, despite the enormous advances that have been made in understanding how the brain functions (Linn, 1986). Of course, one can answer that their longevity is a sign of their success.

Others have argued that intelligence test items really do not measure directly a person's ability to learn or to perform a task rapidly and correctly (e.g., Estes, 1974; Thorndike, 1926). Such items have been incorporated in some tests, and we can argue, as we did in Chapter 2, that the content of a test need not overlap with the predictive criterion, so that a test could empirically predict a person's ability to learn new tasks without necessarily using items that utilize new tasks. Still another criticism is that intelligence tests do not adequately incorporate developmental theories, such as the insights of Piaget, or structural theories such as Guilford's model. Again, some tests do, but the criticism is certainly applicable to most tests of intelligence. Others (e.g., Anastasi, 1983) argue that intelligence, when redefined in accord with what we now know, is a very useful construct.

Finally, it is clear that the terms often associated with intelligence testing, such as "IQ," "gifted," and "mentally defective," are emotionally laden terms and, in the mind of many lay persons, related to genetic connotations. Such terms are being slowly abandoned in favor of more neutral ones.

Intelligent testing. Both Wesman (1968) and A. S. Kaufman (1979a) have argued that intelligence testing should be "intelligent testing," that is that testing should focus on the person not the test, that the skilled examiner synthesizes the obtained information into a sophisticated totality, with sensitivity to those aspects of the client that must be taken into consideration, such as ethnic and linguistic background. This line of thinking is certainly concordant with our definition of a test as a tool; the more sophisticated and well-trained artisan can use that tool more effectively.

Age scale vs. point scale. Assume that as a homework assignment you were given the task to develop an intelligence test for children. There are probably two basic ways you might go about this. One way is to devise items that show a developmental progression – for example, items that the typical 5-year-old would know but younger children would not. If you were to find 12 such items you could simply score each correct answer as worth 1 month of mental age (of course, any number of items would work; they would just be given proportional credit – so with 36 items, each correct answer would be counted one third of a month). A 5-year-old child then, might get all the 5-year-old items correct, plus 3 items at the 6-year level, and 1 item at the 7-year level. That child would then have a mental age of 5 years and 4 months. You would have created an age scale, where items are placed in age-equivalent categories, and scoring is based upon the assignment of some type of age score. This is the approach that was taken by Binet and by Terman in developing the Binet tests.

Another alternative is, using the same items, to simply score items as correct or not, and to calculate the average score for 5-years-old, 6-years-old, and so on. Presumably, the mean for each year would increase, and you could make sense of a child's raw score by comparing that score to the age appropriate group. Now you would have created a *point scale*. This was the approach taken by Wechsler in developing his tests.

The concept of mental age. Just as we classify people according to the number of years they have lived – "he is 18 years old" – it would seem to make sense to describe people according to the level of mental maturity they have achieved. Indeed such a concept has been proposed by many. One of the hallmarks of Binet's tests was that such a concept of *mental age* was incorporated into the test. Thus, a child was considered retarded if his or her performance on the Binet-Simon was that of a younger child. Terman further concretized the concept in the Stanford-Binet by placing test items at various age levels on the basis of the performance of normal children. Thus, with any child taking the Stanford-Binet, a mental age could be calculated simply by adding up the credits for test items passed. This mental age divided by chronological age, and multiplied by 100 to eliminate decimals, gave a ratio called the *intelligence quotient* or *IQ*.

Ever since its creation, the concept of IQ has been attacked as ambiguous, misleading, and limited. It was pointed out that two children with the same mental age but with differing chronological ages were qualitatively different in their intellectual functioning, and similarly two children with the same IQ but with differing chronological and mental ages, might be quite different. In addition, mental age unlike chronological age, is not a continuous variable beyond a certain age; a 42-year-old person does not necessarily have greater mental abilities than a 41-year-old person.

Wechsler (1939) proposed the concept of *deviation IQ* as an alternative to the *ratio IQ*. The deviation IQ consists of transforming a person's raw score on the test to a measuring scale where 100 is the mean and 16 is the standard deviation. Let's assume for example that we have tested a sample of 218 nine-year-olds with an intelligence test. Their mean turns out to be 48 and the SD equals 3. We now change these raw scores to z scores and then to scores that have a mean of 100 and a SD of 16. We can tabulate these changes so that for any new 9-year-old who is tested, we can simply look up in a table (usually found in the manual of the intelligence test we are using) what the raw score is equivalent to. In our fictitious sample, we tested children all of the same age. We could also have tested a sample that was somewhat more heterogeneous in age, for example children aged 5 to 11, and used these data as our norms.

Item selection. You are interested in doing a study to answer the question whether males or females are more intelligent. You plan to select a sample of opposite sex fraternal twins, where one of the twins is male and the other female, because such a sample would presumably control such extraneous and/or confounding aspects as socioeconomic level, child rearing, type of food eaten, exposure to television, and so on. You plan to administer a popular test of intelligence to these twins, a test that has been shown to be reliable and valid. Unfortunately for your plans, your study does not make sense. Why? Basically because when a test is constructed items that show a differential response rate for different genders, or different ethnic groups, or other important variables, are eliminated from consideration. If for example, a particular vocabulary word would be identified correctly for its meaning by more white children than minority children, that word would not likely be included in the final test.

The need for revisions. At first glance, it may seem highly desirable to have tests that are frequently revised, so that the items are current, and so that they are revised or abandoned on the basis of accumulated data obtained "in the field." On the other hand, it takes time not only to develop a test, but to master the intricacies of administration, scoring, and interpretation, so that too frequent revisions may result in unhappy consumers. Each revision, particularly if it is substantial, essentially results in a new instrument for which the accumulated data may no longer be pertinent.

Understanding vs. prediction. Recall that tests can be used for two major purposes. If I am interested in predicting whether Susan will do well in college, I can use the test score as a predictor. Whether there is a relationship or not between test score and behavior, such as performance in class, is a matter of empirical validity. The focus here is on the test score, on the product of the performance. If, however, I am interested in understanding how and why Susan goes about solving problems, then the matter becomes more complicated. Knowing that Susan's raw score is 81 or that her IQ is 123 does not answer my needs. Here the focus would be more on the process, on how Susan goes about solving problems, rather than just on the score.

One advantage of individual tests of intelligence such as the Stanford-Binet or the Wechsler scales, is that they allow for observation of the processes, or at least part of them, involved in engaging in intellectual activities, in addition to yielding a summary score or scores.

Correlation vs. assignment. For most tests, the degree of reliability and validity is expressed as a correlation coefficient. Tests however, are often used with an individual client, and as we discussed in Chapter 3, correlation coefficients represent "nomothetic" data rather than ideographic. Suppose we wanted to use test results to assign children to discrete categories, such as eligible for gifted placement vs. not eligible; how can

we translate such coefficients into more directly meaningful information? Sicoly (1992) provides one answer by presenting tables that allow the user to compute the *sensitivity, efficiency,* and *specificity* of a test given the test's validity, the selection ratio, and the base rate. As we discussed in Chapter 3, sensitivity represents the proportion of low performers (i.e. positives) on the criterion who are identified accurately by a particular test – that is, the proportion of true positives to true positives plus false negatives. Efficiency represents the proportion of true positives – that is, the ratio of true positives to true positives plus false negatives. Finally, specificity represents the proportion of high performers (i.e., negatives) who are identified correctly by the test – that is, the ratio of true negatives to true negatives plus false positives.

We have barely scratched the surface on some of the issues involved in the psychological testing of intelligence, but because our focus is on psychological testing, we need to look at a number of different tests, and leave these basic issues for others to explore and discuss.

THE BINET TESTS

In 1904, the Minister of Public Instruction for the Paris schools asked psychologist, Alfred Binet, to study ways in which mentally retarded children could be identified in the classroom. Binet was at this time a well-known psychologist and had been working on the nature and assessment of intelligence for some time. Binet and a collaborator, Theodore Simon, addressed this challenge by developing a 30-item test, which became known as the 1905 Binet-Simon Scale (Binet & Simon, 1905).

The 1905 Binet-Simon Scale. This scale was the first practical intelligence test. The items on this scale included imitating gestures and following simple commands, telling how two objects are alike, defining common words, drawing designs from memory, and repeating spoken digits (T. H. Wolf, 1973). The 30 items were arranged from easy to difficult, as determined by the performance of 50 normal children aged 3 to 11 and some mentally retarded children. The items were quite heterogeneous but reflected Binet's view that certain faculties, such as comprehension and reasoning, were fundamental aspects of intelligence.

This scale was a very preliminary instrument, more like a structured interview, for which no total score was obtained. The scale was simple to administer and was intended for use by the classroom teacher. The aim of the scale was essentially to identify children who were retarded and to classify these children at one of three levels of retardation, which were called "moron, imbecile, and idiot."

The 1908 Binet-Simon Scale. The Binet-Simon was revised and the 1908 scale contained more items, grouped into age levels based on the performance of about 300 normal children. For example, items that were passed by most 4-year-olds were placed at the fourth-year level, items passed by most 5-year-olds were placed at the fifth-year level, and so on from ages 3 to 13. A child's score could then be expressed as a mental level or mental age, a concept that helped popularize intelligence testing.

The 1911 Binet-Simon Scale. A second revision of the Binet-Simon scale appeared in 1911, the same year that Binet died. This revision had only very minor changes, including the extension to age level 15 and five ungraded adult tests (for specific details on the Binet-Simon scales see Sattler, 1982).

The Binet-Simon scales generated great interest among many American psychologists who translated and/or adopted the scales. One of these psychologists was Terman at Stanford University, who first published a revision of the Binet-Simon in 1912 (Terman and Childs, 1912) but subsequently revised it so extensively that essentially it was a new test, and so the Stanford revision of the Binet-Simon became the Stanford-Binet.

The 1916 Stanford-Binet. The first Stanford-Binet was published in 1916 (Terman, 1916). This scale was standardized on an American sample of about 1,000 children and 400 adults. Terman provided detailed instructions on how to administer the test and how to score the items, and the term "IQ" was incorporated in the test. It was clear that the test was designed for professionals and that one needed some background in psychology and psychometrics to administer it validly.

The 1937 Stanford-Binet. This revision consisted of two parallel forms, forms L and M, a complete restandardization on a new sample of more than 3,000 children, including about 100 children at each half year interval from ages 1 to 5, 200 children at each age from 6 to 14, and 100 children at each age from 15 to 18. The test manual gave specific scoring examples (Terman & Merrill, 1937). The sample was not truly representative however, and the test was criticized for this. Nevertheless, the test became very popular and in some ways represented the science of psychology – quantifying and measuring a major aspect of life.

The 1960 Stanford-Binet. This revision combined the best items from the two 1937 forms into one single form and recalculated the difficulty level of each item based on a sample of almost 4,500 subjects who had taken the 1937 scale between the years 1950 and 1954. A major innovation of this revision was the use of deviation IQ tables in place of the ratio IQ. Test items on this form were grouped into 20 age levels, with age levels ranging from 2 through "superior adult." Representative test items consisted of correctly defining words, pointing out body parts on a paper doll, counting numbers of blocks in various piles, repeating digits, and finding the shortest path in a maze.

The 1972 Stanford-Binet. The 1972 revision made only some very minor changes on two items, but presented new norms based on approximately 2,100 subjects. To obtain a nationally representative sample, the 2,100 children were actually part of a larger stratified sample of 200,000 children who had been tested to standardize a group test called the Cognitive Abilities Test. The 2,100 children were selected on the basis of their scores on the Cognitive Abilities Test, to be representative of the larger sample.

It is interesting to note that these norms showed an increase in performance on the Stanford-Binet, especially at the preschool ages, where there was an average increase of about 10 points. These increases apparently reflected cultural changes, including increasing level of education of parents, the impact of television, especially "Sesame Street" and other programs designed to stimulate intellectual development (Thorndike,

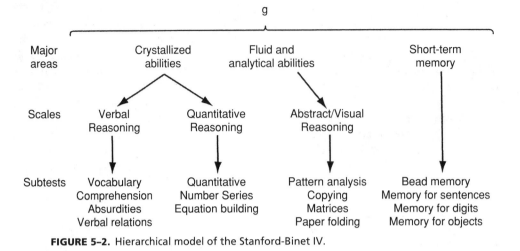

FIGURE 5–2. Hierarchical model of the Stanford-Binet IV.

1977). This form also was criticized with respect to the unrepresentativeness of the standardization sample (Waddell, 1980).

The 1986 Stanford-Binet. This was the fourth revision of the Stanford-Binet and its most extensive to date (Hagen, Delaney, & Hopkins, 1987; Thorndike, Hagen, & Sattler, 1986a; 1986b). So many changes were made on this version, referred to in the literature as the Stanford-Binet IV, that it might as well be considered a new test. The earlier forms were age scales while this revision was a point scale. The earlier forms were predominantly verbal in focus, while the 1986 form contained spatial, quantitative, and short-term memory items as well. This revision was designed for use from the age of 2 to adult. The standardization sample consisted of more than 5,000 persons, from ages 2 to 23, stratified according to the 1980 U.S. Census on such demographic variables as gender, ethnicity, and area of residence. Despite such efforts, the standardization sample had an overrepresentation of blacks, an underrepresentation of whites, and an overrepresentation of children from higher socioeconomic-level homes.

The theory that subsumes the 1986 Stanford-Binet is a hierarchical theory, with *g* at the top of the hierarchy, defined as including information-processing abilities, planning and organizing abilities, and reasoning and adaptation skills. Incorporated into this theory are also the concepts of *crystallized abilities*, which are basically academic skills, and *fluid-analytic* abilities,

which are nonverbal abilities involved in spatial thinking; these concepts were originally proposed by R. B. Cattell (1963). Crystallized abilities are further divided into verbal reasoning and quantitative reasoning, while fluid-analytic abilities translate into abstract/visual reasoning. Finally, there is a short-term memory area. Thus, the 15 subtests of the Stanford-Binet IV are then assigned to these theoretical categories as indicated in Figure 5.2.

As with most other commercially published intelligence tests, the Stanford-Binet consists of a package of products that include the actual test materials (for example, a set of blocks to form into various patterns; a card with printed vocabulary words), a record form that allows the examiner to record and/or keep track of the responses of the subject, often with summarized information as to time limits, scoring procedures, etc., a manual that gives detailed information on the administration, scoring, and interpretive procedures, and a technical manual that gives technical details such as reliability and validity coefficients, etc. Typically, other materials may be available, either from the original publisher, other publishers, or in the literature. These materials might include more detailed guides for specific types of clients, such as the learning disabled, or the gifted, computational aids to estimate standard errors, and computerized procedures to score and interpret the test results.

Description. The 1986 scale is actually composed of 15 subtests. Within each of the subtests, the items are arranged from easy to difficult. Prior to the 1986 revision, Stanford-Binet items included actual toys and objects as part of the materials to be administered. With the 1986 edition, only pictures of such objects were used. As indicated in Figure 5.2, the 15 subtests are subsumed under four content areas: (1) verbal reasoning, (2) abstract/visual reasoning, (3) quantitative reasoning, and (4) short-term memory.

Thus, the Stanford-Binet IV yields a composite score, four area scores, and 15 individual subtest scores.

Some of the subtests range in difficulty from ages 2 to 18; for example the Vocabulary and the Comprehension subtests. Other subtests only cover the older years, from age 10 upwards (for example, the Equation Building and the Paper Folding and Cutting subtests).

Administration. As with other individual intelligence tests, the administration of the 1986 Stanford-Binet requires a highly trained examiner. In fact, the Stanford-Binet can be considered more of a clinical interview than a simple test. There are complex interactions that occur between examiner and subject, and the astute examiner can obtain a wealth of information not only about how the subject uses his or her intellectual capacities, but how well organized the child is, how persistent and confident, what work methods are used, what problem-solving approaches are used, the reaction to success and failure, how frustration is handled, how the child copes with authority figures, and so on.

The 15 subtests are administered in a predetermined and mixed sequence, not as they are listed in Figure 5.2, but with Vocabulary administered first. A number of the subtests have practice items so that the subject has a chance to practice and to understand what is being requested. The Stanford-Binet is an *adaptive* test, that is, not all items are administered to all subjects, but which items and subtests are administered are a function of the subject's chronological age and performance. Where to begin on the Vocabulary subtest is a function of the subject's age. For all the other subtests, the entry level is determined from a chart for which the subject's age and score on the Vocabulary subtest are needed. In administering each of the tests, the examiner must determine the *basal level*, defined as passing four consec-

utive items. If a 10-year-old passes only 2 or 3 of the 4 items, then testing would be continued downward to easier items until four consecutive items are passed. Presumably, items below this basal level are easier and, therefore, would be passed. The examiner must also determine the *ceiling level*, defined when three out of four consecutive items are missed. Testing on the particular subtest would then be discontinued. Note that many tests of intelligence use a basal and a ceiling level, but are not necessarily defined in the same manner as the 1986 Stanford-Binet. Thus, only between 8 and 13 subtests are administered to any one individual subject.

Part of the reason for having such an administrative procedure is so that the test administration begins at an optimal level, not so difficult as to create discouragement or so easy as to result in boredom. Another reason is time; we want to maximize the amount of information obtained but minimize the amount of time required, as well as reduce fatigue in the subject and/or the examiner.

Scoring. Each item is scored as correct or incorrect. Scores on the items for the various subtests are then summed to yield raw scores for each of the subtests. These raw scores are then changed to *standard age scores* or SAS, which are normalized standard scores with mean of 50 and SD of 8, by using the subject's age to locate the appropriate normative tables in the test manual. In addition, SAS can be obtained for each of the four major areas and as a total for the entire test. These summary scores, however, are set so the mean is 100 and the SD is 16, in keeping with the earlier editions of the Stanford-Binet and with most other intelligence tests. What in earlier editions was called a deviation IQ score is now called a *test composite* score. Additional guidelines for administration, scoring, and interpretation of the Stanford-Binet can be found in various publications (such as Delaney & Hopkins, 1987).

Reliability. As you might imagine, there is considerable information about the reliability of the Stanford-Binet, most of which supports the conclusion that the Stanford-Binet is quite reliable. Most of the reliability information is of the internal consistency variety, typically using the Kuder-Richardson formula. At the subtest level, the 15 subtests are reliable, with typical coefficients in the high .80s and low .90s. The one exception to this is the Memory for Objects subtest, which is short and has typical reliability coefficients from the high .60s to the high .70s. The reliabilities of the four area scores and of the total score are quite high, ranging from .80 to .99.

Some test-retest reliability information is also available in the test manual. For example, for two groups of children, 5-year-olds and 8-year-olds, retested with an interval of 2 to 8 months, reliability coefficients of .91 and .90 were obtained for the total score.

Because the Stanford-Binet requires a skilled examiner, a natural question is that of interrater reliability. Would two examiners score a test protocol identically? No such reliability is reported in the test manual, and few studies are available in the literature (Mason, 1992).

With the Stanford-Binet IV, scatter of subtest scores may in fact reflect unreliability of test scores or other aspects such as examiner error or situational variables, all of which lower reliability. Some investigators (Rosenthal & Kamphaus, 1988; Spruill, 1988) have computed tables of confidence intervals that allow the test user to correctly identify when subtest scores for a subject are indeed different from each other and may therefore reflect differential patterning of abilities.

Validity. The assessment of validity for a test like the Stanford-Binet is a complex undertaking, perhaps best understood in terms of construct validity. The development of the 1986 Stanford-Binet was based not just on the prior editions but on a series of complicated analyses of a pool of potential items that were field tested and revised a number of times (Thorndike, Hagen, & Sattler, 1986b). There were three major sources of validity information investigated by the test authors: (1) factor analysis, (2) correlations with other intelligence tests, and (3) performance of "deviant" groups.

The results of various factor analyses indicate support for the notion that the correlations of the 15 subtests can be accounted for by a general factor. In addition, the results are also somewhat consonant with the idea that not only is there one general factor, but there are at least three specific area factors. Because different subtests are administered at different ages, the factor structure of the test varies according to age. For example, the test manual indicates that there are two factors at the preschool level, but four factors at the adolescent/adult level. At the same time, somewhat different factor structures have been reported by different investigators (e.g., Keith, et al., 1988; R. B. Kline 1989; Sattler, 1988). Other investigators have looked at the factor structure of the Stanford-Binet in a variety of samples, from elementary school children to gifted (e.g., Boyle, 1989; Gridley, 1991; T. Z. Keith et al., 1988; R. B. Kline, 1989; McCallum, 1990; McCallum, Karnes & Crowell, 1988; Ownby & Carmin, 1988). At the same time, it can be argued that the results of the factor analyses do not fully support the theoretical model that gave birth to the Stanford-Binet IV. All subtests do load significantly on *g*. Some of the subtests do load significantly on the appropriate major areas, but there are exceptions. For example, the Matrices subtest, which falls under the Abstract/Visual reasoning area, actually loads more highly with the Quantitative reasoning area. Whether these exceptions are strong enough to suggest that the theoretical model is incorrect is debatable (Delaney & Hopkins, 1987).

A second source of validity information are the correlations obtained between scores on the Stanford-Binet and scores on other intelligence tests, primarily with the Wechsler tests and with earlier versions of the Stanford-Binet. The obtained correlation coefficients are too numerous to report here, but in general, show substantial correlation between same type subtests. The correlations between the total Stanford-Binet scores and similar scores on other tests correlate in the .80 to .91 range. Other investigators have compared the Stanford-Binet with the WISC-R in gifted children (e.g., Phelps, 1989; Robinson & Nagle, 1992) and in learning-disabled children (e.g. T. L., Brown, 1991; Phelps & Bell, 1988), with the WAIS-R (e.g., Carvajal, 1987a; Spruill, 1991), with the WPPSI (Carvajal, 1991), with the K-ABC (e.g., Hayden, Furlong, & Linnemeyer, 1988; Hendershott et al., 1990; Knight, Baker, & Minder, 1990; Krohn & Lamp, 1989; Lamp & Krohn, 1990), and with other tests (e.g., Atkinson, 1992; Carvajal, 1987c; 1988; Karr, Carvajal & Palmer, 1992). The Wechsler tests and the K-ABC are discussed below.

Finally, a number of studies with gifted, learning-disabled, and mentally retarded children, show the results to be consonant with group membership. A substantial number of studies are now available in the literature, with most indicating substantial validity of the Stanford-Binet with a variety of subjects (e.g., A. C. Greene, Sapp, & Chissom, 1990; Knight, Baker, & Minder, 1990; Krohn & Lamp, 1989; D. K. Smith, St. Martin, & Lyon, 1989).

Special forms. Assessment of special populations, such as the hearing impaired, or those with learning disabilities, requires different approaches, including the modification of standard techniques. Glaub and Kamphaus (1991) constructed a short form of the 1986 Stanford-Binet by having school psychologists select those subtests requiring the least amount of verbal response by the examinee, and little verbal expression by the examiner. Of the 15 subtests, 5 met the selection criteria. These five subtests are, as a totality, estimated to have a reliability of .95, and correlate .91 with the summary score for the total test.

Jacobson et al. (1978) developed a Spanish version of the Stanford-Binet for use with Cuban children. Abbreviated forms are also available (Carvajal, 1987b; Volker et al., 1999).

Criticisms. The early Binet tests were criticized on a number of grounds including inadequate standardization, a heavy emphasis on verbal skills, items too heavily reflective of school experience, narrow sampling of the intellectual functions assessed, inappropriate difficulty of items with too easy items at the lower levels and too difficult items at the upper levels, and other more technical limitations (Frank, 1983). The 1986 revision has addressed most of the limitations of the earlier versions, but as indicated, the standardization sample is still not fully representative, with an overrepresentation of children from professional-managerial homes and college-educated parents. The results of the factor analyses are also not as uniform as one might hope, and there is a bit of additional confusion generated by the test authors who do not agree as to whether area scores or factor scores should be used (Sattler, 1988; Thorndike, Hagen, & Sattler, 1986b).

THE WECHSLER TESTS

David Wechsler, a psychologist long associated with Bellevue Psychiatric Hospital in New York City, developed a series of three intelligence tests – the Wechsler Adult Intelligence Scale (WAIS), the Wechsler Intelligence Scale for Children (WISC), and the Wechsler Preschool and Primary Scale of Intelligence (WPPSI). These tests have become widely accepted and utilized by clinicians and other professionals and, particularly at the adult level, the WAIS has no competition. The Wechsler tests are primarily clinical tools designed to assess the individual "totally," with the focus more on the process rather than the resulting scores.

The WAIS

Introduction. The WAIS had its beginnings in 1939 as the Wechsler-Bellevue Intelligence Scale. Wechsler (1939) pointed out that the then-available tests of intelligence, primarily the Stanford-Binet, had been designed to assess the intelligence of children, and in some cases had been adapted for use with adults simply by adding more difficult items. He argued that many intelligence tests gave undue emphasis to verbal tasks, that speed of response was often a major component, and that the standardization samples typically included few adults. To overcome these limitations, Wechsler developed the Wechsler-Bellevue, with many of the items adapted from the Binet-Simon tests, from the Army Alpha, which had been used in the military during World War I, and from other tests then in vogue (G. T. Frank, 1983; A. S. Kaufman, 1990).

In 1955, the Wechsler-Bellevue was replaced by the WAIS, which was then revised in 1981 as the WAIS-R, and was again revised in 1997 as the WAIS-3. The items for the WAIS scales were selected from various other tests, from clinical experience, and from many pilot projects. They were thus chosen on the basis of their empirical validity, although the initial selection was guided by Wechsler's theory of the nature of intelligence (Wechsler, 1958; 1975). The WAIS-R revision was an attempt to modernize the content by, for example, including new Information subtest items that refer to famous blacks and to women, to reduce ambiguity, to eliminate "controversial" questions, and to facilitate administration and

Table 5–1. The WAIS-R subtests	
Verbal scale	**Description**
Information	This is a measure of range of knowledge. Composed of questions of general information that adults in our culture presumably know, e.g., in which direction does the sun set?
Digit span	Involves the repetition of 3 to 9 digits, and 2 to 8 backwards. Measures immediate memory and the disruptive effects of anxiety.
Vocabulary	Defining words of increasing difficulty. Measures vocabulary.
Arithmetic (T)	Elementary school problems to be solved in one's head. Presumably measures the ability to concentrate.
Comprehension	Items that attempt to measure common sense and practical judgment.
Similarities	Requires the examinee to point out how two things are alike. Measures abstract thinking.
Performance scale	**Description**
Picture completion	A series of drawings each with a detail that is missing. Measures alertness to details.
Picture arrangement (T)	Sets of cartoon like panels that need to be placed in an appropriate sequence to make a story. Measures the ability to plan.
Block design (T)	A set of designs are to be reproduced with colored blocks. Measures nonverbal reasoning.
Object assembly (T)	Puzzles representing familiar objects like a hand, are to be put together. Measures the ability to perceive part-whole relationships.
Digit symbol (T)	A code substitution task where 9 symbols are paired with 9 digits. The examinee is given a sequence of numbers and needs to fill in the appropriate symbols; has a 90-seconds time limit. Measures visual-motor functioning.

Note: Subtests followed by a T are timed.

scoring by appropriate changes in the Manual. In addition, a new standardization sample was collected.

Description. The WAIS-R is composed of 11 subtests that are divided into 2 areas – the *Verbal* Scale with 6 subtests, and the *Performance* scale with 5 subtests. Table 5.1 lists the subtests and a brief description of each.

Administration. In the 1955 WAIS, the six verbal subtests were presented first, followed by the five performance subtests. In the WAIS-R, they are administered by alternating a verbal and a performance subtest in a prescribed order, beginning with Information. As indicated in Table 5.1, five of the subtests are timed, so that the score on these reflects both correctness and speed.

Scoring. The WAIS-R is an individual test of intelligence that requires a trained examiner to administer it, to score it, and to interpret the results. The test manual gives detailed scoring criteria that vary according to the subtest. For example, for the Information subtest each item is scored as either correct or incorrect. But for the Comprehension subtest and the Similarities subtest, some answers are worth 2 points, some 1 point, and some 0. For the Object Assembly items, scoring is a function of both how many of the puzzle pieces are correctly placed together, plus a time bonus; scores for the hand puzzle for example, can vary from 0 to 11 points. A number of books are available for the professional that give further guidance on administration, scoring, and interpretation (e.g., Groth-Marnat, 1984; Zimmerman, Woo-Sam, & Glasser, 1973).

Raw scores on each subtest are changed into standard scores with a mean of 10 and SD of 3, by using the appropriate table in the test manual. This table is based upon the performance of 500 individuals, all between the ages of 20 and 34. The standard scores are then added up across the six subtests that make up the Verbal scale, to derive a Verbal score; a similar procedure is followed for the five subtests of the Performance scale to yield a Performance score, and the two are added together to yield a *Full Scale* score. Using

Table 5–2. Classification of Wechsler IQs	
IQ	**Classification**
130 & above	Very superior
120–129	Superior
110–119	High average or bright normal
90–109	Average
80–89	Low average or dull normal
70–79	Borderline
69 & below	Mentally retarded or mentally defective

the tables in the manual, these three scores can be changed to deviation IQs, each measured on a scale with mean of 100 and SD of 15. Microcomputer scoring systems that can carry out the score conversions and provide brief reports based on the subject's test performance are now available.

The Full Scale IQs obtained on any of the Wechsler scales are divided into seven nominal categories, and these are listed in Table 5.2.

Reliability. Reliability coefficients for the WAIS are presented for each of nine age groups, separately. Corrected split-half reliabilities for the Full Scale IQ scores range from .96 to .98; for the Verbal IQ scores they range from .95 to .97; and for the Performance IQ scores from .88 to .94 (Wechsler, 1981). Similar coefficients are reported for the WAIS-R: for example, both the Full Scale IQ and the Verbal IQ have coefficients of .97, and for the Performance IQ of .93. For the individual subtests, the corrected split-half reliabilities are lower, but the great majority of the coefficients are above .70. Split-Half reliability is not appropriate for the Digit Symbol subtest because this is a speeded test, nor for the Digit Span subtest, because this is administered as two separate subtests (digits forward and digits backward). For these two tests, alternate form reliabilities are reported, based on comparisons of the WAIS-R with the WAIS, or with the WISC-R (note that the WAIS does not have alternate forms). The WAIS-R manual also includes standard errors of measurement; for the Full Scale IQ and Verbal IQ these are below 3 points, while for the Performance IQ it is 4.1.

Test-retest reliability coefficients, over an interval of 2 to 7 weeks, hover around .90 for the three summary scores (Verbal, Performance, and Full Scale), and in the .80s and .90s for most of

the subtests. Subtests like the Picture Arrangement and Object Assembly seem, however, to be marginal with coefficients in the .60s. Interestingly, average Full Scale IQ seems to increase about 6 to 7 points upon retest, probably reflecting a practice effect.

Validity. Wechsler has argued that his scales have content and construct validity – that is, the scales themselves define intelligence. Thus, the Wechsler manuals that accompany the respective tests typically do not have sections labeled "validity," and the generation of such data, especially criterion validity, is left up to other investigators.

The presence of content validity is argued by the fact that the items and subtests included in the WAIS-R are a reflection of Wechsler's theory of intelligence, and his aim of assessing intelligence as a global capacity. Items were included both on empirical grounds in that they correlated well with various criteria of intelligence, as well as logical grounds in that they were judged to be appropriate by experienced clinicians.

There are however, a number of studies that address the criterion validity of the WAIS and WAIS-R. These have typically shown high correlations between the two tests, and high correlations with the Stanford-Binet and other intelligence tests. Other studies have demonstrated a relationship between WAIS and WAIS-R scores to various indices of academic success, with typical correlation coefficients in the .40s.

Norms. The normative sample consisted of almost 1,900 individuals chosen so as to be representative along a number of dimensions such as race and geographical region of residence, according to U.S. Census data. These individuals were distributed equally over nine age levels, from years 16–17 to years 70–74, and were basically "normal" adults, exclusive of persons with severe psychiatric and/or physical conditions.

Stability over time. Aside from a reliability point of view, we can ask how stable is intelligence over a period of time. A number of studies have used the WAIS with different groups of subjects such as college students, geriatric patients, and police applicants, and retested them after varying periods of time ranging from a few months to 13 years, and have found typical correlation coefficients in the .80s and .90s for the shorter time periods, and in the .70s for longer time periods (e.g., H. S. Brown & May, 1979; Catron & Thompson, 1979; Kangas & Bradway, 1971).

The Deterioration Quotient. A somewhat unique aspect of the WAIS tests is the observation that as individuals age their performance on some of the WAIS subtests, such as Vocabulary and Information, is not significantly impaired, while on other subtests, such as the Block Design and the Digit Symbol, there can be serious impairment. This led to the identification of "hold" subtests (no impairment) and "don't hold" subtests, and a ratio termed the *Deterioration Quotient*, although the research findings do not fully support the validity of such an index (e.g., J. E. Blum, Fosshage, & Jarvix, 1972; R. D. Norman & Daley, 1959).

Wechsler argued that the intellectual deterioration present as a function of aging could also be reflected in other forms of psychopathology and that the Deterioration Quotient would be useful as a measure of such deterioration. In fact, the research literature does not seem to support this point (e.g., Bersoff, 1970; Dorken & Greenbloom, 1953).

Pattern analysis. The use of the Wechsler scales has generated a large amount of information on what is called *pattern analysis*, the meaning of any differences between subtest scaled scores or between Verbal and Performance IQs. For example, we normally would expect a person's Verbal IQ and Performance IQ to be fairly similar. What does it mean if there is a substantial discrepancy between the two scores, above and beyond the variation that might be expected due to the lack of perfect reliability? A number of hypotheses have been proposed, but the experimental results are by no means in agreement. For example, schizophrenia is said to involve both impaired judgment and poor concentration, so schizophrenic patients should score lower on the Comprehension and Arithmetic subtests than on other subtests. Whether there is support for this and other hypothesized patterns is highly debatable (G. H. Frank, 1970). In addition, the same pattern of performance may be related to several diagnostic conditions. For example, a Performance IQ significantly higher than a Vocabulary IQ might be indicative of left hemisphere cerebral impairment (Goldstein & Shelly, 1975), underachievement (Guertin, Ladd, Frank, et al., 1966), or delinquency (Haynes & Bensch, 1981).

Many indices of such pattern or profile analysis have been proposed. Wechsler (1941) suggested that differences larger than two scaled points from the subtest mean of the person were significant and might reflect some abnormality; McFie (1975) suggested three points and other investigators have suggested more statistically sophisticated indices (e.g., Burgess, 1991; Silverstein, 1984).

Part of the difficulty of pattern analysis is that the difference between subtests obtained by one individual may be reflective of diagnostic condition, of less than perfect reliability, or variation due to other causes that we lump together as "error," and we cannot disentangle the three aspects, particularly when the reliabilities are on the low side as is the case with subtests such as Object Assembly and Picture Arrangement.

Factor structure. Whether the Wechsler tests measure *g*, two factors or three factors, is an issue that, at present, remains unresolved, despite energetic attempts at providing a definitive answer (e.g. Fraboni & Saltstone, 1992; Leckliter, Matarazzo, & Silverstein, 1986). Verbal and Performance IQs typically correlate about .80. Scores on the verbal subtests generally correlate higher with the Verbal IQ than with the Performance IQ, while scores on the performance subtests generally correlate higher with the Performance IQ than with the Verbal IQ. (However, the difference in correlation coefficients is typically quite small, of the order of .10.) Factor analytic studies do seem to suggest that there is one general factor in the WAIS, typically called "general reasoning." Many studies however, also find two to three other important factors, typically named "verbal comprehension," "performance," and "memory" (J. Cohen, 1957). A substantial number of studies have factor analyzed the 1955 WAIS, and the results have been far from unanimous; these have been summarized by Matarazzo (1972).

The WAIS-R also has been factor analyzed, and here too the results are equivocal. Naglieri and A. S. Kaufman (1983) performed six factor analyses using different methods, on the

1,880 protocols from the standardization sample, adults aged 16 to 74 years. The various methods yielded anywhere from one to four factors depending on the age group. The authors concluded that the most defensible interpretation was two factors (Verbal and Performance), followed closely by three factors (Verbal, Performance, and Freedom from Distractibility).

Abbreviated scales. Basically, there are two ways to develop a short form of a test that consists of many sections or subtests, such as the WAIS or the MMPI. One way is to reduce the number of subtests administered; instead of administering all 11 subtests of the WAIS-R, for example, we could administer a subset of these that correlate substantially with the total test. This is what has been done with the WAIS. Another way, is to administer all subtests, but to reduce the number of items within the subtests. This second method, the item-reduction method, has several advantages in that a wider sample of test behavior is obtained, and the scores for each subtest can be calculated. Some empirical evidence also suggests that item-reduction short forms provide a more comparable estimate of the full battery total score than do subtest-reduction short forms (Nagle & Bell, 1995).

Short forms have two primary purposes: (1) to reduce the amount of testing time, and (2) to provide valid information. C. E. Watkins (1986) reviewed the literature on the Wechsler short forms (at all three levels of adult, children, and preschool) and concluded that none of the abbreviated forms could be considered valid as IQ measures, but were useful as screening instruments.

For any test then, abbreviated forms are typically developed by administering the original test, and then correlating various subtests or subset of items with the total score on the full form; thus the criterion in determining the validity of a short form is its correlation with the Full Scale IQ. Abbreviated forms of the Wechsler tests have been proposed, by either eliminating items within subtests, or simply administering a combination of five or fewer subtests. Under the first approach, a number of investigators have developed short forms of the Wechsler tests by selecting subset of items, such as every third item. These short forms correlate in the .80 to .90 range with Full Scale IQ (e.g., Finch, Thornton, & Montgomery,

1974; J. D. King & Smith, 1972; Preston, 1978; Yudin, 1966).

Others have looked at a wide variety of subtest combinations. For example, a commonly used abbreviated form of the WAIS is composed of the Arithmetic, Vocabulary, Block Design, and Picture Arrangement subtests. These abbreviated scales are particularly attractive when there is need for a rapid screening procedure, and their attractiveness is increased by the finding that such abbreviated scales can correlate as high as .95 to .97 with the Full Scale IQs (Silverstein, 1968; 1970). McNemar (1950) examined the relationship of every possible combination of subtests, and found that they correlated in the .80 to .90 range with Full Scale IQ. Kaufman, Ishikuma, and Kaufman-Packer (1991) developed several extremely brief short forms of the WAIS-R that seem to be both reliable and valid. Still others have focused on the Vocabulary subtest because for many, vocabulary epitomizes intelligence. Vocabulary subtest scores, either in its regular length or in abbreviated form, typically correlate in the .90s with Full Scale IQ (e.g., Armstrong, 1955; J. F. Jastak & J. R. Jastak, 1964; Patterson, 1946).

Obviously, the use of an abbreviated scale short-circuits what may well be the most valuable aspect of the WAIS, namely an experimental-clinical situation where the behavior of the subject can be observed under standard conditions. It is generally agreed, that such short forms should be administered only as screening tests rather than as an assessment or diagnostic procedure or for research procedures where a rough estimate of intelligence is needed.

Group administration. Although the Wechsler tests are individually administered tests, a number of investigators have attempted to develop group forms, typically by selecting specific subtests and altering the administration procedures so that a group of individuals can be tested simultaneously (e.g., Elwood, 1969; Mishra, 1971). Results from these administrations typically correlate in the .80 to .90 range with standard administration, although again such group administrations negate the rich observational data that can be gathered from a one-on-one administration.

Examiner error. Most test manuals do not discuss examiner error, perhaps based on the assumption that because clear administration and scoring guidelines are given, such error does not exist. The evidence, however, is quite to the contrary. Slate and Hunnicutt (1988) reviewed the literature on examiner error as related to the Wechsler scales, and proposed several explanatory reasons for the presence of such error: (1) inadequate training and poor instructional procedures; (2) ambiguity in test manuals, in terms of lack of clear scoring guidelines, and lack of specific instructions as to when to further question ambiguous responses; (3) carelessness on the part of the examiner, ranging from incorrect calculations of raw scores to incorrect test administration; (4) errors due to the relationship between examiner and examinee – for example, the finding that "cold" examiners obtain lower IQs from their examinees than do "warmer" examiners; and (5) job concerns for the examiner; for example, greater errors on the part of examiners who are overloaded with clients or are dissatisfied with their job.

Criticisms. Despite the frequent use of the Wechsler tests, there are many criticisms in the literature. Some are identical to those of the Stanford-Binet. Some are mild and easily rebuked. Others are much more severe. G. Frank (1983) for example, in a thoughtful and thorough review of the Wechsler tests, concludes that they are like a "dinosaur," too cumbersome and not in line with current conceptualizations of psychometrics and of intelligence; he suggests therefore that it is time for them to become "extinct"!

In spite of such severe judgments, the WAIS-R continues to be used extensively, in both clinical and research practice, and many of its virtues are extolled. For example, contrary to popular opinion, one of the general findings for the Wechsler tests is that they do not have a systematic bias against minority members (e.g., A. R. Jensen, 1976; A. S. Kaufman & Hollenbeck, 1974; D. J. Reschly & Sabers, 1979; Silverstein, 1973).

The WISC

The original Wechsler-Bellevue was developed as an adult test. Once this was done, it was extended downward to assess children, and eventually became the Wechsler Intelligence Scale for Children or WISC. (Seashore, Wesman, & Doppelt,

1950). Many of the items for the WISC were taken directly from the Wechsler-Bellevue and others were simply easier items modeled on the adult items. You might recall that the Stanford-Binet had been criticized because some of its items at the adult level were more difficult versions of children's items! A revised version of the WISC, called the WISC-R was published in 1974. These two scales are quite comparable, with 72% of the WISC items retained for the WISC-R. The WISC-R was again revised in 1991 when it became the WISC-III. Chattin (1989) conducted a national survey of 267 school psychologists to determine which of four intelligence tests (the K-ABC, the Stanford-Binet IV, the WISC-R, and the McCarthy Scales of Children's Abilities) was evaluated most highly. The results indicated that the WISC-R was judged to be the most valid measure of intelligence and the test that provided the most useful diagnostic information.

Description. The WISC-R consists of 12 subtests, 2 of which are supplementary subtests, that should be administered, but may be used as substitute subtests if one of the other subtests cannot be administered. As with the WAIS, the subtests are divided into Verbal and Performance and are very similar to those found in the WAIS. Table 5.3 gives a listing of these subtests.

Administration. As with all the Wechsler tests, administration, scoring, and interpretation requires a trained examiner. Most graduate students in fields such as clinical psychology take at least one course on such tests and have the opportunity to sharpen their testing skills in externship and internship experiences. The WISC-R is particularly challenging because the client is a child and good rapport is especially crucial.

The instructions in the test manual for administration and scoring are quite detailed and must be carefully followed. The starting point for some of the WISC-R subtests varies as a function of the child's age. For most of the subtests, testing is discontinued after a specified number of failures; for example, testing is discontinued on the Information subtest if the child misses five consecutive items.

Scoring. Scoring the WISC-R is quite similar to scoring the WAIS. Detailed guidelines are

Table 5–3. WISC subtests	
Verbal scale	
Information	
Similarities	
Arithmetic	
Vocabulary	
Comprehension	
Digit span*	*Description is identical to that of the WAIS.*
Performance scale	
Picture completion	
Picture arrangement	
Block design	
Object assembly	
Coding (like the Digit Symbol of the WAIS)	
Mazes* (mazes of increasing difficulty)	

*Digit span and Mazes are supplementary tests.

presented in the test manual as to what is considered a correct response, and how points are to be distributed if the item is not simply scored as correct or incorrect. Raw scores are then changed into normalized standard scores with mean of 10 and SD of 3, as compared to a child's own age group. These subtest scores are then added and converted to a deviation IQ with mean of 100 and SD of 15. Three total scores are thus obtained: a Verbal IQ, a Performance IQ, and a Full Scale IQ. As with both the Stanford-Binet and the WAIS, there are a number of sources available to provide additional guidance for the user of the WISC-R (e.g., Groth-Marnat, 1984; A. S. Kaufman, 1979a; Sattler, 1982; Truch, 1989). A. S. Kaufman (1979a), in particular, gives some interesting and illustrative case reports.

Computer programs to score the WISC-R and provide a psychological report on the client are available, but apparently differ in their usefulness (Das, 1989; Sibley, 1989).

Reliability. Both split-half (odd-even) and test-retest (1-month interval) reliabilities are reported in the test manual. For the total scores, they are all in the .90s suggesting substantial reliability, both of the internal consistency and stability over time types. As one might expect, the reliabilities of the individual subtests are not as high, but typically range in the .70s and .80s.

The test manual also gives information on the standard error of measurement and the standard error of the difference between means (which we

discussed in Chapter 3). The SE of measurement for the Full Scale IQ is about 3 points. This means that if we tested Annette and she obtained a Full Scale IQ of 118, we would be quite confident that her "true" IQ is somewhere between 112 and 124 (1.96 times the SE). This state of affairs is portrayed in Figure 5.3.

Validity. Studies comparing WISC scores with various measures of academic achievement such as grades, teachers' evaluations, and so on, typically report correlation coefficients in the .50s and .60s, with Verbal Scale IQs correlating higher than Performance Scale IQs with such criteria. Correlations of WISC scores with scores on the Stanford-Binet are in the .60s and .70s and sometimes higher, again with the Verbal Scale IQ correlating more highly than the Performance Scale IQ, and with the Vocabulary subtest yielding the highest pattern of correlations of all subtests (Littell, 1960).

Studies comparing the WISC-R to the WISC show substantial correlations between the two, typically in the .80s (e.g., K. Berry & Sherrets, 1975; C. R. Brooks, 1977; Swerdlik, 1977; P. J. Thomas, 1980). In addition, scores on the WISC-R have been correlated with scores on a substantial number of other test scores, with the results supporting its concurrent and construct validity (e.g., C. R. Brooks, 1977; Hale, 1978; C. L. Nicholson, 1977; Wikoff, 1979).

Fewer studies have looked at the predictive validity of the WISC-R. Those studies that have, find that WISC-R scores, particularly the Verbal IQ, correlate significantly, often in the .40 to .60 range, with school achievement whether measured by grades, teachers' ratings, or achievement test scores (e.g., Dean, 1979; Hartlage & Steele, 1977; D. J. Reschly & J. E. Reschly, 1979).

Norms. The standardization sample for the WISC-R consisted of 2,200 children, with 100 boys and 100 girls at each age level, from 6½ years

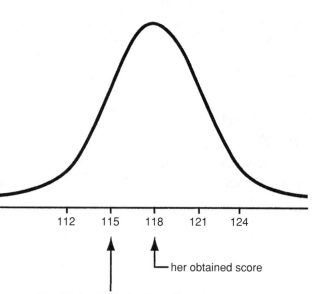

FIGURE 5–3. Annette's theoretical IQ distribution.

her obtained score

The SE (or SD) is 3 points. Therefore we are about 95% confident that her true IQ would not deviate by more than 1.96 standard deviations, or about 6 points.

through 16½ years. These children came from 32 states and represented a stratified sample on the basis of U.S. Census data.

Pattern analysis. As with the WAIS, a number of investigators have looked at pattern analysis on the WISC, with pretty much the same outcome (Lewandoski & Saccuzzo, 1975; Saccuzzo & Lewandoski, 1976). Here the concept of *scatter* is relevant, where the child performs in a somewhat inconsistent manner from the normal expectation – for example, missing some easy items on a subtest but answering correctly on more difficult items, or showing high scores on some of the verbal subtests but low scores on others. Whether such scatter is diagnostic of specific conditions such as emotional disturbance or learning disability remains debatable (e.g., Bloom & Raskin, 1980; Dean, 1978; Hale & Landino, 1981; Ollendick, 1979; Thompson, 1980; Zingale & Smith, 1978).

One measure of scatter is the profile variability index, which is the variance of subtest scores around an examinee's mean subtest score (Plake, Reynolds, & Gutkin, 1981). A study of this index in a sample of children who had been administered the WISC-R, the Stanford-Binet IV, and the K-ABC (see next section) indicated that such an index had essentially no validity (Kline, Snyder, Guilmette, et al., 1993).

Factor structure. Lawson & Inglis (1985) applied principal components analysis (a type of factor analysis) to the correlation matrices given in the WISC-R manual. They obtained two factors. The first was a positive factor, on which all items loaded (i.e., correlated) positively, and was interpreted as *g* or general intelligence. The second factor was a bipolar factor, with a negative loading on the verbal subtests and a positive loading on the nonverbal subtests, a result highly similar to Wechsler's original distinction of verbal and performance subtests. Indeed, many studies of the factor structure of the WISC-R have consistently reported a Verbal Comprehension factor and a Perceptual Organization factor that parallel quite well the division of subtests into verbal and performance (the one subtest that does not conform very well is the Coding subtest). This factor pattern has been obtained with a wide variety of samples that vary in ethnicity, age, clinical diagnosis, and academic status. A third factor is also often obtained, and usually interpreted as a "freedom from distractibility" dimension. Its nature and presence, however, seems to show some fluctuation from study to study, so that perhaps this third factor assesses different abilities for different groups (A. S. Kaufman, 1979a).

Correlations between Verbal Scale IQs and Performance Scale IQs are in the high .60s and low .70s, and indicate substantial overlap between the two areas, but also enough independence to justify the use of the two summary scores.

Other factor analyses of the WISC have suggested a factor structure similar to that of the WAIS, including a general factor, and at least three other substantial factors of verbal comprehension, perceptual-spatial functioning, and a memory or freedom from distractibility factor (Gutkin & Reynolds, 1980; 1981; Littell, 1960; Van Hagan & Kaufman, 1975; Zimmerman & Woo-Sam, 1972). These three factors have also been obtained in studies of learning-disabled children and mentally retarded children (e.g., Cummins & Das, 1980; Naglieri, 1981). The third factor is a rather small factor, and a number of alternative labels for it have been proposed.

Bannatyne (1971) proposed a recategorization of the WISC subtests into four major categories:

verbal-conceptual ability (Vocabulary + Comprehension + Similarities subtests)

acquired information (Information + Arithmetic + Vocabulary subtests)

visual-spatial ability (Block Design + Object Assembly + Picture Completion subtests)

sequencing (Coding + Digit Span + Arithmetic subtests)

The argument for such a recategorization is that the analysis is more meaningful with learning-disabled children, and the results are more easily interpretable to teachers and parents. The focus would not be so much on the IQ, but on the measurement of abilities.

Abbreviated scales. As with the WAIS, a number of efforts have been made to identify combinations of WISC subtests that correlate highly with the Full Scale IQ of the entire WISC (Silverstein, 1968; 1970), or administering every other item, or every third item, but including all subtests (Silverstein, 1967). One such subtest combination consists of the Vocabulary and Block Design subtests; scores here correlate in the .80s with the Full Scale IQ of the entire WISC-R (Ryan, 1981). Typically, quite high correlations (in the .80s and .90s) are obtained between abbreviated forms and the full test, and these abbreviated forms can be useful as screening devices, or for research purposes where only a summary IQ number is needed.

Several investigators have focused on the use of WISC-R short forms to screen and identify intellectually gifted students (e.g., Elman, Blixt, & Sawacki, 1981; Kramer, Shanks, Markely, et al., 1983; Ortiz & Gonzalez, 1989; Ortiz & Volkoff, 1987). Short forms for the WISC-R and the WISC-III for particular use with learning-disabled students are available (Dumont & Faro, 1993).

Use with minority children. We discuss this issue more fully in Chapter 11, but mention should be made that a number of researchers have investigated the validity of the WISC-R with minority children. The results generally support the validity of the WISC-R, but also have found some degree of cultural bias (Mishra, 1983). Studies of the WISC-R with Mexican-American children yield basically the same results as with Anglo children with regard to the reliability, predictive validity, and factor structure (Dean, 1977; 1979; 1980; Johnson & McGowan, 1984). For a Mexican version of the WISC-R see Mercer, Gomez-Palacio, and Padilla (1986). There is also a Mexican form of the WISC-R published (Wechsler, 1984) whose construct validity seems to parallel the American version (Fletcher, 1989). Studies of the WISC-R with black American children also indicate that the test is working as intended, with results similar to those found with white children (Gutkin & Reynolds, 1981).

The WISC-III. The WISC-R was revised in 1991 and became the WISC-III; many of the earlier items were revised, either in actual content or in form, as for example, enlarged printing. Although the word "revision" might convey the image of a single person making some minor changes in wording to a manuscript, revision as applied to a commercially produced test such as the WISC-III is a massive undertaking. Experts are consulted, and the experiences of users in the field are collated and analyzed. Banks of items are submitted to pilot studies and statistically analyzed to identify and minimize any potential sources of bias, especially gender and race. Details such as the layout of answer sheets to equally accommodate right- and left-handed persons, and the use of color art work that does not penalize color blind subjects, are attended to. Considerable reliability and validity data is presented in the test manual, and in the research literature (e.g. Canivez & Watkins, 1998), with results very similar to those obtained with the WISC-R and presented above. Factor analyses of the WISC III yield two factors that seem to correspond to the Verbal and the Performance scales (Wechsler, 1991).

The WPPSI

The Wechsler Preschool and Primary Scale of Intelligence (WPPSI) was published in 1967 (Wechsler, 1967) and covers 4 to $6\frac{1}{2}$ years. It pretty much parallels the WAIS and the WISC in terms of subtests, assessment of reliability, and test format. In fact, 8 of the 11 subtests are revisions or downward extensions of WISC subtests. The WPPSI does contain three subtests that are unique to it: "Animal house," which requires the child to place colored cylinders in their appropriate holes, under timed conditions; "geometric design," which is a perceptual motor task requiring copying of simple designs; and "sentences," a supplementary test that measures immediate recall and requires the child to repeat each sentence after the examiner. The WPPSI was revised in 1989 (Wechsler, 1989) to become the WPPSI-R, with age coverage from 3 to $7\frac{1}{4}$ years, but similar in structure to the WPPSI (see the September 1991 issue of the *Journal of Psychoeducational Assessment*, a special issue devoted to the WPPSI-R).

Administration. It takes somewhere between 1 and $1\frac{1}{2}$ hours to administer the WPPSI, and the manual recommends that this be done in one testing session.

Scoring. As with the other Wechsler tests, raw scores on each subtest are changed to normalized standard scores that have a mean of 10 and a SD of 3. The subtests are also grouped into a verbal and a performance area, and these yield a Verbal Scale IQ, a Performance Scale IQ, and a Full Scale IQ; these are deviation IQs with a mean of 100 and SD of 15. The raw score conversions are done by using tables that are age appropriate. This means, that in effect, older children must earn higher raw scores than younger children to obtain the equivalent standard score.

Reliability. The reliability of the WPPSI is comparable with that of the other Wechsler tests.

The corrected odd-even reliabilities of the WPPSI subtests are mostly in the .80s. For the Verbal and Performance scales reliability is in the high .80s, with Verbal slightly more reliable than Performance; for the Full Scale IQ, reliability is in the low .90s. Similar level reliabilities have been reported in the literature for children representing diverse ethnic backgrounds and intellectual achievement (Henderson & Rankin, 1973; Richards, 1970; Ruschival & Way, 1971).

Validity. The results of validity studies of the WPPSI have produced a wide range of findings (Sattler, 1982; 1988). Scores on the WPPSI have been correlated with a variety of scores on other tests, with typical correlation coefficients between the Full Scale IQ and other test measures in the .50 to .70 range (e.g., Baum & Kelly, 1979; Gerken, 1978; B. L. Phillips, Pasewark, & Tindall, 1978). Keep in mind that for many of these samples, the children tested were homogeneous – for example, retarded – and, as you recall, homogeneity limits the size of the correlation.

As might be expected, scores on the WPPSI correlate substantially with scores on the WISC-R, in the order of .80 (Wechsler, 1974), and with the Stanford-Binet. Sattler (1974) reviewed a number of such studies and reported that the median correlations between the WPPSI Verbal, Performance, and Full Scale IQs and the Stanford-Binet IQ were .81, .67, and .82, respectively. Despite the fact that the tests correlate substantially, it should be noted that the IQs obtained from the WPPSI and from the Stanford-Binet are not interchangeable. For example, Sewell (1977) found that the mean WPPSI IQ was higher than that of the Stanford-Binet, while earlier studies found just the opposite (Sattler, 1974).

Fewer studies are available on the predictive validity of the WPPSI, and these typically attempt to predict subsequent academic achievement, especially in the first grade or later IQ. In the first instance, typical correlations between WPPSI scores and subsequent achievement are in the .40 to .60 range (e.g, Crockett, Rardin, & Pasewark, 1975), and in the second are higher, typically in the .60 to .70 range (e.g., Bishop & Butterworth, 1979). A number of studies have looked at the ability of WPPSI scores to predict reading achievement in the first grade. Typical findings are that with middle-class children there is such a relationship, with modal correlation coefficients in the .50s. With minority and disadvantaged children no such relationship is found – but again, one must keep in mind the restriction of range both on the WPPSI scores and on the criterion of reading achievement (e.g., Crockett, Rardin, & Pasework, 1976; Serwer, B. J. Shapiro, & P. P. Shapiro, 1972; D. R. White & Jacobs, 1979).

Because the term *construct validity* is an umbrella term subsuming other types of validity, all of the studies mentioned so far can be considered as supportive of the construct validity of the WPPSI. A number of other findings might be mentioned here. R. S. Wilson (1975) studied monozygotic (identical) twins and dizygotic (fraternal) twins and found that monozygotic twins were closer in intelligence to each other than were dizygotic twins – a finding that is in line with the view that intelligence has a substantial hereditary/genetic component, and one that supports the construct validity of the WPPSI. Other studies have focused on the relationship of IQ to socioeconomic status (e.g., A. S. Kaufman, 1973), and on language spoken at home (e.g., Gerken, 1978).

Norms. The WPPSI was standardized on a national sample of 1,200 children, with 200 children (100 boys and 100 girls) at each of six half-year age levels, from age 4 to 6. The sample was stratified using census data.

Factor structure. As with the other Wechsler tests, the subtests of the WPPSI and the Verbal and Performance scales intercorrelate with each other significantly. Subtests typically correlate .40 to .60, and Verbal and Performance IQs correlate in the mid .60s. The results of factor analytic studies suggest a general factor, as well as two broad factors, a verbal factor and a performance factor, although the verbal component is a much more important one, and may be interpreted as a general factor (Coates & Bromberg, 1973; Heil, Barclay, & Endres, 1978; Hollenbeck & Kaufman, 1973; Ramanaiah & Adams, 1979). In the younger aged children, the two broad factors are less distinct from each other, a finding that is in line with developmental theories that hypothesize intellectual functioning to evolve as the child grows older, into more specialized and distinct categories. Similar results have been obtained with black children (Kaufman & Hollenbeck, 1974).

Abbreviated scales. A. S. Kaufman (1972) developed a short form of the WPPSI composed of four subtests: Arithmetic and Comprehension from the Verbal Scale, and Block Design and Picture Completion from the Performance Scale. The reliability of this short form was in the low .90s, and scores correlated with the Full Scale IQ of the entire WPPSI in the .89 to .92 range. Other investigators have also developed short forms for both the WPPSI and the WPPSI-R (e.g., Tsushima, 1994).

The WPPSI-R. As with other major tests, while the author may be a single individual, the actual revision is typically a team effort and involves a great many people; and so it is with the WPPSI-R. The WPPSI-R consists of 12 subtests, designed as downward extensions of the WISC-R. Typically, five Verbal and five Performance subtests are administered, with Animal Pegs (formerly Animal House), and Sentences (similar to the Digit Span subtest of the WISC-R) as optional subtests. The Object Assembly subtest is administered first; this is a puzzle like activity that preschoolers usually enjoy, and thus is helpful in establishing rapport. Testing time is about 75 minutes, which may be too long for the typical young child.

The primary purpose of the WPPSI-R is to diagnose "exceptionality," particularly mental retardation and giftedness, in school settings. In addition to the extended age range, the WPPSI-R differs from the WPPSI in several ways. Approximately 50% of the items are new. Several of the subtests have more rigorous scoring rules designed to reduce examiner error and hence increase the reliability of the subtests. The WPPSI-R also includes an Object Assembly subtest, patterned after the same named subtest on the WISC-R and the WAIS-R.

The normative sample for the WPPSI-R consisted of 1,700 children aged 3 years through 7 years-3 months, with equal numbers of boys and girls. The sample was stratified according to U.S. Census data on such variables as race, geographical residence, parental education, and occupation.

Considerable reliability evidence is available. For example, test-retest reliability for a sample of 175 children retested with a mean 4-week period, ranged from .59 to .82 for the subtests, .88 for the Performance IQ, .90 for the Verbal IQ, and .91

for the Full Scale IQ. Split-half reliabilities for the subtests range from .63 to .86 (with a median *r* of .83), and .92 for the Performance IQ, .95 for the Verbal IQ, and .96 for the Full Scale IQ. For four of the subtests, examiners need to make subjective scoring decisions (a response can be given 0, 1, or 2 points); so for these subtests inter-scorer reliability becomes a concern. For a sample of 151 children, two groups of scorers independently scored the protocols. Obtained reliability coefficients for the four subtests were all in the mid .90s.

As with all tests, there are criticisms. The WPPSI-R (as well as other tests like the K-ABC and the DAS) use teaching or demonstration items, which are generally regarded as a strength in preschool measures because they ensure that the child understands what is being asked. The impact of such items on test validity has been questioned (Glutting & McDermott, 1989). Perhaps the major criticism that has been voiced is that the WPPSI-R continues assessment in a historical approach that may well be outdated and does not incorporate findings from experimental studies of cognitive processing. There is no denying that the test works but does not advance our basic understanding of what intelligence is all about (Buckhalt, 1991).

Extensive validity data are also available, including concurrent correlations with other cognitive measures, factor analyses, and studies of group differentiation for gifted, mentally retarded, and learning disabled. Most of the evidence is in line with that obtained with the WPPSI.

OTHER TESTS

The British Ability Scales (BAS)

Both the Stanford-Binet and the Wechsler tests have become very popular, not just in the United States but in other countries as well, including Britain. However, from the British perspective, these were "foreign imports," and in 1965 the British Psychological Society set up a research project to replace the Stanford-Binet and the WISC and develop a measure standardized on a British sample, one that would provide a profile of special abilities rather than an overall IQ. The result was the British Ability Scales (BAS),

which despite receiving highly laudatory reviews in the MMY (Embretson, 1985a; Wright & Stone, 1985), was virtually unknown in the United States until it was "retranslated" and restandardized with an American sample and called the *Differential Ability Scales* (DAS)(Elliott, 1990a).

Description. The BAS is an individual intelligence test designed for ages $2\frac{1}{2}$ to $17\frac{1}{2}$, and contains 23 scales that cover 6 areas and yield 3 IQ scores. The six areas are: (1) speed of information processing, (2) reasoning, (3) spatial imagery, (4) perceptual matching, (5) short-term memory, and (6) retrieval and application of knowledge. The three IQ scores are *General, Visual*, and *Verbal*.

Each of the six areas is composed of a number of subscales; for example, the Reasoning area is made up of four subscales, while the Retrieval and Application of Knowledge area is made up of seven subscales. All of the subscales are appropriate for multiple age levels. For example, the Block Design subscale is appropriate for ages 4 to 17, while the Visual Recognition subscale is appropriate for ages $2\frac{1}{2}$ to 8. Thus, which subscales are used depends on the age of the child being tested.

The BAS is unusual in at least two aspects: it was developed using very sophisticated psychometric strategies, and it incorporates various theories in its subscales. Specifically, the BAS subscales were developed according to the Rasch latent trait model; this is a very sophisticated psychometric theory and has procedures that are beyond the scope of this book (Rasch, 1966). Two of the subscales on the BAS are based on the developmental theories of Piaget, and one subscale, that of Social Reasoning, is based on Kohlberg's (1979) theory of moral reasoning.

Finally, two subtests, Word Reading and Basic Arithmetic, both for ages 5 to 14 and both from the Retrieval and Application of Knowledge area, can be used to estimate school achievement.

Administration and scoring. Administration and scoring procedures are well designed, clearly specified, and hold examiner's potential bias to a minimum. The raw scores are changed to *T* scores and to percentiles and are compared with appropriate age norms.

Reliability and validity. Unfortunately, little data is given in the test manual about reliability and about validity. Embretson (1985a) reports that the results of factor analyses are available, as well as the results of five concurrent validity studies all with positive results, but the details are not given. Similarly, Wright and Stone (1985) indicate that there is "ample evidence" for the internal consistency and construct validity of the scales, but no details are provided. A few studies are available in the literature, but their volume in no way approaches the voluminous literature available on the Stanford-Binet and on the Wechsler tests. For an application of the BAS to learning-disabled children see Elliott and Tyler (1987) and Tyler and Elliott (1988). Buckhalt studied the BAS with black and white children (Buckhalt, 1990) and students from the United States (Buckhalt, Denes, & Stratton, 1989).

Norms. The norms were carefully constructed to create a representative sample for Britain. There are 113 school districts in Britain, and 75 of these participated in the norming effort, which yielded a sample of 3,435 children.

Interesting aspects. Because of the Rasch psychometric approach used in the development and standardization of the items, the BAS can be seen as an "item bank" where the individual examiner can, in effect, add or delete specific items to form their own subtests, without losing the benefits of standardization (Wright & Stone, 1985). Another aspect that follows from the Rasch model is that it is possible to compare subscale differences for a specific child through procedures indicated in the manual.

Criticisms. As Embretson (1985a) stated, the BAS possesses excellent potential and great psychometric sophistication, but the 1985 data on reliability and validity was judged inadequate. For a review of the BAS see Buckhalt (1986).

The Differential Ability Scales. The BAS was introduced in the United States as the DAS and seems well on its way toward becoming a popular test. The DAS is very similar to the BAS; some BAS subtests were eliminated or modified, so that the DAS consists of 20 subtests, 17 of which are "cognitive" and 3 are achievement subtests. The age range goes from 2½ to 17 years, 11 months. One of the major objectives in the development of the DAS was to produce subtests that were homogeneous and hence highly reliable, so that an examiner could identify the cognitive strengths and weaknesses of an examinee. Administration of the DAS requires entry into each subtest at a level appropriate for the age of the subject. Cues on the record form indicate age-related entry levels and decision points for either continuing or retreating to an earlier age level.

Twelve of the DAS cognitive subtests are identified as *core* subtests because they have high loadings on *g*. Groupings of two or three of these subtests result in subfactors called *cluster* scores; these are Verbal and Nonverbal at the upper preschool level, and Verbal, Nonverbal Reasoning, and Spatial ability at the school-age level. An additional five cognitive subtests are labeled *diagnostic* subtests; these have low *g* loadings, but presumably are useful in assessment. These subtests measure short-term memory, perceptual skills, and speed of information processing.

The DAS yields five types of scores: (1) subtest raw scores that are converted to (2) ability scores, using appropriate tables. These are *not* normative scores, but provide a scale for judging performance within a subtest. These ability scores are then converted to (3) *T* scores for normative comparisons. The *T* scores can be summed to obtain (4) cluster scores, which in turn yield (5) the General Conceptual Ability score. *T* scores, cluster scores, and GCA score can be converted to percentiles, standard scores, or age-equivalent scores with use of the appropriate tables.

The subtests cover a range of abilities including both verbal and nonverbal reasoning, visual and auditory memory, language comprehension, speed of information processing, and school achievement in basic number skills, spelling, and word reading. The battery does not yield a global composite score derived from all subtests, as one would find on the WISC-R for example. There is however, a *General Conceptual Ability* (GCA) score, a measure of *g*, based on four to six subtests, depending on the child's age. T. Z. Keith (1990) concluded that the DAS is a robust measure of *g*; that for preschool children the DAS measures Verbal and Nonverbal abilities in addition to *g*, and that for school-aged children the DAS measures verbal ability and spatial-reasoning skill.

Elliott (1990a) not only indicates that the DAS has a broad theoretical basis and could be interpreted from a variety of theories, but also that the term General Conceptual Ability is a better term than IQ or intelligence. The DAS is said to be a "purer" and more homogeneous measure than the global scores used by the Stanford-Binet or the Wechsler scales, primarily because the GCA is composed only of those subtests that had high loadings on *g*, whereas the other tests include in their composite scores subtests with low *g* loadings.

One concept particularly relevant to the DAS, but also applicable to any test that yields a profile of subtest scores, is the concept of *specificity* (note that this is a different use of the word from our earlier discussion). Specificity can be defined as the unique assessment contribution of a subtest. If we have a test made up of three subtests A, B, and C, we would want each of the subtests to measure something unique, rather than to have three subtests that are essentially alternate forms of the same thing. Specificity can also be defined psychometrically as the proportion of score variance that is reliable *and* unique to the subtest. Specificity can be computed by subtracting the squared multiple correlation of each subtest with all other subtests, from the reliability of the subtest. For example, if subtest A has a reliability of .90 and correlates .40 with both subtests B and C, then its specificity will be $.90 - (.40)^2 = .74$. For the DAS, the average specificity for its diagnostic subtests is about .73, while for the WISC-R it is about .30 (Elliott, 1990b).

The DAS was standardized on 3,475 U.S. children selected on the basis of U.S. Census data. An attempt was made to include special-education children such as learning disabled and speech impaired, but severely handicapped children were not included. Gifted and talented children are slightly overrepresented.

Reliability is fairly comparable with that of the Wechsler tests. For example, mean internal reliability coefficients range from .70 to .92 for various subtests; for the GCA they range from .90 to .95. Test-retest reliability, based on 2 to 6 weeks, yielded a GCA coefficient of .90, and interrater reliability for the four subtests that require subjective judgment is in the .90 range.

The DAS manual (Elliott, 1990a) reports several validity studies, including correlations with the WISC-R (mid .80s) and with the Stanford-Binet IV (high .70s to high .80s). The literature also contains a number of studies supportive of the Validity of the DAS (e.g., McIntosh, 1999). Recent reviews of the DAS are quite favorable and point to its technical excellence and potential use with minority children (Braden, 1992).

The Kaufman Assessment Battery for Children (K-ABC)

Kaufman (1983) describes intelligence as the ability to process information effectively to solve unfamiliar problems. In addition, he distinguished between *sequential* and *simultaneous* processing. A number of other theorists have analyzed intellectual functioning into two modes of mental organization. Freud, for example, spoke of *primary* and *secondary* processes. Recently, Guilford (1967b) focused on convergent and divergent thinking, while R. B. Cattell (1963) used the terms fluid and crystallized intelligence, and Wechsler (1958) used verbal and nonverbal intelligence. One dichotomy that has found its way in a number of tests and test interpretations is the notion of sequential (or successive) and simultaneous processing (Luria, 1966). Sequential processing requires the organization of stimuli into some temporally organized series, where the specific order of the stimuli is more important than the overall relationship of these stimuli. For example, as you read these words it is their sequencing that is important for the words to have meaning. Sequential processing is typically based on verbal processes and depends on language for thinking and remembering; it is serial in its nature. Simultaneous processing involves stimuli that are primarily spatial and focuses on the relationship between elements. To understand the sentence "this box is longer than this pencil," we must not only have an understanding of the sequence of the words, we must also understand the comparative spatial relationship of "longer than." Simultaneous processing searches for patterns and configurations; it is holistic. A. S. Kaufman (1979b) suggested that the WISC-R subtests could be organized along the lines of sequential vs. simultaneous processing. For example, Coding and Arithmetic require sequential processing, while Picture Completion and Block Design require simultaneous processing. He then developed the K-ABC to specifically assess these dimensions.

Development. As with other major tests of intelligence, the development of the K-ABC used a wide variety of pilot studies and evaluative procedures. Over 4,000 protocols were administered as part of this development. As with other major tests of intelligence, short forms of the K-ABC have been developed for possible use when a general estimate of mental functioning is needed in a short time period (A. S. Kaufman & Applegate, 1988).

Description. The K-ABC is an individually administered intelligence and achievement measure that assesses styles of problem solving and information processing, in children ages $2\frac{1}{2}$ to $12\frac{1}{2}$. It is composed of five global scales: (1) Sequential processing scale; (2) Simultaneous processing scale; (3) Mental processing composite scale, which is a combination of the first two; (4) Achievement scale; and (5) Nonverbal scale. The actual battery consists of 16 subtests, including 10 that assess a child's sequential and simultaneous processing and 6 that evaluate a child's achievement in academic areas such as reading and arithmetic; because not all subtests cover all ages, any individual child would at the most be administered 13 subtests. The 10 subtests that assess the child's processing include practice items so that the examiner can communicate to the child the nature of the task and can observe whether the child understands what to do. Of these 10 subtests, 7 are designed to assess simultaneous processing, and 3 sequential processing; the 3 sequential processing subtests all involve short-term memory.

All the items in the first three global scales minimize the role of language and acquired facts and skills. The Achievement scale assesses what a child has learned in school; this scale uses items that are more traditionally found on tests of verbal intelligence and tests of school achievement. The Nonverbal scale is an abbreviated version of the Mental Processing composite scale, and is intended to assess the intelligence of children with speech or language disorders, with hearing impairments, or those that do not speak English; all tasks on this scale may be administered in pantomime and are responded to with motor rather than verbal behavior, for example by pointing to the correct response.

The K-ABC is a multisubtest battery, so that its format is quite suitable for profile analysis. In fact, A. S. Kaufman and N. L. Kaufman (1983) provide in the test manual lists of abilities associated with specific combinations of subtests. For example, attention to visual detail can be assessed by a combination of three subtests: Gestalt Closure, Matrix Analogies, and Photo Series.

Administration. Like the Stanford-Binet and the Wechsler tests, the K-ABC requires a trained examiner. Administration time varies from about 40 to 45 minutes for younger children, to 75 to 85 minutes for older children.

Scoring. All K-ABC scales yield standard scores with mean of 100 and SD of 15; the subtests yield scores with mean of 10 and SD of 3. This was purposely done to permit direct comparison of scores with other tests such as the WISC.

Reliability. Split-half reliability coefficients range from .86 to .93 for preschool children, and from .89 to .97 for school-age children for the various global scales. Test-retest coefficients, based on 246 children retested after 2 to 4 weeks, yielded stability coefficients in the .80s and low .90s, with stability increasing with increasing age. As mentioned earlier, specific abilities are said to be assessed by specific combinations of subtests, so a basic question concerns the reliability of such composites; the literature suggests that they are quite reliable, with typical coefficients in the mid .80 to mid .90 range (e.g., Siegel & Piotrowski, 1985).

Validity. The K-ABC Interpretive Manual (A. S. Kaufman & N. L. Kaufman, 1983) presents the results of more than 40 validity studies, and gives substantial support to the construct, concurrent, and predictive validity of the battery. These studies were conducted on normal samples as well as on special populations such as learning disabled, hearing impaired, educable and trainable mentally retarded, physically handicapped, and gifted.

For normal samples, correlations between the K-ABC and the Stanford-Binet range from .61 to .86, while with the WISC-R they center around .80 (A. S. Kaufman & N. L. Kaufman, 1983). For example, the Mental Processing Composite score correlates about .70 with the Full Scale IQ of the WISC-R. You recall that by squaring this coefficient, we obtain an estimate of the "overlap" of the two scales; thus these scales overlap about 50%, indicating a substantial overlap, but also some uniqueness to each measure.

The K-ABC Achievement scale correlates in the .70s and .80s with overall levels of achievement as measured by various achievement batteries. Other sources also support the validity of the K-ABC (e.g., Reynolds & Kamphaus, 1997).

Norms. The K-ABC was standardized on a nation wide stratified sample of 2,000 children, from age 2½ to 12 years, 5 months, 100 at each 6-month interval. A special effort was made to include children from various ethnic backgrounds and children in special education programs, including children with mental disabilities and gifted. Special norms are provided for black and white children, separately, from different socioeconomic backgrounds as defined by parents' education.

Interesting aspects. One of the interesting aspects of the K-ABC is that race differences on the battery, while they exist, are substantially smaller in magnitude than those found on the WISC-R. Typical differences between black and white children are about 7 points on the K-ABC but about 16 points on the WISC-R.

Several investigators (e.g., Barry, Klanderman, & Stipe, 1983; McCallum, Karnes, & Edwards, 1984; Meador, Livesay, & Finn, 1983) have compared the K-ABC, the WISC-R, and the Stanford-Binet in gifted children and have found that the K-ABC yields lower mean scores than the other two tests – results that are also found in children who are not gifted. The indications are that the K-ABC minimizes expressive and verbal reasoning skills, as it was intended to. One practical implication of this is that a school that uses one of these tests as part of a decision-making assessment for identifying and placing gifted children, will identify fewer such children if they use the K-ABC, but may well identify a greater proportion of minority gifted children. For a thorough review of the K-ABC see Kamphaus and Reynolds (1987). It would seem that the K-ABC would be particularly useful in the study of children with such problems as attention-deficit disorder, but the restricted available data is not fully supportive (e.g., Carter, Zelko, Oas, et al., 1990).

Criticisms. The K-ABC has been criticized on a number of issues including its validity for minority groups (e.g., Sternberg, 1984), its appropriateness for preschool children (e.g., Bracken, 1985), its theoretical basis (e.g., Jensen, 1984), and its lack of instructional utility (Good, Vollmer, Creek, et al., 1993).

Aptitude by treatment interaction. One of the primary purposes of the K-ABC was not only to make a classification decision (e.g., this child has an IQ of 125 and therefore should be placed in an accelerated class) but also to be used in a diagnostic or prescriptive manner to improve student academic outcomes. Specifically, if a child is most efficient in learning by sequential processing than by simultaneous processing, then that child ought to be instructed by sequential-processing procedures. Generically, this instructional model is called *aptitude by treatment interaction.*

The Structure of Intellect Learning Abilities Test (SOI-LA)

The SOI-LA (M. Meeker, R. J. Meeker, & Roid, 1985) is a series of tests designed to assess up to 26 cognitive factors of intelligence in both children and adults. Its aim is to provide a profile of a person's cognitive strengths and weaknesses. The SOI-LA is based on Guilford's structure of intellect model that postulates 120 abilities, reduced to 26 for this series. These 26 subtests yield a total of 14 general ability scores. The 26 dimensions do cover the five operations described by Guilford – namely, cognition, memory, evaluation, convergent production, and divergent production.

Description. There are seven forms of the SOI-LA available. Form A is the principal form, and Form B is an alternate form. Form G is a gifted screening form. Form M is for students having difficulties with math concepts and is composed of 12 subtests from form A that are related to arithmetic, mathematics, and science. Form R is composed of 12 subtests from form A that are related to reading, language arts, and social science. Form P is designed for kindergarten through the third grade. Finally, form RR is a reading readiness form designed for young children and "new readers."

Administration. The SOI-LA may be administered individually or in a group format. Forms A and B each require $2\frac{1}{2}$ to 3 hours to administer, even though most of the subtests are 3 to 5 minutes in length. The test manual recommends that two separate testing sessions be held. There are clear instructions in the manual for the administration of the various subtests, as well as directions for making sure that students understand what is requested of them. In general, the SOI-LA is relatively easy to administer and to score, and can easily be done by a classroom teacher or aide.

Scoring. The directions for scoring the subtests are given in the manual and are quite clear and detailed. Most of the subtests can be scored objectively, that is, there is a correct answer for each item. Two of the subtests, however, require subjective scoring. In one subtest, Divergent Production of Figural Units (DPFU), the child is required to complete each of 16 squares into something different. In the second subtest, the Divergent Production of Semantic Units (DPSU), the child is asked to write a story about a drawing from the previous subtest.

Reliability. Test-retest reliability, with a 2- to 4-week interval, ranges from .35 to .88 for the 26 subtests, with a median coefficient of .57, and only 4 of the 26 coefficients are equal to or exceed .75 (J. A. Cummings, 1989). From a stability-over-time perspective, the SOI-LA leaves much to be desired. Because the SOI-LA subtests are heavily speeded, internal consistency reliability is not appropriate, and of course, the manual does not report any. Internal consistency reliability is based on the consistency of errors made in each subpart of a test, but in a speeded test the consistency is of rapidity with which one works.

Because there are two equivalent forms, alternate-form reliability is appropriate. Unfortunately, only 3 of the 26 subtests achieve adequate alternate-form reliability (J. A. Cummings, 1989). These three subtests, incidentally, are among those that have the highest test-retest reliabilities.

For the two subtests that require subjective scoring, interscorer reliability becomes important. Such interscorer reliability coefficients range from .75 to .85 for the DPFU subtest, and from .92 to 1.00 for the DPSU subtest (M. Meeker, R. J. Meeker, & Roid, 1985). These are rather high coefficients, not usually found this high in tests where subjective scoring is a major aspect.

Standardization. The normative sample consisted of 349 to 474 school children in each of five grade levels, from grades 2 to 6, with roughly equivalent representation of boys and girls. Approximately half of the children came from California, and the other half from school districts in three states. For the intermediate levels, samples of children in grades 7 to 12 were assessed; while adult norms are based on various groups aged 18 to 55. Little information is given on these various samples.

Diagnostic and prescriptive aspects. The subtests are timed so that the raw scores can be compared with norms in a meaningful way. However, subjects may be given additional time for uncompleted items, although they need to indicate where they stopped when time was called so the raw score can be calculated. Thus, two sets of scores can be computed: One set is obtained under standard administrative procedures and therefore comparable to norms, and another set reflects ability with no time limit and potentially is useful for diagnostic purposes or for planning remedial action. Whether this procedure is indeed valid remains to be proven, but the distinction between "actual performance" and "potential" is an intriguing one, used by a number of psychologists.

There is available a teacher's guide that goes along with the SOI-LA, whose instructional focus is on the remedial of deficits as identified by the test (M. Meeker, 1985). This represents a somewhat novel and potentially useful approach, although evidence needs to be generated that such remedial changes are possible.

Criticisms. The SOI-LA represents an interesting approach based on a specific theory of intellectual functioning. One of the major criticisms of this test, expressed quite strongly in the MMY reviews (Coffman, 1985; Cummings, 1989), is that the low reliabilities yield large standard errors of measurement, which means that, before we can conclude that Nadia performed better on one subtest than on another, the two scores need to differ by a substantial amount. Because the SOI-LA is geared at providing a profile that is based on subtests differences, this is a rather serious criticism and major limitation. Other criticisms include the lack of representativeness of the standardization sample, not to mention the dearth of empirical validity data.

The School and College Ability Tests, III (SCAT III)

A number of tests developed for group administration, typically in school settings, are designed to assess intellectual competence, broadly defined. The SCAT III is a typical example of such a test. The SCAT III is designed to measure academic aptitude by assessing basic verbal and quantitative abilities of students in grades 3 through 12; an earlier version, the SCAT II, went up to grades 13 and 14. There are two forms of the SCAT III, each with three levels, for use in elementary grades (grades 3.5 to 6.5), intermediate grades (6.5 to 9.5), and advanced grades (9.5 to 12.5). Unlike achievement tests that measure the effect of a specified set of instructions, such as elementary French or introductory algebra, the SCAT III is designed to assess the accumulation of learning throughout the person's life.

The SCAT III was standardized and normed in 1977–1978 and was published in 1979. Its predecessor, the SCAT II was originally developed in 1957, and was normed and standardized in 1966, and renormed in 1970.

Description. Each level of the SCAT III contains 100 multiple-choice test items, 50 verbal in content and 50 quantitative. The verbal items consist of analogies given in a multiple choice format. For example:

arm is to hand as:

(a) head is to shoulder

(b) foot is to leg

(c) ear is to mouth

(d) hand is to finger

Quantitative items are given as two quantitative expressions, and the student needs to decide whether the two expressions are equal, if one is greater, or if insufficient information is given. Thus, two circles of differing size might be given, and the student needs to determine whether the radius of one is larger than that of the other.

Administration. The SCAT III is a group-administered test and thus requires no special clinical skills or training. Clear instructions are given in the test manual, and the examiner needs to follow these.

Scoring. When the SCAT III is administered, it is often administered to large groups, perhaps an entire school or school system. Thus, provisions are made by the test publisher for having the answer sheets scored by machine, and the results reported back to the school. These results can be reported in a wide variety of ways including SCAT raw scores, standard scores, percentile ranks, or stanines. For each examinee, the SCAT III yields 3 scores: a Verbal score, a Quantitative score, and a Total score.

Validity. When the SCAT III test was standardized, it was standardized concurrently with an achievement test battery known as the Sequential Tests of Educational Progress, or STEP. SCAT III scores are good predictors of STEP scores; that is, we have an aptitude test (the SCAT III) that predicts quite well how a student will do in school subjects, as assessed by an achievement test, the STEP. From the viewpoint of school personnel, this is an attractive feature, in that the SCAT and the STEP provide a complete test package from one publisher. Yet one can ask whether in fact two tests are needed – perhaps we need only be concerned with actual achievement, not also with potential aptitude. We can also wonder why might it be important to predict scores on achievement tests; might a more meaningful target of prediction be actual classroom achievement?

There are a number of studies that address the validity of the SCAT III and its earlier forms (e.g., Ong & Marchbanks, 1973), but a surprisingly large number of these seem to be unpublished masters theses and doctoral dissertations, not readily available to the average user. It is also said that SCAT scores in grades 9 through 12 can be used to estimate future performance on the Scholastic Aptitude Test (SAT), which is not surprising because both are aptitude tests heavily focusing on school-related abilities. The SCAT III has been criticized for the lack of information about its validity (Passow, 1985).

Norms. Norms were developed using four variables: geographical region, urban versus rural, ethnicity, and socioeconomic status. In addition to public schools, Catholic and independent schools were also sampled, although separate norms for these groups are not given. Separate gender norms are also not given, so it may well be that there are no significant gender differences. This illustrates a practical difficulty for the potential test user. Not only is test information quite often fragmentary and/or scattered in the literature, but one must come to conclusions that may well be erroneous.

The Otis-Lennon School Ability Test (OLSAT)

Another example of a group intelligence test, also used quite frequently in school systems, is the OLSAT (often called the Otis-Lennon). This test is a descendant of a series of intelligence tests originally developed by Arthur Otis. In the earlier forms, Otis attempted to use Binet-type items that could be administered in a group situation.

There are two forms of the OLSAT, forms R and S, with five levels: primary level for grade 1; primary II level for grades 2 and 3; elementary level for grades 4 and 5; intermediate level for grades 6 to 8; and advanced level for grades 9 through 12. The OLSAT is based on a hierarchical theory of intelligence, which views intelligence as composed, at one level, of two major domains: verbal-educational and practical-mechanical group factors. The OLSAT is designed to measure only the verbal-educational domain. The test was also influenced by Guilford's structure of intellect model in that items were selected so as to reflect the intellectual operations of cognition, convergent thinking, and evaluation.

Description. The test authors began with an initial pool of 1,500 items and administered these, in subsets, to nearly 55,000 students. Incidentally, this illustrates a typical technique of test construction. When the initial pool of items is too large to administer to one group, subsets of items are constructed that can be more conveniently administered to separate groups. In the OLSAT, those items that survived item difficulty and item discrimination analyses were retained. In addition, all items were reviewed by minority educators and were analyzed statistically to assess those items that might be unfair or discriminate against minority group members; items that did not meet these criteria were eliminated.

Reliability. Internal consistency coefficients are reported for the OLSAT, with rather large samples of 6,000 to 12,000 children. The K-R coefficients range from .88 to .95, indicating that the OLSAT is a homogeneous measure and internally consistent. Test-retest correlation coefficients are also given for smaller but still sizable samples, in the 200 to 400 range, over a 6-month period. Obtained coefficients range from .84 to .92. Retest over a longer period of 3 to 4 years, yielded lower correlation coefficients of .75 to .78 (Dyer, 1985). The standard error of measurement for this test is reported to be about 4 points.

Validity. Oakland (1985a) indicates that the OLSAT appears to have suitable content validity, based on an evaluation of the test items, the test format, the directions, and other aspects. Comparisons of the OLSAT with a variety of other measures of scholastic aptitude, achievement test scores, and intelligence test scores indicates moderate to high correlations in the .60 to .80 range, with higher correlations with variables that assess verbal abilities. Construct validity is said to be largely absent (Dyer, 1985; Oakland, 1985a). In fact, while the test is praised for its psychometric sophistication and standardization rigor, it is criticized for the lack of information on validity (Dyer, 1985).

Norms. The OLSAT was standardized in the Fall of 1977 through the assessment of some 130,000 pupils in 70 different school systems, including both public and private schools. The sample was stratified using census data on several variables, including geographic region of residence and socioeconomic status. The racial-ethnic distribution of the sample also closely paralleled the census data and included 74% white, 20% black, 4% Hispanic, and 2% other.

Normative data are reported by age and grade using deviation IQs which in this test are called School Ability Indexes, as well as percentiles and stanines. The School Ability Index is normed with a mean of 100 and SD of 16.

The Slosson Intelligence Test (SIT)

There are a number of situations, both research and applied, where there is need for a "quickie" screening instrument that is easy to administer in a group setting, does not take up much time for either administration or scoring, and yields a rough estimate of a person's level of general intelligence. These situations might involve identifying subjects that meet certain specifications for a research study, or possible candidates for an enrichment program in primary grades, or potential candidates for a college fellowship. There are a number of such instruments available, many of dubious utility and validity, that nevertheless are used. The SIT is probably typical of these.

Description. The SIT is intended as a brief screening instrument to evaluate a person's intellectual ability, although it is also presented by its author as a "parallel" form for the Stanford-Binet and was in fact developed as an abbreviated version of the Stanford-Binet (Slosson, 1963). The SIT was first published in 1961 and revised in 1981, although no substantive changes seem to have been made from one version to the other. It was revised again in 1991, a revision in which items were added that were more similar to the Wechsler tests than to the Stanford-Binet. This latest version was called the SIT-R. The test contains 194 untimed items and is said to extend from age 2 years to 27 years. No theoretical rationale is presented for this test, but because it originally was based on the Stanford-Binet, presumably it is designed to assess abstract reasoning abilities, comprehension, and judgment, in a global way (Slosson, 1991).

Administration. The test can be administered by teachers and other individuals who may not have extensive training in test administration. The average test-taking time is about 10 to 15 minutes.

Scoring. Scoring is quite objective and requires little of the clinical skills needed to score a Stanford-Binet or a Wechsler test. The raw score yields a mental age that can then be used to calculate a ratio IQ using the familiar ratio of $MA/CA \times 100$, or a deviation IQ through the use of normative tables.

Reliability. The test-retest reliability for a sample of 139 persons, ages 4 to 50, and retested over a 2-month interval, is reported to be .97. For the SIT-R, a test-retest with a sample of 41 subjects retested after 1 week, yielded a coefficient of .96.

Validity. Correlations between the SIT and the Stanford-Binet are in the mid .90s, with the WISC in the mid .70s, and with various achievement tests in the .30 to .50 range. For the SIT-R, several studies are reported in the test manual that compare SIT-R scores with Wechsler scores, with typical correlation coefficients in the low .80s.

A typical study is that of Grossman and Johnson (1983) who administered the SIT and the Otis-Lennon Mental Ability Test (a precursor of the OLSAT), to a sample of 46 children who were candidates for possible inclusion in an enrichment program for the gifted. Scores on the two tests correlated .94. However, the mean IQ for the SIT was reported to be 127.17, while for the Otis-Lennon it was 112.69. Although both tests were normalized to the same scale, with mean of 100 and SD of 16, note the substantially higher mean on the SIT. If nothing else, this indicates that whenever we see an IQ reported for a person we ought to also know which test was used to compute this – and we need to remind ourselves that the IQ is a property of the test rather than the person. In the same study, both measures correlated in the .90s with scores on selected subtests (such as Vocabulary and Reading Comprehension) of the Stanford Achievement Test, a battery that is commonly used to assess the school achievement of children.

Norms. The norms for the SIT are based on a sample of 1,109 persons, ranging from 2 to 18. These were all New England residents, but information on gender, ethnicity, or other aspects is not given. Note should be made that the mean of the SIT is 97 and its SD is 20. This larger SD causes severe problems of interpretation if the SIT is in fact used to make diagnostic or placement decisions (W. M. Reynolds, 1979).

The SIT-R was standardized on a sample of 1,854 individuals, said to be somewhat representative of the U.S. population in educational and other characteristics.

Criticisms. Although the SIT is used relatively frequently in both the research literature and in applied situations, it has been severely criticized for a narrow and unrepresentative standardization sample, for lack of information on reliability and validity, for its suggested use by untrained examiners, which runs counter to APA professional ethics, and for its unwarranted claims of equivalence with the Stanford-Binet (Oakland, 1985b; W. M. Reynolds, 1985). In summary, the SIT is characterized as a psychometrically poor measure of general intelligence (W. M. Reynolds, 1985).

The Speed of Thinking Test (STT)

So far we have looked at measures that are multivariate, that assess intelligence in a very complex way, either globally or explicitly composed of various dimensions. There are however, literally hundreds of measures that assess specific cognitive skills or dimensions. The STT is illustrative.

Carver (1992) presented the STT as a test to measure cognitive speed. The STT is designed to measure how fast individuals can choose the correct answers to simple mental problems. In this case, the problems consist of pairs of letters, one in upper case and one in lower case. The respondent needs to decide whether the two letters are the same or different – e.g., Aa vs. aB. Similar tasks have been used in the literature, both at the

theoretical and at the applied level, especially in studies related to reading ability.

The STT is made up of 180 items that use all the eight possible combinations of the letters a and b, with one letter in upper case and one in lower case. There is a practice test that is administered first. Both the practice and the actual test have a 2-minute time limit each. Thus the entire procedure including distribution of materials in a group setting, and instructions requires less than 10 minutes.

The STT was administered, along with other instruments, to 129 college students enrolled in college reading and study skills courses. The test-retest reliability, with a 2-week interval, was .80. Scores on the STT correlated .60 with another measure designed to assess silent reading rate, and .26 (significant but low) with a measure of reading rate, but did not correlate significantly with two measures of vocabulary level. Thus both convergent and discriminant validity seem to be supported. Obviously, much more information is needed.

SUMMARY

In this chapter, we briefly looked at various theories of cognitive assessment and a variety of issues. We only scratched the surface in terms of the variety of points of view that exist, and in terms of the controversies about the nature and nurture of intelligence. We looked, in some detail, at the various forms of the Binet tests, because in some ways, they nicely illustrated the historical progression of "classical" testing. We also looked at the Wechsler series of tests because they are quite popular and also illustrate some basic principles of testing. The other tests were chosen as illustrations, some because of their potential utility (e.g., the BAS), or because they embody an interesting theoretical perspective (e.g., the SOI-LA), or because they seem to be growing in usefulness and popularity (e.g., the K-ABC). Some, such as the SIT, leave much to be desired, and others, such as the Otis-Lennon, seem to be less used than in the past. Tests, like other market products, achieve varying degrees of popularity and commercial success, but hopefully the lessons they teach us will outlast their use.

SUGGESTED READINGS

Byrd, P. D., & Buckhalt, J. A. (1991). A multitrait-multimethod construct validity study of the Differential Ability Scales. *Journal of Psychoeducational Assessment 9*, 121–129.

You will recall that we discussed the multitrait-multimethod design as a way of assessing construct validity, and more specifically, as a way of obtaining convergent and discriminant validity information. This study of 46 rural Alabama children analyzes scores from the DAS, the WISC-R, and the Stanford Achievement Test. The authors conclude that one must be careful in comparing subtests from the DAS and the WISC-R, even though they may have similar content. One may well ask whether this article represents an accurate utilization of the multitrait-multimethod approach – are the methods assessed really different?

Frederiksen, N. (1986). Toward a broader conception of human intelligence. *American Psychologist, 41*, 445–452.

The author argues that current models of intelligence are limited because they do not simulate real-world problem situations, and he reviews a number of studies that do simulate real-world problems.

Kaufman, A. S. (1983). Some questions and answers about the Kaufman Assessment Battery for Children (K-ABC). *Journal of Psychoeducational Assessment, 1*, 205–218.

A highly readable overview of the K-ABC written by its senior author. In addition to a description of the battery, the author covers five basic questions: (1) Why was the age range of $2\frac{1}{2}$ to $12\frac{1}{2}$ years selected? (2) Does the Mental Processing Composite Scale predict future achievement? (3) Do the practice items lower reliability? (4) Why are there more simultaneous than sequential subtests? (5) Is the K-ABC a replacement for the WISC-R?

Keating, D. P. (1990). Charting pathways to the development of expertise. *Educational Psychologist, 25*, 243–267.

A very theoretical article that first briefly reviews the history of the conception of intelligence and then engages in some speculative thinking. The article introduces "Alfreda" Binet, the mythical twin sister of Alfred Binet, who might have done things quite differently from her famous brother.

Weinberg, R. A. (1989). Intelligence and IQ. *American Psychologist, 44*, 98–104.

A brief overview of the topic of intelligence, some of the controversies, and some of the measurement issues.

DISCUSSION QUESTIONS

1. Do you agree that "intelligent behavior can be observed"? What might be some of the aspects of such behavior?

2. Which of the six metaphors of intelligence makes most sense to you?

3. What are some of the reasons why intelligence tests are not good predictors of college GPA?

4. How is the validity of an intelligence test such as the Stanford-Binet IV established?

5. Discuss the validity of any intelligence test in the primary-secondary-tertiary framework we discussed in Chapter 3.

6 Attitudes, Values, and Interests

AIM This chapter looks at the measurement of attitudes, values, and interests. These three areas share much in common from a psychometric as well as a theoretical point of view; in fact, some psychologists argue that the three areas, and especially attitudes and values, are not so different from each other. Some authors regard them as subsets of personality, while others point out that it is difficult, if not impossible, to define these three areas so that they are mutually exclusive.

The measurement of attitudes has been a central topic in social psychology, but has found relatively little application in the assessment of the individual client. Interest measurement on the other hand, particularly the assessment of career interests, probably represents one of the most successful applications of psychological testing to the individual client. The assessment of values has had somewhat of a mixed success, with such assessment often seen as part of personality and/or social psychology, and with some individual practitioners believing that values are an important facet of a client's assessment.

In the area of attitudes we look at some general issues, some classical ways of developing attitude scales, and some other examples to illustrate various aspects. In the area of values, we look at two of the more popular measures that have been developed, the Study of Values and the Rokeach Value Survey. Finally, in the area of interest measurement, we focus on career interests and the two sets of tests that have dominated this field, the Strong and the Kuder.

ATTITUDES

Definition. Once again, we find that there are many ways of defining attitudes and not all experts in this field agree as to what is and what is not an attitude. For our purposes however, we can consider attitudes as a predisposition to respond to a social object, such as a person, group, idea, physical object, etc., in particular situations; the predisposition interacts with other variables to influence the actual behavior of a person (Cardno, 1955).

Most discussions and/or definitions of attitude involve a tripartite model of affect, behavior, and cognition. That is, attitudes considered as a response to an object have an emotional component (how strongly one feels), a behavioral component (for example, voting for a candidate; shouting racial slurs; arguing about one's views), and a cognitive (thinking) component (e.g., Insko & Schopler, 1967; Krech, Crutchfield, & Ballachey, 1962). These three components should converge (that is, be highly similar), but each should also contribute something unique, and that indeed seems to be the case (e.g., Breckler, 1984; Ostrom, 1969; Rosenberg, Hovland, McGuire, et al., 1960). This tripartite model is the "classical" model that has guided much research, but it too has been criticized and new theoretical models proposed (e.g., Cacioppo, Petty, & Geen, 1989; Pratkanis & Greenwald, 1989; Zanna & Rempel, 1988).

Some writers seem to emphasize one component more than the others. For example, Thurstone (1946) defined attitude as, "the degree of positive or negative affect associated with some psychological object." But most social scientists do perceive attitudes as learned predispositions to respond to a specific target, in either a positive or negative manner. As in other areas of assessment, there are a number of theoretical models available (e.g., Ajzen & Fishbein, 1980; Bentler & Speckart, 1979; Dohmen, Doll, & Feger, 1989; Fishbein, 1980; Jaccard, 1981; Triandis, 1980; G. Wiechmann & L. A. Wiechmann, 1973).

Centrality of attitudes. The study of attitudes and attitude change have occupied a central position in the social sciences, and particularly in social psychology, for a long time. Even today, the topic is one of the most active topics of study (Eagly & Chaiken, 1992; Oskamp, 1991; Rajecki, 1990). Part of the reason why the study of attitudes has been so central focuses on the assumption that attitudes will reveal behavior and because behavior seems so difficult to assess directly, attitudes are assumed to provide a way of understanding behavior (Kahle, 1984). Thus the relationship between attitudes and behavior is a major question, with some writers questioning such a relationship (e.g., Wicker, 1969) and others proposing that such a relationship is moderated by situational or personality factors (e.g., Ajzen & Fishbein, 1973; Zanna, Olson, & Fazio, 1980).

Some precautions. Henerson, Morris, and Fitz-Gibbon (1987) suggest that in the difficult task of measuring attitudes, we need to keep in mind four precautions:

1. Attitudes are inferred from a person's words and actions; thus, they are not measured directly.

2. Attitudes are complex; feelings, beliefs, and behaviors do not always match.

3. Attitudes may not necessarily be stable, and so the establishment of reliability, especially when viewed as consistency over time, can be problematic.

4. Often we study attitudes without necessarily having uniform agreement as to their nature.

Ways of studying attitudes. There are many ways in which attitudes can be measured or assessed. The first and most obvious way to learn what a person's attitude is toward a particular issue is to ask that person directly. Everyday conversations are filled with this type of assessment, as when we ask others such questions as "How do you feel about the death penalty?" "What do you think about abortion?" and "Where do you stand on gay rights?" This method of self-report is simple and direct, can be useful under some circumstances, but is quite limited from a psychometric point of view. There may be pressures to conform to majority opinion or to be less than candid about what one believes. There may be a confounding of expressed attitude with verbal skills, shyness, or other variables. A. L. Edwards (1957a) cites a study in which college students interviewed residents of Seattle about a pending legislative bill. Half of the residents were asked directly about their views, and half were given a secret and anonymous ballot to fill out. More "don't know" responses were obtained by direct asking, and more unfavorable responses were obtained through the secret ballot. The results of the secret ballot were also in greater agreement with actual election results held several weeks later.

There are other self-reports, and these can include surveys, interviews, or more "personal" procedures such as keeping a log or journal. Self-reports can ordinarily be used when the respondents are able to understand what is being asked, can provide the necessary information, and are likely to respond honestly.

Observing directly. Another approach to the study of attitudes is to observe a person's behavior, and to infer from that behavior the person's attitudes. Thus, we might observe shoppers in a grocery store to determine their attitudes toward a particular product. The problem of course, is that a specific behavior may not be related to a particular attitude (for a brief, theoretical discussion of the relationship between attitudes and observable behavior see J. R. Eiser, 1987). You might buy chicken not because you love chicken but because you cannot afford filet mignon, or because you might want to try out a new recipe, or because your physician has suggested less red meat. Such *observer-reports* can include a variety of procedures ranging from observational assessment, to interviews, questionnaires, logs, etc. This approach is used when the people whose attitudes are being investigated may not be able to provide accurate information, or when the focus is directly on behavior that can be observed, or when there is evidence to suggest that an observer will be less biased and more objective.

Assessing directly. Because of the limitations inherent in both asking and observing, *attitude scales* have been developed as a third means of assessing attitudes. An attitude scale is essentially a collection of items, typically called *statements*, which elicit differential responses on the part of individuals who hold different attitudes. As with any other instrument, the attitude scale must be shown to have adequate reliability and validity. We will return to attitude scales below.

Sociometric procedures. Mention should be made here of *sociometric procedures*, which have been used to assess attitudes, not so much toward an external object, but more to assess the social patterns of a group. Thus, if we are interested in measuring the social climate of a classroom (which children play with which children; who are the leaders and the isolates, etc.), we might use a sociometric technique (for example, having each child identify their three best friends in that classroom). Such nominations may well reflect racial and other attitudes. Sociometric techniques can also be useful to obtain a *base rate* reading prior to the implementation of a program designed to change the group dynamics, or to determine whether a particular program has had an effect. There are a wide variety of sociometric measures, with two of the more popular consisting of *peer ratings* and *social choices*. In the peer rating method, the respondent reads a series of statements and indicates to whom the statement refers. For example:

____ this child is always happy.
____ this child has lots of friends.
____ this child is very good at playing sports.

In the social choice method, the respondent indicates the other persons whom he or she prefers. For example:

I would like to work with:____
I would like to be on the same team as:____

In general, it is recommended that sociometric items be positive rather than negative and general rather than specific (see Gronlund, 1959, for information on using and scoring sociometric instruments).

Records. Sometimes, *written records* that are kept for various purposes (e.g., school attendance records) can be analyzed to assess attitudes, such as attitudes toward school or a particular school subject.

Why use rating scales? Given so many ways of assessing attitudes, why should rating scales be used? There are at least six major reasons offered in the literature: (1) attitude rating scales can be administered to large groups of respondents at one sitting; (2) they can be administered under conditions of anonymity; (3) they allow the respondent to proceed at their own pace; (4) they present uniformity of procedure; (5) they allow for greater flexibility – for example, take-home questionnaires; and (6) the results are more amenable to statistical analyses.

At the same time, it should be recognized that their strengths are also their potential weaknesses. Their use with large groups can preclude obtaining individualized information or results that may suggest new avenues of questioning.

Ways of Measuring Attitudes

The method of equal-appearing intervals. This method, also known as the Thurstone method after its originator (Thurstone & Chave, 1929), is one of the most common methods of developing attitude scales and involves the following steps:

1. The first step is to select the social object or target to be evaluated. This might be an individual (the President), a group of people (artists), an idea or issue (physician-assisted suicide), a physical object (the new library building), or other targets.

2. Next a pool of items (close to 100 is not uncommon) is generated – designed to represent both favorable and unfavorable views. An assumption of most attitude research is that

attitudes reflect a bipolar continuum ranging from pro to con, from positive to negative.

3. The items are printed individually on cards, and these cards are then given to a group of "expert" subjects (judges) who individually sort the items into 11 piles according to the degree of favorableness (*not* according to whether they endorse the statement). Ordinarily, items placed in the first pile are the most unfavorable, items in the 6th pile are neutral, and items in the 11th pile are the most favorable. Note that this is very much like doing a Q sort, but the individual judge can place as many items in any one pile as he or she wishes. The judges are usually chosen because they are experts on the target being assessed – for example, statements for a religion attitude scale might be sorted by ministers.

4. The median value for each item is then computed by using the pile number. Thus if item #73 is placed by five judges in piles 6, 6, 7, 8, and 9, the median for that item would be 7. Ordinarily of course, we would be using a sizable sample of judges (closer to 100 is not uncommon), and so the median values would most likely be decimal numbers.

5. The median is a measure of central tendency – of average. We also need to compute for each item the amount of variability or of dispersion among scores, the scores again being the pile numbers. Ordinarily, we might think of computing the standard deviation, but Thurstone computed the *interquartile range*, known as Q. The interquartile range for an item is based on the difference between the pile values of the 25th and the 75th percentiles. This measure of dispersion in effect looks at the variability of the middle 50% of the values assigned by the judges to a particular item. A small Q value would indicate that most judges agreed in their placement of a statement, while a larger value would indicate greater disagreement. Often disagreement reflects a poorly written item that can be interpreted in various ways.

6. Items are then retained that (1) have a wide range of medians so that the entire continuum is represented and (2) that have the smallest Q values indicating placement agreement on the part of the judges.

7. The above steps will yield a scale of maybe 15 to 20 items that can then be administered to a sample of subjects with the instructions to check those items the respondent agrees with. The items are printed in random order. A person's score on the attitude scale is the median of the scale values of all the items endorsed.

For example, let's assume we have developed a scale to measure attitudes toward the topic of "psychological testing." Here are six representative items with their medians and Q values:

	Median	Q value
1. I would rather read about psychological testing than anything else	10.5	.68
14. This topic makes you really appreciate the complexity of the human mind	8.3	3.19
19. This is a highly interesting topic	6.7	.88
23. Psychological testing is OK	4.8	.52
46. This topic is very boring	2.1	.86
83. This is the worst topic in psychology	1.3	.68

Note that item 14 would probably be eliminated because of its larger Q value. If the other items were retained and administered to a subject who endorses items 1, 19, and 23, then that person's score would be the median of 10.5, 6.7, and 4.8, which would be 6.7.

The intent of this method was to develop an interval scale, or possibly a ratio scale, but it is clear that the zero point (in this case the center of the distribution of items) is not a true zero. The title "method of equal-appearing intervals" suggests that the procedure results in an interval scale, but whether this is so has been questioned (e.g., Hevner, 1930; Petrie, 1969). Unidimensionality, hopefully, results from the writing of the initial pool of items, in that all of the items should be relevant to the target being assessed and from selecting items with small Q values.

There are a number of interesting questions that can be asked about the Thurstone procedure. For example, why use 11 categories? Why use the median rather than the mean? Could the judges rate each item rather than sort the items? In general, variations from the procedures originally used by Thurstone do not seem to make much difference (S. C. Webb, 1955).

One major concern is whether the attitudes of the judges who do the initial sorting influences how the items are sorted. At least some studies have suggested that the attitudes of the judges, even if extreme, can be held in abeyance with careful instructions, and do not influence the sorting of the items in a favorable-unfavorable continuum (e.g., Bruvold, 1975; Hinckley, 1932).

Another criticism made of Thurstone scales is that the same total score can be obtained by endorsing totally different items; one person may obtain a total score by endorsing one very favorable item or 9 or 10 unfavorable items that would add to the same total. This criticism is, of course, not unique to the Thurstone method. Note that when we construct a scale we ordinarily assume that there is a continuum we are assessing (intelligence, anxiety, psychopathology, liberal-conservative, etc.) and that we can locate the position of different individuals on this continuum as reflected by their test scores. We ordinarily don't care how those scores are composed – on a 100-item classroom test, it doesn't ordinarily matter which 10 items you miss, your raw score will still be 90. But one can argue that it *ought* to matter. Whether you miss the 10 most difficult items or the 10 easiest items probably says something about your level of knowledge or test-taking abilities, and whether you miss 10 items all on one topic vs. 10 items on 10 different topics might well be related to your breadth of knowledge.

Example of a Thurstone scale. J. H. Wright and Hicks (1966) attempted to develop a liberalism-conservatism scale using the Thurstone method. This dimension is a rather popular one, and several such scales exist (e.g., G. Hartmann, 1938; Hetzler, 1954; Kerr, 1952; G. D. Wilson & Patterson, 1968). The authors assembled 358 statements that were sorted into an 11-point continuum by 45 college students in an experimental psychology class (could these be considered experts?). From the pool of items, 23 were selected to represent the entire continuum and with the smallest SD (note that the original Thurstone method called for computing the interquartile range rather than the SD – but both are measures of variability), To validate the scale,

it was administered to college students, members of Young Democrat and Young Republican organizations, with Democrats assumed to represent the liberal point of view and Republicans the conservative.

Below are representative items from the scale with the corresponding scale values:

1.	All old people should be taken care of by the government.	2.30
10.	Labor unions play an essential role in American democracy.	4.84
16.	The federal government should attempt to cut its annual spending.	7.45
23.	Isolation (complete) is the answer to our foreign policy.	10.50

Note that the dimension on which the items were sorted was liberal vs. conservative, rather than pro or con.

The authors report a corrected internal consistency coefficient (split-half) of +.79, and a Guttman reproducibility score of .87 (see following disscussion). The correlation between political affiliation and scale score was +.64, with Young Democrats having a mean score of 4.81 and Young Republicans a mean score of 5.93. These two means are not all that different, and one may question the initial assumption of the authors that democrats equal liberal and republicans equal conservative, and/or whether the scale really is valid. Note also that the authors chose contrasted groups, a legitimate procedure, but one may well wonder whether the scale would differentiate college students with different political persuasions who have chosen not to join campus political organizations. Finally, many of the items on the scale have become outmoded. Perhaps more than other measures, attitude scales have a short "shelf life," and rapidly become outdated in content, making longitudinal comparisons somewhat difficult.

The method of summated ratings. This method, also known as the Likert method after its originator (Likert, 1932), uses the following sequence of steps:

1. and 2. These are the same as in the Thurstone method, namely choosing a target concept and generating a pool of items.

3. The items are administered to a sample of subjects who indicate for each item whether they "strongly agree," "agree," "are undecided," "disagree," or "strongly disagree" (sometimes a word like "approve" is used instead of agree). Note that these subjects are not experts as in the Thurstone method; they are typically selected because they are available (introductory psychology students), or they represent the population that eventually will be assessed (e.g., registered Democrats).

4. A total score for each subject can be generated by assigning scores of 5, 4, 3, 2, and 1 to the above categories, and reversing the scoring for unfavorably worded items; the intent here is to be consistent, so that ordinarily higher scores represent a more favorable attitude.

5. An item analysis is then carried out by computing for each item a correlation between responses on that item and total scores on all the items (to be statistically correct, the total score should be for all the other items, so that the same item is not correlated with itself, but given a large number of items such overlap has minimal impact).

6. Individual items that correlate the highest with the total score are then retained for the final version of the scale. Note therefore that items could be retained that are heterogeneous in content, but correlate significantly with the total. Conversely, we could also carry out an item analysis using the method of item discrimination we discussed. Here we could identify the top 27% high scorers and the bottom 27% low scorers, and analyze for each item how these two groups responded to that item. Those items that show good discrimination between high and low scorers would be retained.

7. The final scale can then be administered to samples of subjects and their scores computed. Such scores will be highly relative in meaning – what is favorable or unfavorable depends upon the underlying distribution of scores.

Note should be made that some scales are called Likert scales simply because they use a 5-point response format, but may have been developed without using the Likert procedure, i.e., simply by the author putting together a set of items.

Are five response categories the best? To some degree psychological testing is affected by inertia

and tradition. If the first or major researcher in one area uses a particular type of scale, quite often subsequent investigators also use the same type of scale, even when designing a new scale. But the issue of how many response categories are best – "best" judged by "user-friendly" aspects and by reliability and validity – has been investigated with mixed results (e.g., Komorita & Graham, 1965; Masters, 1974; Remmers & Ewart, 1941). Probably a safe conclusion here is that there does not seem to be an optimal number, but that five to seven categories seem to be better than fewer or more.

In terms of our fourfold classification of nominal, ordinal, interval, and ratio scales, Likert scales fall somewhere between ordinal and interval. On the one hand, by adding the arbitrary scores associated with each response option, we are acting as if the scale is an interval scale. But clearly the scores are arbitrary – why should the difference between "agree" and "strongly agree" be of the same numerical magnitude as the difference between "uncertain" and "agree"? And why should a response of "uncertain" be assigned a value of 3?

The above two methods are the most common ways of constructing attitude scales. Both are based upon what are called *psychophysical methods*, ways of assessing stimuli on the basis of their physical dimensions such as weight, but as determined psychologically (How heavy does this object feel?). Interested readers should see A. L. Edwards (1957a) for a discussion of these methods as related to attitude scale construction. How do the Thurstone and Likert procedures compare? For example, would a Thurstone scale of attitudes toward physician assisted suicide correlate with a Likert scale of the same target? Or what if we used the same pool of items and scored them first using the Thurstone method and then the Likert method – would the resulting sets of scores be highly related? In general, studies indicate that such scales typically correlate to a fair degree (in the range of .60 to .95). Likert scales typically show higher split-half or test-retest reliability than Thurstone scales. Likert scales are also easier to construct and use, which is why there are more of them available (see Roberts, Laughlin, & Wedell, 1999 for more complex aspects of this issue). We now turn to a number of other methods, which though important, have proven less common.

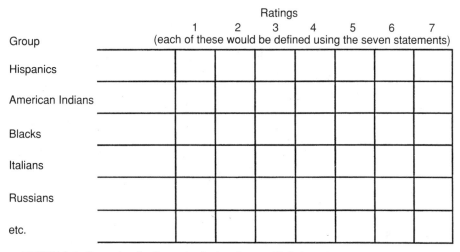

FIGURE 6–1. Example of a Bogardus Scale using multiple targets.

The Bogardus (1925) method. This method was developed in an attempt to measure attitudes toward different nationalities. Bogardus simply asked subjects to indicate whether they would admit members of a particular nationality or race to different degrees of social contact as defined by these seven categories:

1. close kinship by marriage
2. membership in one's club (or as close friends)
3. live on the same street as neighbor
4. employment in the same occupation (or work in same office)
5. citizenship in this country
6. visitor in this country
7. would exclude from this country

The scale forms a continuum of social distance, where at one end a person is willing to accept the target person in a very intimate relationship and at the other extreme would keep the target person as far away as possible. The instructions ask the subject to check those alternatives that reflect his or her reaction and not to react to the best or the worst members of the group that the respondent might have known. The score is simply the rank of the lowest (most intimate) item checked. If the group being assessed is a racial group, such as Blacks, then the resulting score is typically called a *racial distance quotient.* Note that multiple ratings could be obtained by having a bivariate table, with one dimension representing racial groups and the other dimension representing the seven categories. Figure 6.1 illustrates this.

The Bogardus approach is a methodology, but also a unique scale, as opposed to the Thurstone and Likert methods, which have yielded a wide variety of scales. Therefore, it is appropriate here to mention reliability and validity. Newcomb (1950) indicated that split-half reliability of the Bogardus scale typically reaches .90 or higher and that the validity is satisfactory. There have been a number of versions of the Bogardus scale; for example, Dodd (1935) developed an equal-interval version of this scale for use in the Far East, while Miller and Biggs (1958) developed a modified version for use with children. In general however, the Bogardus social distance approach has had limited impact, and its use nowadays seems to be rare.

Guttman scaling. This method is also known as *scalogram analysis* (Guttman, 1944). There is little difficulty in understanding the Bogardus social distance scale, and we can think of the Guttman method as an extension. We can easily visualize how close or far away a particular person might wish to keep from members of a racial group, even though we may not understand and/or condone racial prejudice. Ordinarily, we would expect that if a person welcomes a member of a different race into their own family, they would typically allow that person to work in the same office, and so on. The social distance scale is a univariate scale, almost by definition, where a person's position on that scale can be defined simply by the point where the person switches response mode. Suppose, for example, I have a mild case of racial bias against Venusian Pincos; I would allow them in this country as visitors or citizens, and would not really object to working with them, but I certainly would not want them as neighbors, or close friends, and would simply die if my daughter married one of them. My point of change is from item 4 to item 3; knowing that point of change, you could reproduce all my seven responses, assuming I did not reverse myself. This is in fact what Guttman scaling is all about. In developing a Guttman scale, a set of items that form a scalable continuum (such as social distance) is administered to a group of subjects, and the pattern of responses is analyzed to see if they fit the Guttman model. As an example, let's assume we have only three items: A (on marriage), B (on close friends), and C (on neighbor), each item requiring agreement or disagreement. Note that with the three items, we could theoretically obtain the following patterns of response:

	Item A (marriage)	Item B (close friends)	Item C (neighbor)
Response	Agree	Disagree	Disagree
	Agree	Agree	Disagree
Patterns:	*Agree	Agree	Agree
	*Disagree	Agree	Agree
	*Disagree	Disagree	Agree
	*Disagree	Disagree	Disagree
	Agree	Disagree	Agree
	Disagree	Agree	Disagree

In fact, the number of possible response patterns is 2^N where N is the number of items; in this case 2^3 equals $2 \times 2 \times 2$ or 8. If however, the items form a Guttman scale, there should be few if any reversals, and only the four response patterns marked by an * should occur. The ideal number of response patterns then becomes $N + 1$, or 4 in this example. We can then compute what is called the *coefficient of reproducibility*, which is defined as:

$$1 - \frac{\text{total number of errors}}{\text{total number of responses}}$$

where errors are any deviation from the "ideal" pattern. If the reproducibility coefficient is .90 or above, then the scale is considered satisfactory. Although the matter seems fairly straightforward, there are a number of

complicating issues that are beyond the scope of this book (e.g., A. L. Edwards, 1957a; Festinger, 1947; Green, 1954; Schuessler, 1961).

Guttman scales are not restricted to social distance, but could theoretically be developed to assess any variable. Let's assume I am working with an elderly population, perhaps female clients living in a nursing home, and I wish to assess their degree of independence as far as food preparation is concerned. I might develop a Guttman scale that might look like this:

This client is able to:

(a) plan and prepare a meal on her own

(b) plan and prepare a meal with some assistance

(c) prepare a meal but must be given the ingredients

(d) prepare a meal but needs assistance

(e) she not prepare a meal on her own

We can think of reproducibility as reflecting unidimensionality, and Guttman scales are thus unidimensional scales. Note however, that the method does not address the issue of equal intervals or the arbitrariness of the zero point; thus Guttman scales, despite their methodological sophistication, are not necessarily interval or ratio scales. The Guttman methodology has had more of an impact in terms of thinking about scale construction than in terms of actual, useful scales. Such scales do of course exist, but the majority assess variables that are behavioral in nature (such as the range of movement or physical skills a person possesses), rather than variables that are more "psychodynamic." There are a number of other procedures used to develop attitude scales, which, like the Guttman approach, are fairly complex both in theory and in statistical procedures (e.g., Banta, 1961; Coombs, 1950; Green, 1954; Hays & Borgatta, 1954; Lazarsfeld, 1950, 1954, 1959). In fact, there seems to be agreement that attitudes are multidimensional and that what is needed are more sophisticated techniques than the simple unidimensional approaches of Thurstone and Likert.

The Semantic Differential (SemD). The SemD was developed as a way of assessing word meaning but because this technique has been used quite frequently in the assessment of attitudes it

My ideal self

good	:	:	:	:	:	:	bad
small	:	:·	:	:	:	:	large
beautiful	:	:	:	:	:	:	ugly
passive	:	:	:	:	:	:	active
sharp	:	:	:	:	:	:	dull
slow	:	:	:	:	:	:	fast
dirty	:	:	:	:	:	:	clean

etc.

FIGURE 6–2. Example of a Semantic Differential Scale.

can legitimately be considered here. The SemD is a method of observing and measuring the psychological meaning of things, usually concepts. We can communicate with one another because words and concepts have a shared meaning. If I say to you, "I have a dog," you know what a dog is. Yet that very word also has additional meanings that vary from person to person. One individual may think of dog as warm, cuddly, and friendly while another person may think of dog as smelly, fierce, and troublesome. There are thus at least two levels of meaning to words: the *denotative* or dictionary meaning, and the *connotative* or personal meaning. Osgood (Osgood, Suci, & Tannenbaum, 1957) developed the SemD to measure the connotative meanings of concepts as points in a semantic space. That space is three-dimensional, like a room in a house, and the dimensions, identified through factor analysis, are *evaluative* (e.g., good-bad), *potency* (e.g., strong-weak), and *activity* (fast-slow). Four additional factorial dimensions have been identified: density (e.g., numerous-sparse), orderliness (e.g., haphazard-systematic), reality (e.g., authentic-fake), and familiarity (e.g., commonplace-exceptional) (Bentler & LaVoie, 1972; LaVoie & Bentler, 1974).

The SemD then consists of a series of bipolar adjectives separated by a 7-point scale, on which the respondent rates a given concept. Figure 6.2 gives an example of a SemD.

How does one develop a SemD scale? There are basically two steps. The first step is to choose the concept(s) to be rated. These might be famous persons (e.g., Mother Theresa, Elton John), political concepts (socialism), psychiatric concepts (alcoholism), therapeutic concepts (my ideal self), cultural groups (Armenians), nonsense syllables, drawings, photographs, or whatever other stimuli would be appropriate to the area of investigation.

The second step is to select the bipolar adjectives that make up the SemD. We want the scale to be short, typically around 12 to 16 sets of bipolar adjectives, especially if we are asking each respondent to rate several concepts (e.g., rate the following cities: New York, Rome, Paris, Istanbul, Cairo, and Caracas). Which adjectives would we use? Bipolar adjectives are selected on the basis of two criteria: factor representativeness and relevance. Typical studies of the SemD have obtained the three factors indicated above, so we would select four or five bipolar adjectives representative of each factor; the loadings of each adjective pair on the various factor dimensions are given in various sources (e.g., Osgood, Suci, & Tannenbaum, 1957; Snider & Osgood, 1969). The second criterion of relevance is a bit more difficult to implement. If the concept of Teacher were being rated, one might wish to use bipolar pairs that are relevant to teaching behavior such as organized vs. disorganized, or concerned

SemD Scales	Brand A	Brand B	Brand C	Brand D	Brand E
Table 6–1. SemD ratings from one subject for five brands of beer					
Pleasant-unpleasant	6	2	6	5	3
Ugly-beautiful	5	2	5	5	2
Sharp-flat	6	1	4	6	2
Salty-sweet	7	1	5	6	3
Happy-sad	5	3	5	7	1
Expensive-cheap	6	2	7	7	2
Mean	5.83	1.83	5.33	6.00	2.17

about students vs. not concerned (note that the "bipolar adjectives" need not be confined to one word). However, other bipolar pairs that on the surface may not seem highly relevant, such as heavy-light, ugly-beautiful, might in fact turn out to be quite relevant, in distinguishing between students who drop out vs. those who remain in school, for example.

In making up the SemD scale, about half of the bipolar adjectives would be listed in reverse order (as we did in Figure 6.2) to counteract response bias tendencies, so that not all left-hand terms would be positive. A 7-point scale is typically used, although between 3 and 11 spaces have been used in the literature; with children, a 5-point scale seems more appropriate.

Scoring the SemD. The SemD yields a surprising amount of data and a number of analyses are possible. The raw scores are simply the numbers 1 through 7 assigned as follows:

Good 7: 6: 5: 4: 3: 2: 1 Bad

The numbers do not appear on the respondent's protocol. Other numbers could be used, for example +3 to –3, but little if anything is gained and the arithmetic becomes more difficult.

If we are dealing with a single respondent, we can compare the semantic space directly. For example, Osgood and Luria (1954) analyzed a case of multiple personality (the famous "3 faces of Eve"), clearly showing that each personality perceived the world in rather drastically different terms, as evidenced by the ratings of such concepts as father, therapist, and myself.

Research projects and the assessment of attitudes usually involve a larger number of respondents, and various statistical analyses can be applied to the resulting data. Let's assume for example, we are studying attitudes toward

various brands of beer. Table 6.1 shows the results from one subject who was asked to rate each of five brands:

For the sake of simplicity, let's assume that the six bipolar pairs are all evaluative items. A first step would be to compute and compare the means. Clearly brands A, C, and D are evaluated quite positively, while brands B and E are not. If the means were group averages, we could test for statistical significance perhaps using an ANOVA design. Note that in the SemD there are three sources of variation in the raw scores: differences between concepts, differences between scales (i.e., items), and differences between respondents. In addition we typically have three factors to contend with.

Distance-cluster analysis. If two brands of beer are close together in semantic space, that is rated equivalently, they are alike in "meaning" (for e.g., brands C and D in Table 6.1). If they are separated in semantic space they differ in meaning (e.g., brands D and E). What is needed is a measure of the distance between any two concepts. Correlation comes to mind, but for a variety of reasons, it is not suitable. What is used is the D statistic:

$$D_{ij} = \sqrt{\sum d_{ij}^2}$$

that is, the distance between any two concepts i and j equals the square root of the sum of the differences squared. For example, the distance between brand A and brand B in the above example equals:

$$(6-2)^2 + (5-2)^2 + (6-1)^2 + (7-1)^2 + (5-3)^2 + (6-2)^2 = 106$$
$$\text{and } D = \sqrt{106} \text{ or } 10.3$$

We can do the same for every pair of concepts. If we have n concepts (5 in our example), we will compute

$$\frac{n(n-2)}{2} D \text{ values.}$$

These D values can be written down in a matrix:

	Brand B	C	D	E
Brand A	10.30	3.00	2.65	9.06
B		8.89	10.44	3.16
C			3.16	8.19
D				9.95

Such a D matrix can be analyzed in several ways but the aim is the same: to seek how the concepts cluster together. The smaller the D value the closer in meaning are the concepts. Visually we can see that our five brands fall into two clusters: brands A, C, and D vs. brands B and E. Statistically we can use a variety of techniques including correlation and factor analysis (Osgood, Suci, & Tannenbaum, 1957) or more specific techniques (McQuitty, 1957; Nunnally, 1962).

Although three major factors are obtained in the typical study with the SemD, it is highly recommended that an investigator using the SemD check the resulting factor structure because there may be concept-scale interactions that affect such structure (Piotrowski, 1983; Sherry & Piotrowski, 1986). The evaluative factor seems to be quite consistent across samples, but the other two dimensions, potency and activity, are less consistent.

The SemD has found wide use in psychology, with both adults and children; DiVesta (1965) for example, provides a number of bipolar adjectives that can be used with children. An example of a SemD scale can be found in the study of Poresky, Hendrix, Mosier, et al., (1988) who developed the Companion Animal Semantic Differential to assess a respondent's perception of a childhood companion animal such as a pet dog. They used 18 bipolar sets of adjectives (bad-good, clean-dirty, cuddly-not cuddly) and obtained 164 responses from high-school, college, and graduate students. They used a 6-point scale to score each item, rather than the more standard 7-point. For the entire scale, the Cronbach alpha was .90 indicating substantial reliability. A factor analysis indicated four factors: (1) an evaluative factor

(represented by such items as loving-not loving); (2) a factor related to the monetary value of the animal (e.g., valuable-worthless); (3) a factor related to affective value (kind-cruel); and (4) a factor related to the "size" of the animal (cuddly-not cuddly). When only the items that had substantial loadings were kept, the 18-item scale became a 9-item scale, and the four factors collapsed into one, namely an evaluative factor. Scores on the 9-item scale correlated .96 with scores on the 18-item scale. In case you're wondering of what use might such a scale be, you should know that there is a considerable body of literature and interest on the therapeutic effects of pet ownership on the elderly, the handicapped, coronary-care patients, and others.

One of the major concerns about the SemD is whether in fact the bipolar adjectives are bipolar – are the terms that anchor each scale truly opposite in meaning and equidistant from a true psychological midpoint? Results suggest that for some adjective pairs the assumption of bipolarity is not met (e.g., R. F. Green & Goldfried, 1965; Mann, Phillips, & Thompson, 1979; Schriesheim & Klich, 1991).

Checklists. One way to assess attitudes, particularly toward a large number of issues, is the *checklist* approach. As its name implies, this approach consists of a list of items (people, objects, issues, etc.) to which the respondent is asked to indicate their attitude in some way – by checking those items they endorse, selecting "favorable" or "unfavorable" for each item, indicating approval-disapproval, etc.

This is a simple and direct approach, and because all subjects are asked to respond to the same items, there is comparability of measurement. On the other hand, some argue that the presentation of a number of items can result in careless responding and hence lowered reliability and validity. In addition, the response categories typically used do not allow for degree of preference. (I may favor the death penalty and check that item in the list, but my convictions may not be very strong and might be easily dissuaded.)

An example of the checklist approach in the assessment of attitudes can be found in the work of G. D. Wilson and Patterson (1968) who developed the *conservatism* or C scale.

The C Scale

The liberal-conservative dimension has been studied quite extensively, both as it relates to political issues and voting behavior and a personality syndrome. Many investigators use terms like authoritarianism, dogmatism, or rigidity to refer to this dimension. Perhaps the major scale in this area has been the F (fascist) scale developed in a study called *The Authoritarian Personality* (Adorno et al., 1950). The F scale was for a time widely used, but also severely criticized for being open to acquiescence response set, poor phrasing, and other criticisms. Numerous attempts have been made, not only to develop revised F scales but also new scales based on the approach used with the F scale, as well as entirely different methodologies, such as that used in the C scale.

G. D. Wilson and Patterson (1968) decided that they would use a list of brief labels or "catchphrases" to measure "conservatism," defined as "resistance to change" and a preference for "safe, traditional, and conventional" behavior (G. D. Wilson, 1973). Theoretically, G. D. Wilson and Patterson (1968) identified conservatism as characterized by seven aspects that included religious fundamentalism, intolerance of minority groups, and insistence on strict rules and punishments. On the basis of these theoretical notions, they assembled a pool of 130 items chosen intuitively as reflective of these characteristics. They performed three item analyses (no details are given) and chose 50 items for the final scale. The respondent is asked which items "do you favor or believe in" and the response options are "yes, ?, no." For half of the items, a "yes" response indicates conservatism, and for half of the items a "no" response indicates conservatism. Examples of items (with their conservative response) are: the "death penalty (y)," "modern art (n)," "suicide (n)," "teenage drivers (n)," and "learning Latin (y)."

G. D. Wilson and Patterson (1968) reported a corrected split-half correlation coefficient of .94 based on 244 New Zealand subjects. They also present considerable validity data including age trends (older persons score higher), gender differences (females score slightly higher), differences between collegiate political groups, and between scientists and a conservative religious group.

In a subsequent study, Hartley and Holt (1971) used only the first half of the scale, but found additional validity evidence in various British groups; for example, psychology undergraduate students scored lowest, while male "headmasters" scored higher (female college of education students scored highest of all!). On the other hand, J. J. Ray (1971) administered the scale to Australian military recruits (all 20-year-old males) and found an alpha coefficient of +.63 and a preponderance of "yes" responses. He concluded that this scale was not suitable for random samples from the general population.

Bagley, Wilson, and Boshier (1970) translated the scale into Dutch and compared the responses of Dutch, British, and New Zealander subjects. A factor analysis indicated that for each of the three samples there was a "strong" general factor (however, it only accounted for 18.7 of the variance, or less), and the authors concluded that not only was there a "remarkable degree of cross-cultural stability" for the scale, but that the C scale had "considerable potential as an international test of social attitudes." The C scale was originally developed in New Zealand, and is relatively well known in English-speaking countries such as Australia, England, and New Zealand, but has found little utility in the United States. In part, this may be due to language differences (as Professor Higgins of My Fair Lady sings: English has not been spoken in the United States for quite some time!). For example, one C scale item is "birching" which means "paddling" as in corporal punishment administered by a teacher. In fact, a few investigators (e.g., Bahr & Chadwick, 1974; Joe, 1974; Joe & Kostyla, 1975) have adapted the C scale for American samples by making such item changes.

Although the reliability of the C scale would seem adequate (in the Dutch sample, the split-half was .89), Altemeyer (1981) brings up an interesting point. He argues that coefficient alpha, which you recall is one measure of reliability, reflects both the interitem correlations *and* the length of the test. Thus, one could have a questionnaire with a high coefficient alpha, but that might simply indicate that the questionnaire is long and not necessarily that the questionnaire is unidimensional. In fact, Altemeyer (1981) indicates that the average reliability coefficient for the C scale is .88, which indicates a mean interitem correlation of about .13 – thus, the C scale is criticized for not being unidimensional (see also Robertson & Cochrane, 1973).

Some general comments on rating scales. Like checklists, rating scales are used for a wide variety of assessment purposes, and the comments here, although they focus on attitude measurement, are meant to generalize to other areas of testing. Traditionally, rating scales were used to have one person assess another, for example, when a clinical psychologist might assess a client as to degree of depression, but the rating scales quickly were applied as self-report measures.

One common type of rating scale is *numerical* scale, where the choices offered to the respondent either explicitly or implicitly are defined numerically. For example, to the statement, "Suicide goes against the natural law," we might ask the respondent to indicate whether they (a) strongly agree, (b) agree, (c) are not sure, (d) disagree (e) strongly disagree. We may omit the numbers from the actual form seen by the respondent, but we would assign those numbers in scoring the response. Sometimes, the numbers are both positive and negative as in:

strongly agree	agree	not sure	disagree	strongly disagree
+2	+1	0	−1	−2

In general, such use of numbers makes life more complicated for both the respondent and the examiner. Mention should be made here, that there seems to be a general tendency on the part of some respondents to avoid extreme categories. Thus the 5-point scale illustrated above may turn out to be a 3-point scale for at least some subjects. The extension of this argument is that a 7-point scale is really preferable because in practice it will yield a 5-point scale.

Another type of rating scale is the *graphic* scale where the response options follow a straight line or some variation. For example:

How do you feel about capital punishment? Place a check mark on the line:

_____

1. should be abolished
2. should be used only for serious & repeat offenses
3. should be used for all serious offenses
4. is a deterrent & should be retained
5. should be used for all career criminals

Another example:
Where would you locate President Clinton on the following scale?

An excellent leader.

Better than most prior presidents.

Average in leadership.

Less capable than most other presidents.

Totally lacking in leadership capabilities.

Note that a scale could combine both numerical and graphic properties; essentially what distinguishes a graphic scale is the presentation of some device, such as a line, where the respondent can place their answer. Note also, that from a psychometric point of view, it is easier to "force" the respondent to place their mark in a particular segment, rather than to allow free reign. In the capital punishment example above, we could place little vertical lines to distinguish and separate the five response options. Or we could allow the respondent to check anywhere on the scale, even between responses, and generate a score by actually measuring the distance where they placed their mark from the extreme left-hand beginning of the line. Guilford (1954) discusses these scales at length, as well as other less common types.

Self-anchoring scales. Kilpatrick and Cantril (1960) presented an approach that they called *self-anchoring* scaling, where the respondent is asked to describe the top and bottom anchoring points in terms of his or her own perceptions, values, attitudes, etc. This scaling method grew out of transactional theory that assumes that we live and operate in the world, through the self, both as personally perceived. That is, there is a unique reality for each of us – my perception of the world is not the same as your perception; what is perceived is inseparable from the perceiver.

Self-anchoring scales require both open-ended interviewing, content analysis, and nonverbal scaling. The first step is to ask the respondent to describe the "ideal" way of life. Second, he or she is asked to describe the "worst" way of life. Third, he or she is given a pictorial, nonverbal scale, such as an 11-point ladder:

```
10

 9

 8

 7

 6

 5

 4

 3

 2

 1

 0
```

The respondent is told that a 10 represents the ideal way of life as he or she described it, and 0 represents the worst way of life. So the two anchors have been defined by the respondent. Now the respondent is asked, "where on the ladder are you now?" Other questions may be asked, such as, "where on the ladder were you five years ago," "where will you be in two years," and so on.

The basic point of the ladder is that it provides a self-defined continuum that is anchored at either end in terms of personal perception. Other than that, the entire procedure is quite flexible. Fewer or more than 11 steps may be used; the numbers themselves may be omitted; a rather wide variety of concepts can be scaled; and instructions may be given in written form rather than as an interview, allowing the simultaneous assessment of a group of individuals.

Designing attitude scales. Oppenheim (1992), in discussing the design of "surveys," suggests a series of 14 steps. These are quite applicable to the design of attitude scales and are quite similar to the more generic steps suggested in Chapter 2. They are well worth repeating here (if you wish additional information on surveys, see Kerlinger, 1964; Kidder, Judd, & Smith, 1986; Rossi, Wright, & Anderson, 1983; Schuman & Kalton, 1985; Singer & Presser, 1989):

1. First decide the aims of the study. The aims should not be simply generic aims (I wish to study the attitudes of students toward physician-assisted suicide) but should be specific, and take the form of hypotheses to be tested (students who are highly authoritarian will endorse physician-assisted suicide to a greater degree than less authoritarian).

2. Review the relevant literature and carry out discussions with appropriate informants, individuals who by virtue of their expertise and/or community position are knowledgeable about the intended topic.

3. Develop a preliminary conceptualization of the study and revise it based on exploratory and/or in depth interviews.

4. Spell out the design of the study and assess its feasibility in terms of time, cost, staffing needed, and so on.

5. Spell out the *operational* definitions – that is, if our hypothesis is that "political attitudes are related to socioeconomic background," how will each of these variables be defined and measured?

6. Design or adapt the necessary research instruments.

7. Carry out pilot work to try out the instruments.

8. Develop a research design: How will respondents be selected? Is a control group needed? How will participation be ensured?

9. Select the sample(s).

10. Carry out the field work: interview subjects and/or administer questionnaires.

11. Process the data: code and/or score the responses, enter the data into the computer.

12. Carry out the appropriate statistical analyses.

13. Assemble the results.

14. Write the research report.

Writing items for attitude scales. Much of our earlier discussion on writing test items also applies here. Writing statements for any psychometric instrument is both an art and a science. A number of writers (e.g., A. L. Edwards, 1957a; A. L. Edwards & Kilpatrick, 1948; Payne, 1951; Thurstone & Chave, 1929; Wang, 1932), have made many valuable suggestions such as, make statements brief, unambiguous, simple, and direct; each statement should focus on only one idea; avoid double negatives; avoid "apple pie and motherhood" type of statements that everyone agrees with; don't use universals such as "always" or "never"; don't use emotionally laden words such as "adultery," "Communist," "agitator"; where possible, use positive rather than negative wording. For attitude scales, one difference is that factual statements, pertinent in achievement testing, do not make good items because individuals with different attitudes might well respond identically.

Ambiguous statements should not be used. For example, "It is important that we give Venusians the recognition they deserve" is a poor statement because it might be interpreted positively (Venusians should get more recognition) or negatively (Venusians deserve little recognition and that's what they should get). A. L. Edwards (1957a) suggested that a good first step in the preliminary evaluation of statements is to have a group of individuals answer the items first as if they had a favorable attitude and then as if they had an unfavorable attitude. Items that show a distinct shift in response are most likely useful items.

Closed vs. open response options. Most attitude scales presented in the literature use *closed* response options; this is the case in both the Thurstone and Likert methods where the respondent endorses (or not) a specific statement. We may also wish to use *open* response options, where respondents are asked to indicate in their own words what their attitude is – for example, "How valuable were the homework assignments in this class?" "Comment on the textbook used," and so on. Closed response options are advantageous from a statistical point of view. Open response options are more difficult to handle statistically, but can provide more information and allow respondents to express their feelings more directly. Both types of items can of course be used.

Measuring attitudes in specific situations. There are a number of situations where the assessment of attitudes might be helpful, but available scales may not quite fit the demands of the situation. For example, a city council may wish to determine how citizens feel toward the potential construction of a new park, or the regents of a university might wish to assess whether a new academic degree should be offered. The same steps we discussed in Chapter 2 might well be used here (or the steps offered by Oppenheim [1992] above). Perhaps it might not be necessary to have a "theory" about the proposed issue, but it certainly would be important to identify the objectives that are to be assessed and to produce items that follow the canons of good writing.

VALUES

Values also play a major role in life, especially because, as philosophers tell us, human beings are metaphysical animals searching for the purpose of their existence. Such purposes are guidelines for life or values (Grosze-Nipper & Rebel, 1987). Like the assessment of attitudes, the assessment of values is also a very complex undertaking, in part because values, like most other psychological variables, are constructs, i.e., abstract conceptions. Different social scientists have different conceptions and so perceive values differently, and there does not seem to be a uniformly accepted way of defining and conceptualizing values. As with attitudes, values cannot be measured directly, we can only infer a person's values by what they say and/or what they do. But people are complex and do not necessarily behave in logically consistent ways. Not every psychologist agrees that values are important; Mowrer (1967) for example, believed that the term "values" was essentially useless.

Formation and changes in values. Because of the central role that values occupy, there is a vast body of literature, both experimental and theoretical, on this topic. One intriguing question concerns how values are formed and how values change. Hoge and Bender (1974) suggested that there are three theoretical models that address this issue. The first model assumes that values are formed and changed by a vast array of events and experiences. We are all in the same "boat" and whatever affects that boat affects all of us. Thus, as our society becomes more violence-prone and materialistic, *we* become more violence-prone and materialistic. A second model assumes that certain developmental periods are crucial for the establishment of values. One such period is adolescence, and so high school and the beginning college years are "formative" years. This means that when there are relatively rapid social changes, different cohorts of individuals will have different values. The third model also assumes that values change developmentally, but the changes are primarily a function of age – for example, as people become older, they become more conservative.

The Study of Values (SoV)

The SoV (Allport, Vernon, & Lindzey, 1960; Vernon & Allport, 1931) was for many years the leading measure of values, used widely by social psychologists, in studies of personality, and even as a counseling and guidance tool. The SoV seems to be no longer popular, but it is still worthy of a close look. The SoV, originally published in 1931 and revised in 1951, was based on a theory (by Spranger, 1928) that assumed there were six basic values or personality types: theoretical, economic, aesthetic, social, political, and religious. As the authors indicated (Allport, Vernon, & Lindzey, 1960) Spranger held a rather positive view of human nature and did not consider the possibility of a "valueless" person, or someone who followed expediency (doing what is best for one's self) or hedonism (pleasure) as a way of life. Although the SoV was in some ways designed to operationalize Spranger's theory, the studies that were subsequently generated were only minimally related to Spranger's views; thus, while the SoV had quite an impact on psychological research, Spranger's theory did not.

The SoV was composed of two parts consisting of forced-choice items in which statements representing different values were presented, with the respondent having to choose one. Each of the 6 values was assessed by a total of 20 items, so the entire test was composed of 120 items. The SoV was designed primarily for college students or well-educated adults, and a somewhat unique aspect was that it could be hand scored by the subject.

Reliability. For a sample of 100 subjects, the corrected split-half reliabilities for the six scales range from .84 to .95, with a mean of .90. Test-retest reliabilities are also reported for two small samples, with a 1-month and a 2-month interval. These values are also quite acceptable, ranging from .77 to .93 (Allport, Vernon, & Lindzey, 1960). Hilton and Korn (1964) administered the SoV seven times to 30 college students over a 7-month period (in case you're wondering, the students were participating in a study of career decision making, and were paid for their participation). Reliability coefficients ranged from a low of .74 for the political value scale to a high of .91 for the aesthetic value scale. Subsequent studies have reported similar values.

An ipsative scale. The SoV is also an ipsative measure: if you score high on one scale you must score lower on some or all of the others. As the authors state in the test manual, it is not quite legitimate therefore to ask whether the scales intercorrelate. Nevertheless, they present the intercorrelations based on a sample of 100 males and a sample of 100 females. As expected, most of the correlations are negative, ranging in magnitude and sign from a $-.48$ (for religious vs. theoretical, in the female sample) to a $+.27$ for political vs. economic (in the male sample), and religious vs. social (in the female sample).

Validity. There are literally hundreds of studies in the literature that used the SoV, and most support its validity. One area in which the SoV has been used is to assess the changes in values that occur during the college years; in fact, K. A. Feldman and Newcomb (1969) after reviewing the available literature, believed that the SoV was the best single source of information about such changes. The study by Huntley (1965) although not necessarily representative, is illustrative and interesting. Huntley (1965), administered the SoV to male undergraduate college students at entrance to college and again just prior to graduation. Over a 6-year period some 1,800 students took the test, with 1,027 having both "entering" and "graduating" profiles. The students were grouped into nine major fields of study, such as science, engineering, and pre-med, according to their graduation status. Huntley (1965) then asked, and answered, four basic questions: (1) Do values (i.e., SoV scores) change significantly during the 4 years of college? Of the 54 possible changes (9 groups of students × 6 values), 27 showed statistically significant changes, with specific changes associated with specific majors. For example, both humanities and pre-med majors increased in their aesthetic value and decreased in their economic value, while industrial administration majors increased in both their aesthetic and economic values; (2) Do students who enter different majors show different values at entrance into college? Indeed they do. Engineering students, for example, have high economic and political values, while physics majors have low economic and political values; (3) What differences are found among the nine groups at graduation? Basically the same pattern of differences that exist at entrance. In fact, if the nine groups are ranked on each of the values, and the ranks at entrance are compared with those at graduation, there is a great deal of stability. In addition, what appears to happen is that value differences among groups are accentuated over the course of the four collegiate years; (4) Are there general trends? Considering these students as one cohort, theoretical, social, and political values show no appreciable change (keep in mind that these values *do* change for specific majors). Aesthetic values increase, and economic and religious values decrease, regardless of major.

Norms. The test manual presents norms based on 8,369 college students. The norms are subdivided by gender as well as by collegiate institution. In addition, norms are presented for a wide range of occupational groups, with the results supporting the construct validity of the SoV. For example, clergymen and theological students score highest on the religious value. Engineering students score highest on the theoretical value, while business administration students score highest on the economic and political scales. Subsequent norms included a national sample of high-school students tested in 1968, and composed of more than 5000 males and 7,000 females. Again, given the ipsative nature of this scale, we may question the appropriateness of norms.

Criticisms. Over the years, a variety of criticisms have been leveled at the SoV. For example, Gage (1959) felt that the SoV confounded interests and

values. Others repeatedly pointed out that the values assessed were based on "ideal" types and did not necessarily match reality; furthermore, these values appeared to be closely tied to "middle class" values.

The Rokeach Value Survey (RVS)

Introduction. One of the most widely used surveys of values is the *Rokeach Value Survey* (RVS). Rokeach (1973) defined values as beliefs concerning either desirable *modes of conduct* or desirable *end-states of existence*. The first type of values is what Rokeach labeled *instrumental* values, in that they are concerned with modes of conduct; the second type of values are *terminal* values in that they are concerned with end states. Furthermore, Rokeach (1973) divided instrumental values into two types: moral values that have an interpersonal focus, and competence or self-actualization values that have a personal focus. Terminal values are also of two types: self-centered or personal, and society-centered or social.

Rokeach (1973) distinguished values from attitudes in that a value refers to a single belief, while an attitude concerns an organization of several beliefs centered on a specific target. Furthermore, values transcend the specific target, represent a standard, are much smaller in number than attitudes, and occupy a more central position in a person's psychological functioning.

Description. The RVS is a rather simple affair that consists of two lists of 18 values each, which the respondent places in rank order, in order of importance as guiding principles of their life. Table 6.2 illustrates the RVS. Note that each value is accompanied by a short, defining phrase.

Originally the RVS consisted simple of printed lists; subsequently, each value is printed on a removable gummed label, and the labels are placed in rank order. The two types of values, instrumental and terminal, are ranked and analyzed separately, but the subtypes (such as personal and social) are not considered. The RVS is then a self-report instrument, group administered, with no time limit, and designed for adolescents and adults. Rokeach (1973) suggests that the RVS is really a projective test, like the Rorschach Inkblot technique, in that the respondent has no

Table 6–2. RVS values

Terminal values	Instrumental values
A comfortable life (a prosperous life)	Ambitious (hard-working, aspiring)
An exciting life (a stimulating, active life)	Broadminded (open-minded)
A sense of accomplishment (lasting contribution)	Capable (competent, effective)
A world at peace (free of war and conflict)	Cheerful* (lighthearted, joyful)
A world of beauty (beauty of nature and the arts)	Clean (neat, tidy)
Equality (brotherhood, equal opportunity for all)	Courageous (standing up for your beliefs)
Family security (taking care of loved ones)	Forgiving (willing to pardon others)
Freedom (independence, free choice)	Helpful (working for the welfare of others)
Happiness* (contentedness)	Honest (sincere, truthful)
Inner harmony (freedom from inner conflict)	Imaginative (daring, creative)
Mature love (sexual and spiritual intimacy)	Independent (self-reliant, self-sufficient)
National security (protection from attack)	Intellectual (intelligent, reflective)
Pleasure (an enjoyable, leisurely life)	Logical (consistent, rational)
Salvation (saved, eternal life)	Loving (affectionate, tender)
Self-respect (self-esteem)	Obedient (dutiful, respectful)
Social recognition (respect, admiration)	Polite (courteous, well mannered)
True friendship (close companionship)	Responsible (dependable, reliable)
Wisdom (a mature understanding of life)	Self-controlled (restrained, self-disciplined)

*Note: These values were later replaced by health and loyal respectively.
Adapted with the permission of The Free Press, a Division of Simon & Schuster from *The Nature Of Human Values* by Milton Rokeach. Copyright © 1973 by The Free Press.

guidelines for responding other than his or her own internalized system of values.

How did Rokeach arrive at these particular 36 values? Basically through a clinical process that began with amassing a large number of value labels from various sources (the instrumental values actually began as personality traits), eliminating those that were synonymous, and in some cases those that intercorrelated highly. Thus there is the basic question of content validity and Rokeach (1973) himself admits that his procedure is "intuitive" and his results differ from those that might have been obtained by other researchers.

Scoring the RVS. Basically, there is no scoring procedure with the RVS. Once the respondent has provided the two sets of 18 ranks, the ranks cannot of course be added together to get a sum because every respondent would obtain exactly the same score.

For a group of individuals we can compute for each value the mean or median of the rank assigned to that value. We can then convert these average values into ranks. For example, J. Andrews (1973) administered the RVS to 61 college students, together with a questionnaire to assess the degree of "ego identity" achieved by each student. Students classified as "high identity achievement" ranked the RVS instrumental values as follows:

value	mean ranking
honest	5.50
responsible	5.68
loving	5.96
broadminded	6.56
independent	7.48
capable	7.88
etc.	

We can change the mean rank values back to ranks by calling honest = 1, responsible = 2, loving = 3, and so on.

Another scoring approach would be to summate together subsets of values that on the basis of either a statistical criterion such as factor analysis, or a clinical judgment such as content analysis, seem to go together. For example, Silverman, Bishop, and Jaffe (1976) studied the RVS responses of some 954 psychology graduate students. To determine whether there were differences between students who studied different fields of psychology (e.g., clinical, experimental, developmental), the investigators computed the average of the median rankings assigned to "mature love," "true friendship," "cheerful," "helpful," and "loving" – this cluster of values was labeled "interpersonal affective values." A similar index called "cognitive competency" was calculated by averaging the median rankings for "intellectual" and "logical."

Reliability. There are at least two ways of assessing the temporal stability (i.e., test-retest reliability) of the RVS. One way is to administer the RVS to a group of individuals and retest them later. For each person, we can correlate the two sets of ranks and then can compute the median of such rank order correlation coefficients for our sample of subjects. Rokeach (1973) reports such medians as ranging from .76 to .80 for terminal values and .65 to .72 for instrumental values, with samples of college students retested after 3 weeks to 4 months.

Another way is also to administer the RVS twice, but to focus on each value separately. We may for example, start out with "a comfortable life." For each subject in our sample, we have the two ranks assigned to this value. We can then compute a correlation coefficient across subjects for that specific value. When this is done, separately for each of the 36 values, we find that the reliabilities are quite low; for the terminal values the average reliability is about .65 (Rokeach, 1973) and for the instrumental values it is about .56 (Feather, 1975). This is of course not surprising because each "scale" is made up of only one item. One important implication of such low reliability is that the RVS should *not* be used for individual counseling and assessment.

One problem, then, is that the reliability of the RVS is marginal at best. Rokeach (1973) presents the results of various studies, primarily with college students, and with various test-retest intervals ranging from 3 weeks to 16 months; of the 29 coefficients given, 14 are below .70, and all range from .53 to .87, with a median of .70. Inglehart (1985), on the other hand, looked at the results of a national sample, one assessed in 1968 and again in 1981. Because there were different subjects, it is not possible to compute correlation coefficients, but Inglehart (1985) reported that the stability of rankings over the 13-year period was "phenomenal." The six highest- and six lowest-ranked values in 1968 were also the six highest- and six lowest-ranked values in 1981.

It is interesting to note that all of the 36 values are socially desirable, and that respondents often indicate that the ranking task is a difficult one and they have "little confidence" that they have done so in a reliable manner.

Validity. Rokeach's (1973) book is replete with various analyses and comparisons of RVS rankings, including cross-cultural comparisons and analyses of such variables such as as race, socioeconomic status, educational level, and occupation. The RVS has also been used in hundreds of studies across a wide spectrum of topics, with most studies showing encouraging results that support the construct validity of this instrument. These studies range from comparisons of women who prefer "Ivory" as a washing machine detergent to studies of hippies (Rokeach, 1973). One area where the study of values has found substantial application is that of psychotherapy, where the values of patients and of therapists and their concomitant changes, have been studied (e.g., Beutler, Arizmendi, Crago, et al., 1983; Beutler, Crago, & Arizmendi, 1986; Jensen & Bergin, 1988; Kelly, 1990).

Cross-cultural aspects. Rokeach (1973) believed that the RVS could be used cross-culturally because the values listed are universal and problems of translation can be surmounted. On the other hand, it can be argued that these values are relevant to Western cultures only; for example, "filial piety," a central value for Chinese is not included in the RVS. It can also be argued that although the same word can be found in two languages, it does not necessarily have the same layers of meaning in the two cultures. Nevertheless, a number of investigators have applied the RVS cross-culturally, both in English-speaking countries such as Australia and non-Western cultures such as China (e.g., Feather, 1986; Lau, 1988; Ng et al., 1982).

An example of a cross-cultural application is found in the study by Domino and Acosta (1987), who administered the RVS to a sample of first generation Mexican Americans. These individuals were identified as being either "highly acculturated," that is more American, or "less acculturated," that is more Mexican. Their rankings of the RVS were then analyzed in various ways, including comparisons with the national norms

Table 6–3. Factor structure of the RVS Based on a sample of 1,409 respondents (Rokeach, 1973)

Factor	Example of item with		Percentage of variance
	Positive loading	Negative loading	
1. Immediate vs. delayed gratification	A comfortable life	Wisdom	8.2
2. Competence vs. religious morality	Logical	Forgiving	7.8
3. Self-constriction vs. self-expansion	Obedient	Broadminded	5.5
4. Social vs. personal orientation	A world at peace	True friendship	5.4
5. Societal vs. family security	A world of beauty	Family security	5.0
6. Respect vs. love	Social recognition	Mature Love	4.9
7. Inner vs. other directed	Polite	Courageous	4.0

provided by Rokeach and with local norms based on Anglos. These researchers found a greater correspondence of values between high acculturation subjects and the comparison groups than between the low acculturation subjects and the comparison groups – those that were more "American" in their language and general cultural identification were also more American in their values.

Factor analysis. Factor analytic studies do seem to support the terminal-instrumental differentiation, although not everyone agrees (e.g., Crosby, Bitner, & Gill, 1990; Feather & Peay, 1975; Heath & Fogel, 1978; Vinson et al., 1977). Factor analyses suggest that the 36 values are not independent of each other and that certain values do cluster together. Rokeach (1973) suggests that there are seven basic factors that cut across the terminal-instrumental distinction. These factors are indicated in Table 6.3. One question that can be asked of the results of a factor analysis is how "important" each factor is. Different respondents give different answers (ranks) to different values. This variation of response can be called "total variance." When we identify a factor, we can ask how much of the total variance does that factor account for? For the RVS data reported in Table 6.3, factor 1 accounts for only 8.2% of the total variation, and in fact all seven factors together account for only 40.8% of the total variation, leaving 59.2% of the variation unaccounted for. This suggests that the factors are probably not very powerful, either in predicting behavior or in helping us to conceptualize values. Heath and Fogel (1978) had subjects rate rather than rank the importance of each of the 36 values;

their results suggested eight factors rather than seven.

Norms. Rokeach (1973) presents the rankings for a group of 665 males and a group of 744 females, and these are presented in Table 6.4. Note that of the 36 values, 20 show significant gender differences. Even though the ranks may be identical, there may be a significant difference on the actual rank value assigned. The differences seem to be in line with the different ways that men and women are socialized in Western cultures, with males endorsing more achievement and intellectually oriented values, more materialistic and pleasure seeking, while women rank higher religious values, love, personal happiness, and lack of both inner and outer conflict.

Rank order correlation coefficient. Despite the caveat that the RVS should not be used for individual counseling, we use a fictitious example to illustrate the rank order correlation coefficient, designed to compare two sets of ranks. Let's say that you and your fiance are contemplating marriage, and you wonder whether your values are compatible. You both independently rank order the RVS items. The results for the instrumental values are shown in Table 6.5. The question here is how similar are the two sets of values? We can easily calculate the rank order correlation coefficient (ρ) using the formula:

$$\rho = 1 - \frac{6 \sum D^2}{N(N^2 - 1)}$$

where N stands for the number of items being ranked; in this case $N = 18$. All we need to do is calculate for each set of ranks the difference

Table 6–4. Values medians and composite rank orders for American men and women (Rokeach, 1973)

Terminal value:	Male (n = 665)		Female (n = 744)		Lower rank shown by
A comfortable life	7.8	(4)	10.0	(13)	Males
An exciting life	14.6	(18)	15.8	(18)	Males
A sense of accomplishment	8.3	(7)	9.4	(10)	Males
A world at peace	3.8	(1)	3.0	(1)	Females
A world of beauty	13.6	(15)	13.5	(15)	–
Equality	8.9	(9)	8.3	(8)	–
Family security	3.8	(2)	3.8	(2)	–
Freedom	4.9	(3)	6.1	(3)	Males
Happiness	7.9	(5)	7.4	(5)	Females
Inner harmony	11.1	(13)	9.8	(12)	Females
Mature love	12.6	(14)	12.3	(14)	–
National security	9.2	(10)	9.8	(11)	–
Pleasure	14.1	(17)	15.0	(16)	Males
Salvation	9.9	(12)	7.3	(4)	Females
Self-respect	8.2	(6)	7.4	(6)	Females
Social recognition	13.8	(16)	15.0	(17)	Males
True friendship	9.6	(11)	9.1	(9)	–
Wisdom	8.5	(8)	7.7	(7)	Females

Instrumental values

Ambitious	5.6	(2)	7.4	(4)	Males
Broadminded	7.2	(4)	7.7	(5)	–
Capable	8.9	(8)	10.1	(12)	Males
Cheerful	10.4	(12)	(9.4)	(10)	Females
Clean	9.4	(9)	8.1	(8)	Females
Courageous	7.5	(5)	8.1	(6)	–
Forgiving	8.2	(6)	6.4	(2)	Females
Helpful	8.3	(7)	8.1	(7)	–
Honest	3.4	(1)	3.2	(1)	–
Imaginative	14.3	(18)	16.1	(18)	Males
Independent	10.2	(11)	10.7	(14)	–
Intellectual	12.8	(15)	13.2	(16)	–
Logical	13.5	(16)	14.7	(17)	–
Loving	10.9	(14)	8.6	(9)	Females
Obedient	13.5	(17)	13.1	(15)	–
Polite	10.9	(13)	10.7	(13)	–
Responsible	6.6	(3)	6.8	(3)	–
Self-controlled	9.7	(10).	9.5	(11)	–

Note: The figures shown are median rankings and in parentheses composite rank orders.
The gender differences are based on median rankings.
Adapted with the permission of The Free Press, a Division of Simon & Schuster from *The Nature of Human Values* by Milton Rokeach. Copyright © 1973 by The Free Press.

between ranks, square each difference, and find the sum. This is done in Table 6.5, in the columns labeled D (difference) and D^2. The sum is 746, and substituting in the formula gives us:

$$= 1 - \frac{6\,(746)}{5814} = 1 - \frac{746}{969} = 1 - .77 = +.23$$

These results would suggest that there is a very low degree of agreement between you and your fiance as to what values are important in life, and indeed a perusal of the rankings suggest some highly significant discrepancies (e.g., self-controlled and courageous), some less significant discrepancies (e.g., cheerful and clean), and some near unanimity (ambitious and broadminded). If these results were reliable, one might predict some conflict ahead, unless of course you believe in the "opposites attract" school of thought

Table 6–5. Computational example of the rank order correlation coefficient using RVS data				
Instrumental value	Your rank	Your fiance's rank	D	D²
Ambitious	2	1	1	1
Broadminded	8	9	1	1
Capable	4	2	2	4
Cheerful	12	7	5	25
Clean	15	10	5	25
Courageous	5	16	11	121
Forgiving	6	12	6	36
Helpful	7	17	10	100
Honest	1	11	10	100
Imaginative	18	14	4	16
Independent	11	3	8	64
Intellectual	10	15	5	25
Logical	9	4	5	25
Loving	13	8	5	25
Obedient	14	18	4	16
Polite	16	13	3	9
Responsible	3	6	3	9
Self-controlled	17	5	12	144
			$\sum = 746$	

Penner, Homant, & Rokeach, 1968; Rankin & Grobe, 1980). Interestingly enough, some of the results suggest that rank-order scaling is a better technique than other approaches (e.g., Miethe, 1985).

INTERESTS

We now turn to the third area of measurement for this chapter, and that is interests, and more specifically, career interests. How can career interests be assessed? The most obvious and direct method is to ask individuals what they are interested in. These are called *expressed* interests, and perhaps not surprisingly, this is a reasonably valid method. On the other hand, people are often not sure what their interests are, or are unable to specify them objectively, or may have little awareness of how their particular interests and the demands of the world of work might dovetail. A second way is the assessment of such likes and dislikes through inventories. This method is perhaps the most popular method and has a number of advantages, including the fact that it permits an individual to compare their interests with those of other people, and more specifically with people in various occupations. A third way is to assume that someone interested in a particular occupation will have a fair amount of knowledge about that occupation, even before entering the occupation. Thus we could put together a test of knowledge about being a lawyer and assume that those who score high may be potential lawyers. That of course is a major assumption, not necessarily reflective of the real world. Finally, we can observe a person's behavior. If Johnny, a high school student, spends all of his spare time repairing automobiles, we might speculate that he is headed for a career as auto mechanic – but of course, our speculations may be quite incorrect.

rather than the "birds of a feather flock together" approach.

Criticisms. The RVS has been criticized for a number of reasons (Braithwaite & Law, 1985; Feather, 1975). It is of course an ipsative measure and yields only ordinal data; strictly speaking, its data should not be used with analysis of variance or other statistical procedures that require a normal distribution, although such procedures are indeed "robust" and seem to apply even when the assumptions are violated. Others have questioned whether the RVS measures what one prefers or what one *ought* to prefer (Bolt, 1978) and the distinction between terminal and instrumental values (Heath & Fogel, 1978).

One major criticism is that the rank ordering procedure does not allow for the assessment of intensity, which is basically the same criticism that this is not an interval scale. Thus two individuals can select the same value as their first choice, and only one may feel quite sanguine about it. Similarly, you may give a value a rank of 2 because it really differs from your number 1 choice, but the difference may be minimal for another person with the identical rankings. In fact, several researchers have modified the RVS into an interval measure (e.g., Moore, 1975;

The field of career interest measurement has been dominated by the work of two individuals. In 1927, E. K. Strong, Jr. published the Strong Vocational Interest Blank for Men, an empirically based inventory that compared a person's likes and dislikes with those of individuals in different occupations. The SVIB and its revisions became extremely popular and were used frequently in both college settings and private practice (Zytowski & Warman, 1982). In 1934, G. F. Kuder developed the Kuder Preference Record, which initially used content scales (e.g., agriculture) rather than specific occupational scales. This test also proved quite popular and underwent a number of revisions.

A third key event in the history of career interest assessment occurred in 1959, when John Holland published a theory regarding human behavior that found wide applicability to career interest assessment. Holland argued that the choice of an occupation is basically a reflection of one's personality, and so career-interest inventories are basically personality inventories.

Much of the literature and efforts in career assessment depend on a general assumption that people with similar interests tend to enter the same occupation, and to the degree that one's interests are congruent with those of people in that occupation, the result will be greater job satisfaction. There certainly seems to be substantial support for the first part of that assumption, but relatively little for the second part.

The Strong Interest Inventory (SII)

Introduction. The Strong Vocational Interest Blank for Men (SVIB) is the granddaddy of all career-interest inventories, developed by E. K. Strong, and originally published in 1927. A separate form for women was developed in 1933. The male and female forms were each revised twice, separately. In 1974, the two gender forms were merged into one. The SVIB became the Strong-Campbell Interest Inventory (SCII) and underwent extensive revisions (D. P. Campbell, 1974; D. P. Campbell & J. C. Hansen, 1981; J. C. Hansen & D. P. Campbell, 1985), including the development of occupational scales that were traditionally linked with the opposite sex. For example, a nursing scale for males and a carpenter and electrician scales for women. Recently, the name was changed to the Strong Interest Inventory (SII) (or Strong for short), and a 1994 revision published. To minimize confusion and reduce the alphabet soup, the word *Strong* is used to refer to any of these inventories (except in the rare instances where this would violate the intended meaning).

Description. Basically, the Strong compares a person's career interests with those of people who are satisfactorily employed in a wide variety of occupations. It is thus a measure of interests, not of ability or competence. The Strong contains 325 items grouped into seven sections. The bulk of the items (first five sections) require the respondent to indicate like, dislike, or indifferent to 131 occupations (Would you like to be a dentist? a psychologist?), 36 school subjects (algebra, literature), 51 career-related activities (carpentry; gardening; fund raising), 39 leisure activities (camping trips; cooking), and 24 types of people (Would you like to work with children? the elderly? artists?). Section 6 requires the respondent to select from pairs of activities that they prefer (Would you prefer working with "things" or with people?), and section 7 has some self-descriptive statements (Are you a patient person?). Strong originally used these various types of items in an empirical effort to see which type worked best. Subsequent research suggests that item content is more important than item format, and so the varied items have been retained also because they relieve the monotony of responding to a long list of similar questions (D. P. Campbell, 1974).

The primary aim of the Strong is for counseling high school and college students as well as and adults who are college graduates, about their career choices. It and particularly focuses on those careers that attract college graduates, rather than blue-collar occupations or skilled trades such electrician and plumber. Thus the Strong is geared primarily for age 17 and older. Career interests seem to stabilize for most people between the ages of 20 and 25, so the Strong is most accurate for this age range; it does not seem to be appropriate or useful for anyone younger than 16.

It is not the intent of the Strong to tell a person what career they should enter or where they can be successful in the world of work. In fact, the Strong has little to do with competence and capabilities; a person may have a great deal of similarity of interest with those shown by physicians, but have neither the cognitive abilities nor the educational credentials required to enter and do well in medical school.

There are at least two manuals available for the professional user: the Manual, which contains the technical data (J. C. Hansen & D. P. Campbell, 1985), and the User's Guide (J. C. Hansen, 1984), which is more "user friendly" and more of a typical manual.

Item selection. Where did the items in the Strong come from? Originally, they were generated by Strong and others, and were basically the result of "clinical insight." Subsequently, the items contained in the current Strong came from earlier editions and were selected on the basis of their psychometric properties (i.e., reliability and validity), as well as on their "public relations" aspects – that is, they would not offend, irritate, or embarrass a respondent. As in other forms of testing, items that yield variability of response or *response range* are the most useful. D. P. Campbell and J. C. Hansen (1981), for example, indicate that items such as "funeral director" and "geography" were eliminated because almost everyone indicates "dislike" to the former and "like" to the latter. An item such "college professor" on the other hand yields "like" responses of about 5% in samples of farmers to 99% in samples of behavioral scientists.

Other criteria were also used in judging whether an item would be retained or eliminated. Both predictive and concurrent validity are important and items showing these aspects were retained. For example, the Strong should have content validity and so the items should cover a wide range of occupational content. Because sex-role bias was of particular concern, items were modified (policeman became police officer) or otherwise changed. Items that showed a significant gender difference in response were not necessarily eliminated, as the task is to understand such differences rather than to ignore them. Because the United States is such a conglomeration of minorities, and because the Strong might be useful in other cultures, items were retained if they were not "culture bound," although the actual operational definition of this criterion might be a bit difficult to give. Other criteria, such as reading level, lack of ambiguity, and current terminology, were also used.

Scale development. Let's assume you want to develop an occupational scale for "golf instructors." How might you go about this? J. C. Hansen (1986) indicates that there are five steps in the construction of an occupational scale for the Strong:

1. You need to collect an occupational sample, in this case, golf instructors. Perhaps you might identify potential respondents through some major sports organization, labor union, or other societies that might provide such a roster. Your potential respondents must however, satisfy several criteria (in addition to filling out the Strong): they must be satisfied with their occupation, be between the ages of 25 and 60, have at least 3 years of experience in that occupation, and perform work that is "typical" of that occupation – for example, a golf instructor who spends his or her time primarily designing golf courses would be eliminated.

2. You also need a reference group – although ordinarily you would use the available data based on 300 "men in general" and 300 "women in general." This sample has an average age of 38 years, represents a wide variety of occupations, half professional and half nonprofessional.

3. Once you've collected your data, you'll need to compare for each of the 325 Strong items, the percent of "like," "indifferent," or "dislike" responses. The aim here is to identify 60 to 70 items that show a response difference of 16% or greater.

4. Now you can assign scoring weights to each of the 60 to 70 items. If the golf instructors endorsed "like" more often than the general sample, that item is scored +1; if the golf instructors endorsed "dislike" more often, then the item is scored −1 (for like). If there are substantial differences between the two samples on the "indifferent" response, then that response is also scored.

5. Now you can obtain the raw scores for each of your golf instructors, and compute your normative data, changing the raw scores to *T* scores.

Development. In more general terms then, the occupational scales on the Strong were developed by administering the Strong pool of items to men and women in a specific occupation and comparing the responses of this *criterion* group with those of men, or women, in general. Although the various criterion groups were different depending on the occupation, they were typically large, with Ns over 200, and more typically near 400. They were composed of individuals between the ages of 25 and 55, still active in their occupation, who had been in that occupation for at least 3 years and thus presumably satisfied, who indicated that they liked their work, and who had met some minimum level of proficiency, such as licensing, to eliminate those who might be incompetent.

The *comparison* group, the men-in-general or women-in-general sample is a bit more difficult to define, because its nature and composition has changed over the years. When Strong began his work in the mid-1920s, the in-general sample consisted of several thousand men he had tested. Later he collected a new sample based on U.S. Census Bureau statistics, but the sample contained too many unskilled and semiskilled men. When response comparisons of a criterion group were made to this comparison group, the result was that professional men shared similar interests among themselves as compared with nonprofessional men. The end result would have been a number of overlapping scales that would be highly intercorrelated and therefore of little use for career guidance. For example, a physician scale would have reflected the differences in interests between men in a professional occupation and men in nonprofessional occupations; a dentist scale would have reflected those same differences.

From 1938 to 1966 the in-general sample was a modification of the U.S. Census Bureau sample, but included only those men whose salary would have placed them in the middle class or above. From 1966 onward, a number of approaches were used, including a women-in-general sample, composed of 20 women in each of 50 occupations, and men-in-general samples with occupation membership weighted equally, i.e., equal number of biologists, physicians, life insurance salesmen, etc.

Administration. The Strong is not timed and takes about 20 to 30 minutes to complete. It can be administered individually or in groups, and is basically a self-administered inventory. The

separate answer sheet must be returned to the publisher for computer scoring.

Scoring. The current version of the Strong needs to be computer scored and several such services are available. The Strong yields five sets of scores:

1. Administrative Indices
2. General Occupational Themes
3. Basic Interest Scales
4. Occupational Scales
5. Special Scales

The Administrative Indices are routine clerical checks performed by the computer as the answer sheet is scored; they are designed to assess procedural errors and are for use by the test administrator to determine whether the test results are meaningful. These indices include the number of items that were answered, the number of infrequent responses given, and the percentages of like, dislike, and indifferent responses given for each of the sections. For example, one administrative index is simply the total number of responses given. There are 325 items, and a respondent may omit some items, or may unintentionally skip a section, or may make some marks that are too light to be scored. A score of 310 or less alerts the administrator that the resulting profile may not be valid.

The General Occupational Themes are a set of six scales each designed to portray a "general" type as described in Holland's theory (discussed next). These scales were developed by selecting 20 items to represent each of the 6 types. The items were selected on the basis of both face and content validity (they covered the typological descriptions given by Holland); and statistical criteria such as item-scale correlations.

The Basic Interest Scales consist of 23 scales that cover somewhat more specific occupational areas such as, agriculture, mechanical activities, medical service, art, athletics, sales, and office practices. These scales were developed by placing together items that correlated .30 or higher with each other. Thus these scales are homogeneous and very consistent in content.

The 211 Occupational Scales in the 1994 revision cover 109 different occupations, from accountants to YMCA Directors, each scale developed empirically by comparing the responses of men and/or women employed in that occupation with the responses of a reference group of men, or of women, in general. For most of the occupations there is a scale normed on a male sample and a separate scale normed on a female sample. Why have separate gender scales? The issue of gender differences is a complex one, fraught with all sorts of social and political repercussions. In fact, however, men and women respond differently to about half of the items contained in the Strong, and therefore separate scales and separate norms are needed (J. C. Hansen & D. P. Campbell, 1985). Most of these samples were quite sizable, with an average close to 250 persons, and a mean age close to 40 years; to develop and norm these scales more than 142,000 individuals were tested. Some of the smaller samples are quite unique and include astronauts, Pulitzer Prize-winning authors, college football coaches, state governors, and even Nobel prize winners (D. P. Campbell, 1971). Because these scales have been developed empirically, they are factorially complex, most made up of rather heterogeneous items, and often with items that do not have face validity. The Psychologist Scale, for example, includes items that reflect an interest in science, in the arts, and in social service, as well as items having to do with business and military activities, which are weighted negatively. Thus two people with identical scores on this scale, may in fact have different patterns of responding. Though empirically these scales work well, it is difficult for a counselor to understand the client unless one undertakes an analysis of such differential responding. However, by looking at the scores on the Basic Interest Scales, mentioned above, one can better determine where the client's interests lie, and thus better understand the results of the specific occupational scales.

Finally, there are the Special Scales. At present, two of these are included in routine scoring:

1. The Academic Comfort Scale which was developed by contrasting the responses of high-GPA students with low-GPA students; this scale attempts to differentiate between people who enjoy being in an academic setting and those who do not.

2. The Introversion-Extroversion scale that was developed by contrasting the responses of introverted with those of extroverted individuals, as defined by their scores on the MMPI scale of the same name. High scorers (introverts) prefer working with things or ideas, while low scorers (extroverts) prefer working with people.

Scores on the Strong are for the most part presented as *T* scores with a mean of 50 and SD of 10.

Interpretation of the profile. The resulting Strong profile presents a wealth of data, which is both a positive feature and a negative one. The negative aspect comes about because the wealth of information provides data not just on the career interests of the client, but also on varied aspects of their personality, their psychological functioning, and general psychic adjustment, and thus demands a high degree of psychometric and psychological sophistication from the counselor in interpreting and communicating the results to the client. Not all counselors have such a degree of training and sensitivity, and often the feedback session to the client is less than satisfying (for some excellent suggestions regarding test interpretation and some illustrative case studies, see D. P. Campbell & J. C. Hansen, 1981).

Criterion-keying. When the Strong was first introduced in 1927, it pioneered the use of *criterion-keying* of items, later incorporated into personality inventories such as the MMPI and the CPI. Thus the Strong was administered to groups of individuals in specific occupations, and their responses compared with those of "people in general." Test items that showed differential response patterns between a particular occupational group, for example dentists, and people in general then became the dentist scale. Hundreds of such occupational scales were developed, based on the simple fact that individuals in different occupations have different career interests. It is thus possible to administer the Strong to an individual and determine that person's degree of similarity between their career interests and those shown by individuals in specific careers. Thus each of the occupational scales is basically a subset of items that show large differences in response percentages between individuals in that occupation and a general sample. How large is large? In general, items that show at least a 16%

difference are useful items; for example, if 58% of the specific occupational sample respond "like" to a particular item vs. 42% of the general sample, that item is potentially useful (D. P. Campbell & J. C. Hansen, 1981). Note that one such item would not be very useful, but the average occupational sample scale contains about 60 such items, each contributing to the total scale.

Gender bias. The earlier versions of the Strong not only contained separate scoring for occupations based on the respondent's gender, but the separate gender booklets were printed in blue for males and pink for females! Thus, women's career interests were compared with those of nurses, school teachers, secretaries and other traditionally "feminine" occupations. Fortunately, current versions of the Strong have done away with such sexism, have in fact pioneered gender equality in various aspects of the test, and provide substantial career information for both genders, and one test booklet.

Holland's theory. The earlier versions of the Strong were guided primarily by empirical considerations, and occupational scales were developed because there was a need for such scales. As these scales proliferated, it became apparent that some organizing framework was needed to group subsets of scales together. Strong and others developed a number of such classifying schemas based on the intercorrelations of the occupational scales, on factor analysis, and on the identification of homogeneous clusters of items. In 1974, however, a number of changes were made, including the incorporation of Holland's (1966; 1973; 1985a) theoretical framework as a way of organizing the test results.

Holland believes that individuals find specific careers attractive because of their personalities and background variables; he postulated that all occupations could be conceptualized as representing one of six general occupational themes labeled realistic, investigative, artistic, social, enterprising, and conventional.

Individuals whose career interests are high in the *realistic* area are typically aggressive persons who prefer concrete activities to abstract work. They prefer occupations that involve working outdoors and working with tools and objects rather than with ideas or people. These individuals are typically practical and physically oriented but may have difficulties expressing their feelings and concerns. They are less sociable and less given to interpersonal interactions. Such occupations as engineer, vocational agriculture teacher, and military officer are representative of this theme.

Individuals whose career interests are high in the *investigative* theme focus on science and scientific activities. They enjoy investigative challenges, particularly those that involve abstract problems and the physical world. They do not like situations that are highly structured, and may be quite original and creative in their ideas. They are typically intellectual, analytical, and often quite independent. Occupations such as biologist, mathematician, college professor, and psychologist are representative of this theme.

As the name implies, the *artistic* theme centers on artistic activities. Individuals with career interests in this area value aesthetics and prefer self-expression through painting, words, and other artistic media. These individuals see themselves as imaginative and original, expressive, and independent. Examples of specific careers that illustrate this theme are artist, musician, lawyer, and librarian.

The fourth area is the *social* area; individuals whose career interests fall under this theme are people-oriented. They are typically sociable and concerned about others. Their typical approach to problem solving is through interpersonal processes. Representative occupations here are guidance counselor, elementary school teacher, nurse, and minister.

The *enterprising* area is the area of sales. Individuals whose career interests are high here see themselves as confident and dominant, like to be in charge, and to persuade others. They make use of good verbal skills, are extroverted, adventurous, and prefer leadership roles. Typical occupations include store manager, purchasing agent, and personnel director.

Finally, the *conventional* theme focuses on the business world, especially those activities that characterize office work. Individuals whose career interests are high here are said to fit well in large organizations and to be comfortable working within a well-established chain of command, even though they do not seek leadership positions. Typically, they are practical and sociable, well controlled and conservative. Representative occupations are those of accountant, secretary, computer operator, and credit manager.

As the description of these types indicates, Holland's model began its theoretical life as a personality model. Like other personality typologies that have been developed, it is understood that "pure" types are rare. But the different types are differentiated: A person who represents the "conventional" type is quite different from the person who is an "artistic" type.

Finally, there is a congruence between personality and occupation resulting in satisfaction. An artistic type of person will most likely not find substantial satisfaction in being an accountant. Holland's theory is not the only theory of career development, but has been one of the most influential, especially in terms of psychological testing (for other points of view see Bergland, 1974; Gelatt, 1967; Krumboltz, Mitchell, & Gelatt, 1975; Osipow, 1983; Tiedeman & O'Hara, 1963).

Reliability. The reliabilities associated with the Strong are quite substantial. D. P. Campbell and J. C. Hansen (1981), for example, cite median test-retest correlations, with a 2-week interval the $r = .91$, with a 2- to 5-year interval, the rs range from .70 to .78, and with a 20+ year interval, the rs range from .64 to .72. Not only is the Strong relatively stable over time, so are career interests.

Test-retest reliabilities for the Basic Interest Scales are quite substantial, with median coefficients of .91 for a 2-week period, .88 for 1 month-, and .82 for 3-year periods. Test-retest correlations also vary with the age of the sample, with the results showing less reliability with younger samples, for example 16-year-olds, as might be expected.

Validity. The Basic Interest Scales have substantial content and concurrent validity; that is, their content makes sense, and a number of studies have shown that these scales do indeed discriminate between persons in different occupations. In general, their predictive validity is not as high, and some scales seem to be related to other variables rather than occupational choice; for example, the Adventure Scale seems to reflect age, with older individuals scoring lower.

Strong was highly empirically oriented and developed not just an inventory, but a rich source of longitudinal data. For example, after the

SVIB was published, he administered the inventory to the senior class at Stanford University, and 5 years later contacted them to determine which occupations they had entered, and how these occupations related to their scores on the inventory.

The criterion then for studying the predictive validity of the Strong becomes the occupation that the person eventually enters. If someone becomes a physician and their Strong profile indicates a high score on the Physician scale, we then have a "hit." The problem, however, is that the world is complex and individuals do not necessarily end up in the occupation for which they are best suited, or which they desire. As Strong (1935) argued, if final occupational choice is an imperfect criterion, then a test that is validated against such a criterion must also be imperfect. This of course is precisely the problem we discussed in Chapter 3; a test cannot be more valid than the criterion against which it is matched, and in the real world there are few, if any, such criteria. Nevertheless, a number of studies both by Strong (1955) and others (e.g., D. P. Campbell, 1971; Dolliver, Irwin, & Bigley, 1972) show substantial predictive validity for the Strong, with a typical hit rate (agreement between high score on an Occupational Scale and entrance into that occupation) of at least 50% for both men and women. There is of course something reassuring that the hit rates are not higher; for one thing it means that specific occupations do attract people with different ideas and interests, and such variability keeps occupations vibrant and growing.

Faking. In most situations where the Strong is administered, there is little if any motivation to fake the results because the client is usually taking the inventory for their own enhancement. There may be occasions, however, when the Strong is administered as part of an application process; there may be potential for faking in the application for a specific occupation or perhaps entrance into a professional school.

Over the years, a number of investigators have looked at this topic, primarily by administering the Strong twice to a sample of subjects, first under standard instructions, and secondly with instructions to fake in a specific way, for example, "fake good to get higher scores on engineering" (e.g., Garry, 1953; Wallace, 1950). The results basically support the notion that under such instructions Strong results can be changed. Most of these studies represent artificial situations where captive subjects are instructed to fake. What happens in real life? D. P. Campbell (1971) reports the results of a doctoral dissertation that compared the Strong profiles of 278 University of Minnesota males who had completed the Strong first for counseling purposes and later had completed the Strong a second time as part of their application procedure to the University of Minnesota medical school. Presumably, when the Strong was taken for counseling purposes the respondents completed the inventory honestly, but when the Strong was taken as part of an application process, faking might have occurred, especially on those items possibly related to a career in medicine. In fact, for 47% of the sample, there was no difference on their physician scale score between the two administrations. For 29%, there was an increase, but not substantial. For 24%, there was a substantial increase, enough to have a "serious effect" on its interpretation by an admissions officer. Of course, just because there was an increase does not mean that the individual faked; the increase might well reflect legitimate growth in medical interest. There are three points to be made here: (1) faking is possible on the Strong, (2) massive distortions do not usually occur, (3) the resulting profile typically shows considerable consistency over time.

Inconsistencies. Because the Strong contains different sets of scales developed in different ways, it is not unusual for a client's results to reflect some inconsistencies. R. W. Johnson (1972) reported that some 20% of profiles have at least one or more such inconsistencies between Occupational Scales and Basic Interest Scales. D. P. Campbell and J. C. Hansen (1981) argue that such inconsistencies are meaningful and result in more accurate test interpretation because they force both the counselor and the client to understand the meaning of the scales and to go beyond the mere occupational label. For example, the Basic Interest Scales reflect not only career interests but leisure interests as well (Cairo, 1979).

Unit weighting. The Strong illustrates nicely the concept of unit weights as opposed to variable weights. Let's suppose we are developing a scale

for a new occupation of "virtual reality trainer" (VRT). We administer the Strong, which represents a pool of items and an "open" system, to a group of VRTs and a group of "people in general," and identify those items that statistically separate the two groups.

Let's say for example, that 85% of our VRTs indicate like to the item "computer programmer" vs. only 10% for the general sample, and that 80% of the VRTs also indicate dislike to the item "philosopher" vs. 55% for the general sample. Both items show a significant difference in response pattern and so both would be included in our scale. But clearly, one item is more "powerful," one item shows a greater difference between our two groups, and so we might logically argue that such an item should be given greater weight in the way the scale is scored. That indeed is what Strong originally did; the items were weighted based on a ratio of the response percentage of the specific occupational sample vs. the response percentage of the general sample. And so initially, Strong items were scored with weights ranging from -30 to $+30$. Such scoring, especially in the precomputer days, was extremely cumbersome, and so was simplified several times until in 1966 the weights of $+1$, 0, or -1 were used. Empirical studies of unit weights vs. variable weights show the unitary weights to be just as valid.

Percentage overlap. Another interesting concept illustrated by the Strong is that of *percentage overlap*. Let's assume we have administered the Strong to two groups of individuals, and we are interested in looking at a specific occupational scale for which our theory dictates the two samples should differ. How do we determine whether the two groups differ? Ordinarily we would carry out a *t* test or an analysis of variance to assess whether the means of the two groups are statistically different from each other (you recall, by the way, that when we have two groups, the two procedures are the same in that $t^2 = F$). Such a procedure tells us that yes (or no) there is a difference, but it doesn't really tell us how big that difference is, and does not address the issue of practicality – a small mean difference could be statistically significant if we have large enough samples, but would not necessarily be useful.

A somewhat different approach was suggested by Tilton (1937) who presented the statistic of

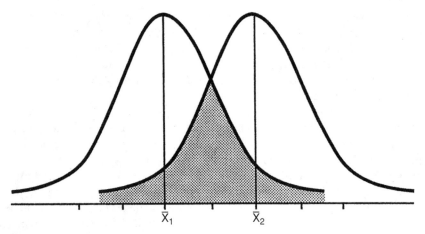

FIGURE 6–3. Two distributions separated from each other by two standard deviations.

percent overlap, which is simply the percentage of scores in one sample that are matched by scores in the second sample. If the two distributions of scores are totally different and therefore don't overlap, the statistic is zero. If the two distributions are identical and completely overlap, then the statistic is 100%. If the intent of a scale is to distinguish between two groups, then clearly the lower the percentage overlap, the more efficient (valid) is the scale. Tilton called this statistic the Q index, and it is calculated as follows:

$$Q = \frac{M_1 - M_2}{2(SD_1 + SD_2)}$$

Once Q is computed, the percent overlap can be determined using Tilton's (1937) table. Essentially, the Q index is a measure of the number of standard deviation units that separate the two distributions. For example, a Q value of 2 represents two distributions that are separated from each other by two standard deviations, and have an overlap of about 32%. Figure 6.3 illustrates this. Note that if our occupational scale were an IQ test, the means of the two groups would differ by about 30 points – a rather substantial difference. The median percent overlap for the Strong occupational scales is in fact about 34%. This is of course a way of expressing concurrent validity. Scales that reflect well-defined occupations such as physicist or chemist, have the lowest overlap or highest validity. Scales that assess less well-defined occupations, such as that of college professor, have a higher degree of overlap and, therefore, lower concurrent validity.

Racial differences. Although racial differences on the Strong have not been studied extensively, and in fact the SVIB Handbook (D. P. Campbell, 1971) does not discuss this topic, the available studies (e.g., Barnette & McCall, 1964; Borgen & Harper, 1973) indicate that the Strong is not racially biased and that its predictive validity and other psychometric aspects for minority groups are equivalent to those for whites.

Item response distribution. D. P. Campbell and J. C. Hansen (1981) indicate that interest measurement is based on two empirical findings: (1) different people give different responses to the individual items; and (2) people who are satisfied with their particular occupation tend to respond to particular items in a characteristic way. Given these two statements, the *item response distribution* for a particular item charts the value of that item and its potential usefulness in the inventory. At the Center for Interest Measurement Research of the University of Minnesota extensive data on the Strong is stored on computer archives, going back to the original samples tested by Strong. For example, D. P. Campbell and J. C. Hansen (1981) show the item response distribution for the item "artist" given by some 438 samples, each sample typically ranging from less than 100 to more than 1,000 individuals in a specific occupation. Both male and female artist samples tend to show near unanimity in their endorsement of "like"; at the other extreme, male farmers show an 11% "like" response, and females in life insurance sales a 32% "like" response.

Longitudinal studies. The Strong has been used in a number of longitudinal studies, and specifically to assess the stability of vocational interests within occupations over long time spans. D. P. Campbell (1966) asked and answered three basic questions: (1) Do Strong scales developed in the 1930s hold up in cross-validation years later? The answer is yes; (2) When Strong scales have been revised, did the revised scales differ drastically from the originals? The answer is not much; (3) Do the individuals of today who hold the same job as the individuals in Strong's criterion groups of the 1930s have the same interest patterns? The answer is pretty much so.

Inventoried vs. expressed interests. "Inventoried" interests are assessed by an inventory such as the Strong. "Expressed" interests refer to the client's direct comments such as, "I want to be an engineer" or "I am going to study environmental law." How do these two methods compare? If for example, the Strong were simply to mirror the client's expressed interests, why waste time and money, when the same information could be obtained more directly by simply asking the subject what they want to be. Of course, there are many people who do not know what career to pursue, and so one benefit of the Strong and similar instruments, is that it provides substantial exploratory information. Berdie (1950) reported correlations of about .50 in studies that compared inventoried and expressed interests. However, Dolliver (1969) pointed out that this deceptively simple question actually involves some complex issues including the reliability and validity of both the inventory and the method by which expressed interests are assessed, attrition of subjects upon follow-up, and the role of chance in assessing such results.

The Kuder Inventories

Introduction. A second set of career-interest inventories that have dominated psychological testing in this area, has been the inventories developed by Frederic Kuder. There are actually three Kuder inventories: (1) the Kuder Vocational Preference Record (KVPR), which is used for career counseling of high-school students and adults; (2) the Kuder General Interest Survey (KGIS), which is a downward extension of the KVPR,

for use with junior and senior high-school students in grades 6 through 12; and (3) the Kuder Occupational Interest Survey (KOIS), designed for grades 10 through adulthood. The first two yield scores in 10 general areas, namely: artistic, clerical, computational, literary, mechanical, musical, outdoor, persuasive, scientific, and social service. The third, the KOIS, yields substantially more information, and our discussion will focus primarily on this instrument. Once again, we use the term "Kuder" as a more generic designation, except where this would violate the meaning.

Development. Initially, the Strong and the Kuder represented very different approaches. The Strong reflected criterion-group scaling while the Kuder represented homogeneous scaling, that is clustering of items that are related. Over the years however, the two approaches have borrowed heavily from each other, and thus have become more convergent in approach and process.

Description. The KOIS takes about 30 minutes to complete and is not timed. It can be administered to one individual or to a large group at one sitting. Like the Strong, it too must be computer scored. The KOIS is applicable to high-school students in the 10th grade or beyond (Zytowski, 1981). In addition to 126 occupational scales, the KOIS also has 48 college-major scales. The KOIS also has a number of validity indices, similar to the Strong's administrative indices, including an index that reflects number of items left blank, and a *verification* score that is basically a "fake good" scale. As with most other major commercially published tests, there is not only a manual (Kuder & Diamond, 1979), but additional materials available for the practitioner (e.g., Zytowski, 1981; 1985).

Scale development. We saw that in the Strong, occupational scales were developed by pooling those 40 to 60 items in which the response proportions of an occupational group and an in-general group differed, usually by at least 16%. The Kuder took a different approach. The Kuder was originally developed by administering a list of statements to a group of college students, and based on their responses, placing the items into 10 homogeneous scales. Items within a scale correlated highly with each other, but not with items in the other scales. Items were then placed in triads, each triad reflecting three different scales. The respondent indicates which item is most preferred and which item is least preferred. Note that this results in an ipsative instrument – one cannot obtain all high scores. To the degree that one scale score is high, the other scale scores must be lower.

Let's assume we are developing a new occupational scale on the Kuder for "limousine driver," and find that our sample of limousine drivers endorses the first triad as follows:

Item #	Most preferred	Least preferred
1	20%	70%
2	60%	15%
3	20%	15%

That is, 20% of our sample selected item #1 as most preferred, 60% selected item 2, and 20% item 3; similarly, 70% selected item #1 as least preferred, 15% item 2, and 15% item 3.

If you were to take the Kuder, your score for the first triad on the "limousine driver" scale would be the proportion of the criterion group that endorsed the same responses. So if you indicated that item #1 is your most preferred and item #2 is your least preferred, your score on that triad would be .20 + .15 = .35. The highest score would be obtained if you endorsed item #2 as most and item #1 as least; your score in this case would be .60 + .70 = 1.30. Note that this triad would be scored differently for different scales because the proportions of endorsement would presumably change for different occupational groups. Note also that with this approach there is no need to have a general group.

In any one occupational group, we would expect a response pattern that reflects homogeneity of interest, as in our fictitious example, where the majority of limousine drivers agree on what they prefer most and prefer least. If we did not have such unanimity we would expect a "random" response pattern, where each item in the triad is endorsed by approximately one-third of the respondents. In fact, we can calculate a total score across all triads that reflects the homogeneity of interest for a particular group, and whether a particular Kuder scale differentiates one occupational group from others (see Zytowski & Kuder, 1986, on how this is done).

Scoring. Scales on the KOIS are scored by means of a "lambda" score, which is a modified biserial correlation coefficient and is essentially an index of similarity between a person's responses and the criterion group for each scale. Rather than interpreting these lambda scores directly, they are used to rank order the scales to show the magnitude of similarity. Thus, the profile sheet that summarizes the test results is essentially a listing of general occupational interests (e.g., scientific, artistic, computational), and of occupations and of college majors, all listed in decreasing order of similarity.

Reliability. Test-retest reliabilities seem quite acceptable, with for example median reliability coefficients in the .80s over both a 2-week and a 3-year period (Zytowski, 1985).

Validity. Predictive validity also seems to be acceptable, with a number of studies showing about a 50% congruence between test results and subsequent entrance into an occupation some 12 to 19 years later (Zytowski & Laing, 1978).

Other Interest Inventories

A large number of other inventories have been developed over the years, although none have reached the status of the Strong or the Kuder. Among the more popular ones are the Holland Self-Directed Search (Holland, 1985b), the Jackson Vocational Interest Survey (D. N. Jackson, 1977), the Career Assessment Inventory (Johansson, 1975), the Unisex edition of the ACT Interest Inventory (Lamb & Prediger, 1981), and the Vocational Interest Inventory (P. W. Lunneborg, 1979).

Interest inventories for disadvantaged. A number of interest inventories have been developed for use with clients who, for a variety of reasons, may not be able to understand and/or respond appropriately to verbal items such as those used in the Strong and the Kuder. These inventories, such as the Wide Range Interest Opinion Test (J. F. Jastak & S. R. Jastak, 1972) and the Geist Picture Interest Inventory (Geist, 1959) use drawings of people or activities related to occupational tasks such as doing laundry, taking care of animals, serving food, and similar activities. Some of these inventories use a forced-choice format, while others ask the respondent to indicate how much they like each activity. Most of these have adequate reliability but leave much to be desired in the area of validity.

Interest inventories for nonprofessional occupations. Both the Strong and the Kuder have found their primary application with college-bound students and adults whose expectations are to enter professions. In fact, most career-interest inventories are designed for occupations that are entered by middle-class individuals. In large part, this reflects a reality of our culture, that perhaps is changing. At least in the past, individuals from lower socioeconomic classes did not have much choice, and job selection was often a matter of availability and financial need. For upper socioeconomic class individuals, their choice was similarly limited by family expectations and traditions, such as continuing a family business or family involvement in government service. A number of other interest inventories have been developed that are geared more for individuals entering nonprofessional occupations.

One example of such inventories is the Career Assessment Inventory (CAI; Johansson, 1986), first introduced in 1975 and subsequently revised several times, recently to include both nonprofessional and professional occupations. The CAI currently contains some 370 items similar in content to those of the Strong and takes about 40 to 45 minutes to complete. For each item, the client responds on a 5-point scale ranging from "like very much" to "dislike very much." Like the Strong, the CAI contains the six general-theme scales that reflect Holland's typology, 25 Basic Interest scales (e.g., electronics, food service, athletics-sports), and 111 occupational scales (such as accountant, barber/hairstylist, carpenter, fire-fighter, interior designer, medical assistant, police officer, and truck driver). Although the CAI seems promising, in that it was well-designed psychometrically and shows adequate reliability, it too has been criticized, primarily for lack of evidence of validity (McCabe, 1985; Rounds, 1989).

Other career aspects. In addition to career interests, there are a number of questionnaires designed to assess a person's attitudes, compe-

tencies, and decision-making skills, all in relation to career choice. For example, the Career Decision Scale (Osipow, 1987) is an 18-item scale designed to assess career indecision in college students, and the Career Maturity Inventory (Crites, 1978) is designed to assess career-choice competencies (such as self-knowledge and awareness of one's interests) and attitudes (such as degree of independence and involvement in making career decisions).

Lack of theory. One criticism of the entire field of career-interest measurement is that it has been dominated by an empirical approach. The approach has been highly successful, yet it has resulted in a severe lack of theoretical knowledge about various aspects of career interests. For example, how do these interests develop? What psychological processes mediate and affect such interests? How do such variables as personality, temperament, and motivation relate to career interests? There is now a need to focus on construct validity rather than criterion validity. To be sure, such questions have not been totally disregarded. For example, Roe (Roe & Klos, 1969; Roe & Siegelman, 1964) felt that career choices reflected early upbringing and that children who were raised in an accepting and warm family atmosphere would choose people-oriented occupations. Others have looked to a genetic component of career interests (e.g., Grotevant, Scarr, & Weinberg, 1977).

New occupational scales. The world of work is not a static one, and especially in a rapidly expanding technology, new occupations are created. Should we therefore continue to develop new occupational scales? Some authors (e.g., Borgen, 1986; Burisch, 1984) have argued that a simple, deductive approach to career interest measurement may be now more productive than the empirical and technical development of new scales. These authors believe that we now have both the theories and the empirical knowledge related to the occupational world, and we should be able to locate any new occupation in that framework without needing to go out and develop a new scale. Indeed, Borgen (1986) argues that occupational scales may not be needed and that a broad perspective, such as the one provided by Holland's theory, is all that is needed.

SUMMARY

We have looked at the measurement of attitudes, values, and interests. From a psychometric point of view these three areas share much in common, and what has been covered under one topic could, in many instances be covered under a different topic. We looked at four classical methods to construct attitude scales; the method of equal appearing intervals or Thurstone method, the method of summated ratings or Likert method, the Bogardus social distance scale, and Guttman scaling. In addition, we looked at the Semantic Differential, checklists, numerical and graphic rating scales, and self-anchoring scales.

In the area of values, we looked at the Study of Values, a measure that enjoyed a great deal of popularity years ago, and the Rokeach Value Survey, which is quite popular now. We also briefly discussed the Survey of Interpersonal Values and the Survey of Personal Values to illustrate another approach. In the area of career interests, we focused primarily on the Strong and the Kuder inventories that originally represented quite different approaches but in recent revisions have become more alike.

SUGGESTED READINGS

Campbell, D. P. (1971). An informal history of the SVIB. In *Handbook for the Strong Vocational Interest Blank* (pp. 343–365). Stanford, CA: Stanford University Press.

This is a fascinating account of the SVIB, from its early beginnings in the 1920s to the mid 1960s, shortly after Strong's death. For those who assume that computers have been available "forever," this chapter has a wonderful description of the challenges required to "machine score" a test.

Domino, G., Gibson, L., Poling, S., & Westlake, L. (1980). Students' attitudes towards suicide. *Social Psychiatry*, 15, 127–130.

The investigators looked at the attitudes that college students have toward suicide. They used the Suicide Opinion Questionnaire, and administered it to some 800 college students in nine different institutions. An interesting study illustrating the practical application of an attitude scale.

Kilpatrick, F. P. & Cantril, H. (1960). Self-anchoring scaling: A measure of individual's unique reality worlds. *Journal of Individual Psychology*, 16, 158–173.

An interesting report where the two authors present the self-anchoring methodology and the results of several studies where such scales were administered to adult Americans, legislators from seven different countries, college students in India, and members of the Bantu tribe in South Africa.

Lawton, M. P. & Brody, E. M. (1969). Assessment of older people: Self-maintaining and instrumental activities of daily living. *The Gerontologist*, 9, 179–186.

Two scales are presented for use with institutionalized elderly. The first scale focuses on physical self-maintenance and covers six areas, toilet use, feeding, dressing, grooming, and physical ambulation. The second scale, Instrumental Activities of Daily Living, covers eight areas ranging from the ability to use the telephone to the ability to handle finances. The scale items are given in this article and clearly illustrate the nature of Guttman scaling, although the focus is on how the scales can be used in various settings, rather than in how the scales were developed.

Rokeach, M. & Ball-Rokeach, S. J. (1989). Stability and change in American value priorities, 1968–1981. *American Psychologist*, 44, 775–784.

Psychological tests can be useful not only to study the functioning of individuals, but to assess an entire society. In this report, the authors analyze national data on the RVS which was administered by the National Opinion Research Center of the University of Chicago in 1968 and again in 1971, and by the Institute for Social Research at the University of Michigan in 1974 and in 1981. Although there seems to be remarkable stability of values over time, there were also some significant changes – for example, "equality" decreased significantly.

DISCUSSION QUESTIONS

1. What are some of the strengths and weaknesses of attitude scales?

2. Which of the various ways of assessing reliability would be most appropriate for a Guttman scale?

3. What might be some good bipolar adjectives to use in a Semantic Differential scale to rate "my best teacher"?

4. What are the basic values important to college students today? Are these included in the Rokeach?

5. Most students take some type of career-interest test in high school. What is your recollection of such a test and the results?

7 Psychopathology

AIM In this chapter we look at testing as applied to psychopathology. We briefly cover some issues of definition and nosology, and then we look at 11 different instruments, each selected for specific purposes. First, we look at two screening inventories, the SCLR-90 and the PSI. Then we look at three multivariate instruments: two of these, the MMPI and the MCMI, are major instruments well known to most clinicians, and the third is new and unknown. Next, we look at an example of a test that focuses on a specific aspects of psychopathology – the schizoid personality disorder. Finally, we look at a measure of anxiety and three measures of depression used quite frequently by clinicians and researchers. More important than each specific test, are the kinds of issues and construction methodologies they represent, especially in relation to the basic issues covered in Chapter 3.

INTRODUCTION

The Diagnostic and Statistical Manual (DSM).
As you are well aware, there is a wide range of physical illnesses that can affect humans. These illnesses are classified, under various headings, in the *International Classification of Diseases*, a sort of dictionary of illnesses which also gives each illness a particular classificatory number. Thus physicians, clinics, insurance companies, governmental agencies, etc., all over the world, have a uniform system for reporting and classifying illnesses.

A similar approach applies to mental illnesses, and here the classificatory schema is called the *Diagnostic and Statistical Manual of Mental Disorders*, or DSM for short. The first DSM was published in 1952, and revisions, are made as needed. This classificatory schema is thus not static but is continually undergoing study and revision. In the DSM, each diagnostic label is numbered, and these numbers coincide with those used in the International Classification of Diseases. Thus for example, if you were to look for pyromania

(fire-setting) in the DSM you would find it listed under "Impulse Control Disorders (not classified elsewhere)," and the number assigned is 312.33. The DSM is based on a medical model of behavioral and emotional problems, which views such disturbances as illnesses. Part of the model is to perceive these problems as residing within the individual, rather than as the result and interplay of environmental, familial, or cultural aspects.

Later revisions of the DSM use a *multiaxial* approach – that is, individuals are classified according to five different axes or dimensions. The first dimension refers to clinical syndromes. The second dimension pertains to developmental disorders and personality disorders. Axis III refers to physical disorders and conditions, axis IV to severity of psychosocial stressors, and axis V to level of adaptive functioning. The DSM is a guide rather than a cookbook; it is intended to assist the clinician in making a diagnosis and in communicating with other professionals (for a reliability and validity analysis of the DSM-IV, see Nelson-Gray, 1991).

Mental disorder. There are many phrases used for the area under consideration, such as "mental illness," "psychopathology," and so on. For our purposes, we will follow the DSM approach and define mental disorder as a psychological pattern associated with distress and/or impairment of functioning that reflects dysfunction in the person.

Psychiatric diagnosis. In the assessment of psychopathology, psychiatric diagnosis has occupied a central position, and often it has become the criterion against which any measuring instrument was matched. In the past, however, psychiatric diagnosis was seen as highly unreliable and was even described as a hopeless undertaking. The development of the DSM with its well-defined and specified criteria, as well as the publication of several structured and semistructured interviews, provided clinicians with the needed tools, so that today diagnostic unreliability is much less of a concern.

Diagnostic classification. Tests are often used to provide a diagnosis for a particular patient or to classify that patient in some way. Traditional psychiatric systems of diagnosis, and indeed the very process of classification, have been severely criticized over the years (e.g., Kauffman, 1989), but classification is both needed and useful. A diagnosis is a shorthand description that allows professionals to communicate, to match services to the needs of the patient, to further understand particular syndromes, and as a statistical reporting device for governmental action, such as allowing funds to be used for the benefit of a client.

Differential diagnosis. Often diagnosis involves the assignment of one of several potentially applicable labels. Diagnoses are often quite difficult to make, particularly in psychological conditions where the indicators of a particular syndrome may not be clearly differentiable from the indicators of another syndrome. Test information can be quite useful in such situations, and the utility of a test can be judged in part from its differential diagnostic validity.

Assessment. Basically there are four ways we can assess an individual. We can ask that person directly (Do you hear voices?). Here we might use an interview or a self-report inventory. A second way is to ask someone else who knows the person (Does your husband hear voices?) Here we can interview spouses, parents, teachers, etc. and/or ask them to complete some rating scale. A third way is to observe the person in their natural environment. This might include home visits, observing a patient interact with others on the ward, or observing children playing in the playground. Finally, we can observe the person in a standardized-test situation. This is probably the most common method and involves tests such as those discussed below. For a compendium of scales that measure specific aspects of psychopathology, following the DSM system, see Schutte and Malouff (1995).

Cost factors. Testing is expensive whether it is done by an in-house professional or an outside consultant. Expensive means not only money that might be associated with the cost of the test itself and the salary of the associated personnel, but also the time commitment involved on the part of the client and staff. That is why, in part, tests that are paper-and-pencil, brief, comprehensive, self-administered, and objectively scored are often preferred by clinicians.

Given these economic concerns, tests are not ordinarily used in a routine fashion but are used only when their potential contribution is substantially greater than their cost. In addition, we need to consider the complexity of the issues concerning potential testing. For example, if a decision needs to be made about placing a client in a long-term institutional setting, as much information as possible needs to be gathered, and test results can be useful, especially when they can provide new information not readily available by other means. Also, tests of psychopathology are often used when there are difficult diagnostic questions about a client, rather than routine "textbook" type decisions. In a sense, the use of psychological tests parallels the use of medical tests – if you have a simple cold, you would not expect your physician to carry out brain scans, spinal taps, or other sophisticated, costly, and invasive procedures.

The use of test batteries. Although tests are used for a variety of purposes in the area of psychopathology, their use often falls into one of two categories: (1) a need to answer a very specific and focused diagnostic question (e.g., does this patient represent a suicide risk?); or (2) a need to portray in a very broad way the client's psycho – dynamics, psychological functioning, and personality structure. The answer to the first category can sometimes be given by using a very specific, focused test – in the example given above, perhaps a scale of suicidal ideation. For the second category, the answer is provided either by a *multivariate* instrument, like the MMPI, or a test *battery*, a group of tests chosen by the clinician to provide potential answers.

Sometimes test batteries are routinely administered to new clients in a setting for research purposes, for evaluation of the effectiveness of specific therapeutic programs, or to have a uniform set of data on all clients so that base rates, diagnostic questions, and other aspects can be determined. The use of a test battery has a number of advantages other than simply an increased number of tests. For one, differences in performance on different tests may have diagnostic significance (a notion similar to scatter discussed in Chapter 5). If we consider test results as indicators of potential hypotheses (e.g., this client seems to have difficulties solving problems that require spatial reasoning), then the clinician can look for supporting evidence among the variety of test results obtained.

The Mental Status Exam (MSE). Traditionally, psychiatric diagnosis is based on the MSE, which is a psychiatrist's analogue to the general physical exam used by physicians. Like a medical exam, the MSE is not rigorously standardized and is highly subjective. Basically the MSE consists of an interview, during which the psychiatrist observes the patient and asks a number of questions. The psychiatrist conducting the MSE tries to obtain information on the client's level of functioning in about 10 areas:

1. Appearance: How does the client look? Is the client's appearance appropriate given his or her age, social position, educational background, etc. Is the client reasonably groomed?
2. Behavior: What is the client's behavior during the MSE? This includes verbal behavior such as tone of voice, general flow, vocabulary, etc., and nonverbal behavior such as posture, eye contact, facial expressions, mannerisms, etc. Does the client act in bizarre or suspicious ways?
3. Orientation: Does the client know who he is, where he is, the time (year, month, day) and why he is there.
4. Memory: Is typically divided into immediate (ability to recall within 10 seconds of presentation), recent (within the recent past, a few days to a few months), and remote memory (such as past employment, family deaths).
5. Sensorium: Is the degree of intactness of the senses (such as vision and touch), as well as to general ability to attend and concentrate.
6. Mood and Affect: Mood refers to the general or prevailing emotion displayed during the MSE, while affect refers to the range of emotions manifested during the MSE.
7. Intellectual functioning: the client's verbal ability, general fund of information, ability to interpret abstract proverbs, etc.
8. Perceptual processes: Is veridical perception of the world vs. hallucinations.
9. Thought content: the client's own ideas about current difficulties; presence of persecutory delusions, obsessions, phobias, etc.
10. Thought process, also known as stream of consciousness: an assessment of the language process as it reflects the underlying thought processes, for example paucity of ideas, giving a lot of irrelevant detail, getting sidetracked, degree of insight shown by the client as to the nature of his or her problems, etc.

The above outline is not rigidly followed, but represents the kind of information that would be elicited during the course of an interview. Although the MSE is widely used, it is not a well-standardized procedure and quite a few variations exist (see Crary & C. W. Johnson, 1975; W. R. Johnson, 1981; Kahn, Goldfarb, Pollack et al., 1960; Maloney & Ward, 1976; Rosenbaum & Beebe, 1975).

MEASURES

The Structured Clinical Interview for DSM-III (SCID)

Brief mention should be made of the SCID because it is an outgrowth of the DSM and is of importance to the assessment of psychopathology. The SCID is a semistructured interview, one of the first to be specifically designed on the basis of DSM-III criteria for mental disorders (Spitzer & Williams, 1983), and subsequently updated to reflect the changes in the revisions of the DSM (Spitzer, Williams, Gibbon, et al., 1992).

The SCID covers nine diagnostic areas including psychotic disorders, mood disorders, anxiety disorders, and eating disorders. The SCID should be administered by trained interviewers who have a background in psychopathology and are familiar with DSM criteria. However, Segal, Hersen, Van Hasselt, et al. (1993), in a study of elderly patients, used master's level graduate students to administer the SCID. These authors argued that in a typical agency it is most likely the less experienced clinicians who do the diagnostic work. In fact, their results showed an interrater agreement rate greater than 85%. The reliability of any structured interview is not a static number, but changes from study to study because it is affected by many variables such as aspects of the interviewers and of the subjects, as well as the reliability of the specific diagnostic criteria (Segal, Hersen, Van Hasselt, et al., 1994; J. B. W. Williams et al., 1992).

There is a shortened version of the SCID for use in settings where psychotic disorders are rare, and a form designed for use with nonpsychiatric patients, such as might be needed in community surveys of mental health. As with other major instruments, there are user's guides and computer scoring programs available.

The Symptom Checklist 90R (SCL-90R)

Introduction. The SCL-90R is probably one of the most commonly used screening inventories for the assessment of psychological difficulties. The SCL-90R evolved from some prior checklists called the Hopkins Symptom Checklist and the Cornell Medical Index (Wider, 1948). As its title indicates, the SCL-90R is a self-report inventory of symptoms, covering nine psychiatric categories such as depression and paranoid ideation, and focusing particularly on those symptoms exhibited by psychiatric patients and, to a lesser extent, by medical patients. A preliminary form was developed in 1973, and a revised form in 1976; in addition there is a brief form available

and two forms for use by clinical observers (Derogatis, 1977).

Development. As indicated, the SCL-90R evolved from other checklists of symptoms that reflected years of diagnostic observations on the part of many clinicians. Factor analytic studies of the Hopkins Symptom Checklist identified five primary symptom dimensions. Four additional, rationally developed, symptom dimensions were added and the result was the SCL-90. An attempt was made to use simple phrases as the checklist items, and to keep the general vocabulary level as simple as possible.

Description. The patient is asked to indicate for each of the 90 items, the degree of distress experienced during the past 7 days, using a 5-point scale (0 to 4) that ranges from "not at all" to "extremely." The SCL-90R can be scored for nine symptom dimensions, and these are presented in Table 7.1. The SCL-90R is primarily applicable to adults, but can be used with adolescents, perhaps even with 13- and 14-year-olds.

Administration. The SCL-90R contains clear directions and is relatively easy to administer, often by a nurse, technician, or research assistant. Most patients can complete the SCL-90R in 10 to 15 minutes. The items on the scale can also be read to the patient, in cases where trauma or other conditions do not permit standard administration. A 3 × 5 card with the response options is given to the patient, and the patient can indicate a response by pointing or raising an appropriate number of fingers.

Scoring. Raw scores are calculated by adding the responses for each symptom dimension, and dividing by the number of items in that dimension. In addition to the nine scales, there are three global indices that are computed. The *Global Severity Index (GSI)*, is the sum of all the nonzero responses, divided by 90, and reflects both the number of symptoms endorsed and the intensity of perceived distress. The *Positive Symptom Total (PST)*, is defined as the number of symptoms out of the 90 to which the patient indicates a nonzero response. This is a measure of the number of symptoms endorsed. The *Positive Symptom Distress Index (PSDI)*, is defined as the PST

Table 7–1 Scales on the SCL-90

No. of items	Name	Definition	Example
12	Somatization	Distress arising from perceptions of bodily dysfunction	Headaches A lump in your throat
10	Obsessive-compulsive	Unwarranted but repetitive thoughts, impulses, and actions	Having to check and double check what you do
9	Interpersonal sensitivity	Feelings of personal inadequacy and inferiority	Feeling shy Feeling inferior to others
13	Depression	Dysphoric mood and withdrawal	Crying easily Feeling blue
10	Anxiety	Nervousness, tension, feelings of apprehension	Trembling Feeling fearful
6	Hostility	Anger	Feeling easily annoyed Shouting/throwing things
7	Phobic anxiety	Persistent and irrational fear response	Feeling afraid of open spaces Feeling uneasy in crowds
6	Paranoid ideation	Suspicious, grandiosity, and delusions	Feeling others are to blame for one's troubles Feeling that most people can't be trusted
10	Psychoticism	Withdrawn, isolated lifestyle with symptoms of schizophrenia	Someone controls my thoughts I hear voices that others do not

Note: If you yourself are a bit "obsessive-compulsive," you will note that the above items only add up to 83. There are in fact 7 additional items to the SCL-90 that are considered to reflect clinically important symptoms, such as poor appetite and trouble falling asleep, that are not subsumed under any of the 9 primary dimensions.

divided by 90; thus, this is a measure of "intensity" corrected for the number of symptoms.

Reliability. The test manual (Derogatis, 1977) provides internal consistency (coefficient alpha) and test-retest (1 week) information. Internal consistency coefficients range from .77 to .90, with most in the mid .80s. Test-retest coefficients range from .78 to .90, again with most coefficients in the mid .80s. Thus from both aspects of reliability, the SCL-90R seems quite adequate.

Validity. The test manual discusses validity findings under three headings: concurrent, discriminative, and construct validity. Under concurrent validity are studies that compare SCL-90R scores with those obtained on other multivariate measures of psychopathology such as the MMPI. These results indicate that the SCL-90R scales correlate .40 to .60 with their counterparts on the MMPI, but the results are somewhat complex. For example, the Psychoticism Scale of the SCL-90R does correlate significantly with the MMPI Schizophrenia Scale (.64), but so does

the SCL-90 Depression Scale (.55), the Obsessive-Compulsive Scale (.57), the Anxiety Scale (.51), and the Interpersonal Sensitivity Scale (.53)!

Under "discriminative" validity are studies where the SCL-90R is said to provide "clinical discrimination" or usefulness in dealing with different diagnostic groups. Thus studies are included in this section, that deal with oncology patients, drug addicts, dropouts from West Point Military Academy, and others. Finally, there is a section on construct validity that presents evidence from factor-analytic studies showing a relatively good match between the original dimensions on the SCL-90R and the results of various factor-analytic procedures. The SCL-90R has been particularly useful in studies of depression (e.g., Weissman, Sholomskas, Pottenger, et al., 1977).

Factorial invariance. How stable are the 9 dimensions in various groups that may differ from each other on selected aspects, such as gender, age, or psychiatric status? In one sense, this is a question of *generalizability* and can be viewed with respect to both reliability and validity. Couched in somewhat different language, it is also the question of *factorial invariance* – does the factor pattern remain constant across different groups? Such constancy, or lack of it, can be viewed as good or bad, depending on one's point of view. Having factorial invariance might indicate stability of dimensions across different groups; not having such invariance may in fact reflect the real world. For example, in psychiatric patients we might expect the various SCL-90R dimensions to be separate symptom entities, but in normal subjects it might not be surprising to have these dimensions collapse into a general adjustment type of factor. The SCL-90R manual suggests that the SCL-90R has such factorial invariance for gender, social class, and psychiatric diagnosis (see Cyr, Doxey, & Vigna, 1988).

Interpretation. The test manual indicates that interpretation of a protocol is best begun at the global level, with a study of the GSI, PSI, and PSDI as indicators of overall distress. The next step is to analyze the nine primary symptom dimensions that provide a "broad-brush" profile of the patient's psychodynamic status. Finally, an analysis of the individual items can provide information as to whether the patient is suicidal or homicidal, what phobic symptoms are present, and so on.

Norms. Once the raw scores are calculated for a protocol, the raw scores can be changed to T scores by consulting the appropriate normative table in the manual. Such norms are available for male ($n = 490$) and female ($n = 484$) normal or nonpatient subjects, for male ($n = 424$) and female ($n = 577$) psychiatric outpatients, and for adolescent outpatients ($n = 112$). In addition, mean profiles are given for some 20 clinical samples ranging from psychiatric outpatients, alcoholics seeking treatment, to patients with sexual dysfunctions.

The Psychological Screening Inventory (PSI)

Introduction. The PSI (Lanyon, 1968) was designed as a relatively brief test to identify psychological abnormality, in particular as an aid to the identification of individuals who may require psychiatric hospitalization or criminal institutionalization. The PSI is not intended to be a diagnostic instrument but is a screening device to be used to detect persons who might receive more intensive attention. For example, a counselor or mental health worker might administer the PSI to a client to determine whether that client should be referred to a psychologist or psychiatrist for further assessment. The PSI consists of 130 true-false items that comprise five scales: two of the scales (Alienation and Social Nonconformity) were designed to identify individuals unable to function normally in society, and two of the scales (Discomfort and Expression) were developed to assess what the author considers major dimensions of personality; one scale (Defensiveness) was designed to assess "fake good" and "fake bad" tendencies. (A sixth scale, Infrequency or Random Response, was later added but is not scored on the profile sheet.)

According to the author (Lanyon, 1968) the Alienation Scale attempts to identify individuals we might expect to be patients in a psychiatric institution; the scale was developed empirically to differentiate between normal subjects and psychiatric patients. The Social Nonconformity Scale attempts to identify individuals we might expect to find in prison. This scale also was developed empirically to differentiate between normal subjects and state-reformatory inmates. The Discomfort Scale is more typically a dimension that is labeled as neuroticism, general maladjustment, or anxiety while the dimension addressed by the Expression Scale is often labeled extraversion or undercontrol. The names of the scales were chosen to be "nontechnical," so they are not the best labels that could have been selected.

Development. The PSI was developed by establishing a pool of items that were face valid and related to the five dimensions to be scaled. These items were brief, in about equal proportions of keyed true and keyed false, and written so as to minimize social desirability. The resulting 220 items were administered to a sample of 200 (100 male and 100 female) normal subjects chosen to be representative of the U.S. population in age and education and comparable in socioeconomic status and urban-rural residence. The Alienation

Scale, composed of 25 items, was developed by criterion groups' analyses between the normal sample and two samples ($N = 144$) of psychiatric patients, primarily schizophrenics; the intent of this scale is to indicate a respondent's similarity of response to those of hospitalized psychiatric patients. Thus this scale is essentially a scale of serious psychopathology. The Social Nonconformity Scale, also made up of 25 items, was developed by a parallel analysis between the normal group and 100 (50 male, 50 female) reformatory inmates; this scale then measures the similarity of response on the part of a client to those who have been jailed for antisocial behavior.

The Discomfort and Expression Scales, each with 30 items, were developed by internal consistency analyses of the items originally written for these scales, using the responses from the normal subjects only. You recall that this method involves correlating the responses on each item with the total scale score and retaining the items with the highest correlations. The Discomfort Scale measures susceptibility to anxiety, a lack of enjoyment of life, and the perceived presence of many psychological difficulties. The Expression Scale measures extraversion-introversion, so that high scorers tend to be sociable extraverted, but also unreliable, impulsive and undercontrolled; low scorers tend to be introverted, thorough, and also indecisive and overcontrolled.

Finally, the Defensiveness scale, composed of 20 items, was developed by administering the pool of items to a sample of 100 normal subjects, three times: once under normal instructions, once with instructions to "fake bad," and once with instructions to "fake good." Items that showed a significant response shift were retained for the scale. High scores therefore indicate that the subject is attempting to portray him or herself in a favorable light, while low scores reflect a readiness to admit undesirable characteristics. This scale appears to be quite similar to the K scale of the MMPI. The above procedures yielded a 130-item inventory. A supplemental scale, Random Response (RA) was developed to assess the likelihood of random responding; this scale is analogous to the MMPI F scale.

Description. Most of the PSI items are of the kind one would expect on a personality test, with some clearly oriented toward pathology (such as hearing strange voices), but many are fairly normal in appearance, such as being healthy for one's age, or being extremely talkative. Versions of the PSI are available in various languages, such as Spanish and Japanese. Most inventories of this type use a separate question booklet and answer sheet. The basic advantage is that the test booklets can be reused, but having a separate answer sheet means the possibility of the client making mistakes, such as skipping one question and having all subsequent responses out of kilter. On the PSI, responses are marked right after each item, rather than on a separate answer sheet.

Administration. The PSI can be self-administered, used with one client or a large group. It takes about 15 minutes to complete, and less than 5 minutes to score and plot the profile.

Scoring. The PSI can easily be scored by hand through the use of templates, and the results easily plotted on a graph, separately by gender. The raw scores can be changed to T scores by either using the table in the manual, or by plotting the scores on the profile sheet. On most multivariate instruments, like the MMPI for example, scores that are within two SDs from the mean (above 30 and below 70 in T scores) are considered "normal." On the PSI, scores that deviate by only 1 SD from the mean are considered significant. Thus one might expect a greater than typical number of false positives. However, the PSI manual explicitly instructs the user on how to determine a cutoff score, based on local norms, that will maximize the number of hits.

Reliability. Test-retest reliability coefficients range from .66 to .95, while internal consistency coefficients range from .51 to .85. These coefficients are based on normal college students, and as Golding (1978) points out, may be significantly different in a clinical population. Certainly the magnitude of these coefficients suggests that while the PSI is adequate for research purposes and group comparisons, extreme caution should be used in making individual decisions.

Validity. The initial validity data are based on comparisons of two small psychiatric cross-validation groups (Ns of 23 and 27), a prison group ($N = 80$), and subjects ($N = 45$; presumably college students) given the fake good and fake bad instructions. In each case, the mean scores on the scales seem to work as they should. For example, the Alienation means for the psychiatric patients are T scores ranging from 66 to 74 (remember that 50 is average), while Social Nonconformity means for the prison subjects are at 67 for both genders. Under instructions to fake good, the mean Defensiveness scores jump to 63 and 67, while under instructions to fake bad the mean scores go down to 31.

The test manual (Lanyon, 1973; 1978) indicates considerable convergent and discriminant validity by presenting correlations of the PSI scales with those of inventories such as the MMPI. Other studies are presented using contrasted groups. For example, in one study of 48 psychiatric patients and 305 normal males, a cutoff score of 60 on the Alienation Scale achieved an 86% overall hit rate, with 17% of the psychiatric cases misidentified as false negatives, and 14% of the normal individuals misidentified as false positives. Incidentally, the criterion for being "normal" is a difficult one – ordinarily it is defined either by self-report or by the absence of some criteria, such as the person has not been hospitalized psychiatrically or has not sought psychological help. These operational definitions do not guarantee that subjects identified as normal are indeed normal.

A number of studies can be found in the literature that also support the validity of the PSI. One example is that of Kantor, Walker, and Hays (1976) who administered the PSI to two samples of adolescents: 1,123 13- to 16-year-old students in a school setting and 105 students of the same age who were on juvenile probation. Students in the first sample were also asked to answer anonymously a questionnaire that contained three critical questions: (1) Did you run away from home last year? (2) Have you been in trouble with the police? (3) Have you stolen anything worth more than $2? A subgroup was then identified of youngsters who answered one or more of the critical questions in the keyed direction. The PSI scales did not differentiate the subgroup from the larger normal group, but the probationary group did score significantly higher on the Alienation, Discomfort, and Social Nonconformity Scales (the results on the Discomfort and Social Nonconformity Scales applied to females only).

Another example is the study by Mehryar, Hekmat, and Khajavi (1977) who administered the PSI to a sample of 467 undergraduate students, of whom 111 indicated that they had "seriously considered suicide." A comparison of the "suicidal" vs. nonsuicidal students indicated significant differences on four of the five PSI scales, with suicidal students scoring higher on Alienation, Social Nonconformity, and Discomfort, and lower on Defensiveness.

Many other studies present convergent and discriminant validity data by comparing the PSI with other multivariate instruments such as the MMPI and CPI, and the results generally support the validity of the PSI (Vieweg & Hedlund, 1984).

Norms. The initial norms were based on a sample of 500 normal males and 500 normal females, with scores expressed as T scores; thus separate norms by gender are given. These subjects came from four geographical states, and ranged in age from 16 to 60. Note that since the basic diagnostic question here is whether a subject is normal, the norms are based on normal subjects rather than psychiatric patients. Norms for 13- to 16-year-olds are presented by Kantor, Walker, and Hays (1976).

Factor analysis. J. H. Johnson and Overall (1973) did a factor analysis of the PSI responses of 150 introductory psychology college students. They obtained three factors which they labeled as introversion, social maladjustment, and emotional maladjustment. These factors seem to parallel the PSI scales of Expression, Social Nonconformity, and a combination of Discomfort and Alienation. Notice that these subjects were college students presumably well-functioning, normal individuals; the results might have been closer to the five dimensions postulated by Lanyon had the subjects been psychiatric patients. Nevertheless, J. H. Johnson and Overall (1973) concluded that their results supported the scoring procedure proposed by Lanyon (i.e., five scales).

Lanyon, J. H. Johnson, and Overall (1974) carried out a factor analysis of the 800 protocols that represented the normative sample of normal adults, ages 16 to 60. The results yielded five factors: Factor I represents a dimension of serious psychopathology, and contains items from 4 PSI scales; Factor II represents an extraversion-introversion dimension, with most of the items coming from the Expression Scale; The third factor seems to be an acting-out dimension, although it is made up of few items and does not seem to be a robust dimension; Factor IV represents the "Protestant Ethic" defined as diligence in work and an attitude of responsibility. It too is made up of items from four of the PSI scales; Finally, Factor V is a general neuroticism factor, made up primarily of items from the Discomfort Scale. Note then, that two of the factors (extraversion and general neuroticism) parallel the two PSI scales that were developed on the basis of factor analysis. Two other factors (serious psychopathology and acting out) show some congruence to the Alienation and Social Nonconformity Scales, but the parallel is not very high.

Overall (1974) did administer the PSI to 126 new patients at a psychiatric outpatient clinic, and compared the results to those obtained on a sample of 800 normal subjects, originally collected as norms by the author of the PSI. What makes this study interesting and worth reporting here is that Overall (1974) scored each PSI protocol on the standard five scales, and then rescored each protocol on a set of five scales that resulted from a factor analysis (presumably those obtained in the Lanyon, J. H. Johnson, and Overall 1974 study cited above). Note that a factor analysis can yield the same number of dimensions as originally postulated by clinical insight, but the test items defining (or loading) each factor dimension may not be the exact ones found on the original scales. Overall (1974) computed a *discriminant* function (very much like a regression equation), which was as follows:

$$Y = +.417\,AL + .034\,Sn + .244\,Di + .046\,Ex$$
$$+ .307\,De$$

For each person then, we would take their scores on the PSI, plug the values in the above equation, do the appropriate calculations, and compute Y. In this case, Y would be a number that would predict whether the individual is normal or a psychiatric patient. By using such an equation, first with the regular PSI-scale scores, and then with the factor-scale scores, we can ask which set of scales is more accurate in identifying group membership? In this study, use of the standard PSI-scale scores resulted in 17.5% of each group being misclassified – or 92.5% correct hits. Use of the factor scores resulted in 21.5% of each group being misclassified. Thus the standard PSI scale-scoring procedure resulted in a superior screening index.

Ethical-legal issues. Golding (1978) suggests that the use of the PSI can raise serious ethical-legal issues. If the PSI is used with patients who are seeking treatment, and the resulting scores are used for potential assignment to different treatments, there seems to be little problem other than to ensure that whatever decisions are taken are made on the basis of all available data. But if the individual is unwilling to seek treatment and is nevertheless screened, for example in a military setting or by a university that routinely administers this to all incoming freshmen, and is then identified as a potential "misfit," serious ethical-legal issues arise. In fact, Bruch (1977) administered the PSI to all incoming freshmen over a 2-year period, as part of the regular freshman orientation program. Of the 1,815 students who completed the PSI, 377 were eventually seen in the Counseling Center. An analysis of the PSI scores indicated that students who became Counseling Center clients obtained higher scores on the Alienation, Social Nonconformity, and Discomfort Scales, and lower scores on the Defensiveness Scale.

Other criticisms. The PSI has been criticized on a number of grounds, including high intercorrelations among its scales and high correlations with measures of social desirability (Golding, 1978). Yet, Pulliam (1975) for example, found support for the idea that the PSI scales are not strongly affected by social desirability. One study that used the PSI with adolescents in a juvenile court related agency, found the PSI to be of little practical use and with poor discriminant validity (Feazell, Quay, & Murray, 1991). For a review of the PSI, see Streiner (1985), Vieweg and Hedlund (1984).

THE MINNESOTA MULTIPHASIC PERSONALITY INVENTORY (MMPI) AND MMPI-2

The MMPI

Introduction. The MMPI was first published in 1943 and has probably had the greatest impact of any single test on the practice of psychology and on psychological testing. Its authors, a psychologist named Starke Hathaway and a psychiatrist J. Charnley McKinley, were working at the University of Minnesota hospital and developed the MMPI for use in routine diagnostic assessment of psychiatric patients. Up to that time diagnosis was based on the mental-status examination, but the psychiatrists who administered this were extremely overworked due to the large numbers of veterans returning from the battlefields of World War II who required psychiatric assistance including, as a first step, psychiatric diagnosis.

Criterion keying. Before the MMPI, a number of personality inventories had been developed, most of which were scored using a *logical* keying approach. That is, the author generated a set of items that were typically face valid ("Are you a happy person?") and scored according to the preconceived notions of the author; if the above item was part of an optimism scale, then a true response would yield 1 point for optimism. Hathaway and McKinley, however, chose to determine empirically whether an item was responded to differentially in two groups – a psychiatric group versus a "normal" group.

Development. A large pool of true-false items, close to 1,000, was first assembled. These items came from a wide variety of sources, including the mental-status exam, personality scales, textbook descriptions, case reports, and consultations with colleagues. This pool of items was then analyzed clinically and logically to delete duplications, vague statements, and so on. The remaining pool of some 500-plus items was then administered to groups of psychiatric patients who had diagnoses such as hypochondriasis, depression, paranoia, and schizophrenia. The pool of items was also administered to normal samples, primarily the relatives and visitors of the psychiatric patients. Scales were then formed by pooling together those items that differentiated significantly between a specific diagnostic group, normal subjects, and other diagnostic groups. Thus items for the Schizophrenia Scale included those for which the response rate of schizophrenics differed from those of normals and those of other diagnostic groups. Scales were then cross-validated by administering the scale to new samples, both normal and psychiatric patients, and determining whether the total score on the scale statistically differentiated the various samples.

Thus eight clinical scales, each addressed to a particular psychiatric diagnosis were developed. Later, two additional scales were developed that became incorporated into the standard MMPI profile. These were: (1) a Masculinity-Femininity (Mf) Scale originally designed to distinguish between homosexual and heterosexual males, but composed primarily of items showing a gender difference; and (2) a Social Introversion (Si) Scale composed of items whose response rate differed in a group of college women who participated in many extracurricular activities vs. a group who participated in few if any such activities. This empirical approach to scale construction resulted in many items that were "subtle" – i.e., their manifest content is not directly related to the psychopathological dimension they are presumed to assess. This distinction between "subtle" and "obvious" items has become a major research focus; it has in fact been argued that such subtle items reduce the validity of the MMPI scales (Hollrah, Schlottmann, Scott, et al., 1995).

In addition to these 10 clinical scales, four other scales, called *validity* scales, were also developed. The purpose of these scales was to detect deviant test-taking attitudes. One scale is the Cannot Say Scale, which is simply the total number of items that are omitted (or in rare cases, answered as both true and false). Obviously, if many items are omitted, the scores on the rest of the scales will tend to be lower. A second validity scale is the Lie Scale designed to assess faking good. The scale is composed of 15 items that most people, if they are honest, would not endorse – for example, "I read every editorial in the newspaper every day." These items are face valid and in fact were rationally derived.

A third validity scale, the F Scale, is composed of 60 items that fewer than 10% of the normal samples endorsed in a particular direction. These items cover a variety of content; a factor analysis of the original F Scale indicated some 19 content dimensions, such as poor physical health, hostility, and paranoid thinking (Comrey, 1958).

Finally, the fourth validity scale is called the K Scale and was designed to identify clinical defensiveness. The authors of this scale (Meehl & Hathaway, 1946) noticed that for some psychiatric patients, their MMPI profile was not as deviant as one might expect. They therefore selected 30 MMPI items for this scale that differentiated between a group of psychiatric patients whose MMPI profiles were normal (contrary to expectations), and a group of normal subjects whose MMPI profiles were also normal, as expected. A high K score was assumed to reflect defensiveness and hence lower the deviancy of the resulting MMPI profile. Therefore, the authors reasoned that the K score could be used as a correction factor to maximize the predictive validity of the other scales. Various statistical analyses indicated that this was the case, at least for 5 of the 10 scales, and so these scales are plotted on the profile sheet by adding to the raw score a specified proportion of the K raw score.

Original aim. The original aim of the MMPI was to provide a diagnostic tool that could be group administered, that could save the valuable time of the psychiatrist, and that would result in a diagnostic label. Thus, if a patient scored high on the Schizophrenia Scale, that patient would be diagnosed as schizophrenic. The resulting MMPI however, did not quite work this way. Depressed patients did tend to score high on the Depression Scale, but they also scored high on other scales. Similarly, some normal subjects also scored high on one or more of the clinical scales. It became readily apparent that many of the clinical scales were intercorrelated and that there was substantial item overlap between scales. Thus it would be unlikely for a patient to obtain a high score on only one scale. In addition, the psychiatric nosology, which in essence was the criterion against which the MMPI was validated, was rather unreliable. Finally, clinicians realized that the diagnostic label was not a particularly important piece of information. In medicine of course, diagnosis is extremely important because a specific diagnosis is usually followed by specific therapeutic procedures. But in psychology, this medical model is limited and misleading. Although diagnosis is a short hand for a particular constellation of symptoms, what is important is the etiology of the disorder and the resulting therapeutic regime – that is, how did the client get to be the way he or she is, and what can be done to change that. In psychopathology, the etiology is often complex, multidetermined, and open to different arguments, and the available therapies are often general and not target specific.

Because in fact, reliable differences in MMPI scores were obtained between individuals who differed in important ways, the focus became on what these differences meant. It became more important to understand the psychodynamic functioning of a client and that client's strengths and difficulties. The diagnostic names of the MMPI scales became less important, and in fact they were more or less replaced by a numbering system. As J. R. Graham (1993) states, each MMPI scale became an unknown to be studied and explored. Thousands of studies have now been carried out on the MMPI and the clinician can use this wealth of data to develop a psychological portrait of the client and to generate hypotheses about the dynamic functioning of that client (see Caldwell, 2001).

Numerical designation. The 10 clinical scales are numbered 1 to 10 as follows:

Scale #	Original name
1	Hypochondriasis
2	Depression
3	Hysteria
4	Psychopathic Deviate
5	Masculinity-Femininity
6	Paranoia
7	Psychasthenia
8	Schizophrenia
9	Hypomania
10	Social introversion

The convention is that the scale number is used instead of the original scale name. Thus a client scores high on scale 3, rather than on hysteria. In addition various systems of classifying MMPI profiles have been developed that use the number designations – thus a client's profile may be a "2 4 7."

The MMPI-2

Revision of MMPI. The MMPI is the most widely used personality test in the United States and possibly in the world (Lubin, Larsen, & Matarazzo, 1984), but it has not been free of criticism. One major concern was the original standardization sample, the 724 persons who were visitors to the University of Minnesota hospital, often to visit a relative hospitalized with a psychiatric diagnosis, were not representative of the U.S. general population.

In 1989, a revised edition, the MMPI-2, was published (Butcher, Dahlstrom, Graham, et al., 1989). This revision included a rewrite of many of the original items to eliminate wording that had become obsolete, sexist language, and items that were considered inappropriate or potentially offensive. Of the original 550 items found in the 1943 MMPI, 82 were rewritten, even though most of the changes were slight. Another 154 new items were added to adequately assess such aspects as drug abuse, suicide potential, and marital adjustment. An additional change was to obtain a normative sample that was more truly representative of the U.S. population. Potential subjects were solicited in a wide range of geographical locations, using 1980 Census data. The final sample consisted of 2,600 community subjects, 1,138 males and 1,462 females, including 841 couples, and representatives of minority groups. Other groups were also tested including psychiatric patients, college students, and clients in marital counseling. To assess test-retest reliability, 111 female and 82 male subjects were retested about a week later.

At the same time that the adult version of the MMPI was being revised, a separate form for adolescents was also pilot tested, and a normative sample of adolescents also assessed. This effort however, has been kept separate.

The resulting MMPI-2 includes 567 items, and in many ways is not drastically different from its original. In fact, considerable effort was made to ensure continuity between the 1943 and the 1989 versions. Thus most of the research findings and clinical insights pertinent to the MMPI are still quite applicable to the MMPI-2. As with the MMPI, the MMPI-2 has found extensive applications in many cultures, not only in Europe and Latin America, but also in Asia and the Middle East (see Butcher, 1996).

New scales on the MMPI-2. The MMPI-2 contains three new scales, all of which are validity scales rather than clinical scales. One is the Backpage Infrequency Scale (Fb), which is similar to the F Scale, but is made up of 40 items that occur later in the test booklet. The intent here is to assess whether the client begins to answer items randomly somewhere after the beginning of the test. A second scale is the Variable Inconsistency Scale (VRIN). This scale consists of 67 pairs of items that have either similar or opposite content, and the scoring of this scale reflects the number of item pairs that are answered inconsistently. A third scale is the True Response Inconsistency Scale (TRIN) which consists of 23 pairs of items that are opposite in content, and the scoring, which is somewhat convoluted (see J. R. Graham, 1993), reflects the tendency to respond true or false indiscriminately.

Administration. The MMPI-2 is easily administered and scored; it can be scored by hand using templates or by computer. It is, however, a highly sophisticated psychological procedure, and interpretation of the results requires a well-trained professional.

The MMPI-2 is appropriate for adolescents as young as age 13, but is primarily for adults. Understanding of the items requires a minimum eighth-grade reading level, and completing the test requires some 60 to 90 minutes on the average. Originally, the MMPI items were printed individually on cards that the client then sorted; subsequently, items were printed in a reusable booklet with a separate answer sheet, and that is the format currently used. The 1943 MMPI was also available in a form with a hard back that could be used as a temporary writing surface. The MMPI-2 is available for administration on a personal computer, as well as a tape-recorded version for subjects who are visually handicapped. The MMPI and MMPI-2 have been translated in many languages.

There is a "shortened" version of the MMPI in that in order to score the standard scales only the first 370 items need to be answered. Subsequent items are either not scored or scored on special scales. Thus the MMPI, like the CPI, represents an "open" system where new scales can be developed as the need arises.

Scoring. Once the scales are hand scored, the raw scores are written on the profile, the *K* correction is added where appropriate, and the resulting raw scores are plotted. The scores for the 10 clinical scales are then connected by a line to yield a profile. The resulting profile "automatically" changes the raw scores into *T* scores. Of course if the test is computer scored, all of this is done by the computer. There are in fact a number of computer services that can provide not only scoring but also rather extensive interpretative reports (see Chapter 17).

Uniform *T* scores. You recall that we can change raw scores to *z* scores and *z* scores to *T* scores simply by doing the appropriate arithmetic operations. Because the same operations are applied to every score, in transforming raw scores to *T* scores we do not change the shape of the underlying distribution of scores. As the distributions of raw scores on the various MMPI scales are not normally distributed, linear *T* scores are not equivalent from scale to scale. For one scale a *T* score of 70 may represent the 84th percentile, but for another scale a *T* score of 70 may represent the 88th percentile. To be sure, the differences are typically minor but can nevertheless be problematic. For the MMPI-2 a different kind of *T* transformation is used for the clinical scales (except scales 5 and 0), and these are called *uniform T scores*, which have the same percentile equivalent across scales (see Graham, 1993 for details).

Interpretation. The first step is to determine whether the obtained profile is a valid one. There are a number of guidelines available on what cutoff scores to use on the various validity scales, but the determination is not a mechanical one, and requires a very sophisticated approach. A number of authors have developed additional scales to detect invalid MMPI profiles, but whether these function any better than the standard validity scales is questionable (e.g., Buechley & Ball, 1952; Gough, 1954; R. L. Greene, 1978).

A second step is to look at each of the clinical scales and note their individual elevation.

Table 7.2 provides a listing of each scale with some interpretive statements. What is considered a high or low score depends upon a number of aspects such as the client's educational background, intellectual level, and socioeconomic status. In general, however, *T* scores of 65 and above are considered high (some authors say 70), and *T* scores of 40 and below are considered low (remember that with *T* scores the SD = 10).

A third step is to use a configural approach, to look for patterns and scale combinations that are diagnostically and psychodynamically useful.

Configural interpretation. The richness of the MMPI lies not simply in the fact that there are 10 separate clinical scales, but that the pattern or configuration of the scales in relation to each other is important and psychodynamically meaningful. Originally, a number of investigators developed various sets of rules or procedures by which MMPI profiles could be grouped and categorized. Once a client's profile was thus identified, the clinician could consult a basic source, such as a handbook of profiles (e.g., Hathaway & Meehl, 1951), to determine what personality characteristics could be reasonably attributed to that profile. Many of the classificatory systems that were developed were cumbersome and convoluted, and their usefulness was limited to only the small subset of profiles that could be so classified. The system developed by Welsh (1948) is one that is used more commonly. Briefly, this involves listing the 10 clinical scales, using their numerical labels, in order of *T* score magnitude, largest first, and then three of the validity scales (L, F, K) also in order of magnitude. If two scales are within 1 *T*-score point of each other, their numbers are underlined; if they are the same numerically, they are listed in the profile order, and underlined. To indicate the elevation of each scale, there is a shorthand set of standard symbols. For example: 6*89"7/ etc. would indicate that the *T* score for scale 6 is between 90 and 99, the *T* scores for scales 8 and 9 are between 80 and 89 and are either identical or within 1 point of each other because they are underlined, and the *T* score for scale 7 is between 50 and 59.

Recently, the interest has focused on 2-scale or 3-scale groupings of profiles. Suppose for example, we have a client whose highest MMPI scores occur on scales 4 and 8. By

Table 7–2. MMPI-2 Clinical Scales

Scale & Number of Items	Scale Description
1. Hypochondriasis (Hs) (32)	Designed to measure preoccupation with one's body (somatic concerns) and fear of illness. High scores reflect denial of good health, feelings of chronic fatigue, lack of energy, and sleep disturbances. High scorers are often complainers, self-centered, and cynical.
2. Depression (D) (57)	Designed to measure depression. High scorers feel depressed and lack hope in the future. They may also be irritable and high-strung, have somatic complaints, lack self-confidence, and show withdrawal from social and interpersonal activities.
3. Hysteria (Hy) (60)	This scale attempts to identify individuals who react to stress and responsibility by developing physical symptoms. High scorers are usually psychologically immature and self-centered. They are often interpersonally oriented but are motivated by the affection and attention they get from others, rather than a genuine interest in other people.
4. Psychopathic Deviate (Pd) (50)	The Pd type of person is characterized by asocial or amoral behavior such as excessive drinking, sexual promiscuity, stealing, drug use, etc. High scorers have difficulty in incorporating the values of society and rebel toward authorities, including family members, teachers, and work supervisors. They often are impatient, impulsive, and poor planners.
5. Masculinity-Femininity (Mf) (56)	Scores on this scale are related to intelligence, education, and socioeconomic status, and this scale more than any other, seems to reflect more personality interests than psychopathology. Males who score high (in the feminine direction) may have problems of sexual identity or a more androgynous orientation. Females who score high (in the masculine direction) are rejecting of traditional female role and have interests that in our culture are seen as more masculine.
6. Paranoia (Pa) (40)	Paranoia is marked by feelings of persecution, suspiciousness, and grandiosity, and other evidences of disturbed thinking. In addition to these characteristics, high scorers may also be suspicious, hostile, and overly sensitive.
7. Psychasthenia (Pt) (48)	Psychasthenic (a term no longer used) individuals are characterized by excessive doubts, psychological turmoil, and obsessive-compulsive aspects. High scorers are typically anxious and agitated individuals who worry a great deal and have difficulties in concentrating. They are orderly and organized but tend to be meticulous and overreactive.
8. Schizophrenia (Sc) (78)	Schizophrenia is characterized by disturbances of thinking, mood, and behavior. High scorers, in addition to the psychotic symptoms found in schizophrenia, tend to report unusual thoughts, may show extremely poor judgment, and engage in bizarre behavior.
9. Hypomania (Ma) (46)	Hypomania is characterized by flight of ideas, accelerated motor activity and speech, and elevated mood. High scorers tend to exhibit an outward picture of confidence and poise, and are typically seen as sociable and outgoing. Underneath their facade, there are feelings of anxiousness and nervousness, and their interpersonal relations are usually quite superficial.
10. Social introversion (Si)	High scorers are socially introverted and tend to feel uncomfortable and insecure in social situations. They tend to be shy, reserved, and lack self-confidence.

Note: Most of the above is based on Graham (1990) and Dahlstrom, Welsh, and Dahlstrom (1972).

looking up profile 48 in one of several sources (e.g., W. G. Dahlstrom, Welsh, & L. E. Dahlstrom, 1972; Gilberstadt & Duker, 1965; J. R. Graham, 1993; P. A. Marks, Seeman, & Haller, 1974), we could obtain a description of the personological aspects associated with such a profile. Of course, a well-trained clinician would have internalized such profile configurations and would have little need to consult such sources.

Content analysis. In the development of the clinical MMPI scales the primary focus was on empirical validity – that is, did a particular item show a statistically significant differential response rate between a particular psychiatric group and the normal group. Most of the resulting scales were quite heterogeneous in content, but relatively little attention was paid to such content. The focus was more on the resulting profile.

Quite clearly, however, two clients could obtain the same raw score on a scale by endorsing different combinations of items, so a number of investigators suggested systematic analyses of the item content. Harris and Lingoes (cited by W. G. Dahlstrom, Welsh, & L. E. Dahlstrom, 1972) examined the item content of six of the clinical scales they felt were heterogeneous in composition, and logically grouped together the items that seemed similar. These groupings in turn became subscales that could be scored, and in fact 28 such scales can be routinely computer scored on the MMPI-2. For example, the items on scale 2 (Depression) fall into five clusters labeled subjective depression, psychomotor retardation, physical malfunctioning, mental dullness, and brooding. Note that these subgroupings are based on clinical judgment and not factor analysis.

A different approach was used by Butcher, Graham, Williams, et al. (1990) to develop content scales for the MMPI-2. Rather than start with the clinical scales, they started with the item pool, and logically defined 22 categories of content. Three clinical psychologists then assigned each item to one of the categories. Items for which there was agreement as to placement then represented provisional scales. Protocols from two samples of psychiatric patients and two samples of college students were then subjected to an internal consistency analysis, and the response to each item in a provisional scale was correlated with the total score on that scale. A number

of other statistical and logical refinements were undertaken (see J. R. Graham, 1993) with the end result a set of 15 content scales judged to be internally consistent, relatively independent of each other, and reflective of the content of most of the MMPI-2 items. These scales have such labels as anxiety, depression, health concerns, low self-esteem, and family problems.

Critical items. A number of investigators have identified subsets of the MMPI item pool as being particularly critical in content, reflective of severe psychopathology or related aspects, where endorsement of the keyed response might serve to alert the clinician. Lachar and Wrobel (1979), for example, asked 14 clinical psychologists to identify critical items that might fall under one of 14 categories such as deviant beliefs and problematic anger. After some additional statistical analyses, 111 such items listed under 5 major headings were identified.

Factor analysis. Factor analysis of the MMPI typically yields two basic dimensions, one of anxiety or general maladjustment and the other of repression or neuroticism (Eichman, 1962; Welsh, 1956). In fact, Welsh (1956) developed two scales on the MMPI to assess the anxiety and repression dimensions, by selecting items that were most highly loaded on their respective factors and further selecting those with the highest internal-consistency values.

Note that there are at least two ways of factor analyzing an inventory such as the MMPI. After the MMPI is administered to a large sample of subjects, we can score each protocol and factor analyze the scale scores, *or* we can factor analyze the responses to the items. The Eichman (1962) study took the first approach. Johnson, Null, Butcher, et al. (1984) took the second approach and found some 21 factors, including neuroticism, psychoticism, sexual adjustment, and denial of somatic problems. Because the original clinical scales are heterogeneous, a factor analysis, which by its nature tends to produce more homogeneous groupings, would of course result in more dimensions. An obvious next step would be to use such factor analytic results to construct scales that would be homogeneous. In fact this has been done (Barker, Fowler, & Peterson, 1971; K. B. Stein, 1968), and the resulting scales seem to be as reliable and as valid as the standard scales. They have not, however, "caught on."

Other scales. Over the years literally hundreds of additional scales on the MMPI were developed. Because the MMPI item pool is an open system, it is not extremely difficult to identify subjects who differ on some nontest criterion, administer the MMPI, and statistically analyze the items as to which discriminate the contrasting groups or correlate significantly with the nontest criterion. Many of these scales did not survive cross-validation, were too limited in scope, or were found to have some psychometric problems, but a number have proven quite useful and have been used extensively.

One such scale is the Ego Strength Scale (Es) developed by Barron (1953) to predict success in psychotherapy. The scale was developed by administering the MMPI to a group of neurotic patients and again after 6 months of psychotherapy, comparing the responses of those judged to have clearly improved vs. those judged as unimproved. The original scale had 68 items; the MMPI-2 version has 52. Despite the fact that the initial samples were quite small ($n = 17$ and 16 respectively), that reported internal-consistency values were often low (in the .60s), and that the literature on the Es Scale is very inconsistent in its findings (e.g., Getter & Sundland, 1962; Tamkin & Klett, 1957), the scale continues to be popular.

Another relatively well known extra MMPI scale is the 49 item MacAndrew Alcoholism Scale (MAC; MacAndrew, 1965), developed to differentiate alcoholic from nonalcoholic psychiatric patients. The scale was developed by using a contrasted-groups approach – an analysis of the MMPI responses of 200 male alcoholics seeking treatment at a clinic, vs. the MMPI responses of 200 male nonalcoholic psychiatric patients. The MAC Scale has low internal consistency (alphas of .56 for males and .45 for females) but adequate test-retest reliability over 1-week and 6-week intervals, with most values in the mid .70s and low .80s (J. R. Graham, 1993). Gottesman and Prescott (1989) questioned the routine use of this scale, and they pointed out that when the base rate for alcohol abuse is different from that of the original study, the accuracy of the MAC is severely affected.

Other scales continue to be developed. For example, a new set of scales dubbed the "Psychopathology Five" (aggressiveness, psychoticism, constraint, negative emotionality, and positive emotionality) were recently developed (Harkness, McNulty, & Ben-Porath, 1995). Similarly, many short forms of the MMPI have been developed. Streiner and Miller (1986) counted at least seven such short forms and suggested that our efforts would be better spent in developing new tests.

Reliability. Reliability of the "validity" scales and of the clinical scales seems adequate. The test manual for the MMPI-2 gives test-retest (1-week interval) results for a sample of males and a sample of females. The coefficients range from a low of .58 for scale 6 (Pa) for females, to a high of .92 for scale 0 (Si) for males. Of the 26 coefficients given (3 validity scales plus 10 clinical scales, for males and for females), 8 are in the .70s and 12 in the .80s, with a median coefficient of about .80.

Since much of the interpretation of the MMPI depends upon profile analysis, we need to ask about the reliability of configural patterns because they may not necessarily be the same as the reliability of the individual scales. Such data are not yet available for the MMPI-2, but some is available for the MMPI. J. R. Graham (1993) summarizes a number of studies in this area that used different test-retest intervals and different kinds of samples. In general, the results suggest that about one half of the subjects have the same profile configuration on the two administrations, when such a configuration is defined by the highest scale (a high-point code), and goes down to about one fourth when the configuration is defined by the three highest scales (a 3-point code). Thus the stability over time of such configurations is not that great, although the evidence suggests that changes in profiles in fact reflect changes in behavior.

The MMPI-2 test manual also gives alpha coefficients for the two normative samples. The 26 correlation coefficients range from a low of .34 to a high of .87, with a median of about .62. Ten of the alpha coefficients are above .70 and 16 are below. The MMPI-2 scales are heterogeneous, and so these low values are not surprising. Scales 1, 7, 8, and 0 seem to be the most internally consistent while scales 5, 6, and 9 are the least internally consistent.

Validity. The issue of validity of the MMPI-2 is a very complex one, not only because we are dealing with an entire set of scales rather than just one, but also because there are issues about the validity of configural patterns, of interpretations derived from the entire MMPI profile, of differential results with varying samples, and of the interplay of such aspects as base rates, gender, educational levels of the subjects, characteristics of the clinicians, and so on.

J. R. Graham (1993) indicates that validity studies of the MMPI fall into three general categories. The first are studies that have compared the MMPI profiles of relevant criterion groups. Most of these studies have found significant differences on one or more of the MMPI scales among groups that differed on diagnostic status or other criteria. A second category of studies try to identify reliable nontest behavioral correlates of MMPI scales or configurations. The results of these studies suggest that there are such reliable correlates, but their generalizability is sometimes in question; i.e., the findings may be applicable to one type of sample such as alcoholics, but not to another such as adolescents who are suicidal. A third category of studies looks at the MMPI results *and* at the clinician who interprets those results as one unit, and focuses then on the accuracy of the interpretations. Here the studies are not as supportive of the validity of the MMPI-based inferences, but the area is a problematic and convoluted one (see Garb, 1984; L. R. Goldberg, 1968).

Racial differences. There is a substantial body of literature on the topic of racial differences on the MMPI, but the results are by no means unanimous, and there is considerable disagreement as to the implications of the findings.

A number of studies have found differences between black and white subjects on some MMPI scales, with blacks tending to score higher than whites on scales F, 8, and 9, but the differences are small and, although statistically significant, may not be of clinical significance (W. G. Dahlstrom, Lachar, & L. E. Dahlstrom, 1986; Pritchard & Rosenblatt, 1980). Similar differences have been reported on the MMPI-2, but although statistically significant, they are less than 5 *T*-score points, and therefore not really clinically meaningful (Timbrook & Graham, 1994).

R. L. Greene (1987) reviewed 10 studies that compared Hispanic and white subjects on the MMPI. The differences seem to be even smaller than those between blacks and whites, and R. L. Greene (1987) concluded that there was no pattern to the obtained differences. R. L. Greene (1987) also reviewed seven studies that compared American Indians and whites and three studies that compared Asian-American and white subjects. Here also there were few differences and no discernible pattern. Hall, Bansal, and Lopez (1999) did a meta-analytical review and concluded that the MMPI and MMPI-2 do not unfairly Portray African-Americans and Latinos as pathological. The issue is by no means a closed one, and the best that can be said for now is that great caution is needed when interpreting MMPI profiles of nonwhites.

MMPI manuals. There is a veritable flood of materials available to the clinician who wishes to use the MMPI. Not only is there a vast professional body of literature on the MMPI, with probably more than 10,000 such articles, but there are also review articles, test manuals, books, handbooks, collections of group profiles, case studies and other materials (e.g., Butcher, 1990; Drake & Oetting, 1959; J. R. Graham, 1993; R. L. Greene, 1991; P. A. Marks, Seeman, & Haller, 1974).

Diagnostic failure. The MMPI does not fulfill its original aim, that of diagnostic assessment, and perhaps it is well that it does not. Labeling someone as schizophrenic has limited utility, although one can argue that such psychiatric nosology is needed both as a shorthand and as an administrative tool. It is more important to understand the psychodynamic functioning of a client and the client's competencies and difficulties. In part, the diagnostic failure of the MMPI may be due to the manner in which the clinical scales were constructed. Each scale is basically composed of items that empirically distinguish normals from psychiatric patients. But the clinical challenge is often not diagnosis but *differential* diagnosis – usually it doesn't take that much clinical skill to determine that a person is psychiatrically impaired, but often it can be difficult to diagnose the specific nature of such impairment. Thus the MMPI clinical scales might have worked better diagnostically had they been developed to discriminate specific diagnostic groups from each other.

Usefulness of the MMPI. There are at least two ways to judge the usefulness of a test. The first is highly subjective and consists of the judement made by the user; clinicians who use the MMPI see it as a very valuable tool for diagnostic purposes, for assessing a client's strengths and problematic areas, and for generating hypotheses about etiology and prognosis. The second method is objective and requires an assessment of the utility of the test by, for example, assessing the hits and errors of profile interpretation. Note that in both ways, the test and the test user are integrally related. An example of the second way, is the study by Coons and Fine (1990), who rated "blindly" a series of 63 MMPIs as to whether they represented patients with multiple personality or not. In this context, rating blindly meant that the authors had no information other than the MMPI profile. Incidentally, when a clinician uses a test, it is recommended that the results be interpreted with as much background information about the client as possible. The 63 MMPI profiles came from 25 patients with the diagnosis of multiple personality, and 38 patients with other diagnoses, some easily confused or coexistent with multiple personality. The overall hit rate for the entire sample was 71.4% with a 68% (17/25) hit rate for the patients with multiple personality. The false negative rates for the two investigators were similar (28.5% and 36.5%), but the false positive rates were different (44.4% and 22.2%), a finding that the authors were at a loss to explain. Such results are part of the information needed to evaluate the usefulness of an instrument, but unfortunately the matter is not that easy.

In this study, for example, there are two nearly fatal flaws. The first is that the authors do not take into account the role of chance. Because the diagnostic decision is a bivariate one (multiple personality or not), we have a similar situation to a T-F test, where the probability of getting each item correct is 50–50. The second and more serious problem is that of the 25 patients diagnosed with multiple personality, 24 were female

and only 1 male; of the 38 other patients 31 were female and 7 were male. Diagnosis and gender are therefore confounded.

Criticisms. Despite the popularity and usefulness of the MMPI, it has been severely criticized for a number of reasons. Initially, many of the clinical samples used in the construction of the clinical scales were quite small, and the criterion used, namely psychiatric diagnosis, was relatively unreliable. The standardization sample, the 724 hospital visitors, was large, but they were all white, primarily from small Minnesota towns or rural areas and from skilled and semiskilled socioeconomic levels. The statistical and psychometric procedures utilized were, by today's standards, rather primitive and unsophisticated.

The resulting scales were not only heterogeneous (not necessarily a criticism unless one takes a factor-analytic position), but there is considerable item overlap, i.e., the same item may be scored on several scales, thus contributing to the intercorrelations among scales. In fact, several of the MMPI scales do intercorrelate. The test manual for the MMPI-2 (Hathaway et al., 1989), for example, reports such correlations as $+.51$ between scales 0 (Si) and 2 (D), and .56 between scales 8 (Sc) and 1 (Hs).

Another set of criticisms centered on response styles. When a subject replies true or, false to a particular item, the hope is that the content of the item elicits the particular response. There are people, however, who tend to be more acquiescent and so may agree not so much because of the item content but because of the response options, they tend to agree regardless of the item content (the same can be said of "naysayers," those who tend to disagree no matter what). A related criticism is that the response is related to the social desirability of the item (see Chapter 16). There is in fact, an imbalance in the proportion of MMPI items keyed true or false, and studies of the social-desirability dimension seem to suggest a severe confounding.

Substantial criticism continues to be leveled at the MMPI-2 in large part because of its continuity with the MMPI. Helmes and Reddon (1993) for example, cite the lack of a theoretical model, heterogeneous scale content, and suspect diagnostic criteria, as major theoretical concerns. In addition, they are concerned about scale overlap, lack of cross-validation, the role of response style, and problems with the norms; similar criticisms were made by Duckworth (1991).

THE MILLON CLINICAL MULTIAXIAL INVENTORY (MCMI)

The MCMI was designed as a better and more modern version of the MMPI. In the test manual, Millon (1987) points out some 11 distinguishing features of the MCMI; 6 are of particular saliency here:

1. The MCMI is brief and contains only 175 items, as opposed to the more lengthy MMPI.

2. The measured variables reflect a comprehensive clinical theory, as well as specific theoretical notions about personality and psychopathology, as opposed to the empiricism that underlies the MMPI.

3. The scales are directly related to the DSM-III classification, unlike the MMPI whose diagnostic categories are tied to an older and somewhat outdated system.

4. The MCMI scales were developed by comparing specific diagnostic groups with psychiatric patients, rather than with a normal sample as in the MMPI.

5. Actuarial base-rate data were used to quantify scales, rather than the normalized standard-score transformation used in the MMPI.

6. Three different methods of validation were used: (1) theoretical-substantive, (2) internal-structural, and (3) external-criterion, rather than just one approach as in the MMPI.

Aim of the MCMI. The primary aim of the MCMI is to provide information to the clinician about the client. The MCMI is also presented as a screening device to identify clients who may require more intensive evaluation, and as an instrument to be used for research purposes. The test is not a general personality inventory and should be used only for clinical subjects. The manual explicitly indicates that the computer-generated narrative report is considered a "professional to professional" consultation, and that direct sharing of the report's explicit content with either the patient or relatives of the patient is strongly discouraged.

Development. In general terms, the development of the MCMI followed three basic steps:

1. An examination was made of how the items were related to the theoretical framework held by Millon. This is called *theoretical-substantive* validity by Millon (1987), but we could consider it as content validity and/or construct validity.

2. In the second stage, called *internal-structural*, items were selected that maximized scale homogeneity, that showed satisfactory test-retest reliability, and that showed convergent validity.

3. The items that survived both stages were then assessed with external criteria; Millon (1987) called this *external-criterion* validity, or more simply criterion validity.

Note that the above represent a variety of validation procedures, often used singly in the validation of a test. Now, let's look at these three steps a bit more specifically.

The MCMI was developed by first creating a pool of some 3,500 self-descriptive items, based on theoretically derived definitions of the various syndromes. These items were classified, apparently on the basis of clinical judgment, into 20 clinical scales; 3 scales were later replaced. All the items were phrased with "true" as the keyed response, although Millon felt that the role of acquiescence (answering true) would be minimal. The item pool was then reduced on the basis of rational criteria: Items were retained that were clearly written, simple, relevant to the scale they belonged to, and reflective of content validity. Items were also judged by patients as to clarity and by mental health professionals as to relevance to the theoretical categories. These steps resulted in two provisional forms of 566 items each (interestingly, the number of items was dictated by the size of the available answer sheet!).

In the second step, the forms were administered to a sample of clinical patients, chosen to represent both genders, various ethnic backgrounds, and a representative age range. Some patients filled out one form and some patients filled out both. Item-scale homogeneity was then assessed through computation of internal consistency. The intent here was not to create "pure" and "independent" scales as a factor-analytic approach might yield, as the very theory dictates that some of the scales correlate substantially

with each other. Rather, the intent was to identify items that statistically correlated at least .30
or above with the total score on the scale they
belonged to, as defined by the initial clinical judgment and theoretical stance. In fact, the median
correlation of items that were retained was about
.58. Items that showed extreme endorsement frequencies, less than 15% or greater than 85% were
eliminated (you recall from Chapter 2, that such
items are not very useful from a psychometric
point of view). These and additional screening
steps resulted in a 289-item research form, that
included both true and false keyed responses, and
items that were scored on multiple scales.

In the third stage, two major studies were carried out. In the first study, 200 experienced clinicians administered the experimental form of the
MCMI to as many of their patients as feasible
(a total of 682 patients), and rated each patient,
without recourse to the MCMI responses, on
a series of comprehensive and standard clinical
descriptions that paralleled the 20 MCMI dimensions. An item analysis was then undertaken to
determine if each item correlated the highest
with its corresponding diagnostic category. This
resulted in 150 items being retained, apparently
each item having an average scale overlap of about
4 – that is, each item is scored or belongs to about
4 scales on average, although on some scales the
keyed response is "true" and on some scales the
keyed response for the same item is "false." Note
however, that this overlap of items, which occurs
on such tests as the MMPI, is here not a function
of mere correlation but is dictated by theoretical
expectations.

The results of this first study indicated that
three scales were not particularly useful, and
so the three scales (hypochondriasis, obsession-
compulsion, and sociopathy) were replaced by
three new scales (hypomanic, alcohol abuse,
and drug abuse). This meant that a new set of
items was developed, added to the already available MCMI items, and most of the steps outlined above were repeated. This finally yielded
175 items, with 20 scales ranging in length
from 16 items (Psychotic Delusion) to 47 items
(Hypomanic).

Parallel with DSM. One advantage of the MCMI
is that its scales and nosology are closely allied
with the most current DSM classification. This is

no accident because Millon has played a substantial role in some of the work that resulted in the
DSM.

Millon's theory. Millon's theory about disorders
of the personality is deceptively simple and based
on two dimensions. The first dimension involves
positive or negative reinforcement – that is, gaining satisfaction vs. avoiding psychological discomfort. Patients who experience few satisfactions in life are *detached* types; those who evaluate
satisfaction in terms of the reaction of others are
dependent types. Where the satisfaction is evaluated primarily by one's own values with disregard
for others we have an *independent* type, and those
who experience conflict between their values and
those of others are *ambivalent* personalities. The
second dimension has to do with coping, with
maximizing satisfaction and minimizing discomfort. Some individuals are *active*, and manipulate or arrange events to achieve their goals; others are *passive*, and "cope" by being apathetic,
resigned, or simply passive. The four patterns
of reinforcement and the two patterns of coping result in eight basic personality styles: active
detached, passive detached, active independent,
and so on. These eight styles are of course assessed
by each of the eight basic personality scales of the
MCMI. Table 7.3 illustrates the parallel.

Millon believes that such patterns or styles
are deeply ingrained and that a patient is often
unaware of the presence of such patterns and
their maladaptiveness. If the maladjustment continues, the basic maladaptive personality pattern
becomes more extreme, as reflected by the three
personality disorder scales S, C, and P. Distortions of the basic personality patterns can also
result in clinical-syndrome disorders, but these
are by their very nature transient and depend
upon the amount of stress present. Scales 12 to 20
assess these disorders, with scales 12 through 17
assessing those with moderate severity, and scales
18 through 20 assessing the more severe disorders. Although there is also a parallel between
the eight basic personality types and the clinical-
syndrome disorders, the correspondence is more
complex, and is not a one to one. For example, neurotic depression or what Millon (1987)
calls dysthimia (scale 15) occurs more commonly among avoidant, dependent, and passive
aggressive personalities. Note that such a theory

Table 7–3. Personality Patterns and Parallel MCMI Scales

Type of personality	MCMI scale	Can become:
Passive detached	Schizoid	Schizotypal
Active detached	Avoidant	Schizotypal
Passive dependent	Dependent	Borderline
Active dependent	Histrionic	Borderline
Passive independent	Narcissistic	Paranoid
Active independent	Antisocial	Paranoid
Passive ambivalent	Compulsive	Borderline &/or Paranoid
Active ambivalent	Passive aggressive	Borderline &/or Paranoid

administered individually, but could be used in a group setting. As the manual indicates, the briefness of the test and its easy administration by an office nurse, secretary, or other personnel, makes it a convenient instrument. The instructions are clear and largely self-explanatory.

focuses on psychopathology; it is not a theory of normality.

Description. There are 22 clinical scales in the 1987 version of the MCMI organized into three broad categories to reflect distinctions between persistent personality features, current symptom states, and level of pathologic severity. These three categories parallel the three axis of the DSM-III; hence the "multiaxial" name. One of the distinctions made in DSM-III is between more enduring personality characteristics of the patient (called Axis II) and more acute clinical disorders they manifest (Axis I). In many ways this distinction parallels the chronic vs. acute, morbid vs. premorbid terminology. The MCMI is one of the few instruments that is fully consonant with this distinction. There are also four validity scales. Table 7.4 lists the scales with some defining descriptions.

The MCMI, like the MMPI and the CPI, is an open system and Millon (1987) suggests that investigators may wish to use the MCMI to construct new scales by, for example, item analyses of responses given by a specific diagnostic group vs. responses given by an appropriate control or comparison group. New scales can also be constructed by comparing contrasted groups – for example, patients who respond favorably to a type of psychotherapy vs. those who don't. The MCMI was revised in 1987 (see Millon & Green, 1989, for a very readable introduction to the MCMI-II). Two scales were added, and responses to items were assigned weights of 3, 2, or 1 to optimize diagnostic accuracy and diminish interscale correlations.

Administration. The MCMI consists of 175 true-false statements and requires at least an eighth-grade reading level. The MCMI is usually

Scoring. Hand scoring templates are not available, so the user is required to use the commercially available scoring services. Although this may seem to be driven by economic motives, and probably is, the manual argues that hand scoring so many scales leads to errors of scoring, and even more important, as additional research data are obtained, refinements in scoring and in normative equivalence can be easily introduced in the computer scoring procedure, but not so easily in outdated templates. The manual does include a description of the item composition of each scale, so a template for each scale could be constructed. Computer scoring services are available from the test publisher, including a computer generated narrative report.

Coding system. As with the MMPI there is a profile coding system that uses a shorthand notation to classify a particular profile, by listing the basic personality scales (1–8), the pathological personality disorder scales (S, C, P), the moderate clinical syndrome scales (A, H, N, D, B, T) and the severe clinical syndrome scales (SS, CC, PP), in order of elevation within each of these four sections.

Decision theory. We discussed in Chapter 3 the notions of hits and errors, including false positives and false negatives. The MCMI incorporates this into the scale guidelines, and its manual explicitly gives such information. For example, for scale 1, the schizoid scale, the base rate in the patient sample was .11 (i.e., 11% of the patients were judged to exhibit schizoid symptoms). Eighty-eight percent of patients who were diagnosed as schizoid, in fact, scored on the MCMI above the cutoff line on that scale. Five percent of those scoring above the cutoff line were incorrectly classified; that is, their diagnosis

Table 7–4. Scales on the MCMI

Scale (number of items)	High scorers characterized by:
A. Basic Personality Patterns. These reflect everyday ways of functioning that characterize patients. They are relatively enduring and pervasive traits.	
1. Schizoid (asocial) (35)	Emotional blandness, impoverished thought processes
2. Avoidant (40)	Undercurrent of sadness and tension; socially isolated; feelings of emptiness
3. Dependent (Submissive) (37)	Submissive; avoids social tension
4. Histrionic (Gregarious) (40)	Dramatic but superficial affect; immature and childish
5. Narcissistic (49)	Inflated self-image
6a. Antisocial (45)	Verbally and physically hostile
6b. Aggressive (45)	Aggressive
7. Compulsive (conforming) (38)	Tense and overcontrolled; conforming and rigid
8a. Passive-Aggressive (Negativistic) (41)	Moody and irritable; discontented and ambivalent
8b. Self-defeating personality (40)	Self-sacrificing; masochistic
B. Pathological Personality Disorders. These scales describe patients with chronic severe pathology.	
9. Schizotypal (Schizoid) (44)	Social detachment and behavioral eccentricity
10. Borderline (Cycloid) (62)	Extreme cyclical mood ranging from depression to excitement
11. Paranoid (44)	Extreme suspicion and mistrust
C. Clinical symptom syndromes. These nine scales represent symptom disorders, usually of briefer duration than the personality disorders, and often are precipitated by external events.	
12. Anxiety (25)	Apprehensive; tense; complains of many physical discomforts
13. Somatoform (31)	Expresses psychological difficulties through physical channels (often nonspecific pains and feelings of ill health)
14. Bipolar-manic (37)	Elevated but unstable moods; overactive, distractable, and restless
15. Dysthymia (36)	Great feelings of discouragement, apathy, and futility
16. Alcohol dependence (46)	Alcoholic
17. Drug dependence (58)	Drug abuse
18. Thought disorder (33)	Schizophrenic; confused and disorganized
19. Major depression (24)	Severely depressed; expresses dread of the future
20. Delusional disorder (23)	Paranoid, belligerent, and irrational
D. Validity scales	
21. Weight factor (or disclosure level). This is not really a scale as such, but is a score adjustment applied under specific circumstances. It is designed to moderate the effects of either excessive defensiveness or excessive emotional complaining (i.e., fake good and fake bad response sets).	
22. Validity index. Designed to identify patients who did not cooperate or did not answer relevantly because they were too disturbed. The scale is composed of 4 items that are endorsed by fewer than 1 out of 100 clinical patients. Despite its brevity, the scale seems to work as intended.	
23. Desirability gauge. The degree to which the respondent places him/herself in a favorable light (i.e., fake good).	
24. The Debasement measure. The degree to which the person depreciates or devalues themselves (i.e., fake bad).	

was not schizoid and, therefore, they would be classified as false positives. The overall hit rate for this scale is 94%.

Base-rate scores. The MCMI uses a rather unique scoring procedure. On most tests, the raw score on a scale is changed into a *T* score or some other type of *standard score*. This procedure assumes that the underlying dimension is normally distributed. Millon (1987) argues that this is not the case when a set of scales is designed to represent personality types or clinical syndromes because they are not normally distributed in patient populations. The aim of scales such as those on the MCMI is to identify the degree to which a patient is or is not a member of a diagnostic entity. And so Millon conducted two studies of more than 970 patients in which clinicians were asked to diagnose these patients along the lines of the MCMI scales. These studies provided the basic base-rate data. Millon was able to determine what percentage of the patients were judged to display specific diagnostic features, regardless of their actual diagnosis, and to determine the relative frequency of each diagnostic entity. For example, 27% of the patient sample was judged to exhibit some histrionic personality features, but only 15% were assigned this as their major diagnosis. Based on these percentages then, *base-rate scores* were established for each of the clinical scales, including an analysis of false positives. Despite the statistical and logical sophistication of this method, the final step of establishing base-rate scores was very much a clinical-intuitive one, where a base-rate score of 85 was arbitrarily assigned as the cutoff line that separated those with a specific diagnosis and those without that diagnosis, a base-rate score of 60 was arbitrarily selected as the median, and a base rate of 35 was arbitrarily selected as the "normal" median. If the above discussion seems somewhat vague, it is because the test manual is rather vague and does not yield the specific details needed.

The idea of using base rates as a basis of scoring is not a new idea; in fact, one of the authors of the MMPI has argued for, but not implemented, such an approach (Meehl & Rosen, 1955). One problem with such base rates is that they are a function of the original sample studied. A clinician working with clients in a drug-abuse residential setting would experience rather different base rates in that population than a clinician working in an outpatient setting associated with a community mental-health clinic, yet both would receive test results on their clients reflective of the same base rate as found in a large research sample.

Reliability. The manual presents test-retest reliability for two samples: 59 patients tested twice with an average interval of 1 week, and 86 patients tested twice with an average interval of about 5 weeks. For the first sample, the correlation coefficients range from .78 to .91 with most of the values in the .80 to .85 range. For the second sample, the coefficients range from .61 to .85, with a median of about .77. Because all the patients were involved in psychotherapy programs, we would expect the 5-week reliabilities to be lower. We would also expect, and the results support this, the personality pattern scales to be highest in reliability, followed by the pathological personality scales, and least reliable, the clinical syndromes (because most changeable and transient).

Internal consistency reliability (KR 20) was also assessed in two samples totaling almost 1,000 patients. These coefficients range from .58 to .95, with a median of .88; only one scale, the 16 item PP scale, which is the shortest scale, has a KR reliability of less than .70.

Validity. A number of authors, such as Loevinger (1957) and Jackson (1970) have argued that validation should not simply occur at the end of a test's development, but should be incorporated in all phases of test construction. That seems to be clearly the case with the MCMI; as we have seen above, its development incorporated three distinct validational stages. We can also ask, in a more traditional manner, about the validity of the resulting scales. The MCMI manual presents correlations of the MCMI scales with scales from other multivariate instruments, namely the MMPI, the Psychological Screening Inventory, and the SCL-90. It is not easy to summarize such a large matrix of correlations, but in general the pattern of correlations for each MCMI scale supports their general validity, and the specific significant correlations seem to be in line with both theoretical expectations and empirically observed clinical syndromes. (For a comparison of the MCMI-II and the MMPI see McCann, 1991).

Norms. Norms on the MCMI are based on a sample of 297 normal subjects ranging in age from 18 to 62, and 1,591 clinical patients ranging in age from 18 to 66. These patients came from more than 100 hospitals and outpatient centers, as well as from private psychotherapists in the United States and Great Britain. These samples are basically samples of convenience, chosen for their availability, but also reflective of diversity in age, gender, educational level, and socioeconomic status.

By 1981, MCMI protocols were available on more than 43,000 patients and these data were used to refine the scoring/normative procedure. For the MCMI-II, a sample of 519 clinicians administered the MCMI and the MCMI-II to a total of 825 patients diagnosed using the DSM-III-R criteria. Another 93 clinicians administered the MCMI-II to 467 diagnosed patients.

Scale intercorrelations. As we have seen, scales on the MCMI do correlate with each other because there is item overlap, and because the theoretical rationale for the 20 dimensions dictates such intercorrelations. Empirically, what is the magnitude of such relationships? The Manual presents data on a sample of 978 patients. Correlating 20 scales with each other yields some 190 coefficients (20×19 divided by 2 to eliminate repetition). These coefficients range from a high of .96 (between scales A and C) to a low of -.01 (between scales B and PP), with many of the scales exhibiting substantial correlations.

A factor analyst looking at these results would throw his or her hands up in despair, but Millon argues for the existence of such correlated but separate scales on the basis of their clinical utility. As I tell my classes, if we were to measure shirt sleeves we would conclude from a factor analytic point of view that only one such measurement is needed, but most likely we would still continue to manufacture shirts with two sleeves rather than just one.

Factor analysis. The MCMI manual reports the results of two factor analyses, one done on a general psychiatric sample ($N = 744$), and one on a substance abuse sample ($N = 206$). For the general psychiatric sample, the factor analysis suggested four factors, with the first three accounting for 85% of the variance. These factors are rather complex. For example, 13 of the 20 scales load significantly on the first factor which is described as "depressive and labile emotionality expressed in affective moodiness and neurotic complaints" (Millon, 1987). In fact, the first three factors parallel a classical distinction found in the abnormal psychology literature of affective disorders, paranoid disorders, and schizophrenic disorders.

The results of the factor analysis of the substance-abuse patients also yielded a four factor solution, but the pattern here is somewhat different. The first factor seems to be more of a general psychopathology factor, the second factor a social acting-out and aggressive dimension related to drug abuse, and a third dimension (factor 4) reflects alcohol abuse and compulsive behavior. These results can be viewed from two different perspectives: Those who seek factorial invariance would perceive such differing results in a negative light, as reflective of instability in the test. Those who seek "clinical" meaning would see such results in a positive light, as they correspond to what would be predicted on the basis of clinical theory and experience.

Family of inventories. The MCMI is one of a family of inventories developed by Millon. These include the Millon Behavioral Health Inventory (Millon, Green, & Meagher, 1982b), which is for use with medical populations such as cancer patients or rehabilitation clients; and the Millon Adolescent Personality Inventory (Millon, Greene, and Meagher, 1982a) for use with junior and senior high-school students.

Criticisms. The MCMI has not supplanted the MMPI and in the words of one reviewer "this carefully constructed test never received the attention it merited" (A. K. Hess, 1985, p. 984). In fact, A. K. Hess (1985) finds relatively little to criticize except that the MCMI's focus on psychopathology may lead the practitioner to overemphasize the pathological aspects of the client and not perceive the positive strengths a client may have. Other reviewers have not been so kind. Butcher and Owen (1978) point out that the use of base rates from Millon's normative sample will optimize accurate diagnosis only when the local base rates are identical. J. S. Wiggins (1982) criticized the MCMI for the high degree of item overlap. Widiger and Kelso (1983) indicated that such built-in interdependence does not allow one to use the MCMI to determine the relationship between disparate disorders. This is like asking "What's the relationship between X and Y?" If one uses a scale that correlates with both X and Y to measure X, the obtained results will be different than if one had used a scale that did not correlate with Y. Widiger, Williams, Spitzer, et al., (1985; 1986) questioned whether the MCMI is a valid measure of personality disorders as listed in the DSM, arguing that

Millon's description of specific personality styles was divergent from the DSM criteria. In fact, Widiger and Sanderson (1987) found poor convergent validity for those MCMI scales that were defined differently from the DSM and poor discriminant validity because of item overlap. (For a review of standardized personality disorder measures such as the MCMI see J. H. Reich, 1987; 1989; Widiger & Frances, 1987). Nevertheless, the MCMI has become one of the most widely used clinical assessment instruments, has generated a considerable body of research literature, has been revised, and used in cross-cultural studies (R. I. Craig, 1999).

OTHER MEASURES

The Wisconsin Personality Disorders Inventory (WISPI)

The DSM has served as a guideline for a rather large number of tests, in addition to the MCMI, many focusing on specific syndromes, and some more broadly based. An example of the latter is the WISPI (M. H. Klein, et al., 1993), a relative newcomer, chosen here not because of its exceptional promise, but more to illustrate the difficulties of developing a well functioning clinical instrument.

Development. Again, the first step was to develop an item pool that reflected DSM criteria and, in this case, reflected a particular theory of interpersonal behavior (L. S. Benjamin, 1993). One interesting approach used here was that the items were worded from the perspective of the respondent relating to others. For example, rather than having an item that says, "People say I am cold and aloof," the authors wrote, "When I have feelings I keep them to myself because others might use them against me." A total of 360 items were generated that covered the 11 personality-disorder categories, social desirability, and some other relevant dimensions. The authors do not indicate the procedures used to eliminate items, and indeed the impression one gets is that all items were retained. Respondents are asked to answer each item according to their "usual self" over the past 5 years or more, and use a 10-point scale (where 1 is never or not at all true, and 10 is always or extremely true).

Content validity. The items were given to 4 clinicians to sort into the 11 personality disorder categories. A variety of analyses were then carried out basically showing clinicians' agreement. Where there was disagreement in the sorting of items, the disagreement was taken as reflecting the fact that several of the personality disorders overlap in symptomatology.

Normative sample. The major normative sample is composed of 1,230 subjects, that includes 368 patients and 862 normals who were recruited from the general population by newspaper advertisements, classroom visits, solicitation of visitors to the University Hospital and so on. Although the authors give some standard demographic information such as gender, education, and age, there is little other information given; for example, where did the patients come from (hospitalized? outpatients? community clinic? university hospital?), and what is their diagnosis? Presumably, patients are in therapy, but what kind and at what stage is not given. Clearly these subjects are samples of convenience; the average age of the normal subjects is given as 24.4 which suggests a heavy percentage of captive college-aged students.

Reliability. Interitem consistency was calculated for each of the 11 scales; alpha coefficients range from a low of .84 to a high of .96, with an average of .90, in the normative sample. Test-retest coefficients for a sample of 40 patients and 40 nonpatients who were administered the WISPI twice within 2 weeks ranged from a low of .71 to a high of .94, with an average of .88. Two forms of the WISPI were used, one a paper-and-pencil form, the other a computer-interview version, with administration counterbalanced. The results suggest that the two forms are equally reliable.

Scale intercorrelations. The scales correlate substantially with each other from a high of .82 (between the Histrionic and the Narcissistic Scales), to a low of .29 (between the Histrionic and the Schizoid Scales); the average intercorrelation is .62. This is a serious problem and the authors recognize this; they suggest various methods by which such intercorrelations can be lowered.

Concurrent validity. Do the WISPI scales discriminate between patients and nonpatients? You recall that this is the question of primary validity (see Chapter 3). Eight of the 11 scales do, but the Histrionic, Narcissistic, and Antisocial Scales do not. Here we must bring up the question of statistical vs. clinical significance. Take for example the Paranoid Scale, for which the authors report a mean of 3.5 for patients ($n = 368$) and a mean of 3.08 for nonpatients ($n = 852$). Given the large size of the samples, this rather small difference of .42 (which is a third of the SD) is statistically significant. But the authors do not provide an analysis of hits and errors that would give us information about the practical or clinical utility of this scale. If I use this scale as a clinician to make diagnostic decisions about patients, how often will I be making errors?

How well do the WISPI scales correlate with their counterparts on the MCMI? The average correlation is reported to be .39, and they range from −.26 (for the Compulsive Scale) to .68 (for the Dependent Scale). Note that, presumably, these two sets of scales are measuring the same dimensions and therefore ought to correlate substantially. We should not necessarily conclude at this point that the MCMI scales are "better," although it is tempting to do so. What would be needed is a comparison of the relative diagnostic efficiency of the two sets of scales against some nontest criterion. The WISPI is too new to evaluate properly, and only time will tell whether the test will languish in the dusty journal pages in the library or whether it will become a useful instrument for clinicians.

The Schizotypal Personality Questionnaire (SPQ)

In addition to the multivariate instruments such as the MMPI and the MCMI, there are specific scales that have been developed to assess particular conditions. One of the types of personality disorders listed in the DSM-III-R is that of schizotypal personality disorder. Individuals with this disorder exhibit a "pervasive pattern of peculiarities of ideation, appearance, and behavior," and show difficulties in interpersonal relations not quite as extreme as those shown by schizophrenics. There are nine diagnostic criteria given for this disorder, which include extreme anxiety in

social situations, odd beliefs, eccentric behavior, and odd speech. A number of scales have been developed to assess this personality disorder, although most seem to focus on just a few of the nine criteria. An example of a relatively new and somewhat unknown scale that does cover all nine criteria is the SPQ (Raine, 1991). The SPQ is modeled on the DSM-III-R criteria, and thus the nine criteria served both to provide a theoretical framework, a blueprint by which to generate items, and a source for items themselves. Raine (1991) first created a pool of 110 items, some taken from other scales, some paraphrasing the DSM criteria, and some created new. These items, using a true-false response, were administered to a sample of 302 undergraduate student volunteers, with the sample divided randomly into two subsamples for purposes of cross-validation. Subscores were obtained for each of the nine criterion areas and item-total correlations computed. Items were deleted if fewer than 10% endorsed them or if the item-total correlation was less than .15.

A final scale of 74 items, taking 5 to 10 minutes to complete, was thus developed. Table 7.5 lists the nine subscales or areas and an illustrative example.

In addition to the pool of items, the subjects completed four other scales, two that were measures of schizotypal aspects and two that were not. This is of course a classical research design to obtain convergent and discriminant validity data (see Chapter 3). In addition, students who scored in the lowest and highest 10% of the distribution of scores were invited to be interviewed by doctoral students; the interviewers then independently assessed each of the 25 interviewees on the diagnosis of schizotypal disorder and on each of the nine dimensions.

Reliability. Coefficient alpha for the total score was computed as .90 and .91 in the two subsamples. Coefficient alpha for the nine subscales ranged from .71 to .78 for the final version. Note here somewhat of a paradox. The alpha values for each of the subscales are somewhat low, suggesting that each subscale is not fully homogeneous. When the nine subscales are united, we of course have both a longer test and a more heterogeneous test; one increases reliability, the other decreases internal consistency. The result, in this

Table 7–5. The Schizotypal Personality Questionnaire	
Subscale	Illustrative item
1. Ideas of reference	People are talking about me.
2. Excessive social anxiety	I get nervous in a group.
3. Odd beliefs or magical thinking	I have had experiences with the supernatural.
4. Unusual perceptual experiences	When I look in the mirror my face changes.
5. Odd or eccentric behavior	People think I am strange.
6. No close friends	I don't have close friends.
7. Odd speech	I use words in unusual ways.
8. Constricted affect	I keep my feelings to myself.
9. Suspiciousness	I am often on my guard.

case, was that internal consistency was increased substantially.

For the 25 students who were interviewed, test-retest reliability with a 2-month interval was .82. Note that this is an inflated value because it is based on a sample composed of either high or low scores, and none in between. The greatest degree of intragroup variability occurs in the mid range rather than at the extremes.

Validity. Of the 11 subjects who were high scorers, 6 were in fact diagnosed as schizotypal; of the 14 low scoring subjects, none were so diagnosed. When the SPQ subscores were compared with the ratings given by the interviewers, all correlations were statistically significant, ranging from a low of .55 to a high of .80. Unfortunately, only the coefficients for the same named dimensions are given. For example, the Ideas of Reference Scale scores correlate .80 with the ratings of Ideas of Reference, but we don't know how they correlate with the other eight dimensions. For the entire student sample, convergent validity coefficients were .59 and .81, while discriminant validity coefficients were .19 and .37.

The State-Trait Anxiety Inventory (STAI)

Introduction. Originally, the STAI was developed as a research instrument to assess anxiety in normal adults, but soon found usefulness with high-school students and with psychiatric and medical patients. The author of the test (Spielberger, 1966) distinguished between two kinds of anxiety. *State* anxiety is seen as a transitory emotional state characterized by subjective feelings of tension and apprehension, coupled with heightened autonomic nervous system activity. *Trait* anxiety refers to relatively stable individual differences in anxiety proneness; i.e., the tendency to respond to situations perceived as threatening with elevations in state anxiety intensity. People suffering from anxiety often appear nervous and apprehensive and typically complain of heart palpitations and of feeling faint; it is not unusual for them to sweat profusely and show rapid breathing.

Development. The STAI was developed beginning in 1964 through a series of steps and procedures somewhat too detailed to summarize here (see the STAI manual for details; Spielberger, Gorsuch, Lushene, et al., 1983). Initially, the intent was to develop a single scale that would measure both state and trait anxiety, but because of linguistic and other problems, it was eventually decided to develop different sets of items to measure state and trait anxiety.

Basically, three widely used anxiety scales were administered to a sample of college students. Items that showed correlations of at least .25 with each of the three anxiety scale total scores were selected and rewritten so that the item could be used with both state and trait instructions. Items were then administered to another sample of college students, and items that correlated at least .35 with total scores (under both sets of instructions designed to elicit state and trait responses) were retained. Finally, a number of steps and studies were undertaken that resulted in the present form of two sets of items that functioned differently under different types of instructional sets (e.g., "Make believe you are about to take an important final examination").

Description. The STAI consists of 40 statements, divided into 2 sections of 20 items each. For the *state* portion, the subject is asked to describe how he or she feels at the moment, using the four response options of not at all, somewhat, moderately so, and very much so. Typical state items are: "I feel calm" and "I feel anxious." For the *trait* portion, the subject is asked to describe how he or she generally feels, using the four response options of almost never, sometimes, often, and almost always. Typical trait items are: "I am happy" and "I lack self-confidence." There are five items that occur on both scales, three of them with identical wording, and two slightly different.

Administration. The STAI can be administered individually or in a group, has no time limit, requires a fifth to sixth grade reading ability, and can be completed typically in less than 15 minutes. The two sets of items with their instructions are printed on opposite sides of a one-page test form. The actual questionnaire that the subject responds to is titled, "Self-evaluation Questionnaire" and the term anxiety is not to be used. The state scale is answered first, followed by the trait scale.

Scoring. Scoring is typically by hand using templates, but one can use a machine-scored answer sheet. For the state scale, 10 of the items are scored on a 1 to 4 scale, depending upon the subject's response, and for 10 of the items the scoring is reversed, so that higher scores always reflect greater anxiety. For the trait scale, only seven of the items are reversed in scoring.

Reliability. The test manual indicates that internal consistency (alpha) coefficients range from .83 to .92 with various samples, and there seems to be no significant difference in reliability between the state and trait components. Test-retest coefficients are also given for various samples, with time periods of 1 hour, 20 days, and 104 days. For the state scale the coefficients range from .16 to .54, with a median of about .32. For the trait scale coefficients range from .73 to .86, with a median of about .76. For the state scale, the results are inadequate *but* the subjects in the 1-hour test-retest condition were exposed to different treatments, such as relaxation training, designed to change their state scores, and the very instructions reflect unique situational factors that exist at the time of testing. Thus for the state scale, a more appropriate judgment of its reliability is given by the internal consistency coefficients given above.

Validity. In large part, the construct validity of the STAI was assured by the procedures used in developing the measure. As we saw with the MCMI, this is as it should be because validity should not be an afterthought but should be incorporated into the very genesis of a scale.

Concurrent validity is presented by correlations of the STAI trait score with three other measures of anxiety. These correlations range from a low of .41 to a high of .85, in general supporting the validity of the STAI. Note here somewhat of a "catch-22" situation. If a new scale of anxiety were to correlate in the mid to high .90s with an old scale, then clearly the new scale would simply be an alternate form of the old scale, and thus of limited usefulness.

Other validity studies are also reported in the STAI manual. In one study, college students were administered the STAI state scale under standard instructions (how do you feel at the moment), and then readministered the scale according to "How would you feel just prior a final examination in an important course." For both males and females total scores were considerably higher in the exam condition than in the standard condition, and only one of the 20 items failed to show a statistically significant response shift.

In another study, the STAI and the Personality Research Form (discussed in Chapter 4) were administered to a sample of college students seeking help at their Counseling Center for either vocational-educational problems or for emotional problems. The mean scores on the STAI were higher for those students with emotional problems. In addition, many of the correlations between STAI scores and PRF variables were significant, with the highest correlation of .51 between STAI trait scores and the Impulsivity Scale of the PRF for the clients with emotional problems. Interestingly, the STAI and the EPPS (another personality inventory discussed in Chapter 4) do not seem to correlate with each other. STAI scores are also significantly correlated with MMPI scores, some quite substantially – for example, an *r* of .81 between the STAI trait score and the MMPI Pt (Psychasthenia) score, and .57 between both the STAI trait and state scores and the MMPI depression scale.

In yet another study reported in the test manual, scores on the STAI trait scale were significantly correlated with scores on the Mooney Problem Checklist, which, as its title indicates, is a list of problems that individuals can experience in a wide variety of areas. Spielberger, Gorsuch,

Table 7–6. Symptom-Attitude Categories of the BDI		
1. Mood	8. Self-accusations	15. Work inhibitions
2. Pessimism	9. Suicidal wishes	16. Sleep disturbance
3. Sense of failure	10. Crying speels	17. Fatigability
4. Dissatisfaction	11. Irritability	18. Loss of appetite
5. Guilt	12. Social withdrawal	19. Weight loss
6. Sense of punishment	13. Indecisiveness	20. Somatic preoccupation
7. Self-dislike	14. Distortion of body image	21. Loss of libido

and Lushene (1970) argue that if students have difficulties in academic work, it is important to determine the extent to which emotional problems contribute to those difficulties. For a sample of more 1,200 college freshmen, their STAI scores did *not* correlate significantly with either high-school GPA, scores on an achievement test, or scores on the SAT. Thus, for college students, STAI scores and academic achievement seem to be unrelated.

Norms. Normative data are given in the test manual for high-school and college samples, divided as to gender, and for psychiatric, medical, and prison samples. Raw scores can be located in the appropriate table, and both T scores and percentile ranks can be obtained directly.

Do state and trait correlate? The two scales do correlate, but the size of the correlation depends upon the specific situation under which the state scale is administered. Under standard conditions, that is those prevailing for captive college students who participate in these studies, the correlations range from .44 to .55 for females, and .51 to .67 for males. This gender difference, which seems to be consistent, suggests that males who are high on trait anxiety are generally more prone to experience anxiety states than are their female counterparts. Smaller correlations are obtained when the state scale is administered under conditions that pose some psychological threat such as potential loss of self-esteem or evaluation of personal adequacy, as in an exam. Even smaller correlations are obtained when the threat is a physical one, such as electric shock (Hodges & Spielberger, 1966).

The Beck Depression Inventory (BDI)

Introduction. Depression is often misdiagnosed or not recognized as such, yet it is a fairly preva-

lent condition affecting one of eight Americans. There is thus a practical need for a good measure of depression, and many such measures have been developed. The BDI is probably the most commonly used of these measures; it has been used in hundreds of studies (Steer, Beck, & Garrison, 1986), and it is the most frequently cited self-report measure of depression (Ponterotto, Pace, & Kavan, 1989). That this is so is somewhat surprising because this is one of the few popular instruments developed by fiat (see Chapter 4) and without regard to theoretical notions about the etiology of depression (A. T. Beck & Beamesderfer, 1974).

Description. The BDI consists of 21 multiple-choice items, each listing a particular manifestation of depression, followed by 4 self-evaluative statements listed in order of severity. For example, with regard to pessimism, the four statements and their scoring weights might be similar to: (0) I am not pessimistic, (1) I am pessimistic about the future, (2) I am pretty hopeless about the future, and (3) I am very hopeless about the future. Table 7.6 lists the 21 items, also called symptom-attitude categories.

These items were the result of the clinical insight of Beck and his colleagues, based upon years of observation and therapeutic work with depressed patients, as well as a thorough awareness of the psychiatric literature. The format of the BDI assumes that the number of symptoms increases with the severity of depression, that the more depressed an individual is, the more intense a particular symptom, and that the four choices for each item parallel a progression from nondepressed to mildly depressed, moderately depressed, and severely depressed. The items represent cognitive symptoms of depression, rather than affective (emotional) or somatic (physical) symptoms.

The BDI was intended for use with clinical populations such as psychiatric patients, and was originally designed to estimate the severity of depression and not necessarily to diagnose individuals as depressed or not. It rapidly became quite popular for both clinical and nonclinical samples, such as college students, to assess both the presence and degree of depression. In fact, there are probably three major ways in which the BDI is used: (1) to assess the intensity of depression in psychiatric patients, (2) to monitor how effective specific therapeutic regimens are, and (3) to assess depression in normal populations.

The BDI was originally developed in 1961 and was "revised" in 1978 (A. T. Beck, 1978). The number of items remained the same in both forms, but for the revision the number of alternatives for each item was standardized to four "Likert" type responses. A. T. Beck and Steer (1984) compared the 1961 and 1978 versions in two large samples of psychiatric patients and found that both forms had high degrees of internal consistency (alphas of .88 and .86) and similar patterns of item vs. total score correlations. Lightfoot and Oliver (1985) similarly compared the two forms in a sample of University students, and found the forms to be relatively comparable, with a correlation of .94 for the total scores on the two forms.

Administration. Initially, the BDI was administered by a trained interviewer who read aloud each item to the patient, while the patient followed on a copy of the scale. In effect then, the BDI began life as a structured interview. Currently, most BDIs are administered by having the patient read the items and circle the most representative option in each item; it is thus typically used as a self-report instrument, applicable to groups. In its original form, the BDI instructed the patient to respond in terms of how they were feeling "at the present time," even though a number of items required by their very nature a comparison of recent functioning vs. usual functioning, i.e., over an extended period of time. The most recent revision asks the respondent to consider how they were feeling over the past few weeks. Incidentally, one advantage of such self-rating procedures is that they involve the patient in the assessment and may thus be therapeutic.

Scoring. The BDI is typically hand scored, and the raw scores are used directly without any transformation. Total raw scores can range from 0 to 63, and are used to categorize four levels of depression: none to minimal (scores of 0 to 9); mild to moderate (scores of 10–18); moderate to severe (19–29); and severe (30–63). Note that while there is a fairly wide range of potential scores, individuals who are not depressed should score below 10. There is thus a *floor effect* (as opposed to a ceiling effect when the range of high scores is limited), which means that the BDI ought not to be used with normal subjects, and that low scores may be indicative of the absence of depression but not of the presence of happiness (for a scale that attempts to measure both depression and happiness see McGreal & Joseph, 1993).

Reliability. A. T. Beck (1978) reports the results of an item analysis based on 606 protocols, showing significant positive correlations between each item and the total score. A corrected split-half reliability of .93 was also reported for a sample of 97 subjects.

Test-retest reliability presents some problems for instruments such as the BDI. Too brief an interval would reflect memory rather than stability per se, and too long an interval would mirror possible changes that partly might be the result of therapeutic interventions, "remission," or more individual factors. A. T. Beck and Beamesderfer (1974) do report a test-retest study of 38 patients, retested with a mean interval of 4 weeks. At both test and retest an assessment of depth of depression was independently made by a psychiatrist. The authors report that the changes in BDI scores paralleled the changes in the clinical ratings of depression, although no data are advanced for this assertion. Oliver and Burkham (1979) reported a test-retest r of .79 for a sample of college students retested over a 3-week interval. In general, test-retest reliability is higher in nonpsychiatric samples than in psychiatric samples, as one might expect, because psychiatric patients would be expected to show change on retesting due to intervening experiences, whether therapeutic or not; such experiences would not affect all patients equally.

Internal consistency reliability seems quite adequate; typical results are those of Lightfoot and Oliver (1985) who reported a coefficient alpha of .87 for a sample of college students. In their review of 25 years of research on the BDI, A. T. Beck, Steer, and Garbin (1988) found that the internal consistency of the BDI ranged from .73 to .95, with a mean alpha value of .81 for nonpsychiatric samples and .86 for psychiatric samples.

Yet, it should be pointed out that a large majority of studies on the BDI do not report any information on reliability. Yin and Fan (2000) carried out a meta-analysis of BDI studies, and found that only 7.5% reported meaningful reliability information. They found that test-retest reliability is lower than internal consistency reliability, and that reliability estimates obtained from studies of substance addicts were lower than those from studies of normal subjects.

Validity. There is a voluminous body of literature on the BDI, most supportive of its validity. In the area of concurrent validity, most studies show correlations in the .55 to .65 and above range of BDI scores with clinicians' ratings of depression (e.g., Metcalfe & Goldman, 1965) and correlations in the .70s with other standardized measures of depression, such as the MMPI D scale (e.g., Nussbaum, Wittig, Hanlon, et al., 1963) and the Zung Self-rating Depression Scale, another well-known measure of depression (Zung, 1965).

With regard to content validity, recent versions of the DSM list nine diagnostic criteria for depression; the BDI covers six of these (P. W. Moran & Lambert, 1983).

A. T. Beck and Beamesderfer (1974) discuss the construct validity of the BDI by relating a series of studies designed to assess such hypotheses as "Are depressed patients more likely to have a negative self-image and more likely to have dreams characterized by masochistic content?" The results of these studies supported such hypotheses and the construct validity of the BDI.

The BDI has been used to differentiate psychiatric patients from normal individuals in both adult and adolescent populations and to differentiate levels of severity of depression. The BDI seems to be sensitive to changes in depression that result from medications and other therapeutic interventions. Scores on the BDI correlate with a variety of conditions, such as suicidal behavior, that might be hypothesized to be related.

Secondary validity. In our discussion of secondary validity (see Chapter 3), we saw that Gough (1965) suggested relating scores on a measure to "important" variables. A. T. Beck and Beamesderfer (1974) undertook just such an analysis and found a small but significant relationship of BDI scores with gender (females scoring higher), none with race, none with age (contrary to the popular belief that older patients are more likely to be depressed), a small but significant relationship with educational attainment (patients with lesser education tended to score higher), a "slight" (but presumably insignificant) correlation with vocabulary scores, and a significant but explainable negative correlation with social desirability, in that depressed patients do select "unfavorable" alternatives.

Cross-cultural studies. The BDI has been used in a substantial number of cross-cultural studies in a variety of countries, ranging from the former Czechoslovakia and Switzerland (A. T. Beck & Beamesderfer, 1974) to Iran (Tashakkori, Barefoot, & Mehryar, 1989) and Brazil (Gorenstein, Andrade, Filho, et al., 1999), and has been translated into a wide range of languages including Chinese, German, Korean, and Turkish (see Naughton & Wiklund, 1993, for a brief review of these studies). The results are supportive of its reliability and validity across various cultures, with some minor exceptions.

Short form. A. T. Beck and Beamesderfer (1974) discuss a brief form of the BDI composed of 13 items, for use by general practitioners and by researchers for the rapid screening of potentially depressed patients. The items were chosen on the basis of their correlation with the total scale and with clinicians' ratings of depression (A. T. Beck, Rial, & Rickels, 1974). The 13-item total score correlated .96 with the total on the standard form. Internal consistency of the short form has ranged from about .70 to .90 (e.g., Gould, 1982; Leahy, 1992; Vredenburg, Krames, & Flett, 1985).

Factor analysis. A variety of investigators have assessed BDI data using factor-analytic techniques, with results reflecting a variety of obtained factors. A. T. Beck and Beamesderfer (1974) report a number of these studies that range from 1 general factor of depression, to 3, 4, and even 10 additional factors. Beck and Beamesderfer (1974) themselves obtained three factors that they labeled as "negative view," "physiological," and "physical withdrawal." Weckowicz, Muir, and Cropley (1967) also found three factors labeled as "guilty depression," "retarded depression," and "somatic disturbance," and corresponding to those factors found by other investigators in more general investigations of depression. Recent studies (e.g., Byrne & Baron, 1994) also have reported three factors but with some cross-cultural differences, at least within French Canadian vs. English Canadian adolescents. Endler, Rutherford, and Denisoff (1999) however, reported two factors for a sample of Canadian students – a cognitive-affective dimension and a physiological dimension. Whether the BDI measures depression in a unidimensional global manner or whether the scale is composed of several replicable factors remains an open issue (e.g., Welch, Hall, & Walkey, 1990).

How high is high? As mentioned earlier psychological measurement is usually relative, and raw scores are of themselves meaningless. Given the possible range of scores on the BDI from 0 to 63, what score indicates the presence of depression? There is no such specific score, since the meaning and usefulness of a specific or cutoff score depends upon a number of aspects. Here again the notions of decision theory (discussed in Chapter 3) are relevant. The usefulness of any particular cutoff score is a function of the relative frequencies of false positives and false negatives. For example, if we wish to minimize false positives (high scorers who are not depressed), and we are not concerned about false negatives (individuals who really are depressed but are not recognized as such by our test), then a "high" cutoff score of at least 21 should be used.

If we are using the BDI as a screening inventory to detect depression among psychiatric patients, A. T. Beck and Beamesderfer (1974) recommend 13. For screening depression among medical patients, a score of 10 is recommended (Schwab, Bialow, Brown, et al., 1967). A score of 10 has also been used in studies of college students (e.g., Hammen, 1980; M. Zimmerman, 1986). Incidentally, M. Zimmerman (1986) found that out of 132 introductory psychology students, 43

scored 10 or more on the initial BDI, but 22 of the 43 scored below 10 upon retesting a week later.

Why use the BDI? Why use an instrument like the BDI, or for that matter any test, rather than depend upon the professional judgment of a clinician? If we think back to the notion of standardization discussed in Chapter 3, then the answer will be obvious. Not all clinicians are highly experienced, and even those who are may in fact be inconsistent in their application of diagnostic criteria. The criteria themselves may be inadequately specified (Ward, Beck, Mendelson, et al., 1962). An instrument such as the BDI is well standardized, economical to use, not dependent on the interviewer's theoretical orientation or clinical sagacity, and yields a score that can be used to assess changes due to medications, psychotherapy, or other treatments.

On the other hand, comparisons between self-ratings and expert ratings often do not produce substantial correlations, as might be expected. For example, Kearns et al. (1982) compared five self-assessment measures of depression, including the BDI, with two interview-based measures. The authors concluded that the self-rating measures showed poor performance and suggested abandoning their use.

Criticisms. No instrument escapes criticism, and the BDI is no exception. Gotlib (1984) has argued that in college students the BDI is a measure of "general psychopathology" rather than just depression (cf. Hill, Kemp-Wheeler, & Jones, 1986). Other authors have pointed out that in its early version, the BDI was administered in a clinical context where both interviewer and patient agreed upon the aim of the interview, i.e., to obtain some factual information about the client's emotional problems. Thus any motivation to dissimulate would have been minimal. Subsequently, however, the BDI has been administered in group settings where the subjects, be they psychiatric patients or college students, may well have different motivational attitudes and may be more likely to distort their responses.

The BDI has also been criticized for its inability to differentiate moderate from severe levels of depression (Bech, et al., 1975).

A somewhat different concern reflects the notion that responses may be in part a function of the structural aspects of the test rather than the content of the items. Dahlstrom, Brooks, and Peterson (1990) administered three forms of the BDI to a sample of college women: the standard form, a backwards form where the response options were presented in reverse order from most pathological to least, and a random form where the response options were scrambled. The random-order BDI resulted in a significantly higher mean depression score (11.01) than for either the standard form (7.93) or the backwards form (6.01). The authors concluded that the standard BDI response format is highly susceptible to a "position response" set, where either the first or the last option tends to be endorsed, rather than careful consideration being given to all four choices. They therefore recommended the use of the random form.

Content validity seems to be an issue also. The BDI items emphasize the subjective experience of depression, and it is estimated that only 29% of the BDI score reflects a physiological factor; other scales of depression seem to have a larger behavioral and somatic component and may therefore be more sensitive to changes in depression as a function of treatment (Lambert, Hatch, Kingston, et al., 1986).

Second edition. A second edition of the BDI was published in 1996 (A. T. Beck, Steer, & Brown, 1996) in part to increase its content validity – i.e., a criticism of the first edition was that the items did not fully cover the DSM diagnostic criteria for depression. A study of the BDI-II concluded that this version shows high internal reliability and factor validity (Dozois, Dobson, & Ahnberg, 1998).

Center for Epidemiologic Studies-Depression (CES-D)

Sometimes, rather than create a new scale, investigators look at the variety of measures that have been developed to assess a particular variable, and select the "best" items as a new scale. The CES-D illustrates this approach. This scale was designed to measure symptoms of depression in community populations (Radloff, 1977); it is basically a screening inventory, designed not as a diagnostic tool but as a broad assessment device. The scale consists of 20 items taken from other depression

scales such as the MMPI D scale and the BDI; these are presumed to reflect the major symptoms of depression such as feelings of loneliness, hopelessness, sleep disturbance, and loss of appetite. The scale however, does not fully match the DSM criteria for depression, does not distinguish between subtypes of depression, and does not include such symptoms as suicidal ideation. The scale can be self-administered, used as part of a clinical interview, and even as a telephone survey.

The respondent is asked to rate the frequency of each of the 20 symptoms over the past week, using one of four response categories, ranging from 0 (rarely or none of the time) to 3 (most or all of the time). Scores can thus range from 0 to 60. Four of the 20 items are worded in a positive direction (e.g., "I was happy"), and 16 are worded negatively (e.g., "I felt depressed").

Reliability. The CES-D is designed to measure current state, and the instructions request the respondent to consider only the past week. In addition, depression is considered to be "episodic," that is, the symptoms vary over time. Therefore, test-retest reliability is expected not to be very high – and indeed it is not. In the original study, test-retest intervals of 2 to 8 weeks produced average test-retest coefficients of .57; greater intervals produced lower coefficients, but shorter intervals did not produce higher coefficients.

Internal consistency measures on the other hand, such as split-half and coefficient alpha, produced coefficients in the high .80s and low .90s (Radloff, 1977; Radloff & Teri, 1986).

Validity. The CES-D discriminates well between clinical patients and general population samples, as well as within various psychiatric diagnostic groups. Scores on the CES-D correlate well with ratings of severity of depression made by clinicians familiar with the patients, as well as with other measures of depression. Radloff and Teri (1986) reviewed studies using the CES-D with the elderly and concluded that the CES-D was as good a measure of depression in older adults as in younger adults. Both reliability and validity findings with the elderly were comparable with those obtained with younger samples. The scale has been used with a wide variety of groups, including homeless persons (Wong, 2000).

The construct validity of the CES-D also seems quite acceptable, but there is some question as to whether the CES-D measures depression, both depression and anxiety, or some other variable. Roberts, Vernon, and Rhoades (1989) suggest for example, that the scale measures "demoralization," which could be a precursor to either depression or anxiety.

Studies of the factor structure of the CES-D have typically found four factors, and although different investigators use different terms, the four factors reflect: (1) depressed affect, (2) positive affect, (3) somatic/vegetative signs, and (4) interpersonal distress – this last factor is composed of only two items and is a "weak" factor psychometrically (Kuo, 1984; Radloff, 1977). Four subscale scores can thus be obtained that include 18 of the 20 items.

Like the BID, the CES-D has been translated into a number of languages including Chinese (Ying, 1988) and Greek (Madianos, Gournas, & Stefanis, 1992), and short forms have been developed (Melchior, Huba, Brown, et al., 1993; Santor & Coyne, 1997).

The Zung Self-Rating Depression Scale (SDS)

The SDS was designed to provide a quantitative, objective assessment of the subjective experience of depression (Zung, 1965). The scale is composed of 20 items that cover affective, cognitive, behavioral, and psychological symptoms of depression. Respondents are asked to rate each item using a 4-point scale from 1 (none or a little of the time) to 4 (most or all of the time), as to how it has applied to them during the past week. The SDS is self-administered and takes about 5 minutes to complete.

The score on the SDS is calculated by summing the item scores, dividing by 80, and multiplying by 100. Scores below 50 are in the normal range, scores between 50 and 59 reflect mild depression, 60 to 69 marked depression, and 70 or above extreme depression.

Although the SDS has been available for some time and has been used in a variety of studies, there is relatively little reliability information available; what is available suggests adequate

reliability (Naughton & Wiklund, 1993). Studies of the validity of the SDS have in general been positive, with some dissent (e.g., Blumenthal, 1975; Hedlund & Vieweg, 1979). Hedlund and Vieweg (1979) concluded that the SDS could be used as a screening tool or as an ancillary measure, but not as a diagnostic measure of depression. As with the BDI, a number of studies have looked at cross-cultural applications of the SDS in various countries such as Finland, Germany, Iran, Italy, and Japan (e.g., deJonghe & Baneke, 1989; Horiguchi & Inami, 1991; Kivela & Pahkala, 1986; Naughton & Wiklund, 1993; Zung, 1969).

Usefulness of self-reports. There is considerable debate about the usefulness of self-report inventories such as the MMPI and the MCMI in the diagnosis and assessment of psychiatric disorders. A number of critics have argued that psychiatric patients, because of the nature of their illnesses, are basically untestable, that is, not able to complete the inventories in a valid manner (e.g., F. K. Goodwin & Jamison, 1990; Walters, 1988). Others have argued that inventories are useful and can provide valuable information (e.g., Bauer, et al., 1991; Wetzler, 1989b). Certainly, the empirical data supports the usefulness of such tests as a major source of data for clinical assessment (e.g., Wetzler, Kahn, Strauman, et al., 1989; Wetzler & Marlowe, 1993).

A core battery. One important role for psychological tests in the area of psychopathology is to measure the efficacy of psychological treatments. Attempts have been made, especially in the assessment of anxiety disorders, personality disorders, as well as mood disorders, to delineate a core battery of tests that could be used by practitioners. This would allow comparisons of different techniques and different programs and would clarify the communication of such results to various agencies, to researchers, and even to the general public. For now, however, there is disagreement as to whether such uniformity is desirable and/or useful and what specific tests might form such a core battery.

Focal assessment. Wetzler (1989a) suggests that in the assessment of psychopathology there is a new movement termed *focal assessment*. Traditionally, a standard battery of projective and intelligence tests was used to assess a psychiatric patient. The battery often included the MMPI, a WAIS, a Rorschach, and perhaps a TAT or other projective instrument. Psychiatric rating scales, structured interviews, or self-report scales were usually relegated to research purposes. Focal assessment involves the use of specialized instruments, of instruments whose focus is much narrower than a broad-based inventory such as the MMPI. This is in sharp contrast to the suggestion made above of a broad-based battery to be given to all patients. For now, most practitioners who use tests use a combination of the twosome, broad-based instruments such the MMPI and/or Rorschach and some specific instruments that measure depression, post-traumatic stress disorder, or other condition.

The Base Rate Problem Revisited

In Chapter 3, we discussed the notion of base rates, the "naturally" occurring rate of something. For example, if out of 500 consecutively admitted patients to a psychiatric hospital, 10 were diagnosed as schizophrenic, the base rate for schizophrenia in that particular setting would be 2% (10/500).

In clinical psychology, the usefulness of a test is often judged by whether the test results can be used to classify a client as having a particular diagnosis vs. some other diagnosis. This validity is often established by comparing contrasted groups – for example, depressed patients vs. non-depressed. Quite often, the two samples are of equal size – a good research strategy designed to maximize the statistical power of such procedures as analysis of variance and facilitating group matching on potentially confounding variables such as age and gender. Note however, that when we assess whether the means of two groups are significantly different on Test X, the typical procedures used, such a t tests or ANOVA, do not indicate whether the size of the difference between two means is large enough for clinical use. Such an answer is provided by the analysis of false positives, false negatives, and hits or, as we indicated in Chapter 3, of sensitivity (the true positive rate) and specificity (the true negative rate). Unfortunately such an analysis is severely influenced by the base rate.

Elwood (1993) gives a clear example. He asks us to imagine that a test to assess depression is given to 100 depressed patients and 100 normal controls. The results are as follows:

		Diagnosis	
		Depressed	Not depressed
Test results	Depressed	90	10
	Not depressed	10	90

Using the test results, of the 100 depressed patients we identify 90 correctly and misidentify 10 (false negatives); of the 100 normal controls we again identify 90 correctly and misidentify 10 (false positives). The predictive value for this test is then 90/100 or 90%, a rather impressive result.

Now imagine that the test is used to screen for depression in a setting where the base rate for depression is 10%; this means that for every 200 patients, 20 are in fact depressed. Administering the test to 200 patients would yield the following results:

		Diagnosis	
		Depressed	Not depressed
Test results	Depressed	18	18
	Not depressed	2	162

Note that both sensitivity and specificity are independent of base rate. So sensitivity stays at 90% and that is why for every 20 depressed patients, the test would correctly identify 18, with 2 false negatives. Specificity also stays at 90%, so of the 180 patients who are not depressed, 90% or 162 are true negatives and the other 18 are false positive. Notice however, what happens to the predictive power. It now becomes 18/36 (true positives/true positives + false positives) or 50%. In effect, we could get the same results by flipping a coin! The solution, of course, is to calculate local base rates and pay attention to them, a point that has been made repeatedly and forcefully (Meehl and Rosen, 1955) and, as we saw, was incorporated in the MCMI.

SUMMARY

We have taken a brief look at a variety of instruments, and through them, at issues that underlie the area of testing for psychopathology. We have seen screening inventories, multivariate tests, and measures of specific dimensions such as anxiety and depression. In the past, a major issue has always been criterion validity, and diagnosis was seen as not highly reliable, and therefore not a valid, even though it was a necessary, criterion. As the focus has changed more to construct validity, the issue has focused more on the sensitivity and predictive power of a test. At the same time, we should not lose sight of the fact that a test, in the hands of a well-trained and sensitive clinician, is much more than a simple diagnostic tool.

SUGGESTED READINGS

Elwood, R. W. (1993). Psychological tests and clinical discriminations: Beginning to address the base rate problem. *Clinical Psychology Review, 13,* 409–419.

We used the arguments and examples given by this author in our discussion of base rates. This article is a very clear exposition of base rates as they affect clinical assessment.

Helmes, E., & Reddon, J. R. (1993). A perspective on developments in assessing psychopathology: A critical review of the MMPI and MMPI-2. *Psychological Bulletin, 113,* 453–471.

The authors perceive the MMPI to be an outmoded instrument and severely criticize it. Although one may not agree with all of the criticisms and the forcefulness with which they are stated, this is a well-written review article that focuses on major aspects of test construction.

Lambert, M. J., Hatch, D. R., Kingston, M. D., & Edwards, B. C. (1986). Zung, Beck, and Hamilton Rating Scales as measures of treatment outcome: A meta-analytic comparison. *Journal of Consulting and Clinical Psychology, 54,* 54–59.

There are three popular depression scales in the psychiatric literature: The Zung, the BDI, and the Hamilton. The first two, discussed in this chapter, are self-rating scales; the Hamilton is completed by the interviewer or clinician. The authors located 85 studies that compared at least two of the three measures and analyzed 36 of these studies through the technique of metaanalysis (explained quite clearly in this article).

Reynolds, W. M., & Kobak, K. A. (1995). Reliability and validity of the Hamilton Depression Inventory: A paper-and-pencil version of the Hamilton Depression Rating Scale clinical interview. *Psychological Assessment, 7,* 472–483.

A very thorough review of a paper-and-pencil version of a depression scale that originally was a semistructured interview measure.

Watson, C. G. (1990). Psychometric posttraumatic stress disorder measurement techniques: A review. *Psychological Assessment, 2,* 460–469.

A review of 12 measures of posttraumatic stress disorder, including a scale developed on the MMPI. The author covers in detail issues of reliability and validity, as well as the utility of such scales.

DISCUSSION QUESTIONS

1. If a test such as the SCL-90R is given to a patient, how do we know that the results are valid?

2. The president of the university decides that all new students are to be given the PSI. What are some of the ethical concerns of such a procedure?

3. Why do you think the MMPI continues to be used widely?

4. What are some of the "unique" aspects of the MCMI?

5. How would you differentiate between state and trait anxiety?

Would the same distinction apply to other variables – for example, depression?

8 Normal Positive Functioning

AIM This chapter looks at a variety of areas that reflect normal positive functioning. The chapter is not intended to be a comprehensive review of normality; it covers a small number of selected areas chosen either because of their importance in psychological testing, or because of some illustrative innovative aspect, and perhaps because of our feeling that some of these areas, although important, are often neglected by instructors. Much of psychological testing has developed within a clinical tradition, with the emphasis on psychopathology. As we saw in Chapter 7, psychologists have developed some fairly sophisticated measures of psychopathology; even intelligence testing covered in Chapter 5, developed originally within the context of assessing retarded children. The assessment of normality has in many ways been neglected, primarily because assessment occurs where there is a need – and the need to "measure" what is normal has not, in the past, been very strong. Keep in mind also that the dividing line between normality and abnormality is not absolute, and so tests of psychopathology such as the MMPI can also be used with presumably mentally healthy college students.

SELF-CONCEPT

Perhaps a first question about normal functioning has to do with a person's self-concept. How do you feel about yourself? Do you like yourself? Do you have confidence in your abilities? Do you perceive yourself as being of value and worth? Or are you doubtful about your own worth, do you have little confidence in yourself and often feel unhappy about yourself? This is the issue of self-esteem and/or self-concept. A person's self-concept is that person's view of self, and it is highly related to a wide variety of behaviors. Other terms such as self-esteem and self-image are used, and authors argue about the differences and similarities. Some differentiate between various self-combinations, and others use all the terms synonymously. Paralleling the development of intelligence measurement, as well as the measurement of many other variables, self-concept research initially emphasized a general or unitary self-concept. Recently it has focused on the multi-dimensionality of the self-concept. For our purposes, we use the term "self-concept" to include both global concept and specific dimensions.

The Tennessee Self-Concept Scale

One of the better well-known scales of self-concept is the *Tennessee Self-Concept Scale* or TSCS (Fitts, 1965); a 1981 bibliography contained some 1,350 relevant references (P. F. Reed, Fitts, & Boehm, 1981). The TSCS consists of 100 self-descriptive items, such as "I am a happy person" and "I do what is right," by means of which an individual indicates what he or she likes, feels, does, and so on. The scale is basically designed to assess a person's self-image, and how realistic or deviant it is. Each item has five response options

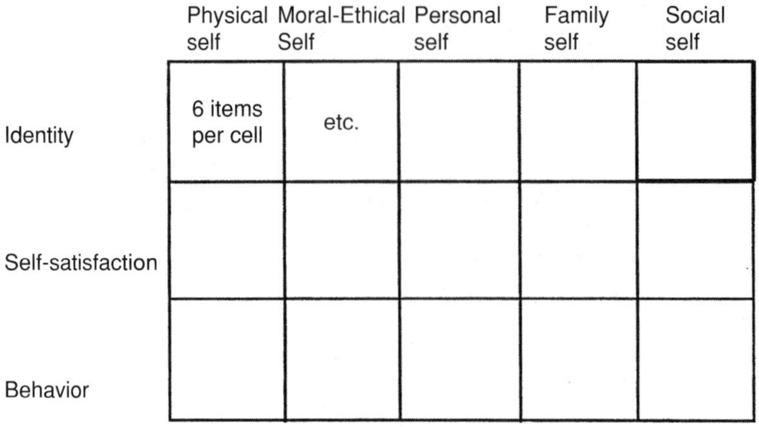

	Physical self	Moral-Ethical Self	Personal self	Family self	Social self
Identity	6 items per cell	etc.			
Self-satisfaction					
Behavior					

FIGURE 8–1. Two-dimensional schema underlying the TSCS.

ranging from "completely false" to "completely true."

Development. The TSCS was developed in 1955 and the first step was to compile a pool of self-descriptive items. These were obtained from other self-concept scales, as well as written self-descriptions of mental-health patients and of nonpatients. These items were then classified into a two-dimensional schema, very much like the taxonomy approach used in content validity. Although the two dimensions are not named explicitly, other than "internal" and "external," one dimension consists of five external aspects of the self such as physical self, moral-ethical self, and family self; the second dimension consists of three internal aspects of functioning, namely identity (what the person is), self-satisfaction (how the person accepts himself or herself), and behavior (how the person acts). Identity can be interpreted as the internal, private, aspect of the self; behavior is the manifestation of the self that is observable to others, and satisfaction can be reframed as the discrepancy between the actual self and the ideal self. Figure 8.1 illustrates the schema.

Items were judged by seven clinical psychologists as to where they belonged in this schema, and whether they were positive or negative. The final 90 items retained for the scale are those where there was perfect agreement on the part of the judges; they are equally divided as to positive and negative items, with six items for each intersection of the two dimensions. An additional 10 items were "borrowed" from the L scale of the MMPI. Note that, in general, the development of this scale follows the pattern outlined in Chapter 2.

Description. The TSCS is self-administered, either individually or in groups, can be used with individuals 12 years or older, and requires about a sixth-grade reading level. Typically it takes about 15 minutes to complete the scale, which can then be scored by hand or machine. There are two forms of the scale, although both forms use the same test booklet and test items. The Counseling form is quicker and easier to score, and the results can be used by the client directly, while the Clinical/Research form is more complicated in terms of scoring, obtained results, analysis, and interpretation.

There is a reusable test booklet and a consumable answer sheet, as well as a consumable test booklet for use in computerized scoring. One of the "interesting" aspects of this test is that the items in the booklet are not listed in the usual numerical order. For example, item 1 is followed by items 3, 5, 19, 21, etc., and the answer sheet matches (somewhat) this numerical progression. This is done so the answer marks go through a carbon paper, onto a scoring sheet in appropriate proximity for each scale. Otherwise the items would either have to be rearranged making their intent even more transparent, or the responses would need to be recopied, or many scoring templates would be needed. (There is of course a simpler solution, and that is to renumber the items in sequence.) Subjects are asked to indicate at what time they began the test and at what time they finished. Although this is not a timed test, the amount of time is used as a score.

Scoring. The TSCS yields a rather large number of scores, 46 total (although only 29 find their way on the profile sheet), and the impression one gets is that every possible combination of items is in fact scored! There is for example, a "Self-Criticism" score, which is the sum of the 10 MMPI items. There is a "Total Positive" score that is a sum of all the 90 items and presumably reflects overall level of self-esteem. The Total Positive score is broken down into eight components, according to each of the eight categories that make up the two-dimensional schema. There is a "Variability" score (actually subdivided into three scores) that assesses the amount of variability or inconsistency from one area of self-perception to another. There are also six empirically derived scales, obtained through various comparisons of a normal group with psychiatric patients, as well as other scores too numerous to mention here. As you might imagine, hand scoring is quite time consuming, although the test manual is fairly clear in the scoring directions given.

Reliability. Test-retest reliability on a sample of 60 college students retested over a 2-week period, yielded coefficients ranging from .60 to .92, with most of the coefficients in the acceptable range. The primary scale, the "total positive," yielded an r of .92.

Validity. The test manual (Fitts, 1965) discusses four types of validity: (1) content validity, (2) discrimination between groups (i.e., concurrent validity), (3) correlation with other personality measures (i.e., criterion validity), and (4) personality changes under particular conditions (i.e., construct validity). Notice that the last two categories implicitly suggest that the TSCS is a personality test.

Content validity is incorrectly interpreted as interrater reliability. That is, Fitts (1965) argues that the TSCS has content validity because the judges agreed in their placement of the retained items, and therefore the scales of the TSCS are "logically meaningful and publicly communicable." As we learned in Chapter 3, the issue of content validity is whether the test adequately covers the variable to be assessed. The two-dimensional

framework used to assign items is of course where the focus of content validity should be, and in this case we might well conclude that what is covered in this test is comprehensive but not exhaustive. For example, we might argue that "academic" self-concept should be included.

Concurrent validity is shown by comparison of TSCS scores for various groups – psychiatric patients, the normative group, and a group of "well-integrated" individuals. Other studies are cited that found significant differences on TSCS scores between delinquents and nondelinquents, between first offenders and repeat offenders, unwed mothers and controls, and alcoholics and controls.

Criterion validity data is presented based on studies of psychiatric patients with the MMPI, high-school students with the Edwards Personal Preference Schedule, and various other measures with college students and other samples. In general, although there are some noticeable exceptions, the pattern of correlations supports the criterion validity of the TSCS. Note, however, that basically the results would be what we would expect if the TSCS were a measure of general adjustment, psychological health, or similar global variable. None of these data exclusively support the notion that the TSCS measures self-concept.

Finally, construct validity is addressed through a number of studies that hypothesize that positive experiences such as psychotherapy should result in an enhancement of self-concept, while negative experiences such as stress or failure result in lowered self-concept. For example, a study of paratrooper trainees is cited in which the trainees underwent physical danger as well as "attitude training," where failure was considered a disgrace. The trainees were administered the TSCS both before and after training, and some trainees passed while some failed the program. However, both pass and fail groups showed "significant score decreases," so it is moot as to whether these results support the validity of the TSCS – we could argue that the brutal training resulted in lowered self-esteem for all, or that the pass group should have shown increased self-concept.

Norms. The original norms were based on a sample of 626 individuals. Little information is given as to the characteristics of these people other than to indicate that the sample is very heterogeneous in age, gender, socioeconomic level, and education. The sample is clearly not random or representative (as might be obtained through census data), so we must conclude that this is a sample of convenience. The author (Fitts, 1965) does argue that large samples from other populations do not differ appreciably from his norms – that is, the norms are representative (even though he indicates that the norm group has an excess of college students). He also argues that there is no need to establish separate norms by age, gender, race, or other variables. We of course would want more than simply the assurance of an author. We would want to look at actual score distributions for separate groups and assure ourselves that indeed they are identical; or at the very least we would want the results of a statistical test such as chi-square to show that the two distributions are not significantly different from each other.

Intercorrelations of scale scores. Because of item overlap among scales and because some scales represent a subtotal of another scale, obtained correlations among scale scores are spuriously high. On the other hand, the major dimensions of self-perception (i.e., self-esteem, self-criticism, variability, certainty, and conflict) are all relatively independent of each other.

Criticisms. It would seem that self-concept would be a valuable dimension to study within the context of normal functioning, and indeed it is. It is somewhat curious then, that much of the focus of the TSCS is based on clinical patients undergoing psychotherapy, who may be lacking in self-esteem or have distorted self-images. In fact, we could have easily discussed the TSCS in Chapter 4 under the topic of personality or in Chapter 7 under the topic of psychopathology.

Despite the fact that this is a commonly used self-concept scale, the TSCS has received substantial criticisms: it is open to social desirability and other response sets, the results of factor-analytic studies do not support its hypothesized dimensions, and the reliability data are considered inappropriate and inadequate (e.g., P. Bentler, 1972; Hoffman & Gellen, 1983; Wylie, 1974). Tzeng Maxey, Fortier, et al. (1985) on the basis of several factor analyses, found that although reliability indices were "exceedingly high," there was no

support for the factors postulated by Fitts, and at best there were only two to four dimensions in the TSCS. The conclusions were that scoring the TSCS according to directions would only "misguide the user" and lead to interpretations that "are simply not warranted," and that the TSCS is "clearly inadequate." Perhaps we can summarize by paraphrasing Marsh and Richards (1988) who indicated that in the 1960s the TSCS perhaps represented one of the best self-concept instruments but, as judged by current test standards, it is a weak instrument.

Primary, secondary, and tertiary validity revisited. In Chapter 3, we discussed a conceptual model to organize information about a specific test. You recall that the model had three steps that we called primary, secondary, and tertiary validity. This model is not used widely in the literature, despite the fact that it provides a very useful framework for the practitioner who is seriously interested in learning about and mastering a specific test. The topic of self-concept allows a useful illustration of this framework.

Years ago, I (G. Domino) carried out a study to assess the effectiveness of a television campaign designed to lower drug abuse among adolescents (G. Domino, 1982). In preparation for that study, we found a 50-item self-concept questionnaire, called the Self-Esteem Questionnaire (SEQ) in the appendix of a drug-education text. Neither the publisher nor the editor could provide any information whatsoever about the questionnaire. We nevertheless used it in our study and found it a relatively interesting measure. We therefore decided to do a series of programmatic studies to generate the type of information needed to evaluate the reliability and validity of this measure, using the tripartite conceptual model (G. Domino & Blumberg, 1987). Table 8.1 gives some illustrative examples of SEQ items.

Table 8–1. Illustrative SEQ Items

I usually feel inferior to others.
I normally feel warm and happy toward myself.
I often feel inadequate to handle new situations.
I usually feel warm and friendly toward all I contact.
I habitually condemn myself for my mistakes and shortcomings.
I am free of shame, blame, guilt, and remorse.

Table 8–2. Mean and SD *T* Scores for Six Groups Presumed to Differ on Self-Esteem		
Group	**Mean**	**SD**
Student leaders	62.3	5.7
Varsity athletes	57.1	5.0
Intro Psych students	51.4	7.3
Counseling Center clients	46.3	5.1
"Problem" students as identified by Dean	43.4	4.8
Students on academic probation	41.4	5.4

The first question is that of reliability, not part of the model because the model addresses only the issue of validity. For a sample of college psychology students a test-retest with a 10-week interval yielded an $r = .76$. For a sample of high-school students, a split-half reliability yielded a corrected coefficient of .81, and an internal consistency analysis, a Cronbach's alpha of .52. These results suggested a modicum of reliability, and a possible hypothesis that the instrument was not homogeneous.

Primary validity. Remember that the task here is to determine how well the test measures what it purports to measure – in this case self-esteem. A good beginning is to determine whether the mean scores for various groups for whom we would theoretically expect a difference, are in fact different. If a test cannot differentiate at the group level, it certainly would not be very useful at the individual level. Six student groups were selected, ranging from student leaders for whom self-esteem should be highest to students on academic probation, for whom self-esteem should be lowest. The results are presented in Table 8.2. Note that the group means form a nice progression along what might be called a sociological continuum. That is, on the basis of sociological theory, we hypothesized that the groups should occupy different positions on this continuum, and indeed the results support this. Note that the means and SDs are expressed as *T* scores, with an expected mean of 50 and a SD of 10. The top three groups can be said to be above the mean on self-esteem, and the bottom three groups below the mean. A biserial correlation between scores on the SEQ and the dichotomy of higher versus lower status yielded an $r = .59$ ($p < .001$). Much more evidence would of course be needed to

establish primary validity, but the above is a good beginning.

Secondary validity. Secondary validity involves a clarification of the underlying dimension of measurement through four steps: (1) a review of the development of the test, (2) an analysis of test items with respect to format and content, (3) an analysis of the relationship between the test and other important variables, and (4) a study of individuals whose scores are diagnostically significant.

As for step one, no information is available on how this test came to be. A perusal of the items suggests that the author(s) had a "humanistic" bent, but that is pure speculation. For step two, a content analysis of the items suggests that they cover the social and emotional aspects of self-concept, but not other aspects such as cognitive and academic components. A factor analysis based on the protocols of 453 students indicated three major factors: a general factor that accounted for 62% of the variance, a specific factor suggesting neurotic defensiveness (11% variance), and a third smaller factor relating to interpersonal competence. Thus a major limitation of this inventory is its unknown conceptual underpinnings and limited content validity.

For step three, a series of studies indicated no gender differences, no ethnic or racial differences, no significant correlations with socioeconomic status or measures of social desirability, no significant correlations with intelligence-test scores, but significant correlations with GPA in both college and high-school students. In addition, scores on this scale correlated significantly with scores on six other self-concept measures, with correlation coefficients ranging from .38 to .73. Of course, this is the kind of data one would expect to find in a test manual or in the professional literature.

The fourth step is to look at high- and low-scoring individuals. That is, if Kathryn obtains a *T* score of 65 on this scale, what else can we say about her, other than that she has high self-esteem? To obtain data to answer this question, high-scoring and low-scoring students were interviewed and the interviews observed by 12 clinical-psychology graduate students. Both interviewer and observer were blind as to the student's score on the SEQ. At the end of the

ACL items		Q sort items
High self-esteem		
Active	Friendly	Has a wide range of interests.
Adaptable	Healthy	Initiates humor.
Ambitious	Humorous	Is productive; gets things done.
Assertive	Intelligent	Is calm, relaxed in manner.
Calm	Natural	Has insights into own motives and behavior.
Capable	Self-confident	Feels satisfied with self.
Confident	Sociable	Has social poise and presence.
Energetic	Talkative	Values own independence and autonomy.
Low self-esteem		
Anxious	Interests narrow	Tends to be self-defensive.
Awkward	Shy	Seeks reassurance from others.
Distractible	Timid	Judges self and others in conventional terms.
Immature	Weak	Is basically anxious.
Inhibited	Withdrawn	Compares self to others.
		Does not vary roles.

Table 8–3. ACL and Q-Sort Items Descriptive of High vs. Low Self-Esteem

interviews, the observers evaluated each of the students by completing an Adjective Checklist (a list of 300 words which the observer checks if descriptive of the client; see section below on creativity), and doing a Q sort (sorting a set of descriptive statements according to the degree that they characterize the client; see Chapter 18).

Table 8.3 indicates which adjectives and which Q-sort statements were used more frequently to characterize high self-esteem students and low self-esteem students.

Note that the portraits presented here of these two types of students are internally consistent, i.e., they make sense, they are coherent. High self-esteem subjects are perceived as confident and productive, as able to relate well interpersonally and to behave in a calm yet active manner. Low self-esteem subjects are seen as timid and conventional, with an almost neurotic need for reassurance.

Tertiary validity. This step involves the justification for using such a measure as the SEQ. For example, if you were not interested in assessing self-esteem, why pay attention to the SEQ? We could of course argue that self-esteem is such a basic variable that it probably is relevant to almost any psychological inquiry. Could the SEQ

however, provide some additional information beyond assessment of self-esteem? In a sample of alcoholics undergoing therapy, scores on the SEQ correlated with staff ratings of improvement; thus the SEQ might have some potential use in studies of the psychotherapeutic process. In another study, two samples of students were assessed. Both samples scored high on a battery of tests of creativity, but one sample showed evidence of actual creative achievement, the other did not. One of the significant differences between the two groups was that the productive students showed a higher mean on self-esteem. Thus the SEQ might be of interest to investigators concerned with creative achievement. Finally, in a sample of male adult professionals, SEQ scores were correlated with a measure of psychological femininity. Thus, although there seem to be no gender differences on this scale, the SEQ might be relevant to studies of androgyny and related aspects.

LOCUS OF CONTROL

One of the major themes of both human and animal behavior is that of control, that is continued attempts to deal effectively with the environment. The experience of achieving mastery over oneself and surrounding circumstances is one of the most fundamental aspects of human experience. There is in fact a voluminous body of literature in psychology on this topic, and a number of experiments have become "classics" that are cited in introductory psychology textbooks. For example, Stotland and Blumenthal (1964) showed that humans made to feel in control in a testing situation tended to be less anxious than those who did not have this belief. Seligman (1975), showed that dogs exhibited "helpless" behavior when exposed to conditions they could not control. Rotter (1966) hypothesized that the degree to which a person perceives rewards to be contingent upon their own efforts vs. controlled by others is an important dimension. He identified belief in *internal* control, as the perception that rewards are contingent upon one's behavior, and *external* control, as the perception that rewards are under the control of powerful others, of luck and chance, or unpredictable. This hypothesis was presented within the context of social-learning theory, where rewards or reinforcements act to strengthen an expectancy that a particular behavior will be followed by that reinforcement in the future. Thus internal-external control of reinforcement is a generalized expectancy that there is more or less a connection between behavior and the occurrence of rewards; this is a continuum rather than a dichotomy.

The Internal-External Locus of Control Scale

Development. The Internal-External Locus of Control (I-E) scale was thus developed by Rotter to operationalize his hypothesis. The I-E scale began as a set of 26 items, using a Likert-type response scale, and developed on a priori grounds – that is, the items were written to reflect the theoretical literature and to be used as is. This scale was used and further refined in two doctoral dissertations by students of Rotter, was then expanded to 60 items, and then through a series of studies, was reduced to a 29-item forced-choice scale, that includes 6 filler items. The I-E scale then presents the respondent with sets of items from which the respondent selects the one that he she most believes in. For example: (a) Becoming a success is a matter of hard work, or (b) Getting a good job depends on being at the right place at the right time. For each pair, one statement represents an internal locus of control and the matching statement an external locus of control. The score is the total number of external choices. Originally, the I-E scale was intended to provide subscale scores in a variety of life areas such as social interactions, political affairs, and academic achievement; however, the subscales were all yielding similar results so it was decided to abandon this effort and measure a single, overall expectancy.

Reliability and validity. Although the details presented by Rotter (1966) on the development of the scale are somewhat sketchy, and one would

need to consult the original doctoral dissertations for specific details, Rotter (1966) provides a rather extensive amount of information on the initial reliability and validity of the I-E scale. In addition, internal vs. external control of reinforcement, often referred to as "locus of control" is probably one of the most studied variables in psychology, and numerous scales of locus of control are available. In fact, the area is so prolific that there are many reviews (e.g., Joe, 1971; Lefcourt, 1966; Strickland, 1989; Throop & MacDonald, 1971), and entire books devoted to the topic (e.g., Lefcourt, 1976; Phares, 1976).

Rotter (1966) reported corrected split-half reliabilities of .65 for males and .79 for females, and Kuder-Richardson coefficients for various samples in the .69 to .76 range. Rotter (1966) felt that the nature of the scale (brief, forced-choice, and composed of items covering a variety of situations) resulted in underestimates of its internal consistency. Test-retest reliability in various samples, with 1- and 2-month intervals, ranged from .49 to .83.

Correlations with a measure of social desirability ranged from −.17 to −.35, with a median of −.22, and correlations with various measures of intelligence essentially were insignificant. Rotter (1966) also reported briefly two factor analyses, both of which suggested one general factor. A number of other studies are presented addressing the construct validity of the scale, such as correlations with story-completion and semistructured interview measures of locus of control, analyses of social-class differences, and controlled laboratory tasks.

The literature is replete with hundreds of studies that support the construct validity of the scale and of the concept. Locus of control scores are related to a wide variety of behaviors such as academic achievement (the more internal the orientation the higher the achievement; e.g., Bar-Tal & Bar-Zohar, 1977) and various aspects of problem solving (e.g., Lefcourt, 1976). A number of studies support the hypothesis that internals show more initiative and effort in controlling both the physical environment and their own impulses (e.g., Joe, 1971).

Popularity of concept. The topic of locus of control has proven to be immensely popular, not only in the United States but also in a cross-cultural context (e.g., Dyal, 1983; Furnham & Henry, 1980; Tyler, Dhawan, & Sinha, 1989; Zea & Tyler, 1994). The concept has been applied to a wide variety of endeavors ranging from beliefs about the afterlife (e.g., Berman & Hays, 1973), to educational settings (e.g., Weiner, 1980), to behavior in organizations (e.g., Spector, 1982), and even dental health (e.g., Ludenia & Dunham, 1983). The scale also gave birth to a large number of additional locus-of-control scales, some for children (e.g., DeMinzi, 1990; Nowicki & Strickland, 1973), some for particular diseases (e.g., Ferraro, Price, Desmond et al., 1987), some multidimensional (e.g., Coan, Fairchild, & Dobyns, 1973; TerKuile, Linssen, & Spinhoven, 1993; K. A. Wallston, B. S. Wallston, & DeVellis, 1978), some for specific arenas of behavior (e.g., Spector, 1988; B. S. Wallston, K. A. Wallston, Kaplan, & Maides, 1976), some brief versions of other scales (e.g., Sapp & Harrod, 1993), and some competing with the Rotter (e.g., Nowicki & Duke, 1974). Levenson (1973; 1974) suggested that locus of control was a multidimensional concept and developed the Multidimensional Locus of Control questionnaire composed of three subscales: Internality, Powerful Others, and Chance. This scale also proved quite popular. Although most of these scales have been developed on the basis of empirical and theoretical guidelines (discussed in Chapter 2), not all have. For example, J. M. Schneider and Parsons (1970), decided, on the basis of a logical analysis, that the Rotter I-E scale actually contained five subscales. They asked judges to sort the items into five *unspecified* categories and found high interrater agreement. The categories were then named "general luck or fate," "respect," "politics," "academics and leadership," and "success."

Criticisms. When the I-E scale was first developed, a typical approach was to administer the scale to a sample and use a median split to obtain groups that would be called internals and externals. At that time, the median (or mean) for college-student samples was typically around 8. In recent studies, the mean has increased by about 0.5 to 1 SD (typical SD runs around 4), to a median of 10 to 12. This means, in effect, that a score of 9 might have been considered an external score in earlier research, but an internal score in recent research.

Given the proliferation of locus-of-control scales, one may well question whether they are all measuring the same variable. Furnham (1987) administered seven such scales to a sample of British adolescents. Although a content analysis of the scales indicated very little overlap – i.e., a look at the items indicated that the scales used different items. The correlations between five of the scales (all measuring locus of control in children) were highly significant, and nearly all greater than .50. Their reliabilities (alpha coefficients) were low and ranged from .33 to .60. However, Furnham (1987) correctly interpreted these results not as lack of reliability, but reflective of the multidimensionality of the scales.

SEXUALITY

As Wiederman and Allgeier (1993) state, "Sexuality is a vital part of being human." Sexuality covers a rather wide variety of variables, such as premarital intercourse, attitudes toward virginity, machismo, pornography, medical conditions, religious and philosophical views, homosexuality, and so on. All types of scales have been developed in this area, ranging from attitude scales toward the use of condoms (e.g., I. S. Brown, 1984) and masturbation (e.g., Abramson & Mosher, 1975) to sexual knowledge questionnaires (e.g., Gough, 1974; Moracco & Zeidan, 1982). From a psychometric point of view, this is a very broad and ill-defined area, and so the examples below cannot be taken as representative in the same way that the Stanford-Binet and the Wechsler tests "represent" intelligence tests.

The sexuality scale. Snell and Papini (1989) developed the Sexuality Scale (SS) to measure what people think and how they feel about their own sexuality. The SS consists of three subscales labeled *sexual-esteem* (e.g., "I am good at sex"), *sexual-depression* (e.g., "I feel depressed about my sex life"), and *sexual-preoccupation* (e.g., "I think about sex constantly"). Sexual-esteem was conceptualized as the capacity to experience one's sexuality in a satisfying and enjoyable way. Sexual-depression reflects a tendency to feel depressed or discouraged about one's capability to relate sexually to another person. Sexual-preoccupation is the persistent tendency to become absorbed and even obsessed with sexual matters.

Ten items were originally written for each of the three subscales, and administered to a sample of undergraduate college students. Respondents indicated degree of agreement with each item on a 5-point scale, where agree equaled +2 and disagree equaled −2. Half of the items in each subscale were reverse keyed. A factor analysis indicated that the three-factor model was reasonable, but two of the sexual-depression items were eliminated because of small factor loadings.

Validity. Snell and Papini (1989) found significantly higher levels of sexual-preoccupation for men than for women, but no gender differences in sexual-esteem or sexual-depression, while Wiederman and Allgeier (1993) found men to score higher on both sexual-esteem and sexual-preoccupation. A basic question that can be asked here is whether each of the subscales measures a variable related to sexuality or related to more general functioning – that is, is the sexual-depression scale a measure of more global depression? In their study, Wiederman and Allgeier (1993) administered the SS scale, the Rosenberg Self-Esteem scale, and the Beck Depression Inventory to a sample of undergraduate college students. They applied a special type of factor analysis and reduced the 30-item scale to 15 items; that is, they constructed a short form that was more reliable and that correlated highly with the original subscales. They found that global self-esteem was only moderately correlated to sexual-esteem, and that depression was only moderately correlated with sexual-depression.

A Guttman scale. In Chapter 6, we briefly discussed Guttman scales as a way of measuring attitudes. You recall that these are unidimensional scales created in such a way that a person's position on the psychological continuum being measured is represented by the point at which the responses of the individual shift from one category to another (for example, from agree to disagree). Guttman scales are relatively rare, but have found particular application in the area of sexuality because sexual behavior and sexual intimacy seem to follow a particular progression. One such scale is that of "intimacy-permissiveness" developed by Christensen and Carpenter (1962). These investigators were interested in exploring the relationship of premarital pregnancy to possible consequences such as having to get married, giving the baby up for adoption, etc., as a function of cultural differences, specifically the "sexually restrictive" Mormon culture of Utah, the more typical United States culture, and the sexually permissive culture of Denmark.

The authors attempted to develop a Guttman type scale to assess "intimacy permissiveness," that is how permissive or restrictive a person's attitudes are toward premarital sexual intimacy. They began with 21 items but eventually reduced these to 10, after some statistical procedures were carried out to test for unidimensionality. The 10 items cover the desirability of marrying a virgin, petting, premarital intercourse, premarital pregnancy, and freedom of access to erotic literature. Presumably someone who has a permissive attitude toward premarital intercourse would also have a permissive attitude toward premarital petting. The subject is required to check each item with which he or she agrees, so scores can go from 0 to 10, with higher scores indicating greater permissiveness.

You recall that in the Guttman scaling, the coefficient of reproducibility is the important statistical procedure. The authors report such coefficients as ranging from .90 to .96 (these are basically reliability coefficients). In terms of validity, the authors present three lines of evidence. The mean for the Danish sample (8.3) is substantially higher than the mean for the U.S. sample (4.1), and the mean for the Mormon sample (2.4). Secondly, males have higher mean scores than females, in all three samples. Finally, the higher the intimacy-permissiveness score the larger the percent having premarital intercourse, again in all three samples. Unfortunately, the authors give no detail on how the original items were developed or on the precise statistical procedures used.

CREATIVITY

Creativity has been of interest to psychologists for quite some time, but a serious effort to study creativity and to develop measures of creativity did not begin until the 1950s, in the work of Guilford at the University of Southern California and the work of various psychologists at the

Institute of Personality Assessment and Research of the University of California at Berkeley. There is at present no clear consensus as to precisely what creativity is and what its specific components are. It is therefore not too surprising that different investigators use different measures and that measures of "creativity," aiming at different subsets of abilities, often do not correlate highly with each other.

Torrance (1966), one of the leading researchers in this area, defines creativity as "a process of becoming sensitive to problems, deficiencies, gaps in knowledge, missing elements, disharmonies, and so on; identifying the difficulty; searching for solutions, making guesses, or formulating hypotheses about the deficiencies; testing and retesting these hypotheses and possibly modifying and retesting them; and finally communicating the results."

It is customary to distinguish between intelligence and creativity, and this theoretical distinction is mirrored in the respective tests. Intelligence tests tend to require *convergent thinking*, that is, coming up with the best single answer, while tests of creativity tend to require *divergent* thinking, that is multiple answers, all of which are "uniquely correct." Thus, tests of intelligence often make use of vocabulary items, facility in solving mathematical problems, reading comprehension, and spatial visualization. Tests of creativity typically require imagination, generation of ideas, asking unusual questions, and coming up with novel responses.

Different perspectives. There are probably at least four ways in which we can study creativity. The first is to focus on creative *persons*. Suppose we were able to identify a group of highly creative individuals, we could ask whether they differed on intelligence, personality, motivation, food preferences, and so on, from their less creative peers. Psychologists have been quite prolific in their study of such persons, and a wide variety of groups have been assessed such as writers, architects, mathematicians, mothers of creative adolescents, and so on. The results suggest that creative persons do differ from their less creative peers in a number of significant ways that transcend field of enterprise (see Barron, 1969; G. A. Davis, 1986).

A second perspective is to study the creative *process*, that is, what happens when that inner light bulb goes on, what happens as a painter creates a painting or a poet writes a poem? The creative process is typically dissected into four stages: (1) preparation, where information is gathered, various solutions are attempted, the challenge may be rephrased; (2) incubation or a turning away from the problem. The person might go for a walk, take a bath, or sleep on it; (3) illumination, the "aha" experience where solutions emerge, often quite complete, detailed, and visual; (4) verification, where the potential solutions are tested and elaborated. This four-stage process was proposed by Wallas (1926) and still seems to be quite applicable, although others have proposed more elaborate versions (e.g., Rossman, 1931).

A third approach is to focus on the creative *product* itself. What distinguishes creative from pedestrian paintings? Are there certain qualities of balance, of asymmetry, of form and motion, that are part-and-parcel of a creative product? Much of the work in this area has been done by artists, art critics, philosophers, and educators, rather than psychologists.

Finally there is a fourth perspective that we might label *press* (to keep our alliteration). Creative press refers to the press or force of the environment on creativity – both the inner psychological environment and the outer physical environment. Here we might be concerned about what motivates a person to create or how the physical environment can promote or dampen creativity.

Torrance Test of Creative Thinking (TTCT)

There are hundreds of measures of creativity that have been proposed in the literature, but most have been presented without the required evidence for their basic reliability and validity. One instrument that has proven quite popular, and in many ways represents a reliable and valid approach, is the TTCT, which is actually a battery of tests (somewhat like the Wechsler tests), containing seven verbal subtests and three figural subtests.

The TTCT was developed by Torrance in 1966, and was intended to measure "creative thinking abilities" rather than creativity. The verbal subtests include an "unusual uses" test ("think of unusual uses for a box"), a "guessing causes" subtest based on a picture to which the examinee generates questions about cause and effect relationships that are not explicitly expressed in the picture, and a "product improvement" subtest, where the respondent generates ideas as how to improve a product such as a toy. The figural subtests ask the subject to construct a picture from given materials, to complete some doodles, and to create drawings from parallel lines.

The TTCT was originally presented as a research instrument, and Torrance (1966) specified five potential uses for the battery: (1) studies of education in order to yield a more "human" education; (2) studies designed to discover effective bases for individualized instruction, where the indications are that more creative children prefer to learn by discovery, experimentation, and manipulation; (3) use of the tests for remedial and psychotherapeutic programs – for example, studies of children with learning disabilities; (4) studies of the differential results of specific educational interventions and/or techniques; (5) use of tests to become aware of potentialities that might go unnoticed – for example, identifying gifted minority children.

The battery is intended for children, although it has been used with adolescents and adults; the subtests are gamelike and designed to catch a child's interest. It is doubtful that most college students and adults would respond with involvement, let alone enthusiasm, to many of the items. There are 5- to 10-minute time limits on the subtests. Note that all of the tasks, even the figural ones, require writing or drawing. Speed is essential but artistic quality is not.

Scoring. Hand scoring the TTCT is tedious and requires a well-trained individual, knowledgeable and experienced with the scoring guidelines. The test manual and scoring guides are quite clear and provide much guidance. There is also the possibility of sending the test protocols to the author for scoring (for a fee).

The subtests can be scored along four dimensions: fluency, flexibility, originality, and elaboration (not every subtest yields all four scores). These dimensions apply to many other creativity measures, especially the Guilford tests,

where they originated as a framework. *Fluency* is often translated into the number of acceptable responses given. *Flexibility* reflects the number of categories of responses. For example, the word "ball" can be defined as a round/oblong object as in baseball or football, but also can be a formal dance, or a colloquial expression for having fun. From a fluency point of view, baseball and football would count as two responses, while from the standpoint of flexibility they would count as one. *Originality* is often translated as statistical infrequency – any response given by fewer than 5 of 100 (or some other ratio) respondents is termed original. Finally, *elaboration* attempts to assess the amount of detail included in the response.

Reliability. Treffinger (1985) reported that test-retest reliability ranges from .50 to .93, with most coefficients in the .60s and .70s. These are marginal figures that suggest the TTCT should not be used for individual decisions, but seem adequate for research or group purposes.

Validity. Treffinger (1985) indicates that scores on the TTCT are positively related to other concurrent criteria, including teacher ratings and observed creative-leadership activities, but that predictive validity is a much more complex and controversial matter. TTCT scores have a modest but significant correlation with later creative achievement criteria (e.g., Torrance, 1981).

In the test manual, Torrance (1966) presents a wide variety of studies covering construct, concurrent, and predictive validity. Many more such studies have been published in the literature since then, and a majority are supportive of the validity of the TTCT. As far as content validity, Torrance (1966) argued that although the TTCT tasks do not sample the entire universe of creative abilities, they do sample a rather wide range of such abilities. The test stimuli were selected on the basis of an analysis of the literature regarding eminently creative individuals and educational theories regarding learning and creativity.

The manual also presents a number of findings that address the issue of whether TTCT scores are correlated with intelligence. The results seem to suggest that there is a very low pattern of correlations with intelligence tests (in the .20s), a slightly higher correlation with tests that assess reading and/or language (mid .20s to mid .30s), but that such patterns also seem to be a function of the characteristics of the sample tested.

Norms. Various group norms are presented by Torrance (1966), ranging from children in public schools to freshmen in a junior college nursing program. Norms are given according to the three or four dimensions (fluency, flexibility, originality, and elaboration), and not for the specific subtests or a total score. Most, if not all, of the samples are samples of convenience, heterogeneous, and somewhat small (fewer than 100). The norms are in many cases somewhat puzzling. For example, on the fluency dimension, a group of seniors in nursing obtains a mean higher by more than 1 SD than a group of male arts college sophomores. Within any one scoring dimension, such as elaboration, the SD can be larger by a factor of 3 from group to group (e.g., 10.5 vs. 34.3).

Criticisms Chase (1985) suggests that the construct validity of the TTCT is weak. In fact, the TTCT was originally intended for research purposes and its focus is clearly on what might be termed "scientific thinking," i.e., developing hypotheses, testing these, and communicating the results (E. Cooper, 1991). Other criticisms have ranged from its low reliability to its poor graphics.

Scores on the various subtests do intercorrelate substantially, with most of the coefficients in the .30 to .50 range. In fact, within the verbal domain, scores on fluency, flexibility, and originality correlate in the high .70s.

Guilford's Tests

When we discussed tests of cognitive abilities in Chapter 5, we mentioned Guilford's structure of intellect model. Briefly, you recall that in this model intellectual functioning involves the application of processes to contents, and this results in products. There were five types of processes including convergent (thinking) production and divergent thinking (see Guilford, 1988, for a revision). Convergent thinking involves problems that have one correct answer: "How much will eight oranges cost if the price is two oranges for 25 cents?" "Who was the ninth president of the United States?" "What is the present capital of Greenland?" and so on. Divergent thinking, on

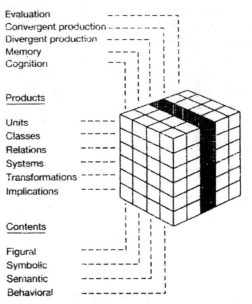

Operations

Evaluation
Convergent production
Divergent production
Memory
Cognition

Products

Units
Classes
Relations
Systems
Transformations
Implications

Contents

Figural
Symbolic
Semantic
Behavioral

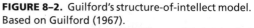

FIGURE 8–2. Guilford's structure-of-intellect model. Based on Guilford (1967).
In Guilford's structure-of-intellect model, the shaded area, divergent production, relates to creativity. From Guilford, 1967. Copyright © 1967 by McGraw-Hill. Reproduced by permission of the publisher.

the other hand, involves problems that have many possible solutions; although some solutions may be more cost effective, aesthetically pleasing, or reasonable than others, there is no one "correct" answer. For example, if you were given $100 to decorate your dorm room, what might you do? Guilford's structure of intellect model can be easily represented by a cube, as is done in Figure 8.2.

Note then, that Guilford's model encompasses both convergent and divergent thinking (Guilford, 1967b). Guilford and his collaborators attempted to develop measures that would assess each of the 120 dimensions of his model, and a number of the measures used to assess divergent thinking became popular as measures of creativity. Figure 8.3 illustrates the "slice" of the cube concerned with divergent thinking and names five of Guilford's tests that have been used in studies of creativity.

Note that the five examples given in Figure 8.3 are not distributed equally across contents and products. Some of the specific cells in Guilford's model have been difficult and/or impossible to translate operationally into reliable

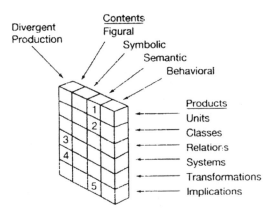

FIGURE 8–3. Some of the Guilford's tests of divergent thinking and their location in the structure-of-intellect model.

1. Consequences – Subject lists consequences of a given event, such as people having three legs.

2. Alternate Uses – Subject states uses for objects.

3. Making Objects – Given simple geometric forms such as a circle and rectangle and others, the subject constructs an object.

4. Match Problems – A configuration made up of short lines (match sticks) is given, and the subject is instructed to remove a specific number of matches to create a new configuration.

5. Possible Jobs – Given an emblem (for example, depicting a light bulb), the subject is to name occupations that might be represented by that emblem.

and valid measures. In Chapter 5, we mentioned the SOI-LA test as based on Guilford's structure-of-intellect model. You might recall that 3 of the 26 subtests of the SOI-LA assess three dimensions of creative thinking: fluency, flexibility, and originality.

The Alternate Uses Test (AUT)

The AUT (R. C. Wilson, Christensen, Merrifield, & Guilford, 1960), earlier called the Unusual Uses Test, involves the naming of a common object, such as a newspaper, and listing a maximum of six uses for that common object – uses that must be different from each other and from the primary use of that object. Thus a newspaper could be used to make up a kidnap note, to line the bottom of drawers, to make a sculpture of papier-mache, or to make a child's play hat. As is characteristic of most of Guilford's tests of divergent thinking, there are several items to the test (nine in the case of AUT) with a very brief time period (for the AUT 4 minutes for each part composed of 3 items). If you look at the Guilford model

as represented in Figure 8.2, you can locate the AUT at the intersection of Divergent production, classes, and semantic content. The test then is presumably a measure of a hypothesized factor of flexibility of thinking.

Scoring. The score is the number of acceptable responses (i.e., fluency), with credit given for no more than six responses per item. Thus the maximum score is 54 (9 items). The question, of course, is what is an acceptable response? In the test manual, the authors provide some guidelines (e.g., an acceptable use should be possible; vague or very general uses are not acceptable), as well as examples of acceptable and unacceptable responses. Thus, the question of interrater reliability is particularly applicable here.

Reliability. The reliability of Guilford's tests of divergent thinking is typically marginal. For example, for the AUT the manual cites ranges of reliability from .62 to .85, although it is not indicated how such reliability was obtained (test-retest?). Interrater reliability is not mentioned in the AUT manual; indeed the term does not appear in the subject index of Guilford's *The Nature of Human Intelligence* (1967b), where these tests are discussed.

Validity. The types of validity we discussed in Chapter 3 are not of interest to Guilford. Rather he is concerned about *factorial* validity. Does a particular measure adequately represent or assess a particular factor dimension? The test manual reports that the factor loadings (very much like correlation coefficients) of the AUT on a factor of spontaneous flexibility have been .51 and .52 for adult samples, and .32 to .45 in samples of ninth graders. In the adult samples, AUT scores also had significant loadings with a factor of originality and a factor of "sensitivity to problems." Tests such as the AUT have actually been used in many studies as de facto valid measures of creativity, but the results suggest that their validity as judged by more traditional methods leaves much to be desired (see E. Cooper, 1991, for a critical review).

The Adjective Check List (ACL)

In one sense, the ACL should have been considered in Chapter 4 because it is primarily a personality inventory, but it is presented in this chapter because its beginnings and its use have been closely interwoven with the field of creativity. The ACL is a very simple device and consists of 300 words, in alphabetical order, from absent-minded to zany. Subjects are typically asked to mark those adjectives that are self-descriptive. As with other personality inventories, the responses of the subject can then be translated into a personality profile over a number of scales.

The ACL actually began its professional life as an observer's checklist used to describe well-functioning subjects, such as architects and writers, who were being intensively studied at the Institute of Personality Assessment and Research (IPAR). The author of the ACL, Harrison Gough, published the 300-item version in 1952. Scales were then developed on the ACL, including a set of 15 scales based on Murray's need system, scales based on Transactional Analysis, and others. A test manual was published in 1965, and revised in 1983 (Gough & Heilbrun, 1983). The ACL has been quite popular, and has been translated into a substantial number of languages, from French to Vietnamese. The ACL can be computer or hand scored. Scoring basically involves subtracting the number of contraindicative items from the number of indicative items for each scale. Raw scores are then converted to T scores, according to both gender and the total number of adjectives checked.

In some ways, the ACL represents an ideal psychometric instrument. It is simple to administer, brief, nonthreatening and noninvasive to the respondent, scorable either by hand or computer, amenable to statistical and logical analyses, useful both as an observer- or self-descriptive instrument, and almost limitless in its range of applications (see Fekken, 1984, for a review). Because it is an open system such as the MMPI and CPI, new scales can be developed as needed, and in fact a number of investigators, including Gough himself, have developed scales of creativity on the ACL (G. Domino, 1994).

The Domino Creativity (Cr) Scale on the ACL.
The Domino Cr scale on the ACL was developed by asking the faculty of an all-male liberal arts college, at the end of the academic year, to identify all freshmen who had shown creative abilities (see G. Domino, 1970, for more specific details). A total of 96 students were nominated and these were matched with a control group as to gender (all males), age (modal age of 18), IQ (means of

128 and 130 respectively), degree of adjustment (as judged by the MMPI profile), and major (all liberal arts).

At the beginning of the second academic year, different faculty members were given names of students in their classes and asked to make a special effort to "observe" these students. At the end of the semester, the faculty were requested to identify each student as creative or not. The observed students were of course the creative nominees and their matched controls. Of the 96 creative nominees, 13 had left the college; of the 83 remaining, 62 were again identified as creative. Of the 96 controls, 6 had left the college and 3 were identified as creative; these were eliminated and a control group of 87 was retained.

At the beginning of the third academic year the same procedure was repeated, but this time after the faculty had observed the specified students for a semester, they were asked to describe each student on the ACL. Of the 300 words, 59 were used more frequently to describe creative students, and these became the Creativity scale. The scale includes such expected items as "artistic," "imaginative," and "inventive" (the ACL does not include the word "creative"), as well as items like "aloof," "argumentative," "dissatisfied," "intolerant," and "outspoken." Globally, the psychometric portrait presented by these items is quite consonant with both empirical findings and theoretical expectations about creative individuals.

Is there any evidence that the students observed by the faculty were indeed creative? One line of evidence is that they were independently nominated as creative by two distinct groups of faculty members. The author (G. Domino, 1970) also compared the creative and control students on three measures of creativity and found that creatives scored higher on all three measures.

Schaefer and Anastasi (1968; Schaefer, 1967), had studied a group of 800 high-school students evenly divided as to creative or control, male vs. female, and field of creativity (science vs. art). These students had filled out a self-descriptive ACL so their protocols were scored for the Domino Cr scale. The results are given in Table 8.4 in T scores.

In each comparison, the ACL Cr scale statistically differentiated between creatives and controls, but showed no significant differences between gender and field of study. Note also, that although the scale was originally developed

Table 8–4. *T* Scores for 800 High-School Students on the ACL Creativity Scale		
Males	**M**	**SD**
Artistic creative	54.48	8.71
Artistic control	45.52	8.94
Scientific creative	54.38	9.72
Scientific control	45.62	7.95
Females	**M**	**SD**
Artistic creative	52.37	9.60
Artistic control	47.63	9.62
Literary creative*	54.14	9.66
Literary control	45.86	8.28

*There were not sufficient numbers of females studying science; hence for females, the fields of study were artistic and literary.

on the basis of observer ratings of male college students, it was cross-validated on self-ratings of both male and female high-school students. Other studies of inventors, of dance and music students, of scientists and architecture students, have supported the validity of the scale (Albaum & Baker, 1977; Alter, 1984; 1989; G. Domino, 1994). The available literature (see G. Domino, 1994) supports the construct and criterion validity of this scale.

Some reliability information, primarily of the internal stability type is available. For example, G. A. Davis and Bull (1978) reported a coefficient of .91 and Ironson and G. A. Davis (1979) of .90 for college students; G. Domino (1994) reported .81 and .86 for samples of scientists and architecture students.

The MBTI revisited. In Chapter 4, we covered the Myers-Briggs Type Indicator. Although the MBTI is a personality inventory, several of its scales are empirically and theoretically related to creativity, and in fact much of the early validational work on the MBTI was carried out at IPAR. In Chapter 3, we mentioned multiple regression as a method of combining test scores, and it might be worthwhile to revisit these two topics at this point.

On the MBTI there is a *creativity index* that can be calculated using the following regression equation (A. Thorne & Gough, 1991):

$$\text{MBTI Creativity Index} = 3SN + JP - EI - .5TF$$

Thus, we administer the MBTI to a subject, score the inventory on its four scales and place the raw scores in the above equation. According to I. B.

Myers and McCaulley (1985), the median score on this index is about 300 (SD = 96.8), with mean scores for various samples ranging from 221 to 365. Scores of 350 or higher are supposedly indicative of creative potential. Fleenor and Taylor (1994) indeed found that scores on this creativity index were substantially correlated to two other "personality type" self-report measures of creativity.

Chinese Tangrams

There are a substantial number of creativity measures available (see the *Journal of Creative Behavior* that publishes lists of these measures at irregular intervals), but few exist that are equally applicable to children as well as adults, that do not involve extensive verbal skills, and that require the subject to produce a potentially creative product without needing technical or specialized skills.

G. Domino (1980) chose a somewhat popular puzzle known as Chinese Tangrams, and explored its feasibility as a test of creativity. The tangram consists of a square, usually made of paper, cut into seven pieces, as illustrated in Figure 8.4.

Tangrams can be used for three major activities: (1) to reproduce a given completed figure using all seven pieces; (2) to solve combinatorial problems, such as the number of different convex polygons that can be generated; and (3) to create "original" pictures, the focus of this effort

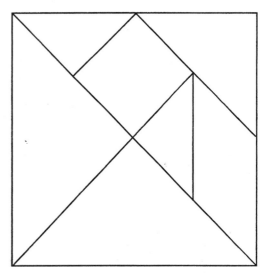

FIGURE 8–4. The Chinese Tangram puzzle.

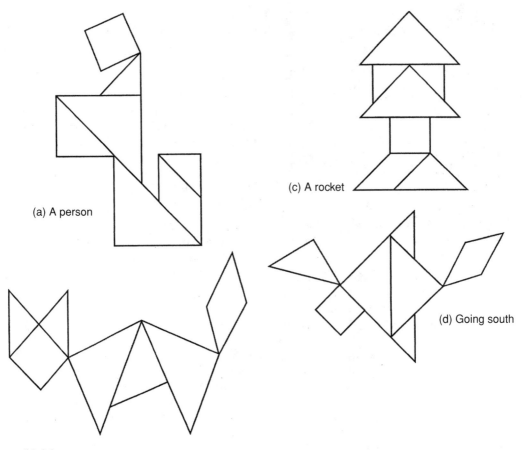

(a) A person

(c) A rocket

(d) Going south

(b) A fox

FIGURE 8–5. Illustrative responses on the Chinese Tangram.

(M. Gardner, 1974). The tangram is presented as a game and its use illustrated by the examiner. Each person is given a tangram and is shown how the seven pieces can be put together to make a person, an animal, an object, or a more abstract idea, as illustrated in Figure 8.5. The examiner then points to the fox and asks what else might that be. Recognizable responses (e.g., a coyote, a skunk, a poodle) are praised. If not indicated by anyone, the examiner suggests that the fox might also be a smiling or jumping cat. The intent is to imply that the seven pieces can result in many configurations including anthropomorphic and animated ones. Subjects are then asked to create their own picture, something creative and original that perhaps no one else will think of, but that others will recognize. The results can be scored on fluency (number of acceptable responses), flexibility (number of response categories), and originality (statistical infrequency).

Interrater reliability ranged from .72 to .96 in a sample of third graders, and from .76 to .92 in a sample of college students. In one study of third graders, children in a gifted class were compared with children in the standard classroom; gifted children scored higher on all three dimensions. In another study, 57 college students were administered the tangram and a battery of creativity measures, including two of Guilford's tests. Of the 15 correlation coefficients, 9 were statistically significant. In addition, scores on the tangram test were not correlated with measures of intelligence or academic achievement (see G. Domino, 1980, for details on all these studies).

General Comments About Creativity Tests

Interscorer and intrascorer reliability. With most tests of creativity, scoring the test protocol requires a fair amount of subjective judgment, and the degree to which specific guidelines, examples, and/or training are provided varies widely. Therefore, with most creativity tests the question of interscorer reliability is important. Would two different individuals scoring a set of protocols independently assign identical (or highly similar) scores? The answer seems to be yes, and typical correlation coefficients can be in the .90s range, provided the scorers focus on the task seriously and are given clear guidelines and/or explicit training.

Given that scoring a test protocol is not the most exciting activity, we need to ask whether the scorer's reliability changes over time as a function of fatigue, boredom, or other aspects. The answer here also seems to be yes, but intrarater stability can be enhanced by not making the task too onerous – e.g., allowing coffee breaks, using aids to summarize scoring rules, keeping the number of protocols scored at one sitting to a minimum, and so on.

In this context, it should be pointed out that interrater reliability in psychological testing seems to be superior to that found in other fields. For example, R. L. Goldman (1992; 1994) reviewed the medical literature on peer assessment of quality of care (the degree to which different physicians agree in their assessment of medical records), and found that such reliability was only slightly higher than the level expected by chance.

Some scoring problems. Conventional scoring methods for many of the tests of creativity present a number of problems. Consider for example the assessment of originality, which seems to be a crucial component of creativity. To assess whether a response is original or not, we have two basic options. One is to collect responses from a large group of individuals (i.e., norms). These responses are tabulated and any infrequent response, for example given by fewer than 5 out of 100 respondents, is classified as original. If we now are scoring a new sample of protocols, we can use the tabulation as a guideline. We will need to make a number of subjective decisions. For example, if our test item is to name round objects that bounce, is a "bowling ball" acceptable or not? Is a "pelota" different from a ball?

A second method is to have raters, for example school teachers, rate the response as original or not. Hocevar (1979) argues that such subjective judgment is better than statistical infrequency as a criterion of originality. Runco and Mraz (1992) argue that both of these methods are unrealistic in that ideas are not produced singly; what is of interest is the ideational potential of the subject. They therefore asked a number of judges to assess a subject's responses in toto, as a unit. They also asked judges to rate "creativity" rather than originality. The results indicated that these ratings had high interrater reliabilities, but unfortunately poor discriminant validity in that ratings of creativity and ratings of intelligence correlated substantially ($r = .58$).

The issues here represent basic questions that need to be asked of any psychological test. To what degree is the scoring of the items objective or subjective? Is the scoring one that assesses individual items or one based on some global assessment? If we score individual items, how can these be placed together to maximize the correlation with some outside criterion? If we use global judgment, how can we make sure that the judgment is not contaminated by extraneous variables?

Measures of creativity have been questioned from a variety of viewpoints. One basic question is whether performance on a test of creativity is related to real-world creativity. Another question is whether performance is a function of the particular stimuli and instructions given to the person; several studies have shown that changes in test instructions result in changes in test performance, such as asking subjects to answer as if they were highly creative (e.g., Lissitz & Willhoft, 1985; S. V. Owen & Baum, 1985). Some have questioned whether the four divergent thinking dimensions of fluency, flexibility, originality, and elaboration are separate aspects of creativity.

IMAGERY

One area that is closely related to creativity is that of imagery, the ability to purposely visualize in one's mind objects that are not present. Because we are not able, at present, to get into someone else's mind, most measures of imagery are self-report questionnaires. Galton (1907) was probably the first psychologist to investigate imagery through a self-report questionnaire, by asking subjects to imagine their breakfast table that morning and noting how vivid that image was.

Marks's Vividness of Visual Imagery Questionnaire (VVIQ)

Today probably the most commonly used measure of imagery is Marks' (1973) Vividness of Visual Imagery Questionnaire (VVIQ), although it has been severely criticized (e.g., Chara & Verplanck, 1986; Kaufman, 1983). This 16-item questionnaire asks the respondent to think, in turn, of a relative or friend seen frequently, a rising sun, a shop, and a country scene, and in each case visualize the picture that comes in the "mind's eye." For each item, the respondent uses a 1 to 5 rating scale, where 1 is defined as "perfectly clear and as vivid as normal vision" and 5 is "no image at all, you only 'know' that you are thinking of the object." The scale is administered twice, once with eyes open and once with eyes closed.

D. F. Marks (1973) reports a test-retest reliability of .74 for a sample of 68 subjects, with no time period indicated, and a split-half reliability of .85. He also reports three different studies, two with college students and one with high-school students, in which in each case the most extreme high scorers were compared with the most extreme low scorers in the degree of recall of colored photographs. In all three experiments "good" visualizers (i.e., low scorers on the VVIQ), were more accurate in recall than "poor" visualizers (i.e., high scorers on the VVIQ). In two of the studies, D. F. Marks (1973) found that females had greater accuracy of recall than males.

Paivio's Individual Differences Questionnaire (IDQ)

Another relatively popular imagery questionnaire is the Individual Differences Questionnaire (IDQ). Paivio (1975) proposed that human thinking involves a continuous interplay of nonverbal imagery and verbal symbolic processes, which are interconnected but functionally distinct; this proposal led to a "dual coding" theory that spells out the implications of such a model. As part of his efforts, Paivio (1971; Paivio & Harshman, 1983) developed the IDQ

to measure imaginal and verbal traits. Basically, Paivio hypothesized that many situations and tasks can be conceptualized either verbally or nonverbally, and that individual persons differ in the extent to which their thinking uses one or another of these modalities. True-false items were then developed, based on the above assumption and on the more formal "dual coding" theory. The items generated (e.g., "I am a slow reader," "I enjoy learning new words," "I use mental pictures quite often") covered various preferences, abilities, and habits. Paivio developed a sample set of items and then asked several graduate students to generate more. The final set of 86 items contained an approximately equal number of items referring to the two symbolic modes and approximately equal numbers of each type keyed true or false. Apparently, the inclusion or exclusion of an item was based on logical grounds and not statistical analyses. The IDQ yields two scores, one an "imaginal" and one on the "verbal" scale. The actual items, instructions, and scoring key can be found in Paivio and Harshman (1983).

In a series of factor analyses on data from 100 college students, both two factors and six factors were obtained. The two factors seem to parallel the imaginal and the verbal dimensions. The six factors were labeled: (1) good verbal expression and fluency (e.g., I express my thoughts clearly); (2) habitual use of imagery (e.g., I often use mental images); (3) concern with correct use of words (e.g., I am very careful about using words correctly); (4) self-reported reading difficulties (e.g., I am a slow reader); (5) use of images to solve problems (e.g., I use images to solve problems); and (6) vividness of dreams, daydreams, and imagination (e.g., my dreams are quite vivid). Note that of the six factors, three are verbal and three reflect imagery. The six factors, however, cover only 47 of the 86 items, and two of the imagery factors are composed of two and four items respectively, so their practical utility is quite limited.

Alpha reliability coefficients for the six factor scales range from a low of .72 to a high of .84 (Paivio & Harshman, 1983). In the initial study, no validity data are presented; the focus is clearly on factor analysis. Subsequent studies have used factor 2, the habitual use of imagery, as a scale with positive results (e.g., B. H. Cohen & Saslona, 1990; Hiscock, 1978).

Hiscock (1978) investigated the IDQ in a series of four studies in which a revised version of the IDQ was compared with other measures of imagery. Cronbach's alpha for the imagery scale was found to be .80, .81, and .87 in three different samples, while for the verbal scale, the obtained values were .83, .86, and .88. Retest reliability, based on a sample of 79 college students retested 2 to 6 weeks later, was .84 for the imagery scale and .88 for the verbal scale. Correlations between the IDQ scales and other measures of imagery were modest at best, ranging from a high of .49 and .56 to several nonsignificant values.

Kardash, Amlund, and Stock (1986) used 34 of the 86 items that met certain statistical criteria and did a factor analysis. Of the 34 items, 27 were verbal and 7 were imagery items. The 27-item verbal scale had an internal consistency reliability of $r = .74$, while for the 7-item imaginal scale, the $r = .52$. The authors concluded that the IDQ is indeed a multifactor instrument that needs improvement but can be interpreted on the basis of either two factors or five factors (the items on the factor "use of images to solve problems" were dropped from consideration because of statistical reasons).

The Verbalizer-Visualizer Questionnaire (VVQ)

A third somewhat popular measure of imagery is the VVQ, developed by A. Richardson (1977) to measure individual differences on a verbal-visual dimension of cognitive style. The 15 items on the scale were selected empirically to discriminate between individuals who habitually move their eyes to the left when thinking vs. eyes to the right because such eye movements are presumably linked to hemispheric brain functions. The items on the VVQ ask whether the subject has good facility of words, whether they think in images, whether their dreams and daydreams are vivid, and so on. The author himself cross-validated the results (A. Richardson, 1978) only to find results that were in the opposite direction from what was expected!

Edward and Wilkins (1981) conducted two studies designed to explore the relationship of the VVQ with measures of imagery and of verbal-visual ability. The results, particularly of the second study, cast considerable doubt on the construct validity of the VVQ. Part of the difficulty may be that the VVQ considers verbal-visual abilities as opposite ends of a continuum, while the literature suggests that these two processes are parallel and independent.

Parrott (1986) also found the VVQ not to relate to visual imagery, spatial-ability level, and examination grades in a sample of mechanical engineering students. Boswell and Pickett (1991) suggested that the problem with the VVQ was its questionable internal consistency. They administered the VVQ to a sample of college students and computed K-R 20 coefficients; these were .42 for males, .50 for females, and .47 for the total sample. They carried out a factor analysis and found six factors, but only the first two were logically meaningful; these were labeled as "vividness of dreams" and "enjoyment of word usage."

General concern about imagery questionnaires. Unfortunately there seems to be a lack of consistent correlation between subjective reports of visual imagery and actual performance on tasks that seem to depend on such visual imagery. Part of the problem may well be the complicated nature of visual imagery, and part of the problem seems to be the assessment devices used in such studies. It may well be that questionnaires such as those by Marks and by Paivio are useful and predictive only under certain circumstances – for example, only when the spontaneous use of such imagery is helpful (e.g., R. G. Turner, 1978). On the other hand, at least one review of such measures concluded that they are reliable and have predictive validity (K. White, Sheehan, & Ashton, 1977).

COMPETITIVENESS

Competitiveness is a salient characteristic of everyday life, particularly in American culture. There are many perspectives one can use in assessing competitiveness, and Smither and Houston (1992) identified four major ones: achievement motivation, sports psychology, experimental social psychology, and personality assessment. Achievement motivation was historically tested by projective techniques, in particular the Thematic Apperception Test, but, subsequently, a large number of objective inventories were developed. A good example is the CPI discussed in Chapter 4, which contains two scales related to achievement motivation. Smither and Houston (1992) argue that competitiveness and achievement motivation are not necessarily the same; they may occur in the same individual, but competitiveness need not be present in a highly achieving person. Competitive behavior is of course central to sports, and a number of questionnaires have been designed to assess competitiveness in the context of sports (e.g., Fabian & Ross, 1984; Gill & Deeter, 1988). In the area of experimental social psychology, competitiveness has been studied extensively by looking at how valued rewards are distributed in a group, or by having subjects engage in games in which they can choose to cooperate or compete. G. Domino (1992), for example, compared Chinese and American children on a game-like task and found that Chinese children were more likely to engage in cooperative responses that maximized group rewards, while American children were more likely to engage in competitive responses that maximized individual gain. Finally, competitiveness can be viewed from the perspective of personality; it may be seen as a pervasive quality present not only in sports but in most human activities.

Smither and Houston (1992) argued that in a review of the literature, they found no measures of competitiveness that were independent of achievement motivation, generalizable rather than focused on athletics and psychometrically sound. They therefore set out to develop such a measure. They generated a set of 67 items designed to identify persons who prefer competitive over cooperative situations (e.g., "I am a competitive person") and administered these items and a scale of achievement motivation to a sample of 84 working adults. Scores on the two scales correlated .68. An item analysis correlating each item to the total score, yielded 41 items with significant correlations. It is not clear exactly what the authors did here because they state that the 41 items "discriminated significantly between high and low scorers," but they indicate that the items were dropped or retained on the basis of the item-total correlation (rather than a contrasted group approach suggested by the quote). They carried out an item analysis on a second, larger sample of undergraduate students and retained 20 items based on item-total correlations larger

than .40. The internal consistency of this 20-item form was .90. Scores on this scale, which the authors call the Competitiveness Index, were significantly correlated with measures of achievement motivation. A factor analysis yielded three factors labeled as "emotion," "argument," and "games." Whether this competitiveness index is useful, remains to be seen.

HOPE

Hope is of particular interest to the fields of health psychology, psychological medicine, and nursing since, anecdotally at least, there seems to be evidence that hope and the course of illnesses such as cancer are intimately related (e.g., J. Dufault & Martocchio, 1985). There is evidence to suggest links between hope and health (e.g., Gottschalk, 1985; Kiecolt-Glaser & Glaser, 1986), hope and psychotherapeutic outcome (e.g., J. Frank, 1968), and even adherence to weight-loss programs (e.g., Janis, 1980). Many writers have suggested that hope is a unidimensional construct that involves an overall perception that goals can be met (e.g., Erickson, Post, & Paige, 1975; Gottschalk, 1974; Mowrer, 1960; Stotland, 1969). As Staats (1989) indicates, philosophers and practitioners have long recognized the importance of hope, but few efforts have been made to assess this construct. We will briefly look at two somewhat recent measures of hope (for other measures see Fibel & Hale, 1978; Obayuwana et al., 1982; Staats, 1989; Staats & Stassen; 1985).

The Miller Hope Scale (MHS)

Miller and Powers (1988) developed a Hope scale based on a broader conceptualization of hope than merely as an expectation for goal achievement. They saw hope as a "state of being," characterized by an anticipation for a continued good or improved state and marked by 10 critical elements such as mutuality-affiliation (i.e., hope is characterized by caring, trust, etc.) and anticipation (i.e., looking forward to a good future).

The Miller Hope Scale (MHS) is a 40-item scale that uses a 5-point response format from "strongly agree" to "strongly disagree" (5 to 1 points). Apparently, the initial item pool consisted of 47 items that were evaluated by four judges as to the degree of "hope information" assessed by each item. Seven items were eliminated. The 40 items were then given to "six experts in measurement" who critiqued the items – but because the scale continued to be 40 items long, it is not clear whether the critiques were used to change the wording of items vs. deleting items, or some other purpose. The MHS was administered to 75 students (primarily nursing students) as a pilot sample and to a convenience sample of 522 students from two universities, who were also administered other scales.

Reliability. For the pilot sample, Cronbach's alpha was computed to be .95, and test-retest reliability over a 2-week interval was .87. For the convenience sample, alpha was .93 and test-retest reliability, also over a 2-week period, was .82. Thus the initial reliability of this scale, viewed from either the point of internal consistency or stability over time is quite good. We would want to round out this picture with samples other than college students and with somewhat greater time intervals.

Validity. Scores on the MHS correlated substantially (.71 and .82) with two measures of psychological well-being that presumably measured purpose and meaning in life, somewhat less (.69) with a one-item self-assessment of hope, and negatively (−.54) with a hopelessness scale. A factor analysis of the MHS suggested that a three-factor solution was the best, which the authors interpreted as satisfaction, avoidance of hope threats, and anticipation of the future.

Note a bit of a problem here. If a scale correlates substantially with other scales that presumably measure different constructs, then we can question whether in fact the scales are measuring the same construct. Here is a hope scale that correlates substantially with measures of psychological well-being; does the MHS measure hope or some other variable, such as purpose in life, psychological health, adjustment, a desire to present one's self favorably? If we could arrive at a consensus – unlikely in reality but thinkable theoretically – that all these scales are measuring hope, then we need to ask why use the MHS? What advantages does this scale have over others? Is it shorter? Does it have better norms? It is more easily available? Does it have higher reliability?

The Snyder Hope Scale (SHS)

Snyder et al. (1991) suggested that hope is made up of two components, encapsulated by the popular saying "Where there is a will there is a way." The "will" has to do with goal-directed agency, while the "way" has to do with pathways. Both agency and pathways are necessary, but neither is sufficient to define hope.

A pool of 45 items written to reflect both agency and pathways aspects of hope were administered to a sample of introductory psychology students. A 4-point response scale (from definitely false to definitely true) was used. Item-total correlations were computed and 14 items with correlations larger than .20 were retained. The senior author then decided to keep the four items that most clearly reflected the agency component (e.g., "I energetically pursue my goals") and the four items that most clearly tapped the pathways component (e.g., "I can think of many ways to get out of a jam"); the final scale then, contains these eight hope items plus four filler items.

Reliability. Cronbach's alphas for the total scale range from .74 to .84, for the agency subscale from .71 to .76, and for the Pathways subscale, they range from .63 to .80. Given that the subscales have only four items each, the results seem quite acceptable. Test-retest reliability was assessed in four samples of college students, with retest intervals ranging from 3 weeks to 10 weeks; the resulting correlation coefficients ranged from .73 to .85.

Validity. Factor analyses across various samples suggest that a two-factor solution parallelling the agency-pathways distinction makes sense; the two factors seem robust in that they account for 52% to 63% of the variance. At the same time, the two factors correlate with each other – with correlation coefficients ranging from .38 to .57. A series of studies assessed convergent validity. Scores on the SHS were positively correlated with measures of optimism, perceived control, and self-esteem, and negatively correlated with measures of hopelessness, depression, and psychopathology, as assessed by the MMPI. A number of other, more complicated studies are presented that address the construct validity of the scale (Snyder et al., 1991). For example, predictions were made that high scorers would maintain their hopefulness in the face of stress ("when the going gets tough, the tough get going"), while low scorers would deteriorate in their hopefulness. Predictions were also made that higher-hope individuals would have a greater number of goals across various life aspects and would select more difficult goals. These and other hypotheses were generally supported. There were no gender differences obtained on this scale, despite the expectation by the authors that there would be.

HASSLES

Life is full of hassles, and how we handle these seems to be an important variable. Some people are able to follow the old adage, "When life gives you lemons, make lemonade."

The Hassles Scale

The Hassles scale (Kanner, Coyne, Schaefer, et al., 1981) consists of 117 minor stressors that occur on a frequent basis. Hassles can involve minor irritations, such as losing things or bigger problems like getting a traffic citation. Respondents to the Hassles Scale are asked to note the occurrence and rate the severity of these daily life hassles on a 4-point scale ranging from none to extremely severe, and a time frame of the "last month." The items are fairly general (e.g., home maintenance; health of a family member) rather than specific (e.g. the roof is leaking and I had to call the apartment manager three times). The Hassles Scale was revised in 1988 (DeLongis, Folkman, & Lazarus, 1988).

Some studies have found that daily hassles are more predictive of self-reported adjustment difficulties than other measures (e.g. DeLongis, Coyne, Dakof, et al., 1982; Wolf, Elston, & Kissling, 1989).

Development of a college form. The Hassles Scale, although used in a number of studies with college students, contains a number of items that do not apply to many college students (e.g., job security, problems with spouse), and so Blankstein, Flett, and Koledin (1991) developed a form for use with college students (for hassles scales developed for particular age groups such as adolescents or the elderly (see Compas, Davis,

Forsythe, et al., 1987; Ewedemi & Linn, 1987; C. K. Holahan & C. J. Holahan, 1987; Kanner, Feldman, Weinberger, et al., 1987). To compile an item pool, the authors asked more than 200 undergraduate students at a Canadian university to list one or two hassles they had recently experienced in nine different areas, such as school, work, family, and financial. The obtained items were classified into the nine areas, tabulated as to frequency, and finally 20 items were selected to represent the nine areas. A new sample of more than 400 students completed this Brief College Student Hassles Scale (BCSHS) along with other measures. The instructions asked the subject to check each item on a 1- to 7-point scale, ranging from no hassle to extremely persistent hassle, and to use the preceding 1 month as a time frame.

Reliability and validity. Reliability was assessed by the alpha coefficient, calculated to be .81 – quite high considering that the items theoretically represent diverse areas. Some minor gender differences were obtained, with women rating the items "academic deadlines," "weight," and "household chores" higher than men. Scores on the BCSHS were negatively correlated with a measure of optimism (greater optimism associated with less persistent hassles), and positively correlated with more persistent problems with negative affect (e.g., anxiety, loneliness, and unhappiness).

LONELINESS

Loneliness has gained recognition as a complex behavior that affects a majority of people. Rubenstein and Shaver (1982) compared loneliness with hunger. Just as our bodies signal a need for food by sensations of hunger, our psyche signals a need for emotionally sustaining ties by the sensation of loneliness. Through a newspaper survey, they found that loneliness was indeed widespread; other researchers indeed agree (e.g., Peplau & Perlman, 1982; R. S. Weiss, 1973). Peplau and Perlman (1982) believe that loneliness is marked by three aspects: (1) It is subjective – being alone is not equal to being lonely; (2) Loneliness is experienced as distressing; (3) Loneliness is marked by a perceived deficiency in social relationships.

As with other areas of research, there are a number of issues upon which there is disagreement. One is the distinction between loneliness and other terms such as aloneness, solitude, and seclusion. Another is whether loneliness is a state or a trait, or both. Still, a third is the differences, if any, between transitory and chronic loneliness.

The UCLA Loneliness Scale (ULS)

One of the most frequently used and psychometrically sound instruments for the measurement of loneliness is the UCLA Loneliness scale, originally presented in 1978 (Russell, Peplau, & Ferguson, 1978) and revised in 1980 (Russell, Peplau, & Cutrona, 1980).

The ULS was initially developed by using 25 items from another longer (75 items) loneliness scale. This pool of items was administered to a sample of UCLA students who were either members of a discussion group on loneliness ($n = 12$), a Social Psychology class ($n = 35$), or in Introductory Psychology ($n = 192$). Correlations between item and total score indicated that 5 of the items correlated below .50 and hence were dropped. The final scale of 20 items was then assessed for reliability and a coefficient alpha of .96 was obtained. A sample of 102 students retested over a 2-month period, yielded a test-retest r of .73. Scores on the ULS correlated .79 with self-ratings of loneliness, and the mean was significantly different for those students who had volunteered for the discussion group on loneliness than for a control sample. Furthermore, scores correlated significantly with self-ratings of depression, anxiety, and endorsement of several adjectives such as "empty" and "shy," and negatively with self-ratings of satisfaction and of happiness.

The ULS is thus a unidimensional measure composed of 20 items, 10 worded positively and 10 worded negatively. Subjects respond on a 4-point scale of never (1), rarely (2), sometimes (3), and often (4). Coefficient alphas are typically in the .80s range for early adolescents (Mahon & Yarcheski, 1990), and in the .90s for college students and adults (Hartshorne, 1993; Knight, Chisholm, Marsh, et al., 1988). The results of factor-analytic studies are however mixed. Some researchers have found one factor (e.g. Hartshorne, 1993), others two factors (e.g., Knight, Chisholm, Marsh, et al., 1988; Zakahi & Duran, 1982), and some, four or five factors (e.g.,

Hays & DiMatteo, 1987; Hojat, 1982). Part of the problem with the ULS is that at least some of the items are worded in a confusing or ambiguous manner (Hartshorne, 1993). Hartshorne (1993) suggests that loneliness as measured by the ULS is a bimodal emotional state; that is, at the time of testing individuals either are or are not lonely.

The ULS has been used in a number of cross-cultural studies. For example, in Japan the ULS was reported to have high internal consistency (alpha of .87, split-half of .83), and reasonable test-retest correlation over a 6-month period ($r = .55$). Lonely Japanese reported more limited social activities and relations and tended to regard their parents as being disagreeable, cold, and untrustworthy; they had lower self-esteem and experienced more medical and psychological problems (Kudoh & Nishikawa, 1983). (For another loneliness scale see N. Schmidt & Sermat, 1983; see also the *Journal of Social Behavior and Personality*, 1987, 2, No. 2; the entire issue is devoted to loneliness).

DEATH ANXIETY

Lives take many forms, but we all share in the reality of our eventual death. Some people are made extremely anxious by this thought, while others are relatively unconcerned, and still others look forward to death as a transition. Thus, death anxiety is an important variable, and a number of investigators have developed scales to assess this concept. Probably, the best known of these scales is the Death Anxiety Scale by Templer (1970).

Death Anxiety Scale (DAS)

Templer (1970) wrote that up to that time three methods of assessment had been used in the measurement of death anxiety: interviews, projective techniques, and questionnaires, but that with the exception of one questionnaire, the reliability and validity of these procedures had not been reported in the literature.

Templer (1970) developed the DAS by devising 40 items on a "rational" basis – that is, because this was his doctoral dissertation, he presumably read the pertinent literature, talked to his committee members, and finally wrote down these items. Four chaplains in a state mental hospital, two graduate students, and one clinical psychologist, rated the face validity of each item; 31 items survived. These items were then embedded in a set of 200 MMPI items to disguise their intent and were administered to three groups of college students. Those items that correlated significantly with total scores in at least two of the three samples were retained. This yielded a scale of 15 items.

The DAS is reported to have adequate test-retest reliability (.83 for a sample of college students retested after 3 weeks) and internal consistency (K-R20 coefficient of .76). Templer (1970) presents a series of small pilot studies. Two of the studies suggest that the DAS is free of nuisance components such as acquiescence and social desirability. Two other studies address the validity of the DAS. In one, psychiatric patients who had spontaneously verbalized fear of death were compared with a control sample: the respective DAS means were 11.62 and 6.77, a statistically significant difference. In another study with college students, scores on the DAS were found to correlate with MMPI measures of general anxiety, with another death-anxiety questionnaire, and with an experimental task designed to assess "number of emotional words."

A number of investigators have used the DAS with varying results. For example, Donovan (1993) translated the DAS into Brazilian Portuguese. This was done by what is called the *back translation* method (Brislin, 1970), where an English language instrument is translated into another language, the other language version is retranslated into English, and then compared with the original English version. Brislin (1970) also suggests that to check the adequacy of translation, one could administer the two forms to a bilingual sample. This was done by Donovan (1993) in a modified manner where some Brazilian students took the odd-numbered items in English and the even-numbered items in Portuguese (form A), and some students took the odd-numbered items in Portuguese and the even-numbered items in English (form B). For form A, the split-half reliability was calculated to be .59, while for form B it was .91. The convergent and discriminant validation of this Portuguese version was carried out by comparing the DAS with various other measures such as the STAI (also in Portuguese). The results were quite similar to those obtained in American samples.

SUMMARY

This chapter looked at a selected number of topical areas to illustrate various uses of tests and some basic issues. In the area of self-concept, the Tennessee Self-Concept Scale illustrates some of the challenges that need to be met. In the area of locus of control, the Rotter scale occupies a central position and gave birth to a multitude of such scales. Sexuality is yet another active field of research where various scales and psychometric methodologies can provide potentially useful results. In the area of creativity, the challenges are many, and the measurement there is, if not still in its infancy, certainly is in its childhood. Other areas such as hope and death anxiety illustrate a variety of approaches and issues.

SUGGESTED READINGS

Barren, F. (1958). The psychology of imagination. *Scientific American, 199,* 151–166.

A fascinating look at the study of creativity as it was undertaken at the Institute of Personality Research and Assessment of the University of California at Berkeley. Barron briefly illustrates a number of techniques used in these assessment studies, including the Welsh Figure Preference Test, a Drawing Completion test, and an inkblot test.

Mednick, S. A. (1962). The associative basis of the creative process. *Psychological Review, 69,* 220–232.

For the area of creativity, this is somewhat of a classic paper in which the author proposes an associative interpretation of the process of creative thinking and presents a test of creativity – the Remote Associates Test – based on the theoretical approach.

O'Donohue, W. & Caselles, C. E. (1993). Homophobia: Conceptual, definitional, and value issues. *Journal of Psychopathology and Behavioral Assessment, 15,* 177–195.

This paper examines the concept of homophobia – negative attitudes, beliefs, or actions toward homosexuals – and in particular looks at a number of scales that have been developed to assess this variable.

Rotter, J. B. (1990). Internal versus external control of reinforcement. A case history of a variable. *American Psychologist, 45,* 489–493.

The author considers why locus of control has become such a popular variable. He identifies four aspects as important: (1) a precise definition of locus of control; (2) the imbedding of the construct in a broader theory; (3) the development of a measure from a broad psychological perspective; and (4) the presentation of the initial scale in a monograph format, rather than a brief journal article, allowing for sufficient detail and data presented from a programmatic effort. Rotter makes a plea for the importance of broad theories in psychology.

Snyder, C. R. (1996). Development and validation of the State Hope Scale. *Journal of Personality and Social Psychology, 70*, 321–335.

A report of four studies to develop and validate a measure of state hope.

DISCUSSION QUESTIONS

1. If you were writing this chapter on psychological tests that measure normal positive functioning, what might be some of the topic areas you would cover and why?

2. What else could have been done to generate primary, secondary, and tertiary validity data for the Self-Esteem Questionnaire?

3. What are some of the aspects of sexuality that might be assessed through psychological tests?

4. Assuming that you have a modest research budget, how would you develop a creativity scale on the ACL?

5. How would you show that the Chinese Tangrams measures creativity rather than say, spatial intelligence?

9 Special Children

AIM This chapter looks at psychological testing in the context of "special" children. We first look at some specific issues that range from the laws that have impacted the psychological testing of handicapped children, to issues of infant intelligence. In the process, we look at several instruments that are broad-based and nicely illustrate some of these issues. Then we look at nine major categories of special children, not exhaustively, but to illustrate various issues and instruments. Finally, we return to some general issues of this rather broad and complicated area.

SOME ISSUES REGARDING TESTING

Special children. Although all children are special, we will use the term "special children" as used in the literature, namely to signify children who have some condition that presents, at least potentially, difficulties in their development and in their learning so that they do not adapt or function at what may be considered the "normal" level.

Need to identify and assess. Recently, there has been a substantial increase in the need to identify and assess such children so that they may be given appropriate assistance. This increase is due to several factors. One is the advance of medical sciences. Children who years ago would have died at birth have now increased survival rates, but often the result is a child with disabilities. A second aspect is the passage in 1975 of Public Law 94–142, the Education for All Handicapped Children Act, which mandates a wide range of services for such children, as well as their right to an education. Finally, parents of special children have become much more vocal in their demands for comprehensive services for their children.

Public Law 94–142. In 1975, Public Law 94–142, or the Education for All Handicapped Children Act was passed by Congress. This law mandated that a "free and appropriate" education be provided to all handicapped children. This necessitated the identification of such children that might be eligible for special educational services. The law also included, for the first time, federal standards for the use of intelligence tests. It specified that test results should be viewed as only one source of information. Furthermore, the law specified that a test should be administered in the child's native language, or at the very least, that linguistic differences should not interfere with the assessment of intelligence. The law however, did not indicate specifically how screening and testing were to be conducted, with the result that each educational entity uses different procedures. As W. L. Goodwin and Driscoll (1980) pointed out, the screening and diagnostic phases have not been kept distinct. Screening requires tests that are valid, but brief and economical. Diagnosis involves in-depth measurement and examination by a team of professionals.

Public Law 99–457. This law is an extension of Public Law 94–142, but it applies to preschool children and infants. Thus, education and school services are mandated to handicapped children aged 3 to 5. In addition, the law created a new program for children from birth to 2 years; children are eligible for the program if they are developmentally delayed or if they are at risk for either developmental, physical, or emotional delays. Both laws have created an impetus for the testing and assessment of these children, as well as for the development of screening instruments. Quite a few instruments are now available, such as the Denver Developmental Screening Test (Frankenburg & Dodds, 1967), the Developmental Indicators for the Assessment of Learning (Mardell, & Goldenberg, 1975), the Comprehensive Identification Process (Zehrbach, 1975), the Minnesota Preschool Inventory (Ireton & Thwing, 1979), and the Preschool Screening System (P. K. Hainsworth & M. L. Hainsworth, 1980).

Challenges in evaluation. In testing special children, three approaches are typically used. One involves the adaptation or modification of existing instruments. Thus, a test such as the Stanford-Binet or WISC-R may be changed in terms of directions, specific items, time limits, or other aspects relevant to the type of handicap present. Clearly, this can invalidate the test or, at the very least, restrict the conclusions that can be made. Such modifications need to be fully reported when the test findings are used in some type of report, like one a school psychologist might prepare. A second approach involves the use of instruments designed specifically for that type of special child. For example, there are tests that have been developed specifically for use with the visually impaired or with hearing impaired. A third approach involves combining a variety of methods and instruments. The problems with this approach are often practical – insufficient time available to the examiner, fatigue for both examiner and subject, and so on.

In evaluating testing of special children, a number of issues must be kept in mind. First, diagnostic criteria are often not well formulated, or is there agreement on what differences, if any, exist among such terms as handicap, disability, defect, and others (e.g., Justen & G. Brown, 1977; Mitchell, 1973).

Second, the assessment of the child is intimately related to the procedures used and the capabilities of the examiner. In the assessment of severity level (e.g., how severe is this child's hearing impairment), there are two basic approaches taken. One is the use of a standardized test, where the judgment of severity is made on the basis of how deviant a child's score is from the mean – for example, an IQ two standard deviations below the mean is taken as possible evidence of mental retardation. A second approach is more of a global or impressionistic procedure in which a professional judgment is made as to the level of severity present. The norms here are often more nebulous and may in large part be a function of the knowledge and experience of the particular clinician. One important aspect of a well-standardized psychological test is that the test provides a common yardstick that supplies every user with an equal amount of experience – i.e., normative data.

A third aspect to consider are the particular conditions for which the child is being tested. Motor and visual impairments, for example, may well interfere with their test performance and mask their capabilities. Medications that the child may be taking to control seizures or other medical conditions may make the child lethargic or may cause side effects that can alter test performance. Children who have multiple handicaps, such as both mental retardation and visual impairment, present special testing challenges (e.g., Ellis, 1978).

Functions of assessment. In this connection, DuBose (1981) indicates that before selecting tests for an assessment battery, the examiner must determine why the child is being assessed. There are two main separate functions of assessment of special children: identification-placement and intervention-programming. The first purpose requires standardized and/or criterion-referenced tests acceptable to the local agencies, schools, etc., that determine eligibility for services and placement. If the testing is being done for intervention and programming purposes, then the tests that are selected need to address the concepts and behaviors to be targeted during the intervention. Most likely, these tests will mirror the curriculum and will be criterion-referenced.

As we have seen, there is probably no test that is free of limitations and criticisms. The utility of a number of tests is severely limited by questions of technical adequacy in their development and in their reliability and validity. Tests that may be quite useful in research settings or with normal children may be of limited use with special children. Even when tests are appropriate, the information they yield may be of limited value to the development of a treatment plan or to the prescription of special educational interventions. Sometimes two instruments that supposedly measure the same functions may yield rather disparate results (e.g., Eippert & Azen, 1978; B. L. Phillips, Pasewark, & Tindall, 1978). Sometimes the same instrument, when revised, can yield substantially different normative interpretations of the same score (e.g., Covin, 1977; R. J. Thompson, 1977).

In Chapter 2, we discussed the notions of age norms and school-grade norms. We noted several problems with these norms, which are particularly acute in the testing of special children. These children are often developmentally delayed. Thus a mentally retarded 8-year-old child may have language abilities that are more appropriate for a normal 3-year-old. But we should not therefore conclude that the child functions at a 3-year-old level. He or she probably functions at different levels in different domains, and most likely his or her language abilities may show more variability of functioning than that of the typical 3-year-old. The challenges to the appropriate use of tests with special children are many, but this is not to say that these tests are useless – far from it. Again, we make the point here that psychometrically valid instruments, in the hands of a well-trained professional, often represent the only objective data available, and they can be extremely useful for a variety of purposes.

Domains of assessment. There are all sorts of tests that can and have been administered to special children, and there are many ways to categorize these tests and/or the underlying domains. One way is to consider the following five categories: (1) infant scales, used to diagnose early developmental delays that may occur in cognitive, physical, self-help, language, or psychosocial development; (2) preschool tests used to diagnose mental retardation and learning disabilities and to assess school readiness; (3) school-age tests of intelligence and cognitive abilities; (4) school-age tests of academic achievement; and

(5) school-age measures of "personality" or affective behavior (Gallagher, 1989).

Simeonsson, Bailey, Huntington et al. (1986) suggest that there are four domains of particular cogency to the testing of special children: cognition, communication, personal-social, and behavior. Although these categories are neither clear-cut nor mutually exclusive, they can serve as a general guide. Under the area of cognition, we would find many of the intelligence tests discussed in Chapter 5, such as the Wechsler tests or the Kaufman ABC. Under the label of communication, we find a number of tests such as the Peabody Picture Vocabulary, to be discussed below. The area of personal-social includes scales of temperament, self-concept scales, locus-of-control scales, personality inventories for children, adaptive-behavior scales, and many others. Finally, under the label of behavior we would typically find checklists and rating scales to be completed by parents or teachers, which assess overt behavior as distinguished from the traits and characteristics under personal-social; a good example is the Child Behavior Checklist (Achenbach & Edelbrock, 1981), discussed next.

Other authors take different approaches. Lichtenstein and Ireton (1984) for example, indicate that there are three major categories of information to be looked at in the testing of young children: physical and sensory functioning, environmental influences, and developmental functioning. In the area of physical and sensory functioning – children who have such conditions as cerebral palsy or vision loss and are typically first identified by health care professionals such as school nurses or pediatricians. It should not be assumed, however, that simply because a child is identified at high risk due to some medical condition, there will necessarily be later developmental problems. R. Lichtenstein and Ireton (1984) argue that health-related screening tests to be included in a typical preschool screening program are justified only if: (1) They relate to conditions that are relatively common in the screening population; (2) The condition allows sufficient lead time between onset and manifestation to make early identification worthwhile; (3) The conditions are relevant to school functioning; and (4) The results have implications for available treatment. Two conditions that would meet these criteria are vision and hearing impairments.

Environmental influences primarily cover the home. A number of studies have documented the role of various aspects of the home environment on subsequent behavior, both in a negative manner (e.g., Lytton, Watts, & Dunn, 1986; Richman, Stevenson, & Graham, 1982; E. E. Werner, Bierman, & French 1971) and in a positive manner (e.g., G. Domino, 1979; Dewing, 1970).

Developmental functioning involves a systematic look at the behavior and progress of a young child in comparison to developmental norms. Such developmental functioning involves a wide variety of domains. Lichtenstein and Ireton (1984) identify nine such domains:

1. Cognitive – e.g., intelligence, reasoning, memory

2. Language – e.g., receptive and expressive

3. Speech/articulation – e.g., quality of voice, stuttering

4. Fine motor – e.g., visual-spatial abilities

5. Gross motor – e.g., hopping, skipping, running

6. Self-help – e.g., adaptive behaviors such as dressing

7. Social-emotional – e.g., temper tantrums, passivity

8. Perceptual and integrative processing – e.g., learning left from right

9. School readiness – e.g., those skills and behaviors needed for school

Obviously, the above categories are not mutually exclusive and different taxonomies can be easily developed.

Self-concept. Although the area of personal-social assessment (as opposed to cognitive) would seem to be of particular importance with special children, it is one that is relatively neglected, with most testing efforts focusing on intellectual capabilities and development. Many authors recommend assessment of self-concept, with many studies suggesting that special children are low on self-esteem, which results in poor adjustment, lack of motivation, a negative self-image, a low tolerance for frustration, and an unwillingness to take risks. There are of course many well-known measures of self-concept such as the Tennessee Self-Concept Scale (Fitts, 1965),

discussed in Chapter 8, the Self-Esteem Inventory (Coopersmith, 1967), the Piers-Harris Self-Concept Scale (Piers & Harris, 1969), and the Self-Perception Inventory (A. T. Soares & L. M. Soares, 1975). The majority of self-concept scales are self-report inventories – the child responds to stimuli by choosing the one that best represents himself or herself. These stimuli may be written statements, statements that are read by the examiner, drawings of children, "happy" faces, etc. (see Coller, 1971; Walker, 1973).

Age differentiation. From birth to 18 months is traditionally considered the infancy stage, while from 18 months to about 5 years are the preschool years. Tests designed for infants and for preschool children usually involve observation, performance items, and/or oral administration rather than the "paper-and-pencil" approach, and need to be administered individually.

Comparability of test scores. When we administer a test to a special child, how do we know that the test is indeed valid for this purpose, given that a test's validity may be based upon "normal" children, and given that the test may have been modified in some way for administration to special children? Willingham (1989) suggests that for a test to be valid, i.e., fair, with handicapped individuals, the scores on the test must be "comparable" between normal and handicapped, along eight dimensions:

1. Comparable factor structure. If a test is modified in some way for administration to special children, it is possible that the test may no longer measure the same construct. A factor analysis of the modified test should yield relevant information as to whether the structure of the test has changed.

2. Comparable item functioning. Even if the overall factor structure is the same for the original test and the modified or nonstandard test, it is possible that specific items may be more (or less) difficult for someone with a particular impairment.

3. Comparable reliability. Obviously, the modified form needs to yield consistent results – i.e., be reliable.

4. Comparable accuracy of prediction. Does the nonstandard test discriminate between successful

and unsuccessful students? Does the test correctly predict academic performance?

5. Comparable admissions decisions. Does the very use of a nonstandard form bias the decision made?

6. Comparable test content. Do the standard and nonstandard test forms have "comparable" content?

7. Are the testing accommodations comparable? Obviously, handicapped individuals may have special requirements such as braille forms, need for a reader, and so on. But insofar as possible, is the situation comparable – i.e. allowing the subject to show what he or she can do?

8. Comparable test timing. Even a power test may have a time limit, if nothing else, imposed by the testing situation (e.g., it is almost lunch time). Nonstandard tests often use very different time limits that in effect may not be comparable.

Although these comparabilities were presented by Willingham (1989) in the context of college-admissions testing, they are equally applicable to tests used for special children and quite clearly represent ideals to strive for.

Issues of measurement of young children. Goodwin and Driscoll (1980) outline a number of issues that concern the measurement and evaluation of young children. The first issue is whether young children should be tested. Some people express fear that the very procedure of testing a young child can be harmful and traumatic. There does not seem to be much evidence to support this, and most professionals believe that the potential benefits of professionally administered tests far outweigh any possible negative effects. Often, fears are raised by misinformed individuals who imagine the wholesale administration of multiple choice exams to preschoolers; they do not realize that most tests at this level are individually administered or require an adult informant. Fleege, Charlesworth, Burts et al. (1992) did report that kindergarten children being given a standardized achievement test exhibited more behaviors that were stress related during the test than before or after the test – but much of the behavior seemed to be related to how the adult authority figures around the children reacted.

A second issue is whether measurement is possible or meaningful with young children. In general, the younger the child, the greater the measurement problems; in addition, the measurement of "affective" constructs seems to be more difficult than the measurement of cognition.

A third issue is whether tests are used appropriately with young children. There is of course a growing dissatisfaction, both by professionals and lay persons, with the use of tests in American schools, but satisfactory substitutes have yet to appear.

Another issue is whether tests used with young children are fair, particularly with regard to ethnic minorities. This is a highly emotional issue, where often facts are distorted to fit preconceived opinions. The issue is by no means an open-and-shut one, and there is much controversy. We take a closer look at this in Chapter 11.

Perhaps of greater concern than the above points is the possible negative consequence of labeling a child with a particular diagnostic label (C. D. Mercer, Algozzine, & Trifiletti, 1979). This also is a highly emotional issue, with little data available. From a psychometric point of view, to test a child merely to obtain a diagnostic label is like purchasing a house to have a mailbox. Although the mailbox may be "central" and may serve a valuable purpose, it is the house that is important.

Infant intelligence. The assessment of infant intelligence is a difficult task. The examiner must not only establish rapport with both the infant and the adult caretaker, but must be a superb observer of behavior that does not appear on command. With older children we can offer them rewards, perhaps reason with them, or use our adult status to obtain some kind of compliance; infants, however, do not necessarily respond in a cooperative manner.

Infant intelligence tests are often assessed from the viewpoint of content validity; that is, do they reflect a sample of behavior that is governed by intellect? They can also be judged by predictive validity, that is, how well they forecast a future criterion. This is a difficult endeavor because intelligence of an infant is primarily exhibited through motor behavior, while the intelligence of a school-aged child is primarily exhibited through verbal school achievement. Finally, tests of infant intelligence can be judged from the more global aspect of construct validity – i.e., we can perceive the behavior of an infant as a stage that is part of a maturational or developmental sequence.

Most tests of preschool intellectual functioning use similar items, and most of these items go back to the work of Gesell and the Gesell Developmental Schedules (Gesell, Halveron, & Amatruda, 1940). This is somewhat peculiar because Gesell did not believe that intelligence could be assessed but was more interested in measuring the general maturation or developmental level of the child.

We take a brief look at the Gesell Developmental Schedules, followed by a good example of a scale for infant intelligence, namely the Bayley Scales of Infant Development.

The Gesell Developmental Schedules. As the title indicates, these are developmental schedules or frameworks, that is, they are not tests in the strict sense of the word, but a timetable of what is to be expected of a child in five areas of behavior: adaptive behavior, gross motor movement, fine motor movement, language, and personal-social behavior. The schedules provide a standardized means by which a child's behavior can be observed and evaluated; they are particularly useful to pediatricians and child psychologists who need to observe and evaluate young children.

The scales were developed by Gesell (Gesell, Halveron, & Amatruda, 1940) and revised a number of times by various investigators (Ames, Gillespie, Haines, et al., 1979; Gesell, Ilg, & Ames, 1974; Knobloch & Pasamanick, 1974; Knobloch, Stevens, & Malone, 1980). The scales cover an age range of 4 weeks to 5 years and are basically a quantification of the qualitative observations that a pediatrician makes when evaluating an infant. The scales are used to assess developmental status, either from a normal normative approach, or to identify developmental abnormalities that might be the result of neurological or other damage. In fact, part of the value of these schedules is their focus on neuromotor status, which covers such things as posture, locomotion, and muscle tone, and can provide valuable quantitative information for the identification of neuromotor disabilities.

The items in the schedules are organized in terms of three *maturity zones*, namely supine, sitting, and locomotion, which serve as starting points for the examination. Developmental quotients are calculated for each of the five areas of behavior. These quotients parallel the old ratio IQs and use the formula of maturity age/chronological age × 100.

Because these scales involve an observer, namely the examiner, we might ask about interrater reliability. The evidence suggests that with appropriately trained examiners, such reliability can exceed .95 (Knobloch & Pasamanick, 1974).

A number of other scales for infant assessment have been developed; among these might be mentioned the Griffiths Scales of Development (Griffiths, 1970) and the Vulpe Assessment Battery (Vulpe, 1982).

The Bayley Scales of Infant Development. One of the best known tests of infant development is the Bayley (Bayley, 1969). The Bayley is composed of three scales: a *mental* scale, which assesses such functions as problem solving and memory; a *motor* scale, which assesses both gross-motor abilities such as walking and finer motor skills such as finger movement; and an *Infant Behavior Record* (IBR) which is a rating scale completed by the examiner at the end of testing and designed to assess "personality" development in 11 areas such as social behavior, persistence, attention span, cooperation, fearfulness, and degree of activity. The scales cover the ages of 2 months to 30 months. The mental scale consists of 163 items arranged chronologically beginning at a 2-month level and ending at the 30-month level. The nature of the items changes with progressive age. At the earliest levels, the items assess such aspects as visual tracking and auditory localization. Later items assess such functions as the purposeful manipulation of objects, early language development, memory, and visual discrimination. The motor scale consists of 81 items also arranged chronologically that assess both fine- and gross-motor abilities, such as grasping objects and crawling. The test stimuli for the mental and motor scales include a variety of objects such as a mirror, a ball, a toy car, a rattle, crayons, and cups.

The Infant Behavior Record consists of 30 items, most of which are rated on a 5- or

9-point Likert-type response scale. The items assess such variables as the infant's responsiveness to the examiner, the degree of happiness and fearfulness, attention span, gross bodily movement, degree of excitability to the environment, sensory activities such as exploration with hands, and muscle-movement coordination.

The Bayley was revised in 1993 and is now known as the Bayley II. The revision included new normative data based on a representative sample of 1,700 children, an extended age range from 1 month to 42 months, and some item changes, but the nature of the test has not changed any. For a comparison of the original and revised versions see Gagnon and Nagle (2000).

Administration. The Bayley requires a well-trained examiner, who is not only familiar with the scales themselves, but who is comfortable with infants, and has a good knowledge of what is and is not a normal pattern of development. Although the items are arranged chronologically, test items that have similar content, as for example involving wooden cubes, are administered consecutively. As with the Stanford-Binet and other tests, there is a basal level and a ceiling level. The basal level is defined as 10 consecutive items that are passed; the child then gets credit for earlier items even though they were not administered. A ceiling level is defined as 10 consecutive items that are not passed. Pass-fail criteria for each item are stated clearly in the test manual, but there is still a considerable amount of subjective judgment needed. The examiner usually begins by administering items 1 month below the child's chronological age, unless there are indications a lower level might be more appropriate. As with other major tests, ancillary materials are available for the examiner, such as a supplementary manual (Rhodes, Bayley, & Yow, 1984).

For testing to be successful, there has to be good rapport between child and examiner. The child needs to be interested in the testing and cooperative so that the testing can be completed.

Scoring. Scores on the mental and motor scales are expressed as normalized standard scores with a mean of 100 and a SD of 16, similar to the Stanford-Binet. These are called the Mental Development Index and the Psychomotor Development Index and can vary from 50 to 150. For the IBR, there is no total score. Matheny (1980) developed five subscales on the IBR based on factor analysis. He called these task orientation, test affect (introversion-extraversion), activity, audiovisual awareness, and motor skill. The Bayley has been quite useful in a variety of areas, including the early detection of sensory and neurological impairments. As the author herself has pointed out, the scales should be used to assess current developmental status and not to predict future ability level (Bayley, 1969). The Bayley can, however, provide a baseline against which later evaluations can be compared to assess developmental progress in both mental and motor areas.

Reuter, Stancin, and Craig (1981) developed a scoring adaptation for the Bayley that leads to developmental-age scores for five domains: cognitive, language, social, fine motor, and gross motor. This approach is particularly useful when assessing special children such as mentally retarded or those with developmental-language disorders.

Reliability. In general, the reliability of the Bayley is acceptable and fairly consistent throughout the age periods covered. But reliabilities for the motor scale tend to be lower for the first 4 months. Interrater reliability ranges from 67% to 100% agreement by two separate raters, with most of the items showing interrater correlations greater than .60 (Matheny, 1980). Split-half reliabilities for the mental scale range from .81 to .93 with a median of about .88; for the motor scale they range from .68 to .92 with a median of .84.

Validity. The correlations between the mental and motor scales vary considerably and tend to decrease with age; that is, motor and mental development are different and should be assessed separately in young children. Early developmental functioning has little predictive validity in terms of later intelligence, except for those children who are clearly developmentally deficient.

The concurrent validity of the Bayley seems good, with strong positive correlations between the Bayley and the Stanford-Binet.

There really is not much validity information available on the Infant Behavior Record, in part because the behavior measured is rather narrow in its specificity to a situation, i.e., the test situation. Thus for example, items on the IBR do not correlate highly with items on another infant inventory as filled out by the mothers (Burg, Quinn, & Rapoport, 1978). In addition there is no total score on the IBR, and single item scores are considered too unreliable.

Norms. The 1969 scale norms were based on 1,262 children, approximately equally distributed between the ages of 2 months and 30 months. The standardization sample was selected to be representative of the U.S. population on a variety of demographic aspects, such as geographic region of residence, gender, race, and educational level of the head of the household. The norms are presented separately for different age groups – from 2 to 6 months in $\frac{1}{2}$-month intervals, and from 6 to 30 months in 1-month intervals. Because children can show dramatic increases in abilities within a short time span, such specific norms are both needed and quite valuable. These norms, however, do not include children who were institutionalized or born prematurely.

Social-emotional behavior. Much of the assessment of infants and young children has, from a psychometric point of view, focused on cognitive development as shown by motoric behavior and coordination. The assessment of noncognitive aspects that might be labeled "social skills," "personality," "social-emotional behavior," or similar labels has seen substantially less emphasis. There are numerous reasons for this. One is, as we've learned before, tests are developed usually in response to some need. With infants, there has been a need to identify those children with possible developmental difficulties such as mental retardation; with school children, the emphasis has been on behaviors related to learning problems, discipline, hyperactivity, and so on. Another reason was the active role of behaviorism in American psychology, a movement in which the emphasis was on behavior that could be observed rather than such theoretical concepts as personality. Psychoanalysis also has played a role. Although its emphasis has been on early childhood and on the notion that a person's personality was well established in the first 5 years of life, its focus was not on psychometrics.

It is only recently, beginning in the 1960s and 1970s that there has been an increased focus on special-education programs in schools, with an increased emphasis on the identification of children who either have or are at risk for developmental handicaps. And only very recently have researchers begun to explore, in a systematic and longitudinal manner, the relationship between infant behavior and subsequent manifestations (e.g., A. Thomas & Chess, 1977).

Why assess preschool children in terms of social-emotional behavior? Martin (1988) suggests four reasons:

1. As an outcome measure, that is, to determine the effects of a particular set of conditions such as stress, a congenital disease, or child abuse, on the infant;

2. As a concurrent measure, to describe the current status of a child objectively, so that the information can be used by the parents. For example, although most children go through a phase commonly called "the terrible twos," there may be need to assess a particular child to determine whether their oppositional behavior is normal or symptomatic of a more serious condition;

3. As a predictive measure, to identify children who are at risk for some condition, so that therapeutic and/or preventive procedures can be initiated;

4. As a research tool, to relate infant characteristics to other aspects, such as future interactions in the classroom.

This area of testing is of course very broad and encompasses a wide range of variables, many that might be called "temperament," such as mood, degree of persistence, distractibility, activity level, and so on. Assessment of these is typically done through observation by the examiner, interview of the child's caregiver, or completion of a questionnaire by an adult familiar with the child. The Infant Temperament Questionnaire (Carey & McDevitt, 1978) and the Colorado Childhood Temperament Inventory (Rowe & Plomin, 1977) are examples of such measures. Unfortunately, most of these measures have been criticized for not meeting basic psychometric standards (e.g., Hubert, Wachs, Peters-Martin, et al., 1982).

Other scales assess social competence, self-help skills, or other related aspects. Indeed these may well be considered part of the more general label of adaptive behavior. The Cain-Levine Social Competency Scale (Cain, Levine, & Elzey, 1977) is a good example of such a scale. Others that are mentioned in the literature with some frequency are the Brazelton Behavioral Assessment Scale (Brazelton, 1973), the Rothbart Infant Behavior Questionnaire (Rothbart, 1981), and the Fullard Toddler Temperament Scale (Fullard, McDevitt, & Carey, 1984). The Brazelton in particular, has been used in a wide variety of studies, including the assessment of cross-cultural differences in neonates (e.g., Brazelton, Robey, & Collier, 1969; D. G. Freedman & N. Freedman, 1969). However, none of these scales come close in popularity and psychometric sophistication to the Bayley Scales of Infant Development, discussed earlier.

There are hundreds of such measures available and, although there are individual exceptions, most are unpublished, lack basic validity data, and in particular are weak as to their construct validity. For a review of 10 such scales, see Bracken (1987). One scale that has found a certain degree of popularity is the Personality Inventory for Children (Wirt, Lachar, Klinedinst, et al., 1990).

The Personality Inventory for Children (PIC). At first glance, the PIC should be described as a behavior-rating scale. It is, however, listed as a personality test in such places as the *Mental Measurements Yearbook* because of its rating format (true-false) and scale-construction methods (empirical correlates between scale scores and other independent measures). In fact, the PIC is sometimes characterized as the childhood equivalent of the MMPI.

The PIC is an objective personality-assessment inventory developed for use with children and adolescents, aged 3 to 16, to provide descriptions of "child behavior, affect, and cognitive status, as well as family characteristics" (Wirt, Lachar, Klinedinst, et al., 1984; 1990).

The test was originally published in 1958, and norms were then collected between 1958 and 1962. In 1977, the first manual was published, and in 1979, an interpretive guide appeared. In 1984, two manuals were published, and the PIC was "revised" in 1990; the revised PIC consists of the same items, scales, norms, etc., as its predecessor, but what was changed is the order of

the items (Knoff, 1989; Wirt, Lachar, Klinedinst, et al., 1990). In its current format, the PIC consists of 600 true/false items completed by an adult informant, typically the child's mother.

The PIC scales were developed either through empirical methods or through rational methods, where expert judges rated specific items as to scale membership. It is a test that is easy to administer and score, but interpretation of the results is quite complex.

One of the interesting aspects of the PIC, from a psychometric point of view, is the sequence of items. The first 131 items include a lie scale and four broad-band factor scales: undisciplined-poor self-control, social incompetence, internalization-somatic symptoms, and cognitive development. The first 280 items include the above scales, a shortened version of two other validity scales, a general screening scale of adjustment, and 12 clinical scales, such as achievement, depression, delinquency, anxiety, and social skills. The first 420 items include the four broad-band factor scales, and the full versions of all the validity, screening, and clinical scales. Finally, the entire 600 items contain all of the above scales plus some 17 supplemental scales. Thus, the examiner in administering the test has four choices of increasing length: administer items 1 to 131, 1 to 280, 1 to 420, or all 600.

Reliability. Three test-retest reliability studies are reported in the manual, covering a psychiatric sample and two normal samples, with retest intervals from 2 weeks to about 7 weeks. The mean correlation coefficients are in the low .70s to the high .80s, with some individual scales showing coefficients in the low .40s. One internal consistency study is reported on a large clinic sample of more than 1,200 children, with a mean alpha coefficient of .74. Mother-father interrater reliabilities are also reported; typical coefficients tend to cluster in the high .50s to mid .60s range.

Validity. A substantial number of studies are presented, both in the test manuals and in the literature, that support the validity of the PIC, particularly the concurrent, convergent, and discriminant validity. As Knoff (1989) stated, these studies provide an excellent basis for the PIC, but additional work is needed, especially a more sophisticated and broader-based restandardization (i.e., new norms).

Norms. The PIC was normed between 1958 and 1962 on a sample of 2,390 children from the greater Minneapolis area, with approximately 100 boys and 100 girls at each of 11 age levels, between the ages of $5\frac{1}{2}$ and $16\frac{1}{2}$ years. Additional norms were obtained for a small group of children aged 3 to 5. For scoring purposes, the norms are actually separated into two age levels – 3 to 5, and 6 to 16.

The norms are based on the responses of mothers whose children were being evaluated. Thus the completion of the PIC by any other person, such as the father, may or may not be meaningful in terms of the available norms, particularly because the interrater reliability between mothers and fathers is not that high. Knoff (1989) indicates that the original norms are now "unacceptable."

Criticisms. Despite its relative popularity, the PIC has been criticized on a number of grounds. The items are responded on a true-false basis, rather than a Likert-type scale, which would give greater variability and perhaps sensitivity to individual differences. The directions do not specify a time frame; the mother is asked to rate her child's behavior, but there is no indication as to the past week, past year, since the beginning of the school year, and so on. It is quite possible that different mothers may implicitly use different time frames. Some of the items involve "guessing" (e.g., "My child is a leader in groups"). These may be minor issues, but together they can seriously limit the utility of an instrument.

The testing environment. Recall that we used the analogy of an experiment as a way of thinking about tests. This is particularly true in testing special children, and we want the testing environment to be free of extraneous conditions. Ideally, the testing room should be well lit, free from noise, distractions, and interruptions. The furniture should be appropriate for the child. A number of authors (e.g., Blau, 1991) have described what the ideal testing environment should be like, but the reality is that testing often takes place in whatever room is available in the school or clinic, with interruptions, scheduling

conflicts, and other negative aspects par for the course.

Demands on the examiner. Perhaps more than with any other type of client, the testing of special children places a great burden on the examiner and requires a great deal of patience, adaptability, and understanding. The examiner needs to be highly sensitive to the needs and state of the child. If the child becomes quite fidgety, for example, it may well signal that a trip to the bathroom or a change in activity is in order, but the skilled examiner should "sense" this before the change is actually needed (for an excellent discussion see Chapter 4 in Kamphaus, 1993).

Infants of 7 to 10 months of age typically show anxiety about strangers, and the examiner needs to be particularly sensitive to this. In general, the examiner needs to create a relaxed and informal atmosphere to make sure that the child is comfortable and not overly anxious, yet also establish a structured situation in which the necessary tasks get accomplished. The examiner should be friendly but calm; too much enthusiasm can scare or overwhelm a child. For many children, the closest out-of-home experience they have had is a visit to a physician's office, which may have been difficult and perhaps even traumatic. A visit to a psychologist's office may resurrect anxieties and fears. Children typically do not understand what a psychologist is, or why they are being tested. They may or may not have been prepared prior to the testing; they may perceive the testing as a "punishment" for their misbehavior or a reflection of parental displeasure.

The examiner needs to be thoroughly familiar with the test materials. Tests such as the Stanford-Binet and the WISC-R involve a "kit," a briefcase filled with blocks, beads, picture plates, and other materials. These need to be out of the child's line of sight so they are not a distraction, but readily available to the examiner. The examiner should attempt to present the various test tasks in a standard manner, but should be flexible enough to deviate when necessary, and compulsive enough to carefully document such deviations. The entire test procedure should "flow" well. (For a useful guide to interviewing children see J. Rich, 1968.)

DuBose (1981) points out that from a developmental testing perspective, most theoretical work as exemplified by Jean Piaget, and most applied work as seen in the work of pediatrician, Arnold Gesell, has focused on normal children rather than those who are developmentally impaired. In the training of psychologists, both in developmental psychology and in psychological testing, the emphasis is on normal development; they are poorly prepared to assess special children. In fact, a survey of clinical psychology graduate programs indicated that training in child diagnostic assessment focused largely on intelligence and personality using a narrow range of instruments; the author concluded that training at the predoctoral level is insufficient in preparing professionals to assess the competence and special needs of a broad spectrum of exceptional children (Elbert, 1984).

Characteristics of the child. Quite often, children who are referred for testing present a particular challenge in that they may have poor self-concept, difficulties in maintaining attention, lack of motivation, substantial shyness, poor social skills, and so on. These deficits of course, affect not only the child's coping with the demands of school, but may well affect their test performance. Thus, establishing good rapport is particularly important.

Children are highly variable. Not only do they differ substantially from each other, but differ within themselves from day to day and from behavior to behavior. Their emotional states are highly volatile – a child may be very happy at 10 in the morning and very unhappy an hour later. Children's behaviors are often specific to a particular situation; a child may have great difficulties with school peers but may get along well with siblings at home. A particular child may be advanced motorically but may lag in social skills; another child may be more easily distracted, and a third may fatigue easily in the testing situation. In fact, it is generally recommended that children be tested in the morning when they are well rested and alert.

Young children have a short attention span so that sustained effort, such as that required by a test, can be difficult. Children's responses to a test can sometimes be more reflective of their anxiety or attempts to cope with a task they don't understand; thus a child may reply "yes" regardless of the questions asked. Young children also may have limited (or no) reading and writing skills, so that the usual testing procedures used with older children and adults may not be applicable. They do not have the personal history and perspective to make social comparisons (e.g., "In comparison to others, I am more intelligent"). Their observational abilities are limited and they may not have the maturity to reflect on their own behavior or the family interactions that occur. The behavior of young children is also more directly affected by the immediate circumstances. Hunger, fear, boredom, fatigue, etc., can all disrupt a young child's behavior.

On the plus side, most children are curious and self-directed; they are eager to explore and discover, and may well find the testing situation interesting and fun.

Test aspects. There are many recommendations concerning the tests to be administered. They should be selected so that the information obtained answers the referral question. Often agencies and practitioners use the same standard battery for every child, simply because "that's the way it's been done." The measures selected should have a range of difficulty levels and should assess cognitive, affective, and psychomotor aspects. Their selection should reflect the child's age, the ability to use expressive and receptive language, the ethnic-linguistic background, and the examiner's familiarity with specific instruments.

Blau (1991) suggests that a complete psychological test battery should include tests that cover these four areas: (1) the child's intellectual capacities and learning styles; (2) neuropsychological development and status; (3) the child's achievement levels in major school activities; and (4) personality and character.

Sources of information. In testing young children, three sources of information can be used. One involves administering a standardized test to the child directly; clearly a major concern here would be the reliability and credibility of young children's reports (Bruck, Ceci, & Hembrooke, 1998). Second, we can give the parents a checklist or other instrument to fill out, to systematize their knowledge of their child. Third, we can use various procedures to observe the child directly, specifically behavior checklists filled out by the examiner or a teacher.

CATEGORIES OF SPECIAL CHILDREN

We can probably identify some nine major categories of special children, although these categories are not mutually exclusive and, for some specific purposes, we may wish to use different divisions.

Mental Retardation

Mental retardation is typically defined as below-average general intellectual functioning with deficits in adaptive behavior, and which manifests itself during the developmental period. A 28-year-old who sustains massive brain damage in a motorcycle accident and can no longer function intellectually at his preaccident level would not be labeled as mentally retarded. In terms of psychological testing, there are two major areas of concern: intellectual functioning and adaptive behavior. We have already considered intellectual functioning in Chapter 5. We focus here on adaptive behavior.

Adaptive behavior. The term *adaptive behavior* was introduced and defined in 1959 by the American Association on Mental Deficiency (retardation); it refers to the effectiveness of an individual in coping with environmental demands (Nihira, Foster, Shellhass, et al., 1974). This term was introduced in part because of the dissatisfaction of diagnosing mental retardation solely on the basis of intelligence test results. Thus, mental retardation is currently diagnosed based on both subaverage general intellectual functioning and deficits in adaptive behavior. There are however those who believe that adaptive behavior is an elusive concept, difficult to define and hence to measure, and that retardation should be defined only in cognitive terms (e.g., Zigler, Balla, & Hodapp, 1984).

There are a number of scales designed to measure adaptive behavior that are particularly applicable to mentally retarded children. Among these scales may be mentioned the Adaptive Behavior Inventory for Children (J. Mercer & Lewis, 1977), the AAMD Adaptive Behavior Scale (Nihira, Foster, Shellhass, et al., 1974), the Children's Adaptive Behavior Scale (Richmond & Kicklighter, 1980), and the Vineland Adaptive Behavior Scale, formerly known as the Vineland Social Maturity Scale (Sparrow, Balla, & Cicchetti, 1984). For an overview of the measurement of adaptive behavior, see Meyers, Nihira, and Zetlin (1979). We take a closer look at the Vineland as an example of an "old" instrument that has been revised.

The Vineland Adaptive Behavior Scale. The Vineland is probably the best known measure of social competence or adaptive behavior. It assesses self-help skills, self-direction, and responsibility in individuals from birth to maturity. The Vineland Social Maturity Scale was first published in 1935 and subsequently revised in 1947, 1953, and 1965. A technical manual was initially published in 1953 (Doll, 1953). Finally, in 1984 it was restandardized, substantially changed, and rebaptized as the Vineland Adaptive Behavior Scales (Sparrow, Balla, & Cicchetti, 1984).

Development. The Vineland was developed at the Training School at Vineland, New Jersey, a well-known institution for the retarded, still in existence. When the scale was introduced, its author suggested five ways in which the scale could be useful: (1) as a standard measure of normal development to be used repeatedly for the measurement of growth or change; (2) as a measure of individual differences, specifically extreme deviation that may be significant in the study of mental retardation, juvenile delinquency, and related areas; (3) a qualitative index of variation in development in "abnormal" subjects such as maladjusted individuals; (4) a measure of improvement following special treatment; and (5) as a schedule for reviewing developmental histories in the clinical study of retardation. Although the Vineland is not an intelligence test, it can be used to obtain developmental data when a child is unable or unwilling to be tested directly. Care must be exercised however, in going from adaptive behavior to conclusions about cognitive functioning.

Description. The old scale consisted of 117 items arranged serially in increasing order of difficulty. The placement of each item is based on the average age when the item was achieved by the standardization sample; this average age is called the life-age. Table 9.1 illustrates the nine areas of the Vineland, with illustrative items and their

Table 9–1. The Vineland Adaptive Behavior Scales		
Area	**Examples of items**	**Life age**
Self-help general	Asks to go to toilet	1.98
	Tells time to quarter hour	7.28
Self-help eating	Drinks from cup or glass unassisted	1.40
	Uses table knife for spreading	6.03
Self-help dressing	Dries own hands	2.60
	Exercises complete care of dress	12.38
Self-direction	Is trusted with money	5.83
	Buys own clothing accessories	13.00
Occupation	Uses skates, sled, wagon	5.13
	Performs responsible routine chores	14.65
Communication	Uses names of familiar objects	1.70
	Communicates by letter	14.95
Locomotion	Moves about on floor	.63
	Walks downstairs one step per tread	3.23
Socialization	Plays with other children	1.50
	Plays difficult games	12.30

corresponding life-age. Each of the items is more fully defined in the test manual.

Revised Vineland. There are three forms of the revised Vineland: a *survey* form, an *expanded* form, and a *classroom* edition. Each form assesses adaptive behavior in four areas: communication, daily living skills, socialization, and motor skills. The first two forms also have an optional scale of maladaptive behavior and are suitable for clients from birth to 19 years, including low-functioning adults. The classroom edition is used for children aged 3 to 13. Each of the four areas is further divided into subareas. For example, the communication area consists of receptive, expressive, and written communication.

Within each of the areas, the items are listed in order according to developmental level, and suggested starting points for each age are indicated. Thus, as we have seen with other tests, there is a basal and a ceiling level, so that every item need not be completed.

The survey form includes 261 items to assess adaptive behavior and 36 items to assess maladaptive behavior. This form covers ages 0 to 19, and is available in Spanish as well.

The expanded form is a longer version of the survey form, and contains 577 items, including the 297 items of the survey form. Basically, this form offers a more comprehensive assessment of adaptive behavior, but the scales and subscales are the same, except that items are grouped together not just within scales, but also within subclusters.

The classroom edition is designed for administration to the teachers and by the teacher – that is, it is a questionnaire completed by a teacher. The classroom edition contains 244 items, some identical to those of the other forms. The scales and subclusters are the same as on the other two forms.

Administration. The scale is to be completed by the examiner based on information obtained from an informant who knows the subject well. The manual, however, cautions that this is not a rating scale and scores are not to be based on mere opinions. Although the items are printed in order on the scoring sheet, the intent is not to follow their order precisely, but to adapt the order to the circumstances. This is akin to an interview, where the information supplied by the informant is "translated" into the test items. Thus, despite the apparent simplicity of the Vineland, the examiner needs to be well qualified – in fact, the manual equates the skills needed here as equivalent to the skills needed for administering the Stanford-Binet. The examiner asks broad questions of the informant (e.g., "How is Amy doing at school?") and where necessary, can follow up with more specific details. Administration time is about 20 minutes for the classroom edition, 20 to 60 minutes for the survey form, and 60 to 90 minutes for the longer expanded form.

Scoring. Scoring is a bit complicated in that items can be scored as habitually performed, formerly performed, no opportunity to perform, occasionally performed, and not performed. Scores at the two extremes are counted 1 and 0 respectively, but items scored in the middle categories may be given full, partial, or no credit. The revised edition uses a 2, 1, 0 scale, but retains the complexity of scoring. The total score, which is the sum of the items, is converted to an age score (social age) by interpolation using the age placement of the items. A ratio social quotient can be calculated by dividing the child's social age by the chronological age and multiplying by 100. One can also compute a deviation social quotient (Silverstein, 1971). Scores on the Vineland increase up to age 25.

Scoring also involves a basal and a ceiling score, defined as two consecutive passes or failures, respectively. In the revised survey form edition, ceiling is defined as seven consecutive failures.

In the revised Vineland, raw scores are changed to standard scores (mean of 100, SD = 15) on each of the four domains, and the four domains are averaged to obtain an Adaptive Behavior Composite, also with a mean of 100 and SD = 15. Scores can also be changed to various other derived scores such as z scores, percentile rankings, stanines, and so on.

Reliability. Split-half reliability coefficients for the survey form range from .89 to .98 for the Adaptive Behavior Composite, and from .77 to .88 for the Maladaptive Behavior area. For the four adaptive behavior domains, median split-half reliability coefficients range from .83 to .90.

Interrater reliability based on a sample of 160 clients interviewed by two different interviewers, with an interval of 1 to 14 days between interviews, yielded coefficients in the .70s, except for the Socialization area which yielded a .62 coefficient.

The test-retest reliability of the Vineland seems satisfactory. Test-retest coefficients with a 2- to 4-week interval are in the .80s and .90s. However, teachers and mothers differ in their ratings, with mothers typically reporting information that results in higher social quotients (e.g., Kaplan & Alatishe, 1976).

These coefficients suggest adequate reliability, but some concern remains about the interview method that is at the basis of this scale, i.e., higher interrater reliability would probably be obtained if in fact the individual items were administered individually.

Validity. A careful analysis of content validity was done on an initial pool of 529 items to make sure that the items that were retained were of appropriate difficulty level, had adequate discriminative ability, and were in correct developmental sequence.

Criterion-related validity was assessed, in part, by comparing total scores on the revised edition with those on the older edition, i.e., the Adaptive Behavior Composite vs. the Deviation Social Quotient. The two correlated only .55, and were higher in samples of mentally retarded adults and hearing-impaired children. One would expect the two versions of the "same" scale to correlate substantially higher, although the authors argue that the revised scale is in fact significantly different.

Similarly, scores on the survey form were correlated with the parallel scores on the classroom edition. This yielded correlation coefficients of .31 to .54; lower correlations were obtained on a sample of preschool children in a Head Start program, and higher correlations were obtained in a sample of mentally retarded students. Because the classroom edition contains some of the exact items as the survey form, we would expect typical correlations to be higher, if for no other reason than item overlap. The relatively low correlations suggest various possibilities: that the two groups of informants, parents and teachers, perceive the same child quite differently; that adaptive behavior is not highly stable across situations, and what is observed at home is in fact different from what is observed at school; that adaptive behavior is a meaningful variable for mentally retarded children but not for normal children; that the two scales use different methodologies (interview vs. questionnaire) that create different results.

Several studies have compared scores on the survey form with other measures of adaptive functioning. Most of the obtained coefficients are in the mid range, from about .20 to .70, with lower and higher coefficients obtained depending upon the nature of the sample, the test form used, and other aspects.

Correlations with standard measures of cognitive functioning are also relatively low, typically in the .20 to .50 range. This, of course, supports the idea that the Vineland is measuring something different than, yet related to, cognitive functioning.

Construct validity is supported in a number of ways. For example, the results of factor analyses suggest one major factor at various ages and support the use of the Adaptive Behavior Composite as an overall measure of adaptive skills. Support is also found for the separate use of the various areas. It is interesting to note that gender differences in the original items were reported to be so small as to be negligible.

In general, the survey form seems to be relatively valid. The expanded form takes most of its validity by "association" – that is, because the survey form is valid, the expanded form must also be valid. The classroom edition seems to be the questionable one. (For a review, see Bailey-Richardson, 1988.)

The manual provides considerable information on the interpretation of scores, as well as the use of the Vineland in conjunction with the K-ABC. This is a plus because the two tests then represent a "package" for which scores can be directly compared.

Norms. The original Vineland was standardized on 620 white male and female residents of New Jersey, including 10 males and 10 females at each year of age from birth to 30 years. The norms for the revised Vineland are based on a national sample of 3,000 individuals, with about 100 persons in each of 30 age groups between birth and 19 years. The sample was stratified on a number of dimensions according to the 1980 U.S. Census data. Many of the children in this sample also participated in the standardization of the K-ABC. These children were basically "normal." In addition, seven samples of handicapped children were also assessed. Each sample contained from 100 to significantly more than 1,000 individuals. Norms are thus given for several special populations, such as mentally retarded adults in residential facilities, visually handicapped, and hearing-impaired children. Norms are provided at 1-month age intervals for infants between birth and 2 years, at 2-month age intervals for children aged 2 through 5, at 3-month intervals for children aged 6 through 8, and at 4-month intervals for children aged 9 through 18.

Norms for the classroom edition were developed using a rather different method, which we need not discuss here (the interested reader should consult the test manual by Sparrow, Balla, & Cicchetti, 1984).

Use with handicapped children. The Vineland makes provisions for specialized interpretation of handicapped children, and separate scales have been developed for visually-impaired, hearing-impaired, and emotionally disturbed children in residential settings.

Behavioral-Emotional Disorders

This is a broad, ill-defined area of children whose behavior deviates from what is expected or typical. These may cover problems of conduct, that is, children who behave in ways that are unacceptable to a particular culture (for example, juvenile delinquents, truants), or it may involve children who are severely emotionally disturbed. Such problems may exist within the context of other conditions, such as mental retardation, or may exist by themselves. One category of children sometimes listed under this label are autistic children. Autistic children have often been considered "untestable," but a number of authors have in fact shown that testing is not only possible but quite useful to plan for appropriate treatment (e.g., A. F. Baker, 1983; B. J. Freeman, 1976; Rutter, 1973). Traditional intelligence tests such as the Wechsler scales, the McCarthy scales, and the Bayley have been used with autistic children, as well as specialized instruments designed specifically for this population (e.g., Flaharty, 1976; Schopler & Reichler, 1979). In addition, some excellent resources are available in the literature on assessment of autistic children (e.g., Baker, 1983; Wing, 1966).

Learning Disabilites

Perhaps more than any of the other categories, this is one that is filled with controversy as to definition and scope. Usually, these disabilities involve difficulties in the understanding and use of spoken or written language, not associated with the other categories (such as mental retardation), but presumably related to dysfunctions of the central nervous system.

Children with hyperactivity (formally known as Attention Deficit Hyperactivity Disorder) might be listed under this label. Some authors believe that traditional standardized testing with hyperactive children is of limited value, and that what is needed is a more multimodal intervention-oriented strategy (e.g., DuPaul, 1992). A number of scales have been developed to assess this condition, including the Conners scales discussed below, the McCarney Attention

Deficit Disorders Evaluation Scale (McCarney, 1989) and the Attention Deficit Disorder-Hyperactivity Comprehensive Teacher's Rating Scale (Ullmann, Sleator, & Sprague, 1991).

Motor Impairments

These are neuromuscular conditions that affect such aspects as fine motor control affecting holding a pencil to write, mobility, and posture. Some of the more common conditions include cerebral palsy, a central nervous system lesion that leads to motor dysfunction of the limbs; spina bifida, which is an incomplete closure of the spinal cord that results in a lesion and in some degree of neurologic impairment; and muscular dystrophy, which represents a wide range of conditions involving muscle degeneration and weakness. The impairment may be present as part of multiple handicaps, or it may exist by itself.

Cerebral palsy involves "encephalopathic conditions culminating in muscular incoordination and may further include convulsive states, intellectual deficits, impairment in ability to think, and specialized hearing deficits" (Allen & Jefferson, 1962). Although cerebral palsy has a low incidence, with only 1 or 2 per 1,000 children with this condition, approximately 25,000 children are born each year with it. In addition, one half to three fourths of these children have speech disorders, one half have visual impairments, one third hearing defects, one third convulsive disorders, about two thirds suffer from severe emotional stress, and a full 50% are mentally retarded (Barnett, 1982).

Children with cerebral palsy, for example, often show a marked degree of incoordination and stiffness, and they often perform motor tasks in a slow and laborious manner. For example, they may not be able to manipulate test materials as is required in several of the Wechsler subtests or may not be able to respond within the stated time limits. Katz (1955) pointed out, for example, that the standard administration of the Stanford-Binet to children with cerebral palsy underestimated the child's intellectual abilities "in proportion to the child's severity of handicap." Thus care must be exercised in selecting a testing instrument that does not confound receptive with expressive skills, for example, or motoric with verbal responses. Studies of the intellectual functioning of cerebral palsied children indicate that about 50% score below an IQ of 70 – that is, they are also mentally retarded. Quite often these children also have visual-perceptual or visual-motor problems that compound the challenge of testing.

In assessing a child with motor impairment, the examiner should be aware of any medications or other medical conditions, such as recent surgery, that might affect test performance. Because intelligence is so often assessed through language, the examiner needs to be particularly careful not to come to conclusions that are either incorrect or not appropriate to the available data. The examiner needs to be sure that the testing situation is as objective as possible. For example, if a parent needs to be present during testing, the examiner needs to make sure that there is no visual contact between the child and parent that might provide extraneous cues or expectations. The examiner needs to be particularly sensitive to the needs of the child. For example, handicapped children may be more susceptible to fatigue in a standardized testing situation. Children with motor impairments may need special positioning to show optimal performance (Stephens & Lattimore, 1983).

These children may find it difficult to respond to tests that are timed or that require the manipulation of objects, such as some of the subtests of the Wechsler. Alternative tests such as the Pictorial Test of Intelligence (J. L. French, 1964), the Columbia Mental Maturity Scale (Burgemeister, Blum, & Lorge, 1972), or the Peabody Picture Vocabulary Test (L. M. Dunn & L. Dunn, 1981) discussed next, are recommended. There are various measures of gross motor functioning mentioned in the literature. Among these might be listed the Bruininks-Oseretsky Test of Motor Proficiency (Bruininks, 1978), the McClenaghan and Gallahue Checklist (1978), and the Vulpe Assessment Battery (Vulpe, 1982).

When tests are modified, it is difficult to know whether such modifications make available norms inapplicable. Modifications can involve using eye movements instead of pointing, presenting items in a multiple-choice format, steadying the child's hand, and other procedures. Some authors (e.g., Sattler & Tozier, 1970) argue that new norms using the modified procedure need to be established; they reviewed test modifications used with various handicapped groups and found only a handful of studies that assessed such modifications. Most of these studies were judged inadequate, but the findings were of nonsignificant differences between standard and modified administrations. Regular standardized instruments such as the Stanford-Binet can be used with some children with motor impairments. In fact, some testers prefer the Stanford-Binet over the Wechsler because of its modifiability and its higher proportion of verbal over perceptual-performance items. On the other hand, you recall that the WISC-R yields separate scores for verbal and performance scales; this allows an assessment of difficulties with such aspects as information processing and attention, often found in the cerebral palsied individual. Also the fact that the WISC-R yields a profile of scores based on subtests allows more directly for an analysis of weaknesses and strengths (Simeonsson, Bailey, Huntington et al., 1986).

Needless to say, when any child, "special" or not, is to be tested for clinical purposes, the examiner should have as much information as possible about the child's background, academic history, medical status, and so on. Testing is not to be treated as a parlor game where the test is administered in a blind fashion to see whether the results correspond with reality.

The Peabody Picture Vocabulary Test-Revised (PPVT-R). The PPVT-R (L. M. Dunn & L. Dunn, 1981) is one of the better known measures to assess receptive vocabulary. It was originally published in 1959 and presented as a screening measure of general intellectual ability, and then revised in 1981. It is nonverbal in nature and yields mental age and IQ indices. The PPVT is composed of two equivalent forms, L and M, with 175 items per form. Each item consists of a page (or plate) with four line drawings. The examiner says a word and the child points to the drawing that "matches" the word. The PPVT-R covers the age range of 2 to 18, with basal and ceiling rules to determine which items are administered to the client. It is not a timed test, takes approximately 10 to 20 minutes to administer, and the availability of the two alternate forms is a plus. The test can be used for normal children, but it is particularly applicable to special children for whom standard tests such as the Stanford-Binet may not be suit-

able. The score is simply the number of correct responses. Raw scores are converted to standard scores, with mean of 100 and SD = 15.

Development. The items were originally selected by the author to represent unbiased common words used in the United States. Of the 300 words contained in the two forms, only 111 (or 37%) were retained for the revised edition. Words that had any type of bias, racial, geographical, cultural, or regional, were eliminated. Subsequent research has shown that these efforts to eliminate potentially biased items were quite successful, particularly with form M (Reynolds, Willson, & Chatman, 1984).

Reliability. For form L internal consistency *rs* range from .67 to .88, and for form M they range from .74 to .86. Similar coefficients are reported for test-retest, in which one form was followed by a different form. Alternate form reliability on a sample of 642 subjects yielded *rs* ranging from .71 to .89. In general then, the reliability indices are somewhat lower than ideal. Related to this, the SE of measurement is about 7 points, twice the size as that found on standard tests of intelligence, such as the WISC. Bochner (1978) reviewed 32 reliability studies on the PPVT, most done on Head Start children. She reported a median reliability coefficient of .72 and concluded that for average children in the elementary grades and for retarded individuals of all ages, the PPVT showed acceptable equivalence of forms (i.e., alternate forms reliability) and stability (test-retest).

Validity. The test manual primarily addresses content validity, indicating that the test items were carefully chosen according to various criteria. Bracken, Prasse, and McCallum (1984) published a comprehensive review of the PPVT-R and indicated correlations in the .70s and low .80s between scores on the PPVT-R and other tests of intelligence, although in some individual studies the results were not as positive. The results seem to be variable, as a function of the instruments used, the nature of the samples, and other aspects. They noted that scores on the PPVT-R tended to be lower than those obtained on the Stanford-Binet or the WISC-R. Thus, the concurrent validity with standard tests of intelligence is quite good, and sometimes the PPVT has been used as a substitute for a test of general intelligence. However, the evidence indicates that the PPVT-R, although useful as a screening instrument, should not be substituted for a more comprehensive measure of cognitive functioning. Some evidence suggests that PPVT IQs are lower than those obtained on the Stanford-Binet in the case of minority children, but they are higher for children that come from well-educated and verbally articulate families.

An example of a concurrent validity study is that by Argulewicz, Bingenheimer, and Anderson (1983) who studied a sample of Anglo-American and Mexican-American children in first through fourth grade. They found the Mexican-American children to score almost a standard deviation below Anglo-American children on both forms of the PPVT-R. Only Form L correlated significantly with achievement measures of reading and mathematics in both groups (.31 and .41 with reading, and .29 and .36 with mathematics, for Mexican-American and Anglo-American, respectively), with group differences not statistically significant.

The PPVT-R has also been used with adults, both mentally retarded (e.g., Prout & Schwartz, 1984) and normal (e.g., Altepeter & Johnson, 1989). The results are rather mixed and inconsistent, but the conclusion is the same – caution should be used when the PPVT-R is used with adults.

Norms. The original normative sample consisted of some 4,000 white persons residing in or around Nashville, Tennessee. Norms for the revised edition, however, are quite extensive, based on stratified samples of 4,200 children and adolescents and 828 adults, according to U.S. Census data. The adults were tested in groups using slides of the test plates.

Adaptations. Adaptations of the PPVT have been made. Although the PPVT only requires a pointing response, which is part of the response repertoire of most children over the age of 1, there are some children such as autistic children who do not exhibit such a response. Levy (1982) administered both the standard form and a cut-up version to 10 normal 4- to 6-year-olds, as well as 10 autistic 5- to 7-year-old children. In the cut-up version, the instructions were to "give me

the — ," using the stimulus word. The performance of the normal children remained essentially the same on the two forms, but the autistic children showed significant improvement on the modified form.

The PPVT-R and decision theory. If the PPVT-R is used as a screening instrument, how correct are the decisions that are made? Part of the answer is supplied by F. B. Hayes and Martin (1986) who studied the effectiveness of the PPVT-R in identifying young gifted children. They tested 100 children aged 2 to 6 who had been referred to a university's preschool assessment project. Referral meant that someone, typically the parent, thought that the child had exhibited early intellectual and/or language development and could possibly participate in programs for the intellectually gifted.

Children were administered both the PPVT-R and the Stanford-Binet. One of the analyses presented by the authors assumes that the Stanford-Binet IQ is in fact the criterion to be used for possible identification as gifted. Therefore, we can ask if we used a score of 130 as the cut off score on the PPVT-R, how many children would we correctly identify? In fact, the hit rate was 69%, which included 64 children "correctly" identified as having Stanford-Binet's lower than 130, and 5 children with IQs higher than 130. Unfortunately, there were also 31 errors, including a 30% false negative rate of children who scored lower than 130 on the PPVT-R but higher than 130 on the Stanford-Binet, and 1 false positive. Various other cut-off scores did not produce highly different results. The authors concluded that the use of the PPVT-R to identify young gifted children is "questionable."

Criticism. In general, the PPVT-R seems to be a useful measure because it is brief, simple to administer and score, and essentially nonthreatening to the client. The literature is very clear in indicating that its usefulness should be limited to its use as a screening instrument.

Speech Impairments

These are a wide variety of conditions and symptoms that interfere with spoken communication. Communication skills are extremely important in normal development, and their assessment quite basic. Often such skills are categorized into receptive and expressive areas, or in terms of structure of language, contents, and use or context (e.g., Bloom & Lahey, 1978). Receptive language refers to understanding language that is spoken or written by others. This requires reading, listening skills, and the understanding of various communication channels such as nonverbal gestures. Expressive language refers to the skills necessary to express one's ideas; this may be done by speaking, writing, or gesturing. A number of scales have been developed specifically to assess such communication skills; for example, the Receptive and Expressive Emergent Language Scale (Bzoch & League, 1971), the Reynell Developmental Language Scales (Reynell, 1969), and the Clark-Madison Test of Oral Language (Clark & Madison, 1984). Such skills can also be assessed in a more global manner by such tests as the Stanford-Binet. Other useful tests are the Detroit Tests of Learning Aptitude (Baker & Leland, 1959), the Illinois Tests of Psycholinguistic Abilities (S. A. Kirk, McCarthy, & W. D. Kirk, 1968), the Northwestern Syntax Screening Test (L. Lee, 1971), the Carrow Elicited Language Inventory (Carrow, 1973), and the Bracken Basic Concept Scale (Bracken, 1984).

Early identification of language delay in children is very important because such children are likely to exhibit not only linguistic deficits later on, but also academic and social difficulties. The characteristics of a good screening test for language development include short administration time, assessment of various levels of linguistic functioning, and the ability to measure linguistic skills rather than academic development (Cole & Fewell, 1983). A representative test is the Token Test (DeRenzi & Vignolo, 1962), which consists of a number of tokens, in different shapes, sizes, and colors. The examiner asks the child to "touch a blue square," "touch a small one," and so on.

The Boehm Test of Basic Concepts. A somewhat more restricted test, but one fairly popular in the literature is the Boehm Test of Basic Concepts. The Boehm was originally published in 1971 and revised in 1986. This test is designed to assess a child's mastery of those basic concepts necessary to understand verbal instruction and to achieve in the early school years. The test covers kindergarten to grade 2, and has three forms, two that are alternate forms, and one that is an "applications" form designed to assess mastery of basic concepts used in combination with other basic concepts. These concepts involve such basic notions as left and right, first and last, more and less, whole vs. part, and so on. There is a version of the test for use with blind children. The Boehm can serve as a screening test to identify children who have deficiencies in those basic concepts, and therefore might need special attention from the teacher.

Each of the alternate forms is divided into two booklets, with each booklet having 3 practice items and 25 operational pictorial items arranged in approximate order of increasing difficulty. The child looks at a picture composed of three objects, such as an ice cream cone, a piece of pie, and a shirt, and the teacher asks, "Which of these should a child never eat?" School-aged children can mark their answers with a pencil or crayon, while preschool children can simply point. The two alternate forms use the same concepts but different illustrations.

The manual is quite clear in its instructions, and the black and white line drawings are quite unambiguous. The test can actually be administered to a small group of children, with the teacher reading each question, but more typically individual administration is needed. If a child has a short attention span, the test can be divided into sections, with each section administered separately. Administration of this test does not require a high degree of training or expertise.

Scoring. Scoring is straightforward. A single test protocol can be used for all children tested in one class; this permits an analysis of the frequency of errors made by the children so the teacher can focus on those concepts that were more frequently missed. Scoring is done by hand, one page at a time, and takes some 5 to 10 minutes per booklet; this is a considerable amount of time when one considers scoring a handful of them.

Reliability. The Boehm has reasonable split-half and alternate forms reliability at the kindergarten and grade 1 levels (low to mid .80s coefficients), but fares less well at the second grade level – there the split-half coefficients are .64 and .73 for the two forms, and the alternate form reliability is .65. The reason for these lowered coefficients is a *ceiling* effect, that is, the test becomes so easy for second graders that it does not provide differentiation between children, except for the lowest scoring students. The result is that the distribution of scores has a high negative skew and a small variance.

Validity. Content validity seems to be the strong area for this test. Test items were chosen because of their frequency of use in school and by teachers. Substantial criterion-related validity is presented in the form of correlations with other tests such as achievement tests; the coefficients range from about .24 to about .64, with a median in the low .40s. The Boehm does seem to be a good predictor of early school success (Estes, Harris, Moers, et al., 1976). It has been criticized as being culturally biased, but Reynolds and Piersel (1983), in fact, found no empirical evidence for such bias in a study of white and Mexican-American children.

Norms. Students from 15 states were tested, but the norms are said to be representative of the national school population, and were selected according to U.S. Census data. The 1983 norms are based on approximately 10,000 children.

Hearing Impairments

Children with hearing impairments can be classified into two broad categories: the hard of hearing and the deaf. The difference essentially lies in whether their hearing level can or cannot be enhanced and used. Many other terms have been used to try and distinguish among various types of hearing impairment. One major distinction is that of congenitally deaf (i.e., born deaf) and adventitiously deaf (i.e., became deaf later in life because of illness, accident, etc.). Another distinction is whether the person has hearing that is nonfunctional for conducting ordinary aspects of everyday life (i.e., deaf) vs. those whose hearing is functional with or without a hearing aid (i.e., hard of hearing). Another distinction is whether the impairment occurred before or after the development of language (i.e., prelingually or postlingually deaf).

Hearing impairments are caused by all sorts of etiological aspects ranging from trauma to viral infections such as meningitis and, in general, affect language skill acquisition more severely than other skill areas. These special children have very limited, if any, linguistic skills, and testing presents a particular challenge. In a way, English is typically a second language for these children. All the caveats that apply to the testing of minority or culturally different children, apply particularly to hearing-impaired children. Hearing impairment can vary from mild to profound. About two out of three children who are enrolled in special education programs have either a profound or severe hearing loss. Approximately three of four of these children had a hearing loss present at birth. One out of two hearing-loss children have additional handicapping conditions, such as cerebral palsy (Meadow, 1983; Scherer, 1983). At the same time, it needs to be pointed out that hearing-impaired children are not a homogeneous group. In one study, for example, significant differences in WISC-R Performance Scale scores were obtained in hearing impaired children when they were subdivided according to the etiology of their impairment (for example, genetic vs. multiple handicapped; Sullivan, 1982).

Sullivan and Vernon (1979) present an excellent overview of psychological tests and testing procedures with hearing-impaired children. They point out, for example, that most deaf children only understand about 5% of what is being said by lipreading – and that such things as a mustache or beard on the face of the speaker can make lipreading even more difficult if not impossible.

In testing hearing-impaired children, nonverbal-performance items are essential. Testing should be carried out in a well-defined, distraction-free area. The test materials should be brightly colored, multifunctional, and multisensory. The examiner should be demonstrative in gestures and facial expressions, should provide demonstrations with sample items, and manually guide the child through the practice items. The examiner is encouraged to use smiles, touch, and claps to reward the child's efforts. Rapport building is particularly important because hearing-impaired children may often be socially withdrawn, shy, and hesitant (Bagnato & Neisworth, 1991).

Often, hearing-impaired children are evaluated by using nonverbal tests that have been standardized on the hearing population – for example, the performance portion of the WISC-R or an adaptation of the WPPSI for deaf children (Ray & Ulissi, 1982). There are a number of difficulties with this approach. If only one scale or subtest is used, the obtained information is quite limited. Second, hearing-impaired and normal-hearing children do not differ solely in their capacity to hear. They have had different experiences with language, which is intimately related to problem solving as well as a host of other aspects such as social skills. Even though performance tests are "nonverbal," they still have verbal components such as the ability to understand instructions or to respond within a time limit.

McQuaid and Alovisetti (1981) surveyed psychological services for hearing-impaired children in a portion of the northeastern United States and found that the Wechsler scales, especially the performance scale of the WISC-R, were commonly used. One of the measures also used that has been developed specifically for the hearing impaired is the Hiskey-Nebraska Test of Learning Aptitudes, which we discuss next. (For an overview of the assessment of auditory functioning, see Shah & Boyden, 1991.)

Hiskey-Nebraska Tests of Learning Aptitude. This test was first published in 1941 and was originally designed as a measure of learning ability for deaf children. In 1955, it was standardized on hearing children to provide a measure of intelligence for children who might be at a disadvantage on highly verbal tests of ability. The age range covers $2\frac{1}{2}$ to $17\frac{1}{2}$, with five subtests applicable to ages 3 to 10, four subtests applicable to ages 11 to 17, and three subtests that range across all age ranges. Table 9.2 indicates the 12 subtests that make up the Hiskey.

Instructions on each subtest may be presented orally or by pantomime, depending on the child's hearing acuity. The items were selected on the basis of several criteria. They needed to reflect school experience, but to be adaptable for use in a nonverbal test and administrate by pantomime. Performance on the item needed to be correlated with acceptable criteria of intelligence, and not be influenced by time limits. In some ways the

Table 9–2. Hiskey-Nebraska Tests of Learning Aptitude

Subtest name	Appropriate age range
Bead patterns	3 to 10
Memory for color	3 to 10
Picture identification	3 to 10
Picture association	3 to 10
Paper folding	3 to 10
Visual attention span	All ages
Block patterns	All ages
Completion of drawings	All ages
Memory for digits	11 to 17
Puzzle blocks	11 to 17
Picture analogy	11 to 17
Spatial reasoning	11 to 17

Description of subtests:

1. Bead patterns: At the younger levels, the child strings beads as rapidly as possible. At the older levels, the child reproduces a string of beads, matches the pattern of round, square, and rectangular beads, and may do so from memory.

2. Memory for color: The child selects from memory one or more color chips to match the chip(s) presented by the examiner.

3. Picture identification: The child is required to select one of several pictures that matches the target picture.

4. Picture association: The child selects a picture that "goes with" a pair of pictures presented by the examiner.

5. Paper folding: The child imitates from memory paper folding sequences shown by the examiner.

6. Visual attention span: The child reproduces a series of pictures from memory.

7. Block patterns: The child reproduces block construction patterns.

8. Completion of drawings: The child draws the missing parts of geometric forms or pictures of objects.

9. Memory for digits: The child is required to reproduce from memory a series of visually presented numerals, by using black plastic numerals.

10. Puzzle blocks: The child puts together puzzle pieces that make a cube.

11. Picture analogy: The child completes a visually presented analogy by selecting the correct answer from five alternatives.

12. Spatial reasoning: The child identifies from four alternatives the geometric figures that could be put together to form the target figure.

Hiskey is analogous to the WISC; it is a broad-based measure of intellectual functioning, composed of a number of subtests.

Development. The Hiskey was standardized on more than 1,000 deaf children and 1,000 hearing children, aged $2\frac{1}{2}$ to $17\frac{1}{2}$. The hearing sample was a stratified sample according to parental occupation as an indicator of social class, but other information is lacking. Most likely, the deaf children represent samples of convenience.

Administration. As with most other intelligence tests that cover a developmental span, which tasks are presented to the child is a function of the child's chronological age. Testing is discontinued after a specific number of consecutive failures. Instructions for each task can be presented orally or in pantomime. Three of the subtests (bead memory, block patterns, and puzzle blocks) have time limits on individual items. Total testing time is between 45 and 60 minutes.

Scoring. The manual provides clear scoring criteria, although they are a bit complicated because each subtest uses somewhat different scoring procedures. For each of the subtests, a mental age is obtained and a median mental age is then computed as an overall rating of intelligence. The median is used on the subtests as well (rather than a raw score sum) because the author believes that deaf children often tend to score poorly on initial items of a task because they fail to understand completely what they are to do. The median rating can then be converted to a deviation IQ, with mean of 100 and SD = 16. For deaf children, however, the scoring procedure is slightly different. The median age is converted to a learning quotient using the ratio of:

$$\frac{\text{learning age}}{\text{chronological age}} \times 100$$

You will recognize this as the old Stanford-Binet procedure, abandoned for the deviation IQ. In fact, the Hiskey seems, in some ways, to be an adaptation of the Stanford-Binet.

Reliability. The manual reports split-half coefficients in the .90s for both deaf and hearing children (Hiskey, 1966). Test-retest reliability is reported by B. U. Watson (1983) to be .79 for a sample of 41 hearing-impaired children retested after a 1-year interval.

Validity. The test manual gives minimal information on validity, basically addressing only concurrent validity for hearing children. Correlation coefficients in the high .70s and low to middle .80s are reported with the Stanford-Binet and the WISC.

B. U. Watson and Goldgar (1985) assessed 71 hearing-impaired children and reported a correlation coefficient of .85 between the learning quotient of the Hiskey and the WISC-R Full Scale. Phelps and Branyan (1988) studied 31 hearing-impaired children and found correlations of .57 with the K-ABC nonverbal scale and .66 with the WISC-R Performance score.

Norms. The norms are based on a standardization sample of 1,079 deaf children and 1,074 hearing children, ranging in age from $2\frac{1}{2}$ to $17\frac{1}{2}$. The majority of the deaf children attended schools for the deaf, while the hearing sample was stratified according to parental occupation to match U.S. Census figures. Norms for individuals older than 17 are based on extrapolation and cannot be considered reliable.

Criticisms. Some authors feel that the Hiskey is "psychometrically inadequate and cannot be recommended for use" (e.g., Kamphaus, 1993). Some authors do not recommend this test because the norms are not representative and may be outdated. Some suggest that the nonverbal scale of the K-ABC is a better instrument that can be administered to deaf children with pantomimed instructions (Aylward, 1991). The Hiskey continues to be used, in part, because psychologists working with hearing-impaired children have relatively few choices.

Visual Impairments

Here also two major categories may be distinguished: those who are blind and those with partial vision. If the loss of vision is congenital, that is, present at birth, the child may lag developmentally in several areas including gross-motor behavior and other visually dependent behaviors such as smiling (e.g., Fraiberg, 1977). Often these conditions are part of a total picture that may involve sensory and emotional deficits, disorders of learning and development, or even include mental retardation and/or other deficits. Sometimes blind children are misdiagnosed as mentally retarded because standard intelligence tests "discriminate" against visually impaired children. Blindness has a great impact on sensorimotor development and has less of an impat on verbal and cognitive skills.

Visual acuity is typically measured by the well known Snellen chart or scale (National Society to Prevent Blindness, 1974) with clients who can read, or with an adaptation that uses only the letter E with the "arms" pointing in different directions. Other scales are also available such as the Parsons Visual Acuity Test (Cibis et al., 1985) and test procedures that assess preferential looking (e.g., Cress, 1987).

Hansen, Young, and Ulrey (1982) suggest that when the professional is testing visually impaired children, he or she should distribute the testing over time rather than doing it at one sitting; this gives the child time to become familiar with the surroundings and with the test items, and enables the tester to be familiar with what is normal behavior in visually impaired children and be flexible with the testing procedures.

Many of the tests used with visually handicapped persons have been standardized on normal samples rather than on special children. Where there are norms for visually impaired groups, the samples are typically "atypical" – that is, they may be small, unrepresentative, too homogeneous (children with a particular condition being assessed in a special program), or too heterogeneous (all types of visual impairment lumped together).

Usually, tests need to be modified for use with visually impaired clients. The modifications can vary from using braille to substituting objects for words. From its early days, changes were made to the Binet-Simon for possible use with the visually impaired. For example, Irwin (1914) simply omitted those items that required vision. Hayes (1929) did the same for the Stanford-Binet and eventually developed the Hayes-Binet, which was widely used for assessment of the visually impaired. A recent version consists of the Perkins-Binet (Davis, 1980), which provides a form for children who have some usable vision and a form for children who do not.

The Wechsler scales have also been used with the visually impaired, quite often by modifying items, or by omitting subtests. Despite the fact that the Wechsler scales seem to be the most frequently used cognitive test with visually impaired clients (Bauman & Kropf, 1979), there is relatively little known about the reliability and validity of these scales with the visually impaired. In general, the reliability seems to be adequate (e.g., Tillman, 1973), and the concurrent validity as assessed by correlations of the Binet with the Wechsler scales is substantial (e.g., Hopkins & McGuire, 1966).

Many of the subtests of standardized tests such as the WPPSI, the Stanford Binet, and the McCarthy Scales assess perceptual-motor development either directly or indirectly. Other tests that can be listed here include the Developmental Test of Visual-Motor Integration (Beery & Buktenica, 1967) and the Grassi Basic Cognition Evaluation (Grassi, 1973). Listings of tests that are appropriate for visually impaired individuals can be found in the literature. For example, Swallow (1981) lists 50 assessment instruments commonly used with the visually impaired.

Children with Chronic Illnesses

There are a number of diseases such as asthma, diabetes, and epilepsy that present special challenges and may interface with the educational experience, creating special problems and the need for identification and assessment to provide ameliorative services.

A child's understanding of illness in general and of his or her own condition, in particular, is an important area of assessment because that understanding is potentially related to how well the child copes with aspects such as hospitalization and treatment (Eiser, 1984; Reissland, 1983; Simeonsson, Buckley, & Monson, 1979).

Gifted

It may seem strange to have this category among a list of categories that primarily reflect deficits or disturbances in functioning, but from an educational point of view this is also a "deviant" group that presumably requires special educational procedures. Giftedness is defined in various ways, but in most practical situations it is operationalized as high scores on an intelligence test. In some instances, evidence of creativity, originality, and/or artistic talent is also sought out. Marland (1972) defined gifted children as those capable of high performance in one or more of six areas: general intellectual ability, specific academic aptitude, creative or productive thinking, leadership ability, visual and performing arts, and psychomotor ability. Sternberg and Davidson (1986) used a fourfold classification of superior abilities: intellectual skills, artistic skills, niche-fitting skills (e.g., a mechanically inclined child), and physical skills.

Many states require multiple-selection criteria for the identification of the gifted or talented. Typically measures of intelligence and of achievement are used, in addition to teacher nominations. Criticisms of these procedures, however, have been made by many in that the process seems to be dominated by the assessment of convergent thinking rather than divergent thinking (e.g., Alvino, McDonnel, & Richert, 1981).

Teacher ratings of the giftedness of their pupils have been criticized (e.g., J. J. Gallagher, 1966; Gear, 1976), although the limitations may reflect lack of instruction as to what creativity really is, as well as problems inherent in the rating forms. In an attempt to make teacher ratings more objective and systematic, Renzulli and his colleagues (Renzulli, Hartman, & Callahan, 1971; Renzulli, Smith, White, et al., 1976) developed the scales for Rating the Behavioral Characteristics of Superior Students. Unfortunately, subsequent research has not supported the validity of these scales (e.g., Gridley & Treloar, 1984; Houtz & Shaning, 1982; Rust and Lose, 1980).

A number of authors have developed checklists of characteristics, traits, or behaviors supposedly related to giftedness; typical items are "this child is curious," "this child is a rapid reader," "he or she learns easily and readily" (Denton & Postwaithe, 1985; Martin, 1986; Tuttle & Becker, 1980). Unfortunately, most of these checklists are no better than the checklists found in popular magazines. They are the fictional product of an author's imagination and biases, devoid of any reliability and validity. The items are often vague or apply to almost any child; quite often they reflect the behavior of children who are highly intelligent but not necessarily creative.

SOME GENERAL ISSUES ABOUT TESTS

Readability. Rating scales, checklists, and self-report inventories have become popular screening instruments, used by school psychologists among others, because of their efficiency and minimal cost. Harrington and Follett (1984) argue, however, that despite improvements in the reliability and validity of these measures, there may be a basic flaw – individual respondents, whether children or adults, may have difficulty reading the instructions and the items. They analyzed the readability of 18 widely used instruments including the Child Behavior Checklist (to be discussed) and the Personality Inventory for Children, discussed earlier. Their analyses, based on computing various reading difficulty indices, suggested that for the CBCL the average reading level required is that of an eighth grader (the author of the CBCL indicates fifth grade), while for the PIC it was a seventh grader. For the PIC, the authors stated that because of its length, it is "arduous if not overwhelming for a poor reader to complete." They propose that the readability of a self-report test be considered an essential component of a well-designed test.

Minimizing verbal aspects. Instruments such as the Stanford-Binet or the WPPSI are well-standardized instruments, and quite useful with many types of special children. One of their problems, however, is that they tend to be highly verbal in nature, and special children often have verbal deficits. As a result, a number of tests have been developed that minimize verbal skills by using nonverbal items such as matching of patterns. Several of these tests have also been presented as "culture-fair" tests – that is, they can presumably be used with children in or from different cultures. Many of these tests, such as the Leiter International Performance Scale (Leiter, 1952) or the Coloured Progressive Matrices (J. C. Raven, Court, & J. Raven, 1977) have respectable concurrent validities, often in the .70s range with standard verbal IQ tests. However, scores on these tests are often lower than their counterparts on the Stanford-Binet or WPPSI; caution needs to be exercised if such scores are used for placement purposes. Thus a particular child may have an IQ of 76 on the Stanford-Binet but an IQ of 68 on a nonverbal test; knowing only the score on the nonverbal test might lead to erroneous decisions. That, of course, is not a criticism solely of nonverbal tests. Scores on the Stanford-Binet and the WISC-R, for example, can be quite discrepant with mentally retarded and learning-disabled children (e.g., A. S. Bloom, Reese, Altshuler, et al., 1983).

Other tests use cartoons as the items and ask the child to respond by pointing to a "thermometer" response format, happy faces, or similar nonverbal stimuli (for an example see Praver, DiGiuseppe, Pelcovitz, et al., 2000).

Testing the limits. This phrase, often associated with the Rorschach (see Chapter 15), refers to the notion of psychologically "pushing" the subject to see what the limits of that person's abilities might be. This procedure can be useful with special children, indeed with almost any subject. Once a test has been administered in a standardized manner, the examiner can return to specific items that the child missed, for example, and provide cues and encouragement for the child to complete the item. Here the intent is to see whether in fact a particular child can use cues to solve a problem, whether encouragement and support can allow the child to really show and stretch his or her abilities. Budoff and his colleagues (e.g., Budoff & Friedman, 1964) have in fact taken testing to the limits and changed it into a strategy to assess learning potential.

Test-retest stability of preschool measures. One major concern is the low stability of measurement associated with infant behavior. When cognitive tests are administered to children as they enter school at age 6 and are readministered a year later, we typically obtain coefficients in the .70s or higher. But with infants and preschoolers, such correlations over a year-time-span range from zero to the high .50s. Interestingly, these coefficients are substantially higher for handicapped children (Kamphaus, 1993). The instability is a reflection of the behavior rather than the measure, but nevertheless creates problems.

Neuropsychological assessment. There are two major approaches to neuropsychological assessment in children. The first is to use a standardized battery of tasks that were designed to identify brain impairment. The field seems to be dominated by two such batteries: the Reitan Batteries, i.e., the Halstead-Reitan Neuropsychological Test Battery for children 9 to 14, the Reitan-Indiana Test Battery for children aged 5 through 8 (Reitan 1969; Reitan & Davison, 1974), and the Luria-Nebraska Children's Battery (Golden, 1981). We illustrate the Luria-Nebraska next. This approach has been criticized because of the time and cost requirements, because many of the important behaviors are evaluated only in a cursory manner, and because the procedures used tend to be redundant (e.g., Goldstein, 1984; Slomka & Tarter, 1984; Sutter & Battin, 1984).

A second approach consists of using a combination of traditional psychological and educational tests. Tests such as the K-ABC, the Stanford-Binet, and the WISC-R are often used as the main measure, together with other scales that may measure oral and written language skills (e.g., the Peabody Picture Vocabulary Test), motor and visual-motor skills (e.g., the Developmental Test of Visual Motor Integration), academic achievement (discussed in Chapter 13), and aspects of social-emotional behavior (e.g., the Child Behavior Checklist).

A third approach, of course, is to combine the two. For example, Bigler and Nussbaum (1989) describe the test battery used at a neurological clinic in Texas. The battery includes selected sub-tests from the Halstead-Reitan batteries, the Reitan-Aphasia Screening Battery, the Wide Range Achievement Test, the Boder Test of Reading and Spelling Patterns, the Durrell Analysis of Reading Difficulty, the Beery Test of Visual/Motor Integration, Raven's Coloured Progressive Matrices, the WISC-R, a family history questionnaire, the Child Behavior Checklist, the Personality Inventory for Children, projective drawings, and a behavioral observation inventory; additional measures, such as the K-ABC, are included as needed. For a thorough and sophisticated critique of measurement and statistical problems associated with neuropsychological assessment of children, see Reynolds (1989).

The Luria-Nebraska Children's Neuropsychological Test Battery. The Luria-Nebraska assesses brain-behavior relationships in children 8 to 12 years. It was first published in 1980 and then revised in 1987. The battery is based on the neurodevelopmental theory of A. R. Luria, a Russian physician and psychologist (e.g., Luria, 1966), and consists of 11 neuropsychological tests, with 3 additional scales developed subsequently (Sawicki, Leark, Golden, et al., 1984). Although the Luria-Nebraska is modeled on an adult version, the tasks used take into account the neurological development of children and are not merely downward extensions of adult items.

This battery consists of 149 items that assess functioning in 11 areas, such as motor skills as for example, touching fingers with thumb in succession, rhythm skills as in repeating a pattern of taps, visual skills as in the recognition of objects, and intelligence, with items similar to those found on the WISC-R.

Development. The Luria-Nebraska was developed by administering the adult version to children aged 5 to 12. Initially the authors found that children 8 years and older could do a majority of the procedures in the adult battery, and that for 13- and 14-year-olds the adult battery was quite appropriate. The authors therefore decided to create a children's battery for ages 8 to 12. This was done by eliminating difficult items from the adult battery, substituting easier items where possible, and adding new items where needed. Three versions of the battery were investigated, and the fourth version was published (Golden, 1989).

The assignment of each item to one of the 11 basic scales was done on the basis of the authors' clinical judgment, followed by a correlational analysis. A further factor analysis on a separate sample of brain-damaged and normal children, seemed in general to substantiate item placement. However, further factor analyses of each scale alone resulted in the creation of a new set of 11 scales that, judging by their titles, have some overlap but are not identical with the original 11 scales.

Each of the 11 scales is said to be multifactorial in structure. Each scale covers not just a specific skill but a domain of skills in a given area. For example, the motor scale measures fine motor speed as well as unilateral and bilateral coordination, imitation skills, verbal control of motor movements, and construction skills.

Administration. The Luria-Nebraska requires a skilled examiner and is typically used to assess children who have known or suspected brain damage. Testing time is about 2 hours. The results can be used in conjunction with other data, or as a baseline against which future evaluations can be made to assess amount of deterioration or effectiveness of specific therapeutic procedures such as medications or surgery. Most of the items in the battery cannot be used with children who have sensory or motor handicaps.

Scoring. Scoring of test items is based on normative data for the 8- to 12-year-old age group. Each item is scored as zero if the performance is equal to or less than 1 SD below the mean; it is scored 1 for performance between 1 and 2 SDs below the mean, and scored 2 for performance more than 2 SDs below the mean. Thus higher scores indicate more severe deficit. Scoring is fairly straightforward and objective, although subjective judgment is required in many aspects of the test. The raw scores for each of the scales are transformed to T scores using the appropriate table provided in the test booklet.

Validity. Neuropsychological assessment of children with learning disabilities is now fairly common, given that the definition of learning disabilities includes minimal brain dysfunction. So it is quite appropriate to ask questions about the validity of the Luria-Nebraska with such children. Several studies have obtained findings supportive of the validity of the Luria-Nebraska (e.g., Geary & Gilger, 1984; Nolan, Hammeke, & Barkley, 1983), but primarily with the language and academic achievement subtests, that are adequately assessed by other instruments (Hynd, 1988).

A rather interesting study is reported by Snow and Hynd (1985a). They administered the Luria-Nebraska, the WISC-R, and an achievement test, to 100 children who had been previously identified as learning disabled on the basis of a discrepancy between aptitude and achievement – that is, they achieved less than what their abilities would predict. The authors analyzed the results using Q-factor analysis. In this type of factor analysis, rather than seek out the fewest dimensions among the test variables, the Q-technique analysis clusters subjects with similar test score patterns. The intent then is to identify subgroups of subjects who "belong together" on the basis of the similarity of their test scores. The authors found statistically three subgroups of children, that included 72 of the 100 children. Unfortunately the three subtypes did not appear to be markedly different on the intelligence and achievement tests, and the authors concluded that the Luria-Nebraska has a strong language component across most of its subtests, and that therefore its construct validity is poor.

The construct validity of the Luria-Nebraska has been questioned both on the basis of the relationship of the battery to Luria's theory on which it is based, and also as to its factor structure (Snow & Hynd, 1985b; Hynd, 1988).

Norms. Initially, the Luria-Nebraska was normed on 125 "normal" children, 25 at each of five age levels.

The Luria-Nebraska and decision theory. One basic way to validate a neuropsychological assessment procedure is to determine the procedure's ability to discriminate between brain-damaged and nonbrain-damaged individuals. The brain-damaged individuals are usually diagnosed on the basis of a neurological exam and other evidence, while the normal subjects are usually identified by exclusion, such as not having obvious head trauma. Several studies have looked at this with quite positive results. For example, Wilkening, Golden, MacInnes, et al. (1981) studied a sample of 76 brains-damaged and 125 normal controls and found an overall accuracy hit rate of 81.6% for the Luria-Nebraska (91.3% for the normal controls and 65.3% for the brain-damaged subjects).

Geary, Jennings, Schultz, et al. (1984) studied the diagnostic accuracy and discriminant validity of the Luria-Nebraska by comparing 15 learning-disabled children with 15 academically normal children. The obtained neuropsychological profiles were rated as normal, borderline, or abnormal on the basis of cutoff scores, with the last two categories considered as presumable evidence of a learning disability. A comparison of this categorization based on test results with actual group status, indicated that 28 of the 30 children were correctly identified, with two of the normal children falsely identified as learning disabled. Thus, for this study, the overall hit rate was 93.3%, the number of false positives was 13.3%, and there were no false negatives. Sensitivity is therefore 100% and specificity is 86.7% (see Chapter 3 if you've forgotten what these terms mean).

Levels of interpretation. Golden (1989) points out that in interpreting the Luria-Nebraska or other batteries, there are several levels of interpretation that differ based on both the needs of the situation and the expertise of the examiner. Level 1 aims at ascertaining whether there is significant brain injury in the child to differentiate neuropsychological from other disorders. Obviously, if it is known that the child has a significant brain injury, this question is not appropriate, At this level, the battery is used basically as a screening procedure.

Level 2 concerns the description of the child's behavior – what the child is able to do and not do. There is no interpretation or integration of the findings, but merely a description. Level 3 requires the identification of the probable causes that underlie the child's behavior. This requires a thorough knowledge of brain-behavior relationships. Level 4 involves the integration of the findings and conclusions into a description of how the brain of the subject is and is not functioning. This involves an understanding of the effects and implications of specific brain injuries.

Drawing techniques. There are a number of procedures such as the Draw-A-Person and the House-Tree-Person that involve having the client produce a drawing. These techniques were typically developed initially as measures of intellectual functioning, but soon became measures of personality. These are subsumed under the topic of projective techniques is discussed in Chapter 15. They have been used not only as assessment devices but also as ancillary procedures to be used in therapy, or as screening procedures to evaluate readiness for school or the effectiveness of special training programs.

Adults typically become somewhat defensive when asked to draw, but children do so often with great pleasure and little discomfort. For children, drawings are a way of portraying the world, as they see it and as they wish it were. Thus if the examiner can distinguish between what is fact and what is fiction, what is fantasy and what is fear, the drawings can become powerful sources of information. In addition, because the structure of drawing is minimal, much can be learned about the way a child responds to authority, to ambiguity, and to their own inner resources. Finally, for the well-trained and sensitive examiner, drawings can be a source of observation and information about the child's impulsivity, self-worth, motor dexterity, and so on.

Unfortunately, from a psychometric perspective, the picture presented by drawings is quite different. Although we should be leery of dumping together a set of techniques and evaluating them wholesale, reviews of such techniques lead to the conclusion that although a clinician may be able to arrive at certain conclusions about a child's emotional disturbance and intellectual level on the basis of drawings, such tests seem to have little value in assessing personality and/or psychodynamic functioning (e.g., Cummings, 1986). They are quite useful to establish rapport, but drawing skills per se affect the performance, as well as the child's intellectual level and degree of normality.

A number of measures involve the reproduction of drawings rather than the creation of a picture. Such tasks are, of course, part of standard tests such as the Stanford-Binet, and indeed one might question whether a separate test is necessary. But these tests exist and are often used as part of a comprehensive neuropsychological battery. The Developmental Test of Visual-Motor Integration (VMI) is a good example.

The Developmental Test of Visual-Motor Integration. The VMI was originally published in 1967, revised in 1982 and 1989, and is based on the author's observation that there is a significant relationship between children's abilities to copy geometric forms and their academic achievement (Beery, 1989). The VMI is designed as a screening instrument to identify difficulties that a child may have in visual-spatial processing and/or visual-motor integration that can result in learning and behavioral problems.

The test consists of 24 drawings of geometric designs that the child copies in designated spaces. The drawings cover a wide range of difficulty, from a simple vertical line to a six-pointed star. The items are copied in order, only one attempt per drawing is allowed, and erasing is not permitted. The test is discontinued after three consecutive failures. The VMI can be administered individually or in small groups. Both the test booklet and the instructions have been carefully designed to avoid any extraneous aspects that might affect the child's performance. For example, the test booklet is not to be turned at an angle, and the child begins on the last page and works toward the front of the booklet – this latter avoids impressions on subsequent pages. The test is not timed, and typical administration takes about 10 to 15 minutes. The test is relatively easy to administer and score, and theoretically at least, it can be used with preschool children through adults, although the norms only go up to $17^{11}/_{12}$ years. There is a short form of the VMI composed of the 15 easiest items, for use with children aged 2 to 8, while the full set of items is suitable for children aged 2 to 15.

Scoring. Each item is scored as passed or failed. Passed items may be scored from 1 to 4 points, with higher point values given to the more difficult designs. The manual provides clear scoring criteria, together with examples. Total raw scores are converted to standard scores, with a mean of 100 and SD of 15. These scores can also be converted to percentiles, T scores, scores with a mean of 10 and SD equal to 3, an age equivalent score, and others.

Reliability. Interrater reliability is particularly important for this test because the scoring is ultimately based on the examiner's judgment; obtained coefficients range from .58 to .99, with a median r of about .93. Internal consistency alphas range from .76 to .91, with a median of .85, and test-retest reliabilities range from .63 (with a 7-month interval) to .92 (2-week interval), with a median of about .81. These results suggest that the reliability is adequate and that it increases with well-trained examiners. Unfortunately, the manual gives little information on the studies done to establish such reliability.

Validity. Concurrent validity of the VMI has been assessed by correlating VMI scores with a wide variety of other measures of visual-spatial and visual-motor skills, both as tests and as behavior (e.g., as in handwriting). Correlations vary quite widely, from the high .20s to the low .90s, but in general do support the concurrent validity of the VMI.

Correlations between VMI scores and standard tests of intelligence such as the WISC-R correlate about the mid .50s, somewhat lower with verbal than with performance indices. Similarly, correlations between VMI scores and school-readiness tests correlate about .50 as do correlations between measures of academic achievement as, for example, reading; these latter ones are somewhat higher for younger children than for older children.

Beery (1989) also reports studies of predictive validity, for example correlations of VMI scores at the beginning of kindergarten with later measures of school achievement. In general, the predictive validity of tests such as the VMI is better with younger children than older children. Unfortunately, for most studies reported in the manual there is little information given as to sample size or other details that would allow the reader to critically judge the results; many of the samples seem quite small and atypical. Whether the VMI measures the integration of the visual and the motor functions rather than either separately is debatable (W. L. Goodwin & Driscoll, 1980).

Norms. Norms are based on three samples of children tested at three different times, with the total N close to 6,000 children. Only the third sample is "representative," but the results from the three samples do not appear to be significantly different. These norms cover the ages of 4 years through 17 years 11 months, although the actual ages of the children tested exceeded these limits.

Behavior rating scales. Since the 1970s, there has been increased interest and use of behavior rating scales as a method of assessment of children. Behavior rating scales essentially provide a standardized format in which information supplied by an informant who knows the child well is integrated and translated into some judgment (Merrell, 1994). Thus, behavior rating scales measure perceptions of specified behaviors rather than firsthand direct observation.

Behavior rating scales have a number of advantages. Merrell (1994) lists six: (1) They usually require less training and less time than direct behavioral observations; (2) They can provide information on infrequent behaviors; (3) They are more reliable than some other approaches such as unstructured interviews; (4) Because they utilize observer information, they can be used to assess individuals who may not be cooperative; (5) They reflect observations made over a period of time in a natural setting, i.e., home or school; (6) They capitalize on the judgment and observations of "experts," those who know the child best.

These scales can be particularly useful as screening instruments to identify children who might benefit from some type of intervention or who might need to be more carefully assessed with individual tests or other procedures.

They also have a number of limitations. One of the major problems has to do with interrater agreement. Low interrater agreement is often found between parents and between parent and teacher. In a way, this is not surprising because the demands and challenges of a home environment may be quite different from that of the classroom. The issue here is not whether one source is more accurate than another, but that the obtained information comes from different sources. A number of rating scales now include separate versions for the parents and for teachers to account for such differences. Higher agreement is obtained on scales that use items where a behavior is operationally defined, rather than require the rater to make some inference. For example, consider an item such as, "gets into many fights" vs. "is an aggressive child"; the first item is one of observation, the second item requires an inference.

There may be bias on the part of the informants. For one, the ratings may reflect a *halo effect* – e.g., because Linda is so cute she must also be bright, outgoing, and well adjusted. Or the raters may be overly critical or lenient in their perceptions, or may be "middle of the road," unwilling to endorse extreme responses. Worthen, Borg, and White (1993) point out that when a rater completes a rating scale there is a tendency for both recent and more unusual behaviors to be given greater weight.

The ratings may also reflect *error variance.* There are at least four sources of such variance: (1) source variance – different informers have different biases; (2) setting variance – behavior may be situation specific (Billy is horrid in math class but quite reasonable in art); (3) temporal variance – both the behavior and the informant can change from point A to point B; and (4) instrument variance – different rating scales may measure closely related behaviors but use different items, wording, and so on.

Rating scales (or checklists) completed by a sensitive informant can yield very useful information. In fact, such scales can often provide a better picture than the child's own perception. These scales are easy to administer, can cover a substantial amount of ground, and can focus on global characteristics as well as specific behaviors. They can be more useful than an interview in assuring that all relevant areas are covered and can provide quantifiable information. Among the better known instruments may be mentioned the Behavior Problem Checklist (H. C. Quay & Peterson, 1967) and the Denver Developmental Screening Test (Frankenburg & Dodds, 1967). We look at two scales: the Child Behavior Checklist and the Conners Rating Scales (for general reviews see Barkley, 1988; Cairns & Green, 1979; Edelbrock & Rancurello, 1985; McMahon, 1984).

The Child Behavior Checklist (CBCL). The Child Behavior Checklist (CBCL; Achenbach, 1991) actually consists of six different forms: (1) the CBCL/4-18, which is for use by parents of children aged 4 to 18; (2) the CBCL/2-3, for use by parents of children aged 2 to 3; (3) the Teacher's Report form, for use by the child's teacher, covering ages 5 to 18; (4) the Youth Self-Report, to be used by adolescents, aged 11 to 18; (5) the Direct Observation Form, to be used by an observer, after direct observation of the child in the classroom; and (6) the Semistructured Clinical Interview for Children, completed by the interviewer following an interview, and suitable for ages 6 to 11. Most of the comments to follow are applicable to the first two forms, although a full exploration of reliability, validity, and norms has been done on the first form only.

The CBCL yields five scale scores, three for social competence (activities, social, and school) and two for behavior problems (internalizing and externalizing). Internalizing refers to "overcontrol" problems while externalizing refers to "undercontrol" problems. An additional nine "narrow-band" syndrome scales are also available; these scales were developed on the basis of factor analysis for a sample of almost 4,500 protocols of children referred to clinics. A fac-

tor analysis of the nine syndrome scales yielded two "super" factors (called second-order factors) that resulted in the Internalizing and Externalizing scales.

The CBCL is designed to assess in a standardized manner the behavioral problems and social competencies of children, as reported by parents. The form can be administered by an interviewer or answered directly by a parent. The checklist consists of 118 behavior problem items (e.g., disobedient at home), each rated on a 3-point scale from not true to often true. There are an additional 20 items that cover social competencies, such as the child's involvement in sports, hobbies, jobs, and friends.

The items are clearly written, require about a fifth-grade reading level, and are nontechnical in nature. The manual is clear and well written, and the CBCL is easily administered and scored. Administration does not necessarily require a well-trained examiner, although as Freeman (1985) points out "a checklist is only as good as the clinician who uses it." The CBCL can be hand scored, although the procedure is tedious and typically requires longer than 15 minutes. Computer scoring programs are available.

Reliability. The CBCL manual reports item reliabilities greater than .90 between mothers' reports, mothers' and fathers' reports, and reports from three different interviewers. Given that item statistics are often unstable, these are rather impressive figures. The stability of the CBCL over a 3-month period is reported as .84 for behavior problems and .97 for social competencies. Test-retest reliabilities over a 1-week interval are in the .80s to mid .90s range, but are lower for longer intervals. Interrater reliabilities between teachers and teacher aides range from .42 to .72. Interrater reliabilities between mothers and fathers is in the mid .60s.

Validity. Several studies support the construct validity of the CBCL, such as studies comparing "normal" children with children referred to a clinic. The discriminative power of the test is fairly high. By using the 90th percentile of the behavior-problem scores, and the 10th percentile of the social-competence scores, the authors were able to correctly classify 91.2% of the normal children and 74.1% of the referred children.

Concurrent validity results, by way of correlations with other rating scales, are also quite positive, with typical coefficients in the high .80s and low .90s. The CBCL is a very popular instrument and has been used in hundreds of studies.

Norms. The original CBCL provided norms on children between ages 4 and 16, but the 1991 revision was extended upward through age 18, and a separate form for 2- and 3-year-old children was developed. The norms are based on some 1,300 children, and T scores can be obtained for the subscales.

Evaluation. Reviewers of the CBCL see this instrument as "well-documented psychometrically with adequate reliability and validity" (B. J. Freeman, 1985) and as "one of the best standardized instruments of its kind" (M. L. Kelley, 1985), and others characterize the CBCL as one of the most sophisticated and well-researched broad-spectrum behavior Rating Scales (Merrell, 1994).

The Conners Rating Scales. Another set of scales that has also proven popular is the Conners Rating Scales. Conners also developed separate scales for parents and for teachers, designed to identify behavior problems in school-aged children. The CRS (Conners, 1990) consists of four scales, two parent and two teacher rating scales, that have many items in common and are also conceptually similar. The scales vary in length from 28 to 93 items. Originally developed in 1969 (Conners, 1969), they have been widely used since then and have been revised as the need arises and as research findings accumulate (Conners, Sitarenios, Parker, et al., 1998). For parents then, there is the CPRS-93 (Conners parent's rating scale with 93 items) and the CPRS-48. For teachers, there is the CTRS-28 and the CTRS-39. The CPRS-48 and the CTRS-39 seem to be the most widely used versions. The rating scales were originally developed within an applied research setting, Johns Hopkins University Hospital, and were intended as norm-referenced instruments to be used widely. A practical result of this is that in reading the literature, one finds different versions of these scales, sometimes with different results as in the number of factors reported.

The Conners Parent's Questionnaire, or CPRS-93 (Conners, 1970), consists of 93 items that assess a number of behavior problems ranging from hyperactivity to bowel problems. Each item is rated by the parent on a 4-point scale ranging from 0, not at all, to 3, very much (all four scales use this format). Factor analysis of this scale yielded six factors labeled as: aggressive-conduct disorder, anxious-inhibited, antisocial, enuresis-encopresis, psychosomatic, and anxious-immature. However, the actual scale is scored on five dimensions: conduct problem, learning problem, psychosomatic, impulsive-hyperactive, and anxiety.

The Conners Teacher Rating Scale, or CTRS-39 (Conners, 1969), consists of 39 items that cover three areas: classroom behavior, group participation, and attitude toward authority. It also includes six subscales such as hyperactivity, conduct problems, and daydream-attention problem. The longer version (CTRS-48) contains only five subscales, such as conduct problems, similar to those on the CTRS-39, but with different others such as psychosomatic. The teacher rates each item on a 4-point scale, identical to the one used by parents. Factor analysis suggests four clusters: conduct problem, inattentive-passive, tension-anxiety, and hyperactivity. An abbreviated 10-item scale, using the items from the longer version that are most frequently checked by teachers, is also available. These 10 items include such aspects as restless, impulsive, short attention span, easily frustrated, and has temper outbursts; the scale seems quite useful in identifying hyperactive children.

Reliability. Test-retest for the CTRS-39, at 1-month intervals, ranges from .72 to .91, but drops to .33 to .55 at 1-year intervals (R. A. Glow, P. A. Glow, & Rump, 1982).

Interrater agreement on the CTRS-39 ranges from a low of .39 to a high of .94 on different subscales. Agreement between parents on the CPRS-48 averages in the low .50s. Sandberg, Wieselberg, & Shaffer (1980) reported an alpha coefficient of .92 for the 10-item Hyperactivity Index.

Validity. Numerous studies have supported the ability of the Conners scales to differentiate various diagnostic groups from their normal counterparts, such as learning disabled, hyperactive, and juvenile delinquents (e.g., Merrell, 1990).

Some evidence of their predictive validity is also available. For example, in one study behavior ratings obtained at age 7 were highly predictive of hyperactivity at age 10 (I. C. Gillberg & I. C. Gillberg, 1983). Convergent validity data is also available in a variety of studies that have correlated a Conners scale, typically the CTRS-39, with other comparable instruments and have reported significant correlations (e.g., Sandoval, 1981).

Norms. The norms for the CPRS-48 are for children aged 3 to 17, while those for the CTRS-39 are for these aged 3 to 14. Raw scores on each subscale are converted to T scores, but a total score is not computed. The answer sheet is specially designed so that scoring requires a minimum of time. Computer programs that provide administration, scoring, and interpretation of results are also available. The factor structure and normative data for the CTRS-39 is based on a sample of almost 10,000 Canadian children, presented as a stratified and random sample. For the CPRS-48, the sample is much smaller (570 children and from the Pittsburgh, Pennsylvania, area).

Criticisms. Some critics feel that evaluating the reliability and validity of the Conners scales is difficult because of the many forms, and they believe that other instruments such as the CBCL are psychometrically superior (e.g., Witt, Heffer, & Pfeiffer, 1990). The response choices of "just a little," "pretty much," and "very much" have been criticized as ambiguous and ill defined – what may be "pretty much" to one person may be "just a little" or "very much" to another. Many of the scale items have also been criticized because they are too abstract (e.g., "submissive"), or contain two separate aspects (e.g., "temper outbursts, explosive and unpredictable behavior").

McCarthy Scales of Children's Abilities. Finally, let's take a look at the McCarthy Scales of Children's Abilities (D. McCarthy, 1972). The McCarthy is an individually administered test of young children's intellectual functioning, has been used with both normal and special children, and seems to be a very useful measure, falling short of the Stanford-Binet and the Wechsler tests in popularity. Unfortunately, the author died at the time that the test was being published, so studies of the test are up to other researchers.

Description. The McCarthy Scales consist of 18 tests grouped into 6 scales: Verbal, Perceptual-Performance, Quantitative, General Cognitive, Memory, and Motor. These scales are overlapping – for example, the General Cognitive score is actually based on 15 of the 18 tests, and thus represents a global measure of intellectual development. The 18 subtests include block building, word knowledge (i.e., vocabulary), pictorial memory (recalling names of objects pictured on cards), and leg coordination (e.g., motor tasks such as standing on one foot). Although the McCarthy is standardized for children ages $2\frac{1}{2}$ to $8\frac{1}{2}$, it is probably most useful for children aged 3 to 6.

The McCarthy Scales use highly attractive test materials, so that the typical child finds the procedure relatively enjoyable. In fact, great care was taken to build within the testing procedure a number of steps designed to obtain a child's optimum performance. For example, several nonverbal tasks are presented before the child is asked to verbalize. When the child is asked to talk, the required responses are one-word, so the child can overcome what anxiety there might be in talking to a stranger. As another example, in the middle of the tests there are a number of activities, such as skipping, designed to give the child a break from the more scholastic type of items.

The 18 subtests are administered consecutively, most starting at a beginning level (there is no basal level) and progressing to a point where a child has made a number of errors. The administration, however, allows the examiner both to model successful performance and to complete tasks that the child cannot to minimize anxiety and frustration.

Testing time requires somewhere between 45 and 60 minutes, in part depending on the age of the child. As with tests such as the Stanford-Binet or the K-ABC, the McCarthy requires a well-trained examiner. In fact some reviewers believe that the McCarthy Scales are more difficult to learn to administer than the WISC-R or the K-ABC (e.g., T. Keith, 1985).

Scoring. The test manual presents scoring criteria for each item and provides many examples to minimize the amount of subjectivity involved. Scores on the separate scales are normalized standard scores with a mean of 50 and a SD of 10, and scores can range from 22 to 78. The score on the General Cognitive Scale, which is called the General Cognitive Index (GCI), is a normalized standard score with a mean of 100 and a SD of 16. Scores on the GCI can range from 50 to 150. Incidentally, the McCarthy was one of the first popular tests of intelligence that did not use the term IQ.

A profile can be drawn to summarize the six scales, and these scores can be converted to percentiles. Instructions are also provided for assessing the child's laterality (i.e., left-or right-handedness), based on the child's eye and hand preference on several subtests.

Reliability. Split-half reliabilities for the six scales range from .79 to .93, with the GCI averaging .93 across various age levels. Test-retest reliabilities over a 1-month interval range from .69 to .90, again with the GCI having one of the highest values, a not-surprising finding because it encompasses most of the subtests. In general, the reliability of the GCI and of the first four cognitive scales seems to be adequate. The results on the Motor scale, however, need to be interpreted cautiously. The reliability of the 18 subtests is not reported in the test manual.

Validity. The original test manual gives relatively little validity data, but subsequent studies in the literature have provided the needed information. The results of factor analytic studies indicate three major factors at all ages: a general cognitive factor, a memory factor, and a motor factor (e.g., A. S. Kaufman, 1975). The results also suggest that the same task may require different abilities at different ages.

No significant gender differences have been reported and few ethnic differences; socioeconomic status seems more important than race as an influence on performance on this test (A. S. Kaufman & N. L. Kaufman, 1975). The McCarthy correlates moderately to strongly with tests of achievement and cognitive skills, both in concurrent and predictive validity studies (e.g., Bracken, 1981; A. S. Kaufman, 1982; Nagle, 1979).

Norms. The original standardization sample consisted of 1,032 children between the ages of $2\frac{1}{2}$ and $8\frac{1}{2}$. At each age level, $\frac{1}{2}$-year steps below $5\frac{1}{2}$ and 1-year steps above, there were approximately 100 children, with an equal number of boys and girls, and selected in accord with U.S.

Census characteristics such as geographic region, race, urban vs. rural residence, and so on. These children were "normal" children – children that were institutionalized or had obvious physical handicaps were excluded.

Short forms. A. S. Kaufman (1977) proposed a short form of the McCarthy for rapid screening of preschool, kindergarten, and first-grade children; Taylor, Slocumb, and O'Neill (1979) have proposed another short form by identifying the six subtests that correlated most highly with the GCI, in a sample of 50 kindergarten children. For a comparison of three short forms see Harrington and Jennings, (1986). A set of six subtests has also been published as a "separate" test called the McCarthy Screening Test (McCarthy, 1978).

Interesting aspects. One interesting aspect of the McCarthy is that the various subtests can be clustered into different areas of intellectual functioning than those originally proposed; for example, one such area might be visual-organizational abilities. Age-equivalent scores can be calculated for these areas (A. S. Kaufman & N. L. Kaufman, 1977). In addition to the test manual, much information about the McCarthy is available in journal articles and textbooks (one excellent source is A. S. Kaufman & N. L. Kaufman, 1977). For a review of the McCarthy Scales, see Bracken (1991).

SUMMARY

The needs of special children present challenges and require instruments over and beyond those discussed in Chapter 9 with nonhandicapped children. The testing of these special children requires a great deal of innovative thinking and flexibility on the part of all concerned. Yet such innovativeness can in some ways go counter to the basic psychometric canons. What we have looked at in this chapter is a wide variety of issues and instruments representing, in some aspects, clear and innovative solutions and, in others, inadequate attempts that are far from acceptable.

SUGGESTED READINGS

Czeschlik, T. (1992). The Middle Childhood Temperament Questionnaire: Factor structure in a German sample. *Personality and Individual Differences, 13*, 205–210.

In this study, the cross-cultural validity of a temperament questionnaire was assessed through factor analysis. The results do not support the validity of this instrument. The author concludes that if temperament research is to make progress, there is need for sound measuring instruments.

Glascoe, F. P., & Byrne, K. E. (1993). The accuracy of three developmental screening tests. *Journal of Early Intervention, 17*, 368–379.

The authors indicate that developmental screening tests are widely used for early identification, but few studies look at the percentage of children with and without problems that are correctly detected, i.e., the "hit" rate. In this article, the authors assess three such screening tests.

Scarr, S. (1981). Testing for children. *American Psychologist, 36*, 1159–1166.

Scarr argues that in addition to cognitive functioning, children should be assessed as to motivation and adjustment, that these are important components of intellectual competence. Above all, she points out that testing should always be used in the interests of the children tested.

Waksman, S. A. (1985). The development and psychometric properties of a rating scale for children's social skills. *Journal of Psychoeducational Assessment, 3*, 111–121.

A readable article, illustrating the development of a rating scale to assess children's social skills. You might want to compare and contrast this article with the one by Clark, Gresham, and Elliott (1985), who also developed a children's social-skills measure.

Witt, J. C., & Martens, B. K. (1984). Adaptive behavior: Tests and assessment issues. *School Psychology Review, 13*, 478–484.

As the authors indicate, the assessment of adaptive behavior was rare prior to the mid 1960s, but today it is almost routine. The authors review the reasons for this change, discuss various definitions of adaptive behavior, and point out that half of the available tests of this construct lack the most rudimentary psychometric data.

DISCUSSION QUESTIONS

1. How do we know that a test is valid when used with a "special" child?

2. How would you describe the Vineland Adaptive Behavior Scale to someone with little testing background?

3. How were the items for the Peabody Picture Vocabulary Test originally selected? Can you think of other ways that might be better?

4. The Hiskey-Nebraska is characterized as "psychometrically inadequate". How might such inadequacy be remedied?

5. Of the several categories of special children discussed in this chapter, which might be the most challenging to test?

10 Older Persons

AIM This chapter looks at testing older persons. We first discuss some basic issues such as defining who is an older person, practical issues of testing, and some general comments related to personality, cognitive, and attitude testing. Then we look at a number of specific areas of relevance: attitudes toward older persons, anxiety about aging, life satisfaction, marital satisfaction, morale, coping, death and dying, neuropsychological assessment, memory, and depression.

SOME OVERALL ISSUES

Currently, there is great interest in older persons, in part, because the number of older persons and their relative frequency within the general population has increased substantially (John, Cavanaugh, Krauss-Whitbourne, 1999). Exactly who is an "older person"? Chronological age is often used as the criterion, with age 65 as the cutoff point. Terms such as the *young-old* (ages 65 to 74) vs. the *old-old* (75 years and older) have been proposed (Neugarten, 1974), as related to various physical and sociopsychological characteristics. The term *aging*, as J. E. Birren and B. A. Birren (1990) so well state, implies something that is associated with chronological age but not identical with it. Thus the term is used in two ways – as an independent variable used to explain other phenomena (e.g., there are changes that occur in intellectual processes as one gets older) and as a dependent variable explained by other processes (e.g., lack of support by others creates aging difficulties). In contrast to chronological age, functional age has been suggested (Salthouse, 1986), i.e., the person's ability to be involved in directed activities, intellectual pursuits, and so on.

The fact that the population of the United States is aging presents a number of challenges directly relevant to psychological testing. For one, we know relatively little about the "oldest-old," those over age 80; such information about how, for example, mental abilities change might provide useful information in terms of the maintenance of independent functioning vs. more effective long-term care.

Older people when they are tested by psychologists, often present a complaint that may have wider ramifications – for example, "difficulty on the job" may be related to marital difficulties, medical problems, lowered self-esteem, anxiety about personal competence, and so on. Many of the applications of testing to the elderly are problem- or diagnostic-oriented. Thus, for example, there are hundreds of studies on Alzheimer's in the elderly, but very few studies on creativity in the elderly.

At the same time, we should remember that many older people do experience difficulties that may affect their test performance. For example, it is not unusual for an older person to experience visual difficulties that may range from quite severe to simply annoying, such as taking a bit longer to adapt to a change in illumination. These difficulties may affect their performance on particular tests, especially when some visual component of the test, such as print size is important.

257

Testing problems. D. Gallagher, Thompson, and Levy (1980) point out that among the major problems involving the use of tests with older persons are: improper standardization, lack of normative data, poor reliability and external validity, ambiguous instructions, inappropriate items, and inability of tests to discriminate at lower levels of functioning. They also point out that traditionally, clinical psychologists have been trained to evaluate intellectual processes, personality, psychopathology, and other relevant areas, but that in testing older persons there is need to focus on such aspects as physical health, leisure-time use, and life satisfaction.

Equivalence of tests. Many measures used with older persons were originally developed using younger samples, and so a basic question is: Are such tests equivalent when used with elders? By equivalent we mean that they should be reliable and valid when used with older persons and, to a lesser degree, whether such aspects as item difficulty and factor structure are also the same. A different factor structure in middle-aged samples and in elderly samples would of course not necessarily invalidate a test. Keep in mind that a factor structure is basically a statistical "fiction" we impose on reality to attempt to explain that reality. Different factor structures in different samples may in fact reflect important aspects of reality.

Most tests now used with older persons show equivalence in reliability and validity. Early studies of the equivalence of factor structure were contradictory, but recent studies with more sophisticated techniques of confirmatory factor analyses seem to suggest equivalence in factor structure as well (Hertzog & Schear, 1989).

Practical issues. In Chapter 9, a number of practical issues were discussed with regard to testing children. Many of these issues apply to older persons as well. The test environment, for example, needs to have adequate lighting. Many elderly individuals have hearing impairments, so directions need to be clearly audible, and the testing room needs to be free of those acoustical problems that can affect the understanding of instructions. The test format must be suitable for the physical limitations the clients may have – printed items need to be in print large enough to be read comfortably, and oral administration must be clearly heard. The test must have face validity in that the client must feel that the test is appropriate and useful.

Good rapport is also quite important. Many elderly individuals may not be "test wise," and may find multiple-choice answer sheets and similar forms confusing; at the same time, they may not be willing to admit their quandary to a younger examiner. Often, older individuals are tested clinically because of the possible presence of some problem or condition – dementia, for example – and the individual needs to be reassured so that anxiety about the testing and the potential findings does not interfere with the performance, and so that self-esteem is not lowered by what may be perceived as failure or incompetence (Crook, 1979). Ideally, the testing situations should be nonthreatening and the client should leave feeling a sense of accomplishment and enhanced self-worth.

Although many people, particularly younger adults such as college students, are relatively comfortable taking tests, the elderly can be intimidated by them, and they may act in highly cautious ways that might negatively affect their performance.

Fatigue is also a problem. Often older persons are assessed with a multivariate test such as the WAIS, or an entire test battery composed of many such tests, and the examiner needs to be sensitive to this aspect. If fatigue takes place, the client may perceive the testing procedure as a failure on his or her part and may feel depressed and/or inadequate. Tests for the older person need to be brief, not only because of fatigue but also because of a briefer attention span (Wolk, 1972).

Aiken (1980) suggested eight procedures to be implemented when testing older persons: (1) Give ample time for the client to respond, (2) Give practice items, (3) Test in several short sessions rather than a few long ones, (4) Recognize and be sensitive to fatigue on the part of the client, (5) Be aware of and make appropriate accommodations for any sensory deficits (such as hearing) the client may have, (6) Make sure the testing environment is free of distractions, (7) Give lots of encouragement, and (8) do not pressure the client to continue if the client refuses.

Self-assessment vs. performance-assessment. Suppose that we wanted to assess someone's ability to swim. We could ask them a relevant set of questions, either in interview form, or as a rating scale, e.g., Can you swim? How good a swimmer are you? Are you certified by the Red Cross? and so on. This type of assessment is called self-assessment and recently, a number of writers have questioned the validity of such methods. We could also assess the person's ability to swim by having them swim. This is called performance assessment, also variously called "direct," "objective," "behavioral" assessment (E. L. Baker, O'Neill, & Linn, 1993).

At first glance, such performance assessment would seem to be superior to self-assessment. A. M. Myers, Holliday, Harvey, et al. (1993) compared the two methods in a sample of adults, aged 60 to 92. They asked these adults to complete a series of tasks that included measures of motor capacity (e.g., using a dynamometer, moving limbs, etc.); of manual ability (e.g., spooning beans into a can); self-care activities (e.g., using the telephone, writing a check), and other activities, such as opening a medication container, following a simple recipe, and picking up a penny from the floor. These tasks were all administered in a standardized form. They also asked the participants to complete a self-assessment questionnaire that addressed the same activities. They found that although 182 subjects were willing and able to complete the self-assessment questionnaire, only 99 attempted at least one of the performance tasks. These authors reported that the performance measures were not more acceptable to the participants than the self-report measure, that some participants found some of the tasks silly or demeaning, and that some found the procedure of being observed as they undertook a task rather disruptive. Based on this and a variety of other analyses, the authors concluded that functional performance measures do provide different information but should not be viewed as psychometrically superior.

Tests of personality. In Chapter 4, we discussed tests of personality, and much of what was discussed there is applicable to the testing of older persons. Most tests of personality such as the MMPI, the CPI, and the Edwards Personal Preference Schedule, are applicable to the elderly, although in some cases (such as the EPPS) there is the question of the appropriateness of the available norms. There are also changes that do occur as a function of aging and concomitant aspects.

For example, a number of studies have been done on the MMPI with older persons, with the general conclusion that the scales measuring somatic complaints (scale 1), depression (scale 2), denial (scale 3), and social introversion (scale 0) are generally higher in the aged, and scales measuring rebelliousness (scale 4) and energy level (scale 9) are generally lower (Gynther, 1979; Swenson, 1985).

Cognitive functioning. In Chapter 5, we discussed tests of cognition. Standard tests of adult intelligence, such as the WAIS, are certainly applicable to older adults. The challenge is not so much in the test itself but in the available norms. Most tests of cognitive functioning are normed on younger adults, and the norms may not be appropriate for older adults. Secondly, comparisons of adult groups of various ages to assess, for example, intellectual decline with advancing age, often compare groups that are different in more ways than just age. In the United States, for example, older groups tend to be less educated and more likely to be of immigrant background than younger groups. It is also important to remember that for many categories of tests, such as tests of cognitive functioning and rating scales, their reliability and validity is closely dependent on the skills of the examiner who uses the scale (Overall & Magee, 1992).

Values and attitudes. In Chapter 6, we discussed the measurement of values and attitudes, and much of our discussion is applicable to older persons. A typical example of the type of study that has been done with elders is that by Kogan and Wallach (1961) who used the semantic differential to assess age changes in attitudes and values. They compared the responses of 137 college students vs. those of 131 older men and women, members of a gerontological research association, with a mean age of about 70 to 71. The two samples were similar in education and verbal-intelligence level. The semantic differential used in this study consisted of 25 bipolar pairs of adjectives; the participants rated 28 different concepts representing work and leisure, majority and minority groups, family and interpersonal relations, self-concept, and other areas. A factor analysis yielded a strong evaluative factor (as one would expect). Approximately one third of the concepts yielded significant age differences, with older subjects rating concepts like "retirement" and "old age" more favorably and concepts such "future" and "life" less favorably.

Another concept that we discussed in Chapter 6 was that of Guttman scales. This type of scaling has been used with the elderly, particularly in the context of assessing "activities of daily living" or degree of disability present. For example, Katz, Ford, Moskowitz, et al. (1963) developed a hierarchy of activities of daily living with seven levels:

1. those without any disability;

2. those with one disability;

3. those with two disabilities who have difficulty bathing;

4. those with three disabilities, including difficulty in bathing and dressing themselves;

5. those with four disabilities including difficulty in bathing, dressing, and toileting;

6. those with five disabilities, including difficulty in bathing, dressing, toileting, and transferring from bed;

7. those who have difficulty performing all activities of daily living.

This scale has been useful in studies of older persons (e.g., Siu, Reuben, & Hayes, 1990), although some authors question the invariance of such a progression (e.g., Lazaridis, Rudberg, Furner, et al., 1994). Another area of the elderly where Guttman scales have been useful is in the study of morale (see Kutner's seven-item morale scale in Kutner, Fanshel, Togo, et al., 1956).

ATTITUDES TOWARD THE ELDERLY

One area of research that has generated a number of instruments focuses on attitudes toward older persons, on the part of younger people as well as older individuals themselves. One technique that has been used quite frequently is the semantic differential, as illustrated in the Kogan and Wallach study (see also Eisdorfer & Altrocchi, 1961; Rosecranz & McNevin, 1969). Even more popular is the use of Likert-type scales, using the standard Likert responses (strongly agree to strongly disagree) or some other format.

One of the earliest scales using a yes-no format was by Tuckman and Lorge (1952). Originally, their scale was developed to investigate attitudes of college students toward old age. This scale consisted of 137 statements that covered 13 different categories such as "conservatism" (e.g., they are set in their ways), "mental deterioration" (e.g., they are absent-minded), and personality traits (e.g., they are kind). The items were developed through a series of unstructured interviews with a small sample of adults, as well as discussions with social workers, study of case records of elderly clients, and a review of the literature. However, no item statistics are given as to how the final items were selected.

The scale can be administered in a group setting. There is no time limit and completion typically takes 15 to 30 minutes. The authors experimented with a response scale of 0 to 100, where the respondent was instructed to use these numbers as percentages, i.e., "If you think that 90% of older people are characterized by this statement, give that statement a response value of 90." The authors concluded that a yes no response format was preferable, as it took less time and simplified the instructions.

Although the scale and various subsets of items were used in a variety of studies with samples ranging from college undergraduates to older persons, the authors did not seem particularly concerned about reliability, and so little reliability evidence is available (Axelrod & Eisdorfer, 1961; Bekker & Taylor, 1966; Kilty & Feld, 1976; Lane, 1964; Tuckman & Lorge, 1953; 1958). In one study, the scale was administered at the beginning of a course on the psychology of the adult and a subset of 30 items readministered with the final examination; the obtained r was .96. Spearman-Brown reliability coefficients from .73 to .88 are also reported.

Although this scale has been used in one form or another in a variety of studies, the studies were typically "isolated" and do not present the cohesive portrait required by construct validity. In part, the difficulty may lie in the lack of a well-articulated theory about attitudes toward older persons. Axelrod and Eisdorfer (1961) administered the scale to a class of college students, with random fifths of the class asked to respond to different age groups (35, 45, 55, 65, and 75). If we assume that the negative stereotype of aging increases with the age of the stimulus target, then the sensitivity of the scale to such increases could be seen as evidence of the construct validity of

Table 10–1. Multidimensional Model of Anxiety About Aging (Lashen & Faulkender, 1993)			
	Fears		
Dimensions of anxiety	**of aging (process of aging)**	**of being old (state of being old)**	**of old people (perception of others)**
1. Physical – e.g., perceived changes in physical appearance as one gets older; worries about health			
2. Psychological – e.g., self-esteem and life satisfaction; degree of personal control; fear of memory loss			
3. Social – e.g., economic and social losses; worries about retirement			
4. Transpersonal – e.g., search for meaning of life; religious issues			

the scale. In fact, 96 of the 137 items showed such monotonic increases in percentage endorsement.

ANXIETY ABOUT AGING

Lasher and Faulkender (1993) proposed that anxiety about aging is a separate dimension from other forms of anxiety such as death anxiety or state-trait anxiety. They felt that this concept of "aging anxiety" has importance both because it helps to understand how we react to the elderly, and it has not been adequately researched.

These authors began the development of their scale with a theoretical model composed of two major dimensions, as illustrated in Table 10.1 The intersection of the two dimensions yields 12 cells, and the authors used this theoretical blueprint to generate 7 items per cell, for a total of 84 items. These items used a Likert 5-point response scale, with half of the items phrased positively and half of the items phrased negatively. The authors then asked three psychology graduate students to sort the items in terms of the two dimensions. This was done twice and the authors concluded that no new items were needed, although no statistical data is offered in support of this conclusion. Note that this represents a variation from the usual procedure where a pool of items is first developed and then a subset of the "best" items is chosen, on the basis of some preliminary decision rules.

The 84-item Aging Anxiety Scale (AAS) was then administered to 312 volunteers, ranging in age from below 25 to over 74. A series of factor analyses were performed, and finally 20 items were retained, reflecting 4 factors, each composed of 5 items: fear of old people; psychological concerns; physical appearance; and fear of losses (it is interesting to note that only 6 of the 20 items are worded negatively and that 5 of these 6 occur on the fear-of-losses factor).

Although these results do not support the initial theoretical framework, the authors felt that the obtained 20-item AAS is a potentially useful scale. Total scores on the scale show higher mean scores on the part of males than females, and the four factors intercorrelate with each other, but not substantially, with coefficients ranging from .20 to .39. Scores on the AAS correlate significantly with two other measures of aging, and the overall pattern does suggest some construct validity.

LIFE SATISFACTION

One of the active areas of research with older persons has to do with their perceived life satisfaction (subjective well-being, happiness, etc.). There are a number of interesting issues in this area, such as how happy are older Americans relative to some comparison group, what are the sources of satisfaction and dissatisfaction, and what are the dimensions and relative importance of such life satisfaction (Doyle & Forehand, 1984).

A number of studies have found a negative relationship between age and self-reported happiness, that is, life satisfaction decreases with age (e.g., Bradburn & Caplovitz, 1965; Robinson & Shaver, 1973). However, other researchers (Herzog & Rodgers, 1981) have reported that such relationship can be positive, that obtained correlation coefficients tend to be small, and that whether the results are positive or negative tends to be a function of how the variables are defined. For example, A. Campbell, Converse, and Rodgers (1976) found that younger people reported feeling happier than older persons, but reported lower life satisfaction.

A number of investigators have attempted to define and measure the psychological well-being of older people, quite often with the intent of using such a measure as an operational definition of successful aging. Two basic approaches seem to have been used. In one, the focus has been the overt behavior of the individual, and the criterion has been one of success or competency, usually in a social context. A second approach focuses on the person's internal frame of reference, i.e., the person's own evaluation of satisfaction, happiness, accomplishments, and so on. Many studies, of course, combine the two approaches.

Neugarten, Havighurst, and Tobin (1961) developed a set of scales for rating "life satisfaction," using a sample of 177 adults aged 50 to 90 that were participating in a longitudinal study. These individuals were interviewed regarding their life activities – such things as what they did every day and on the weekend, questions about work, religion, attitudes toward illness, etc. A rational analysis of the available literature led the investigators to postulate that psychological well-being was composed of: zest vs. apathy, resolution and fortitude, congruence between desired and achieved goals, positive self-concept, and mood tone. An individual was seen as having psychological well-being to the extent that he or she took pleasure from everyday activities, regarded life as meaningful, felt success in achieving major goals, held a positive self-image, and maintained happy and optimistic attitudes and mood.

The interview data was then used as the basis for rating each of the five components on a 5-point scale; total scores could then range from 5 to 25, with higher scores indicating greater life satisfaction. For the sample of 177 interviews, the interrater reliability for the total score was .78, with 94% of the judgments showing either exact agreement or agreement within one step of the 5-step response scale. The five components do intercorrelate with each other, from a low of .48 (for resolution vs. mood tone) to a high of .84 (for zest vs. mood tone), with a median r of about .71. In this sample, there was no relationship between total life satisfaction and either age or gender, but there was a relationship (.39) with socioeconomic status, and with marital status (married persons having higher scores). The interview ratings were correlated with ratings made by a clinician who actually interviewed the participants, with a resulting correlation of .64.

Because the above scale is based on interview material, its use would be time consuming and limited to those occasions where a participant is,

in fact, interviewed. Interviews can of course vary in length, topics covered, and so on, so that the reliability and validity of the scale is intimately bound with the interview procedure. The authors therefore developed two self-report instruments by selecting 60 cases and analyzing the interview materials of those who were high scorers and those who were low scorers on the initial life satisfaction measure. They also added items as needed, and the results were two scales: (1) the Life Satisfaction Index A consisting of 25 attitude items for which an agree or disagree response is required (e.g., These are the best years of my life); and (2) the Life Satisfaction Index B consisting of 17 open-ended questions and checklist items to be scored on a 3-point scale [e.g., As you get older, would you say things seem to be better or worse than you thought they would be? – better (2 points); about as expected (1 point); worse (0 points)]. These scales were administered to 92 respondents along with an interview. The scales were then revised with the result that scores on scale A correlated .55 with the life satisfaction ratings, while scores on scale B correlated .58 with the life satisfaction ratings. Correlations of the scale scores with a clinician's ratings based on interview were .39 and .47, respectively. (For a critique of the Life Satisfaction Index, see Hoyt & Creech, 1983).

Lohmann (1977) administered seven of the most frequently used measures of life satisfaction, adjustment, and morale, including the two scales discussed above, and the Lawton scale to be discussed below, to a sample of 259 adults over the age of 60. All scales correlated significantly with each other, with coefficients ranging from a low of .24 to a high of .99 and a median correlation of .64. The two Neugarten scales correlated .63 with each other and .76 and .74 with the Lawton scale.

Doyle and Forehand (1984) studied survey data that had been collected in 1974 with a nationally representative sample of noninstitutionalized Americans aged 18 and older. The survey was designed specifically to facilitate comparisons between three age groups: those aged 18 to 54, 55 to 64, and 65 and older. As part of the survey, respondents were administered a version of the Neugarten Life Satisfaction Index discussed above. They found that life satisfaction decreased with advanced age, although the decline was very apparent only in those who were in their 70s and

80s. Lowered life satisfaction was a function of poor health, loneliness, and money problems. Thus age correlates with life satisfaction, but it is not age per se, but rather some of the concomitants, such as lesser income and greater health problems, that create such a relationship.

There is quite a lot of research on the concept of self-perceived quality of life among older persons but the psychometric adequacy of the measures themselves has not been studied extensively. Illustrative concerns can be found in Carstensen and Cone (1983) who administered the Neugarten Life Satisfaction Index and the Philadelphia Geriatric Center Morale Scale (see below) to a sample of 60 persons, aged 66 to 86. The two scales correlated .64 with each other. Both scales also correlated significantly with a measure of the tendency to represent oneself in a socially favorable light (discussed in Chapter 16). The authors wondered if life satisfaction really decreases with age, or if people are merely willing to endorse less desirable item content as they get older.

MARITAL SATISFACTION

The life satisfaction of older people is substantially related to their marital relationships (e.g., Dorfman & Mofett, 1987; Medley, 1980). S. N. Hayes and his colleagues (1992) felt that the marital satisfaction inventories available were not fully appropriate for older individuals, and therefore carried out a series of five studies to develop such a questionnaire, which they called the MSQFOP (Marital Satisfaction Questionnaire for Older Persons).

Study 1. The first step was to generate a pool of items based on the available literature, on other available questionnaires, and structured interviews with a small sample of older individuals and professional workers. This procedure yielded an initial pool of 120 items that were then reviewed to remove redundancies, etc., and resulted in a preliminary version of 52 items answered on a 6-point response scale from very dissatisfied to very satisfied. Note that the even number of responses was chosen purposely to minimize a "central response" tendency. The 52-item version was then administered to 110 older married persons, whose mean age was 69.9 years. An item analysis was then undertaken and items were eliminated if less than 5% of the sample

indicated dissatisfaction (a rating of 3 or less) on that item, or if the correlation between the item and the total (i.e., internal consistency) was less than .65. These procedures resulted in a 24-item scale, that can be completed in 6 to 8 minutes, with 20 items that address specific areas of marital distress (e.g., the day-to-day support my spouse provides: very dissatisfied to very satisfied). These 20 items when summed generate a marital-satisfaction scale score.

Study 2. Here the MSQFOP was administered to 40 married persons (mean age of 63 years), who were then retested some 12 to 16 days later. Test-retest correlations for the individual items ranged from .70 to .93 and was .84 for the total score.

Study 3. The MSQFOP was administered to a sample of 56 persons (mean age of 63.5 years) along with the Locke-Wallace Marital Adjustment Test (Locke & Wallace, 1959), which is a frequently used marital satisfaction inventory. The total scores on the two inventories correlated .82.

Study 4. The aim of this study was to develop norms for the MSQFOP and to examine its factor structure, homogeneity, and construct validity. The MSQFOP and several other measures were administered to a sample of 313 married persons, with a mean age of 66 years. A factor analysis suggested one major factor, composed of 16 of the 20 items, that accounted for 58% of the variance, and two smaller factors accounting for 6% and 5% of the variance; these factors were labeled as communication/companionship, sex/affection, and health. As the authors point out, given that the items were initially retained based on their item-total correlation, it is not surprising that there is one major factor.

Homogeneity was assessed by computing the Cronbach coefficient alpha – the obtained value was .96 for men separately, and also for women. Thus the 20-item scale seems to be quite homogeneous for both genders, in line with the results of the factor analysis. A number of gender differences were however obtained, with men scoring higher than women on the total score, and on the communication/companionship factor. Finally, correlations between the MSQFOP and other related measures were almost all statistically significant, and in many cases they were substantial and supportive of the construct validity of this measure.

Study 5. In this study, 26 couples with mean age of 65, were videotaped as they discussed an important marital problem. These tapes were then rated as to overall positiveness vs. negativity of the spouses' actions toward the partner. Scores on the MSQFOP correlated significantly with such ratings, somewhat higher for men than for women. Although the authors presented this as evidence for predictive validity, the results are probably best understood in the context of construct validity.

MORALE

Sauer and Warland (1982) criticized instruments in the area of morale as lacking conceptual clarity, i.e., the measured concept is not well defined and the items generated are therefore not tied to a specific definition. Because of this, instruments in this area have little in common with each other. They also often lack adequate reliability, both at the initial steps when the author should produce such evidence and at subsequent stages when users should also generate such information. Validity information is also often lacking. We briefly look at two scales in this area that are somewhat better than most others and have found widespread use in a variety of studies.

The Philadelphia Geriatric Center Morale Scale (PGC Morale Scale; Lawton, 1972). Lawton believes that morale is a multidimensional concept composed of a basic sense of satisfaction with oneself, a feeling that there is a place in the environment for oneself, and an acceptance of what cannot be changed. Originally, 50 items were written or taken from existing scales to represent the content areas thought to be related to morale. Several revisions of the content of the items resulted in a 41-item scale. These items were administered in small group sessions to 208 tenants of an apartment dwelling for the independently aged, whose average age was 77.9, and to 92 residents of a home for the aged, whose mean age was 78.8. As a criterion for morale, a psychologist and a nurse familiar with the patients in the first sample were provided with a detailed definition of morale; they were asked to rank order the 107 subjects they were familiar with into 8 groupings, according to the degree of judged morale. The two observers agreed .45 in their rankings (after

"consultation" this was raised to .68). A similar procedure was used with the second sample.

The 41 items of the scale were then correlated with these rankings and, on the basis of various statistical analyses, 22 items with a yes no response format were retained. Morris and Sherwood (1975) revised the scale to 15 items, while Lawton (1975) revised the scale to 17 items.

The scale is purposely short so as not to fatigue the respondent. It can be administered in written or oral form, individually or in groups. Examples of items are: "I have as much pep as I did last year," and "Life is hard for me most of the time." The original sample consisted of some 300 residential clients, mostly female, with an average age of 78.2 years. Lawton's (1975) revision involved a sample of more than 1,000 residents, while Morris and Sherwood (1975) assessed almost 700 elderly persons.

Lawton (1972) factor analyzed the 22 items and came up with 6 factors: (1) surgency (i.e., activity and freedom from anxiety and depression); (2) attitude toward own aging; (3) acceptance of status quo; (4) agitation; (5) easygoing optimism; and (6) lonely dissatisfaction. These six factors intercorrelate moderately with each other, with most coefficients in the .30s, and ranging from .16 to .52. Morris and Sherwood (1975) were only able to replicate factors 1, 2, and 6 and thus suggested dropping five of the items. The revised 17 items were then factor analyzed and two factors obtained: (1) tranquillity, and (2) satisfaction with life progression. Lawton (1975) carried out several factor analyses and felt that a three-factor solution was the best: (1) agitation, (2) attitude toward own aging, and (3) lonely dissatisfaction.

The reliability of the scale is somewhat marginal. For the 22-item scale, split-half reliability is reported to be .79, and K-R reliability .81. Incidentally, the split-half reliability was not computed by the usual method of odd-vs.-even items, but by dividing the scale into two subsets of items matched in content. Test-retest coefficients with intervals ranging from 1 week to 3 months, varied from a low of .22 for the surgency factor to a high of .89 for the attitude-toward-own-aging factor, with only one of six coefficients above .70 in one sample, and four of the six above .70 in a second sample. For the 17-item revision, all three factors show Cronbach's alphas of .81 to .85. For the 15-item revision, the tranquillity factor shows K-R 20 coefficients of .73 and .78, and .58 and .65 for the satisfaction-with-life progression factor. Part of the problem, as you might guess, is that the scale is brief, and the factors are even briefer, ranging from two to five items each.

Validity is also problematic, and some critics (e.g., Sauer & Warland, 1982) question whether the scale adequately measures the domain of morale and feel that additional work, both theoretical and empirical, is needed. Among the validity data available, we might mention correlations of .43 and .53 of total scores with Q-sort evaluations of morale, by judges familiar with the subjects, and a correlation of .57 with another measure of morale (Lawton, 1972). Lohmann (1977) correlated the PGC Morale Scale with nine other measures of psychological well-being and obtained correlations ranging from .47 to .79. Clearly, morale and psychological well-being are related concepts, but are they identical?

COPING OR ADAPTATION

Coping or adaptation basically involves the efforts of an individual in solving real-life problems (E. Kahana, Fairchild, & B. Kahana, 1982). Often the focus is on problems that represent everyday life stresses or major life crises. A good example of an instrument in this area is the Geriatric Scale of Recent Life Events (E. Kahana, Fairchild, & B. Kahana, 1982). Of the 55 items on this scale, 23 were taken directly from the Holmes and Rahe (1967) Social Readjustment Rating Scale (see Chapter 15), and 8 more items were altered in various ways. Additional items particularly relevant to older persons were then added. The scale is thus composed of items such as "minor illness," "death of a close friend," "change in residence," "retirement," and "marriage of a grandchild." Respondents are asked to indicate whether the event has occurred in their lives, and the degree of readjustment or change required by a given event, on a 0 to 100 scale. The scale can be administered as a questionnaire or as an interview. The authors suggest that with older subjects the interview format is preferable.

The initial normative sample consisted of 248 individuals aged 60 years or older, with a mean age of 70.8 years. To score the questionnaire and obtain a total "stress" score, the "stress weights"

for items (events) that are checked are simply summed. For example, a "minor illness" has a weight of 27 (one of the lowest weights), a "financial difficulty" has a weight of 59, and "death of a spouse" has a weight of 79 (one of the highest weights). E. Kahana, Fairchild, and B. Kahana, (1982) report correlations of .51 to .84 between the stress weights obtained in their study and those originally reported by Holmes and Rahe (1967). They label this "reliability," but it can be argued whether this is in fact evidence for the reliability of this scale.

The use of such life events is a popular one, with specific scales developed for various target groups such as college students and the elderly. Higher total scores are reflective of greater stress and may be predictive of subsequent events, such as becoming physically ill. We discuss some of the relevant issues when we discuss the Holmes and Rahe (1967) scale which began this whole field (see Chapter 15).

DEATH AND DYING

Death and dying is a central concern for all of us, but is particularly salient for older persons, if for no other reason than the increase in ill health and the more frequent death of others in the lives of older persons. Much of the focus has been on scales that measure the fear of death (see Chapter 8), Marshall (1982) reviewed 32 instruments having to do with death and dying and divided them into 5 topical categories: measures of the experience of death; measures of awareness of impending death; measures of death anxiety (the largest category); measures of other attitudes toward death; and measures of behavior and planning in response to death. As an example, although not necessarily a typical one, let us look at the death-images scale developed by Back (1971). This author selected 25 metaphors or phrases to describe death, such as "an infinite ocean," "a falling curtain," and "a bursting rocket." Each of these items is printed on a separate card and the respondent is asked to sort the 25 cards into 5 piles, ranging from most appropriate to least appropriate as images for death. This is done in a two-step procedure, where the respondent first selects the best five images, then the worst five images, and then five "fairly bad" images. The instructions are incomplete, but presumably the respondent goes on to select five images that are "fairly good" and the five that remain are "neutral." Placement of each item in a pile is then numerically translated so that 1 = best, 2 = fairly good, 3 = neutral, 4 = fairly bad, and 5 = worst.

This instrument was used in a larger study of some 502 adults aged 45 to 70. Seven of the items showed a gender difference, with three items liked more by males and four items liked more by females. Five of the items showed a relationship with age, but Marshall (1982) indicates that none of the death factors had a relationship to age, and no reliability or validity data is presented. In a subsequent study, Ross and Pollio (1991) used this set of metaphors as an interview procedure to study the personal meaning of death. Although most of their data is impressionistic and does not directly address the reliability and/or validity of this instrument, the results nevertheless can be seen as supportive in the context of construct validity. The use of metaphors as test items is intriguing and potentially useful, but very few investigators have used this method. Knapp and Garbutt (1958) used it with time imagery, and more recently Domino used it with cancer imagery (G. Domino, Affonso, & Hannah, 1991; G. Domino & Lin, 1991; G. Domino, Fragoso, & Moreno, 1991; G. Domino & Lin, 1993; G. Domino & Pathanapong, 1993; G. Domino & Regmi, 1993).

NEUROPSYCHOLOGICAL ASSESSMENT

Neuropsychological assessment basically involves the assessment of cognitive and behavioral factors that reflect neurological disease. As Kaszniak (1989) states, neuropsychological evaluation is playing an increasingly important role in the assessment of older adults. A wide variety of measures and approaches are used in neuropsychological testing, but at the risk of oversimplification, we can identify the following major categories of tests (as listed in Schmitt & Ranseen, 1989):

1. Brief screening procedures. A number of procedures have been developed that are brief and are used primarily as screening procedures to be followed by more extensive testing where appropriate. At the same time, these procedures are often used for other purposes, ranging from the assessment of changes over time to

differential diagnosis. Many of these procedures are actually brief mental-status exams. Examples of such procedures are the Mini-Mental State Examination (M. D. Folstein, S. E. Folstein, & McHugh, 1975), the Short Portable Mental Status Questionnaire (Pfeiffer, 1975), and the Cognitive Capacity Screening Examination (Jacobs, Bernhard, Delgado, et al., 1977).

2. Mental status exams. These exams are longer than the screening tests mentioned above and typically take closer to 1 hour to administer. Typical of these exams is the Mattis Dementia Rating Scale (Mattis, 1976), which consists of five subtests that evaluate attention, initiation and perseveration, constructional ability, conceptualization, and memory. Other scales representative of instruments in this category are the Alzheimer's Disease Assessment Scale (Rosen, Motts, & Davis, 1984) and the Neurobehavioral Cognitive Status Examination (Kiernan, Mueller, Langston, et al., 1987).

3. Neuropsychological screening batteries. Schmitt and Ranseen (1989) cite three approaches under this heading. The first consists of standard tests or subtests from different batteries. For example, Filskov (1983) used various subtests from the WAIS and the Halstead-Reitan Neuropsychological Test Battery. A second approach is illustrated by the work of Benton and his colleagues (Benton, Hamsher, Varney, et al., 1983; Eslinger, Damasio, Benton, et al., 1985), who developed a battery of tests for the assessment of dementia. A third approach is illustrated by the work of Barrett (Barrett & Gleser, 1987; Barrett, Wheatley, & La Plant, 1983), who developed a "brief" (2 hour) neuropsychological battery modeled on the Halstead-Reitan Neuropsychological Test Battery.

4. Neuropsychological batteries. There are basically two major neuropsychological batteries available: the Halstead-Reitan Neuropsychological Test Battery and the Luria-Nebraska Neuropsychological Battery. Both of these are rather extensive to administer and require a welltrained clinician to interpret the results. Both instruments have been widely used, and there is a substantial body of literature that generally supports their reliability and validity (see Chapter 15).

5. Tests of memory functioning. As Schmitt and Ranseen (1989) state, an adequate memory test should assess both input and output

functions that are involved in the registration, storage, and retrieval of information that is to be remembered. Such assessment should cover various spheres, such as visual memory, auditory memory, and spatial memory. Both recall and recognition need to be assessed. The most commonly used measure, despite a number of limitations, is the Wechsler Memory Scale. Other measures in this category are the Benton Visual Retention Test (Benton, 1974), the Randt Memory Test (Randt, Brown, & Osborne, 1980), and the Denman Neuropsychology Memory Scale (Denman, 1984).

6. Measures of functional abilities. These measures cover a wide variety of activities of daily living, such as the ability to use the telephone, personal grooming, dressing, and managing one's financial affairs.

Basically all of the tests listed above rest on the reasonable assumption that organic brain damage results in the deterioration of psychological functioning, and that the measurement of such functioning will reflect the nature and degree of brain impairment. The tasks that are used to assess such deterioration require a skilled examiner and are usually multivariate, i.e., they contain many subtests and thus require extensive time to administer. Two important questions relevant to the validity of these tests are: (1) Do the test scores differentiate brain-damaged older persons from non-brain-damaged older persons? (2) Do the test scores differentiate brain-damaged older persons from those who are functionally disordered, i.e., those who have a disorder such as depression, which presumably serves a function.

Alzheimer's. Dementia is a disorder of cognition. That is, it involves grossly impaired thinking, memory lapses, and faulty reasoning. Thus the term dementia does not refer to a single illness, but to a group of conditions all of which involve the same basic symptoms, namely a progressive decline in intellectual functions. Two of these conditions account for most of the patients: one is Alzheimer's where the neurons of the brain cells deteriorate, and the other is multi-infarct dementia (an infarct is a small stroke, and this condition is due to the effects of many small strokes that damage brain tissues).

Many current efforts are aimed at the diagnosis of Alzheimer's. For example, Volicer, Hurley, Lathi, et al. (1994) presented a scale to measure the disease severity in patients with advanced dementia of the Alzheimer type. They argued that currently there are no such instruments and one is needed to make decisions related to health-care policies as well as planning. They also point out that the first symptoms of Alzheimer's are often cognitive deficits, which if serious enough severely limit the usefulness of cognitive tests. There are a number of measures of activities of daily living, but these authors felt that the measures are more suitable for patients in the early and middle stages of Alzheimer's, rather than the advanced patients they are interested in. Because of these concerns, Volicer, Seltzer, Rheaume, et al. (1987) developed the Bedford Alzheimer Nursing Scale; based on that scale they developed a seven-item scale to measure severity. The seven items cover dressing, sleeping, speech, eating, mobility, muscles, and eye contact, and each item presents four descriptors from which the rater checks the one that is most appropriate. For example, the eating item contains these four choices: (1) eats independently, (2) requires minimal assistance and/or coaxing, (3) requires moderate assistance and/or coaxing, and (4) completely dependent. Thus the scale is brief and easily completed by nursing personnel. The items are scored on a 1 to 4 basis, so that a total score of 7 indicates no impairment, and a score of 28 indicates complete impairment.

For 3 samples with a total of 77 patients, internal consistency alphas were reported to be between .64 and .80. Two raters were involved in this study, and the interrater reliability ranged from .82 to .87. The construct validity of the scale was assessed by comparing the scores to various indices of dependence-independence in activities of daily living, cognitive impairment, and language abilities. In general, the correlations ranged from the low .40s to the mid .60s. One could easily argue that these results represent criterion validity rather than construct validity, as no theoretical rationale is presented.

Memory assessment. Although concern about failures of memory in everyday life is a topic that intrigued the pioneers of psychology such as William James and Sigmund Freud, a concentrated effort to study everyday memory did not occur until the 1970s. One approach was the development of self-reported memory questionnaires. If responses to the questionnaires could be shown to correspond to observed behavior, then the questionnaires could provide a valuable tool. In addition, the questionnaires, whether or not they parallelled behavior, could provide valuable insights into a person's belief about their memory and memory loss (Herrmann, 1982). Older adults do complain of memory difficulty more than younger adults (Zelinski, Gilewski, & Thompson, 1980). Unfortunately, questionnaires that assess the subjective frequency of everyday memory failures in older adults have typically very poor test-retest reliability and low internal consistency (Gilewski & Zelinski, 1986). In addition, the relationship between subjective reports of memory difficulty and actual performance on verbal memory tests seems to be a function of other factors, such as diagnostic status. For example, depressed older adults tend to complain about memory difficulty, but may show no memory performance deficits, while somewhat of the opposite pattern may be true of patients with Alzheimer's disease (Kaszniak, 1989).

Herrmann (1982) reviewed 14 memory questionnaires. Although he concluded that as a group these questionnaires were reliable, a more careful analysis of the data presented might lead to a more pessimistic conclusion. Of the 15 instruments (one has a short version that is listed separately), 7 do not have reliability data reported. For the 8 that do, the reliability coefficients (mostly test-retest) range from .46 to .88, with 6 of the coefficients below .70.

Two major limitations of many memory tests is that, first, they do not reflect the current state of knowledge about memory because they were developed years ago, and, second, they bear little resemblance to the tasks of everyday life (Erickson & Scott, 1977). More relevant assessments are beginning to be available, at least on a research basis. For example, Crook and Larrabee (1988) developed a test battery that is fully computerized and uses laser-disk technology to simulate memory and learning tasks encountered everyday, such as dialing telephone numbers and the recall of a person's name.

The Wechsler Memory Scale (WMS) The WMS has been the most frequently used clinical instrument for the assessment of memory. The scale was developed in 1945 and revised in 1987

(Wechsler, 1987), when it was standardized on a nationally representative sample of adults from aged 16 through 74. The WMS was intended as a rapid, simple, and practical memory examination. It consists of seven subtests: personal and current information (How old are you? Who is the President of the United States?); orientation (What day of the month is this?); mental control (i.e., sustained attention, such as counting backwards from 20 to 1); logical memory (a brief passage is read and the subject is asked to recall the ideas in the passage); digit span (recall of digits forward and backward); visual reproduction (simple geometric figures are presented for 10 seconds each; the subject is asked to draw them from memory); and associate learning (word pairs are read, such as cat-window, and the subject is asked to recall the second word when the first is presented). However, scores on the seven subtests are combined into a single summary score called the Memory Quotient, so that it is difficult to compare the various aspects of memory performance. Norms were initially available for adults up to age 64, and subsequently extended to include those 80- to 92-years-old (Klonoff & Kennedy, 1965, 1966; Meer & Baker, 1965). The WMS was also intended to identify organic problems associated with memory disorders, but subsequent studies showed that the scale did not differentiate among psychotic, neurotic, and organic patients when age and IQ were controlled (J. Cohen, 1950). The WMS was criticized for a number of limitations, including the preponderance of verbal stimuli and inadequate interrater agreement on two of the subtests (Erickson & Scott, 1977; Prigatano, 1978). In 1987, the WMS was revised (Wechsler, 1987) and now consists of 13 subtests, including 3 new nonverbal subtests.

The WMS-R was standardized on a sample of approximately 300 individuals aged 16 to 74 designed to match the general population with respect to race, geographic region, and educational level. The sample was stratified as to age, with about 50 subjects in each of six age groups, and with approximately equal numbers of men and women within each age group. The scale and subtests are composed of a variety of items that include counting backwards, identifying previously shown abstract geometric designs, recalling two stories immediately after they are read by the examiner as well as at the end of the testing, a learning of word pairs for subsequent recall, and repeating the examiner's performance on a series of colored squares that are touched in sequence.

The WMS-R contains not only an expanded number of subtests, but also nonverbal subtests and delayed recall measures (e.g., remembering items from stories read earlier by the examiner). Two of the subtests are used for screening purposes and are kept separate from the rest of the scale. In addition, the revised scale allows the report of separate scores for various components of memory performance. The WMS-R yields two major scores, the General Memory Index, and the Attention/Concentration Index. In addition, the General Memory Index can be subdivided into a Verbal Memory Index and a Visual Memory Index. Finally, there is a Delayed Recall Index. Unlike many other test revisions where what is changed is typically minor and often cosmetic, the WMS became in its revision a vastly superior scale (Robertson-Tchabo & Arenberg, 1989; and for a review of the WMS-R compared with another memory scale, see Zielinski, 1993).

Self-rating scales. Self-rating scales also are used widely in the study and assessment of memory. Gilewski and Zelinski (1986) gave four important reasons for using self-rating scales to assess memory in older adults. They pointed out that there is a relationship between memory complaints and memory performance in healthy older individuals. Second, complaints of memory impairment may be early signs of a subsequent dementia, although in advanced stages of Alzheimer's, for example, there may be no relationship between complaint and actual performance, in that the patient may deny memory deficit. Third, complaints of memory deficit may be diagnostically related to depression, and may in fact serve as a useful differential diagnostic sign between depression and dementia. Finally, memory complaints may be good indicators of how a person perceives their general cognitive functioning as they become older.

As an example of the self-rating memory scales that are available, consider the Memory Assessment Clinics Self-Rating Scale (MAC-S; Winterling, Crook, Salama, et al., 1986). The MAC-S was developed because the authors felt that available scales had either inadequate normative data, used poor wording of items, or did not consider the multivariate nature of memory. The original MAC-S consisted of 102 items that described specific memory tasks or problems encountered in everyday life – for example, whether the person remembered turning off the lights and appliances before leaving home, or which door they came in when shopping in a large department store or mall. The items were divided into two subscales of equal length: (1) *ability*, with items indicative of the ability to remember specific types of information, for example, the name of a person just introduced; and (2) *frequency of occurrence*, with items indicative of how often specific memory problems occurred, for example, going to a store and forgetting what to purchase. On the ability scale, the response format was a Likert-type scale from very poor to very good, while on the frequency of occurrence the response choices ranged from very often to very rarely.

On the basis of factor analysis the MAC-S was reduced to 49 items. Crook and Larrabee (1990) administered the scale to 1,106 healthy volunteers, with a mean age of 56 and a range from 18 to 92. The protocols were factor analyzed and the authors obtained five factors for the Ability scale and five factors for the Frequency of Occurrence scale. These are listed in Table 10.2.

The authors found essentially the same factor structure when the total group was analyzed according to various age subgroups. They also found a lack of association between MAC-S scores and both age and gender. (To see how another memory scale was developed see Gilewski, Zelinski, & Schaie, 1990.)

DEPRESSION

There seems to be agreement that depression represents a major public health problem and that depression can and does occur late in life, with high rates of depression in clients over the age of 65. Thus, depression seems to be the most common functional psychiatric disorder among older persons, although there is some question whether the prevalence of depression increases with age. A number of authors point out that what is called depression in older persons may in fact represent reactions to the economic and social difficulties they encounter, grief over the loss of friends and family, and reactions to physical illness and problems.

Table 10–2. Factors on the Memory Assessment Clinics Self-Rating Scale	
Ability Scale	**Example**
Factor	
1. Remote personal memory	Holiday or special-occasion memory
2. Numeric recall	Telephone numbers
3. Everyday task-oriented memory	Turn off lights
4. Word recall/semantic memory	Meaning of words
5. Spatial/topographic memory	How to reach a location
Frequency of Occurrence Scale	
1. Word and fact recall or Semantic Memory	Forgetting a word
2. Attention/concentration	Having trouble concentrating
3. Everyday task-oriented memory	Going into a room and forgetting why
4. General forgetfulness	Forgetting an appointment
5. Facial recognition	Failing to recognize others

The literature suggests that somatic complaints are more prominent in older depressed patients than in younger individuals. However, complaints of fatigue, pain, or lack of energy, which in a person may be reflections of depression, may in an older person be realistic evidence of being old, and not necessarily depressed. Part of the complexity of assessing depression in older persons is that many self-report scales of depression contain items that have to do with somatic symptoms, such as sleep disturbances and diminished energy levels. Because older persons do tend to have more physical illnesses, endorsement of these items may not necessarily be reflective of depression (Blazer, Hughes, & George, 1987; Himmelfarb, 1984; Newman, 1989).

A wide variety of procedures are used to assess depression in older persons. These include the depression scales discussed in Chapter 7 and others, particularly the three most common scales, the Beck Depression Inventory (A. T. Beck, Ward, Mendelson, et al., 1961), the Hamilton Rating Scale for Depression (Hamilton, 1960), and the Zung Self-Rating Depression Scale (Zung, 1965). Other approaches include multivariate instruments such as the MMPI, projective tests such as the Gerontological Apperception Test (R. L. Wolk & R. B. Wolk, 1971) and structured interviews, such as the Schedule for Affective Disorders and Schizophrenia (Spitzer & Endicott, 1977).

SUMMARY

Psychological testing of older persons presents a number of challenges from both a psychometric

and a clinical point of view. Although this area of testing is relatively young, a number of advances have taken place, but much more needs to be done. The areas that have been presented in this chapter are illustrative of the various issues and challenges faced by both practitioners and researchers alike.

SUGGESTED READINGS

Costa, P. T., & McCrae, R. R. (1984). Concurrent validation after 20 years: The implications of personality stability for its assessment. In N. W. Shock, R. G. Greulich, R. Andres, D. Arenberg, P. T. Costa, E. G. Lakatta, & J. D. Tobin (Eds.), *Normal human aging: The Baltimore longitudinal study of aging* (NIH Publication No. 84-2450). Washington, D.C.: U.S. Public Health Service.

What happens to personality as a person ages? One answer was given by what is called the Kansas City Studies (see Neugarten & Associates, 1964): As people aged they became more preoccupied with themselves, more emotionally withdrawn – what eventually became known as disengagement theory. This suggested reading, covering what is known as the Baltimore study, gives a different answer – there is personality stability as one ages.

Gallagher, D. (1986). The Beck Depression Inventory and older adults. *Clinical Gerontologist*, 5, 149–163.

This article reviews the development and utility of the BDI with particular emphasis on the use of the BDI with older persons. The author discusses the usage of the BDI, the reliability, validity, factor structure, and other aspects of one of the most popular measures of depression.

Herrmann, D. J. (1982). Know thy memory: The use of questionnaires to assess and study memory. *Psychological Bulletin*, 92, 434–452.

The author reviews 14 questionnaires designed to assess people's beliefs about their memory performance in natural circumstances. Research findings suggest that responses to these questionnaires are reliable but they correspond only moderately with a person's memory performance, suggesting that people's beliefs about their memory performance are stable but not very accurate.

Lewinsohn, P. M., Seeley, J. R., Roberts, R. E., & Allen, N. B. (1997). Center for Epidemiologic Studies Depression Scale (CES-D) as a screening instrument for depression among community-residing older adults. *Psychology and Aging*, 12, 277–287.

A study of more than 1,000 older adults designed to assess the CES-D scale (covered in Chapter 7), as a screening instrument. The article presents data and uses such concepts as sensitivity and specificity, which we discussed. A bit advanced in its use of statistical analyses, but worth reading.

Libman, E., Creti, L., Amsel, R., Brender, W., & Fichten, C. S. (1997). What do older good and poor sleepers do during periods of nocturnal wakefulness? The Sleep Behaviors Scale: 60 +. *Psychology and Aging*, 12, 170–182.

An instructive example of the development of a scale within a clinical context, for use with older persons.

DISCUSSION QUESTIONS

1. You have been assigned to test some elderly people living in a nursing home, while your classmate is testing individuals of the same age living in a retirement community. How might the two experiences differ in terms of testing?

2. Consider the concept of "psychological well-being". What might be the components of such a concept?

3. How might you validate the MSQFOP?

4. How would you develop a memory scale for use with the elderly?

5. What do you consider to be the three major points of this chapter?

11 Testing in a Cross-Cultural Context

AIM What are the problems associated with using psychological tests with minority individuals and those of another culture? If for example, we wish to administer the WISC-R to a black child, or we translate the test into French for use with French children, will the test still be valid? Basically, this is the issue we look at in this chapter.

INTRODUCTION

In this chapter, we look at cross-cultural testing, that is, at some of the ways in which culture and testing can interact. We use the term "culture" in two different ways: (1) to delineate people living in different countries, for example, the United States vs. the People's Republic of China; and (2) to refer to minority groups within a particular country, for example, blacks and Hispanics living in the United States. There are of course many ways of defining culture. For our purpose, we can define culture as a set of shared values and behaviors that include beliefs, customs, morals, laws, etc., that are acquired by a person, shared in common with other members who are typically in close proximity, but different from those held by others who often live in a different geographical setting (D. W. Sue & D. Sue, 1990).

MEASUREMENT BIAS

The issue of test or measurement bias is a central one for all who are concerned with developing and using tests. There is a substantial body of literature on the topic, with some rather complex statistical issues, and even entire books devoted to the topic (e.g., Berk, 1982; Osterlind, 1983). Most concerns about test bias are related to tests of intelligence and, to a lesser degree, to tests of aptitude, ability, and achievement; we can use the broader label of cognitive-ability tests to cover these various aspects.

During the 1960s, the use of standardized tests with ethnic minorities became a major issue. Critics claimed that standardized tests: (1) were loaded with items based on white middle-class values and experiences; (2) penalized children who had linguistic styles different from that of the majority culture; (3) assessed cognitive styles often substantially different from those found in low-income families; (4) fostered a dual educational system by excluding minority children from regular educational programs; (5) were of no use in formulating instructional programs; and (6) were culturally biased and discriminated unfairly against racial and ethnic minorities (P. Henry, Bryson, & C. A. Henry, 1990).

Blacks vs. whites. Much of the controversy on test bias revolves around the performance of blacks on cognitive-ability tests and, to a lesser extent, around the performance of Hispanics, primarily Mexican-Americans. As the Hispanic population in the United States continues to grow, the concern of possible test bias has become more salient with this population, particularly with the issue of bilingualism (Olmedo, 1981). Asian minority groups seem to do well on cognitive-abilities tests and on academic achievement, so the issue of test bias is not brought up. Indeed, differences in average cognitive performance between white and black students in the United States do exist, and often they approach a full standard deviation. This means that a level of performance that is achieved by about 84% of white students is achieved by only 50% of their black peers. Most psychologists would argue that such results do not reflect test bias, but rather the cumulative effects of societal bias.

We can talk about bias at three different stages: (1) before the test, referring to those societal and environmental aspects that result in discrimination, lower self-esteem, poorer nutrition, fewer opportunities, etc.; (2) in the test itself as a measuring instrument; and (3) in the decisions that are made on the basis of test scores. Most psychologists would argue that it is far more likely for bias to occur in the first and last stages than in the second stage.

Messick and Anderson (1970) indicate that there are three possible sources for the typical finding that minority children do less well than majority children on tests of cognitive abilities:

1. The test may measure different things for different groups. To assess this, the reliability and validity of the test needs to be studied separately for each group, and the results need to be comparable to conclude that the test is not biased. Construct validity needs to be assessed by looking at the pattern of correlations between the test and other measures; comparability of results across different groups would be evidence for lack of test bias.

2. The test may involve irrelevant difficulty – for example, an answer sheet that is confusing or difficult to use, testing conditions that may increase anxiety more for one group than for another, or items that differentially favor one group over the other. In fact, such issues are of concern to test constructors, and most well-standardized tests cannot be faulted on such aspects.

3. The test may accurately reflect ability or achievement levels. Lower scores on the part of a minority group do not necessarily reflect bias in measurement, but may reflect the effects of poverty, prejudice, and inequality of educational opportunities.

The cultural test-bias hypothesis. This hypothesis contends that group differences on mental tests are due to artifacts of the tests themselves and do not reflect real differences between groups that differ on such demographic variables as ethnicity, race, or socioeconomic status. There is, in fact, almost no evidence to support such a hypothesis with tests that have been carefully designed, such as the Stanford-Binet or the Wechsler tests (A. R. Jensen, 1980).

Eliminate tests. In the 1970s, black psychologists demanded an immediate moratorium on all testing of black persons (R. L. Williams, 1970), with the assumption that most, if not all tests, were intrinsically biased against minorities (Messick & Anderson, 1970). The typical response to this demand was to argue that tests per se were not biased, but that tests were misused. Some argued that both questions – whether a test is valid or not, and whether a test should be used in a specific context – needed to be addressed. The first question is a scientific one: the answer can be found in the psychometric properties of a test. The second question is an ethical one whose answer can be found in terms of human values. Messick and Anderson (1970) argued that not using tests would not eliminate the need to make decisions, and that alternate decision-making mechanisms such as interviews and/or observations would be more costly, more biased, and less valid. Others have argued rather convincingly that the social consequences of not using tests are far more harmful than the consequences of using tests to make educational decisions (e.g., Ebel, 1963). There are also some arguments for using tests. Cognitive tests are of value in documenting patterns of strengths and weaknesses in all children and are useful in documenting change and progress. Tests represent an objective standard free of examiner prejudice. Tests are equally good predictors of future performance for white and for minority children. Tests can be useful for securing and evaluating special services in the schools, such as Head Start programs. Without appropriate evaluations, children may not receive the services they are entitled to (Wodrich & Kush, 1990). Another general criticism that is made of intelligence tests is that they ignore the multicultural aspects of American society, that they treat individuals as if they were culturally homogeneous (Samuda, 1975).

Somewhat more specific arguments against the testing of minority children are also expressed, and most of these can be subsumed under four categories:

1. Cognitive tests are biased because they have been developed to mirror middle-class, white values and experiences. The counterargument is that in fact there is no evidence that cognitive tests are biased against minority members.

2. Minorities are not represented in the norms and therefore score interpretation is inappropriate. Although this argument may apply to some tests, it does not apply to the major cognitive measures such as the Stanford-Binet or the WISC, whose norms are representative of the general population according to census parameters.

3. Minority students do not have the appropriate test-taking skills, sophistication, or orientation (e.g., awareness of the need to answer rapidly on a timed test). Poor test-taking skills are of course not the sole province of minority children; non-minority children can be just as deficient. The issue here is of competence in administering tests. The examiner should be aware and recognize individual factors that may interfere with or limit the child's performance, regardless of the ethnicity of the child. Test results for a particular child may indeed be limited and even invalid, although the test itself may be valid from a psychometric point of view.

4. Most examiners are white and use standard English with detrimental effects on minority children's scores. The literature indicates that the effect of examiner race on cognitive test scores is negligible (Sattler & Gwynne, 1982). Fewer studies have been done on the effects of using standard English vs. Black dialect, but the results here also suggest negligible differences (L. C. Quay, 1974).

Extraneous variables. It is sometimes argued that certain types of test items are biased against particular groups. In particular, there is concern that what are nonessential characteristics of particular test items may result in poorer performance for minority children. For example, if we wish to measure arithmetic skills and the problems are presented as vignettes (e.g., John has six

oranges . . .), the use of words that are less familiar to one group than another may result in a biased item. If it were a matter of only vocabulary then possible solutions might be relatively easy. However, the matter becomes more complex because aspects such as test anxiety or differences in motivation may interact with aspects of the test items. Such interactions can in fact be studied experimentally, and recently approaches based on item response theory (see Chapter 2) have been used (e.g., Linn & Harnisch, 1981). Ultimately, one must ask why is a particular test item "biased"? If it is a matter of vocabulary, for example, might that not reflect an "instructional" or a learning bias rather than a test-item bias? In many ways, test bias is similar to the concept of test validity in that there is no one index or procedure that in and of itself allows us to say, "this test is biased." Rather bias, like validity, is arrived at through the gathering of substantial evidence, and an objective analysis of that evidence (Sandoval, 1979).

Limited English proficiency. English is not the first language for a substantial number of students in the United States, and they have limited English proficiency. Their number seems to be growing and, because of increased use of standardized tests in school systems, there is great concern that test results for these students may either be less valid or misused.

Lam (1993) indicates that test developers, particularly of standardized achievement tests, make five assumptions: (1) test takers have no linguistic barriers that might interfere with their performance on the test, i.e., they can follow instructions, understand the test items, and have adequate time to complete the test; (2) the test content is suitable and of appropriate difficulty level for the test taker; (3) test takers have the required test sophistication for taking standardized achievement tests; (4) test takers are properly motivated to do well on the test; and (5) test takers do not have strong negative psychological reactions (such as anxiety or feeling stressed) to testing.

Lam (1993) feels that these assumptions may at least be questionable with language minority students, and therefore their test results may not be as reliable and valid. This issue is a well-recognized one and in fact is incorporated in the *Standards for Educational and Psychological*

Testing discussed in Chapter 1. Part of the solution consists of strategies that reduce the probability that any of the five assumptions are violated. These include translating tests into the child's native language, developing ethnic specific norms, developing tests that accommodate the cultural differences of various people, extending time limits, using items that are relevant to the minority culture, and so on.

Matluck and Mace (1973) presented a number of suggestions regarding tests to be used with Mexican-American children. With regard to format, such tests should assess separately the child's receptive ability (e.g., listening comprehension) vs. productive ability. The test should use appropriate stimuli – for example, for younger children pictorial-visual stimuli are most likely appropriate, but verbal-auditory stimuli are not. Similarly, the number of items and the administration time should be appropriate – for example, for most children 15 to 25 minutes is considered appropriate. With regard to content, the items should be simple in language and not require linguistic skills that are beyond the child's age. Items should not have language or cultural bias. Concerning test materials, the authors point out that sometimes "impressionistic" or sketchy line drawings are used as stimuli, and a child may not have the appropriate experiential background to deal with such materials; actual objects or photographs might be better. Finally, with respect to the test examiner, the authors point to a need to be sensitive as to whether the examiner's gender, degree of experience, physical appearance as to ethnicity, and so on might influence the test performance of the child.

External vs. internal criteria. A number of authors define test bias in terms of validity and distinguish between validity that focuses on external criteria and validity that focuses on internal criteria. Thus A. R. Jensen (1974; 1976), for example, identified two general strategies for determining bias in tests, one based on external criteria and the other on internal criteria. External criteria involve predictive validity, and assessing the test's predictive validity in minority and majority samples. Internal criteria involve content and construct validity, an analysis of the test in terms of the item content and the overall theoretical rationale. An example of an external criterion study is that by Reschly and Sabers (1979), while an example of an internal criteria study is that of Sandoval (1979). Incidentally, both of these studies found the WISC-R not to be biased against minority children including blacks and Mexican-Americans.

A similar discussion is presented by Clarizio (1982) who also defined test bias in terms of external and internal criteria. From an external or predictive validity point of view, a test is unbiased if the prediction of criterion performance is of equal accuracy in the two samples, i.e., equivalent regression equations or standard errors of estimate. From an internal or construct validity point of view, a test is unbiased if it behaves the same way for different groups. Evidence of such "unbias" might focus on test homogeneity, rank ordering of item difficulty, loadings on "g," and the relative frequencies in choice of error distractors, for the two groups being compared.

In general, investigations of internal measures of validity have typically found no evidence for test bias, whether in terms of differential reliability, rank order of item difficulty, factor structure, or other psychometric concerns. Similarly, investigations of external measures of validity have typically found no evidence for such bias. Regression equations to predict a particular outcome show no differential validity, and appear to be relatively valid for different ethnic and/or socioeconomic groups. C. R. Reynolds (1982) concludes that psychological tests, especially aptitude tests, function in essentially the same manner across race and gender. Differential validity does not seem to exist.

Many "external" studies of test bias use achievement test scores as the criterion – thus for example, WISC-R IQs are correlated with scores on an achievement-test battery; the results of such test batteries are often routinely available in students' folders. Critics question the use of such achievement test scores as the criterion and argue instead that "actual behavior" should be the criterion. The problem seems to be that no one is willing to define concretely what such actual behavior might be, other than school grades.

Eliminating test bias in test development. A number of steps can be taken to attempt to eliminate bias as a test is being developed. First, a sensitive and knowledgeable test writer can eliminate obviously biased items. Item statistics can be easily collected, and those items that are related to race, gender, or other irrelevant variables can be eliminated. Sometimes, matched samples are used for this purpose – that is, the pool of items is administered to a black sample and a white sample that have been matched on ability. The difficulty level of each item is computed for the two samples separately, and items that show a difference in difficulty rates are eliminated. It should be obvious, however, that when we match the samples we no longer have representative samples; also an item that has different difficulty rates in different groups is not necessarily a biased item. We can compute the correlation of an item with the criterion and determine whether the item predicts the criterion equally well in the two samples (although item-criterion correlations are typically quite low).

Test bias. Specifically, what are the problems that are perceived to be present in using tests with minorities? C. R. Reynolds (1982) lists six:

1. Inappropriate test content; test items are used that reflect primarily white middle-class experiences to which minority children have had little or no exposure.

2. Inappropriate standardization samples; the samples are either all white or ethnic-minorities are underrepresented.

3. Examiner and language bias; lower test scores for minority children reflect their intimidation with a white examiner who speaks standard English.

4. Inequitable social consequences; because of bias in tests, minority group members who are already at a disadvantage in the marketplace, are subject to further discrimination.

5. Tests measure different constructs in minority children than they do in majority children.

6. Tests have differential predictive validity; they may be valid for white middle-class children, but they are not valid for minority children.

APA Committee study and report. In 1968, the American Psychological Association Board of Scientific Affairs appointed a committee to study the issue of test bias. The Committee prepared a report (Cleary, Humphreys, Kendrick, et al.,

1975) and offered a definition of test bias that focused on predictive validity, although both content and construct validity were also considered important. The Committee stated that "a test is considered fair for a particular use if the inference drawn from the test score is made with the smallest feasible random error and if there is no constant error in the inference as a function of membership in a particular group" (Cleary, Humphreys, Kendrick, et al., 1975, p. 25).

This definition is based on earlier work by Cleary (1968) whose definition of test bias in terms of errors of prediction has become almost universally accepted. Given a particular test and a particular criterion, we can compute the regression line by which we use test scores to predict that criterion. If the criterion score that is predicted from the common (i.e., for both blacks and whites) regression line is consistently too high or too low for members of a subgroup, then the test is said to be biased.

A broader view. Others have taken a broader view of test bias. One way to define test bias is to consider those aspects that prevent a test from being valid when used with a particular individual in a particular instance (Bradley & Caldwell, 1974). Three sources of potential bias can then be identified: (1) bias due to the test itself (e.g., the test is not valid, or the test is unduly influenced by social desirability); (2) bias due to the client (e.g., the client does not pay attention); and (3) bias due to the situation (e.g., interfering noise from an airplane while the test is administered). Note that in this approach bias becomes lack of validity; to the extent that such lack is related to a minority group, then we have test bias. In fact, most experts would include only the first bias under "test bias" and would place categories 2 and 3 under some other label such as error, lack of experimental control, individual differences, etc. To the extent that they affect testing, they need to be controlled, eliminated, or accounted for.

A narrower view. Are there differences in mean performance on a particular test among groups that differ in ethnicity? If there are, this is taken as evidence of test bias. This particular point of view is based on the implicit notion that all people are equal on the particular variable being measured.

But the reality is quite different. We may well accept the notion of "all people are created equal" in terms of human dignity and respect, but all of the scientific evidence points to the fact that people are quite different from each other in all sorts of ways.

Some believe that a test is culturally or racially biased when a child's performance on the test is compared against a culturally or racially different reference group that has a higher mean score. Thus, a test given to Mexican-American children is considered biased if the children's performance is compared to Anglo norms. This is the view that is promulgated by Mercer (1976), who argues for the use of "pluralistic" norms (see the discussion that follows on the SOMPA). Many have argued that such reasoning is fallacious (e.g., Clarizio, 1982).

Some critics assume that if a test is standardized on a particular ethnic group, such as whites, it therefore must be biased if used with another ethnic group. The answer is obvious: the reliability and validity of a test that is used with different groups needs to be investigated empirically.

The psychometric perspective. Psychometrically, if a test is biased that test results in systematic error related to one group but not to another. Specifically, there are two situations that can occur. The first is differential validity or *slope bias*. Here we have a situation where the relationship between test scores and criterion scores (for example, SAT scores and predicted GPA) is substantially greater in one ethnic group than in another. Because the correlation, or regression line, is represented statistically by the slope of graphed data, this is called slope bias. In fact, the literature suggests that slope bias is the result of poor experimental procedure, differences in sizes of samples from majority and minority populations, or chance findings (e.g., J. E. Hunter, Schmidt, & R. F. Hunter, 1979).

To examine slope bias we look at group differences by using a regression equation to predict from test scores (e.g., IQ) to criterion scores (e.g., GPA). Two questions are typically asked here: (1) Can the same regression equation be used for the two different groups? and (2) Does the regression equation overpredict or underpredict for either group?

Underprediction means that the estimated criterion value is lower than the actual value, while overprediction means that the estimated criterion value is higher than the actual value. If under- or overprediction occurs in a systematic way, there is bias present.

In the second situation, the majority group obtains a higher mean score on the test than the minority group; the bias comes in that both groups do equally well on the criterion. Thus for example, if we could show that on a college entrance exam whites obtained a mean score of 600 and blacks obtained a mean score of 400, and both groups did equally well on academic achievement as measured by grades, for example, then we would have what is called *intercept bias* (the term again referring to the regression line in a bivariate graph). In this case, the predictive validity coefficients for each sample would be approximately equal, so that test scores would be equally predictive of criterion performance. However, if a college admissions committee were to use a particular cutoff score to admit or reject applicants, a greater proportion of minority applicants would be rejected. In fact, there is no evidence that supports intercept bias, and some studies have shown that there is a slight to moderate bias in *favor* of the minority group (e.g. Duran, 1983; J. E. Hunter, Schmidt, & Rauschenberger, 1977).

Intercept bias is often assessed through the analysis of item difficulty. Obviously, if there are mean differences between samples, there will be differences in item difficulty; in fact, we can think of the mean as reflecting average difficulty. To determine item bias we look for items that do not follow the expected pattern. Thus, for a minority sample, one item may be substantially more difficult than similar items; such an item needs to be inspected to determine what is causing these results, and it should possibly be eliminated from the test.

In fact, when these procedures are used in an objective, scientific manner, the finding is that cognitive tests are generally not biased against minorities.

Bias and decision theory. Tests are used by educational institutions and by some businesses to screen applicants for admission or hiring. Not entirely for unselfish reasons, most of these institutions would like to make decisions that are culturally and/or ethnically fair. Petersen and Novick (1976) discuss this process and the various models for culture-fair selection. They point out that the selection situation is basically the same; we have a group of applicants about whom decisions are to be made on the basis of some information. The information is processed by some strategy, some set of rules, leading to a decision to either admit or not admit, hire or not hire. There are consequences that result from that decision, not only in terms of the individual who may find himself with or without a job, but also in terms of the outcome – the individual's performance after the assignment. Several different models assess whether the selection strategy is indeed culture fair. The four main models are:

1. *The regression model.* This is probably the most popular and usually associated with Cleary (1968). This model defines fairness as identical regression lines for each sample (e.g., blacks and whites) and therefore the use of a common regression equation. In effect what this means is that we disregard race. For example, if we believe that SAT scores are the most objective and valid predictor of grades, then we will admit those applicants who score highest on the SAT regardless of their ethnic background.

2. *The constant ratio model.* Thorndike (1971) pointed out that it is not enough to consider the regression line; we need to also consider the proportion of applicants admitted from each sample. For example, we might find that the SAT predicts GPA equally well for blacks and for whites, but that blacks as a group score lower on the SAT than whites. If we select the top-scoring applicants on the SAT, we will select proportionally more whites than blacks. We need to take into account such an outcome, essentially by using different decision rules for each sample, based on either statistical criteria or "logical" criteria (e.g., if 25% of applicants are black, then 25% of admissions should also be black). Thorndike (1971) argued that a test is fair if it admits or selects the same proportion of minority applicants who would be selected on the criterion itself. For example, if we know that 40% of minority applicants to our college equal or exceed the average majority-group member in GPA, then if we select 50% of the majority applicants on the basis of their SAT scores, we need to select 40% of minority applicants. In terms of decision theory

(see Chapter 3), this model looks at the number of false negatives and false positives as related to the number of true negatives and true positives. This approach, which seems as reasonable as the definition given above, leads to rather different conclusions (Schmidt & Hunter, 1974).

3. *Conditional probability model.* Cole (1973) argued that all applicants who, if selected, are capable of being successful on the criterion should be guaranteed an equal opportunity to be selected, regardless of ethnic membership. The focus is on the criterion: if a person can achieve a satisfactory criterion score (e.g., GPA of C or above), then that person should have the same probability of being selected, regardless of group membership. In terms of decision theory, this model looks at the number of true positives in relation to the number of true positives plus false negatives (i.e., sensitivity).

4. *The equal probability model.* This model argues that all applicants who are selected should be guaranteed an equal chance of being successful, regardless of group membership. This model looks at the true positives compared with the true positives and false positives (i.e., predictive value).

These approaches are highly statistical and involve sophisticated analyses that go beyond the scope of this book.

Logical solutions. Not all theoretical models regarding test bias are psychometric in nature. Darlington (1976) for example, suggested that selection strategies be based upon "rational" rules rather than "mechanical" ones. He felt, for example, that a college should determine the number of minority applicants to admit in much the same way that it determines the number of athletes to admit. In other words, the strategies are to be determined by the policymakers rather than by "psychometric technicians."

Nature vs. nurture. Central to the issue of bias is the question of nature vs. nurture. For example, is intelligence determined by our genes (i.e., nature), or is it heavily influenced by educational experiences, family setting, and other environmental aspects (i.e., nurture). These are the two major perspectives that are used to explain racial differences on cognitive measures, although other perspectives have been presented (e.g., J. E. Helms, 1992). A basic point is that the question, "Is it nature or nurture?" is not a good question to ask. Any complex behavior such as that reflected in our label of intelligence is the result of myriad influences, including both hereditary and environmental aspects that interact with each other in complex ways. To go over the various historical issues and findings associated with this controversy would take us far afield and not serve our purposes; the story has been told countless times and the reader can consult such sources as Samuda (1975) for an overview.

Some findings. A number of studies have shown that the mean score on cognitive tests for blacks in the United States is significantly and consistently lower than that of whites. These results are fairly factual and, in general, are not disputed. What is disputed is the interpretation. On one side, individuals attempt to explain such findings as reflecting "nature," that is hereditary and/or genetic differences. On the other side, are those who attribute the findings to "nurture," to aspects such as differences in nutrition, school environments, role models, etc. In the middle, are the interactionists who believe that such mean differences are the reflection of both nature and nurture as they interact in ways that we are barely beginning to understand. Off to one side, are those that believe that such findings are an artifact, that they reflect inadequacies and biases inherent in our instruments. Still others believe that there is a conspiracy afoot with testing serving as a gate-keeping function, a way of keeping minorities "in their place."

Studies that support one particular point of view are both easy and hard to find – easy because research results can sometimes be interpreted in accord with one's preferred theoretical stance, and hard because studies that control for possible confounding aspects are difficult to carry out. The Coleman Report (Coleman et al., 1966) was a survey of schools attended by blacks and by whites. The authors showed that ethnic differences in tests of intelligence and in tests of academic achievement were not related to differences in school curricula, physical facilities, or teacher characteristics. The authors concluded that when socioeconomic background is controlled for, there is little difference in test performance that can be attributed to the schools

themselves. Thus the differences that do exist in mean test scores are not reflective of ethnicity per se, but of socioeconomic status. Poor whites and poor blacks do less well than their more advantaged peers. Yet the fact remains that carefully done reviews of the literature point to heredity as a major source of variation in intelligence scores (A. R. Jensen, 1969), and sober-minded reflections suggest that most criticisms of tests as culturally biased are the result of prejudice and preconceptions (Ebel, 1963).

A historical note. Unfortunately, much of the literature on this topic seems to be severely flawed. Early studies such as those of Goddard (1913; 1917), who tested immigrants to the United States and found 80% of them to be "feeble-minded," did not take into account such obvious aspects as lack of knowledge of English. More current studies make sweeping generalizations and often reflect political vehemence rather than scholarly deliberation (R. L. Williams, 1971).

Most test authors have been aware of the limitations and potential misuses of their instruments; Binet himself cautioned professionals on the limitations of his newly developed measure of intelligence. Unfortunately, many of the pioneers in the field of intelligence testing in the United States, notably Terman and Goddard (see Chapter 19), were not as "scientific" as they ought to have been. Goddard, for example, administered the translated Binet-Simon to arriving European immigrants and concluded that 83% of Jews, 80% of Hungarians, 79% of Italians, and 87% of Russians were feeble-minded. In opposition to such misguided "findings," a number of early studies can be cited where the authors were sensitive to the limitations of their instruments. For example, Yerkes and Foster (1923) argued that the interpretation of a person's IQ score should be made in the context of the person's socioeconomic background, as well as educational and familial history.

Some investigators concluded that nonverbal measures of intelligence were the appropriate instruments to use with minority children (e.g., Garth, Eson, & Morton, 1936), while others pointed to differences in home environments, educational deficits, and other differential aspects between Anglo and minority children (e.g., G. Sanchez, 1932; 1934). Other investigators administered the same test in an English format and a Spanish format to Spanish-speaking children, and found that the children scored significantly higher on the Spanish version than on the English version (e.g., Mahakian, 1939; A. J. Mitchell, 1937), although later studies that controlled for degree of bilingualism found just the opposite results (e.g., Keston & Jimenez, 1954).

Finally, other investigators began to look at the administrative aspects of tests as possible sources of bias. R. R. Knapp (1960) for example, administered the Cattell Culture Fair Intelligence Test to Mexican boys, with no time limit, and found that they scored higher than an Anglo sample where the test was given with the standard time limit.

Diagnostic discrimination. It is sometimes argued that test bias is not so much a matter of the test being biased; the bias occurs in the use of test results to label minority children and to place a disproportionate number of these in special-education programs, that is, to label these children as mentally retarded. In fact, the empirical evidence argues just the opposite. A number of studies show that black and low-socioeconomic-class children are *less* likely to be recommended for special-education-class placement than their white or higher-socioeconomic-class peers (C. R. Reynolds, 1982).

Language and examiner bias. Some studies have shown significant increases in mean scores of black children when a test has been administered using standard vs. nonstandard English (e.g., Hardy, Welcher, Mellits, et al., 1976) but others have not (e.g., L. C. Quay, 1974). C. R. Reynolds (1982) points out that such studies do not include experimental and control groups of *white* children. Jencks (1972) concluded that there was no evidence to support the hypothesis that black children are more disadvantaged on verbal tests where language is important than on nonverbal tests where language is at a minimum. Others (e.g., Oakland & Matuszek, 1977) have concluded that having a white examiner does not alter the validity of test results for minority children.

Special-education children. One particular concern might be with children who are tested because of possible retardation and/or

educational difficulties. Perhaps, tests are fair when used with average children but biased when used with lower-functioning children. In a typical study Poteat, Wuensch, and Gregg (1988) reviewed 83 black and 85 white students, referred for special-education evaluations. These children ranged in age from 6 to 16, with a median age of 10 and represented some 20 different schools. Of these students, 41% were eventually placed in programs for learning disabled, 10% were identified as educable mentally handicapped, and 11% as needing other forms of special education.

For the black students, the mean WISC-R IQ was 79.5 while for the white students it was 94.1. Similarly, the mean GPA for black students was 2.73 and for white students 3.09. A significant mean difference was also obtained on average scores on the California Achievement Test. WISC-R Full Scale IQs were significantly correlated with GPA for both black students ($r = .32$) and for white students ($r = .42$), with differences in the regression line not significant. A variety of other statistical analyses again indicated no significant differences between black and white students in the differential validity of the WISC-R.

Determining item bias. One approach is to determine item difficulty separately for the majority group and for the minority group. In fact, item bias is now called "differential item functioning" to reflect this perspective. If any item seems to be particularly difficult for one group, relative to other items on the test, then the item is considered potentially biased. When in fact such items are identified during test construction, there seem to be two possible explanations: (1) the items are poorly written and of low reliability, and hence ought to be removed; (2) the items seem well written, with adequate reliability, and do *not* share any common characteristics that might provide a reasonable explanation. When such items are eliminated from a test, the results are not particularly different from those that are obtained with the items retained. What seems to occur is that the test becomes slightly more difficult for everyone because the eliminated items typically have moderate to low difficulty (C. R. Reynolds, 1982).

Another approach is to have expert minority group members review proposed test items and to eliminate any items the experts judge to be biased, either in content, wording, scoring, or other aspect. Unfortunately, the research literature indicates that such judgments show little relationship to actual empirical findings. Sandoval and Mille (1979, cited by C. R. Reynolds, 1982), for example, asked a sample of 100 judges from Mexican-American, Anglo, and black backgrounds to judge which of 30 WISC-R items would be of greater difficulty for specific ethnic groups. The authors concluded that judges are not able to identify items that are more difficult for a minority child than for an Anglo child; both minority and nonminority experts were equally incorrect in their subjective judgments vis-à-vis, empirical data.

When there is such cultural bias in test items, it is usually related to the specificity of item content. For example, an item that requires the identification of the capital of Pakistan may be biased in favor of individuals who live in that part of the world. Such bias can best be established by objective analysis based on item statistics, rather than subjective judgment (Clarizio, 1982).

Intent of the test. One question often neglected by critics of tests concerns the intent of a test. In Chapter 9, for example, we discussed the Boehm Test of Basic Concepts. This test has been criticized as being culturally biased because the language of the items is "unfamiliar" to black children. For example, the item "mark the toy that is behind the sofa" should be changed to "mark the toy that is in back of the sofa." Such arguments neglect the intent of the test. The Boehm assesses a child's knowledge of specific language concepts that are used by teachers in the classroom. If the concept were "in back of" then the change would be appropriate; but the concept that is assessed is "behind" (C. R. Reynolds, 1982).

Separate or racial norming. One solution that is sometimes proposed to perceived test bias is that of separate norms, also called racial or subgroup norming (D. C. Brown, 1994). This involves interpreting a person's test score in comparison to norms based on an ethnically relevant sample. For example, the SAT scores of a black candidate for admission to a university would be compared to norms based on black individuals. A good argument can be made for using appro-

priate norms. If we are assessing how depressed a psychiatric patient is, it would make sense to compare that person's score on the depression inventory we used with norms based on psychiatric patients. If the subject were a college student, then more appropriate norms might be based on college students. The appropriateness of norms must be determined by their relevance to a criterion. If there were no difference in criterion performance, i.e., depression, between college students and psychiatric patients, then separate norms would not be appropriate.

In effect, using racial norms prejudges the question and assumes that the minority group will do less well on the criterion. This approach is exemplified by the work of Mercer on the SOMPA (see section below). The counterargument to the issue of separate norms is that the typical child will need to function in a pluralistic setting and will be working in a world that includes people from many different cultures. In addition, cultural groups are not "pure"; there are many children who have parents of mixed ethnicity, parents who come from different geographical locations (e.g., an American father and a Vietnamese mother), and may have different cultural and linguistic backgrounds. It is not possible to develop such specific norms, and at any rate, the criterion is not one's ethnic group but one's peers in the school system and in the world of work.

Some general conclusions. There is a considerable body of literature on test bias, particularly with the better known tests of cognitive functioning such as the WISC-R and the Raven (for representative illustrative studies see Dean, 1980; McShane, 1980; McShane & Plas, 1982; Reschly, 1978). The literature is complex, sometimes contradictory, and sometimes it is difficult to disentangle what is factual evidence vs. subjective judgment. However, we can come to some conclusions. In general, studies of intelligence tests have shown that these tests do not have bias against blacks or other minority groups (e.g., C. R. Reynolds, 1982; C. R. Reynolds, Willson, & Chatman, 1985). More specifically, from an internal criterion point of view, studies show factorial equivalence of tests such as the WISC-R in Hispanics, blacks, and Anglos and equivalent indices of internal consistency in these various groups. In other words, the bulk of the evidence suggests that well-designed cognitive tests are not biased. At the same time, the evidence suggests that nonverbal cognitive measures such as the Raven show no bias, but that verbal tests may show some possible bias for Mexican-Americans; Mexican-American children, particularly those who are bilingual, do better on performance and nonverbal items than on verbal items. The language of the examiner and/or of the test seems to have some impact with Mexican-American children. For example, Mexican-American children tend to score higher on such tests as the WISC and the Stanford-Binet when these are given in Spanish rather than English.

From an external point of view, the literature indicates that standardized tests such as the WISC-R are just as predictively accurate with minority children as with Anglo children, particularly when the criterion is a standardized achievement test. The data is less convincing (and also more limited) when the criterion consists of teachers' grades. Such conclusions also apply to the testing of adults. For example, a number of studies have shown that the predictive validity of the SAT for blacks attending black colleges is as high as that for whites (e.g., Stanley & Porter, 1967).

On the basis of a literature review, Clarizio (1982) came to the following conclusions:

1. Nonverbal tests such as the Performance scale of the WISC-R provide valid measures of the intellectual functioning of Mexican-American children.

2. Verbal intelligence scales have about as good validity for Mexican-American children as they do for Anglos, in predicting short-term achievement. However, because a specific language factor may depress the performance of bilingual children on verbal scales, care needs to be exercised in arriving at specific decisions.

3. Consideration should be given in testing a bilingual child in both languages by an examiner who is fluent in both languages.

CROSS-CULTURAL ASSESSMENT

When psychological tests were first developed, particularly those of intelligence, researchers attempted to develop measures that would not be affected by differing cultural factors such as language, literacy (i.e., ability to read), test sophistication, and so on. For example, if test items could be developed that did not require language, such items could be used in a test that could be administered to groups having different languages, and such tests would then be "culture-free." Eventually, it became apparent that valid culture-free tests could not be developed. Behavior does not exist in a vacuum, and culture is not simply an outside veneer that can be discarded at will. Thus, in the measurement of intelligence there was a shift from "culture-free" tests to "culture-fair" tests that need to be evaluated and validated within each culture.

Culture-fair tests tend to be nonverbal in nature. They use items such as those depicted in Figure 11.1. These items often consist of completing patterns, classification tasks, finding one's way out of a paper maze, and so on. Such items, which are typically pictorial or involve performance, rather than verbal, often involve abstract reasoning and the solution of novel problems rather than the more traditional verbal items that reflect school knowledge. Sometimes the items are selected because they are equally unfamiliar to different cultures, and sometimes they are presumed to be of equal familiarity. Instructions may be verbal, but can often be given orally, in the appropriate language, or through pantomime.

Unfortunately, establishing the validity of culture-fair tests is problematic in part because validity must ultimately rest on criteria that are not free of culture. For example, academic achievement occurs in a school setting with all the demands, expectations, prejudices, values, etc., that clearly reflect a particular culture.

Problems in cross-cultural testing. There are many problems associated with cross-cultural research and particularly with the use of specific tests in different cultures. For example, translations from one language to another may result in instruments that are not really equivalent. Psychological constructs such as depression, ego-strength, or intelligence may not necessarily be equivalent across languages and/or cultures. There may be crucial differences from one culture to another in terms of test sophistication and

1. Which item on the right completes the pattern on the left?

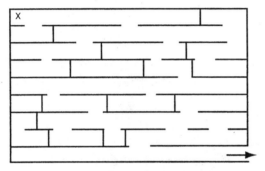

2. Find the correct way out of the maze.

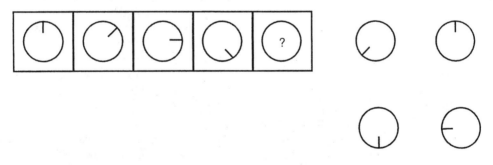

3. Select the correct choice.

FIGURE 11–1. Illustrations of items used in Culture-Fair Tests.

test-taking behavior. A test may well have content validity in one country, but not in another. Holtzman (1968) divides such potential problems into three categories: (1) cross-national differences, (2) cross-language differences, and (3) subcultural differences (such as ethnic origin and degree of urbanization). He suggests that studies can be undertaken that control for one or more of these categories. For example, a comparison of college students in Mexico, Venezuela, and Peru on the CPI would presumably control for cross-language differences – although colloquialisms and other aspects may still be different. (For a brief review of many of the measurement problems involved in cross-cultural testing see Hui and Triandis, 1985.)

Translating from one language to another. If we wanted to determine the utility of a particular test that was developed in the United States in another country, such as Venezuela, for example, we would translate the test into Spanish and carry out the necessary assessments of reliability and validity in Venezuela. In fact, most of the major commercially published tests, such as the Stanford-Binet, the WISC, the MMPI, and the CPI, are available in various languages. However, translation is not a simple matter of looking up the equivalent words in a dictionary. Common objects in one culture may be uncommon in another; bland words in one language may have strong affective meanings in another. Phrases may be translated correctly in a literary sense, but not be colloquially correct; maintaining the language equivalence of an instrument across languages can be difficult.

Brislin (1970) suggested that the procedure to be used, called the *back translation method*, follow certain steps. The items to be translated should be simple, not use hypothetical phrasings or subjunctive mood, avoid metaphors and colloquialisms. The items are translated from the source language to the target language by a bilingual person. A second bilingual person translates the items back from the target language to the source language. The two source language versions are then compared; any discrepancies hopefully can be resolved.

There is also a process known as *decentering*, which refers to the translation process in which both the source and the target language versions are equally important – i.e., both the source and the target versions contribute to the final set of questions, and both are open to revisions.

A number of other procedures are also used. In addition to the back translation, bilinguals can take the same test in both languages. Items that yield discrepant responses can easily be identified and altered as needed or eliminated. Rather than use only two bilingual individuals to do the back translation, several such individuals can be used, either working independently or as a committee. It is also important to pretest any translated instruments to make sure that the translated items are indeed meaningful.

Quite often, tests that are developed in one culture are not simply translated into the target language, but they are changed and adapted. This is the case, for example, with the Cuban version of the Stanford-Binet (Jacobson, Prio, Ramirez, et al., 1978).

Etic and emic approaches. Two words that are used by linguists, "phonetic" and "phonemic," refer to language. Phonetic refers to the universal rules for all languages, while phonemic refers to the sounds of a particular language. From these terms, the words "etic" and "emic" were derived and used in the cross-cultural literature. Etic studies compare the same variable across cultures. For example, we might be interested in depression and might administer a depression scale to nationals of various countries. Emic studies focus on only one culture and do not attempt to compare across cultures. We might administer a depression questionnaire to a sample of Malaysian adults, for example, and determine how scores on the questionnaire are related to everyday behaviors in that culture.

A good example of an emic study is that by Laosa (1993) who studied what family characteristics are related to a child's school readiness in Chicano children. He studied normal young children in 100 two-parent Chicano households of widely varied socioeconomic levels. This was a longitudinal study with data collected when the children were 30 months, 42 months, and 48 months of age. The data collection involved interviews with the mother, administration of the Culture Fair Intelligence Test (see discussion that follows) to both parents, and administration of a preschool achievement test to the children as a measure of school readiness. Among the many findings were that children's school readiness was related to the father's and the mother's levels of schooling ($r = .54$ and $.46$), and to the father's and mother's scores on the Culture Fair Intelligence Test ($r = .52$ and $.32$). In other words, children who were better prepared to enter school had better educated and more intelligent parents. In particular, the results of this study suggest an important influence of Chicano fathers on their children's learning and development. For another interesting emic study, see M. King and J. King (1971) who studied more than 1,100 freshmen at a university in Ethiopia to see what variables correlated most with academic achievement.

MEASUREMENT OF ACCULTURATION

Assessing acculturation. What is meant by acculturation? Although it is a straightforward question, there is no simple answer. As Olmedo

(1979) stated, the term *acculturation* is one of the most elusive yet ubiquitous constructs in the behavioral sciences. For our purposes, acculturation involves all the myriad aspects and processes that impinge on an individual from one culture as that person enters a different culture for an extended period of time. The process of acculturation refers to the changes in behavior and values that occur in minority individuals as they are exposed to the mainstream cultural patterns. Acculturation can be seen as a group phenomenon, which is how anthropologists and sociologists study it, or as an individual phenomenon, which is how psychologists see it. However defined, acculturation is a multifaceted and gradual process. Concrete objects such as clothing can be adopted rather rapidly, but changes in values may take longer, or never occur. Acculturation is an important variable, not only intrinsically, but because it is related to a variety of physical and psychological conditions ranging from alcoholism, educational achievement, suicide, mortality rates, willingness to use counseling, and others (e.g., Leighton, 1959; Hong & Holmes, 1973; Padilla, 1980; Ruesch, Loeb, & Jacobson, 1948; R. Sanchez & Atkinson, 1983).

There seems to be substantial agreement in the literature that the major dimension underlying acculturation and acculturation scales is language use. If a person speaks Spanish but little or no English, then that person is assumed not to be acculturated. Another major dimension underlying acculturation is generational distance, defined by where the respondent and family members were born. A first generation person is someone whose parents, grandparents, and self were born outside the United States, while a second generation person was born in the United States with both parents and grandparents born outside of the United States. (Third generation Mexican-Americans are assumed to be more acculturated than second generation, who in turn are more acculturated than first.) Generational distance is often used as a criterion for determining the construct validity of acculturation scales.

Acculturation scales typically use one or more of three types of items: linguistic, psychological, and sociocultural. Almost all scales use linguistic items, having to do with language use, proficiency, and preference. Psychological items deal with values, attitudes, knowledge, and behavior. Sociocultural items typically cover occupational status, educational level, family size, degree of urbanization, and similar aspects.

A number of scales to measure acculturation have been developed, primarily for Hispanics (e.g., Cuellar, Harris, & Jasso, 1980; Deyo, Diehl, Hazuda, et al., 1985; Franco, 1983; Mendoza, 1989; Olmedo, J. L. Martinez, & S. R. Martinez, 1978; Olmedo & Padilla, 1978; Ramirez, Garza, & Cox, 1980; Triandis, Kashima, Hui, et al., 1982); a smaller number of scales have been developed for Asians (Suinn, Ahuna, & Khoo, 1992; Suinn, Rikard-Figueroa, Lew, et al., 1987). A few investigators have developed scales to measure specific subgroups within the broader labels, such as, for Cubans. Szapocznik, Scopetta, Aranalde, et al., (1978) developed a 24-item behavioral-acculturation scale for Cubans, with a high degree of internal reliability (alpha = .97) and test-retest stability over a 4-week period ($r = .96$). Garcia and Lega (1979) developed an 8-item Cuban Behavioral Identity Questionnaire; one interesting but somewhat burdensome aspect of this scale is that responses to this scale, given on a 7-point Likert format, are placed in a regression equation to obtain a total score. Most of these scales are applicable to adolescents and adults, but some have been developed specifically for children (e.g., Martinez, Norman, & Delaney, 1984).

Most acculturation scales assume acculturation to be a unipolar variable, i.e., a person is more or less acculturated. Some investigators see acculturation as a bipolar variable – a person can also be bicultural, equally at ease in both cultures. For example, Szapocznik, Kurtines, and Fernandez (1980) developed separate scales to measure "Hispanicism" and "Americanism" in an attempt to measure *biculturalism*, the degree to which the person identifies with both cultures.

The Marin scale. A representative example of an acculturation scale for Hispanics is the one developed by G. Marin (G. Marin, Sabogal, & B. V. Marin, 1987). The authors selected 17 behavioral-acculturation items from previously published acculturation scales. These items measured proficiency and preference for speaking a given language in various settings (e.g., what language(s) do you read and speak: (a) only Spanish, (b) Spanish better than English, (c) both equally, (d) English better than Spanish, (e) only English. Other questions with similar response options ask what language(s) are spoken at home, with friends, as a child, etc.). The items were placed within the context of a 16-page questionnaire, and administered to a sample of 363 Hispanics and 228 non-Hispanic white. Both English and Spanish versions were available.

The responses for the two samples were factor analyzed separately. For the Hispanic sample three factors were obtained. The first accounted for 54.5% of the variance and was called "language use and ethnic loyalty." This factor was made up of seven items that measured language use and the ethnicity of important others. The second factor accounted for only 7% of the variance and included four items on preference for media (e.g., Spanish language TV). The third variable accounted for 6.1% of the variance and included four items that measured the ethnicity of friends for self and for one's children. Similar results were obtained for the non-Hispanic white sample, except that the second and third factors accounted for a greater portion of the variance. On the basis of some additional statistical decisions, the authors chose 12 items as their final scale. The 12-item scale was then analyzed for reliability (alpha coefficient = .92) and for validity. Scores on the scale correlated significantly with generational distance, with length of residence in the United States (taking age into account), and with the respondent's own evaluation of their degree of acculturation.

The Olmedo, Martinez, & Martinez (1978) Scale. This is a two part paper-and-pencil inventory that started with 127 items. The first part consists of a semantic differential in which four concepts (mother, father, male, and female) are rated on a set of 15 bipolar adjectives, all reflective of a potency dimension (e.g., hard-soft, weak-strong). The second part consists of 18 items that cover background information such as gender, place of birth, family size, and language spoken at home. The scale was originally administered to some 924 high-school students, of which about 27% were Chicanos. A series of analyses yielded a set of 20 variables (9 semantic and 11 sociocultural) that were correlated with ethnicity. The

most significant item was, "only English spoken at home," with affirmative responding subjects likely to be Anglo. Conversely, those endorsing the item "mostly Spanish spoken at home" were likely to be Chicano.

Test-retest reliability over a 2- to 3-week period for a group of 129 junior college students was reported to be .89 for Chicanos and .66 for Anglos. A factor analysis of the 20 items indicated 3 factors: factor I was labeled a Nationality-Language factor, factor II a socioeconomic status factor, and factor III a semantic factor. This scale has been used in a number of studies, with college students (Padilla, Olmedo, & Loya, 1982), and with community adults (Kranau, Green, & Valencia-Weber, 1982; Olmedo & Padilla, 1978). The scale has been cross-validated (Olmedo & Padilla, 1978), and a Spanish version developed (Cortese & Smyth, 1979).

The ARSMA. Another popular acculturation scale is the Acculturation Rating Scale for Mexican Americans, or ARSMA (Cuellar, Harris, & Jasso, 1980). The ARSMA consists of 20 questions each scored on a 5-point scale, ranging from Mexican/Spanish to Anglo/English. For example, one item asks what language you prefer. Available responses are (a) Spanish only; (b) mostly Spanish, some English; (c) Spanish and English about equally; (d) mostly English, some Spanish; (e) English only. The total scores on this scale yield a typology of five types: very Mexican; Mexican-oriented bicultural; "true" bicultural; Anglo-oriented bicultural; and very Anglicized. Four factors have been identified on the scale: (1) language preference; (2) ethnic identity and generation removed from Mexico; (3) ethnicity of friends and associates; (4) direct contact with Mexico and with ability to read and write in Spanish. Both internal reliability (alpha = .88), and test-retest reliability (.80 for 4- to 5-week period) are adequate. This scale and its factors was cross-validated (Montgomery & Orozco, 1984) and used in a variety of studies (e.g., Castro, Furth, & Karlow, 1984). Some of the items have been incorporated into a semistructured interview measure of acculturation (Burnam, Telles, Karno, et al., 1987).

SL-ASIA. Most of the acculturation scales that have been developed are for Hispanics. One scale that was developed for Asians but modeled on the ARSMA is the Suinn-Lew Asian Self-Identity Acculturation Scale or SL-ASIA (Suinn, Rickard-Figueroa, Lew, et al., 1987). The SL-ASIA consists of 21 multiple-choice items, written to mimic the ARSMA items, and covering such aspects as language preference, identity, and generational background. Suinn, Ahuna, and Khoo (1992) administered the SL-ASIA and a demographic questionnaire to a sample of 284 Asian-American college students, with a mean age of 24.4 years.

Internal consistency estimates across several studies range from .88 to .91 (Atkinson & Gim, 1989; Suinn, Ahuna, & Khoo, 1992; Suinn, Rickard-Figueroa, Lew, et al., 1987). Scores on the SL-ASIA correlated significantly with such demographic variables as total years living in the United States ($r = .56$), total years attending school in the United States ($r = .61$), years lived in a non-Asian neighborhood ($r = .41$), and self-ratings of acculturation ($r = .62$). A factor analysis indicated five factors, three of which were identical to those found on the ARSMA. These factors were: (a) reading/writing/cultural preference (accounting for 41.5% of the variance), (b) ethnic interaction (10.7% of the variance), and (c) generational identity (5.9% of the variance). The two additional factors were: (d) affinity for ethnic identity and pride (6.6% of the variance), and (e) food preference (5%). These 5 factors involve 17 items, so each factor is made up of 2 to 5 items. Again, the one major factor involves language.

SOME CULTURE-FAIR TESTS AND FINDINGS

The Cattell Culture-Fair Intelligence Test

This test was first published in 1944 and was one of the first attempts to develop an intelligence measure free of cultural influences. The test was presumed to be a measure of "g" and reflect R. B. Cattell's theory of *fluid* intelligence and *crystallized* intelligence. Fluid intelligence is made up of abilities that are nonverbal, that do not depend on specific exposure to school or other experiences, and therefore are relatively culture free; basically, fluid intelligence is general mental capacity for problem solving, especially in novel situations. Crystallized intelligence refers to acquired skills

and knowledge, reflecting particular educational experiences, and it is therefore culture related (R. B. Cattell, 1963; 1987). Crystallized intelligence develops through the use of fluid intelligence, and the two are in fact highly correlated.

R. B. Cattell's test is composed of three scales: Scale I for ages 4 to 8, Scale II for ages 8 to 12 and "average adults," and Scale III for high-school students and superior adults. Scale I consists of eight subtests that involve mazes, copying of symbols, identifying similar drawings, and other nonverbal tasks. Both Scales II and III are composed of four subtests: (1) a Series subtest where a sequence of drawings is completed by choosing among response options; (2) a Classifications subtest, where the respondent selects the one drawing that is different from the other drawings; (3) a Matrices subtest that requires completing a matrix or pattern; and (4) a Conditions subtest, that requires the respondent to identify which of several geometric drawings fulfills certain specified conditions. Two forms are available, forms A and B, which are combined and administered as a single scale in the standardization process. Karnes, May, and Lee (1982) report a correlation of .59 between scores on Form A and scores on Form B for a sample of economically disadvantaged children.

Almost as soon as the Cattell was published, it was criticized. For example, Marquart and Bailey (1955) argued that performance on the items of Scale I was in fact influenced by socioeconomic status, just as much as on verbal measures like the Stanford-Binet.

On the other hand, there is a substantial body of literature that suggests that culture-fair tests such as the Cattell fulfill not only theoretical and social concerns but practical needs as well. For example, juvenile courts often require screening of intellectual ability in a population that is overrepresented with minority groups. Smith, Hays, and Solway (1977) compared the Cattell Culture-Fair Test and the WISC-R in a sample of juvenile delinquents, 53% of whom were black or Mexican-American. The results indicated significant ethnic differences, with whites scoring 17.9 points higher on the WISC-R and 11.4 points higher on the Cattell than their minority peers. Scores on the Cattell correlated .76 with the WISC-R Full Scale IQ, .71 with the Verbal IQ, and .70 with the Performance IQ. The authors concluded that the Cattell is a better measure of intelligence for minority groups than the WISC-R, as it lessens the effect of cultural bias and presents a "more accurate" picture of their intellectual capacity.

Raven's Progressive Matrices

The Raven's PM consists of a series of three tests: the Standard Progressive Matrices (SPM; J. C. Raven, 1938), the Coloured Progressive Matrices (CPM, J. C. Raven, 1947a), and the Advanced Progressive Matrices (APM, J. C. Raven, 1947b). These tests are based on Spearman's two-factor theory, which distinguished between *g* or general intelligence and *s* or specific factors. Spearman's theory also distinguished between "eductive" and "reproductive" thinking processes, and the Progressive Matrices are designed to assess a person's ability to educe relationships rather than reproduce learned material. We might prefer to use the term *inductive* reasoning and consider the Raven's as such measures, in that the examinee is presented with a collection of elements, needs to infer a rule or rules that relate such a collection, and then needs to verify the rule by selecting an appropriate new element that fits the rule(s). Others might call this "analytical" intelligence, the ability to deal with novelty, to adapt one's thinking to a new cognitive problem (Carpenter, Just, & Shell, 1990), while still others might prefer to use Cattell's term of "fluid intelligence."

Each of the Raven's PM yields only one score, namely the number of items answered correctly. These tests can be used with children, adolescents, and adults, although the evidence suggests that the PM are of limited value and questionable reliability for children aged under 7. In general, there do not seem to be gender differences on any of the three PM (Court, 1983). The Raven's PM have achieved a high degree of popularity and have been used in significantly more than 1,600 published studies (Court, 1988). In particular, the Raven is used with groups such as children and the elderly, for whom language processing may need to be kept at a minimum. As with many of the other popular tests, short forms have also been developed (e.g., W. Arthur & Day, 1994; Wytek, Opgenoorth, & Presslich, 1984).

Because of its relationship to the concept of *g*, there is the temptation to consider that whatever the Raven's measures it is immutable and hereditary, but the evidence is quite to the contrary. For example, Irvine (1969) reports on a series of studies of eithth and tenth graders in Central Africa. He reports that when special introductory procedures were used involving the teaching of sample problems, there was a decrease in the variance of the scores and an increase in the mean. There were also differences in mean scores between specific schools, and in item difficulty levels among specific ethnic groups.

Despite the popularity of the Raven's PM, they have been criticized rather substantially. For example, Bortner (1965) indicated that the diagnostic value of a test of cognitive functioning comes from an analysis of the errors made by the subject, and from observations of the subject's attempts to deal with the task. The PM does not allow for such analyses and observations and hence is of limited value.

The Standard PM (SPM). The SPM (J. Raven, J. C. Raven, & Court, 1998) is probably the most widely used of the three progressive matrices tests; it consists of 60 problems in 5 sets of 12. The tests are called progressive because each problem in a set, and each set, are progressively more difficult. Each problem consists of a geometric design with a missing piece; the respondent selects the missing piece from six or eight choices given.

Originally, the SPM was developed together with a vocabulary test (the Mill Hill Vocabulary Scale) to assess the two components of general intelligence as identified by Spearman; the SPM was a measure of eductive ability, while the Mill Hill was a measure of reproductive ability. The two scales correlate about .50, suggesting that the two measures are somewhat distinct. While the Mill Hill Vocabulary Test is widely known and used in England, it is practically unknown in the United States.

The SPM is untimed and can be group-administered. The test was originally standardized in 1938 and restandardized in 1979 on British school children, and with norms on ages 6 to 65. The reliability of the SPM is quite solid. Split-half reliabilities are in the .80s and .90s, with median coefficients hovering near .90.

For example, H. R. Burke and Bingham (1969) reported a corrected split-half reliability of .96. Similarly, test-retest reliabilities range from the .70s to the .90s, with median coefficients in the .80s. Extensive norms are available for the SPM, both for English-speaking groups from countries such as Canada, England, Ireland, and the United States, and for other countries such as China and the former Czechoslovakia. For example, H. R. Burke (1972) gives norms based on a sample of 567 male American veterans that allow one to change the SPM score into an estimated WAIS IQ. There is a substantial cross-cultural literature on the SPM (e.g., Abdel-Khalek, 1988; A. Moran, 1986).

Much of the concern about the validity of the SPM centers on Spearman's theory. In the United States, the concept of g has never been popular, with American theorists preferring a multifactor approach, that is, theories that suggest intelligence is made up of a number of separate dimensions. In England and other countries, Spearman's theory has had greater impact and acceptance. A number of studies that have factor-analyzed SPM data have indeed obtained one major factor, although some studies have found a variety of other factors.

Concurrent validity of the SPM with standard tests of intelligence such as the Stanford-Binet or the WISC, shows correlations that range from the .50s to the .80s. Predictive validity, especially predicting academic achievement, is generally low. The test appears to be a "culturally fair" measure and not to have gender bias, although the results of different studies are contradictory.

S. Powers and Barkan (1986) administered the SPM to 99 Hispanic and 93 non-Hispanic seventh graders and compared their scores with the scores on a standardized norm-referenced achievement test (California Achievement Test). SPM scores correlated .40 with reading achievement scores, .45 with language achievement, and .49 with mathematics achievement, with no significant differences between Hispanic and non-Hispanic students in the magnitude or pattern of correlations.

Among the criticisms leveled at the SPM is that it tends to overestimate IQ compared with tests such as the Wechsler and has a restricted ceiling, that is, it may be too easy for a number of subjects (Vincent & Cox, 1974).

The Coloured PM (CPM). The CPM was designed for use with young children aged 5 to 11, with the mentally handicapped, and with the elderly. The CPM contains 36 problems printed in different colors, but is the same as the SPM in other respects. In fact, two subsets of items are identical with those found on the SPM (except for the color). There is also a vocabulary test (the Crichton Vocabulary Scale) to be used in conjunction with the CPM, but it is not, at least in the United States.

The reliability of the CPM also is adequate, with split-half coefficients between .82 and .99, and test-retest coefficients between .67 and .86 (Court & J. C. Raven, 1982). Concurrent validity with tests such as the Stanford-Binet and the WISC varies widely, with correlation coefficients ranging from the .20s to the .80s. In general, higher correlations are found with older children (ages 11 and 12). How important is the color aspect? Tuddenham, Davis, Davison, et al. (1958) reproduced the items in black and white on throw-away sheets, rather than using the more expensive color-printed reusable booklets of the commercial version; and obtained identical results to those obtained under standard administration. The CPM has been criticized for unrepresentative norms, but it is considered a useful instrument, particularly in the assessment of minority children. In one study of Chicano and Anglo children (Valencia, 1979), the investigator reported that when socioeconomic status and language were held constant, Chicano children did almost as well as Anglos.

In another study (J. S. Carlson & C. M. Jensen, 1981), the CPM was administered individually to some 783 children aged $5\frac{1}{2}$ to $8\frac{1}{2}$; these children included 301 Anglo, 203 black, and 279 Hispanic. For all children together, the alpha reliability was .82, the K-R reliability was .82, and the corrected split-half reliability was .85. However, for the youngest children ($5\frac{1}{2}$ to $6\frac{1}{2}$) these coefficients were .57, .64, and .65, respectively. When the results were analyzed by ethnicity, the authors concluded that the CPM appeared to be equally reliable for all three ethnic groups. However, the coefficients they report are as follows: for Anglo .83, .83, and .87; for Hispanic .76, .76, and .77; and for blacks .76, .76, and .81, suggesting slightly lower reliability for non-whites.

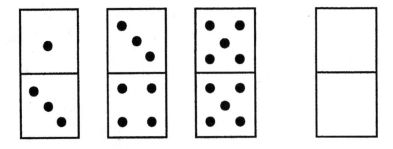

(Solution: blank item should be zero and 6)

FIGURE 11–2. An example of a D–48 item.

The Advanced PM (APM). The APM consists of 48 items similar to those on the SPM, but considerably more difficult; the test is intended for children aged 11 and older of above-average intellectual ability. The test consists of two sets of items. Set 1 can be used either as a practice test for Set 2 or as a rough screening test. Set 2 can be used either as a test of "intellectual capacity" when administered without a time limit or as a test of "mental efficiency" when used with a time limit. Although the APM has been used in a number of studies (e.g., Ackerman, 1992), there seems to be relatively little psychometric information available. What is available suggests that the APM is much like the other two forms in terms of reliability and validity. One major difference between the APM and the other two is the lack of norms. The test manual reports "estimated" norms rather than actual norms. Another possible difference concerns the dimensionality of this form. Because the underlying theory is that of Spearman, a construct validity approach would require the PM to be unidimensional, i.e., a "pure" measure of g. That seems to be the case for the SPM and the CPM, but there seems to be some question about the APM: some studies have reported a single factor (e.g., Alderton & Larson, 1990; Arthur & Woehr, 1993), while others have reported two (Dillon, Pohlmann, & Lohman, 1981). A 12-item short form is also available (Arthur & Day, 1994).

The D–48. Like the Progressive Matrices, the D–48 began its life in the British Army, during the Second World War, as a parallel test to the PM. This test, in various forms, is used widely in England and in various South American countries, but is lesser known in the United States. The D–48 is a nonverbal-analogies test also designed to

measure g. It consists of 48 sequences of dominoes (4 are used as practice examples) in which the subject must determine the pattern and/or sequence, and fill in the blank item. Figure 11.2 illustrates an item.

In the first study to appear in the U.S. literature, the D–48 was administered to 86 fifth- and sixth-grade students, and their scores compared to grades and to achievement test scores (G. Gough & Domino, 1963). D–48 scores correlated .58 and .45 with grades in the fifth- and sixth-grade classes. Scores on the D–48 also correlated significantly with achievement test scores, from a low of .27 to a high of .51. In both groups of children scores on the D–48 correlated more highly with grades than did the scores on the achievement tests, and in the sixth-grade sample scores on the D–48 were a better predictor of grades than the grades those children had obtained the prior year.

As we discussed above, in assessing test bias one concern is the difficulty level of the items across various groups. Gough and G. Domino (1963) calculated the difficulty level of each of the items on the D–48 for their sample of children and changed these indices to ranks (the easiest item was given a rank of 1, etc.). They then compared these ranks with those obtained by other investigators. For example, they obtained a correlation of +.83 between the ranks for these American children and the ranks for a sample of Italian university students; .89 with ranks for a sample of French college students; .95 with those for a sample of Lebanese men; and .91 with ranks for a sample of Flemish children. Thus the relative difficulty level of the D–48 items is rather constant for different age groups and for testing in different countries and in different languages.

Most of the validity information for the D–48 is of the concurrent type. For example, Welsh (1966) administered the D–48, the Terman Concept Mastery Test (a verbal intelligence test), and a measure of creativity to gifted high-school students. Scores on the D–48 correlated .49 with scores on the Terman (note that this is just about identical with the correlation of the Raven with a vocabulary test), and did not correlate with the measure of creativity. Boyd and Ward (1967) administered the D–48, the Raven PM, and a group intelligence test to a sample of college students. D–48 scores correlated .20 with GPA, .39 with the Raven's, and .57 with the intelligence test. The D–48 did slightly better than the Raven's in predicting GPA, but not as well as the group intelligence test.

These results are in accord with might be called differentiation theories of cognitive functioning. These theories postulate that cognitive abilities become more differentiated as the child matures. At the preschool level the notion of g appears sensible. As cognition develops with age, g becomes differentiated into specific abilities. Thus, at the younger school grades we would expect a measure of g to correlate more substantially with achievement than at the upper school levels. Such a view is indeed supported by factor-analytic studies of instruments such as the Stanford-Binet (Thorndike, Hagen, & Sattler, 1986a).

Only future research can indicate how useful this test might or might not be, but Gough and G. Domino (1963) list five reasons to pay attention to the D–48: (1) American psychologists should be aware of what psychologists in other countries are doing; (2) the D–48 uses stimuli (domino sequences) that are familiar to people of most cultures; (3) the D–48 is almost entirely nonverbal; (4) the British literature suggests that the D–48 is more highly loaded on g than even the Raven's; and (5) the D–48 is easy to administer and score, requires a brief time period (30 minutes), and can be administered individually or in groups.

The System of Multicultural Pluralistic Assessment (SOMPA)

The SOMPA (J. R. Mercer, 1976; J. Mercer & Lewis, 1977) is really a test battery designed to assess children from culturally different backgrounds. It is composed of six tests to be administered to the child and three instruments administered to the parent. These tests were selected to reflect a tripartite model that includes a medical perspective, a social system perspective, and a pluralistic perspective.

There are six measures on the SOMPA that reflect the medical perspective. These include: (1) the Physical Dexterity Tasks (behaviors used by physicians to assess sensorimotor coordination) are used to screen for possible neurological or central nervous system anomalies; (2) the Bender Visual Motor Gestalt Test (see Chapter 15), a widely used measure of perceptual and neurological aspects, involves the copying of a series of designs; (3) the Health History Inventory, a series of questions about the child's birth and medical history (asked of the parent); (4) weight; (5) height; and (6) visual acuity, as measured by the Snellen charts. These last three measures are usually available in nursing records. Basically, the intent of all these tasks is to identify potential medical and physical problems.

The social system perspective fundamentally focuses on social deviance, which is defined as specific behaviors in terms of norms appropriate to a specific group. There are two instruments that reflect this perspective. One is the Adaptive Behavior Inventory for Children (ABIC), which was developed on the basis of extensive interviews with mothers of children from the Anglo, black, and Hispanic cultures. The parent is asked to evaluate the child's competence in six areas such as family role and student role; the intent here is to obtain an estimate of how the child meets specific cultural demands for independent functioning, as judged by a parent. The test is said to be culturally fair because ethnic and gender differences in mean scores are negligible. The second test under this perspective is the WISC-R. However, the test is not used as a measure of ability, but as a measure of functioning in school.

The pluralistic perspective uses four sociocultural scales to determine how much an individual's world differs from the Anglo core culture. These scales assess socioeconomic status, degree of Anglo cultural assimilation, and degree of integration into Anglo social systems. Multiple regression procedures are then used to predict a normal distribution of WISC-R scores for a particular sociocultural group. A child's relative standing then provides an index of "estimated learning potential." Note then, that scores on the WISC-R are not compared with test norms, but with specific sociocultural norms, so that a child's performance is compared with that of members of his or her own sociocultural or ethnic group; that is what the term "pluralistic" in the title of the SOMPA refers to.

What is unique about the SOMPA – and a source of controversy – is the theoretical rationale, the way norms are used, and the structure of the battery. The SOMPA comes out of a pluralistic view of American society, that is, American society is composed of a dominant Anglo core culture as well as many identifiable unique cultural groups that vary in their degree of identification with Anglo culture. The argument is then made that the more distinct and homogeneous the ethnic group, the greater the difference in the life experiences of children from this group vs. the Anglo group, and so the ethnic child needs to be assessed with norms that are "appropriate," that is, reflective of the child's sociocultural group (Figueroa, 1979). The assessment devices that make up the SOMPA were selected on the basis of the social and educational philosophy held by the author. As Humphreys (1985) indicates, the assumptions that underlie this rationale reflect values rather than psychometric principles.

The SOMPA was designed to assess the cognitive abilities, perceptual-motor skills, and adaptive behaviors of children from aged 5 to 11, with a particular emphasis in identifying deficits such as mental retardation. The standardization group consisted of 2,100 California children, aged 5 through 11, representing black, Anglo, and Hispanic children. In part, the intent of the SOMPA was to separate the effects of physical and sociocultural aspects and to assess cognitive potential by taking into account such circumstances. The SOMPA was greeted with much anticipation, perhaps too much, but the criticisms of this battery and its approach have been many, and they indicate that its usefulness is quite limited (cf. F. Brown, 1979; Humphreys, 1985; C. R. Reynolds, 1985; Sandoval, 1985).

If we accept the notion that a significant mean difference between ethnic groups on a test is reflective of test bias, then there are a number of options. Of course, one is to label tests as racist and not to use them. Another is to equate test performance. Such equating can be done in a variety of ways, from assigning extra points to the scores of minority members to the use of separate norms. The SOMPA system in fact provides a corrected estimate of intellectual abilities labeled as the *estimated learning potential* by providing separate norms based on ethnicity (black, Hispanic, and white) and various cultural characteristics such as family structure.

The SOMPA has been criticized on a number of grounds ranging from specific psychometric issues such as an inadequate standardization sample, low test-retest correlations of some of the components, and lack of validity data, to issues having to do with the assumptions underlying the approach, such as the concept of "innate ability" (that lurking within each of us is a "true IQ" whose expression is hampered by poverty, ethnic membership, parental example, and so on). The Hispanic group that was part of the normative sample was 95% Mexican-American children; in other parts of the United States, Hispanic may refer to Puerto-Rican, Cuban, or of South American descent. The data obtained on the "medical" scales is not normally distributed, but the scoring procedures assume such normality (F. Brown, 1979). Information on many of the psychometric aspects, such as the reliability of the sociocultural scales, is lacking. There are also practical problems – the battery of tests is extensive and may require more time and knowledge than the typical school psychologist may have. Many of the SOMPA scales use a transformation of raw scores to a mean of 50 and a SD of 15, rather than the more usual T scores or IQ scores. C. R. Reynolds (1985) concludes that the SOMPA was an innovative effort, but that its conceptual, technical, and practical problems are too great. (For a sober review of the SOMPA see F. Brown, 1979; for a review by several authors and a rebuttal of their criticisms see the Winter 1979 issue of the *School Psychology Digest*.)

Culture-Specific Tests

One reaction to the difficult issues of culture-fair tests has been to develop tests that are culture-specific. Perhaps the best known example is that of the Black Intelligence Test of Cultural Homogeneity, abbreviated as BITCH-100 (R. L. Williams, 1975). This test is composed of 100 multiple-choice items that assess knowledge about black culture and "street wiseness." The test was actually standardized on black high-school students. In one of the few studies designed to assess the validity of the BITCH-100, the test and the WAIS were administered to 116 white and 17 black applicants to a police department (Matarazzo & Wiens, 1977). As expected, the black applicants performed better on the BITCH-100 and less well on the WAIS than the white applicants. Scores on the two tests did not correlate, and the mean BITCH-100 score for the black applicants fell below the average of the standardization sample of high-school students, despite the fact that these police applicants were better educated and more intelligent as a group than the standardization sample. It would seem that the BITCH-100 is not a valid measure of intelligence, even within the black population, and may not even be a valid measure of street wiseness or knowledge of black slang (A. R. Jensen, 1980). In general, such culture-specific tests do yield higher mean scores for members of that minority, but they have little if any predictive validity. From the viewpoint of understanding they can yield useful, if restricted, information. From the viewpoint of prediction, for example of scholastic attainment, they are typically not valid.

The TEMAS

An example of a more useful test is TEMAS (the initials of tell-me-a-story) and meaning "themes" in Spanish; (Costantino, Malgady, & Rogler, 1988; Costantino, Malgady, Rogler, & Tsui, 1988; Malgady, Costantino, & Rogler, 1984). The TEMAS is a projective technique based on the Thematic Apperception Test (see Chapter 15) and is composed of 23 chromatic pictures that depict black and Hispanic characters in interpersonal situations where there is some psychological conflict. The pictures were chosen to elicit themes such as aggression, sexual identity, and moral judgement. There is also a nonminority version of the TEMAS with white characters (R. Flanagan & DiGiuseppe, 1999).

STANDARDIZED TESTS

We should not lose sight of the fact that there is a rather substantial body of literature that supports the utility of standard tests such as the Stanford-Binet and the WISC-R with minority students. A typical example is the study by D. L. Johnson and McGowan (1984) who evaluated the school performance of low-income Mexican-American children. These children were tested with the Stanford-Binet at age 3, with the Stanford-Binet and the McCarthy Scales of Children's Abilities at age 4, and with the WISC-R at age 7 to 9. These tests were administered by bilingual examiners using back-translation Spanish versions. Scores on these tests were then compared with measures of school performance in first or second grade; these measures included school grades and scores on the Iowa Tests of Basic Skills. Scores on the Stanford-Binet at age 3 correlated significantly with both grades (correlation coefficients ranging from .27 to .34) and Iowa Tests results (correlation coefficients ranging from .23 to .34). The Stanford-Binet given at age 4 showed a somewhat similar pattern. Neither the McCarthy Scales nor the WISC-R correlated significantly with school grades, but did correlate significantly with the Iowa measures of reading and of mathematics, and less so with the Iowa language measure. In general, there is a modest relationship between assessment of general intellectual functioning and evidences of that functioning in specific areas in school, regardless of the child's ethnic background. Keep in mind that school grades, especially at the lower grades, reflect much more than simply cognitive functioning. (For a review of selected studies on the WISC-R, see A. S. Kaufman, 1979a.)

College Entrance Tests

Much of the discussion so far has centered on assessment instruments used with children. What about adolescents, specifically those high-school seniors who take the Scholastic Aptitude Test (see Chapter 13) as part of the application procedure for college? Most studies of Mexican-American or Puerto Rican students (e.g., Astin, 1982; R. D. Goldman & Hewitt, 1976; Pennock-Roman, 1990) have shown that there is a difference of about 80 points on the

SAT between minority and non-Hispanic whites (recall that the SAT scores are on a measurement scale where 500 is the mean, and 100 is the SD); even when social, academic, or other variables are held constant, a smaller discrepancy continues to exist. Yet most of the evidence also suggests that the SAT has equal predictive validity for both groups and is, therefore, not biased (e.g., Duran, 1983; Pennock-Roman, 1990). The lower scores are assumed to reflect the more limited English verbal skills and the poorer academic status of Hispanics (Pearson, 1993).

At the same time, a convincing argument can be made against the use of the SAT. Pearson (1993) studied Hispanic and non-Hispanic white students attending the University of Miami, a private, medium-sized university. These Hispanic students, most of whom came from middle- and upper-middle professional families, were primarily U.S. born and of Cuban ancestry. Academically, they did as well as their non-Hispanic white peers. Despite equivalent college grades, the SAT means for the Hispanic sample were 42 points lower on the verbal portion, and 49 points lower on the math portion. Thus poorer test performance is not related to poorer academic performance, at least in this sample. Pearson (1993) postulated that the difference in SAT scores may be related to the information processing required when one knows two languages, or it may be related to working under a time limit. The data she presents suggest that the SAT contributes very little to the prediction of college GPA, compared to high-school grades and biographical material – a conclusion supported by other studies (e.g., Crouse, 1985; R. D. Goldman & Widawski, 1976) (see Chapter 13).

Another illustrative example is a study by McCormack (1983) who examined two successive entering classes at a large urban state university, each class totaling more than 2,400 students. First-semester GPA was predicted from high-school GPA and from a SAT composite of verbal + mathematics divided by 100. The following regression equation was developed on white students in one class:

$$\text{Predicted GPA} = \text{high-school GPA } (.73555)$$
$$+ \text{ SAT composite } (.08050)$$
$$- .67447$$

Table 11–1. Comparison of Predicted GPA Using Regression Equation vs. Actual GPA (McCormack, 1983)

Group	First cohort	Second cohort
White	.38	.42
Asian	.57	.54
Hispanic	.35	.52
Black	.36	.40
American-Indian	.40	.42

Note that the high-school GPA has a greater weight (.73) than the SAT composite (.08), and the last number is merely a constant needed for the numbers to come out on the GPA scale of 4 to 0.

An analysis of the actual data showed that white students obtained higher SAT scores and higher mean GPA than Hispanics, blacks, and Asian students, although the differences were quite small, and only the differences with the black students were statistically significant. Using the regression equation, the author found correlations of predicted GPA with actual GPA as indicated in Table 11.1. These results indicate that the majority equation overpredicted (by a very small amount) the GPA of black, Hispanic, and Asian students in both cohorts, but that the predictive accuracy of the equation was moderately low in all groups, both majority and minority. The use of first-semester GPA as the criterion severely limits this study. First-semester college GPA is relatively unstable and may reflect to a greater degree than any other semester problems of adjustment to a relatively novel environment; a much better criterion would have been the four-year cumulative GPA.

The Graduate Record Examination (GRE)

Similar concerns can be expressed about the GRE (see Chapter 13), which has been used in graduate-school admission decisions for many years, despite substantial criticisms and low correlations between GRE scores and graduate-school performance. In 1988, the Educational Testing Service, the company that publishes the GRE, reviewed 492 validity studies that had been done on the GRE between 1983 and 1988. Correlations between GRE scores and graduate grades ranged from .15 to .31 (Staff, 1988).

Whitworth and Barrientos (1990) studied 952 students admitted over a 5-year period to graduate studies at the University of Texas at El Paso; these included 320 Hispanics and 632 Anglos. Anglos scored significantly higher than Hispanics on undergraduate and graduate GPA as well as on the three scores that the GRE yields – verbal, quantitative, and analytic. An analysis (using multiple regression) to predict graduate grades indicated a correlation of .19 for Hispanic students and .27 for Anglos; these correlations were based on both undergraduate GPA and all three GRE scores. In fact, most of the correlation was due to undergraduate grades, and GRE scores did not predict graduate grades in either group. The authors listed several limitations of their study including restriction of range in the variables studied and graduate grade inflation because usually only grades of A or B are assigned, but nevertheless concluded that the GRE appeared to discriminate against Hispanics when compared to Anglos.

The MMPI with Minorities

A number of studies, especially in the 1960s and 1970s, raised questions about the use of the MMPI as a diagnostic tool with minorities, especially with blacks. Many of these studies found that blacks responded differently than Anglos to many MMPI items and that norms based upon primarily white groups were misleading (e.g., Baughman & Dahlstrom, 1972; Gynther, 1972; Gynther, Fowler, & Erdberg, 1971; D. Miller, Wertz, & Counts, 1961). Reviews of MMPI studies (e.g., Dahlstrom, Lachar, & Dahlstrom, 1986; Pritchard & Rosenblatt, 1980) reported that significant differences on MMPI profiles between blacks and whites were found, that usually these involved blacks scoring higher than whites on scales F (deviant response), 8 (schizophrenia), and 9 (hypomania), that these differences tended to be of 1- or 2-raw points magnitude, and when groups were equated for such variables as education, socioeconomic status, and age, the differences often disappeared. However, other researchers either found no significant racial differences (e.g., J. Flanagan & Lewis, 1969; Stanton,

1956) or concluded that the obtained differences were a function of differences in socioeconomic status and/or education (e.g., W. E. Davis, 1975; W. E. Davis, Beck, & Ryan, 1973). Fewer studies have been done on other minorities such as Hispanics, but the issues and the findings seem to be the same (e.g., McGill, 1980; Plemons, 1977; Reilly & Knight, 1970). Despite the substantial popularity of the MMPI and the importance of possible test bias, there is little evidence to interpret the racial differences that have been obtained. What data there is suggests that these differences are related to differences in personality and/or behavior rather than test bias (J. R. Graham, 1987).

SUMMARY

The issue of testing in a cross-cultural context is a difficult one. Unfortunately it cannot be divorced from the political, economic, and social consequences of decisions that need to be made. If there is one message, it is that those who consider tests to be totally useless are as misguided as are those who consider tests to be totally valid. With appropriate cautions and careful application based on the canons of acceptable reliability and validity, tests can be useful but limited tools.

SUGGESTED READINGS

Bracken, B. A., & Fouad, N. (1987). Spanish translation and validation of the Bracken Basic Concept Scale. *School Psychology Review, 16*, 94–102.

An interesting article that illustrates several steps that can be taken to assure that a test that is translated from a source to a target language remains equivalent across cultures.

Holtzman, W. H. (1968). Cross-cultural studies in psychology. *International Journal of Psychology, 3*, 83–91.

Although somewhat simplistic in approach, this is a very readable article that illustrates some of the challenges and stumbling blocks of doing cross-cultural research.

Huebner, E. S., & Dew, T. (1993). An evaluation of racial bias in a Life Satisfaction Scale. *Psychology in the Schools, 30*, 305–309.

A typical study that looks at the possible presence of racial bias in a scale that measures overall satisfaction with life. The findings of no bias when this scale is used with black adolescents are also quite typical.

Lam, T. C. M. (1993). Testability: A critical issue in testing language-minority students with standardized achievement tests. *Measurement and Evaluation in Counseling and Development, 26*, 179–191.

The concept of testability refers to the degree to which a test is appropriate and valid for a particular subgroup, in this case individuals who have limited English proficiency. An interesting and well-written article that discusses testing issues relevant to language-minority students.

Schwarz, P. A. (1963). Adapting tests to the cultural setting. *Educational and Psychological Measurement, 23*, 673–686.

Although this report is rather old, it still offers interesting insights into the challenges faced by an investigator who wishes to use tests in a different cultural context – in this case, Africa.

DISCUSSION QUESTIONS

1. Why do you think minority children do less well on tests of cognitive abilities than majority children?

2. If all tests such as intelligence tests, college entrance exams, etc., were eliminated, what might be some of the consequences?

3. Could you explain slope bias and intercept bias to someone who has not studied statistics?

4. What do you think of racial norming?

5. Imagine that you have decided to move to Mexico (or some other country that you might be familiar with). What would be involved in your becoming "acculturated"?

12 Disability and Rehabilitation

AIM This chapter looks at testing in the context of disability and rehabilitation. Although we talk about the entire life span, the focus is on adults, as opposed to Chapter 9 where the focus was explicitly on children. We look at three major categories of disability: visual impairment, hearing impairment, and physical impairment. For each category, we look at some of the basic principles and some specific examples as illustrations of these principles.

SOME GENERAL CONCERNS

Who are the disabled? The International Center for the Disabled undertook three national surveys between 1986 and 1989 to obtain some fundamental information. They reported that in the United States there are some 27 million individuals, aged 16 and older, who are disabled. Approximately 66% are not working, but two thirds of these say they would like a job. Among the major barriers to employment were lack of marketable skills, lack of accessible or affordable transportation, and feelings that employers do not recognize the fact that they are capable of doing full-time jobs. As a matter of fact, a subsequent survey of employers and managers indicated that disabled employees typically received good or excellent job ratings.

Categories of disability. The four major categories of disabilities – vision impairment, hearing impairment, physical or motor disabilities, and learning disabilities – account for the majority of occasions where the application of standard tests presents a challenge, both from a psychometric and a clinical perspective. We take a look at the first three of these categories. With regard to the fourth, the term *learning disabilities* refers to a variety of neurological problems that affect

how a person organizes sensory information; as a result, test performance is affected. Others define learning disability more in the context of difficulties in the basic processes involved in the use of spoken or written language. The diagnosis however, is often made on the basis of self-reported or observed behaviors (e.g., not doing well on classroom tests when all else points to average or above-average capabilities), rather than neurological findings. Learning disabilities may manifest themselves in a wide variety of problems and may relate to listening, thinking, speaking, reading, writing, spelling, or doing mathematical calculations. Because this topic is complex in terms of etiology and other aspects and, at present, the source of much controversy, we do not consider it here (see Feldman, 1990; Gaddes, 1994; Rourke & Fuerst, 1991; or Westman, 1990, for some current views).

Vocational evaluation. In rehabilitation settings, the focus is often on helping the client be a productive and contributing member of the community, i.e., helping her or him obtain employment commensurate with his or her abilities and needs. A basic assumption of our culture is that everyone is entitled to the most productive life of which they are capable. Such goals are often achieved by vocational evaluation, which may involve psychological tests or other procedures such as *work samples,* where the client is evaluated using a simulated work activity or by actual on-the-job evaluation. A number of experts in this area feel that testing is quite limited. Clearly, a variety of approaches need to be used, and the criterion of validity is paramount. Tests can provide relatively objective, reliable, and valid indices and, compared to other approaches such as on-the-job evaluation, are less expensive and time consuming. Tests are typically more comprehensive and can provide more varied assessment data. At the same time, there are a number of legitimate constraints and criticisms that can be made of tests, as we will see.

Vocational placement. Vocational placement is not simply a matter of placing the "proper peg in its round hole"; the matter is complicated, given the complexities of the labor market, the technological advances that have revolutionized many jobs, and the nature of the disabilities a client may have. In addition, there are a number of psychological aspects to consider. For example, adults who have disabilities have often been sheltered and overprotected by their families and may have had little exposure to the world of work. The specific use of vocational or career interest tests may be of differential utility in young clients with a history of disability vs. older clients who, because of some accident, can no longer pursue their former occupation (A. B. Meyer, Fouad, & Klein, 1987).

Challenge of testing the handicapped. Individuals with disabilities present a number of challenges with regard to tests. Because such disabilities can involve a wide range of conditions, such as mental retardation, visual impairments, chronic health problems, and so on, the challenges are numerous and varied. For example, typical paper-and-pencil inventories require a fair degree of hand and finger dexterity, so often clients cannot complete these without assistance. Often, disabilities can result in poor self-esteem, a high degree of frustration, depression, denial, poor adjustment, and other psychological aspects that may interfere with and/or color the results of a psychological test. Simeonsson, Huntington, and Parse (1980) stated that, "it is an unfortunate

irony that valid assessment is extremely difficult to achieve with children for whom it is essential" (p. 51). These authors indicate that with disabled children there are four major goals of testing: (1) to predict future status, (2) to prescribe an appropriate treatment, (3) to assess progress and/or program evaluation, and (4) to develop a comprehensive data base across time and/or across children. It is interesting to note that although studies of normal children find relatively poor predictability from infancy to later periods, studies of disabled children find substantial stability – typically 70% to 90% of the children tested retain their diagnostic classification upon later testing (e.g., DuBose, 1976; Vandeveer & Schweid, 1974).

A. B. Meyer, Fouad, and Klein (1987) point out that in addition to the usual concerns about reliability and validity, there are three aspects of importance in the use of tests with rehabilitation clients:

1. The readability level of the instrument is especially important because such clients may have limited educational skills, often as a result of the very disability.
2. The test should be appropriate for the client; this applies particularly to time limits and to performance aspects that may not be suitable for the particular client.
3. The test should have a validity scale that indicates whether the client is responding randomly or not and consistently (tests such as the MMPI and CPI have such scales as part of the inventory).

Wide range of impairment. Even within one category of disability, there may be a wide range of impairment. For example, individuals who are motorically impaired and are in a wheelchair, may have no upper body limitations, mild limitations, or moderate to severe limitations. In a testing situation, the degree of limitation would dictate whether the individual can respond on a standard answer sheet, requires additional breaks, or uses special equipment. Thus, testing of rehabilitation clients requires a thorough knowledge and awareness of that client's particular abilities and disabilities and a sensitivity to individual differences.

Common sense guide. Often, testing of the disabled requires a great deal of common sense, which frequently seems to be a precious commodity. The U.S. Office of Personnel Management has put together a guide for administering employment tests to handicapped individuals (S. M. Heaton, Nelson, and Nester, 1980). If the client is blind, for example, the examiner should speak directly to the person, should not avoid phrases such as, "it's nice to see you," should not pet or distract the guide dog, and should let the blind person take their arm. With a deaf client, it is important to determine the best means of communication. The examiner should speak clearly and distinctly in a normal speed and tone, but with expression because facial expressions, gestures, and body movements can help clarify the meaning of what is said. If the client is in a wheelchair, the examiner should not hold on to the wheelchair. If possible, the examiner should also be seated because it is uncomfortable for a seated person to look straight up for a long period.

A multivariate approach. There is a strong suggestion in the literature that a multivariate approach is best in the testing of disabled individuals. One aspect of such an approach is to use instruments that yield subscale scores (such as the MMPI, the WAIS, etc.). Another approach is to use a battery of instruments, so that hypotheses generated by one test result can be corroborated in other test results. Finally, we should not lose sight of the fact that tests are but one source of information, and in assessment there is need for various sources of information (Simeonsson, Huntington, & Parse, 1980).

Diagnostic assessment. Hartlage (1987) describes four stages in the process of diagnostic assessment with rehabilitation clients. The first is to determine the relevant issue or question, that is, what are the goals of assessment for this particular client. Often, a battery of tests is administered routinely to all clients. Although such data may be quite useful for research purposes or may provide valuable local norms, the usefulness of such an approach for a particular client may be quite limited.

The second stage involves obtaining the necessary background data. This can involve medical records that can yield valuable information about a client's disabilities, or prior testing results that may dictate a different or more circumspect approach. For example, a client may already have been tested with a particular instrument, and retesting may be less valid or useful.

The third stage is the selection of appropriate instruments. Ordinarily, these include measures of intellectual functioning, assessment of hemispheric dominance, assessment of academic skills, assessment of special characteristics such as visual-motor coordination, career interests, personality, and aptitudes.

In the area of intellectual functioning, a wide number of tests can be useful, ranging from broad-based tests such as the Wechsler to more narrow and limited tests such as the D–48. The area of hemispheric dominance represents a newer concern. The research so far suggests that the two cerebral hemispheres control different abilities; language and sequential skills are controlled by the left hemisphere, and spatial and simultaneous thinking abilities are controlled by the right hemisphere. In a large number of adults, perhaps as many as 75%, there are anatomic asymmetries of the cerebral hemispheres that may be related to differential performance in a variety of areas (Geschwind and Levitsky, 1968). Evidence of hemispheric dominance can be obtained from a variety of sources, including tests such as the WAIS (verbal vs. performance scores) or neuropsychological test batteries such as the Halstead-Reitan (see Chapter 15). In rehabilitation clients, the cerebral dominance may be particularly important whether it occurred naturally or whether it was the result of injury, either at birth or subsequent to birth (as in a motorcycle accident). In the area of academic skills, such test information may already be part of the client's file, such as test scores from routine school testing. Sometimes such information when compared with more current test results can yield evidence of intellectual deterioration. A comparison of academic skills with intellectual functioning can also be quite informative from a diagnostic point of view.

The fourth stage involves placing the results into a specific rehabilitation plan. The information obtained from testing needs to be translated into decisions and actions for the benefit of the client.

MODIFIED TESTING

In testing clients with disabilities, the examiner often needs to modify the test and/or testing procedure, to be consonant with the client's capabilities and needs. Tests can be modified in a variety of ways, but most changes can be subsumed under one of three categories: changes in testing medium, changes in time limits, and changes in test content.

Testing medium. In most tests, test information is presented in the English language. Changes in testing medium therefore can refer to using braille, large print, audiotapes, or a reader or *amanuensis* (a person who writes or marks the answers for the test taker), and so on. Ordinarily these changes do not present any problems from a psychometric perspective, but there are some circumstances that need to be considered. For example, long reading passages may be more difficult when presented orally than in their printed version. Figural materials such as charts can also be a problem. A figure can be presented by embossing, but the tactual sense required to understand the embossed figure is quite different from the visual sense needed to understand the original. Thus the "same" item may be measuring quite different functions in a sighted person than in a visually impaired person.

Time limits. We saw the distinction between power and speed tests in Chapter 1. Changing time limits especially with speed tests creates problems psychometrically. Many tests that are power tests are actually "speeded power" tests, in that a considerable number of people are unable to attempt every question. Having additional time, as might be done with a disabled subject, gives an "unfair" advantage, but typically people with disabilities do need additional time. Nester (1993) suggests that the ideal solution is to eliminate the use of speeded power tests.

Test content. Changes in test content might include changes in individual test questions, changes in the question type being used, or changes in one of the variables being measured (for example, by dropping a subtest). From a construct validity point of view, changes in a specific test question are acceptable because presumably the underlying construct is still being measured. Changes in question type or in the variables being measured are much more problematic, and most experts would agree that evidence would be needed to show that such changes did not alter the reliability and validity of the test.

Item content. For some tests, the meaning of a particular item may in fact be a different stimulus for the disabled. The MMPI (see Chapter 7) provides a good illustration of how the presence of a disability or physical illness can affect the meaning of test scores. The MMPI contains a number of items that relate to physical complaints and physical health, items such as, "I frequently suffer from constipation," and "My health is not as good as it use to be." With individuals who do not have major disabilities, endorsement of such items may be indicative of psychological difficulties, such as preoccupation with his or her body or the presence of physical symptoms that reflect psychological conflicts and inadequate adjustment. With individuals who do have disabilities, such endorsement may well reflect the physical reality rather than any psychopathology.

Small samples. Much work has gone into modifying tests and testing procedures for use with disabled individuals. At the same time, there have been fewer efforts to determine the effects of such modifications on the reliability and validity of specific tests. In part, a major reason offered for the paucity of such studies is the availability of only small, atypical samples, while psychometric procedures to assess reliability and validity typically require large and representative samples.

A Panel on Testing of Handicapped People, formed because of the Rehabilitation Act of 1973, examined various issues concerning the use of standardized tests in making decisions about people with disabilities and made a number of specific suggestions (Sherman & Robinson, 1982). With regard to the validity of tests, the Panel urged that validity information on disabled samples was urgently needed. In particular, information on the effects of modifying tests and test administration procedures on reliability, validity, and other aspects of test performance, was needed. Furthermore, the Panel suggested that techniques to validate tests with small samples needed to be developed and used. Other possibilities, such as pooling of data from several samples, needed to be explored. With regard to the testing situation, the Panel pointed out that little was known about the relationship of aspects of the disabled person and the testing situation as reflected in such questions as: Why do some disabled persons take the standard form of a test, such as the SAT, rather than the modified version? Are there other approaches besides paper-and-pencil tests? How does the attitude of the examiner affect the test scores of the disabled person? How do coaching and training in test-taking strategies affect the performance of disabled persons? Finally, with regard to the actual decision-making process, how are test scores actually used in making decisions about disabled individuals, and how do "flagged" (i.e., the results of a nonstandard test administration identified as such) test scores influence the decision-making process? The Panel also concluded that tests can provide good objective measures of merit and provide the opportunity to show that a person has the required abilities. At the same time, members of the Panel felt that psychometric technology simply was not advanced enough to ensure that tests could measure skills independent of disabling conditions, and they recommended that multiple sources of information to supplement test scores should be used.

Note that when we ask how changes in a test affect that tests's reliability and validity, the implication is that the potential result is to lower the reliability and validity. Quite legitimately, we can ask what happens if we administer a test with no modification to a disabled individual. In many cases, the test would be invalid.

ETS studies. The major source of information about the reliability and validity of modified testing was compiled by researchers at Educational Testing Service (ETS). From 1982 to 1986, ETS conducted a series of studies on the performance of individuals with disabilities on the SAT and the GRE. Four types of disabilities were considered: visual impairment, hearing impairment, physical impairment, and learning disabilities. The results of these studies were described in a comprehensive report (Willingham, Ragosta, Bennett, et al., 1988). These researchers assessed the comparability of standard and nonstandard (i.e.,

modified) test administrations using a variety of indices including test reliability, factor structure, how test items functioned, admissions decisions, and so on. Although there were a number of specific findings, the general conclusion was that the nonstandard versions of the SAT and the GRE were generally comparable to the standardized versions in most important aspects. What these studies do show is that carefully thought-out test accommodations can be successful in preserving the reliability and validity of tests (Nester, 1993).

SOME GENERAL RESULTS

Basic issues. In testing disabled clients, there are a number of basic issues to keep in mind. Tests that are administered individually, such as the WAIS, allow the examiner to observe the client and gather clinically relevant information. Group-administered tests, although more economical and usually easier to administer, do not usually provide such information. Sometimes, tests that were originally developed for group administration are given on an individual basis, especially by computer (see Chapter 17).

Speed of performance is sometimes an integral part of a test. For example, in the assessment of intelligence, some tests use items that have a time limit. Handicapped clients often do less well on timed tests, and their disability may interfere with rapidity of response. The crucial question here is whether the person's ability is underestimated by a speeded test.

Finally, we must note that the frequency of some disabilities seems to be greater among minority and/or disadvantaged groups. So here we have the questions of potential test bias and of appropriate norms.

Test sources. In general, not much is available to the tester who needs to assess disabled clients. Many textbooks do not mention such a topic, and appropriate journal articles are scarce and scattered throughout the literature. One useful source is the book by Bolton (1990), which covers a collection of 95 instruments for use with disabled clients.

Career assessment. Individuals who are disabled often have great difficulties in obtaining employment. Although some of these difficulties are due to prejudice, stereotypes, or realistic demands of a specific occupation, some of the difficulties are due to the nature of the disability and its concomitant conditions (e.g., lower self-esteem). Vocational guidance then becomes very important, and the use of career-interest tests potentially useful. The results of career-interest tests can: (1) provide a focus for vocational evaluation and planning; (2) yield information that the client can use to achieve career goals; (3) identify occupations and interest areas that the client might not have considered; (4) provide both the counselor and the client with useful information about the client's orientation toward work and level of vocational maturity; and (5) provide valuable information as to the selection of a college major or appropriate educational pathway, such as technical institute, community college, or apprenticeship (L. K. Elksnin & N. Elksnin, 1993).

In Chapter 6, we discussed the two major career-interest inventories – the Strong Interest Inventory and the Kuder inventories. These can be very useful with some disabled clients, but also have limited utility with other disabled clients; they require not only the ability to read, but to read at a fairly sophisticated level, with instructions typically requiring high-school or college-level reading comprehension.

A number of career-interest inventories have been developed that eliminate reading by using drawings that typically show individuals engaged in different occupations. Typical of these *picture-interest inventories* is the Geist Picture Interest Inventory-Revised (GPII-R; Geist, 1988). The GPII-R is designed to assess 11 masculine and 12 feminine general-interest areas of individuals who have limited reading/verbal skills. These areas include mechanical, music, outdoors, social service, and personal service (such as beautician). The GPII-R is composed of 44 picture triads in which each drawing depicts a person engaged in work activities that reflect a particular interest area. For each triad, the client is asked to indicate which activity he or she is most interested in doing. The GPII-R is suitable for normal children in grades 8 to 12 and with adults who have limited verbal skills. It is untimed, requires hand scoring, and can be administered to both individuals or groups. The inventory requires that the client circle the drawing of choice, but presumably this

can be done by the examiner if necessary, without altering the test.

Test-retest reliability over a 6-month period seems adequate to marginal, with most coefficients falling below .80; predictive validity information is not given.

The GPII-R has been criticized that its black-and-white line drawings appear dated, that some are ambiguous, and that many occupations covered reflect gender stereotypes. Some other picture interest inventories are the Wide-Range Interest-Opinion Test (J. F. Jastak & S. Jastak, 1979), the Pictorial Inventory of Careers (Kosuth, 1984–1985), and the Reading-Free Vocational Interest Inventory-Revised (R. L. Becker, 1988). Many of these picture inventories have inadequate standardization and/or normative samples; some samples are quite small, others are atypical, and still others are not described adequately in terms of demographic variables. Sometimes, current norms are not available. Thus, the examiner is often left without the necessary information needed to make an informed decision about the meaning of the client's scores. In general, many if not most of these instruments are technically inadequate, and their results should be confirmed through other sources of information (L. K. Elksnin & N. Elksnin, 1993).

A more basic issue has to do with the developmental aspects of career interests. In normal subjects, career interests begin to stabilize around ages 17 to 18, and testing of younger subjects to elicit their career interests yields limited and unstable data. Clients who have developmental disabilities, for example, those born blind, may also experience delays in the development and stability of their career interests, or may be deprived of the kind of experiences such as after-school work that crystallize into career interests. Such delays and deprivations may make career-interest test results invalid. In addition, the most technically competent career-interest tests are geared for professions or occupations that require a fair amount of education. Often, clients in rehabilitation settings may be more realistically oriented towards lower-level occupations, and tests available for these are not as psychometrically sophisticated.

Admissions testing. Most colleges, graduate-school programs, medical and law schools, and other professional programs require some test such as the SAT (Scholastic Aptitude Test), GRE (Graduate Record Exam), or MCAT (Medical College Admission Test) as part of the admissions procedure. A number of disabled applicants take these tests each year, and most of these tests have special provisions for such applicants. How well do such test scores predict the performance of disabled students? There is relatively little data available, but Sherman and Robinson (1982) give some representative examples. In one study of disabled students (type of disability not specified), both their high-school and college grades were somewhat lower than for nondisabled students (e.g., 0.17 grade point lower for first year of college). The correlation between the college entrance exam (ACT in this case) and college freshman grades was .46, while the correlation between high-school grades and college-freshman grades was .43. For nondisabled students, the correlations were quite similar, except that for nondisabled students high-school grades were a slightly, better predictor of college grades than were test scores. Some studies have indicated that tests such as the SAT are as good a predictor of college grades for both disabled and nondisabled students, while other studies suggest that measures specifically designed for a disabled population are better predictors.

World of work. Licensing or certification procedures that include a test are required for many occupations. In addition, civil-service systems rely heavily on screening through testing. Thus, disabled individuals may encounter such tests, especially in rehabilitation agencies that assist them with training and obtaining employment.

Employment testing has been under close scrutiny since the mid 1960s when it was observed that the use of such tests tended to screen out minority-group members. Such close scrutiny had three major consequences: (1) The importance of tests in the total hiring process was overestimated. It is rare that decisions to hire are primarily driven by test results, and test results are typically seen as just one of many sources of information. (2) Much effort has been invested in employment testing, including litigation of results. (3) Use of tests in the world of work has declined, in large part because of confusion about legal and federal guidelines and, in part, because of fear of legal suits.

Aptitude and achievement tests. Rehabilitation personnel who do counseling rely heavily on both aptitude and achievement tests, which happen to be categories of tests that have achieved excellent technical levels and high degrees of reliability and validity.

Originally, aptitudes were seen as basically innate, while achievement reflected knowledge and skills that were learned. Recently however, the distinction between the two has become somewhat blurred, and the notion of "innate" has been rejected. Most experts define aptitudes as the result of lifelong learning, while achievement refers to a specific learning experience. Thus, playing tennis would be considered an achievement, the result of specific training, while the ability to play sports in general would be more of an aptitude, or the result of many influences that could encompass physique, parental expectations, upbringing, role models, and so on.

The reliability of such tests is typically high with median reliability coefficients of achievement test batteries in the low .90s and of aptitude batteries in the high .80s.

Ghiselli (1966) reviewed the professional literature to assess the general level of validity of occupational aptitude tests. He classified the aptitude tests used in personnel selection and placement into five major types: (1) tests of intellectual abilities, measuring such aspects as memory and arithmetic computation; (2) tests of spatial and mechanical abilities; such tests are of limited use with visually handicapped clients beacause they require a fair degree of vision; (3) tests of perceptual accuracy; these usually involve sets of items where the subject needs to decide if they are the same or different, or items where the client is required to cancel out something, for example the letter "e" in a paragraph of prose. Some of these procedures can be administered through braille; (4) tests of motor abilities, for example, tests that require manual dexterity where blocks and cylinders are moved as rapidly as possible into different configurations; (5) personality tests, including both paper-and-pencil inventories like the MMPI and CPI, and projective tests such as the Rorschach and Thematic Apperception Test. Some of these are useful even with visually handicapped clients; for example, E. L. Wilson (1980) reports on the use of the TAT with totally blind clients, where the stimulus picture is described to the client.

The findings of Ghiselli's review are rather complex, but we can summarize some of the major conclusions. Training, as reflected by criteria such as grades in occupational-training courses, was predicted well by tests of intellectual abilities, spatial and mechanical abilities, and perceptual accuracy. Proficiency, as reflected by criteria such as supervisors' ratings or measures of dollar volume of sales, was less successfully predicted, with most correlation coefficients in the .20s, except for sales and service occupations where personality tests seemed substantially more valid predictors. Overall, Ghiselli concluded that tests possessed sufficient predictive power to be of considerable value in personnel selection. Recent studies using metaanalysis do suggest that tests of cognitive abilities correlate from the low .30s to the mid .70s for predicting training success, and from the .30s to the low .60s for predicting job proficiency (J. E. Hunter & R. F. Hunter, 1984). These results come from studies of "normal" subjects, but presumably would generalize to studies of rehabilitation clients.

LEGAL ISSUES

Full participation. In the United States, many of the important decisions made about an individual such as placement in particular educational programs, admission to college and professional schools, military assignment, and so on, are made in part upon the basis of test results. One can argue that such use of tests is suspect and negative, and that tests ought to be banned. It can also be argued that denying a person the opportunity to take a test and to show in an objective and standardized manner what the person can do, is an infringement of that person's civil rights (Sherman & Robinson, 1982).

Full participation in American society has become a major goal of the disabled, one that has been supported through a variety of federal legislative acts. Thus, children with special-educational needs are no longer segregated, but where possible are "mainstreamed" in the regular classroom, and such decisions are made in part on the basis of test results.

From a legal standpoint, it is assumed that disabled people can be tested in a way that will not reflect the effects of their disability, and that the obtained scores will be comparable with those of people who are not physically challenged. Whether in fact such assumptions can be met psychometrically, is debatable.

Minimum competency testing. There has been widespread concern in the United States that graduating high-school seniors have not received an adequate education. One response on the part of many states is to mandate some form of minimum competency testing. That is, before a student is promoted or awarded a diploma, he or she must show minimum competencies as assessed by a battery of achievement tests. Such programs have become major political issues in some communities, especially because such tests often show differential racial performance. Another issue has to do with disabled students. Should they be exempted from such tests? Should they be allowed extended time, the use of readers, or other nonstandard procedures? Should different tests be used that are tailored to the needs of the student? Such issues are not easy to resolve because they transcend psychometric issues (Haney & Madaus, 1978; Sherman & Robinson, 1982).

Which norms? The issue of nondiscrimination against persons with disabilities is relatively new in the area of psychometrics, and very little research has been devoted to it. In the past, most assessment efforts were devoted to placement in settings where the disabled individual would not compete with "normal" persons, and therefore the question of norms was not an important one. Typically, available test norms are for "normal" groups, perhaps a captive group working in a specific industry, such as 62 assembly-line workers at a General Motors plant in Michigan. Such norms may well represent a group that has already been screened, where incompetent workers were not hired, and the group has survived a probationary period; it most likely contains few, if any individuals, with disabilities. Sometimes published norms are available for particular subgroups of disabled clients, perhaps tested at a rehabilitation agency or at a training school. Sometimes the local agency where a client is tested develops its own in-house norms, and sometimes it does follow up clients to determine the relationship between test scores and subsequent on-the-job competence. In general, however, much remains to be done to provide practitioners with better, well-defined norms.

When we compare a client's raw score on a test with norms, we are in effect describing that client's level of performance relative to some comparison group. Thus, Rebecca takes the WAIS-R and her raw score is translated, through norms, into an IQ of 126. Ordinarily, however, we are not content in simply describing, but also wish to forecast future behavior. We might want to predict, for example, how well Rebecca will do in college. But such prediction needs to be made not just on the basis of descriptive data, i.e. norms, but on the basis of predictive evidence, such as expectancy tables or regression equations. For rehabilitation clients, such data is not readily available.

Governmental efforts. Two governmental agencies have been involved in the testing of the disabled and in efforts to solve various legal/psychometric problems. One agency is the U.S. Civil Service Commission (now known as the U.S. Office of Personnel Management, or OPM), and the other is the U.S. Department of Labor. The OPM develops tests used to select people for jobs in the federal government. Beginning in the 1950s, they developed tests to select blind applicants for industrial jobs, studied the validity of these tests simultaneously for blind and for sighted persons, and have continued various studies up to the present.

The U.S. Department of Labor has, among other activities, investigated the scoring patterns of deaf, emotionally disturbed, and mentally retarded persons on the *General Aptitude Test Battery* (*GATB*), an instrument used by state employment services for a wide range of jobs (Nester, 1993); in fact, the GATB is the most widely used test for state and local government hiring and private-sector job referral. The GATB consists of 12 tests that measure 9 aptitudes:

1. *General learning ability* (or intelligence), defined as the ability to understand instructions, to reason, and to make judgments.

2. *Verbal aptitude*, the ability to understand words, to use them effectively, to understand relationships between words, to present ideas clearly.

3. *Numerical aptitude*, the ability to perform arithmetic operations accurately and with rapidity.

4. *Spatial aptitude*, the ability to visualize objects in three dimensional space.

5. *Form perception*, the ability to perceive details and differences in different objects.

6. *Clerical perception*, the ability to proofread correctly, to perceive pertinent details.

7. *Motor coordination*, the ability to coordinate visual and motor movements, to make movements accurately and rapidly.

8. *Finger dexterity*, the ability to manipulate small objects rapidly and accurately.

9. *Manual dexterity*, the ability to work with one's hands easily and skillfully.

The first seven aptitudes use paper-and-pencil measures; the last two aptitudes are assessed through performance tests. The original edition of the GATB was published in 1947 (Dvorak, 1947) and was based on a factor-analytic approach – namely, there is a basic set of aptitudes, and different occupations require different combinations of such aptitudes. A battery of some 50 tests was thus factor analyzed; the resulting 9 aptitudes could then be measured by just using 12 of the 50 subtests. The chosen tests were selected on the basis of their factorial validity and their empirical validity against some external criterion (Droege, 1987). The 12 tests were then administered to a sample of workers in a wide variety of occupations. The data from this sample was used to develop tables to convert raw scores into standardized scores with a mean of 100 and SD of 20 (Mapou, 1955). Incidentally, the Labor Department routinely uses *race norming* on this test, that is, the percentile scores of whites, blacks, and Hispanics are computed within each racial group.

Administration of the entire battery requires about 2 hours and 15 minutes. One of the unique aspects of the GATB is that there are occupational-aptitude patterns that indicate the aptitude requirements for various occupations, so that a specific client's scores can be matched against specific patterns. There is a tremendous amount of technical material on the GATB, ranging from a very hefty test manual to government reports and studies in the scientific literature. For a description of other aspects of this program, see Droege (1987). Like other tests, the GATB is not free of criticism, and despite its wide use, it seems to have some significant weaknesses (see Keesling, 1985). We will return to this test in Chapter 14.

The "Standards." The *Standards for Educational and Psychological Testing* issued in 1985 (see Chapter 1) contain a chapter on testing people with disabilities. The chapter stresses that caution must be used in interpreting the results of modified tests because of lack of data; it encourages the development of tests for people who are disabled. These standards include the requirement that the examiner have psychometric expertise and knowledge about the interaction of handicap and test modification, that such modifications be pilot-tested, that empirical procedures be used to establish time limits, and that the effects of modifications on reliability and validity be investigated. In addition, general population norms or specific norms, i.e., disabled, be used depending on the purposes of testing. Other experts have, however, expressed the concern that the legal and regulatory requirements of the Americans with Disabilities Act of 1990 go beyond the state of the science of testing.

One of the basic principles of measurement, as we saw in Chapter 2, is that of standardization. The use of modified testing procedures departs from this principle and may affect measurement in an unknown way. Another issue of concern is whether test scores from nonstandard administrations of standardized tests, such as the SAT, should be "flagged" to indicate the non-standard administration. Federal regulations prohibit inquiry about a disability before employment or during admission procedures, but "flagging" in fact alerts the selection officials that the candidate has a disability.

Civil Rights Act of 1964 (PL 88–352). This well known legislative act made it illegal to discriminate among people on the basis of "race, color, religion, sex, or national origin." The Act addressed five major areas in which blacks had suffered unequal treatment: (1) political

participation; (2) access to public accommodations, such as restaurants; (3) access to publicly owned facilities, such as parks; (4) education; and (5) employment. Much of the language of the Act was prohibitory in nature (thou shalt not . . .), but there were a number of provisions (called titles) for implementing various sections of the Act. Title VII for example, enumerated unlawful employment practices and established the Equal Employment Opportunity Commission as a means of implementing its provisions. Most legal challenges to the use of standardized tests have fallen under this Title. In effect, Title VII indicates that if a test results in a proportionally lower selection rate for minorities and females than for white males, the procedure is considered discriminatory, unless the test can be validated in accord with specific guidelines called the technical validation requirements.

Rehabilitation Act of 1973. This act extended civil rights protection to people with disabilities and was a direct descendant of the Civil Rights Act. One section of the 1973 Act, Section 504, specifically indicates that a disabled individual shall not be subjected to discrimination. Unfortunately, this act was enacted without specific indications of how the law was to be implemented. Eventually, guidelines for ending discrimination in areas such as education and employment practices on the basis of disability were developed. For example, employers cannot use tests that tend to screen out disabled individuals unless: (1) it can be shown that the test is job-related, and (2) alternative tests that do not screen out disabled individuals are not available (see Sherman & Robinson, 1982, for a detailed discussion).

With regard to admission to postsecondary educational institutions (such as college), Section 504 guidelines eventually evolved to cover four psychometric aspects:

1. A test that has a disproportionate adverse effects on disabled applicants may not be used, unless the test has been validated specifically for the purpose in question, or unless alternative tests with less adverse effects do not exist.

2. Tests are selected and administered so that the results reflect the disabled applicant's capabilities on the variable being measured, rather than

the applicant's impaired skills (unless the test is measuring those skills).

3. An institution may not inquire before admission whether a person is disabled; that is, test scores for a disabled person should be reported in identical manner to those of nondisabled persons.

4. Prediction equations may be based on first-year college grades, but periodic validity studies against the criterion of overall success in the education program in question will be carried out.

These four provisions have generated a fair amount of psychometric research, although the overall picture is far from complete or comprehensive.

These governmental regulations then, require reasonable accommodation to the needs of disabled persons, including appropriate adjustment or modifications to tests. Furthermore, as stated above, these regulations prohibit the use of a selection criterion that tends to screen out disabled persons unless that criterion has been shown to be job-related, and there is no alternative procedure. Finally, these regulations state that tests should be selected and administered so that sensory and speaking disabilities do not interfere with effective measurement (Nester, 1984; 1993).

These issues become particularly crucial in a competitive employment situation where standardized assessment instruments are used to compare applicants and to select the most qualified. People who have physical disabilities will be at a disadvantage, if their disability interferes with the accurate measurement of their abilities. The bottom line is that tests must not discriminate and must reflect the intended construct rather than the disability.

Public Law 94–142. As we saw in Chapter 9, this law, the Education for All Handicapped Children Act, mandates that a full and individual evaluation of a child's educational needs be carried out before the child is assigned to a special-education program. However, the specifics of the evaluation are not spelled out, so that the number and nature of tests used can differ quite widely from one setting to another. The Act also mandates that tests and procedures used for the evaluation and placement of disabled children

be used in a nondiscriminatory manner. These tests must be administered in the client's "native language," which for hearing-impaired children is their "normal" mode of communication, i.e., sign language, oral communication, mime, finger spelling, or other method. The tests must also be selected and administered so that children with impaired skills are not penalized for their lack of language ability. This means, in effect, that the examiner must be not only an expert test administrator, but must also be expert in the method of communication.

THE VISUALLY IMPAIRED

Types of tests. Tests that are used with the visually impaired seem to fall into one of four categories: (1) tests that were developed for the general population of normally sighted individuals and are simply used with the visually impaired; (2) tests developed for the general population, but with specific norms for the visually impaired; (3) tests adapted for the visually impaired by the use of braille, large print, or other procedure; (4) tests developed specifically for the visually impaired.

Visual nature of testing. Many problems complicate the assessment of the visually impaired person. A major problem is that most tests involve sight because of the visual nature of the test items themselves, such as on the WAIS-R, or because of the way the measure is administered under standard conditions, as with the printed booklet of the MMPI. (There are braille versions of the MMPI, e.g., O. H. Cross, 1947.)

Visual impairment. There are many degrees of visual impairment; some individuals who are "legally" blind may have sufficient vision to read large print, with or without corrective lenses. Blindness can also be present from birth (the congenitally blind) or can occur any time after birth (the adventitiously blind).

Visual impairment in the elderly. For the individual with normal vision, there are two major causes of visual impairment as the person gets older. One of these is *cataracts*, a clouding of the lens of the eye and a condition that is now amenable to corrective surgery. The second is *macular* degeneration. The macula is the central region of the retina responsible for fine visual acuity; degeneration of the macula affects vision, and in particular, the ability to read.

Modified testing. Quite often, the test changes that are needed to assess a visually handicapped person involve changes in the administration method. For example, test items may need to be presented in large print, braille, or on an audio tape. Or a sighted reader may be required, one who reads and enunciates well. These procedures require more time than the standard method, and so usually speed tests are not appropriate for visually impaired persons. When there are time limits on power tests, these limits are usually for administrative convenience, so unlimited time could, at least theoretically, be given to all candidates, impaired or not.

There is also concern about the test content. In general, verbal tests such as the verbal portions of the Wechsler tests are appropriate for administration. Nonverbal items present a challenge. In fact, verbal cognitive tests seem to be valid predictors of work or academic success for the visually impaired. What limited evidence there is seems to support the criterion validity of such tests (e.g., Suinn, Dauterman, & Shapiro, 1967).

Some recommendations. In testing blind clients, it is recommended that the blind client be given whatever information a sighted client would have by nature of their sight (Cautilli & Bauman, 1987). Thus, the examiner should describe the test materials and, where appropriate, encourage the client to explore the materials by touch. If the test items are to be presented by braille, then the braille reading ability of the client needs to be determined. Having poor or no vision does not automatically guarantee proficiency in braille reading.

If the items are presented orally, dichotomous items, such as true-false, can be read orally by the examiner or a reader and the answers recorded for the client. Multiple-choice items represent more of a challenge because they require that the client keep in mind the various options. At the same time, if the answers are recorded by the examiner, there is less privacy for the blind client than there would be for a sighted client.

Need for special norms. Standard test norms, usually developed on sighted samples, can be used only with great caution because administration of a test to a blind client is often substantially different from that of a sighted client. Norms based on visually impaired are sometimes available, but often they are neither random nor representative. Quite often, blind clients who participate in testing for normative purposes may be captive clients of an agency that serves a particular segment of the population, for example, ambulatory blind clients being retrained for a new job. In addition, the term "blind" encompasses a rather wide range of amount of useful vision, so the normative sample needs to be carefully designated in terms of such vision. Finally, if the goal of testing is to provide information about the client in terms of competitive employment, then the more useful information is that based on the sighted individuals with whom the client will compete.

The need for special norms for the visually impaired is well illustrated by the Minnesota Rate of Manipulation Test (MRMT; American Guidance Service, 1969). This test consists of a form-board on which there are 40 round blocks, each nestled in a hole. The task is to turn the blocks over as rapidly as possible, as well as to move them in various prescribed ways. The test is designed to assess various aspects of motor coordination, and scores on it are related to success in various industrial-type jobs. The test was developed and normed on normal-sighted individuals, but the manual states that scores of blind persons correspond closely with the normative data. However, Needham and Eldridge (1990) showed that blind persons do score significantly below the norms of sighted persons. They suggested that its use as a predictor of motor skills in the blind may be limited, but that the test seems to be of value as a neuropsychological tool to identify brain-damaged, visually impaired persons.

Cognitive abilities. The cognitive abilities of the visually impaired are often measured by verbal tests, such as the verbal portions of the WAIS-R. In fact, the verbal portions of the Wechsler scales are particularly useful. They can be administered to the blind client exactly as with a sighted client, and therefore the regular norms can be used. A number of authors have argued that nonverbal

Table 12–1. WAIS Verbal Subtests Findings on Visually Impaired (Vander Kolk, 1982)								
WAIS Verbal Subtest	Adventitious		vs.	Congenitally Blind		No vision		Partial vision	
	Mean	SD		Mean	SD	Mean	SD	Mean	SD
Information	10.36	2.25		10.02	2.10	10.59	4.31	9.87	4.35
Comprehension	10.91	2.23		10.05	2.54	9.81	4.18	10.29	2.68
Arithmetic	11.47	3.12		9.63	2.28	8.72	3.79	10.35	2.71
Similarities	11.99	3.20		10.90	2.24	11.04	4.17	11.30	2.75
Digit Span	9.68	3.33		10.59	2.30	11.69	3.44	10.28	2.40
Vocabulary	10.85	2.56		9.86	2.14	10.45	3.70	9.85	2.28

abilities should also be assessed because the results yield complementary information with respect to general intelligence, are less influenced by extraneous factors such as poor socioeconomic background, may provide opportunities to observe qualitative aspects of behavior, and may possibly be of diagnostic significance, if there is a discrepancy between verbal and nonverbal abilities (Dekker, Drenth, Zaal, et al., 1990).

Studies of visually impaired students who take special administrations of college admission tests, such as the SAT and the ACT, suggest that their mean scores do not differ significantly from those of their normal-vision peers, to the degree that the test is untimed. Studies of such tests as the WISC and the WAIS, also suggest that mean scores of the visually impaired are equivalent to those of the sighted population. On the other hand, performance on achievement tests is significantly below that of normal-sighted students (Willingham et al., 1988). Very few studies exist on the validity of cognitive tests for visually impaired students.

A representative study is that of Vander Kolk (1982). He studied 597 legally blind clients of two rehabilitation agencies who had been administered the WAIS verbal subtests. Vander Kolk found that the verbal IQ scores for various subgroups within this sample averaged from 104 to 107, all in the normal range, and indeed higher than the normative 100.

Comparisons of subtest mean scores were made between clients who were adventitiously blind vs. those who were congenitally blind, as well as between subjects with no light perceptions vs. those with some partial vision. The results are presented in Table 12.1.

Recall that on the Wechsler tests, the subtests are normed so that the mean is 10 and the SD is

3. Adventitiously blind persons obtained average scale scores somewhat above sighted norms on the Arithmetic and Similarities subtests, while the congenitally blind group scored essentially in the normal range. Individuals who had no useful vision scored higher than the norm on Similarities and Digit Span, and lower on Arithmetic. Those with partial vision scored essentially at the norm, but higher on Similarities. Overall, the subgroup with no light perception seems more variable (note the larger SDs).

The results of this study indicate that the visually impaired do not differ on intelligence subtest scores from their sighted counterparts. These results must be taken with some caution for several reasons. First of all, we don't know whether these clients are representative of the population of visually impaired. Those who seek out the services of a rehabilitation agency may be more intelligent than those who do not seek out community resources to aid them with their disability. Second, the comparisons presented in Table 12.1 do not account for any potential differences in education, age, or other variables between subgroups that might covary with intelligence; that is, there is no indication in the study that the samples were equated.

The Perkins-Binet. The intellectual functioning of visually impaired children is typically assessed with modified versions of standardized tests such as the Stanford-Binet or the Wechsler tests. However, a modification of a test may be such as to actually result in a new test, rather than just a slightly altered form. An example of this is the Perkins-Binet Test of Intelligence for the Blind (C. Davis, 1980). Perkins is a school for the blind in Watertown, Massachusetts. In the Perkins-Binet a number of items have been altered, instructions have been changed, and time limits omitted. There are two forms available: form N for children aged 4 through 18 with nonusable vision, and form U for children aged 3 through 18 with some usable vision.

The test was standardized on low-vision and blind school children, and measures performance as well as verbal abilities. This test represents a valiant but somewhat limited effort, and many criticisms have been voiced. First of all, some degree of judgment is required to select the appropriate form. Secondly, the instructions may be altered to fit the particular testing situation; although this is a realistic approach, the fact that the examiner is permitted to alter such instructions may introduce an additional source of error variance. There also seem to be a number of discrepancies between what the test manual says and the actual test materials (Genshaft & Ward, 1982). Gutterman (1985) examined the correlation of the Perkins-Binet with the verbal scale of the WISC-R and an achievement test in a sample of 52 low-vision children, and concluded that the Perkins was not appropriate for these children because it was psychometrically inadequate and lacked reliability and validity.

A Dutch cognitive test. Over the years, a few investigators have attempted to develop standardized tests of cognitive abilities for the visually impaired, as opposed to modifying available tests such as the Stanford-Binet. A group of Dutch investigators (Dekker, Drenth, Zaal, et al., 1990) set out to construct just such a test series for blind and low-vision children, aged 6 to 15. They used the Primary Factors theory of Thurstone (1938) which identified seven primary factors or components of intelligence: verbal comprehension, memory, numerical fluency, verbal fluency, reasoning, perceptual speed, and spatial ability. For each of these dimensions (except for numerical fluency), they either borrowed a test from a standardized instrument (e.g., the WISC-R vocabulary subtest as a measure of verbal comprehension) or developed a new test. An example of the latter is the Perception of Objects subtest, designed to measure perceptual speed and consisting of a series of five small three-dimensional objects such as buttons, which are presented to the child. The object on the far left is identical to one of the four others that the child is asked to identify.

The total test battery consisted of 13 of these subtests, covering both verbal abilities and "haptic" (i.e., active tactual perception) abilities. Because the battery is intended for use with children who are totally blind as well as with children who have low vision, the authors used dark or light gray test materials to minimize any vision a child may have. As part of the test battery, they used the Dot test, using 10 cards, each of which has a number of dots, from 0 to 5, printed on it. The child is asked to indicate the number of dots on each card; one or more correct responses would indicate that the child has some usable vision.

The investigators studied this battery with 106 Dutch and Belgian children without usable vision and 49 with usable vision. They report considerable data including the fact that for both verbal and haptic subtests the mean difficulty level was .50, with alpha reliability coefficients ranging from .76 to .94, with a median value of .86, and no evidence of item bias. Correlations between total scores and various measures of academic achievement were typically in the .40s and low .50s, comparable to the coefficients reported in studies of normally sighted children.

Tactual forms. Another approach is to use tactual forms of standardized tests; that is, paper-and-pencil type items are changed into concrete objects or embossed items that can be physically felt. For example Rich and Anderson (1965) developed a tactual form of the Raven's Coloured Progressive Matrices (see Chapter 5); they reported high reliability and moderate validity coefficients in a group of 115 blind children.

Another example is the study by G. Domino (1968), who developed a tactual version of the D-48 (see Chapter 5), utilizing commercially available three-dimensional dominoes. Each D-48 item was then presented individually to 30 male adults, aged 20 to 46, all totally blind from birth, following the same sequence of the standard D-48 but with no time limit. The subjects were also administered the verbal portion of the WAIS, an interview that was subsequently rated as to intellectual efficiency and observer ratings on two scales measuring motivational and adjustment aspects.

A split-half reliability, with the halves composed of items of comparable difficulty, yielded a

Spearman-Brown coefficient of .87. A comparison of the difficulty level of the test items for these blind subjects vs. a sample of sighted children who took the standard form, yielded a coefficient of .93, indicating a very close correspondence in the two samples of which items were difficult and which were easy. However, the mean obtained by these blind adults was substantially lower than the means obtained by fifth- and sixth-grade sighted children. The tactual form of the D-48 proved to be a difficult task, as shown by the mean score on the WAIS Verbal IQ of 108.9.

The results indicated that scores on the D-48 correlated significantly with WAIS Verbal IQ ($r = .58$), with observers' ratings on personal adjustment ($r = .39$), with interview ratings of intellectual efficiency($r = .84$), with age ($r = .39$), and with educational level ($r = .42$). Thus, the validity of the D-48 with blind adults seems substantial. The task, however, proved to be a rather frustrating situation for many clients. From a psychometric point of view, this is a negative aspect, but from a clinical point of view, the D-48 may well provide a situation where the ability to tolerate frustration and to cope can be observed.

Perceptual-motor assessment. The assessment of perceptual-motor development and abilities is a complex field, strongly affected by theoretical viewpoints, as well as the difficulty of relating research findings to practical applied procedures in the classroom.

From a theoretical point of view, the study of perception, and particularly visual perception, has been dominated by the theoretical positions of *nativism* and of *empiricism*. The nativist position views visual perception as genetically determined and basically a passive process in which external stimulation falls on the retina; the image is then transmitted to the brain. This point of view gives little attention to perceptual development because it is assumed that infants perceive their environment as adults do (Wertheimer, 1958). Empiricists consider perception as an acquired ability. The perceptual world of the infant is seen as unpredictable and changeable; only through learning does the chaos become orderly. Either position does not seem adequate to explain perception fully, and a number of attempts have been made to combine the two into a better explanatory framework (e.g., Gibson, 1966; Piaget, 1967).

The Frostig Developmental Test of Visual Perception. A test that is illustrative of some of the issues and problems in the area of visual perception is the Frostig (Frostig, Lefever, &Whittlesey, 1966; Maslow, Frostig, Lefever, et al., 1964). This test was developed based on the observation that children who had school difficulties often experienced difficulty in processing visual stimuli. These difficulties seemed to fall into five major areas: (1) eye-motor coordination (assessed by drawing lines between boundaries); (2) figure-ground (assessed by such items as hidden figures); (3) form constancy (discriminating specific geometric figures from other shapes); (4) position in space (correctly identifying rotated figures); and (5) spatial relationships (on the Frostig assessed by copying of patterns by linking dots).

The Frostig can be administered individually or in small groups and requires somewhere between 30 to 60 minutes to administer. The 1963 standardization sample consisted of California children aged 4 to 8, with 93% coming from "middle class" homes, and including very few minority children. Thus the sample does not seem to be representative. The test yields three sets of scores:

1. A perceptual-age score for each subtest and for the total test is defined in terms of the performance of the average child in each age group.

2. A scaled score is also available for each subtest, but these scores are not standard scores as found on tests like the WISC, and their rationale is not indicated; some authors recommend that such scores *not* be used (e.g., Swanson & Watson, 1989).

3. A perceptual quotient can also be obtained as a deviation score based on the sum of the subtest scale scores corrected for age variation. Because this quotient is based on the scaled scores, it too is suspect.

Three test-retest reliability studies are reported by the test authors. In two of the studies, the examiners were trained psychologists, and the obtained test-retest coefficients ranged from .80 to .98 for the total test score, and from .42 to

.80 for the subtest scores. In the third study, the examiners were not psychologists; the test-retest correlation coefficients were .69 for the total test score, and from .29 to .74 for the subtest scores. Split-half reliability for the total test score ranged from .89 at 5 and 6 years of age to .78 at 8 and 9 years of age. In general, the reliability of the total test is adequate, but the subtest coefficients are too low to be used for individual differential diagnosis.

A number of factor-analytic studies of the Frostig by itself have reported a single factor rather than the five hypothesized by the test authors (e.g., Corach & Powell, 1963). Other studies that included additional tests, such as an intelligence test, found multiple factors, with various of the Frostig subtests loading on different factors, but either way the results do not support the authors' initial theoretical framework (e.g., Becker & Sabatino, 1973).

Vision testing. One of the most common devices used to assess vision is the familiar Snellen chart or test. Such charts use rows of letters of gradually diminishing size, the letter E in various positions, a broken circle with the opening in various positions, or other stimuli. Rabideau (1955) reported split-half reliabilities of .98 for the Snellen letter series under carefully controlled conditions; Guion (1965a) indicated that under the nonlaboratory conditions in which the Snellen chart is typically used, its reliability may be as low as .20.

Bibliographies. Various bibliographies of tests that can be used with the visually impaired are available. An example is the book by Scholl and Schnur (1976), which provides a listing and references for a wide variety of measures, from tests of cognitive functioning to measures of personality.

HEARING IMPAIRED

General issues

Prelingual onset. Hearing impairment can also cover a wide range of impairment from mild losses that are barely perceptible to total deafness, and thus the population subsumed by this label is rather complex and defined by multiple criteria. For example, one criteria is degree of hearing loss; ranging from hard of hearing to deaf. Heredity

accounts for about 40% to 60% of all childhood deafness; in about half of these cases there are other disabilities as well. Other causes of deafness include rubella (German measles), meningitis (infection of the membranes that surround the brain), and premature birth (Vernon & Andrews, 1990). A crucial variable in the hearing impaired is the age at which the person became deaf. There are those who become deaf *prelingually,* as infants, before they develop skills in spoken language; as a consequence they do not achieve normal competence in that language. Often the result is not only a deficit in verbal language but in reading, writing, speaking, and hearing. (There are also individuals who are *postlingually deaf, prevocationally deaf,* and *late deafened.*)

In the assessment of intelligence, it is important to use nonverbal rather than verbal tests. In fact, nonverbal tests of intelligence typically show that the intelligence of the hearing impaired is normally distributed, while verbal intelligence tests show a decline of about one standard deviation below the norm. In general, the use of verbal language to measure intelligence, personality, aptitudes, or other domains, may not be valid for the hearing impaired because the results may well reflect the person's language limitations. In many hearing-impaired individuals, the picture is also complicated by the presence of additional handicaps that include neurological damage, as well as cultural and attitudinal aspects (Holm, 1987).

Early identification. The early identification of language-related deficits such as hearing impairment is of substantial importance. Not only is language central to most human activities, but it is probably the major aspect of most education and becomes increasingly important as the child progresses developmentally. The gap between the language-impaired child and the normal child widens with age. Early language deficit is also related to subsequent learning and behavioral problems.

Usually, a preschool or kindergarten screening program will use a test or test battery for language assessment, as well as teacher rating scales. There are quite a few such tests; for example, Swanson and Watson (1989) list 91, and the interested reader might wish to consult more specialized sources (e.g., Illerbrun, Haines, & Greenough, 1985; Schetz, 1985).

Very often, the use of different instruments results in different children being identified as needing remedial work. Here the concepts of false positive and false negative are particularly relevant. In using a screening test, to what extent do we tolerate errors of identification? Are we willing to label certain children as having language deficits when in fact they may not? Is it worse not to identify the child who indeed needs that remedial work?

American Sign Language (ASL). In the United States, the native language of the deaf is American Sign Language (ASL), which has grammar and syntax different from English; it can be argued that deaf people are a minority language group, and many of the issues discussed in Chapter 11 are appropriate here.

Just because there is a qualified interpreter, who translates questions that are presented orally into American Sign Language, does not mean that the testing situation has now been made equivalent to that of a hearing person. For one, there needs to be almost constant eye contact between the deaf subject and the gestures being made by the interpreter. Such eye contact can be easily broken by all sorts of distractions. Second, ASL is a vehicle for informal social discourse and not necessarily for formal presentation. Finally, ASL is really a language of its own, rather than representing a strict translation. Thus, if the language is structured so as to conform to the English syntax, the result may be an awkward or garbled translation (Hoemann, 1972).

Limitations of agencies and examiners. Quite often, hearing-impaired clients who come to the attention of some agency, perhaps in a school setting or a vocational rehabilitation agency, are sent to a private psychologist for testing. The staff at the agency often lacks either the time or the expertise to do specialized testing; unfortunately many private psychologists lack testing experience with the hearing impaired. It is not surprising that the literature suggests great caution and limited effectiveness of tests with the hearing impaired (e.g., M. Vernon & D. W. Brown, 1964; Vescovi, 1979; Watson, 1979). Surveys of agencies that serve the hearing impaired, other than school facilities, in fact indicate that very little testing is done, and very few tests are available that

have been validated on hearing-impaired samples (E. S. Levine, 1971; 1974; McCrone & Chambers, 1977).

Understanding test instructions. For people who are hearing impaired, probably the most important testing consideration is how well they understand spoken instructions, and how well they speak. In testing hearing-impaired persons, it is important to make sure that they understand the test instructions (M. Vernon, 1970). Although many tests have written instructions, this does not necessarily mean that the hearing-impaired person will understand. Studies have shown that in the population of deaf adults there is a disproportionate number of people with low reading levels (Nester, 1984). Thus, a sign language interpreter may be needed. In fact, in testing the hearing impaired the major difficulty experienced by professionals concerns the tests themselves – problems of administration, interpretation, and the lack of norms (E. S. Levine, 1974).

Prelingually deaf people tend to have a deficiency in verbal language skills, which presents a problem. If the test is one that measures verbal language skills, then the performance of the hearing-impaired person will reflect the degree of deficiency. But if the test is measuring something else, for example, self-esteem, through verbal items, then the result may to an extent reflect the language deficit rather than the variable of interest.

How can these challenges be met? One way is to use nonverbal items, for example, the performance subtests of the WAIS rather than the verbal subtests. The majority of studies on methods to assess the hearing impaired draw attention to the fact that instruments used must have nonverbal performance-type responses and must also contain nonverbal directions (e.g., Berlinsky, 1952; Goetzinger, Wills, & Dekker, 1967; M. Reed, 1970). Another approach is to rewrite the verbal items in language appropriate for the deaf, i.e., language that reflects the grammatical structure used in sign language; this approach however, is quite limited. Still a third approach is to translate the test items into sign language by the use of a sign-language interpreter (e.g., Hoemann, 1972).

Administration of tests to the hearing impaired should be done by trained examiners, those who have had experience working with the hearing impaired. Group testing is probably not a valid or useful procedure, except perhaps for screening purposes.

Bragman (1982) found that different methods of conveying test instructions – for example, pantomime vs. demonstration – affect deaf children's performance, at least on pattern-recognition tasks. How generalizable these results are to other testing domains is at present not known.

Lack of norms and appropriate tests. Bragman (1982) listed 22 tests commonly used with the hearing impaired. These tests covered three domains: intelligence (e.g., the Wechsler tests), achievement (e.g., the Stanford Achievement Test), and personality (e.g., the 16 PF). Of the 22, only one, the Hiskey-Nebraska Test of learning aptitude, was originally developed for hearing-impaired individuals. For 14 of the 22 tests, modifications were made for use with the hearing impaired, but for only 4 were these modifications standardized and for only 3 were norms available for the hearing impaired.

Careful use of norms needs to be made. Hearing norms are appropriate if we wish to obtain some knowledge of how the person might function in a competitive environment. Same-group norms are more appropriate if we wish to obtain a profile of the person's strengths and weaknesses.

Modified tests for hearing impaired. Some instruments, particularly performance tests that have simple directions, are used as is with normal hearing norms. Good examples are the performance subtests from the Wechsler or the Raven's Progressive Matrices. Other instruments are also used as is, or with minor modifications, but offer norms based on hearing-impaired samples. With few exceptions, these norms are based on small and atypical samples that often represent the captive clientele of a particular agency. An example is the 16 PF (Trybus, 1973), for which norms of hearing-impaired college students are available. Even with a well-established test such as the 16 PF, the literature suggests that it may not be reliable or valid with the hearing impaired (e.g., Dwyer & Wicenciak, 1977; Jensema, 1975a, b). As with the visually impaired, tests to be used with the hearing impaired often need to be modified, for example, the verbal items from the WAIS (Sachs, Trybus, Koch, & Falberg, 1974) or the Rotter

Locus of Control Scale (Koelle & Convey, 1982). Such modifications can take various forms. For example, Leigh, Robins, Welkowitz, et al. (1989) used the Beck Depression Inventory in a study of depression in deaf individuals. They modified the items by rewriting them with a fourth-fifth grade vocabulary level. A different example involves the K-ABC where the child is asked to identify a picture such as that of a typewriter. The typewriter is similar in appearance to a telecommunication device for the deaf (TDD), so a response of TDD was also judged acceptable (Ulissi, Brice, & Gibbins, 1989).

Among the test modifications that have been used are the omission of verbal items, addition of practice items, addition of demonstrations of task strategies (i.e., ways of trying to solve test items), testing the limits, use of additional printed or signed instructions, or the use of pantomime for instructions. The most frequent modification seems to be changes in the test instructions, through pantomime or sign language, for example (Bragman, 1982). Although such modifications can be quite useful both for research purposes and for individual assessment, it must once again be recognized that such modifications can change the meaning of the available norms and of the client's obtained score. Basically it is important to determine the effect of such modifications – yet little information is available on this topic.

In testing the hearing impaired more time is often required. There is a need for examples and introductory trials before beginning the actual testing. Quite often test forms, especially those developed on normal samples, do not have these examples. An alternative procedure is to use items from an alternate form of the test as trial items (one more reason why alternate forms of tests can be useful).

In a few cases, tests have been developed specifically for use with the hearing impaired. Sometimes these tests are not readily available because they were developed for use at a specific agency, and sometimes when they are available, they are severely criticized for their inadequacies (e.g., the Geist Picture Interest Inventory; see Farrugia, 1983).

Schemas. Tests sometimes use stories, vignettes, or written material such as a sentence, as test items. The child may be asked to agree or disagree, to complete a story, to come to some conclusion, or in general to process the material in some way. Some researchers have concluded that to comprehend and recall such material, the child needs to actively construct meaning by applying prior knowledge and experiences rather than passively receive the information (e.g., Chan, Burtis, Scardamalia, et al., 1992). This prior knowledge is stored in memory structures that are called *schemas*. For example, there is a story schema, an expectation that a story has a setting, an initiating event, a series of episodes, and a resolution. Studies suggest that children who read below their grade level have poorly developed story schemas. There is some suggestion that hearing-impaired children have less well-developed schemas than those of hearing children (Schirmer, 1993). Such findings have repercussions not only for educational practices such as teaching reading comprehension to deaf children, but also for testing practices.

Why test the hearing impaired? Given all the difficulties and the test limitations, one might well wonder why make an effort to test the hearing impaired? There are a number of obvious answers including the need for appropriate educational placement, the identification of skills and aptitudes, and the goal of having impaired individuals participate more fully in mainstream activities. A serious attempt is being made in the United States to identify children with significant hearing impairment during their first year of life. Children who are thus identified and receive early intervention achieve greater receptive- and expressive-language scores than children who receive later or no intervention (Barringer, Strong, Blair, et al., 1993).

One purpose that may not be so self-evident is illustrated by Aplin (1993), who describes a British medical program where the cochlea is implanted in deaf adults to ameliorate their deafness. A battery of psychological tests is used to assess the suitability of the patient for implant, as well as to monitor the psychological progress of the patient and to assist when the patient may become disheartened at the perceived lack of progress. Most of the tests used in this program are tests we discussed, including selected scales from the British Ability Scales, the Wechsler, and the Hiskey-Nebraska.

Some Selected Findings

Measures used. What are the tests that are used for testing the hearing impaired? S. Gibbins (1989) conducted a national survey of school psychologists who serve the hearing impaired. Among the most popular measure of cognitive abilities were the WISC-R Performance Scale, the Leiter International Performance Scale, the WAIS-R Performance Scale, the Hiskey-Nebraska Test of Learning Aptitude, the WISC-R Verbal Scale, the Ravens Progressive Matrices, and the Stanford-Binet, in that order. The Vineland Adaptive Behavior Scale was the most commonly used test to assess adaptive behavior, and the Wide Range Achievement Test was the most common test of educational achievement. Figure drawings were among the most common measures of social-emotional status. This use of various psychological tests reflected little change from earlier reports, and probably current usage is much the same.

Projective drawings. Projective drawings are among the most popular assessment techniques used with the hearing impaired. Cates (1991) suggests three reasons for this: (1) they are easy to administer, (2) they are basically a visual-spatial technique and so seem to be appropriate for a population that relies predominantly on visual-spatial cues, and (3) they show consistently high reliability (some would disagree with this point). Unfortunately, there is little evidence of validity of these measures with the hearing impaired, and most clinicians who use these techniques assume that if they are valid for the normal hearing then they must be valid for the hearing impaired.

Cognitive tests. Early studies of the intelligence of the hearing impaired suggested that as a group, these individuals averaged 10 to 15 IQ points below normal. Later studies indicated that if appropriate nonverbal or performance measures were used, the average scores were comparable with those of the hearing population. At the same time, it has been suggested that there are differences between hearing impaired and normal on the qualitative aspects of intelligence, for example, that the hearing impaired are more concrete and less creative in their thinking.

The need for reliable and valid tests for the evaluation and guidance of hearing-impaired children has long been recognized, with many attempts to modify tests for use with this population. The studies of Pintner and Paterson (1915) with the Binet scale represent one of the earliest studies to test the intelligence of deaf children. These investigators found that deaf children scored in the mentally retarded range, but attributed this to language deprivation, and developed a nonlanguage test (the Pintner Nonlanguage Test; Pintner, 1924). However, later studies showed that deaf children continued to score significantly below the norm of hearing children (M. Vernon, 1968).

Subsequent research indicated that verbal tests of intelligence were inappropriate, that group tests of intelligence were of questionable validity with the hearing impaired, and that appropriate instruments must have nonverbal performance type of items as well as nonverbal directions (M. Vernon, 1968). The Stanford-Binet is not generally recommended by experts for use with the hearing impaired, because of its heavy emphasis on language ability.

Braden (1985) showed that the factorial structure of nonverbal intelligence is basically identical in hearing-impaired and normal hearing subjects, with one major factor g explaining much of the variance. These results suggest that the nonverbal intelligence of the hearing impaired does not differ qualitatively from that of normal hearing, as some theories have suggested (for a different conclusion, see Zwiebel & Mertens, 1985).

The Wechsler tests and the hearing impaired. The Wechsler Performance Scales are the most popular test for assessing deaf children and adults and seem to demonstrate adequate reliability and validity with deaf subjects (e.g., Braden, 1984; Hirshoren, Hurley, & Kavale, 1979; Lavos, 1962).

There are several reasons why the Wechsler scales are so popular. First, they represent a series of "equivalent" tests, so that a young child may be tested with the WISC and several years later retested with the WAIS. Second, most school counselors and psychologists are trained on the Wechsler and have Wechsler kits readily available, whereas tests such as the Hiskey-Nebraska are not used with normal children and often are not readily available in the school setting.

Braden (1990) did an analysis of the literature and located 21 studies where a version of the Wechsler Performance Scale was administered to deaf subjects, and means were given for at least 5 subtests. A meta-analysis of these 21 studies indicated that although deaf persons have mean Performance IQs slightly below normal-hearing norms, they are well within the average range. The only exception occurs on the Coding/Digit Symbol subtest, where the mean score is markedly lower (a mean of 8.77 versus the expected 10). These findings were quite consistent across studies. The significantly lower mean on Coding/Digit Symbol was consistent across gender, degree of hearing loss, and version of the Wechsler used, but was increased by the type of administration procedure used (e.g., standard vs. oral administration), the presence of additional handicapping conditions, and the use of norms based on deaf persons. Several explanations for this finding have been proposed, including the failure of the person to understand the speeded nature of the task, underdeveloped language skills needed to mediate the task, the prevalence of neuropsychological deficits among deaf persons, and even test bias (Braden, 1990).

In discussing the Wechsler tests in Chapter 5, we discussed the concept of subtest variability. At a theoretical level, we would expect a person to perform equally well, or equally poorly, across all subtests, but in fact we typically obtain variability, i.e., a person might do better on some subtests and less well on others. We saw that there have been attempts to relate such variability to diagnostic status. Hearing-impaired individuals show a typical group profile. They perform relatively well on the Picture Completion subtest, suggesting above-average ability to discern essential and unessential details. They perform somewhat below average on the Picture Arrangement subtest that requires the subject to correctly place in order a sequence of "cartoon" panels to make a story. Whether this reflects poorer social skills based on more restricted social experiences, or poorer sequential skills that reflect the lack of continuous auditory stimulation, is debatable. The hearing impaired perform above average on the Block Design subtest, where a design is to be reproduced using wooden blocks, and on the Object Assembly subtest, essentially a series of puzzles. They do less well on the Coding subtest, which requires a number of skills. Whether this "typical" profile reflects more "concrete" abilities and lower capacity to deal with abstract material is a moot question (D. W. Hess, 1969).

A typical study is that by D. R. Ross (1970), who administered the WAIS to deaf students aged 16 to 21, by both manual and verbal communication. The mean Performance IQ was 106, but the mean Verbal IQ was 72.

It should be noted that, although there are many articles on the WISC-R as applied to deaf children, there are relatively few studies of the WAIS-R with hearing-impaired adolescents or adults (Ensor & Phelps, 1989).

The WISC-R and deaf children.

The WISC-R Performance scale (PS) is probably the intelligence test used most often by psychologists assessing deaf children. Despite this, there are actually few studies of the validity of the WISC-R PS with deaf children. Hirshoren, Hurley, & Hunt (1977) administered the PS and the Hiskey-Nebraska to a sample of 59 prelingually deaf children, average age about 10. The average IQ on the WISC-R PS was 88, with IQs ranging from 52 to 129. The intercorrelations among PS subtests were quite similar to those obtained with hearing children. Scores on the PS correlated .89 with the Hiskey-Nebraska learning quotient scores; this and other analyses indicate the two tests are fairly interchangeable. Braden (1989) compared the WISC-R PS scores for a sample of 33 prelingually severely deaf children, with their scores on the Stanford Achievement Test (hearing-impaired edition). The correlations between the two sets of scores were rather low, ranging from a high of .37 to a low of −.08, with a median r of about .14. In a second study, a number of nonverbal tests of intelligence (such as the Hiskey-Nebraska) were also used. Again, the correlation between nonverbal IQ and achievement was rather low. The author questions the criterion validity of the WISC-R PS with deaf children, but also points out that academic achievement may not be an appropriate criterion measure for nonverbal IQs; each involves different psychological processes, and academic achievement is attenuated (i.e., lowered) by hearing loss.

On the other hand, the WISC-R is one of the few standardized tests for which there is a standardized version, of the performance subscales only, for deaf children, based on a sample of more than 1,200 deaf children (R. D. Anderson & Sisco, 1977). Older studies (e.g., E. E. Graham & Shapiro, 1963) administered the performance scale of the WISC by pantomime, with positive results.

Culture-fair tests.

Culture-fair tests, and particularly the Raven Progressive Matrices (see Chapter 5) have been used quite frequently to assess the intellectual level of deaf persons, with results that correlate relatively well with Performance IQs on the Wechsler (e.g., Naglieri & Welch, 1991).

The Peabody Picture Vocabulary Test (PPVT).

Another cognitive test that has been useful with the hearing impaired is the PPVT (see Chapter 9), which consists of a series of plates with drawings on them. A word is given by the examiner and the child identifies the corresponding drawing. Forde (1977) describes its use at a Canadian school as a screening device, with two modifications: where necessary the printed vocabulary word was used rather than the spoken one, and rather than stop testing after six out of eight errors, it was up to the examiner to determine when the test should be discontinued. For a sample of hearing-impaired students tested during a 6-year period ($N = 196$), the average IQ was 104 (SD = 15). Correlations of the PPVT with scores on the Stanford Achievement Tests ranged from a low of .49 (with Arithmetic Computation) to a high of .70 (with Language).

Stanford Achievement Test-Special Edition.

In 1974, the Office of Demographic Studies of Gallaudet College (a famous college for the hearing impaired) developed a special edition of the 1973 Stanford Achievement Test for use with hearing-impaired students (SAT-HI; Trybus & Karchmer, 1977). This special edition was standardized nationally on a stratified random sample of almost 7,000 hearing-impaired children and adolescents. Like the Stanford, this form is a full-range achievement test, composed of six different levels or batteries – from primary level through advanced levels, covering grades 1 to 9. There are four core-subject areas: vocabulary, reading comprehension, mathematics concepts, and mathematics computation.

The SAT-HI is a group test to be administered in the classroom using whatever method of communication is normally used. Practice tests are provided for each level and subtest. The test is designed for ages 8 to 21, and the norms are based on students in 119 special-education programs throughout the United States.

The results of nationwide applications of this special edition show that for hearing-impaired students aged 20 or above, the median reading score is equivalent to a grade norm of 4.5; that is, half of hearing-impaired students can barely read at a newspaper literacy level. For math computation, the results are somewhat better, with the median score equivalent to just below the eighth-grade level. As the authors indicate, the overwhelming majority of hearing-impaired children leave school in their late teens at a very substantial educational disadvantage compared with their normal-hearing peers (Trybus & Karchmer, 1977).

The average test-retest correlation coefficient is about .83, and the standard error of measurement is about 3. The test-retest reliability of this special edition was assessed over a 5-year period for a national sample of hearing-impaired students (Wolk & Zieziula, 1985). Despite this rather extended time period, the results indicated substantial stability over time. Interestingly, the test-retest coefficients were consistently lowest for black hearing-impaired students. Because the test items of the SAT-HI are identical to those of the Stanford, it is assumed that the validity of the Stanford (which is generally excellent) also applies to the SAT-HI.

The SAT and the hearing impaired. Ragosta and Nemceff (1982) studied the SAT performance of hearing-impaired students who had taken the nonstandard administration of the SAT. As a group, their means were between .5 and 1.2 standard deviations below the means of hearing students, with verbal scale performance more discrepant than mathematical scores. D. H. Jones and Ragosta (1982) investigated the validity of the SAT vs. the criterion of first-year college grades. For a sample of deaf students attending a California state university, the SAT verbal correlated .14 with grades, while the SAT mathematical correlated .41; for hearing students the coefficients were .38 and .32, respectively.

Self-concept. In Chapter 8, we discussed self-concept and the Tennessee Self-Concept Scale

(TSCS; Fitts, 1965). Self-concept is basically the sum total of the perceptions an individual has about him or herself. A positive but realistic self-concept seems to be associated with optimal development. Self-concept is an important variable for disabled individuals as well, with a number of studies looking at self-concept and its ramifications for individuals with specific disabilities such as hearing impairment (e.g., H. B. Craig, 1965; Farrugia & Austin, 1980; Loeb & Sarigiani, 1986; Yachnick, 1986). Typical findings of lowered self-esteem in the hearing impaired may, in part, be a function of the instruments used because such instruments are typically developed on normal samples.

There is a wide variety of self-concept measures, most useful with individuals who have disabilities. At the same time, there are at least two concerns: (1) the reading level required; and (2) use of inappropriate items in relation to a particular disability (e.g., "I can hear as well as most other people"). If these concerns seem strong enough, then there are two alternatives: to revise existing instruments, which would mean determining the reliability and validity of the revised form (see Jensema, 1975a, for an example) or creating a new instrument specifically designed for a particular disabled population.

Gibson-Harman and Austin (1985) revised the TSCS by simplifying the language structure of the items, shortening sentences, and lowering the vocabulary level required. Of the 100 TSCS items, 79 were thus changed. These investigators then studied three samples of individuals: normal-hearing persons, deaf persons, and hard-of-hearing persons. The normal-hearing persons were administered the original TSCS followed by the revised TSCS, some 2 to 4 weeks later (one half received the revised first and then the original). The deaf and hard-of-hearing persons were administered the revised form and retested some 2 to 4 weeks later. For the normal-hearing group, the correlation of total scores between original and revised forms was .85, indicative that the two forms are fairly equivalent. For the deaf and hard-of-hearing samples, the test-retest correlations were .76 and .89, indicative of adequate test-retest reliability.

Oblowitz, Green, and Heyns (1991) chose to develop a new instrument, specifically for the hearing impaired. The Self-Concept Scale for the

Hearing Impaired (SSHI) is a 40-item Likert-type self-report scale. These items were selected from a pool of 80 statements that had been written on the basis of a literature review, with a number of items adapted from existing scales. The basis for selection was primarily a logical, judgmental one, rather than based on statistical criteria. Each item consists of three pictures of young people, identical except for their facial and bodily expressions; the first picture portrays a happy expression, the second, a neutral expression, and the third, a sad expression, with the order of the three expressions different from item to item. Each of the drawings has a statement in a cartoon like fashion, such as, "I do not want to wear my hearing aid." There are two forms of the questionnaire, one with male drawings and one with female drawings. The 40 items cover 4 areas of self-concept: personal, physical, academic, and social, although the distribution of items is not equivalent. There are only 4 items that cover personal self-concept but there are 24 items that cover social self-concept. Items that differ only slightly in meaning are included to check for consistency of response, although the number and nature of such items is not indicated. Students mark the picture in each triad that best represents their response choice. The SSHI is not timed, with an average completion time of about 30 minutes. Scoring uses a 3-point scale, with 3 points assigned to positive items, 2 points to neutral, and 1 to negative items. You might wish to review our discussion of nominal, ordinal, interval, and ratio scales, (Chapter 1), and consider the rationality of this scoring scheme. A total score can be computed on the SSHI, as well as scores for the four subareas.

The SSHI was administered to 253 hearing-impaired children at three different special schools, with children ranging in age from 11 to 19. Test-retest reliability coefficients over an interval of about 1 month were .70 for the total scale and from .49 to .68 for the 4 subareas. The reliability seemed to be higher for those children whose hearing loss was minimal, as well as for those children whose communication skills were good, with no gender differences.

Correlations between scores on the SSHI and ratings by professionals on the same dimensions were relatively poor, ranging from a low of .08 for the personal dimension to a high

of .32 for the total score. In particular, when ratings were made by school teachers rather than by professionals experienced in making such judgments, the resulting coefficients were lower. Other approaches, such as administering the SSHI to a group of normal-hearing adolescents together with other self-concept scales, yielded more promising results. A factor analysis yielded 10 factors that the authors interpreted as "corresponding reasonably well to the dimensions of the self-concept" included in this test. Incidentally, the authors of this test are from Italy and South Africa, but no mention is made whether the SSHI was developed in the United States or where the subjects came from. Although more efforts like this need to be made, the SSHI illustrates the difficulties of doing good research and some of the challenges associated with the development of tests for special populations.

Personality functioning. The literature suggests that there are a number of personality characteristics associated with hearing impairment, such as neurotic tendencies, excessive anxiety, social withdrawal, lack of sociability, depression, suspiciousness, social immaturity, and emotional instability. To what degree these findings reflect attempts to cope with the deafness or realistic repercussions of being hearing impaired, or limitations in the instruments used, is an unresolved issue.

Paper-and-pencil inventories such as the MMPI and the 16 PF require a fairly high reading level, and also use idiomatic expressions that hearing-impaired persons may not understand. However, Brauer (1993) translated the MMPI into American Sign Language (ASL) and reported some basic data showing the linguistic equivalence of the ASL and English versions of the MMPI, adequate reliability, but no validity data. Rosen (1967) showed that hearing-impaired persons, whose academic achievement scores were sufficient to understand MMPI items, in fact did not understand many of these items due to their idiomatic nature; in addition, some of the MMPI test items are not appropriate for hearing-impaired persons. Thus, a number of researchers have turned to projective tests. Many of these projective techniques are of limited use because they emphasize language and communication, as in the Rorschach and the TAT. Drawing tasks are used quite often, but psychometric issues abound with these measures. Unfortunately, much of the research also is rather flawed.

A typical example is the study by Ouellette (1988), who administered the House-Tree-Person (HTP; Buck, 1966) to a sample of 33 severely hearing-impaired young adults. The HTP requires the subject to draw pictures of a person, a person of the opposite gender, a house, and a tree. The test was administered using both sign language and voice. Three psychologists were then asked to rate each subject, on the basis of the drawings, on eight personality traits culled from the literature as particularly applicable to the deaf, namely aggression, anxiety, dependency, egocentricity, feelings of inadequacy, immaturity, impulsivity, and insecurity. The psychologists' ratings were then compared with counselors' ratings on the same eight dimensions, except that the counselors' ratings were based on direct knowledge of the clients. The first question asked concerned the interrater reliability, that is, how well did the three psychologists agree with each other? The answer unfortunately is "not very well." The 24 correlation coefficients that were computed range from a high of .72 to a low of $-.14$, with a median of about .32. Although the author argues that for four of the scales there was adequate interrater reliability because the correlation coefficients were statistically significant, for none of the scales were the coefficients consistently above .70.

The author of the study then compared the psychologists's ratings to the counselors' ratings by using T tests and found no significant differences in mean ratings for five of the eight dimensions. However, this was not the appropriate analysis. Two individuals could rate a group of subjects in drastically different ways, yet still give the same average rating. What would have been appropriate is the correlation coefficient.

Creativity. Hearing-impaired persons have often been described in the literature as rigid and concrete, lacking imagination, and having limited abstract and divergent thinking (Myklebust, 1964). Recent research suggests that some of these findings are more reflective of the linguistic limitations of hearing-impaired children rather than a reflection of their abilities. Nevertheless, few studies have looked at the creativity of hearing-impaired children and fewer still at strategies for developing creative abilities in such individuals. Laughton (1988) studied 28 profoundly hearing-impaired children aged 8 to 10. All of the children were given the figural nonverbal part of the Torrance Tests of Creative Thinking (see Chapter 8), and then half of the children were exposed to a curriculum designed to enhance their creativity, while the other half met for traditional art class. The results indicated significant improvement in flexibility and originality for the experimental group.

The Vineland Adaptive Behavior Scale. You recall from Chapter 9 that this test is a revision of the Vineland Social Maturity Scale. Dunlap and Sands (1990) administered the Vineland to 118 hearing-impaired persons, with an average age of 20.7 years. On the basis of a cluster analysis (like a factor analysis), three subgroups of subjects were identified, having low, middle, or high scores on the Vineland. Additional analyses indicated that the three groups differed in communication skills, daily-living skills, and degree of socialization. It is interesting to note that the "low" group did not have the most severe hearing losses, as might be expected, but did have more members with physical impairments and with low IQ scores. The authors suggest that a classificatory scheme based on functional ability may be more useful than one based on hearing loss. Other adaptive and behavioral scales that can be quite useful for the hearing impaired are the American Association of Mental Deficiency Adaptive Behavior Scale (1974) and the Cain-Levine Social Competency Scale (Cain, Levine, & Elzey, 1977), both of which were standardized on the mentally retarded.

Behavioral rating scales. These scales, such as the Behavioral Problem Checklist (H. C. Quay & Peterson, 1967), can be quite useful, especially when there are norms available based on hearing-impaired samples. The value of these scales lies in part on the fact that they reflect the evaluation of an observer who typically has had extensive contact with the client, and they force the observer to report his or her observations in a standardized manner.

Test guides. A number of test guides listing tests that are suitable for the hearing impaired are also available. One example is by Zieziula (1982), which covers a wide variety of tests from academic achievement measures to work evaluation systems. Often these guides are superficial, and they become rapidly outdated.

PHYSICAL-MOTOR DISABILITIES

Nature of physical disabilities. From a psychometric perspective, physical disabilities present a much more heterogeneous set of conditions, some requiring no particular modifications in test or test administration and others presenting substantial challenges. Even within a particular disability, clients may differ dramatically from each other in their test-taking capabilities.

Three of the major categories of physical disabilities that can present challenges in the testing situation are those due to neuromuscular diseases, major physical injuries, and severe chronic health problems. Neuromuscular diseases include conditions such as cerebral palsy and muscular dystrophy. These often involve troublesome involuntary movements, clumsy voluntary movements, impaired mobility, and sometimes evidence of brain injury as reflected in impairments in verbal skills and in motor coordination. Physical injuries can also be quite varied and may involve paralysis due to spinal-cord injury or orthopedic disabilities, such as injuries to a limb. Finally, chronic health problems can range from cancer to severe allergies to conditions such as diabetes and asthma.

Motor impairment. In this chapter, we include motor impairments under the more generic label of physical disabilities. Motor disabilities refer to impairment in moving parts of the body, such as hands or arms, and cover a wide variety of conditions such as cerebral palsy and quadriplegia. What test modifications are needed is, of course, a function of the specific motor impairments. For some clients, no change from standardized procedures are necessary. Considerations needed by others follow next.

Some considerations. There are three major areas of concern regarding the testing of physically disabled individuals: psychological, physical, and psychometric (K. O. White, 1978).

Psychological considerations include sensitivity to the fact that some disabled individuals have limited opportunities for social interactions; for these individuals, the testing situation may be frightening and strange, and their test anxiety may well cloud the results.

Physical considerations involve the verbal contents of a test and the performance requirements. The content of some items may be inappropriate for disabled individuals – for example, a personality test item that reads, "I am in excellent health." The test itself may be inappropriate in that it may require speed of performance or other aspects not in keeping with the client's coordination, strength, or stamina. When standard instruments are used with disabled individuals, often they are modified to meet the requirements of the specific situation. There may be a need for a comfortable work space designed to accommodate a wheelchair, or assistance in some of the manual tasks involved in a test such as turning the pages of the test booklet, indicating responses by gestures, pointing, or pantomime, perhaps longer and/or more frequent test breaks, or extra time. Speed tests may also be inappropriate.

Psychometric considerations involve the impact that modifications of administration have on both the normative aspects of the test (e.g., Does the same raw score obtained under a time limit vs. untimed mean the same?), and on the psychometric aspects, such as validity.

The client is the focus. Most experts agree that the examining procedures for physically disabled individuals need to be modified to reduce the physical barriers that can interfere with appropriate testing. Keep in mind that the aim of testing is typically to obtain a picture of what the individual can do. The examiner should be aware of the nature and extent of the client's disabilities, and the client should be contacted prior to testing to determine what testing modifications, if any, are required. As always, rapport is important. Patience, calmness, adaptability, and tact are desirable examiner characteristics, as well as eye contact, emphasis on ability as opposed to disability, and acceptance of the client as an independent, fully functioning individual (K. O. White, 1978).

Disabilities and personality. Years ago, some efforts were made to determine whether there were specific personality types associated with various disabilities. Mental health professionals often spoke of the "ulcer personality," the "tuberculosis personality," and even the "multiple sclerotic personality." In fact, the evidence suggests that no such personality types exist (e.g., A. H. Canter, 1952; Harrower & Herrmann, 1953; Linde & Patterson, 1958).

SAT and GRE as examples. Developing fair and valid tests for individuals who are physically impaired poses unique and complex measurement questions. Some of these issues can be illustrated by the Scholastic Aptitude Test (SAT), used in college admissions, and the Graduate Record Examination (GRE) used in graduate-school admissions.

A major goal of an admissions-testing program is to provide standardized assessment of scholastic ability and achievement that is objective and fair for all applicants. But how are we to test those that are disabled? A standard test and the same test in braille, as we have seen require different sensory skills, and thus may not be equivalent. Some individuals may have disabilities whose effects cannot be distinguished from the abilities and skills that a test attempts to measure – for example, how do we separate reading disability from reading comprehension?

As mentioned above, researchers at ETS have looked at the extensive data available on the nonstandard versions of the SAT and the GRE. In general, the results indicate that the nonstandard versions of the SAT and GRE appear to be generally comparable with the standard tests with respect to reliability, factor structure, and how items function. As to predicting academic performance, for example in college, it turns out that the academic performance of physically impaired students tends to be somewhat less predictable than that of normal students. In addition, the nonstandard SAT and GRE were not comparable with the standard versions with respect to timing – i.e., disabled examinees were more likely to finish the test than their nondisabled peers, and some test items near the end of the test were relatively easier for disabled students. These results, of course, reflect the fact that nonstandard versions of the SAT and GRE basically give the disabled candidate as much time as needed.

Spinal-cord injury. There are an estimated 250,000 people with spinal-cord injury in the United States, and an additional 8,000 sustain such injury each year (Trieschmann, 1988). There are thus a number of studies on this population, using measures of such variables as adjustment (e.g., Hanson, Buckelew, Hewett, & O'Neal, 1993), depression (e.g., Tate, Forchheiner, Maynard, et al., 1993), and employment (e.g., McShane & Karp, 1993). A typical study is that of Krause and Dawis (1992) who administered the Life Situation Questionnaire (LSQ) to a sample of 286 persons who had suffered from spinal-cord injury. These individuals were basically middle aged (mean of 41.9 years), but had suffered the injury as young adults (mean of 23.4 years at injury). Most (81%) were male, and 61% were quadriplegic.

The LSQ was developed specifically to measure mostly objective information on a broad range of areas relevant to persons with spinal-cord injury. Items include asking participants to indicate the number of weekly visitors, number of nonroutine doctor visits, overall self-assessed adjustment, and degree of satisfaction in various areas of one's life.

The Ostomy Adjustment Scale. Some instruments such as the Wechsler tests or the MMPI are designed for a rather broad segment of the population – for example, all "normal" individuals who are at least 16, or all psychiatric patients. Nonetheless, they can be quite useful with specific populations, such as the physically disabled. Some instruments, however, are designed specifically for a target population, a somewhat narrower segment; an example of this is the Ostomy Adjustment Scale (Olbrisch, 1983).

More than 1.5 million persons in the United States and Canada have undergone ostomy surgery, with approximately 110,000 new ostomies performed each year. A *stoma* is a passage way that is surgically constructed through the abdominal wall as an exit for body waste. There are several specialized procedures here, including a colostomy which is a rerouting of the large intestine, often performed with older persons who have been diagnosed with colorectal cancer. One of the key issues in recovery from this surgical procedure is the patient's emotional adjustment and acceptance of the stoma.

Olbrisch (1983) attempted to develop a reliable and valid measure of adjustment to ostomy surgery to evaluate that process of adjustment and the effectiveness of mutual aid groups for ostomy patients. The first step was to generate a pool of potential items based on a review of the literature, as well as the contributions of three ostomy patients and three expert professionals. From this pool of items, 39 were selected that reflected a wide range of situations, applicability to most potential respondents, and readability. The items were worded so they could be responded to on a 6-point Likert scale (e.g., "I can lead a productive and fulfilling life despite my ostomy," and "I feel embarrassed by my ostomy, as though it were something to hide"). The scale, together with several other instruments, was mailed to a sample of 120 ostomy patients; of these, 53 returned usable questionnaires. These patients ranged in age from 19 to 83, included 29 males and 24 females, with the average time since surgery of about $2\frac{1}{2}$ years.

Five of the items were eliminated because of low item-total correlations or low variances, suggesting that the items were being misinterpreted or did not discriminate among participants. For the 34 remaining items, the Cronbach alpha was .87 indicating high internal consistency. A test-retest analysis with an interval ranging from 2 to 6 weeks yielded an r of .72.

Discriminant validity was established by showing that scores on the scale were not significantly correlated with measures of social desirability and measures of self-esteem. Convergent validity was shown by small but significant correlations with such variables as number of months elapsed since surgery, whether the surgery had been elective or emergency, and whether the patient was able to work or not.

An exploratory factor analysis yielded 12 factors, with the first 5 factors accounting for 69% of the variance. These factors cover such dimensions as normal functioning and negative affect. Based on the factor analysis and other considerations, the author divided the items into two alternate forms of 17 items each.

SUMMARY

In this chapter, we looked briefly at three types of disabilities: visual impairment, hearing impairment, and physical impairment. The overall picture is that tests can be very useful with these individuals, but great care needs to be exercised because quite often tests need to be modified in ways that may significantly alter the test results. The evidence suggests that such modified tests are comparable with the original format, that reliability can be quite satisfactory, but the validity in most cases has not been investigated adequately.

SUGGESTED READINGS

Fabiano, R. J., & Goran, D. A. (1992). A principal component analysis of the Katz Adjustment Scale in a traumatic brain injury rehabilitation sample. *Rehabilitation Psychology, 37,* 75–86.

This is a prototypical study that takes a scale originally developed for one population and asks whether that scale is applicable and useful with another population. Here the authors take an adjustment scale and explore its utility with patients who were participating in a rehabilitation program following traumatic brain injury.

Freeman, S. T. (1989). Cultural and linguistic bias in mental health evaluations of deaf people. *Rehabilitation Psychology, 34,* 51–63.

This article discusses what the author calls a "cultural minority" that is distinguished by its language – namely, the deaf. An interesting article that focuses on psychological testing of the deaf.

Head, D. N., Bradley, R. H., & Rock, S. L. (1990). Use of home-environment measures with visually impaired children. *Journal of visual impairment and blindness, 84,* 377–380.

A brief article that focuses on the assessment of the home environment of visually impaired children. Although the authors do not discuss specific measures in any detail, contrary to what they state in the abstract, they make some interesting observations about the topic.

Morgan, S. (1988). Diagnostic assessment of autism: A review of objective scales. *Journal of Psychoeducational Assessment, 6,* 139–151.

Although the focus of this chapter was on "physical" disabilities, there are a number of other diagnostic entities that could have been included: autism is a good example and the focus of this article. This is a review of five scales for the diagnosis of autism, and is a good example of many articles that review a well-defined set of scales for a specific population.

Nester, M. A. (1993). Psychometric testing and reasonable accommodation for persons with disabilities. *Rehabilitation Psychology, 38,* 75–85.

An excellent article that covers the legal and psychometric issues related to nondiscriminative testing of persons with disabilities. The author is a psychometrician with the United States Office of Personnel Management, who has written extensively on the topic.

DISCUSSION QUESTIONS

1. What are some of the basic issues involved in testing disabled clients?

2. In interpreting the test score of a disabled individual, we can use general norms based on a "random" sample or selected norms based on specific samples (e.g., blind college students). Which is more meaningful? Is this situation different from using ethnic-specific norms (e.g., based on black students only)?

3. Compare and contrast testing the visually impaired vs. the hearing impaired.

4. How might the Semantic Differential (discussed in Chapter 6) be used with physically disabled individuals? (For an example, see Thomas, Wiesner, & Davis, 1982).

5. One of the conclusions of this chapter is that the validity of most measures has not been investigated adequately. How can this be remedied?

13 Testing in the Schools

AIM Because much testing occurs in a school setting, this chapter looks at testing in the context of school, from the primary grades through professional training. For each level, we look at a representative test or test battery, as illustrative of some of the issues, concerns, and purposes of testing. The intent here is not to be comprehensive, but to use a variety of measures to illustrate some basic issues (see R. L. Linn, 1986).

PRESCHOOL ASSESSMENT

At least in the United States, testing in the schools is quite prevalent. Tests are used for accountability, for instructional improvement, and for program evaluation, as well as for individual student diagnosis and/or placement, advancement, and graduation determinants. In any one year, more than one third of all children (about 14 to 15 million) are tested, with about 70% of the tests using multiple-choice items (Barton & Coley, 1994).

Entrance into school represents a major transition point for most children in the United States and in most other cultures. The transition is often facilitated by a variety of preschool programs. Testing can provide a partial answer to a number of key questions such as the readiness of the child to enter school, the identification or diagnosis of conditions that may present special educational challenges, and the assessment of a child's abilities and deficiencies. Recently in the United States, there has been a marked trend to evaluate children as early as possible in order to plan educational interventions and remediation.

Objectives of Preschool Assessment

Preschool assessment involves a variety of efforts, from comprehensive developmental assessment

to the screening of high-risk children. The general objective of assessment in educational settings is to make appropriate decisions about children that will facilitate their educational and psychological development (Paget & Nagle, 1986). Among the various purposes for testing preschool children might be: (1) screening of children at risk – here the concepts of false positive and false negative are particularly relevant; (2) diagnostic assessment to determine the presence or absence of a particular condition, often for the purpose of establishing eligibility for placement in a special program, as well as to formulate intervention and treatment recommendations; and (3) program evaluation, where the test results are used to document and evaluate specific programs.

Neisworth and Bagnato (1986) indicate that decisions based on assessment typically include diagnosis, i.e., assignment to a clinical category, and prognosis, i.e., projection of status, and program planning. Succinctly, testing can be used to place, to predict, or to prescribe.

In the past, the focus has been on diagnostic testing. However, it is now recognized that this approach is both difficult and unproductive at the preschool level because the young child has not yet developed stable behavior, shows intraindividual variance, is difficult to test, and changes rapidly. Some authors argue that assessment should be prescriptive and should provide information relevant to school instruction (Neisworth & Bagnato, 1986). These authors advocate a "test-teach-test" approach, where test items become instructional objectives and vice versa. They urge the use of curriculum-based assessment measures, which are basically criterion-referenced tests that use the curricular items themselves as the assessment content.

Some general problems. Testing preschoolers can represent quite a challenge. Most preschool children cannot read, and written self-report measures, which probably represent the most common testing approach, cannot be used. Their verbal and visual-motor response capabilities are also restricted – thus a preschool child may be unable to tell a story in response to pictures. Similarly, their information-processing skills may be quite limited and their responses to questions may reflect such limitations. Preschool children may not be familiar with a "testing" situation and may be fearful and apprehensive. Preschool children also have a relative inability to understand the demand characteristics of the testing situation, and may not understand the need to be motivated in answering "test" questions. They may find the smiles of the examiner not particularly reinforcing, and it may be difficult to assess whether the child lacks the ability to answer correctly or does not wish to cooperate (D. Martin, 1986).

Assessment approaches. There seem to be five major approaches within the tradition of psychometric testing:

1. Interviews of the parents and teachers are probably the most widely used method to assess the social-emotional functioning of the preschool child. Interviews, particularly of the child directly, are quite limited from a psychometric point of view, often yielding low reliability and validity.

2. Direct behavioral observation is considered to be one of the most valuable assessment methods for young children. In part, this is due to the fact that young children are ordinarily not bothered by observation as are older children, and in part due to their limited verbal repertoire. When such observation is done systematically,

the interobserver reliability can be substantial (R. P. Martin, 1986), and a number of such observation systems where behavior can be coded have been developed.

3. Rating scales, filled out by the parent and/or teacher are relatively inexpensive and require little time to complete and to score. These scales are limited by three types of errors that produce unwanted variation in scores or *error variance.* The first is interrater variance – different people filling out a rating scale for the same child will often give different ratings. Usually, this is not a reflection of the poor reliability of the scale, but rather reflects the different perspectives that different people have. A second source of error is setting variance. The parent sees the child at home, while the teacher sees the child at school. These different settings may elicit different behaviors. Finally, there is temporal variance, which reflects the effect of taking a measure at one time as opposed to another (D. Martin, 1986, gives a brief review of 12 such rating scales, including the Conner's Parent Rating Scale).

4. Projective techniques such as producing drawings or story telling in response to a specific picture are also used. These techniques are severely limited for preschool children. Most require a fair degree of verbal skills that the child does not yet possess. For example, in producing a drawing the child is asked to tell what the drawing represents, what feelings are associated with the drawing, etc. Often the drawings and other productions of young children are either very limited or not easily interpretable.

5. Traditional tests that have been normed on children this age. The literature seems to be dominated by four such tests: the Stanford-Binet, the WPPSI, the McCarthy Scales of Children's Abilities, and the Kaufman Assessment Battery for Children.

Available methods. From a somewhat different and perhaps broader point of view, we can consider four methods available to assess preschool children:

1. individual tests, such as the Stanford-Binet;

2. multidimensional batteries; a wide variety of measures exist in this category, many covering such domains as fine and gross motor

movement, language, cognition, self-help, and personal-social-emotional aspects;

3. adaptive skill assessment measures, which focus on specific skills; and

4. adaptive process measures; these involve the assessment of complex competencies (e.g., eye contact) that can simultaneously involve social, adaptive, and cognitive abilities. (For a review of 28 such measures see Neisworth & Bagnato, 1986.)

Psychometric tests. Schakel (1986) argued that most standardized assessment tests normed on preschool age children, such as the Stanford-Binet and the WPPSI, are based on a psychometric approach, and are useful in making classification and placement decisions, but are of limited use in truly understanding a child's cognitive development. In addition to these scales based upon a "psychometric" approach, there are also the following:

1. Piagetian-based scales. The cognitive developmental theory of Piaget has served as a springboard for several scales (e.g., the Concept Assessment Kit, Goldschmidt, & Bentler, 1968), that attempt to measure the child's cognitive level in accord with the various stages proposed by Piaget. Such scales however, have been criticized (e.g., Dunst & Gallagher, 1983), and have not found widespread use.

2. Comprehensive Developmental Assessment Tools. These are typically checklists of items drawn from descriptions of normal child development. They usually cover several domains of development, including the cognitive domain. Some of these checklists involve standardized administration, while others involve informal administration by observing the child and/or interviewing the parent. One example of this type is the Brigance Inventory of Early Development (Brigance, 1978). Items that are failed on these tests typically are targeted for intervention because the items usually reflect observable behaviors that reflect specific skills.

3. Process-oriented assessment approaches. The main assumption of these approaches is that the identification of cognitive strategies is necessary to understand cognitive performance, i.e., what is important is not the answer but how one arrives

at the answer. Thus, testing is not seen as static, but as part of the test-teach-test sequence. Many of these techniques involve allowing the child to learn from the testing experience.

Equivalence of instruments. In Chapter 4, we discussed a number of instruments, such as the Stanford-Binet, the Wechsler, and the K-ABC, that can be used with this age range. From a psychometric point of view, one concern is the equivalence of such instruments. Note that part of the answer is provided by the correlation coefficient – that is, do scores on one test correlate with scores on the other test? But this is only part of the answer. Scores on the two tests could correlate substantially, yet one test might produce consistently higher IQs than the other test. If the IQ score was then used to make practical decisions, such as placing a child in a special program, use of different tests would produce different decisions.

Two of the tests discussed in Chapter 4 are the Stanford-Binet and the K-ABC, both quite useful with preschool children. In one study, the Stanford-Binet IV and the K-ABC were administered to 36 preschool children, aged 3 to 5 (Hendershott, Searight, Hatfield, et al., 1990). The authors obtained no significant differences between the overall mean composite scores on the two tests, and scores on most dimensions across the two tests were moderately to highly intercorrelated. Thus, the two tests seem fairly equivalent.

Gerken and Hodapp (1992) compared the Stanford-Binet L-M with the WPPSI-R in a group of 16 preschoolers, all of whom had been referred for assessment as to whether they were eligible for special-educational services. The children ranged in age from 3 to 6. The average S-B IQ for these children was 77.93, vs. a WPPSI-R mean IQ of 75.62, with 10 of the 16 children obtaining higher IQs on the S-B than on the WPPSI-R. However, scores on the two tests correlated .82. Equivalence then is a function not only of the test forms used but the nature of the child tested.

Lowered reliability. One of the general findings is that the reliability of tests administered to young children is often quite low, even though the same instrument with older children will achieve quite respectable levels of reliability. Paget and Nagle (1986) indicate that the lowered reliability should not be taken as evidence of psychometric weakness, but rather reflective of the rapid developmental changes characteristic of this age group. Preschool children comprise a "unique" population, and not simply a younger version of school-aged children. There is wide variability in their experiential background in terms of exposure to adults, preschool environments, peers, demands for responsible behavior, and so on.

Test requirements. As we discussed in Chapter 12, certain children present special challenges, and a test that may be quite useful with normal children may be of limited use with special populations. Bagnato (1984) indicates that the major dilemma when assessing preschoolers who are handicapped is finding scales that are technically adequate, yet appropriate for the child's disabilities, practical for planning interventions, and sensitive for monitoring developmental progress.

Assessing social and emotional functioning. This area of measurement is a relatively new one, and dates to the 1960s when compensatory-education programs such as Head Start were begun. These programs were based on the premise that children who presumably were not ready for first grade because of their disadvantaged background, must receive preschool experiences so that they would become "school ready." Thus the assessment of school readiness, defined not only in cognitive terms, but also in personal and social terms, such as self-confidence, self-discipline, and positive attitudes toward others, became a set of expectations against which to compare the behavior of the school child (R. P. Martin, 1986).

Preparing for testing. Romero (1992) suggests a number of preparatory steps be taken before testing a preschool child. First, the examiner needs to have a clear and specific referral question. Often the referral is made in very general terms – for example, "assess this child for educational placement," and so the referral source needs to be interviewed to determine what information is wanted and how findings and recommendations can be related to remedial action or placement decisions. A second step is to study the available data determining, for example, whether the child has certain medical conditions such as

vision problems that may alter the testing procedure. A third step is to identify all the relevant persons who need to be involved in the assessment, such as parents, school nurse, pediatrician, teachers, and so on. The fourth step is to determine which areas of assessment need to be emphasized. Testing often covers such areas as cognitive functioning, social-emotional behavior, motor coordination, adaptive competencies, and language – but in specific cases some of these may be of paramount importance. Finally, an overall testing strategy is developed. The examiner decides which specific tests will be used, in what order they will be administered, and what specific adaptations will need to be made. (See Nuttall, Romero, & Kalesnik, 1992, for an excellent overview on assessing and screening preschoolers.)

ASSESSMENT IN THE PRIMARY GRADES

The various concerns we have discussed typically continue to be relevant as the child advances into the primary grades. However, a new focus appears, and that is how much the child achieves in school. Thus, achievement test batteries become important. A typical example is the California Achievement Tests (CAT) battery.

The California Achievement Tests (CAT)

The CAT is one of several nationally standardized, broad-spectrum achievement test batteries designed to assess the basic skills taught in elementary and secondary schools. The CAT measures basic skills in reading, language, spelling, mathematics, study skills, science, and social studies, and is designed for use in kindergarten through the twelfth grade. This test battery was first used in 1943 and has undergone a number of revisions, with the fifth edition published in 1992. There are two major uses for the CAT: first, to determine which specific skills students have or have not mastered, and second, to compare students' performance with that of a national sample.

Description. The items in the CAT are multiple-choice items, most with four response choices. They range in difficulty level, with an average difficulty level of about 50%. The items are printed in test booklets, and beginning with grade 4, there are separate answer sheets. At the primary-grade levels the test administrator reads both the directions and the items aloud to the students. At the upper-elementary and secondary-grade levels, only the directions are read aloud. This is a group-administered test battery designed to be administered by classroom teachers, with the help of proctors.

There are three formats or combinations to the CAT: the Basic Skills Battery, the Complete Battery, and the Survey Tests. These formats differ in the number of items per subtest, and in the kind of scores that are reported. The Basic Skills Battery provides both norm-referenced and curriculum-referenced results for reading, spelling, language, mathematics, and study skills. The Complete Battery has two parallel forms and covers the same areas as the Basic Skills Battery, plus science and social studies. Subtests in both the Basic Skills Battery and the Complete Battery contain 24 to 50 items. The Survey Tests provide norm-referenced scores for the same areas as the Complete Battery, but each subtest is composed of fewer items, in other words, the Survey Tests can be considered a "short" form of the Complete Battery. The drawback is that the Survey Tests do not provide curriculum-referenced scores, and because they are shorter, the standard error of measurement is larger.

Each subtest has time limits, although the CAT is not intended to be a speed test. Subtest time limits vary from 14 to 50 minutes, and administration of the Complete Battery takes anywhere from $1\frac{1}{2}$ to more than 5 hours, depending on the level used.

Locator tests. Within a particular classroom, there may be a fairly wide range of achievement. If the exact test were administered to all pupils, the brightest might well be bored and not challenged, while the less competent may well be discouraged. To minimize this, the CAT uses "locator tests" that consist of 20 multiple-choice vocabulary items and 20 multiple-choice mathematics items; the child's performance can be used as a guideline on which level of the CAT to administer.

Some special features. The CAT has been praised for a variety of aspects that reflect a highly professional product. For example, the test

booklets are easy to read and use, and the type and graphics are legible and attractive (Carney & Schattgen, 1994). The test manuals, including the directions for administration, are very clearly written and provide comprehensive directions. There are practice tests that allow students experience in taking a standardized test. Braille and large-type editions are available for visually impaired examinees.

The tests at different school levels are "linked" together, both statistically and theoretically as well as by actual items, so that continuity is assured. Thus a child can be tested in the fifth grade, and retested in the seventh grade, with assurance that the test scores are comparable, rather than reflecting two different tests.

There is a vast amount of material available on the CAT, including a guidebook for the classroom teacher, a guide for test directors, comprehensive technical summaries, and test reviews in sources such as the *Mental Measurements Yearbook*.

Scoring. Booklets for kindergarten through grade 3, and answer sheets for grades 4 through 12 are available in both hand-scorable and computer-scorable formats. The publisher offers computer scoring services with a number of reporting options that provide scores for the individual student as well as for specific units, such as classrooms and grades. The individual student reports contain clear and comprehensive explanations of the results, so that teachers and parents can readily understand the test results. Test scores are reported on a scale that ranges from 0 to 999 and, because of the way it was developed using item-response theory, is actually an equal interval scale.

Interrelationship of subtests. Do the CAT subtests measure different domains? In fact, the subtests intercorrelate substantially with each other, with coefficients in the .50 to .80 range. There is thus substantial overlap, suggesting that perhaps the test battery is really assessing a general construct (g?) (Airasian, 1989). In fact, scores on the CAT tend to correlate substantially with scores on tests of cognitive abilities, with coefficients in the .60 to .80 range. This could be a troublesome aspect, particularly because the newest edition of the CAT is said to measure more general understanding, skills, and processes, rather than factual content; it is not clear, at a conceptual level, whether we have an achievement or an aptitude test.

Reliability. In general, the reliability estimates of the CAT seem satisfactory (Carney & Schattgen, 1994). Much of the focus is on internal consistency, with K-R 20 reliability coefficients ranging from about .65 to .95; most of the coefficients are in the .80s and .90s. The lower reliabilities occur at the younger grades and with the shorter subtests. Alternate form reliability coefficients are in the .75 to .85 range, and test-retest reliability coefficients in the .80 to .95 range.

Content validity. As mentioned in Chapter 3, content validity is of major importance to educational tests, and so it is not surprising that authors of achievement test batteries place great emphasis on content validity, often at the expense of other types of validity.

The content validity of the CAT was built into the test from the beginning, as it should have. Educational objectives to be measured were specified by reviewing curriculum guides, instructional programs, textbooks, and other relevant materials. Individual items were written by professional item writers, with vocabulary difficulty and readability closely monitored. Both teachers and curriculum experts reviewed the items, and special steps were taken to ensure that gender, ethnic, or racial bias were avoided. For the fifth revision, new items were administered and cross-validated with representative samples of students, and the results analyzed using item-response theory.

Unfortunately, there is less information available on other types of validity. For example, the test manuals contain evidence that mastery of a particular content area, as assessed by the CAT, increases within a grade level from Fall to Spring, and increases across grade levels.

Norms. Both Fall and Spring norms are available, so that depending on the time of test administration, a better comparison can be made. The norms are based on sizable samples of pupils at each level (typically around 10,000), selected on the basis of a stratified random-sampling procedure, with minority groups well represented, with Catholic and private schools included, and

with an overall normative sample in excess of 300,000 students.

The Lake Wobegon effect. One of the reasons why achievement test batteries are revised frequently is the need for current norms. Garrison Keillor, a humorist with a popular radio program, talks about a community where, "all the men are good looking, all the women are strong, and all the children are above average." This "Lake Wobegon effect" was applied to the results of national achievement tests where most school districts using the test were reporting above-average results. The reason for this, in part, has to do with the recency of available norms. Because children are learning more, a comparison of their performance vs. "older" norms will yield a more positive comparison than using more recent norms (Linn, Grave, & Sanders, 1990). Unfortunately, the results of a test battery like the CAT often take on a life of their own and are misused as a yardstick against which to measure the performance of teachers and the whole community. (As I write this, the newspapers report a national scandal in which teachers altered the answers of their pupils to obtain higher test scores.)

Overall evaluation. Carney and Schattgen (1994) note that the development of the CAT was carried out in a very thorough and professional manner, and that efforts to achieve content validity were "first-rate." The CAT is also praised for its clarity and ease of use, and for the variety of score reports available, so that a particular school system can choose what best fits its needs.

The CAT is generally seen as a well-constructed state-of-the-art battery, that compares very favorably to other achievement-test batteries such as the Iowa Tests of Basic Skills, the Metropolitan Achievement Tests, and the Stanford Achievement Tests. However, it is faulted for not providing complete information on test-retest reliability and construct validity (e.g., Wardrop, 1989).

Teacher Rating Scales

These rating scales of childhood behavior problems are used widely by school psychologists.

They are easy to administer and score, and can provide a summary evaluation of the child's behavior in the setting where they spend most of their time – the classroom. These scales can be quite useful for direct measurement and can provide a guide for later interviews with the teacher, parent, or for direct observation. These scales can also be used to evaluate treatment programs, such as the effect of medications or of behavioral interventions. Many teacher-rating scales have been developed, often with a specific focus that is different from scale to scale.

Neeper and Lahey (1984) undertook a study to determine what the common dimensions of teacher-rating scales might be, and whether these dimensions might be related to well-established factors of maladaptive behavior. They developed a 60-item teacher-rating scale designed to reflect a broad range of childhood behavior problems and cognitive deficits. They asked 26 teachers to rate a total of 649 children in the second through fifth grades. A factor analysis indicated five meaningful factors:

I. A Conduct disorders factor accounted for 60.9% of the common variance and was defined by such items as "disrespectful to teacher" and "fights with other children."

II. Inattentive-perceptual factor accounted for 15.2% of the common variance and was defined by such items as "starts to work before making sure of directions" and "confuses visually similar words or numbers."

III. Anxiety-depression accounted for 9% of the common variance and was defined by such items as "appears tense or nervous" and "seems depressed."

IV. Language processing accounted for 7.9% of the common variance and was defined by such items as "does not speak clearly and fluently" and "doesn't seem to think in a coherent, logical fashion."

V. Social competence accounted for 7.2% of the common variance and was defined by such items as "is able to join in ongoing group activities easily" and "cooperates actively with other children in a group."

These five factors were used to develop five corresponding scales. A subsample of 45 children was re-rated 2 weeks later and test-retest correlation coefficients computed; these ranged from a low of .69 to a high of .89, indicating adequate reliability. A correlational analysis indicated that some of the scales correlated significantly with each other, with correlation coefficients ranging from a low of $-.13$ (between factors 4 and 5), to a high of .64 (between factors 1 and 2). One of Neeper and Lahey's conclusions was that currently published teacher-rating scales are not sufficiently comprehensive.

HIGH SCHOOL

Social Competence. One of the critical aspects of adolescence is the development of social competence. This is a complex construct that probably involves such aspects as achieving age-appropriate goals and having good social skills.

Cavell and Kelley (1994) developed a self-report measure of social competence to identify adolescents experiencing significant interpersonal difficulties. They first asked a large sample of 7th, 9th, and 11th graders to answer an open-ended questionnaire and describe situations that "did not go well" in a variety of areas. They obtained a total of 4,005 such problem descriptions that were then sorted into single categories, with redundant items eliminated. This yielded a pool of 157 discrete problem situations (e.g., Friend ignores you; Sibling refuses to let you borrow something). Adolescents were then asked to rate each situation on 5-point Likert response scales as to how often the situation had occurred (frequency) and how difficult it had been to deal with the situation (difficulty). A factor analysis yielded seven factors that comprised 75 items. These factors were labeled: (1) Keep Friends (e.g., Friend tells others your secrets); (2) Problem Behavior (e.g., You want to drink alcohol, but your parents object); (3) Siblings (e.g., Sibling embarrasses you in front of your friends); (4) School (e.g., Teacher is mean to everyone including you); (5) Parents (e.g., Parents are too nosy); (6) Work (e.g., You dislike your job and your boss, but you need the money); (7) Make Friends (e.g., Peers don't like you because of your appearance).

Each of the seven scales could then be scored for frequency and for difficulty. Internal consistency, coefficient alpha, for the seven scales seem substantial. For the frequency scores alphas ranged from .79 to .90 (median $\alpha = .86$), and for difficulty scales they ranged from .87 to .90 (median $\alpha = .89$). These coefficients are, as the authors indicate, somewhat inflated because they were computed on the same sample used for the factor analysis. The individual scales were inter-correlated with one another, some to a substantial degree. For example, Keep Friends and Make Friends correlated .68; Siblings and Work, on the other hand, correlated .16.

The authors report a number of interesting findings. For example, situations involving parents and siblings were the most frequently occurring, whereas situations involving problem behavior and work were relatively infrequent events. Situations involving parents and current friends were seen as the most difficult, and problem behavior and work as least difficult. Two of the scales, Problem Behavior and Work showed significant gender differences as to frequency, with male adolescents rating these situations as more common. Three scales – Parents, School, and Keep Friends – showed significant gender differences as to difficulty, with females rating these problem situations as more difficult.

In a second study, the authors revised the scoring procedure slightly and combined the frequency and difficulty ratings into one score, and found that this seemed to be a more accurate assessment of adolescents' social performance. In a third study, they assessed the concurrent validity of their scale, by comparing scale scores with peer nominations of most liked and least liked, with teachers' ratings of peer acceptance, and with a standardized measure of parent-adolescent conflict.

In this third study, reliability was also assessed. Internal consistency yielded a median α of .81, but for the Problem Behavior scale, α was .58. Test-retest reliability over a 2-week period ranged from .72 for Work to .86 for School, with a median coefficient of .78. Adolescents who were seen by peers and teachers as popular were compared with those seen as unpopular. Unpopular adolescents scored significantly higher on Parents, School, and Make Friends, and generally endorsed more overall problem situations. Similarly, adolescents who scored higher on the measure of parent-adolescent conflict scored higher on five of the seven scales. These findings support the construct validity of this questionnaire.

Tests of General Educational Development (GED Tests)

The GED tests, developed by the American Council on Education, are used throughout the United States and Canada to award high-school level equivalency credentials to adults who did not graduate from high school. Specific score requirements are set by each state or Canadian province. More than 700,000 adults take the GED tests each year, and nearly 470,000 are awarded a high school equivalency diploma (Whitney, Malizio, & Patience, 1986).

Description. The GED battery contains five tests: (1) writing skills; (2) social studies; (3) science; (4) reading skills; and (5) mathematics. Because of the nature of this battery, new forms of each test are continually produced, so questions about reliability and validity can either focus on a specific form, or more usefully, on the test itself regardless of form.

Reliability. Whitney, Malizio, and Patience (1986) present K-R coefficients for different forms used in 1980, for both large samples of U.S. graduating high-school seniors, and for samples of GED examinees. The results are summarized in Table 13.1. These coefficients reflect a high degree of reliability for the various forms and for both samples. As you see, the K-R 20 coefficients are slightly lower for the GED examinees, reflecting their lesser variability in their scores.

During the 1980 standardization study, samples of high-school seniors took two different forms of the GED tests. This allowed the computation of alternate forms reliability; obtained coefficients ranged from .76 to .89, with the majority of the coefficients in the low to mid .80s, again suggesting substantial reliability. These

Table 13–1. Range of K-R 20 Coefficients for the GED Tests (Whitney, Malizio, & Patience, 1986)		
GED test	**High-School seniors**	**GED examinees**
Writing skills	.93 to .94	.88 to .94
Social studies	.91 to .93	.86 to .94
Science	.90 to .93	.86 to .93
Reading skills	.89 to .92	.85 to .93
Mathematics	.90 to .93	.81 to .92

coefficients are somewhat lower than the K-R 20 coefficients because different forms of the tests were used and were administered on different days, thus introducing two additional sources of error variation.

Content validity. Because the GED tests are intended to measure "the major and lasting outcomes of a high school program of study," the authors argue that content validity is of greatest importance. You recall that content validity is carried out primarily by logical analyses of test items, and that ordinarily it is built into the test rather than analyzed afterwards. Items from the GED tests are written by teams of experienced educators, and test content is carefully analyzed by other teams of curriculum specialists and related professionals.

Concurrent validity. As indicated above, the GED tests are also administered to national samples of high-school graduating seniors, even though the tests are intended for adults who have left the high-school environment without obtaining the degree. One reason for doing this is to ascertain that the decision made on the basis of the GED test scores is equivalent to the decision made by high schools, that is, the test scores truly reflect a high-school equivalency performance. Considering the typical GED scores required by most states, somewhere between 27% and 33% of currently graduating high-school seniors would be considered to have failed the GED tests. Thus, the standards used in the GED testing program are somewhat more stringent than those employed by high schools.

Another aspect of concurrent validity concerns the correlations between tests. The GED tests do correlate substantially with each other: correlation coefficients range from .63 for the Mathematics vs. Writing Skills to .82 for Science versus Social Studies. All of the tests require that the examinee read and interpret written material, and four of the tests involve the use of written passages followed by a series of questions. Therefore, it is not surprising that the tests correlate significantly with each other. We would hope that these correlation coefficients are somewhat lower than the parallel forms reliability – i.e., the Writing Skills test should correlate more with itself

(different form) than with another GED test, and that seems to be the case.

There is a substantial body of literature available, although most of it is in American Council on Education publications, indicating that correlations between GED tests and tests in other batteries designed to assess similar or identical variables are quite substantial and generally support the validity of this battery.

Predictive validity. Predictive validity is somewhat more difficult to document in this case because the test battery is not designed to measure a specific variable for which specific predictions can be made, but rather assesses the equivalency of a broad educational procedure, i.e., high school. One aspect of predictive validity can be found in nationwide follow-up studies of GED graduates who indicate that passing the GED tests led to improvements in pay, acceptance into training programs, and other benefits. Of course, such data is somewhat suspect because we don't know to what degree the responses were elicited by the questions asked, or do we know what happened to individuals who did not take the GED tests.

The National Assessment of Educational Progress (NAEP)

The NAEP is a Congressionally mandated survey of American students' educational achievement; it was first conducted in 1969, annually through 1980, and biennially since then. The goal of the NAEP is to estimate educational achievement and changes in that achievement over time, for American students of specific ages, gender, and demographic characteristics (E. G. Johnson, 1992).

The items used by the NAEP are similar to those in teacher-made classroom tests and standardized achievement tests. However, such tests are designed to measure the proficiencies of an individual. The NAEP is designed to measure the distribution of proficiencies in student populations. Thus, not every student is tested, nor are the tested students presented with the same items.

The NAEP covers a wide range of school-subject areas such as reading, mathematics, writing, science, social studies, music, and computer competence. Students are tested at ages 9, 13, and 17 corresponding somewhat to grades 4, 8, and

12. Some subject areas, such as reading and mathematics, are assessed every 2 years, while other areas are assessed every 4 or 6 years. For sample items and an overview of the development of the NAEP, see Mullis (1992).

The items or exercises for each content area were developed using a consensus approach, where large committees of experts including concerned citizens specified the objectives for each content area. The test results are then analyzed using item-response theory.

The NAEP was conceived as an information system that would yield indicators of educational progress, just as the Consumer Price Index is one indicator of economic health (R. L. Linn & Dunbar, 1992). Rather than report global test scores, analyses of the NAEP are based on the individual items or exercises; thus the basic scoring unit is the percentage of test takers who successfully complete a particular exercise.

Essay vs. Multiple Choice

Tests composed of multiple-choice items are quite often vilified with the arguments that they merely test factual knowledge rather than the ability to think, to produce arguments, to organize factual material, and so on. From a psychometric and a practical point of view, multiple-choice items are preferable because they are easy to score by machine, do not involve the measurement error created by subjective scoring, are more reliable and more amenable to statistical analyses. In addition, well-written multiple-choice items can indeed assess the more complicated and desirable aspects of cognitive functioning.

Bridgeman and Lewis (1994) addressed this issue by looking at Advanced Placement (AP) examinations in the fields of American History, European History, English, and Biology, which contain both multiple-choice and essay sections. The AP examinations are taken by high-school students who are seeking college credit or placement into advanced college courses. Thus, content validity of these exams is of importance. Bridgeman and Lewis (1994) tabulated the AP scores for a nationwide sample of more than 7,000 students from 32 colleges, and compared these to GPA obtained in the same topic-area courses. It is interesting to note the differences in

reliability between the essay and multiple-choice sections for these exams. For example, the K-R 20 reliability for the American History exam, multiple-choice section was .90 and .89 for two yearly samples vs. a coefficient alpha of .54 for the essay section. The correlations between the multiple-choice and essay sections were .48 and .53; similar findings were obtained on all other AP exams. In other words, scores on the essay sections are not reliable and do not correlate highly with the scores on the multiple-choice sections. What about correlations with GPA? Multiple-choice scores from the American History and Biology examinations were more highly correlated with freshman GPA than were essay scores. For the European History and English examinations, the differences between correlation coefficients from multiple-choice sections and essay sections were not significant, and a composite of the two sections was a better predictor of GPA than either section by itself.

ADMISSION INTO COLLEGE

The Scholastic Aptitude Test (SAT)

Historical note. In 1900, 12 colleges and universities joined the College Entrance Examination Board, an organization created by an association of colleges, to bring some order into the chaotic world of admission examinations, which up to that time varied substantially from institution to institution (M. R. Linn, 1993). The first examinations prepared by this Board were essay type, but in 1926 the Board presented the Scholastic Aptitude Test (SAT). Some 8,040 candidates were tested in that year, versus the 1 million plus who are tested currently. At first, only a total score was provided, but subsequent analyses indicated that verbal and mathematical scores did not correlate highly, and so the two scores were kept separate.

The SAT was actually intended to fight discrimination in the college admission process. At that time, selective colleges such as the Ivy League schools had relationships with specific college preparatory academies, so that students from those schools could be admitted readily without too much regard for their academic credentials, but with emphasis on their social and ethnic characteristics. By introducing a test such as the SAT into the admission process, equal opportunity was presented to all.

From the early years, the standard score system with a mean of 500 and SD of 100 was used. However, this did not permit comparison of one year's candidates with those of the following year because each test form contained different items, but the mean was always equated to 500. It was decided to use the candidates who took the April 1941 test as the normative sample. This was made possible because each subsequent form does contain some identical items to the prior form, and thus statistically, it is possible to equate the scores on such forms.

Prior to 1958, test scores on the SAT were not given to the students, and so it was quite easy for admission officers to indicate that a student had been rejected because of low SAT scores, whereas in fact the rejection might be based on marginal high-school grades or other aspects.

In terms of college admissions, the Scholastic Aptitude Test clearly dominates the field, followed by the Academic Tests of the American College Testing Program, known as the ACT.

Description. The content of the SAT has changed very little since its inception. From the beginning there have been two major content areas: verbal and quantitative. The current SAT Verbal section consists of four item types: antonyms, analogies, sentence completion, and reading comprehension. The antonyms have been used since 1926 and the other three since the mid 1940s (Bejar, Embretson, & Mayer, 1987).

The SAT quantitative (or SAT-M) appears to be unidimensional, so there is little empirical justification for dividing the SAT-M score into subscores. The SAT-V however, seems to be composed of two distinct but highly related dimensions: a reading dimension and a vocabulary dimension (Dorans & Lawrence, 1987).

Each of the 85 verbal and 60 mathematical items is a five-option multiple-choice task, scored by a formula intended to offset any gain in score that might be expected from blind guessing (R. M. Kaplan, 1982).

The SAT can be described as an outcome-oriented test, as opposed to a process-oriented test. In an outcome oriented test, what matters is the total score that reflects the number of correct answers. With a process-oriented test, the focus is on both the correct and incorrect answers, and the emphasis is on diagnostic utility, i.e., the pattern of responses is related to a diagnosis. Thus, the SAT is not intended to be a diagnostic tool.

Revisions. In one sense, the SAT is continually being revised because new forms are generated for every test administration. Revision in the sense of major changes does not occur too frequently. The SAT was revised in 1994 and these revisions include longer reading comprehension passages with questions that ask students to focus more on the context of the reading; math questions that require students to generate their own answers; and more time per question on the test, so there is less time pressure.

A number of changes were also made on the Achievement Tests, such as the inclusion of a 20-minute essay in the English Achievement Test. These achievement tests are now called SAT IIs, to emphasize that they supplement the SAT, now called the SAT I.

Part of the 1995 revision involved "recentering" the scores. Theoretically, although the mean for the SAT is supposed to be 500, for 1993 college-bound seniors the verbal mean was 424 and the math mean was 478. Such recentering involves statistical calculations that increase the scores but do not change the percentile ranking – very much like adding X number of points to each score to make the average come out to be 500 (Educational Testing Service, 1994).

More recent revisions include essay portions and different scoring procedures.

Multiple-choice items. Perhaps more than any other test, the SAT represents the stereotypical use of multiple-choice items, which are praised by test experts, but criticized by critics. Multiple-choice items are advantageous not only because they can be scored by machine and thus are relatively inexpensive, but because they permit a much wider sampling of the subject matter and the student's abilities. In the same amount of time, we can ask a student to answer four or five short essay questions on American History, or we can administer 100+ multiple-choice items. A test made up of multiple-choice items can be planned carefully by specifying what is to be covered in terms of content and of abilities. Thus, the content validity of multiple-choice tests is usually substantially higher than that of essay tests. Finally, multiple-choice items can be studied systematically to determine which items work as designed.

Test sophistication. One of the concerns that test developers have is the degree of test sophistication or test-taking familiarity a person may have. We want a test score to reflect a person's standing on the variable tested, and not the degree of familiarity the subject has with multiple-choice items. This is a particular concern with tests such as the SAT where, on the one hand, sophisticated examinees should not "beat the test" and, on the other hand, naive examinees should not be penalized (D. E. Powers & Alderman, 1983).

Two approaches are usually taken to remove sophistication as an extraneous variable. The first is to make sure that the test items and directions are easy to read, not complicated, and do not have extraneous clues that can help test-wise examinees. The second approach is to make sure that all examinees are equally sophisticated by teaching all of them the precepts of good test-taking strategies (e.g., budget your time; don't spend too much time on any one item, etc.), and by providing practice examples of test items. In 1978, the College Board introduced a booklet called *Taking the SAT*, designed to familiarize students with the SAT and provide all candidates with the same basic information about the test. Before the booklet was made available to all students, pre-publication copies were sent to a random sample of SAT candidates. A comparison was then made of the effects of the booklet on test scores. The results indicated that, although the booklet was useful, reading it had a minimal effect on subsequent test scores.

Gender gap. There is currently an average difference of about 59 points on the combined score on the SAT between men and women, in favor of men. This is somewhat peculiar because the outcome that the SAT is supposed to predict, college-freshman year GPA, is consistently slightly higher for women than for men. This gender gap is primarily made up of lower mean scores on the math section for women; since the 1960s male students have scored an average of 46 points higher than female students (College Entrance Examination Board, 1988). But since 1972 it is also reflected in

lower SAT-V scores. As a rule, women score better on verbal tests than men. Therefore, the implication is that there may be something "unusual" about the SAT.

There is a substantial body of literature on gender differences in mathematical ability indicating that female students outperform male students on measures of mathematical ability at the elementary and middle-school levels, but male students outperform female students at the high-school and college levels (e.g., L. R. Aiken, 1987). There is also evidence that the gender difference in a variety of math tests has become smaller over time, so the persistent gender difference on the SAT is quite puzzling (Byrnes & Takahira, 1993; Hyde, Fennema, & Lamon, 1990).

These test differences do not appear to be related to such aspects as choice of a college major, different career interests, or different courses taken in high school. One suggested possibility is that the gender gap is due to the increasing number of women, particularly minority women, who are taking the test.

As a predictor of college success, the SAT underpredicts the performance of women (their predicted GPA is lower than their actual GPA) and overpredicts that of men (their predicted GPA is higher than their actual GPA, Clark & Grandy, 1984). Sheehan and Gray (1991) compared results on the SAT with the results on a standardized algebra exam taken by entering freshmen and transfer students at American University, a private university in Washington, D.C. The mean combined SAT score for women students was 1,096 and for men students 1,132. Their mean college GPA however, was 3.01 for women and 2.89 for men. Scores on the algebra test had a higher correlation with college GPA than did the SAT scores, but all the correlations were lower than .30. The results of this study indicated no gender gap on the algebra test, but a gender difference on the combined SAT and on the GPA. The authors felt that this gender difference was not due to the hypothesis that women choose less difficult majors, or that more women with fewer economic and intellectual advantages take the SAT, or that women have more difficulty with multiple-choice tests. They also concluded that the SAT is not a valid predictor of academic achievement, and that a better approach might be to use achievement tests.

Byrnes and Takahira (1993) suggested that the gender difference on the SAT reflects the fact that male students perform certain cognitive operations more effectively than female students. In an experimental study of high-school students, they tested and found support for the hypothesis that performance on SAT items was due to differences in cognitive skills such as the ability to define the problem and avoid misleading alternatives.

Minority bias. The use of standardized tests in the selection of applicants for admission to college theoretically benefits both the institution and the individual. By identifying students who potentially will fail, the institution is less likely to waste its resources, and so is the individual. Both false negatives (a selected individual who fails) and false positives (a potentially successful student who is rejected) are of concern, however.

Thorndike (1971) argued that if members of a minority group tend, on the average, to score lower on the predictor (i.e., the SAT) than on the criterion (i.e., GPA) as compared with the majority, then there will be a relatively higher incidence of false negatives, if the test is used as a selection device. R. D. Goldman and Widawski (1976) analyzed student scores at four universities and found that the use of the SAT in selection of black and Mexican-American students shifted the number of errors from the false positive category to the false negative category.

A number of studies have shown that minority or disadvantaged students, when admitted to college, can do quite well academically, despite relatively low Scholastic Aptitude Test scores. These findings raise issues about the validity of such scores for minority students, and a number of studies have shown that high-school achievement is a better predictor of college achievement than are test scores. In general, high-school GPA correlates about .30 with college GPA, with test scores adding little to the prediction.

Houston (1980) studied a small sample ($n =$ 61) of black students given "special" admission to a university. A comparison of those students who had graduated within eight semesters vs. those who had been dismissed for academic reasons indicated significant differences in high-school rank, college GPA, and SAT-M scores, but not on SAT-V. Although the difference was in the "right" direction of 371 vs. 339, the sample size was too

Table 13–2. Correlations between Predicted GPA and Obtained GPA (McCormack, 1983)

Group	Year 1	Year 2
White	.38	.42
Asian	.57	.54
Hispanic	.35	.52
Black	.36	.40
Indian	.40	.42

small and the variation too large to obtain significance.

McCormack (1983) studied the issue of minority bias on the SAT by analyzing the SAT scores and scholastic records of students at a large state university in California. He first developed a regression equation to predict first semester college GPA for white students only. The equation looked like this:

$$\text{College GPA} = .73555 \text{ high-school GPA} + .08050 \text{ SAT-Total}/100 - .67447$$

Note that high-school GPA is a better predictor than the SAT-Total as indicated by its larger weight. The last number in the equation is simply a mathematical "correction" to make the two sides of the equation equal.

For each person in the sample, we can compute the expected GPA using this equation and compare the expected GPA to the actual obtained GPA. To the degree that the prediction is accurate, the two GPAs should be equal, i.e., the average error should be zero. If the equation systematically underpredicts, that is, if the predicted GPA is lower than the actual GPA, then the average error should be positive; conversely, overprediction should result in a negative error.

How well did the equation work for white students and for minority students? Table 13.2 gives the correlations between the predicted GPA and the obtained GPA for two cohorts of freshmen.

Note that the regression equation seems to work relatively well in both cohorts for all ethnic groups, including minority groups, and especially for Asian students. What about the SAT taken individually and high-school GPA taken individually? How did these variables correlate with actual GPA? Table 13.3 provides the answers.

Table 13–3. Correlations between SAT and High-School GPA with Actual College GPA (McCormack, 1983)				
	SAT		High-school GPA	
Group	Year 1	Year 2	Year 1	Year 2
White	.22	.24	.35	.37
Asian	.26	.53	.56	.45
Hispanic	.16	.44	.34	.47
Black	.29	.39	.29	.37
Indian	.04	.23	.40	.32

Note that with the possible exception of black students, high-school GPA is a better predictor than SAT scores (keep in mind that high-school GPA summarizes 4 years of behavior, whereas the SAT reflects a few hours). Note also that there is a fair amount of variability from one cohort to the other, but generally the results of the regression equation are better than either variable by itself. A statistical analysis did in fact indicate a small overprediction for minority groups, except for American Indians.

J. Fleming and Garcia (1998) studied black students attending predominantly black and predominantly white colleges. Although their findings are too complex to summarize here, they suggest that any racial differences in the predictive validity of the SAT may be more a function of adjustment problems than inherent bias in the SAT.

The SAT and Mexican-Americans. Goldman and Richards (1974) analyzed SAT scores and academic performance, as defined by second quarter college GPA, for a sample of Mexican-American and Anglo-American students attending a large California university. On the SAT-V, SAT-M, and GPA, the Anglo students scored higher. For the Mexican-Americans, SAT-V correlated .33 with GPA, and SAT-M correlated .12 (corresponding correlations for the Anglo group were .40 and .37). A regression equation developed on the Anglo group correlated .44 with GPA. When this regression equation was applied to the Mexican-American sample, there was an overprediction of GPA; the actual average GPA was 2.28, but the predicted GPA was 2.66. The entire study was replicated on a subsequent larger sample with similar results.

The authors concluded that if the SAT is used to predict the grades of Mexican-American students, using a regression equation developed on Anglos, the result will be overprediction of grades, that is, the students will do less well than what is predicted. If however, the equation is based on Mexican-American norms, the predictive validity of the SAT will be similar for Mexican-American students as for Anglo students.

Utility or validity? One of the major investigators in the area of using aptitude and achievement tests in college admissions has been James Crouse, who has recommended that colleges abandon the SAT and use standardized achievement tests, instead, to select incoming students (Gottfredson & Crouse, 1986).

Part of Crouse's argument is that the focus should be on the utility of a test rather than on its validity. Even if a test is unbiased and predicts desired criteria well, it does not necessarily mean that it should be used. Crouse argues that the practical benefits of the SAT for college admissions are minimal because the SAT provides predictions of success that are largely redundant with those made from high-school grades alone. SAT scores and high-school rank are moderately correlated (in the .40 to .50 range) with each other and with educational outcomes such as college GPA, so that outcomes predicted from high-school rank alone have a part-whole correlation of at least .80 with outcomes predicted from high-school rank plus SAT scores.

Crouse argues that achievement tests should be substituted for the SAT in that such tests are "no worse" than the SAT in predicting academic success. Their advantage is that they would promote "diligence" in high school. The SAT is seen as a measure of how smart a person is, presumably, in part, an innate characteristic. The achievement tests, however, would reflect how hard a person is willing to work (see Crouse, 1985, and a rebuttal by Hanford, 1985).

Aptitude vs. achievement. In addition to the SAT, some colleges, particularly the more selective ones, require applicants to present scores on the CEEB achievement tests. There are a number of these, and often the candidate has some degree of choice in which ones to take, so that not all candidates present the same achievement tests.

Schrader (1971) assessed the validity of these achievement tests and found, by adding such test scores to the information already provided by high-school GPA and SAT scores, the prediction of college grades increased by about .05 for women and .03 for men. K. M. Wilson (1974) studied several liberal arts colleges for women. In these colleges, the combination of SAT-V + SAT-M correlated with first-year college grades from .13 to .53, median of about .26. By adding high-school rank, the correlations ranged from .23 to .59, with an average increase of about .12. Adding achievement test scores (an average of whatever the student had taken), the correlations ranged from .28 to .60, with an average increase of about .07.

Using a slightly different statistical analysis however, K. M. Wilson (1974) was able to show that knowing the high-school rank and the achievement test scores, the SAT scores did not improve the prediction of college GPA. In fact, he argued that the achievement tests overall average is a more valid predictor of college grades than the SAT. Baron and Norman (1992) studied close to 4,000 students who entered the University of Pennsylvania. In general, they found that both high-school class rank and average achievement-test scores added significantly to the overall prediction of cumulative GPA, but SAT scores did not.

Are aptitude/intelligence tests different from achievement tests? Kelley (1927) argued that they are not because such measures correlate substantially with each other. The argument is still unresolved.

High-school achievement tests. Should high-school achievement test results be used to predict college GPA? Because these tests are routinely given in high school, and most are nationally normed tests such as the California Achievement Tests, we might omit the SAT altogether, if we can show as a first step, that high-school achievement test scores do indeed correlate with collegiate GPA. G. Halpin, G. Halpin, and Schaer (1981) studied more than 1,400 college freshmen who had taken either the SAT or the ACT, and while in high school had taken the California Achievement Tests. How did these tests

Table 13–4. Correlations of Four Predictors with College GPA (Halpin et al., 1981)

Predictor	Correlation
High-school GPA	.49
SAT	.42
Calif. Achievement Tests	.38
ACT	.37

correlate with freshman college GPA? Table 13.4 provides the answer. When high-school GPA was combined with each of the test scores individually, the correlation with college GPA went up to .53. The authors concluded that high-school GPA was a better predictor of college grades than either the ACT, the SAT, or the CAT. Combining high-school GPA with any of the test measures increased the predictive efficiency about 18.5%, with basically no differences between tests. Therefore, the authors concluded that the CAT could be used in lieu of the SAT or the ACT.

Intelligence vs. aptitude. Feingold (1983) asked an interesting question: Are measures of intelligence, specifically the information and vocabulary subtests of the WAIS, better predictors of college achievement than are tests such as the SAT? He was able to locate four relevant studies and summarized the results, given in Table 13.5. Note that in the first two studies, the WAIS subtests are better predictors of college GPA than are achievement-test scores. In one sense, this is not at all surprising. Academic achievement is a function of the broad intellectual capabilities one has, rather than a specific degree of knowledge.

Decline in SAT scores. Because the SAT is used, or misused, to somehow assess the state of our

Table 13–5. Correlations with College GPA (Feingold, 1983)

	Achievement test[*]	WAIS information	Vocabulary
Study 1	.38	.48	.46
Study 2	.30	.43	.38
Study 3	.46	–	.45
Study 4	.25	.19	.25

[*] Note: Different achievement tests were used in the different studies; study 3 used the SAT.

educational system, the observed decline in SAT scores from year to year has been the focus of much debate and concern. A substantial number of hypotheses have been advanced to account for the decline in SAT scores; Wharton (1977) listed 79. These hypotheses cover such reasons as inadequate teacher training, changes in family values, growing anti-intellectualism, food additives, and changing family patterns. Zajonc and Bargh (1980) postulated that the decline might be due to changes in family configuration, specifically birth order and family size, since the U.S. birthrate increased steadily from the late 1940s to the early 1960s; however, the data they collected did not support such a hypothesis. Although a definitive answer cannot be given, the observed decline seems to reflect democracy at work: Each year the number of students who apply to college are less elite and more heterogeneous.

Coaching. Can special preparation, i.e., coaching, have a significant impact on SAT test scores? A large number of companies provide coaching services to a substantial group of paying students each year. D. E. Powers (1993) indicates that a positive answer would have three major implications. First, if coaching is effective but not reasonably available to all test takers, then some test takers may have an unfair advantage. Second, if such short-term preparation that essentially emphasizes test-taking strategies is effective, then the validity of the test as an index of general academic ability is called into question. Third, because such special preparation through commercial services can be quite expensive, it may detract from students' participation in other worthwhile academic activities.

The term coaching may actually subsume three somewhat different types of activities. At the most superficial level, coaching means giving subjects a test-taking orientation, that is making sure that the subject is familiar with the general procedures involved in taking a particular test. At a second level, we have the usual procedure which is to practice on items that are similar to those in the test. At a third level, coaching involves teaching broadly applicable cognitive skills.

N. Cole (1982) suggested that coaching can affect the validity of a test in three ways: (1) Coaching could increase a person's score above their "true" level, thus invalidate the test; (2)

Coaching could allow a person to do their best rather than their typical. Because such coaching would not be available to all, the validity of the test would suffer; and (3) Finally, if coaching affects test performance on a test that supposedly measures stable traits, then again validity is compromised.

Coaching can cover a variety of procedures and goals. It can aim at increasing confidence or decreasing anxiety, or it can teach specific test-taking strategies or skills. It can involve short-term cramming or long-term instruction.

Coaching companies often suggest that their services can increase retest scores by a minimum number of points. Increases in test scores on retest however, can be due to practice effects, real growth in abilities over the ensuing time period, or measurement error. Simply retaking the SAT improves test scores by about 15 points on the verbal portion, and about 12 points on the math portion. Some very limited evidence suggests a yearly average improvement of about 50 points (D. E. Powers, 1993). Measurement error can increase or decrease scores, and Powers estimates that typically 1 in 25 SAT takers will gain 100 or more total points, and about 1 in 110 will lose 100 or more points in retesting.

A substantial number of studies have looked at the question of coaching on the SAT and have come up with a variety of conclusions. Numerous study findings suggest negligible gains for students who do take such preparatory courses (e.g., Kulik, Bangert-Drowns, & Kulik, 1984; Messick & Jungeblut, 1981). These studies have also been analyzed through meta-analysis, and D. E. Powers (1993) summarizes the results of these meta-analyses. Overall, for the typical coaching program, the average increase in SAT test scores is about 15 to 25 points each on the verbal and on the mathematics sections. More specifically, Powers indicates the following conclusions: (1) The effects of coaching are somewhat greater for the mathematics than for the verbal section; (2) Longer coaching programs yield somewhat greater effects than do shorter ones, but diminishing returns set in rather quickly, e.g., doubling the effort does not double the effect; (3) More rigorous studies, in which possible confounding results are controlled, yield substantially smaller effects – estimated to be 9 points for the SAT-V and 19 points for the SAT-M; and (4) The average effect of coaching for a variety of other aptitude tests is estimated to be nearly three times the average effect for the SAT.

A typical study is that by Alderman and P. E. Powers (1980) who found an average gain of 8 points due to coaching; or that of Smyth (1989) who found that high-school students who had taken some formal preparation for the SAT scored 6 points higher on the verbal section and 32 points higher on the math than their peers who had not taken such courses. However, the analyses showed that the scores of students who took the SAT a second or third time tend to improve significantly, and that coached students do tend to take the SAT more than once. In general such coaching shows a negligible impact on verbal scores and a relatively small improvement on math (for an interesting review of some of the claims made by coaching companies see Smyth, 1990).

The criterion: First year GPA. The SAT predicts about 10% to 15% of the observed variance in first-year college grades, and so we might ask about the remaining 85% to 90%. Wainer (1993) suggests that part of the problem is that the criterion is neither well defined nor all that important – we ought to be more interested in predicting who will be a good engineer or a good social worker. One major point to keep in mind is that college grades are a very fallible criterion, and grading standards vary substantially across different majors and different institutions (e.g., R. D. Goldman & Slaughter, 1976).

Because the SAT was specifically designed to predict first-year college grades, most studies use that as the criterion. A smaller number of studies focus on total GPA. For example, J. French (1958), in a study of eight institutions, reported mean correlations of .43 and .27 between cumulative senior GPA and SAT-V and SAT-M scores. Hills, Bush, & Klock (1964) found a multiple correlation of .66 between cumulative senior GPA and a predictor composed of SAT-V, SAT-M, and high-school GPA. Mauger and Kolmodin (1975) reported correlations of .52 and .43 between "terminal" GPA and SAT-V and SAT-M scores, in a sample of students where only 32% had graduated. In a sample of graduating seniors, where the range of grades was restricted, the correlations dropped to .26 and .22 respectively.

Reliability. Test-retest, internal consistency, and alternative form reliability coefficients for the SAT range from the high .80s to the low .90s; the KR-20 reliability for the SAT-V is about .91 and for the SAT-M is about .92.

Validity. Most of the validity information is predictive validity, and most consists of correlations of SAT scores with first-year college GPA. These coefficients vary widely depending on a number of variables, such as major and institution, with coefficients ranging from the .10s to the mid .60s, but with most studies reporting a correlation near .40 between SAT scores and first-year college GPA.

Validity generalization. Traditionally, research on admission testing has emphasized the results of local validity studies, that is, using data from individual institutions. The assumption was made that validity differences from one study to another reflect the unique characteristics of different institutions and of the different applicants they attract.

The approach called *validity generalization* (see Chapter 3) has in fact shown that much of the variation in results from study to study is due to statistical artifacts, especially error from the use of small samples, and institutional differences in such things as how reliable the criterion is. Boldt (1986) studied three national samples of students who had taken the SAT, students who had applied to a particular college, and students who were admitted to a college. These samples were quite large – from 65,000 to almost 350,000. Boldt (1986) found that the internal reliability of the SAT ranged from .90 to .92 for both the verbal and the mathematics portions. The two sections correlated .68 with each other. He also concluded that the average validity for either SAT-V or SAT-M, when various sources of error were statistically controlled, was about .55.

Family income. In 1980, Ralph Nader, the well-known consumer advocate criticized the SAT, and more generally ETS, stating that the SAT was not a valid predictor of college success, and that SAT scores reflected family income more than scholastic potential (Nairn & Associates, 1980). These arguments were in part fallacious and not supported by empirical findings (Kaplan, 1982).

Although there was a time when only the wealthy and well-to-do could gain entrance to major universities, most college admission boards would argue that prospective students are evaluated on the basis of merit rather than economic background. SAT scores and parental income do correlate in the .20s; the Nader report however, incorrectly used grouped data and found an r of .96 between the two variables. Kaplan (1982) calculated the correlation between mean SAT scores and mean GPA using grouped data and found an r of .999! The point here is that computing a correlation on grouped data is misleading; what is needed is not more politically misleading propaganda, but rigorous empirical analysis.

Fair or unfair? Testing for admissions to educational institutions is a topic that generates a fair amount of heated controversy. Despite the horror stories one frequently hears about the unfairness of such tests, and how Jane did not get into her favorite university because of low test scores, surveys of test takers in fact show that most believe tests such as the SAT and the GRE are fair, that their test scores did not influence where they applied, and that they believe that institutions pay more attention to grades and other academic aspects (Baird, 1987); that indeed seems to be the case.

THE GRADUATE RECORD EXAMINATION

Purpose of the GRE. The GRE General Test and Subject Tests are designed to assess academic knowledge and skills relevant to graduate study. The GRE is designed to offer a global measure of the verbal, quantitative, and analytical reasoning abilities acquired over a long period of time and not related to a specific field of study. GRE scores are to be used in conjunction with other information to determine admissibility to graduate study. GRE scores are suitable for selection of applicants for admission to graduate school, selection of graduate fellowship applicants for award, selection of graduate teaching or research assistants, and for guidance and counseling for graduate study. However, in the *GRE Guide*, a yearly publication of the GRE Board, specific mention is made that multiple sources of information, in addition to GRE scores, should be used in making decisions about specific candidates.

The GRE has two primary limitations: (1) It does not measure all the qualities that are important in predicting success in graduate study; and (2) It is an inexact measure, that is, only score differences between candidates that exceed the standard error of measurement can serve as a reliable indicator of differences in knowledge or abilities.

Widespread use. How widely used is the GRE? Oltman and Hartnett (1984) reported that of the more than 7,000 programs in the United States that offered the master's degree, almost 47% required the GRE General Test, and an additional 18% recommended or required the test for specific programs. Of nearly 5,500 doctoral programs, some 63% required it, and an additional 24% recommended or required the test for specific programs. Wide variations in practice were found among different academic areas; for example, 82% of biological sciences programs required or recommended the GRE General Test vs. 52% in the fine and applied arts. A study of 1972 vs. 1981 program requirements showed almost no overall change in the requiring of the GRE. A survey of a smaller number of departments indicated that the primary use of GRE scores seemed to be to compensate for otherwise weak applicant credentials, and that, in making admission decisions, graduate departments weighted most heavily undergraduate grades followed by letters of recommendation, and then by GRE scores.

The General Test. The General Test yields separate scores for verbal, quantitative, and analytical abilities. The verbal portion uses four types of questions: antonyms (identify words opposite in meaning), analogies, sentence completions, and reading-comprehension questions. These questions cover a variety of content areas, such as arts and humanities, physical and biological sciences, social studies, everyday life, and human relationships and feelings.

The quantitative portion used three types of questions: discrete quantitative questions that test basic mathematical skills, data interpretation items that use charts and graphs, and comparisons that require the evaluation of the relative size of two expressions or quantities. The mathematics that is required does not extend beyond that usually covered in high school, and covers arithmetic, algebra, geometry, and data analysis.

The analytical portion contains questions related to analytical reasoning, logical reasoning, and analysis of explanations. These questions attempt to assess such abilities as evaluating arguments, recognizing assumptions, and generating explanations.

Each form of the GRE consists of seven sections of 30 minutes duration: two verbal, two quantitative, two analytical, and one for research purposes, such as trying out items that might be included in future forms.

The three portions of the General Test are correlated with each other. The average correlation between verbal and quantitative is .45, between verbal and analytical is .65, and between quantitative and analytical is .66. By 1999, the GRE General test contained a new writing test and a new mathematical reasoning test. The five tests were packaged in two different combinations of four tests each.

Subject Tests. Currently there are Subject Tests in several areas ranging from biochemistry to sociology. Each subject test yields a total score, and seven subject tests yield subscores. For example, the biology test yields three subscores: (1) cellular and molecular biology; (2) organismal biology, and (3) ecology and evolution. Each subject test differs in the number of questions. For example, the computer science test contains about 80 questions while the psychology test contains about 220 questions (these numbers can change from form to form).

Scores on the GRE. Raw scores on the GRE are changed to both standard scores (mean of 500 and SD of 100) and percentiles. In the feedback given to candidates, these scores are based on two normative groups. The first group is all examinees who took the test during the past 3 years; the second is a subgroup of college seniors or recent college graduates who have not yet enrolled in graduate school. In addition, percentile ranks on the General Test are available for specific fields such as biology and psychology. For the General Test the raw score is the number of questions answered correctly. For all the subject tests (except music), the raw score is the number of

questions answered correctly minus one fourth of the number of questions answered incorrectly.

On the General Test, scores can range from 200 to 800, with a theoretical mean of 500 and SD of 100. The actual range of scaled scores for the subject tests varies from test to test. Theoretically, the scores should range from 200 to 800, but in fact they range from 200 to 990. On the Biochemistry Subject Test, the 99th percentile is equivalent to a score of 760, while the first percentile is equivalent to a score of 300. By contrast, on the Physics Subject Test, the 97th percentile is 990 (highest score), and the first percentile is equivalent to 400.

Although all the Subject Tests use the same scaling procedure, quite clearly scores on one Subject Test cannot be directly compared with scores on another Subject Test. Not only do the tests measure different content, but the score distributions are different, and the tests are taken by different examinees.

Practice. Descriptive booklets that contain sample and practice questions are available free from ETS for both the General Test and for the Subject Tests. In addition, older test forms for the Subject Tests are available for purchase. Finally, a number of publications are available designed to assist students in preparing for these exams, thereby reducing any differences in test sophistication among candidates.

Development. Questions for the General Test are written primarily by ETS staff members, with degrees and background appropriate to the subarea they are working on. There is also a technical advisory committee composed of university professors specializing in fields such as mathematics, linguistics, and psychological measurement; this committee advises the staff on various aspects, such as content specifications.

Each item is reviewed by specialists both on the staff of ETS and outside ETS, and intensive discussions are held. Once the items are judged as appropriate, they are assembled into clusters and are included in an actual test administration. These questions do not contribute to the examinee's scores, but the data is used to statistically analyze the items. Those items that perform satisfactorily become part of a pool of items from which new forms of the General Test are assembled.

The same basic procedure is also used for the Subject Tests, except that the items are written primarily by experts in that field. For both General Test and Subject Tests there is an extensive and careful procedure that has evolved over the years, in which each item is scrutinized multiple times both by itself and in the context of other items. Part of the review and of the subsequent statistical analyses is to ensure that items are not biased, sexist, or racist, or show unfair relationship to minority group membership.

Multiple scores. Candidates can take the GRE more than once and therefore may present multiple scores in their application. Studies have shown that individuals who repeat the General Test show on average a score gain of about 25 to 30 points – but these individuals are a self-selected group who believe that repeating the test will increase their scores. ETS suggests that multiple scores can be averaged, or only the most recent or highest score be used.

Computer version. In 1992, the GRE program began administering a computerized version of the General Test. The computer version contains the same sections and methodology as the standard version, but has different time limits, and a minimal number of questions must be answered for a score to be generated. In 1993, a computer adaptive form of the General Test was introduced. In an adaptive test, the selection of questions is tailored to an examinee's ability level. Initially, the examinee is presented with questions of average difficulty; subsequent questions are then a function of the examinee's pattern of responding. Correct answers lead to more difficult questions; incorrect questions lead to easier questions. Computer-delivered versions of the General Test and of many Subject Tests are now offered at many test centers, and their number and availability will increase substantially; eventually all GRE tests will be delivered by computer, and the candidate will receive the test scores at the close of the testing session.

Reliability. Reliability, as measured by the K-R, is in the low .90s for both the verbal portion and the quantitative portion, and in the high .80s for the analytical portion. These coefficients might be somewhat inflated because speed plays a slight role in the GRE. For the subject tests, the coefficients range from a low of .80 for a subtest in geology, to .96 for literature in English, and for sociology, with most test coefficients in the low .90s and most subtest coefficients in the mid to high .80s.

Validity. Most studies report fairly low validity coefficients for the verbal and quantitative sections, regardless of academic department and criterion used in measuring academic achievement. Typical coefficients range from .20 through the low .30s. GRE Subject Tests tend to be better predictors of first-year GPA for specific departments than the GRE General Test, and GRE quantitative scores tend to be better predictors in the mathematical and physical sciences. Validation studies by ETS (1977) show median validity coefficients that range from .02 to .36 for the verbal section and from .06 to .32 for the quantitative section. Jaeger (1985) reported that the median predictive validity coefficients for the verbal score ranged from .02 to .36 across nine major fields of study, while corresponding coefficients for the quantitative score ranged from .06 to .32. A 1988 review (Staff, 1988) of 492 validity studies done between 1983 and 1988 indicated that correlations between GRE scores and graduate grades were low and ranged from .15 to .31. When GRE scores were combined with undergraduate GPA, the correlations rose somewhat to a high of .44. Jaeger (1985) pointed to a time trend in the correlation between GRE and undergraduate GPA with graduate GPA. In studies done in the 1950s and 1960s the median r was about .45; in the 1970s it was .39, and in the 1980s it was about .35. The suggested explanation was restriction of range due to grade inflation.

How does the GRE predict graduate first-year GPA? The ETS Guide yields substantial information based on large national samples, and some results are summarized in Table 13.6.

Note that undergraduate GPA is a better predictor of graduate GPA than are the GRE subtests, taken either individually or in combination. However, the best prediction is obtained when both undergraduate GPA and GRE scores are placed in a composite (essentially a regression equation). A similar pattern shows up when

Table 13–6. Correlations with Graduate First-Year GPA

Variable	
Undergraduate GPA	.37
GRE Verbal	.30
GRE Quantitative	.29
GRE Analytical	.28
Composite of Verbal, Quantitative & Analytical	.34
Composite of Above + Undergraduate GPA	.46

individual subject tests are considered. Table 13.7 gives some examples.

Four examples are given below from more extensive data available in the GRE Guide. Note that in each case, the correlation between scores on the Subject Test and the graduate GPA is higher than the corresponding correlation between undergraduate GPA and graduate GPA, or between GRE Verbal and graduate GPA. As we discussed with the SAT, the evidence suggests that achievement tests are indeed better predictors.

Validity issues. There are two major issues related to the validity of the GRE. One is the criterion problem – that is, how do you operationally define graduate school success? (see Harnett & Willingham, 1980). A second problem is that of range restriction, or to put it another way, a very low selection ratio. In graduate psychology programs for example, the mean selection ratio is .11 (only 11% of the applicants are actually accepted), although in fact for most programs the selection ratio is under .09 (Chernyshenko & Ones, 1999). Thus GRE validation studies typically involve only students who were accepted into graduate school – a highly restricted sample as far as GRE scores. When a validity coefficient is computed between GRE scores and some criterion of graduate performance such as GPA, that

Table 13–7. Correlations with Graduate First-Year GPA

Subject test	r	Undergraduate GPA	GRE Verbal
Biology	.37	.33	.24
Chemistry	.51	.36	.27
Economics	.43	.31	.22
Psychology	.37	.37	.29

coefficient is really an underestimate of the correlation for the entire group of applicants. There are however, statistical formulae to estimate the correlation for the entire sample. When this is done, the obtained correlation coefficients are quite respectable – in the .35 to .70 range.

Restriction of range. Various issues are involved in why the validity coefficients for the GRE are so low, and why there is substantial variation from study to study. One issue is that of restriction of range. Cohn (1985) indicated that the GRE was "the best documented instrument of its type," and that restriction of range was a major consideration in the small validity coefficients obtained. Dollinger (1989) analyzed the GRE scores for 105 clinical psychology students admitted without regard for their GRE scores. Restriction of range of GRE scores was not a problem in this sample; GRE-V scores ranged from 340 to 800 and GRE-Q ranged from 260 to 770. Dollinger (1989) used two criteria: (1) number of failed preliminary examinations, and (2) a composite that incorporated the failure plus several criteria on timely progression in the program and faculty judgment. All three GRE scores (V, Q, and Advanced) correlated significantly with both criteria, with correlation coefficients ranging from .33 to .46, and better than graduate GPA. However, when the data were analyzed for minority students, the coefficients dropped substantially, and the only significant result was that GRE Advanced Test scores did correlate significantly with the criteria for both majority and minority students.

Huitema and Stein (1993) report an interesting study of 204 applicants to the Department of Psychology at Western Michigan University, where GRE scores were required but ignored in the admissions process. The authors show that the variation in GRE scores for those 138 applicants who were accepted was essentially the same as for the total pool of applicants, that is, there was no restriction of range. Under these circumstances, GRE total scores correlated between .55 and .70 with four criteria of graduate achievement, such as exam scores in Advanced Statistics courses and faculty ratings. Correlations between undergraduate GPA and the four criteria were all nonsignificant. The authors argue that restriction of range in fact severely limits the validity of the

GRE. For example, the GRE Total correlated .63 with faculty ratings for the total sample, but only .24 for those whose GRE Total was at least 1200, a typical cutoff score.

Restriction of range can also refer to the criterion, which is often GPA. Graduate GPA is usually expressed on a 4-point scale, and in many graduate courses only As and Bs are awarded, and in some graduate programs "remedial" retesting is allowed if the initial examination score is below the A level. In fact, in the Huitema and Stein (1993) study, GPA was not even considered because it was felt that assigned grades did not reflect the variation in the academic skills of the students.

Validity in psychology. There have been many studies of the predictive validity of the GRE with regard to graduate students in psychology. Typically the predicted criterion consists of grades, either overall or in specific courses, or examination performance (e.g., Boudreau, Killip, MacInnis, et al., 1983; Federici & Schuerger, 1974; House, J. J. Johnson, & Tolone, 1987).

Marston (1971) briefly reviewed the validity of the GRE. He reported that correlations of the GRE-V and/or the GRE-Q scores correlated with graduate school grades in Psychology from .23 to .64. Correlations with faculty ratings ranged from .29 to .57. In one study covering seven different psychology departments, correlations with the criterion of success versus failure in graduate school ranged from −.39 to −.55, with a median r of about .18, and with the high correlation coefficient reflecting the contribution of undergraduate GPA as well.

Several studies have looked at degree completion as the criterion. For example, Merenda and Reilly (1971) found that GRE scores in combination with undergraduate GPA, psychology courses GPA, and ratings of the quality of students' undergraduate institution, were able to successfully discriminate among students who earned their doctoral degrees without delay from those who earned the degree with some delays, and those who failed to complete their degrees. However, another study found that GRE scores alone were unable to differentiate between students who completed advanced degrees and those who did not (J. R. Rawls, D. J. Rawls, & Harrison, 1969).

Marston (1971) decided to examine post-PhD success by analyzing the GRE scores of 11 students and identifying their number of subsequent professional publications, which in psychology is considered evidence of professional achievement. For the clinical psychology students, the correlation between combined GRE scores and number of postdoctoral publications was −.05, and for nonclinical PhDs, it was .18. Additional analyses generally supported the lack of relationship between GRE scores and publication rates. Marston (1971) concluded that it was time to have a nationwide review of the effectiveness of the GRE and to seek better alternatives.

House and J. J. Johnson (1993b) analyzed the predictive validity of the GRE by dividing graduate students into those enrolled in professional psychology areas, such as clinical and counseling vs. those in experimental or general psychology. A regression analysis of GRE scores and undergraduate GPA to predict whether the student had completed the master's degree or not, indicated that GRE Verbal scores were the best predictor for professional psychology students, but the worst predictor for experimental or general students. GRE Quantitative scores were however, the best predictor for the experimental or general students (for a recent study see Sternberg & W. M. Williams, 1997).

Advanced Psychology Test. Although the predictive validity of the GRE Verbal and Quantitative sections have been studied extensively, there are substantially fewer studies on the Advanced tests. In the area of Psychology, as an example, Advanced Psychology Test scores have been significant predictors of grades and performance on comprehensive examinations (e.g., Kirnan & Geisinger, 1981), but not of faculty ratings (e.g., Hackman, Wiggins, & Bass, 1970).

House and J. J. Johnson (1993b), in the study mentioned above, looked at GRE Advanced Psychology Test scores for 293 graduate students in master's programs. For the entire sample, test scores were significantly correlated with grades ($r = .41$), but the correlation coefficients showed substantial variation across program areas, from a low of .10 for clinical psychology students, to .56 for counseling psychology students (see Kalat & Matlin, 2000 for an overview of this test).

Table 13–8. Correlations with Scores on a Master's Comprehensive Exam (Kirnan & Geisinger, 1981)

Variable	Clinical students	Experimental students
GRE Verbal	.44[*]	.32[*]
GRE Quantitative	.31[*]	.07
GRE Advanced Test – Psychology	.35[*]	.03
Miller Analogies Test	.42[*]	.13[*]
Undergraduate GPA	.07	.05

[*] Statistically significant coefficients

Alternatives to the GRE. Are there other tests that could be used in lieu of the GRE? Potentially there are, but the only one of note that is used is the Miller Analogies Test.

Kirnan and Geisinger (1981) studied 114 graduate students at a private university enrolled in either clinical or experimental psychology. All students had taken the GRE as well as the Miller prior to admission, and as part of their studies had taken a Master's Comprehensive Exam. How did these variables correlate with the scores on the master's exam? Table 13.8 provides the answer.

Note that the GRE Verbal does a commendable job of predicting comprehensive exam scores. The Miller also does well for the clinical students but not for the experimental students. Undergraduate GPA does not correlate significantly with exam scores. Whether these findings generalize to other institutions needs to be investigated, but for now we must conclude that the position of the GRE is not threatened by other tests.

GPA as the criterion. A basic question is whether first-year graduate GPA is the criterion measure that ought to be used. Perhaps, whether a person obtains their degree or not is a more appropriate criterion of success. E. L. Goldberg and Alliger (1992) undertook a metaanalysis of the literature, identifying 27 studies dealing with counseling and/or psychology departments. Their analysis indicated that the GRE Advanced Test in Psychology did correlate with graduate school success measured by multiple criteria, but the typical validity coefficient was about .19; neither the GRE-V nor the GRE-Q did as well. When graduate GPA was the criterion, the GRE did not demonstrate adequate predictive validity.

The GRE-Q did predict grades in quantitative courses, and the GRE-V did predict comprehensive exam performance. The authors suggested that what is needed is not necessarily to throw out the GRE, but to focus on the criterion. That is, we should define whether we are trying to predict graduation, scientific productivity, or something else, and operationalize such criteria.

What criterion to use? How can successful performance be defined? Hartnett and Willingham (1980) categorized three broad classes of criterion measures: (1) traditional criteria such as grades; (2) evidence of professional accomplishment such as publications; and (3) specially developed criteria such as faculty ratings.

Traditional criteria include variables such as grades, degree attainment, time to complete degree, performance on comprehensive examinations, and quality of dissertation. Grades have been used more than any other criteria in studies of graduate-school success and the validity of the GRE. Grades are readily available and are common to most institutions. Although grades reflect a variety of aspects, it is reasonable to treat them as reflective of an underlying dimension of "academic success." On the negative side, the range of grades, particularly in graduate studies, is quite restricted, and grading standards vary substantially from setting to setting.

Whether a student obtains a degree is a most important outcome of graduate studies, and many regard this as the best criterion. Clearly, however, students drop out of graduate school for many reasons that have nothing to do with competence or academic skills. Time to degree is another criterion used as a measure of success in graduate school. Here, too, one can argue that speed of completion reflects a wide variety of circumstances that are unrelated to academic competence (House & J. J. Johnson, 1993a).

Part of graduate studies involves qualifying and/or comprehensive examinations, written and/or oral. The nature and form of these exams varies substantially across departments, with many departments never having defined precisely the nature and purpose of such exams. The scoring of these exams is frequently a highly subjective matter, and the reliability associated with such a criterion can be easily questioned. Dissertation quality presents other problems.

The dissertation is basically evidence that the student is able to conduct scholarly research in a sound and competent manner. On the one hand, this represents a potentially useful criterion; on the other, there are a number of problems such as separating what portions reflect the student's work vs. the mentor's work.

In terms of evidence of professional accomplishment, there are a number of criteria that could be used, such as papers published or presentations at professional conferences. Such criteria have a number of problems. First, they may not be routinely collected and thus may not be available for analysis. Second, such accomplishments may mirror a variety of factors other than professional competence. Finally, such criteria are typically not normally distributed but are highly positively skewed.

Among the specially constructed criteria might be considered global faculty ratings and performance work samples. Ratings are relatively easy to obtain and provide a fairly convenient criterion. At the same time, ratings are limited, may show restriction of range, and are open to bias such as the "halo" effect, where ratings are influenced by the observer's general impression of the person being rated. With regard to work samples, graduate students are being trained both for specific tasks germane to their discipline, such as analysis of water contamination, and for more generic tasks such as research, scholarly work, and teaching. Theoretically, at least, one could develop work samples that could be used as criterion measures. In reality, such work samples are quite rare and present a number of both practical and theoretical difficulties (Hartnett & Willingham, 1980).

GRE with Hispanics. Whitworth and Barrientos (1990) compared Anglo and Hispanic graduate students on their respective performances on the GRE-V, GRE-Q, and GRE Analytic test scores, and their undergraduate and graduate grades, to see how these variables predicted graduate academic performance. The sample were students admitted to graduate studies at the University of Texas at El Paso during a 5-year period; the sample consisted of 320 Hispanics and 632 Anglos. A statistical analysis indicated that Anglos scored higher than Hispanics on all three GRE variables and on both undergraduate and graduate GPA.

The differences in GPA were somewhat small, but the differences on the GRE scores were more substantial. Regression equations were then computed with the predictor being graduate GPA. For Hispanics, the regression equation correlated with graduate GPA only .19, and the only variable that had some predictive power was undergraduate GPA. Essentially the same results were obtained with Anglo students, with the regression equation correlating .27 with graduate GPA; again undergraduate GPA was the only significant variable. The authors concluded: (1) there is both an intercept bias (Anglos score higher on the GRE) and a slope bias (although the regression equations were poor predictors for both groups, they were slightly worse for the Hispanic group) on the GRE; and (2) continued use of the GRE for graduate-school selection is a questionable practice.

ENTRANCE INTO PROFESSIONAL TRAINING

The Medical College Admission Test (MCAT)

Purpose. The purpose of the Medical College Admission Test (MCAT) is to "measure achievement levels and the expected prerequisites that are generally relevant to the practice of medicine" (Association of American Medical Colleges, 1977).

The new MCAT. In 1977, a revised version of the MCAT consisting of six subtests (Biology, Chemistry, Physics, Science Problems, Skills Analysis: Reading, and Skills Analysis: Quantitative) replaced the original MCAT which contained only four subtests (Science, General Information; Verbal Ability; and Quantitative Ability).

Validity. There is a substantial body of literature on the MCAT, with a great emphasis on its criterion validity as a predictor of first-year medical school grades, and to a lesser extent as a predictor of scores on the National Board of Medical Examiners examinations, particularly part I (NBME-I), which examines knowledge of the basic sciences, and less frequently part II (NBME-II), which examines knowledge of the "clinical" sciences (R. F. Jones & Adams, 1982). R. F. Jones and Thomae-Forgues (1984) indicate that there are five sets of questions regarding the validity of the MCAT:

1. How do MCAT scores compare in predictive validity with undergraduate GPA?

2. Do MCAT scores contribute unique information not already provided by undergraduate GPA?

3. What is the relative predictive validity of the individual MCAT scores in relation to overall performance in the basic medical sciences?

4. What is the relative predictive validity of the individual MCAT scores in relation to performance in specific areas of the medical school curriculum?

5. How well does the MCAT predict medical school competence?

To answer these questions, R. F. Jones and Thomae-Forgues (1984) analyzed data from some 20 medical schools and concluded the following:

1. When the criteria were medical school course grades, MCAT-combined scores were similar to undergraduate GPA in their predictive value. However, no single MCAT score tended to be correlated with medical school grades as highly as undergraduate science GPA. When the criteria were NBME-I examination scores, MCAT scores in combination were substantially better predictors of performance than undergraduate grades.

2. How much predictive validity do the MCAT scores contribute? The increase in the average multiple correlation when MCAT scores were added to the GPA was .11 to .14, when medical-school course grades were the criterion, and .29, when NBME-I examination scores were the criterion. The authors indicated that the MCAT scores improved predictability by as much as 90% with course grades, and by nearly 300% with NBME examination scores.

3. Of the various subtests, Chemistry had the highest average correlation with medical-school grades, with Biology and Science Problems slightly less. In more than two thirds of the samples studied, either the subtest of Chemistry or of Biology was the best predictor of medical school grades and NBME-I exam scores.

4. The pattern of correlations between MCAT subtest scores and performance in specific areas of the medical-school curriculum tended to be consistent with content similarities – for example, the Chemistry MCAT subtest correlated .41 with grades in course work in Biochemistry (the Biology subtest correlated .31), while scores on the Biology MCAT subtest correlated .29 with grades in Microbiology (the Physics subtest correlated .08).

5. How well does the MCAT do? The authors point out that despite its simplicity, this is a complex question, and one needs to take into account: (1) the restricted range of the examinees – students who have been accepted into medical school, rather than applicants who have taken the MCAT; (2) restricted range of medical-school GPA; (3) restricted reliability of some of the classroom exams on which medical-school GPA is calculated. Given these restrictions, the authors conclude that MCAT scores show "fairly strong" predictive validity with first-year medical-school grades, and "extremely strong" predictive validity with NBME-I examination scores. In general, these results are quite similar to those obtained by other graduate- and professional-school admission test programs.

Overall, one can conclude that the MCAT has significant predictive validity for medical-school grades in the first 2 years, and for scores on the NBME-I. In particular, the Biology and Chemistry subtests seem to be the most valid across medical schools. MCAT scores also add unique predictive information to other variables such as undergraduate GPA.

Admissions vs. advising. Most studies of the validity of the MCAT are carried out to assess how well the MCAT predicts medical-school performance, typically defined in terms of GPA and/or scores on the NBME. These findings are of use to the admissions committees who may or may not place substantial weight on the MCAT scores of a potential applicant.

Donnelly et al. (1986) went one step further. They first studied a variety of variables, such as gender, undergraduate GPA, and other demographic aspects, to determine which would correlate significantly with scores on the NBME-I at their institution. They found that the best prediction was achieved with a regression equation

Table 13–9. Actual vs. Predicted Performance on NBME-I (Donnelly et al., 1986)				
Actual performance	**Predicted performance**			
	High pass	**Average pass**	**Low pass**	**Fail**
High pass ($n = 76$)	26 (92.9%)	50 (24.2%)	0 (0.0%)	0 (0.0%)
Average pass ($n = 179$)	2 (7.1%)	140 (67.6%)	27 (42.9%)	10 (14.7%)
Low pass ($n = 65$)	0 (0.0%)	16 (7.7%)	30 (47.6%)	19 (27.9%)
Fail ($n = 46$)	0 (0.0%)	1 (0.5%)	6 (9.5%)	39 (57.4%)
Totals:	28	207	63	68

composed of the MCAT (average of four sub-tests) and grades in anatomy courses (four such courses). The equation was cross-validated and then the results were sent to the currently enrolled medical students who had not yet taken the NBME-I. This was meant as a counseling device so that students for whom failure was predicted could take remedial steps. Incidentally, the regression equation correlated .85 with NBME-I scores, and .90 when it was cross-validated (this is somewhat unusual, as more typically correlation coefficients drop in value when cross-validated). How well did the regression equation predict actual NBME-I scores? Table 13.9 gives the results. The percentages indicate the conditional probabilities. For example, 57.4% of those for whom the regression equation predicted failure, in fact did fail, while 27.9% of those for whom the equation predicted failure did obtain a low pass. Notice that overall the results indicate a high degree of accuracy (92.6%), but that the accuracy is greater in predicting those who do pass rather than those who do fail.

Generalizability of regression equations. To have any practical value, a specific regression equation should be applicable to more than just one group or class. If a regression equation is used for admission decisions, the results obtained with one class must be generalizable to the next class.

In the area of employment testing, considerable variability in the validity coefficients is observed from one study to another, even when the tests and the criteria used seem to be essentially identical. A series of studies showed that such variability was due to various statistical and research artifacts, such as sampling error, unreliability of the criteria used, and restriction of range; the conclusion is that validity results are quite generalizable (e.g., Pearlman, Schmidt, & Hunter, 1980; Schmidt & Hunter, 1977; Schmidt, Hunter, Pearlman, et al., 1979).

An analysis of 726 validity studies of the Law School Admissions Test (LSAT) as a predictor of first-year grades in law school, indicated that the "average true validity" was estimated to be .54, although the values varied substantially across different law schools and as a function of when the study was conducted (R. L. Linn, Harnisch, & Dunbar, 1981). Although a similar analysis is not as yet available for the MCAT, it is most likely that the results would be about the same.

Method effect. Nowacek, Pullen, Short et al., (1987) studied all students who entered the University of Virginia School of Medicine in the years 1978 through 1984 ($n = 974$). They determined that MCAT scores predicted the NBME-I scores well (rs in the .40 to .50 range), and predicted medical-school course grades less well (rs in the .30 to .40 range). Undergraduate science GPA predicted medical-school course grades well (rs in the .40 range), but predicted NBME-I scores less well (rs in the .30 range). These authors suggested that there might be a method effect present; both the MCAT and the NBME-I are long, multiple-choice, paper-and-pencil, standardized tests. Both undergraduate and graduate GPA include laboratory work, test data of various types, subjective ratings, group projects, and other less well-defined activities. The correlational pattern may well reflect the underlying nature of these variables.

Interstudy variability. There is a great deal of variability in the predictive results reported from study to study. For example, with first-year medical-school grades as the criterion, in one study the Physics subtest correlated .12 (C. M. Brooks, Jackson, Hoffman, et al., 1981), in another .02 (M. E. Goldman & Berry, 1981), and .47 in yet another (McGuire, 1980).

Performance in the clinical years. Most studies of the validity of the MCAT focus on prediction of grades in the first 2 years of medical school, designated as the basic science years, and on the parallel part I of the NBME.

Carline, Cullen, Scott, et al. (1983) focused on the last 2 years of medical school, designated as the clinical years, and on the parallel part II of the NBME. The validity coefficients of the MCAT with the NBME-II ranged from .03 to .47, with most coefficients in the high .20s to mid .30s range. Although these are not particularly high, as expected given the homogeneity of third- and fourth-year medical students, they were generally higher than the correlations between undergraduate science GPA and performance on the NBME-II.

New MCAT vs. original MCAT. We have basically considered only studies with the new MCAT. The literature suggests that the new MCAT has better predictive validity than the original MCAT. McGuire (1980) for example, reports a multiple regression of MCAT scores and undergraduate science GPA as correlating .57 with class rank in medical school, slightly better than the .50 obtained with the original MCAT. In this study, MCAT subtests correlated from a low of .25 to a high of .47 with class rank (median r of about .43), whereas science undergraduate GPA correlated .41 with class rank in medical school.

Differential validity. Does the validity of MCAT scores in predicting academic performance in medical school vary for students from different undergraduate institutions? Zeleznik, Hojat, and Veloski (1987) studied students from 10 undergraduate universities who were all attending the same medical school. GPA for first and second year of medical school as well as scores on the NBME exams were used as criteria. Obtained correlations ranged from a low of .03 to a high of .66 with significant differences between institutions. The MCAT was more or less valid, depending on the students' undergraduate institution. Incidentally, for all 10 institutions, combined MCAT scores correlated .32 with first-year GPA, .27 with second-year GPA, .39 with NBME-I scores, and .37 with NBME-II scores.

MCAT with black students. D. G. Johnson, Lloyd, Jones, et al. (1986) studied medical students at Howard University College of Medicine, a predominantly black institution. The criterion of performance consisted of grades in all 4 years of medical school and scores on both parts I and II of the NBME exams. In general, the predictive validities of the MCAT scores and of undergraduate GPA were found to be similar to those of studies with white medical students, and the results supported the use of the MCAT as an admissions criterion.

Coaching. Although most of the studies on coaching have focused on the SAT, and to a lesser extent on the Law School Admission Test (LSAT), there is also concern about the MCATs. N. Cole (1982) listed six components of test preparation programs (or coaching), and each of these components has rather different implications for test validity:

1. supplying the correct answers (as in cheating)
2. taking the test for practice
3. maximizing motivation
4. optimizing test anxiety
5. instruction in test-taking skills
6. instruction in test content

Each of these components has a different impact depending upon whether the targeted test is an aptitude test or an achievement test. Aptitude tests are designed to measure abilities that are developed over a long period of time, and therefore should be relatively resistant to short-term intervention. Achievement tests reflect the influence of instruction, and performance on them should in fact be altered by well-designed courses of instruction.

R. F. Jones (1986) studied national samples of students who had taken the MCAT and compared the test scores of those who had been coached with those who had not. Coached examinees did better on the Biology, Chemistry, Physics, and Science Problems subtests, and equally well on the Skills Analysis: Reading subtest. Mixed results were obtained on the Skills Analysis:

Quantitative subtest. The effect was small, however, and attributable to the science review component of these coaching programs.

The Dental Admission Testing Program (DAT)

The Dental Admission Testing Program (DAT) is administered by the Council on Dental Education of the American Dental Association, and has been in place on a national basis since 1950. The DAT is designed to measure general academic ability, understanding of scientific information, and perceptual ability. The test results are one of the sources of information that dental schools use in their admission procedures. The DAT is intended for those who have completed a minimum of 2 years of collegiate basic science study.

Description. The current DAT contains four sections:

1. A subtest of 100 multiple-choice questions covers the natural sciences – specifically the equivalent of college courses in biology and in chemistry (both organic and inorganic). This section requires the simple recall of basic scientific information and is called Survey of Natural Science.
2. The Perceptual Ability subtest contains 90 multiple-choice items that require the subject to visually discriminate two- and three-dimensional objects.
3. The Reading Comprehension subtest consists of 50 multiple-choice items based on a reading passage, similar to reading material in dental school.
4. The Quantitative Reasoning subtest contains 50 multiple-choice questions that assess the person's ability to reason with numbers and to deal with quantitative materials.

Scoring. The test scores for the DAT are reported on a standard scale score that ranges from -1 to $+9$, with a mean of 4 and SD of 2. A total of 10 scores are reported including three composite scores: total science (based on section 1), academic average (based on sections 1, 3, and 4), and perceptual ability (based on section 2).

Reliability. K-R reliability coefficients typically range in the .80s. However, the DAT may place too much emphasis on speed; test-retest or parallel form reliabilities would be more appropriate, but these are not reported (DuBois, 1985).

Validity. Scores on the Total Science and the Academic Average typically correlate in the .30s both with first-year grades in dental school and with later performance on the National Boards for Dentistry exams. The DAT seems to be as good a predictor of first-year dental-school grades as is undergraduate GPA. DuBois (1985) points out that the reported validity coefficients may be attenuated (i.e., lowered) by the fact that they are computed on admitted students rather than the broader group of those who take the exam, that grades in dental school typically show a restricted range, and that data from various institutions that have somewhat different curricula are lumped together – in other words, the same concerns expressed with the MCATs.

Criticism. The DAT may be assessing academic skills rather than the combination of psychomotor skills and problem solving that are required in the everyday practice of dentistry (Cherrick, 1985). Another criticism is that because the specific form of the DAT changes regularly, there are no data published to show that the different forms of the DAT are equivalent (DuBois, 1985).

TESTS FOR LICENSURE AND CERTIFICATION

In the United States approximately 800 occupations are regulated by state governments, including occupations such as barber, physician, and psychologist. Other occupations, travel agent or auto mechanic, for instance, are regulated by various boards and agencies (Shimberg, 1981). For many of these occupations, licensure or certification involves a test or series of tests. Licensure is a process whereby the government gives permission to an individual to engage in a particular occupation. The granting of the license reflects minimal competency, and usually there are definitions of what a licensed practitioner may do. Furthermore, it is illegal for someone who is not licensed to engage in any of the defined practices.

Certification is the recognition that a person has met certain qualifications set by a credentialing agency and is therefore permitted to use a designated title. Individuals who are not certified are not prohibited from practicing their occupation. For some occupations, both licensing and certification may be pertinent. For example, in order to practice, a physician must be licensed by the state. In addition, she or he may wish to be certified by one of a number of medical specialty boards, such as pediatrics or psychiatry. Often, certification standards reflect higher degrees of competency than those of licensure.

A rather wide variety of tests are used for licensing and certification purposes, some national in scope, and others developed locally, some the result of national test organizations such as Educational Testing Service or Psychological Corporation, others reflecting the work of local boards. The format of many of these tests consists of multiple-choice items because they are economical to score, especially with large number of candidates, and the results can be readily tabulated. Often these exams are accompanied by work samples, e.g., a flying test for airplane pilots.

The purpose of licensing exams, and to some degree, certification tests, is to protect the public's welfare and safety, rather than to predict job success. Therefore, these tests should assess basic skills and abilities to carry out professional or occupational tasks safely and competently. Typically, licensing exams deal with an applicant's knowledge and skill at applying relevant principles, laws, rules, and regulations (Shimberg, 1981). Rather than assess a full range of difficulty, such tests will use items that assess minimal competency and thus should be relatively easy for individuals in that occupation. Sometimes licensing and certification tests yield only a total score, so that a candidate who is weak in area A can compensate by doing quite well in area B. Other tests yield subtest scores and may specify the required passing score for each subtest.

A more complicated issue is the setting of the cutoff score. On some tests the cutoff score is a relative standard; for example, the top 80% will pass and the bottom 20% will fail, no matter what the score distribution is. On other tests, the cutoff score represents an absolute standard, and theoretically every examinee could pass or fail.

Validity. This is a challenging issue for licensing/certification tests. Certainly content validity is very important, and in a certain sense, relatively easy to establish. These tests are usually designed to assess knowledge and skills in a particular area and are usually put together by experts in that area, often on the basis of a job or performance analysis. Thus content validity is often built into the test.

Criterion validity is more difficult to assess. Consider psychologists, for example. Some work in a private psychotherapeutic setting, and may see patients who are highly motivated to change their lifestyle. Other psychologists work in mental hospitals where they may see patients with multiple disabilities and for whom the hospital contact may represent a mechanism for the maintenance of the status quo. Some teach and carry out research in university settings, while others may be consultant to business organizations. What criteria could apply to these diverse activities?

Similarly, construct validity is difficult to apply. Most licensing and certification tests are not concerned with global and personological concepts such as adjustment, competence, or even professionalism.

Cutoff scores. A cutoff score is that score used to separate those who pass a test from those who do not. In school courses, a cutoff score on exams is typically pegged at 70%. Cutoff scores are used widely in a variety of settings, from schools to personnel decisions. Sometimes cutoff scores are set on the basis of clearly defined criteria, and sometimes they are set quite arbitrarily (for a detailed discussion see Cascio, Alexander, & Barrett, 1988).

What is an appropriate cutoff score? Legal challenges have resulted in a series of cases involving cutoff scores on tests, where the conclusion was that a cutoff score should be consistent with the results of a job analysis, it should permit the selection of qualified candidates, and it should allow an organization to meet its affirmative action goals. Cutoff scores should be based upon aspects such as reliability, validity, and utility, and should relate to the proficiency of the current work force.

How are cutoff scores set? There are two basic ways that parallel norm-referenced vs. criterion-referenced approaches. Thorndike

(1949) suggested the "method of predictive yield" which now would be called a human-resources planning approach (Cascio, Alexander, & Barrett, 1988). That is, information regarding projected personnel needs, the past history of the proportion of offers accepted, and a large sample distribution of applicants' test scores are all studied to set a cutoff score on a test that will yield the number of applicants needed. For example, if I have 400 applicants for 20 positions, and in the past 60% of applicants who were offered employment accepted, then the cutoff score will be one that identifies the top 34 individuals.

Another way to determine a cutoff score is simply to base it on the distribution of applicants' test scores, such as at the mean, the 80th percentile, $1\frac{1}{2}$ standard deviations above the mean, etc. Norm-referenced methods like these are relatively simple and minimize subjective judgment. They may be acceptable where there is a need to create a list of eligible applicants; but they would probably not be acceptable in situations where minimum competency needs to be identified.

There are basically two methods to set criterion-referenced cutoff scores. In one, the experts provide the judgments about the test items, and in the other a judgment is made about the criterion performance of individuals. When experts are asked to provide the judgments, the procedure used typically includes one or more of the methods proposed by Angoff (1971), Ebel (1972) or Nedelsky (1954).

The method that is often used is called the Angoff method (Angoff, 1971), after its author. Angoff suggested that the minimum raw score for passing can be developed on a test by looking at each test item and deciding whether a "minimally acceptable person," i.e., a barely qualified person, could answer each item correctly. A related variation of this procedure, also suggested by Angoff, is to state the probability, for each item, that the "minimally acceptable person" would answer the item correctly. The mean probability would then represent the minimally acceptable score. These judgments could be made by a number of judges and an average computed. The computed cutoff score, under this method, is rather stringent; for example, in a study of the National Teacher Examination, 57% of the examinees would have failed the exam (L. H. Cross, Impara, Frary, et al., 1984). G. M. Hurtz and N. M. R. Hertz (1999) recommend that 10 to 15 judges be used to establish cutoff scores.

The Ebel procedure is similar, but judges are also asked to rate the relative importance of each item. The Nedelsky method requires the test judges to identify those distractors of a multiple-choice question that a "minimally competent" examinee would recognize as incorrect. Then the expected chance score over the remaining choices is computed, and these scores are averaged across judges. Thus the cutoff score represents an above chance score that takes into account the obvious distractors. Such a standard is quite lenient. All three methods have rather poor interjudge reliability and are time consuming (for reviews see Berk, 1986; Shepard, 1980).

In the second criterion-referenced method, contrasted-groups analysis is used. A group of clearly competent individuals is compared with group of either marginally competent or not competent individuals. Once these two groups have been identified, the cutoff score is defined as the point of intersection of the two test-score distributions.

Cascio, Alexander, and Barrett (1988) suggest that it is unrealistic to expect to determine a single best method of setting cutoff scores, and the process should begin with a careful job analysis. They also suggest that cutoff scores be set high enough to ensure the meeting of minimum standards of job performance and to be consistent with normal expectations of acceptable proficiency within the work force.

SUMMARY

Tests are used in the school context for a variety of purposes, many of which were discussed in Chapters 9 and 12. In this chapter, we looked at the California Achievement Tests as applicable to both elementary and secondary schools. At the high-school level we illustrated several content areas, including the assessment of social competence, the GED tests used to award high-school equivalency diplomas, and the NAED used as a national thermometer of school achievement. For college, the focus was on the SAT, while for graduate school it was the GRE. Finally, we briefly covered some of the tests used for admission into professional schools and some of the issues concerned with licensure and certification.

SUGGESTED READINGS

Green, B. F., Jr. (1978). In defense of measurement. *American Psychologist, 33,* 664–670.

A well-written review of many of the criticisms of psychological tests, especially as they apply to educational settings.

Kaplan, R. M. (1982). Nader's raid on the testing industry. *American Psychologist, 37,* 15–23.

A rebuttal of two arguments used by Nader and others as a criticism of the SAT, namely that the SAT is no better than chance in predicting college performance and that the use of SAT scores denies low-income students the opportunity to be admitted to college.

Menges, R. J. (1975). Assessing readiness for professional practice. *Review of Educational Research, 45,* 173–207.

A review of how readiness for professional practice can be measured in a variety of ways, especially with regard to the helping professions.

Powers, D. E. (1993). Coaching for the SAT: A summary of the summaries and an update. *Educational Measurement: Issues and Practice, 12,* 24–39.

A review of some of the key issues about coaching and of several meta-analyses that have been done.

Wainer, H. (1993). Measurement problems. *Journal of Educational Measurement, 30,* 1–21.

An excellent article that looks at 16 unsolved problems in educational measurement and what might be potential solutions.

DISCUSSION QUESTIONS

1. Why are tests less reliable when administered to young children?

2. How would you make sure that a teacher rating scale has adequate content validity?

3. What was your experience with the SAT or other college-admission procedure?

4. This chapter mentions outcome-oriented tests vs. process-oriented tests. Think back to the various tests you are now familiar with. How would you classify each of these? Could a test be both?

5. As this chapter indicates, there is a gender gap on the SAT. What might be some of the reasons? What evidence could be obtained to shed light on this situation?

14 Occupational Settings

> **AIM** This chapter looks at some issues and examples involved in testing in occupational settings, including the military and the police. Many of the tests that are used are tests we have already seen – for example, tests of personality such as the CPI (Chapter 4), tests of intelligence such as the WAIS (Chapter 5), or tests to screen out psychological problems such as the MMPI (Chapter 7). Our emphasis here will be on issues and tests not discussed before.

SOME BASIC ISSUES

Purposes of Testing

In the world of work, testing can serve a number of purposes including the following:

1. To determine potential for success in a program. For example, if a program to train assembly-line workers requires certain basic mathematical and reading skills, candidates who do not have such skills could be identified, and remediation given to them.
2. To place individuals programs. This involves matching the candidates' abilities and competencies with the requirements of specific training programs.
3. To match applicants with specific job openings.
4. To counsel individuals, for career advancement, or career changes, for example.
5. To provide information for program planning and evaluation.

Preemployment Testing

Preemployment testing generally serves two purposes: (1) to elicit a candidate's desirable and undesirable traits, and (2) to identify those characteristics of the candidate that most closely match the requirements of the job (D. Arthur, 1994). Sometimes tests are used to screen out candidates; those who pass the individual testing are then given individual interviews. Sometimes tests are used after the interview, generally to confirm the interview findings.

Employment Testing

Employment testing is often used to evaluate the promotability of an employee. Sometimes they are used to identify employees that have certain specific skills, or for career advising. Most tests seem to be administered to middle managers and supervisors, followed by clerical workers, executives, and professionals (D. Arthur, 1994).

Government Regulations

Formal governmental regulation of testing began in 1968 when the U.S. Secretary of Labor signed the first Testing and Selection Order that indicated that government contracts were required to specify that the contractor could not discriminate against job applicants because of race, color, religion, gender, or national origin. This applied to selection procedures including testing.

In 1978, a Uniform Guidelines on Employee Selection Procedures was adopted. These guidelines provide a framework for determining the proper use of tests when used for employment decisions (D. Arthur, 1994). The guidelines recognized the three major categories of validity, i.e., criterion, content, and construct.

Personnel Selection

In the area of personnel selection, there seem to be five major themes in the literature, all of them basically relevant to the issue of criterion validity (Schmitt & Robertson, 1990): (1) job analysis – much of this research has focused on the nature and quality of job-analysis ratings; (2) predictor development and measurement – the focus here has been on such predictors as assessment centers, interviews, biodata, and personality tests, as well as other selection procedures; (3) criterion development and measurement – much of the focus here has been on job performance ratings, issues such as what variables increase or decrease the accuracy and validity of ratings; (4) validity issues – such as the nature of validity and the use of metaanalysis; (5) Implications of implementing a selection strategy – for example, how can adverse impact be minimized.

What Methods Are Used?

A. M. Ryan and Sackett (1987a) surveyed about 1,000 industrial and organizational psychologists regarding individual assessment practices. One of the questions asked was what methods were used in assessing managerial potential. The results are presented – next.

Method	Used by
interview	93.8%
personal history form	82.7%
ability tests	78.4%
personality &/or interest tests	77.8%
simulation exercises	38.2%
projective tests	34.0%

The most frequently used test was the Watson-Glaser Critical Thinking Appraisal. Among the most frequently used personality tests were the 16 PF, the CPI, and the MMPI (discussed in Chapter 4). Of the simulation exercises, the most frequent was the "in-basket" (to be discussed below). When asked to rank various procedures as to validity, simulations, ability tests, and personal history forms were ranked as the most valid, while personality tests and projective techniques as least valid.

Instruments Used in Industry

Typically, textbooks (such as Guion, 1965a) list five major types of tests that are used in occupational settings:

1. General measures of intellectual ability. These include individual tests such as the WAIS (discussed in chapter 5), or group screening measures such as the Wonderlic Personnel Test (discussed below).

2. Measures of specific intellectual abilities. These might involve clerical aptitude tests, measures of spatial relations, measures of creativity, of abstract reasoning, and of numerical reasoning. Many of these tests are packaged as batteries that assess multiple aptitudes.

3. Measures of sensory and psychomotor abilities including vision testing, tests of coordination, and of manual dexterity. Many of these tests involve apparatus rather than paper-and-pencil. For example, in the O'Connor Tweezer Dexterity Test the subject uses tweezers to pick up pins and place them as rapidly as possible in a board that has 100 holes. In the Purdue Hand Precision Test, there is a revolving turntable with a small hole in it. As the turntable revolves, the subject inserts a stylus in an attempt to touch target holes beneath the turntable. The apparatus records the number of correct responses, number of attempts, and time elapsed.

4. Measures of "motivation," often used as a catchall phrase to include interest inventories such as the SVIB (see Chapter 6), personality inventories such as the CPI (see Chapter 4), and projective techniques (see Chapter 15).

5. Specially derived measures such as biographical inventories (or biodata), standardized interviews, and work samples.

How Is Job Success Measured?

Tests are often validated against the criterion of job success, but there are many ways of defining such a global variable, all of which have limitations (Guion, 1965a):

1. Quantity and/or quality of production. In a factory situation, quantity might be measured by the actual number of units produced within a time period. Quality might be assessed by the number of units that do not pass inspection or meet specific engineering criteria. In the area of sales, quantity might be defined in terms of dollar amounts, and quality in terms of client contacts per sale. The possibilities are quite numerous and may differ drastically from each other.

2. Personnel records. These might provide operational criteria such as absenteeism, number of industrial accidents, etc.

3. Administrative actions, which may be included in personnel records, might cover such processes as promotions, pay increases, resignations, and so on.

4. Performance ratings, made on rating scales of various types.

5. Job samples, a standardized sample of work for which all persons perform the same tasks. The performance of the applicants can then be compared directly and ranked. Such job samples are often used as preemployment tests, for example, typing tests.

The Criterion Problem

Do different methods of measuring job performance, such as work samples, ratings by supervisors, self-ratings, measures of production output, etc., result in different validity results for the same tests?

Nathan and Alexander (1988) conducted metaanalyses of validity coefficients from tests of clerical abilities for five criteria: supervisor ratings, supervisor rankings, work samples, production quantity, and production quality. They found that for the first four criteria, high test validities were obtained, with validities resulting from rankings and from work samples on the average higher than the validities resulting from ratings and from quantity of production. Only the fifth criterion, quality of production, had low validity and did not generalize across situations.

Criteria Are Dynamic

Ghiselli and Haire (1960) suggested that the criteria against which tests are validated are dynamic,

that is, they change over time. In a typical study, a test is administered to a sample of applicants or new employees, and the test is then validated against some measure of job performance during an initial period of employment, perhaps after 3 or 4 months. What is of interest, however, is performance over a much longer period of time. It is not unusual for performance to increase over time, but not all individuals improve at the same rate or in the same amount.

Ghiselli and Haire (1960) studied 56 men who had been hired as taxicab drivers, none of them having had prior experience in this type of work. At the time of hiring, these men were given a battery of tests ranging from arithmetic, speed of reaction, distance discrimination, and interest in occupations dealing with people. The criterion of job performance was dollar volume of fares. Such data were collected for each of the first 18 weeks of employment. The results showed that during the 18 weeks there were significant changes in average productivity (greater in the last 3 weeks than in the first 3 weeks), in the range of individual differences (larger standard deviation in the last 3 weeks), and in the order of individuals ($r = .19$ between productivity on the 1st week and productivity on the 18th week). The validity of the tests also changed substantially over the time period. For example, the inventory designed to measure interest in dealing with people correlated .42 against the criterion for the first 3 weeks, but dropped to .13 against the criterion of the last 3 weeks. In fact, the tests that correlated significantly with the criterion for the first 3 weeks were different from those that correlated significantly with the criterion of the last 3 weeks. An analysis of productivity over all 18 weeks, and of rate of improvement in production, showed that those tests that predicted one of the criteria would be poor in predicting the other criteria.

The Method Problem

Quite often, different results are obtained in different studies because different methods were used. For example, in the area of market research, questions (i.e., test items) are often presented either verbally or pictorially. Weitz (1950) wondered whether the two methods would yield equal results. A sample of 200 adult women was surveyed. One half were asked verbal questions about the design of a cooking range (e.g., Do you prefer a table top oven or a high oven?), and the other half were shown sketches of the various options. All subjects were interviewed by the same interviewer, and the two subsamples were matched on socioeconomic background. For eight of the nine choice questions, there were significant differences between the two groups. For example, when asked whether they preferred the burner controls on the back or the front panel, 91 of the 100 verbal responses indicated a preference for the back panel, but for the pictorial responses only 73 of 100 gave such a preference. Weitz (1950) concluded that these two questionnaire techniques are not interchangeable, and that data obtained from the two methods should not be equally evaluated.

SOME BASIC FINDINGS

Predicting Job Performance

Schmidt and Hunter (1981) argued that:

1. Professionally developed cognitive ability tests are valid predictors of performance on the job and in training for all jobs in all settings.
2. Cognitive ability tests are equally valid for minority and majority applicants.
3. Cognitive ability tests are fair to minority applicants in that they do not underestimate the expected job performance of minority groups.
4. The use of cognitive ability tests for selection in hiring can produce substantial savings for all types of employers.

Numerous studies have calculated that the use of valid tests in selecting individuals for specific jobs saves companies, the federal government, and the armed forces, millions of dollars (e.g., J. E. Hunter & R. F. Hunter, 1984; Schmidt, Hunter, Pearlman, et al., 1979). J. E. Hunter and R. F. Hunter (1984) applied metaanalysis to literally thousands of studies. Here are some of their conclusions:

1. Cognitive-ability tests have a mean validity of about .55 in predicting training success, across all known job families.
2. There is no job for which cognitive ability does not predict training success.

3. The validity of psychomotor-abilities tests can vary on average from .09 to .40 across job families; thus, under some circumstances the validity of psychomotor tests may be very low.
4. Even the smallest mean validity of cognitive tests (such as .27 for sales clerks) is large enough to result in substantial labor savings, if such tests are used for selection.
5. As job complexity decreases, the validity of cognitive tests decreases, but the validity of psychomotor tests increases.
6. If general, cognitive ability alone is used as a predictor, the average validity across all jobs is .54 for a training success criterion and .45 for a job proficiency criterion.
7. For entry-level jobs, predictors other than tests of cognitive ability have lower validities.
8. Validity could be increased by using, in addition to cognitive tests, other measures such as social skills and personality that are relevant to specific job performance.

A classic example is that of General Electric, which because of government pressure abandoned the use of job-aptitude tests in hiring. The company eventually realized that a large percentage of the people hired without use of such tests were not promotable. Thus "adverse impact" had been merely shifted from the hiring stage to the promotion stage (Schmidt & Hunter, 1981).

Job Performance: Cognitive and Biodata

Overall, the two most valid predictors of job performance are cognitive ability tests and biodata forms. J. E. Hunter and R. F. Hunter (1984) reviewed the available literature and estimated the average validity of general cognitive-ability tests against the criterion of supervisory ratings of overall job performance to be .47, and for biodata forms to be .37. The literature also indicates that such findings are generalizable, thus the results of biodata forms are not limited to one specific situation.

g as a Predictor of Occupational Criteria

Ree and Earles (1991) studied some 78,000 airmen in 82 job specialties and found that *g* or general cognitive ability was the most valid predictor of technical school grades. In Project A, another large military study (McHenry, Hough, Toquam et al., 1990), g was the best predictor of Army performance measures. Ree, Earls, and Teachout (1994) in a study of Air Force enlistees who took the ASVAB found that g was the best predictor of job performance, with an average r of .42. Olea and Ree (1994) studied Air Force navigator and pilot students. Again, g was the best predictor of criteria such as passing or failing the training, grades, and work samples.

Cognitive Ability and Minorities

Although cognitive-ability tests are valid indicators for on-the-job performance, they present a serious challenge, namely that in the United States blacks score, on the average, about one SD lower than whites (J. E. Hunter & R. F. Hunter, 1984). If such tests are used to select applicants, the result is what the courts called adverse impact. When this problem arose in the 1960s, the solution seemed relatively straightforward: if cognitive tests were unfair to black applicants, one only needed to make the tests fair, that is, to remove the items that were culturally biased.

The evidence collected since then has not supported this approach. As discussed in Chapter 11, any test that is valid for one racial group is valid for the other. Single-group validity, where a test is valid for one group but not another, and differential validity, where the test is less valid for one group than for another, are artifacts of small sample size. If tests were in fact culturally biased, that would mean that the test scores for blacks would be lower than their true ability scores, and so their job performance would be higher than what is predicted by their test scores. In fact, however, the regression equations for blacks are either equal to those of whites or overpredict the performance of blacks. The overwhelming evidence is that differences in average test scores reflect real differences in abilities. These differences are likely the result of societal forces such as poverty and prejudice. Eliminate these and the test differences should be eliminated.

Minimizing Adverse Impact

McKinney (1987) suggests that to maximize both predictive efficiency and affirmative action, one should select the best-scoring individuals from each racial subgroup in proportions that equal their representation in the applicant pool. The U.S. Employment Service in fact does this with scores on the General Aptitude Test Battery (see discussion that follows).

RATINGS

Supervisors' Ratings

A supervisor's rating is probably the most common measure of job performance, and the most common criterion against which tests are evaluated. These ratings are used not only to validate tests, but for issues such as promotions and pay raises, as well as to assess the impact of training programs. Other more "objective" criteria such as salary or promotion history can be used instead of ratings, but most of these criteria have some serious shortcomings. Rating scales can be constructed from a variety of points of view, and the literature has not clearly identified one form as superior to others (e.g., Atkin & Conlon, 1978; Dickinson & Zellinger, 1980).

Lawler (1967) suggested that the multitrait-multimethod approach (see Chapter 3) might be a useful one for performance appraisal, where the multimethod is replaced by multi-rater. Rather than use a single supervisor's ratings, this approach calls for multiratings – i.e., ratings by supervisors, by peers, by subordinates, and by the individual – anyone who is familiar with the aspects to be rated of the individual's performance.

The multitrait requirement is met by rating somewhere around three to five traits. One rating should be a global one on quality of job performance. The nature of the other ratings depends upon the purpose of the rating procedure and the particular types of behaviors relevant to a specific job. Lawler (1967) suggests that whatever these behaviors are, the rating scales should be behavior-description anchored scales. Rather than rate dimensions such as friendliness and adaptability (which cannot be rated reliably), what should be rated is effort put forth on the job and ability to perform the job.

Lawler (1967) gives as an example some data based on a group of managers, where superiors', peer, and self-ratings were obtained on three

Table 14–1. An Example of the Multitrait-Multimethod(rater) Approach (Lawler, 1967)

Ratings by:	Superiors			Peers			Self	
	1	2	3	4	5	6	7	8
Superiors								
1. Quality of job performance								
2. Ability to perform the job	.53							
3. Effort put forth on the job	.56	.44						
Peers								
4. Quality of job performance	(.65)	.38	.40					
5. Ability to perform the job	.42	(.52)	.30	.55				
6. Effort put forth on the job	.40	.31	(.53)	.56	.40			
Self								
7. Quality of job performance	(.01)	.01	.09	.01	.17	.10		
8. Ability to perform the job	.03	(.13)	.03	.04	.09	.02	.43	
9. Effort put forth on the job	.06	.01	(.30)	.02	.01	.30	.40	.14

Note: The larger squares include the heterotrait-monorater coefficients; the smaller circles include the monotrait-heterorater coefficients – i.e., the validity coefficients. The remaining coefficients are the heterotrait-heterorater coefficients.

dimensions: quality of job performance, ability to perform the job, and effort put forth on the job. The results are presented in Table 14.1.

Note that the validity coefficients, that is, the correlations on the same trait by different raters, should be highest of all. In this case, the ratings by superiors and by peers do show such convergent validity, but the self-ratings do not. These validity ratings are higher than the heterotrait-heterorater coefficients, even in the case of the self-ratings – as they should be to show discriminant validity. Finally, the validity coefficients should be higher than the heterotrait-monorater coefficients – which they are.

Self- vs. Other Ratings

The use of multiple sources for performance ratings has gained considerable acceptance due to several advantages, among them greater reliability and a stronger legal standing. Often however, there is a lack of agreement between self-ratings and those provided by peers and by supervisors. For example, Harris and Schaubroeck (1988) conducted a metaanalysis of the literature and computed the average correlation between self-and peer ratings to be .36, between self-and supervisor ratings to be .35, and between peer and supervisor ratings to be .62. Some view such lack of agreement as expected because different raters observe different aspects

of a person's performance or have different views of what effective performance is.

Others view the lack of agreement as reflective of bias in the self-ratings. That is, when individuals are asked to rate their own performance they may tend to inflate their ratings on such aspects as self-esteem.

Rating Errors

Traditionally, ratings are subject to two types of errors, identified as *halo* and *bias*. Halo refers to the tendency to rate an individual high or low on all dimensions because the person is outstandingly high or low on one or a few dimensions. Thus, if I like you because you are particularly friendly, I might be tempted to also automatically rate you as high on interpersonal skills, leadership ability, intelligence, etc. Halo has always been regarded as a rating error, something that could potentially be controlled through training of raters or through better rating forms. In fact, halo may not be an error but may result in *increased* validity coefficients – perhaps halo serves to ensure that raters consider the "person as a whole" rather than pay attention to specific but perhaps unrepresentative critical incidents (Nathan & Tippins, 1990). The literature also indicates that halo can be analyzed into two components: a true or valid component and an illusory or invalid component. That is, if the ratings across dimensions correlate substantially, this is taken as evidence of the halo effect. Such high correlations reflect, in part, the real overlap among such dimensions (i.e., true halo) and irrelevant factors such as memory errors on the part of the rater (i.e., invalid halo). Because of such halo error, it is assumed that the obtained correlations among dimensions are larger than the "true" correlations. Murphy, Jako, and Anhalt (1993) reviewed the literature on the halo error and concluded that the halo effect is not all that common, that such an effect does not necessarily detract from the validity of ratings, and that it is probably impossible to separate true from invalid components. (For another review, see Balzer & Sulsky, 1992.)

Rater bias refers to the tendency of raters to pile up their ratings – one rater may be lenient and rate everyone as above average, another rater may be tough and rate everyone as below average, and a third rater may restrict the ratings to the middle (often called the *leniency* error or the error of *central tendency*). The broader term of "rater bias" covers all these cases.

Some techniques have been developed to counter these errors. One is the *forced distribution* method where the rater is instructed to have the ratings follow a specified distribution, usually based on the normal curve. We could for example, force a rater to make 5% of the ratings fall in the highest category and 5% in the lowest, 20% in the above average category and 20% in the below average categories, and 50% in the average category.

Another approach is to rank the individuals being rated. This is a feasible procedure when the number of individuals is somewhat small. A variation of the ranking method is called *alternation-ranking* where the rater selects the best and the poorest person on the rating dimension, then the next best and next poorest, and so on, until all persons have been ranked. Because ranks do not form a normal distribution, but a rectangular one, they must be converted to normalized standard scores for statistical analyses. Tables for doing this are available (see Albright, Glennon, & Smith, 1963, pp. 172–173 for an example that converts ranks to T scores).

A third method is the *paired comparison* system (Lawshe, Kephart, & McCormick, 1949). The rater is given a deck of 3 × 5 cards, each card bearing the names of two individuals to be rated. The rater checks the one name who performs the job (or whatever the dimension being rated is) better. ALL possible pairs of names are presented. The number of pairs can be computed by the formula:

$$N(N-1)/2$$

where N is the number of persons. Thus, if there were 12 persons being rated, there would be 66 pairings. Clearly the usefulness of this technique is limited by the size of N, although there are techniques available for larger groups (see Albright, Glennon, & Smith, 1963; Guion, 1965a).

Despite their ubiquity, ratings have a number of potential limitations. Some of the limitations stem from the situation in which ratings are used. Often, for example, the supervisors have not had the opportunity to carefully observe the required behavior. Or there may be "demand" characteristics in the situation – for example, a supervisor who needs to discuss the ratings with each person rated may not be willing to give extremely low ratings. Rating forms may also be at fault in not providing clear and unambiguous behaviors to be rated.

Behavioral Anchors

One strategy to reduce bias is to use rating scales that have concrete behavioral anchors that illustrate the performance aspects to be rated. Such behavioral anchors provide a standard framework by which to evaluate a person's performance and provide examples of specific behaviors that might be expected from good, average, or poor performers. On the other hand such behavioral anchors may bias the ratings given by making the described behavior more salient for the rater (K. R. Murphy & Constans, 1987). An example of a rating scale item with behavioral anchors, can be found in Figure 14.1.

P. C. Smith and Kendall (1963) proposed the use of continuous graphic rating scales, arranged vertically, with behavioral descriptions as anchors. The person making the ratings can place a check at any position on the line and may also indicate some actual observed behaviors to support the check made. The approach used by these investigators was not to trick the rater by using forced-choice items, but to help the rater to make accurate ratings by using anchors

Variable to be related: list making

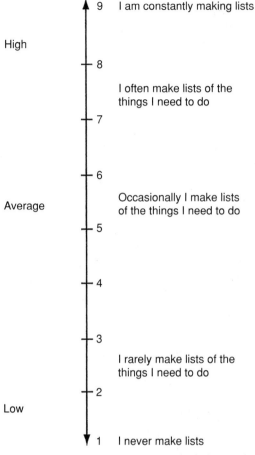

FIGURE 14–1. A rating scale with behavioral anchors.

that reflect observable behaviors rather than inferences.

Cultural Differences in Ratings

The literature indicates that self-ratings are typically one half SD higher than supervisory ratings. Subordinates tend to be more lenient in evaluating themselves than do their supervisors (M. M. Harris & Schaubroeck, 1988). Farh, Dobbins, and Cheng (1991) studied self-ratings vs. supervisory ratings in the Republic of China (Taiwan). Their results indicated a "modesty" bias – that is, Chinese employees rated their job performance less favorably than did their supervisors. Quite clearly, Western individualism stresses individual achievement, self-sufficiency,

and self-respect, while in collectivistic cultures like Taiwan, individuals are discouraged from boasting about their individual accomplishments and are expected to be more modest in their self-ratings.

THE ROLE OF PERSONALITY

Personality as Predictor of Job Performance

It is often stated that individual personality variables are relatively poor predictors of job performance.

B. Schneider (1983) proposed an attraction-selection-attrition framework for understanding organizational behavior. That is, individuals select themselves into and out of organizations, and different types of people make up different types of organizations. Thus personality variables should be important in determining not only which persons are seen as leaders, but also the likelihood that a person will fit in and stay with a particular company. (For a test of Schneider's hypothesis, see Bretz, Ash, & Dreher, 1989.)

In the 1960s, a number of reviewers indicated that the validity of personality measures for personnel selection purposes, and specifically as a predictor of job performance, was low, although most of the studies on which this conclusion was based were one-shot studies lacking a theoretical or conceptual framework (Guion & Gottier, 1965). In fact, however, personality measures are widely used in employee selection, and the general conclusion about their lack of validity has changed. Which personality characteristics are important for on-the-job performance depend upon the specific job, among other things – we would not expect accountants, for example, and circus performers to exhibit the same pattern of relationships between on-the-job performance and personality aspects.

Barrick and Mount (1991) analyzed the literature with regard to three job performance criteria – job proficiency, training proficiency, and personnel data, for five occupational groups that included police, managers, and sales persons. They analyzed the personality measures in terms of the "Big Five" model discussed in Chapter 4, i.e., extraversion, emotional stability, agree-ableness, conscientiousness, and openness to experience. The results indicated that conscientiousness showed consistent relations with all job-performance criteria for all occupational groups. Extraversion was a valid predictor for managers and sales, the two occupational fields that involve social interaction. And both openness to experience and extraversion were valid predictors of the training proficiency criterion across occupations.

Tett, Jackson, and Rothstein (1991) also conducted a meta-analysis of the literature. They found that personality variables did correlate significantly with job criteria, although the "typical" value of .24 was somewhat low. In addition, they found higher values as a function of several variables. For example, where job analyses were used to select predictors, in studies of applicants vs. incumbents (i.e., people holding the job), and in military vs. civilian samples. These authors concluded that current validational practices have a number of correctable weaknesses; specifically, they pointed to the need to carry out job analyses and use valid personality measures. In general, most correlations between well-designed personality inventories and job-effectiveness criteria fall in the .40 to .60 range.

The Big Five revisited. As discussed in Chapter 4, the five-factor model of personality has received rather wide, but not unanimous, support, and a number of investigators have urged its use in the area of personnel selection (e.g., Barrick & Mount, 1991; Cortina, Dortina, Schmitt et al., 1992). Some researchers have noted that the five-factor model is too broad to have predictive usefulness (e.g., Briggs 1992, Mc Adams, 1992). One study for example (Mershon & Gorsuch, 1988) found that 16 factors were better predictors of various occupational and psychiatric criteria than six scales that assessed the five-factor model. Another study (Hough, 1992) showed that a nine-factor model had higher validities than the five-factor model in predicting job performance. Schmit and Ryan (1993) administered a 60-item version of the NEO-PI (see Chapter 4) to a sample of college students and a sample of job applicants. A confirmatory factor analysis indicated that the five-factor model fit the student data well, but not the job-applicant data. In the data obtained from the job applicants, the largest factor was one that was made

up of items from four of the five subscales – a dimension which the authors labeled as an "ideal employee" factor. They suggested that this dimension represents the hypothesis that respondents present themselves in a manner that they see as appropriate to the situation, i.e., as job applicants, without deliberately falsifying their answers.

Hogan (1990) cites a meta-analysis done to determine the relationship between the five personality dimensions and various organizational outcomes. Among the conclusions of this study, are the following:

1. The dimension of extraversion or social ascendancy is correlated with performance in sales and management.

2. The dimension of emotional stability (also called adjustment and self-esteem) is correlated with upward mobility and leadership status.

3. The dimension of agreeableness or likability is correlated with supervisors' ratings of job performance.

4. Conscientiousness or dependability is correlated positively with academic performance and negatively with indices of delinquency.

5. Finally, openness to experience or new ideas is correlated with intellectual performance and rated creativity.

Repeated administrations. The use of personality tests as screening devices, especially in high-risk or sensitive occupations such as police officer jobs, seems to be increasing. Without a doubt, the MMPI has dominated the field. Given that the MMPI is so frequently given, it is not unlikely that a police officer, for example, may take the test several times. What is the effect of such repeated administrations on the obtained test scores? Note that this question is closely related to, but different from, the question of test-retest reliability. As discussed in Chapter 7, the long-term test-retest reliability of the MMPI, where the intervening period ranges from several months to several years, is significantly lower than its short-term reliability. Graham (1987) indicates that for normal samples, typical MMPI test reliabilities for retest periods of a day or less are about .80 to .85, for periods of 1 to 2 weeks they are .70 to .80, and for periods of a year or more they are .35 to .45.

There are several possible explanations for the increased change in scores – possible changes in personality, or placing different interpretations on the meaning of items over a longer period of time, or the results of practice effects.

P. L. Kelley, Jacobs, and Farr (1994) looked at the MMPI profiles of almost 2,000 workers in the nuclear-power industry. Each of the participants had completed the MMPI several times as a result of regular employment procedures, most from two to five times. The results indicated that the obtained differences from one testing point to another were small, but for some MMPI scales, there were significant changes. The authors found that scale reliabilities tended to increase, and the result was more "normal" test profiles, perhaps because candidates became more "testwise."

Values. As our world shrinks, business individuals find themselves more frequently dealing with persons from different cultures. Problems can arise because what is highly valued in one country may not be valued in another, yet individuals tend to behave in accord with their own values, especially when making difficult or complex decisions.

Bond and a group of international colleagues (Chinese Culture Connection, 1987) developed an instrument, the Chinese Value Survey (CVS), to assess values of importance in eastern countries such as China. The CVS consists of 40 items such as "filial piety," "solidarity with others," "patriotism," and "respect for tradition." Each item is answered on a 9-point Likert-type scale that ranges from "extreme importance" to "no importance." The CVS assesses four factor-analytic dimensions labeled as: (1) integration or social stability – i.e., being in harmony with oneself, one's family, and colleagues; (2) Confucian work dynamism, reflecting the teachings of Confucius such as maintaining the status quo and personal virtue; (3) human heartedness – having compassion and being people-oriented; (4) moral discipline – i.e., self-control.

In one study (Ralston, Gustafson, Elsass et al., 1992), the CVS was administered to managers from the United States, Hong Kong, and the People's Republic of China (PRC). The results indicated that on the Integration dimension there were no differences between U.S. and Hong Kong managers, but both groups scored significantly higher than the PRC managers. On the Confucian Work Dynamism, PRC managers scored the highest, next the Hong Kong managers, and lowest of all the U.S. managers. On the Human heartedness dimension, where higher scores reflect a greater task orientation, U.S. managers scored highest, followed by Hong Kong managers, and lowest of all the PRC managers. Only on Moral Discipline were there no significant differences among the three groups.

BIOGRAPHICAL DATA (BIODATA)

There is a saying in psychology that the best predictor of future behavior is past behavior. This does not necessarily mean that people will behave in the future as they have in the past, but rather that earlier behavior and experience will make some future behaviors more likely (Mumford & Owens, 1987). Past behavior can be assessed through biographical data or what is called *biodata*. Biodata forms consist of a variety of items, some of which are quite factual and verifiable (e.g., what was your undergraduate GPA), and others that are more subjective and less verifiable (e.g., what is your major strength?). Quite often, such biodata forms are administered as job-application blanks, that contain both descriptive information (e.g., the person's address and phone number), and biodata items. The items or questions are then weighted or scored in some manner, and the resulting score used for classification or predictive purposes. The literature uses a number of labels for biodata such as background data, scored autobiographical data, or job-application blanks.

Biodata forms have been used quite successfully in a variety of areas ranging from creativity to executive evaluations. In the early 1920s, there were a number of studies in the literature showing that such weighted application blanks could be useful in distinguishing successful from unsuccessful employees in a variety of occupations. During and after the Second World War, such items were formulated in a multiple-choice format that was quite convenient and efficient. In general, these measures show relatively high validity, little or no adverse impact, and job applicants typically respond positively. One major source of concern is to what degree they are susceptible to faking (Kluger, Reilly, & Russell, 1991).

Many biodata forms are in-house forms developed by business or consulting companies for use with specific client companies and not available for public browsing. Others are made available to professionals. For example, the Candidate Profile Record (CPR) is a 145-item biodata form used to identify high-potential candidates for secretarial and office personnel. All items are multiple-choice and cover aspects such as academic history, work history, work-related attitudes, and self-esteem. The CPR is untimed and can be administered individually or in groups, with an administration time of about 30 to 45 minutes. The CPR can be computer scored (Pederson, 1990). For those who prefer to build their own, there is a vast body of literature on biodata forms, including a dictionary of biodata items (Glennon, Albright, & Owens, 1966).

Items. Items for biodata forms typically reflect two approaches: (1) items that center on a particular domain or criterion – for example, items that have to do with job-related knowledge and skills; (2) items that reflect previous life experiences, such as prior job experiences or attitudes toward particular work aspects. An example of the first type of item might be the following: How many real-estate courses have you completed? The response options might go from none to five or more. An example of the second item might be: At what age did you begin working? The response options might go from 14 and younger to "never."

The nature of biodata items. It is not quite clear how biodata items differ from items found on other tests, such as personality tests, although one difference is that biodata items do not represent general descriptions of behavioral tendencies (e.g., I am a friendly person), but rather focus on prior behavior and experiences in specified, real-life situations. Mael (1991) suggests that biodata items pertain to historical events that may have shaped a person's behavior and identity. Furthermore, he argues that biodata items should reflect external events, be limited to objective and first-hand recollections, be potentially verifiable, and measure discrete events.

Constructing a biodata form. In general, the construction of biodata follows the same general steps discussed in Chapter 2. An item pool is first put together and potential items are reviewed both rationally and empirically. Rational review might involve judges or subject matter experts. Empirical review might involve administering the pool of items to samples of subjects and carrying out various statistical analyses. For example, items that lack sufficient variability or show skewed response distributions might be eliminated. Intercorrelations and factor analyses can be carried out to determine whether clusters of items that conceptually ought to go together, indeed do so statistically.

Scaling Procedures

How is a set of biodata items turned into a scale? There are basically four procedures: (1) empirical keying, (2) rational scaling, (3) factor analysis, and (4) subgrouping.

1. Empirical keying. This represents the most common method, and is essentially identical to the procedure used for personality tests such as the MMPI and CPI, discussed in Chapters 4 and 7. The pool of potential items is administered to a group or groups of subjects, and the scoring is developed against some criterion. For example, we might administer the pool of items to a large sample of job applicants, hire them all, and at the end of a year identify the successful vs. the unsuccessful through supervisors' ratings, records of sales, or some other criteria. Items in the biodata protocols are then analyzed statistically to see which ones show a differential pattern of responding either in the two contrasted groups (i.e., successful vs. unsuccessful) or against the continuous criterion of amount of sales. Items that correlate significantly with the criterion can then be cross-validated and those that survive form the scoring key.

One of the crucial aspects of this procedure is the criterion – its reliability, validity, and utility. To the extent that the criterion measures are well defined, measured accurately, and free of any confounding aspects, to that degree will the empirical key work (Klein & Owens, 1965; Thayer, 1977).

In most tests, of personality, for example, where the key is constructed empirically, items are given unit weights – thus an item responded to in the keyed direction is assigned a scoring weight of $+1$. Might we not enhance the usefulness or validity of our test if we used different weights for different items (or even for different response options to the same item), perhaps to reflect each item's ability to discriminate between the *criterion* group members (e.g., the successful employees) from the *reference* group members (e.g., the job applicants). In fact, this is what is often done, and the result is called a *weighted* biodata questionnaire (see Mumford & Owens, 1987 for a brief discussion of various procedures).

Mumford and Owens (1987) review several studies of the reliability and validity of the empirical keying approach and concluded that empirically keyed biodata measures are among the best available predictors of training and job performance criteria. In addition, empirically developed biodata forms show considerable cross-cultural validity and a relative lack of ethnic differences.

A major criticism of the empirical keying approach, aside from its dependence on the criterion, is that the scoring pattern may lack psychological meaningfulness (construct validity). Thus we may find that an item dealing with infrequent church attendance may discriminate between successful and less successful employees, and we may be at a loss to theoretically explain why this item works. Those who focus on the use of tests as a means of *understanding* human behavior see this as a major limitation; those who see tests as a way of *predicting* behavior are less bothered.

2. Rational scales. Mumford and Owens (1987) identify two major strategies here, which they label as the direct and the indirect approaches. In the direct approach, a job analysis is undertaken to define the behaviors that are related to differential performance. Items are then developed to presumably measure such behaviors as they appeared in the respondent's earlier life. For example, let's assume that part of being a successful life insurance salesperson is that the individual occupies a highly visible role in the activities of the community. We might develop biodata items that would address the respondent's earlier role in his or her community, such as participation in vol-

unteering activities, leadership roles, participation in one's religious faith, etc. The indirect approach also attempts to identify the information that describes performance on the criterion (e.g., sales volume) but an attempt is made to identify the psychological constructs that might underlie such a performance (e.g., sales motivation, feelings of inferiority, sociability, etc.). and items are developed to reflect such constructs.

Usually, items for rational scales are retained based on their internal consistency – i.e., does the item correlate with other items and/or total score. A particular biodata form may have several such clusters of items. In general, a number of studies seem to suggest that such rationally developed scales have adequate reliability and substantial predictive validity, although studies comparing rational vs. empirical scaling techniques show the empirical scales to have higher initial criterion related validity and similar results when cross-validated (Hornick, James, & Jones, 1977; see below). This approach has not received much attention, although it would seem to be most useful when content and construct validity are of concern.

3. Factorial scales. Here the pool of biodata items is administered to a sample of respondents and various factor analytic techniques are used to determine the smallest number of dimensions (i.e., factors) or groupings of items that are also psychologically meaningful. Items that load (i.e., correlate) .30 on a particular dimension are usually retained and scored either with unitary weights (e.g., $+1$), or weights that reflect the size of the loading.

Given that most item pools are quite heterogeneous and that specific items do not correlate highly with each other, this approach is limited because its usefulness depends upon homogeneity of item content and high internal consistency. On the other hand, the results of a limited number of studies do suggest that factor-analytic results yield fairly stable factor structures across time, across various groups, and even across cultures. Mumford and Owens (1987) point to the paucity of studies on this approach, and suggest that factorial scales may not be as effective as empirically keyed scales, but may display greater stability and generality.

4. Subgrouping. This is a somewhat complicated technique, that also begins with a pool of items administered to a large sample of subjects. Item responses are then analyzed separately for men and for women, and a special type of factor analysis carried out to determine the basic components or dimensions. For each person then, a profile of scores is generated on the identified dimensions. These profiles are then analyzed statistically to determine subgroups of individuals with highly similar profiles. These subgroups are then analyzed to determine how they differ on the various biodata item responses. Much of this approach has been developed by Owens and his colleagues, and most of the studies have been carried out with college students, although the results seem quite promising (Mumford & Owens, 1987).

Scoring. The scoring of empirical biodata forms is relatively simple and was first outlined by Goldsmith in 1922. This is the empirical keying method discussed in Chapter 4 concerning personality inventories. A sample of individuals is administered the pool of items, in this case biodata items. The sample is then separated into two or more subgroups on the basis of some criterion we wish to predict – for example, life-insurance salespersons are divided into those who sell X amount of insurance vs. those who sell less. The responses of the two subgroups to the biodata items are then compared, and a scoring key formed on the basis of items whose responses distinguish the two groups. For example, suppose that we find that 86% of our super salespersons indicate a large eastern city as their birthplace, whereas only 12% of our "poor" salespersons do so. That item would be subsequently scored in a positive direction to predict sales performance. Obviously, the procedure would need to be cross-validated to eliminate what might be chance results.

Such biodata scales generally work quite well and are relatively easy to develop. As with personality inventories like the MMPI and CPI, the pool of biodata items represents an open system – the same pool of items can be used to develop different scales. At the same time, biodata forms have the same criticism that some psychologists aim at any empirically derived measure, that is, they lack a unifying theoretical background that permits understanding of why the items work as they do. Such empirical item-keying is based on the assumption that there is a linear relationship between the item option and the criterion. Thus with a 5-point Likert-type response, the various options will be given weights of 1, 2, 3, 4, and 5.

A second scoring alternative is called option-keying, where each response alternative is analyzed separately and is scored only if it correlates significantly with the criterion. For a Likert-type item (or any item with several response options), we might use contrasted groups and analyze the frequency with which each response option was chosen within each group. Options that statistically differentiate the two groups would then be scored plus or minus, and options that do not differentiate the two groups are scored zero. The advantage of the option-keying approach is that it can reflect both linear and nonlinear relationships and may be more resistant to faking (Kluger, Reilly, & Russell, 1991).

Empirical vs. rational. Biodata questionnaires can be classified as either empirical or rational (Mosel, 1952). Empirical biodata questionnaires are developed using criterion validity. Items are typically multiple choice and the scoring weights are based on the empirical relationship between the item and the criterion. Rational biodata questionnaires are developed using content validity. Items usually require narrative responses that typically focus on previous job experiences. The responses are evaluated by raters with the help of predetermined standards.

A basic question is to ask which method is better? T. W. Mitchell and Klimoski (1982) developed a biodata form for real-estate salespersons, and administered it to a sample of more than 600 enrollees in a course on real-estate principles. Two scoring keys were then developed, one based on an empirical approach, the other on a rational approach, against the criterion whether the individual had or had not obtained a license to sell real estate.

The empirical approach involved comparing the response frequencies of the two groups and translating these frequencies into scoring weights. T. W. Mitchell and Klimoski (1982) illustrate this procedure with one item that inquires about the person's living arrangements:

Do you:	Licensed	Not Licensed	Difference	Weight
own your home?	81%	60%	21	5
rent a house?	3%	5%	-2	-1
rent an apartment?	9%	25%	-16	-4
live with relatives?	5%	10%	-5	-2

The first two columns indicate the percentage of responses by those who obtained the license and those who did not. The third column is simply the difference. These differences are then translated into scoring weights (shown in column four) using standard tables that have been developed for this purpose. Thus an individual who indicates he or she owns their home would get +5 points, whereas a person who rents an apartment would receive −4 points.

In the rational approach, the intent is to identify items that measure a theoretically meaningful set of constructs. Item-response choices are then scored according to a hypothesized theoretical continuum. For example, in the item given above, it might be theoretically assumed that as a person becomes more economically independent they move from living with relatives, to renting an apartment, to renting a house, and finally to owning a home. In this approach, these four response choices would be given scoring weights of 1, 2, 3, and 4, respectively.

For each person in the sample and in a cross-validation sample, the two scores were correlated against the criterion of licensing, with the following results:

	Original sample	Cross-validation sample
Empirical score	.59	.46
Rational score	.35	.36

Note that the empirical approach was superior to the rational even though the empirical approach showed shrinkage (i.e., loss of validity) upon cross-validation, whereas the rational approach did not.

Accuracy. Biodata items rely on the self-report of the respondent as to their past behavior and experiences. There is concern that item responses may be distorted by selective recall, either purposive or "unconscious." A number of studies have looked at this issue with mixed results; some studies have found substantial agreement between what the respondent reported and objective verification of that report, whereas other studies have found disagreement (e.g., Cascio, 1975; I. L. Goldstein, 1971; Weiss & Dawis, 1960).

Mumford and Owens (1987) believe that the discrepancy among studies may reflect the methodology used, and that although there may be a general self-presentation bias, there is accuracy of item responses when there is no motive for faking. They also indicate that there are three techniques that can be used to minimize faking: (1) use items that are less sensitive to faking; (2) develop scoring keys that predict faking; and (3) use faking keys in the scoring (see Chapter 16).

Reliability. The reliability of biodata items can be enhanced by a number of approaches:

1. Make the items simple and brief.

2. Give the response options on a numerical continuum [e.g., What was your salary range in your last position? (a) less than $ 10,000; (b)$ 10,000 to 15,000 etc.].

3. Provide an *escape* response option if all the possible alternatives have not been included (e.g., in the above item we might include the option "I did not receive a salary").

4. Make the items positive or neutral (for example, instead of saying "I was fired from my last job because ...," we might ask, "What was the length of service in your last job?") (Owens, Glennon, & Albright, 1962).

A number of studies have indicated that well-developed biodata questionnaires show relatively low item intercorrelations – i.e., the items are relatively independent (e.g., Owens, 1976; Plag & Goffman, 1967). Therefore, we would expect relatively low internal consistency coefficients, and that indeed is the case, with typical coefficients in the range of .40 to .80. Test-retest reliability on the other hand, seems more than adequate, even with rather substantial time intervals of several years.

Validity. Because biodata forms differ from each other, and are compared with a variety of criteria, the issue of validity can be quite complex.

In general, however, the literature indicates that biodata forms are valid in a wide variety of settings and samples (see Mumford & Owens, 1987). Reilly and Chao (1982) reviewed a number of studies and found the average correlation between biodata forms and on-the-job productivity to be .46.

One might expect that the validity of biodata forms to be somewhat limited over a long period of time. For example, a form developed in the 1950s to select successful candidates for a specific position, might not work very well in the 1990s. Such indeed seems to be the case, although few longitudinal studies exist. A notable exception is a study by A. L. Brown (1978) who investigated the long-term validity of a biodata scoring key developed in 1933 for a sample of life-insurance agents; the results some 38 years later indicated that little, if any, validity was lost.

Two other findings need to be mentioned: (1) significant black-white differences have not been obtained in most studies (Mumford & Owens, 1987); (2) typically, correlations between information provided by an applicant and the same information obtained from previous employers are very high, with coefficients in the .90s (e.g., Mosel & Cozan, 1952).

Biodata and creativity. Biodata has been particularly useful in studies of the identification and prediction of scientific competence and creativity (e.g., Albright & Glennon, 1961; Kulberg & Owens, 1960; McDermid, 1965; Schaefer & Anastasi, 1968; M. F. Tucker, Schmitt Cline, & Schmitt, 1967).

Tucker, Cline, and Schmitt (1967) for example, administered a 160-item biographical inventory, originally developed with NASA scientists, to a sample of 157 scientists working for a pharmaceutical company. Information on a variety of criteria was also collected; these included supervisory and peer ratings on creativity and overall work performance, as well as employment records such as length employed by the company and number of salary increases. High intercorrelations among the criteria indicated were interpreted by the authors as reflecting the influence of a halo effect. Peer ratings and supervisory ratings on the same dimensions did not correlate very highly. Subsets of items on the biodata inventory

however, when cross-validated, correlated significantly (.36 and .42) with criteria of creativity.

Biodata with unskilled workers. Scott and R. W. Johnson (1967) reported an interesting study with unskilled workers in a small canning factory. The company experienced substantial losses of unfilled contracts due to rapid employee turnover – therefore "tenure" was of great importance and tantamount to worker effectiveness. They first identified 75 workers who had been at the factory for at least 6 months (long-tenure group), and 75 who had been there for 1 month or less (short-tenure group). Apparently, all of these workers had filled out a job-application form that contained 19 items. From each of the two samples, 50 applications were selected randomly, and item responses were analyzed. Differential weights of 0, 1, or 2 were assigned to items as a function of their ability to discriminate the two samples. Of the 19 items, 12 were given different weights; a cross-validation with the 25 employment forms in each group not used in the initial analyses, indicated a hit rate of 72%, and a correlation coefficient between scores on the biodata form and tenure of .45.

A regression equation using just six items was then developed:

$$\text{Tenure} = .30(\text{age})$$
$$+ 8.82(\text{gender})$$
$$- .69(\text{milesfromplant})$$
$$+ 5.29(\text{typeofresidence})$$
$$+ 2.66(\text{numberofchildren})$$
$$+ 1.08(\text{yearsonlastjob})$$
$$- 1.99.$$

Gender was scored as male $= 0$ and female $= 1$, and type of residence was scored as 0 if the person lived with parents or in a rented room and 1 if they lived in their own home. Using this regression equation in the cross-validation groups yielded a hit rate of 70% and a correlation coefficient of .31. Both the regression equation and a subsequent factor analysis point to two major themes: family responsibility and convenience. Long-term employees are married, provide for one or more dependents, live in their own home, and worked a relatively long period of time in their last job. Unskilled females who live fairly close to work were likely to stay on the job at this factory longer.

(For a biodata study on college students, see Holland & Nichols, 1964).

ASSESSMENT CENTERS

This approach was originally developed to select military officers during World War II, but was made popular in the 1950s by the American Telephone and Telegraph Company, and refers to a method of assessment rather than actual physical place (Thornton & Byham, 1982). The first step in this method involves a job assessment, that is, an analysis of what qualities, skills, dimensions, etc., are relevant to a specific job. Then job candidates are observed and assessed for a given period of time, which may last several days. Multiple assessment or simulation methods are used, including leaderless group discussions, in-basket tests (see below), problem-solving exercises, as well as standard tests believed to be useful in inferring managerial skills and abilities (Brannick, Michaels, & Baker, 1989). There are usually multiple assessors whose judgments, typically in the form of ratings, are pooled to produce an overall evaluation. Because of the time and expense involved, assessment centers are usually used for managerial and executive personnel, for either selection or training purposes. (For an overview of what assessment centers are all about, see Bray, 1982.)

Uniqueness of dimensions. The dimensions and tasks used are not standard and vary from one assessment center to another. Reilly, Henry, and Smither (1990) for example, report eight dimensions that include leadership, problem solving, work orientation, and teamwork. Two group exercises are briefly described. In one, the candidates had to arrive at an assembly procedure for a flashlight or a simple electrical device. In another, the group was required to organize and plan an approach to construct a prototype of a robot, after being shown a model and given tools and parts. Three assessors were assigned two candidates each to observe and rate. T. H. Shore, Thornton, and L. M. Shore (1990) used 11 dimensions falling into two major domains: the interpersonal style domain that included "amount of participation" and "understanding of people," and the performance style domain that included "originality," "work drive (i.e., persistence)," and "thoroughness of performance."

Some tasks seem to be used more frequently, such as leaderless group discussions and the in-basket test.

Validity. Meta-analytic reviews support the validity of assessment centers from a predictive-validity perspective, but less so from a construct-validity point of view. In other words, less is known about why assessment ratings predict later performance than the fact that they do (Gaugler, Rosenthal, Thornton, et al., 1987; Klimoski & Brickner, 1987; N. Schmitt, Gooding, Noe, et al., 1984).

A number of researchers have reported lack of evidence to support the convergent and discriminant validity of the specific dimensions assessed: correlations within the same exercise are higher than the correlations for the same dimension across different exercises, that is, the multitrait correlation coefficients are higher than the multimethod ones (e.g., Sackett & Dreher, 1982). Others have shown that using behavior checklists increases the average convergent validity and decreases the average discriminant validity (Reilly, Henry, & Smither, 1990). Sackett (1987) points out that the content validity leaves much to be desired – it is not enough to pay attention to the construction of the exercises; how these exercises are presented and evaluated is also crucial.

Why do they work? There is substantial evidence that assessment centers are useful predictors of subsequent managerial success. The main issue is not so much whether they work, but why they work (i.e., predictive vs. construct validity).

Typical conclusions are that assessment centers are useful tools to predict the future success of potential managers, regardless of educational level, race, gender, or prior assessment-center experience (Klimoski & Brickner, 1987). They seem to work in a wide variety of organizational settings ranging from manufacturing companies to educational and governmental institutions; they can be useful not only for selection and promotion purposes, but also for training, for career planning, and for improving managerial skills.

Why do these centers work? The traditional answer is that they are standardized devices to allow assessment of traits that are then used to predict future success on the job. They work because they do a good job of measuring and integrating information regarding a person's traits and qualities. However, the evidence suggests that assessment center ratings do not reflect the dimensions they are supposed to and may at best represent a global rating, something like a "halo" effect. Other alternative explanations range from the hypothesis that promotions in organizations may be partially based on ratings of assessment-center performance (i.e., those who do well get promoted) to the hypothesis that the ratings obtained reflect the level of intellectual functioning of candidates.

The In-Basket Technique

Probably the best known situation or simulation exercise used in assessment centers is the in-basket technique (Frederiksen, 1962). In this technique the candidate is given an "in-basket" that contains letters, memos, records of phone calls, etc., and the candidate is asked to handle these as he or she would in an everyday job. The behavior (i.e., the actions and decisions the candidate makes) is scored according to content and to style; content refers to *what* was done and style to *how* a task was completed. Content scoring procedures typically involve a simple counting – for example, the number of memos completed or number of decisions made. Stylistic scoring procedures evaluate the quality of the performance, the quality of the decisions made. Unfortunately, the technique is not standardized and a variety of assessment materials and scoring procedures are used.

Reliability. Three types of reliability have been investigated: interrater reliability, alternate-form reliability, and split-half reliability. Interrater reliability coefficients vary substantially: in one study, for example, they varied from .47 to .94 and in another study from .49 to .95. Median *rs* however appear to be fairly substantial: in one study, the median *r* was .80, and in another it was .91. Schippmann, Prien, and Katz (1990), concluded that, despite the fact that none of the studies they reviewed used more than 4 raters and sample sizes are typically quite small, scorers and raters are responding fairly consistently to the data.

Few studies have looked at alternate-form reliability, but the few that have report fairly abysmal results. Typical correlations are only in the high .10s and low .20s, suggesting either that individuals are not consistent in their performance across forms, or that different versions of the in-basket are eliciting different behaviors.

Split-half reliabilities have also been disappointing, with typical reliability coefficients in the .40s to .50s range.

Validity. Schippmann, Prien, and Katz (1990) argue that the available literature confuses face validity with content validity. Thus, although a number of studies suggest that the in-basket procedure is valid because of its contents, none uses content validity procedures to construct an in-basket form.

Criterion validity is a bit more complex to summarize. There are various criteria that can be used, such as supervisory ratings, ratings obtained as part of the assessment-center evaluation, or various indices of career progress such as occupational title and salary. A very wide range of correlation coefficients are reported in the literature that range from nonsignificant to coefficients in the .50 to .70 range. Clearly, some of the evidence supports the validity of the procedure, but just as clearly there is need to study what aspects are confounding the results.

Very few studies have looked at the construct validity of this procedure. Studies that use factor analysis yield a fair amount of congruent results, but the evidence is too sparse to come to any conclusions. In general, Schippmann, Prien, and Katz (1990) conclude that the use of the in-basket technique is based more on "belief" about its value than on empirical evidence.

An experimental study. Brannick, Michaels, and Baker (1989) used two alternate forms of the in-basket exercise. Each in-basket presented a series of tasks such as phone messages, complaints from managers, and schedule conflicts that the candidate needed to act on. The responses were scored on five dimensions: organizing and planning; perceptiveness; delegation; leadership; and decision making. Scoring keys for these dimensions were developed by collecting the responses of about 20 students and managers and rating each response as positive, neutral, or negative on each of the five dimensions. A prior study indicated that the interrater correlation for this scoring procedure was .95, so it appears to be reliable.

A sample of 88 business students, both graduate and undergraduate, were then administered both forms. Interjudge reliability of the scoring of the two forms ranged from a low of .71 for organizing and planning, to a high of .89 for decision making, and a high of .91 and .94 for the total sum of Form A and of Form B. Internal reliability coefficients ranged from a low of .35 to a high of .72, with only one of the 12 coefficients (two forms with five dimensions and one total per form) above .70. More surprising was that scores across the two forms for the same dimensions did not correlate very highly – the coefficients ranged from .21 to .43. As the authors indicate, these results call into question the validity of inferences about managerial traits that are made on the basis of in-basket scores.

ILLUSTRATIVE INDUSTRIAL CONCERNS

Work Samples

A work sample is a replica of the position for which someone has applied. For example, someone applying for a position as typist might be asked to type a letter from dictation. Clearly for some jobs it is relatively easy to put together a work sample, but for others it is a bit more difficult. Work samples are sometimes called situational exercises, particularly when only a specific aspect of a job is being sampled. Thus, with candidates for a management position we might put them through situational exercises where they might need to show their ability to solve a personnel problem, their evaluation of a written document such as a contract, or their ability to write a business letter.

Expectancy Tables

Industrial psychologists are often concerned with predictive validity. In addition, they need to communicate such validity results to individuals who are not necessarily trained in statistics or psychometrics who may have difficulty understanding the meaning and limitations of a correlation coefficient. As discussed in Chapter 3, a useful device to communicate such results is an expectancy table, essentially a graphic display of data that

shows the relationship between a predictor (such as scores on a test) and a criterion (such as amount of sales), and allows the determination of the likelihood that a person with a specific score on the predictor will achieve a particular level of performance on the criterion.

Banding

When a sample of applicants is given a test, they are then typically ranked on the basis of their test scores, and the top-scoring applicants are then selected. Because of some of the issues discussed in Chapter 11, such a procedure may have adverse impact on members of specific minority groups. Ideally, a selection method should reduce adverse impact but not reduce the utility of such a procedure. One strategy is to adjust test scores to reduce or remove group differences, such as using separate norms for blacks and for whites. However, such a strategy is not only illegal in that it is forbidden by the Civil Rights Act of 1991 (see Chapter 15), but it is difficult to support rationally.

Another approach is that of test score *banding* (Cascio, Outtz, Zedeck, et al., 1991). Banding involves specifying differences in test scores that might be observed for two individuals who do not differ on the construct measured by the test (K. R. Murphy, 1994). For example, if the width of a test score band is 8 points, then someone who scores 28 should not be treated differently than someone who scores 22 because a difference of less than 8 points in this example, does not reliably indicate a difference on the construct measured. Note that this is very much like the concept of standard error for the difference between two means, discussed in Chapter 3, and indeed the formula for computing the bandwidth involves the reliability of the test and the standard error of measurement (see K. R. Murphy, 1994, for the actual formula).

Basically, banding defines a range of scores that should be treated as if they were identical; the selection decision must be made using additional information. For example, let's assume we have administered test X, where the highest obtained score is 120, and we have computed the bandwidth to be 5. Then scores between 120 and 115 are treated as essentially equal. Let's say we need to hire 8 applicants and we have a pool of 12 who scored 115 and above. In this case we would need to use additional information to select the 8 out of the 12. Suppose, however, only 5 applicants scored above 115. We would hire all of them as well as 3 applicants from the next bandwidth, namely 110 to 115.

Banding is not without criticism. Quite obviously, the procedure requires that we ignore the numerical differences within a band but not across bands – in the example above, differences between 115 and 120 are ignored, but 114 is treated as different from 115. This of course is not unusual. In college classes such a procedure is used implicitly when numerical scores are translated into letter grades – scores of 93 to 100 might for example, all be given As, while a score of 92 might be equated to a B (F. L. Schmidt, 1991).

Synthetic Validity

Lawshe introduced the concept of *synthetic* validity to refer to the notion that tests can be validated, not against a single overall criterion, but against job elements (Guion, 1965b; Lawshe, 1952; Lawshe & Steinberg, 1955). These job elements may be common to many dissimilar jobs. By using tests that are valid for specific job elements, one can create a tailor-made battery of tests, even for a new unique job.

Guion (1965b) presents an interesting application of this method. He studied an electrical wholesaler firm composed of 48 people, from president to stock boy. In no case were more than 3 persons doing the same job. Clearly, a traditional approach where test scores are related to a criterion would not work here. A detailed analysis of the various jobs and job descriptions indicated that there were seven major job elements, such as sales ability, creative business judgment, leadership, and work organization. The president and vice president of the company were then asked to rate the employees on the seven major job elements, as well as to give an overall rating. The procedure used attempted to eliminate any halo ratings, and only employees for whom a particular job element was relevant were rated on that dimension. The interrater reliability was quite high, ranging from a low of .82 to a high of .95, with most of the coefficients in the high .80s. Employees were subsequently administered a test battery that yielded 19 scores. These scores were then compared to the seven

job-element ratings, with the result that for five of the seven job-element ratings there were specific tests that correlated significantly with each job-element dimension. An application of these results to 13 new employees showed the system to be working well, and that consideration of specific job elements was better than the use of an overall criterion. (For other examples of synthetic validity studies, see Drewes, 1961; Griffin, 1959).

Time Urgency

How persons keep track of and use time has been a major topic of interest for industrial-organizational psychologists. One's time orientation seems to be related to a significant number of behaviors and outcomes, including the possibility of experiencing greater stress and subsequent cardiovascular disease.

Time urgency, or the tendency to perceive time as a scarce commodity, seems to be a particularly important variable. Like other complex psychological variables, time urgency is probably multidimensional. In one study, seven such dimensions were identified, including eating fast, impatience, and doing many things at once (Edwards, Baglioni, & Cooper, 1990).

Landy, Rastegary, Thayer, et al. (1991) took the items from four different scales, eliminated duplicate items and eventually developed a "new" scale of 33 items, all responded to in a Likert-type format. These items seemed to fall into five factors labeled as: competitiveness, eating behavior, general hurry, task-related hurry, and speech pattern. These five factors had coefficient alpha reliabilities ranging from a low of .69 to a high of .89, and intercorrelated with each other low to moderate, with correlation coefficients ranging from .17 to .39.

In a second study, Landy, Rastegary, Thayer, et al. (1991) undertook to develop a new test of time urgency by using behaviorally anchored rating scales (P. C. Smith & Kendall, 1963). Using a brainstorming technique, nine dimensions of time urgency were developed, such as "awareness of time," "eating behavior," and "speech patterns." For each of these nine dimensions, specific behavior anchors were then written; these were then submitted to various logical and statistical analyses, until there were two parallel rating scales for each of six dimensions, and a single-rating scale for a seventh dimension (two other dimensions were dropped). The resulting 13 scales were administered to a sample of introductory psychology college students, who were retested 4 weeks later. Test-retest reliabilities ranged from a low of .63 to a high of .83, with most values in the acceptable range. Parallel-form reliabilities ranged from .60 to .83, again also in the acceptable range. Inter-correlations among the seven dimensions are quite low, with the majority of coefficients in the .10s or below. The authors also present evidence for the construct validity of the scales.

Excessive Turnover

Excessive turnover is a serious problem for many companies. Whether an employee quits voluntarily or fails a probationary period or is fired, the economic loss to the employer can be substantial. There are a number of ways to combat this problem, but one strategy is to identify such "short tenure" personnel before hiring. One method is through the use of personal-history items, often found on standard application blanks.

Schuh (1967) reviewed the available literature and concluded that biographical items had predictive validity as related to turnover, although his conclusion was later criticized (e.g., D. P. Schwab & Oliver, 1974).

Cascio (1975) studied the application blanks of 160 female clerical employees of a large insurance company that was experiencing a 48% turnover rate within a year after hire – i.e., of every two employees hired only one would remain longer than a year. Of the total group, 80 were minorities, primarily Spanish speaking, and 80 were not. Within each group 40 had voluntarily terminated within a year (short tenure) and 40 had remained on the job 12 months or longer (long tenure). Sixteen items were chosen from the application blank, on the basis that previous research had shown they were valid predictors of tenure. These items were scored, and the resulting total scores analyzed for minority and nonminority group members separately, and cross-validated. Ten items survived the item analyses, including such items as age, marital status, education, tenure on previous job, and location of residence.

Differences in total scores between short-tenure and long-tenure employees were significant, within each racial group, but differences across groups were not significant. Point-biserial correlations between application-blank scores and the dichotomy of long vs. short tenure was .77 for the nonminority group and .79 for the minority group. These coefficients dropped slightly to .56 and .58 on the cross-validation samples, as expected. By using an expectancy chart of the combined data, Cascio (1975) could increase the predictive accuracy to 72%, as opposed to the base rate of 52%.

Occupational Choice

How are occupational choices made? There are a number of theories that attempt an explanatory framework. Some emphasize the economic aspect – people choose jobs that give them the best economic advantage. Others emphasize chance – most occupational choices are made on the basis of serendipity and happenstance. Still others emphasize the values and goals that a person learns from society and family. Many psychological theories attempt to explain vocational choice in terms of the differences in aptitudes, interests, and personality traits among people.

Ginzberg (1951) conceptualized vocational choice as a developmental process spanning the entire period of adolescence, and felt that specific events or experiences played a major role. Other theorists also have emphasized the role of specific life experiences, and the usefulness of biodata in predicting vocational choice. A typical study is that of Neiner and Owens (1985) who administered a 118-item biographical inventory to entering college freshmen. Some 3 to 5 years after graduation, these students were contacted and asked, as part of a questionnaire, their current job title and job description. These jobs were then coded into one of the six groupings proposed by Holland – i.e., artistic, investigative, conventional, realistic, social, and enterprising (see Chapter 6). A statistical analysis indicated that the biodata factor dimensions did correlate significantly with post-college job choice. For example, males who entered investigative type jobs tended to score higher on the biodata dimensions of academic achievement (e.g., higher standing on academic grades; more successful in academic situations), social introversion (e.g., fewer dates, fewer casual friends), and scientific interest (e.g., enjoyed science courses, the use of scientific apparatus).

TESTING IN THE MILITARY

As you might imagine, there is a substantial amount of testing that takes place in the military. We cover a few examples, just to illustrate some of the basic issues (for a brief history of testing in the military, see Haney, Madaus, & Lyons, 1993).

The Navy Basic Test Battery

In 1943, during World War II, a battery of tests known as the Basic Test Battery was developed by Navy psychologists for the purpose of classifying enlisted personnel into occupational specialties; originally there were nine tests, but three were dropped, and three were combined into one. The remaining four subtests included in the battery were: (1) The General Classification Test, originally developed as a test of verbal reasoning; (2) the Arithmetic Reasoning Test, containing verbally stated problems that require arithmetic solutions; (3) the Clerical Aptitude Test containing items that require alphabetizing, name checking, and letter checking (i.e., are these two names or words the same); (4) A Mechanical Test, composed of aptitude and knowledge sections, designed to measure the ability to apply mechanical principles to the solution of problems and to assess knowledge of mechanical and electrical tools.

This test battery has been used to select enlisted personnel for training as apprentices in a variety of naval occupations. The primary validational criteria for these tests have been final school-grade averages for the trainees at the end of their training period; these have varied from .03 to .72. Kuder-Richardson reliability ranged from .77 to .96 with a median of .87.

Merenda (1958) reported a study of two samples of candidates for advancement to petty officer. The first sample was used to derive multiple-regression equations, and the second sample to cross-validate such regression equations against the criterion of scores on a promotion examination. The obtained correlation coefficients between scores on the Basic Test Battery and scores on the promotion examination ranged from .28 to .67, with a median coefficient of .45. The obtained correlation coefficients between actual promotion examination scores and predicted examination scores ranged from a low of .10 to a high of .82, with a median of .48. For only one Navy occupation was the correlation not statistically significant, indicating that scores on the Basic Test Battery were useful in the assignment of Navy personnel.

The Army Selection and Classification Project (Project A)

Between 1983 and 1988, Project A was developed to create a selection and classification system for all 276 entry level positions in the United States Army. The primary instrument used in this project was the Armed Services Vocational Aptitude Battery (ASVAB), made up of 10 subtests; 4 of the subtests comprise a test of their own called the Armed Forces Qualification Test (AFQT). For each of the entry-level positions, critical scores on the appropriate subtests were developed, and if an individual scored above those critical scores, that person would be assigned to the position, depending on Army needs, individual preference, and other aspects. Basically, Project A was one of the largest validational studies ever conducted; 19 of the entry-level positions, such as "motor transport operator" and "combat engineer" were studied with samples of 500 to 600 individuals in each position (see J. P. Campbell, 1990, for overall details, McHenry, Hough, Joquam, et al., 1990, for specific validity results and Drasgow & Olson-Buchanan, 1999, for the history of a computerized version of the ASVAB).

The Dot Estimation Task (DOT)

In 1983, the United States Air Force Human Resources Laboratory began administering an experimental test battery to new flight-training candidates to select and classify pilots (Lambirth, Gibb, & Alcorn, 1986). One component of the battery was the Dot Estimation Task (DOT) in which the subject is simultaneously presented with two fields containing an arbitrary number of dots ranging from 1 to 50; one of the two fields contains one more dot than the other. The candidate is required to determine as rapidly as possible

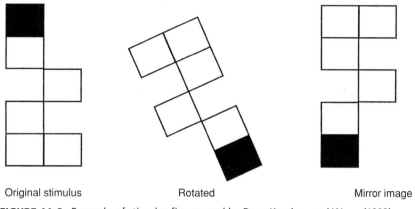

Original stimulus   Rotated   Mirror image

FIGURE 14–2. Example of stimulus figure used by Dror, Kosslyn, and Waag (1993).

which of the two fields contains the greater number of dots. This is a self-paced test lasting 6 minutes and containing a maximum of 50 trials. The DOT was intended to measure compulsivity vs. decisiveness, with the underlying assumption that compulsive individuals will either actually count the dots or vacillate in their estimates and thus have longer response time and attempt fewer trials in a given time period. Decisive individuals will presumably work quickly and make their estimates with some rapidity. Lambirth, Gibb, and Alcorn (1986) administered the DOT and a personality measure of obsessive-compulsive behavior to 153 students and retested them 4 weeks later. The reliability of the DOT was low: .64 for number of trials attempted, .46 for number of correct trials, and .64 for the number of incorrect trials. All validity coefficients – that is all correlations between DOT scores and scores on the obsessive-compulsive measure were essentially zero, thus indicating that the DOT cannot be used as a nonverbal indicator of obsessive-compulsive traits.

Visual-spatial abilities of pilots. In this textbook, we have emphasized paper-and-pencil tests. Tests however come in many forms, and sometimes the line between what is a test and what is an experimental procedure can be quite blurred. In Chapter 1, however, we suggested that one useful way to think of a test is as a laboratory procedure, and so we can consider laboratory procedures as tests, that is, needing to show reliability and validity.

Dror, Kosslyn, and Waag (1993) studied the visual-spatial abilities of pilots in a series of five experiments. In one of them, a shape similar to that in Figure 14.2 was presented on a computer screen to the individual pilot. Then a second shape was presented, and the pilot had to decide as fast as possible whether the second shape represented a rotation of the first or a mirror-reversed version. Sixty-four such trials were conducted. The authors did not consider reliability of the task directly, although they did eliminate any responses where the response time was greater than 2.5 times the mean of the other responses. They did ask the question whether the task was measuring what "they thought it was," and answered by looking at whether response time varied with degree of rotation (does it take longer to analyze a rotated figure that has been rotated a lot than one that has been rotated a little?). The data did indicate that in fact, the task was assessing mental rotation ability, and they found that pilots were faster overall than non-pilots, but equally accurate.

PREDICTION OF POLICE PERFORMANCE

A substantial number of studies have assessed law-enforcement candidates in an effort to identify those who are ill suited for such jobs. There are two major reasons why testing might be useful: the economic issue, to screen out recruits who subsequently might fail the training, the probationary period, or actual job performance, and the legal-social issue, to identify those candidates who might misuse their training and position.

The process of selecting the best qualified applicants has been, and in many instances still is, based on subjective evaluation and clinical impressions often made by administrators rather than mental-health specialists. A 1967 Presidential advisory committee on law enforcement was critical of such techniques and recommended the use of clinical psychologists and psychiatrists, as well as batteries of appropriate assessment devices (J. J. Murphy, 1972).

Some problems. Once again the criterion problem looms large. Police departments vary substantially, and the demands made on an urban police officer may be quite different from those made on a rural county sheriff. The base-rate problem also complicates the picture. Inappropriate use of force, for example, is actually a relatively rare behavior despite the publicity it receives.

Police departments have increasingly turned to the use of standardized tests with the MMPI as a very popular choice, even though Butcher (1979) in a review of the MMPI literature reported that the relationship of MMPI scores to job performance was modest at best. In addition, it should be kept in mind that the MMPI was not designed to select police officers. Some authors (e.g., Saxe & Reiser, 1976) have argued that most police applicants score in the normal range on the MMPI and hence the predictive value of the MMPI is limited. Other authors (e.g., Saccuzzo, Higgins, & Lewandowski, 1974), while agreeing that scores are often normal, also argue that the pattern and elevation of the MMPI profile are distinguishable against various criteria, and therefore the MMPI can still be used.

The Inwald Personality Inventory (IPI)

The Inwald Personality Inventory (Inwald, Knatz, & Shusman, 1983), a 310-item true-false inventory yielding 26 scales, was developed specifically for use by law-enforcement agencies in selecting new officers. The IPI attempts to assess the psychological and emotional fitness of recruits, with items that are relevant to police work. In addition to the 26 basic scales, the IPI yields a "risk" score, which is a weighted combination of several IPI scales. Studies of the IPI have yielded favorable results (e.g., Scogin, Schumacher, Gardner, et al., 1995). The manual reports that in one study, the IPI predicted accurately 72% of the male officers and 83% of the female officers who were eventu-

ally terminated, compared with 62% and 66% for the MMPI (for critical reviews see Bolton, 1995; Lanyon, 1995).

Racial differences. Baehr, Saunders, Froemel et al. (1971) reported on a study to design and validate a psychological test battery to select police patrolmen. The battery consisted of 14 tests that covered four broad domains: motivation, mental ability, aptitude, and behavior. For motivation, measures of background and experience were used. Mental ability used standard tests of reasoning, language facility, and perception. Aptitude covered "creative potential" and social insight. And behavior was assessed by various aspects of temperament and personality. The test battery was administered to 540 patrolmen who represented both the upper-rated third and the lower-rated third in a large urban police department. The sample reflected the racial composition of the department: 75% white and 25% black.

The authors attempted to answer four basic questions: (1) Are there any racial differences on the predictor (i.e., test) variables? Significant differences in group means were obtained in three of the four areas, with white subjects scoring higher on motivation, mental ability, and behavior – only on the aptitude area was there no difference. (2) Are there any racial differences on the criterion (i.e., job performance) variables? The criteria used here were semiannual performance ratings by supervisors, as well as variables such as number of arrests made and disciplinary actions taken against the patrolman. Only four criterion variables showed consistent results. White and black officers did not differ on tenure (i.e., amount of time on the police force) or absenteeism. Black patrolmen made significantly more arrests and had significantly more disciplinary actions taken against them, a result that might simply reflect the area of their patrol. (3) Do such differences lead to discrimination? Using complex statistical procedures, the authors found that the best predictive validity was obtained when the test data on a given racial group were used to predict criterion scores for members of that same group; the poorest predictive validity was obtained when predicting across racial groups. When the groups were treated separately statistically, better prediction resulted for the black group. The authors argued that these results are good evidence for computing separate prediction equations and that since the same level of performance is associated with a lower test score for the black group as compared to the white, a greater number of black applicants can be hired. (4) Which tests and variables are most related to effectiveness as a police officer, regardless of race? The authors were able to describe the more successful patrolman as having early family responsibilities (i.e., married and established a home), as having stability in both childhood and occupational environment, and better-than-average health. The successful patrolman has at least average mental functioning and good visual-perceptual skills. In interpersonal situations he tends to be cooperative rather than withdrawn or aggressive. He has good impulse control, is personally self-reliant, and has a work orientation rather than a social orientation. In a word – stable.

EXAMPLES OF SPECIFIC TESTS

The Job Components Inventory (JCI)

In England, Banks, Jackeon, Stafford, et al. (1983) developed the Job Components Inventory (JCI), designed to assist young people in their vocational preparation and training. The JCI contains five sections: (1) Tools and equipment; covers the use of 220 tools and pieces of equipment ranging from small hand tools such as chisels to large pieces of equipment such as forges. (2) Perceptual and physical requirements; 23 items that deal with such aspects as dexterity, physical strength, and reaction time. (3) Mathematical requirements; 127 items that cover mathematics up to algebra and trigonometry, with emphasis on practical applications such as work with drawings. (4) Communication requirements; 22 items that deal with the preparation of reports and letters, dealing with complaints, and other interpersonal communication aspects. (5) Decision making and responsibility; nine items that deal with decisions in the context of work.

It is not clear what response the examinee makes, but usually such inventories ask the candidate to indicate whether a particular task is performed, how frequently, and how important the task is, in the context of a specific occupation or task. The JCI takes about an hour or less to administer, is easily understood by individuals with limited educational skills, and provides wide coverage of job elements.

The JCI was administered to 100 individuals in eight different job groups falling under one of two occupational areas – engineering jobs, such as drilling machine operator, and clerical jobs, such as mailroom clerk. For six of the eight job groups, it was possible to have supervisors complete the JCI as well. The overall pattern of results indicated a high level of agreement between the ratings given by the job holders and their supervisors, with most correlation coefficients above .50. Correlations between composite ratings for the entire JCI were higher in general than the correlations for the individual sections of the JCI.

A comparison of the engineering vs. clerical occupational areas indicated significant differences on both the total score and three of the five JCI sections. Clerical jobs required a wider variety of tools and equipment and used more mathematical and communication components. In addition, significant differences were obtained across job groups within the same occupational area.

The Supervisory Practices Test (SPT)

Bruce and Learner (1958) developed the SPT to predict success in supervisory, managerial, and executive work. They first prepared a 100-item experimental form of the test with items drawn from the literature as well as from individuals in managerial and supervisory positions. The items are essentially miniature vignettes followed by several choices; for example, "If I were too busy to teach a new procedure to a subordinate, I would: (a) ask the subordinate to learn it on his own; (b) have another person teach it to the subordinate; or (c) make time in my next day's schedule."

The form was administered to 285 subjects who included 51 executives, 71 managers, and 163 persons in a variety of nonsupervisory jobs. Of these 100 items, 64 were retained on the basis of a dual criteria: (1) each of the distractors was endorsed by at least 15% of the sample; and (2) the item discriminated between supervisors and nonsupervisors. A cross-validation with a second sample resulted in a final form of 50 items.

Item weights were determined by a rather complicated procedure. A new sample of 200 supervisors and 416 nonsupervisors was tested. The sample was then divided into two ways. The first was supervisors vs. nonsupervisors. The second was in accord to the majority response for each item; that is, for each subject the number of responses agreeing with the majority was calculated. Then the entire sample was dichotomized into the 50% choosing the greatest number of majority responses, and the 50% choosing the least number of majority responses. The majority view was thus combined with the supervisors' view to develop positive weights for "good" responses, and negative weights for "poor" responses.

Reliability. For a sample of 112 nonsupervisors who were retested with an interval of seven months, the obtained r was .77. The authors argued that for this sample the range of test scores was restricted (although they varied from 11 to 126), and a more correct estimate of reliability was .86. Split-half reliability for a sample of 177 individuals was .82.

Validity. The final form was administered to various samples of supervisors vs. nonsupervisors across a wide range of industries, and in each case the mean scores between groups were significantly different. In one sample of foremen who were also ranked by two supervisors on the basis of overall competence, the correlation between SPT scores and supervisor ratings was .62. In a sample of 174 individuals, the SPT and a test of intelligence were administered. Correlations between the SPT and various portions of the test of intelligence ranged from a low of .18 to a high of .35 (median r of about .25), indicating a low and positive correlation between the SPT and intelligence. Finally, in another sample, the SPT was correlated with another supervisory practices measure. The overall correlation was .56 indicating significant overlap between the two measures.

The General Aptitude Test Battery (GATB)

In the years 1942 to 1945, the U.S. Employment Service decided to develop a "general" aptitude battery that could be used for screening applicants for many occupations, with an emphasis on occupational counseling. An analysis of both job requirements across many jobs and the 100 or so occupation-specific tests that were then available led to the identification of nine basic aptitudes that seemed to be relevant to many jobs. Thus what was unique about the GATB at its inception was that it was a comprehensive battery – clients did not need to be assessed with a variety of single purpose tests. Drawing on existing tests, a battery of 12 subtests was put together in 1947. Table 14.2 lists the nine dimensions and the 12 tests that make up the battery. Initially, there were two forms of the GATB, Form A reserved for use in employment offices and Form B used for retesting, validation research, and made available to other authorized users. In 1983 two other forms, C and D, were developed. A Spanish version has been available since 1978.

The GATB consists of 12 separately timed subtests that are combined to form nine aptitude scores. Eight of the tests are paper-and-pencil, and four are apparatus tests. Six subtests are intended to measure aptitudes that involve speed of work as a major component. The score on each subtest is the number correct, with no correction for guessing.

The individual subtests are listed below:

1. *Name comparison.* This subtest contains two columns of 150 names, and the examinee is required to indicate whether each pair of names are the same or different. The subtest has a time limit of 6 minutes.

2. *Computation.* Composed of 50 multiple-choice items that require arithmetic, such as addition or multiplication of whole numbers. Each item contains 5 choices, the last being "none of these." The time limit is 6 minutes.

3. *Three dimensional space.* Composed of 40 items, each with a stimulus figure and four options. The stimulus figure represents a flat piece of material that could be folded or bent into a three-dimensional figure – the four options present such figures, with only one correct. The time limit is 6 minutes.

4. *Vocabulary.* Contains 60 multiple-choice items, each item with four choices. Correct answer involves which two choices mean the same (or the opposite). The time limit is 6 minutes.

5. *Tool matching.* Composed of 49 items, each containing a stimulus drawing and four choice drawings, of simple shop tools, such as pliers and hammers. Different parts of the stimulus drawing

Factor symbol	Aptitude	Specific subtests
G	General intelligence	Three-dimensional space; vocabulary; arithmetic reasoning
V	Verbal aptitude	Vocabulary
N	Numerical aptitude	Computation; arithmetic reasoning
S	Spatial aptitude	Three-dimensional space
P	Form perception	Tool matching; form matching
Q	Clerical perception	Name comparison
K	Motor coordination	Mark making
F	Finger dexterity	Assemble and disassemble
M	Manual dexterity	Place; turn

Table 14–2. Composition of the General Aptitude Test Battery

are black or white, and the examiner matches the identical drawing from the available choices. The time limit is 5 minutes.

6. *Arithmetic reasoning.* Twenty-five verbal mathematical problems (e.g., If I buy eight oranges at 25 cents each . . .), with possible answers given in multiple-choice form with 5 choices, the fifth being "none of these." The time limit is 7 minutes.

7. *Form matching.* Composed of two groups of variously shaped line drawings. In one group, each drawing is identified by a number, and in the other by a letter. The drawings are jumbled up, and the examinee needs to match each figure in the second group with the identical figure in the first group. There are 60 such drawings, and the time limit is 6 minutes.

8. *Mark making.* Consists of 130 drawn squares; for each square the examinee must make a mark of three lines (II). The time limit is one minute.

9. and 10. *Place and turn.* Two subtests use a rectangular pegboard, divided into two sections, each with 48 holes. The upper section contains 48 cylindrical pegs. For the *place* subtest, the pegs are removed from the upper part and inserted in the corresponding holes of the lower section, two at a time. This is done three times (3 trials), with a time limit of 15 seconds per trial. The score is the sum of pegs moved over the 3 trials. For the *turn* subtest, the 48 pegs, each of which is painted half red and half white, are turned over and replaced in the same hole, using one's preferred hand. Three trials are also given, 30 seconds for each trial. The score is the total number of pegs turned over, for the three trials.

11. and 12. *Assemble and disassemble.* Two subtests use a small rectangular finger dexterity board that contains two sets of 50 holes and a supply of small metal rivets and washers. In the *assemble* subtest, the examinee assembles rivets and washers and places each unit in the designated hole as rapidly as possible. The subtest has a 90-second time limit. In the *disassemble* subtest, rivets and washers are disassembled and placed in designated areas; the time limit is 60 seconds. Both tests are measures of finger dexterity.

Scoring. Protocols can be hand scored locally or scored by computer services. For each subtest, the raw score, defined as number of items correct, is calculated. Raw scores are then converted to scores that are referenced on the norming population. The specific conversion depends upon the form of the GATB used, the type of answer sheet used, and the purpose for which the subtest score will be used. For example, the arithmetic reasoning subtest is used both in the calculation of intelligence and in the calculation of numerical aptitude; the same raw score will be converted differently for each of these purposes.

Raw scores are thus converted into aptitude scores, with a mean of 100 and SD of 20. These aptitude scores can be further converted to composite scores because the nine basic dimensions form three composites: a cognitive composite (G + V + N), a perceptual composite (S + P + Q), and a psychomotor composite (K + F + M). These three composites are then given different relative weights to predict each of five job families, that is, these are regression equations developed empirically. Finally, percentile scores for the sum of the composites can be calculated in accord with separate race norms for blacks, Hispanics, and others.

Reliability. Temporal stability of the cognitive aptitudes (G, V, and N) is quite acceptable, with correlation coefficients typically above .80, and seems to decline slightly as the test-retest interval increases. In general, the results compare quite well with those of similar measures in other test batteries.

For the perceptual aptitudes (S, P, and Q), test-retest coefficients are in the .70s and .80s, while for the psychomotor aptitudes (K, F, and M) the test-retest coefficients are in the high .60s and low .70s. In general, reliability is higher for samples of adults than for samples of ninth and tenth graders, probably reflecting the lack of maturation of the younger examinees.

Equivalent-form reliability in general parallels the test-retest reliability findings, with most coefficients in the .80s and .90s. Internal-consistency reliability is not appropriate to assess the reliability of speeded tests, and because the GATB is so heavily dependent on brief time limits, internal consistency is not an appropriate reliability estimate.

Validity. The GATB has been studied intensively, with more than 800 validity studies available in the literature. Much of the validity information on the GATB can be interpreted in light of construct validity – i.e., does each subtest measure the particular designated construct? The GATB manual (U.S. Department of Labor, 1970) presents considerable evidence comparing results on the GATB to a variety of other aptitude and vocational interest measures. Jaeger, Linn, and Tesh (1989) report that of the 51 convergent validity coefficients for the G composite, the correlation coefficients ranged from .45 to .89, with a median value of .75. Other representative results are a median value of .47 for form perception, and a median value of .50 for clerical perception. In general, the results strongly support the construct validity of the cognitive aptitudes; there is less support for the construct validity of the perceptual aptitudes, and no conclusion can be made on the psychomotor aptitudes because, surprisingly, there is little available data.

In terms of criterion validity, the overall conclusion is that the GATB has small but relatively consistent positive correlations with ratings of job performance and other relevant criteria.

Criticisms. One of the concerns is the sheer amount of score conversion that takes place, to the point where even experts are not able to reconstruct the nature and logic of the various statistical steps (Hartigan & Wigdor, 1989). For other criticisms of this battery, see Kirnan and Geisinger (1990).

How Supervise?

The How Supervise? test is a 70-item inventory designed to assess a respondent's knowledge of supervisory practices. The test was developed as a doctoral dissertation, became quite popular in the 1950 to 1975 period, but then began to languish, primarily because it was not revised. This is a clear example of a successful product whose marketing efforts did not support its usefulness.

As with most other tests, the How Supervise? began as a pool of 204 items generated to represent good supervisory practices. These items were then judged by groups of experts who identified ambiguous items, as well as "correct" responses. A scoring key was constructed to represent the modal correct response.

The pool of items was then administered to a sample of 577 supervisors, who had been rated as to effectiveness by their superiors. A contrasted groups analysis of the top and bottom 27% of the sample indicated that 23 items statistically discriminated the two subsamples. However, 140 items were retained, and two forms of the test, each with 70 items distributed over three sections, were developed. All responses are indicated by desirable, undesirable, or? for the first two sections, and agree, disagree, or? for the third section.

The first section is called Supervisory Practices and requires the respondent to indicate whether specific supervisory practices are or are not desirable. The second section, Company Policies, requires the respondent to indicate the desirability of various policies, such as concerning labor unions or promotion policies. The third section, called Supervisor Opinions, requires the respondent to indicate agreement or disagreement with various supervisory opinions, in particular whether workers are motivated by external punishments and rewards. Although the three subsections are scored separately, the scores are summed into a single total.

The 1971 manual provides norms for 12 samples of supervisors in a variety of industries, with median scores showing rather wide variability from industry to industry.

Note that the How Supervise? measures knowledge and not necessarily behavior. Knowing what is a good supervisory practice does not necessarily mean that the person will behave in a consonant manner. Furthermore, a number of investigators have argued that the How Supervise? is basically an intelligence test (Millard, 1952).

Reliability. Reliability seems adequate. Both alternate form and split-half reliabilities are typically in the .80s range.

Validity. Three types of validity studies are available (Dobbins, 1990). One type involves the comparison of scores obtained by individuals who occupy different levels of supervision, such as higher-level vs. lower-level supervisors. In general, the results are that higher-level supervisors score higher than lower-level supervisors, although confounding aspects such as age and intelligence are typically not accounted for. A second type of study looks at concurrent validity with on-the-job ratings. Typical correlation coefficients are low but significant, in the .20s and .30s range, although a number of studies also report no significant correlations. A third group of studies focuses on the convergent and discriminant validity of the How Supervise?, showing that scores on this instrument are indeed significantly correlated with measures of intelligence. A typical study is that by Weitz and Nuckols (1953), who used a modified version of the How Supervise? with district managers in a life insurance company. Scores were compared with various criteria that reflected volume of sales, as well as personnel turnover. None of the correlation coefficients were significant, except for a correlation of .41 between number of right answers on section 1 and educational level.

Work Orientation scale of the CPI (WO). One of the major themes in the study of managerial performance is that there are two motivational aspects related to high-quality managerial success. These aspects are given different names by different researchers, but one refers to a "need for advancement," for seeking more demanding levels of responsibility, and the other refers to the degree to which a person espouses high personal standards of performance.

Gough (1984; 1985) attempted to develop two scales on the CPI (see Chapter 4) that parallel these motives; he called them the Managerial Potential and the Work Orientation scales. Two samples of subjects were used, married couples and correctional officers. On the basis of several statistical criteria (see Gough, 1985, for details), a 40-item Work Orientation (WO) scale was developed. Alpha coefficients for two other samples were .75, and test-retest correlations over a 1-year period were .62 and .70. A comparison of English and French versions of the CPI given to the same sample of bilingual high-school students yielded an interform correlation of .76 for males and .78 for females.

An analysis of WO scale scores with a variety of other instruments indicated that high-scoring persons on the WO are well organized, optimistic, dependable individuals, who do not necessarily have exceptional intellectual abilities. The major goal of the WO scale is to identify those individuals who possess self-discipline, dependability, perseverance, efficiency – essentially those qualities that are incorporated under the rubric of the "Protestant ethic." Indeed, in a study of fraternity and sorority members, higher-scoring individuals on the WO scale were characterized as responsible, reliable, reasonable, moderate, dependable, clear thinking, optimistic, stable, efficient, and mature.

The Wonderlic Personnel Test (WPT)

The WPT was first published in 1938 and was designed to test adult job applicants in business and industrial settings. New forms have been developed and extensive norms have been collected since then, but the nature of the test has not changed. The WPT is a 50-item, 12-minute test of general mental ability, named "personnel" so as to reduce the candidate's recognition that this is a test of intelligence and the fear that may be associated with taking a mental ability test. The WPT was standardized on samples of adults ranging in age from 20 to 65, with a total sample of more than 50,000 individuals. A recent manual indicated that there are 16 alternate forms available, including a large-print version for the visually handicapped; it provided extensive normative data by age, race, gender, industry, type of job, and educational level. The items are of various types such as yes-no, multiple choice, and requiring a numeric answer, and cover a broad range of cognitive abilities that include analogies, definitions, geometric figures, and so on. The items are intermingled and presented in order of difficulty, with an average difficulty level of about 60%.

Administration. The test manual includes directions for administration with both a 12-minute time limit and with unlimited time, although the usual procedure and the norms are based on the timed administration.

Scoring. Handscoring of the test is very simple with the use of a scoring key – the score is simply the number of items answered correctly. Although the manual recommends that raw scores be used, these can be converted to the more familiar IQs.

Reliability. Test-retest reliability coefficients are in the .82 to .94 range, and interform reliabilities go from a low of .73 to a high of .95. Even internal consistency coefficients are high, primarily in the mid .80s to mid .90s range.

Validity. The literature does indicate that reliable measures of general mental ability are valid as predictors of job performance in a wide variety of occupational areas, and the WPT has been validated in a large number of studies (Schmidt, 1985). Correlations with educational level and academic achievement are quite substantial, with coefficients ranging from .30 to .80. An example is the study by Dodrill and Warner (1988) who administered the WAIS and the WPT to four groups of subjects: hospitalized psychiatric patients, hospitalized nonpsychiatric seizure-disorders patients, psychiatric epileptic patients, and normal control subjects. Correlations between test scores on the two tests ranged

from .85 to .91, and between 81% and 94% of the subjects in each group had IQs from the two tests within 10 points of each other. These results do support the value of the WPT as a measure of general intelligence; in many ways, it is a useful screening instrument.

Norms. The test manual recommends that separate norms by race and ethnic group be used. Thus, what is recommended is that candidates' test scores be converted to percentiles separately for each ethnic group based on that group's norms. Selection or hiring of candidates is then made within each group.

Although cutoff scores need to be established by a particular industry, based in part upon the number of available candidates, the test manual does suggest minimum scores for various occupations as general guidelines. These range from a 30 for statistician and engineer, to 25 for foreman and private secretary, to 8 for unskilled laborer and janitor.

Because older individuals tend to do less well on the WPT than younger persons, the manual recommends adding a certain number of points to the raw score, to reflect that person's age. For example, a person aged 40 to 44 would receive 4 extra points, whereas a person aged 60 to 69 would receive 11 points.

Legal issues. We discussed some legal issues in Chapter 5, but mention might be made here of the case of Griggs v. Duke Power (1971). In 1971 the U.S. Supreme Court ruled that the tests used by Duke Power, a utility company, were inappropriate, in that these tests failed to measure the applicant for the job and adversely impacted protected groups; one of the tests was the Wonderlic. However, another company, PPG Industries, also used the WPT and in a 1983 court case, was able to establish the validity of the selection battery that included the WPT (Schoenfeldt, 1985).

INTEGRITY TESTS

These tests, also known as honesty tests, are paper-and-pencil inventories used for personnel selection to identify potentially dishonest or "counterproductive" employees. Usually these tests contain items that assess the applicant's attitude toward theft and inquire about any past thefts. Such tests are typically proprietary tests purchased from a publisher who provides such services as scoring and guidelines for score interpretation. The development of most such tests has taken place largely outside mainstream psychological testing, so that these tests are not available for professional perusal, nor are their psychometric properties evaluated in the forum of the scientific literature. Relatively little psychometric information is available about integrity tests, and many of them seem to have been developed by individuals who have a minimum of psychometric training. What is available often is contained in in-house reports rather than public scientific journals.

American businesses lose anywhere from $15 to $25 billion per year because of employee theft, and 30% of all business failures are attributed to employee theft (Camara & Schneider, 1994). Despite such impressive figures, the base rate for a behavior like employee theft is very low in most settings – usually less than 5% (Hollinger & Clark, 1983). As discussed Chapter 3, when base rates are low, accurate detection by tests is minimal (Dawes, 1962). Integrity tests then fulfill a major need and represent a major industry; in 1984 Sackett and Harris estimated that more than 5,000 firms were using such tests. These tests are used particularly in settings where employees may have access to cash or merchandise, such as banks and retail stores. They are used for both entry-level personnel, such as clerks and cashiers, and for higher-level positions, such as supervisory and managerial ones (for overviews of this field see D. Arthur, 1994, and J. W. Jones, 1991).

Camara and Schneider (1994) were able to identify 46 publishers or developers of integrity tests and requested their cooperation in completing a survey; 65% ($n = 30$) responded. Camara and Schneider (1994) reported that the majority of these tests are computer scored by the test publisher or are scored on-site using software provided by the publisher, and typically both a total score and subtest scores can be obtained. Scores are often reported in standard or percentile form, indicating the risk level for theft by the individual applicant. Cutoff scores are provided by 60% of the tests studied. Computer-generated narrative reports are available for most tests, although most of these reports cover only basic results. Actual

scoring keys are typically closely guarded by the publisher.

Types of integrity tests. Two distinct types of tests fall under the rubric of integrity tests. The first are overt integrity tests that inquire directly about attitudes toward theft and about prior dishonest acts. The second are broader-oriented measures that are less transparent and perceive theft as one aspect of a broader syndrome of deviant behavior in the workplace (Sackett, Burris, & Callahan, 1989). These tests may include scales designed to measure drug use, job satisfaction, the prediction of burnout, and related variables.

Overt integrity tests usually have two sections – one that deals with attitudes toward theft and other forms of dishonesty and one dealing with admissions of theft and other illegal activities such as drug use. Perhaps the three most common of these tests are the *London House Personnel Selection Inventory, the Reid Report,* and the *Stanton Survey.*

The broader personality-oriented measures are designed not as measures of honesty per se, but as predictors of a wide variety of counterproductive work behaviors. Some of these measures assess such personality aspects as nonconformance, irresponsibility, lack of conscientiousness, degree of socialization, and so on.

Cutoff scores. Although most test manuals indicate that scores on the integrity test should not be used as the only criterion for not hiring an individual, most also provide cutoff scores that separate the score distribution into two areas, such as pass and fail, or three areas, such as high, medium, and low risk.

Reliability. Reliability of most of these tests seems to be consistently high, with reported test-retest coefficients typically above .70, and internal consistency coefficients often in the .90s range.

Validity. Sackett and Harris (1984) reviewed the validity data for 10 integrity tests, with a focus on criterion validity. Five categories of studies were available: (1) comparisons with polygraph (lie-detecting machine) results; (2) measures of future behavior, such as being discharged for theft; (3) admission of past theft, where tests are administered under conditions of anonymity; (4) shrinkage reduction – i.e., a store is monitored for amount of loss, then the integrity testing program is introduced, and subsequent rates of loss are compared to previous losses; (5) contrasted groups – for example, convicts vs. a control group are tested.

What are the results? (1) *Polygraph studies.* When both attitude and admission portions are used, correlation coefficients between test scores and polygraph results range from .72 to .86, with an average of .78. When only the attitude section is used, the range of coefficients goes from .27 to .76, with an average of .49. Thus integrity-test scores correlate significantly with polygraph results and even more so when admissions are incorporated into the procedure. (2) *Future behavior.* In general, the correlations between test scores and future behavior are rather low, often in the .20s, but there are a number of methodological problems including the fact that the base rate (the number of employees dismissed for stealing) is rather low. (3) *Admissions.* Integrity test scores consistently correlate with admissions of past theft, whether such data is collected as part of a preemployment procedure, or anonymously by current employees. (4) *Shrinkage reduction.* The small amount of evidence available indicates that the introduction of integrity tests into a company's procedures lowers the amount of employee shoplifting. Whether in fact such changes are due to unknown other variables, to concurrent changes in company policy, or to perceived change in a company's tolerance of dishonest behavior, is not clear. In fact, one of the common confounding aspects is that the introduction of integrity testing in a company may be perceived by the employees as a change in the company's tolerance of theft. (5) *Contrasted groups.* Studies of convicts vs. the general public indicate substantial mean-score differences on typical integrity tests. Often the assumption is that convicts "fake good" on these tests to increase their chances of parole, and therefore the tests are somewhat resistant to faking in that they still show significant group differences.

It should be pointed out that the above results were based on only 14 studies, many of which were severely flawed from an experimental point of view. Subsequently, Sacket, Burris, and Callahan (1989), were able to locate 24 studies. One of the findings is that little theft is detected. Thus, although the score differences between those individuals who are detected for theft and those who are not are substantial, the correlation coefficient is very small due to the lack of variance on the criterion, i.e., few employees are detected for theft.

An APA Task Force (Goldberg, Grenier, Guion, et al., 1991) reviewed some 300 studies and concluded that for those few tests for which validity information was available, their predictive validity was supported. In part, this may have been due to the fact that validity criteria for integrity tests were expanded to cover such aspects as absenteeism, personnel turnover, behavioral indicators such as grievances, and supervisory ratings. However, validity information was available for only a few of the tests, and much of what was available was judged to be fragmented and incomplete. It was suggested that integrity tests predict more validly at the untrustworthy end of the scale than at the trustworthy end.

Ones, Viswesvaran, and Schmidt (1993) also conducted a meta-analysis of the validity of integrity tests. They concluded that the best estimate of the mean true validity was .41, when the criterion is supervisory ratings of overall job performance. They also concluded that the validity for predicting counterproductive behavior on the job (such as theft and absenteeism) is also fairly substantial, but that validity is affected by several moderator variables such as whether the sample is composed of applicants or current employees.

Most integrity tests do not correlate significantly with measures of intelligence, with available coefficients typically in the −.10 to +.10 range. When scores on the attitude and the admissions subsections are correlated with each other, significant coefficients are obtained, often in the .50 to .70 range.

Construct validity. This is a much more complex type of validity to establish, in part because the construct is ill defined, and different integrity tests reflect different definitional points of view. In general, however, the available evidence seems congruent with construct validity. People known to be dishonest, such as convicted thieves, do less well on these tests than the general population does. Males do worse than females, and younger people do worse than older people (Goldberg, Grenier, Guion, et al., 1991).

The employer's viewpoint. The APA Task Force indicated that there were three concerns of interest to employers. The first is the extent to which the use of integrity tests leads to a generally improved workforce, e.g., having greater job satisfaction. Some studies do indeed present such evidence. A second concern might be the usefulness of integrity tests in predicting the occurrence of such events as theft. The conclusion here is that few predictive studies are free from methodological difficulties and that most integrity tests have not been used in predictive studies. For a few tests, however, the available evidence would support their predictive validity. A third concern is the extent to which losses due to employee theft are actually decreased. Although the picture is far from complete, the available evidence suggests that for some integrity tests there is documentation available to support their utility in this respect.

Faking. A major concern with integrity tests is their resistance to faking. Three lines of inquiry are relevant here (Sackett, Burris, & Callahan, 1989): (1) the effects of direct instructions to fake good; (2) the correlation of test scores with various indices of social desirability and "lie" scales (see Chapter 16); and (3) studies that statistically separate the effects of lying from the obtained validity coefficients. Few studies exist in each category, and at least for category (1) the results are contradictory – although in both studies the instructions to fake did result in significantly different mean scores. For the second category, most available studies do show significant correlations between integrity test scores and various measures designed to assess faking. Under category (3) the very limited evidence suggests that integrity tests do measure something beyond the mere ability to fake.

Factor analysis. Studies of factor analyses of integrity tests suggest that the instruments are not unidimensional, but little is known about the utility and validity of the individual factor scores.

On the Reid Report, for example, the evidence suggests that high scorers are emotionally stable, relatively optimistic about human nature, flexible in their beliefs and attitudes, and motivated to excel because of the intrinsic satisfaction that work provides (Cunningham, Wong, & Barbee, 1994).

Adverse impact. A few studies have looked at adverse impact. The available evidence indicates that there are no significant gender and/or race differences on such tests; when differences are obtained, they typically favor females and blacks.

Alternatives. Alternatives to integrity tests have innumerable drawbacks (Goldberg, Grenier, Guion, et al., 1991). Unstructured interviews are time consuming and have lower reliability and validity. Structured interviews do use many of the items identical to those found in integrity tests, but have limited validity and utility as a stand-alone screening instrument. Background checks are expensive and elicit legal concerns. Surveillance can be quite expensive and may be counterproductive to morale and productivity. The use of polygraphs in employment screening is prohibited by the Employee Polygraph Protection Act of 1988. However, there are exceptions such as for governmental employees, agencies that are involved in national security and defense, and other agencies. Incidentally, the passage of this act resulted in an increased use of integrity tests. Even if polygraph examinations were not illegal, they are of questionable validity.

Legal aspects. Many psychological tests have been curtailed in their use by court actions and legal issues (see Chapter 16). Integrity tests may be the only category of tests whose use is actually enhanced by legal concerns. As the APA Task Force pointed out (Goldberg, Grenier, Guion, et al., 1991), under the "negligent hiring" legal doctrine, an employer may be held liable if an "unfit" employee is hired who later causes harm to coworkers or others, if the employer could have either reasonably foreseen the risk of hiring such a person or had failed to conduct a reasonable inquiry into the employee's fitness. Integrity tests may serve as protection against such charges.

A typical study. Collins and Schmidt (1993) looked at white-collar crime – i.e., nonviolent crimes for financial gain that utilize deception and are usually carried out by an individual rather than an organization. They wondered whether integrity and personality measures could discriminate between white-collar criminals and their nonoffender colleagues.

They studied 329 federal prison inmates who had been convicted of white-collar crimes, who volunteered for the study, and 320 individuals employed in white-collar positions of authority. All subjects were administered the CPI, a biodata questionnaire, and an integrity scale; all three instruments yielded a total of 37 scores for each subject.

For the statistical analyses, the total sample was randomly divided into a validation sample and a cross-validation sample. The statistical analyses were conducted in three steps. First, the number of variables was reduced to 16 in the validation sample. Second, a discriminant function was developed in the validation sample. Third, the discriminant function was cross-validated. Among the top four variables that discriminated between criminals and noncriminals was the Performance subscale of the integrity test (the Performance scale is said to measure conscientious work attitudes and behavior). The other three variables were scales from the CPI: Socialization, Responsibility, and Tolerance. As dicussed in Chapter 4, the Socialization scale measures the degree to which individuals adhere to social norms; the Responsibility scale measures the degree to which an individual is conscientious, responsible, and attentive to duty; the Tolerance scale assesses the degree to which a person is tolerant and trusting. The authors suggested that the common theme underlying these four scales is that of "social conscientiousness."

SUMMARY

In this chapter, we have looked at a variety of issues, findings, and specific tests as they apply to testing in the world of work. The overall picture is one of positive findings, with substantial cautions. There are many tests and applications that are potentially useful, yet the test practitioner must be careful and mindful, not only of the basic issues of reliability and validity, but also legal and public relations issues.

SUGGESTED READINGS

Binning, J. F., & Barrett, G. V. (1989). Validity of personnel decisions: A conceptual analysis of the inferential and evidential bases. *Journal of Applied Psychology, 74*, 478–494.

An excellent theoretical discussion of the concept of validity as it pertains to personnel selection and decisions.

Cascio, W. F. (1995). Whither industrial and organizational psychology in a changing world of work? *American Psychologist, 50*, 928–939.

Although not directly related to psychological testing, this is an excellent overview of the current and future state of the world of work. The author discusses key changes in such a world and some of the research questions that must be answered. A careful reading of this article will indicate many areas where the judicious appli-cation of psychological testing could be most useful.

Cunningham, M. R., Wong, D. T., & Barber, A. P. (1994). Self-presentation dynamics on overt integrity tests: Experimental studies of the Reid Report. *Journal of Applied Psychology, 79*, 643–658.

The Reid Report is one of the most popular integrity tests. The authors conducted a series of three experiments to study the effects of instructions and monetary reward on faking of the Reid Report.

Day, D. V., & Silverman, S. B. (1989). Personality and job performance: Evidence of incremental validity. *Personnel Psychology, 42*, 25–36.

An investigation of the relationship between specific personality variables, as measured by the Jackson Personality Research Form, and job performance as rated by seven managers, for a sample of accountants. Three personality scales were significantly related to important aspects of job performance.

Haire, M. (1950). Projective techniques in marketing research. *Journal of Marketing, 14*, 649–656.

This is somewhat of a classic study in which two samples of subjects were asked to characterize a woman, based only on her grocery shopping list. The shopping list presented to the two samples was identical except for one item – in one sample the item referred to instant coffee, in the other to regular coffee. The results are intriguing.

DISCUSSION QUESTIONS

1. Have you ever been given a test as part of a job? What was the experience like?

2. Consider the following two occupations: nurse in an operating room vs. teacher of fifth-grade children. How might job success be defined in each of these?

3. How might you answer someone who states that, "psychological tests are useless in the world of work"?

4. Do you think that applicants for police work should be psychologically tested?

5. If you had to indicate the three major themes of this chapter, what might they be?

15 Clinical and Forensic Settings

AIM This chapter looks at testing in two broad settings: testing in clinics or mental health centers, and testing in forensic settings, settings that are "legal" in nature such as jails, courtrooms, etc. Obviously, the two categories are not mutually exclusive. A clinical psychologist may for example, evaluate a client, with the evaluation mandated by the courts. Under clinical settings, we look at neuropsychological testing, projective techniques, some illustrative clinical issues and clinical syndromes, as well as applications in the area of health psychology. Under forensic settings, we look at some illustrative applications of testing, as well as how legislation has affected testing.

CLINICAL PSYCHOLOGY: NEUROPSYCHOLOGICAL TESTING

This field formally began toward the end of the Second World War in the early 1940s when clinical psychologists were asked to test brain-injured soldiers to determine whether their behavior and difficulties reflected an "organic brain syndrome." At first, available tests such as the Rorschach and the Wechsler were used for this purpose because they were already used for the routine assessment of psychiatric patients. Subsequently, Halstead and his student Reitan, developed a battery of tests designed specifically to assess the presence or absence of brain dysfunction. The Halstead-Reitan Neuropsychological Test Battery had a profound impact and expanded the focus from whether there was a brain lesion present to the determination of the nature, location, and behavioral consequences of such lesions (Prigatano & Redner, 1993). At present, there is only one other major neuropsychological test battery, called the Luria-Nebraska (Golden, Purisch, & Hammeke, 1985; see Franzen, 1987, for a review).

The Halstead-Reitan Neuropsychological Battery

In 1935, at the University of Chicago, Halstead established one of the first neuropsychology laboratories to study the impact of impairment in brain functions on behavior. He developed a number of tests to be used in this endeavor. One of his students, Reitan, subsequently modified and expanded the battery in his own laboratory. The result is three separate batteries, one for young children (aged 5 to 8), one for older children (aged 9 to 14), and one for adults. Each battery includes a minimum of 14 subtests, as well as the age-appropriate Wechsler test of intelligence, a broad-range academic achievement measure, and for adults, the MMPI.

The test batteries have undergone extensive research and revisions throughout the years. The adult battery contains five of the original Halstead tests. Two examples are:

1. The Category Test consists of 208 photographic slides of geometric figures that are projected one at a time on a screen. The slides are divided into subsets, and the items in a subset

follow a particular "rule" or category (e.g., all figures have a missing portion in the upper left quadrant). The patient tries to figure out the rule by pressing one of four levers associated with one of four choices. If the response is correct, a bell sounds; if the response is incorrect, a buzzer sounds. Patients are told when a new subset of slides is to begin.

Basically, this is a learning task that requires a high level of new problem-solving skills. Individuals impaired on this task because of brain lesions or other aspects, often show deficits in abstract learning, judgment, and concept formation, and lack the ability to concentrate over a period of time.

Scoring is simply the number of errors, with a score of 50 to 51 discriminating well between neurologically impaired and neurologically intact individuals.

2. The Tactual Performance Test uses a wooden board with spaces for 10 geometrically shaped blocks, such as a square, a triangle, and a cross. The patient is blindfolded and does not see the board or the blocks. He or she is guided to use the dominant hand to locate the board and the blocks and is told to place the blocks in their proper spaces as rapidly as possible. A second trial is done with the nondominant hand and a third trial with both hands. The board and blocks are then removed, the patient's blindfold is removed, and the patient is asked to draw a picture of the board on a sheet of paper.

Both the administration and scoring of this subtest are complicated. For example, the patient must be correctly blindfolded so that "peeking" cannot take place. Scoring is the time taken for completion of each trial, but there is a time limit of 15 minutes; however, extra time may be given if the patient was near completion. Scoring of the memory drawing requires a fair amount of subjectivity. The subtest is a measure of problem solving, specifically right-left differences in tactile, kinesthetic, and motor abilities in the absence of visual cues. It also measures incidental memory, the ability to remember things even when not explicitly told to do so.

Other subtests in the battery include a finger tapping test (tapping a telegraph type key) and a trail making test, which resembles a connect-the-dots procedure. The results are recorded on protocol sheets, with a summary sheet available so that all test results can be studied with a minimum of paper shuffling. The entire battery takes some 5 hours to administer, more or less depending on the patient's age, degree of brain damage, and other aspects.

The aim of the Halstead-Reitan is not simply to diagnose whether there is brain injury, but to determine the severity of such injury, the specific localization of the injury, the degree to which right or left hemisphere functioning is affected, and to provide some estimate of the effectiveness of rehabilitation.

The battery requires some rather expensive and bulky materials, so unlike the MMPI and WAIS, it is not a portable test. Such testing is usually carried out in a clinic. Numerous modifications of the battery are available; for example, in the Category Test individual stimulus cards rather than slides can be used.

Most of the subtests used in the Halstead-Reitan are actually "borrowed" from other procedures and tests. On the one hand, this means that available psychometric information as to reliability and validity should generalize to this "new" use. On the other hand, the entire field of neuropsychological assessment has paid little attention to such psychometric issues (Davison, 1974).

Perhaps more than any other test we have considered, the utility of the Halstead-Reitan is closely related to the competence of the test administrator. This is not an easy test to administer, score, and interpret. Although most clinical psychologists now receive some training in neuropsychological assessment, administration, and interpretation of the Halstead-Reitan requires considerable knowledge of neuropsychology and supervised training.

Validity. The validation of the Halstead-Reitan has primarily focused on concurrent validity, and specifically on the ability of the battery to correctly identify brain-damaged patients from non-brain-damaged controls. As Whitworth (1987) states, the reliability and validity of the Halstead-Reitan are higher than for almost any other type of psychometric procedure (see Heveren, 1980, and Sherer, Parsons, Nixon, et al., 1991, for examples of validity studies). Whether such a broad and uncritical endorsement is warranted remains to be seen, but certainly, the reliability and validity of this battery in differentiating between impaired and intact brain function is well established (Franzen, 1989; Heveren, 1980).

Criticisms. There are many criticisms of the Halstead-Reitan in the literature, some substantive and some less so. The apparatus is not mass produced and is seen by many as clumsy and very expensive. Test administration is long and can be stressful; the length of the text means, in part, that it is a costly procedure to administer or may not be appropriate for a patient whose medical condition places severe limits on their capacity to complete extensive testing. The scoring is characterized as simplistic and primarily aimed at assessing whether there is organicity or not, rather than using a more normative approach. Individual practitioners often modify the battery or use only part of it, so that standardization is not followed. Finally, the problem of false negatives can be a significant one (Whitworth, 1987).

Some criticisms may not be fully deserved. For example, there are normative scores based on age, education, and gender that allow the test results to be changed to *T* scores for comparative purposes (R. R. Heaton, Grant, & Matthews, 1991). Other criticisms may not really be criticisms. For example, the Halstead-Reitan does not reflect a particular theory of brain functioning; the subtests were chosen empirically because they seemed to work. Some see this as a weakness, others as a strength. A theoretical framework is now available (e.g., Reitan & Wolfson, 1985).

Neuropsychological tests in general have a number of limitations. Prigatano and Redner (1993) identify four major ones: (1) not all changes associated with brain injury are reflected in changed test performance; (2) test findings do not automatically indicate the reason for the specific performance; (3) neuropsychological test batteries are long to administer and therefore expensive; and (4) a patient's performance is influenced not just by brain dysfunction but also by a variety of other variables such as age and education.

PROJECTIVE TECHNIQUES

For many years, the primary testing tool of clinical psychologists were projective techniques such as the Rorschach Inkblot Technique. These techniques have in common the presentation of ambiguous and malleable stimuli to which a large number of different responses can be made. Presumably, the specific responses given by a client reflect something about that individual's psychodynamic functioning. Projective techniques no longer occupy the dominant position they did years ago, but nevertheless continue to be used in clinical practice and research.

Most projective techniques fall into one of five categories (Lindzey, 1959):

1. *Associative* techniques; the subject responds to a particular stimulus, such as an inkblot or a word, by indicating what the stimulus suggests. The Rorschach Inkblot Technique is a prime example.

2. *Construction* techniques; the subject constructs a response, usually in the form of a story, to a stimulus, usually a picture. The prime example here is the Thematic Apperception Test (TAT).

3. *Ordering* techniques; involve placing a set of stimuli in a particular order. Typically the stimuli are a set of pictures, very much like the panels of a newspaper comic strip but the panels are presented in random order, and they need to be placed in order to make a coherent sequence. The Picture Arrangement subtest of the WAIS is sometimes used as an ordering technique.

4. *Completion* techniques; the subject responds to a "partial" stimulus. For example, the subject may be given the beginning of a story to complete, or a set of sentence stems (e.g., I am always . . .) to complete. Sentence completion tests are a prime example here.

5. *Expressive* techniques; the subject engages in some "creative" activity, such as drawing, finger painting, acting out certain feelings or situations (as in psychodrama). The Draw-A-Person test is a good example.

Controversy. Perhaps more than any other area of testing, projective techniques are a source of controversy and argument. Some psychologists swear by these techniques and some swear at them! Some see them as valuable ways to assess the psychodynamic complexities of the human psyche, and others see them as closely related to superstitious behavior, tea readings, handwriting analysis, astrology, and other systems that lack scientific proof.

Clinical usefulness. There is little doubt that in the hands of a skilled and sensitive clinician, projective techniques can yield useful information and individual practitioners can utilize these measures to elicit superb psychodynamic portraits of a patient, and to make accurate predictions about future behavior. Given this, why is there need for scientific validation? MacFarlane and Tuddenham (1951) provided five basic answers to this question:

1. A social responsibility. Projective tests are misused, and we need to know which types of statements can be supported by the scientific literature and which cannot.

2. A professional responsibility. Errors of interpretation can be reduced and interpretive skills sharpened by having objective validity data.

3. A teaching responsibility. If we cannot communicate the basis for making specific inferences, such as "this type of response to card 6 on the Rorschach typically means that . . .," then we cannot train future clinicians in these techniques.

4. Advancement of knowledge. Validity data can advance our understanding of personality functioning, psychopathology, etc.

5. A challenge to research skills. As scientists, we ought to be able to make explicit what clinicians use intuitively and implicitly.

Basic assumptions. In general, psychologists believe that behavior is determined or can be explained by specific principles. If we observe a person verbally or physically attacking others, we label the behaviors as aggressive and we seek explanations for the behavior, perhaps postulating "frustration" or looking for childhood developmental explanations or antecedent conditions. With projective tests, the assumption is that specific responses reflect the person's personality and/or psychodynamic functioning. This is based, however, on the questionable assumption that the test protocol presents a sufficiently extensive sampling of the client.

Second, we know that specific behaviors can be strongly influenced by transitory aspects. A person can do well academically in all courses except one, with performance in that course influenced by a dislike for the instructor or some other "chance" factor. Projective tests however, assume

that each and every response is indeed basic and reflective of some major personal themes.

The projective viewpoint further assumes that perception is an active and selective process, and thus what is perceived is influenced not only by the person's current needs and motivation, but by that person's unique history and the person's habitual ways of dealing with the world. The more ambiguous a situation the more the responses will reflect individual differences in attempting to structure and respond to that situation. Thus, projective tests are seen as ideal miniature situations, where presentation can be controlled and resulting responses carefully observed.

Reliability. Standard reliability procedures, discussed in Chapter 3, are applicable to quantitative scores, such as those obtained on a typical test. With projective techniques, the end result is a protocol, perhaps containing stories or inkblot responses. To assess the reliability of such qualitative data, two general methods are used:

1. Determine the accuracy to which protocols can be matched (the degree of agreement to which a judge can match protocols with diagnosis) e.g., of these 50 protocols, which belong to individuals diagnosed with schizophrenia and which belong to controls? Or given test-retest protocols, can we accurately match protocols to the same person? Or can protocols be correctly matched with the interpretations given? Most of these questions can be empirically answered, but they confound the reliability of the test with the reliability of the judgment process used. Thus we may establish that a particular judge is able (or not) to match protocols with diagnosis, but we don't know that the same results apply to other clinicians, nor do we know what specific aspects of the protocol lead to particular judgments.

2. We can therefore select specific aspects of protocols, and use rating scales to assess the reliability of such aspects. In Rorschach protocols, for example, we might assess the number of cloud responses, or the number of depressive responses, or the overall "affective tone"; that is, we can go from a very concrete specific counting procedure to a more abstract and inferential level. This approach also presents many problems. What categories are we to select? Instead of cloud responses should we score animal responses, kitchen utensils, or – ? Quite possibly, the

categories that might be reliably counted might not be particularly meaningful. If we select the more abstract levels, we again confound the reliability of the test with the reliability of the rater.

In general then, the establishment of reliability is problematic. Test-retest seems incongruent with the notion that whatever projective techniques measure (personality?), changes over time. Alternate-forms reliability is often not applicable because even when there are two forms of a test, the individual stimuli can be quite different. Internal consistency is typically not applicable because it can only be applied to homogeneous items that are directly scorable.

Validity. Validity is even more problematic because most projective tests are designed to assess rather broad domains such as "personality," rather than more specific questions, such as "Is the number of human movement responses on the Rorschach indicative of creative output?" Thus, although specific questions can and have been studied, often with nonsupportive results, the clinician argues that projective techniques are global or holistic in nature and that such piecemeal validation violates the spirit of such measures.

The Rorschach Inkblot Technique

The Rorschach was developed in 1921 by Hermann Rorschach, a Swiss psychiatrist. Originally, the test consisted of some 15 inkblots that had been created by dropping blobs of ink on pieces of paper and folding these to form somewhat symmetrical figures. Printing was in its infancy then, and only 10 inkblots could be printed because of budgetary constraints (in fact, the publisher went broke after publishing the inkblots with an accompanying monograph). The theoretical background of the Rorschach was Jungian and psychoanalytic, but much of the evidence was empirical. Rorschach had administered inkblots to different patients and people he knew and had retained those whose responses and patterns of responses seemed to be related to personality and psychodynamic functioning. In the United States, the Rorschach became extremely popular due to primarily five psychologists: Samuel Beck, Marguerite Hertz, Bruno Klopfer, Zygmunt Piotrowski, and David Rapaport, each of whom

developed a slightly different scoring system. Exner (1974) combined these approaches and developed a "comprehensive system" which is now used quite widely. He united a number of theoretical trends and aspects of the various scoring systems, provided extensive norms, and basically a common language. Exner attempted to develop the Rorschach into more of an objective and less a projective test (Exner, 1999).

Description. The Rorschach consists of 10 symmetrical inkblots each printed on a separate $6\frac{1}{2} \times 9\frac{1}{2}$ inch plate. Five of the inkblots are black and gray, and five have other colors, all on white backgrounds. Often the instructions are not standardized but simply require the subject to tell what the blots remind him or her of, or what they might represent, or what they could be (B. Klopfer, Ainsworth, W. G. Klopfer, et al., 1954). The inkblots are presented one at a time, in the same order. This presentation is called the "free association" or response phase. Questions that the subject may have are typically responded to in a noncommittal way (e.g., however you like). The inkblots are then presented a second time for the "inquiry" phase. Here the examiner asks whatever questions are necessary to determine *what* precisely the response was, *where* in the inkblot it was seen, and *why* it was seen – i.e., what aspects of the inkblot contributed to the perception. The information obtained here is to be used primarily for scoring the responses. Sometimes, a third administration of the inkblots is used (called "testing the limits") where the examiner explores whether other kinds of responses might be elicited; for example, if the patient gave originally only bizarre responses, could that patient perceive more "normal" aspects?

Scoring. There are five scores that are obtained for each response:

1. Location – Does the response cover the whole of the blot, or part of it? If only a part, is that detail large or small, usual or unusual?

2. Determinant – What aspects of the inkblot, at least as perceived by the subject, determined the response? Was it the form of the inkblot, the color, the shading?

3. Content – Each response is classified according to content. For example, did the person see a

human figure, an animal, a geographical concept, food, clouds, man-made objects, . . . ?

4. Popularity or originality (sometimes this is subsumed under content) – Is the response given a popular one or is it original? Popularity can be defined by a list of 10 responses given by B. Klopfer, Ainsworth, W. G. Klopfer, et al., (1954), and originality is a response that appears no more than once in a 100 protocols. There are also normative tables that one can use to make these judgments.

5. Form quality or accuracy of percept – Each response can be scored on a rating scale as to the extent to which the response fits the blot, and the extent to which a response is elaborated (for example, a "dog" vs. a "Scottish terrier sitting up begging"). In the Klopfer system the scale goes from −2 to +5.

Once the responses are scored, various percentages are tabulated because the number of responses can vary from person to person. For example, a "typical" protocol will have less than 5% responses that use uncommon small details. A "typical" schizophrenic protocol will have a higher percentage of these responses, typically about 1 in 5. Once these percentages are tabulated, the psychologist weaves these results into an overall interpretation, combining clinical skill and art with normative data, experience, and internal norms.

Approach. Originally, many psychologists considered the Rorschach as providing an "X-ray" view of the internal psychodynamics of the patient. Recently, the Rorschach is considered a perceptual cognitive task that presents ambiguous visual stimuli. The responses are thought to represent the strategies used by the patient in dealing with the world. Note that Rorschach himself did not emphasize the imaginative or content aspects of the responses to the inkblots, but rather focused on the perception aspects (those aspects of the response that reflected the form of the response, whether the entire inkblot was being used or just a small detail). Under the Exner approach, the Rorschach is seen as a problem-solving task and the responses as reflective of styles of coping behavior. That is, how the subject responds to the Rorschach is seen as evidence of how the subject responds to the world, especially to ambiguity and challenge.

Basic issues. The Rorschach is used for multiple purposes, from providing a psychiatric diagnosis to assessing a person's level of creativity. Thus, the issue of validity becomes rather complex – validity for what?

Another major issue is whether the Rorschach is a test and therefore accountable as to reliability and validity, or a technique or method to generate information about personality functioning that transcends psychometric issues.

Psychometric views. As I. Weiner (1977) indicated, there are three types of opinions regarding the psychometric status of the Rorschach. The first holds that the Rorschach should be discarded as an assessment procedure because it has no demonstrated validity. The second point of view holds that the Rorschach is not a test but a technique whose utility is a function of the examiner's skills and intuition, and therefore the usual psychometric criteria do not apply. A third approach represents something of a middle ground – the Rorschach is a test and its utility needs to be assessed objectively, but the challenge is to develop more sophisticated experimental designs that reflect the complexity of the Rorschach and of the clinical decisions that are made.

I. B. Weiner (1994) argues that the Rorschach is not a test because it does not test anything, i.e., a test is designed to measure whether something is present or not and in what quantity. The Rorschach is a method of generating data that describe personality functioning, and thus it should be called the Rorschach Inkblot Method.

The Rorschach itself can be seen from two validity perspectives. From the viewpoint of *criterion* validity, the focus is on how specific Rorschach variables or signs are related to actual criteria, such as psychopathology or coping styles. This is the approach of Exner and his colleagues. From the viewpoint of *construct* validity, the focus is more on the Rorschach as reflective of personality functioning, particularly from a psychoanalytic point of view. This has been the classical or traditional approach. (For an excellent discussion of these issues, see H. Lerner & P. M. Lerner, 1987.)

Perceptual vs. content approaches. One of the major distinctions in the area of assessment is that of nomothetic and idiographic approaches. The nomothetic approach has as its aim the discovery of general laws, while the idiographic approach focuses on individual differences and the uniqueness of the individual (see Chapter 19).

Aronow, Reznikoff, and Moreland (1995) argue that there is another distinction to be kept in mind when dealing with the Rorschach – perceptual vs. content approaches. Those who favor the perceptual approach emphasize those aspects of *how* the subject perceives, such as location, form level, and determinants. Those who emphasize the content approach emphasize *what* the subject perceives. These two dimensions can result in four "theoretical" stances: (1) the perceptual nomothetic; (2) the content nomothetic; (3) the content idiographic; and (4) the perceptual idiographic.

The perceptual nomothetic approach is how Rorschach began. He felt that the scoring of the determinants was most important, and the scoring of content, the least important. Subsequently, however, Rorschach shifted his orientation to a more content and psychoanalytic approach that focused on projection rather than perception. Most scoring systems of the Rorschach taught in American graduate schools emphasize this perceptual nomothetic approach, and the Exner system would fall here also.

The content nomothetic approach focuses on the categories of content to be scored, such as human responses, animal responses, etc. A number of content scales have been developed to measure a variety of variables such as depression and primary process thinking. According to Aronow and Reznikoff (1976), these content scales have shown better psychometric properties than perceptual scores, but because of inadequate reliability are not recommended for use with individual subjects in clinical settings.

The content idiographic approach focuses on the content, the responses of the individual, and what these responses indicate about this particular individual. The approach here is a psychodynamic one that focuses on the unconscious aspects of mental functioning. From this approach, the very strength of the Rorschach is the unlimited freedom the subject has to respond, or not, as well as the ambiguous nature of the inkblots and the visual aspects of the task. The fourth possibility, the perceptual idiographic approach has never come about (Aronow, Reznikoff, & Moreland, 1995).

Faking. Still another issue is the susceptibility of the Rorschach to faking. In a classical study done by Albert, Fox, and Kahn (1980), Rorschach protocols were given to experts to judge. Some of the protocols came from paranoid schizophrenic patients, some were from normal individuals, and some were from college students who had been instructed, to varying degrees, to fake the responses as if they were paranoid schizophrenics. More of the protocols from the faking subjects were identified as psychotic (from 46% to 72%); 48% of the schizophrenic protocols were diagnosed as psychotic, as well as 24% of the normal protocols. Although in the usual application of the Rorschach diagnostic status is not the aim, these findings are somewhat disturbing.

Limitations. From a psychometric point of view, the Rorschach leaves much to be desired. There are only 10 items (inkblots), so its reliability is inherently limited. Different individuals can and do give differing number of responses, so that conclusions and interpretations are made using different databases. There is only one form of the Rorschach, so alternate form reliability cannot be computed, and pre- and poststudies are limited to using the same form.

Reliability and validity. When there are many studies on one topic, and their results seem conflicting – as occurs with the Rorschach – a useful procedure is to analyze overall trends through a metaanalysis. Parker (1983) conducted such an analysis on 39 studies; studies that had been published between 1971 and 1980 in one journal, and that met certain experimental criteria. He reported that reliabilities in the order of .83 and higher, and validity coefficients of .45 and higher, can be expected with the Rorschach when hypotheses supported by empirical or theoretical rationales are tested using reasonably powerful statistics (for an example of a specific study, see Bornstein, Hill, Robinson, et al., 1996). Hiller, Rosenthall, Bornstein, et al., (1999) concluded that the validity of the Rorschach is not significantly different from that of the MMPI, with both instruments showing mean validity coefficients of about .29 to 30. An opposite conclusion however, was reached by Garb, Florio, and Grove (1998) – that the Rorschach is not as valid as the MMPI.

Percentage of agreement. Percentage of agreement is a poor measure of reliability. If a test has perfect reliability, we would expect 100% agreement among scorers. If the test has zero reliability, however, the lowest chance level of agreement is not zero, but 50%. If for example, the judgment is required in a yes-no format (e.g., Is this response an aggressive response? Does this Rorschach protocol show evidence of psychotic thinking? etc.), with two raters giving completely blind guesses, we have four possible results: one rater says "yes" and the other "no" and vice versa; both say "yes" or both say "no." With four possibilities, two or 50% represent agreement (regardless of correctness). Furthermore, if either or both raters make a particular judgment more often than 50%, the rate of agreement will increase. Suppose, for example, that two Rorschach raters each have a tendency to label 80% of the responses as aggressive in nature, their rate of chance agreement will actually be about 68%, a rather respectable figure, although in this case it would reflect biased blind guessing. Wood, Nezworski, and Stejskal (1996) soundly criticize the Exner system on this basis, and show that even a percentage agreement of 92% could reflect no agreement on the part of any two raters.

Grønnerød (1999) computed percentage agreement, correlations, and Kappa coefficients, and found Kappa to be "conservative and reliable"; this author recommends Kappa as a standard estimate of interrater agreement (see his article for the formulas to compute Kappa).

Representative study. A representative study using the Exner Comprehensive System is that by Haller and Exner (1985). They administered the Rorschach to 50 patients, mostly women, with complaints and symptoms of depression. Three to four days later they were retested. At retest, one half of the sample were given special instructions to remember what responses they had given the first time, and to give different responses. Thirty percent of the protocols were scored by two psychologists, with percentage of interscorer

agreement ranging from 88% to 100%. Experimental group subjects (with special instructions) repeated about one third of their responses, while control subjects (standard instructions) repeated about two thirds of their responses.

The protocols were scored on 27 different variables, with only 5 variables showing significant changes from test to retest. Most of the test-retest correlations were above .70, even for the experimental group which was instructed to give different responses.

G. J. Meyer (1997) concluded that Exner's Comprehensive system has excellent interrater reliability with a mean coefficient of .86, but Wood, Nezworks, and Stejskal (1997) strongly disagreed.

The Holtzman Inkblot Technique (HIT)

The HIT (Holtzman, Thorpe, & Swartz, 1961) was designed to overcome most of the psychometric limitations of the Rorschach. The HIT consists of two sets of 45 inkblot cards (Forms A and B), and the subject is required to give only one response per card. Exact wording of instructions is not given to avoid "stiffness" and maintain rapport, but three points should be made: (1) the inkblots are not made to represent something in particular; (2) different people see different things; and (3) only one response is required per card. Following each response, a brief inquiry is made to determine the location of the percept, the determinants, and a general question to encourage elaboration (what else can you tell me?).

Development. Literally hundreds of inkblots were created as an item pool. Blots were then selected on the basis of a number of principles having to do with such aspects as shading and color, and the degree to which they elicited different responses. Eventually, three sets of 45 inkblots each were developed and administered to samples of college students and psychotic patients. The responses were then analyzed, ultimately on six dimensions, and inkblots retained both on the basis of whether responses could be discriminated between the two samples, and other considerations such as reliability.

Scoring. Each response is scored on 22 variables, each variable carefully defined, using a numerical scale. These variables range from reaction time (the time between presentation of the inkblot to the beginning of the response), to a 3-point location score (0 for whole blot, 1 for large areas, and 2 for smaller areas), to "pathognomic verbalization" (i.e., deviant autistic responses), such as "a person with the head of a chicken").

Reliability. Four major types of reliability studies were carried out by Holtzman and his colleagues: (1) studies of intra-scorer consistency (the degree of agreement when the same protocols are scored twice by the same individual); (2) inter-scorer reliability (the degree of agreement between two or more different scorers); (3) intra-subject stability (the degree of internal consistency); and (4) delayed intra-subject stability (the degree of agreement between alternate forms, with varying test retest time intervals).

These studies were carried out on a wide variety of samples, from 5-year-olds to depressed patients. In general, intra-scorer reliability coefficients were high, typically in the mid .90s. Inter-scorer reliability was also high, with coefficients in the .80s and .90s. Internal consistency also was high, with typical coefficients in the high .80s and low .90s; some coefficients were substantially lower but these typically were on variables where the scores were not normally distributed (for example, the variable of "space," responses based on the white space, which are infrequent). Finally, test-retest studies showed close comparability of the two forms, with most variables showing stability over time.

Validity. There are hundreds of studies that have looked at the validity of the HIT, typically by comparing diagnostic groups, such as psychotic vs. normal, or correlating specific HIT variables with personality test scores. In general, the results support the validity of the HIT, although the results are typically modest. Although the HIT has been useful in research projects, it has not caught on with clinicians. Those clinicians who are likely to use an inkblot test, tend to select the Rorschach.

The Thematic Apperception Test (TAT)

When we read a story, we not only learn about the fictitious characters but also about the author.

The personality of a Truman Capote is distinctly different from that of a Charles Dickens, and one need not have a doctorate in literature to perceive the major differences between these two authors from their writings. It was this type of observation that led Murray and Morgan to develop the TAT, where the respondent is asked to make up stories in response to a set of pictures. Like the Rorschach, the TAT is used extensively and also has received a great deal of criticism. The TAT was introduced in 1935 and consists of a series of 31 pictures, most of which are relatively ambiguous. The subject is shown a picture and asked to make up a story that reflects what is going on, what has happened, what will happen, and the feelings of the various characters depicted. The resulting stories are assumed to reflect the person's needs, emotions, conflicts, etc., at both the conscious and unconscious levels.

Variations. Many variants of the TAT approach have been developed, including sets of cards that depict animal characters for use with children (e.g., the Children's Apperception Test, Bellak, 1975), a specific animal character, the dog Blacky, in situations depicting crucial psychoanalytic concepts such as castration anxiety (the Blacky Pictures Test, G. S. Blum, 1950), sets for use with the elderly (the Gerontological Apperception Test, R. L. Wolk & R. B. Wolk, 1971), with families (Julian, Sotile, Henry, et al., 1991), with specific ethnic or cultural groups (Bellak, 1986), and sets developed according to standard psychometric procedures (e.g., the Picture Projective Test, Ritzler, Sharkey, & Chudy, 1980; and the Roberts Apperception Test for Children, McArthur & Roberts, 1982).

Description. Twenty of the TAT cards are designated as appropriate for either boys or girls, or for adult males or females; eleven of the cards have no designation, with one of these being a blank card. (See Morgan, 1995 for a detailed description of each of these pictures and their historical origin). It was intended that 20 cards be selected for a particular subject, 10 of which would be appropriate for the person's age and gender. Typically, most clinicians use somewhere between 6 and 10 cards, selected on the basis of the clinician's judgment that the card will elicit thematic information related to the client's functioning or sometimes on the basis of published recommendations (e.g., Arnold, 1962; see A. A. Hartman, 1970, for a popularity ranking of TAT cards).

The pictures are quite varied. In one for example, which is traditionally used as the first card, there is a seated young boy contemplating a violin that rests on a table in front of him. Another picture shows four men in overalls lying on a patch of grass; still another is of a man clutched from behind by three hands.

Administration. Although theoretically the TAT could be used with children, it is typically used with adolescents and adults. The original manual (H. A. Murray, 1943) does have standardized instructions, but typically examiners use their own versions. What is necessary is that the instructions include the points that: (1) the client is to make up an imaginative or dramatic story; (2) the story is to include what is happening, what led to what is happening, and what will happen; (3) finally, it should include what the story characters are feeling and thinking.

As part of the administration, the examiner unobtrusively records the response latency of each card, i.e., how long it takes the subject to begin a story. The examiner writes down the story as accurately as possible, noting any other responses (such as nervous laughter, facial expressions, etc.). Some examiners use a tape recorder, but such a device may significantly alter the test situation (R. M. Ryan, 1987).

Often, after all the stories have been elicited, there is an inquiry phase, where the examiner may attempt to obtain additional information about the stories the client has given. A variety of techniques are used by different examiners, including asking the client to identify the least preferred and most preferred cards.

Pull of TAT cards. TAT cards elicit "typical" responses from many subjects, somewhat like the popular responses on the Rorschach. This is called the "pull" of the card (e.g., Eron, 1950), and some have argued that this pull is the most important determinant of a TAT response (Murstein, 1963). Many of the TAT cards are from woodcuts and other art media, with lots of shadings and dark, sometimes indistinguishable details. Because of this stimulus pull, many of the cards

elicit stories that are gloomy or melancholic (Goldfried & Zax, 1965). There is some evidence to suggest that the actual TAT card may be more important than the respondent's "projections" in determining the actual emotional tone of the story (e.g., Eron, Terry, & Callahan, 1950).

Scoring. H. A. Murray (1938) developed the TAT in the context of a personality theory that saw behavior as the result of psychobiological and environmental aspects. Thus not only are there *needs* that a person has (both biological needs, such as the need for food, and psychological, such as the need to achieve or the need for control), but there are also forces in the environment, called *press*, that can affect the individual. Presumably, the stories given by the individual reflect the combination of such needs and presses, both in an objective sense and as perceived by the person.

In most stories, there is a central figure called the hero, and it is assumed that the client identifies psychologically with this hero. Both the needs and the presses are then identified, and each is scored on a 1- to 5-point scale in terms of intensity and how central their expression. Murray (1938) originally identified some 36 needs, but others have reduced or increased this list. Following Murray's example, there were a number of attempts to develop comprehensive scoring systems for the TAT. A number of manuals are available that can be used (e.g., W. E. Henry, 1956; M. I. Stein, 1981), although none have become the standard way, and ultimately the scoring reflects the examiner's clinical skills and theoretical perspective.

A number of scoring procedures have been developed for these stories (e.g., Bellak, 1986; Shneidman, 1951), but typically in clinical settings, as opposed to research studies, the interpretation is based not on quantitative analysis, but on a qualitative assessment, often couched in psychodynamic theory. Analysis of TAT protocols is often impressionistic – a subjective, intuitive approach where the TAT protocol is perused for such things as repetitive themes, conflicts, slips of the tongue, degree of emotional control, sequence of stories, etc. As with the Rorschach, the interpretation is not to be done blindly but in accord with other information derived from interviews with the client, other test results, etc.

In effect then, the utility of the TAT is, in large part, a function of both the specific scoring procedure used and the talent and sensitivity of the individual clinician.

Many specific scoring guidelines have also been developed that focus on the measurement of a specific dimension, such as gender identity (R. May, 1966) or achievement motivation (McClelland, Atkinson, Clark, et al., 1953). A recent example is a scoring system designed to measure how people are likely to resolve personal problems; for each card a total score as well as four subscale scores are obtained, and these are aggregated across cards (Ronan, Colavito, & Hammontree, 1993).

What does the TAT measure? First and foremost TAT stories are samples of the subject's verbal behavior. Thus, they can be used to assess the person's intellectual competence, verbal fluency, capacity to think abstractly, and other cognitive aspects. Second, the TAT represents an ambiguous situation presented by an "authority" figure, to which the subject must somehow respond. Thus some insight can be gained about the person's coping resources, interpersonal skills, and so on. Finally, the TAT responses can be assumed to reflect the individual's psychological functioning, and the needs, conflicts, feelings, etc., expressed in the stories are presumed to reflect the client's perception of the world and inner psychodynamic functioning.

TAT stories are said to yield information about the person's: (1) thought organization, (2) emotional responsiveness, (3) psychological needs, (4) view of the world, (5) interpersonal relationships, (6) self-concept, and (7) coping patterns (Holt, 1951).

Holt pointed out that the responses to the TAT not only are potentially reflective of a person's unconscious functioning, in a manner parallel to dreams, but there are a number of "determinants" that impact upon the responses obtained. For example, the situational context is very important. Whether a subject is being evaluated as part of court-mandated proceedings or whether the person is an introductory psychology volunteer can make a substantial difference. The "directing set" is also important, i.e., the preconceptions that the person has of what the test, tester, and testing situations are like.

Research uses. The TAT has also been used for research purposes with perhaps the best known example as a measure of need achievement (McClelland, Atkinson, Clark, et al., 1953; see Heckhausen, 1967, for a review).

Manuals. There is an extremely large body of literature on the TAT, not just in terms of journal articles, but also scoring manuals, chapters in books on projective techniques, entire books on the TAT, and critical reviews (see Varble, 1971).

Reliability. The determination of the reliability (and validity) of the TAT is a rather complex matter because we must ask which scoring system is being used, which variables are scored, and perhaps even what aspects of specific examinees and examiners are involved.

Eron (1955) pointed out that the TAT was a research tool, one of many techniques used to study the fantasy of normal individuals, but that it was quickly adopted for use in the clinic without any serious test of the reliability and validity of the many methods of analysis that were proposed. He pointed out that there are as many ways of analyzing TAT stories as there are practitioners, and that few of these methods have been demonstrated to be reliable.

Some would argue that the concept of reliability is meaningless when applied to projective techniques. Even if we don't accept that argument, it is clear that the standard methods of determining reliability are not particularly applicable to the TAT. Each of the TAT cards is unique, so neither split-half nor parallel-form reliability is appropriate. Test-retest reliability is also limited because on the one hand the test should be sensitive to changes over time, and on the other, the subject may focus on different aspects of the stimulus from one time to another.

The determination of reliability also assumes that extraneous sources of variation are held in check, i.e., the test is standardized. This is clearly not the case with the TAT, where instructions, sequence of cards, scoring procedure, etc., can vary.

Validity. Validity is also a very complex issue, with studies that support the validity of the TAT and studies that do not. Varble (1971) reviewed this issue and indicated that: (1) the TAT is not well suited or useful for differential diagnosis; (2) the TAT can be useful in the identification of personality variables, although there are studies that support this conclusion and studies that do not; (3) different reviewers come to different conclusions ranging from "the validity of the TAT is practically nil" to "there is impressive evidence for its validity."

Holt (1951) pointed out that the TAT is not a test in the same sense that an intelligence scale is, but that the TAT really reflects a segment of human behavior that can be analyzed in many ways. One might as well ask what is the reliability and validity of everyday behavior. It is interesting to note that Bellak's (1986) book on the TAT, which is quite comprehensive and often used as a training manual, does not list either reliability or validity in its index. But the TAT continues to be of interest to both practitioners and researchers (e.g., Cramer, 1999).

Gender differences. A. J. Stewart and Chester (1982) reviewed a number of studies of gender differences on the TAT and concluded that gender differences were "inconclusive," in part, because many of the studies administered different cards to male subjects than those used for female subjects. Worchel, Aaron, and Yates (1990) administered both male and female cards to both male and female subjects. Their analyses indicated that female TAT cards elicited more responses on a "general concerns" dimension, and that female subjects gave more responses on an "interpersonal relations" scale. Thus, they obtained both a gender difference between types of TAT cards and between subjects of different gender.

TAT in an applied setting. An interesting application of the TAT can be found in the study of McClelland and Boyatzis (1982), who studied the TAT protocols of 237 managers at the American Telephone and Telegraph Company. The TAT had been administered to them when they joined the company, and the investigators correlated various TAT variables to the levels of promotion attained after 8 and 16 years. A leadership motive pattern, defined as a moderately high need for power, a lower need for affiliation, and a high degree of self-control, was significantly associated with managerial success after 8 and 16 years for non-technical managers. Need for achievement was also associated with success, but only at the lower managerial levels. None of the variables was associated with success for technical managers who had engineering responsibilities.

TAT in research setting. K. L. Cooper and Gutmann (1987) used five TAT cards to assess pre- and post-empty-nest women (women whose children were still living at home vs. women whose children had left). The results were in line with the theoretical expectations of the authors in that the TAT stories of post-empty-nest women showed more active "ego mastery."

Are instructions the key? The TAT is the focus of much controversy, with advocates finding the test quite useful, and critics pointing out the lack of reliability and validity. Lundy (1988) suggested that these divergent views may be a reflection of the way the test is administered. He administered four TAT cards to samples of adolescents using one of four instructional sets: (1) neutral, standard instructions; (2) following a personality test; (3) with emphasis that the TAT is a personality test; and (4) with nonthreatening but structured instructions. Comparisons with various criteria indicated that the stories written after the neutral instructions were valid predictors of the three need dimensions that were scored, but with the other instructional sets nonsignificant results were obtained.

Sentence Completion Tests

A sentence completion test consists of a number of incomplete sentences where only the stem is presented; the client is asked to complete each sentence, typically with the first response that comes to mind. Sometimes stems are selected for their potential response value (e.g., "My father . . ."), and sometimes they are quite open ended (e.g. "I always . . ."). Presumably, the responses reflect the person's personality, psychodynamic functioning, motivation, conflicts, degree of adjustment, and so on. As with most other projective techniques, the results are interpreted by an impressionistic, subjective, intuitive approach, and less usually by scoring the completions and using the obtained scores in a normative fashion.

Many sentence completion tests are available, and it is not unusual for individual clinicians or agencies to use their own form, which typically lacks standardization and psychometric data as to reliability and validity, as well as appropriate norms. Over the years, a number of sentence completion tests have also been published commercially, some for use with specific samples such as older persons, and some to assess specific variables such as self-concept, attitudes toward authority figures, etc.

Although no one sentence completion test dominates the market, among the best known currently in use are the Washington University Sentence Completion Test (Loevinger, 1976; 1979), which assesses ego development and is primarily a research tool, and the Rotter Incomplete Sentences Blank (Rotter, 1946; Rotter & Rafferty, 1950), which is a measure of adjustment often used in clinical settings such as college counseling centers (Holaday, Smith, & Sherry, 2000).

The Rotter contains 40 sentence stems, with 3 forms: for high school, college, and adults. The test can be easily administered, has no time limit, can usually be completed in less than 30 minutes, and can be administered individually or in a group setting. It probably takes longer to score the test than to administer it! Each response is scored in a two-step sequence. First, the response is categorized as: omission (i.e. no response), conflict (indicative of hostility), positive, or neutral (e.g. "I . . . am answering this test"). Then positive responses are scored 0, 1, or 2 and conflict responses are scored 4, 5, or 6, using explicit definitions and examples given in the test manual. Total scores can vary from 0 to 240, with the mean score reported to be 127 (SD of 14).

The reliability of this scoring system is quite good with interscorer reliability coefficients in the .90s. Split-half reliability is also quite good, with typical coefficients in the .80s. Validity however, is somewhat questionable. Although there are studies that used the Rotter as a screening device to identify delinquent youths, for example, the number of false negatives (delinquent youths not identified as delinquents) and the number of false positives (nondelinquent youths "identified" as delinquents) can be quite high. This indicates that the test cannot be used for individual clients (Cosden, 1987). Correlations between scores on the Rotter and various indices of adjust-

ment are typically in the .20 to .50 range, modest at best.

Normative data on the Rotter are based on a medium-sized sample (about 300) of college students, and are probably no longer current; by 1981, significantly different mean scores were being reported (Lah & Rotter, 1981).

Clinicians who use tests such as the Rotter see its value as allowing the client to respond more freely than if the same questions were asked in an interview; thus, some see the Rotter as a semi-structured interview that gives the client more freedom to indicate, at least at a surface level, some of the conflicts they experience and how they perceive aspects of the world. Other clinicians see sentence completion tests as good starting points; they can ask the client "what did you mean by item 6" or "tell me more about item 12" and have the responses be the basis for a productive therapeutic session. At the same, time, there is recognition, supported by research, that the responses to sentence completion tests are less "deep" than ones elicited by the Rorschach or other less structured projective tests. Some investigators have argued that responses to the Rotter are heavily affected by social desirability, but others have not found support for this (e.g., Janda & Galbraith, 1973; McCarthy & Rafferty, 1971). For a review of some of the basic issues involved in sentence completion tests, see Goldberg (1965). See the Miner Sentence Completion Scale intended to measure the "motivation to marriage"; this scale also appears useful in studies of employee selection (Carson & Gilliard, 1993; Miner, 1964).

Drawings

There are a number of projective tests that request the client to draw something, for example, a person (Machover, 1949), or a house, a tree, and a person (Buck, 1966), their own family (Hammer, 1978), and so on. Some of these procedures evolved out of attempts to measure intelligence from a developmental perspective, using stimuli that could be applied cross-culturally with a minimum of verbal skills required either to understand the instructions or respond to the task. Eventually these procedures were expanded to assess personality, especially within a psychodynamic framework.

Despite the fact that such procedures are quite popular and often used by clinicians as part of a battery of tests, the experimental and psychometric literature does not, in general, support their reliability and validity as measures of personality and/or psychopathology. A typical reliability example is the study by S. Fisher and R. Fisher (1950), who evaluated the drawings of 32 paranoid schizophrenics; they found that the interrater reliability of trained psychologists was no better than for untrained raters, and that for both the interrater reliability was quite poor. Validity studies fare no better, with many studies reporting inconclusive or negative findings. Yet these techniques continue to be popular and attempts are made to integrate research findings with clinical practice (e.g., Riethmiller & Handler, 1997).

Draw-A-Man Test and the DAP. Originally developed by Goodenough (1926), this was a simple test based on even simpler assumptions. The child was required to draw a man (rather than a woman, because women's clothing was much more variable and thus difficult to quantify). It was assumed that children draw what they know rather than what they see, and that up to age 10 the quality of a child's drawing reflected intellectual development. Given the historical context, Goodenough's efforts were indeed good enough – she collected a normative sample of almost 4,000 children and used standardized procedures. She developed a scoring scale that could be used to assess the child's drawing in terms of cognitive development, and so an IQ could actually be computed.

A revision of this test came about in 1963 (the Goodenough-Harris Draw-A-Person Test (DAP); D. B. Harris, 1963), where a drawing of a woman was added, and an attempt was made to extend the scale to the adolescent years. In 1968, Koppitz developed a scoring system that became very popular, and in 1988, Naglieri presented a revision and update, in which three drawings (a man, a woman, and oneself) are produced and scored on 64 aspects that include the number of body parts, their location, and their proportion. The result of this quantitative scoring system is a standardized score for each of the drawings as well as a total test score, with a mean of 100 and SD of 15, just like most intelligence tests. The Naglieri scoring system was normed on more than 2,600 individuals aged 5 through 17, representative of U.S. Census data on a variety of variables.

With these newer revisions, reliability is generally satisfactory although low-median internal consistency coefficients range from .56 to .78 (median of .70) for each of the drawings and a median of .86 for the total test score; test-retest coefficients range from .60 to .89, and interrater reliability is typically in the mid .90s (Kamphaus & Pleiss, 1991). Validity correlations are substantially lower, with a median correlation coefficient of .57 between the draw-a-person and standard measures of intelligence. Wisniewski and Naglieri (1989) obtained a correlation of .51 between DAP total scores and WISC-R Full Scale IQ in a sample of 51 school children; their mean IQ on the WISC-R was 99.5 and on the DAP it was 95.2. Thus, from the perspective of intelligence or cognitive development, the DAP can be a legitimate part of the clinician's repertoire of instruments. It is nonthreatening and can be a good "conversation opener" with a young client. Psychometric difficulties arise however, when the test (or a variant) is used as a projective technique to elicit information about the client's functioning.

Gender-role identification. The DAP is frequently used as a measure of gender role identification. That is, it is assumed that the "normal" response to the instructions of "draw a person" is to draw a figure of one's own gender. Most of the time this is a reasonable assumption supported by the research literature. However, opposite gender drawings are frequently obtained from women as well as from young school-aged boys. Numerous explanations have been proposed, including the notion that women in our culture are ambivalent about their gender identification. Farylo and Paludi (1985) point out a number of methodological problems including the observation that masculinity-femininity is often assumed to be a bipolar dimension (vs. the notion of several types including androgynous and undifferentiated individuals), that the gender of the administrator has an impact, and that in our culture "draw a person" may well be equated with "draw a man."

The DAP has also found substantial use in studies of attitudes toward target groups such as dentists (S. Phillips, 1980), scientists (Chambers, 1983), and computer users (Barba & Mason, 1992).

The Bender Visual Motor Gestalt Test

Introduction. As with drawings, the Bender-Gestalt is used for two distinct purposes with adult clients: a measure of neuropsychological functioning and a projective test to assess personality functioning. From a psychometric point of view, the evidence supports its use as a measure of neuropsychological functioning, but substantially less so as a projective device. With children, it is also used for two purposes: a test of visual-motor development and a projective personality technique. There is considerable evidence to support the validity of the Bender-Gestalt as a measure of visual-motor development (Tolor & Brannigan, 1980), but less so for its use to assess children's affective or behavioral disorders (Dana, Feild, & Bolton, 1983). Visual-motor development parallels various aspects of intelligence such as memory, visual perception, spatial aspects, and so on, so the test is potentially an indicator of the intellectual status of a child from a developmental perspective.

The Bender-Gestalt is one of the most widely used tests; in fact, in a 1969 survey, it was used more frequently than the WAIS or the Rorschach (Lubin, Wallis, & Paine, 1971). Why this popularity? There are probably four major reasons: (1) the test is easy to administer and relatively brief; (2) the Bender-Gestalt has, as mentioned above, two distinct purposes; (3) the test can be useful as a screening device to determine if more in-depth assessment is needed; and (4) the clinician can obtain considerable information from the test situation by carefully observing the client's behavior (see Piotrowski, 1995).

Development. The Bender-Gestalt was developed in 1938 to investigate how concepts from Gestalt psychology applied to the study of personality and brain injury and was initially administered to many different clinical samples such as mentally retarded, and brain-damaged individuals (Bender, 1938). However, there was no standard scoring procedure presented or any systematic data analysis of the results.

Description. The test consists of nine geometric designs, originally developed to illustrate the tendency of the perceptual system to organize visual stimuli into whole figures or "gestalts." Each design is on an individual card and presented one at a time; the subject is asked to copy it on a piece of paper. Bender (1938) believed that the quality of the reproduction of the designs varied according to the level of motivation of the subject and according to the pathological state of the subject, such a state being "organic" (i.e., the result of damage to the central nervous system) or "functional" (i.e., no actual brain damage but the abnormal behavior serving some psychological purpose). The test was originally used as a clinical and research instrument with adults, but in the 1950s began to be used with children and was presumed to measure visual-motor integration.

Administration. Although there are no standard directions, various authors have provided guidelines (e.g., Lezak, 1983). For example, the client is ordinarily told that there will be nine such cards. The test is considered appropriate for all age groups, from 3 years through adult, and can be administered on an individual or group basis (e.g., Keogh & Smith, 1967; Siebel, W. L. Faust, & M. S. Faust, 1971). Sometimes, the Bender-Gestalt is used as a "warm up" test, before administering an entire battery, because it is fairly simple and non-threatening.

Scoring. A variety of scoring systems have been developed for the Bender-Gestalt, primarily concerned with the accuracy and organization of the drawings. Some of the aspects that are considered are the relative size of the drawings compared to the stimuli, their location on the sheet of paper, and any inversions or rotations of the figure. The Pascal and Suttell (1951) scoring system for adult subjects is one of the better known and includes 106 different scorable features of the drawings, where each abnormal response is given a numerical value. Typical test-retest reliabilities over a short time period of 24 hours are in the .70s, and interscorer reliability of trained scorers is typically in the .90s.

Another popular scoring system, this one for the protocols of children, was developed by Koppitz (1964; 1975). Koppitz identified a group of 13 "pathognomonic" signs that she felt were indicators of emotional disturbance in children, each of these signs being relatively independent of the child's visual-motor functioning. Some of these indicators include the use of dashes rather than dots, and the size of the drawing in comparison to the actual figure. The presence of three or more of these signs in a child's protocol indicated serious emotional disturbance. The Koppitz scoring system takes into account that the number of errors decreases rapidly between ages 5 and 8; the decrease levels off between ages 9 to 11, and so there is some dispute as to whether the scoring system is applicable to children beyond age 8 or 10 (R. L. Taylor, Kauffman, & Partenio, 1984). There is some support however, for the validity of the 13 pathognomonic signs. Rossini and Kaspar (1987) for example, studied three groups of children, 40 in each group aged 7 to 10. The three groups were presumably normal children, children with mild problems, and children with chronic psychological problems. All Bender-Gestalt protocols were scored by an experienced clinician, and 32 were independently scored by a second clinician. The interscorer reliability was reported to be .92, and both groups of problem children produced significantly more emotional indicators than the normal children, although the two problem groups could not be differentiated from each other. An analysis of the 13 specific indicators, showed that only 3 were significantly related to psychopathology. Hutt (1977) developed a scoring system to measure severity of psychopathology, and several other modifications and scoring systems are available (e.g., Brannigan, Aabye, Baker, et al., 1995; E. O. Watkins, 1976). These systems seem to have adequate test-retest reliability and high interscorer reliability with trained scorers. For example, for the Koppitz system interscorer correlations are mostly in the high .80s and low .90s, and test-retest coefficients are typically in the .50 to .90 range, with periods ranging from 1 day to 8 months.

Norms. The 1974 norms presented by Koppitz are said to reflect a socioeconomic cross section, and include blacks, orientals, and Hispanics. In general however, the normative data available to the clinician is quite limited and not as extensive or representative as what is available on tests such as the Stanford-Binet and the Wechsler series.

Validity. The validity of the Bender-Gestalt as a measure of neuropsychological functioning was reviewed by Tolor and Brannigan (1980) who concluded that the test was remarkably effective in discriminating between psychiatric patients, brain-damaged patients, and normal controls, with hit rates typically above 70%. However, the validity of the Bender-Gestalt as a measure of personality and/or emotional disturbance seems to be typical of other projective techniques – difficult to prove psychometrically, with mixed results at best (Whitworth, 1984). Clearly, the Bender-Gestalt has "face" validity as a measure of visual-motor integration, and factor-analytic studies do support its structure as a measure of visual-motor perception (e.g., Becker & Sabatino, 1973). A number of studies suggest that scores on the Bender-Gestalt are related to a wide variety of variables, such as achievement in reading and in arithmetic, general intellectual competence, and various other measures of visual-motor integration (e.g., Aylward & Schmidt, 1986; Breen, Carlson, & Lehman, 1985; D. Wright & DeMers, 1982). In at least one study, it was found that students with high Bender-Gestalt scores tended to do well academically, but a prediction could not be made of students with low scores (Keogh & Smith, 1967).

A classical study. L. R. Goldberg (1959) took 30 Bender-Gestalt protocols from the files of a Veterans Administration (VA) hospital. For 15 of these protocols there was substantial evidence that the patients had organic brain damage; for 15 of the patients there was no such evidence. He gave the protocols to three groups of judges: 4 clinical psychologists, 10 psychology trainees, and 8 nonpsychologists (e.g., secretaries), and asked each to indicate whether the protocol was "organic" or not and how confident they were in their judgment. Goldberg points out that for the psychologists and the trainees that is precisely the task that they encounter in their professional work, and all of them were familiar with the Bender-Gestalt, an instrument designed to assess this diagnostic question. How correct were the psychologists? 65%. Not bad. How correct were the psychology trainees? 70%. And the nonpsychologists? 67%! Interestingly, the nonpsychologists were more confident in their judgment than the psychologists or the trainees, and the trainees were more confident than the psychologists. In addition, there was no relationship between a person's diagnostic accuracy and their degree of confidence. Goldberg also asked a Bender-Gestalt "expert" to diagnose the 30 protocols – the expert's diagnostic accuracy was 83%. L. R. Goldberg makes two points: (1) By rating all protocols as nonorganic, one could have obtained an accuracy of 80%; (2) By scoring the protocols according to the Pascal-Suttell method, one could also have obtained an 80% accuracy rate. These results do not necessarily argue against the usefulness of the Bender-Gestalt, but do support the notions that psychometric analysis is better than impressionistic formulations, and that a test's usefulness is limited by the capabilities of the test user.

A recent study. Bornstein (1999) carried out a meta-analysis of studies that compared objective/self-report measures of interpersonal dependency vs. projective measures of the same variable, and found that projective tests such as the Rorschach and the TAT correlated higher with external indices of dependency-related behavior than did the objective tests (mean correlations of .37 vs .31). More studies like this one are needed before we can objectively come to a conclusion about the value of specific projective techniques for specific domains of inquiry.

SOME CLINICAL ISSUES AND SYNDROMES

Clinical vs. Statistical Prediction

Given the same information, which might include or exclusively be test scores, how can that information be combined so as to maximize the correctness of our prediction? For example, Mary is an applicant to graduate school. As an undergraduate, her GPA was 3.06, her GRE Verbal score was 650, and her letters of recommendation contain 46 glowing adjectives. We can put this information together using our clinical judgment and intuition, noting that although her GPA is somewhat low for graduate work, her GRE score is quite respectable, and her letters of recommendation quite positive. We conclude that she should be accepted with the prediction that she will do relatively well. Or we can place her scores, as

well as those of other candidates, into a regression equation, and in fact compute her predicted GPA in graduate school. We can then accept or reject her on the basis of the regression-equation results. These two methods are known as clinical and statistical prediction methods.

Meehl (1954) wondered about the relative accuracy of clinical judgment when compared to statistical prediction, particularly because studies of psychiatric diagnoses showed that such diagnoses were often somewhat unreliable, that is, there was less than unanimous agreement among psychiatrists. In diagnosing general conditions such as psychosis, agreement ranged from mid 60% to mid 80%, but for specific conditions the agreement ranged from about mid 30% to mid 60%. Meehl (1954) found 19 studies relevant to this issue. Nine of the studies found statistical prediction to be more accurate; 10 of the studies found no difference between clinical and statistical methods. No studies found the clinical method to be superior. A later study reviewed 45 such studies and essentially supported Meehl's findings (Sawyer, 1966). An analysis of 136 studies (Grove, Zald, Lebow, et al., 2000) indicated that on average "mechanical prediction techniques" (e.g., using regression equations) were about 10% more accurate than clinical (i.e., subjective) techniques. Mechanical prediction outperformed clinical prediction in 33% to 47% of the studies examined, while in only 6% to 16% were clinical predictions more accurate than mechanical predictions.

The Effective Therapist

One of the crucial issues in clinical psychology, as well as in other fields where direct service is provided to clients, is the degree to which the effectiveness of the treatment is related to the effectiveness of the practitioner. Thus, it becomes important to identify effective therapists. Whitehorn and Betz (1960) did exactly that by comparing SVIB (see Chapter 6) responses of therapists who were successful with schizophrenic patients and therapists whose improvement rates with their patients were low. The result was a 23-item scale called the AB scale, in this case, type A referring to successful psychotherapists and type B to less successful. Type A therapists scored high on the Lawyer and CPA scales of the

SVIB, and low on the Printer and Mathematics-Physical Science Teacher scales, whereas type Bs showed the opposite pattern. Type A were thus seen as individuals characterized by a problem-solving approach, one that included genuineness and respect, an ability to understand the patient's experiences, and an expectation of responsible self-determination.

Eventually, the hypothesis was suggested, based on some empirical evidence, of an interaction between therapist-type and client diagnosis, such that type A therapists were more successful with schizophrenic patients, and type B therapists were more successful with neurotic patients. Whether this is the case is debatable (Chartier, 1971; Razin, 1971). Unfortunately, the research in this area has been complicated by the fact that there are nine different versions of this scale, and it is not always clear which version is being used, although at least four of the scales are so highly intercorrelated that they can be considered alternate forms (Kemp & Stephens, 1971).

Alcoholism

The assessment of patients with alcoholism serves at least three purposes: (1) The test information can result in individualized treatment to meet the patient's needs, coping skills, psychodynamic strengths, risk factors, and so on; (2) The test information can allow a better match between client and available treatment options; and (3) The test results can serve to monitor the course of therapeutic progress or lack of it (Allen & Mattson, 1993).

Allen and Mattson suggest that assessment instruments for alcoholism can be subsumed under nine categories:

1. *Screening* tests to determine, for example, whether an in depth evaluation is required.

2. *Diagnostic* tests to determine diagnostic status of, for example, alcohol-related conditions, such as drug abuse and brain deterioration.

3. *Triage* tests (triage being a medical term referring to the assignments of patients to specific treatments) whose results might be used to determine the appropriate setting, such as hospitalization vs. out-patient treatment, and the intensity of the treatment.

4. *Treatment* planning where the test results are used to establish treatment goals and strategies appropriate to the patient.

5. Outcome *monitoring*, for example, to assess at the end of a specified time period whether the patient requires further treatment.

6. *Program evaluation* measures to assess the therapeutic program itself rather than the individual client.

7. Scales for *family* and *marital* functioning.

8. *General* psychological tests, such as the MMPI, to assess general emotional adjustment, neuropsychological functioning, degree of psychopathology present, and so on.

9. *In-process* measures used to assess specific aspects of the treatment program and the client's progress in that program, for example, the degree of acceptance that one has a drinking problem.

Quite clearly, specific tests can be used in several of these categories. A number of such instruments (in addition to the old standards such as the MMPI) are available to assess alcoholism and/or drug abuse, such as the Alcohol Expectancy Questionnaire (S. A. Brown, Goldman, Inn, et al. 1980), the Alcohol Use Inventory (Horn, Wanberg, & Foster, 1987), and the Personal Experience Inventory (Winters & Henley, 1989) (see Lettieri, Nelson, & Sayer, 1985, for a listing of 45 such instruments).

Probably the most popular type of scale is the self-report concurrent measure i.e., use of inventories that assume that alcoholics differ from nonalcoholics, and that they therefore respond in consistently different ways to selected self-report items. There are two major test construction strategies used here (W. R. Miller, 1976). The first, or *indirect scale* strategy, involves the administration of a large pool of items, such as the MMPI, items which have little or no obvious relationship to drinking behavior. The responses of alcoholic and control samples are then statistically analyzed and a scale compiled of items whose responses are statistically different in the two groups (this is of course the empirical approach discussed in Chapter 4). The second strategy is the *direct scale* strategy, where the pool of items is directly relevant to drinking and related behaviors i.e., items have face validity.

Table 15-1. Dimensions on the EDI

Subscale	Definition
1. Drive for thinness	The wish to lose weight and the fear to gain weight
2. Bulimia	The tendency to binge and to purge
3. Body dissatisfaction	Believing specific body parts to be too large
4. Ineffectiveness	Feelings of general inadequacy
5. Perfectionism	Excessive personal expectations
6. Interpersonal distrust	A sense of alienation
7. Interoceptiveness awareness	Lack of confidence in one's ability to recognize and identify hunger and satiation
8. Maturity fears	Fear of the demands of adulthood

A good example of the first approach is the McAndrew (1965) scale of alcoholism derived from the MMPI. This is a 49-item scale, with the keyed items indicating that alcoholics report themselves to be outgoing and social, to have few problems with self-image, to have had school problems, and to experience physical problems due to excessive alcohol intake. The two statistically most discriminating items on this scale were face valid items (e.g., "I have used alcohol excessively") and were thus *eliminated* from the scale. An example of the second approach is the Michigan Alcoholism Screening Test (MAST; Selzer, 1971), which contains 25 items with a high degree of face validity (e.g., "Do you have troubles with drinking?"). The validity of both of these scales remains an open issue.

A second type of scale is based on the notion that there is an alcoholic "personality," and thus standard scales of personality, from the MMPI to measures of depression, have been used. Such studies have typically found significant differences between alcoholics and controls, to the point that Keller (1972) concluded that the study of *any* trait in alcoholics "will show that they have either more or less" of that trait! Mention should also be made of the physiological measures, such as dependence on alcohol, metabolic rates, or effects on memory and sleep, which can be used diagnostically.

Allen and Litten (1993) reviewed a broad range of psychological as well as laboratory tests (such as blood tests that assess biochemical markers for alcoholism), to identify and treat alcoholics. These authors point out that such measures have several advantages in addition to their primary use as screening instruments; these include enhancement of the patient's motivation to change their behavior, and reinforcement of patient progress. They also point out some

limitations; such instruments do not measure motivation or beliefs about the benefits of recovery and some other variables that may be related to success in treatment. In addition, most alcoholism measures have been developed with adult patients, rather than with adolescents. Most normative groups do include women and minority patients, but separate norms for these groups are rarely available.

Eating Disorders

As the name implies, eating disorders involve abnormal eating behaviors. Two major categories are identified: anorexia, which involves extreme restriction of food intake, and bulimia which involves bouts of binge eating followed by vomiting and/or laxative use. Two subtypes of anorexia are currently recognized: bulimic anorexics who engage in binge eating, and restrictor anorexics who severely restrict their food intake. In the assessment and research of eating disorders, a wide variety of scales are used. Some have to do with body dissatisfaction, others represent survey checklists of weight reduction methods, and still others are self-report questionnaires of eating attitudes and behaviors.

The Eating Disorder Inventory-2 (EDI-2). The EDI-2 (Garner, 1991) is a 91-item self-report measure of the symptoms, behaviors, and feelings related to bulimia and anorexia. The original EDI (Garner & Olmsted, 1984) consisted of 64 items scored on 8 subscales, and was developed with the recognition that eating disorders are multidimensional; the 8 scales are listed in Table 15.1. The initial pool of items consisted of 146 items generated by clinicians familiar with eating disorders. Items were retained that discriminated between anorexic patient and control samples, that correlated with the relevant sub-scale more than with other subscales, and that had alpha coefficients above .80. The EDI-2 contains an additional 27 items scored on 3 provisional subscales, as well as expanded norms totaling almost 1,000 patients. The EDI-2 items cover both specific eating behaviors, such as dieting, and more adjusted-oriented aspects, such as meeting parental expectations. Responses are given on a 6-point scale, ranging from "always," through "often" and "sometimes," to "never," although the actual scores range from 0 to 3, with responses of "never," "rarely," or "sometimes" all given a zero weight. The scores are recorded on a profile form that allows direct comparison with patient and female college-student norms.

The primary purpose of the EDI-2 is to aid clinicians to assess patient symptoms, to plan treatment, and to evaluate the effectiveness of therapeutic interventions. It can also be used as a screening inventory to identify at-risk individuals, to assess the incidence of symptoms in a target sample, or to study from a research point of view what specific changes may be related to various therapeutic modalities.

The EDI-2 is relatively easy to administer and score. It is appropriate for both males and females, primarily for adolescents and adults, but can be used for children as young as 12. The EDI-2 takes about 20 minutes and can be administered individually or to groups. The answer sheet contains a carbon page that allows a direct translation of chosen responses into scores on the appropriate scales. Scoring is thus simply a clerical task. The obtained raw scores can be changed to percentile ranks using patient or nonpatient norms.

For the eight original EDI scales, internal consistency reliability is quite adequate ranging from the low .80s to the low .90s for patient samples both in the United States and in other countries (e.g., Norring & Sohlberg, 1988). For the three provisional scales, the reliabilities are significantly lower, with internal-consistency alpha coefficients falling below .70 for two of the three scales. Test-retest reliability is also adequate, with coefficients in the mid .80s for short periods (1 to 3 weeks), and substantially lower for longer time periods.

Much of the validity of the EDI-2 is criterion-related validity, with several studies showing eating disorder patient samples scoring significantly higher than control samples. A number of studies

have also shown that specific subscales show significant changes in patient samples as a function of specific treatments. Concurrent validity data is also available that shows scores on the eight original subscales to correlate significantly with scores on other eating-disorder inventories, with clinical ratings on the same dimensions, and with body-image measures. A representative study is that by Gross, Rosen, Leitenburg, et al. (1986) who administered the EDI and another eating attitudes test to 82 women diagnosed as bulimic. Both instruments discriminated bulimic patients from control subjects, despite the fact that many subscales on both tests did not correlate significantly with each other; for example, the EDI subscale of "bulimia" did not correlate significantly with the other test's subscale of "dieting." Many of the subscales also did not correlate significantly with behavioral measures such as the amount of calories consumed during three standardized meals. The authors concluded that both self-report measures and direct behavioral measures of eating and vomiting would be needed, and that their results supported the criterion validity of the tests, but showed only partial support for the concurrent validity.

Some construct-validity data is also available; for example, several studies have obtained eight factors on the EDI that correspond to the eight original scales, but some have not (e.g., Welch, Hall, & Norring, 1990). Investigators in New Zealand administered the EDI to three samples of nonpatient women: 192 first-year psychology students, 253 student nurses, and 142 aerobic dance-class enrollees. A factor analysis did not confirm the original eight scales, but indicated three factors in each of the samples: a factor focusing on concern with body shape, weight, and eating, a factor of self-esteem, and a factor of perfectionism (Welch, Hall, & Walkey, 1988). Not all EDI scales show equal degree of validity, and further research is needed to indicate which scales are indeed valid and useful.

HEALTH PSYCHOLOGY

Psychology and medicine. Originally, the interface between psychology and medicine occurred in the area of mental health, but recently there has been great concern with the behavioral factors that affect physical health and illness. Thus in the 1970s the field of health psychology developed in a very vigorous way into a subarea of psychology that is in many ways distinct from clinical psychology (Stone, Cohen, & Adler 1979). Health psychology includes a variety of aspects, ranging from the study of the processes by which behavior is linked to physical disease, to the study of the physiological effects of stressors that can influence susceptibility to disease.

Primary focus. Health psychology is primarily concerned with the psychological aspects related to the maintenance and promotion of good health, and the prevention and treatment of illness, as well as with issues such as health-care systems and health-policy formulation (Matarazzo, 1980). Among the major questions asked by health psychologists are how to keep people healthy (especially in terms of diseases such as lung cancer and alcohol and drug abuse), the role of personality factors and coping styles in the development of illness, the role of stress, and the benefits of social supports (see Stokols, 1992, and S. E. Taylor, 1990, for comprehensive overviews).

The healthy person. In the 1940s, Abraham Maslow began to study psychologically healthy individuals, as he believed that one could not understand mental illness unless one understood mental health first. Eventually, he was able to describe the "fully functioning" person and to label this process as self-actualization (Maslow, 1970). Shostrom (1963; 1964) developed a personality inventory called the Personal Orientation Inventory, that was based on Maslow's ideas, and operationalized self-actualization (Knapp, 1976; R. R. Knapp, Shostrom, & L. Knapp, 1978).

A somewhat different but related approach is represented by the work of Suzanne Kobasa (1979) who developed the Hardiness Test. People become ill for a wide variety of reasons, ranging from genetic defects or predispositions to environmental happenstance, such as becoming exposed to someone with a contagious illness. Stressful life events do contribute to the development of physical illness, although some people seem to be less vulnerable to such negative effects. One explanatory approach is to postulate that such resistance is due to "hardiness," a constellation of personality characteristics (e.g., Hull, Van Treuren, & Virnelli, 1987; Kobasa, Maddi, & Kahn, 1982). There are three characteristics that

seem central to this constellation: a hardy person is committed to his or her work and activities (i.e., has a sense of belief in himself or herself and the community), has a sense of control (i.e., the belief that he or she can influence the course of events), and sees life as a challenge (that changes are an opportunity to grow rather than a threat to security). The hypothesis is that hardiness mediates or acts as a buffer of stressful life events, or perhaps alters the way in which stressful life events are perceived (Alfred & Smith, 1989). Originally, the Hardiness Test was composed of six scales from other tests that were considered reliable and valid. Raw scores for each of the scales were changed to standard scores and these standard scores added into a total score, so each scale was given equal weight. The six scales actually made up three dimensions: control, commitment, and challenge. These three dimensions had internal consistency, reliability, and test-retest reliabilities all near .70 (Kobasa, Maddi, & Kahn, 1982). Subsequently the Hardiness Test was revised and shortened to 50 items, on the basis of factor analysis. A study comparing the Hardiness Test with two scales from the Personal Orientation Inventory, reported modest correlations between the two instruments, and the authors concluded that there was a relationship between the two instruments (J. M. Campbell, Amerikaner, Swank, et al., 1989).

Questions as to whether hardiness is a unidimensional or multidimensional construct have not been resolved, and indeed the very concept is a debatable one (e.g., Funk & Houston, 1987).

Physical fitness. Another major area under the topic of health psychology, and interfacing with other areas like sports psychology, is the relationship of physical fitness training to improvements in psychological functioning, and in particular to variables such as body image, cognitive functioning, self-concept, sleep, the reduction of anxiety, and so on. The vast majority of these studies use psychological tests to either categorize the independent variable, such as degree of physical fitness, or assess the dependent variables such as increases in self-esteem (see Folkins & Sime, 1981, for a review of some issues in this area).

Self-reports revisited. A psychologist named Woodworth developed the Personal Data Sheet during World War I, as a self-report inventory designed to screen out emotionally unstable recruits. This was the prototype of all subsequent self-report instruments, and although current ones are much more psychometrically sophisticated, they still reflect much of Woodworth's approach.

As I have noted before, self-reports are economical in that they do not require a well-trained professional for administration and scoring, and are amenable to psychometric treatment, such as scoring and interpretation by computer. They are typically brief, usually inexpensive, and reflect the client's experience through their own assessment rather than through an observer. This last point can of course be detrimental, in that some professionals are skeptical about the accuracy of self-reports. For an overall review of self-report measures of stress see Derogatis (1987).

Stress. One area of health psychology concerns the relationship between stress and subsequent susceptibility to disease. All individuals experience events or changes in their lives that may be potential stressors because they require coping, readjustment, and adaptation. The energy used to cope with such stressors is assumed to rob the body of resistance to disease, and thereby increase the probability of physical illness and interpersonal dysfunction. The field of stress is rather heterogeneous, but for our purposes we can classify theories of stress into three categories (Lazarus, 1966):

1. Stimulus-oriented theories view stress as being in selected aspects of the environment. Tests that reflect this point of view, attempt to catalog and assess aspects, such as the "life events" that a person experiences such as school exams, automobile accidents, divorce, and so on. Perhaps the best known measure that illustrates this approach is the Holmes and Rahe Schedule of Recent Experience, discussed next. Other life event measures include the Life Experience Survey (Sarason, Johnson, & Siegel, 1979), and the Impact of Life Event Scale (Horowitz, Wilner, & Alvarez, 1979).

2. Response-oriented theories define or focus on stress as the response of the individual. Tests and inventories here focus on the affect or mood of the person, their coping patterns, and so on. Almost all the measures of psychopathology that

we discussed in Chapter 7 could be listed here as examples of response-oriented measures – such as the MMPI, the Beck Depression Inventory, and the Spielberger State-Trait Anxiety Inventory.

3. A third group of theories might be labeled as "interactionists." They see the person as being the major mediating link between the characteristics of the environment and the responses made. The approach here is that not only does the environment have an impact on the individual, but the individual can have an impact on the environment. Because this is a rather complex and dynamic point of view, psychometric assessment has so far not reflected this approach in any significant way, with some exceptions. One such exception is the Jenkins Activity Survey to measure "Type A" behavior, discussed next.

Health Belief Model. The theory that has probably generated the most instruments to measure attitudinal components of health behaviors is the Health Belief Model, developed in the 1950s and 1960s (e.g., Janz & Becker, 1984; Rosenstock, 1974). The model developed out of social psychological concerns as to why people were not using newly developed procedures for the detection of cancer, rheumatic fever, and other illnesses. The model postulated that the likelihood of a person taking action to avoid disease was a function of subjective beliefs along several dimensions: *susceptibility* to the disease, *severity* of consequences of the disease, *benefits* of taking the recommended health action, and the *barriers* related to that action. Other dimensions, such as motivation, were later added.

Unfortunately, many of the scales developed to empirically assess facets of this model were not evaluated for reliability and validity, and were criticized for their psychometric limitations (e.g., Champion, 1984).

Life-events research. The notion that life events, such as marriage or an illness, can have an impact on the individual is not a new idea; the focus on measurement goes back to the 1950s and the work of Holmes, Rahe, and their colleagues (Hawkins, Davies, & Holmes, 1957; Holmes & Rahe, 1967; Rahe, Meyer, Smith, et al., 1964). These investigators proposed that the readjustment required by major life changes such as a divorce or a change in jobs substantially increased the risk of physical illness (Holmes & Rahe, 1967). They developed the Schedule of Recent Experience (SRE), a 43-item questionnaire designed to measure the incidence or occurrence of life events, which were as a total, significantly associated with physical illness onset. In fact, these items were generated from a larger list of life events that were clinically observed to cluster at the time of disease onset; these events were taken from the charts of more than 5,000 medical patients. This instrument underwent a number of changes (e.g., B. S. Dohrenwend & B. P. Dohrenwend, 1978; Ross & Minowsky, 1979) including name changes (e.g., the Social Readjustment Rating Scale); it has been central to a research program on the effects of life changes on subsequent physical, medical, and psychological conditions ranging from cardiovascular disease and death (e.g., Adler, MacRitchie, & Engel, 1971; Rahe & Lind, 1971), the onset of diabetes (S. P. Stein & Charles, 1971), complications with birth and pregnancy (e.g., Gorsuch & Key, 1974), to more general susceptibility to illness (e.g., Marx, Garrity, & Bowers, 1975). However, the evidence suggests that the relationship between major life changes and health outcomes is modest at best, with the average correlation coefficient about .12 (Rabkin & Streuning, 1976).

The list of items was originally given to 394 subjects, who were asked to rate each item as to how much social readjustment was required for each event. As an anchor, they were told that marriage was given an arbitrary value of 500. These values or ratings were termed "LCUs" or life change units. The mean score for each life event was then calculated and divided by 10 in order to have the items fall on a scale from a theoretical 0 to 100. Thus marriage has a value of 50. The highest-rated items were "death of a spouse" at 100, and "divorce" at 73. Average items were "son or daughter leaving home" and "trouble with in-laws," both rated at 29. Lowest items were "Christmas" at 12, and "minor violations of the law" at 11. Ratings of the various items were fairly consistent among different subgroups, such as men vs. women, or older vs. younger subjects.

The fundamental assumption of this approach is that major life-change events result in stress. Experiencing such changes requires adjustments that inhibit the body's natural resistance to illness, with the end result being physical and/or psychological symptoms. Part of the original theoretical framework was that life events, whether positive or negative, were stressful. Subsequent research has shown that the impact is a function of the degree of aversiveness of the event. Two events such as marriage and divorce, may reflect equal amounts of disruption, but the stressfulness is related to the negative event and not the positive one. Indeed, an important component is how the individual perceives the event (e.g., Horowitz, Wilner, & Alvarez, 1979; Zeiss, 1980).

Another issue is the weighing of the individual items. Originally, different weights were used through a technique called "direct magnitude estimation" in which each item was assigned a mean "life change" score. Several investigators have shown that alternative scoring schemes, using unitary weights (i.e., every item endorsed is counted as one), or using factor weights (i.e., items are scored to reflect their loading on a factor) are just as predictive, if not more so (e.g., Grant, Sweetwood, Gerst, et al., 1978; Lei & Skinner, 1980). In most studies where different scoring techniques are compared, weighted scores and unitary weight scores typically correlate in the low to mid .90s (e.g., G. R. Elliot & Eisdorfer, 1981; M. Zimmerman, 1983). Might the weights of the individual items change across time? Scully, Tosi, and Banning (2000) found that 14 of 43 events did show a significant shift in weight, but there was a correlation of .80 between the original and new weights.

A third issue concerns the dimensionality of these life-event questionnaires. Originally, they were presented as unidimensional, with endorsed events contributing to an overall stress score. Subsequent studies have presented evidence of the multidimensionality of such scales (e.g., Skinner & Lei, 1980).

How stable are life-change scores over time? In a 2-year study, the rank ordering of the amount of readjustment required by life events remained quite consistent for both male psychiatric patients and normal controls, with correlation coefficients ranging from .70 to .96. There was also stability in the absolute weights given, but only in the normal controls. These results suggest that for normal individuals, the perception of the impact of life changes is relatively stable, but the same cannot be said for psychiatric patients (Gerst, Grant, Yager, et al., 1978).

What about cross-cultural results? Holmes and Rahe (1967) suggested that the items in their scale were of a universal nature and should therefore be perceived similarly in different cultures. There is some support for this, with studies of Japanese (Masuda & Holmes, 1967), Mexican-Americans (Komaroff, Masuda, & Holmes, 1968), and Swedes (Rahe, Lundberg, Bennett, et al., 1971), with samples yielding fairly similar results.

P. Baird (1983) criticized the Holmes and Rahe scale as including too few categories of life events (i.e., lacking content validity), being biased against unmarried persons (more than 15% of the items pertain to spouse or marital circumstances), having many vague items, and having some items that could reflect the consequence of illness rather than the cause (for example, severe illness could result in difficulties on the job and not necessarily the other way around).

The publication of the Holmes & Rahe scales was followed by a huge amount of research, as well as substantial debate about the adequacy of this and alternative approaches (e.g., Moos & Swindle, 1990; Raphael, Cloitre, & Dohrenwend, 1991; Sandler & Guenther, 1985). As criticisms were made, newer versions of such checklists were developed; M. Zimmerman (1983), for example, cited 18 such life-event inventories.

Turner and Wheaton (1995) identified nine key issues regarding checklists to measure stressful life events:

1. How does one define and select life events to be included in a checklist? This includes the issue of content validity, the notion that different subsets of items may not be germane to specific samples – for example "death of a spouse" may be quite relevant to the elderly but of relative rare occurrence among college students.

2. Is change per se, whether positive or negative in nature, what matters? Or is it the undesirability of an event? For example, many scales include items such as "vacation" or "promotion" which for most people would be quite positive in nature. The evidence does suggest a pattern of positive relationships between eventual illness and the occurrence of negative events, whereas the pattern is weak and contradictory in relation to positive events (Zautra & Reich, 1983).

3. A number of items that appear on checklists are themselves indicators or symptoms of illness. There is thus a confounding of events with outcomes that might then result in spuriously high correlations; basically, this is a variation of criterion contamination discussed in Chapter 3. Specifically, Hudgens (1974) argued that 39 of the 43 life events could be viewed as symptoms or consequences of illness rather than precipitating events.

4. Internal reliability also presents a challenge here. The experience of one event, for example a vacation, is not intrinsically or theoretically related to the experience of another event, for example getting a divorce. Because the test items are independent we would not expect a high Cronbach's alpha. On the other hand, it can be argued that subsets of events are linked together as a function of a person's "ecological niche." Thus, an uneducated individual living in the inner city is more likely to experience unemployment, divorce, poor living conditions, and so on.

5. A related problem is that the potential occurrence of stressful events is related to one's role, "occupancy." As R. J. Turner and Wheaton (1995) point out, the person who is unemployed is not at risk of being fired or having conflicts with the boss.

6. The original instructions on the Holmes & Rahe scale asked the respondent to consider what they had experienced during the "past year." In some ways this was an arbitrary time period, but in part it was assumed that the effects of increased stress would show up in about a year's time. In fact, the assumption appears questionable, and the empirical evidence suggests higher correlations between events and physical illness when the time frame is longer than 1 year.

7. R. J. Turner and Wheaton (1995) note that events are salient for their stress-evoking potential for varying periods of time. Some events are very discrete and others are much more enduring. For example, a vacation is typically brief, whereas financial difficulties often can be more chronic. Some events are discrete, such as the death of a spouse, but the effect is much more chronic. Thus, an effective checklist should assess not just the occurrence of the event, but also its time duration.

8. Issue of weights. The two most common approaches to weighing of items is to use the average LCU weight assigned by a sample of raters, or to use the individual's subjective ratings of

such LCU. Neither approach however, results in a more significant result than a simple counting of the number of events endorsed. From a psychometric point of view this makes sense – all items are equal. But from a theoretical or logical point of view, the argument that the death of a spouse and a vacation produce equal amounts of stress is somewhat awkward.

9. Finally, there is the issue of reliability. Most of the concerns discussed in Chapter 3, such as the effect of memory on short test-retest periods, apply to these checklists. You recall that the usual procedure for test-retest reliability is to compare total scores obtained at two points in time. Total scores that are equal may, however, reflect different constellations of endorsed items, and so R. J. Turner and Wheaton (1995) argue that reliability should be considered at the individual item level rather than at the total score. Yet, recall that reliability reflects test length, and the reliability of one item can be quite low (see Kessler & Wethington, 1991, for a different approach to assessing reliability). Despite all these criticisms, the Social Readjustment Rating Scale continues to be one of the most widely cited instruments in the stress literature and is judged to be a useful tool (Scully, Tosi, & Banning, 2000).

Hassles and uplifts. Another approach is represented by the work of Lazarus and his colleagues (e.g., Lazarus, 1980), who focus on the relatively minor stresses and pleasures of everyday life – what they call the hassles and uplifts (Kanner, Coyne, Schaefer, et al., 1981). These investigators developed a hassles scale and an uplifts scale. You recall from Chapter 8 that the hassles scale consists of a list of 117 hassles such as, "troublesome neighbors," "too many responsibilities," and "the weather." These were simply generated by the research staff, using predetermined categories such as work, health, and family but with no indication of how the final items were selected. Respondents are asked to rate each item first on whether the hassle occurred during the past month, and second, using a 3-point scale on the severity of the hassle (somewhat, moderately, or extremely severe).

The uplifts scale consists of a list of 135 uplifts, ranging from "daydreaming" to "looking forward to retirement." Items on this list are also circled if they occurred in the past month, and also rated on intensity (i.e., how often: somewhat, moderately, or extremely often). Here also, no indication is given as to what psychometric considerations, if any, entered into the construction of the scale.

The two scales were administered once a month for 9 months to a sample of 100 adults. For the hassles scale, the average month-to-month reliability coefficient was .79 for the frequency score and .48 for intensity; for the uplifts scale the coefficients were .72 and .60, respectively. Thus, these subjects experienced roughly the same number of hassles and uplifts from month to month, but the amount of distress or pleasure varied considerably. From a psychometric point of view, these coefficients might be considered test-retest coefficients, and at least for intensity they fall short of what is required. Hassles and uplifts scores are also related to each other – with a mean r of .51 for frequency and .28 for intensity perhaps reflecting a response style (see Chapter 16) or a tendency for people who indicate they have many hassles also to indicate they have many uplifts. These investigators and others (e.g., Weinberger, Hiner, & Tierney, 1987) have reported that hassles are better predictors of health status than major life-change events.

Health Status

Since the 1970s, a number of measures have been developed to assess the physical and psychological health of populations. Although the concept of "health" is a fairly simple one, it is also complex to define particularly because health care has changed from a focus on increasing longevity to the "quality of life" that people have. Most of these instruments are designed to assess groups of individuals such as persons living in a particular community; thus, they are typically short, simple, and easily administered. Their focus is typically the absence of ill health rather than the presence of good health, that is, the focus is on how ill the person is rather than how well. Some of the measures are very general; they assess health status quite broadly. Others are very specific in that they focus on the presence or absence of a particular condition, such as cancer.

From a measurement point of view, there are a number of major problems and challenges to be met. One is that the same terms are often used differently by different investigators, and different terms are used as synonyms. For example, some investigators equate measures of quality of life with measures of health status, and some do not. Another issue is the sensitivity of these scales to clinical change. That is, a measure of health status should not only show the usual reliability and validity, but should also be sensitive to detect those differences that may occur as a function of treatment, such as chemotherapy with cancer; in fact, the evidence suggests that many brief measures of health status are sensitive to such changes (e.g., J. N. Katz, Larson, Phillips, et al., 1992). Another issue is length. Even a 15-minute questionnaire may be too long when one is assessing the elderly, the infirm, people undergoing surgical treatments, and so on.

These health-status measures have generally four purposes: (1) to examine the health of general populations; (2) to examine the effects of clinical interventions; (3) to examine changes in the health-care delivery system; and (4) to examine the effects of health-promotion activities (Bergner & Rothman, 1987). Among the better known health status measures are the Activities of Daily Living (Katz, Ford, Moskowitz, et al., 1963), the General Health Survey (A. L. Stewart, Hays, & Ware, 1988), and the Sickness Impact Profile (Bergner, Bobbitt, Carter, et al., 1981; Bergner, Bobbitt, Kressel, et al., 1976); for a review of the major scales see R. T. Anderson, Aaronson, and Wilkin (1993).

The Short-Form General Health Survey (SF-36).
Originally, this was developed as a 20-item form and later expanded to 36 items (A. L. Stewart, Hays, & Ware, 1988; Ware & Sherbourne, 1992). The SF-36 has two aims: to represent the multidimensional concept of health, and to measure the full range of health states. The SF-36 was actually one of several forms developed as part of a medical outcomes study, a large-scale study to monitor the results of medical care. The test manual and U.S. norms have recently been published (J. E. Ware, Snow, Kosinski, et al., 1993).

The SF-36 contains eight subscales: physical functioning (10 items); role limitations due to physical problems (4 items); bodily pain (2 items); mental health (5 items); role limitations due to emotional problems (4 items); social functioning (2 items); vitality (4 items); and general health perceptions (5 items).

The validity of the subscales has been largely determined using criterion groups of medical and psychiatric patients, as well as against the long-form version. In one study (McHorney, Ware, & Raczek, 1993), four groups of patients were compared: patients with minor chronic medical conditions; patients with serious chronic medical conditions; patients with psychiatric conditions; and patients with both serious medical and psychiatric conditions. The results indicated that the SF-36 functioned as hypothesized, in discriminating between degree of medical conditions (i.e., severely ill, moderately ill, and healthy groups), and between medical and psychiatric conditions.

It is too early to tell about the cross-cultural validity of this scale. There is a project underway designed to study the applicability of the SF-36 in 15 different countries (Aaronson, Acquadro, & Alonso, 1992).

Some studies have reported limitations of this scale. For example, there is a "floor" effect in severely ill samples, where 25% to 50% of the sample obtained the lowest possible score, and scores on some of the subscales do not correlate highly with the criterion when the criterion (e.g., degree of control over diabetes) is measured on something other than a categorical (e.g., yes or no) scale (R. T. Anderson, Aaronson, & Wilkin, 1993). Content validity can also be questioned. For example, the physical activity items cover only gross-motor activities, such as walking and kneeling, and not activities such as cleaning and shopping that may be influenced by the presence of illness.

The Sickness Impact Profile (SIP)

The SIP is designed to measure the changes in behavior that occur as a function of sickness, and focuses on behavior and the respondent's perception. The test is clearly geared for medical patients, particularly the elderly, who may be struggling with chronic diseases and other major illnesses.

The SIP covers a wide range of functioning in 12 areas by presenting a set of 136 yes or no statements. The areas include eating, sleep, alertness, body care, and mobility. Scores are obtained for each area, three summed indices, as well as an overall score. Lower scores indicate more desirable outcomes; with items weighted by the severity of health impact. The standard form of the SIP is administered by an interviewer and takes about 30 minutes; there is also a self-administered form and a mail version, although the interviewer form is more reliable (Pollard, Bobbitt, Bergner, et al., 1976). One of the somewhat unique aspects of the SIP is that test administrators need to undertake a self-training procedure, as outlined in the test's training manual.

Handscoring of SIP protocols is awkward at best. Consider for example the item, "I sit during much of the day." If endorsed, this item is worth 4.9 points; the score for each area is calculated by adding the scale values for each item endorsed within that category and dividing by the maximum possible "dysfunction" score for that category. This maximum value is provided; for the item above, for example, which falls in the "Sleep and Rest" category, the maximal value is 49.9. The resulting score is then multiplied by 100 to obtain the category score. Fortunately, computer scoring is available.

Although there are 12 areas or subscales, the SIP actually measures three dimensions: psychosocial functioning, assessed by the sum of 4 scales; physical functioning, assessed by the sum of 3 scales, and independent aspects, assessed by the sum of 5 scales.

The SIP has been used in many studies, with a wide variety of medical and psychiatric patients, and the results have supported its reliability and validity. For example, scores on the SIP psychosocial component correlate moderately (rs of .40 to .60) with more traditional measures of anxiety and of depression. It appears that the SIP may be more sensitive to declines in health-related quality of life than in improvements. The SIP is available in several languages including French, German, and Norwegian, and studies in different countries have yielded basically similar findings.

The original test manual has a thorough discussion of how to administer the test, but the discussion of reliability and validity consists simply of enumerating various approaches that have been taken, without giving specific results. The interested user of this test then, must dig through the literature to obtain any relevant data.

The McGill Pain Questionnaire (McGill PQ)

The McGill PQ, published by Melzack, a psychologist at McGill University, was designed to provide a quantitative profile of clinical pain. Originally, it was intended as a way to evaluate the effectiveness of different pain therapies, but it is often used both clinically and in research applications as a diagnostic tool (Melzack, 1975). The McGill PQ stems from a theoretical basis that postulates three major psychological dimensions to pain: a sensory-discriminative dimension (for example, how long the pain lasts), a motivational-affective dimension (for example, the fear associated with pain), and a cognitive-evaluative dimension (for example, how intense the pain is).

Melzack realized that the experience of pain is a highly personal experience, influenced by individual differences, perceptions, and cultural aspects, and developed a "gate control" theory of pain to explain how the "gating" or modulation of pain is possible (Melzack & Wall, 1965). This theory is at the basis of the McGill PQ, although use of this test does not necessarily require acceptance of the theory.

The first step in the development of the McGill PQ was to establish an item pool, a set of 102 descriptive words related to pain, obtained from the literature, patients' pain descriptions, and other questionnaires. These words were sorted into the three categories, and then further sorted within each category into subgroups. For example, the word "throbbing" was categorized in the temporal category, which is part of the sensory dimension; similarly, the word "shooting" is part of the spatial category and also part of the sensory dimension (Melzack & Torgerson, 1971). Patients and physicians were then asked to rate each item as to intensity using a 5-point numerical scale from least to worst. In addition to the pain descriptor words, there are other components on the McGill PQ (e.g., questions about the patient's diagnosis, an anatomical drawing on which to indicate the location of pain), but these are not scored. On the actual test protocol, the items are presented in 20 groupings of 2 to 6 items each, listed in order of intensity. For scoring purposes, the 20 groupings are divided into

4 categories: sensory, affective, evaluative, and miscellaneous.

The McGill PQ takes 5 to 15 minutes to complete. Originally, it was intended to be used as an interview so unfamiliar words could be explained, but it is typically self-administered. The instructions indicate that the patient is to describe his or her present pain, and only one word in each grouping is to be circled. In research use and in clinical applications the instructions may vary – the patient may be asked to describe their current pain, their average pain, their most intense pain, and so on.

Scoring. In addition to the three dimensions, there is a fourth "miscellaneous" category. Pain-rating scores can be obtained for each of the four areas, as well as for the total. There are also four indices that can be obtained: (1) Pain Rating Index, based upon the mean scale values of the words endorsed; (2) Pain Rating Index of ranks, based upon the ranks of the words endorsed; (3) Total number of words checked; and (4) Present Pain Intensity, based on the rating scale of 0 (for no pain) to 5 (for excruciating pain). As might be expected, the first two indices correlate substantially (in excess of .90) and thus only the Pain Rating Index of ranks is used because it is simpler to compute. Number of words chosen also correlates quite high with the two pain ratings ($r = .89$ and above), while the ratings of present pain intensity correlate less substantially with the other three indices. The initial scoring system was weak, and suggestions have been made to improve it (Kremer, Atkinson, & Ignelzi, 1982; Melzack, 1984).

Reliability. Test-retest reliability is difficult to measure because low reliability may in effect mirror the test's sensitivity – pain in its various sources and manifestations does change over time. The evidence in fact seems to suggest that the scale is sensitive to changes in pain over time (e.g., C. Graham, Bond, Gerkovich, et al., 1980).

Factor analysis. Studies of the factor structure of the McGill PQ have typically provided support for a sensory dimension, an affective-evaluative dimension, and a sensory-affective dimension, with different studies finding from two to seven factors (Prieto & Geisinger, 1983). In general there appears to be support for the three dimensions postulated by Melzack, though the dimensions are substantially intercorrelated (Turk, Rudy, & Salovey, 1985).

Validity. There are various lines of evidence that support the validity of the McGill PQ. One such line is that the responses of patients with different pain syndromes, such as menstrual pain vs. toothache, result in different word constellations (Dubuisson & Melzack, 1976). Another line are studies that show the sensitivity of the McGill PQ following cognitive or behavioral interventions to reduce pain (e.g., Rybstein-Blinchik, 1979).

The McGill PQ has been translated into numerous languages, and studies done in such countries as Germany, The Netherlands, and Kuwait generally support the cross-cultural usefulness of this measure (Naughton & Wiklund, 1993).

Criticisms. Three disadvantages of the McGill PQ are the time required to administer and score (in excess of 30 minutes for what seems like a simple questionnaire), the need for trained personnel to administer it because it is confusing to many patients, and the fact that a number of words are unfamiliar to many patients (e.g., lancinating and rasping).

Modifications. Several modifications of the McGill PQ have been proposed, such as a card sort method (Reading & Newton, 1978) or rating the words through other methods than rating scales (e.g., Gracely, McGrath, & Dubner, 1978; Tursky, 1976). There is also a short form of the McGill PQ available in which respondents are asked to pick the one word from each category that is most applicable (Melzack, 1987).

The Jenkins Activity Survey (JAS)

The JAS was constructed to measure Type A behavior. Type A behavior, the coronary-prone behavior pattern, is an overt behavioral syndrome or style of living characterized by extreme competitiveness, striving for achievement, aggressiveness, impatience, restlessness, and feelings of being challenged by responsibility and under the pressure of time. In addition to providing a Type A score, the JAS also provides separate factor scores for three components of Type A behavior: a speed and impatience factor, a job-involvement factor, and a hard-driving and competitive factor.

The JAS is based on the work of M. Friedman and R. Rosenman, two cardiologists who conducted a series of studies on the role of behavior and the central nervous system in the development of coronary disease. They defined the coronary-prone behavior pattern Type A and focused on the excesses of aggression, hurry, and competitiveness, all of which are manifestations of a struggle to overcome environmental barriers. The pattern is neither a personality trait nor a standard reaction to a challenging situation, but rather the reaction of a characterologically predisposed person to a situation that challenges him or her.

Initially, Type A behavior was assessed through a structured interview, which although apparently valid, required rather rigorous training (Friedman & Rosenman, 1959; C. D. Jenkins, Rosenman, & Friedman, 1967). Other measures were also developed, including a semantic-differential approach, experimental-performance tests, and voice analysis. The JAS was developed in an effort to provide a more standard psychometric procedure accessible to individual practitioners and researchers.

Development. The first experimental form was developed in 1964 and drew heavily from the Rosenman Structured Interview. This form (64 multiple-choice questions) was administered to 120 male employees of a large corporation and the results compared with the Structured Interview. Forty questions statistically discriminated Type A from Type B (i.e., not A) individuals. These 40 questions plus 21 new ones were then published as the first edition of the JAS in 1965. There followed a series of sophisticated studies that essentially computed weights for each item based on that item's ability to discriminate Type As from Type Bs and placed these items into discriminant function equations. The samples used were substantial (a total of almost 3,000) and the procedures cross-validated more than once. The results indicated that a 19-item discriminant

equation best combined efficiency of prediction with brevity.

A second edition of 57 items was published in 1966. Again a series of analyses were undertaken with a resulting 26-item discriminant equation. At this point, a series of factor analyses were undertaken, and the three factors named above were identified. A third revision came out in 1969, and discriminant equations were developed using each of the factor scores. In 1972, a fourth revision came out, with items revised in language so that JAS items could be appropriate for housewives, medical students, and other groups, rather than simply for the employed, middle-class, middle-aged men of prior studies. In 1979, a fifth edition came out (Form C) that consists of 52 items.

Here are two items to illustrate the JAS:

1. Do you ever have trouble finding time to get your hair cut or styled?
(a) never
(b) occasionally
(c) almost always
(if you select (a), you receive 3 points on the Speed and Impatience factor, (b) = 16 points, and (c) = 40 points)

2. Is your everyday life filled mostly by
(a) problems needing a solution?
(b) challenges needing to be met?
(c) a rather predictable routine of events?
(d) not enough things to keep me interested or busy?
(a) = 11 points; (b) = 10; (c) = 1; (d) = 12 points for Type A scale. For Job Involvement, however, (a) = 24 points, (b) = 26; (c) = 2, (d) = 9)

The manual clearly indicates that JAS scores should not be used alone to predict individual risk of coronary heart disease. The Type A pattern is one of several important risk factors, but none of these risk factors is sufficiently sensitive to permit individual prediction. In general, however, Type A people have a higher probability of developing coronary heart disease.

The JAS was standardized on the male participants of a longitudinal study on cardiovascular diseases, who held middle-to-upper level occupations in 10 large California corporations; they ranged in age from 44 to 64 years. The JAS is primarily applicable to male, employed subjects, although initial evidence suggests it is equally applicable to employed women. A number of questions refer to salaried employment, and thus the JAS may not be applicable to students, retired persons, or self-employed individuals. It is *not* applicable to adolescents and children.

The JAS requires an eighth-grade reading level, and 15 to 20 minutes to complete. Hand scoring is possible, but it is a time consuming task (about 25 minutes per protocol), subject to clerical errors. Computer scoring is available and preferable. Raw scores are converted to standard scores with a mean of 0 and a SD of 10. The manual presents a table of means and SDs for 35 different samples, most with sizable Ns; there is also a table of percentile equivalents, and a table of correlations with CPI scales.

Reliability. Reliability was assessed by internal-consistency methods. The resulting coefficients range from .73 to .85. Test-retest correlations with intervals of 1 to 4 years fall mostly between .60 and .70. However, many of the coefficients are based on successive modifications of the JAS and thus reflect both change over time and differences between forms.

Validity. There are several lines of evidence that support the construct validity of the JAS. First, there is high agreement between the JAS and a structured interview (e.g., Jenkins & Zyzanski, 1980). Second, several studies have found a significant relation between Type A behavior and coronary heart disease; these studies have typically compared patients with coronary disease with a control group, in a retrospective design (e.g., Jenkins, Rosenman, & Zyzanski, 1974). Third, the manual cites one prospective study, which is the normative study. Analysis of JAS scores of 2,750 healthy men showed the Type A scale to distinguish the 120 future clinical cases of coronary heart disease. In another analysis, three risk factors discriminated between the 220 men surviving a single coronary event and the 67 having recurring events: the Type A score, number of daily cigarettes, and serum cholesterol level. Finally, the manual cites a study where male patients suffering from a variety of cardiovascular disorders and undergoing coronary angiography completed the JAS on admission to the hospital. Fifty-five men, with two or more main coronary

arteries obstructed 50% or more, scored significantly higher on all four JAS scales than the other 36 men with lesser atherosclerosis.

The JAS has been translated into numerous languages and has been the focus of a voluminous body of literature (see reviews by Glass, 1977, and by Goldband, Katkin, & Morell, 1979).

FORENSIC PSYCHOLOGY

In the area of forensic psychology, two of the major applications of psychological testing involve *competence to stand trial* (i.e., assessing the defendant's ability to understand and participate in legal proceedings), and *criminal responsibility* or insanity (i.e., the defendant's mental status at the time of the crime). A number of surveys of forensic psychologists and psychiatrists indicate that most practitioners perceive psychological testing to be highly essential to these forensic procedures, and that tests such as the MMPI and the WAIS are used by the vast majority, with other tests such as the Rorschach and the Halstead-Reitan used with lesser frequency (Borum & Grisso, 1995; Grisso, 1986; Lees-Haley, 1992).

Heilbrun (1992) suggested criteria for selecting, using, and interpreting psychological tests in a forensic setting. These included the availability of the test and reviews of its properties (e.g., listed in the *Mental Measurements Yearbook*); exclusion of a test with a reliability coefficient less than .80; relevancy of the test to the forensic issue (supported with published, empirical data); likelihood of replicating an ideal and standardized testing environment, as close to the conditions under which the test was normed; appropriateness of the test to the individual and situation; consideration of clinical data in lieu of or in conjunction with actuarial data; and assessment of the individual's response style and its impact on testing results.

Competency to stand trial. In a 1960 legal case (Dusky v. United States [1960]), the legal standard for competency to stand trial was established. Such a standard holds that the defendant must have sufficient present ability to consult with his or her lawyer and have a rational as well as factual understanding of the legal proceedings. Mental-health professionals are often asked to undertake such evaluations, and they often use either traditional instruments such as the MMPI or instruments developed specifically to make a determination of competency. Two such instruments are the Competency Screening Test and the Georgia Court Competency Test (see Nicholson, Briggs, & Robertson, 1988, who include the items for both scales in their article). Both of these measures show excellent interscorer agreement greater than .90, and substantial agreement with forensic staff decisions regarding competency to stand trial.

The Competency Screening Test consists of 22 sentence-completion stems, such as "If I am found guilty, I . . ." The stems describe hypothetical legal situations for which the respondent must provide appropriate responses. Thus, this is not a projective device, in that there isn't the freedom of responding found in projective sentence-completion tests. Responses are scored from 0 to 2 to reflect competency. The test can be administered orally but is intended as a written test.

The Georgia Court Competency Test (GCCT) consists of 17 questions that cover four areas: (1) understanding of court procedures, (2) knowledge of the charge, (3) knowledge of possible penalties, and (4) ability to communicate rationally with an attorney. A representative item is, "What does the jury do?" Items are scored according to different weights and can add up to 50 points. Total scores are multiplied by 2. Factor analysis initially indicated two principal factors labeled as "legal knowledge" and "defendant's style of responding," but further factor analyses did not replicate these results (see Rogers, Ustad, Sewell, et al., 1996).

The GCCT revised version (the GCCT-Mississippi State Hospital Revision) contains 21 items and is similar in format and administration to its predecessor. The GCCT-MSH has been criticized regarding its limited utility with diverse populations (Mumley, Tillbrook, & Grisso, 2003) and the lack of focus on a defendant's decision-making abilities (Zapf & Viljoen, 2003).

Another competency instrument, the MacArthur Competence Assessment Tool Criminal Adjudication (MacCAT-CA), requires approximately 30 minutes to administer its 22 items. The MacCAT-CA uses a vignette to assess an individual's reasoning abilities and knowledge of legal proceedings, and questions to assess a defendant's appreciation of their specific situation.

Mental illness. A substantial number of individuals who are in jail awaiting trial show evidence of mental illness. Such prevalence rates range from about 5% to 12% for severe mental illness and from 16% to 67% for any mental illness (Teplin, 1991). Hart, Roesch, Corrado, et al. (1993) point out that mentally ill inmates present two major concerns to corrections administrators: (1) jails have a legal responsibility to provide some health care, including mental-health care, to inmates or face civil suits; (2) such inmates typically require different institutional procedures and routines, such as segregation from other inmates and more intense supervision. There is therefore a need for the identification of such individuals through rapid and accurate procedures; unfortunately, the very setting and its limitations result at best in a quick and routine screening.

Teplin and Swartz (1989) developed a Referral Decision Scale (RDS) composed of 18 questions, later collapsed into 15 items. Most of the questions ask whether the respondent had experienced specific symptoms such as feeling poisoned or had loss of appetite. These symptoms, taken from a diagnostic interview, were predictive of three conditions: schizophrenia, bipolar disorder (mania), and major depressive disorder. The RDS was intended for use by correctional officers rather than by psychologists or other mental-health professionals. Scoring is simple: the number of items endorsed in each of the three symptom areas, plus a total score.

The RDS was administered to a sample of 790 pretrial defendants in the Vancouver, Canada area. Of these, 40.7% of defendants were found to exhibit symptoms of mental disorder. The results of this study indicated excellent interjudge reliability and acceptable validity as a screening measure. However, a substantial number of false positive errors were made, as compared to other assessments.

The polygraph. In the 1920s, the first forerunner of the modern polygraph was constructed – a machine that made continuous recordings of blood pressure, pulse rate, and respiration. The assumption was that these physiological correlates of emotions could be used as an index of lying.

Some authors consider the polygraph a psychological test, very much like all the other instruments we have discussed, and thus needing to meet reliability and validity standards. Unfortunately the reliability of the polygraph is usually reported as total percentage of agreement between two or more raters, or between test and retest results. Although these rates are typically in the 80% to 90% range, these results are open to the same criticism discussed earlier regarding the Rorschach (Kleinmuntz & Szucko, 1984). The validity of polygraph tests is a highly contested issue, perhaps even more acrimonious than the issue of validity of the Rorschach.

Voir dire. Voir dire is the process of jury selection, particularly the elimination of potential jurors whom the attorneys feel may be biased against the defendant or may not be open minded to what is to be presented in the courtroom. Studies of jury selection attempt to identify those variables that can reliably predict juror verdicts. This is not only an important practical issue of interest to lawyers who may wish to maximize the possibility of obtaining a specific verdict, but is also an important theoretical issue because understanding how people arrive at a verdict may be applicable to the understanding of how individuals arrive at solutions in general, and how such aspects as personality interface with cognitive abilities. A wide variety of procedures are used in this process. In terms of psychological testing, there are three major categories: (1) scales that have been developed to measure attitudes and/or personality; (2) scales developed specifically for the voir dire process; and (3) biodata questionnaires (Saks, 1976).

Under category (1) measures of authoritarianism have proven to be popular, with many studies showing that potential jurors high on authoritarianism are more likely to convict or punish the defendant (e.g., McAbee & Cafferty, 1982). Under category (2) a number of instruments have been developed, but many of these also seem to focus on authoritarianism (e.g., Kassin & Wrightsman, 1983). Under category (3) studies that use biodata information generally show significant correlations between biographical variables such as age and judicial outcome, but these correlations tend to be modest at best.

The authoritarian personality is a constellation of characteristics that includes a desire to be part of an orderly, powerful society, with well-defined rules and authoritative leadership, a preference for more conventional norms, hostility toward out-group members, and a belief in the rightness of power and control. It has been hypothesized that individuals high on authoritarianism, if selected to be jurors on a trial, would be likely to convict the defendant if the defendant is perceived to reject legitimate authority. There are a number of personality scales that have been developed to measure authoritarianism, with the California F (fascism) scale being quite popular, especially in the 1950s and 1960s. Other researchers have developed measures of legal authoritarianism, with the item content focusing on beliefs about the legal system. For example, the Legal Attitudes Questionnaire (LAQ; V. R. Boehm, 1968) contains 30 items arranged in triads, in which one item is authoritarian, one is antiauthoritarian, and one is equalitarian. Consider as an example the following triad:

(a) If a person is obviously guilty, they should be given a speedy trial.

(b) Most people who are arrested are innocent.

(c) Simply because a person does not testify on their behalf, should not be taken as evidence of their guilt.

Authoritarian items are those that are essentially punitive in nature or accept the role of legal authority without question. Antiauthoritarian items place the blame for crime on the fabric of society and reject the actions of legal authority, while equalitarian items endorse nonextreme positions or reflect the possibility that more than one answer is possible.

The subject is asked to indicate for each triad, which item he or she agrees with the most, and which the least. These responses are recoded as ranks, with the positive item given a rank of 3, the unselected item a rank of 2, and the negatively marked item a rank of 1. The ranks assigned to the 10 authoritarian items are summed (or averaged) to obtain the authoritarian subscale score. The antiauthoritarian and the equalitarian subscale scores are computed in the same manner. The author hypothesized that scores on the authoritarian scale would be positively correlated with the tendency to convict, scores on the antiauthoritarian scale would be negatively correlated, and scores on the equalitarian scale not correlated. Indeed this was the case in a sample of 151 college students who were presented with vignettes of a murder case. A handful of studies that have used this questionnaire with different types of subjects and different experimental designs have generally found support for the validity of the authoritarian subscale, mixed support for the antiauthoritarian scale, and absent or ambiguous results for the equalitarian scale (Kravitz, Cutler, & Brock, 1993).

Note a couple of "peculiar" aspects about this questionnaire. First, this is a forced-choice format where the subject is "forced" to make a particular type of response. Second, the unselected items are scored 2 points. Third, because of the way the items are scored, the scales are not independent; if a person endorses the authoritarian items, for example, the scores on the other two subscales must perforce be lower.

Kravitz, Cutler, and Brock (1993) administered both the LAQ, a revised version of the LAQ requiring a Likert-type response, and several other scales to a sample of undergraduate psychology students. One of their first findings was that the internal reliability (coefficient alpha) for the LAQ subscales and the revised version was "abysmal," ranging from .19 to .71, with six of the seven coefficients below .70. Despite such low reliability, the construct and concurrent validity seemed satisfactory. Authoritarian scores, for example, correlated with other measures of authoritarianism and with attitudes toward the death penalty, as well as with attending religious services and believing in a "just world" (i.e., people deserve what happens to them). On the basis of these results, Kravitz, Cutler, and Brock (1993) dropped the items with low item-total correlations and obtained a 23-item scale, with an internal reliability of .71. Several factor analyses of this 23-item form failed to indicate factors that were reliable and clearly interpretable. When compared to the other measures collected in the study, the authors concluded that the 23-item form had better concurrent validity but poorer discriminant validity. The 23-item version was then administered to a sample of adults. Internal consistency was now .83, but again the validity results were mixed, supportive of the authoritarian dimension, but not the other two. For another example of how a juror scale was constructed, in this case, to measure the pretrial biases a juror may have, see Kassin and Wrightsman (1983).

Narby, Cutler, and Moran (1993) conducted a metaanalysis of studies that looked at authoritarianism and the juror's perception of defendant culpability. They did find a relationship, although the estimated average r was .16, a modest effect at best. The effect was a bit stronger when legal authoritarianism was considered vs. personality measures of authoritarianism.

LEGAL STANDARDS

What are the legal standards applicable to psychological testing? There are two such sets. One is the "Federal Rules of Evidence (or FRE) that require mental-health professionals to offer evidence (e.g. results of psychological testing) that "is reasonably relied upon by such professionals."

A second set is known as the Daubert standard that evidence presented by experts must be reliable (testable, subject to peer review, with known rate of error, and/or generally accepted within the field) and relevant (applicable to the specific case and helpful to the fact finders in resolving the legal question).

LEGAL CASES

A number of legal acts and court cases have had substantial impact on the practice of psychological testing. We have discussed some of these in the context of testing children (Chapter 9) and testing in occupational settings (Chapter 14). Here we briefly mention a few of the better known ones.

Title VII of the Civil Rights Act of 1964

This act, commonly known as the Equal Employment Opportunity Act, is probably the best known piece of civil-rights legislation. This act created the Equal Employment Opportunity Commission, which eventually published guidelines concerning standards to be met in the construction and use of employment tests. Title

VII of this act makes discrimination against any individual on the basis of race, color, religion, sex, or national origin illegal. If testing is used as a condition for employment, then testing cannot discriminate. In essence, this act also dictates that tests should be prepared by experts and be validated according to the standards indicated in the Uniform Guidelines on Employee Selection Procedures.

It should be noted here that in-house tests (such as the integrity tests we discussed in Chapter 14) are usually more difficult to validate than professionally researched tests (such as the MMPI and the WAIS), and hence their use might be considered discriminatory. This act led to a number of court cases of which the following are the most relevant:

Myart v. Motorola (1966). This was one of the first cases to focus on employment testing discrimination. Mr. Myart was a black applicant for a job at a Motorola factory; he alleged that the qualifying test he was asked to take was discriminatory in that it required familiarity with white, middle-class culture. The Illinois Fair Employment Practices Commission agreed that the test was discriminatory, but the Illinois Supreme Court overturned the examiner's ruling.

Griggs v. Duke Power Company (1971). The hiring requirements of Duke Power Company included satisfactory scores on the Wonderlic Personnel Test and a mechanical aptitude test; these were challenged by blacks as arbitrary and not job-related. The trial court ruled that the tests did not violate Title VII, but the U.S. Supreme Court disagreed, and in fact criticized employment testing in general. The court ruled that broad, general testing devices could not be used, but that measures of the knowledge or skills required by a specific job could be used.

Albemarle Paper Company v. Moody (1975). In this case, the company also required satisfactory scores on two tests, but had hired a psychologist to conduct a validity study of the tests on their current employees. The Supreme Court concluded, however, that having a psychologist claim validity was not sufficient.

Connecticut v. Teal (1982). An employer required employees to pass a written test to qualify for promotion. The written test had not been validated, and the proportion of blacks to whites who passed the test was 68%. However, passing the test did not guarantee promotion, and a greater percentage of blacks than whites was promoted. The U.S. Supreme Court ruled, however, that the test still had to be validated and might be discriminatory.

Watson v. Fort Worth Bank and Trust (1988). Ms. Watson, a black woman, sued because she was denied a promotion based on work evaluations by white supervisors. Although both the district court and the appeals court dismissed the case, the U.S. Supreme Court accepted Watson's evidence that blacks received lower average performance ratings and fewer promotions than did whites, and concluded that subjective employment practices must meet the same objective standards as tests.

Daubert v. Merrell Dow Pharmaceuticals (1993). This case, along with existing Federal Rules of Evidence, provided the Court with guidelines to assess the appropriateness, relevancy, and admissibility of scientific expert testimony (e.g., psychological testing). Specifically, it was recognized that the admissibility of expert testimony should be judged on its reliability (e.g., testability, subjection to peer review and publication, with a known error rate, and/or general acceptance within the field) and relevancy to the legal issue (e.g., helpful to the trier-of-fact). A 1999 case (Kumho Tire Company v. Carmichael [1999]) noted that the "Daubert criteria" applies to the testimony of all experts, not just "scientists," and that the Court may consider one or more of these factors in their determination of admissibility.

Tests in Educational Settings

A number of court cases have had an impact on the use of tests in educational settings. The following are some of the better known examples:

DeFunis v. Odegaard (1971). Mr. DeFunis applied for admission to the University of Washington Law School, but was not admitted. He had an undergraduate GPA of 3.71, had been elected to Phi Beta Kappa, and had taken the Law School Admission Test three times with scores of 512,

566, and 668. He had also applied and had been admitted to two other law schools. He sued the University of Washington Law School (Odegaard was the President) on the grounds that other persons with lesser qualifications had been admitted. The Superior Court of the State of Washington held that the admission procedure was racially discriminatory and ordered that DeFunis be admitted to the law school. The Washington Supreme Court, however, reversed the judgment of the Superior Court. By the time that several legal maneuvers had been played, DeFunis was completing his degree and the case was declared "moot"; no decision was made.

Breland and Ironson (1976) present an interesting discussion of this case, considering the actual admission process used by the law school vs. what psychometric models would consider fair. It is interesting to note that the admission procedure used admitted 53% of selected ethnic groups, but only 15% of whites.

Debra P. v. Turlington (1981). Minimal competency legislation refers to individual state laws that typically result in a formal testing program designed to assess the minimum competencies that youngsters must have before being issued a high-school diploma or other educational endorsements. In 1976, the State of Florida passed the Educational Accountability Act designed, in part, to ensure that the state's educational system in fact educated students, at the very least, to meet certain minimum competencies. What better way to assess this than through minimum competency testing? The result was a number of pro and con opinions (e.g., B. Lerner, 1981; Popham 1981), and a number of legal challenges including the court case of Debra P. The minimum competency test was challenged on grounds of racial bias (20% of black students failed the exam vs. only 2% of white students) and questionable "instructional validity" (i.e., was the test a fair representation of what was taught in the classroom?). This is not a closed issue, with some states having minimum competency tests and others facing legal challenges on the issue.

Truth-in-testing legislation. These laws give examinees the right to know more about examinations, particularly tests such as the SAT and the GRE. They cover issues as privacy, information about the test's development, how test scores are to be used, and the right to examine individual test items.

Other Legislative Actions

In addition to the Civil Rights Act of 1964, there have been a number of major legislative actions that have impacted psychological testing. The major ones are:

Public Law 94–142 (1975). In 1975, Congress passed the Education for All Handicapped Children Act, known as Public Law 94–142, and recently as the Individuals with Disabilities Education Act. This law is intended to ensure a free and appropriate public education, and all related educational services, to children with disabilities. Thus the law mandated that children with possible mental or physical handicaps are to be identified through the use of screening instruments, evaluated, and a specific educational plan designed to meet the child's special educational needs. This law has had a tremendous impact on assessment, and more specifically, on psychological testing, because the law mandates, in part, that a child be assessed with "valid tests" that are culturally and racially appropriate. In 1990, a new amendment to this act replaced the term "handicapped" with the term "disability."

The Rehabilitation Act of 1973. This act protects qualified disabled individuals against discrimination in employment. Note first the term "qualified" – that is, the person must be capable of performing the essential functions of the job. Second, note that disability is a fairly broad term that includes conditions such as alcoholism and drug addiction (unless current drug use interferes with the job performance), muscular dystrophy, epilepsy, cancer, tuberculosis, AIDS, and many more. This act not only protects but also requires affirmative action to employ qualified disabled individuals. One of the practical aspects of this act with regard to testing, is that an applicant who contends that because of their disability they cannot demonstrate the required skills on a test, but argues that they can perform the job, must be given alternate means for demonstrating job suitability.

The Americans with Disabilities Act of 1990. This act prohibits all employers from discriminating against disabled employees or job candidates; however, the federal government, Indian tribes, tax-exempt private membership clubs, and religious organizations, are exempt. Here too disabled is a rather broad category, although some specific conditions such as bisexuals, compulsive gamblers, and kleptomaniacs are excluded. This act requires that testing be conducted in a place and manner accessible to persons with disabilities – for example, test using Braille with visually impaired. One consequence is that tests used in employment selection must measure the skills essential to a particular job, rather than intelligence in general, and not reflect a person's disability. Thus an item on a personality test such as, "As a child I was sickly" would be in violation if that test were used for employment purposes.

The Civil Rights Act of 1991. This act was designed to facilitate worker lawsuits based on job discrimination. In terms of testing, the act prohibits the use of race norming and places employers in a quandary. On the one hand, employers can hire whomever they choose; if they use a test they can hire the most qualified (i.e., highest scoring) individuals. But given the differences in test scores between whites and minority members, such a procedure would have an adverse impact.

These various acts also resulted in a number of legal challenges and counter challenges. Some illustrative examples are:

Gaines v. Monsanto (1983). A relatively new form of liability sustained by court decisions happens when an employer fails to exercise "reasonable care" in hiring an employee who subsequently commits a crime or does harm to others. In this case, a mailroom clerk who had a prior record of rape and conviction, followed a secretary home and murdered her. The parents of the victim sued Monsanto for negligent hiring. Quite clearly, the employer needs to take preventive measures that might include additional testing, yet such testing may well be challenged as discriminatory.

Target Stores 1989. A class action suit was filed, also in California, against Target Stores who used the CPI and the MMPI to screen prospective security guards. The plaintiffs argued that the questions, such as "I am fascinated by fire," were not only bizarre but violated sexual, religious, and racial discrimination laws. The store settled without admitting legal wrongdoing.

Bilingual children. At least two court cases have focused on the misdiagnosis of bilingual children: Diana v. State Board of Education of California (1970) and Guadalupe v. Tempe Elementary District (1972). In both suits the argument was that improper assessment with IQ tests led to an over representation of minority children in classes for the educable mentally retarded. The Diana case involved nine Spanish-speaking children who were placed in classrooms for the educable mentally retarded on the basis of their performance on tests of intelligence that were administered in English. These children had in fact been misdiagnosed. In the Diana case, the court directed that minority children be tested in both native language and English and that cognitive assessment be carried out primarily with nonverbal tests. In Guadalupe, the court again directed that testing be carried out using the child's native language, but also that IQ could not be used as the only basis for making placement decisions about a minority child; adaptive behavior and/or other areas needed also to be assessed.

Larry P. v. Riles (1972). Larry P. was a black child "erroneously" classified as mentally retarded, while Wilson Riles was the Superintendent of Public Instruction in California. Because of this trial, intelligence tests were found to be biased against African American children, and the San Francisco public schools were prohibited from using such tests. This trial provided considerable impetus for the study of test bias.

In the Larry P. v. Riles (1972, 1974, 1979) case, the issue was again over-representation of minority children in classes for the educable mentally handicapped, but the focus was on black children. Much of the case revolved around the issue of whether the WISC-R was biased when used with black children, and the judge did find the test biased. In California then, IQ testing of all black children was prohibited, regardless of what program the child was being considered for (e.g., gifted), and whether or not the parents gave permission. Interestingly enough, in a 1980 case just the opposite conclusion was reached. In Parents in Action on Special Education (PASE) v. Hannon, in the Chicago public school system, the WISC-R and the Stanford Binet were found not to be biased against black children.

Sharif v. New York State Education Department (1989). The N.Y. State Education Department used SAT scores to award state-funded scholarships. The American Civil Liberties Union brought suit charging sex discrimination because the SAT "underpredicts the academic ability of women." The judge agreed and, as a result, scholarships were awarded on the basis of both SAT scores and high-school GPA.

SUMMARY

We have taken a brief look at testing in the context of clinical and forensic settings. The examples chosen were illustrative rather than comprehensive. We devoted a substantial amount to projective techniques, although these, as a group, seem to be less popular than they were years ago. However, they are, if nothing else, of historical importance and do illustrate a number of issues and challenges. Testing in the health psychology area is growing and substantial headway is being made in applying psychological principles and techniques to the maintenance of good health and the understanding of how the human "body and psyche" actually function in unison. Testing is also increasing in forensic settings, while at the same time being regulated and challenged by a number of court decisions.

SUGGESTED READINGS

Aronow, E., Reznikoff, M., & Moreland, K. L. (1995). The Rorschach: Projective technique or psychometric test? *Journal of Personality Assessment, 64*, 213–228.

An excellent review of the idiographic-nomothetic and the perceptual-content approaches as they pertain to the Rorschach. The authors argue that the value of the Rorschach is in its being a projective technique rather than a psychometric test.

Blankstein, K. R., Flett, G. L., & Koledin, S. (1991). The Brief College Students' Hassles Scale: Development, validation, and relation with pessimism. *Journal of College Student Development, 32*, 258–264.

Presents a hassles scale developed specifically for college students. High scores on this scale are associated with a pessimistic outlook and more persistent symptoms of poor psychological adjustment.

Foster, G. D., & Wadden, T. A. (1997). Body image in obese women before, during, and after weight loss treatment. *Health Psychology, 16*, 226–229.

A major variable in the field of eating disorders is that of body image. Over the years, many scales have been developed to assess this dimension, from Rorschach responses to self-report inventories, from standardized body silhouettes to experimental laboratory procedures. This is a fairly representative study that uses two scales from a multidimensional questionnaire.

Kleinmuntz, B., & Szucko, J. J. (1984). Lie detection in ancient and modern times. *American Psychologist, 39*, 766–776.

The authors assume that the polygraph is basically a psychological test, although of questionable psychometric merit. They discuss the history of this technique, as well as a number of psychometric issues.

Lambert, N. M. (1981). Psychological evidence in Larry P. v. Wilson Riles. *American Psychologist, 36*, 937–952.

This article presents a brief history of this landmark case, and argues convincingly that the court's decisions were erroneous.

DISCUSSION QUESTIONS

1. Why use batteries like the Halstead-Reitan when brain functioning can now be assessed through a number of medical procedures?

2. You have been admitted to graduate school to pursue a doctorate in clinical psychology. You have the option to take a course on projective techniques. Would you and why (or why not)?

3. You are testing an incarcerated 26-year-old male who has a history of sexual and physical aggression toward women. Which one projective technique would you choose and why?

4. If someone asked, "Is the Rorschach valid" how would you answer?

5. Scales that measure authoritarianism appear to be useful to screen potential jurors in the "voir dire" process. What other scaled variables might be relevant?

16 The Issue of Faking

AIM In this chapter we begin by asking, "What can interfere with the validity of a particular test score? If Rebecca scores at the 95th percentile on a test of vocabulary, can we really conclude that she does possess a high level of vocabulary?" While there are many issues that can affect our conclusion, in this chapter we focus mainly on just one – faking. We take a brief look at two additional issues – test anxiety and testwiseness. We use a variety of tests, such as the MMPI and CPI, to illustrate some basic points; you have met all of these tests in earlier chapters.

SOME BASIC ISSUES

Response sets. As discussed in Chapter 2, a test is typically constructed from an appropriate item pool by selecting the items that meet certain rational and/or empirical and statistical criteria. Basically, what a test measures is determined by the content of the items, yet the final score for a person reflects not only the item content, but also the item and response formats – aspects which Cronbach defined as response sets. In a pioneering article, Cronbach (1946) defined response sets as any tendency that might cause a person to consistently give different responses to test items than he or she would have given if the same content was presented in a different form. He then listed a number of such response sets that included:

1. The tendency to gamble. Cronbach described this as the tendency to respond to an item when doubtful, to omit responses, to be cautious, to answer with a neutral response alternative rather than an extreme alternative (as in Likert scales choosing "unsure" rather than strongly agree or strongly disagree). Such guessing can increase the reliability of a test because it results in greater individual differences (some guess

and some don't) but tends to reduce validity. Under this label, Cronbach listed several response sets that others have subsequently considered as separate.

2. Definition of judgment categories. Most tests require the subject to respond using given response categories, such as the Likert response scale. But different subjects give different meanings to the response options, e.g., the meaning assigned to such response categories as "frequently": Does that mean every day? Six times a day? Once a week?

3. Inclusiveness. When the subject can make as many responses as he or she likes, some individuals make more responses than others. This occurs not only on essay exams, where one person's answer may be substantially longer, but also on tests such as the Rorschach, where one person may see many more percepts on an inkblot, or the Adjective Check List, where one person may endorse substantially more items as self-descriptive.

4. Bias or acquiescence. This is the tendency to endorse "true" or "yes" to dichotomous response items. Such response tendencies affect an answer only when the student is to some degree uncertain about the item content. Thus, acquiescence tends

to make false items more valid and true items less valid.

5. Speed vs. accuracy. Where speed of response is an important element, the respondent can answer carefully, sacrificing speed, or can answer rapidly, sacrificing accuracy.

6. Response sets on essay tests. Cronbach argued that there were many such response sets that involved how organized, fluent, detail oriented, etc., the person might be.

Cronbach argued that there were individual differences in these response sets (e.g., some people are more willing to guess if unsure than others are), and these individual differences were reliable. He pointed out that response sets have the greatest impact on a test score when the items are ambiguous or unstructured (another reason to stay away from essay-type items). In fact, Cronbach (1946; 1950) suggested the use of multiple-choice items as a way to reduce response sets.

Since that time, a number of these response sets (sometimes also called response biases) have been studied (see Broen & Wirt, 1958, for a listing of 11 such sets), including primarily the following:

1. social desirability bias (or faking good)

2. faking bad

3. acquiescence (or yea saying)

4. opposition (or nay saying)

5. positional set (extremity and mid-point response sets)

6. random responding (carelessness and/or inconsistency)

These response sets are seen as potential threats to the reliability and validity of self-report measures, and a number of efforts have been made to deal with such biases. Three such ways are

1. Have one or more measures of response bias incorporated in the self-report measure – this is illustrated by the CPI and the MMPI among others.

2. Compare (typically correlate) the results of a self-report measure with a measure of such bias. For example, if we were to administer a self-esteem measure, we might also include a response bias scale as part of our administration.

3. Determine how susceptible a scale is to faking, typically by having subjects complete the task under different directions (e.g., standard directions vs. fake bad), and see to what degree the responses differ.

Note, however, that such response styles not only can confound test results, but also represent legitimate dimensions that may reflect personality traits. A person who is more likely to guess on a multiple-choice exam, may in real life be more of a gambler, willing to take risks, perhaps more impulsive, and so on. Thus, these two aspects – error variance in content scores and reliable variance for "stylistic" personality measures – represent two separate domains. These domains can be assessed independently by a variety of techniques such as factor analysis (see Messick, 1962).

Cognitive styles. There are consistent individual differences in the way different persons typically perceive, think, remember, solve problems, or perform other intellectual operations. These have typically been called *cognitive styles*, and a substantial number of them have been identified. For example, in decision making, some individuals prefer to take risks while others prefer to be cautious. In the area of memory, some individuals are "levelers" and others are "sharpeners," i.e., they either assimilate or exaggerate stimulus differences. If you ask a leveler what they did on their vacation, they'll reply, "I went to the beach"; if you ask a sharpener, they will give you all the details.

Although such dimensions are considered "cognitive," they in fact involve not only cognition, but personality, affect, temperament, etc., as well as interpersonal domains. Research on some cognitive styles, such as field dependence vs. field independence, or reflection vs. impulsivity, have a fairly substantial base; other cognitive styles have not been investigated to any degree.

Obviously, these styles can interact with test performance, yet at the same time they probably reflect the person's behavior. For example, an impulsive individual may do poorly on a multiple-choice test by not considering the alternatives carefully – but in fact, that's how they may well behave in work situations.

We will not consider cognitive styles further, although they are very important, and a number of scales have been developed to assess specific cognitive styles. A consideration of these would simply take us too far afield. For a recent overview of cognitive styles see Sternberg and Grigorenko (1997).

Faking. There are many types of faking and different sets of terms. One such term is *malingering*, which is seen as intentional faking to obtain some external incentive such as monetary compensation, avoiding punishment for criminal behavior, or avoiding military duty (APA, 1987). Faking basically refers to deliberate systematic distortion of the responses given to test items because the respondent wishes to create a particular impression. This impression may be made up of two components: an emphasis on socially desirable characteristics and/or a denial of negative characteristics. Various terms are used in the literature to discuss this topic, including "impression management" (e.g., Edwards, 1970) and "response bias" (e.g., Orvik, 1972).

Rogers (1984) distinguishes four patterns of responding to questionnaire items: (1) honest responding, where a sincere attempt is made to be accurate in responding; (2) irrelevant responding, where the response given is not relevant to item content, such as answering randomly; (3) defensiveness, where there is conscious denial or minimization; and (4) malingering, which is conscious fabrication or exaggeration.

Incidence of faking. When we instruct subjects to take a test first under standard conditions, and then under instructions to fake, we are looking at asking "Can a test be faked?" A separate question however is, "Does faking occur in practice?" The first question has received considerable attention, and the answer seems to be a rather strong, "yes." The second question has received much less attention, and the answer seems to be, "depends."

When faking or cheating does take place, we ordinarily do not find out about it, so it is difficult if not impossible, to estimate the incidence. Furthermore, the incidence varies depending upon a number of variables, such as the type of test, the rewards and punishments associated with cheating, the procedures in place to eliminate or detect cheating and so on.

Some writers feel faking is quite rare (e.g., Bigler, 1986), while others feel it is quite common (e.g., R. K. Heaton, Smith, Lehman, et al., 1978). A literature review cited incidence estimates ranging from 1% to 50% (P. I. Resnick, 1988). Binder (1992) argues that the only sensible procedure for the clinician is to consider the possibility of malingering on neuropsychological exams in every patient, when there is a monetary or external incentive. The usual premise is that faking is commonplace, but the evidence for such faking is usually indirect.

Lanning (1989) studied CPI archives (at the University of California Berkeley's Institute of Personality Assessment and Research) and reported the incidence of faking good as ranging from 0%, in various samples studied, to 10.7%, in a sample of male police applicants. The protocols of psychiatric patients were most likely to be identified as fake bad (11.8% in one sample) and random (7.3%). Male prison inmates yielded a 2% frequency of fake bad, and male military academy students gave a 6.5% frequency of random responses. Thus, the prevalence of invalidity reflects the circumstances of test administration as well as sample characteristics.

It is estimated that the base rate for malingering is 33% among mild head-trauma patients who sought financial compensation (Binder, 1993), and as high as 77% among accused criminals who sought a finding of mental incompetence (Frederick, Sarfaty, Johnston, et al., 1994). As another indicator, we may consider the finding that between 40% and 90% of all college students cheat (K. M. May & Loyd, 1994).

At least under a number of circumstances, faking is an infrequent phenomenon. As we discussed in Chapter 3, detecting infrequent events, that is, those with a low base rate – is a difficult problem. Nevertheless, the literature is replete with successful studies, with success being greater when sophisticated analyses such as regression equations are used (Lanning, 1989). Certainly, the research shows that subjects, when instructed to do so, are quite capable of faking good (e.g., Dunnette, McCartney, Carlson, et al., 1962; Hough, Eaton, Dunnette, et al., 1990).

Most faking that occurs "naturally" is probably fairly unsophisticated and detectable. Many years ago, Osipov (1944) argued that every malingerer is an actor portraying his or her interpretation of an illness and that, in assuming this role, the malingerer goes to extremes, believing that the more eccentric the responses given, the more disordered he or she will be judged to be.

Legal issues. The topic of faking is particularly relevant to a number of legal issues (H. V. Hall & Pritchard, 1996). For example, the malingering of psychosis is of special concern as a defendant may be found legally insane or incompetent to stand trial based on such a diagnosis. However, there is little empirical research on the prevalence of malingering in a criminal forensic population, in part, because of the criterion problem – what are we to use as a standard of "truth" against which we match our test results?

Cornell and Hawk (1989) found an incidence of diagnosed malingering of psychosis of 8% (25 cases out of 314) in criminal defendants who were referred for evaluation of competency to stand trial and/or insanity. Malingerers did differ from genuine psychotics on a number of variables which, when placed in a discriminant function analysis, correctly classified 89.1% of the cases. No tests were used in this study although many of the symptoms, such as disturbed affect and delusions, could be easily assessed by a test such as the MMPI.

Another issue is that, traditionally, clinicians have worked for the client; if testing is to be administered it is for the joint effort of clinician and client to help the client. However, in forensic situations, the clinician often assumes a neutral role that may be perceived as adversarial by the defendant – i.e., the client is being tested to determine insanity, not necessarily because the client is to be helped, but because such an evaluation is mandated by the court or the legal proceedings.

Lack of insight. In discussing faking, three major issues are of concern: (1) motivation to distort the results in a particular way, such as faking mental illness or attempting to look more positive than one really is; (2) random responding in a conscious effort to sabotage the testing situation; and (3) inaccurate reporting of one's abilities, beliefs, etc., through lack of self-insight. Although all three are major issues, much of the literature and research efforts focus on the first issue.

Demand characteristics. Although much of the focus in this chapter is on faking, faking can be seen as part of a broader question that has to do with "demand" characteristics – i.e., are there aspects of the testing situation, such as the instructions, that do influence a person's response?

Content vs. style. In the area of personality assessment, we can distinguish, at least theoretically, between what a person says or does (content) and how a person acts (style). In reality, the *what* and the *how* are often intertwined and integrated. If we now apply this distinction to how a person responds on a personality inventory, we find that people can respond to the content of an item, or to what is considered a "response set," some aspect of the form of the item – for example, they may tend to answer true regardless of content.

In most applications of personality inventories, we assume that the responses reflect content – i.e., if the scale is one of responsibility we assume that a high score reflects a high degree of responsibility. In constructing such a scale however, we take appropriate steps to reduce, eliminate, or control for such stylistic patterns. For example, we would try to have half of our scale items keyed true and half keyed false. Some investigators have argued that test results are heavily influenced by such stylistic approaches; D. N. Jackson and Messick (1958), for example, argued that acquiescence was a major source of variance in the CPI.

Set vs. style. Rorer (1965) distinguished between "set," which refers to a conscious or unconscious desire to respond in such a way as to create a certain image (e.g., to fake good) vs. "style," which refers to a tendency to select some response category a disproportionate amount of the time, independent of the item content. Acquiescence, for example, can be both in that it can refer to a general tendency to be "agreeably passive" or to a preference for endorsing "true" or "agree" categories. Others (e.g., D. N. Jackson & Messick, 1958; McGee, 1967) have defined the two somewhat differently, but much of the literature uses these terms as synonyms.

Is response set error? There are at least two points of view here. Some writers think that response sets in fact represent meaningful dimensions of behavior to be assessed (e.g., Cronbach, 1946; 1950), while others think that response sets need to be corrected for or eliminated from tests (e.g., A. L. Edwards, 1957b; Fricke, 1956). Just considering validity, there are also two perspectives. From the viewpoint of predictive validity, it can be argued that if response set increases the predictive validity, then it is not error. Such an example occurs on the California F (fascist) Scale, where content of the items and acquiescence of response were confounded (Gage, Leavitt, & Stone, 1957). From the viewpoint of construct validity, such confounding is error, because it interferes with our understanding of the underlying nature of the construct (Messick & Jackson, 1958).

Faking is more than faking. In many instances, scales to assess faking also can yield valuable information in their own right. For example, on the CPI the three validity scales can also be useful in interpreting the individual's personality structure and dynamics. As an example, in high-school males (but not females) random answering on the CPI is related to a lower probability of going on to college, a lower GPA, and a greater likelihood of being perceived as delinquent (Lanning, 1989).

Faking good and faking bad. Traditionally, faking good and faking bad were thought to represent opposite poles of a unitary dimension, but recently, the two concepts are seen as different dimensions to be assessed separately. Faking good is seen as composed of two independent concepts, typically labeled as "self-deceptive enhancement" and "impression management." Are there also two components in faking bad? At present, the answer is unclear, but the two major scales in this area, the MMPI F scale and the CPI Sense of Well-being scale seem to reflect two different approaches. In general, the detection of faking good seems to be more difficult than the detection of faking bad (R. L. Greene, 1988).

How does one fake good? Basically, by endorsing test items that portray personal honesty and virtue. The MMPI L scale was developed to detect this strategy. Another strategy of the test taker is to overendorse items indicative of especially good adjustment or mental health. The MMPI Mp (positive malingering) scale was developed to detect this strategy (Cofer, Chance, & Judson, 1949). Faking good is often manifested by a failure to acknowledge commonly held weaknesses and endorsement of a constellation of unusual virtues. If one considers self-deception vs. other deception, faking good focuses more on

other deception – that is, the person who fakes good knows that he or she is making incorrect claims.

How does a test taker fake bad? One strategy is to overendorse symptoms. Scales such as the MMPI F scale and the F-K index attempt to detect this strategy. Another strategy is to endorse specific symptoms that represent the respondent's concept of what mental illness is all about. The CPI Sense of Well-being scale (originally called the Dissimulation scale) was developed to detect such a strategy (Gough, 1954). Faking bad, at least on personality tests, reflects a desire to appear poorly adjusted, perhaps mentally ill. Faking bad may represent a cry for help, a negativistic stance, or a manipulative attempt to gain a particular goal (for example, ending up in a psychiatric hospital rather than prison).

Most scales developed to measure deception, particularly the MMPI scales, were developed empirically and/or rationally, but are heterogeneous in content, like most other personality scales developed empirically. For example, a fake-good scale will typically have both items that represent excessive virtue and items that involve the endorsement of superior adjustment.

Random responding. Random responding also needs to be considered. This may be the result of an honest error, such as placing answers incorrectly on an answer sheet, lack of understanding as with a person of borderline intelligence, or willful behavior, such as someone who is passive-aggressive and does not wish to answer a personality inventory.

Personality tests. There are probably three major ways in which personality test scores may be distorted: (1) deliberate faking, (2) an idealized presentation of oneself as opposed to a more realistic presentation, and (3) an inaccurate presentation because of lack of insight. These aspects involve habits and attitudes. Habits are usually more focused on the mechanics of the test – for example, a person may have the habit of selecting the first plausible answer in a multiple-choice item, rather than closely considering all the alternatives. Attitudes, as we saw in Chapter 6, are broader. In terms of testing, such habits and attitudes that may influence test scores are subsumed under the term "response sets."

SOME PSYCHOMETRIC ISSUES

Scale-development strategies. Most scales to detect faking have been developed using one of three strategies:

1. One group – one instruction. Here, an item pool is administered to one group, usually normal individuals, under standard instructions, and the rate of endorsement for each item is calculated. For example, we might find that only 7% endorse the item, "I am extremely honest in all my dealings." We might then form a scale of such items with low endorsements. High scorers on this scale would tend to reflect unusual claims.

2. One group – two instructions. Here a group of subjects, often captive college students, take the item pool under standard instructions, and then retake it under faking instructions. The instructions may be quite generic (e.g., fake good), or much more specific (e.g., answer as if you were a chronic alcoholic). Items that show significant response shifts under the two sets of instructions are retained for the faking scale. For example, if the item, "I am a wonderful person" is endorsed as true by 16% of the sample under standard instructions, but by 62% under the faking instructions, then that item would be retained for the scale.

3. Two groups – two instructions. Here a group that is "deviant," such as psychiatric patients, is administered the item pool under standard instructions. A second group, usually normal, is asked to fake as if they were psychiatric patients. Items that show differential endorsement are retained. For example, the item, "I hear voices" might be endorsed by 28% of psychiatric patients, and by 86% of normal individuals instructed to fake mental illness; that item would be retained for the faking scale.

Faking psychopathology. To develop procedures to detect the faking of psychopathology, the task is to find ways to distinguish between persons who actually have psychopathology and persons who pretend that they do. Dannenbaum and Lanyon (1993) indicate that two types of items are relevant: Type 1 items have predictive validity but low or no face validity; Type 2 items have face validity but no predictive validity.

Type 1 items might be like the "subtle" MMPI items (except for the fact that research indicates that the MMPI subtle scales have no predictive validity). An item that illustrates this type comes from studies of deception in interviews; the item "disturbed affect – flat/blunted or inappropriate" is in fact characteristic of most psychotics, but has a low endorsement rate for malingerers (Cornell & Hawk, 1989).

Type 2 items are endorsed by malingerers, but not by psychiatric patients. An example is the item, "visual hallucinations." Few psychotic patients actually report such symptoms, but many malingerers endorse this item.

One approach then is to empirically identify sets of items that statistically discriminate between individuals who are truly mentally ill and individuals who are instructed to answer as if they were suffering from mental illness. Thus, if only 2% of mentally ill persons respond true to the item, "I hear voices," but 86% of normals instructed to fake bad do so, then the item would be an excellent candidate for a fake bad scale. If an individual we are testing endorses the item, the probabilities are quite low that the person is truly mentally ill, but quite high that the person is faking.

Generic vs. specific scales. One approach is to develop a scale (or scales) that are "generic." Thus, a fake bad scale should detect faking bad wherever if might occur. This is the implicit belief that many researchers have when they include an MMPI validity scale as part of their battery of questionnaires.

A second approach lies in developing scales that are specific to a content area. For example, the three factors identified in the Timmons, Lanyon, Almer, et al. (1993) study are germane to the detection of malingering on a sentence completion test used to examine claims of disability.

Scales used as a correction. Validity scales, such as those on the MMPI, were developed primarily for the purpose of identifying suspect protocols, that is, respondents who may have deliberately distorted their answers. Occasionally, validity scales are also used to "correct" the scores on the other scales. Christiansen, Goffin, Johnston, et al. (1994) studied the 16 PF where fake good and fake bad scales can be used to add or subtract points to the other scales. These corrections basically treat the faking scales as suppressor variables – a suppressor variable is one that removes the variance that is assumed to be irrelevant to accentuate the relationship between the predictor scale and the criterion. A suppressor variable is one that is significantly associated with a predictor, but not associated with the criterion for which the predictor is valid. For example, if we have a personality scale that predicts leadership behavior well, we have a predictor (the scale) that correlates well with the criterion (leadership behavior, however defined). Suppose however, our scale is heavily influenced by acquiescence – i.e., our scale correlates with acquiescence, but the predictor does not. If we can remove the acquiescence, then the correlation between our scale and the predictor should increase. Generally, if we can identify and measure the suppressor variable, then the validity between our predictor and our criterion should increase. The Christiansen, Goffin, Johnston, et al. (1994) study of assessment-center candidates indicated that correction for faking had little effect on criterion-related validity (performance data based on job analyses), but would have resulted in different hiring decisions than those made on the basis of uncorrected scores. These authors concluded that faking is not a serious threat to the validity of personality tests and that the use of faking corrected scores may be unwarranted.

Oblong trapezoids. A rather different and potentially useful approach is illustrated by Beaber, Marston, Michelli, et al. (1985) who developed a test to measure malingering in schizophrenic persons. The test consists of three subscales, including a malingering subscale composed of beliefs that cannot be true because they are nonexistent (e.g., "God has revealed to me the truth about oblong trapezoids") or that present atypical hallucinations and delusions (e.g., "I see colored triangles in my field of vision"). The test identified 87% of true negatives (schizophrenic patients) and 78% true positives (normal individuals instructed to malinger). However in two cross-validations, the test did not work as well and a revision was proposed (Rogers, Bagby, & Gillis, 1992).

Stylistic scales. How useful are stylistic scales, that is, personality scales that attempt to measure one's personality style, such as impulsivity?

Research on the CPI provides some interesting answers. Hase and Goldberg (1967) compared standard CPI scales with several sets of "new" CPI scales developed through different methods (such as rational rather than empirical), as well as a set of stylistic scales. They used a rather complex validational procedure with 13 validity criteria, such as peer ratings and behavioral indices. They found that the various sets of scales did not differ from each other in overall validity, except that the stylistic scales were the least valid and were not useful predictors of nontest behaviors.

It can be argued that the variation in test scores due to such stylistic variables is error variance and, therefore, needs to be identified and eliminated. This can be done by considering such scales as suppressor variables. Dicken (1963) did so by comparing the correlations between standard CPI scales and a variety of criteria vs. the correlations obtained when the stylistic scales are considered and their influence analyzed statistically. He concluded that statistically correcting personality scores for stylistic response did not increase validity.

We can consider stylistic scales from another point of view, as a moderator variable. Let's say we have a scale, such as leadership, and a criterion such as participation in collegiate activities like being treasurer of a social club. We might find that in a sample of American college students scores on the scale predict the criterion quite well, but in a sample of Chinese students the relationship is minimal at best. The variable of culture would moderate the relationship between the scale and the criterion. Similarly then, we might find that CPI scales predict well in subjects who do not respond in a stylistic manner (i.e., who score low on such scales), but that the relationship is attenuated (i.e., lowered) for subjects who do respond stylistically (i.e., who score higher on such scales). In fact, L. R. Goldberg, Rorer, and Greene (1970) undertook such an analysis with the CPI and found that the predictive validity of the standard CPI scales was not increased by using any of 13 stylistic scales as either suppressor or moderator variables.

Detection of faking. From a statistical point of view, there are basically two methods to detect faking. When we ask a sample of subjects to take an inventory first under standard directions and then a second time by faking, we can compare the mean differences in scores obtained under the two conditions. If there are constant discrepancies across subjects attributable to faking, then the difference between means should be statistically significant.

From a research point of view this is a useful and well-used design, but the procedure doesn't tell us anything about individual differences in faking. To address this issue, we need to look at the variance (i.e., SD^2) of the differences between scores, or we need to correlate the scores obtained under the two conditions. If there are individual differences in faking, then the rank order of individuals should change over the two conditions (see Gordon & Gross, 1978; Lautenschlager, 1986).

TECHNIQUES TO DISCOURAGE FAKING

Intentional distortion. When instructed, people are able to distort their responses on personality tests in the desired direction. Several approaches have been used to deal with such intentional distortion:

1. Instructions or warnings that distortion can be detected and/or punishment will follow (e.g., Schrader & Osburn, 1977). Such warnings do seem to reduce the amount of intentional distortion, but the research support is limited. There is evidence that indicates that different types of instructions do result in different amounts of faking (e.g., Longstaff & Jurgensen, 1953).

2. Use of forced-choice items that are equated on social desirability. Such scales are however, still open to fakability, and the use of such items does not seem to be the solution (e.g., Longstaff & Jurgensen, 1953; Waters, 1965).

3. The use of subtle vs. obvious items, i.e., items for which the underlying construct is not apparent.

4. Use of validity scales. Most personality inventories contain such scales; for example, the MMPI, CPI, and Personality Research form discussed previously all have such scales.

Disguised titles. Individual scales, as opposed to multivariate instruments such as the MMPI or CPI, sometimes do use disguised titles so as not to establish in the client a "set" that might lead to distortion of responses. For example,

the Maslach Burnout Inventory is administered with the title of "Human Services Survey," presumably to eliminate potential bias that the term "burnout" might activate (Maslach & S. E. Jackson, 1981).

Filler items. A number of scales, particularly when they are relatively brief and/or when their intent is quite obvious, use filler items, items inserted throughout the scale that are not scored. For example, Rotter's (1967) Interpersonal Trust Scale, not only has a disguised title (the General Opinion Survey), but of its 40 items, 15 are fillers designed to further obscure the purpose of the scale.

There is little data available on whether the use of disguised titles and/or filler items does prevent faking or distortion of responses. At least in the case of Rotter's Interpersonal Trust Scale, the innocuous title and filler items seem to have no significant impact on its reliability and validity (Kumar, Rehill, Treadwell, et al., 1986). Given that filler items can be difficult to write, increase the length of a test, and make scoring of the test somewhat more cumbersome, research needs to be undertaken on the usefulness of this approach.

Forced-choice format. One of the problems with a forced-choice format is that it results in lowered reliability. If a response set is operating, the result will be increased reliability – the person who picks "true" as the answer will continue to do so across test items and/or test administrations. If we now eliminate this response set, reliability will also be reduced. Most of the time, this is of little concern because the reduction will be minor (not all people respond true all of the time), and there may well be an increase in construct validity – i.e., we are measuring more of what the test really is measuring. If however, the reduction in reliability is substantial, then with low reliability we may not be able to achieve validity. This is in fact a criticism that was leveled at the EPPS, which uses forced-choice items to control for social desirability (Levonian, Comrey, Levy, et al., 1959).

Developing faking scales. There are two basic approaches that parallel the approaches in developing any personality scales. The first is the empirical approach, where the items chosen for a scale are chosen because they show differential endorsement.

The second is the rational approach. Here the items that are to comprise a potential malingering scale are selected on the basis of their content. For example, items that reflect highly improbable behavior (e.g., I read every editorial column in the paper every day), claims of exceptional virtue (I have never lied in my life), nonexistent behaviors (I am one of the few persons who understands the concept of relative reciprocal tropism). The items are then tested empirically to see if, in fact, they work.

Cross-cultural perspective. Several studies have looked at cross-cultural differences in response styles. They have been able to document a preference for choosing the extreme categories in a response scale (extreme response set) or for choosing a "yes" response (acquiescence) among ethnic or racial minorities such as Hispanics and African Americans in the United States (e.g., Bachman & O'Malley, 1984; Hui & Triandis, 1989).

Marin, Gamba, and Marin (1992) analyzed the responses given to four large data sets (e.g., questions answered in a study of variables associated with cigarette smoking) by Hispanics and non-Hispanic whites. Hispanics preferred extreme responses to a greater degree (e.g., selecting strongly agree or strongly disagree on Likert response scales) and answered more items in an acquiescent manner (i.e., endorsing extreme agreement such as "very likely"). Such response styles were related to acculturation and to education, so that the more acculturated and more highly educated Hispanics tended to make less extreme or acquiescent responses.

In general, Latinos obtain higher average scores on social desirability scales than do Euro-Americans. One possible explanation is the concept of "simpatia," a cultural value that focuses on the enhancement of smooth interpersonal relationships and the minimization of conflict (e.g., Booth-Kewley, Rosenfeld, & Edwards, 1992).

Shultz and Chavez (1994) administered an 11-item social desirability scale to a large sample of job applicants for an unskilled manual-labor position. Some 1,900 applicants completed an English form of this scale, and some 600 used the Spanish form. Not only was the mean on the English version significantly lower than that for the Spanish version, but a factor analysis indicated that the factor structures were somewhat different for the two versions. For the English version, two factors were obtained, a factor of "impression management" that reflected overreporting of desirable behaviors and underreporting of undesirable behaviors, and a factor of "self-deceptive enhancement," reflecting a belief that one is better than he or she really is. In the Spanish version, these two factors also appeared, as well as an additional two factors (both composed of too few items to consider here).

Symptom validity testing. This approach involves the presentation of repeated two-alternative, forced-choice, discrimination problems (e.g., Binder & Willis, 1991). The probability of a given outcome, assuming no knowledge of the correct responses, will conform to a binomial distribution. If one avoids giving correct answers (malingers), the score obtained will be markedly below chance. This is akin to having a blind-folded person identify the way a coin lands over a large number of coin tosses. If the person is truly blindfolded, their guesses should be correct about half of the time. If they are peeking through the blindfold, their responses will show a greater degree of correctness than we would expect on the basis of the binomial distribution. Similarly, if they are being negativistic and say "heads" when they peek and see "tails," in the long run their response correctness will be below chance level.

RELATED ISSUES

Does format alter scores? In most personality inventories that assess many variables, the scale items are listed randomly, rather than grouped together. Why randomize items? Presumably such randomization reduces biases such as social desirability. However, there are some disadvantages. If a subject is answering a questionnaire whose intent is not clear, there may be a lack of trust and less motivation to answer honestly. It can also be argued that shifting from one item in one domain to another in a different domain creates an intellectual demand that may not be met. There is some evidence available, but these issues have not been investigated thoroughly.

In the area of reliability, for example, Solomon and Kopelman (1984) looked at three different item-presentation modes for life-satisfaction scales and the hypothesized changes in reliability. They found that grouping items increased internal consistency somewhat, but grouping items and labeling the subscale resulted in very modest increases in reliability. In the area of validity, Baehr (1953) assessed the impact of grouping together vs. randomly distributing items on attitude scales and found that test format had no impact on the discriminant validity of the scales. Schriesheim and DeNisi (1980) and Schriesheim (1981) looked at leadership scales and found that grouping the items did impair discriminant validity.

Positional response bias. This bias refers to selecting one response position on multiple-choice tests significantly more often, regardless of the item content. The few studies that have been done on positional response bias are inconclusive because of various methodological problems, such as failure to randomize the position of the keyed responses. In one study with 62 university students, positional response bias was found in 6 students (about 10%), but degree of positional bias did not significantly correlate with test scores (Fagley, 1987).

Use of discriminant functions. Regression equations and discriminant functions (like regression equations that predict a categorical variable, such as neurotic vs. psychotic or faking vs. not faking) are very useful analyses to assess faking. Schretlen, Wilkins, VonGorp, and Bobholz (1992) developed a discriminant function from combined MMPI, Bender-Gestalt, and malingering scale scores that correctly identified 93.3% of their subjects, which included 20 prison inmates instructed to fake insanity and 40 nonfaking control subjects. The discriminant function included only three variables: the F − K index from the MMPI, a Vocabulary subset of the malingering scale, and the sum of five Bender-Gestalt indicators of faking.

Dissimulation about neuroticism. One of the earliest studies of dissimulation was carried out by Gough (1954), the author of the CPI. He began with the observation that both lay persons and professionals held a stereotype of neuroticism that is, in fact, quite discrepant from the actual behavior of these patients. He analyzed the MMPI protocols completed by four samples of neurotic patients with those obtained from three samples of normal subjects, primarily college students, who were instructed to answer as if they were neurotic patients. Altogether, 74 MMPI items were identified that statistically discriminated between patients and dissimulators. These items had to do with multiple physical complaints, feelings of being misunderstood and being victimized, anxiety and fear, sexual preoccupations, and other aspects. One item, for example, was "I usually feel that life is worth while." From 59% to 79% of the patients endorsed the item "true," but only from 10% to 36% of the dissimulators said "true" (44 of the 74 items were incorporated in the CPI as a dissimulation scale later called the Sense of Well-being Scale).

The 74 items, considered as a scale, were analyzed on a new set of samples. Clinical samples (i.e., patients) did not differ from normal samples (high-school students), but both differed substantially from samples instructed to fake. In fact, by using a cutoff score of 35, 93% of the dissimulators were correctly identified, but only 6% of the clinical cases and 2% of the normal cases scored at or above this point.

Can clinicians detect faking? There are many studies available on the capacity of subjects to "fake good" or "fake bad," especially on personality tests, and the evidence clearly indicates that subjects can fake quite well, but that in most cases the validity scales to detect such faking also work well. There are, however, very few studies on the ability of clinicians to detect such faking.

The "classic" study is one done by Albert, Fox, and Kahn (1980), who showed that experienced clinicians could not distinguish Rorschach protocols of psychotic patients from those of normal individuals who were instructed to fake. On the other hand, Bruhn and Reed (1975) showed that clinicians could accurately identify such dissimulation on the Bender-Gestalt, and Goebel (1983) obtained the same results on the Halstead-Reitan.

Yet, consider the following: Faust, Hart, and Guilmette (1988) tested three normal youngsters with the WISC-R and the Halstead-Reitan. The children were instructed to "perform less well than usual but not to be so obvious" that their faking would be detected. Of the 42 clinical neuropsychologists who reviewed the test protocols, 93% diagnosed abnormality (from two given choices: normal or abnormal), and of these 87% attributed the abnormality to cortical dysfunction (from three given choices: cortical dysfunction, malingering, or functional factors). No clinicians attributed the results to malingering.

Though each of these studies is limited, for now we must conclude that clinicians, when judging test protocols impressionistically are not very good at detecting faking. The answer quite clearly is to use psychometric scales, signs, or indices to detect malingering because their batting average is substantially higher.

How important are response sets? Distortion of self-report through response-style bias has long been recognized as a potential major source of systematic error in psychological testing, especially in the assessment of personality and of psychopathology. But how important are such response sets as social desirability and acquiescence? Dicken (1963) used the CPI and assessed the role of SD and acquiescence as suppressor variables; he found that, on the CPI, significant gains in validity by accounting for good impression and social desirability were rare and that no gain in validity resulted from suppressing acquiescence. He thus concluded that the importance of these variables in personality inventories may have been overemphasized.

Rorer (1965) reviewed much of the early literature on acquiescence as related to the MMPI and other measures and concluded that the inference that response styles are an important variable in personality inventories was simply not warranted. (For a very different conclusion, see D. N. Jackson & Messick, 1958.)

Some criticisms. Much of the research in this area is limited by a number of design restrictions. Many studies use college students rather than samples of individuals who may be more likely to malinger. Scores of subjects asked to fake are compared with scores of subjects answering under standard conditions, rather than with those of individuals who are genuinely disturbed. Typically, no incentive is provided to subjects

Table 16–1. Mean Scores on the MMPI Validity Scales under Different Instructions (Cassisi & Workman, 1992)			
	MMPI scales		
	L	F	K
Group instructed to:			
Be honest	50	54	48
Fake good	70	49	52
Fake bad	55	114	41

Note: Remember that these are *T* scores, where 50 is the expected mean and 10 is the standard deviation.

instructed to fake, whereas in real-life situations such incentives may well be present.

How effective are instructions to fake? In most studies, instructions to fake are usually explicit, and typically indicate that the subject should do a "believable" job, that is, not be extreme and bizarre. Sometimes incentives are offered to "fool" the judge who might potentially analyze the results. The findings from such studies do indicate that subjects given different instructions do produce different results. For example, typical mean scores on the MMPI validity scales are shown in Table 16.1.

Note that these are *T* scores and we would expect average scores to be about 50. That is exactly the case with the standard-instructions group. Note the elevation of the L scale for the fake-good group, and the elevation of the F scale for the fake-bad group.

THE MMPI AND FAKING

General comments. The original MMPI included scales designed to identify subjects who might claim symptoms and problems they did not have (i.e., fake bad), or claim positive characteristics they did not have (fake good), or deny symptoms and problems they really had (fake good also); these scales are collectively known as the "validity" scales (as opposed to the clinical scales).

Many MMPI studies have been carried out to determine the effectiveness of these validity scales. A typical design involves a "normal" group such as college students who are administered the test twice, first with regular instructions and then with instructions to fake in a specific direction. In most studies, the validity scales are able to differentiate between valid and invalid profiles with typical accuracy rates of 80% to 98%.

Another common approach, which seems more appropriate, is to compare the MMPI protocols of individuals who have been diagnosed as mentally ill vs. the protocols of normal subjects who are asked to fake bad. The results here, although typically supportive of the usefulness of the MMPI validity scales and indices, are less impressive.

Validity scales. The term "validity scales" refers to a specific set of scales that are used to determine whether a specific administration of the test is valid (that is, appropriate or acceptable). The term is different from the use discussed in Chapter 3, yet it is the same – here we consider validity for the individual client rather than validity of the scale.

The MMPI contains three basic validity scales: the ? scale, the L scale, and the F scale. The ? is simply the number of items omitted by the respondent. If too many items are not answered, the interpretation of the results is questionable. The L scale detects those who have probably lied in the fake-good direction. The F scale consists of items where 90% or more of the normative group gave an identical answer; high scores on this scale reflect endorsement of rare answers, presumably the result of faking and/or random answering.

The Cannot Say or ? scale. Although ordinarily subjects are encouraged to answer all items on a questionnaire, the standard MMPI instructions indicate that items that do not apply can be omitted. Because omitting many items automatically lowers the raw scores on the other scales, it is important to make sure that most items have, in fact, been answered. J. R. Graham (1990) recommends that protocols with more than 30 items omitted not be interpreted. Raw scores on this scale, which reflect the number of items not answered, are changed to T scores, but the transformation is done arbitrarily rather than statistically. Thus raw scores below 30 are equated to a T score of 50, and raw scores of 110 are equated to a T score of 70.

Items can be omitted for a wide variety of reasons discussed in detail in the MMPI Handbook (W. G. Dahlstrom, Welsh, & L. E. Dahlstrom, 1972). The Handbook suggests that if there is an elevated Cannot Say score, the subject be interviewed to determine the reason (e.g., suspiciousness, lack of understanding, depression, fear of loss of privacy, etc.).

The Lie (L) scale. This 15-item scale is designed to identify deliberate efforts to lie on the test. The items involve denial of aggression, prejudices, poor self-control, etc., that in fact are rather common and that most people are willing to admit. All the keyed responses are false. High scores on the L scale represent a rather unsophisticated attempt to fake good, and so scores on this scale are related to socioeconomic level, intelligence, and education, with more sophisticated persons from higher socioeconomic levels scoring lower. Higher scorers on this scale tend to be rigid, overly conventional, socially conforming individuals who are moralistic and unoriginal.

The F scale. The earliest validity index on the MMPI was the F scale, designed by the authors to detect deviant response sets. The F scale was derived from a set of 64 items endorsed by less than 10% of the normal normative group. The keyed responses are the infrequent answers; a high score presumably reflects falsification or random answering. The content of the items is quite diverse, covering some 19 different areas such as hostility, poor physical health, feelings of isolation, and atypical attitudes toward religion and authority. The scale does not assess *why* a person is endorsing the rare answers. Does the person not understand the directions? Is there a deliberate intent to fake? Does the person's mental status interfere with honest completion of the test? (Scores on the F scale do correlate with scores on the schizophrenia scale.)

The F scale has often been used to detect the presence of faking bad (e.g., Cofer, Chance, & Judson, 1949). In one study, the F scale by itself was the most effective index for identifying faking bad subjects (Exner, McDowell, Pabst, et al., 1963).

One problem with the F scale is that elevated scores are also associated with blacks, maladjusted individuals, individuals of lower

Table 16–2. Clinical Diagnosis			
		Clinical diagnosis	
		Normal	Abnormal
MMPI test results	Normal	True Negatives	False Negatives
	Abnormal	False Positives	True Positives

socioeconomic status, highly individualistic persons, marginal reading proficiency, a different cultural background, poor cooperation and inattention (Hathaway & McKinley, 1943; Schretlen, 1988). Several attempts have been made to refine the F scale, to take these concerns into account; for example, one was the F-K index.

Another major problem with the F scale and similar indices is that different studies report substantially different cutoff scores (the score above which faking is presumably present). Such scores would be expected to differ depending on the setting where the testing is done (e.g., a clinic vs. a university counseling center), nature of the client sample (e.g., neurotic vs. psychotic), and other aspects.

The K scale. The first three validity scales,?, L, and F, were part of the original MMPI when it was published. These scales were, however, fairly "obvious" and did not detect more subtle types of faking. A number of different scales were eventually developed that approached the identification of invalid protocols from different directions. One of these was the K scale. Recall from Chapter 3 the discussion of false positives and false negatives. If we use the simple dichotomy of test results vs. clinical diagnosis, we again have our fourfold classification, as shown in Table 16.2.

The intent of the K scale is to minimize both false negatives and false positives, without altering the number of true positives and true negatives.

The 30-item K scale was developed empirically by comparing the responses of psychiatric patients whose MMPI profiles were normal (but whose L score was at least 60) with the item responses of a group of normal subjects. The items incorporated into the K scale also cover a wide range of content areas, but are quite subtle in content so that their intent is not readily identified.

Once the K scale is scored, it is also used as a "correction" factor (i.e., as a suppressor variable) for 5 of the 10 MMPI clinical scales. For example, a person's MMPI schizophrenia scale score is composed of the raw score on that scale *plus* the raw score on the K scale (see the MMPI Handbook for a detailed discussion).

Not surprisingly, the K scale is psychologically a rather complex scale. Scores on the K scale are related to defensiveness, but moderate elevations in well-educated individuals can reflect "ego strength," that is, self-reliance, the ability to cope with challenges, and good interpersonal skills. High scores on the K scale may reflect a person who has responded false to most items, or tried to fake good, or who lacks self-insight. In a normal individual, a high score may reflect above-average positive characteristics. Low scores on the K scale may reflect a "true" response bias or a fake-bad response set. They may reflect confusion or suspicion or a person who is socially awkward and conforming.

Although the MMPI profile and practice is to routinely incorporate the K correction, there is actually little evidence that K-corrected scores are more valid predictors than uncorrected scores (J. R. Graham, 1990).

The F minus K index. Gough (1947; 1950) determined that individuals who fake on the MMPI and try to create an image of severe psychopathology score considerably higher on the F scale than on the K scale. He therefore suggested and empirically evaluated that the difference in raw scores between the two scales, i.e., F minus K, could be a useful index to detect fake-bad profiles. In one of the earliest studies of faking on the MMPI, Gough (1947) asked 11 professionals (psychiatrists and clinical psychologists) to take the MMPI three times: under standard instructions, while attempting to simulate severe psychoneurosis, and while attempting to simulate paranoid schizophrenia. These profiles were then compared with those of actual psychiatric patients with the same diagnoses. The faked neurotic profiles were in fact fairly similar to those

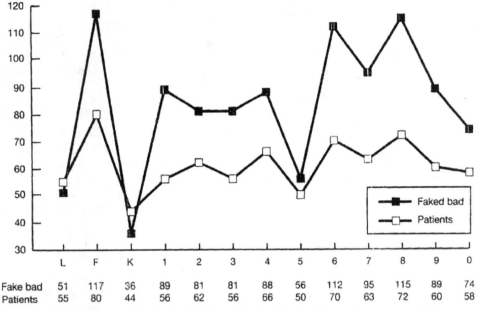

	L	F	K	1	2	3	4	5	6	7	8	9	0
Fake bad	51	117	36	89	81	81	88	56	112	95	115	89	74
Patients	55	80	44	56	62	56	66	50	70	63	72	60	58

FIGURE 16–1. Comparison of MMPI-2 profiles for fake bad instructions vs. psychiatric patients (*T* scores, rounded to nearest whole number). [Based on J. R. Graham, D. Watts, & R. E. Timbrook (1991). Detecting fake-good and fake-bad MMPI-2 profiles. *Journal of Personality Assessment, 57*, 264–277. Reprinted with permission of the publisher; Minnesota Multiphasic Personality Inventory-2 (MMPI-2) Profile for Basic Scales. Copyright 1989 the Regents of the University of Minnesota. All rights reserved. "Minnesota Multiphasic Personality Inventory-2" and "MMPI-2" are trademarks owned by the University of Minnesota. Reproduced by permission of the University of Minnesota Press.]

of the neurotic patients, but the F-K index identified 9 out of the 11 (82%) as faked. Four judges (including three of the original MMPI authors) were able to correctly identify from 55% to 73% of the 11 profiles as faked. For the psychotic profiles, the F-K index again identified correctly 9 of the 11 (82%) faked profiles, with the four judges achieving success rates from 91% to 100%.

In general, differences greater than +10 on the F-K index are associated with faking bad, and differences less than -10 are associated with faking good, although the specific cutoff score varies from sample to sample.

MMPI-2. Initial results on the MMPI-2 show that the same procedures to identify faking on the MMPI are also quite applicable to the MMPI-2. For example, J. R. Graham, Watts, and Timbrook (1991) administered the MMPI-2 twice to a sample of college students, first with standard instructions, and secondly with either fake-bad or fake-good instructions. These protocols were compared with those of a psychiatric patient

sample with varying diagnoses. Figure 16.1 presents the results. As is typical, normal subjects who tried to fake bad overreported symptoms and difficulties compared to psychiatric patients; their entire MMPI profile was elevated. Most of the MMPI indices designed to detect faking bad worked quite well. The detection of fake-good profiles was more difficult, but the L scale seemed to work relatively well.

As mentioned in Chapter 7, several additional validity scales were developed for the MMPI-2. These include (1) a Back-page Infrequency Scale. This 40-item scale parallels the original F scale in development and was meant to correct the limitation that all of the F-scale items appeared early in the test booklet; (2) a Variable-Response Inconsistency Scale, composed of 67 pairs of items with either similar or opposite content. The score reflects the number of pairs of items that are answered inconsistently, presumably reflecting random answering; (3) a True Response Inconsistency Scale, that consists of 23 pairs of items that are opposite in content. The total score is computed by subtracting the number of pairs of items to which the client gives two false responses from the number of pairs of items to which the client gives two true responses with either pattern reflecting inconsistency. A constant of 9 is added to the score to remove potentially negative raw scores, so that the final scores can range from 0 to 23. Higher scores reflect a tendency to give true responses indiscriminately, and lower scores indicate a tendency to give false responses indiscriminately. These scales are relatively new but available studies support their utility (e.g., Arbisi & Ben-Porath, 1998; L. A. R. Stein & J. R. Graham, 1999).

Consistency of response. Buechley and Ball (1952) pointed out that the F scale is based on items from the first 300 MMPI items, and not from the latter 266 items. Because boredom is of a progressive nature, a person may well obtain a "normal" F score, yet still answer randomly on the latter set of items. Buechley and Ball therefore developed the Tr (test-retest) scale on the MMPI, which consists of 16 items that are repeated in the original test booklet. These items were originally repeated, not to catch individuals who are inconsistent, but to allow the early test-scoring machines to keep track of the scores. In a sample of 137 juvenile delinquents, presumably uncooperative and poorly motivated, the F and Tr scales correlated +.63, and the authors argued that the Tr scale provides a basis for identifying subjects who respond randomly vs. subjects whose responses are valid but consistently bizarre. One advantage of this scale over the F scale, is that it is unaffected by psychopathology.

Another consistency-type scale consists of 12 pairs of items that were judged to be psychologically opposite in content (R. L. Greene, 1978). Both this scale and the one just described are of interest when "person reliability" becomes an issue, and they have been useful in identifying MMPI protocols that were the result of random responding, but have not been used widely (Grigoriadis & Fekken, 1992). This scale also, is independent of psychopathology.

Rogers, Harris, and Thatcher (1983) conducted a discriminant analysis of MMPI protocols, using the above scales as well as the MMPI validity scales, and found accuracy rates of 90% or better at correctly classifying random MMPI

profiles. They also checked on the accuracy of "decision rules" – for example, the rule that if the F scale is greater than 80, then call this protocol a random protocol. Such decision rules were also quite accurate, with half of them correctly identifying 100% of the random protocols, and more than 90%, the nonrandom protocols.

Subtle and obvious keys. Another approach to detect faking is illustrated by the work of Wiener (1948), who developed subtle vs. obvious keys for five of the MMPI scales. Basically, this was done by the author and a colleague on the basis of the manifest content of the items. Items that were relatively easy to detect as indicating emotional disturbance if endorsed were considered "obvious" items. It was assumed that obvious items differentiate best between abnormal and normal groups, whereas subtle items differentiate best between gradations of normal personality. Using this distinction, Wiener rationally divided five MMPI scales into obvious and subtle subscales, and he hypothesized that those who faked bad on the MMPI would endorse more obvious than subtle items, while those who faked good would endorse fewer obvious than subtle items. In general, Wiener (1948) reported that obvious scales were highly correlated with each other and had no correlations with subtle scales. Subtle scales showed low positive correlations with each other.

Although these scales have become quite popular in the MMPI literature, several reviews raise considerable doubt as to the ability of these scales to identify faked profiles (e.g., D. T. R. Berry, Baer, & Harris, 1991; Dubinsky, Gamble, & Rogers, 1985; Schretlen, 1988). In addition, there is evidence that the standard validity scales of L and F appear to be more useful to identify faked profiles (Timbrook, Graham, Keiller, et al., 1993).

One of the findings that has been consistently reported is that when subjects fake bad on the MMPI, the "subtle" items tend to be endorsed in the opposite of the keyed direction for psychopathology (e.g., Burkhart, Christian, & Gynther, 1978; E. Rosen, 1956). This seems to be due to the face validity for these items, which is opposite to the keyed direction for psychopathology (Dannenbaum & Lanyon, 1993).

Faking good vs. faking bad. A number of studies have concluded that the detection of faking

Table 16–3. Percentages of Correct and Incorrect Identifications (Cassisi & Workman, 1992)

	Identified as:		
	Honest	Fake good	Fake bad
Actual instructions:			
Be honest	80%	10%	10%
Fake good	35%	55%	10%
Fake bad	5%	0%	95%

(Modified from Gough & Bradley, 1996)

bad on the MMPI can be fairly accurate, but the detection of faking good is less so. A typical study is that of Austin (1992), who administered the MMPI-2 to college students with instructions that were either standard, fake good, or fake bad. Five indicators of faking were looked at – the L, F, and K scales, the Gough F-K index, and the difference between obvious and subtle subscales. The F-K index was the best indicator of fake good, correctly identifying 90% of the fake good protocols, *and* the best indicator of fake bad, correctly identifying 100% of the fake bad protocols. However, this index misclassified more than one third of those who were instructed to respond honestly.

Out of context. If an investigator or clinician is concerned with possible faking, a common procedure is to administer, in addition to the usual tests that do not have a faking index (such as the Beck Depression Inventory), one or more scales to measure the possible presence of such faking; such scales often come from the MMPI.

At least two questions come to mind. First, how valid are such scales when they are not embedded in their original instrument? And second, how well do these scales work compared to each other?

Cassisi and Workman (1992) asked college students to take the complete MMPI-2, and an additional short form that included the 102 items that comprise the L, F, and K scales. They then scored these two sets of scales (those in the standard MMPI and those in this short form). They found correlations of .78 for the L scale, .87 for the F scale, and .83 for the K scales; these coefficients are quite equivalent to the test-retest correlation coefficients reported in the test manual. They then asked another sample of students to take the 102-item form, under either standard

instructions, fake good, or fake bad. Using a *T* score of 70 (2 SDs above the mean), which is the standard decision rule on the MMPI, they classified the protocols as valid or invalid. Their results appear in Table 16.3. However, the three groups were not significantly different on the K scale, and the F-K index yielded an extremely high false positive rate: 55% of the standard-instructions group were misidentified as either faking good or faking bad (of course, simply because the subjects were instructed to "answer honestly" doesn't mean they did!).

Does social desirability equal mental illness? Furnham (1986) argued that the reason why tests such as the MMPI that measure mental health are so susceptible to faking (i.e., correlated with measures of social desirability), is that giving socially desirable responses is, in and of itself, an index of mental illness. This is an interesting idea, but seems to be counter to the findings from other tests.

Random and positional response sets. In both adult and adolescent populations, invalid MMPI profiles, due to either random endorsement or tendencies to endorse all items as true or as false, are relatively easy to detect (e.g., Archer, Gordon, & Kirchner, 1987; R. L. Greene, 1980; Lachar, 1974).

General conclusions. There is an extensive body of literature on faking on the MMPI; the above studies are just examples. What can we conclude? H. V. Hall and Pritchard (1996), concluded the following:

1. Normal individuals who fake psychosis can be detected fairly readily.

2. Psychotics who feign normality can be detected fairly readily.

3. Psychotics who exaggerate their condition can be detected.

4. MMPI indices are better at discriminating between normal MMPI profiles and the profiles of normal subjects instructed to fake psychopathology than they are at discriminating

genuine patients and normal subjects instructed to fake psychopathology.

5. MMPI indices are even less able to discriminate between honest genuine patients and patients who exaggerate.

6. Some MMPI indices are consistently better than others.

7. A universal cutoff score to distinguish genuine from faked MMPIs is not available. Specific cutoff scores must be established to take into account the population of interest and other aspects.

THE CPI AND FAKING

Sense of Well-being (Wb) scale. This scale, originally called the Dissimulation scale, was developed through external criterion analyses that compared the *MMPI* responses of actual neurotics with the responses of normal subjects who were asked to fake neurosis. In the current CPI (Form 434; Gough & Bradley, 1996) the Wb contains 38 items; these items originally showed large differences between the neurotic samples and dissimulation samples, but the items also have identical rates of endorsement between patients and normals. The original scale was used with the MMPI, but when the CPI was published, the scoring was reversed and the scale retitled "Well-being."

Very low scores on this scale are indicative of faking bad. The scale however is not simply a validity scale but also reflects personological aspects. Thus, high scores tend to be associated with behaviors that reflect productivity, self-confidence, getting along well with others – in short, a person who has good health and a positive outlook on life.

Good impression (Gi) scale. The Gi scale consists of 40 items obtained from a pool of 150 items that were administered to high-school students twice – first under standard instructions, and second as if they were applying for a very important job. Those items that showed significant response shifts under the two sets of instructions were retained for the scale. Most of the item content reflects obvious claims to favorable attributes and virtues, or denial of negative aspects such as failings. As with other CPI scales, there is also a rather complex layer of personological implications attached to scores,

other than their relationship to social desirability. Thus above-average scorers may be characterized as considerate, cooperative, conscientious, and industrious. Low scorers are seen as rebellious, critical, self-indulgent, and distrustful (Gough & Bradley, 1996).

The Communality (Cm) scale. The Cm scale was developed in a parallel manner to the MMPI F scale, and was originally called the Infrequency scale. The scale consists of 38 items chosen because they are answered in the keyed direction by 95% or more of the normative subjects. Low scores then raise the possibility of random or "nonnormative" responses. In general, high scores confirm the validity of the protocol, and they also suggest that the subject "fits in," that the person endorses the values and goals of the culture; higher scores thus suggest undue conventionality and conformity. Low scores not only can reflect invalidity of the protocol, but may point to feelings of alienation, not "fitting in"; moderately low scores can thus be indicative of a creative, independent individual.

The use of regression equations. The CPI has always been marked by a rather sophisticated approach to test construction and psychometric aspects, and the same can be said about its validity scales. Lanning (1989) developed three regression equations to identify invalid CPI protocols, which are applied in a "decision tree" format. The first equation is applied to a test protocol. If the test is declared "valid" then the second and third equations are applied.

The equations for the CPI-434 are given in Table 16.4. To use these equations, one simply uses the raw scores found in the client's protocol.

On the first equation, if the total score is 60.6 or greater, then the protocol is considered to reflect fake good. If not, then the next two equations are taken together and the following decisions are made: (1) if the score on the fake bad equation is equal to or greater than 59.5 *and* the score on the random equation is less than 48.01 then the protocol is classified as fake bad; (2) if the score on the fake bad equation is equal to or greater than 59.5 *but* the score on the random equation is equal to or greater than 48.01, then the protocol is identified as random; (3) If the protocol does not fit any of the above, then it is considered valid.

Table 16–4. Regression Equations to Identify Invalid CPI Protocols

Fake good:	41.225 +.273 Do +.198 Em +.538 Gi −.255 Wb −.168 Fx
Fake bad:	86.613− 1.000 Cm −.191 Wb +.203 Ac −.110 Fx
Random:	34.096 +.279 Gi +.201 Wb +.225 Py +.157 Fx

Note that these equations involve the three validity scales, and in addition the Dominance (Do), Empathy (Em), Flexibility (Fx), Achievement via Conformance (Ac), and Psychological Mindedness (Py) scales. The initial number in each equation represents a weight so that the equation "balances." (Lanning, 1989).

How well does this procedure work? These equations were applied to sets of protocols produced by faking good or faking bad instructions or by the use of tables of random numbers or by computer-generated random responses. The results are given in Table 16.5.

Note that each equation worked as it ought-to – the fake-bad equation identified most of the fake-bad protocols, etc. These figures suggest that by using such equations, fake-good protocols will be correctly identified about 64% of the time, fake-bad protocols about 84% of the time, and random protocols about 87% of the time.

The CPI manual gives considerable data on the application of these equations to a wide variety of samples. The incidence of identified faking is extremely small in most samples. The highest incidence of fake good, for example, was 7.5% in a large sample of male applicants for the position of police officer. Faking good, faking bad, and random responding appear to be highly infrequent phenomena.

Stylistic scales. In addition to the standard scales discussed above, other investigators have

Table 16–5. Outcome of CPI Regression Equations

	Identified by equation as:		
	Fake bad	**Fake good**	**Random**
Instructions:			
Fake bad			
Males	84%	0%	2%
Females	78%	0%	4%
Fake good			
Males	0%	68%	0%
Females	0%	58%	0%
Random			
Table	24%	0%	66%
Computer	22%	0%	65%

developed "stylistic" scales. For example, Dicken (1963) developed a 32-item social desirability scale, and Lovell (cited by Hase & Goldberg, 1967) developed nine scales such as a "deviance" scale (items with low rates of endorsement and low social desirability) and a "hyper-communality" scale (items with high rates of endorsement and high social desirability). Such scales have been used in a very limited way in research projects.

SOCIAL DESIRABILITY AND ASSESSMENT ISSUES

The concept of social desirability as applied to personality assessment represented a major controversy in the 1960s, suffered relative obscurity in the 1970s, and seems to have once again come to the fore. Social desirability is generally defined as the tendency for subjects to respond to personality-test items in a manner that consistently presents the self in a favorable light.

A. L. Edwards (1957b) indicated that personality-inventory items represent desirable and undesirable characteristics and that people have learned to evaluate the behaviors represented by the test items, whether or not they actually behave in accordance with these evaluations. He proposed a social-desirability continuum on which individual statements could be placed and their social-desirability scale value determined. These values are normative values in that they represent the average judgment of a large number of judges. Very simply, individuals are asked to rate personality-inventory items on a 9-point rating scale, in which all anchors are labeled, ranging from 1 = extremely undesirable, through 5 = neutral, to 9 = extremely desirable. The rating is based on how desirable or undesirable the item is when used to describe another person.

Once we have a pool of items that have been rated as to their social desirability, we can administer these items to another sample under standard instructions, that is, "Answer true or false as the item applies to you." For each item, we can then determine the proportion of individuals who endorsed that item. Edwards

(1957b) showed that the proportion of endorsement was highly correlated to the social desirability. Edwards (1957b) then developed social-desirability scale of 39 MMPI items, each item keyed for socially desirable response. Thus, individuals who obtain high scores on the social-desirability scale have endorsed a relatively large number of socially desirable responses, and those with low scores have given few socially desirable responses.

Ratings of social desirability are highly reliable, whether we compare different groups of judges rating the same items, or the same group of judges rating the same items on two occasions, with typical coefficients in the .90s. In fact, even when the groups of judges are quite different, such as college students vs. schizophrenic patients, or they come from different cultures (e.g., Japan and the United States), the degree of correspondence is quite high (Iwawaki & Cowen, 1964; J. B. Taylor, 1959).

Meaning of social desirability. The concept of social desirability has been interpreted in two major ways. In the past, social desirability has generally been interpreted as a contaminant; that is, individuals scoring high on a social-desirability scale are assumed to be faking good, and therefore their test scores on the other scales are considered invalid. Thus, self-report scales that correlate highly with social-desirability scales are considered invalid. Not as extreme is the view that although social desirability is a contaminant, it can be held in check by statistically computing that portion of variance due to it. Zerbe and Paulhus (1987) argue that social-desirability can be considered contamination only when the construct of social desirability is unrelated to the construct of interest. A good argument can be made that there are a number of constructs, such as adjustment, which on theoretical grounds we would expect to correlate substantially with social desirability.

Furthermore, social desirability is in and of itself a meaningful personality dimension that correlates with a variety of behaviors. For example, high social desirability individuals, at least in the United States, are less aggressive, more likely to avoid social interactions, and less argumentative (Chen, 1994). Thus, whether or not social-desirability scales are useful as a suppressor variable to correct scores on other scales, they are in fact personality measures; they are not measuring a response set but a personality trait (Furnham, 1986; McCrae & Costa, 1983a).

Individual differences. J. S. Wiggins (1968) pointed out that social desirability can be seen as a property of scale items or as a variable that reflects individual differences. In fact, scale items do differ in the desirability of their responses, and such response rates (i.e., how many people endorse an item) are correlated to estimates of desirability; more "desirable" items are endorsed by greater numbers of people.

The concern of social desirability typically focuses more on individual differences – whether social desirability reflects conscious lying, unconscious defensiveness, or a need for approval, self-report instruments will be influenced. Individuals who are high on social-desirability will score higher on measures of adjustment, conscientiousness, and similar variables. Scales of such traits will also be correlated, not necessarily because the traits are, but because social desirability will cause some individuals to score higher on all scales and some to score lower.

How can we determine if a subject is dissimulating? One way is to check the self-report against objective external criteria. If the subject says true to the item, "I am an excellent swimmer" we can observe his or her performance in the swimming pool. For most items however, such objective evidence is difficult or impossible to obtain. A second approach is to assume that high endorsement of socially desirable items represents malingering. However, such a result could be due to other factors. Maybe the person *is* well adjusted and conscientious. McCrae and Costa (1983a) argue that the evidence of several studies does not support the hypothesis that social-desirability scales measure individual differences in social desirability, and that suppressing the variation in test scores does *not* increase the predictive validity of a test score. They analyzed the test scores on 21 personality traits of a sample of adults and used spouse ratings as the criterion. Self-report and spouse ratings correlated from .25 to .61; however, when these correlations were corrected for social desirability, for most traits the correlations between test scores and spousal ratings decreased; for only two of the traits was there an increase, but these were trivial (e.g., from .35 to .36). In fact, McCrae and Costa (1983a) presented evidence that individuals who scored higher on the social-desirability scale were better adjusted, friendlier, and more open to experience.

Scales of social desirability. At least 15 scales have been developed to measure social desirability (Paulhus, 1984), but there are three major ones: the Edwards scale (A. L. Edwards, 1957b), the Marlowe-Crowne scale (Crowne & Marlowe, 1960), and the Jackson scale (D. N. Jackson, 1984).

The Edwards social desirability scale evaluates the tendency of subjects to give socially desirable responses. It consists of 39 MMPI items that were unanimously responded to in a socially desirable fashion by 10 judges, and correlated substantially with scale total (i.e., the scale is internally consistent).

The Marlowe-Crowne SD scale measures the tendency to give "culturally approved" responses, and consists of 33 true-false items selected from various personality inventories, items that describe culturally approved behaviors with a low probability of occurrence. These items reflect cultural approval, avoid the psychopathological content of the MMPI, are keyed for social desirability on the basis of agreement by at least 9 out of 10 judges, and also showed substantial correlation with scale total.

Finally, Jackson's social desirability scale is a scale from his Personality Research Form (see Chapter 4); it assesses the tendency to describe oneself in desirable terms and to present oneself favorably. This scale consists of 20 nonpsychopathological items selected from a larger pool of items scaled for social desirability. These items were chosen to avoid substantial content homogeneity, as well as extreme endorsement probabilities.

Intercorrelation of social-desirability scales. Presumably, all three scales measure the same phenomenon and so should intercorrelate substantially. In fact they do not. In one study of 402 Canadian college students (Holden & Fekken, 1989) the three scales correlated as follows: Edwards vs. Marlowe-Crowne .26; Edwards vs. Jackson .71; Jackson vs. Marlowe-Crowne .27.

The authors conducted a factor analysis and concluded that the Edwards and the Jackson scales assess a dimension of social desirability that they labeled as "a sense of own general capability," and that the Marlowe-Crowne assessed a separate dimension of "interpersonal sensitivity," thus suggesting that SD has a "self" component and an "another" component.

Components of social desirability. The various measures of social desirability can be incorporated within a two-factor model, with at least two such models present in the literature. In one, the two dimensions are attribution vs. denial – i.e., claiming socially desirable characteristics for oneself and denying undesirable characteristics (e.g., Jacobson, Kellogg, Cauce, et al., 1977). A second model argues that the two dimensions are self-deception vs. impression management – in self-deception the respondent actually believes the positive self-report, whereas in impression management, there is conscious faking (e.g., Paulhus, 1986). Thus self-deception is a response style that involves an unconscious tendency to see oneself in a favorable light, whereas impression management is a conscious presentation of a false front (Zerbe & Paulhus, 1987). Most of the social desirability scales address impression management, or a combination of the two. Studies suggest that the impression management style of responding is in fact used by few job applicants and has a negligible effect on criterion validity (Schmit & Ryan, 1993).

Ganster, Hennessey, and Luthans (1983) argued that there are actually three types of social desirability effects: spuriousness, suppression, and moderation. Social desirability may create spurious or misleading correlations between variables, or suppress (that is, hide) the relationship between variables, or moderate (that is, interact with) relationships between variables. In spuriousness, social desirability is correlated with both the predictor and the criterion. Any observed correlation between the two results from the shared variance in social desirability rather than some other aspect. Statistically, we can partial out the effects of such social desirability. In suppression, the social desirability masks the true relationship. By statistically controlling for social desirability, the relationship between predictor and criterion increases in magnitude.

In moderation, there is an interaction between the independent variable and social desirability. Here too, this can be assessed statistically.

Can a social-desirability scale be faked? Apparently, the Edwards social-desirability scale itself is influenced by fake good instructions (Furnham & Henderson, 1982); thus, it may not be a good instrument by which to measure the response bias of other scales.

Reducing social desirability. Five basic suggestions to reduce social desirability can be found in the literature:

1. Use a forced-choice format (as in the EPPS), where the subject must select one of two paired items equal in social desirability. Unfortunately, this does not eliminate social desirability. For one, the items' social desirability is judged by mean rating, but may not be equal for a particular individual.

2. Use items that are neutral in respect to social desirability. Such items are rare and may not address important personality dimensions. On the other hand, items that are so socially "obvious" (e.g., "I am basically an honest person") may not be particularly useful from an empirical validity point of view.

3. Create a situation where the subject is led to believe that whether they are truthful or not can be detected; this is called the "bogus pipeline" technique (E. E. Jones & Sigall, 1971). The ethical implications of this approach are bothersome, even though there is some evidence that this approach works.

4. Use a lie scale. That is, if you administer a test that does not have built-in validity keys, you should also administer such scales.

5. Ignore the issue. Some writers (e.g., P. Kline, 1986) argue that if a test was properly constructed and shows adequate validity, the effects of response sets are minimal.

The Marlowe-Crowne. Crowne and Marlowe (1960; 1964) criticized the Edwards social-desirability scale because of its origin in MMPI items. They asked that if a subject denied that "their sleep is fitful and disturbed," did the response reflect social desirability or a genuine absence of such symptoms? They therefore developed their scale from non-MMPI type items. Their initial item pool consisted of 50 items drawn from a variety of personality instruments. They retained those items where there was at least 90% agreement on the part of raters as to the socially desirable response direction, and they also retained those items that discriminated between low and high scorers. The final scale consisted of 33 items, 18 keyed true and 15 keyed false, for example, "I always try to practice what I preach" (true) and "I like to gossip at times" (false).

Reliability. Crowne and Marlowe (1960) computed the internal consistency reliability (K-R 20) to be .88 in a sample of 39 college students, and the test-retest (1-month interval) to be .89 on a sample of 31 college students.

Validity. In the original article (Crowne & Marlowe, 1960) which includes the scale items, the Marlowe-Crowne correlated only .35 with the Edwards in a sample of 120 college students. They also compared both the Marlowe-Crowne and the Edwards scale with the standard MMPI scales. The results indicated positive correlations between social desirability and the MMPI validity scales, and negative correlations with most of the MMPI clinical scales. The pattern of correlations was significantly greater for the Edwards than for the Marlowe-Crowne scale; the authors interpreted these results as indicative that the Edwards scale measured the willingness to endorse neurotic symptoms.

Rather than use this scale as a way of showing that other scales are confounded by social desirability (as was done with the Edwards), the authors have attempted to show the construct validity of their scale by relating scores on this scale to motor skills, attitude changes, self-esteem, and so on.

Ballard, Crino, and Rubenfeld (1988) investigated the construct validity of the Marlowe-Crowne scale and recommended caution in the use of this scale. They reported that few of the scale items were sensitive enough to discriminate between high and low scorers, and that many of the items were no longer keyed in the original direction.

The Marlowe-Crowne was developed originally as a measure of social desirability response style and has been used extensively for this purpose. In addition, a number of studies indicated that the Marlowe-Crowne could be also used as a predictor of defensive behavior, such as early termination from psychotherapy (e.g., Strickland & Crowne, 1963), or willingness to accept negative test feedback (e.g., Mosher, 1965). R. G. Evans (1982) concluded that the scale could be used in a variety of clinical assessment contexts and reviewed evidence for several psychotherapy-related behaviors.

The scale has been conceptualized as having two dimensions, a responsiveness to social pressure as well as defensiveness, or attribution (the tendency to attribute social desirable characteristics) vs. denial (the tendency to deny socially undesirable characteristics). Unfortunately, all of the attribution items are keyed true, while all of the denial items are keyed false; thus the theoretical separation is confounded psychometrically. Furthermore, Ramanaiah and H. J. Martin (1980) argued that the two subscales are measuring the same construct and should not be used separately.

Attesting to the popularity of this scale is that a number of short forms have been developed. Strahan and Gerbasi (1972) produced two 10-item and one 20-item forms. C. R. Reynolds (1982) developed three short forms with 11 to 13 items; others divided the original items into subsets of attribution items (that reflect the tendency to attribute socially approved but improbable statements to oneself) and denial items (that reflect the tendency to deny socially disapproved but probably true statements about oneself, e.g., Paulhus, 1984). See Fischer and Fick (1993) for which of these scales seems most valid.

Goldfried (1964) "cross-validated" the procedure used by Crowne and Marlowe, but used different judges, different instructions, a reduced item pool, and different criteria for item retention. Not surprisingly, the results were quite different.

ACQUIESCENCE

This term was originally used by Cronbach (1942; 1946) to denote a tendency to agree more than to disagree. Cronbach was concerned about the effect of guessing on objective classroom achievement examinations. If there is no penalty for guessing, the student who fails to guess is penalized. It is therefore common practice to correct for chance, success by some subtractive weighing of wrong answers from right answers. If however, the number of true and false keyed items is not equal, then a student would still be penalized, depending on whether they tended to guess "true" or "false," when in doubt and the number of such items.

Cronbach hypothesized, and found experimental support for the notion, that "acquiescent" students (who guess true more often than false) should score higher on the true item portion than on the false item portion. Such guesses on true items will increase their score, but on false items will decrease their score. Furthermore, poor students should guess more often than good students. The net effect is that the reliability and validity of the score computed on false keyed items will be greater than that of scores based on true keyed items, and these two total scores on a test will correlate to a negligible degree.

Subsequently, Cronbach (1946) defined acquiescence as a response set, a tendency to agree with an item regardless of the content of that item. Rorer (1965) argued quite convincingly that there is no evidence to support the existence of acquiescence as defined this second way. All we can say is that individuals have somewhat stable guessing habits, that there are reliable individual differences in such habits, and that in a two-choice situation such as true-false items, individuals do not respond 50-50.

A number of scales have been developed to measure acquiescence (e.g., Bass, 1956; Couch & Keniston, 1960), but most of these scales seem to have substantial correlations with measures of social desirability, even when these scales are made up of neutral items. A. L. Edwards and Diers (1963) were able to create a 50-item scale that correlated only .08 with scores on the Edwards social desirability scale, but this scale (as with most others) has not been used widely.

Controlling for acquiescence. D. N. Jackson (1967) argued that acquiescence should be controlled or eliminated when the test is being developed, rather than afterwards, and primarily through careful construct validation. In general, to the degree that there is an imbalance in the true-false keying of the items in a scale, the scale is susceptible to acquiescent responding. Thus the solution, at least on the surface, would appear simple: any test constructor should attempt to reduce such an imbalance. Items can be rewritten, so that "I am happy" becomes "I am not happy." There is, however, evidence that "regularly" worded items are the most reliable and that negative and polar-opposite items (e.g., "I am sad") may in fact lower the reliability, if not the validity, of a test (e.g., Benson & Hocevar, 1985; Schriesheim, Eisenbach, & Hill, 1991).

Another way to reduce acquiescence is to make sure that test items are clear, unambiguous, and anchored in specific behaviors. "Do you like food?" is an item that almost requires a positive answer, but "Do you eat four or more meals per day?" is much more specific and unambiguous.

A number of statistical procedures have also been suggested as a way to measure and control acquiescence. Logically, for example, we could derive two scores from a scale, one based on the keyed items, and one based on the number of "true" responses given regardless of the keyed direction. D. N. Jackson (1967) argued that such procedures do not generally control acquiescence.

We could also of course, not use true-false items, but use other variants such as forced-choice or multiple-choice procedures, where the various alternatives are matched for endorsement frequency.

One way to assess whether acquiescence plays a role on a particular scale, is to rewrite the items so that the keyed response is false, and to administer both the original items and the rewritten items. This has been done for the MMPI, and the correlations of the original scales with their corresponding reversed forms are similar to their test-retest reliabilities, that is, acquiescence does not seem to play a major role (E. Lichtenstein & Bryan, 1965).

OTHER ISSUES

Variance in personality tests. J. S. Wiggins (1968) placed the matter in perspective by indicating that the variance associated with response sets and/or styles covers, at best, 16% of the variance of any socially relevant criterion measure.

Why do scores on a personality scale differ from person to person? The question may seem trite and the answer obvious – people differ from each other, that is, variance is due to individual differences on the trait being measured. However, there are other sources of variance, such as: (1) variance due to the particular strategy used to construct the scale, (2) variance due to the specific item characteristics, and (3) variance due to response styles (J. S. Wiggins, 1968).

1. Different strategies. Despite the proliferation of instruments devised by different strategies, there is very little by way of systematic comparison among different strategies. The study by Hase and Goldberg (1967) is somewhat unique. You recall that they compared four strategies of scale construction, all using the common item pool of the CPI. The results indicated the four main strategies to be equivalent.

2. Analyses of the variance due to specific item characteristics have in large part focused on social desirability. The procedure here, initiated by Edwards (1957b), is to have judges estimate the social-desirability scale value of specific items using a Likert-type scale. These ratings are then averaged across judges to provide a mean rating for each item. Such ratings are quite reliable and show a fair amount of consistency for different groups of judges. There are, at the same time, significant individual differences on these ratings.

3. Variance due to stylistic consistencies or response styles refers to aspects such as the tendency to be critical, extreme, acquiescent, and so on. Here also, the focus is social desirability, but this time the scale of Social Desirability developed by Edwards (1957b) is typically used. This 39-item scale was developed from the MMPI item pool and from the Taylor Manifest Anxiety Scale (which is itself comprised of MMPI items). In fact, 22 of the 39 items come from the TMAS. Because anxiety is in fact the major dimension found in tests such as the MMPI, it is not surprising that the Social Desirability scale (composed of anxiety items) should correlate significantly with almost any MMPI scale. It is thus not surprising that Edwards could predict a person's MMPI scores by equations derived solely from social-desirability indices.

Acquiescence has also been studied. Part of the problem is that different measures of acquiescence tend not to correlate with each other and to be factorially distinct (Wiggins, 1968).

Single vs. multiple approaches. Much of the earlier literature used direct but simple approaches to determine the occurrence of faking. Thus, the investigator either had a predetermined decision rule (e.g., all profiles that have an F score of above 80 are to be classified as fake) or looked at a distribution of results and determined which cutoff score would give maximum correct identification of profiles as either faked or not. Recent studies combine indices, sometimes from different tests, to assess faking. A representative example of a well-done empirical study is that by Schretlen and Arkowitz (1990), who gave a series of tests, including the MMPI and the Bender Gestalt, to two groups of prison inmates who were instructed to respond as if they were either mentally retarded or insane. Their responses were compared with those of three criterion groups: psychiatric inpatients, mentally retarded adults, and prison-inmates controls, all taking the tests under standard conditions. Based on discriminant analyses, 92% to 95% of the subjects were correctly classified as faking or not faking.

Response set vs. item format. The bias of a response set can reside in the individual (and most of the above discussion makes this assumption) or can be a function of the item format, that is, a specific item may have a certain "pull" for a response bias. Nunnally and Husek (1958) identified two types of statements: frequency-type statements and causal-type statements. For example, the item, "Most individuals who attempt suicide are depressed" is a frequency statement, whereas "Depression leads to suicide" is a causal statement. Each of these types of statements can be further subdivided into four types: total (all depressed individuals attempt suicide), unspecified (depressed individuals are suicidal), qualified (some depressed individuals are suicidal) and possible (depressed individuals may be suicidal). These authors wanted to know whether the structure of a statement, independent of the meaning, affected subjects' responses. To answer this they created a phony language examination with key words in German (e.g., "Blocksage can do Hohn-lachter"), each item requiring a 7-point Likert-like response scale. The German words were randomly chosen from a dictionary, but the meaning of the statements was actually nonsensical, and the subjects did not speak German.

They found that the type of statement significantly affected the type of response, with causal statements and particularly causal total statements, eliciting disagreement. Greater education on the part of the subject also elicited greater disagreement with causal statements.

Faking with Other Tests

The Edwards Personal Preference Schedule. The EPPS, which we discussed in Chapter 4, is somewhat unique in that its author (the same one who spearheaded the social-desirability controversy) attempted to control for social desirability by having each test item consist of two statements, equated for social desirability. The subjects select one statement from each pair as self-descriptive. Corach et al. (1958) argued that such a procedure did not eliminate social desirability. They showed that there is a "contextual" effect; the social desirability of a single item can differ when that item is paired with another, as is done in the EPPS. Furthermore, they showed that the degree to which a choice in each pair was made was highly related ($r = .88$) to an index of social desirability. On the other hand, Kelleher (1958) concluded that social desirability played an insignificant role on the EPPS!

Messick (1960) argued that pairing items equated in social desirability would be effective only if social desirability were a unitary dimension and showed that there were nine dimensions or factors underlying social desirability.

Other Lie scales. Besides the MMPI L scale, there are other lie scales that have been developed. For example, the Eysenck Personality Questionnaire (H. J. Eysenck & S. B. G. Eysenck, 1975) contains a Lie scale, but several studies suggest that the scale does not adequately discriminate between subjects who answer honestly and those who don't (e.g., Dunnett, Koun, & Barber, 1981; Gorman, 1968); other researchers conclude just the opposite, finding that the Lie scale is able to detect both positive and negative faking (e.g., Furnham & Henderson, 1982).

The semantic differential. K. Gibbins (1968) suggested that two response styles operated in the semantic differential: (1) a tendency to use the neutral response category either frequently or rarely; and (2) a tendency to make judgments consistently often in one evaluative direction (i.e., to judge targets as either relatively good or relatively bad). Gibbins administered a semantic differential to a sample of British college women who were asked to rate 28 "innocuous" targets such as lace curtains, on six bipolar evaluative scales, such as good-bad, presented in random order. Some support for the hypothesized relationship was obtained, although the actual correlation coefficients were modest. The question here is not one of faking, but of the influence of response style.

Faking on the Beck Depression Inventory (BDI). The Beck Depression Inventory (see Chapter 7) was originally a structured interview in which the examiner read to the client 21 sets of statements. For each set, the client chose the one out of 4 or 5 alternatives that most accurately described the client's feelings at the moment, with the alternatives presented in order of increasing disturbance. This interview was presented as an advance over self-administered instruments or other interview-based rating methods, and the validational data seems to support this claim, even though now the BDI is routinely used as a self-report scale rather than as a structured interview.

The initial validational studies were conducted on patients, individuals who had implicitly or explicitly admitted that they were experiencing difficulties. The motivation to dissimulate in some way was probably minimal. In more recent applications of the BDI, it may be administered to large samples of subjects in either research or applied settings where the motivation to dissimulate may be enhanced, for example, in mass testing of entering college students by student health staff or required participation in an experiment as part of an introductory psychology course.

Kornblith, Greenwald, Michelson, et al. (1984) hypothesized that college students might be less willing to endorse depressive items if they thought the BDI measured severe pathology rather than everyday problems; they also hypothesized that the order of the items (with more

severe symptomatology at the beginning) might influence the subjects' responses. A sample of students were then given the BDI twice, once under standard instructions and a retest under one of four conditions: (1) with an instructional set that the BDI measures clinical depression; (2) with an instructional set that the BDI measures "how you feel with everyday difficulties"; (3) using standard sequence of items; (4) using sequence of items from most to least severe symptoms. The results indicated that item sequence did not affect students' scores, but the clinical-depression instructions did have an inhibitory effect, although very small (the BDI mean for the depression-instruction group was 5.51 compared to a mean of 6.67 for the everyday-problem instruction sample).

W. G. Dahlstrom, Brooks, and Peterson (1990) developed two alternate forms of the BDI – a backwards form, where the alternatives were presented in reverse order, and a random form, where the alternatives were presented in a random sequence. These forms, together with other instruments, were administered to college undergraduate women. The random order BDI resulted in a significantly higher mean depression score: 11 vs. 8 for the original form and 6 for the backwards form. These results suggest that the traditional BDI format is susceptible to a "position" response set, where the subject selects the first (or last) alternative, rather than carefully thinking about which of the various alternatives best describes his or her current situation. At the same time, the pattern of correlations between each of the three versions of the BDI and several other instruments, such as the Depression scale of the MMPI, was highly similar, suggesting that the random scale may be a methodological improvement, yet add little to the criterion validity.

The Millon Clinical Multiaxial Inventory (MCMI). Another test discussed in Chapter 7 was the MCMI, which has become recognized as one of the best instruments to assess personality disorders. A number of investigators have looked at susceptibility to faking on the MCMI, including the use of subtle vs. obvious subscales, with generally positive results for most but not all of the MCMI subscales (e.g., Bagby, Gillis, & Dickens, 1990; VanGorp & R. Meyer, 1986; Wierzbicki & Daleiden, 1993).

The Psychological Screening Inventory (PSI). Lanyon (1993) developed four scales to assess deception on the PSI (see Chapter 7), two to assess faking bad (symptom overendorsement and erroneous psychiatric stereotype) and two to assess faking good (endorsement of superior adjustment and endorsement of excessive virtue).

The Symptom Overendorsement scale consists of 26 items and attempts to assess the extent to which a person in a normal population may indiscriminately endorse symptoms of psychopathology. The chosen items empirically discriminated between responses of introductory psychology students asked to answer under standard instructions and under instructions to fake bad. These items have face validity (that is, they are obvious in their nature, such as "hearing voices"). Malingerers who indiscriminately endorse psychopathology would be expected to score higher than actual patients, who endorse only the psychopathology items that apply to them. This scale is like the F scale of the MMPI, except that MMPI items have a low frequency of endorsement by normals (less than 10%).

The Erroneous Psychiatric Stereotype scale, also made up of 26 items, aims to distinguish between actual psychiatric patients and persons who claim to be psychiatrically disturbed. These items empirically discriminated the responses of college students instructed to fake bad and the responses of a sample of psychiatric inpatients, mostly schizophrenics.

The Endorsement of excessive virtue scale began with 42 PSI items identified by expert judges to be consistent with a claim of excessive virtue. These items reflected claims of being completely above reproach in behavior, being thoroughly trustworthy and honest, and so on. The percentage of endorsement for these items by the expert judges were computed. Then the percentage of endorsement of each item given by the original normative group (1,000 individuals chosen to represent some aspects of Census data) was computed and compared. Items where the judges' endorsement and the normative endorsement differed by at least 40% were retained. This yielded a 34-item scale – i.e., items judged to represent excessive virtue and, in fact, selected by few individuals.

The Endorsement of superior adjustment scale consists of 27 items, and attempts to identify normal individuals who deliberately attempt to claim very superior mental-health adjustment. These items showed significant response shifts from the standard instructions to the fake-good instructions for a sample of 100 college students.

Lanyon (1993) showed that for each of these scales, simulated deception (i.e., instructions to fake) significantly altered the mean scores, that the correlations between the fake-good and fake-bad scales were negative, and the correlations within each domain (e.g., fake good) were positive, although in part the magnitude of the correlation was due to item overlap between scales.

Integrity tests. In Chapter 14 we discussed integrity tests, tests used to identify potentially dishonest employees. How susceptible to faking are such tests? A firm answer cannot be given because such tests are not easily available to interested researchers, but the literature does contain some illustrative studies.

Sackett and Harris (1984) reviewed the literature on personnel honesty testing and concluded that research was needed to determine the fakability of such tests.

Ryan and Sackett (1987b) administered an honesty test they developed for their study, under three conditions: respond honestly, fake good, or respond as if applying for a job. The honesty test, modeled after "real" honesty tests, contained three subscales: a theft attitude scale, a social desirability or lie scale, and an admission scale. Scores of college students in the fake-good condition differed from the scores in the other two conditions, while the scores of participants in the "respond honestly" and "respond as job applicant" differed only on the theft attitude scale. Thus subjects responding as if they were applying for a job basically seem to respond truthfully.

A related issue is the relationship between integrity tests and intelligence. The hypothesis suggests that more intelligent applicants presumably are more likely to understand the purpose of the test and therefore attempt to appear more honest; but in fact, there is no relationship between indices of intelligence and scores on integrity tests (S. H. Werner, Jones, & Steffy, 1989).

K. M. May and Loyd (1994) administered a trustworthiness scale and an attitude-about-honesty scale to college students in one of two conditions: respond as honestly as possible or respond as if applying to graduate school or for a job. No significant differences were obtained for the trustworthiness scale, but the results indicated that students modified slightly their responses on one of the four subscales of the attitude scale under the condition of applying to graduate school, but not under the condition of applying for a job. Although the authors interpret their findings as supportive of the hypothesis that students modify their responses based on the purpose of the testing, in fact the support is minimal, and the results are more in line with the conclusion that such tests are fairly robust as far as faking good is concerned.

Cunningham, Wong, and Barbee (1994) conducted three experiments to assess "impression management" on the Reid Report. In the first experiment, subjects were encouraged to try and present themselves as honestly as possible; their responses were compared with those of a sample participating in a research project and a sample of employment applicants. The instructed sample scored higher than the research sample, but not higher than the job-applicant sample.

In a second study, subjects were offered a monetary reward for obtaining high scores, and different types of instructions providing specific information about the constructs involved in the Reid Report were used. Again, subjects who were instructed scored higher than control subjects, but no different from job applicants. Finally, in the third study, subjects were instructed to respond as if "they seriously wanted a job." After the test, they were overpaid for their participation, and note was made as to whether they returned the overpayment. High scorers were significantly more likely to display integrity by returning the overpayment. The authors concluded that integrity tests possess predictive validity, despite the possibility of some response distortion associated with impression management.

Alliger and Dwight (2000) analyzed 14 studies and concluded that overt integrity tests were susceptible to fake good and coaching instructions, while personality-based measures were more resistant.

Biodata. You will recall that biodata instruments can contain either or both verifiable and nonverifiable items. Some studies on the fakability of these items have found little response bias (e.g., Cascio, 1975; Mosel & Cozan, 1952), while others have (e.g., Goldstein, 1971; S. P. Klein & Owens, 1965; Schrader & Osburn, 1977; D. J. Weiss & Dawis, 1960). Some studies have reported that subjects can improve their scores when instructed to do so, while other studies show that, in actual practice, relatively little faking occurs, particularly on biodata items that can be verified (T. E. Becker & Colquitt, 1992). Mumford and Owens (1987) speculated that such differences may be due to the item-keying strategies used in scoring the particular biodata questionnaire.

There are two major strategies used – the *item-keying* strategy and the *option-keying* strategy. In the item-keying strategy the alternatives to each item are scored in such a way that assumes a linear relationship between item and criterion. Thus, if the choices are the typical Likert responses – e.g., "I am a take-charge person" – strongly agree, agree, not sure, disagree, strongly disagree – the item is scored from 5 to 1 if there is a positive correlation with the criterion (and 1 to 5 if the correlation is negative).

With the option-keying strategy, each alternative is analyzed separately, and scored only if that alternative significantly correlates with the criterion. Typically, we might analyze the responses given by contrasted groups (e.g., successful insurance salespeople vs. unsuccessful ones), and score those specific alternatives that show a differential response endorsement with either unit weights (e.g., 1) or differential weights (perhaps reflecting the percentage of endorsement or the magnitude of the correlation coefficient).

Although both scoring procedures seem to yield comparable results from a validity point of view, items scored with the option-keying procedure are less amenable to faking because the respondent does not know which option yields the maximal score for that item. That is, this procedure could well yield items where a "strongly agree" response is scored zero, but an agree response is scored +1.

Kluger, Reilly, and Russell (1991) investigated the fakability of these two procedures, as well as the fakability under two types of instructions: general instructions of applying for a job vs. specific instructions of applying for the job of retail-store manager. Their results indicated that when subjects simulated responding to biodata items as general job applicants, their responses were distorted in a socially desirable direction. Item-keyed scores were susceptible to inflation due to socially desirable responding and to specific job-title instructions; option-keyed scores were not.

These authors suggest that key developers should routinely check whether a combination of both types of keys, improves the validity of a specific biodata questionnaire. They also suggested that the effects of faking on validity may depend on the specific job performance being predicted; jobs that require socially desirable behavior (e.g., working with others) may be better predicted by item-keying strategies, while jobs that do not require such behavior may be better predicted by option-keying strategies.

A different approach was taken by J. B. Cohen and Lefkowitz (1974) who administered a biodata questionnaire and the MMPI-K scale to a sample of 118 job applicants. They used the K score as a measure of faking and analyzed the biodata results for those scoring above the median on the K scale vs. those scoring below the median. They obtained 14 biodata items that differentiated the two, which when taken as a scale correlated .66 with the K score. They interpreted these biodata items as predictive of fakability. Note, however, that the biodata profile of a supposed dissimulator is that of a person who endorses the following: married man, considers himself "middle-of-the-road" politically, is not bothered when interrupted in his work, tends to ignore the bad habits of others, masters difficult problems by independent reading, has not achieved in sports, has parents who are in business and are satisfied with their home, and called a physician when he was ill. While this portrait may not be an "exciting" one, it suggests middle-class stability and solid adjustment, rather than a scheming faking approach to the world, and in fact it supports the validity of the K scale as a measure of "ego strength." (For other studies see T. E. Becker & Colquitt, 1992; S. P. Klein & Owens, 1965.)

Faking on the Rorschach. Early studies on the Rorschach seemed to suggest that the Rorschach could not be faked. One of the earliest investigators was Fosberg (1938, 1941, 1943), who

concluded that the Rorschach could not be faked, but used flawed statistical methodology (Cronbach, 1949). In the 1950s and 1960s, several studies concluded that there was some degree of susceptibility to faking; for example, Carp and Shavzin (1950) indicated that under instructions to fake good or fake bad, subjects could vary the results.

Seamons, Howell, Carlisle, et al. (1981) administered the Rorschach to prison inmates, many with a diagnosis of schizophrenia, with instructions to fake good or fake bad. A number of response aspects on the Rorschach were influenced by the instructions, but expert judges were able to differentiate correctly between the protocols of those who were asked to appear normal or asked to fake psychosis. As indicated in Chapter 15, at least one recent study found that the Rorschach is indeed subject to malingering, at least in the case of paranoid schizophrenia. A further study by the same authors (M. Kahn, Fox, & Rhode, 1988) indicated that computer analysis of Rorschach protocols was as susceptible to faking as the results of their earlier study; the computer scoring system only identified 10% of the psychotic protocols as psychotic, and still misdiagnosed from 53% to 80% of the faked protocols as psychotic. (For criticism of this study see J. B. Cohen [1990] and M. Kahn, Fox, & Rhode's reply [1990].)

Perry and Kinder (1990) reviewed the literature and concluded that (1) when subjects are instructed to malinger on the Rorschach, they give fewer responses; (2) because analyses of responses on the Rorschach depend on how many responses are given, further analyses must control for this, but they do not. Hence, any findings reported in the literature are for now inconclusive; (3) no reliable pattern of responding has been found to be related to malingering across studies; and (4) college students instructed to fake cannot be equated to patients who might be motivated, for a variety of reasons, to fake.

Sentence-completion tests. Of the various projective techniques, sentence-completion tests seem to be among the most valid, yet also most susceptible to faking. Timmons, Lanyon, Almer, et al. (1993) administered a 136-item sentence-completion test to 51 subjects involved in personal-injury litigation. Based on the literature, they developed 12 categories of malingering characteristics such as exaggerated confidence in the doctor, excessive focus on problem severity, and so on. They scored the protocols and carried out a factor analysis. Three factors were identified: one that represented a posture of anger and resentment, a second that represented a disability too severe for future employment, and a third that reflected exaggerated claims of compliance and honesty. Correlations with MMPI items and a cross validation seemed to show both convergent and discriminant validity for these three scales. Thus, as we saw in the MMPI and CPI, scales designed to assess faking can also have additional personological implications of their own.

Neuropsychological testing. Neuropsychological testing is often performed when there are questions of head trauma, perhaps due to automobile or industrial accidents, and thus the issue of financial compensation may be of importance. Under such circumstances the possibility of malingering or, at the very least, exaggerating of symptoms is a very real one.

The issue is a very complex one, but a general conclusion is that impaired levels of neuropsychological test performance can be simulated by individuals who attempt to fake the symptoms of head trauma, but convincing patterns of impaired test performance may be more difficult to fake (Mittenberg, Azrin, Millsaps, et al., 1993).

In this area of testing also, the typical approach is to have samples of normal subjects who take the specific tests under standard instructions vs. samples who are asked to simulate malingering. Memory disorder is likely to be a prominent head-trauma symptom. Several investigators have focused on susceptibility of malingering on such tests, particularly on the identification of patterns of performance that may be used to identify invalid protocols.

Bernard, Houston, and Napoli (1993), for example, administered a battery of five neuropsychological tests that included the Wechsler Memory Scale-Revised (see Chapter 15) to a sample of college students, with approximately half taking the tests under malingering instructions. Two discriminant equations were calculated and used to identify protocols as either "standard instructions" or "malingering." The overall accuracy rate for the two equations were 88% and 86%.

The discriminant function based on the Wechsler Memory Scale-Revised was able to identify correctly all 26 standard-instruction subjects, and misidentified 7 of the 31 malingering subjects as standard. Similar results are reported by Mittenberg, Azrin, Millsaps, et al. (1993).

Intelligence is also often affected in patients who have sustained head trauma, and therefore a comprehensive neuropsychological examination, such as the Halstead-Reitan, usually includes the administration of an intelligence test, typically the WAIS. A number of studies have shown that malingered and valid WAIS profiles can be distinguished on the basis of configural aspects (subtest patterns). In one study (Mittenberg, Theroux-Fichera, Zielinski, et al., 1995), WAIS-R protocols obtained from a sample of nonlitigating head-injured patients (and therefore lacking motivation to fake bad) were compared with those of a sample of normal subjects instructed to malinger head-trauma symptoms. A discriminant function was able to accurately classify 79% of the cases, with 76% true positives, and 82% true negatives. A discriminant function based on the difference between only two subtests, Vocabulary and Digit Span, also was successful in 71% of the cases.

Binder (1992) concluded that normal subjects if instructed to simulate brain damage can do so relatively well, but not completely. On some tests quantitative and qualitative differences do exist between genuine brain-damaged patients and normal simulating subjects. Binder also concluded that clinicians have poor rates of detection of malingering on traditional neuropsychological measures.

The Halstead-Reitan battery. As discussed in Chapter 15, the Halstead-Reitan battery is used to assess cognitive impairment due to head trauma, often in situations where liability or criminal responsibility may be at issue; thus there may be substantial financial or other incentives to fake, especially fake bad.

Several studies have shown that simulated and actual impairment can be distinguished by significant differences on several of the subtests, but the results vary somewhat from study to study, in part because of small sample fluctuations. Mittenberg, Rotholc, Russell, et al. (1996) did study a sizable sample (80 patients and 80 normal subjects with instructions to malinger) and did find that a discriminant function with 10 variables correctly identified 80% of the protocols, with 84% true positives and 94% true negatives. Other more complex approaches, including identifying test results that are significantly below chance, have been developed with promising results (e.g., Binder & Willis, 1991; Pankratz, Fausti, & Peed, 1975; Prigatano & Amin, 1993)

Other instruments. Studies of the fakability of other instruments do not fare as well. For example, on the Philadelphia Geriatric Center Morale Scale (discussed in Chapter 10), scores correlated .70 with the Edwards Social Desirability Scale in one study (Carstensen & Cone, 1983). As the authors indicated, it is to be expected that a measure of psychological well-being should correlate with social desirability because it is socially desirable to be satisfied with life and experience high morale. But such a high correlation calls into question the construct validity of the scale.

TEST ANXIETY

Test anxiety, like anxiety in general, is an unpleasant general emotion, where the individual feels apprehensive and worried. Test anxiety is a general emotion attached to testing situations, situations which the individual perceives as evaluative. Test anxiety is a major problem for many individuals; it can also be a major problem from a psychometric point of view, because it can lower a student's performance on many tests.

During the 1950s, there was a proliferation of scales designed to assess general anxiety (Sarason, 1960). One of the major ones was the Taylor Manifest Anxiety Scale (J. A. Taylor, 1953). This scale was a somewhat strange product. Clinical psychologists were asked to judge which MMPI items reflected a definition of anxiety and these became the Taylor, but the scale was really designed to measure "drive" – an important but generic concept in learning theory. Subsequently, the research focused on specific types of anxiety, such as social anxiety and test anxiety. Seymour Sarason and his colleagues (Sarason, Davidson, Lighthall, et al., 1960) developed the Test Anxiety Scale for Children, which became the first widely used test-anxiety instrument.

I. Sarason (1980) suggested that there are five characteristics of test anxiety:

1. The test situation is seen as difficult and threatening.
2. The person sees himself or herself as ineffective to cope with the test.
3. The person focuses on the undesirable consequences of being personally inadequate.
4. Self-deprecation interferes with possible solutions.
5. The person expects and anticipates failure and loss of regard by others.

Thus, the test-anxious individual performs more poorly under evaluative and stressful situations, such as classroom exams. If the situation is not evaluative or stressful, then there seem to be no differences between high- and low-test-anxious individuals (Sarason, 1980). For a review of the measurement and treatment of test anxiety, see Tryon (1980).

The Test Anxiety Questionnaire. The first measure to be developed was the Test Anxiety Questionnaire, originally a 42-item scale, later revised to 37 items (Sarason & Mandler, 1952). The respondent indicates for each item the degree of discomfort experienced. Reliability for this measure is excellent (e.g., .91 for split-half), and its construct validity is well supported in the literature.

The Test Anxiety Scale. I. Sarason (1958) developed a 37-item Test Anxiety Scale that has also become a popular scale. This scale has undergone several changes, but originally consisted of items rewritten from the Test Anxiety Questionnaire. Typical items are: "I get extremely worried when I take a surprise quiz" and "I wish taking tests did not bother me as much." This scale, in turn, resulted in at least three other instruments: the Worry-Emotionality Questionnaire (Liebert & Morris, 1967), the Inventory of Test Anxiety (Osterhouse, 1972), and best known, the Spielberger Test Anxiety Inventory (Spielberger, 1980).

Test anxiety is seen by some researchers as a special case of general anxiety. One popular theoretical model is the state-trait model of test anxiety (Spielberger, 1966) where state anxiety is seen as a transitory phenomenon, a reaction to a particular situation, whereas trait anxiety refers to a relatively stable personality characteristic. There seems to be general agreement that test anxiety results from the child's reactions to evaluative experiences during the preschool and early school years (Dusek, 1980). A number of studies have shown a negative relationship between test anxiety and performance on achievement tests, although some have not (e.g., Tryon, 1980).

The Test Anxiety Scale for Children (TASC). The TASC is probably the most widely used scale to assess test anxiety in children. The scale consists of 30 items to which the child responds "yes" or "no." The examiner reads the questions out loud, and the TASC can be group-administered. The scale seems to have adequate reliability and validity (e.g., K. T. Hill, 1972; Ruebush, 1963).

One basic issue concerns a child's willingness to admit to anxiety. Sarason and his colleagues developed two scales – a Lie scale composed of 11 questions related to anxiety to which the majority of children answer "yes" (e.g., "Do you ever worry?"), and a Defensiveness scale composed of 27 items that assess a child's willingness to admit to a wide range of feelings (e.g., "Are there some persons you don't like?"). These two scales are highly correlated and are usually given together as one questionnaire. The child's total defensiveness score is the number of items answered "no." Such scores do correlate about −.50 with TASC scores, that is, highly defensive children tend to admit to less anxiety. Therefore, it is suggested that, in a research setting, the scores of those children who score above the 90th percentile of defensiveness not be considered.

The TASC is clearly a multidimensional instrument, with most studies identifying some four factors; yet at the same time, only the total score is considered (Dusek, 1980).

Sarason and his colleagues (e.g., K. T. Hill & Sarason, 1966) conducted a 5-year longitudinal study of first and second graders, who were administered the TASC and the two lie-defensiveness scales in alternate years. Test-retest correlations over a 2-year period were modest (primarily in the .30s); over a 4-year period

the coefficients were very low, indicating lack of stability, but is the lack of stability a function of the test or a function of the construct? Does a test-anxious child stay anxious, or does that child learn to cope and conquer the anxiety?

In general, test anxiety seems to be composed, at least theoretically, of two separate aspects: worry and emotionality (e.g., Deffenbacher, 1980). Self-report scales to measure these two components have been developed (e.g., Liebert & Morris, 1967; Osterhouse, 1972).

The Test Anxiety Inventory (TAI). This Inventory (Spielberger, 1980) is one of the major measures used to assess test anxiety. The TAI yields a total score, as well as two separate subscores indicating worry and emotionality. The TAI has been used widely with both high-school and college students (Gierl & Rogers, 1996) and has been translated or adopted into many languages including Italian (Comunian, 1985) and Hungarian (K. Sipos, M. Sipos, & Spielberger, 1985); these versions seem to have adequate reliability and construct validity (see DeVito, 1984, for a review).

TESTWISENESS

Testwiseness or test sophistication refers to a person's ability to use the characteristics and format of a test or test situation, to obtain a higher score independent of the knowledge that the person has. Put more simply, there are individual differences in test-taking skills. Research suggests that test-wiseness is not a general trait, is not related to intelligence, but is clue-specific, that is, related to the particular type of clue found in the test items (Diamond & Evans, 1972; T. F. Dunn & Goldstein, 1959). Apparently, even in sophisticated college students, individual differences in testwiseness may be significant; Fagley (1987) reported that in a sample studied, testwiseness accounted for about 16% of the variance in test scores.

Millman, Bishop, and Ebel (1965) analyzed testwiseness into two major categories – those independent of the test and those dependent on it. Independent aspects include strategies to use test time wisely, to avoid careless errors, to make a best guess, and to choose an answer using deductive reasoning. Dependent aspects include strategies to interpret the intent of the test constructor and the use of cues contained within the test itself.

Experimental test. One of the tests developed to measure testwiseness is the Gibb (1964) Experimental Test of Testwiseness, which is composed of 70 multiple-choice questions. The questions appear to be difficult history items, but can be answered correctly by using cues given within the test question or the test itself. There are seven types of cues, including alliterative association cues in which a word in the correct answer alternative sounds like a word in the item stem, and length cues where the correct alternative is longer than the incorrect alternatives. The reliability of the test is adequate though low −.72 for K-R20 and .64 for a test-retest with a 2-week period (Harmon, D. T. Morse, & L. W. Morse, 1996). The validity has not yet been established, although a factor analysis suggested that the test could be characterized as tapping a general proficiency in testwiseness (Harmon, D. T. Morse, & L. W. Morse, 1996).

Eliminating testwiseness. Testwiseness is primarily a reflection of poorly written items and can be substantially if not totally eliminated by:

1. Avoiding use of a name or phrase repeated in both the stem and the correct alternative. For example: "The German psychologist Wundt was affiliated with the university of: (a) Leipzig, Germany (b) Zurich, Switzerland . . . etc."
2. Not using specific determiners (such as "all," "never") in the distractors. For example: "Wundt: (a) never visited other universities, (b) disliked all French psychologists . . . etc."
3. Not using a correct alternative that is longer. For example: "Wundt was: (a) French, (b) a neurosurgeon, (c) considered the father of experimental psychology . . ."
4. Not giving grammatical clues in the stem. For example: "Cattell was a ___ of Wundt. (a) acquaintance, (b) enemy, (c) student . . ."
5. Not using overlapping distractors. For example: "Wundt had at least ___ doctoral students. (a) 5, (b) 10, (c) 15 . . ."

SUMMARY

We have looked at the issue of faking in some detail. In part, because there is a rather large body of literature on this topic, and in part because a common concern about tests is whether they can be faked. The evidence suggests that the incidence of faking is rather low, and well-constructed questionnaires can indeed identify various types of faking with some degree of success. At the same time, our discussion should alert us to the need to get a subject's full cooperation, to act for the benefit of the client, and yet maintain a healthy prudence when we use test results.

SUGGESTED READINGS

Cofer, C. N., Chance, J., & Judson, A. J. (1949). A study of malingering on the Minnesota Multiphasic Personality Inventory. *Journal of Psychology, 27*, 491–499.

This is an "old" but fairly representative study of the early research in this area. The authors used the ubiquitous students in an introductory psychology course (N = 81) who took the MMPI under standard instructions and under malingering instructions (fake good or fake bad). The article is quite readable, and the statistical operations simple and easy to follow.

Ganellen, R. J. (1994). Attempting to conceal psychological disturbance: MMPI defensive response sets and the Rorschach. *Journal of Personality Assessment, 63*, 423–437.

The subjects of this study were commercial airline pilots who were required to undergo an independent psychological evaluation after completing a treatment program for alcohol or substance abuse. Because the results of the evaluation would have a bearing on whether their pilots' licenses would be reinstated, there was considerable incentive to fake good. Did they? Did the potential defensive response set affect the MMPI and the Rorschach? Read the article to find out!

Heilbrun, K., Bennett, W. S., White, A. J., & Kelly, J. (1990). An MMPI-based empirical model of malingering and deception. *Behavioral Sciences and the Law, 8*, 45–53.

This study is also in many ways illustrative of the current research on the MMPI and malingering and makes a nice contrast with the Cofer et al. (1949) article.

Lees-Haley, P. R., English, L. T., & Glenn, W. J. (1991). A fake bad scale on the MMPI-2 for personal injury claimants. *Psychological Reports, 68*, 203–210.

The scale developed in this study was "inspired" by Gough's Dissimulation Scale, which, as we have seen, was originally developed on MMPI items, but is part of the CPI rather than the MMPI.

DISCUSSION QUESTIONS

1. How would you define "stylistic" variables?

2. One technique to discourage faking is the use of filler items. How might you go about determining whether such a technique works?

3. Compare and contrast the F scale and the K scale of the MMPI.

4. Do you think that most people fake when they are taking a psychological test such as a personality inventory?

5. Is the nature of faking different for different types of tests? (e.g., consider a career-interest test such as the Strong vs. an intelligence test such as the WAIS).

17 The Role of Computers

AIM This chapter looks at the role of computers in psychological testing. Computers have been used as scoring machines, as test administrators, and recently as test interpreters. We look at the issue of computer-based test interpretation (CBTI) and questions about the validity of such interpretations. We consider ethical and legal issues, as well as a variety of other concerns. The role of computers in testing is a very "hot" topic currently, with new materials coming out frequently. Entire issues of professional journals are devoted to this topic (e.g., December 1985 issue of the *Journal of Consulting and Clinical Psychology* and the *School Psychology Review*, 1984, *13*, [No. 4]), and there are entire journals that focus on computers and psychology (e.g., *Computers in Human Behavior*). At the same time, this is a relatively new field, and many issues have not yet been explored in depth.

HISTORICAL PERSPECTIVE

Computers have been involved in some phase of psychological testing ever since the mid 1950s when computer centers were established on university campuses. One of the first uses of campus computers was to score tests that previously had been hand scored or mechanically scored.

Although a wide variety of tests were involved in this phase, from achievement tests to personality inventories, much of the early impetus focused on the MMPI.

A second area of computer and testing interface involved the direct administration of the test by computer. Many tests are now available for computerized administration, but here too, much of the pioneer work involved the MMPI.

A third area involved the increased use of computers to provide not just test scores but actual test interpretation; this function, too, was enhanced by the work of a number of psychologists at the University of Minnesota, who had been developing and refining the MMPI. One such event was the publication of an atlas

of MMPI profiles; a clinician testing a patient with the MMPI could code the resulting profile and look up in the atlas similarly coded profiles together with a clinical description of those clients. This was the beginning of the *actuarial* method of test prediction – interpretation of the meaning of a test score based upon empirical relationships rather than clinical subjective judgment.

The first computer-assisted psychological testing program was used in the early 1960s at the Mayo Clinic in Minnesota. The clinic had a large number of patients but a small psychology staff. There was a strong need for a rapid and efficient screening procedure to determine the nature and extent of psychiatric problems and symptoms. A solution was the administration of the MMPI using IBM cards, which could be read by a computer as answer sheets. A program was written that scored 14 MMPI scales, changed the raw scores to standard scores, and printed a series of descriptive statements, depending on the patient's scores. These statements were the kind of elementary statements that a clinician might make (e.g., a score of 70 or above on scale X suggests a great degree of anxiety). This program was simple, ignored configural patterns such as specific combinations of scales, but worked relatively well (R. D. Fowler, 1967, 1985). Similar work on the MMPI was also going on at the Institute of Living in Hartford, Connecticut (Glueck & Reznikoff, 1965).

A number of other computer-based test interpretation systems were then developed, each one more sophisticated than the earlier one, using data based on configural patterns, special scales and indices, taking into account whether the client is a psychiatric patient or a college student, and other aspects. Basically the procedure remains the same: There is a library of descriptive statements that are matched to particular scores or combinations of scores. By the 1980s, there were commercially available interpretive programs for a variety of personality inventories, the MMPI, the CPI, the Millon CMI, the Cattell 16 PF and others, but for practically all of them, no information was available as to how the computer program had been developed and whether the resulting descriptions were valid.

The entire process of testing can now be automated, from initial instructions, presentation of test items, scoring and transformation of raw scores, to the final narrative interpretation, and it will probably be automated in the future.

Currently, a number of other areas of interfacing are being explored, limited only by our creativity and ingenuity. One is the assessment of reaction time, another the use of test-item formats not found on the traditional paper-and-pencil (p-p) test, such as interactive graphics, movement, and speech – all possible on a computer screen.

Computer functions. Recapping briefly, three major roles that computers play in psychological testing are: (1) They can quickly and efficiently score tests and transform the raw scores into various forms, such as percentiles, T scores, etc.; (2) They can present and administer the test directly; (3) They can be programmed to generate interpretations of the test results.

Two additional functions that also have an impact on psychological testing, namely:

(1) They can store large amounts of information such as normative data or "banks" of items; and (2) they can control other pieces of equipment such as optical scanners, videodisc presentations, and so on.

The Mayo Clinic MMPI program. The computer program initially developed at the Mayo Clinic consisted of a scoring portion and an interpretation portion. The scoring simply tabulated the responses according to keyed responses for each scale. The interpretive portion consisted of simple narrative statements associated with specific scores. For example, a raw score between 11 and 14 on the Paranoia scale was associated with the statement "sensitive, alive to opinions of others." A score of 15 to 19 elicited the statement, "touchy, overly responsive to opinions of others. Inclined to blame others for own difficulties." A score of 20 or more elicited the statement "Resentful and suspicious of others, perhaps to the point of fixed false beliefs" (Kleinmuntz, 1977).

In addition to some 49 such descriptive statements, there were also a number of statements related to specific profile patterns. For example, if the person was older than 69 and had a hypomania score of less than 15, instead of printing the statement associated with a low hypomania score, the computer would print "low energy and motivation typical for age" (Hartman, 1986; Rome, et al., 1962).

COMPUTER SCORING OF TESTS

In general, there is relatively little controversy about the scoring of tests by computer. For many tests, the scoring can be done locally, sometimes using "generic" answer sheets that, for example, can be read by a Scantron machine. For other tests, the scoring sheets must be returned, either electronically or by mail, to the original publisher, or to another scoring service. Clearly, at least in objective-test items, the scoring reliability is perfect because computers do not get tired or inattentive, as humans do.

Optical scanners. Many tests can be scored using optical scanners that detect and track pencil marks. These marks are translated into data, the data is stored, and it can then be analyzed with the appropriate software programs. The scanner can also be combined directly with a microcomputer and a printer, so that the sequence from scoring to output is more fully automated. We can also entirely eliminate the paper-and-pencil format and place the entire test and its scoring key directly into the computer.

Configural scoring. In this book, we have considered test items as having a keyed response, and each response to an item is independent, yet added to responses on other items to obtain a total score on a scale. Other possibilities exist, and one of these is configural scoring, with the simplest case based on two items. Consider the following true-false items:

1. I like vanilla ice cream better than chocolate ice cream.
2. Most people are dishonest if they can get away with it.

Considered as a unit, there are four possible response patterns to these items: both items can be answered as true, both as false, the first one as true and the second as false, and vice versa. Let's assume that empirically we find that 80% of student leaders give a false-false response, whereas only 20% of student nonleaders do so. We now have the possibility of scoring the two items as a pattern indicative of some real-life behavior (assuming we rule out chance and other possibilities). Essentially that is what *configural* or *pattern* scoring is all about, and the computer can be extremely useful in carrying out such calculations, which might be prohibitive if done by hand. For a good example of a review of a computer scoring program (in this case for the Luria-Nebraska Neuropsychological Battery), see Hampton, 1986.

COMPUTER ADMINISTRATION OF TESTS

Type of service. Generally speaking there are three types of service currently available:

1. Local processing. Here a test is administered locally, often with software that can score and interpret the test. Such software is typically obtained from the test publisher, and it may have a built-in limit. For example, after 25 adminis-

trations, the software "expires" and new software must be purchased. This type of service is in many ways the most flexible and least time consuming, but may be too expensive for the individual practitioner, or may not be available for many tests.

2. Terminal to mainframe computer. Here the test is administered through a local terminal (microcomputer), the data is then transmitted to a central-location computer by phone lines or electronic means, and the test results are returned to the local terminal and printed there. This eliminates the need for a separate answer sheet, and results are available almost immediately.

3. Remote central location. Here the test is administered in the traditional paper-and-pencil (p-p) mode, and the special answer sheet is mailed to a central location such as the test publisher, where the test is processed. The scored sheet and/or test results are then sent back to the original administrator, by mail or fax. Currently, this is probably the most common yet most antiquated method; the main problem is the time lag.

Essentially, the administration of a test on a computer terminal is not very different from a paper-pencil standard presentation. Usually, there are instructions presented and the examinee must indicate understanding by pressing a particular key. Often there are demonstration or practice items, with feedback as to whether the answer given is correct or not. Responses can be given through a keyboard, a clicking device (mouse), a light pen, by touching the screen manually, and in the future, by voice response. Other possibilities are technically feasible and limited only by our imagination. For example, S. L. Wilson, Thompson, and Wylie (1982) used a dental plate activated by the tongue to permit handicapped individuals who lack the capacity for speech or the use of limbs, to select from five distinct responses per item. For an example of an early automated system to administer the WAIS, see Elwood and Griffin, (1972).

One major advantage of the computer in test administration is that the computer demands an active response to the instructions and to the practice problems. It is therefore not possible to begin testing until there is evidence that the respondent has mastered the instructions and understands what is to be done.

Paper-and-Pencil (p-p) vs. Computer Format (cf)

When we take a p-p test and administer it through a computer, we haven't simply changed the medium, but we have potentially changed the test. Thus, we cannot assume that existing norms and evidence of the reliability and validity of the p-p format apply automatically to the cf; equivalence of the two needs to be established.

There are at least four potential ways in which a cf test can differ from the original p-p version:

1. The method of presentation: for example, a graph may be more readable and clearer on the original p-p version than on the cf version.

2. The requirements of the task: for example, on a p-p version the examinee can go back and review earlier items and answers; on the cf version this may not be possible.

3. The method of responding: for example, the p-p version of the ACL requires the examinee to check those items that are self-descriptive and items that are not are left blank. The computer version cannot accept a blank response, and each item must be responded to as self-descriptive or not.

4. The method of interpretation: for example, norms available for a p-p version may not be fully applicable to the cf version (Noonan & Sarvela, 1991).

Evidence for equivalence. Equivalence is present if: (1) The rank order of scores on the two versions closely approximate each other; and (2) The means, variability, and shape of score distribution are approximately the same, or have been made the same statistically. Empirically, when p-p tests are changed to cf, two types of evidence are usually investigated to show that the two forms are equivalent: (1) The means under the two conditions should be the same; and (2) The inter-correlations, such as among subtests, should also be the same. Occasionally, a third type of evidence is presented – the correlational pattern between cf version and relevant criteria are of the same magnitude as the p-p version. Sometimes, it is somewhat difficult to determine whether there is equivalence or not because we would expect some random fluctuations in means. For example, an arithmetic reasoning test was given to a large number of Navy recruits, either p-p or cf. The mean score on the cf was significantly lower by 1.04 raw-score points – but is such a difference of practical import?

Equivalence can also be defined more broadly as equivalence in construct validity – specifically equivalence in factor structure, and equivalence of factor loadings. W. C. King and Miles (1995) assessed this type of equivalence in four noncognitive instruments and found that administration mode had no effect on equivalence.

Theoretical aspects. From a theoretical point of view, there are two major approaches to assessing the equivalence of p-p and cf versions (F. R. Wilson, Genco, & Yager, 1985):

1. Classical test theory. Here we wish to show that the two versions yield equal means and variances, and that the pattern of correlations with other measures, as in criterion validity, is essentially identical. We may also wish to assess the convergent-discriminant validity of the two forms.

2. Generalizability theory. Here we wish to ask the questions whether obtained results are generalizable across different conditions; i.e., if we wish to diagnose an individual as having a particular psychiatric syndrome, it should not make any difference whether the MMPI was administered as a cf or as a p-p instrument, and what is more important, we can identify various sources of potential variability. (For an example that combines the two approaches, see F. R. Wilson, Genco, & Yager, 1985.)

Issues of test construction. Although it would seem an easy matter to change a p-p test into a cf, there are a number of issues, many related to the question of equivalence between the two forms (see Noonan & Sarvela, 1991).

On a paper-and-pencil test, the instructions and sample items are typically presented at the beginning, and the examinee can go back to them at any time. On a computer, these options have to be explicitly programmed.

On a paper-and-pencil format, there are a number of ways to indicate a response, but most involve a simple mark on an answer sheet. On the computer, responses can be indicated by pressing a key, clicking a mouse, touching the screen, and so on. After the response is entered, the computer can be programmed to present the next item or to present an option such as, "are you sure? yes or no." This would require a double keystroke response for every item, which may safeguard against "accidental" responses, but prolongs testing time and may, for some examinees, become an aversive feature.

When students change an answer on a p-p test, research seems to suggest that it is more likely that the change involves going from an incorrect answer to a correct one rather than the other way (L. T. Benjamin, 1984). Should a computerized test then be programmed so that the respondent is allowed to return to an earlier item? In adaptive testing, this would create difficulties.

On a p-p test, examinees often will answer easy items, skip the more difficult items, and then go back to answer the more difficult ones. To program these options into a computer is quite difficult, and requires a certain amount of interaction between examinee and machine that may alter the nature of the test.

At present, computer screens cannot comfortably present a full page of writing. If the test item is a matching exercise, this could present difficulties.

The nature of the test, whether it is a diagnostic test or a mastery test, interacts with the nature of the computer to create some challenges. Diagnostic or placement tests, when implemented on a computer system, ordinarily use branching (see discussion that follows), where the testing sequence is directly related to the responses given on earlier items. In a mastery test, such as an achievement or "classroom" type test, items are usually presented sequentially, although branching could also take place.

When to discontinue testing also can differ between diagnostic or mastery testing. In a diagnostic test, failure at one level might move the examinee to less difficult material. In a mastery test, testing is stopped once the examinee has answered a minimal number of items either correctly or incorrectly (you will recall our discussion of basal and ceiling levels with cognitive tests in Chapter 5).

Finally, in diagnostic tests we are typically interested in obtaining a full picture of the individual, not just a diagnosis that this person is psychotic, but a detailed analysis of the strengths and difficulties the person experiences. In mastery testing, we are usually more interested in global scores, such as knowing that this examinee scored at the 87th percentile on mastery of elementary algebra.

The type of test item also interacts with the computer format. For now, computers are quite adept at using selected-response items (such as multiple choice and T-F), but are much less able to cope with constructed-response items such as essays.

The size of the item pool is also something to consider. At least theoretically, computers could handle any number of items, but some types of tests such as diagnostic tests, or some procedures such as branching would generally require larger item pools.

For the present, most efforts that have become applied involve true-false and/or multiple-choice items, and we have not as yet taken advantage of the computer's capability of presenting visual and changing stimuli. No doubt in the future, we will have tests of mechanical aptitude for example, which might present moving machines that need to be altered in some way, automobile engines that need to be fixed, and so on. Sound and animation may well be an integral part of future cf tests.

General findings. Most studies of the comparability or equivalence of p-p tests with their cf versions indicate a great degree of comparability with such tests as the MMPI, CPI, Strong-Campbell Interest Inventory, and others in a wide variety of samples such as gifted children, children and adolescents, college students, and geriatric patients (e.g., Carr, Wilson, Ghosh, et al., 1982; Finger & Ones, 1999; L. Katz & Dalby, 1981; Scissons, 1976; Simola & Holden, 1992; Vansickle & Kapes, 1993). Despite this, the results should not be taken as a blanket assumption of equivalence. Schuldberg (1988) pointed out that most previous research used statistical designs that were not very sensitive to possible differences between p-p and cf administrations; however, using such sensitive statistical analyses, he found few differences or differences that were small in magnitude on the two versions of the MMPI.

There may well be differences in various subgroups of individuals, and the computerized procedure may well interact with personality, attitudinal, or psychopathological variables. For example, Finegan and Allen (1994) compared a variety of cf questionnaires, such as attitude and personality scales, with their p-p versions. Basically the two modes of presentation were highly correlated in their Canadian college-student subjects, but there was some evidence that computer administration increased slightly socially desirable responding among subjects with little computer experience. Waring, Farthing, and Kidder-Ashley (1999) found that impulsive students answered multiple choice questions more quickly and less accurately than reflective students.

In fact, a handful of studies that have incorporated other variables into their equivalence design, suggest that cf result in lesser social desirability, more extreme responses, more self-disclosure, more interest, and greater awareness of thoughts and feelings. Other studies do report greater social desirability and reduction in candor (King & Miles, 1995). Clearly, this is not a closed issue.

In addition, much of the research reports the equivalence results in terms of correlation coefficients between the p-p version scores and the cf version scores. Keep in mind that a high correlation coefficient can be obtained even if the scores on one format are consistently higher or lower than on the other format.

At the same time, if a cf version of a test is not equivalent to the p-p version, that does not mean that the cf version is useless and should be thrown out. It may well be that the cf version is *more* reliable and valid than the p-p format, but this needs to be determined empirically.

Some studies have not found equivalence. For example, in a study of the Raven's Progressive Matrices, the scores on the cf version were significantly different from the p-p version, and the authors concluded that separate norms were needed (Watts, Baddeley, & Williams, 1982).

One potential difference between p-p and cf is that more items are endorsed on the cf version. One hypothesized explanation is that individuals "open up" more to a computer than to a live examiner. Another possibility is that the cf version requires a response to be given to every item, whereas on the p-p version, items can be left blank or skipped.

Equivalence of reliability. Few studies have addressed this issue. D. L. Elwood and Griffin (1972) compared the p-p and the cf version of the WAIS through a test-retest design, and found the results to be virtually identical.

Equivalence of speeded tests. Many clerical and perceptual tests are highly speeded. They consist of items that are very easy, such as crossing out all the letter e's in a page of writing, but the score reflects the ability to perform the task rapidly; if sufficient time were given, all examinees would obtain perfect scores. With such tests, there are a number of potential differences between the p-p version and the cf version. In general, marking a bubble on an answer sheet takes considerably longer than pressing a computer key. Several studies do indicate that with speed tests, subjects are much faster in the cf version, that the reliability of scores obtained on the cf presentation is as high as that of the p-p version, and that despite the differences in mean performance, the correlation between the two forms (reflecting the rank order of individuals) can be quite high (e.g., Greaud & Green, 1986; Lansman, Donaldson, Hunt, et al., 1982).

One possible advantage of the cf is that a fixed number of items can be administered, and time elapsed can be tracked simultaneously with number of items attempted. This is much more difficult to do with p-p tests. Whether such information can be used in a predictive sense (e.g., to predict job performance) remains to be seen.

Even with tests that are not highly speeded, equivalence can be problematic if speed is involved. For example, Van de Vijver and Harsveld (1994) analyzed the equivalence of the General Aptitude Test Battery as administered to Dutch applicants to a military academy. You recall from Chapter 14 that the GATB is a general intelligence speed test that uses a multiple-choice format and is composed of seven subtests, such as vocabulary and form matching. Differences between the p-p and cf versions were "small though noticeable," with the cf subtests producing faster and more inaccurate responses, with simple clerical tasks affected more than complex tasks.

A meta-analysis of the equivalence of p-p versus cf versions of cognitive ability tests indicated a significant difference between speeded tests and power tests. For power tests, the typical correlation was .97, whereas for speeded tests it was .72. Keep in mind that the definitions of speeded and of power tests, such as the one we gave in Chapter 1, are "idealized" types; most tests are somewhere in between. Many power tests, such as the SAT and the GRE, do in fact have significant time limits.

Equivalence of checklists. Checklists may present problems also. On a p-p version, the respondent checks those items that are pertinent and leaves the rest blank. The cf forces the respondent to read all items and respond to each one as, "Yes" or "No." On the ACL, for example, people tend to select many more adjectives as self-descriptive when they respond to the cf version, and most of the additional adjectives checked are favorable ones (B. F. Green, 1991).

Equivalence of computers. One of the issues that has not been fully explored is the equivalence of different computers, specifically the degree of resolution of the screen (i.e., how clear the image is on the monitor) and the range of color available. The same test may not be the same when presented on two different computer screens, and this needs to be assessed.

Report of results. When a test is administered through computer, it is relatively easy to program the computer to calculate the raw scores and to change such scores into standard scores or derived scores, such as T scores and percentiles. The computer is an ideal instrument to carry out such calculations based on extensive normative data that can be programmed.

Do examinees like the computer? Initially, there was a great deal of concern that computers might be seen as impersonal and cold, and that examinees would respond negatively to the experience, and perhaps alter their test answers. In fact, the research indicates that in most cases, if not all, examinees like computer testing. These studies have obtained similar results with a variety of clients and a variety of tests (e.g., M. J. Burke, Normand, & Raju, 1987; Klingler, Johnson, & Williams, 1976; N. C. Moore, Summer, & Bloor, 1984; F. L. Schmidt, Urry, & Gugel, 1978).

There is however, the phenomenon of "computer anxiety," an emotional fear or discomfort that some individuals experience when interacting with computers. Studies suggest that female college undergraduates are more anxious than males, older people are more anxious, and that computer anxiety is inversely related to computer experience (Chua, Chen, & Wong, 1999).

Preference of p-p or cf. In most studies where this is assessed, subjects typically prefer the cf over the p-p format. For example, in one study of the MMPI, 77 of 99 subjects preferred the cf (D. M. White, Clements, & Fowler, 1986). Most of these studies however, use American-college students, who are fairly sophisticated computer users.

Test preparation. As part of test administration by computer we might consider the possible role of the computer as a mentor. H. V. Knight, Acosta, and Anderson (1988) compared the use of microcomputers vs. textbook materials as aids in the preparation of high-school students to take the ACT (a college entrance examination along the lines of the SAT). They found that students in the computer group scored significantly higher on the composite and math subtests but not on the science subtest.

Issue of disclosure. One of the earliest studies on the effect of computer administration on subjects' responses involved patients at an alcohol-abuse treatment clinic who tended to report greater amounts of alcohol consumption in a computer-administered interview than in face-to-face psychiatric interviews (Lucas, Mullin, Luna, et al., 1977). The results of this study were widely interpreted as an indication that subjects will be more frank and disclosing, especially about personal and negative matters, in the more impersonal computer-administered situation. Subsequent studies supported this interpretation, but some did not (e.g., Carr, Ghosh, & Ancil, 1983; T. Reich, et al., 1975; Skinner & Allen, 1983).

Issues of test security. Although computer testing would seem to provide greater security than the traditional format of p-p tests, there are a number of issues that need to be faced.

Achievement tests such as course examinations that are available on computer illustrate some issues. Should such exams be made available at any time for the student to take? What kind of monitoring, if any, is needed to prevent cheating or misuse of the system? Should examinees be allowed to "preview" a test or only some examples? Should the examinee be given feedback at the end of the test; if so, what kind? For example, should the feedback simply include the score with some normative interpretation ("your score of 52 equals a B+") or more detailed feedback as to which items were missed, and so on.?

COMPUTER-BASED TEST INTERPRETATIONS (CBTI)

We now come to the third area of computer usage, where the test results are interpreted by the computer. Obviously, it is not the computer that does the interpretation. The computer is programmed to produce such an interpretation based on the test results. Such CBTIs are commercially available on a significant number of tests, especially personality inventories; for example, on the MMPI there are at least 14 such computer-based scoring systems (Eyde, Kowal, & Fishburne, 1991).

Types of CBTIs. CBTI systems can be characterized along two dimensions – the amount of information they provide and the method used to develop the program (Moreland, 1991).

In terms of amount of information, reports can vary substantially, from a simple presentation of scores, to graphs, information on what the scores mean, and interpretive and integrated descriptions of the client. For our purposes, we can distinguish at least three levels:

1. Descriptive reports. In these reports each of the test scales is interpreted individually without reference to the other scales, and the comments made are directly reflective of the empirical data and are usually fairly brief. For example, a high score on a depression scale might be interpreted as, "Mr. Jones reports that he is very depressed." These reports, though limited, can be useful when a multivariate instrument (such as the MMPI) has many scales or when there are many protocols to be processed.

2. Screening reports. These are somewhat more "complicated" in that the computer narrative reflects scale relationships rather than the individual scales taken one at a time. Thus a descriptive statement tied to a particular high score on a depression scale might appear only if a second scale is also high; if the second scale score is low, then a different statement might be printed out.

3. Consultative reports. These are the most complex and look very much like the report a clinician might write on a client who has been assessed. The intent of these reports is to provide a detailed analysis of the test data, using professional language, and typically written for professional colleagues. This type of report is analagous to having a consultation with an expert on that test, a consultation that would ordinarily not be available to the typical practitioner. This type of report is produced by scoring services for multivariate instruments such as the MMPI and the CPI. To see what CBTI reports look like for a wide variety of tests, see Krug (1987).

Actuarial vs clinical. In terms of development, there are basically two methods at present, by which such computer software is developed. One is the *actuarial* method, and the other is the *clinical* method.

1. The actuarial method. Historically, this approach was given great impetus by P. E. Meehl, a Minnesota psychologist who in various publications (e.g., Meehl 1954; 1956) argued that test results could be automated into standard descriptions by the use of a computer. In 1956, Meehl called for a good "cookbook" for test interpretation, just as a cook "creates" a dish by following a set of instructions. The idea was simply to determine empirically the relationship between test scores and nontest criteria and to use this actuarial data to make predictions for a specific client. Thus, if on test X of depression, we find that 85% of clients who score above 70 attempt suicide within a year, we can now predict that Mr. Jones, who scored 78, will most likely attempt suicide. There are in fact a few examples of this approach in the literature, most notably on the Personality Inventory for Children (Lachar & Gdowski, 1979).

As one might expect, there have been several attempts to produce such actuarial cookbooks for the MMPI (e.g., Drake & Oetting, 1959; Gilberstadt & Duker, 1965; P. A. Marks & Seeman, 1963), but these systems have failed when applied to other samples than those originally used. One of the major problems is that a large number of MMPI profiles cannot be classified following the complicated rules that such MMPI cookbooks require for actuarial interpretation.

2. The clinical method. The clinical method involves one (or more) experts who certainly would use the results of the research literature and actuarial data and basically combine these data with his or her own acuity and clinical skills to generate a library of potential interpretations associated with different scale scores and combinations. A variety of such clinical computer-based interpretive systems are now available for a wide variety of tests, but primarily for the MMPI.

One argument present in the literature (e.g., Matarazzo, 1986) is that the same test scores, as on the MMPI, can be interpreted differently given different demographic factors. For example, a high paranoia-scale score would be interpreted one way if obtained by a 45-year-old patient with schizophrenia, but rather differently if obtained by a 21-year-old college student. The clinician attempts to take into account the unique characteristics of the client, whereas the computer can only be programmed in a nomothetic fashion, for example, if the client is older than 28, it interprets *this* way, if younger, it interprets *that* way.

Unfortunately, the literature suggests that in attempting to take into account the individual uniqueness of the client, the validity of clinical reports generated by clinicians usually decreases, primarily because clinicians are inconsistent in their judgment strategies, whereas computers are consistent. Virtually all the 100 or so studies that compare the clinical vs. the actuarial methods, show that the actuarial methods are equal to or exceed the accuracy of the clinical methods. The greater the extent to which clinicians rely on empirically established methods of data interpretation and collection, the greater their overall accuracy. The computer has tremendous potential to play a major role in increasing the accuracy of psychological evaluations and predictions, as the programing becomes more sophisticated in evaluating an individual's test scores.

Automated vs. actuarial. Note that automated or computerized test interpretation is not equivalent to actuarial. Meehl (1954) specified that an actuarial method must be prespecified; that is, it must follow a set procedure and be based on empirically established relations. A computerized test interpretation may simply model or mimic subjective clinical judgment, or it may actually be based on actuarial relationships. As a matter of fact, very few computerized-report programs are based solely on actuarial relationships. Why is that? In large part because, at present, actuarial rules on tests such as the MMPI would tend to classify few protocols at best.

Study the clinician. Because we basically want the computer to do what an expert clinician does, we can start by studying expert clinicians. One example is the work of Kleinmuntz (1969) who asked several experienced MMPI interpreters to sort 126 MMPI profile sheets, which had been previously identified as belonging to adjusted or maladjusted college students. The expert who achieved the highest hit rate was then asked to think aloud as he sorted MMPI profiles. His verbalizations were tape recorded, and specific decision rules were then devised. For example, the first rule used by the clinician was that if there were 4 or more MMPI scales higher than 70, that profile would be called maladjusted. A second rule was that if all the clinical scales were below 60, if the Hypomania scale (scale 9) was below 80, and Mt (a maladjustment scale) was below a raw score of 10, then the profile would be called adjusted (see Kleinmuntz, 1969, for the set of 16 rules used). These rules were then programmed into a computer to be used to score MMPI profiles. In a follow up study, the computer program did as well as the best MMPI clinician, and better than the average clinician.

Reliability of CBTIs. In one sense, the reliability of CBTIs is perfect. If the same responses, say for the MMPI, are entered and then reentered, the computer will produce the same exact report. This is not the case with a clinician, who may interpret the same MMPI profile somewhat differently on different occasions. On the other hand, if the same protocol is submitted to several scoring services, the result may not be the same.

However, at present, aside from the MMPI, such choice is not available for most tests.

The validity of CBTIs. As with the Rorschach, and indeed with almost every test, we cannot simply ask, "Are CBTIs valid?" We must ask, "Which CBTI and for what purpose?" Not many studies are available to answer these questions, but hopefully they will be in the future. Ideally, to evaluate a CBTI, we need to evaluate the library of item statements and the interpretive rules by which statements are selected. Very few studies have been done where experts are asked to look at the interpretive system and evaluate the accuracy of the decision rules that lead to the interpretive statements (e.g., Labeck, Johnson, & Harris, 1983). Such information is typically not available, and thus most studies evaluate the resulting CBTI, either in toto or broken down into sections.

A number of studies can be subsumed under the label of "consumer satisfaction," in that clinicians are asked to rate the accuracy of such reports, using a wide variety of experimental approaches, some of which control possible confounding effects and some of which do not (see Labeck, Johnson, & Harris, 1983; J. T. Webb, Miller, & Fowler, 1970, for examples). Moreland (1987) listed 11 such studies (although many others are available especially on the MMPI) with accuracy ratings ranging from a low of 32% to a high of 91%, and a median of 78.5%. Although this consumer satisfaction approach seems rather straightforward, there are a number of methodological problems with this approach (see D. K. Snyder, Widiger, & Hoover, 1990). A general limitation of these studies is that high ratings of satisfaction do not prove validity.

In a second category of studies, clinicians are asked to complete a symptom checklist, a Q sort, or some other means of capturing their evaluation, based on a CBTI. These judgments are then compared to those made by clinicians familiar with the client or based on some other criteria, such as an interview. Moreland (1987) listed five such studies, with mean correlations between sets of ratings (based on CBTI vs. based on knowledge of the client) between .22 and .60, with the median of 18 such correlation coefficients as .33. Such studies now are relatively rare (see Moreland, 1991, for a review of such studies).

Such findings essentially show that there is moderate agreement between clinicians – the clinicians who are asked to judge the CBTI and the clinician who originally supplied the test interpretation. Such agreement may well be based on clinical "lore"; although the clinicians may agree with each other, both could be incorrect.

A third set of studies are external criterion studies, where the accuracy of CBTI is matched against some criterion. As Moreland (1987) points out, these studies have all sorts of problems, and the results are mixed. However, at least for the MMPI, the results look fairly good, and the validity coefficients of computerized reports are fairly comparable with those found in the literature for conventional MMPI reports. Yet, we must consider Faust and Ziskin (1989) who concluded, "that there is little scientific basis for determining the validity of CBTIs." (For a critical response, see Brodsky, 1989.)

Perceived validity. It is quite possible that simply seeing that a report is computer generated may make that CBTI more acceptable as correct and objective.

Honaker, Hector, and Harrell (1986) asked psychology graduate students and practicing psychologists to rate the accuracy of MMPI interpretive reports that were labeled as generated by either a computer or a licensed clinician. There was no difference in accuracy ratings between the two types of reports. In addition, some reports contained a purposefully inaccurate statement, and these reports were rated as less valid. Experienced clinicians tended to perceive reports labeled computer generated as less useful and less comprehensive than the same reports labeled clinician generated. Thus, this study failed to support the claim that computer-generated interpretations are assigned more credibility than is warranted.

L. W. Andrews and Gutkin (1991) asked school personnel to rate identical reports that differed only in terms of authorship – computer vs. school psychologist. The results indicated that authorship had virtually no effect in how the reports were perceived as to overall quality, credibility, and diagnostic interpretation.

Usefulness of CBTIs. CBTIs can provide unique quantitative assistance to the test user (Roid,

1985). In particular, CBTI reports can assist in answering four questions:

1. How should the results of the test be tempered in light of the client's background, demographic variables such as age, base rates of possible diagnostic conditions, and so on. In particular, CBTI programs can help the clinician become more aware of moderator variables that may affect test interpretation for a particular client.

2. How would experts on the test analyze and interpret the patterns of observed scores, indices, etc.?

3. What research findings have implications for this particular client?

4. How usual or unusual are the client's scores, patterns of diagnostic signs, and so on?

Potential limitations. Two major potential limitations of CBTIs have been identified. First there is the potential for misuse. CBTIs are widely available, may be used by individuals who do not have the appropriate training, or be uncritically accepted by professionals. Second, there is the issue of excessive generality, or what is sometimes called "the Aunt Fanny" report – a report that is so general that its contents could apply to anyone's Aunt Fanny. That is, CBTIs are basically built on modal descriptions or generic types.

The Barnum effect. One of the major problems in trying to study the validity of CBTIs is the Barnum effect. The "Barnum effect" (named after the P. T. Barnum circus which had a little something for everyone) refers to the phenomenon of accepting a personality interpretation that is comprised of vague statements that have a high base rate in the population (Meehl, 1956). For a review of this topic, see C. R. Snyder, Shenkel, & Lowery, 1977.

Here is a typical Barnum-effect study. College students were administered the 16 PF and were subsequently provided with a CBTI. One sample of students received a CBTI and a "Barnum" interpretation, while another sample also received a third interpretation labeled a "prosecuting attorney" interpretation. The CBTI was based on a library of some 1,500 possible statements associated with different scores on the 16 PF. The Barnum version, identical in appearance to the CBTI, was made up of generic statements that tend to be true of most people (such as "He has a great deal of potential that is not well utilized"). The prosecuting attorney reports were essentially identical to the Barnum reports but contained a lot of clinical jargon (for example, the word "potential" became "libidinal energy used in maintaining defenses"). Each student had to select which interpretation was most accurate and which they liked best. In general, the Barnum interpretation was perceived as the most accurate and the prosecuting attorney as the least accurate. There was no difference in liking between the actual interpretation and the Barnum one, but the prosecuting attorney was generally disliked (O'Dell, 1972).

It is not surprising that the Barnum report was seen as high in accuracy, after all it consisted of statements that are true of almost everyone. The point is that to judge the accuracy of a CBTI we need to assess that accuracy against a benchmark – in this case, that obtained through a Barnum report.

A number of studies use real and bogus CBTIs that are rated as to perceived accuracy. The difference between average ratings for the real CBTI and for the bogus CBTIs expressed as a "percentage correct" increment is used as the perceived discriminant accuracy of the CBTI (Guastello & Rieke, 1990). For example, in one study, undergraduates completed a personality questionnaire and received a CBTI. Approximately half of the students received a CBTI based on their test scores, while half received a bogus CBTI, and both were asked to rate their relative accuracy. The real CBTIs were rated as 74.5% accurate while the bogus CBTIs were rated as 57.9% accurate. The authors concluded that the amount of rated accuracy associated with the Barnum effect was 66.2% (S. J. Guastello, D. D. Guastello, & Craft, 1989; for other studies, see Baillargeon & Danis, 1984; S. J. Guastello & Rieke, 1990).

Obviously, how favorable the statements in the CBTI are affects the ratings, and this must be controlled experimentally and/or statistically. There are also many ways to make up a bogus report. The bogus report may be a randomly selected real report that belongs to someone else, or it may be made up partially or totally. One can use an average test profile as the source for the bogus report, or one can create a bogus report simply by reversing extreme T scores – for example, a T

score of 30 (two SDs below the mean) would be fed to the computer as a T score of 70 (two SDs above the mean). S. J. Guastello & Rieke (1990) had college students take the 16 PF and subsequently rate their CBTI, as well as a bogus one based on the average 16 PF class profile. The real CBTI were rated as 76.3% accurate overall, while the bogus report was rated as 71.7% – thus the real reports were judged better than the bogus report by a very small margin.

CBTI vs. the clinician. As yet, there is little evidence of how CBTIs compare to the traditional report prepared by the individual clinician. In one study that compared the two, CBTIs were judged substantially superior in writing style, accuracy, and completeness (Klingler, Miller, Johnson, et al., 1977). In another study, both types of reports were judged to be mediocre in accuracy and usefulness (Rubenzer, 1992). However, most of the studies in this area involve only one case and are anecdotal in nature (see Moreland, 1991). It can also be argued that a clinician's report is not a good criterion against which to judge the validity of the CBTI.

Test X vs. Test Y. It would seem natural to compare the relative accuracy and usefulness of different tests and their CBTI, but almost no studies exist on this. C. J. Green (1982) compared two CBTIs on the MMPI with the CBTI on the Millon Clinical Multiaxial Inventory (MCMI). Twenty-three clinicians, such as psychiatrists, social workers, and clinical psychologists, rated the CBTIs for 100 of their patients, on the basis of how adequate was the information, how accurate, and how useful (i.e., how well organized) was the report. One of the two MMPI report systems was judged as substantially less satisfactory on almost all aspects, and the MCMI was judged more accurate on interpersonal attitudes, personality traits and behaviors, self-images, and styles of coping.

SOME SPECIFIC TESTS

Criticisms of MMPI CBTIs. Butcher (1978) listed five criticisms of CBTI for the MMPI:

1. Computerized reports are not an adequate substitute for clinical judgment, and a computerized report does not do away with the need for a trained clinician.

2. Reports may be incorrect because they fail to take into account relevant demographic aspects such as age or educational background.

3. Once something is computerized, it often becomes "respected" even though it was not validated to begin with.

4. Computerized interpretation systems may not be kept current.

5. The validity of computer-generated narratives has not been adequately established.

Accuracy of MMPI CBTIs. As we have seen above, this is a complex issue. One aspect is that the CBTI may not necessarily identify the major themes pertinent to a specific client. A good illustration is a study cited by Schoenfeldt (1989) in which an MMPI protocol was submitted to four different companies that provide computer-based interpretations. The results were compared with a blind analysis of the MMPI profile by a clinician and with information obtained during a clinical interview. The four computer narratives failed to identify several important problems of the client that included depression, alcohol abuse, and assaultive behavior.

The Millon Clinical Multiaxial Inventory (MCMI). Eight clinical psychologists rated the accuracy of CBTI for the MCMI. For each client a clinician received two reports: one generated by the computer and one generated randomly, and these reports were rated as accurate or inaccurate for each of the seven sections of the report. Percentage of accuracy ranged from 62% to 78% (median of 73%) for the real report and from 32% to 64% (median of 39%) for the random report, with two sections of the report judged as no more accurate than those of the randomly generated report. Thus, although the results supported the judged accuracy of the MCMI, this study points out the need for a "control" group to determine whether the obtained results yield findings over and above those generated by random procedures (Moreland & Onstad, 1987; Piersma, 1987).

The Marital Satisfaction Inventory (MSI). For each of the MSI scales, low, moderate, and high, ranges of scores have been determined empirically. These ranges differ from scale to scale, so that a clinician would need to know that, for example, a *T* score of 65 on one scale might well represent a moderate score, while on another scale it would represent a high score. The test author (D. K. Snyder, 1981) developed a CBTI composed of more than 300 interpretive paragraphs based on individual scale elevations as well as configural patterns, both within and across spouses. (For an interesting case study and an example of a CBTI, see D. K. Snyder, Lachar, & Wills, 1988.)

Neuropsychological Testing and Computers

Report = work. A neuropsychological report represents a great deal of professional time, and so it would be most advantageous if such reports could be computer generated. Also there is research that indicates a greater diagnostic accuracy for mechanical/statistical methods of data combination vs. human clinical judgment, and so the diagnostic accuracy of a well-designed computer program should exceed that of clinicians.

However, at present this potential has not been realized. Adams and Heaton (1985; 1987) point out that there are several obstacles to the development of computer programs to interpret neuropsychological test results:

1. There is little uniformity in clinical neuropsychology. The specific tests, the types of interpretations and recommendations, as well as the type of diagnostic decisions made are so varied, that computer programs have great difficulty in incorporating all these parameters.

2. We have an incomplete state of knowledge about brain-behavior relationships. Most research studies are based on samples that have well-defined conditions, but in most clinical settings the patients who need a diagnostic workup have conditions that are not so clearly defined.

3. In normal adults, performance on neuropsychological tests is correlated positively with education and negatively with age, indicating that such demographic variables are important in neuropsychological test interpretation. We do not yet have the adequate norms to incorporate such corrective data in our computerized decision systems. There are other factors that complicate interpretation of neuropsychological test results, such as low intelligence. A clinician can consider the unique combination of variables present in a client but, for now, a computer cannot.

4. Finally, the use of such computer programs can be considered premature and possibly unethical at this time.

Test scoring. Many neuropsychological tests are quite simple to score in that they require a simple correct-not correct decision or time taken to perform a certain task, and so on. Thus computer scoring of neuropsychological tests would not necessarily provide a major advantage.

For some tests, there are scoring corrections to be made depending upon the subject's age, education, or other variable – for example, add 3 points if the subject is older than 65. Such scoring corrections are usually easy to calculate, but for many tests such corrections are simply not available as part of the normative data. One major exception is the Luria-Nebraska Neuropsychological Battery, for which computer-scoring programs are available and quite useful.

One area where computerized scoring could be very helpful is to compare scores across tests. In neuropsychological assessment, a battery like the Halstead-Reitan or the Luria-Nebraska is often given in conjunction with other measures, such as the WAIS and the MMPI, as well as measures of receptive and expressive language skills, memory, and so on. Each of these tests has often been normed on different samples, and scores are often not directly comparable from instrument to instrument. What is needed are computer programs that can analyze such disparate data and yield comparable scores.

Test administration. Neuropsychological patients as a group have difficulties with aspects such as following directions and persisting with a task. Also, qualitative observations of the testing are very important in the scoring and test interpretation. Thus, the kind of automation that is possible with a test such as the MMPI may not be feasible with neuropsychological testing, more because of the nature of such assessment than because of any test aspects themselves.

Test interpretation. In general, most attempts to develop a computer program that would take the raw data and interpret the results, focus on three questions: (1) Is there brain damage present? (2) Where is the damage localized? and (3) Is the damage acute or chronic? The results have been quite limited and disappointing. One study found that three computerized scoring systems did reasonably well in identifying the presence of brain damage, but were less accurate in localizing such damage (Adams, Kvale, & Keegan, 1984). Such systems, however, were not compared to the results obtained by clinicians. One study that compared a computer program with the accuracy of skilled psychologists found that the two experts were more accurate than the computer program in predicting the presence of brain lesions, their laterality, but not their chronicity (R. K. Heaton, Grant, Anthony, et al., 1981).

The Halstead-Reitan. A number of computer programs have been developed to do an actuarial analysis of the Halstead-Reitan Neuropsychological Test Battery. The early investigations of these systems produced inconsistent results, and it was questioned whether these programs could be as accurate as experienced clinicians in determining the presence or absence of brain damage and related aspects. Adams, Kvale, and Keegan (1984) studied a sample of 63 brain-damaged patients on which there was reliable diagnostic information – what was wrong with the patients was well documented. Each patient had taken a number of tests such as the WAIS, MMPI, and many of the Halstead-Reitan subtests. The computer program essentially involved a statistical comparison of an index of WAIS subtest scores that presumably are resistant to mental deterioration (see Chapter 5), vs. an index on the Halstead-Reitan presumably showing degree of impairment. Basically, the computer program correctly identified 57% of those with left-hemisphere brain damage, 81% with right-hemisphere damage, and 90% with diffuse damage. The authors concluded that all three computer programs they tested were inadequate as comprehensive neuropsychological report mechanisms.

ADAPTIVE TESTING AND COMPUTERS

The advent of computers into psychological testing has resulted in a number of advances, perhaps most visibly in the area of adaptive testing. In a typical test, all examinees are administered the same set of items. In Chapter 2 we discussed the bandwidth-fidelity dilemma. Do we measure something with a high degree of precision, but applicable to only some of the clients, or do we measure in a broad perspective, applicable to most, but with little precision? Adaptive testing solves that dilemma. In an adaptive test, different sets of items are administered to different individuals depending upon the individual's status on the trait being measured (Meijer & Nering, 1999; D. J. Weiss, 1985). For example, suppose we have a 100-item multiple-choice vocabulary test, with items ranging in difficulty from the word "cat" to the word "gribble." Rather than starting everybody with the word cat, if we are testing a college student, we might begin with a word of middle difficulty such as "rickets." If the person gets that item correct, the next item to be presented would be of slightly higher difficulty. If the person answers incorrectly, then the next item to be presented would be of lower difficulty. Thus the computer calculates for each answered item whether the answer is right or wrong, and what the next appropriate item would be. As the person progresses through the test, the calculations become much more complex because, in effect, the computer must calculate a "running average" plus many other more technical aspects. The person might then experience a slight delay before the next appropriate item is presented. However, the computer is programmed to calculate the two possible outcomes – the answer is right or the answer is wrong – while the person is answering the item. When the answer is given, the computer selects the pertinent alternative and testing proceeds smoothly.

There are many synonyms in the literature for adaptive testing, including tailored, programmed, sequential, and individualized testing. Generic adaptive testing is of course efficient and can save considerable testing time. They are also more precise, and at least potentially, are therefore more reliable and valid.

Adaptive testing actually began with the Binet-Simon tests and its principles were incorporated into the Stanford-Binet. Thus, the administrator begins the Stanford-Binet not at the same question for everybody, but at a point appropriate for the particular child; with a bright 8-year-old, we might start testing at the 9th- or 10th-year level. As items are administered they are also scored, so the examiner can determine whether to continue, stop, or return to easier items. Currently, most adaptive administration strategies are based on item-response theory and have been primarily developed within the areas of achievement and ability testing. Item-response theory, however, requires scales of items that are unidimensional. Most personality tests such as the MMPI and the CPI have multidimensional scales.

Branching. A variation of adaptive testing with particular potential in personality assessment is that of branching. Let's say we wish to assess an individual on more than 25 different areas of functioning, and we have some 50 items per area. In the area of depression, for example, we might have items about hopelessness, lack of libido, loss of weight, suicidal ideation, and so on. If the responses to the first four or five items clearly indicate that for this client suicide is not a concern, we could move or branch to the next area where more items might be appropriately administered.

The countdown method. Butcher, Keller, and Bacon (1985) have proposed the countdown method as a way to adaptively administer the MMPI. Essentially, this method terminates item administration on a particular scale once sufficient information for that scale is obtained. Suppose, for example, that we have a 50-item scale and that an elevated score (for example, a T score of 70 or above) is obtained once the client answers 20 items in the keyed direction. At that point, administration of further items could be terminated. Similarly, if the client answers 31 items in a nonkeyed direction, the test administration could also be stopped because scale elevation could not be obtained with the remaining 19 items. Because degree of elevation might be important, we could continue testing in the first case but not in the second.

In one study (Roper, Ben-Porath, & Butcher, 1995), 571 college students were randomly assigned to one of three groups, and adminis-

tered the MMPI-2 twice, 1 week apart. One group took the standard booklet form, one group the standard form and a retest with a computerized adaptive form, and the third group a standard computerized form and retested with the adaptive computerized form. The results showed a high degree of similarity indicating that the three forms of the MMPI-2 were quite comparable. The subjects were also administered a variety of other scales such as the Beck Depression Inventory; the results again supported the comparability of the three forms. The administration of the computer adaptive form achieved about a one-third time savings.

Item banking. Computerized testing in general, and adaptive testing specifically, often require large item pools. This is an advantage that computers have because large item pools can be easily stored in a computer's memory. These item pools are referred to as item "banks" (for a view of item banking in Holland and in Italy, see LecLercq & Bruno, 1993). The computer allows subsets of items with specific characteristics (e.g., all items testing material from Chapter 14, or all items on scale X, or all items that are empirically correlated with GPA) to be called and selected – these can then be modified and printed or presented as a test. CBTIs also require extensive pools of interpretive statements called "libraries." For example, one MMPI computer-based test interpretation system contains more than 30,000 sentences (cited in Moreland, 1991).

A computer with a large item bank can be programmed to randomly select a subset of items as a test, so that each person to be tested gets a different test. This can be useful in academic settings, as well as in situations where retesting might be needed. This should, of course, be distinguished from adaptive testing.

Purposes of testing. We discussed the basic purposes of testing in Chapter 1; these purposes can interact with computer methodology. For example, if a test is to be used for diagnostic or placement purposes, then branching could be fully used so that the testing can become a teaching tool. (However, if the basic purpose is to assess mastery, then such branching may not be appropriate.)

Advantages and Disadvantages of Computer Use in Testing

Advantages. In addition to the advantages already mentioned above (such as the increased scorer reliability) there are a number of advantages to using computers in the testing process:

1. Better use of professional time. Paper-and-pencil tests are often administered by clinicians who could better use their time and expertise in diagnostic and/or therapeutic activities or in conducting the research needed to validate and improve tests. Tests on computers allow the use of trained "assistant psychometricians" or even clerks who would not require extensive educational background or professional training.

2. Reduced time lag. In most clinical and/or client settings there is a serious lag between test administration and availability of results – whether we refer to achievement test batteries given in the primary grades, tests given to psychiatric patients, tests used in an applied settings such as preemployment assessment, or other tests. The use of a computer can make "instant" feedback a reality in most situations. Scores can be provided quickly not only to the examinee, but also to various agencies, for example in the case of GRE scores that may need to be sent to a dozen or more universities.

3. Greater availability. Tests on computers can be administered when needed, with fewer restrictions than the traditional p-p format. For example, a student wishing to take the GRE can do so only on one of several dates in p-p format, but computer administration can be scheduled more frequently.

4. Greater flexibility. Individuals can be tested in a computer setting individually or in groups, usually in more user-friendly environments than the large classroom-auditoriums where tests such as the SAT and the GRE have been administered traditionally. The computer format is also much more flexible than the printed page; for example, split screens could show stimuli such as a picture, as well as the possible responses. In addition, the computer format allows each examinee to work at his or her own pace, much more so than the p-p version.

5. Greater accuracy. Computers can combine a variety of data according to specific rules; humans are less accurate and less consistent when they attempt to do this. Computers can handle extensive amounts of normative data, but humans are limited. Computers can use very complex ways of combining and scoring data, whereas most humans are quite limited in these capabilities. Computers can be programmed so that they continuously update the norms, predictive regression equations, etc., as each new case is entered.

6. Greater standardization. In Chapter 1, we saw the importance of standardizing both test procedures and test interpretations. The computer demands a high degree of such standardization and, ordinarily, does not tolerate deviance from such standardization.

7. Greater control. This relates to the previous point, but the issue here is that the error variance attributable to the examiner is greatly reduced if not totally eliminated.

8. Greater utility with special clients or groups. There are obvious benefits with computerized testing of special groups, such as the severely disabled, for whom p-p tests may be quite limited or inappropriate.

9. Long-term cost savings. Although the initial costs of purchasing computer equipment, of developing program software, etc., can be quite high, once a test is automated it can be administered repeatedly at little extra cost.

10. Easier adaptive testing. This approach requires a computer and can result in a test that is substantially shorter and, therefore, more economical of time. The test can also be individualized for the specific examinee.

Are advantages really advantages? In reading the above list, you may conclude that some advantages may not really be advantages. There may be some empirical support for this, but relatively little work has been done on these issues. For example, immediate feedback would typically be seen as desirable. S. L. Wise and L. A. Wise (1987) compared a p-p version and two cf versions of a classroom achievement test with third and fourth graders. One cf version provided immediate item feedback and one did not. All three versions were equivalent to each other in mean scores. However, high math-achievers who were administered the cf version with immediate feedback showed significantly higher state anxiety; the authors recommended that such feedback not be used until its effects are better understood.

Disadvantages. In addition to the disadvantage just discussed, we might consider that computerized testing reduces the potential for observing the subject's behavior. As we have seen, one of the major advantages of tests such as the Stanford-Binet is that subjects are presented with a set of standardized stimuli, and the examiner can observe directly or indirectly the rich individual differences in human behavior that enhance the more objective interpretation of test results. With computerized testing, such behavior observation is severely limited.

ETHICAL ISSUES INVOLVING COMPUTER USE

The use of computers involves a number of issues that are potentially ethical and/or legal. R. D. Fowler (1985) identified four basic questions:

1. Do computers "dehumanize" the assessment process? While this seemed to be a major concern when computers first became available, it no longer seems to be an issue. For example, White (cited in Fowler, 1985) found that 80% of college students preferred taking the MMPI by computer. J. H. Johnson and Williams (1980) reported that 46% of their subjects said they were more truthful when responding to the computer than to a clinician.

2. What are the ethical implications? For example, when test scoring and test reporting were first offered by mail, some psychologists believed this might be a violation of the American Psychological Association (APA) policy against mail-order testing.

3. Who is qualified to use CBTI reports? Many test publishers have restricted the sales of tests to qualified purchasers, often broadly defined. Such policies have, in some cases applied to the sale of computer-generated services.

4. How valid are CBTIs? Quite clearly the validity of the CBTI is intrinsically related to the validity of the test upon which the CBTI is based. If the test has poor validity to begin with, the CBTI will also have poor validity. In the 1980s, a number of writers pointed out that there was no evidence

that such CBTIs were valid (e.g., Lanyon, 1984; Matarazzo, 1983).

There are in fact a number of such ethical-legal issues (N. W. Walker & Myrick, 1985). One centers on unauthorized access to records and violations of confidentiality. There is the possibility that computers promote the indiscriminate storage of personal information and may result in violations of privacy. Equipment does fail, and there may be loss of information as a result of such failures. Many of the issues center on CBTIs. Some people may show blind acceptance of computer interpretations, although the limited data suggest this is not the case. A major unresolved issue is who is responsible for the CBTI? Is it the individual clinician who submitted the client's protocol? Is it the clinician(s) who originally developed the interpretive program? Or is it the company who sells the scoring service? These are not simply "academic" concerns; but they are voiced in applied settings, such as schools (Jacob & Brantley, 1987). Some of the concerns are somewhat less tangible. For example, Matarazzo (1986) wrote that when the Binet-Simon test was first developed, it was developed within a philosophy that emphasized the worth of the individual; most assessment today is carried out with sensitive concern for the client but such sensitivity is easily neglected with computerized technology.

The CBTI guidelines. It is generally agreed that computer technology in the area of psychological testing be applied with the same ethical and professional standards as traditional tests – but this may not always happen. At least two states (Colorado and Kansas) have published standards for computerized psychological assessment, and in 1986 the APA developed *Guidelines for Computer-Based Tests and Interpretations* (APA, 1986), known as the CBTI Guidelines.

The CBTI Guidelines are an extension of the *Standards for Educational and Psychological Testing* (1999) and are designed to guide test developers to establish and maintain the quality of their products, and to assist professionals to use CBTI in the best interests of clients and the public (Schoenfeldt, 1989).

The CBTI Guidelines distinguish four participants in the testing process: (1) the test developer, (2) the test user, (3) the test taker, and (4) the test administrator. Test users are defined as qualified professionals who have (1) knowledge of psychological measurement, (2) a background in the history of the tests being used; (3) experience in the use of the test and familiarity with the associated research; and (4) knowledge of the area of intended application. The CBTI Guidelines recognize that nonpsychologists such as physicians and lawyers, may have legitimate need to use psychological tests and computerized test reports, but require that they also have sufficient knowledge to serve the client public.

There are nine guidelines for test users that cover two areas: administration and interpretation. For administration, the main concern is standardization of procedures – that the conditions of computerized testing be equivalent to those in which normative, reliability, and validity data were obtained. In terms of interpretation, the CBTI Guidelines state that, "computer-generated interpretive reports should be used only in conjunction with professional judgment." Basically, this reflects the APA policy that computer-based interpretations are considered professional-to-professional consultations.

There are 31 guidelines under the heading of test developer, and these relate primarily to two issues: (1) the computer-based administration issues (such as the client having the opportunity to change a test answer); and (2) psychometric issues, such as establishing the equivalence between p-p and cf versions of the same test (see Schoenfeldt, 1989). A full copy of the CBTI Guidelines can be found in B. F. Green (1991).

OTHER ISSUES AND COMPUTER USE

Legal issues. Psychologists are often called upon as expert witnesses in the courtroom. Unfortunately, studies that evaluate the accuracy of diagnosis and prediction show mixed results and cast substantial doubts as to whether psychological evaluation can meet the legal standards for expertise. Ziskin and Faust (1988) cite 1,400 studies and articles that cast doubt on the reliability and validity of clinical evaluations conducted for legal purposes. Why is the reliability and validity of such psychological evaluations so limited? Faust and Ziskin (1989) cite several reasons: (1) Psychological theory is not so advanced as to permit precise behavioral prediction; (2) Available

information that is potentially useful is often misused, by disregarding base rates and by reliance on subjective rather than objective procedures; and (3) Clinicians, like people in general, have a limited capacity to manage complex data. These reasons once again point to the future potential of using CBTIs.

Computer tests. For now, much effort has been devoted to "translating" p-p versions to cf versions, and relatively little effort has been devoted to creating new computer-administered tests. A number of tests have however been developed specifically for computerized use, and some of these take advantage of the graphic possibilities of the computer (e.g., Davey, Godwin, Mittelholtz, 1997). As one might imagine, psychologists in the military, both in the U.S. and other countries including England, have pioneered many such techniques (B. F. Green, 1988). For example, one technique used with Navy personnel is an "Air Defense Game" that involves a simulated radar screen with hostile air targets approaching one's ship. The examinee has to defend the ship by launching missiles. The effects of stress and other aspects on such "test" performance can be easily studied (Greitzer, Hershman, & Kelly, 1981).

These approaches would seem to be particularly useful in the assessment of perceptual-motor coordination and decision-making aspects, as well as other domains of human abilities (Fleishman, 1988).

Barrett, Alexander, Doverspike, et al. (1982) reported on a battery of information-processing tests developed specifically for computer testing (although p-p versions of these tests are also available). For example, in the Linear Scanning test, 20 equilateral triangles are presented in a row. Each triangle has a line through it, with the exception of one to four triangles. The row of triangles is presented for 1.5 seconds and erased, and the subject needs to indicate how many triangles did not have a line through them. The split-half reliability for most of these measures was above .80 but test-retest reliability with a 2-week to a 1-month interval, was rather low, with none of the 15 reported correlation coefficients higher than .60, and in most cases substantially lower. To be sure these measures are more "complex" in structure than the type of items found on personality inventories or traditional cognitive tests, but the results are disappointing, nevertheless. (See Van den Brink and Schoonman, 1988, for an example of computerized testing in the Dutch Railway personnel system; and N. Schmitt, Gilliland, Landis, et al., 1993, for an example of computerized testing for the selection of secretarial applicants.)

A LOOK AT OTHER TESTS AND COMPUTER USE

The CPI. Despite the fact that the CPI is a well-researched personality inventory, and that its CBTIs are widely available and used, there is very little research currently on computerized applications. Sapinkopf (1978) computerized the CPI and used an adaptive-testing approach that essentially presented 67% fewer items and thus took less time to administer. However, the reliability of this computerized version was lower than the p-p version.

Projective techniques. Attempts have been made to computer score such projective techniques as the Rorschach and the Holtzman Inkblot Test (e.g., Gorham, 1967; Gorham, Moseley, & Holtzman, 1968; Piotrowski, 1964), but in general these do not seem to be widely used by clinicians.

As you might expect, computer administration and computer interpretation of projectives presents major challenges, but an interesting example comes from a sentence-completion test. Veldman (1967) administered 36 sentence stems to more than 2,300 college freshmen; these stems required a one-word response. He thus obtained a response pool of more than 83,000 responses. By eliminating all words with frequencies of less than 1%, a pool of 616 "common" responses was kept. Veldman then developed a computer program that administers each sentence stem and waits for the subject to respond. If the response is a rare word, the computer program requests a synonym. A second rare response results in another request; if the third response is also rare, then the second sentence stem is presented. If the response is a common word – that is, one in the computer's memory – then followup questions are presented. For example, if the sentence stem "My work has been __" is responded with the word "hard" or "difficult," the computer asks, "What do you find difficult about it?" If the response is "good," the

computer asks, "To what do you attribute your success?" Although such an approach has little utility at present (for one, note that only 616 of the 83,000 responses can be handled by the computer), it points to future developments.

The Beck Depression Inventory. Steer, Rissmiller, Ranieri, et al. (1994) administered the BDI in a cf to 330 inpatients diagnosed with mixed psychiatric disorders. The coefficient alpha was reported as .92, and the BDI significantly differentiated patients diagnosed with mood disorders from those with other psychiatric disorders. Scores on the BDI correlated significantly from pretest to posttest some 9 days later, and correlated significantly with scores on the Hopelessness scale. Scores were not significantly related to gender, ethnicity, or age. Thus the reliability and validity of the BDI cf seems comparable with that of the p-p version.

However, in a different study with college students (Lankford, Bell, & Elias, 1994), the results showed that students high on computer anxiety scored higher on the BDI cf than p-p format. The authors concluded that the use of computer-administered personality tests may not be a valid procedure in assessing personality dimensions because: (1) Elevated computer anxiety is related to elevated scores on tests that measure negative affect and to lowered scores on tests that measure positive affect; and (2) scores of female subjects on computer-administered tests were altered more than scores of male subjects, and this was not due simply to higher computer anxiety. Therefore, these authors recommended that standardized normative distributions may not be applicable to computerized personality tests.

Behavioral assessment. Kratochwill, Doll, and Dickson (1985) point out that microcomputers have, both actually and potentially, revolutionized behavioral assessment. First, behavioral assessment can be time-and personnel-intensive, and microcomputers can reduce the cost associated with this. Second, microcomputer technology can be applied to the full range of behavioral-assessment techniques such as psychophysiological recordings, direct observation, and self-monitoring. Third, behavioral assessment has in the past lacked standardization;

the use of computers can aid substantially in this respect. Fourth, because microcomputers are now readily available, the dissemination of behavioral-assessment techniques is facilitated. Finally, microcomputers have the potential to strengthen the relationship between assessment and treatment.

Miscellaneous Issues Involved in Computer Use

The disabled. A number of studies have investigated the use of light pens, joysticks, and other mechanical-electronic means of responding to test items for disabled individuals who are not able to respond to tests in traditional ways. The results suggest substantial equivalence across response modes (e.g., Carr, Wilson, Ghosh, Ancill, & Woods, 1982; Ridgway, MacCulloch, & Mills, 1982). (See S. L. Wilson, 1991, for a description of a microcomputer-based psychological assessment system for use with the severely physically disabled, as used in a British medical facility, and see S. L. Wilson, Thompson, & Wylie, 1982, for examples of automated psychological testing for the severely physically disabled.)

Response time. Computers can easily assess response time, that is, how fast a subject responds. Response time (or reaction time, response latency) to questionnaire items could be a useful additional measure in a number of research areas (Ryman, Naitoh, Englund, et al., 1988). Some authors, for example, have argued that such latencies can potentially be indicative of meaningful variables. On a personality test, longer latencies may reflect more "emotional" items (Space, 1981). Response time brings up two issues: (1) Are the individual differences associated with such responding related to different behaviors (e.g., are faster responders more emotional?); and (2) Are items that are responded to more rapidly different from those that require a longer reaction time, either within the individual (e.g., If I take longer to respond to item X is that item more conflict-laden for me?), or within groups (e.g., Are items that take longer to respond to more complicated or confusing?)

T. G. Dunn, Lushene, and O'Neil (1972) administered a computerized version of the MMPI to college students. Response times were averaged across students and entered as the dependent variable in a regression analysis to determine whether response time is related to item characteristics, such as item length and ambiguity. They found that item length accounted for about half of the variance, that is, for the subjects as a group, response time was clearly a function of item length.

Additional concerns. As with any technological revolution, there are problems and challenges to be met, some of which we have discussed above, some of which we have ignored because they would take us too far afield, and some of which we are not even as yet aware. J. A. Cummings (1986) relates an interesting series of studies done by him and his colleagues. They wanted to use CBTIs to generate early detection of emotional distress in medical patients of primary-care physicians, so that the physicians could refer these patients to psychotherapy. They studied more than 10,000 patients who were seen by 36 primary-care physicians. All of the patients took a 3-hour automated multiphasic health screening that included a computerized psychological questionnaire. For a random half of the patients, the physicians received a computer printout, with the suggestion (if appropriate) that the patient be referred for psychotherapy. The results indicated that the computerized report and suggestion elicited no more referrals than those in the group with no report.

The authors speculated that perhaps the report did not contain sufficient information to motivate the primary-care physician; they repeated the study, this time by providing three types of reports, ranging from a relatively brief description of the computerized findings to an extensive detailed description of the patient's emotional distress and personality. In this case, the report worked. Not only were there more referrals in the experimental than the control (no report) group, but as the complexity of the report increased, the percentage of referrals increased. In a subsequent study, increased information in the report not only increased the likelihood of referral for psychotherapy, but also increased the number of missed medical diagnoses; that is, the symptoms of the patient were initially ascribed by the physician to emotional distress, but were subsequently rediagnosed as a physical illness.

Acceptability to clients. Originally, some psychologists feared that computerized testing depersonalized the client. As we have seen, the literature indicates rather strongly that clients react favorably to computerized testing, that such acceptability increases as the topic of the test becomes more "sensitive," and that any anxiety induced by the computer is usually brief, especially if adequate practice is provided (see M. J. Burke & Normand, 1987).

Response bias. It is reasonable to suppose that computer administration of tests might increase the honesty of response, particularly to "sensitive" types of questions – i.e., response bias ought to be reduced. The view here is that acquiescence, social desirability, and so on, operate primarily because the test situation is perceived as embarrassing and not confidential; thus, a computer would be seen as more anonymous and confidential. In one study, three groups of college students were administered questionnaire items, either in a p-p format, an interview format, or via computer. The questionnaire included embarrassing questions. The computer group answered more questions in the keyed direction (i.e., admitted "true" to more embarrassing questions) and scored in the less defensive direction on the MMPI K scale (although the differences between groups were not statistically significant D. Koson, Kitchen, M. Kochen, & Stodolosky, 1970).

Social desirability. Some studies on the equivalence of p-p and cf questionnaires have found that respondents on the cf admit to more anxiety symptoms, score lower on lie scales, and endorse fewer socially desirable responses. Other studies however, find that the two modes of administration yield similar results as far as social desirability is concerned (Booth-Kewley, Edwards, & Rosenfeld, 1992).

Familiarity with computers. Just as in Chapter 16 we were concerned about testwiseness, here we need to be concerned about computer wiseness or sophistication. If a child is brought up in a home environment where a computer is part of the furniture or in a school that uses computers extensively, will that child be at an advantage in taking computerized tests? Will women

be handicapped, because of a stereotype that males are more interested and better at computer-related activities? Prior familiarity with computers can affect performance on at least some tests. For example, D. F. Johnson and White (1980) administered a computerized version of the Wonderlic Personnel Inventory (an intelligence test frequently used in employment screening) to 20 elderly volunteers. Ten of the participants received 1 hour of training on the computer terminal and 10 did not. Those who received the training scored about 5 points higher (approximately one SD). However, initial studies indicate no differences in performance between boys and girls, between African-Americans and Anglos, and between those with different levels of prior experience.

Achievement tests. Classroom exams have been traditionally administered to the entire class at one sitting, and make-up exams represent a major headache for the instructor because either a new form has to be created, or the student has to be prevented from talking with any other student in the class. With on-line testing, each student can take a test at a microcomputer terminal, where the test items may well be unique to that administration, and randomly selected from an item bank.

Can the computer generate tests? In some areas, the answer is, "Yes." For example, the sentence verification technique is used to construct valid tests of language comprehension. Traditionally, language comprehension has been assessed by presenting a prose passage and then asking the subject a number of questions, often in a multiple-choice format. The sentence verification technique also presents a passage, but the task requires the subject to recognize rather than recall textual information by responding to sentences that either correspond to the original meaning of a sentence in the passage, or do not. These sentences could be either identical sentences or paraphrased sentences; in either case the keyed response would be, "Yes." Or the sentences could be sentences that have been changed from the original passage (e.g., "My dog is white" changed to, "My dog is not white") or sentences that are related but were not in the original passage; in either case, the keyed answer is "No."

For an example of computer software that automates and simplifies the process of constructing such a test, see Walczyk (1993).

THE FUTURE OF COMPUTERIZED PSYCHOLOGICAL TESTING

It is probably foolhardy to look into our crystal ball and predict what the future of psychological testing will be like with the computers of the future. We can however, look at what is available now and use that as a limited and probably myopic view of the future.

Constructed responses. At present, computerized applications work best when the items are selected-response items (e.g., multiple-choice items). Constructed-response items, such as essay exams or sentences given as responses, present much more of a challenge.

Voice output. Voice output devices are now available so the computer can "speak" to the examinee, and for example, present administrative instructions. The potential of this for blind subjects or those with limited reading skills is only now beginning to be explored.

Voice input. Voice analysis indicators are potentially related to a variety of variables, such as stress and deception. By having subjects respond orally rather than by clicking a mouse, such indicators could be related to various test characteristics.

Interactive video tests. An example of future direction is presented by Dutch researchers from their National Institute for Educational Measurement (Bosman, Hoogenboom, & Walpot, 1994), who developed an interactive video test for pharmaceutical chemists' assistants. The test offers six cases that simulate real-life situations in a pharmacy. The assistant needs to (1) answer questions of the patient, (2) ask the patient relevant questions, (3) handle the administrative-computer program, (4) make the right choice of medicines written on the prescription, and (5) deliver the medicines with the right information.

The six cases were developed to cover a wide variety of situations, including dangerous interactions of different medicines, specific ways of handling medicines, and so on. The examinee works independently, and it takes about 1 hour to complete each case. The test is essentially composed of three different types of items: (1) multiple-choice questions; (2) open-questions, where the patient asks a question and the examinee types an answer. The program checks the answer with a prerecorded list of possible responses; and (3) open-actions. Here the examinee initiates the response, by typing on the prescription or consulting with the physician (all on the computer screen).

The program is basically a branching program where at each decision point there are different alternatives. The path taken by each examinee can be quite different, but there is in fact an ideal, most efficient, correct pathway. One interesting aspect of this test is that feedback is provided both during the test and at the end of the test. In fact, each case can be replayed showing the correct pathway, and providing comments on the student's particular responses that deviated from this pathway.

Scoring is somewhat complicated to explain, but very easy for the computer. The scoring system covers five categories: (1) accepting the prescription, (2) handling the computer program, (3) preparing the medicine, (4) managing the medical supplies, and (5) delivering the prescription. For each of these, there, are two scores: on effectiveness (i.e., was the problem solved regardless of how the solution was reached) vs. efficiency (did the examinee follow the ideal path). Unfortunately, for a sample of 143 pharmacy students, the alpha coefficient was only .58. In part, this is understandable because both the cases and the scoring procedures are heterogeneous. This is a pioneering effort with many challenges yet to be faced, but it is a good illustration of ingenuity and what the future might hold.

SUMMARY

In this chapter, we discussed how computers interface with psychological tests. Specifically, we looked at computers as test-scoring machines, as test administrators, and as test interpreters. One of the major issues is that of equivalence: Is the computer version of a paper-and-pencil test equivalent to the original test? Another major issue is the validity of computer-based test interpretations. The MMPI has played a central role in the development of computer use in testing, but other tests are also involved. Neuropsychological testing presents special challenges and adaptive testing some potentially novel solutions. Although the advantages of computer use far outweigh the disadvantages, there are ethical and other issues that we need to be concerned about.

SUGGESTED READINGS

Fowler, R. D. (1985). Landmarks in computer-assisted psychological assessment. *Journal of Consulting and Clinical Psychology, 53,* 748–759.

An interesting review of the history and development of computer-based test interpretation by a talented psychologist who was a pioneer in this area.

Klee, S. H., & Garfinkel, B. D. (1983). The computerized continuous performance task: A new measure of inattention. *Journal of Abnormal Child Psychology, 11,* 487–496.

An example of a study of a test administered by computer, with such aspects as sensitivity and specificity discussed.

Matarazzo, J. D. (1986). Computerized clinical psychological test interpretations. *American Psychologist, 41,* 14–24.

An excellent thought-provoking article about the potential and the problems associated with CBTIs, written by one of the leading clinical psychologists in the United States (See the February 1986 issue of the *American Psychologist,* pp. 191–193, for some rejoinders to this article.)

Schoenfeldt, L. F. (1989). Guidelines for computer-based psychological tests and interpretations. *Computers in Human Behavior, 5,* 13–21.

A review and discussion of many of the guidelines included in the APA "Guidelines."

Tennar, B. A. (1993). Computer-aided reporting of the results of neuropsychological evaluations of traumatic brain injury. *Computers in Human Behavior, 9,* 51–56.

Reports on a computer program, the TBI Report Assistant, designed to be used with patients known to have suffered traumatic brain injury. A program that basically describes a patient's current performance on several tests, including the WAIS-R and the Wechsler Memory Scale-Revised, and compares that performance to the patient's peers.

DISCUSSION QUESTIONS

1. The book discusses three types of service associated with computer administration of tests. What is available on your college campus or community? Do these services deviate from the three categories presented?

2. How might you carry out a study to determine whether a personality variable (such as impulsivity, for example), interacts with some aspects of computerized presentation of a test?

3. To assess the validity of a CBTI one could compare a clinician's judgment based on the CBTI vs. a second clinician's judgment based on personal knowledge of the client. What do you think of this procedure? What are some of the potential problems?

4. Could adaptive testing be used in the exams you take in this class?

5. What are some of the ethical issues involved in using computers in psychological testing?

18 Testing Behavior and Environments

> **AIM** This chapter looks at a particular point of view called *behavioral assessment* and contrasts this with the more traditional point of view. We look at a variety of instruments developed or used in behavioral assessment to illustrate various issues. We then turn our focus to four broad areas of assessment that transcend the individual: program evaluation, the assessment of environments, the assessment of family functioning, and finally, some broad-based, flexible techniques.

TRADITIONAL ASSESSMENT

Much of traditional personality assessment and therefore testing is based upon psychodynamic theory, as found in Freud's writings, for example, and trait theory, as the work of Gordon Allport and of Raymond B. Cattell, for example. Both of these approaches view personality as the central aspect to understand, predict, or alter behavior. Both of these approaches assume that there are a number of dimensions called traits (or drives, needs, motives, etc.) that exist within the individual, are relatively stable, and give consistency to behavior – that is, knowing that a person is high on aggression allows us to predict with some accuracy that the individual will behave in certain ways across a number of situations. In both of these approaches, we infer that certain dimensions exist and that behavior is a "sign" of such underlying dimensions. Thus, the responses of a subject to the Beck Depression Inventory are seen as evidence that the subject is (or is not) depressed. The test performance is an indicator, a sign of the underlying hypothesized construct.

Behavioral assessment, on the other hand, does not use such inferences, but looks at the specific variables that control or affect behavior in a specific situation (e.g., Goldfried & Kent, 1972). Behavior has both antecedents and consequences. For example, the antecedent may be a stimulus, such as seeing a snake, and consequences, what occurs after the response, may be being rewarded by attention as one tells how one met the great rattlesnake. In behavioral assessment, problem behaviors such as fear of snakes are not seen as a sign of an underlying trait of phobic personality or maladjustment, but is the problem itself. The test responses are not a "sign" but rather a sample of behavior to be interpreted directly. In behavioral testing, the focus is to assess the behavior directly rather than a hypothesized trait. Originally, such assessment did not use questionnaires or tests, but focused on direct behavioral observation. Psychological tests were viewed with distrust and not used (Greenspoon & Gersten, 1967). Eventually, however, even behavioral assessment began to develop questionnaires, rating scales, and so on.

Another aspect of behavioral assessment is that trait labels are translated into operational definitions. Thus, a behavioral assessment questionnaire would not ask, "are you depressed?" but would ask, "how many times in the past month did you have crying episodes?" Similarly, alcoholism might be translated into number of beverages consumed per day and insomnia as number of hours spent sleeping.

Today, many psychologists would argue that the two approaches differ in their assumptions about behavior rather than necessarily in the specific techniques. In the traditional view, behavior is seen as the result of relatively stable causal variables, assumed to exist within the person – personality. Thus, the focus of assessment is on what the person *has*. By contrast, behavioral assessment focuses on what the person *does* in a particular context. Behavior is seen as the result of both organismic variables, such as biological and genetic influences, and the current environment.

BEHAVIORAL ASSESSMENT

Beginning in the late 1940s, there was a marked shift in the United States from a psychodynamic approach to a behavioral approach in the treatment of maladaptive behaviors. Various techniques of behavior therapy were developed and promulgated. These techniques required the assessment of the specific client behaviors (such as phobias) that needed to be changed, as well as specification of what variables elicited and maintained the maladaptive behaviors. Traditional assessment procedures such as the MMPI or projective techniques were seen by some as not useful, and so alternative approaches were developed that are now called *behavioral assessment.*

Although behaviorism is not a new idea, the application of behavioral principles as a therapeutic procedure or as an intervention strategy really began in the late 1960s and early 1970s. At first, these efforts did not focus on assessment, but eventually assessment became a major priority. Early behavioral assessment focused on motor behavior, but today behaviorists view all activities as behavior. Behavioral assessment has broadened its scope and readily includes such aspects as physiological-emotional behavior and cognitive-verbal behavior (Nelson & Hayes, 1979). Some behaviorists even believe that projective techniques, which would seem to be the antithesis of behavioral assessment, can be useful with a behavior assessment framework (e.g., Prout & Ferber, 1988).

If the 1960s were the beginning of behavioral assessment, the 1970s can be considered the honeymoon period. This was followed by a period of disillusionment (S. C. Hayes, Nelson, & Jarrett, 1986), due in particular to three findings:

(1) Different measures presumably of the same behavior, did not correlate significantly with each other, even when these consisted of direct observation; (2) There was a proliferation of nonstandardized behavioral assessment techniques, many of which were not psychometrically sound; and (3) The available techniques did not result in differential diagnosis, that is, in ways of classifying clients into discrete groupings.

Motoric, Cognitive, and Physiological Behavior Assessment

Behavioral assessment focuses on behavior, and behavior has been traditionally categorized as either motoric, cognitive, or physiological. Motoric responses are probably the most commonly assessed, in part because they can be relatively easy to observe. Cognitive responses are, from a behavioral assessment point of view, more difficult to define and measure. Typically these responses involve either thought or emotion, and only the outward result can be observed. The thoughts and feelings are "private" events, even though they can be verified empirically. If Brian says, "I'm angry," we watch his facial expressions, or we observe him kicking the chair.

Physiological responses such as heart rate, galvanic skin response, respiration, etc., can be somewhat easier to measure provided we have the right equipment, but difficult to measure outside of medical or research settings.

It is interesting to note that typically there is only a moderate correlation between measures of the same variable in the three categories. For example, the verbal report of anxiety may be present even though the physiological signs are not existent.

One way to categorize the techniques used in behavioral assessment is to label them as direct or indirect, based on the degree to which the actual target behavior is measured in a particular setting, that is the degree to which the responses observed match the behavior of interest (Cone, 1977; 1978).

Direct Assessment Methods

1. Observation. Direct observation is preferred by behaviorists because observations are empirically verifiable and do not require any inference.

Behavioral observations can take place in a natural setting, such as a playground or a classroom (and are called naturalistic observations), or in an "analog" setting, such as a laboratory task that tries to simulate a real-life procedure. The observation may be "obtrusive," where the subject is aware that they are being observed, or "unobtrusive." Unobtrusive observations often focus on aspects of the environment rather than the person, for example, counting the number of empty beer bottles in someone's thash as an indicator of drinking behavior. From a practical point of view, such observations can be easy in some cases and nearly impossible in others. We can easily observe a child on the playground or in the classroom to assess his or her aggressiveness, but it would be more difficult, for example, to observe an adult executive as he or she interacts with subordinates and peers to assess anxiety. From a psychometric point of view, however, there are a number of challenges. Is what is to be observed so specific that two observers will agree as to the occurrence of the behavior (i.e., interrater reliability)? Does the act of observing alter the behavior, e.g., "If Alberto knows he is being observed, will he throw that spitball?" What is to be recorded? Is it the occurrence of a behavior (Alberto throws a spitball), the frequency (Alberto threw six spitballs in the past hour), the antecedents (Alberto throws spitballs when the teacher ignores him), etc.? What coding system shall be used (e.g., Is "throwing spitballs" an instance of "aggressive behavior"?) (See Wahler, House, & Stanbaugh, 1976, for an example of a coding scale that covers 24 categories of behavior, for the direct observation of children in home or school settings.) In studies of behavioral assessment, direct observation is the most common assessment procedure used, followed by self-report (Bornstein, Bridgwater, Hickey, et al., 1980).

2. Self-monitoring. Here the subject observes his or her own behavior and records the results, for example, the amount of food eaten. Subjects may be asked to observe not only the behavior but the contingencies surrounding the behavior: Where does the eating take place? Who else was there? What were the thoughts and feelings associated with the eating? Although this appears to be a simple procedure, from a psychometric point of view there are also a number of challenges (e.g.,

J. L. Jackson, 1999). The accuracy with which an individual records his or her own behavior is an issue, with some studies report a high degree of accuracy, and other studies, a low degree of accuracy (e.g., Nelson, 1977). Self-monitoring also introduces the problem of reactivity; the behavior may change because it is being monitored. For example, cigarette smoking may decrease simply by having the subject record how many cigarettes he or she smokes and under what conditions.

3. Role playing. Sometimes direct observation is disruptive, difficult to implement, costly, or simply not practical. Although we can observe children in the classroom, it is more difficult to observe adults in the workplace. Role playing can then be used by setting up artificial situations, for example, in a therapy context the therapist may play the role of the boss. Such role playing has also been translated to tests where vignettes or instructions to the respondent to pretend that they are in a specific situation are used. Responses, either open-ended, or choice among options, can then be scored (see Reardon, Hersen, Bellack, et al., 1979, for an example of assessing social skills in children). The basic assumption of these tests is that the way the client responds in this simulation is the way the client will respond in the real-life situation. Whether that is in fact the case, is debatable (e.g., Bellak, Hersen, & Lamparski, 1979).

In addition to these three approaches, behavioral assessment uses a wide variety of techniques, such as laboratory tasks and psychophysiological measures that are beyond the scope of this chapter.

Indirect Assessment

Here the behavior of interest is not observed directly, but the subject, or someone who knows the subject well, is asked about the behavior. Thus one must make behavioral inferences about the data collected and must empirically verify the data.

1. Interviews. This is perhaps the most frequently used technique in behavioral assessment. Interviewing is in and of itself a major topic with a voluminous body of literature. If one considers interviewing as essentially an oral test, then it is legitimate to ask questions about reliability and validity. Interestingly, there is relatively little information about the reliability and validity of behavioral interviewing. One major exception is the work of Bergan and his colleagues who have developed a behavioral-consultation model, which sees interviewing as a series of verbal exchanges. These exchanges can be described in specific, operational terms, and the type and quantity of specific types of verbal statements can be coded and monitored, thus allowing for assessments of reliability and validity (see Bergan, 1977; Bergan & Kratochwill, 1990).

S. N. Haynes and Wilson (1979) indicate that the interview is the most frequently used, the least systematically applied, and the least frequently evaluated behavioral-assessment instrument. Recall that in Chapter 1 we suggested a test could be usefully considered as an interview. We can now turn that around and consider the interview as a test.

In behavioral settings, interviews are often used to screen clients for possible participation in specific therapeutic interventions and as diagnostic instruments. Interviews can also be used to identify subjects for research and/or clinical studies, or to obtain information from clients as to the cognitive components of their behavior disorders because altering such cognitive components (e.g., negative self-thoughts) can, in effect, ameliorate the disordered behavior. Finally, interviews can be used to evaluate intervention outcomes.

There is a vast body of literature on interviews, both from the behavioral-assessment aspect and from a more general perspective; to review such literature would take us far afield. Studies that have been conducted on the validity of the interview are not particularly encouraging. For example, in one study (Sarbin, 1943) academic success was predicted for a sample of college freshmen on the basis of tests and interviews. Validity coefficients for the tests alone were .57 for men and .73 for women. When interview data was added, the coefficients were .56 and .73, in other words, the interview added nothing. However, we can arrive at some general conclusions:

1. In spite of the ubiquity of the interview, there is relatively little literature on its reliability and validity.

2. Interviews are conducted for different purposes, in different ways, by different examiners. Therefore, issues of reliability and validity cannot address interviewing in general, but must pay attention to the various aspects and circumstances. This is a clear situation where generalizability theory (as discussed in Chapter 3) could be useful.

3. Reliability would seem important to establish, but very few studies do so. In the area of behavioral assessment, a number of studies have looked at interrater agreement, for example, by taping interviews and scoring such interviews along specified dimensions, by independent observers. Such interrater agreement is often relatively high.

4. Internal-consistency reliability, for example, by repeating items within the same interview, is rarely evaluated.

5. A number of studies have looked at criterion-related validity, where interview results are compared with data from other assessment instruments. Results differ widely, with some studies reporting high validity coefficients and others low; what is needed is to determine under what conditions valid results are obtained.

6. Content validity seems particularly appropriate and adequate in structured interviews, which essentially represent a set of questions (much like the MMPI) read aloud by the examiner.

7. The validity of interviews can also be evaluated in a pre-post design, where an interview precedes and follows an experimental or therapeutic intervention. To the extent that the interview is valid, the data obtained in the interview should covary with the results of the intervention.

8. There are many potential sources of error in interviews; not only are these self-reports, but interactions between such aspects as the gender and ethnicity of the interviewer vs. the interviewee can introduce considerable "error" variance.

9. In general, from a psychometric point of view, interviews are less preferable.

Structured vs. unstructured interviews. Interviews can vary from very unstructured to highly structured. In an unstructured interview, there is a goal (e.g., Is this a good candidate for this position?), but the format of the interview, the sequence of questions, whether a topic is covered or not, are all unstructured. Unstructured interviews are often used in therapeutic settings, for example when a clinician conducts an initial interview with a client. The unstructured interview allows a great deal of flexibility and the potential to go in new or unplanned for directions.

In a highly structured interview, the goal may be the same, but the procedure, questions, etc., are all predetermined and standardized. Thus, the structured interview lacks flexibility but provides standardization. From a psychometric point of view this is a preferable strategy because it permits quantification and comparability across interviewers, situations, and clients.

Types of interviews. There are, of course, numerous types of interviews and different ways of categorizing them. There are employment interviews whose goal is generally to decide on a person's qualifications as to a particular position. There are psychiatric intake interviews where initial information about a client is obtained. There is the mental status exam, which is an interview that ascertains what abnormalities are present in the client (see Chapter 7). There are exit interviews, polls, case histories, and various other types of interviews.

Regardless of the type of interview, we can conceptualize the interview as made up of three aspects: the interviewer, the interviewee, and the interview process itself. Each of these three aspects also represents a source of error in terms of reliability and validity.

2. Checklists and rating scales. These are used widely in behavioral assessments and are completed either by the individual as a self-report or by someone else as an observer's report. Both the Child Behavior Checklist (Achenbach, 1991) and the Conners rating scales (Conners, 1990), which we covered in Chapter 9, are good examples of behavioral checklists and rating scales. Both focus on specific behaviors rather than hypothesize personality traits. In general, self-report scales that emanate from a behavioral perspective differ in two major ways from their more traditional counterparts. First, the items typically focus on behavior and use behavioral terms. Second, many (but not all) have been developed informally so that their psychometric structure does not

have the degree of sophistication and complexity found in instruments such as the MMPI or the SVIB. When behavioral-assessment instruments first became popular, there was a tendency to reject classical psychometric principles of reliability and validity, and to be more concerned with other issues more directly relevant to behavioral observation. Subsequently, psychometric concepts were seen as quite applicable, and while traditional testing was "rejected," traditional psychometric concepts were not.

Checklists and rating scales are economical, can be easily administered, and serve to focus subsequent interviewing and observational efforts. They are useful to quantify observations. In addition, these are typically normative instruments; they allow for the comparison of a specific child with norms. They also can be used to quantify any change that is the result of intervention efforts. At the same time, because they are indirect measures of behavior, behaviorists tend to be suspicious of them and are concerned that the obtained data may be affected by social desirability, situational aspects, and a host of other limitations.

We used the terminology of bandwidth and fidelity earlier, and there is a parallel between these terms and the direct-indirect dichotomy. Indirect methods are essentially broad-band, low fidelity, whereas direct methods are narrowband, high fidelity. Broad-band low fidelity methods provide more information, but at a lower quality.

Note also, that these indirect methods could be considered as "self-reports." From a behavioral assessment point of view, self-report has several advantages. The observer, who is also the subject, is always present when a specific behavior occurs, and the observer can observe "internal" events (thoughts and feelings).

Concerns. From a psychometric point of view, substantial concern has been voiced that the procedures used in behavioral assessment have not been subjected to the scrutiny that typically accompanies the creation of a new scale. What is more important, is the concern that the methodology used in behavioral assessment is relatively unsophisticated and does not take advantage of psychometric principles that could make it more useful.

Behavior modification. Much of what is done under the rubric of behavioral assessment is for the purpose of behavior modification: the application of learning principles such as reinforcement and extinction to change behavior, specifically to eliminate unwanted behavior, such as fear of snakes, and to strengthen positive behavior, such as doing well academically. Most of the questionnaires developed focus on behavioral dysfunctions rather than, for example, the enhancement of creative achievement, happiness, superior intellectual functioning, and so on.

TRADITIONAL VS. BEHAVIORAL ASSESSMENT

Both approaches attempt to predict human behavior, but there are a number of differences between the two. One difference is that the assessment information obtained should be directly relevant to the specific goals of the assessment. If a client has a snake phobia, behavioral assessment attempts to identify the day-to-day conditions related to the phobic behavior. Traditional testing would attempt a broader perspective and determine what type of person this individual is, and so on. The concepts of fidelity and bandwidth are again relevant here.

A second difference is that traditional assessment depends on the notion of intervening variables. That is, between stimulus and response, the assumption is that there are personality traits, motivational needs, and so on. Thus, the aim of traditional testing is to map these inferred constructs to predict overt behavior. In behavioral assessment, the focus is on the behavior itself, and the aim of testing is to obtain a sample of that behavior without making inferences about the underlying constructs.

A third difference is that behavioral assessment is based on learning principles that include both specificity and generality. A behavioral anxiety scale would try to determine under what conditions and in what situations the client experiences the symptoms of anxiety. Traditional testing assumes that behavior is fairly consistent across situations – a person who is anxious when giving a talk to a class will also be anxious on a blind date – thus the items of a traditional anxiety scale are generic (e.g., I am anxious most of the time).

A fourth difference is that behavioral assessment typically uses multiple sources of data collection. Not only are interviews conducted, but behavioral observations are made, and checklists and questionnaires used.

Another difference is that in behavioral assessment there is typically a rather strong insistence on clarity of definition and precision of measurement. These are of course highly desirable, but in traditional testing they may be absent or not as strongly emphasized.

Finally, traditional assessment typically either precedes treatment or uses a pre-post design. For example, a patient is assessed as depressed, is given 6 months of psychotherapy and medications and is again evaluated at the end of 6 months. With behavioral assessment, the assessment is typically ongoing and multiple in nature. For a more detailed analysis of the differences between traditional and behavioral approaches, see D. P. Hartmann, Roper, and Bradford (1979).

VALIDITY OF BEHAVIORAL ASSESSMENT

In Chapter 3, we discussed validity – specifically content – criterion – predictive and concurrent – and construct validity. Initially, a number of behaviorists argued that these traditional concepts did not apply to behavioral assessment, but the more acceptable view now is that they do (e.g., Cone, 1977).

Content validity is very important in behavioral assessment because it basically reflects adequate sampling (the observations made must be representative of the behavior of interest). Another way to look at this issue is to determine to what degree an observed behavior is specific to a particular situation (the same issue discussed under generalizability).

Predictive validity refers to the accuracy of a test to predict specific types of behaviors. This also is important in behavioral assessment, particularly in the use of checklists and rating scales. In a number of studies, the predictive validity of such scales, as defined by correlations with real-life behaviors, has been less than adequate.

In behavioral assessment, concurrent validity is often defined as how well a particular scale or observational method correlates with other scales or methods designed to assess the same behavior. Concurrent validity data is frequently available and seems to be a common technique in behavioral assessment.

Finally, there is construct validity that looks at the underlying dimension that a test is supposedly measuring. This type of validity, as discussed earlier, is theory-driven and requires inferential thinking and hypothetical variables. This seems to be not entirely applicable to behavioral assessment because the focus is on direct observation and not on underlying constructs. On the other hand, in dealing with concepts such as "social skills," the notion of construct validity seems quite germane.

Social validity. In the area of behavioral assessment, there is an additional type of validity called "social validity" that refers to the effectiveness of a behavior change as assessed by its utility. For example, we could easily teach a child to increase eye contact with others. However, such a change would not necessarily increase that child's social skills or alter the nature of his or her interaction with peers, so the behavior change would have little social validity (Kazdin, 1977). Social validity can be assessed in a number of ways, for example, by assessing "consumer satisfaction" or comparing the experimental group to a control group which did not receive a treatment (Shapiro, 1987). Social validity really refers to applied intervention programs rather than to the tests that might be used to assess the efficacy of such interventions. Kazdin (1977) defined social validation as consisting of two procedures. First, the behavior of the target subject is compared with the behavior of peers who have not been identified as problematic. Second, subjective evaluations of the person's behavior are obtained, either from the subject, or better still from "objective" observers.

Generalizability. As discussed in Chapter 3, an alternate way to consider reliability and validity is through generalizability theory. That is, the relationships of a given measure with either itself (reliability) or other criteria (validity) reflect the fact that a given score can be generalized in different ways. Cone (1977) suggests that generalizability theory can provide a way to evaluate behavioral assessment techniques and indicates that there are six aspects to such generalizability:

(1) scorer, (2) item, (3) time, (4) setting, (5) method, and (6) dimension.

1. Scorer generalizability refers to the degree to which data obtained from one observer or scorer matches that obtained from a second observer. Interrater reliability would be an example, as well as the degree to which the father's ratings of a child compare with the mother's ratings. Note also that two observers could agree with each other, yet both could be wrong.

2. Item generalizability can be translated into internal consistency – i.e., do all of the items measure the same phenomenon or behavior?

3. The issue of time is one of stability – i.e., test-retest correlation. The concern here is about to what extent data obtained at one point in time are comparable with those obtained at other points in time.

4. Setting generalizability refers to the degree to which data obtained in one situation are representative of that obtained in other situations. From a traditional point of view, personality tests attempt to assess the typical way in which a person behaves, although it has been argued that behavior is not consistent across situations.

5. Method generalizability refers to the degree that data obtained by different methods are in fact comparable. Do responses on a self-report measure correspond to responses on a behavioral-avoidance test?

6. Dimension generalizability refers to the comparability of data on two or more different behaviors – i.e., essentially construct validity. An example here might be whether scores on a measure of assertiveness are inversely related to scores on a measure of anxiety.

Self-reports. The reliability and validity of information gathered from an individual, i.e., self-report, has always been a controversial topic within psychology. For psychoanalysts, self-reports based on such techniques as free association ("what comes to mind when . . .") and retrospection ("tell me about your childhood"), were presumed to be reliable, that is replicable, but not particularly valid because what the patient said was distorted by ego defenses, needs, early childhood experiences, and so on. For the behaviorists, as exemplified by John B. Watson, self-report was basically rejected – the focus was on behavior, on what the client *did* rather than what the client *said*. Those who believed in the trait approach, on the other hand, saw self-report inventories as the way to go, with the assumption that subjects could provide reliable and valid responses on such tests. Even when the possibility of distortion was accepted, the solution was to create self-report scales, such as the MMPI, that could detect such faking.

Overall score. When one has a questionnaire, it is tempting to develop an overall score, a total. As Bellack and Hersen (1977) point out however, the use of an overall score to summarize typical behavior or to predict some outcome is a trait concept.

Reliability and validity of observations. For observations to be valuable, they must be reliable and valid. In general, reliability is increased when the observer is trained, when the behavior to be observed is well defined, when the observations are specific (Tommy hits the other child) rather than general (Tommy shows aggressive behavior), and when the observations are recorded using an unambiguous system.

Evaluating behavioral assessment techniques. Behavioral-assessment techniques need to be evaluated as with any instrument, primarily in terms of reliability and validity. In addition, there are a number of other issues relevant to traditional tests that seem somewhat more visible in the area of behavioral assessment:

1. Sensitivity. To what degree does the test reflect changes in the behavior? If for example, through behavior therapy, we change a person's behavior so that they are now comfortable in visiting a snake exhibit at the local zoo, does our scale reflect this change?

2. Reactivity. This refers to changes in the behavior as a function of the measurement. For example, if we ask someone to self-record the amount of food they eat on a daily basis, will the very monitoring result in lesser food consumed? If we watch little Johnny in the classroom, will he engage in more or less disruptive behavior than is typical? S. N. Haynes and Wilson (1979) reviewed a number of studies showing that obser-

vational procedures can affect the behavior of the observed subjects. In some studies, subjects showed a greater degree of behavior when observed than when not observed, but in other studies, just the opposite effect was obtained. Thus, reactivity may be influenced by a number of variables including how obtrusive the observational procedure is, the expectancies of the subjects, the types of behaviors being observed, and so on.

3. Expectancy. If for example, we are conducting behavior therapy with a child who is hyperactive and ask the teacher to fill out a post-treatment questionnaire, the expectancies that the teacher has about the effectiveness of the therapeutic procedure may well influence the ratings.

Interobserver agreement. The accuracy of observations is typically assessed by interobserver agreement, raising the issue of interrater reliability. In addition to the Pearson correlation coefficient, there are a number of other indices used such as percentage agreement, discussed in Chapter 15. There are a number of statistical issues that complicate the picture (see the 1977 *Journal of Applied Behavior Analysis*). One of the issues is that of chance agreement. If two observers are independently observing the same behavior, they may agree on the basis of chance alone. The *kappa statistic* (J. Cohen, 1960), takes into account such chance agreement.

BEHAVIORAL CHECKLISTS

Although behavioral checklists and rating scales are somewhat different, the two terms are sometimes used as synonymous. A behavioral checklist consists of a list of fairly specific behaviors, and the person completing the checklist indicates the presence or absence of each behavior, thus checklists require a series of binary decisions. A rating scale on the other hand, typically involves making a judgment where the available responses are at a minimum three (e.g., is this person low, average, or high on honesty?), and where the judgment made typically reflects a global score that summarizes a number of observations. For example, as a teacher, if I am asked to rate Johnny on how attentive he is in class, using a 5-point scale from very inattentive to very attentive, my judgment will be a global judgment, hopefully summarizing a large number of observations.

There are a large number of behavioral checklists and behavioral rating scales used both for research purposes and in applied settings. In 1973 a group of researchers (Walls, Werner, Bacon, et al., 1977) placed an ad in various professional publications to locate behavior checklists that could be used with mentally retarded, psychiatric patients, children, or other populations. They were able to obtain and tabulate more than 200 such instruments, differing quite widely in their psychometric structure, reliability, and validity. These instruments differed from each other along a variety of dimensions. McMahon (1984) identifies three such dimensions:

1. Informants – i.e., who fills the scale out? It could be the client, peers, teachers, parents, co-workers, ward personnel, therapist, and so on. Some scales have been developed for use with specific informants; some scales may have parallel forms for use by different informants, and some scales can be used by any informant.

2. Scope – i.e., does the instrument cover a variety of behaviors or only one type? Is the age range covered broad (e.g., children) or more restricted (e.g., preschool children)?

3. Structure – this refers to a variety of aspects. For example, some scales are composed of only one item whereas others are quite lengthy. Some items can be very specific and others quite global. Some checklists require yes-no responses, others provide more options, such as a 7-point response scale. Anchors can be very specific or more global (e.g., "at least three or more headaches every day" vs. "I suffer from headaches frequently"). The time period which the informant uses as a frame of reference (and typically included as part of the instructions) can vary – e.g., "how many headaches have you had in the past 6 hours" vs. "how many headaches have you had in the past year?"

Reliability of checklists. Test-retest, internal consistency, and interrater reliability are probably the most pertinent types of reliability for behavioral checklists and for rating scales. If the behavior to be rated is very specific (e.g., Johnny pulls his little sister's pony tail), then test-retest

reliability may be low and, in essence, inappropriate. Where appropriate, test-retest reliability is generally higher the shorter the time period between test and retest. We also need to distinguish, at least theoretically, between test-retest reliability and a pre-post research design where the instrument is given twice to assess the effectiveness of an intervention. Good research practice would require the use of a control group as well, which typically would yield a better measure of reliability.

Internal consistency is relevant only to the degree that the particular scale measures a unitary dimension or factor.

Interrater reliability can also, in an applied situation, be confounded with other aspects. For example, the ratings of teachers may not fully coincide with those given by mothers. However, such differences may not necessarily represent low interrater reliability or error, but may be legitimate sources of information.

Validity of checklists. Content validity as well as criterion-related validity (both concurrent and predictive) would seem to be of essence.

What affects the validity of behavioral checklists? S. N. Haynes and Wilson (1979) identified eight types of variables that could affect the validity:

1. Response bias. The response to one item may be affected by the responses to other items. Response bias means that different item arrangements may generate different responses, thus affecting validity. We saw an example of this with the Beck Depression Inventory.

2. Social desirability. In behavioral checklists, this might likely take the form of overreporting positive behaviors and underreporting negative behaviors.

3. Demand factors. Because behavioral checklists are often used in therapeutic situations to decide on a therapeutic intervention, for example, the situation may result in "different" scores than if there were no such demand factors – e.g., anonymous conditions.

4. Expectancies. Similarly, the client or respondent may have certain expectancies. Teachers for example, who fill out the checklist on children to be referred to a school psychologist, may have certain expectancies about what services will be

Table 18–1. Examples of Behavioral Questionnaires

Reference	Questionnaire	Assesses
Lang & Lazovik (1963)	Fear Survey Schedule	Common fears
Thorne (1966)	Sex Inventory	Deviant sexual behaviors
Lanyon (1967)	Social Competence	Heterosexual interactions
Wollersheim (1970)	Eating Patterns Questionnaire	Eating patterns
J. P. Galassi & M. D. Galassi (1974)	College Self-expression Scale	Assertiveness
Denney & Sullivan (1976)	Spider Anxiety	Fear of spiders
Behar (1977)	Preschool Behavior Questionnaire	Preschool behavior
R. L. Weiss & Margolin (1977)	Marital Conflict Form	Marital problem areas
Gresham & Elliott (1990)	Social Skills Rating System	Social skills
T. M. Fleming et al. (1991)	Roommate Relationships	Roommate relationships
Gillespie & Eisler (1992)	Feminine Gender Role Stress	Gender role stress
Greenbaum, Dedrick & Lipien (2004)	Child Behavior Checklist	Children's Behaviors

provided and what ratings may be required to initiate such services.

5. Population characteristics. A checklist may have been validated on one group, such as college students, but may not necessarily be valid with another group, such as counseling-center clients.

6. Observer reactivity. Although there is a substantial body of literature on the reactive effects of self-monitoring, substantially less is known about reactivity associated with self-report. For example, does reporting that one often gets into fights with one's spouse make the subject take pause and try to alter that behavior?

7. Situational and behavioral specificity. This refers to the items in a particular checklist. The less specific and concrete an item, the greater the probability that the item can be interpreted (and misinterpreted) in a variety of ways.

8. Scale length. As a general rule, the longer the test, the greater the reliability, and to a lesser degree, the greater the validity. However, there may well be situations where a shorter checklist of carefully chosen items, or a checklist requiring more limited but better defined responses (e.g., a three-way judgment of below average, average, or above average vs. a 15 item response) may result in greater validity.

BEHAVIORAL QUESTIONNAIRES

A large number of questionnaires are now available to assess a variety of behaviors such as sexual behaviors, interpersonal behaviors like assertiveness, phobias, alcohol and drug abuse, marital interactions, and so on. There are literally hundreds of such questionnaires available. Table 18.1 lists some examples of such questionnaires. Perhaps the largest category of questionnaires falls under the rubric of problem behaviors, which include a wide variety of behaviors such as school-conduct problems, aggressiveness, suicidal intent, obsessive-compulsive behaviors, hyperactivity, lack of assertiveness, and so on. For an excellent review of behavioral questionnaires in a wide variety of areas, see Chapter 6 in S. N. Haynes and Wilson (1979).

Measurement of Anger

One of the very common problems of children seen for psychological or psychiatric services is the management of anger. Anger is a subjective, internal experience that may or may not be reflected in aggressive behavior. Thus, self-report would seem to be the most direct method of measurement (Finch & Rogers, 1984).

One such scale is the *Children's Inventory of Anger* (CIA; Finch & Rogers, 1984), a 71-item self-report inventory where each item is a mini-vignette (e.g., "the bus driver takes your name for acting up on the bus, but so was everyone else"). The child responds by selecting one of four "happy" faces that portray four reactions from happy to angry. Each face also has a verbal descriptive anchor.

A study of emotionally disturbed children over a 3-month period, indicated a test-retest reliability of .82. Spearman-Brown reliability for a much larger sample of normal and emotionally disturbed children yielded a coefficient of .91 for split-half and a coefficient of .95 for odd-even; Kuder-Richardson reliability was .96. Thus reliability, especially of the internal-consistency type, is exceptionally high.

Concurrent validity was assessed by comparing CIA scores to peer ratings with significant findings and by comparing CIA scores with results on another checklist of acting-out behavior; these latter results were modest at best. A factor analysis indicated six factors such as injustice and sibling conflict. Use of the scale with individual children in treatment suggested that the scale reflected the changes in anger management brought about by the therapeutic treatment.

The Daily Child Behavior Checklist (DCBC)

To assess problems of child behavior, mental-health specialists often depend on parental reports, usually in the form of behavioral checklists. As we have said, checklists have several advantages; they are economical, easy to administer, and easy to score. Checklists can be used to help define specific problems and can be used to jog the informant's memory.

Furey and Forehand (1983) criticized available checklists as containing items that were not equal (for example "shy" vs. "wets the bed at night"), that focused on negative behaviors, and that aimed at global perceptions over a substantial time period. They set out to develop a checklist that (1) contained both positive and negative behaviors; (2) might be used daily; (3) used specific and objective items that, and (4) focused on factual events rather than attitudes, emotions, and so on.

The resulting checklist contains 65 items, 37 positive (e.g., "gave parent a hug") and 28 negative (e.g., "refused to go to bed when asked"). The items were gathered from a variety of sources, but little information is given as to how specific items survived selection. Three scores are obtained from the DCBC: (1) total number of pleasing (positive) behaviors checked; (2) total number of displeasing behaviors checked; and (3) total score (pleasing minus displeasing behaviors).

Test-retest reliability over a 2-week interval was .19 for the pleasing score, .59 for the displeasing score, and .66 for the total score. The authors concluded that the DCBC has "satisfactory" reliability – but one would certainly question that conclusion, although quite clearly the nature of the variable (i.e., specific behaviors) is not necessarily temporally stable – if Daniel whines on Tuesday, will he also whine 2 weeks later?

According to the authors, content validity was established by having graduate students and mothers sort the original pool of 68 items into pleasing and displeasing categories. The 65 retained items were those that showed at least 90% agreement in both groups. A second sample of mothers completed the DCBC for their child. No significant correlations were obtained with demographic variables such as age and gender of the child, socioeconomic status, or number of siblings. Pleasing scores correlated .65 and displeasing scores correlated $-.78$ with total behavior scores. The two subscales however did not correlate with each other ($r = -.07$). Concurrent validity was assessed by comparing the DCBC scores with four subscales of a Parent Attitude Test. A significant pattern of correlations was obtained, supportive of concurrent validity.

Laboratory procedures. In this textbook, we have emphasized paper-and-pencil tests because these are the largest category of tests, they are the ones that you most likely would meet either as a professional or as a lay person, and they are the ones that most clearly illustrate basic issues, such as reliability and validity. However, there are many tests and procedures used in psychological research and assessment with formats different from paper-and-pencil. For example, in the area of sleep, researchers use the electroencephalogram to determine the stages of sleep; they may also be interested in measuring body temperature, heart rate, respiration, penile erection, postural changes, and so on. These instruments also need to be evaluated from the perspectives of reliability and validity (see W. W. Tryon, 1991, for an excellent review of activity measurement). As an example of these procedures, let us take a brief look at penile tumescence measurement, typically used as a measure of sexual arousal in males.

Penile Tumescence Measurement (PTM)

Penile measurement techniques provide information about a male's sexual interests by measuring penile response to various categories of sexual stimuli. One type of penile gauge is a device that involves the encasement of the penis in a glass cylinder. Sexual arousal of the penis causes air displacement in the glass cylinder, and thus volume changes can be recorded (McConaghy, 1967). Other types of gauges have also been developed (see R. C. Rosen & Beck, 1988).

O'Donohue and Letourneau (1992) reviewed the psychometric properties of such gauges in samples of child molesters, although fully realizing that sexual arousal to children is neither a necessary nor a sufficient condition for sexual offending. At the onset we should ask, as these investigators did, what kind of assessment method does PTM represent? Is this a norm-referenced test where the results for a subject are compared to those for a group of subjects? Is PTM a criterion-referenced test where we have some criterion of what is healthy or deviant, and we can assess an individual accordingly? Or is PTM not really a test, but a direct observation of behavior? If the latter, then the major criterion is whether this sample of behavior is representative and what can we infer from it. The writers assumed that standard psychometric criteria (i.e., reliability and validity) were indeed relevant.

Reliability. Studies of child molesters usually have few subjects, and the range of scores of PTM is often quite restricted. Both of these aspects tend to result in lower reliability coefficients. From a reliability perspective, we would want consistency of response to similar stimuli; in fact the level of sexual arousal may be affected by a variety of factors such as time since last orgasm and drug use.

An illustrative reliability study is that of Frenzel and Lang (1989), who studied heterosexual and homosexual sex offenders as well as a control group of heterosexual volunteers. The stimuli were 27 film clips that were shown three times to assess test-retest reliability. The film clips varied as to gender and age of subject shown, and three items were sexually neutral. Coefficient alpha was .93 for the 27 stimuli. A factor analysis of the data resulted in four factors: general heterosexuality, general homosexuality, adult heterosexuality, and neutral stimulation. This was interpreted by the authors as showing satisfactory internal consistency. A number of the stimuli were repeated; the test-retest correlations for these items ranged from .71 to .86 for female stimuli, with a mean r of .82, and from .21 to .74 with a mean r of .61 for male stimuli.

Alternate-forms reliability. The three major types of gauges presumably measure the same variable, penile tumescence, taken as an indicator of sexual arousal. O'Donohue and Letourneau (1992) reviewed four studies and concluded that these different devices do not correlate highly and therefore cannot be considered as alternate forms of the same measurement procedure.

Criterion validity. Validity criteria commonly used are arrest records, criminal convictions, self-report, and the reports of others. All of these criteria are fallible. For example, O'Donohue and Letourneau cite one study where the investigators interviewed 561 nonincarcerated paraphiliacs (sex offenders); they found a ratio of arrests to commission of rape and child molestation to be 1 to 30, indicating a very high rate of false negatives (i.e., people who have not been arrested but have committed a sexual offense).

An illustrative study is that of Freund (1965), who used colored slides of nude males and females of different ages to compare two groups: 20 heterosexual pedophiles and 20 heterosexual patients in an alcohol-abuse program. All subjects showed the greatest sexual arousal to female slides; sex offender subjects showed the greatest arousal to slides of children and least arousal to slides of adults. Of the 20 sex offenders, the results misclassified only 1 subject, and of the controls, only 1 subject was misclassified as a pedophile. In general, studies in this category show that child molesters can be differentiated from normal controls, and there is good sensitivity in general with few false positives and fewer false negatives (Blanchard, Klassen, Dickey, et al., 2001).

Differential diagnosis. One validity question is whether PTM can distinguish sexual offenders from normal controls, and the above suggests that the answer is, "Yes." Another question is that of differential diagnosis. Can the procedure be used to differentiate among various diagnostic groups, in this case, for example, between child molesters and rapists?

Unfortunately, the answer is complicated by the fact that many paraphiliacs engage in multiple paraphilic acts. O'Donohue and Letourneau (1992) report a study where in a sample of 561 nonincarcerated paraphiliacs, 20% had offended against both male and female targets, and 42% had offended against individuals in more than one age group. Of those who had been arrested for pedophilia, 33% had also engaged in acts of exhibitionism and 16% in acts of voyeurism. Of those who had been arrested for rape, 44% reported acts of female pedophilia. Thus, there does not seem to be the existence of mutually exclusive subgroups of sexual offenders. Therefore, it is not surprising that results of such validity studies present rather mixed findings.

Predictive validity. A few studies have examined the predictive validity of PTM to assess sex-offense relapse. The results are somewhat promising – in one study, 71% of the sample were correctly classified.

Faking. Can PTM be faked? The answer seems to be "Yes." For example, in one study subjects instructed to pretend to prefer adult women had significantly lower arousal to child stimuli. Other studies report that 80% of child molesters and rapists can control their sexual arousal when asked to do so.

Anxiety. Although there is disagreement about anxiety and how it should be defined, it is generally agreed that anxiety is diffuse (as opposed to fear, which is specific). Therefore, anxiety does not result in a specific behavior (such as in fear of flying where one avoids airplanes). Anxiety is an emotional reaction that centers on a subjective feeling of distress; there may be physiological arousal (e.g., sweating) and motor disturbances (e.g., stiffness of posture).

Because the subjective feeling of distress is at the core of anxiety, then self-report is highly relevant. Basically, there are three types of anxiety scales: (1) those that measure anxiety as a trait – i.e., as a general and stable disposition to become anxious. The trait part of the State-Trait Anxiety Scale discussed in Chapter 7 (as well as the

Beck Anxiety Inventory) would be examples; (2) those that measure anxiety as a state, that is as a response to a particular situation (e.g., how anxious do I feel right now as I'm about to take a final exam). The state part of the State-Trait Anxiety Scale would be an example; and (3) those that measure specific types of anxiety, such as test anxiety or anxiety about public speaking. These inventories could well be classified under the label of "fear."

Depression

Depression can be seen as a behavioral disorder characterized by dysphoric mood, accompanied by motoric changes (e.g., walking slowly) and physiological concomitants such as loss of appetite (see Lewinsohn & Graf, 1973). The Pleasant Event Schedule (PES; MacPhillamy & Lewinsohn, 1976) was developed specifically from a behavioral point of view and reflects Lewinsohn's theory about depression, which essentially sees depression as a lack of positive reinforcement. The PES is intended to assess the amount of external positive reinforcement the individual receives.

Lewinsohn (1976) believes that the general goal for the behavioral treatment of depressed individuals is to restore an adequate schedule of positive reinforcement for the individual. Specific intervention techniques can vary from person to person, and one approach is to use activity schedules to increase the patient's rate of behaviors that are likely to be reinforced by others or are intrinsically reinforcing for that patient.

The PES consists of 320 events that were elicited from various groups of subjects; several forms of the PES were developed, but form III with 320 items seems to be the standard one. The PES is used as a retrospective report of the events of the last 30 days, as well as a daily log for ongoing behavior. Lewinsohn (1976) describes how the PES can be administered to a patient: a subgroup of PES items judged to be most pleasant are targeted, and the patient is asked to indicate at the end of each day which activities he or she has engaged in.

In using the PES as a retrospective report, subjects are asked to indicate how frequently each item occurred within the last 30 days, on a 3-point scale: 0 (not happened); 1 (a few, 1 to 6 times);

and 2 (often, 7 or more times). Subjects then go through the PES a second time and indicate how pleasant each event was, also using a 3-point scale: 0 (not pleasant); 1 (somewhat pleasant); and 2 (very pleasant). From these two sets of ratings, three scores are obtained: Activity Level which is the sum of the frequency ratings; Reinforcement Potential, which is the sum of the pleasantness ratings; and Obtained Reinforcement, which is the overall sum. Representative PES items are: going to a rock concert, wearing clean clothes, being at the beach, playing golf, and sitting in the sun.

Test-retest reliability for a sample retested over a 4 to 8 week period was .85, .66, and .72 for the three scores; alpha coefficients were .96, .98, and .97 (Hersen & Bellack, 1981).

Evidence for the validity of the instrument has been presented by Lewinsohn and his colleagues in studies where the PES discriminates between depressed individuals and psychiatric or normal controls, and studies where various psychotherapeutic interventions with depressed patients result in parallel changes in the PES. Most of the validity would then be considered construct validity. For example, Lewinsohn and Graf (1973) found that the number of pleasant activities engaged in was significantly related to mood ratings of depression (more activities, less depression), and depressed subjects engaged in fewer pleasant activities. The 49 PES items that were significantly related to mood seemed to fall into three categories: (1) incompatible affects (e.g., laughing, being relaxed); (2) social interactions (e.g., kissing, being with friends); and (3) ego supportive (e.g., doing a job well, driving skillfully).

Bouman and Luteijn (1986) took the 49 PES items from the above study and used them as a scale in a sample of Dutch psychiatric patients, who also completed other questionnaires. Scores on this PES Mood related scale correlated significantly with other questionnaires of depression and of neuroticism; for example, −.58 with the Beck Depression Inventory, −.46 with the State Anxiety and −.39 with the Trait Anxiety scores of the Spielberger State-Trait Anxiety Inventory. However, when amount of depression was statistically removed, the correlations between PES and nondepression scores became insignificant – i.e., the PES Mood scale is related to depression and not other variables. When the sample of patients was divided into three diagnostic groups (major depression, nonmajor depression, and no depression), significant mean differences on the PES Mood scale were obtained, with lower scores associated with greater depression.

In keeping with the behaviorist orientation, the various published studies on the PES do not mention reliability or validity. The focus is on the relationship of pleasant events to various behavioral issues, rather than concern with the psychometric aspects of the scale.

Lewinsohn also developed an Unpleasant Events Schedule, a 320-item scale somewhat parallel to the PES, but designed to assess stressful life events (Lewinsohn, Mermelstein, Alexander, et al., 1985).

Hersen and Bellack (1981) indicate that such activity schedules, and the PES in particular, are good examples of behavioral measures that have been subjected to careful psychometric development and analysis. Unfortunately, most of the data that would be of interest from a psychometric point of view (e.g., reliability, results of factor analyses, etc.) is in unpublished manuscripts rather than in the public domain.

Social Skills

One of the major areas of deficit studied by behavior modification has been that of social skills, generally involving the ability to express both positive and negative feelings appropriately in interpersonal situations. The label "social skills" stands for a variety of behaviors that usually have an interpersonal component (i.e., relating to others) and an evaluative component (i.e., how effective the person is in relation to others). From a behavioral-assessment stance, we might perceive social skills as the abilities to emit behaviors that are positively reinforced by others and not emit behaviors that are punished by others. Among these skills, assertiveness and heterosexual dating skills have been the focus of much research and many self-report scales (for an early review of several self-report techniques used in the social-skills area, see Hersen & Bellack, 1977).

Assertiveness

Assertiveness involves the direct expression of one's feelings, preferences, needs, and opinions. Assertiveness is thus positively related to social dominance and negatively related to "abasement." It is different from aggression, in that aggression involves threats or punishment. Assertiveness seems to be a major problem for many people, and especially from a behavioral-assessment point of view, there is a need for reliable and valid instruments for use with adult samples, and a number have been proposed (e.g., McFall & Lillesand, 1971; Rathus, 1973). Most of assertiveness inventories ask the subject to indicate whether or not they engage in specific behaviors. Thus the questions are typically quite specific and are therefore less likely to be distorted by general attitudes and more likely to be directly related to the outside criterion.

The Rathus Assertiveness Schedule (RAS)

Rathus (1973) felt the need for an instrument to measure behavioral change in assertion training programs, and presented a 30-item Assertiveness Schedule, which subsequently became quite popular in the assertiveness literature.

The subject is asked to rate each of the 30 items on a 6-point scale, ranging from "very characteristic of me, extremely descriptive" to "very uncharacteristic of me, extremely undescriptive." The items cover such issues as whether the person complains in a restaurant if the service is poor or the food is not prepared satisfactorily, whether the person has difficulties saying no, and whether he or she finds it embarrassing to return merchandise. The items were obtained from other scales, as well as from students' diaries.

Test-retest reliability for a sample of 68 college students with a time interval of 8 weeks, was .78. Odd-even reliability for a sample of 67 subjects was .77. Split-half reliability coefficients reported in the literature generally range from .73 to .91 for various subgroups of patients.

Validity was originally established by comparing RAS scores to semantic differential ratings given by acquaintances. Five of the ratings covered an assertiveness factor, and these ratings correlated with RAS scores as follows: boldness .61; outspokenness .62; assertiveness .34; aggressiveness .54 confidence .33.

Semantic differential items such as smart-dumb, happy-unhappy, did not correlate significantly, indicating that RAS scores are not confounded by social desirability.

In a second study with 47 college coeds, their RAS scores were compared with their audiotaped responses to five vignettes that could be resolved by assertive behavior. These responses were rated blindly by judges who showed high interrater reliability ($r = .94$). RAS scores and ratings from these audiotaped responses correlated .70.

An item analysis indicated that 27 of the items correlated significantly with the total RAS score, and 19 of the 30 items correlated significantly with the semantic differential items indicating assertiveness. However, Rathus, 1973 suggested retaining all 30 items because they provide useful information.

Concurrent validity of the RAS is high. For example, in one study (Rathus & Nevid, 1977) scores for a sample of psychiatric patients correlated .80 with therapists' ratings of assertiveness using a semantic differential scale. Discriminant validity also is good. For example, the RAS differentiates between assertive and nonassertive male and female students (Nietzel, Martorano, & Melnick, 1977).

Adult Self-Expression Scale (ASES)

Gay, Hollandsworth, and Galassi (1975) set out to develop an assertiveness scale. They first developed a blue-print to guide their efforts by describing assertiveness along two dimensions. One dimension specified interpersonal situations in which assertive behavior might occur, such as in interactions with parents or with friends; six such situations were specified. The second dimension specified assertive behaviors that might occur in these interpersonal situations such as refusing unreasonable requests or expressing negative feelings; seven such behaviors were specified. This 6×7 format became a specification table for item selection.

A pool of 106 items, most coming from other scales, were administered to 194 adult subjects attending a community college. Items were then retained on the basis of item analyses which looked at item discrimination and item-total correlations. Forty-eight items were retained that covered 40 of the 42 cells in the specification table.

The ASES uses a 5-point Likert response format, with 25 of the items positively worded and 23 negatively worded. Test-retest reliability coefficients for 2-week and 5-week intervals are .88 and .91. In another study, test-retest reliability with a 1-week interval ranged from .81 to .89, and odd-even reliability was .92 (Hollandsworth, Galassi, & Gay, 1977).

Construct validity was established by correlating scale scores with ACL scores and with other measures of anxiety and of locus of control. The pattern of results supported the construct validity of the scale. For example, high scorers described themselves more favorably, as more self-confident and spontaneous, more achievement oriented, and more often seeking leadership roles. A factor analysis suggested 14 factors that the authors interpreted as supporting the two dimensional descriptive model used in the construction of the scale.

Hollandsworth, Galassi and Gay (1977) reported two validational studies of the ASES using a multitrait-multimethod procedure. In the first study, three samples (adults attending a technical institute, students in a graduate course in counseling, and psychiatric inpatients) were administered the ASES, the ACL, and an observer-rating scale on assertiveness. In the second study, convicted male felons were administered the ASES, the Rathus Assertiveness Schedule, and a self-report of aggressiveness; their criminal records were also rated for previous assaultive behavior.

Scores on the ASES correlated positively with dominance (.35 to .68) and negatively with abasement ($-.46$ to $-.72$) across all samples. Scores on the ASES also correlated significantly with other measures of assertiveness; thus, convergent validity using the same method of assessment was supported. However, when convergent validity as assessed by different methods was analyzed, the results for the relationship between assertiveness and abasement supported the hypothesis, but the results for the relationship between assertiveness and dominance were significant for only one sample. Finally, the analysis of discriminant validity only partially supported the hypotheses. In general however, the authors concluded that the results do support the utility of the ASES as a measure of assertive behavior.

Children's Assertive Behavior Scale (CABS)

There are many self-report measures of assertiveness for use with adult subjects, but relatively few for children. Michelson and Wood (1982)

developed the CABS designed to assess not only children's assertive behavior, but also their passive and aggressive modes of responding. The authors first identified various content areas of assertive behavior. Items were then developed for each content area and were examined by graduate students for their content validity. Other judges were then asked to assess the validity of the "continuum of responses" for each item (e.g., "is choice D more aggressive than choice B on the sample item below?"). Mean percentage of agreement was 94%.

The CABS is composed of 27 multiple-choice items, where the stem sets up a situation, followed by five response options. For example: "You are working on a project and someone says 'what are you doing?' Usually you would reply: ___"

-1 (a) Nothing really.

$+1$ (b) Don't bother me. Can't you see I'm busy?

-2 (c) Continue working and ignore the person.

$+2$ (d) It's none of your business.

0 (e) You would stop and explain what you were doing.

The scoring weights given above would of course not appear on the test protocol. Of the five responses, one is very passive (a), one is passive (c), one is assertive (e), one is aggressive (B) and one is very aggressive (d). Each of the response options is given a scoring weight, and three scores are generated: a passive score that is the sum total of the minus answers, an aggressive score that is the total of the positive scores, and a total score that is the absolute value of the passive and aggressive scores.

Significant concurrent validity was obtained with ratings of social competence by peers, parents, and teachers. The CABS also discriminated children who had participated in social-skills training vs. those who had not.

Hobbs and Walle (1985) asked a sample of primary school children to complete some sociometric procedures in which they indicated their three best friends, as well as three children whom they would most wish to be like (i.e., admired). The children also completed the CABS, which was scored for passivity, aggressiveness, and assertiveness. Children who scored high on positive peer nominations responded less aggressively than children who received low scores on peer nominations. Black children showed greater aggressive responding than white children, and boys were more aggressive but less assertive than girls. The findings were significant only for the measure of aggression and not the measure of passivity, but the authors concluded that the findings supported the validity of the CABS.

Sensitivity. One major line of evidence for the validity of such assertiveness questionnaires is their sensitivity to changes in behavior as a function of therapeutic interventions. Such studies usually use a pre-post format, where the questionnaire is administered to a sample of subjects, typically clients seeking help; then the clients are given behavior therapy, and are reassessed. In general, such studies support the validity of assertiveness scales.

Other studies look at the concurrent validity of such scales, by comparing scale scores with scores on other questionnaires, or look at discriminant validity by comparing assertive vs. nonassertive individuals. Still other studies have looked at the factor structure of such questionnaires.

Criticism. One of the problems with many assertiveness scales is that they confound assertiveness and aggressiveness, i.e., scores on the assertiveness scale correlate not only with indices of assertiveness, but also with indices of aggression (e.g., DeGiovanni & Epstein, 1978).

Phobias

It is estimated that in the United States more than 15 million individuals are affected by phobias at any given time, which makes phobias the most common "mental disorder." Thus a number of scales have been developed to measure such phobias.

The fear thermometer. One of the first self-report measures of fear was developed in the context of evaluating parachute jumpers (Walk, 1956). This was called the fear thermometer in which a thermometer like figure was divided into 10 equal parts; the trainee was asked to indicate his fear of jumping from a 34-foot mock tower, by placing a mark on the fear thermometer, with the height of the mark indicating the degree of fear experienced.

The Fear Survey Schedule (FSS)

There are various forms of the FSS that range in items from 50 to 122. The first form of the FSS, FSS1 was a list of 50 common fears to be rated by subjects on a 7-point scale (Lang & Lazovik, 1963). The items were developed on the basis of subjective judgment (i.e., the author chose the items), as part of a doctoral dissertation (Akutagawa, 1956). The focus was a clinical one; the FSS was designed to provide the therapist with a brief overview of the fears a client might have. FSS2 was constructed empirically for research purposes by selecting 51 items from open-ended questionnaires, with considerable psychometric data (Geer, 1965). FSS3 was developed within a clinical setting and consisted of a large number of items (the literature cites from 72 to 108) to be used for clinical purposes (Wolpe & Lang, 1964; 1977). Other forms representing different combinations of items have also been presented in the literature (e.g., Braun & Reynolds, 1969; Lawlis, 1971; Tasto & Hickson, 1970; Wolpe, 1973).

The FSS has been used in many studies, but because different forms that have different degrees of overlap have been used (e.g., FSS2 and FSS3 overlap by 20 items), it is difficult to generalize the results.

Different FSS forms have been factor analyzed and, not surprisingly, different numbers of factors have been obtained – sometimes as few as 3 and sometimes as many as 21. Sometimes the factors were replicated on a second sample and sometimes they were not. Sometimes different factors emerged for males than for females. Many studies have used the ubiquitous college students taking introductory psychology, but some have used psychiatric samples, with different results. Tasto (1977) suggested that if we consider only studies of college students and go beyond the different factor labels that different authors use, there is a fair amount of agreement across studies, with four major factors present: (1) fears related to small animals; (2) fears related to death, physical pain, and surgery; (3) fears about aggression; and (4) fears of interpersonal events.

Reliability. Hersen (1973) pointed out that few studies have looked at reliability, but those that have, have reported substantial reliability.

Internal-consistency estimates where reported, seem to be high – typically in the low to mid .90s. Test-retest reliability is lower but still acceptable; typical coefficients reported are in the mid .70s to mid .80s, with test-retest intervals of 1 to 3 months.

Validity. A behavioral assessment procedure such as the FSS was developed because other instruments, for example the MMPI, were seen as not adequate from either a theoretical point of view or an applied point of view. To then turn around and correlate the FSS with such measures would seem somewhat strange. If low correlations are obtained, one could argue that the instrument lacked construct validity, even though construct validity does not seem as germane to behavioral assessment techniques as it does to more traditional tests. If high correlations were obtained, then one could argue that the new measure was superfluous. In fact, studies that have looked at such correlations find coefficients in the mid-range, for example, correlations in the .40s with measures of anxiety in samples of therapy clients and/or college students.

From a behavioral point of view, validity is best established by comparing verbal reports to overt behavior and/or physiological indices. The fear thermometer mentioned above showed that parachute trainees who passed the course rated themselves as less fearful than those who did not. Within those who passed, lower fear ratings were related to achieving correct jump techniques earlier in training. Fazio (1969) validated a fear survey with actually picking up a cockroach.

Geer (1965) conducted a number of validational studies of the FSS. In one, subjects were required to approach a German Shepherd. For females, scores on the FSS were related to behavioral indices such as distance and latency (i.e., how close and how fast they approached the dog), but not for males. In another study, latency was longer for low-fear subjects than for high-fear subjects, contrary to what one would predict. In general, many of the results reported in the literature suggest that great caution needs to be exercised as there may well be confounding factors present when one attempts to validate such measures.

Because scales such as the FSS are used in the context of behavioral treatment, there are a number of studies in which the FSS is used with experimental and control groups, and a pre-post treatment design. If one is interested in the efficacy of the treatment, we can assume that the FSS is valid, and we can use significant pre-post changes in scores in the experimental group as evidence that the treatment works. We can also consider such sensitivity as evidence that the FSS is valid (see Tasto, 1977, for discussion of such studies).

A number of factor-analytic studies have been done, with the results reflecting the composition (i.e., the number and type of items) on the particular scale being analyzed. A number of authors have suggested that factor scores be used rather than subtotal scores of discrete items.

One of the major problems, especially with FSS3, is that it generates a large number of false positives. Klieger and McCoy (1994) developed a modified version of the FSS3 by decreasing the ambiguity of the items, including specific anchors for each item, and including instructions that separated emotions, such as disgust, from fear. They then administered the modified FSS3 to undergraduate students. To evaluate the scale, a behavioral-avoidance task (or BAT) was used. For example, one such BAT consisted of a harmless snake housed in a terrarium. The student walked toward the terrarium and stopped when he or she felt anxious. The floor was marked in 1-foot increments, so the distance traveled could easily be determined. As an example of the results, responses on the modified FSS3 correlated .33 for females and .64 for males with scores on the BAT that involved approaching the closed terrarium, removing the lid, and touching an upright log. In an earlier study (Klieger & Franklin, 1993), no significant differences on BATs were obtained between high-fear and no-fear students. For example, all 20 no-fear students approached the snake terrarium, as did 17 of the 20 high-fear students. A number of studies have indeed found low correlations (e.g., in the .20s and .30s) between FSS scores and various behavioral indices. Thus, cognitive and behavioral indices of fear are independent of each other, and it may well be that the FSS is not an effective classificatory tool. There may also be a number of confounding aspects, such as the demand characteristics of the experimental situation.

Gender differences. One of the consistent findings is that of gender differences, with females reporting higher degrees of fear than males. One argument to account for this difference is that social desirability inhibits males from admitting to fears, whereas in females social expectations are of greater fear.

Normative data. A variety of studies report normative data, typically in the form of means, and often separately by gender because women rate themselves as more fearful than men. In addition z score equivalents are also available (Tasto & Hickson, 1970), as well as an MMPI-like profile sheet that allows a person's scores on five FSS factors to be plotted using T scores (Tasto, Hickson, & Rubin, 1971).

The Fear Questionnaire (FQ)

Another popular measure is the FQ, a brief 15-item instrument that requires the subject to rate his or her avoidance of specific situations (I. M. Marks & Mathews, 1979). Typical items are: sight of blood, going into crowded shops, being criticized. Three subscales are available blood/injury, agoraphobia, and social, as well as a total score. This scale is probably one of the most frequently used self-report instruments in the treatment of agoraphobia (Trull, Neitzel, & Main, 1988). In clinical samples, the FQ has excellent test-retest reliability, normative data is available (Mizes & Crawford, 1986; Trull & Hillerbrand, 1990), and the scale has been translated into a number of languages including French, Italian, and Spanish (H. B. Lee & Oei, 1994).

Trull and Hillerbrand (1990) studied a sample of college students and a volunteer sample of community adults (surveyed by phone). For the collegiate sample, females scored higher than males on the blood/injury and agoraphobia subscales, as well as the total phobia score. For the community sample, females scored higher on all three subscales, as well as the total score. Community subjects scored higher than college students on the social and agoraphobia subscales, as well as on the total score. In both samples, the three subscales intercorrelated significantly, with coefficients from .28 to .48. Internal consistency (Cronbach's alpha) ranged from .44 to .73. A confirmatory factor analysis indicated that the three-factor model was not appropriate for either sample; exploratory factor analysis indicated a four-factor solution for the college sample, and a five-factor solution for the community sample.

H. B. Lee and Oei (1994) investigated the applicability of the FQ in a sample of Chinese college students in Hong Kong. Coefficient alpha for the total score was .83. Individual items correlated with total score from .15 to .59, with a mean r of .45. A factor analysis indicated three major factors that accounted for 37% of the variance. Factor 1, labeled agoraphobia, consisted of 5 items such as "walking alone in busy streets" and "traveling alone by bus or coach." Factor 2, social phobia, consisted of items such as "speaking or acting to an audience," and "talking to people in authority." Factor 3, blood-injury phobia, contained items such as "injections or minor surgery" and "hospitals."

No gender differences were obtained on these three factors and modest correlations with various measures of anxiety. The three-factor scales were found to be correlated with each other, contrary to the findings of other studies that the three factors are independent. Quite clearly, there may be significant cultural differences. Another obvious source of variation may be the nature of the sample; healthy college students are different from neurotic patients seen in a clinic, and it is therefore not surprising that different studies yield different results.

PROGRAM EVALUATION

Tests can also be used to evaluate programs rather than individuals. There are many ways to do this. We could, for example, ask individuals to complete rating scales that focus on a particular program. For example, if you have ever evaluated a course by filling out a questionnaire, you were basically participating in a program evaluation where you were one of the evaluators. We could also administer questionnaires to individuals, typically in a pre- versus post-design to evaluate the effectiveness of a program. If we wish to evaluate the effectiveness of a therapeutic program, we can assess the mental health of the patients before entering the program, and then again some 6 months later. Here the focus would not be on how psychologically healthy the person is at post-test, but rather on the changes that have occurred, presumably reflective of the effectiveness of the program. Sometimes, tests are misused in this way. The teaching effectiveness of a school and its staff is often evaluated based on how the children do on a standardized achievement battery, without considering the fact that the scores on these tests may be more highly related to the socioeconomic background of the children than to the expertise and efforts of the teachers.

National programs such as Head Start have had massive evaluations, although the conclusions derived from such evaluations do not necessarily reflect unanimous agreement (see W. L. Goodwin & Driscoll, 1980).

Program evaluations can vary from rather simple approaches where a single rating scale is used, as in the typical course evaluation conducted on collegiate campuses, to complex multiphasic approaches that use cognitive measures, assessment of psychomotor changes, economic indicators, direct observation, use of archival data, and so on. Thus, in evaluating a graduate program in clinical psychology, the evaluating team looks not only at information such as the publications of the faculty, their rank, their teaching evaluations, etc., but also interviews graduate students, deans and other administrators, obtains architectural information about the amount of space available, library resources, and so on.

An excellent example and case study is the evaluation of *Sesame Street*, an extremely popular children's television program geared for children ages 3 to 5. The program was originally developed as a remedial program, especially for disadvantaged children, to prepare them for school. The intent was not only to entertain but to increase intellectual and cultural development (Ball & Bogatz, 1970). The first year of *Sesame Street* was evaluated through a large sample of children that included disadvantaged inner-city children, Spanish-speaking children, and rural-area children. A special battery of tests was developed for this program evaluation, basically consisting of 12 major tests (such as Numbers and Sorting Skills) that took an average of 2 hours to administer. The alpha coefficients for the subtests ranged from .17 to .93, with a median of .66 (see W. L. Goodwin & Driscoll, 1980, for a synopsis). To the extent that psychological tests are used in such program evaluations, we need to be mindful of the psychometric requirements of the instruments used.

ASSESSMENT OF ENVIRONMENTS

Measuring the Home Environment

You recall that Public Law 91-230, the Handicapped Children's Act (Chapter 12) mandated the establishment of preschool and early-childhood programs for disabled and high-risk children. Thus, these children need to be identified, and there is a need for instruments. Traditional intelligence tests such as the Wechsler or the Stanford-Binet can be quite useful, but "at risk" involves more than simply cognitive deficit. There is a need to identify environmental aspects that can either directly affect development, or can interact with other variables such as intelligence, to produce greater developmental delay. Scientists often use socioeconomic status (SES) as an index of environmental quality. Although SES works and is used widely, it is also a fairly limited index. Within an SES grouping, for example, families differ widely in the kinds and amounts of stimulation they provide their children.

Caldwell and her colleagues (e.g., Bradley & Caldwell, 1977, 1979) pointed out that there is a need to develop screening and diagnostic procedures that identify children at risk. A child's developmental environment can be hypothesized to play a major role, and thus should be included as a major assessment dimension. In particular, a child's developmental environment can be indexed by *process* measures, that is the day-to-day, moment-to-moment transactions of the child with the environment – the type of language stimulation received, the kind of play materials available, the types of punishment and rewards, etc. They therefore developed the Home Observation for Measurement of the Environment (HOME) Inventory, which consists of items (different numbers in different versions) that cover such aspects as the emotional and verbal responsivity of the mother to the child, whether there are appropriate play materials, and so on. The HOME inventory is administered in the home by a trained observer and requires about 60 minutes.

Bradley and Caldwell (1979) presented validity data for the preschool version of the HOME

Table 18–2. Use of HOME Inventory in a Sample of 91 Families			
	Predicted group membership based on discriminant function of HOME Inventory		
Actual IQ group	Low	Low average	Average to superior
Low	12	5	0
Low average	9	14	11
Average to superior	7	8	25

Inventory. This version was designed to assess the quantity and quality of the social, emotional, and cognitive support available for children aged 3 to 6 within their home. Originally, all the items developed for the HOME Inventory were based on direct observation of actual transactions between mother and child. As the inventory was refined, however, additional items based on interview data were added. Several forms were produced, including a 144-item version, an 80-item version, and a 55-item version, with items scored as present or absent.

The 80-item version was administered to 232 volunteer families, including both black and white participants. A factor analysis indicated 7 factors, and items that loaded significantly on one of these factors were retained, as well as 9 items that correlated with academic achievement, yielding a 55-item scale. Some of the factors were (1) stimulation through toys, games, and reading materials; (2) language stimulation; and (3) stimulation of academic behavior. An item analysis indicated that item correlations with total score or total subscale score were moderate to high (.20 to .70). In most instances, the correlation between an item and its subscale score was greater than the correlation between an item and the total scale score.

Internal consistency coefficients (KR 20) for the subscales ranged from .53 to .83. Test-retest stability over 18 months ranged from .05 to .70. However, these are not really reliability coefficients, but may in fact reflect the kind of changes that occur in the home over such a time span.

Validity was assessed by correlating HOME subscale scores with indices of socioeconomic status (such as maternal and paternal education, and occupation), and Stanford-Binet IQ. In general, correlations with mother's or father's occupation was negligible, but correlations with mother's and father's education, as well as with the amount of crowding in the home, were significant (the more crowded the home, the lower the child's score). HOME scores were substantially related to Stanford-Binet scores.

A discriminant analysis of the HOME inventory in relation to Stanford-Binet scores indicated that low IQ (below 70) was associated with poorer organization of the environment, fewer appropriate play materials available, and less maternal involvement with the child. Table 18.2 presents the results for a sample of 91 families, where the families were divided into low IQ child (IQ below 70), low average (70 to 89), and average to superior (90 and above). Note that the sensitivity of the HOME Inventory for the low IQ group is high with 71% (12 of 17) correctly identified. There is less sensitivity for the low average group, where 14 of 34 or 62% are correctly identified. For the average to superior group, 25 of 40 or 62.5% were correctly identified. Specificity within the low IQ group (the number of homes incorrectly identified as being associated with low IQ, i.e., false positives) is high. Thus, the procedure identifies 28 as low IQ, with 16 being incorrect. By comparison, the specificity associated with average to superior IQ is good – 25 of 40 were correctly identified, so 15 were false negatives. When screening for retardation, it can be argued that sensitivity is more important than specificity – that is, we really want to identify those children who do need special and/or remediation programs.

Bradley, Caldwell, and Elardo (1977) studied the ability of the HOME inventory and SES to predict IQ, and found that across both white and black children, as well as male and female, the HOME inventory was a more accurate index of environmental quality, and predicted IQ better than did SES, with correlation coefficients between .58 to .79.

Measuring Classroom Environments

It is generally believed that the classroom, especially in the primary grades and the high-school years is a critical setting not only for educational development but also for psychosocial and interpersonal development. It is also believed that there are individual differences between classrooms, and that classrooms do have distinct climates or atmospheres. Thus, there has been a lot of research on classroom climate.

The Classroom Environment Scale (CES)

Moos and his colleagues (e.g., Moos 1968; 1972; Moos & Houts, 1968; Trickett & Moos, 1970), have devoted considerable effort to the measurement of environments in a variety of settings, such as university dormitories, psychiatric wards, and high-school classrooms. Trickett and Moos (1973) developed a Classroom Environment Scale (CES) to assess the psychosocial environment of junior high- and high-school classrooms. They began by analyzing the literature on the topic, and based on the theoretical notions found in the literature, decided there were three major sets of variables: (1) interpersonal relationship variables, which include affective aspects of student-student and teacher-student interactions; (2) structural aspects of the classroom; and (3) goal-orientation variables.

Given this theoretical framework, the authors then searched the educational literature, conducted structured interviews with both teachers and students, and observed a wide range of classes. This led to the identification of conceptual dimensions (e.g., student involvement) and to the writing of test items presumably indicative of each conceptual dimension. Note again the close correspondence between the steps taken and those outlined in Chapter 2. Although having a strong basement doesn't mean that the rest of the structure will necessarily be solid, a strong foundation is a necessary first step.

Once the original pool of items was constructed, items were independently evaluated as to conceptual dimension by two raters. If the raters did not agree, the item was discarded. The initial version of the CES consisted of 242 items representing 13 conceptual dimensions. On each dimension, approximately half of the items were keyed true and half were keyed false. For each item (e.g., "The teacher is very strict"), the respondent answers true or false depending on whether the statement is seen as a general characteristic of the classroom.

This initial version was given to 504 students in 26 different classrooms, in seven high schools, along with the Marlowe-Crowne Social Desirability Scale (see Chapter 16). All of the items showed very low correlations (.20 or less) with scores on the Marlowe-Crowne, but item analyses showed that some items either did not correlate with dimension scores, or were too highly correlated with other items. After a number of statistical analyses were carried out, and additional observations made, a 208-item form was developed and administered to 443 students in 22 different classrooms.

Most of the items (89%) discriminated between classrooms, and most of the items correlated highly with their subscale scores. This and other statistical considerations led to the development of a 90-item form that covers nine dimensions (such as affiliation, competition, and teacher control) with 10 items per dimension. The internal consistency (Cronbach's alpha) for these nine dimensions ranged from .67 to .86, showing acceptable internal consistency. All 9 scales differentiated the 22 classrooms, with most of the scales having relatively low intercorrelations with each other (average was .26). Two of the classrooms were retested after a 2-week period, with test-retest correlations ranging from .91 to .98. The CES then, provides something like a personality profile, not of a person but of a classroom, as perceived by the respondents.

The Individualized Classroom Environment Questionnaire (ICEQ)

In the 1980s, education within Great Britain underwent a number of dramatic changes that created and accompanied a shift in thinking – from a traditional approach that explained scholastic success and failure as located "within the child" to explanations that concentrate on evaluating the total context in which learning is expected to occur – that is, an evaluation of the classroom environment.

Fraser (Burden & Fraser, 1993; Rentoul & Fraser, 1979) developed the Individualized Classroom Environment Questionnaire in Australia, and cross-validated the questionnaire in British schools. There are two forms of the questionnaire (presumably using the same items): one is the actual form where the child rates the actual classroom, and a "preferred" form where the child indicates what he or she would prefer. The forms can also be completed by the teacher so a total of four combinations can be obtained. Representative items are, "the teacher talks with each student," and "there is classroom discussion." Each item is responded to on a Likert-like scale of 1 (almost never) to 5 (very often). The 25 items are divided into five subscales: Personalization, Participation, Independence, Investigation, and Differentiation (i.e., whether different students use different materials or engage in different projects).

Burden and Fraser (1993) present alpha reliability coefficients on children in eight classrooms. These coefficients range from .62 to .85, with 6 out of the 10 coefficients above .70. In a study of 34 classrooms in Australia, alpha coefficients ranged from .61 to .90, indicating satisfactory reliability. The scales themselves intercorrelate from .09 to .36, suggesting adequate discriminant validity. Test-retest reliability is from .67 to .86. Several studies of predictive and criterion validity support the initial validity of the ICEQ (Fraser, 1981). A comparison of the ICEQ with scores on a locus of control scale indicated small but significant correlations with three of the five scales. The authors also give a case study where the actual and preferred forms were administered in one science class, with appreciable difference between the two. The teacher then made a number of changes based on the students' comments, and 4 weeks later the forms were readministered, showing substantial changes.

Classroom environments have been assessed in terms of student or teacher perceptions of psychosocial dimensions such as cohesiveness and degree of competition; see Moos (1979) for an introduction to the assessment of educational environments. A number of popular instruments in this area exist in addition to the Classroom Environment Scale (Moos & Trickett, 1974), such as the Learning Environment Inventory (G. J. Anderson & Walberg, 1976). In general, when classroom environment perception is used as independent variable, there is considerable validity in that this variable (and its components) accounts for an appreciable amount of the variance in cognitive and affective outcomes (such as degree of learning and customer satisfaction), often more than what can be attributed to student characteristics, such as their general ability (Fraser, 1981). When used as a dependent variable, classroom environment perception also shows validity in that such perception shows differences between classrooms that differ in class size, type of school, and so on.

College environments. Pace and Stern (1958) began with the theoretical framework proposed by Henry Murray, whose personality theory was based on the notion of personal needs (motives, goals, etc.) as well as environmental press, i.e., aspects of the environment that impinge upon human behavior. They constructed the College Characteristics Index, composed of 300 true-false items organized into 30 ten-item subscales. The scales basically reflect needs such as need affiliation, but these are presses (statements about the college environment); in this case, the aspects of the college environment that would promote affiliation. Respondents answer true or false if they believe the item is or is not characteristic of this particular college environment (e.g., "Spontaneous student demonstrations occur frequently" might reflect the press of impulsiveness).

The initial instrument was given to a sample of 423 college students and 71 faculty members at five different collegiate institutions. Differences between student and faculty responses were minor, and rank order correlations across the 30 presses for students vs. faculty correlated .88 and .96, showing substantial agreement. Case studies of different institutions are presented to support the validity of the instrument (which was subsequently revised).

Thistlethwaite (1960) took a revised form of the College Characteristics Index and studied a sample of 1,500 National Merit Scholars, college students who had done extremely well on the SAT. He found that stability of students' study plans were related to such aspects as role models for imitation. Decisions to seek advanced degrees were often based on the perception of faculty as enthusiastic and informal and on their stressing achievement and independence. (For a different approach to the measure of college environments, see Astin & Holland, 1961.)

Measuring the Physical Environment

Rating the taste of water. From a psychological testing perspective, the assessment of the psychological components of a physical environment are of greater interest than assessing the physical components. Take water for example. We could measure its mineral content, degree of pollution, viscosity, etc., but we usually leave such measurements to physical scientists. But the psychological perception is another matter. Bruvold (1968) presented four rating scales to evaluate the taste of water. These scales were developed using the Thurstone method of equal-appearing intervals, and for each of the scales, nine items were retained. The first scale, called the "hedonic" scale, consists of nine items that range from, "I like this water extremely" to "I dislike this water extremely." The second scale, the "quality" scale, consists of nine items that range from, "This water has an excellent taste" to "This water has a horrible taste." The third scale is the "action tendency" scale, and its nine items range from, "I would be very happy to accept this water as my everyday drinking water" to "I can't stand this water in my mouth and I could never drink it." Finally, the fourth scale, called the "combination" scale, has nine items that range from, "This water tastes real good. I would be very happy to have it for my everyday drinking water" to "This water has a terrible taste. I would never drink it."

Reliability of these scales was assessed in a laboratory study where 24 employees of the California State Department of Public Health rated 10 water samples, with order of water sample presentation randomized, as well as a number of other experimental controls. For each subject there were 28 reliability correlation coefficients computed, but the average intercorrelations between and within scales ranged from .62 to .77. The validity of the scales was assessed by comparing mean ratings for samples of respondents from different towns, and by showing an inverse relationship between favorability toward water and mineral content of the water.

Environmental preferences. People differ in their preferences for different environmental settings. The Environmental Preference Questionnaire (EPQ; R. Kaplan, 1977) was designed to explore individual differences in such environmental preferences. The 1977 form of the EPQ contains seven scales developed on the basis of responses made by several hundred people, and as a result of various factor-analytic procedures. The seven EPQ scales are described next:

1. Nature: this scale deals with the preference for woodland areas, lakes, wilderness, and other natural settings;

2. Romantic escape: this scale also reflects a preference for natural settings, but adds a dislike for urban places;

3. Modern development: this one reflects a preference for modern housing developments and industrial areas;

4. Suburbs: here the focus is on ownership of property and law and order;

5. Social: this scale shows preference for people activities such as parties and conversation;

6. Passive reaction to stress: here the preference for sleeping, eating, pleasant smells like perfume is indicated;

7. City: this scale expresses a preference for bustle and excitement of a large city.

The EPQ consists of six questions or areas of concern; for example, question 1 asks the respondent to indicate their preference for each of 11 settings, such as "the bustle and excitement of a large city" and "a woodland area." Responses are made using a 5-point agree-disagree scale. A total of 60 items are thus rated. The seven EPQ scales range in length between 4 and 12 items. Internal consistency alpha coefficients range from .63 to .83, with five of the scales falling in the .70s.

In a study of high-school students, R. Kaplan (1977) found some significant but modest correlations between EPQ scales, self-esteem, and motivations for different recreation activities, supportive of the construct validity of the scale. It could be argued, however, that this scale is really a personality inventory. After all, saying that "I like a bright sunny day" vs. "I like collecting pine cones" could easily be items from an MMPI- or CPI-like instrument.

ASSESSMENT OF FAMILY FUNCTIONING

The majority of tests considered in earlier chapters have the individual as their focus. That is, whether we administer an intelligence test, a personality inventory, a checklist of values, a measure of creativity, etc., we are assessing an individual. Tests can also be used to assess the psychosocial and/or physical environment, such as a college campus as we discussed earlier, or as we will see next, the relationships between individuals as family members or the family as an organized system.

The earliest attempts at assessment of couples were primarily based on self-reports, and focused on such aspects as satisfaction and marital adjustment (e.g., E. W. Burgess & Cottrell, 1939). Beginning in the 1960s, as movie cameras and later video cameras became available and affordable, observational techniques through filmed interactions became more popular. This led to the development of coding systems to assess the filmed interactions, at first primarily the verbal interactions of parents and their children. Beginning in the 1980s, a number of self-report measures of family functioning began to be available, such as the Family Adaptability and Cohesion Evaluation Scales (Olson, et al., 1985) considered by some to represent a benchmark in family assessment (Halverson, 1995).

Family measurement has been affected by many disciplines who bring to the field their own particular points of view and preferred measurement techniques. For example, sociologists depend more on survey and interview methods, whereas psychologists use self-report inventories, or those with a behaviorist bent use observational techniques. Currently, the emphasis seems to be on multiple measurement strategies.

In the area of family and marriage, reliability and validity of measurement was ignored until the 1960s when several publications began to focus on this issue. As B. C. Miller, Rollins, and Thomas (1982) state so well, "What we know and how we know it are inextricably linked." Still, reliability and validity are often ignored in the family literature even today.

In assessing family behavior through direct observation, for example, a key issue is at what level of behavior do we observe and analyze? For example, we could observe behaviors such as hugging, expressing approval, and joking, or we could combine such behaviors into a behavioral construct of warmth. The limited evidence suggests that a broader level of analysis, the warmth level, is more reliable and valid than a more specific level of behavior; similarly, rating scales that basically summarize a variety of observational events are more reliable and valid than individual observations (A. L. Baldwin, Cole, & C. Baldwin, 1982). Not everyone agrees; D. C. Bell &

L. Q. Bell (1989) for example, argue that "micro" coding of smaller units of behavior is always better than "macro" coding inferences made from the behavior. Much of family research is based on self-report, however (for a review of methods to study families, see B. C. Miller, Rollins, & Thomas, 1982).

General problems. There are a number of problems in the area of family assessment vis-à-vis measurement. Halverson (1995) cites seven:

1. Most research in this area is small-scale research that is never replicated.

2. There are too many measures measuring too many constructs. Some 80% of available measures have never been used more than once, and there is no consensus on what are the most important constructs in family assessment. Even the scales that are used widely have met with a lot of criticism (e.g., Conoley & Bryant, 1995; Norton, 1983; Sabatelli, 1988).

3. Most measures are of unknown reliability and validity.

4. There are few, if any, studies that compare the usefulness of various constructs within the same study, such as by using a multitrait-multimethod approach.

5. Most of the measures we have are self-reports, instruments that elicit information from individuals who report on their family's functioning.

6. Family assessment measures have been developed on relatively small and restricted samples.

7. Most instruments lack normative data.

Family-Systems Rating Scales

Many family-systems rating scales have been developed, although a substantial number lack appropriate psychometric information as to their reliability and validity. Carlson and Grotevant (1987) reviewed eight rating scales used in the assessment of family functioning and concluded that these scales demonstrated both strengths and limitations, as well as differences in their reliability and validity. They concluded that such rating scales were the "method of choice" in family assessment, even though their research utility and usefulness were questionable.

Rating scales can be improved if what is to be rated is a single dimension clearly defined and anchored with specific behaviors. If the rating to be made requires a high level of inference, the results usually show lower reliability and validity. Rating scales can also be improved if the rater is well trained. Note that a rater is not simply an accurate observer; he or she takes the observations and dynamically integrates them into a rating.

Cohesion and control. Two major theoretical dimensions in the area of family assessment are cohesion and control. Given their importance, there have been a number of attempts to operationalize these by specific measures. Unfortunately, different measures of these constructs do not correlate highly with each other, even when they use the same method, such as self-report; they correlate even less across methods, such as self-report vs. behavioral measures (e.g., Oliveri & Reiss, 1984; Olson & Rabunsky, 1972; Schmid, Rosenthal, & Brown, 1988).

Marital quality. There are a number of marital-quality scales, a term that subsumes marital adjustment, satisfaction, and happiness. Some of these scales, such as the Locke-Wallace Marital Adjustment Test (Locke & Wallace, 1959) and the Dyadic Adjustment Scale (Spanier, 1976), are very well known and used in many studies, while many other scales have languished in relative obscurity. In general, most of these scales show substantial psychometric limitations. Even when the overall reliability and validity are acceptable, there is controversy about the factor structure (as in the case of the two scales mentioned above) or other aspects.

Impression management. A basic assumption in studying marital or cohabiting partners is that the information they provide on self-report scales is veridical. As we have seen in Chapter 16, a major concern in the area of personality has been social desirability, and as we have also seen, social desirability can be conceptually divided into self-deception (where the person really believes the distorted evidence he or she is presenting) vs. impression management, which is a positively biased response designed to enhance one's self-image as presented to others.

Hunsley Vito, Pinsent, et al. (1996) studied the relationship of impression management to various marital-relationship measures. They found that impression management biases did not affect women's self-reports. It did affect men's self-reports, but controlling for such bias statistically did not alter the results – that is, such biases when present are minor and do not affect the self-reports given, at least when it comes to "commonplace" aspects of marriage such as communication, as opposed to physical violence. However, other studies have found modest correlations (above .30) between measures of social desirability, such as the Marlowe-Crowne scale, and various measures of marital adjustment or satisfaction (e.g., Roach, Frazier, & Bowden, 1981).

The McMaster Family-Assessment Device (FAD)

The FAD is a 60-item self-report instrument developed on the basis of *systems theory*. Applying systems theory, the family is a system, where the various parts of the family are interrelated, and the whole does not simply equal the sum of the parts; the focus is on relationships, on how the family operates as a system (Epstein, Baldwin, & Bishop, 1983). Thus, the FAD assesses family functioning, theorized to follow six dimensions: problem solving, communication, roles, affective involvement, affective responsiveness, and behavior control. There is also an overall General Functioning scale. Each dimension is rated on a 7-point scale with three defined anchor points: 1 = severely disturbed; 5 = nonclinical; and 7 = superior. Ratings of 1 through 4 indicate family dysfunction, and therefore the need for intervention. Kabacoff, Miller, Bishop, et al. (1990) present psychometric data on this scale using large psychiatric, normal, and medical samples. The internal reliability (Cronbach's alpha) for the subscales ranges from .57 to .80, and from .83 to .86 for the overall General Functioning scale. Two lines of evidence are presented for the construct validity of this instrument. First, families with a psychiatric member reported significantly greater difficulties on all six subscales; no significant differences were obtained between medical families and normal families. Second, confirmatory factor analysis supported the hypothesized theoretical structure of six factors. For examples of other recently developed marital scales, see Arellano and Markman (1995) and Baucom, Epstein, Rankin, et al. (1996).

Projective instruments. One approach to family assessment is to use projective instruments. You recall that the distinguishing feature of projective tests is the presentation of relatively unstructured stimuli that allow for an almost unlimited number of possible responses. How a person perceives and interprets these ambiguous stimuli presumably reflects fundamental aspects of the person's psychological makeup and motivational dynamics.

One of the major projective techniques is the Thematic Apperception Test (see Chapter 15). Although the TAT was developed for use with individual clients, it has been used to study family functioning and dynamics (e.g., Winter, Ferreira, & Olson, 1966). It has also given rise to a number of special sets of cards that portray family scenes. One such set of 21 cards is the Family Apperception Test (Julian, Sotile, Henry, & Sotile, 1991). Seven of the cards show scenes of nuclear family members engaged in group interaction; seven cards show interactions between an adult and a child, and the other seven depict a variety of situations. The scoring guide covers seven basic concepts, such as conflict and quality of relationships, and these yield nine scoring categories. Reliability is reported primarily by percentage of agreement, with Cohen's Kappa coefficients ranging from a low of .28 to a high of .77. Several studies of discriminant validity show statistically significant differences between clinical and nonclinical subjects. This test is criticized, however, for lack of content validity – the nine scoring categories do not cover many of the topics central to family theory. Several of the scoring categories that are included are poorly conceptualized, and 14 of the 21 cards may elicit responses that have nothing to do with family themes. As the reviewer indicates, the validity of this instrument has not been demonstrated (Bagarozzi, 1991).

Semi-projective techniques. There are a number of techniques that are somewhat more difficult to categorize because they combine various aspects of projective and objective techniques. One category are figure placement techniques, which presumably reflect an individual's or a family's perception of how the family is organized. Most of these instruments have, however, lacked standardization and have, at best, modest reliability and validity (Bagarozzi, 1991). An example, is the Family Systems Test (FAST) developed in Germany, originally in a German version, but also in English. The FAST is based on a specific family theory that considers cohesion and hierarchy as two important dynamic aspects of family functioning. The FAST consists of a board divided into 81 squares, with 6 male and 6 female figures, 18 cylindrical blocks of 3 sizes, and 1 male and 1 female figure each in orange, violet, and green. The respondent, an individual, a couple, or an entire family, arranges the figures on the board to indicate cohesion, and elevates the figures with blocks to indicate hierarchy. This is done three times to represent a typical situation, an ideal situation, and a conflict situation. Cohesion is operationally translated as proximity of figure placement, and hierarchy as the differences in height between figures. Cohesion and hierarchy scores are combined to reflect family structure in each situation, or can be combined across situations to assess perceived family flexibility. There are two additional options that involve using figures of varying colors, and indicating degree of eye contact between figures.

In a study of California adolescents, test-retest reliability with a 1-week period was adequate (.63 to .87) with higher coefficients associated with older adolescents. Test-retest reliability over a 4-month interval was poor (.42 to .59). The construct validity of the FAST is mixed. Some findings are supportive of hypothesized relationships and some are not. There are a number of concerns about this technique, which potentially may be useful.

Assessment of couples. What are the purposes of couple assessment? Fruzzetti and Jacobson (1992) suggest that there are three purposes:

1. To obtain information to be used for clinical intervention. Typically, these are couples who are about to enter psychotherapy, and the assessment is often broad aimed at understanding the couple within an overall context.

2. As part of a research assessment, perhaps a study of basic relational processes. Often, these

are more focused endeavors and are typically theory driven.

3. Both clinical and research needs are present – as for example in a study of couples in therapy, where there is need to evaluate the changes that occur as a function of therapeutic interventions.

Fruzzetti and Jacobson also point out that there are many different factors that influence the functioning of a couple, and thus assessment may be aimed at one of several aspects. Among the major categories:

1. Individual aspects. There are many personal or individual aspects that each person brings to a relationship that can affect that relationship. These may involve psychiatric conditions, such as depression or substance abuse, or limited interpersonal skills, such as the inability to communicate clearly, to express emotions appropriately, to be sensitive to the other person's needs, and so on. In this area of assessment, inventories such as the MMPI and CPI can be quite useful.

2. Contextual aspects. These refer to the physical and psychological environment or context that the couple finds themselves in – essentially the question of, "What is their life as a couple like?" Are there children present? are there elderly infirm parents? Are there money concerns? What is their living environment like? Is there a support system? These contextual aspects are typically assessed through interviews rather than psychometric measures, although instruments do exist to assess specific aspects such as social support.

3. Conflicts and satisfactions. How partners think and feel about their relationship is of primary importance, and often therapy is sought out because of real or perceived dissatisfactions. A substantial number of questionnaires have been developed in this area, such as the Marital Satisfaction Inventory (D. K. Snyder, 1979). In general, these questionnaires seem to have adequate reliability and moderate validity.

4. Interactional processes. A couple is not simply a sum of two individuals; most theorists in this area assume that there is an interactive effect, that the couple is a system with properties that go beyond a simple summation of the parts. Among the more important interactive processes, Fruzzetti and Jacobson list violence, communication, and physiological arousal, as well as the structural dynamic aspects of such interactions, such as the degree of demand-withdrawal (i.e., as one partner makes greater demands, the other withdraws emotionally).

BROAD-BASED INSTRUMENTS

Most of the instruments we have covered in this text are fairly specific in their objective; some, for example, attempt to measure depression, intelligence, or neuroticism. There are however a number of techniques that by their very nature are quite flexible and can be used in a variety of endeavors. The Semantic Differential, for example, discussed in Chapter 6, is one such technique. We will briefly take a look at three other techniques as illustrative: sociometric procedures, adjective checklists, and Q sets.

Sociometric Procedures

These procedures, developed in the 1930s (e.g., Koch, 1933) are one of the most frequently used methods for measuring a child's status within a peer group (i.e., the child's popularity or degree of acceptance). These procedures essentially ask children to nominate children who have certain attributes – for example, who are the three most intelligent children in this classroom? The questions can take a variety of forms, the nominations may be positive or negative, the responses may be open-ended or use a paired comparison (e.g., do you prefer Tommy or Billy to be on your basketball team). Thus, there is no one procedure, but a rather broad array of procedures. In general, three types of procedures are more commonly used (Hops & Lewin, 1984):

1. Restricted nominations. Here children in a classroom are asked to choose a number of classmates for a specific situation (e.g., which three children do you like the most?). Positive nominations for each child can be easily tabulated as an index of friendship. Negative nominations can also be used (e.g., which 3 children do you like the least?) as an index of rejection. Such procedures usually ask the child to write the names down, but younger children can also be asked individually to select photographs of classmates. Various analyses can then be undertaken – for example, children who receive no positive nominations are "isolates," whereas children who receive a lot of negative nominations are rejected children.

2. Peer rating scales, which involve a Likert-type rating scale. Typically, the children are provided with a roster of their classmates, and rate each child on a 5-point scale indicating, for example, how much they like that child. Sometimes the verbal anchors are accompanied by or replaced with various sequences of happy faces.

3. Paired-comparison procedure. Here each child is asked to choose between every possible pair of children (excluding oneself) again in terms of a particular situation. If we have a classroom of 25 children, then each child will make 253 such judgments; that is the major drawback, although short cuts are available (for illustrative studies see Asher, Singleton, Tinsley et al., 1979; Deutsch, 1974; LaGreca, 1981).

Because there are so many variations in sociometric techniques, it is difficult to generalize about the reliability and validity of these techniques. At the risk of oversimplifying, however, we can make some general tentative conclusions. First as to reliability:

1. Reliability generally seems to be adequate.

2. Reliability is greater with older children than with younger children.

3. Reliability of positive nominations is greater than that of negative nominations.

4. As usual, test-retest reliability decreases as the time interval gets longer.

5. Peer rating procedures seem somewhat more reliable than restricted nomination procedures.

6. Lack of reliability may not necessarily represent "error" as in the classical test theory model, but may reflect legitimate sources of variation. For example, sociometric ratings made by less popular children are less stable; they may simply reflect their inability to form stable friendships.

With regard to validity the following applies

1. In general, there is a moderate to low relationship between sociometric indices and various indices of behavior. Positive correlations are typically found between indices of social acceptance and prosocial behavior, and between indices of rejection and negative aggressive social behavior. For example, rejected children are twice as likely to engage in aggressive behavior on the playground.

2. Acceptance and rejection are not inversely related – i.e., they are basically independent dimensions rather than the opposite ends of a continuum.

3. Peer ratings are only moderately related to teachers' ratings.

Adjective Checklists

Natural language. Adjectives represent a natural descriptive language with relevance and utility for both lay persons and scientists. Several adjective checklists are available in the psychological testing literature ranging from broad-based personality assessment techniques such as the Adjective Check List (ACL; Gough & Heilbrun, 1965), to lists developed for specific populations such as children and the mentally retarded (G. Domino, 1965; G. Domino, Goldschmid, & Kaplan, 1964; Lipsitt, 1958), or to measure specific variables such as affect and mood (Lorr, Daston, & Smith, 1967; Zuckerman & Lubin, 1965), depression (Lubin, 1965; 1967) or complexity-simplicity (Jackson & Minton, 1963).

Assessing environments. Craik (1971) reviewed the assessment of environments and argued that the development of standard techniques for the assessment of environmental settings was a prime requirement for the advancement of environmental psychological research. There are in fact a wide variety of techniques in this area, from adjectival descriptions (e.g., G. Domino, 1984; Kasmar, 1970), to measures of environmental participation (Mathis, 1968), to standardized questionnaires designed to assess social climates (Moos & Gerst, 1974), and to more complex rating techniques (Craik, 1971).

A number of investigators have taken standard psychological instruments and successfully applied them to the study of the environment. For example, Canter (1969) used the semantic differential to assess architectural plans and drawings. Driver and Knopf (1977) used the Personality Research Form in a study of outdoor recreation, while Schiff (1977) used Rotter's Locus of Control Scale. Others have developed specific instruments, often modeled on personality inventories, but designed to measure environmental dispositions; for example, Sonnenfeld (1969) developed the Environmental Personality Inventory, while McKechnie (1975) developed a Leisure Activities Blank.

The Environmental Check List (ECL)

The ECL was developed using the steps outlined in Chapter 2. The first step was to obtain from 304 volunteers, open-ended written descriptions of various geographical localities where the respondent had lived for at least three years. These volunteers included college students, business executives, and community adults in 11 different settings in both the United States and Canada. The localities they described covered 42 states and 23 foreign cities, and included large cities, villages, and even a psychiatric hospital and a nudist camp!

From these descriptions the author (G. Domino, 1984) culled an initial list of 288 adjectives, by eliminating synonyms, esoteric words, foreign terms, or words with dual connotations (like "cool"). The initial list was then given to two samples of college students. In one sample, students checked the words they were familiar with and could define, and the second sample checked those words that were descriptive of any geographical setting they were familiar with. Items checked by at least 70% in both samples were retained, resulting in a 140-item list.

The ECL then consists of 140 adjectives in alphabetical order from attractive to young. Representative items are: bustling, crowded, easy going, expensive, green, large, safe, and windy. The instructions simply ask the subject to "check items that describe ___," with the examiner specifying the target, such as "New York City," "your hometown," "the college library," "your ideal retirement place," and so on.

Reliability. The ECL was administered twice to a sample of college students over a 21-day interval, to describe the one place where they had lived most of their lives. The test-retest correlation of the individual items ranged from .18 to .98, with a mean of .67; for the entire ECL the test-retest correlation was .82.

In a second study, two samples who had filled out the ECL to describe Tucson were treated as a unit and a score obtained for each ECL item.

For example, if 14 out of the 20 subjects checked the word "delightful," then a score of 14 would be assigned to that word. Scores for the two samples were then correlated across all ECL items, with a resulting coefficient of .78; this might be considered an interrater reliability. A similar procedure, with two other samples who described a new library building, yielded a coefficient of .86.

Validity. Three validity studies are reported by the author (G. Domino, 1984). In the first study, a sample of 108 newcomers to Tucson filled out the ECL twice, first to describe Tucson and then to describe their prior place of residence. A year later they were recontacted and again filled out the ECL twice. Two questions were then asked of the data: (1) How did the perception of a new environment (Tucson) differ from the perception of a familiar environment? (prior residence), and (2) What changes took place over the year's time? The results indicated that newcomers had a highly positive reaction to Tucson, both initially and a year later. However, the year later description was less positive and probably reflected the actual physical changes that had taken place in rapidly growing Tucson, with increased traffic, construction, and concerns about water quality and availability. There were also a number of changes in the perception of their prior residence, with negative words checked more frequently upon retest.

In the second study, five psychologists were asked to check ECL items that reflected a positive evaluation. Forty-three such items were identified by at least four of the five raters. These items were then used as a scale to score the protocols of the Tucson newcomers. It was hypothesized that those whose initial reaction to the desert environment of Tucson was extreme, either in a positive or negative manner, should experience subsequent difficulties because such extreme reactions would be indicative of poor reality testing, and these individuals would be more likely to leave Tucson. Indeed, of 98 respondents, 26 had left within a 5-year period, and a statistical analysis of their initial ECL endorsements supported the hypothesized relationship.

A third study involved a sample of adults who completed the ECL to describe Tucson, and in addition indicated for each item checked whether that item was positive or negative. Thus, two individuals may both check the word "hot" to describe Tucson. But one person may love the heat and see it as a positive feature, while the second person may hate that heat. In addition, subjects completed two scales from McKechnie's (1975) Environmental Response Inventory: (1) the Urbanism scale which measures enjoyment of city living, and (2) the Need for Privacy scale, which measures the preference for solitude and isolation. Finally, ECL items were identified to parallel the Urbanism (e.g., bustling and cosmopolitan) and Need for Privacy (e.g., quiet and rural) scales. The hypothesis was that subjects high on urbanism, as defined by McKechnie's scale, would not necessarily perceive Tucson as more urban, but as more positively urban, while low-scoring subjects would see Tucson as less positively urban. A similar hypothesis applied to the need for privacy dimension. Both hypotheses were supported. For example, scores on McKechnie's Urbanism scale correlated .22 with number of urban items checked on the ECL, but correlated .58 with positive urban items checked.

The Adjective Check List (ACL)

The best known of all adjective check lists is the ACL (Gough & Heilbrun, 1983) which was initially developed in 1949 as a method of recording the observations and reactions of the staff of the Institute of Personality Assessment and Research of the University of California (Berkeley), as the staff studied subjects participating in various assessment programs. Thus, the ACL was an observer instrument; it quickly evolved however into a personality inventory as a self-report measure, which contains some 37 scales, some developed rationally and some empirically. Although this instrument could have been presented in Chapter 4 on personality, I include it here because of its broad applicability to various areas, including the assessment of environments.

Fifteen of the 37 scales assess needs, as reflected in H. A. Murray's (1938) need-press theory, of personality. These scales were developed by asking 19 graduate students in psychology to check which adjectives if endorsed would indicate a particular need, such as need Dominance. If at least 9 of the 19 judges agreed on a word, then that word was included in the scale. Once the scales were developed, various statistical analyses were carried out to minimize the overlap of items from scale to scale and to maximize the correlations between individual items and total score. Other scales assess such aspects as Counseling Readiness, Personal Adjustment, and Military Leadership.

The ACL Manual (Gough & Heilbrun, 1983) gives a considerable amount of data on normative samples, reliability, social desirability, factor analysis, case illustrations, and other issues. The ACL has been used in hundreds of studies, including many cross-cultural applications, and in the study of environments. In one study reported in the Manual, introductory psychology students were asked to complete the ACL to describe the cities of Rome and of Paris. Both males and females saw these cities in an unfavorable light, with females being somewhat more favorable toward Rome. Both cities were seen as vain, self-indulgent, and indifferent to the feelings and wishes of others. Rome was seen as more tenacious, while Paris was more flamboyant and more feminine.

Q Sorts and Q Sets

Introduction. In Chapter 8 and above we talked briefly about the Adjective Check List, a list of 300 words in alphabetical order from absent-minded to zany (Gough & Heilbrun, 1965). Imagine that we took a random subset of these words, say 100 of them, and printed each word on a 3 × 5 index card. We could now give the deck of cards to a subject and ask that person to sort the 100 items into 9 separate piles or categories to describe someone (the person doing the sorting, or their ideal self, or their spouse, or their ideal spouse, or the "typical" alcoholic, etc.), along a dimension of representativeness, with most characteristic items in pile 9 and least characteristic items in pile 1. The person has now done a Q sort, and the deck of cards is called a Q set (although you will find the term Q sort applied both to the set and to the sort). If this procedure has a deja vu feeling, it is because this is the same procedure that was used in the Thurstone method of equal-appearing intervals to create an attitude scale (see Chapter 6).

There is nothing sacred about the number 9, so we could instruct the subject to use 5, 7, 11, or 681 categories. Ordinarily, we would use an odd number of categories (9 rather than 10) so that there is a midpoint, and we would use a number that is not too onerous a task (681 would definitely be out), and does not collapse the data into few categories (e.g., 3 categories would not be a wise decision). As with any other rating task, it is better to have each category labeled, rather than just the extreme ones.

We could allow our sorter complete freedom in placing any number of statements in any one pile, as is done in the Thurstone method, but this freedom is not a particularly good psychometric procedure. Therefore we would instruct the sorter as to how many statements are to be placed in each category. For a 100-item Q set, using 9 categories, we would use the following distribution: 5, 8, 12, 16, 18, 16, 12, 8, and 5. Note that the distribution is symmetrical around the center point; indeed these numbers come from the normal or bell-shaped distribution.

You realize by now that a Q-set is an ipsative measure, and therefore a total score and normative interpretation of that score are not appropriate. However, we do have a set of 100 items distributed along 9 categories, so that for each item that item's score is the number of the category. If I place the word "intelligent" as one of the 5 items in pile number 9 as most descriptive of me, then the word intelligent can be assigned a score of 9. Note that by convention we use higher numbers for most descriptive items and lower numbers for least descriptive items. How can Q sorts be used psychometrically? There are actually a number of ways, from an impressionistic point of view as well as psychometrically.

Impressionistic analyses. Suppose we ask John, a college student seeking assistance at the Student Counseling Center, to do a Q sort. We can then go over with him his placement of the items, obtain a lot of psychodynamic impressions (for example, he describes himself as nervous and peculiar, and places the items creative and innovative in pile number 1, and even discuss his choices as a therapeutic starting point.

Consider this other example. Professionals from different fields that work in school or clinical settings often come together in a case conference to discuss a particular client. In an elementary school the school psychologist, counselor, special ed teacher, school nurse, principal, etc.,

might meet to discuss a new child with multiple handicaps. Often communication does not move forward as well as it ought to because each specialist has different information, a different perspective, different jargon, etc. If each were to do a Q sort on the child and the different Q sorts were compared, the results could provide a common language and perspective.

Psychometric analyses. We ask Dr. Smith to do a Q sort to describe Richard, who is a patient in therapy. Dr. Smith uses a standardized Q set, namely the California Q set which is probably the best known Q set (Block, 1961). We can now correlate Dr. Smith's Q sort with one provided in Block's monograph, on the optimally adjusted personality, that reflects the modal sorting by nine clinical psychologists. Block (1961) provides a convenient formula to use, which is a derivative of the standard formula for the correlation coefficient:

$$r = 1 - \frac{\sum d^2}{2N(SD^2)}$$

where $\sum d$ = the sum of the squared differences between Q values of corresponding items

N = the number of items in the Q set

SD = the standard deviation of the Q set

To calculate the $\sum d^2$ we would compare placement of items, such as in the example below:

item	Category by Dr. Smith	Category optimally adjusted	d	d²
warm	8	9	1	1
dependable	6	8	2	4
etc.				
				SUM:__

Nature of items. The items of a Q set need not necessarily be personality type items. They could be for example, attitudinal statements sorted on an approval-disapproval continuum, statements dealing with career and vocational aspects (e.g., Kunert, 1969), study habits (Creaser, 1960), or even artistic drawings sorted on aesthetic dimensions (Stephenson, 1953). In fact, Q sorts have been applied to a rather wide number of domains such as attitudes about abortion (P. D. Werner, 1993), defense mechanisms (Davidson & MacGregor, 1996), criminology (J. H. Carlson & Williams, 1993), and marital functioning (Wampler & Halverson, 1990).

Psychometric aspects. To obtain statistical stability and acceptable reliability, the number of items in a Q set should probably be substantial, maybe 80 to 100, but not much larger or it becomes a rather onerous task.

Most Q sets are what Kerlinger (1986) labels as unstructured; that is, they consist of a set of items like personality statements that have been put together without specific regard to a structure that might underlie such items. A structured Q set is one where the items have been selected to reflect a specific theoretical or empirical structure. For example, a Q set designed to assess differential diagnosis between two distinct personality types would contain an equal number of items pertinent to each type. As another example, Kerlinger (1986) reports a study in which a 90-item Q set was used, where each item reflected one of the six major values in Spranger's theory (see Chapter 19). For example, words such as God and church represented the Religious value, and words such as science and reason represented the Theoretical value. Subjects like ministers presumably high on the Religious value, and musicians presumably high on the Aesthetic value, were then asked to sort the items according to the degree to which they favored or did not favor the words, with 15 items representing each of the 6 values.

Wide applicability. Q sets have found wide application not just in psychology but in other fields such as political science (e.g., S. R. Brown, 1980) and nursing (e.g., Dennis, 1986). Q sorts can be done not only by adults but by children as well. For example, V. D. Bennett (1964) developed two forms of a self-concept Q set, each made up of 26 statements, and administered these to sixth-grade students. Each child was asked to sort the items into five categories from "most like me" to "most unlike me," with the Q cards placed in designated pockets rather than in piles. Q sets have also been used with the elderly in gerontological research (e.g., Hayslip, 1984).

An example. Q sorts not only can yield useful empirical data but, perhaps more important, can provide a useful methodology to test theoretical ideas. For example, Metzger (1979) attempted through Q methodology, to assess a theory proposed by Kübler-Ross (1969) who hypothesized that a dying person goes through stages of denial, anger, bargaining, depression, and acceptance in coming to grips with impending death. Metzger developed a 36-item structured Q set from a larger pool of items – items such as "Why did God let this happen to me?" and "I pray to be well." She administered the Q set to two couples, in which the wife had a potentially terminal medical diagnosis. Although the results did not support Kubler-Ross' stage theory, the author concluded that the Q methodology was a useful procedure to investigate terminal illness.

SUMMARY

In this chapter, we looked at behavioral assessment, various basic issues, and illustrative instruments like the Pleasant Events Schedule and the Fear Survey Schedule. We also looked at how tests can be used in program evaluation, the assessment of environments, and the assessment of systems like the family. Finally, we looked at sociometric techniques, adjective checklists, and Q sets – all broad-based techniques that can be used in a variety of ways.

SUGGESTED READINGS

Calvert, J. D., Moore, D. W., & Jensen, B. J. (1987). Psychometric evaluation of the Dating Anxiety Survey: A self-report questionnaire for the assessment of dating anxiety in males and females. *Journal of Psychopathology and Behavioral Assessment, 9,* 341–350.

This article evaluates an instrument designed to assess dating anxiety. The authors report the results of two studies in which a factor analysis, an assessment of reliability (internal consistency), and concurrent validity, were investigated.

Cautela, J. R. (1994). The use of the Anxiety Meter to reduce anxiety. *Behavior Modification, 18,* 307–319.

Describes the Anxiety Meter in treating anxiety reactions, especially in agoraphobia and panic reactions. A good illustration of behavioral assessment and therapeutic application.

Goldfried, M. R., & Kent, R. N. (1972). Traditional vs. behavioral personality assessment: A comparison of methodological and theoretical assumptions. *Psychological Bulletin, 77,* 409–420.

A review of the assumptions that underlie traditional vs. behavioral assessment, as these assumptions impact the selection of test items and the interpretation of the responses to the test.

Greenspoon, J., & Gersten, C. D. (1967). A new look at psychological testing: Psychological testing from the point of view of a behaviorist. *American Psychologist, 22,* 848–853.

Perhaps more of historical interest, this paper proposes a "new look" at psychological testing, contrasting the classical psychodynamic view with what, in 1967, was a new point of view – that of the behaviorist.

Holm, J. E., & Holroyd, K. A. (1992). The Daily Hassles Scale (Revised): Does it measure stress or symptoms? *Behavioral Assessment, 14,* 465–482.

A study of the Daily Hassles Scale-Revised from a factor-analytic perspective.

DISCUSSION QUESTIONS

1. Compare and contrast classical with behavioral assessment.

2. What are some of the limitations of direct observation?

3. The chapter discusses penile tumescence measurement. Can you think of other techniques that are or might be used as behavioral assessments?

4. Many people have a phobia, or at the very least, an uncomfortable feeling with hypodermic needles. How might you go about assessing such a fear?

5. Using the three Moos categories of classroom environments (interpersonal relationships; structural aspects; and goal orientation) how would you classify your classroom?

19 The History of Psychological Testing

AIM In this chapter we take a brief look at the history of psychological testing and a peek at the future. For didactic purposes, we consider the current status of psychological testing as reflecting four major strands: the French clinical tradition, the German nomothetic tradition, the British idiographic tradition, and the American applied tradition.

INTRODUCTION

When you meet a new person at a party, for example, you want to know their name and a little bit about their background – what's their family like, where did they grow up, and so on. In this text, you have "met" psychological testing; it is time to take a brief look backwards. Psychological testing is, in American society, at least, quite ubiquitous. Children are tested in a variety of ways, from preschool days through middle-school graduation. High-school adolescents are given aptitude tests to determine what they can master, achievement tests to assess what they have mastered, minimum competency exams to determine whether their diploma should be granted, interest tests to help them choose careers, and college-entrance examinations to allow them to progress in the educational stream. Similarly, college students come face to face with a variety of educational and psychological exams, and if you think college graduation means the end of testing, you are in for a big surprise!

Psychological testing is a recent phenomenon, closely interwoven with 20th-century American culture, yet the use of systematic procedures for comparing and evaluating individuals is quite old. In China for example, in the year 2200 B.C., public officials were examined every three years and were either promoted or dismissed on the basis of these examinations, which covered such areas as writing, music, archery, and ceremonial rites (P. H. DuBois, 1966). Bowman (1989) argues that such formal testing procedures may go back "only" 2000 years rather than 4000; but the conclusion is the same.

The Book of Judges, in the Old Testament, tells of what might be considered the first situational test. Gideon, a hero of the Israelites, is selecting an army to fight the Midianites. As a result of Gideon's pep talk on the hazards of war, his 32,000 volunteers are reduced to 10,000, a number that for tactical reasons is, however, still too large. God then advises Gideon to take his prospective soldiers to the river for a drink; those that lap the water are to be accepted, but those that kneel to drink and hence expose their backs to any potential enemy, are to be rejected. Only 300 passed this test and went on to victory over the Midianites – clear evidence of validity! The same Biblical book also provides another example of testing – a one-item verbal test that involved pronouncing the word "shibboleth." Ephraimites pronounced the initial sh as "s" and were thus identified and executed on the basis of that linguistic giveaway (Wainer, 1987). The ancient Greeks also made use of tests, both individual and group, primarily to assess physical achievement (K. O. Doyle, 1974).

African tribal life also contains numerous examples of ritualized procedures aimed at evaluation, which might in a loose sense be considered tests. For example, in Kenya, witch doctors often place a live toad in the patient's mouth to determine whether the patient is really sick or merely malingering. If the patient is faking, the toad presumably will jump down his throat.

Today, psychological tests have become an intrinsic part of our lives, despite the intensive criticisms they have received. From aviation cadets to zoologists, there are relatively few individuals who have not, at one time or another, been tested. Despite this pervasiveness of psychological tests, their direct historical antecedents are rather short. We take a brief look at some of the historical figures and ideas that have shaped the present status of psychological tests, although we have already met a number of these. Psychology does not exist in a vacuum but represents the work of specific people living in a particular culture at a particular point in time. Although the individual names are important, what is more important are the societal movements that both impinge on the activities of individuals and are, in turn, changed by these activities.

As stated in the Introduction, four distinct but related movements are of primary concern to a historical understanding of today's psychological testing: (1) the French clinical tradition, (2) the German nomothetic approach, (3) the British idiographic approach, and (4) the American applied orientation.

THE FRENCH CLINICAL TRADITION

Every student of abnormal psychology knows of *Philippe Pinel* (1745–1826), the French physician who, when placed in charge of the Bicetre Hospital for the Insane in 1793, freed the patients from their chains: Pinel's action represents a turning point from a demonological explanation of mental illness (the insane are possessed by the Devil) to a medical and humanitarian one (the insane are ill); more basically, his action reflected the possibility of explaining behavior by natural rather than supernatural causes, a possibility that in the area of psychopathology was explored in detail by many French physicians.

Jean Esquirol (1772–1840) was one of these physicians. A pupil of Pinel, he is perhaps best remembered for a text on *Des Maladies Mentales*, which for several decades remained a fundamental text of psychopathology. Esquirol was one of the first to sketch the main forms of insanity and to apply elementary statistical methods to his clinical descriptions, mainly in the form of tabulations of causative categories. He was one of the first to explicitly differentiate between the mentally ill and the mentally deficient, and to propose that various degrees of mental deficiency could be distinguished on the basis of the patient's use of language. (See A. S. Kaufman, 2000)

Another famous French physician was *Edouard Seguin* (1812–1880), a pioneer in the field of mental deficiency. Seguin emphasized the importance of training the senses in the education of the mentally deficient and developed many procedures to enhance their muscular control and sensory abilities. Some of these procedures were later incorporated into tests of intelligence.

Hysteria and hypnosis. *Ambroise-Auguste Liebeault* (1823–1904), *Hippolyte Bernheim* (1840–1919), *Jean Charcot* (1825–1893), and *Pierre Janet* (1859–1947) are well-known protagonists in the history of hysteria (physical symptoms such as blindness without the underlying organic damage, due to psychological factors) and hypnosis, and they too reflect the French clinical tradition. Liebeault and Bernheim, physicians in the city of Nancy, proposed that hypnotism and hysteria were related, and both due to suggestion. Charcot, a leading neurologist and superintendent of the Salpetriere Hospital in Paris, disagreed and argued that organic factors were also operative in hysteria. It was to Charcot's clinic that a young Viennese physician by the name of *Sigmund Freud* (1856–1939) came to study, and it was the work of the French physicians on the use of hypnosis on hysterical patients that led Freud to postulate such concepts as the unconscious. (See Libbrecht & Quackelbeen, 1995, on the influence of Charcot on Freud.)

Janet also came under the influence of Charcot. He is perhaps best known for establishing the dissociation school of psychopathology, a theoretical view of the mind as a system of forces in equilibrium, whose dissociation or splitting off would be reflected in pathological behavior. Janet was a keen observer whose rich clinical experiences were transformed into vivid descriptions; his description of hysteria, for example, is considered a classic.

Although sweeping generalizations are of their very nature incorrect, it can be said that the efforts of French investigators were in general heavily grounded on clinical observations. This resulted in perceptive and detailed descriptions of various types of mental aberrations, but little concern over quantification of these clinical insights. Psychological testing must begin with sensitive observations of human behavior, and the French clinical tradition provided this; but additional steps must be taken.

Alfred Binet. Additional steps were taken by *Alfred Binet* (1857–1911), a French psychologist who occupies a central position in the history of testing. Although Binet is best known for the scale of intelligence he devised in 1905, he made many other contributions, including the establishment of the first French psychological laboratory in 1889, and the first French psychological journal, called *L'Annee psychologique*, in 1895.

Binet held that differences among individuals were due to differences in mental functioning, particularly in faculties such as reasoning, imagination, attention, persistence, and judgment. He began a thorough investigation of what techniques might be used to measure these faculties. Although German and British investigators had already developed a variety of procedures, Binet criticized these as emphasizing sensory aspects and reflecting simple, rather than complex, intellectual functions.

Binet's work culminated in the 1905 Binet-Simon scale, the first successful test of general intelligence, whose aim was to identify those school children who could not profit from regular school instruction. Although earlier tests than this scale existed, they were not standardized, so Binet's work is recognized as first (Bondy, 1974). As discussed in Chapter 5, the 1905 scale contained some 30 questions ranging from psychophysical tasks such as comparing two weights to making rhymes and following a moving object with one's eyes. The 1905 Binet-Simon scale was an empirical scale; the thirty tests that made up

the scale were chosen because they were related to age, school attainment, and teachers' judgments of intelligence of the pupils, not because they reflected the theoretical preconceptions of the investigator. The Binet-Simon scale clearly demonstrated the greater accuracy of objective measurement over clinical and personal intuition, an issue that is basic to psychological testing.

As you know, in 1908 Binet and Simon published a revision of their scale, and in 1911 Binet published another revision involving a number of technical refinements (a detailed description of these scales can be found in Peterson, 1926). Although Binet had devoted much effort to the investigation of separate mental faculties, his scales reflected a global approach to intelligence, with no attempt to measure the relative contribution of each faculty to the total functioning of a child (T. H. Wolf 1969a, 1969b).

In summary, modern psychological tests owe to the French tradition an emphasis on pathology, a clinical descriptive approach and, mainly because of Binet's work, a practical, empirical orientation (for a review of intelligence testing in France after Binet, see W. H. Schneider, 1992).

THE GERMAN NOMOTHETIC APPROACH

Germany gave us, in 1692, the earliest instance of the use of rating scales in personality evaluation and the first documented use of numerical scales to represent psychological variables (McReynolds & Ludwig, 1984; 1987), but our story begins with a later and much more central protagonist.

As every psychology student knows, the science of psychology was born in 1879 at the University of Leipzig, Germany, with *Wilhelm Wundt* (1832–1920) as both puerpera and midwife (apparently a strong case can be made for 1875 rather than 1879; see Boring, 1965; R. I. Watson, 1966). The work and contributions of Wundt and his students comprise a basic chapter in the history of experimental psychology (see Boring, 1957, for a review, and Bringmann, Balance, & Evans, 1975, for a brief biographical sketch). There are at least four major reasons why their work is of importance to the development of psychological testing:

1. Their experimentation marks the turning point from a philosophical, armchair, speculative approach about human nature to an empirical approach based on quantification. French investigators were already looking at abnormal behavior from a medical-scientific viewpoint, yet they were relatively unconcerned with systematic experimentation, or with investigating *normal* behavior.

2. There was a heavy emphasis on the measurement of sensory functions, such as differential sensitivity to various modes of stimulation. This was later reflected in the early mental tests that included measures of weight discrimination, pain sensitivity, reaction time, and other functions. These were the tests that Binet criticized as too sensory.

3. The use of complex brass instruments in their psychological experiments and their emulation of the physiologists and physicists underscored the need for standardization of procedures and experimental conditions. Modern psychological tests are characterized by such standardization, where all subjects are exposed to essentially the same task, with the same instructions and scoring standards.

4. Wundt was a university professor, and testing, as well as most of psychology, grew up as an academic discipline. The role of the psychologist became primarily that of a scholar-researcher, and the practitioner aspects were added very slowly.

A few German psychologists, most of whom were pupils of Wundt, did assemble test batteries designed to measure complex functions. *Emil Kraepelin* (1855–1926) for example, investigated the psychological effects of fatigue in psychiatric patients and made extensive use of the free-association method, a task requiring the subject to respond to a stimulus word with the first word that comes to mind. Kraepelin also published a diagnostic classification regarded as the precursor of our current *Diagnostic and Statistical Manual of Mental Disorders* (Zilboorg, 1941). *Herman Ebbinghaus* (1850–1909), well known for his monumental investigations of memory, administered tests of arithmetic, memory span, and sentence completion to groups of school children. In 1891, *Hugo Munsterberg* (1863–1916) described various tests he had given to school children such

as naming three different smells, reading aloud as fast as possible, and stating as quickly as possible the colors of ten objects. Munsterberg was later brought to Harvard University by *William James* (1842–1910) and became a dedicated practitioner of the applications of psychology to law and industry.

Germany has also contributed a longer tradition of viewing a problem in both its philosophical ramifications and its taxonomic potential (Misiak & Sexton, 1966). A well-known example of this is the work of *Eduard Spranger* (1882–1920). Spranger postulated that there are six main types of values, and that individuals tend to center and organize their lives around one or more of these values. The six values are: (1) the theoretical, aimed at the discovery of truth; (2) the economic, characterized by utility; (3) the aesthetic, centering on form and harmony; (4) the social, focused on love of people; (5) the political, interested primarily in power; and (6) the religious, directed toward understanding the totality of being.

The Allport-Vernon-Lindzey Study of Values, originally published in the United States in 1931, represents an attempt to measure the relative prominence of these six basic orientations and was for many years a test used widely in social psychology.

The approach of the German psychologists was a *nomothetic* one, aimed at discovering the fundamental laws that govern the human mind. Investigative efforts were directed toward determining the fundamental workings of visual perception, auditory sensation, reaction time, and other similar problems. Differences between individuals in their reaction time or in their ability to discriminate sounds were regarded as nuisance. In fact, much experimental control was applied to the elimination of these individual differences.

THE BRITISH IDIOGRAPHIC APPROACH

The British, on the other hand, were vitally interested in these individual differences and viewed them not as error, but as a fundamental reflection of evolution and natural selection, ideas that had been given a strong impetus by the work of *Charles Darwin* (1809–1882). It was Darwin's cousin, *Sir Francis Galton* (1822–1911), who united the French clinical tradition, the

German experimental spirit, and the English concern for variation, when he launched the testing movement on its course (A. R. Buss, 1976).

Galton studied eminent British men and became convinced that intellectual genius was fixed by inheritance. He then developed a number of tests to measure this inherited capacity and to demonstrate individual differences. He established a small anthropometric laboratory in a London museum where, for a small fee, visitors could undergo tests of reaction time, hearing acuity, color vision, muscular strength, and other basic sensorimotor functions. To summarize the information he collected on approximately 10,000 persons, Galton made use of or himself developed statistical procedures. He also realized that a person's score could be expressed in a *relative* rather than an *absolute* manner (e.g., John is taller than these 18 men, rather than John is 6 feet tall). This is an extremely important and fundamental concept in psychological measurement, yet one that can easily be neglected.

Galton's ultimate objective was the early identification of geniuses so that they could be encouraged to reproduce and thus improve the intellectual level of the human race. This grandiose idea, however, was not supported by the test results, for although sensorimotor functions demonstrated individual differences, they showed little relationship to other criteria of intelligence.

Factor analysis. Although it was Galton who laid the groundwork for the application of statistical methods to psychological and educational measurement, many others made important contributions as well. One of these was *Charles Spearman* (1863–1945), best known for his two-factor theory of intelligence, which stated that all cognitive activities are a reflection of general intelligence, labeled as *g*, and specific abilities or factors. Because specific factors are specific to a particular test or activity, testing efforts should concentrate on measuring general intelligence. Spearman's statistical support for his theory, the intercorrelations between tests, represents a first step in the application of factor analysis. Spearman also contributed the concept of test reliability. He considered a test score to be the sum of truth and error, truth being the individual's actual standing on the variable being measured,

and error being the work of a myriad influences that resulted in an increased or decreased test score (see Spearman, 1930, for an autobiography). This concept, aside from its basic importance in testing, did much to revive interests in tests, an interest that had been demoralized by the lack of relation between test scores and school grades.

Cyril L. Burt (1883–1971), an outstanding contributor to educational psychology, wrote books on testing and on factor analysis. He also published an English revision of the Binet scale in 1921, designed for children aged 3 and older (see A. D. Lovie & P. Lovie, 1993, on how Burt was influenced by Spearman). After his death, Burt became rather controversial as he may have committed fraud in his famous studies of the intelligence of separated twins (Joynson, 1989; Osborne, 1994; W. H. Tucker, 1994; 1997). *Godfrey H. Thompson* (1881–1955) developed a number of tests for the measurement of school achievement; he also supervised testing programs, conducted large population surveys, and played a major role in British educational psychology. *Karl Pearson* (1857–1936), a statistician and associate of Galton, made a large number of contributions; his name is perhaps best associated with the correlation coefficient. Pearson was one of the first to apply correlational analysis to the study of parent-child resemblance; for example, he measured the height and arm span of parents and of their children and reported a correlation of approximately .50, a result that Pearson interpreted as reflecting the contribution of heredity.

Ronald A. Fisher (1890–1962) was another outstanding contributor to the development of factor analysis; he is best known for developing techniques for the analysis of variance and small-sample statistics. Fisher was a statistician and geneticist whose contributions made statistics a tool at the disposal of psychology (Porter, 1986).

It is interesting to note that the British approach to the organization of abilities still emphasizes Spearman's *g* factor, while American psychologists consider *g* as of secondary importance and prefer to talk about group factors – factors common to many activities, but not all. Mention might also be made that early in the 19th century, the British established a civil-service examination system, which was heavily influenced by the British missionaries and foreign-service personnel who had lived in China and had observed the extensive Chinese examination system.

The Scottish surveys. At the time of Galton, the British considered themselves the pinnacle of evolution. They were concerned however, that the nobility which obviously represented high levels of intelligence, had smaller families than the lower classes, who also obviously had lower intellectual capabilities. Because there had been found a negative correlation between intelligence and family size, with children from larger families tending to have lower IQs than those from smaller families, there was concern that, in several generations, the lower classes would gain the upper hand at least numerically, and Englnd would thus become a nation of "morons." Several large scale intelligence testing programs were undertaken. Mention might be made of the so-called Scottish surveys, carried out in Scotland under the direction of the Scottish Council for Research in Education. The first survey in 1932 was an attempt to test all 11-year-old children. Approximately 87,500 children, or 90% of all 11-year-olds, were administered a group test of 76 verbal and 9 pictorial items. A subgroup of 1,000 children was also given the 1916 Stanford-Binet.

In 1947, the same group test was again administered to all 11-year-olds, this time to approximately 71,000. One of the interesting results of this survey was to indicate a small, but statistically significant increase in mean test score from the 1932 survey. This finding was contradictory to the postulated decline.

THE AMERICAN APPLIED ORIENTATION

Despite Wundt's view of individual differences as error, one of his assistants was vitally interested in variation and, in fact, wrote his doctoral dissertation on individual differences in reaction time. This assistant was *James McKeen Cattell* (1860–1944), an American who is credited with being the first to use the term "mental test" in an 1890 paper in which he presented in some detail a series of 10 tests to measure a person's intellectual level. These 10 tests involved such procedures as the estimation of a 10-second interval,

the reaction time for a sound, and the measurement of dynamometric pressure (the pressure exerted by one's grip). Cattell felt that differences in sensory acuity, reaction time, and similar functions would result in differences in intellectual achievement; hence he administered his tests to Columbia University college freshmen in the hope of predicting their college achievement (Sokal, 1987). Incidentally, Cattell and his wife had seven children, one of whom named "Psyche" also became a well-known psychologist (Sokal, 1991).

Cattell's 1890 paper resulted in a tremendous interest in mental testing. Psychologists at various institutions began developing similar tests and in 1895 the American Psychological Association formed a committee to investigate the possibility of having various psychological laboratories cooperate in the collection of data.

Other American investigators. Cattell was not the first nor the only American investigator concerned with testing. *Joseph Jastrow* (1863–1944), a student of G. Stanley Hall, and holder of the first PhD in psychology awarded in the United States, had developed a set of 15 tests that he demonstrated to visitors at the 1893 Columbian Exposition held in Chicago. These tests, with a heavy Wundtian flavor, included weight discrimination, reproduction of letters after tachistoscopic presentation, tests of color blindness, and tests of reaction time (see Jastrow, 1930, for an autobiography).

Lightner Witmer (1867–1956) who also studied with Wundt, established the first psychological clinic in the United States, in 1896 at the University of Pennsylvania (McReynolds, 1987; O'Donnell, 1979). As the number of clients referred to the clinic grew, Witmer began collecting tests and using these in diagnostic evaluations (for a survey of the clinic's activities from 1896 to its closing in 1961, see Levine & Wishner, 1977). Soon other university clinics were established, and diagnostic evaluation based on psychological test results became part of the clinical approach. Until the late 1920s, a large portion of the clinic psychologist's activities consisted of administering intelligence tests. Beginning in the 1930s however, the psychological horizons expanded, and the use of projective tests to study the deeper aspects of personality became a more important function. Most of these clinics served children rather than adults, with the result that psychologists often became identified as child experts.

Interest in testing was also reflected by the increasing number of reports related to testing that appeared in psychological and educational journals. Three reports can be considered representative. In 1892, T. Bolton reported a comparison of children's memory span for digits with teachers' estimates of their general mental ability. J. A. Gilbert in 1894 administered several tests (including reaction time, memory, and sensory discrimination) to about 1,200 Connecticut children and compared the results with teachers' estimates of general ability. Both studies indicated a correspondence between some tests and teachers' estimates, although the correspondence was low and of little practical significance. W. C. Bagley in 1901 compared the mental abilities of school children as evidenced by school marks and test scores and found an inverse relationship between these two types of abilities.

In 1903 *Helen Thompson* published the results of a study of sex differences. In this study, she used sensory acuity tests, associative reaction time, a general information test, tests of ingenuity (problem solving), and various other measures. She reported a number of sex differences, such as men scoring higher in the ingenuity tests whereas women scoring higher on tests of memory.

In the area of educational testing, mention might be made of *Horace Mann* (1796–1859), the famous educator, who took what might be the first major step toward standardized testing when, in 1845, he replaced the oral interrogation of Boston school children with a written examination that presented to all children a uniform set of questions. Unfortunately, this work had negligible impact on educational practices.

Joseph M. Rice (1857–1934) made, in 1895, lists of spelling words as well as arithmetic and language tests, and administered these to thousands of children in an effort to objectively evaluate the relative effectiveness of teachers. This work also did not receive the attention it deserved.

One of the most outstanding contributors to psychological and educational measurement was *Edward Lee Thorndike* (1874–1949) of Columbia University (Joncich, 1966). In 1904, he published the first textbook on educational measurement, *An Introduction of the Theory of Mental and Social Measurement.* This book presented many statistical concepts based on the work of Galton and Pearson, in relatively easy-to-understand language. Thorndike also developed a number of psychological tests and wrote voluminously on measurement. His work made Columbia University a center for the investigation of mental testing, even though his concern was not specifically aimed toward the measurement of general intelligence (see the article written by his grandson, R. M. Thorndike, 1990).

In the 1860s, several United States legislators introduced bills to establish a civil-service examining commission, modeled on the British one. By the late 1800s, several examinations had been developed to assess postal clerks, trademark examiners, and other occupations.

Back to Cattell. The great enthusiasm about testing generated by Cattell's work was, however, of short duration and was soon dampened by the lack of interest on the part of several well-known psychologists, such as William James, and more importantly, by the results of two research papers, one published by Stella Sharp and the other by Clark Wissler (F. S. Freeman, 1984).

S. E. Sharp (1898–1899) administered a battery of mental tests to seven students. These tests, which were administered repeatedly, were more complex than those of Cattell and involved tests of imagination, memory, and other "higher" functions. She reported that, in general, there was little self-consistency in the test results, i.e., low reliability.

Wissler (1901) compared Cattell's psychological tests with anthropometric measures (e.g., height, weight, arm span) and with college grades. He reported that Cattell's tests did not correlate highly with either the anthropometric measures or the college grades. In fact, they did not correlate with one another! For example, the correlation between strength of hand and class standing was –.08, while reaction time and class standing correlated –.02. Grades in various courses however correlated substantially with each other – for example, Latin and Math correlated +.58.

Although both studies had serious methodological limitations, and they were not meant by their authors to be indictments of testing, they were nevertheless taken by many as proof that mental measurement could not be a reality. As a result, when the 1905 Binet-Simon scale appeared, psychologists in American universities exhibited little interest; however, psychologists and educators working in clinics and schools, faced with the same practical problems of mental classification that Binet was struggling with, were quite receptive and rapidly enthusiastic.

Mental deficiency. One such man was *Henry Goddard* (1866–1957), Director of Research at the Vineland Training School, a New Jersey institution for the mentally defective. At Vineland, Goddard founded the first laboratory for the psychological study of the retarded and was also a pioneer in using a team approach to research, involving house mothers, psychometricians, and others. Goddard translated the Binet scale into English and became an outspoken advocate of Binet's approach. In working with mental defectives, Goddard had become acutely aware of the fact that their potential for learning was extremely limited and apparently physiologically determined. It was an easy, though incorrect, step to assume that intelligence was therefore unitary and largely determined by heredity. Hence everyone could, and should, be measured with the Binet scale and assigned a place in society commensurate with their mental level. This was Goddard's gospel, despite the fact that Binet himself was opposed to the view of intelligence as a genetically fixed quantity. Goddard's views were not unique. It was widely believed at that time that the "feeble minded" were responsible for most social problems, that they reproduced at an alarming rate, and that it was important to restrict immigration especially from Southern and Eastern Europe (Gelb, 1986).

Goddard is also remembered for his study of the Kallikak family, an account of two lines of descendants of Martin Kallikak (a pseudonym), an American soldier in the Revolutionary War who impregnated a feebleminded bar maid and then, after the war, married a "good" girl. The differential incidence of criminals, prostitutes, tubercular victims, and mental retardates in these two family branches were taken by Goddard and others as clear evidence of the hereditary nature of these conditions (Fancher, 1987; J. D. Smith, 1985).

Lewis M. Terman (1877–1956). Although Goddard's translation of the Binet-Simon scale and his passionate proselytizing statements made the Binet-Simon scale a popular and well-known test, it was the work of Lewis M. Terman, for 20 years (1922–1942) head of the Psychology department at Stanford University, that made the Binet test not only the best-known intelligence test, but a yardstick against which new tests were subsequently compared (see Terman, 1932, for an autobiography).

Terman's revision of the Binet test, which included a restandardization on an American sample of more than 2,000 subjects, was not merely a translation, but virtually resulted in a new test, the 1916 Stanford-Binet. As we saw, one of the major innovations of this test was the use of the IQ, the ratio of mental age to chronological age, a concept that had been proposed by *William Stern* (1871–1938), a German psychologist (Stern, 1930). Unfortunately, the subsequent popularity of the IQ concept made it synonymous with intelligence and was soon considered a property of the person rather than of the test. In addition, the concept of IQ reinforced the notion that intelligence was relatively constant and genetically fixed.

The Stanford-Binet represented a practical screening method and was enthusiastically received because it met a pressing need. Perhaps more importantly, the Stanford-Binet was proof that mental measurement was possible, and thus it led to both the development of other psychological tests and to public acceptance of testing. Terman is also well known for his longitudinal series of studies of California gifted-children, known as the Genetic Studies of Genius (and its participants affectionately dubbed "termites"), the development of a masculinity-femininity test, and a study of the psychological factors involved in marital happiness. His work was heavily grounded in empiricism and his careful approach in many ways became a model to be emulated (Hilgard, 1957; Sokal, 1987).

Other adaptations of the Binet. In addition to the work of Goddard and Terman, there appeared several revisions or adaptations of the Binet scales. Notable among these were the Kuhlmann-Binet, one of the first preschool tests of intelligence that made it possible to test children as young as 3 months, and the Hayes-Binet, adapted for use with the blind. Mention might also be made of the Yerkes Point Scale, a 20-item test (19 of which came from the Binet) that was scored in terms of points rather than in terms of mental age credit.

G. Stanley Hall (1846–1924). By 1910, testing had grown to the extent that G. M. Whipple could publish a *Manual of Mental and Physical Tests*, discussing 54 available tests. The growth of psychological testing was, in great part, a reflection of the general growth in American psychology. For example, by 1894 there were 24 psychological research laboratories at such universities as Columbia, Chicago, Johns Hopkins, Stanford, and Yale.

A major force in this growth was *Granville Stanley Hall*, a central figure in the establishment of child psychology. Hall's endeavors, reflected in his writings and organizational undertakings, were voluminous. He established several psychological journals, wrote extensively on a variety of topics including adolescence, religious experience, and senescence. He organized and was first president of the American Psychological Association, and in 1909 invited Freud and Jung to the United States to help celebrate the 20th anniversary of Clark University; thus, he introduced the psychoanalytic movement to American psychologists. For the history of testing, however, his major contributions were the development of an extensive series of questionnaires covering topics such as fears, dreams, and foods, for the study of children's thinking, and for his great teaching influence – both Goddard and Terman, for example, were pupils of Hall (Averill, 1990; R. B. Evans & J. B. Cohen, 1987; E. C. Sanford, 1987; Sokal, 1990; Wapner, 1990).

The Healy-Fernald Tests. In 1911, *William Healy* and *Grace Fernald* published a series of tests to be used in the evaluation of delinquent children. Although the 1908 Binet-Simon scale was available, Healy and Fernald were interested not simply in obtaining a picture of the child's general mental level as reflected by a total score, but also

an awareness of the child's specific strengths and weaknesses. Thus, the child's performance on the various single tests was kept separate. The emphasis was not on what score the child obtained, but on how the child approached the various tasks and what the child's general behavior was. It was the process rather than the outcome that was of primary concern to Healy and Fernald. In keeping with this aim, the scoring and administrations of the tests were not spelled out precisely.

The series of tests was quite varied and included puzzles of various kinds, a "testimony" test in which the child was shown a picture of a butcher shop, the picture was then removed, and the child was asked to recall various details, including an attempt to measure the degree to which the child yielded to suggestion; the tests also included a game of checkers, arithmetic problems, and drawing of designs from memory. It is interesting to note that while the Binet test underwent several revisions and is still one of the most commonly used tests of intelligence, the Healy-Fernald series is now only of historical interest. Perhaps this was due to its subjectivity and lack of standardization which in many ways ran counter to the spirit of the time, so engrossed in quantifying mental processes.

In 1917, the Pintner-Patterson Performance Scale was published. This test is of interest because it represents the first major attempt to standardize a test that required no language on the part of either the examiner or the subject.

In the same year, Helen Boardman published a monograph titled, *Psychological Tests, a Bibliography*; like Whipple's efforts of 1910, this was an attempt to survey the field of psychological tests. Boardman divided her references into two areas, those that referred to the Binet-Simon and those that referred to other tests, mostly intelligence tests.

World War I and testing needs. The beginning of World War I in 1917 created a pressing need for mental tests as selection and placement devices; there was need not only to screen out men whose intellectual capabilities were too limited for military service, but also to determine which men could be given specialized training or admitted to officer programs. The answer to these needs were two intelligence tests, the *Army Alpha* and the *Army Beta*, the latter designed for illiterates or nonEnglish speaking recruits. The Army Alpha consisted of eight tests including a directions test that required the examinee to follow oral directions given by the examiner, a multiple-choice test of common sense where the examinee indicated, for example, why we use stoves, and what to do if given too much change by the grocer, and an information test that asked the subject to identify the location of certain cities, the manufacturer of shoes, and other cultural items. These tests held an advantage over the Stanford-Binet in that they could be administered to many subjects at one sitting; almost two million men were tested (Von Mayrhauser, 1989).

Another World War I instrument developed in response to military, needs was the Woodworth Personal Data Sheet (Woodworth, 1920), a self-report inventory of 116 yes-no questions concerning neurotic symptoms, designed as a rough screening device for identifying recruits with serious psychological difficulties, who would be emotionally unsuited for military service. Sample questions were: Do you feel tired most of the time? Did you have a happy childhood? Is it easy to make you laugh? Do you often feel miserable and blue? Basically, the Personal Data Sheet was a paper-and pencil version of a psychiatric interview, although it also contained some interesting empirical aspects: for example, items endorsed by 25% or more of a normal sample were omitted, and only symptoms that occurred twice as frequently in a neurotic group than in a normal group were included. Recruits who endorsed many symptoms could then be further assessed in a psychiatric interview. The Personal Data Sheet subsequently became the prototype for many personality inventories dealing with mental health and adjustment. Judged by modern standards, the Personal Data Sheet was unsophisticated, lacked norms, and did not address issues of reliability and validity; but it was successful, fulfilled a need, and provided a good role model; it was the forerunner of some 100 such inventories (Kleinmuntz, 1967).

The postwar period. Although the practical contribution of these tests to the war effort was minor (Samelson, 1977), the tremendous success of the mass application of psychological tests in World War I resulted in an upsurge of interest in testing (Pastore, 1978). After World War I the use of psychological tests rapidly became an integral part of our culture. The Army Alpha and Beta were released for general use and were widely used in schools and some industrial settings. Many new tests were devised, including many tests to serve special needs such as the testing of the deaf or the measurement of personality characteristics. Testing, which prior to World War I had been mainly confined to educational settings, now found applications in other areas, and the role of the psychologist expanded to include the assessment of human potential and abilities.

A safe world. The first World War was the war to end all wars. The world was then considered a safe place and anthropologists and other social scientists took off for "exotic" parts of the world like Samoa and Egypt. In 1921, *Florence Goodenough* published her "draw-a-man" test, an attempt to develop a method of intelligence testing that would reflect a child's intellectual maturity from the drawings of a man (Goodenough, 1926). Because the test required only a piece of paper and a pencil, could be administered in pantomime, it quickly became a favorite cross-cultural tool. In the late 1930s and 1940s, this test was expanded to the measurement of personality and became a popular tool of clinical and child psychologists.

The Rorschach. Also in 1921, *Hermann Rorschach* (1884–1922), a Swiss psychiatrist, published a series of ten inkblots to be used as a diagnostic technique in the study of psychiatric patients. Rorschach was not the first to investigate the use of inkblots as a tool to study personality. Binet, for example, had already written on this topic. American psychologists such as Dearborn (1898), Sharp (1899), and Kirkpatrick (1900) had also published studies dealing with inkblots. But Rorschach's contribution was a systematic and in-depth approach, so that the Rorschach Inkblot became rapidly popular in the United States; several scoring systems were developed despite the fact that, in general, academic psychology criticized the Rorschach "cult" for its lack of scientific discipline. As we saw, today the Rorschach is still one of the most widely used tests and the focal point of much research and controversy.

The Stanford Achievement Test. In 1923, Terman and others published the Stanford Achievement Test, a battery of standardized tests to measure achievement in elementary-school subjects. The content of this test battery reflected a careful sampling of the actual material being taught in schools across the United States. As in the Stanford-Binet, the items had been carefully tested to determine their validity, and extensive norms had been gathered. In the field of educational testing, it was the Stanford Achievement Test that made large-scale testing a practical reality.

The Downey Will Temperament Test. In 1923, the Downey Will Temperament Test appeared, a test requiring the subject to write under various conditions, for example as fast as possible, or with eyes closed. This test attempted to measure various personality aspects such as flexibility, interest in detail, and reaction to contradiction, but most research studies that used this test obtained negative results. The Downey test was an interesting but unsuccessful reflection of the behavioristic demand for "objectivity."

Several tests of aptitude in the areas of music, clerical skills, and mechanical ability also appeared in the early 1920s and subsequently found wide application in industry and civil service.

Louis L. Thurstone (1887–1955). Largely as the result of the work of *L. L. Thurstone*, at the University of Chicago, the global approach to intelligence as reflected in the Stanford-Binet and the Army Alpha and Beta, was complemented by a "primary mental abilities" approach that attempted to develop tests to measure distinct and basic mental abilities. Thus Spearman's approach, popular in Britain, was replaced in the United States by the multiple-factor approach (although the pendulum seems to be swinging back to primacy of the *g* factor – see A. R. Jensen, 1998). Thurstone also was a pioneer in the measurement of attitudes, and his techniques for the construction of attitude scales are still widely used (see Chapter 6).

Thurstone was an engineer and inventor of a movie projector that eliminated the flicker of projectors then in use by having a continuous moving film. He demonstrated this to Thomas Edison who was impressed and offered him a position in Edison's New Jersey laboratory. Soon, Thurstone became more interested in educational than engineering problems and returned to the academic world. He made many basic contributions to topics such as factor analysis, and despite the fact that many of his papers deal with highly complex and esoteric statistical issues, his primary concern was with practical problems (see Thurstone, 1952, for his autobiography).

Arnold Gesell (1880–1961). In 1925, *Arnold Gesell*, a pupil of G. Stanley Hall, began publishing a series of developmental schedules for infants and preschool children. These schedules were essentially an inventory of spontaneous and elicited behaviors that occurred in children's motor, adaptive, language, and personal-social behavior. Given such an inventory, their time of occurrence in a specific child could be compared with the "typical" time of occurrence. The work of Gesell is well known and represents a pioneering effort in the field of infant testing. Subsequent tests for young children have often used the Gesell Schedules as one of their main sources of material.

The Berkeley Growth Study. In 1928, *Nancy Bayley*, a psychologist at the University of California (Berkeley) began the Berkeley Growth Study (her doctoral dissertation) – a longitudinal study of a sample of 61 newborns, devoted to the investigation of mental and motor development and physical growth and maturing. Each newborn was studied intensively and was seen monthly for the first 15 months, and then at 3-month intervals until age 3 and less frequently after that. Mental and motor test scores, anthropometric measures, observations of mother and child, interview data, and projective test data were collected. Reports from this study have been numerous and have contributed much to our understanding of psychological development (Bayley, 1968; 1986; 1991).

Other developments. Situational tests in the study of personality were also developed. These tests involved the close observation of a subject engaged in a task whose purpose was often disguised. A classical example is the series of investigations conducted by Hartshorne and May

(1928) concerned with cheating, stealing, and other behaviors in school children.

All of these developments reflected a rapid shift in psychology from a pre-Wundtian philosophical orientation to a scientific one grounded in measurement. This shift was paralleled in the field of education. Many bureaus of educational research were established and their findings were rapidly disseminated. Surveys of instructional efficiency were made and tests of intelligence and achievement became a routine part of school life. Various professional educational societies were established, and articles in scientific journals dealing with educational measurement became more common.

Textbooks in the area of educational measurement began to appear in 1916 and 1917 and were quickly followed by others. In 1926, the Scholastic Aptitude Test was introduced as part of a college-admissions program.

In 1935, *C. D. Morgan* and *H. A. Murray* published the Thematic Apperception Test, a series of semistructured pictures to which the subject responds by telling a story (see Chapter 15). The TAT rapidly joined the Rorschach in terms of research studies and number of controversies that it generated (see W. G. Klopfer, 1973, for a brief history of projective techniques, and H. A. Murray, 1967, for an autobiography; see also M. B. Smith, 1990, M. B. Smith & Anderson, 1989).

In 1935 also, *Oscar K. Buros* published a 44-page bibliography of tests. In 1936, the list was expanded to 83 pages. In 1938, this list became the *First Mental Measurements Yearbook*, some 400 pages long covering about 4,000 tests, the first volume of a series that contains not only a compendium of commercially available tests, but also test information such as price, number of forms available, etc., and critical reviews.

In 1938, *Lauretta Bender* presented the Visual Motor Gestalt test, commonly known as the Bender-Gestalt, that consists of nine simple designs that the subject is instructed to copy. The rationale of this test was that perception is a total integrative process, and the subject's reproductions would reflect maturational level, personality organization, and pathological states. As discussed in Chapter 15, the Bender-Gestalt has found wide use both as an indicator of possible brain damage and as a reflection of psychodynamic aspects.

In a 1939 paper, *L. K. Frank* introduced the label—projective techniques to refer to materials, such as inkblots, which the subject can respond to in such a way that the responses are taken to reflect needs, motives, past experiences, etc. – i.e., the individual presumably "projects" his or her personality into the perceptual organization. As discussed in Chapter 15, projective techniques became quite popular, not only among clinical psychologists who used these techniques to assess clients, but also among anthropologists and other behavioral scientists, who saw in these techniques a method to quantify observations across cultures. By way of contrast, the use of tests in the Soviet Union was banned by a 1936 decree (Brozek, 1972).

Nature vs. nurture. To be sure, the growth of testing was not without its pains. A large number of tests eagerly placed on the market did not live up to the user's expectations and often resulted in a negative attitude toward all testing. Many individuals with little or no psychological training used complex instruments to make decisions that often were not valid. For example, many school teachers were taught administration of the Binet scale during one summer course and would then become official community examiners, frequently being labeled as psychologists. In 1914, surveys published by J. E. Wallin indicated that the majority of psychological examiners were teachers, principals, and even medical personnel, most with very little training in psychology.

Acrimonious controversies over technical issues also did not help. A classical example is the Stanford-Iowa controversy over the constancy of the IQ – i.e., the question of whether intelligence is a fixed personal attribute based on hereditary givens, or a characteristic that not only reflects one's culture and upbringing but can also be altered by environmental manipulations such as coaching, nursery experiences, intensive teaching, and others (see McNemar, 1940; R. L. Thorndike, 1940; Wellman, Skeels, & Skodak, 1940). Again, this was not a new question, but one that went back to the time of Gallon (Fancher, 1983). In 1932, *Beth Wellman* of Iowa published the first of a series of studies reporting marked changes in the IQs of children attending the Iowa University Elementary School. The evidence to support this contention consisted in mean IQ increases from 110 to 119 and 124 on subsequent testing of a large group of children. Subsequent reports by Wellman and her co-workers presented additional evidence that the stimulation in a child's environment is an important factor in mental development (see Minton, 1984).

Criticisms of the Iowa studies were swift and often violent. B. R. Simpson published an article in 1939, entitled "The wandering IQ: Is it time to settle down?" in which he bitterly denounced the work of Wellman as "worse than nonsense." Florence Goodenough, also in 1939, published "A critique of recent experiments on raising the IQ," a thoughtful evaluation based on the more rational arguments of unreliability, examiner bias, and statistical regression.

David Wechsler. In 1939, *David Wechsler* (1896–1981) pointed out that available adult tests of intelligence had typically been developed from children's tests, and therefore their content was often inappropriate for adults. He also indicated that available tests overemphasized speed and verbal abilities, and their standardization rarely included adults. To correct these and other weaknesses, Wechsler created the Wechsler-Bellevue Intelligence Scale, an individual point-scale for adults. The Wechsler-Bellevue scale won wide acceptance and was soon ranked second in frequency of use, following the Stanford-Binet. In particular, the Wechsler-Bellevue found great use in military hospitals during World War II. Ten years later Wechsler published the Wechsler Intelligence Scale for Children, and in 1955 the Wechsler-Bellevue was replaced by the Wechsler Adult Intelligence Scale (see Chapter 5).

World War II. World War II also made extensive demands on the skills and ingenuity of psychologists and further stimulated psychological testing. The successful placement of personnel into specialized war activities, such as radar observers, airplane navigators, and radio operators, became a crucial goal that generated much systematic and sophisticated research. Problems of adjustment, morale, and psychopathology also stimulated interest in testing, particularly in the use of projective techniques as tools for clinical psychologists. The high rate of draftee difficulties emphasized the severity of the mental-health problem and made greater demands upon clinical psychologists. These demands were further intensified by the fact that, at the end of the War, more than 50% of the patients in Veterans Administration Hospitals were neuropsychiatric patients. Clinical psychologists began to perform services such as psychotherapy, which previously had been restricted to medical personnel. Testing played a greater part in the clinical psychologists' activities, although often a wide gulf developed between the use of a particular test and experimental proof of its validity.

The Army Alpha of the first world war was replaced by the *Army General Classification Test* that contained vocabulary, arithmetic, reasoning, and block-counting items (Harrell, 1992). Noteworthy also, was the extensive use of situational tests made by the Office of Strategic Services (now called the Central Intelligence Agency) in their program designed to select spies, saboteurs, and other military intelligence personnel (OSS Assessment Staff, 1948).

The MMPI. In 1940, *Starke Hathaway*, a psychologist, and *J. C. McKinley*, a psychiatrist, at the University of Minnesota presented the Minnesota Multiphasic Personality Inventory, a collection of 550 items to aid in the diagnosis of clinical patients. The MMPI was instrumental in creating and fostering the profession of clinical psychology because it was seen as evidence that psychologists could not only diagnose but also provide therapy, functions which up till then were the province of psychiatry. The MMPI resulted in a veritable deluge of research publications, many of them aimed at developing new MMPI scales, or applying standard scales to a wide variety of constructs. This intensity of research, as well as the applicability of the MMPI to a wide range of problems, made the MMPI the best-known personality inventory.

Postwar period. At the end of World War II, the federal government actively supported the training of clinical psychologists. This resulted both in great interest in psychological tests designed to measure the "inner" aspects of personality, and in a reaction against the identification of clinical psychology as applied psychometrics. The young clinicians felt they were not "just testers" and often disavowed any connections with tests in their attempts at creating a professional "doctor" image.

On the other hand, some psychologists produced evidence that tests could be a valuable avenue to the understanding of personality dynamics. Of note here is the work of *David Rapaport* and his collaborators (notably Merton Gill and Roy Schafer) at the Menninger Foundation. In their 1945 publication *Diagnostic Psychological Testing*, they presented a unified clinical diagnostic approach, demonstrating that psychological tests could contribute to our understanding of personality functioning.

The federal government also supported vocational and educational training, with the result that the profession of guidance and counseling made heavy demands on the development and use of vocational tests, tests of aptitude, interests, personality, and intelligence.

SOME RECENT DEVELOPMENTS

The development and application of psychological tests has increased enormously; they are routinely used in education, the military, civil service, industry, even religious life. The number of tests available commercially is truly gigantic, but probably surpassed by noncommercial tests. Large-scale testing involving thousands of subjects are relatively common. Complex statistical analyses, not possible before computers, have now become routine matters. It is somewhat difficult to single out recent contributions as historically noteworthy because the objectivity of time has not judged their worth, but the following are probably illustrative.

The Authoritarian Personality. One of the major issues of concern to social scientists, follwing World War II, was to try to understand how and why the Nazi movement had taken place, and whether such a movement might be possible in the United States. The answer was a book published in 1950 called *The Authoritarian Personality*. This psychoanalytically oriented investigation identified allegiance to authoritarianism as the culprit; this complex personality syndrome resulted from rigid and punitive child-rearing practices (Baars & Scheepers, 1993). The book also presented the F (fascist) scale, a self-inventory designed to assess authoritarianism. The F scale became one of the best

known and most heatedly debated personality scales, with much of the focus on methodological issues.

The three faces of intellect. *J. P. Guilford* and his coworkers at the University of Southern California developed a unified theory of the human intellect that organizes various intellectual abilities into a single system called the structure of intellect (Guilford, 1959a; 1967b). As discussed in Chapters 5 and 8, Guilford's model is a three-dimensional one that classifies human intellectual abilities according to the type of mental operations or processes involved, the kind of content, and the type of outcome or product. Given five categories of operations, four kinds of content, and six kinds of products, the theory can be represented by a cube subdivided into 120 ($4 \times 5 \times 6$) smaller cubes. Based on this model and a factor-analytic approach, Guilford and his coworkers developed a large number of tests, each designed to be a pure measure of a particular intellectual ability. Under the operation dimension of divergent thinking, a number of measures have been developed and used in the area of creativity, despite their limited validity (see Guilford, 1967a, for his autobiography).

The 1960s. The launching of the Soviet Sputnik in October 1957 brought to the consciousness of the American public the possibility that the United States was no longer number one, at least in some areas of endeavor. As always, the high-school educational system was criticized and a flurry of legislative actions resulted in a search for talented students who could once again bring the United States to the forefront of science and technology. These searches involved large-scale testing, exemplified by the National Merit Scholarship Corporation program. Such programs were facilitated by various technological advances that permitted machine scoring of large number of answer sheets. This in turn facilitated the use of multiple-choice items, as opposed to essay questions, which could not be scored by machine.

The result was dual. On the one hand, teams of experts devoted their considerable talents to the development of multiple-choice items that would assess more than memory and recognition. On the other hand, a number of critics protested rather vocally against these tests, particularly the ones used to make admission decisions in higher education. One of the most vocal critics was *Banesh Hoffman* who, in a 1962 book titled *The Tyranny of Testing*, argued that multiple-choice tests were not only superficial but penalized the brighter and creative students who, rather than select the simplistically correct choice defined by the test constructor, would select incorrect options because they were able to perceive more complex relationships between question and answer.

The 1960s also saw a major controversy over the use of personality tests in the selection of personnel, especially, in the use of the MMPI for assessment of Peace Corps volunteers. This led to a Congressional investigation of psychological testing, a special issue of the *American Psychologist* (November, 1965) devoted to this topic, and a proliferation of books strongly critical of psychological testing [e.g., Hillel Black (1962) *They Shall Not Pass*; Martin Gross (1962) *The Brain Watchers*]. While much of the criticism generated more smoke than heat and was accompanied more by irrational conclusions than empirical evidence, the antitest movement, like most movements, had some benefits. For one, psychologists became more aware of the issue of privacy, and the need to communicate to and instruct the lay public as to the nature and limitations of psychological testing. For another, it made psychologists more critical of their tests and therefore more demanding of evidence to support the validity of such tests.

The 1970s: The IQ controversy. For many years, it had been observed and documented that minority children, especially black children, did not do as well in school as their Anglo counterparts. In an effort to redress this, the Federal Government had begun a massive program, the Head Start program, designed to provide minority children remedial and enrichment opportunities to given them a compensatory headstart in the scholastic race. Although the program was received enthusiastically, a number of critics suggested that such interventions were of little value (Zigler & Muenchow, 1992).

In 1969, *Arthur Jensen*, a psychologist at the University of California at Berkeley, published an article in the *Harvard Educational Review* titled, "How much can we boost IQ and scholastic achievement?" In this article,

Jensen very carefully reviewed the literature and concluded that differences in intelligence and scholastic achievement within white children were primarily attributable to genetic aspects. He then concluded that the differences in intelligence between black and white children were also the result of genetic differences between the two races. The conclusion was the product of a scholarly mind and was based on a careful review of some rather complex issues, but it was certainly an unpopular conclusion that resulted in a barrage of criticisms, not only of Jensen's article, but also of psychological testing. Once again, it became clear that the enterprise of psychological testing is intertwined with societal, political, and philosophical values, and that their use transcends the application of a scientific instrument. Psychological testing, especially intelligence testing, has been closely entwined in the United States with racism (A. J. Edwards, 1971; S. J. Gould, 1981; Urban, 1989). The entire controversy associated with intelligence testing is still unresolved and still very much with us. In 1994, Richard Herrnstein and Charles Murray published *The Bell Curve*, a book subtitled "Intelligence and class structure in American life," and once again reignited a century-old controversy (Zenderland, 1997).

The 1970s: Educational testing. Another major development of the 1970s concerned three aspects of educational testing (Haney, 1981; Resnick, 1982). The first concerned a decline from 1963 to 1977 of average SAT verbal scores by nearly 50 points, and of SAT math scores by about 30 points. A variety of causes for the decline were discussed, with the result that once again testing was brought to the public's consciousness.

A second development was minimum competency testing, the specification of standards to be achieved to be promoted from one grade to another and to graduate from high school (B. Lerner, 1981). Although the idea seemed simple and popular with the American public, implementation was not as easy, and it contained a number of legal ramifications. For example, in Florida such a testing program was declared unconstitutional because 20% of blacks but only 2% of white high-school seniors would have failed such standards, despite the fact that the test was judged to have adequate content and construct validity (Haney, 1981).

The third development was the truth-in-testing legislation. Just as there are a variety of laws that protect the consumer when a product is purchased or used, so a number of legislative efforts were made, particularly in relation to admissions tests for professional and graduate programs, to allow the test taker to have access to his or her test results, to have publicly available information on the psychometric aspects of the test, and to give full disclosure to the test taker prior to testing as to what use will be made of the test scores. The basic rationale for such legislation was to permit the test taker the opportunity to know explicitly the criteria by which decisions are made about that individual; public disclosure would presumably make the test publisher and test administrator more accountable and, hence, more careful. The intent was good, but the results, it may be argued, punished test takers by resulting in higher fees and fewer administrative dates (for a fascinating chronology of noteworthy events in American psychology, many relevant to testing, see Street, 1994).

The 1980s also saw a number of major attacks of both specific tests and psychological testing more generally, with the publication of books such as *The Reign of ETS: The Corporation that Makes Up Minds* (Nairn & Associates, 1980), *The Testing Trap* (Strenio, 1981), *None of the Above: Behind the Myth of Scholastic Aptitude* (D. Owen, 1985).

A peek at the future. Following the example of Matarazzo (1992), I can hazard eight guesses about testing in the 21st century:

1. Current tests that are popular and have survived the rigors of scientific critique, will still be with us. These should include tests such as the Stanford-Binet, the Wechsler series, and yes, even the MMPI.

2. Testing will be marked by a broader sensitivity to the individual aspects of the client. For example, versions of the tests will be available in a wide variety of languages, such as Vietnamese and Croatian.

3. There will be much greater use of physiological measures of intelligence, using a variety of biological indices such as reaction time (shades of Wundt!), velocity of nerve conduction, and the rate at which glucose is metabolized in the brain.

4. Studies from cognitive psychology, especially how information from each test item is processed, will provide us with much information on cognitive abilities, new theoretical models to guide our thinking, as well as new types of test items and test forms.

5. Neuropsychological tests, along the lines of the Halstead-Reitan, will be much more sophisticated and will provide complex analyses of the processes that underlie various cognitive functions.

6. There will be even wider use of personality type tests to assess various phenomena discussed in Chapter 8 (normal positive functioning) and Chapter 15 (health psychology), such as Type A behavior, hassles in everyday living, and optimism toward one's own health.

7. There will be more tests designed to assess positive functioning and abilities such as personal competence and quality of life, rather than the past emphasis on deficits.

8. Computers and technology will play a major role in testing, from administration to interpretation.

9. New statistical techniques, and in particular the Item Response Theory model, will result in drastically new approaches. For example, one of the commandments of psychometric testing has always been that all subjects taking test X must respond in the same way – if test X is a 100-item multiple-choice vocabulary test, we do not let John answer some items and Tom answer different items. In the future this will change (it has already through adaptive testing) and not only will we be able to compare John's performance with Tom's, even though based on different subsets of items, but also allow each to answer whatever items they wish, and to use their choice in useful predictive ways.

10. Testing has been dominated by multiple-choice items. Such items can be and are very useful and have been unjustly maligned. However, their dominance in the future will recede as other forms of tests such as portfolios, essay exams, and virtual reality situations are developed and their utility explored.

A final word. Perhaps the obvious needs to be stated. Psychologists themselves have been the most critical of all about psychological testing;

if you don't believe me simply browse through the test reviews found in the *Mental Measurements Yearbook*! A reflection of their criticality was the development of the *Standards for educational and psychological tests* (see Chapter 1), a code of recommended practices and ethical principles involved in testing. Another reflection is the steady stream of articles published in professional journals that are critical of either specific tests, aspects of testing, or the whole totality of testing.

In the 1960s and 1970s, a number of graduate programs in psychology began to deemphasize testing in the training of future psychologists, and for some, such deemphasis reached crisis proportions and hindered the advancement of psychology as a science (Aiken et al., 1990; N. M. Lambert, 1991; Meier, 1993). The pendulum seems to be swinging in the other direction; *Time* magazine, for example, reported (July 15, 1991) that in the United States, 46 million students from kindergarten through high school are subjected to more than 150 million standardized tests each year. For better or for worse, psychological testing is a part of our everyday life, and a number of recent advances, from the development of more sophisticated psychometric models to the ubiquity of microcomputers, will probably make testing an even more important endeavor. With education and a firm understanding of both the potential and the limitations of tests, we can use tests judiciously as part of an effort to create a better world. I hope this textbook has provided the beginnings of such a foundation.

SUMMARY

We have taken a quick look at the history of psychological testing and a very brief peek at its potential future. Testing has a rather long past, perhaps because it seems to be an intrinsic human activity. But testing today seems to have evolved primarily due to the French clinical tradition and the work of Binet, the German nomothetic tradition as represented by the work of Wundt, the British idiographic approach, especially that of Sir Francis Galton, and the American emphasis on pragmatism.

SUGGESTED READINGS

Baars, J., & Scheepers, P. (1993). Theoretical and methodological foundations of the Authoritarian Personality. *Journal of the History of the Behavioral Sciences, 29*, 345–353.

A fascinating review by two Dutch social scientists of the background, theoretical ideas, and methodological contributions that resulted in the classic study of the "Authoritarian Personality."

Buchanan, R. D. (1994). The development of the Minnesota Multiphasic Personality Inventory. *Journal of the History of the Behavioral Sciences, 30*, 148–161.

A review of how the MMPI came to be. Very readable and an interesting look at a chapter in the history of psychology that in many ways revolutionized psychological testing.

Dennis, P. M. (1984). The Edison Questionnaire. *Journal of the History of the Behavioral Sciences, 20*, 23–37.

Thomas A. Edison, the famous inventor, developed a questionnaire of 48 questions to be administered to applicants for positions as industrial chemists in his laboratories. The questions included: "What countries bound France?" "What is copra?" and "Who was Plutarch?" Although now unknown, the questionnaire actually had quite an impact on the public's perception of psychological testing.

Landy, F. J. (1992). Hugo Munsterberg: Victim or visionary? *Journal of Applied Psychology, 77*, 787–802.

Munsterberg was an early leader in the applied study of psychology and was, indeed, one of the pioneers in the development of psychology in the United States. Yet in many ways he was, and is, an obscure figure.

Matarazzo, J. D. (1992). Psychological testing and assessment in the 21st century. *American Psychologist, 47*, 1007–1018.

The author, a very distinguished psychologist, looks into the crystal ball and gives us a glimpse of the future of testing.

DISCUSSION QUESTIONS

1. From a historical perspective which one person had the most impact on the development of psychological testing as a field?

2. If you could invite one person from those mentioned in the chapter to visit your class, which one would it be?

3. If you are familiar with the musical "My Fair Lady" (or the book *Pygmalion* on which it is based) you might want to discuss the major themes as they applied to England at the time of Sir Francis Galton.

4. Could you take the work of Galton and of Goddard and argue for an environmental explanation?

5. Are there any recent events that in the future may be incorporated in a chapter on the history of psychological testing?

Table to Translate Difficulty Level of a Test Item into a *z* Score

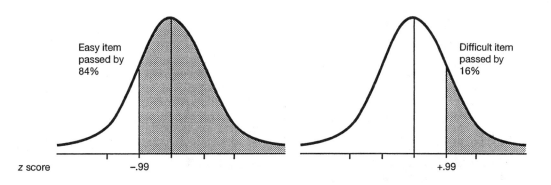

	Difficulty level (area to the right)	Equivalent *z* score	Difficulty level (area to the right)	Equivalent *z* score
	99%	−2.33	50%	.00
	98	−2.05	49	+.03
very	97	−1.88	48	+.05
easy	96	−1.75	47	+.08
items	95	−1.65	46	+.10
	94	−1.56	45	+.13
	93	−1.48	44	+.15
	92	−1.41	43	+.18
	91	−1.34	42	+.20
	90	−1.28	41	+.23
	89	−1.23	40	+.25
	88	−1.17	39	+.28
	87	−1.13	38	+.31
	86	−1.08	37	+.33
	85	−1.04	36	+.36
	84	−.99	35	+.39
	83	−.95	34	+.41
	82	−.92	33	+.44
	81	−.88	32	+.47
	80	−.84	31	+.50
	79	−.81	30	+.52
	78	−.77	29	+.55
	77	−.74	28	+.58
	76	−.71	27	+.61
	75	−.67	26	+.64
	74	−.64	25	+.67

Difficulty level (area to the right)	Equivalent z score		Difficulty level (area to the right)	Equivalent z score
73	−.61		24	+.71
72	−.58		23	+.74
71	−.55		22	+.77
70	−.52		21	+.81
69	−.50		20	+.84
68	−.47		19	+.88
67	−.44		18	+.92
66	−.41		17	+.95
65	−.39		16	+.99
64	−.36		15	+1.04
63	−.33		14	+1.08
62	−.31		13	+1.13
61	−.28		12	+1.17
60	−.25		11	+1.23
59	−.23		10	+1.28
58	−.20	very	9	+1.34
57	−.18	difficult	8	+1.41
56	−.15	items	7	+1.48
55	−.13		6	+1.56
54	−.10		5	+1.65
53	−.08		4	+1.75
52	−.05		3	+1.88
51	−.02		2	+2.05
			1	+2.33

Note: Because of rounding error and lack of interpolation, the values are approximate, and may not match normal curve parameters (e.g., the value for 84% is given as .99 rather than the expected 1).

References

Aaronson, N. K., Acquadro, C., Alonso, J., et al. (1992). International Quality of Life Assessment (IQOLA) project. *Quality of Life Research, 1,* 349–351.

Abdel-Khalek, A. (1988). Egyptian results on the Standard Progressive Matrices. *Personality and Individual Differences, 9,* 193–195.

Abramson, P. R., & Mosher, D. L. (1975). Development of a measure of negative attitudes toward masturbation. *Journal of Consulting and Clinical Psychology, 43,* 485–490.

Achenbach, T. M. (1991). *Manual for the Child Behavior Checklist and 1991 profile.* Burlington, VT: University of Vermont Department of Psychiatry.

Achenbach, T. M., & Edelbrock, C. S. (1981). Behavioral problems and competencies reported by parents of normal and disturbed children aged 4 through 16. *Monographs of the Society for Research in Child Development, 46,* Serial Nos 1 & 188.

Ackerman, P. L. (1992). Predicting individual differences in complex skill acquisition: Dynamics of ability determinants. *Journal of Applied Psychology, 77,* 598–614.

Adams, K. M., & Heaton, R. K. (1985). Automated interpretation of neuropsychological test data. *Journal of Consulting and Clinical Psychology, 53,* 790–802.

Adams, K. M., & Heaton, R. K. (1987). Computerized neuropsychological assessment: Issues and applications. In J. N. Butcher (Ed.), *Computerized psychological assessment.* (pp. 355–365). New York: Basic Books.

Adams, K. M., Kvale, V. I., & Keegan, J. F. (1984). Relative accuracy of three automated systems for neuropsychological interpretation. *Journal of Clinical Neuropsychology, 6,* 413–431.

Adler, R., MacRitchie, K., & Engel, G. L. (1971). Psychologic process and ischemik stroke. *Psychosomatic medicine, 33,* 1–29.

Ado Rno, T. W., Frenkel-Brunswick, E., Levinson, D. J., & Sanford, R. N. (1950). *The Authoritarian Personality.* New York: Harper & Row.

Aiken, L. R. (1980). Problems in testing the elderly. *Educational Gerontology, 5,* 119–124.

Aiken, L. R. (1987). *Assessment of intellectual functioning.* Boston, MA: Allyn & Bacon.

Aiken, L. S., West, S. G., Sechrest, L., Reno, R. R., Rodiger, H. L. III, Scarr, S., Kazdin, A. E., & Sherman, S. J. (1990). Graduate training in statistics, methodology, and measurement in psychology: A survey of PhD programs in North America. *American Psychologist, 45,* 721–734.

Airasian, P. W. (1989). Review of the California Achievement Tests. In J. C. Conoley & J. J. Kramer (Eds.), *The tenth mental measurements yearbook* (pp. 126–128). Lincoln, NE: University of Nebraska Press.

Ajzen, I., & Fishbein, M. (1973). Attitudinal and normative variables as predictors of specific behaviors. *Journal of Personality and Social Psychology, 27,* 41–57.

Ajzen, I., & Fishbein, M. (1980). *Understanding attitudes and predicting social behavior.* Englewood Cliffs, NJ: Prentice Hall.

Akutagawa, D. A. (1956). *A study in construct validity of the psychoanalytic concept of latent anxiety and a test of projection distance hypothesis.* Unpublished doctoral dissertation, University of Pittsburgh.

Albaum, G., & Baker, K. (1977). Cross-validation of a creativity scale for the Adjective Check List. *Educational and Psychological Measurement, 37,* 1057–1061.

Albert, S., Fox, H. M., & Kahn, M. W. (1980). Faking psychosis on the Rorschach: Can expert judges detect malingering? *Journal of Personality Assessment, 44,* 115–119.

Albright, L. E., & Glennon, J. R. (1961). Personal history correlates of physical scientists' career aspirations. *Journal of Applied Psychology, 45,* 281–284.

Albright, L. E., Glennon, J. R., & Smith, W. J. (1963). *The use of psychological tests in industry.* Cleveland: Howard Allen Inc.

Alderman, A. L., & Powers, P. E. (1980). The effects of special preparation on SAT verbal scores. *American Educational Research Journal, 17,* 239–251.

Alderton, D. L., & Larson, G. E. (1990). Dimensionality of Raven's Advanced Progressive Matrices items. *Educational and Psychological Measurement, 50,* 887–900.

Alfred, K. D., & Smith, T. (1989). The hardy personality: Cognitive and physiological responses to evaluative threat. *Journal of Personality and Social Psychology, 56,* 257–266.

Allen, J. P., & Litten, R. Z. (1993). Psychometric and laboratory measures to assist in the treatment of alcoholism. *Clinical Psychology Review, 13,* 223–239.

Allen, J. P., & Mattson, M. E. (1993). Psychometric instruments to assist in alcoholism treatment planning. *Journal of Substance Abuse Treatment, 10,* 289–296.

Allen, M. J., & Yen, W. M. (1979). *Introduction to measurement theory.* Monterey, CA: Brooks-Cole.

Allen, R. M., & Jefferson, T. W. (1962). *Psychological evaluation of the cerebral palsied person.* Springfield, IL: Charles C Thomas.

Alliger, G. M., & Dwight, S. S. (2000). A metaanalytic investigation of the susceptibility of integrity tests to faking and coaching. *Educational and Psychological Measurement, 60,* 59–72.

Allport, G. W. (1937). *Personality: A psychological interpretation.* New York: Holt, Rinehart and Winston.

Allport, G. W. (1961). *Pattern and growth in personality.* New York: Holt, Rinehart and Winston.

Allport, G. W., & Odbert, H. S. (1936). Trait-names: A psycholexical study. *Psychological Monographs, 47,* (1, whole No. 211).

Allport, G. W., Vernon, P. E., & Lindzey, G. (1960). *Study of values* (3rd ed.). Boston: Houghton-Mifflin.

Altemeyer, B. (1981). *Right-wing authoritarianism.* Manitoba, Canada: University of Manitoba Press.

Altepeter, T. S., & Johnson, K. A. (1989). Use of the PPVT-R for intellectual screening with adults: A caution. *Journal of Psychoeducational Assessment, 7,* 39–45.

Alter, J. B. (1984). Creativity profile of university and conservatory dance students. *Journal of Personality Assessment, 48,* 153–158.

Alter, J. B. (1989). Creativity profile of university and conservatory music students. *Creativity Research Journal, 2,* 184–195.

Alvino, J., McDonnel, R. C., & Richert, S. (1981). National survey of identification practices in gifted and talented education. *Exceptional Children, 48,* 124–132.

American Association on Mental Deficiency. (1974). *Adaptive Behavior Scale: Manual.* Washington, DC: Author.

American Educational Research Association, American Psychological Association, and National Council on Measurement in Education. (1999). *Standards for educational and psychological testing.* Washington, DC: American Educational Research Association.

American Guidance Service, Inc. (1969). *The Minnesota Rate of Manipulation Tests, examiner's manual.* Circle Pines, MN: Author.

American Psychological Association. (1986). *Guidelines for computer-based tests and interpretations.* Washington, DC: Author.

American Psychological Association. (1987). General guidelines for providers of psychological services. *American Psychologist, 42,* 712–723.

American Psychological Association. (1992). Ethical principles of psychologists and code of conduct. *American Psychologist, 47,* 1597–1611.

American Psychological Association, Task Force on the Delivery of Services to Ethnic Minority Populations. (1993). Guidelines for providers of psychological services to ethnic, linguistic, and culturally diverse populations. *American Psychologist, 48,* 45–48.

American Psychological Association Committee on Psychological Tests and Assessment. (1996). Statement on the disclosure of test data. *American Psychologist, 51,* 644–648.

Ames, L. B., Gillespie, B. S., Haines, J., & Ilg, F. L. (1979). *The Gesell Institute's child from one to six: Evaluating the behavior of the preschool child.* New York: Harper & Row.

Anastasi, A. (1983). Evolving trait concepts. *American Psychologist, 38,* 175–184.

Anastasi, A. (1988). *Psychological testing* (6th ed.). New York: Macmillan.

Anastasi, A., & Schaefer, C. E. (1969). Biographical correlates of artistic and literary creativity in adolescent girls. *Journal of Applied Psychology, 53,* 267–273.

Anderson, G. J., & Walberg, H. J. (1976). *The assessment of learning environments.* Chicago, IL: University of Illinois.

Anderson, R. D., & Sisco, F. H. (1977). *Standardization of the WISC-R for deaf children* (series T, No. 1). Washington, DC: Gallaudet College, Office of Demographic Studies.

Anderson, R. T., Aaronson, N. K., & Wilkin, D. (1993). Critical review of the international assessments of health-related quality of life. *Quality of Life Research, 2,* 369–395.

Andrews, J. (1973). The relationship of values to identity achievement status. *Journal of Youth and Adolescence, 2,* 133–138.

Andrews, L. W., & Gutkin, T. B. (1991). The effects of human vs. computer authorship on consumers' perceptions of psychological reports. *Computers in Human Behavior, 7*, 311–317.

Angoff, W. H. (1971). Scales, norms, and equivalent scores. In R. L. Thorndike (Ed.), *Educational Measurement* (pp. 508–600). Washington, DC: American Council on Education.

Aplin, D. Y. (1993). Psychological evaluation of adults in a cochlear implant program. *American Annals of the Deaf, 138*, 415–419.

Arbisi, P. A., & Ben-Porath, Y. S. (1998). The ability of Minnesota Multiphasic Personality Inventory-2 validity scales to detect fakebad responses in psychiatric inpatients. *Psychological Assessment, 10*, 221–228.

Archer, R. P., Gordon, R. A., & Kirchner, F. H. (1987). MMPI response-set characteristics among adolescents. *Journal of Personality Assessment, 51*, 506–516.

Arellano, C. M., & Markman, H. J. (1995). The Managing Affect and Differences Scale (MADS): A self-report measure assessing conflict management in couples. *Journal of Family Psychology, 9*, 319–334.

Argulewicz, E. N., Bingenheimer, L. T., & Anderson, C. C. (1983). Concurrent validity of the PPVT-R for Anglo-American and Mexican-American students. *Journal of Psychoeducational Assessment, 1*, 163–167.

Arizmendi, T., Paulsen, K., & Domino, G. (1981). The Matching Familiar Figures Test: A primary, secondary, and tertiary evaluation. *Journal of Clinical Psychology, 37*, 812–818.

Armstrong, R. G. (1955). A reliability study of a short form of the WISC vocabulary subtest. *Journal of Clinical Psychology, 11*, 413–414.

Arnold, M. B. (1962). *Story sequence and analysis.* New York: Columbia University Press.

Aronow, E., & Reznikoff, M. (1976). *Rorschach content interpretation.* New York: Grune & Stratton.

Aronow, E., Reznikoff, M., & Moreland, K. L. (1995). The Rorschach: Projective technique or psychometric test? *Journal of Personality Assessment, 64*, 213–228.

Arrasmith, D. G., Sheehan, D. S., & Applebaum, W. R. (1984). A comparison of the selected-response strategy and the constructed-response strategy for assessment of a third-grade writing task. *Journal of Educational Research, 77*, 172–177.

Arthur, D. (1994). *Workplace testing.* New York: American Management Association.

Arthur, W., Jr., & Day, D. V. (1994). Development of a short form for the Raven Advanced Progressive Matrices Test. *Educational and Psychological Measurement, 54*, 394–403.

Arthur, W., Jr., & Woehr, D. J. (1993). A confirmatory factor analytic study examining the dimensionality of the Raven's Advanced Progressive Matrices. *Educational and Psychological Measurement, 53*, 471–478.

Asher, S. R., Singleton, L. C., Tinsley, B. R., & Hymel, S. (1979). A reliable sociometric measure for preschool children. *Developmental Psychology, 15*, 443–444.

Association of American Medical Colleges (1977). *New Medical College Admission Test interpretive manual.* Washington, DC: Association of American Medical Colleges.

Astin, A. W. (1982). *Minorities in American higher education.* San Francisco: Jossey-Bass.

Astin, A. W., & Holland, J. L. (1961). The environmental assessment technique: A way to measure college environments. *Journal of Educational Psychology, 52*, 308–316.

Atkin, R. S., & Conlon, E. J. (1978). Behaviorally anchored rating scales: Some theoretical issues. *Academy of Management Review, 3*, 119–128.

Atkinson, D., & Gim, R. (1989). Asian-American cultural identity and attitudes toward mental health services. *Journal of Counseling Psychology, 36*, 209–212.

Atkinson, L. (1992). Concurrent validities of the Stanford Binet (4th ed.), Leiter, and Vineland with developmentally delayed children. *Journal of School Psychology, 30*, 165–173.

Austin, J. S. (1992). The detection of fake good and fake bad on the MMPI-2. *Educational and Psychological Measurement, 52*, 669–674.

Averill, L. A. (1990). Recollections of Clark's G. Stanley Hall. *Journal of the History of the Behavioral Sciences, 26*, 125–130.

Axelrod, S., & Eisdorfer, C. (1961). Attitudes toward old people: An empirical analysis of the stimulus-group validity of the Tuckman-Lorge Questionnaire. *Journal of Gerontology, 16*, 75–80.

Aylward, E. H. (1991). *Understanding children's testing.* Austin, TX: Pro-ed.

Aylward, E. H., & Schmidt, S. (1986). An examination of three tests of visual-motor integration. *Journal of Learning Disabilities, 19*, 328–335.

Baars, J., & Scheepers, P. (1993). Theoretical and methodological foundations of the authoritarian personality. *Journal of the History of the Behavioral Sciences, 29*, 345–353.

Back, K. W. (1971). Metaphors as test of personal philosophy of aging. *Sociological Focus, 5*, 1–8.

Bachman, J. G., & O'Malley, P. M. (1984). Yea-saying, nay-saying, and going to extremes: Black-white differences in response styles. *Public Opinion Quarterly, 48*, 491–509.

Baehr, M. E. (1953). A simplified procedure for the measurement of employee attitudes. *Journal of Applied Psychology, 37*, 163–167.

Baehr, M. E., Saunders, D. R., Froemel, E. C., & Furcon, J. E. (1971). The prediction of performance for black and for white police patrolmen. *Professional Psychology, 2,* 46–58.

Bagarozzi, D. (1991). The Family Apperception Test: A review. *American Journal of Family Therapy, 19,* 177–181.

Bagby, R. M., Gillis, J. R., & Dickens, S. (1990). Detection of dissimulation with the new generation of objective personality measures. *Behavioral Sciences and the Law, 8,* 93–102.

Bagley, C., Wilson, G. D., & Boshier, R. (1970). The Conservatism scale: A factor structure comparison of English, Dutch, and New Zealand samples. *The Journal of Social Psychology, 81,* 267–268.

Bagnato, S. J. (1984). Team congruence in developmental diagnosis and intervention: Comparing clinical judgment and child performance measures. *School Psychology Review, 13,* 7–16.

Bagnato, S. J., & Neisworth, J. T. (1991). *Assessment for early intervention: Best practices for professionals.* New York: Guilford Press.

Bahr, H. M., & Chadwick, B. A. (1974). Conservatism, racial intolerance, and attitudes toward racial assimilation among whites and American Indians. *Journal of Social Psychology, 94,* 45–56.

Bailey, K. D. (1988). The conceptualization of validity: Current perspectives. *Social Science Research, 17,* 117–136.

Bailey-Richardson, B. (1988). Review of the Vineland Adaptive Behavior Scales, Classroom ed. *Journal of Psychoeducational Assessment, 6,* 87–91.

Baillargeon, J., & Danis, C. (1984). Barnum meets the computer: A critical test. *Journal of Personality Assessment, 48,* 415–419.

Baird, L. L. (1985). Do grades and tests predict adult accomplishment? *Research in Higher Education, 23,* 3–85.

Baird, L. L. (1987). Do students think admissions tests are fair? Do tests affect their decisions? *Research in Higher Education, 26,* 373–388.

Baird, P. (1983). Assessing life events and physical health: Critique of the Holmes and Rahe scale. *Psychology, 20,* 38–40.

Baker, A. F. (1983). Psychological assessment of autistic children. *Clinical Psychology Review, 3,* 41–59.

Baker, E. L., O'Neill, H. F., Jr., & Linn, R. L. (1993). Policy and validity prospects for performance-based assessment. *American Psychologist, 48,* 1210–1218.

Baker, H. J., & Leland, B. (1959). *Detroit Tests of Learning Aptitude.* Indianapolis, IN: Bobbs-Merrill.

Baker, R. L., Mednick, B. R., & Hocevar, D. (1991). Utility of scales derived from teacher judgements of adolescent academic performance and psychoso-cial behavior. *Educational and Psychological Measurement, 51,* 271–286.

Baldessarini, R. J., Finkelstein, S., & Arana, G. W. (1983). The predictive power of diagnostic tests and the effects of prevalence of illness. *Archives of General Psychiatry, 40,* 569–573.

Baldwin, A. L., Cole, R. E., & Baldwin, C. (1982). Parental pathology, family interaction, and the competence of the child in school. *Monographs of the Society for Research in Child Development, 47,* (Number 5).

Ball, S., & Bogatz, G. A. (1970). *The first year of Sesame Street: An evaluation.* Princeton, NJ: Educational Testing Service.

Ballard, R., Crino, M. D., & Rubenfeld, S. (1988). Social desirability response bias and the Marlowe-Crowne Social Desirability Scale. *Psychological Reports, 63,* 227–237.

Balzer, W. K., & Sulsky, L. M. (1992). Halo and performance appraisal research: A critical examination. *Journal of Applied Psychology, 77,* 975–985.

Banks, M. H., Jackson, P. R., Stafford, E. M., & Warr, P. B. (1983). The Job Components Inventory and the Analysis of Jobs requiring limited skill. *Personnel Psychology, 36,* 57–66.

Bannatyne, A. D. (1971). *Language, reading, and learning disabilities.* Springfield, IL: Charles C Thomas.

Banta, T. J. (1961). Social attitudes and response styles. *Educational and Psychological Measurement, 21,* 543–557.

Barba, R. H., & Mason, C. L. (1992). Construct validity studies for the Draw-A-Computer User Test. *Computers in Human Behavior, 8,* 231–237.

Barker, H. R., Fowler, R. D., & Peterson, L. P. (1971). Factor analytic structure of the short form MMPI in a VA hospital population. *Journal of Clinical Psychology, 27,* 228–233.

Barkley, R. A. (1988). A review of Child Behavior Rating Scales and checklists for research in child psychopathology. In M. Rutter, H. Tuma, & I. Lann (Eds.), *Assessment and diagnosis in child and adolescent psychopathology.* New York: Guilford Press.

Barnett, A. J. (1982). Designing an assessment of the child with cerebral palsy. *Psychology in the Schools, 19,* 160–165.

Barnette, W. L., Jr., & McCall, J. N. (1964). Validation of the Minnesota Vocational Interest Inventory for vocational high school boys. *Journal of Applied Psychology, 48,* 378–382.

Baron, J. (1985). *Rationality and intelligence.* Cambridge, UK: Cambridge University Press.

Baron, J., & Norman, M. F. (1992). SATs, Achievement Tests, and High-School class rank as predictors of college performance. *Educational and Psychological Measurement, 52,* 1047–1055.

Barrett, E. T., & Gleser, G. C. (1987). Development and validation of the cognitive status examination. *Journal of Consulting and Clinical Psychology, 55,* 877–882.

Barrett, E. T., Wheatley, R. D., & LaPlant, R. J. (1983). A brief clinical neuropsychological battery: Clinical classification trails. *Journal of Clinical Psychology, 39,* 980–984.

Barrett, G. V., Alexander, R. A., Doverspike, D., Cellar, D., & Thomas, J. C. (1982). The development and application of a computerized information-processing test battery. *Applied Psychological Measurement, 6,* 13–29.

Barrick, M. R., & Mount, M. K. (1991). The big five personality dimensions and job performance: A meta-analysis. *Personnel Psychology, 44,* 1–26.

Barringer, D. G., Strong, C. J., Blair, J. C., Clark, T. C., & Watkins, S. (1993). Screening procedures used to identify children with hearing loss. *American Annals of the Deaf, 138,* 420–426.

Barron, F. (1953). An Ego-Strength Scale which predicts response to psychotherapy. *Journal of Consulting Psychology, 17,* 327–333.

Barron, F. (1969). *Creative person and creative process.* New York: Holt, Rinehart and Winston.

Barry, B., Klanderman, J., & Stipe, D. (1983). Study number one. In A. S. Kaufman & N. L. Kaufman (Eds.), *Kaufman Assessment Battery for Children: Interpretive manual* (p. 94). Circle Pines, MN: American Guidance Service.

Bar-Tal, D., & Bar-Zohar, Y. (1977). The relationship between perception of locus of control and academic achievement: Review and some educational implications. *Contemporary Educational Psychology, 2,* 181–199.

Barton, P. E., & Coley, R. J. (1994). *Testing in America's schools.* Princeton, NJ: Educational Testing Service.

Bass, B. M. (1956). Development and evaluation of a scale for measuring social acquiescence. *The Journal of Abnormal and Social Psychology, 53,* 296–299.

Baucom, D. H. (1985). Review of the California Psychological Inventory. In J. V. Mitchell, Jr. (Ed.), *The ninth mental measurements yearbook* (Vol. 1, pp. 250–252). Lincoln, NB: University of Nebraska Press.

Baucom, D. H., Epstein, N., Rankin, L. A., & Burnett, C. K. (1996). Assessing relationship standards: The Inventory of Specific Relationship Standards. *Journal of Family Psychology, 10,* 72–88.

Bauer, M. S., Crits-Christoph, P., Ball, W. A., Dewees, E., McAllister, T., Alahi, P., et al. (1991). Independent assessment of manic and depressive symptoms by self-rating: Scale characteristics and implications for the study of mania. *Archives of General Psychiatry, 48,* 807–812.

Baughman, E. E., & Dahlstrom, W. G. (1972). Racial differences on the MMPI. In S. S. Guterman (Ed.), *Black psyche.* Berkeley, CA: Glendessary Press.

Baum, D. D., & Kelly, T. J. (1979). The validity of Slosson Intelligence Test with learning disabled kindergarteners. *Journal of Learning Disabilities, 12,* 268–270.

Bauman, M. K., & Kropf, C. A. (1979). Psychological tests used with blind and visually handicapped persons. *School Psychology Digest, 8,* 257–270.

Bayley, N. (1968). Behavioral correlates of mental growth: Birth to thirty-six years. *American Psychologist, 23,* 1–17.

Bayley, N. (1969). *Bayley Scales of Infant Development.* New York: Psychological Corporation.

Bayley, N. (1986). Behavioral correlates of mental growth: Birth to thirty-six years. *Advances in Infancy Research, 4,* 16–37.

Bayley, N. (1991). Consistency and variability in the growth of intelligence from birth to eighteen years. *Journal of Genetic Psychology, 152,* 573–604.

Beaber, R., Marston, A., Michelli, J., & Mills, M. (1985). A brief test for measuring malingering in schizophrenic individuals. *American Journal of Psychiatry, 142,* 1478–1481.

Beaver, A. P. (1953). Personality factors in choice of nursing. *Journal of Applied Psychology, 37,* 374–379.

Bechtoldt, H. P. (1959). Construct validity: A critique. *American Psychologist, 14,* 619–629.

Bech, P., Gram, L. F., Dein, E., Jacobsen, O., Vitger, J., & Bolwig, T. G. (1975). Quantitative rating of depressive states: Correlations between clinical assessment, Beck's Self Rating Scale and Hamilton's Objective Rating Scale. *Acta Psychiatrica Scandinavia, 51,* 161–170.

Beck, A. T. (1967). *Depression.* New York: Harper & Row.

Beck, A. T. (1978). *Beck inventory.* Philadelphia, PA: Center for Cognitive Therapy.

Beck, A. T., & Beamesderfer, A. (1974). Assessment of depression: The depression inventory. In P. Pichot (Ed.), *Psychological measurement in pharmacopsychiatry* (Vol. 7). Basel: S. Karger.

Beck, A. T., Rial, W. Y., & Rickels, K. (1974). Short form of depression inventory: Cross validation. *Psychological Reports, 34,* 1184–1186.

Beck, A. T., & Steer, R. A. (1984). Internal consistencies of the original and revised Beck Depression Inventory. *Journal of Clinical Psychology, 40,* 1365–1367.

Beck, A. T., Steer, R. A., & Brown, G. K. (1996). *Beck Depression Inventory manual* (2nd ed.). San Antonio, TX: Psychological Corporation.

Beck, A. T., Steer, R. A., & Garbin, M. G. (1988). Psychometric properties of the Beck Depression

Inventory: Twenty-five years of evaluation. *Clinical Psychology Review, 8,* 77–100.

Beck, A. T., Ward, C. H., Mendelson, M., Mock, J., & Erbaugh, J. (1961). An inventory for measuring depression. *Archives of General Psychiatry, 4,* 561–571.

Beck, M. D., & Beck, C. K. (1980). Multitrait-multimethod validation of four personality measures with a high-school sample. *Educational and Psychological Measurement, 40,* 1005–1011.

Becker, J. T., & Sabatino, D. A. (1973). Frostig revisited. *Journal of Learning Disabilities, 6,* 180–184.

Becker, R. L. (1988). *Reading-free Vocational Interest Inventory-Revised.* Columbus, OH: Elbern.

Becker, T. E., & Colquitt, A. L. (1992). Potential vs. actual faking of a biodata form: An analysis along several dimensions of item type. *Personnel Psychology, 45,* 389–406.

Beery, K. (1989). *The VMI (Developmental Test of Visual-Motor Integration) administration, scoring, and teaching manual.* Cleveland, OH: Modern Curriculum Press.

Beery, K. K., & Buktenica, N. A. (1967). *Developmental Test of Visual-Motor Integration.* Chicago, IL: Follett Educational Corporation.

Behar, L. B. (1977). The Preschool Behavior Questionnaire. *Journal of Abnormal Child Psychology, 5,* 265–276.

Bejar, I. I., Embretson, S., & Mayer, R. E. (1987). Cognitive psychology and the SAT: A review of some implications. *ETS Research Report,* #87–28.

Bekker, L. D., & Taylor, C. (1966). Attitudes toward the aged in a multigenerational sample. *Journal of Gerontology, 21,* 115–118.

Bell, D. C., & Bell, L. G. (1989). Micro and macro measurement of family systems concepts. *Journal of Family Psychology, 3,* 137–157.

Bellack, A. S., & Hersen, M. (1977). Self-report inventories in behavioral assessment. In J. D. Cone & R. P. Hawkins (Eds.), *Behavioral assessment* (pp. 52–76). New York: Brunner/Mazel.

Bellack, A. S., Hersen, M., & Lamparski, D. (1979). Role play tests for social skills: Are they valid? Are they useful? *Journal of Consulting and Clinical Psychology, 47,* 335–342.

Bellak, L. (1975). *The T.A.T., C.A.T. and S.A.T. in clinical use* (3rd ed.). New York: Grune & Stratton.

Bellak, L. (1986). *The Thematic Apperception Test, the Children's Apperception Test, and the Senior Apperception Technique in clinical use* (4th ed.). Orlando, FL: Grune & Stratton.

Bender, L. (1938). A visual motor gestalt test and its clinical use. American Orthopsychiatric Association, *Research Monographs,* No. 3.

Bendig, A. W. (1959). Score reliability of dichotomous and trichotomous item responses on the Maudsley Personality Inventory. *Journal of Consulting Psychology, 23,* 181.

Benjamin, L. S. (1993). Every psychopathology is a gift of love. *Psychotherapy Research, 3,* 1–24.

Benjamin, L. T. (1984). Staying with initial answers on objective tests: Is it a myth? *Teaching of Psychology, 11,* 133–141.

Bennett, R. E., & Ward, W. C. (1993). *Construction versus choice in cognitive measurement: Issues in constructed response, performance testing, and portfolio assessment.* Hillsdale, NJ: Erlbaum.

Bennett, V. D. C. (1964). Development of a self concept Q sort for use with elementary age school children. *Journal of School Psychology, 3,* 19–25.

Benson, J., & Hocevar, D. (1985). The impact of item phrasing on the validity of attitude scales for elementary school children. *Journal of Educational Measurement, 22,* 213–240.

Bentler, P. (1972). Review of the Tennessee Self Concept Scale. In O. K. Buros (Ed.), *The seventh mental measurements yearbook* (pp. 366–367). Highland Park, NJ: Gryphon Press.

Bentler, P. M., & LaVoie, A. L. (1972). An extension of semantic space. *Journal of Verbal Learning and Verbal Behavior, 11,* 174–182.

Bentler, P. M., & Speckart, G. (1979). Attitude organization and the attitude-behavior relationship. *Journal of Personality and Social Psychology, 37,* 913–929.

Benton, A. L. (1974). *The Visual Retention Test.* New York: Psychological Corporation.

Benton, A. L., Hamsher, K. de S., Varney, N. R., & Spreen, O. (1983). *Contributions to neuropsychological assessment: A clinical manual.* New York: Oxford University Press.

Berdie, R. F. (1950). Scores on the SVIB and the Kuder Preference Record in relation to self-ratings. *Journal of Applied Psychology, 34,* 42–49.

Berg, I. A. (1955). Response bias and personality: The deviation hypothesis. *Journal of Psychology, 40,* 60–71.

Berg, I. A. (1959). The unimportance of test item content. In B. M. Bass & I. A. Berg (Eds.), *Objective approaches to personality assessment* (pp. 83–99). Princeton, NJ: D. Van Nostrand.

Bergan, J. R. (1977). *Behavioral consultation.* Columbus, OH: Charles E. Merrill.

Bergan, J. R., & Kratochwill, T. R. (1990). *Behavioral consultation in applied settings.* New York: Plenum Press.

Bergland, B. (1974). Career planning: The use of sequential evaluated experience. In E. L. Herr (Ed.), *Vocational guidance and human development.* Boston, MA: Houghton Mifflin.

Bergner, M., Bobbitt, R. A., Carter, W. B., Gilson, B. S. (1981). The Sickness Impact Profile: Development and final revision of a health status measure. *Medical Care, 19*, 787–785.

Bergner, M., Bobbitt, R. A., Kressel, S., et al. (1976). The Sickness Impact Profile: Conceptual foundation and methodology for the development of a health status measure. *International Journal of Health Service, 6*, 393–415.

Bergner, M., & Rothman, M. L. (1987). Health status measures: An overview and guide for selection. *Annual Review of Public Health, 8*, 191–210.

Berk, R. A. (1982). *Handbook of methods for detecting test bias*. Baltimore, MD: Johns Hopkins University Press.

Berk, R. A. (Ed.) (1984). *A guide to criterion-referenced test construction*. Baltimore, MD: Johns Hopkins University Press.

Berk, R. A. (1986). A consumer's guide to setting performance standards on criterion-referenced tests. *Review of Educational Research, 56*, 137–172.

Berlinsky, S. (1952). Measurement of the intelligence and personality of the deaf: A review of the literature. *Journal of Speech and Hearing Disorders, 117*, 39–54.

Berman, A., & Hays, T. (1973). Relation between belief in after-life and locus of control. *Journal of Consulting and Clinical Psychology, 41*, 318.

Bernard, L. C., Houston, W., & Natoli, L. (1993). Malingering on neuropsychological memory tests: Potential objective indicators. *Journal of Clinical Psychology, 49*, 45–53.

Berry, D. T. R., Baer, R. A., & Harris, M. J. (1991). Detection of malingering on the MMPI: A meta-analysis. *Clinical Psychology Review, 11*, 585–598.

Berry, J. W. (1974). Radical cultural relativism and the concept of intelligence. In J. W. Berry & P. R. Dasen (Eds.), *Culture and cognition: Readings in cross-cultural psychology* (pp. 225–229). London: Methuen.

Berry, K., & Sherrets, S. (1975). A comparison of the WISC and WISC-R for special education. *Pediatric Psychology, 3*, 14.

Bersoff, D. N. (1970). The revised deterioration formula for the Wechsler Adult Intelligence Scale: A test of validity. *Journal of Clinical Psychology, 26*, 71–73.

Beutler, L. E., Arizmendi, T. G., Crago, M., Shanfield, S., & Hagaman, R. (1983). The effects of value similarity and clients' persuadability on value convergence and psychotherapy improvement. *Journal of Social and Clinical Psychology, 1*, 231–245.

Beutler, L. E., Crago, M., & Arizmendi, T. G. (1986). Research on therapist variables in psychotherapy. In S. L. Garfield & A. E. Bergin (Eds.), *Handbook of psychotherapy and behavior change* (pp. 257–310). New York: Wiley.

Bigler, E. D. (1986). Forensic issues in neuropsychology. In D. Wedding, A. M. Horton, Jr., & J. Webster (Eds.), *The neuropsychology handbook* (pp. 526–547). Berlin: Springer-Verlag.

Bigler, E. D., & Nussbaum, N. L. (1989). Child neuropsychology in the private medical practice. In C. R. Reynolds & E. Fletcher-Janzen (Eds.), *Handbook of clinical child neuropsychology* (pp. 557–572). New York: Plenum Press.

Binder, L. M. (1992). Deception and malingering. In A. E. Puente & R. J. McCaffrey (Eds.), *Handbook of neuropsychological assessment* (pp. 353–374). New York: Plenum Press.

Binder, L. M. (1993). Assignment of malingering after mild head trauma with the Portland Digit Recognition Test. *Journal of Clinical and Experimental Neuropsychology, 15*, 170–182.

Binder, L. M., & Willis, S. C. (1991). Assessment of motivation after financially compensable minor head trauma. *Psychological Assessment, 3*, 175–181.

Binet, A., & Simon, T. (1905). Methodes nouvelles pour le diagnostic du niveau intellectual des anormaux. *Annee Psychologique, 11*, 191–244.

Birren, J. E., & Birren, B. A. (1990). The concepts, models, and history of the psychology of aging. In J. E. Birren, & K. W. Schaie (Eds.), *Handbook of the psychology of aging* (3rd ed., pp. 3–20). New York: Academic Press.

Bishop, D., & Butterworth, G. E. (1979). A longitudinal study using the WPPSI and WISC-R with an English sample. *British Journal of Educational Psychology, 49*, 156–168.

Blanchard, R., Klassen, P., Dickey, R., Kuban, M. E., & Blak, T. (2001). Sensitivity and specificity of the Phallometric test for pedophilia in nonadmitting sex offenders. *Psychological Assessment, 13*, 118–126.

Blankstein, K. R., Flett, G. L., & Koledin, S. (1991). The Brief College Student Hassles Scale: Development, validation, and relation with pessimism. *Journal of College Student Development, 32*, 258–264.

Blau, T. H. (1991). *The psychological examination of the child*. New York: Wiley.

Blazer, D., Hughes, D. C., & George, L. K. (1987). The epidemiology of depression in an elderly community population. *The Gerontologist, 27*, 281–287.

Block, J. (1957). A comparison between ipsative and normative ratings of personality. *Journal of Abnormal and Social Psychology, 54*, 50–54.

Block, J. (1961). The Q-sort method in personality assessment and psychiatric research. Springfield, IL: Charles C Thomas.

Block, J. (1978). *The Q-sort method*. Palo Alto, CA: Consulting Psychologists Press.

Block, J. (1981). Some enduring and consequential structures of personality. In A. I. Rabin (Ed.), *Further explorations in personality*. New York: Wiley InterScience.

Block, J., Weiss, D. S., & Thorne, A. (1979). How relevant is a semantic similarity interpretation of ratings? *Journal of Personality and Social Psychology*, 37, 1055–1074.

Bloom, A. S., & Raskin, L. M. (1980). WISC-R Verbal-Performance IQ discrepancies: A comparison of learning disabled children to the normative sample. *Journal of Clinical Psychology*, 36, 322–323.

Bloom, A. S., Reese, A., Altshuler, L., Meckler, C. L., & Raskin, L. M. (1983). IQ discrepancies between the Binet and WISC-R in children with developmental problems. *Journal of Clinical Psychology*, 39, 600–603.

Bloom, B. (Ed.) (1956). *Taxonomy of educational objectives. Handbook 1: Cognitive domain*. New York: Longmans, Green & Co.

Bloom, L., & Lahey, M. (1978). *Language development and language disorders*. New York: Wiley.

Blum, G. S. (1950). *The Blacky Pictures*. Cleveland, OH: The Psychological Corporation.

Blum, J. E., Fosshage, J. L., & Jarvix, L. F. (1972). Intellectual changes and sex differences in octogenarians: A twenty-year longitudinal study of aging. *Developmental Psychology*, 7, 178–187.

Blumenthal, M. (1975). Measuring depressive symptomatology in a general population. *Archives of General Psychiatry*, 34, 971–978.

Bochner, S. (1978). Reliability of the Peabody Picture Vocabulary Test: A review of 32 selected research studies published between 1965 and 1974. *Psychology in the Schools*, 15, 320–327.

Boehm, A. E. (1971). *Boehm Test of Basic Concepts*. New York: The Psychological Corporation.

Boehm, V. R. (1968). Mr. Prejudice, Miss Sympathy, and the authoritarian personality: An application of psychological measuring techniques to the problem of jury bias. *Wisconsin Law Review*, 734–750.

Bogardus, E. S. (1925). Measuring social distance. *Journal of Applied Sociology*, 9, 299–308.

Boldt, R. F. (1986). Generalization of SAT validity across colleges. *ETS Research Report*, #86–24.

Bolt, M. (1978). The Rokeach Value Survey: Preferred or preferable? *Perceptual and Motor Skills*, 47, 322.

Bolton, B. (Ed.) (1990). *Special education and rehabilitation testing: Practical applications and test reviews*. Austin, TX: Proed, Applied Testing Series.

Bolton, B. (1995). Review of the Inwald Personality Inventory. In J. C. Conoley & J. C. Impara (Eds.), *The twelfth mental measurements yearbook* (pp. 501–503). Lincoln, NB: The University of Nebraska Press.

Bondy, M. (1974). Psychiatric antecedents of psychological testing (before Binet). *Journal of the History of the Behavioral Sciences*, 10, 180–194.

Booth-Kewley, S., Edwards, J. E., & Rosenfeld, P. (1992). Impression management, social desirability, and computer administration of attitude questionnaires: Does the computer make a difference? *Journal of Applied Psychology*, 77, 562–566.

Booth-Kewley, S., Rosenfeld, P., & Edwards, J. E. (1992). Impression management and self-deceptive enhancement among Hispanic and non-Hispanic white Navy recruits. *Journal of Social Psychology*, 132, 323–329.

Borgatta, E. F. (1964). The structure of personality characteristics. *Behavioral Science*, 9, 8–17.

Borgen, F. H. (1986). New approaches to the assessment of interests. In W. B. Walsh & S. H. Osipow (Eds.), *Advances in vocational psychology* (Vol. 1, pp. 83–125). Hillsdale, NJ: Erlbaum.

Borgen, F. H., & Harper, G. T. (1973). Predictive validity of measured vocational interests with black and white college men. *Measurement and Evaluation in Guidance*, 6, 19–27.

Boring, E. G. (1957). *A history of experimental psychology*. New York: Appleton-Century-Crofts.

Boring, E. G. (1965). On the subjectivity of important historical dates: Leipzig, 1879. *Journal of the History of the Behavioral Sciences*, 1, 5–9.

Bornstein, P. H., Bridgwater, C. A., Hickey, J. S., & Sweeney, T. M. (1980). Characteristics and trends in behavioral assessment: An archival analysis. *Behavioral Assessment*, 2, 125–133.

Bornstein, R. F. (1999). Criterion validity of objective and projective dependency tests: A metaanalytic assessment of behavioral prediction. *Psychological Assessment*, 11, 48–57.

Bornstein, R. F., Hill, E. L., Robinson, K. J., Calabrese, C., & Bowers, K. S. (1996). Internal reliability of Rorschach Oral Dependency Scale scores. *Educational and Psychological Measurement*, 56, 130–138.

Bortner, M. (1965). Review of the Progressive Matrices. In O. K. Borum, R., & Grisso, T. (1995). Psychological test use in criminal forensic evaluations. *Professional Psychology*, 26, 465–473.

Borum, R., & Grisso, T. (1995). Psychological test use in criminal forensic evaluations. *Professional Psychology: Research and Practice*, 26, 465–473.

Bosman, F., Hoogenboom, J., & Walpot, G. (1994). An interactive video test for pharmaceutical chemist's assistants. *Computers in Human Behavior*, 10, 51–62.

Boswell, D. L., & Pickett, J. A. (1991). A study of the internal consistency and factor structure of the Verbalizer-Visualizer Questionnaire. *Journal of Mental Imagery, 15,* 33–36.

Boudreau, R. A., Killip, S. M., MacInnis, S. H., Milloy, D. G., & Rogers, T. B. (1983). An evaluation of Graduate Record Examinations as predictors of graduate success in a Canadian context. *Canadian Psychology, 24,* 191–199.

Bouman, T. K., & Luteijn, F. (1986). Relations between the Pleasant Events Schedule, depression, and other aspects of psychopathology. *Journal of Abnormal Psychology, 95,* 373–377.

Bowman, M. L. (1989). Testing individual differences in ancient China. *American Psychologist, 44,* 576–578.

Boyd, M. E., & Ward, G. (1967). Validities of the D-48 test for use with college students. *Educational and Psychological Measurement, 27,* 1137–1138.

Boyle, G. J. (1989). Confirmation of the structural dimensionality of the Stanford-Binet Intelligence Scale (4th ed.). *Personality and Individual Differences, 10,* 709–715.

Bracken, B. A. (1981). McCarthy Scales as a learning disability diagnostic aid: A closer look. *Journal of Learning Disabilities, 14,* 128–130.

Bracken, B. A. (1984). *Bracken Basic Concept Scale.* San Antonio, TX: The Psychological Corporation.

Bracken, B. A. (1985). A critical review of the Kaufman Assessment Battery for Children (K-ABC). *School Psychology Review, 14,* 21–36.

Bracken, B. A. (1987). Limitations of preschool instruments and standards for minimal levels of technical adequacy. *Journal of Psychoeducational Assessment, 5,* 313–326.

Bracken, B. A. (1991). The assessment of preschool children with the McCarthy Scales of Children's Abilities. In B. A. Bracken (Ed.), *The Psychoeducational assessment of preschool children* (2nd. ed., pp. 53–85). Boston, MA: Allyn & Bacon.

Bracken, B. A., Prasse, D. P., & McCallum, R. S. (1984). Peabody Picture Vocabulary Test-Revised: An appraisal and review. *School Psychology Review, 13,* 49–60.

Bradburn, N. M., & Caplovitz, D. (1965). *Reports on happiness.* Chicago, IL: Aldine.

Braden, J. P. (1984). The factorial similarity of the WISC-R Performance Scale in deaf and hearing samples. *Journal of Personality and Individual Differences, 4,* 403–410.

Braden, J. P. (1985). The structure of nonverbal intelligence in deaf and hearing subjects. *American Annals of the Deaf, 130,* 496–501.

Braden, J. P. (1989). The criterion-related validity of the WISC-R Performance Scale and other nonverbal IQ tests for deaf children. *American Annals of the Deaf, 134,* 329–332.

Braden, J. P. (1990). Do deaf persons have a characteristic psychometric profile on the Wechsler Performance Scales? *Journal of Psychoeducational Assessment, 8,* 518–526.

Braden, J. P. (1992). The Differential Ability Scales and Special Education. *Journal of Psychoeducational Assessment, 10,* 92–98.

Bradley, R. H., & Caldwell, B. M. (1974). Issues and procedures in testing young children. *Eric TM Report, #37.* Princeton, NJ: Educational Testing Service.

Bradley, R. H., & Caldwell, B. M. (1977). Home observation for measurement of the environment: A validation study of screening efficiency. *American Journal of Mental Deficiency, 81,* 417–420.

Bradley, R. H., & Caldwell, B. M. (1979). Home observation for measurement of the environment: A revision of the Preschool Scale. *American Journal of Mental Deficiency, 84,* 235–244.

Bradley, R. H., Caldwell, B. M., & Elardo, R. (1977). Home environment, social status, and mental test performance. *Journal of Educational Psychology, 69,* 697–701.

Bragman, R. (1982). Effects of different methods of conveying test directions on deaf children's performance on pattern recognition tasks. *Journal of Rehabilitation of the Deaf, 16,* 17–26.

Bragman, R. (1982). Review of research on test instructions for deaf children. *American Annals of the Deaf, 127,* 337–346.

Braithwaite, V. A., & Law, H. G. (1985). Structure of human values: Testing the adequacy of the Rokeach Value Survey. *Journal of Personality and Social Psychology, 49,* 250–263.

Brannick, M. T., Michaels, C. E., & Baker, D. P. (1989). Construct validity of in-basket scores. *Journal of Applied Psychology, 74,* 957–963.

Brannigan, G. G., Aabye, S. M., Baker, L. A., & Ryan, G. T. (1995). Further validation of the qualitative scoring system for the modified Bender-Gestalt Test. *Psychology in the Schools, 32,* 24–26.

Brauer, B. A. (1993). Adequacy of a translation of the MMPI into American Sign Language for use with deaf individuals: Linguistic equivalency issues. *Rehabilitation Psychology, 38,* 247–260.

Braun, P. R., & Reynolds, D. N. (1969). A factor analysis of a 100-item fear survey inventory. *Behaviour Research and Therapy, 7,* 399–402.

Bray, D. W. (1982). The assessment center and the study of lives. *American Psychologist, 37,* 180–189.

Brazelton, T. B. (1973). *Neonatal Behavioral Assessment Scale* (Clinics in Developmental Medicine, No. 50). Philadelphia, PA: J. B. Lippincott.

Brazelton, T. B., Robey, J. S., & Collier, G. (1969). Infant development in the Zinacanteco Indians of Southern Mexico. *Pediatrics, 44,* 274–293.

Breckler, S. J. (1984). Empirical validation of affect, behavior, and cognition as distinct components of attitude. *Journal of Personality and Social Psychology, 47,* 1191–1205.

Breen, M. J., Carlson, M., & Lehman, J. (1985). The revised developmental test of visual-motor integration: Its relation to the VMI, WISC-R, and Bender Gestalt for a group of elementary aged learning disabled students. *Journal of Learning Disabilities, 18,* 136–138.

Breland, H. M., & Ironson, G. H. (1976). DeFunis reconsidered: A comparative analysis of alternative admissions strategies. *Journal of Educational Measurement, 13,* 89–99.

Brennan, R. L. (1983). *Elements of generalizability theory.* Iowa City, IO: ACT Publications.

Bretz, R. D., Jr., Ash, R. A., & Dreher, G. F. (1989). Do people make the place? An examination of the attraction-selection-attrition hypothesis. *Personnel Psychology, 42,* 561–581.

Bridgeman, B., & Lewis, C. (1994). The relationship of essay and multiple-choice scores with grades in college courses. *Journal of Educational Measurement, 31,* 37–50.

Brigance, A. H. (1978). *Brigance Diagnostic Inventory of Early Development.* Billerica, MA: Curriculum Associates.

Briggs, S. R. (1992). Assessing the five-factor model of personality description. *Journal of Personality, 60,* 253–293.

Bringmann, W. G., Balance, W. D. G., & Evans, R. B. (1975). Wilhelm Wundt 1832–1920: A brief biographical sketch. *Journal of the History of the Behavioral Sciences, 11,* 287–297.

Brislin, R. W. (1970). Back-translation for cross-cultural research. *Journal of Cross-Cultural Psychology, 1,* 185–216.

Brodsky, S. (1989). Advocacy in the guise of scientific objectivity: An examination of Faust and Ziskin. *Computers in Human Behavior, 5,* 261–264.

Brody, N. (1985). The validity of tests of intelligence. In B. B. Wolman (Ed.), *Handbook of intelligence* (pp. 353–389). New York: Wiley.

Broen, W. E., Jr., & Wirt, R. D. (1958). Varieties of response sets. *Journal of Consulting Psychology, 22,* 237–240.

Brooks, C. M., Jackson, J. R., Hoffman, H. H., & Hand, G. S., Jr. (1981). Validity of the new MCAT for predicting GPA and NBME Part 1 Examination Performance. *Journal of Medical Education, 56,* 767–769.

Brooks, C. R. (1977). WISC, WISC-R, SB L & M, WRAT: Relationships and trends among children ages six to ten referred for psychological evaluation. *Psychology in the Schools, 14,* 30–33.

Brown, A. L. (1978). Knowing when, where, and how to remember: A problem of metacognition. In R. Glaser (Ed.), *Advances in instructional psychology* (Vol. 1, pp. 77–165). Hillsdale, NJ: Erlbaum.

Brown, D. C. (1994). Subgroup norming: Legitimate testing practice or reverse discrimination? *American Psychologist, 49,* 927–928.

Brown, F. (1979). The SOMPA: A system of measuring potential abilities? *School Psychology Digest, 8,* 37–46.

Brown, F. G. (1976). *Principles of educational and psychological testing* (2nd ed.). New York: Holt, Rinehart and Winston.

Brown, H. S., & May, A. E. (1979). A test-retest reliability study of the Wechsler Adult Intelligence Scale. *Journal of Consulting and Clinical Psychology, 47,* 601–602.

Brown, I. S. (1984). Development of a scale to measure attitude toward the condom as a method of birth control. *The Journal of Sex Research, 20,* 255–263.

Brown, S. A., Goldman, M. S., Inn, A., & Anderson, L. R. (1980). Expectations of reinforcement from alcohol: Their domain and relation to drinking patterns. *Journal of Consulting and Clinical Psychology, 48,* 419–426.

Brown, S. H. (1978). Long-term validity of a personal history item scoring procedure. *Journal of Applied Psychology, 63,* 673–676.

Brown, S. R. (1980). *Political subjectivity: Application of Q methodology in political science.* New Haven, CT: Yale University Press.

Brown, T. L. (1991). Concurrent validity of the Stanford-Binet (4th ed.) Agreement with the WISC-R in classifying learning disabled children. *Psychological Assessment, 3,* 247–253.

Brozek, J. (1972). To test or not to test: Trends in the Soviet views. *Journal of the History of the Behavioral Sciences, 8,* 243–248.

Bruce, M. M., & Learner, D. B. (1958). A supervisory practices test. *Personnel Psychology, 11,* 207–216.

Bruch, M. A. (1977). Psychological Screening Inventory as a predictor of college student adjustment. *Journal of Consulting and Clinical Psychology, 45,* 237–244.

Bruck, M., Ceci, S. J., & Hembrooke, H. (1998). Reliability and credibility of young children's reports. *American Psychologist, 53,* 136–151.

Bruhn, A. R., & Reed, M. R. (1975). Simulation of brain damage on the Bender-Gestalt Test by college students. *Journal of Personality Assessment, 3,* 244–255.

Bruininks, R. H. (1978). *Bruininks-Oseretsky Test of Motor Proficiency, examiner's manual*. Circle Pines, MN: American Guidance Service.

Bruvold, W. H. (1968). Scales for rating the taste of water. *Journal of Applied Psychology, 52*, 245–253.

Bruvold, W. H. (1975). Judgmental bias in the rating of attitude statements. *Educational and Psychological Measurement, 35*, 605–611.

Buck, J. N. (1966). *The House-Tree-Person technique: Revised manual*. Beverly Hills, CA: Western Psychological Services.

Buckhalt, J. A. (1986). Test review of the British Ability Scales. *Journal of Psychoeducational Assessment, 4*, 325–332.

Buckhalt, J. A. (1990). Criterion-related validity of the British Ability Scales Short-Form for black and white children. *Psychological Reports, 66*, 1059–1066.

Buckhalt, J. A. (1991). Test review of the Wechsler Preschool and Primary Scale of Intelligence – Revised. *Journal of Psychoeducational Assessment, 9*, 271–279.

Buckhalt, J. A., Denes, G. E., & Stratton, S. P. (1989). Validity of the British Ability Scales Short-Form for a sample of U.S. students. *School Psychology International, 10*, 185–191.

Budoff, M., & Friedman, M. (1964). "Learning potential" as an assessment approach to the adolescent mentally retarded. *Journal of Consulting Psychology, 28*, 433–439.

Buechley, R., & Ball, H. (1952). A new test of "validity" for the group MMPI. *Journal of Consulting Psychology, 16*, 299–301.

Burden, R. L., & Fraser, B. J. (1993). Use of classroom environment assessments in school psychology: A British perspective. *Psychology in the Schools, 30*, 232–240.

Burg, C., Quinn, P. O., & Rapoport, J. L. (1978). Clinical evaluation of one-year-old infants: Possible predictors of risk for the "hyperactivity syndrome." *Journal of Pediatric Psychology, 3*, 164–167.

Burgemeister, B. B., Blum, L., & Lorge, I. (1972). *Columbia Mental Scale*. New York: Harcourt, Brace, Jovanovich.

Burger, G. K. (1975). A short form of the California Psychological Inventory. *Psychological Reports, 37*, 179–182.

Burgess, A. (1991). Profile analysis of the Wechsler Intelligence Scales: A new index of subtest scatter. *British Journal of Clinical Psychology, 30*, 257–263.

Burgess, E. W., & Cottrell, L. S. (1939). *Predicting success or failure in marriage*. New York: Prentice Hall.

Burisch, M. (1984). Approaches to personality inventory construction. *American Psychologist, 39*, 214–227.

Burke, H. R. (1972). Raven's Progressive Matrices: validity, reliability, and norms. *The Journal of Psychology, 82*, 253–257.

Burke, H. R., & Bingham, W. C. (1969). Raven's Progressive Matrices: More on construct validity. *The Journal of Psychology, 72*, 247–251.

Burke, M. J., & Normand, J. (1987). Computerized psychological testing: Overview and critique. *Professional Psychology: Research and Practice, 18*, 42–51.

Burke, M. J., Normand, J., & Raju, N. S. (1987). Examinee attitudes toward computer-administered ability testing. *Computers in Human Behavior, 3*, 95–107.

Burkhart, B. R., Christian, W. L., & Gynther, M. D. (1978). Item subtlety and the MMPI: A paradoxical relationship. *Journal of Personality Assessment, 42*, 76–80.

Burnam, M. A., Telles, C. A., Karno, M., Hough, R. L., & Escobar, J. I. (1987). Measurement of acculturation in a community population of Mexican Americans. *Hispanic Journal of Behavioral Sciences, 9*, 105–130.

Buros, O. K. (Ed.). *The sixth mental measurements yearbook* (pp. 762–765). Highland Park, NJ: The Gryphon Press.

Buss, A. H. (1989). Personality as traits. *American Psychologist, 44*, 1378–1388.

Buss, A. R. (1976). Galton and the birth of differential psychology and eugenics: Social, political, and economic forces. *Journal of the History of the Behavioral Sciences, 12*, 47–58.

Buss, D. M., & Scheier, M. F. (1976). Self-consciousness, self-awareness, and self-attribution. *Journal of Research in Personality, 10*, 463–468.

Butcher, J. N. (1978). Automated MMPI interpretative systems. In O. K. Buros (Ed.), *Eighth mental measurements yearbook* (pp. 942–945). Highland Park, NJ: Gryphon Press.

Butcher, J. N. (1979). Use of the MMPI in personnel selection. In J. N. Butcher (Ed.), *New developments in the use of the MMPI*. Minneapolis, MN: University of Minnesota Press.

Butcher, J. N. (1990). *MMPI-2 in psychological treatment*. New York: Oxford University Press.

Butcher, J. N. (Ed.) (1996). *International adaptations of the MMPI-2*. Minneapolis, MN: University of Minnesota Press.

Butcher, J. N., Dahlstrom, W. G., Graham, J. R., Tellegen, A., & Kaemmer, B. (1989). *Manual for administration and scoring: Minnesota Multiphasic Personality Inventory-2: (MMPI-2)*. Minneapolis: University of Minnesota Press.

Butcher, J. N., Graham, J. R., Williams, C. L., & Ben-Porath, Y. S. (1990). *Development and use of the MMPI-2 content scales*. Minneapolis, MN: University of Minnesota Press.

Butcher, J. N., Keller, L. S., & Bacon, S. F. (1985). Current developments and future directions in computerized personality assessment. *Journal of Consulting and Clinical Psychology*, 53, 803–815.

Butcher, J. N., & Owen, P. (1978). Objective personality inventories: Recent research and some contemporary issues. In B. B. Wolman (Ed.), *Clinical diagnosis of mental disorders: A handbook* (pp. 475–546). New York: Plenum.

Byrne, B. M., & Baron, P. (1994). Measuring adolescent depression: Tests of equivalent factorial structure for English and French versions of the Beck Depression Inventory. *Applied Psychology: An International Review*, 43, 33–47.

Byrnes, J. P., & Takahira, S. (1993). Explaining gender differences on SAT-Math items. *Developmental Psychology*, 29, 805–810.

Bzoch, K. R., & League, R. (1971). *Assessing language skills in infancy: A handbook for multidimensional analysis of emergent language*. Gainesville, FL: Tree of Life Press.

Cacioppo, J. T., Petty, R. E., & Geen, T. R. (1989). Attitude structure and function: From the tripartite to the homeostasis model of attitudes. In A. R. Pratkanis, S. J. Breckler, & A. G. Greenwald (Eds.), *Attitude structure and function* (pp. 275–309). Hillsdale, NJ: Erlbaum.

Cain, L. F., Levine, S., & Elzey, F. F. (1977). *Manual for the Cain-Levine Social Competency Scale*. Palo Alto, CA: Consulting Psychologists Press.

Cairns, R. B., & Green, J. A. (1979). How to assess personality and social patterns: Observations or ratings? In R. B. Cairns & J. A. Green (Eds.), *The analysis of social interactions*. Hillsdale, NJ: Erlbaum.

Cairo, P. C. (1979). The validity of the Holland and Basic Interest Scales of the Strong Vocational Interest Blank: Leisure activities vs. occupational membership as criteria. *Journal of Vocational Behavior*, 15, 68–77.

Caldwell, A. B. (2001). What do the MMPI scales fundamentally measure? Some hypotheses. *Journal of Personality Assessment*, 76, 1–17.

Camara, W. L., & Schneider, D. L. (1994). Integrity tests: Facts and unresolved issues. *American Psychologist*, 49, 112–119.

Campbell, A., Converse, P. E., & Rodgers, W. L. (1976). *The quality of American life*. New York: Russell Sage Foundation.

Campbell, D. P. (1966). The stability of vocational interests within occupations over long time spans. *Personnel and Guidance Journal*, 44, 1012–1019.

Campbell, D. P. (1971). *Handbook for the Strong Vocational Interest Blank*. Stanford, CA: Stanford University.

Campbell, D. P. (1974). *Manual for the Strong-Campbell Interest Inventory*. Stanford, CA: Stanford University.

Campbell, D. P., & Hansen, J. C. (1981). *Manual for the SVIB-SCII* (3rd ed.). Stanford, CA: Stanford University.

Campbell, D. T. (1960). Recommendations for APA test standards regarding construct, trait, and discriminant validity. *American Psychologist*, 15, 546–553.

Campbell, D. T., & Fiske, D. W. (1959). Convergent and discriminant validation by the multitrait-multimethod matrix. *Psychological Bulletin*, 56, 81–105.

Campbell, J. M., Amerikaner, M., Swank, P., & Vincent, K. (1989). The relationship between the Hardiness Test and the Personal Orientation Inventory. *Journal of Research in Personality*, 23, 373–380.

Campbell, J. P. (1990). An overview of the Army selection and classification project (Project A). *Personnel Psychology*, 43, 231–239.

Canfield, A. A. (1951). The "sten" scale – A modified C scale. *Educational and Psychological Measurement*, 11, 295–297.

Canivez, G. L., & Watkins, M. W. (1998), Long-term stability of the Wechsler Intelligence Scale for Children – Third Edition. *Psychological Assessment*, 10, 285–291.

Canter, A. H. (1952). MMPI profile in multiple sclerosis. *Journal of Consulting Psychology*, 15, 353–356.

Canter, D. (1969). An intergroup comparison of connotative dimensions in architecture. *Environment and Behavior*, 1, 37–48.

Cardno, J. A. (1955). The notion of attitude: An historical note. *Psychological Reports*, 1, 345–352.

Carey, W. B., & McDevitt, S. C. (1978). Stability and change in individual temperament diagnoses from infancy to early childhood. *Journal of the American Academy of Child Psychiatry*, 17, 331–337.

Carline, J. D., Cullen, T. J., Scott, C. S., Shannon, N. F., & Schaad, D. (1983). Predicting performance during clinical years from the New Medical College Admission Test. *Journal of Medical Education*, 58, 18–25.

Carlson, C. I., & Grotevant, H. D. (1987). A comparative review of family rating scales: Guidelines for clinicians and researchers. *Journal of Family Psychology*, 1, 23–47.

Carlson, J. G. (1985). Recent assessments of the Myers-Briggs Type Indicator. *Journal of Personality Assessment*, 49, 356–365.

Carlson, J. H., & Williams, T. (1993). Perspectives on the seriousness of crimes. *Social Science Research*, 22, 190–207

Carlson, J. S., & Jensen, C. M. (1981). Reliability of the Raven Colored Progressive Matrices Test: Age and ethnic group comparisons. *Journal of Consulting and Clinical Psychology, 49*, 320–322.

Carlyn, M. (1977). An assessment of the Myers-Briggs Type Indicator. *Journal of Personality Assessment, 41*, 461–473.

Carmines, E. G., & Zeller, R. A. (1979). *Reliability and validity assessment.* Beverly Hills, CA: Sage.

Carney, R. N., & Schattgen, S. F. (1994). California Achievement Tests (5th ed.). In D. J. Keyser, & R. C. Sweetland (Eds.), *Test critiques* (Vol. X, pp. 110–119). Austin, TX: Pro-ed.

Carp, A. L., & Shavzin, A. R. (1950). The susceptibility to falsification of the Rorschach psychodiagnostic technique. *Journal of Consulting Psychology, 14*, 230–233.

Carpenter, P. A., Just, M. A., & Shell, P. (1990). What one intelligence test measures: A theoretical account of the processing in the Raven Progressive Matrices Test. *Psychological Review, 97*, 404–431.

Carr, A. C., Ghosh, A., & Ancil, R. J. (1983). Can a computer take a psychiatric history? *Psychological Medicine, 13*, 151–158.

Carr, A. C., Wilson, S. L., Ghosh, A., Ancill, R. J., & Woods, R. T. (1982). Automated testing of geriatric patients using a microcomputer-based system. *International Journal of Man-Machine Studies, 17*, 297–300.

Carraher, S. M. (1993). Another look at the dimensionality of a learning style questionnaire. *Educational and Psychological Measurement, 53*, 411–415.

Carrier, M. R., Dalessio, A. T., & Brown, S. H. (1990). Correspondence between estimates of content and criterion-related validity values. *Personnel Psychology, 43*, 85–100.

Carroll, J. B. (1952). Ratings on traits measured by a factored personality inventory. *Journal of Abnormal and Social Psychology, 47*, 626–632.

Carroll, J. B. (1982). The measurement of intelligence. In R. J. Sternberg (Ed.), *Handbook of human intelligence* (pp. 29–120). Cambridge, MA: Cambridge University Press.

Carrow, E. (1973). *Carrow Elicited Language Inventory.* Austin, TX: Learning Concepts.

Carson, K. P., & Gilliard, D. J. (1993). Construct validity of the Miner Sentence Completion Scale. *Journal of Occupational and Organizational Psychology, 66*, 171–175.

Carstensen, L. L., & Cone, J. D. (1983). Social desirability and the measurement of psychological well-being in elderly persons. *Journal of Gerontology, 38*, 713–715.

Carter, B. D., Zelko, F. A. J., Oas. P. T., & Waltonen, S. (1990). A comparison of ADD/H children and clinical controls on the Kaufman Assessment Battery for children (K-ABC). *Journal of Psychoeducational Assessment, 8*, 155–164.

Caruso, J. C. (2000). Reliability generalization of the NWO Personality scales. *Educational and psychological measurement, 60*, 236–254.

Carvajal, H. (1987a). Correlations between scores on Stanford-Binet IV and Wechsler Adult Intelligence Scale-Revised. *Psychological Reports, 61*, 83–86.

Carvajal, H. (1987b). 1986 Stanford-Binet abbreviated forms. *Psychological Reports, 61*, 285–286.

Carvajal, H. (1987c). Relationship between scores of young adults on Stanford-Binet IV and Peabody Picture Vocabulary Test-Revised. *Perceptual and Motor Skills, 65*, 721–722.

Carvajal, H. (1988). Relationships between scores on Stanford-Binet IV and scores on McCarthy Scales of Children's Abilities. *Bulletin of the Psychonomic Society, 26*, 349.

Carvajal, H. (1991). Relationships between scores on Wechsler Preschool and Primary Scale of intelligence-Revised and Stanford-Binet IV. *Psychological Reports, 69*, 23–26.

Carver, R. P. (1974). Two dimensions of tests: Psychometric and edumetric. *American Psychologist, 29*, 512–518.

Carver, R. P. (1992). Reliability and validity of the Speed of Thinking test. *Educational and Psychological Measurement, 52*, 125–134.

Cascio, W. F. (1975). Accuracy of verifiable biographical information blank responses. *Journal of Applied Psychology, 60*, 767–769.

Cascio, W. F., Alexander, R. A., & Barrett, G. V. (1988). Setting cutoff scores: Legal, psychometric, and professional issues and guidelines. *Personnel Psychology, 41*, 1–24.

Cascio, W. F., Outtz, J., Zedeck, S., & Golstein, I. L. (1991). Statistical implications of six methods of test score use in personnel selection. *Human Performance, 4*, 233–264.

Casey, T. A., Kingery, P. M., Bowden, R. G., & Corbett, B. S. (1993). An investigation of the factor structure of the Multidimensional Health Locus of Control Scales in a health promotion program. *Educational and Psychological Measurement, 53*, 491–498.

Cassisi, J. E., & Workman, D. E. (1992). The detection of malingering and deception with a short form of the MMPI-2 based on the L, F, and K scales. *Journal of Clinical Psychology, 48*, 54–58.

Castro, F. G., Furth, P., & Karlow, H. (1984). The health beliefs of Mexican, Mexican American, and Anglo American women. *Hispanic Journal of Behavioral Sciences, 6*, 365–383.

Cates, J. A. (1991). Comparison of human figure drawings by hearing and hearing-impaired children. *The Volta Review. 93*, 31–39.

Catron, D. W., & Thompson, C. C. (1979). Test-retest gains in WAIS scores after four retest intervals. *Journal of Clinical Psychology, 35*, 352–357.

Cattell, R. B. (1943). The description of personality: I. Foundations of trait measurement. *Psychological Review, 50*, 559–594.

Cattell, R. B. (1950). *Personality: A systematic theoretical and factual study.* New York: McGraw-Hill.

Cattell, R. B. (1963). Theory of fluid and crystallized intelligence: A critical experiment. *Journal of Educational Psychology, 54*, 1–22.

Cattell, R. B. (1986). Structured tests and functional diagnoses. In R. B. Cattell & R. C. Johnson (Eds.), *Functional psychological testing.* New York: Brunner-Mazel.

Cattell, R. B. (1987). *Intelligence: Its structure, growth and action.* New York: North Holland.

Cattell, R. B., Cattell, A. K., & Cattell, H. E. (1993). *Sixteen Factor Questionnaire* (5th ed.). Champaign, IL: Institute for Personality and Ability Testing.

Cattell, R. B., Eber, H. W., & Tatsuoka, M. M. (1970). *Handbook for the Sixteen Personality Factor Questionnaire.* Champaign, IL: Institute for Personality and Ability Testing.

Cautilli, P. G., & Bauman, M. K. (1987). Assessment of the visually impaired client. In B. Bolton (Ed.), *Handbook of measurement and evaluation in rehabilitation* (2nd ed., pp. 249–262). Baltimore, MD: Paul H. Brookes.

Cavell, T. A., & Kelley, M. L. (1994). The Checklist of Adolescent Problem Situations. *Journal of Clinical Child Psychology, 23*, 226–238.

Chambers, D. W. (1983). Stereotypic images of the scientist: The Draw-A-Scientist Test. *Science Education, 67*, 255–265.

Champion, V. (1984). Instrument development for health belief model constructs. *Advances in Nursing Science, 6*, 73–85.

Chan, C. K. K., Burtis, P. J., Scardamalia, M., & Bereiter, C. (1992). Constructive activity in learning from text. *American Educational Research Journal, 29*, 97–118.

Chara, P. J., Jr., & Verplanck, W. S. (1986). The Imagery Questionnaire: An investigation of its validity. *Perceptual and Motor Skills, 63*, 915–920.

Chartier, G. M. (1971). A-B therapist variable: Real or imagined? *Psychological Bulletin, 75*, 22–33.

Chase, C. I. (1985). Review of the Torrance Tests of Creative Thinking. In J. V. Mitchell, Jr. (Ed.), *The ninth mental measurements yearbook* (pp. 1486–1487). Lincoln, NB: University of Nebraska.

Chattin, S. H. (1989). School psychologists' evaluation of the K-ABC, McCarthy scales, Stanford-Binet IV, and WISC-R. *Journal of Psychoeducational Assessment, 7*, 112–130.

Chen, G. M. (1994). Social desirability as a predictor of argumentativeness and communication apprehension. *The Journal of Psychology, 128*, 433–438.

Chernyshenko, O. S., & Ones, D. S. (1999). How selective are psychology graduate programs? The effect of the selection ratio on GRE score validity. *Educational and Psychological Measurement, 59*, 951–961.

Cherrick, H. M. (1985). Review of Dental Admission Test. In J. V. Mitchell, Jr. (Ed.), *The ninth mental measurements yearbook* (Vol. 1, pp. 448–449). Lincoln: University of Nebraska Press.

Chinese Culture Connection. (1987). Chinese values and the search for culture-free dimensions of culture. *Journal of Cross-Cultural Psychology, 18*, 143–164.

Christensen, H. T., & Carpenter, G. R. (1962). Value-behavior discrepancies regarding pre-marital coitus in three Western cultures. *American Sociological Review, 27*, 66–74.

Christiansen, N. D., Goffin, R. D., Johnston, N. G., & Rothstein, M. G. (1994). Correcting the 16PF for faking: Effects on criterion-related validity and individual hiring decisions. *Personnel Psychology, 47*, 847–860.

Chua, S. L., Chen, D., & Wong, A. F. L. (1999). Computer anxiety and its correlates: A metaanalysis. *Computers in Human Behavior, 15*, 609–623.

Cibis, G. W., Maino, J. H., Crandall, M. A., Cress, P., Spellman, C. R., & Shores, R. E. (1985). The Parsons Visual Acuity Test for screening children 18 to 48 months old. *Annals of Ophthalmology, 17*, 471–478.

Clarizio, H. F. (1982). Intellectual assessment of Hispanic children. *Psychology in the Schools, 19*, 61–71.

Clark, J. B., & Madison, C. L. (1984). *Manual for the Test of Oral Language.* Austin, TX: Pro-ed.

Clark, L., Gresham, F. M., & Elliott, S. N. (1985). Development and validation of a social skills assessment measure. *Journal of Psychoeducational Assessment, 3*, 347–356.

Clark, M. J., & Grandy, J. (1984). Sex differences in the academic performance of Scholastic Aptitude Test takers. *College Board Report No. 84–8.* New York: College Board Publications.

Cleary, T. A. (1968). Test bias: Prediction of grades of Negro and white students in integrated colleges. *Journal of Educational Measurement, 5*, 115–124.

Cleary, T. A., Humphreys, L. G., Kendrick, S. A., & Wesman, A. (1975). Educational uses of tests with disadvantaged students. *American Psychologist, 30*, 15–41.

Coan, R. W., Fairchild, M. T., & Dobyns, Z. P. (1973). Dimensions of experienced control. *The Journal of Social Psychology, 91*, 53–60.

Coates, S., & Bromberg, P. M. (1973). Factorial structure of the Wechsler Preschool and Primary Scale of

Intelligence between the ages of 4 and 6 1/2. *Journal of Consulting and Clinical Psychology, 40,* 365–370.

Cofer, C. N., Chance, J., & Judson, A. J. (1949). A study of malingering on the Minnesota Multiphasic Personality Inventory. *The Journal of Psychology, 27,* 491–499.

Coffin, T. E. (1941). Some conditions of suggestion and suggestibility: A study of certain attitudinal and situational factors influencing the process of suggestion. *Psychological Monographs, 53* (Whole No. 241).

Coffman, W. E. (1985). Review of the Structure of Intellect Learning Abilities Test. In J. V. Mitchell, Jr. (Ed.), *The ninth mental measurements yearbook* (pp. 1486–1488). Lincoln, NE: University of Nebraska Press.

Cohen, B. H., & Saslona, M. (1990). The advantage of being an habitual visualizer. *Journal of Mental Imagery, 14,* 101–112.

Cohen, J. (1950). Wechsler Memory Scale performance of psychoneurotic, organic, and schizophrenic groups. *Journal of Consulting Psychology, 14,* 371–375.

Cohen, J. (1957). The factorial structure of the WAIS between early adulthood and old age. *Journal of Consulting Psychology, 21,* 283–290.

Cohen, J. (1960). A coefficient of agreement for nominal scales. *Educational and Psychological Measurement, 20,* 37–46.

Cohen, J., & Cohen, P. (1983). *Applied multiple regression/correlation analysis for the behavioral sciences* (2nd ed.). Hillsdale, NJ: Erlbaum.

Cohen, J., & Lefkowitz, J. (1974). Development of a biographical inventory blank to predict faking on personality tests. *Journal of Applied Psychology, 59,* 404–405.

Cohen, J. B. (1990). Misuse of computer software to detect faking on the Rorschach: A reply to Kahn, Fox, and Rhode. *Journal of Personality Assessment, 54,* 58–62.

Cohn, S. J. (1985). Review of Graduate Record Examination. In J. V. Mitchell, Jr. (Ed.), *The ninth mental measurements yearbook* (Vol. 1, pp. 622–624). Lincoln: University of Nebraska Press.

Cole, D. A. (1987). Utility of confirmatory factor analysis in test validation research. *Journal of Consulting and Clinical Psychology, 55,* 584–594.

Cole, K. N., & Fewell, R. R. (1983). A quick language screening test for young children: The token test. *Journal of Psycoeducational Assessment, 1,* 149–154.

Cole, N. (1982). The implications of coaching for ability testing. In A. Wigdor & W. Garner (Eds.), *Ability testing: Uses, consequences, and controversies.* (pp. 389–414). Washington, DC: National Academy Press.

Cole, N. S. (1973). Bias in selection. *Journal of Educational Measurement, 10,* 237–255.

Coleman, J. S. (1966). *Equality of Educational Opportunity.* Washington, DC: U.S. Department of Health, Education, and Welfare.

College Entrance Examination Board. (1988). *1988 profile of SAT and achievement test takers.* New York: Author.

Coller, A. R. (1971). *Self-concept measures: An annotated bibliography.* Princeton, NJ: Educational Testing Service.

Collins, J. M., & Schmidt, F. L. (1993). Personality, integrity, and white collar crime: A construct validity study. *Personnel Psychology, 46,* 295–311.

Compas, B. E., Davis, G. E., Forsythe, C. J., & Wagner, B. M. (1987). Assessment of major and daily stressful events during adolescence: The Adolescent Perceived Events Scale. *Journal of Consulting and Clinical Psychology, 55,* 534–541.

Comrey, A. L. (1958). A factor analysis of items on the F scale of the MMPI. *Educational and Psychological Measurement, 18,* 621–632.

Comunian, A. L. (1985). The development and validation of the Italian form of the Test Anxiety Inventory. In H. M. Van Der Ploeg, R. Schwarzer, & C. D. Spielberger (Eds.), *Advances in Test Anxiety Research* (Vol. 4, pp. 215–220). Lisse, Netherlands: Swets & Zeitlinger.

Cone, J. D. (1977). The relevance of reliability and validity for behavioral assessment. *Behavior Therapy, 8,* 411–426.

Cone, J. D. (1978). The Behavioral Assessment Grid (BAG): A conceptual framework and a taxonomy. *Behavior Therapy, 9,* 882–888.

Cone, J. D., & Foster, S. L. (1991). Training in measurement: Always the bridesmaid. *American Psychologist, 46,* 653–654.

Conners, C. K. (1969). A Teacher Rating Scale for use in drug studies with children. *American Journal of Psychology, 126,* 884–888.

Conners, C. K. (1970). Symptom patterns in hyperkinetic, neurotic, and normal children. *Child Development, 41,* 667–682.

Conners, C. K. (1990). *Conners Rating Scales manual.* North Tonawanda, NY: Multi-Health Systems.

Conners, C. K., Sitarenios, G., Parker, J. D. A., & Epstein, J. N. (1998). The revised Conner's Parent Rating Scale (CPRS-R): Factor structure, reliability, and criterion validity. *Journal of Abnormal Child Psychology, 26,* 257–280.

Conoley, J. C., & Bryant, L. E. (1995). Multicultural family assessment. In J. C. Conoley & E. B. Werth (Eds.), *Family assessment* (pp. 103–129). Lincoln, NE: Buros Institute of Mental Measurements.

Coombs, C. H. (1950). Psychological scaling without a unit of measurement. *Psychological Review, 57,* 145–158.

Coons, P. M., & Fine, C. G. (1990). Accuracy of the MMPI in identifying multiple personality disorder. *Psychological Reports, 66,* 831–834.

Cooper, E. (1991). A critique of six measures for assessing creativity. *Journal of Creative Behavior, 25,* 194–204.

Cooper, K. L., & Gutmann, D. L. (1987). Gender identity and ego mastery style in middle-aged, pre- and post-empty nest women. *The Gerontologist, 27,* 347–352.

Coopersmith, S. (1969). A method of determining types of self-esteem. *Journal of Abnormal Psychology, 59,* 87–94.

Coopersmith, S. (1967). *The antecedents of self-esteem.* San Francisco, CA: W. H. Freeman.

Corach, N. L., Feldman, M. J., Cohen, I. S., Gruen, W., Meadow, A., & Ringwall, E. A. (1958). Social desirability as a variable in the Edwards Personal Preference Schedule. *Journal of Consulting Psychology, 22,* 70–72.

Corach, N. L., & Powell, B. L. (1963). A factor analytic study of the Frostig Developmental Test of Visual Perception. *Perceptual and Motor Skills, 16,* 39–63.

Cornell, D. G., & Hawk, G. L. (1989). Clinical presentation of malingerers diagnosed by experienced forensic psychologists. *Law and Human Behavior, 13,* 375–383.

Cornwell, J. M., Manfredo, P. A., & Dunlap, W. P. (1991). Factor analysis of the 1985 revision of Kolb's Learning Style Inventory. *Educational and Psychological Measurement, 51,* 455–462.

Cortese, M., & Smyth, P. (1979). A note on the translation to Spanish of a measure of acculturation. *Hispanic Journal of Behavioral Sciences, 1,* 65–68.

Cortina, J. M. (1993). What is coefficient alpha? An examination of theory and applications. *Journal of Applied Psychology, 78,* 98–104.

Cortina, J. M., Doherty, M. L., Schmitt, N., Kaufman, G., & Smith, R. G. (1992). The "Big Five" personality factors in the IPI and MMPI: Predictors of police performance. *Personnel Psychology, 45,* 119–140.

Cosden, M. (1987). Rotter Incomplete Sentences Blank. In D. J. Keyser, & R. C. Sweetland (Eds.), *Test critiques compendium.* Kanas City, MO: Test Corporation of America.

Costa, P. T., Jr., & McCrae, R. R. (1980). Still stable after all these years: Personality as a key to some issues in adulthood and old age. In P. B. Baltes & O. G. Brim, Jr. (Eds.), *Life span development and behavior* (Vol. 3, pp. 65–102). New York: Academic Press.

Costa, P. T., Jr., & McCrae, R. R. (1985). *The NEO Personality Inventory manual.* Odessa, FL: Psychological Assessment Resources.

Costa, P. T., Jr., & McCrae, R. R. (1989). *NEO-PI/FFI manual supplement.* Odessa, FL: Psychological Assessment Resources.

Costa, P. T., Jr., & McCrae, R. R. (1992). Normal personality assessment in clinical practice: The NEO Personality Inventory. *Psychological Assessment, 4,* 5–13.

Costantino, G., Malgady, R., & Rogler, L. H. (1988). *Tell-Me-a-Story-TEMAS-Manual.* Los Angeles, CA: Western Psychological Services.

Costantino, G., Malgady, R. G., Rogler, L. H., & Tsui, E. C. (1988). Discriminant analysis of clinical outpatients and public school children by TEMAS: A Thematic Apperception Test for Hispanics and Blacks. *Journal of Personality Assessment, 52* 670–678.

Couch, A., & Keniston, K. (1960). Yeasayers and naysayers: Agreeing response set as a personality variable. *Journal of Abnormal and Social Psychology, 60,* 151–174.

Court, J. H. (1983). Sex differences in performance on Raven's Progressive Matrices: A review. *The Alberta Journal of Educational Research, 29,* 54–74.

Court, J. H. (1988). *A researcher's bibliography for Raven's Progressive Matrices and Mill Hill Vocabulary scales* (7th ed.). Cumberland Park, South Australia: author.

Court, J. H., & Raven, J. C. (1982). *Research and references: 1982 update.* London: H. K. Lewis.

Covin, T. M. (1977). Comparison of WISC and WISC-R full scale IQs for a sample of children in special education. *Psychological Reports, 41,* 237–238.

Craig, H. B. (1965). A sociometric investigation of the self-concept of the deaf child. *American Annals of the Deaf, 110,* 456–474.

Craig, R. J. (1999). Overview and current status of the Millon Clinical Multiaxial Inventory. *Journal of Personality Assessment, 72,* 390–406.

Craik, K. H. (1971). The assessment of places. In P. McReynolds (Ed.), *Advances in psychological assessment* (Vol. 2, pp. 40–62). Palo Alto, CA: Science & Behavior Books.

Cramer, P. (1999). Future directions for the Thematic Apperception Test. *Journal of Personality Assessment, 72,* 74–92.

Crary, W. G., & Johnson, C. W. (1975). The mental status examination. In C. W. Johnson, J. R. Snibbe, & L. E. Evans (Eds.), *Basic psychopathology: A programmed text* (pp. 50–89). New York: Spectrum.

Creaser, J. W. (1960). Factor analysis of a study-habits Q-sort test. *Journal of Counseling Psychology, 7,* 298–300.

Cress, P. J. (1987). Visual assessment. In M. Bullis (Ed.), *Communication development in young children with deaf-blindness: Literature Review III*. Monmouth, OR: Teaching Research Division of Oregon State System of Higher Education.

Crites, J. O. (1978). *Career Maturity Inventory*. Monterey, CA: CTB/McGraw-Hill.

Crockett, B. K., Rardin, M. W., & Pasewark, R. A. (1975). Relationship between WPPSI and Stanford-Binet IQs and subsequent WISC IQs in Headstart children. *Journal of Consulting and Clinical Psychology, 43*, 922.

Crockett, B. K., Rardin, M. W., & Pasewark, R. A. (1976). Relationship of WPPSI and subsequent Metropolitan Achievement Test scores in Headstart children. *Psychology in the Schools, 13*, 19–20.

Cronbach, L. J. (1942). Studies of acquiescence as a factor in the true-false test. *Journal of Educational Psychology, 33*, 401–415.

Cronbach, L. J. (1946). Response sets and test validity. *Educational and Psychological Measurement, 6*, 475–494.

Cronbach, L. J. (1949). Statistical methods applied to Rorschach scores: A review. *Psychological Bulletin, 46*, 393–429.

Cronbach, L. J. (1950). Further evidence on response sets and test design. *Educational and Psychological Measurement, 10*, 3–31.

Cronbach, L. J. (1951). Coefficient alpha and the internal structure of tests. *Psychometrika, 16*, 297–334.

Cronbach, L. J. (1970). *Essentials of psychological testing* (3rd ed.). New York: Harper & Row.

Cronbach, L. J. (1980). Validity on parole: How can we go straight? *New Directions in Test Measurement, 5*, 99–108.

Cronbach, L. J. (1988). Five perspectives on the validity argument. In R. Wainer, & H. I. Braun (Eds.), *Test validity* (pp. 3–17). Hillsdale, NJ: Erlbaum.

Cronbach, L. J., & Gleser, G. C. (1965). *Psychological tests and personnel decisions*. Urbana, IL: University of Illinois Press.

Cronbach, L. J., Gleser, G. C., Rajaratnam, N., & Nanda, H. (1972). *The dependability of behavioral measurements*. New York: Wiley.

Cronbach, L. J., & Meehl, P. E. (1955). Construct validity in psychological tests. *Psychological Bulletin, 52*, 281–302.

Crook, T. H. (1979). Psychometric assessment in the elderly. In A. Raskin & L. F. Jarvik (Eds.), *Psychiatric symptoms and cognitive loss in the elderly: Evaluation and assessment techniques* (pp. 207–220). Washington, DC: Hemisphere.

Crook, T. H., & Larrabee, G. J. (1988). Interrelationships among everyday memory tests: Stability of factor structure of age. *Neuropsychology, 2*, 1–12.

Crook, T. H., & Larrabee, G. J. (1990). A self-rating scale for evaluating memory in everyday life. *Psychology and Aging, 5*, 48–57.

Crosby, L. A., Bitner, M. J., & Gill, J. D. (1990). Organizational structure of values. *Journal of Business Research, 20*, 123–134.

Cross, L. H., Impara, J. C., Frary, R. B., & Jaeger, R. M. (1984). A comparison of three methods for establishing minimum standards on the National Teacher Examinations. *Journal of Educational Measurement, 21*, 113–129.

Cross, O. H. (1947). Braille adaptation of the Minnesota Multiphasic Personality Inventory for use with the blind. *Journal of Applied Psychology, 31*, 189–198.

Crouse, J. (1985). Does the SAT help colleges make better selection decisions? *Harvard Educational Review, 55*, 195–219.

Crowne, D. P., & Marlowe, D. (1960). A new scale of social desirability independent of psychopathology. *Journal of Consulting Psychology, 24*, 349–354.

Crowne, D. P., & Marlowe, D. (1964). *The approval motive: Studies in evaluative dependence*. New York: Wiley.

Cuellar, I., Harris, L. C., & Jasso, R. (1980). An acculturation scale for Mexican American normal and clinical populations. *Hispanic Journal of Behavioral Sciences, 2*, 199–217.

Cummings, J. A. (1986). Projective drawings. In H. M. Knoff (Ed.), *The assessment of child and adolescent personality* (pp. 199–244). New York: Guilford Press.

Cummings, J. A. (1989). Review of the Structure of Intellect Learning Abilities Test. In J. C. Conoley & J. J. Kramer (Eds.), *The tenth mental measurements yearbook* (pp. 787–791). Lincoln, NE: University of Nebraska Press.

Cummings, N. A. (1986). Assessing the computer's impact: Professional concerns. *Computers in Human Behavior, 1*, 293–300.

Cummins, J. P., & Das, J. P. (1980). Cognitive processing, academic achievement, and WISC-R performance in EMR children. *Journal of Consulting and Clinical Psychology, 48*, 777–779.

Cunningham, M. R., Wong, D. T., & Barbee, A. P. (1994). Self-presentation dynamics on overt integrity tests: Experimental studies of the Reid Report. *Journal of Applied Psychology, 79*, 643–658.

Cureton, E. E. (1960). The rearrangement test. *Educational and Psychological Measurement, 20*, 31–35.

Cureton, E. E. (1965). Reliability and validity: Basic assumptions and experimental designs. *Educational and Psychological Measurement, 25*, 327–346.

Cureton, E. E., Cook, J. A., Fischer, R. T., Laser, S. A., Rockwell, N. J., & Simmons, J. W. (1973).

Length of test and standard error of measurement. *Educational and Psychological Measurement, 33,* 63–68.

Cyr, J. J., Doxey, N. C. S., & Vigna, C. M. (1988). Factorial composition of the SCL-90R. *Journal of Social Behavior and Personality, 3,* 245–252.

Dahlstrom, W. G. (1993). Tests: Small samples, large consequences. *American Psychologist, 48,* 393–399.

Dahlstrom, W. G., Brooks, J. D., & Peterson. C. D. (1990). The Beck Depression Inventory: Item order and the impact of response sets. *Journal of Personality Assessment, 55,* 224–233.

Dahlstrom, W. G., Lachar, D., & Dahlstrom, L. E. (1986). *MMPI patterns of American minorities.* Minneapolis: University of Minnesota Press.

Dahlstrom, W. G., Welsh, G. S., & Dahlstrom, L. E. (1972). *An MMPI handbook: Vols. 1 and 2,* Minneapolis: University of Minnesota Press.

Dana, R. H., Feild, K., & Bolton, B. (1983). Variations of the Bender Gestalt Test: Implications for training and practice. *Journal of Personality Assessment, 47,* 76–84.

D'Andrade, R. G. (1965). Trait psychology and componential analysis. *American Anthropologist, 67,* 215–228.

Dannenbaum, S. E., & Lanyon, R. I. (1993). The use of subtle items in detecting deception. *Journal of Personality Assessment, 61,* 501–510.

Darlington, R. B. (1976). A defense of "rational" personnel selection, and two new methods. *Journal of Educational Measurement, 13,* 43–52.

Das, J. P. (1989). Review of the Explorer. In J. C. Conoley & J. J. Kramer (Eds.), *The tenth mental measurements yearbook* (pp. 888–889). Lincoln, NE: University of Nebraska Press.

Das, J. P., Kirby, J. R., & Jarman, R. F. (1979). *Simultaneous and successive cognitive processes.* New York: Academic Press.

Das, J. P., Naglieri, J. A., & Kirby, J. R. (1994). *Assessment of cognitive processes: The PASS.* New York: Allyn & Bacon.

Davey, T., Godwin, J., & Mittelholtz, D. (1997). Developing and scoring an innovative computerized writing assessment. *Journal of Educational Measurement, 34,* 21–41.

Davidson, K., & MacGregor, M. W. (1996). Reliability of an idiographic Q-sort measure of defense mechanisms. *Journal of Personality Assessment, 66,* 624–639.

Davis, C. (1980). *Perkins-Binet Tests of Intelligence for the Blind.* Watertown, MA: Perkins School for the Blind.

Davis, G. A. (1986). *Creativity is forever* (2nd ed.). Dubuque, IA: Kendall-Hunt.

Davis, G. A., & Bull, K. S. (1978). Strengthening affective components of creativity in a college course. *Journal of Educational Psychology, 70,* 833–836.

Davis, W. E. (1975). Race and the differential "power" of the MMPI. *Journal of Personality Assessment, 39,* 141–145.

Davis, W. E., Beck, S. J., & Ryan, T. A. (1973). Race-related and educationally-related MMPI profile differences among hospitalized schizophrenics. *Journal of Clinical Psychology, 29,* 478–479.

Davison, L. A. (1974). Current status of clinical neuropsychology: In R. M. Reitan & L. A. Davison (Eds.), *Clinical neuropsychology: Current status and applications.* New York: Hemisphere.

Davison, M. L. (1985). Multidimensional scaling versus components analysis of test intercorrelations. *Psychological Bulletin, 97,* 94–105.

Dawes, R. M. (1962). A note on base rates and psychometric efficiency. *Journal of Consulting Psychology, 26,* 422–424.

Dean, R. S. (1977). Reliability of the WISC-R with Mexican-American children. *Journal of School Psychology, 15,* 267–268.

Dean, R. S. (1978). Distinguishing learning-disabled and emotionally disturbed children on the WISC-R. *Journal of Consulting and Clinical Psychology, 46,* 381–382.

Dean, R. S. (1979). Predictive validity of the WISC-R with Mexican-American children. *Journal of School Psychology, 17,* 55–58.

Dean, R. S. (1980). Factor structure of the WISC-R with Anglos and Mexican-Americans. *Journal of School Psychology, 18,* 234–239.

Dearborn, G. V. (1898). A study of imaginations. *American Journal of Psychology, 9,* 183–190.

Debra P. v. Turlington, 644 F. 2d 397 (5th Cir. 1981).

Deffenbacher, J. L. (1980). Worry and emotionality in test anxiety. In I. G. Sarason (Ed.), *Test anxiety: Theory, research, and applications* (pp. 111–128). Hillsdale, NJ: Erlbaum.

DeFrancesco, J. J., & Taylor, J. (1993). A validational note on the revised Socialization scale of the California Psychological Inventory. *Journal of Psychopathology and Behavioral Assessment, 15,* 53–56.

DeGiovanni, I. S., & Epstein, N. (1978). Unbinding assertion and aggression in research and clinical practice. *Behavior Modification, 2,* 173–192.

deJonghe, J. F. M., & Baneke, J. J. (1989). The Zung Self-Rating Depression Scale: A replication study on reliability, validity and prediction. *Psychological Reports, 64,* 833–834.

Dekker, R., Drenth, P. J. D., Zaal, J. N., & Koole, F. D. (1990). An intelligence test series for blind and low vision children. *Journal of Visual Impairment and Blindness, 84,* 71–76.

Delaney, E. A., & Hopkins, T. F. (1987). *Examiner's handbook: An expanded guide for fourth edition users.* Chicago, IL: Riverside.

Delhees, K. H., & Cattell, R. B. (1971). *Manual for the Clinical Analysis Questionnaire (CAQ).* Champaign, IL: Institute for Personality and Ability Testing.

DeLongis, A., Coyne, J. C., Dakof, G., Folkman, S., & Lazarus, R. S. (1982). Relationship of daily hassles, uplifts, and major life events to health status. *Health Psychology, 1,* 119–136.

DeLongis, A., Folkman, S., & Lazarus, R. S. (1988). The impact of daily stress on health and mood: Psychological and social resources as mediators. *Journal of Personality and Social Psychology, 54,* 486–495.

DeLuty, R. H. (1988–1989). Physical illness, psychiatric illness, and the acceptability of suicide. *Omega, 19,* 79–91.

DeMinzi, M. C. R. (1990). A new multidimensional Children's Locus of Control Scale. *The Journal of Psychology, 125,* 109–118.

Denman, S. (1984). *Denman Neuropsychological Memory Scale manual.* Charleston, SC: Author.

Denney, D. R., & Sullivan, B. J. (1976). Desensitization and modeling treatments of spider fear using two types of scenes. *Journal of Consulting and Clinical Psychology, 44,* 573–579.

Dennis, K. E. (1986). Q methodology: Relevance and application to nursing research. *Advances in Nursing Science, 8,* 6–17.

Denton, C., & Postwaithe, K. (1985). *Able children: Identifying them in the classroom.* Philadelphia, PA: Nfer-Nelson.

DeRenzi, E., & Vignolo, L. (1962). The Token Test: A sensitive test to detect receptive disturbances in aphasics. *Brain, 85,* 665–678.

Derogatis, L. R. (1987). Self-report measures of stress. In L. Goldberger & S. Breznitz (Eds.), *Handbook of Stress* (pp. 270–294). New York: The Free Press.

Derogatis, L. R. (1977). *The SCL-90 manual: Scoring, administration, and procedures for the SCL-90.* Baltimore, MD: Johns Hopkins University School of Medicine, Clinical Psychometrics Unit.

Derogatis, L. R. (1983). *SCL-90R: Administration, scoring and procedures manual II.* Townson, MD: Clinical Psychometrics Research.

Detterman, D. K. (1992) (Ed.), *Current topics in human intelligence: Vol. 2. Is mind modular or unitary?* Norwood, NJ: Ablex.

Deutsch, F. (1974). Observational and sociometric measures of peer popularity and their relationship to egocentric communication in female preschoolers. *Developmental Psychology, 10,* 745–747.

DeVito, A. J. (1984). Review of Test Anxiety Inventory. In D. J. Keyser & R. C. Sweetland (Eds.), *Test Critiques* (Vol. 1, pp. 673–681). Kansas City, MO: Test Corporation of America.

DeVito, A. J. (1985). Review of Myers-Briggs Type Indicator. In J. V. Mitchell, Jr. (Ed.), *The ninth mental measurements yearbook* (Vol. 2, pp. 1030–1032). Lincoln, NB: University of Nebraska Press.

Dewing, K. (1970). Family influences on creativity: A review and discussion. *The Journal of Special Education, 4,* 399–404.

Deyo, R. A., Diehl, A. K., Hazuda, H., & Stern, M. P. (1985). A simple language-based acculturation scale for Mexican Americans: Validation and application to health care research. *American Journal of Public Health, 75,* 51–55.

Diamond, J. J., & Evans, W. J. (1972). An investigation of the cognitive correlates of testwiseness. *Journal of Educational Measurement, 9,* 145–150.

Diamond, J. J., & Evans, W. J. (1973). The correction for guessing. *Review of Educational Research, 43,* 181–191.

Dicken, C. (1963). Good impression, social desirability, and acquiescence as suppressor variables. *Educational and Psychological Measurement, 23,* 699–720.

Dickinson, T. L., & Zellinger, P. M. (1980). A comparison of the behaviorally anchored rating and mixed standard scale formats. *Journal of Applied Psychology, 65,* 147–154.

Digman, J. M. (1989). Five robust trait dimensions: Development, stability, and utility. *Journal of Personality, 57,* 195–214.

Digman, J. M. (1990). Personality structure: Emergence of the five-factor model. *Annual Review of Psychology, 41,* 417–440.

Digman, J. M., & Inouye, J. (1986). Further specification of the five robust factors of personality. *Journal of Personality and Social Psychology, 50,* 116–123.

Digman, J. M., & Takemoto-Chock, N. K. (1981). Factors in the natural language of personality: Re-analysis, comparison, and interpretation of six major studies. *Multivariate Behavioral Research, 16,* 149–170.

Dillon, R. F., Pohlmann, J. T., & Lohman, D. F. (1981). A factor analysis of Raven's Advanced Progressive Matrices freed of difficulty factors. *Educational and Psychological Measurement, 41,* 1295–1302.

Di Vesta, F. (1965). Developmental patterns in the use of modifiers as modes of conceptualization. *Child Development, 36,* 185–213.

Dobbins, G. H. (1990). How Supervise? In J. Hogan & R. Hogan (Eds.), *Business and Industry Testing* (pp. 472–477). Austin, TX: Pro-ed.

Dodd, S. C. (1935). A social distance test in the Near East. *American Journal of Sociology, 41*, 194–204.

Dodrill, C. B., & Warner, M. H. (1988). Further studies of the Wonderlic Personnel Test as a brief measure of intelligence. *Journal of Consulting and Clinical Psychology, 56*, 145–147.

Dohmen, P., Doll, J., & Feger, H. (1989). A component theory for attitude objects. In A. Upmeyer (Ed.), *Attitudes and behavioral decisions* (pp. 19–59). New York: Springer-Verlag.

Dohrenwend, B. S., & Dohrenwend, B. P. (1978). Some issues in research on stressful life events. *Journal of Nervous and Mental Disease, 166*, 7–15.

Doll, E. A. (1953). *The measurement of social competence. A manual for the Vineland Social Maturity Scale.* Philadelphia: Educational Test Bureau.

Dollinger, S. J. (1989). Predictive validity of the Graduate Record Examination in a Clinical Psychology Program. *Professional Psychology, 20*, 56–58.

Dolliver, R. H. (1969). Strong Vocational Interest Blank vs. expressed vocational interests: A review. *Psychological Bulletin, 72*, 95–107.

Dolliver, R. H., Irwin, J. A., & Bigley, S. E. (1972). Twelve-year follow-up of the Strong Vocational Interest Blank. *Journal of Counseling Psychology, 19*, 212–217.

Domino, G. (1965). Personality traits in institutionalized mongoloids. *American Journal of Mental Deficiency, 69*, 541–547.

Domino, G. (1968). A non-verbal measure of intelligence for totally blind adults. *The New Outlook for the Blind, 62*, 247–252.

Domino, G. (1970). The identification of potentially creative persons from the Adjective Check List. *Journal of Consulting and Clinical Psychology, 35*, 48–51.

Domino, G. (1979). Creativity and the home environment. *Gifted Child Quarterly, 23*, 818–828.

Domino, G. (1980). Chinese Tangrams as a technique to assess creativity. *Journal of Creative Behavior, 14*, 204–213.

Domino, G. (1982). Get high on yourself: The effectiveness of a television campaign on self-esteem, drug use, and drug attitudes. *Journal of Drug Education, 12*, 163–171.

Domino, G. (1984). Measuring geographical environments through adjectives: The Environmental Check List. *Psychological Reports, 55*, 151–160.

Domino, G. (1992). Cooperation and competition in Chinese and American children. *Journal of Cross-Cultural Psychology, 23*, 456–467.

Domino, G. (1994). Assessment of creativity with the ACL: An empirical comparison of four scales. *Creativity Research Journal, 7*, 21–33.

Domino, G., & Acosta, A. (1987). The relation of acculturation and values in Mexican Americans. *Hispanic Journal of Behavioral Sciences, 9*, 131–150.

Domino, G., & Affonso, D. D. (1990). A personality measure of Erikson's life stages: The Inventory of Psychosocial Balance. *Journal of Personality Assessment, 54*, 576–588.

Domino, G., Affonso, D., & Hannah, M. T. (1991). Assessing the imagery of cancer: The Cancer Metaphors Test. *Journal of Psychosocial Oncology, 9*, 103–121.

Domino, G., & Blumberg, E. (1987). An application of Gough's conceptual model to a measure of adolescent self-esteem. *Journal of Youth and Adolescence, 16*, 179–190.

Domino, G., Fragoso, A., & Moreno, H. (1991). Cross-cultural investigations of the imagery of cancer in Mexican nationals. *Hispanic Journal of Behavioral Sciences, 13*, 422–435.

Domino, G., Goldschmid, M., & Kaplan, M. (1964). Personality traits of institutionalized mongoloid girls. *American Journal of Mental Deficiency, 68*, 498–502.

Domino, G., & Hannah, M. T. (1987). A comparative analysis of social values of Chinese and American children. *Journal of Cross-Cultural Psychology, 18*, 58–77.

Domino, G., & Hannah, M. T. (1989). Measuring effective functioning in the elderly: An application of Erikson's theory. *Journal of Personality Assessment, 53*, 319–328.

Domino, G., & Lin, J. (1991). Images of cancer: China and the United States. *Journal of Psychosocial Oncology, 9*, 67–78.

Domino, G., & Lin, W. Y. (1993). Cancer metaphors: Taiwan and the United States. *Personality and Individual Differences, 14*, 693–700.

Domino, G., & Pathanapong, P. (1993). Cancer imagery: Thailand and the United States. *Personality and Individual Differences, 14*, 693–700.

Domino, G., & Regmi, M. P. (1993). Attitudes toward cancer: A cross-cultural comparison of Nepalese and U.S. students. *Journal of Cross-Cultural Psychology, 24*, 389–398.

Donnelly, M., Yindra, K., Long, S. Y., Rosenfeld, P., Fleisher, D., & Chen, C. (1986). A model for predicting performance on the NBME Part I Examination. *Journal of Medical Education, 61*, 123–131.

Donovan, J. M. (1993). Validation of a Portuguese form of Templer's Death Anxiety Scale. *Psychological Reports, 73*, 195–200.

Dorans, N. J., & Lawrence, I. M. (1987). The internal construct validity of the SAT. *ETS Research Report*, No. 87–35.

Dorfman, L., & Mofett, M. (1987). Retirement satisfaction in married and rural women. *The Gerontologist, 27*, 215–221.

Dorken, H., & Greenbloom, G. H. (1953). Psychological investigation of senile dementia. II. The Wechsler-Bellevue Adult Intelligence Scale. *Geriatrics, 8*, 324–333.

Doyle, D., & Forehand, M. J. (1984). Life satisfaction and old age. *Research on Aging, 6*, 432–448.

Doyle, K. O., Jr. (1974). Theory and practice of ability testing in ancient Greece. *Journal of the History of the Behavioral Sciences, 10*, 202–212.

Dozois, D., Dobson, K., & Ahnberg, J. L. (1998). A psychometric evaluation of the Beck Depression Inventory-II. *Psychological Assessment, 10*, 83–89.

Drake, L. E., & Oetting, E. R. (1959). *An MMPI codebook for counselors.* Minneapolis: University of Minnesota Press.

Drasgow, F., & Olson-Buchanan, J. B. (Eds.). (1999). *Innovations in computerized assessment.* Mahwah, NJ: Erlbaum.

Drewes. D. W. (1961). Development and validation of synthetic dexterity tests based on elemental motion analysis. *Journal of Applied Psychology, 45*, 179–185.

Driver, B. L., & Knopf, R. C. (1977). Personality, outdoor recreation, and expected consequences. *Environment and Behavior, 9*, 169–193.

Droege, R. C. (1987). The USES Testing Program. In B. Bolton (Ed.), *Handbook of measurement and evaluation in rehabilitation* (2nd ed., pp. 169–182). Baltimore, MD: Paul H. Brookes.

Dror, I. E., Kosslyn, S. M., & Waag, W. L. (1993). Visual-spatial abilities of pilots. *Journal of Applied Psychology, 78*, 763–773.

Dubinsky, S., Gamble, D. J., & Rogers, M. L. (1985). A literature review of subtle-obvious items on the MMPI. *Journal of Personality Assessment, 49*, 62–68.

DuBois, L. M. (1985). Review of Dental Admission Test. In J. V. Mitchell, Jr. (Ed.), *The ninth mental measurements yearbook* (Vol. 1, pp. 449–450). Lincoln: University of Nebraska Press.

DuBois, P. H. (1966). A test-dominated society: China 1115 B.C. – 1905 A.D. In A. Anastasi (Ed.), *Testing problems in perspective* (pp. 29–36). Washington, DC: American Council on Education.

DuBose, R. F. (1976). Predictive value of infant intelligence scales with multiple handicapped children. *American Journal of Mental Deficiency, 81*, 388–390.

DuBose, R. F. (1981). Assessment of severely impaired young children: Problems and recommendations. *Topics in Early Childhood Special Education, 1*, 9–21.

Dubuisson, D., & Melzack, R. (1976). Classification of clinical pain descriptions by multiple group discriminant analysis. *Experimental Neurology, 51*, 480–487.

Duckworth, J. C. (1991). The Minnesota Multiphasic Personality Inventory-2: A review. *Journal of Counseling and Development, 69*, 564–567.

Dufault, K. J., & Martocchio, B. (1985). Hope: Its spheres and dimensions. *Nursing Clinics of North America, 20*, 379–391.

Dumont, R., & Faro, C. (1993). A WISC-III short form for learning-disabled students. *Psychology in the Schools, 30*, 212–219.

Dunlap, W. R., & Sands, D. I. (1990). Classification of the hearing impaired for independent living using the Vineland Adaptive Behavior Scale. *American Annals of the Deaf, 135*, 384–388.

Dunn, L. M., & Dunn, L. (1981). *Peabody Picture Vocabulary Test-Revised.* Cicle Pines, MN: American Guidance Service.

Dunn, T. F., & Goldstein, L. G. (1959). Test difficulty, validity, and reliability as functions of selected multiple-choice item construction principles. *Educational and Psychological Measurement, 19*, 171–179.

Dunn, T. G., Lushene, R. E., & O'Neil, H. F. (1972). Complete automation of the MMPI and a study of its response latencies. *Journal of Consulting and Clinical Psychology, 39*, 381–387.

Dunnett, S., Koun, S., & Barber, J. (1981). Social desirability in the Eysenck Personality Inventory. *British Journal of Psychology, 72*, 19–26.

Dunnette, M. D., McCartney, J., Carlson, H. C., & Kirchner, W. K. (1962). A study of faking behavior on a forced-choice self-description checklist. *Personnel Psychology, 15*, 13–24.

Dunst, C. J., & Gallagher, J. L. (1983). Piagetian approaches to infant assessment. *Topics in Early Childhood Special Education, 3*, 44–62.

DuPaul, G. J. (1992). Five common misconceptions about the assessment of attention deficit hyperactivity disorder. *The School Psychologist, 10*, 14–15.

Duran, R. P. (1983). *Hispanics' education and background: Predictors of college achievement.* New York: College Entrance Examination Board.

Dusek, J. B. (1980). The development of test anxiety in children. In I. G. Sarason (Ed.), *Test anxiety.* Hillsdale, NJ: Erlbaum.

Dvorak, B. J. (1947). The new USES General Aptitude Test Battery. *Occupations, 26*, 42–44.

Dwyer, C., & Wicenciak, S. (1977). A pilot investigation of three factors of the 16 P. F., Form E, comparing the standard written form with an Ameslan videotape revision. *Journal of Rehabilitation of the Deaf, 10*, 17–23.

Dyal, J. A. (1983). Cross-cultural research with the locus of control construct. In H. M. Lefcourt (Ed.), *Research with the locus of control construct: Vol. 3.*

Extensions and limitations (pp. 209–306). New York: Academic Press.

Dyer, C. O. (1985). Review of the Otis-Lennon School Ability Test. In J. V. Mitchell, Jr. (Ed.), *The ninth mental measurements yearbook* (Vol. 2, pp. 1107–1111). Lincoln, NE: University of Nebraska Press.

Eagly, A. H., & Chaiken, S. (1992). *The psychology of attitudes.* San Diego, CA: Harcourt Brace Janovich.

Ebel, R. L. (1963). The social consequences of educational testing. *Proceedings of the 1963 Invitational Conference on Testing Problems.* (pp. 130–143). Princeton, NJ: Educational Testing Service.

Ebel, R. L. (1969). Expected reliability as a function of choices per item. *Educational and Psychological Measurement, 29,* 565–570.

Ebel, R. L. (1972). *Essentials of educational measurement.* Englewood Cliffs, NJ: Prentice Hall.

Edelbrock, C. S., & Rancurello, M. D. (1985). Childhood hyperactivity: An overview of rating scales and their applications. *Clinical Psychology Review, 5,* 429–445.

Educational Testing Service. (1977). *Graduate Record Examinations technical manual.* Princeton, NJ: Author.

Educational Testing Service. (1994). College Board to recenter scoring scale for PSAT/NMSQT and SAT I. *ETS Developments, 39,* 1–3.

Edward, J. E., & Wilkins, W. (1981). Verbalizer-Visualizer Questionnaire: Relationship with imagery and verbal-visual ability. *Journal of Mental Imagery, 5,* 137–142.

Edwards, A. J. (1971). *Individual Mental Testing.* Part I History and theories. Scranton, PA: Intext Educational.

Edwards, A. L. (1957a). *Techniques of attitude scale construction.* New York: Appleton-Century-Crofts.

Edwards, A. L. (1957b). *The social desirability variable in personality assessment and research.* New York: Dryden.

Edwards, A. L. (1959). *The Edwards Personal Preference Schedule* (Rev. ed.). New York: Psychological Corporation.

Edwards, A. L. (1970). *The measurement of personality traits by scales and inventories.* New York: Holt, Rinehart and Winston, Inc.

Edwards, A. L., & Diers, C. J. (1963). Neutral items as a measure of acquiescence. *Educational and Psychological Measurement, 23,* 687–698.

Edwards, A. L., & Kilpatrick, F. P. (1948). A technique for the construction of attitude scales. *Journal of Applied Psychology, 32,* 374–384.

Edwards, J. R., Baglioni, A. J., Jr., & Cooper, C. L. (1990). Examining relationships among self-report measures of Type A behavior pattern: The effects of dimensionality, measurement error, and differences in underlying constructs. *Journal of Applied Psychology, 75,* 440–454.

Eichman, W. J. (1962). Factored scales for the MMPI: A clinical and statistical manual. *Journal of Clinical Psychology, 18,* 363–395.

Eippert, D. S., & Azen, S. P. (1978). A comparison of two developmental instruments in evaluating children with Down's syndrome. *Physical Therapy, 58,* 1066–1069.

Eisdorfer, C., & Altrocchi, J. (1961). A comparison of attitudes toward old age and mental illness. *Journal of Gerontology, 21,* 455–457.

Eiser, C. (1984). Communicating with sick and hospitalized children. *Journal of Child Psychology and Psychiatry, 25,* 181–189.

Eiser, J. R. (1987). *The expression of attitude.* New York: Springer-Verlag.

Ekman, P. (1965). Differential communication of affect by head and body cues. *Journal of Personality and Social Psychology, 2,* 726–735.

Ekstrom, R. B., French, J. W., & Harman, H. H. (1979). Cognitive factors: Their identification and replication. *Multivariate Behavioral Research,* No. 79–2.

Elbert, J. C. (1984). Training in child diagnostic assessment: A survey of clinical psychology graduate programs. *Journal of Clinical Child Psychology, 13,* 122–133.

Elksnin, L. K., & Elksnin, N. (1993). A review of picture interest inventories: Implications for vocational assessment of students with disabilities. *Journal of Psychoeducational Assessment, 11,* 323–336.

Elliot, G. R., & Eisdorfer, C. (1981). *Stress and human health: Analysis and implications of research.* New York: Springer-Verlag.

Elliott, C. D. (1990a). *Differential Ability Scales: Introductory and technical handbook.* San Antonio, TX: Psychological Corporation.

Elliott, C. D. (1990b). The nature and structure of children's abilities: Evidence from the differential ability scales. *Journal of Psychoeducational Assessment, 8,* 376–390.

Elliott, C. D., & Tyler, S. (1987). Learning disabilities and intelligence test results: A principal components analysis of the British Ability Scales. *British Journal of Psychology, 78,* 325–333.

Ellis, D. (1978). Methods of assessment for use with the visually and mentally handicapped: A selective review. *Childcare, Health and Development, 4,* 397–410.

Elman, L., Blixt, S., & Sawacki, R. (1981). The development of cutoff scores on a WISC-R in the multidimensional assessment of gifted children. *Psychology in the Schools, 18,* 426–428.

Elwood, D. L. (1969). Automation of psychological testing. *American Psychologist, 24,* 287–289.

Elwood, D. L., & Griffin, R. H. (1972). Individual intelligence testing without the examiner: Reliability of an automated method. *Journal of Consulting and Clinical Psychology, 38,* 9–14.

Elwood, R. W. (1993). Psychological tests and clinical discriminations: Beginning to address the base rate problem. *Clinical Psychology Review, 13,* 409–419.

Embretson, S. (1985a). Review of the British Ability Scales. In J. V. Mitchell, Jr. (Ed.), *The ninth mental measurements yearbook* (Vol. 1, pp. 231–232). Lincoln, NE: University of Nebraska Press.

Embretson, S. E. (1985b). Introduction to the problem of test design. In S. E. Embretson (Ed.), *Test design* (pp. 3–17). New York: Academic Press.

Endler, N. S., & Magnusson, D. (1976). *Interactional psychology and personality.* New York: Wiley & Sons.

Endler, N. S., Rutherford, A., & Denisoff, E. (1999). Beck Depression Inventory: Exploring its dimensionality in a nonclinical population. *Journal of Clinical Psychology, 55,* 1307–1312.

Ensor, A., & Phelps, L. (1989). Gender differences on the WAIS-R Performance Scale with young deaf adults. *Journal of the American Deafness and Rehabilitation Association, 22,* 48–52.

Epstein, N., Baldwin, L., & Bishop, D. (1983). The McMaster family assessment device. *Journal of Marital and Family Therapy, 9,* 171–180.

Epstein, S. (1979). The stability of behavior. I. On predicting most of the people much of the time. *Journal of Personality and Social Psychology, 37,* 1097–1126.

Erickson, R. C., Post, R., & Paige, A. (1975). Hope as a psychiatric variable. *Journal of Clinical Psychology, 31,* 324–329.

Erickson, R. C., & Scott, M. (1977). Clinical memory testing: A review. *Psychological Bulletin, 84,* 1130–1149.

Erikson, E. H. (1963). *Childhood and society* (2nd ed.). New York: Norton.

Erikson, E. H. (1980). *Identity and the life cycle.* New York: Norton.

Erikson, E. H. (1982). *The life cycle completed: A review.* New York: Norton.

Eron, L. D. (1950). A normative study of the Thematic Apperception Test. *Psychological Monographs, 64* (No. 9).

Eron, L. D. (1955). Some problems in the research application of the Thematic Apperception Test. *Journal of Projective Techniques, 19,* 125–129.

Eron, L. D., Terry, D., & Callahan, R. (1950). The use of rating scales for emotional tone of TAT stories. *Journal of Consulting Psychology, 14,* 473–478.

Eslinger, P. J., Damasio, A. R., Benton, A. L., & Van Allen, M. (1985). Neuropsychologic detection of abnormal mental decline in older persons. *Journal of the American Medical Association, 253,* 670–674.

Estes, G. D., Harris, J., Moers, F., & Wodrich, D. L. (1976). Predictive validity of the Boehm Test of Basic Concepts for achievement in first grade. *Educational and Psychological Measurement, 36,* 1031–1035.

Estes, W. K. (1974). Learning theory and intelligence. *American Psychologist, 29,* 740–749.

Evans, R. B., & Cohen, J. B. (1987). The American Journal of Psychology: A retrospective. *American Journal of Psychology, 100,* 321–362.

Evans, R. G. (1982). Clinical relevance of the Marlowe-Crowne Scale: A review and recommendations. *Journal of Personality Assessment, 46,* 415–425.

Ewedemi, F., & Linn, M. W. (1987). Health and hassles in older and younger men. *Journal of Clinical Psychology, 43,* 347–353.

Exner, J. E., Jr. (1974). *The Rorschach: A comprehensive system* (Vol. 1). New York: Wiley.

Exner, J. E., Jr. (1993). *The Rorschach: A comprehensive system: Vol. 1,* Basic Foundations (3rd ed.). New York: Wiley.

Exner, J. E., Jr. (1999). The Rorschach: Measurement concepts and issues of validity. In S. E. Embretson & S. L. Hershberger (Eds.), *The new rules of measurement.* Mahwah, NJ: Erlbaum.

Exner, J. E., McDowell, E., Pabst, J., Stackman, W., & Kirk, L. (1963). On the detection of willful falsifications in the MMPI. *Journal of Consulting Psychology, 27,* 91–94.

Eyde, L. D., Kowal, D. M., & Fishburne, F. J., Jr. (1991). The validity of computer-based test interpretations of the MMPI. In T. B. Gutkin & S. L. Wise (Eds.), *The computer and the decision-making process* (pp. 75–123). Hillsdale, NJ: Lawrence Erlbaum.

Eysenck, H. J. (1985). Review of the California Psychological Inventory. In J. V. Mitchell, Jr. (Ed.), *The ninth mental measurements yearbook* (Vol. 1, pp. 252–253). Lincoln, NE: University of Nebraska Press.

Eysenck, H. J., & Eysenck, S. B. G. (1975). *The Eysenck Personality Questionnaire manual.* London: Hodder & Stoughton.

Fabian, L., & Ross, M. (1984). The development of the Sports Competition Trait Inventory. *Journal of Sports Behavior, 7,* 13–27.

Fagley, N. S. (1987). Positional response bias in multiple-choice tests of learning: Its relation to test-wiseness and guessing strategy. *Journal of Educational Psychology, 79,* 95–97.

Fancher, R. E. (1987). Henry Goddard and the Kallikak family photographs. *American Psychologist, 42,* 585–590.

Fancher, R. E. (1983). Alphonse de Candolle, Francis Galton, and the early history of the nature-nature controversy. *Journal of the History of the Behavioral Sciences, 19,* 341–352.

Farh, J. L., Dobbins, G. H., & Cheng, B. S. (1991). Cultural relativity in action: A comparison of self-ratings made by Chinese and U.S. workers. *Personnel Psychology, 44,* 129–147.

Farmer, R., & Sundberg, N. D. (1986). Boredom Proneness – The development and correlates of a new scale. *Journal of Personality Assessment, 50,* 4–17.

Farrugia, D. (1983). A study of vocational interests and attitudes of hearing impaired clients. *Journal of Rehabilitation of the Deaf, 17,* 1–7.

Farrugia, D., & Austin, G. F. (1980). A study of social-emotional adjustment patterns of hearing-impaired students in different educational settings. *American Annals of the Deaf, 125,* 535–541.

Farylo, B., & Paludi, M. A. (1985). Research with the Draw-A-Person Test: Conceptual and methodological issues. *The Journal of Psychology, 119,* 575–580.

Faust, D., Hart, K., & Guilmette, T. J. (1988). Pediatric malingering: The capacity of children to fake believable deficits on neuropsychological testing. *Journal of Consulting and Clinical Psychology, 56,* 578–582.

Faust, D., & Ziskin, J. (1989). Computer-assisted psychological evaluation as legal evidence: Some day my prints will come. *Computers in Human Behavior, 5,* 23–36.

Fazio, A. F. (1969). Verbal and overt-behavioral assessment of a specific fear. *Journal of Consulting and Clinical Psychology, 33,* 703–709.

Feather, N. T. (1975). *Values in education and society.* New York: Free Press.

Feather, N. T. (1986). Cross-cultural studies with the Rokeach Value Survey: The Flinders program of research on values. *Australian Journal of Psychology, 38,* 269–283.

Feather, N. T., & Peay, E. R. (1975). The structure of terminal and instrumental values: Dimensions and clusters. *Australian Journal of Psychology, 27,* 151–164.

Feazell, D. M., Quay, H. C, & Murray, E. J. (1991). The validity and utility of Lanyon's Psychological Screening Inventory in a youth services agency sample. *Criminal Justice and Behavior, 18,* 166–179.

Federici, L., & Schuerger, J. (1974). Prediction of success in an applied M. A. psychology program. *Educational and Psychological Measurement, 34,* 945–952.

Feingold, A. (1983). The validity of the Information and Vocabulary Subtests of the WAIS for predicting college achievement. *Educational and Psychological Measurement, 43,* 1127–1131.

Fekken. G. C. (1984). Adjective Check List. In D. J. Keyser & R. C. Sweetland (Eds.), *Test critiques* (Vol. 1, pp. 34–40). Kansas City, MO: Test Corporation of America.

Feldman, K. A., & Newcomb, T. M. (1969). *The impact of colleges on students: Vol. 1. An analysis of four decades of research.* San Francisco, CA: Jossey-Bass.

Feldman, W. (1990). *Learning disabilities: A review of available treatments.* Springfield, IL: Charles C Thomas.

Fenigstein, A., Scheier, M. F., & Buss, A. H. (1975). Public and private self-consciousness: Assessment and theory. *Journal of Consulting and Clinical Psychology, 43,* 522–527.

Ferketich, S. L., Figueredo, A. J., & Knapp, T. R. (1991). The multitrait-multimethod approach to construct validity. *Research in Nursing and Health, 14,* 315–320.

Ferraro, L. A., Price, J. H., Desmond, S. M., & Roberts, S. M. (1987). Development of a diabetes locus of control scale. *Psychological Reports, 61,* 763–770.

Festinger, L. (1947). The treatment of qualitative data by "scale analysis." *Psychological Bulletin, 44,* 149–161.

Feuerstein, R. (1979). *The dynamic assessment of retarded performers: The learning potential assessment device, theory, instruments, and techniques.* Baltimore, MD: University of Maryland Press.

Fibel, B., & Hale, W. D. (1978). The generalized expectancy for success scale – A new measure. *Journal of Consulting and Clinical Psychology, 46,* 924–931.

Figueroa, R. A. (1979). The system of Multicultural Pluralistic Assessment. *The School Psychology Digest, 8,* 28–36.

Filskov, S. B. (1983). Neuropsychological screening. In P. Q. Keller & L. G. Writt (Eds.), *Innovations in clinical practice: A sourcebook* (Vol. II, pp. 17–25). Sarasota, FL: Professional Resource Exchange.

Finch, A. J., & Rogers, T. R. (1984). Self-report instruments. In T. H. Ollendick & M. Hersen (Eds.), *Child behavioral assessment* (pp. 106–123), New York: Pergamon Press.

Finch, A. J., Thornton, L. J., & Montgomery, L. E. (1974). WAIS short forms with hospitalized psychiatric patients. *Journal of Consulting and Clinical Psychology, 42,* 469.

Finegan, J. E., & Allen, N. J. (1994). Computerized and written questionnaires: Are they equivalent? *Computers in Human Behavior, 10,* 483–496.

Finger, M. S., & Ones, D. S. (1999). Psychometric equivalence of the computer and booklet forms of the MMPI: A metaanalysis. *Psychological Assessment, 11,* 58–66.

Fischer, D. G., & Fick, C. (1993). Measuring social desirability – Short forms of the Marlowe-Crowne

Social Desirability scale. *Educational and Psychological Measurement, 53*, 417–424.

Fishbein, M. (1980). A theory of reasoned action: Some applications and implications. In M. M. Page (Ed.), *Nebraska Symposium on Motivation, 1979* (pp. 65–115). Lincoln, NE: University of Nebraska Press.

Fisher, S., & Fisher, R. (1950). Test of certain assumptions regarding figure drawing analysis. *Journal of Abnormal and Social Psychology, 45*, 727–732.

Fitts, W. H. (1965). *Manual for the Tennessee Self-Concept Scale.* Nashville, TN: Counselor Recordings and Tests.

Flaharty, R. (1976). EPEC: Evaluation and Prescription for Exceptional Children. In E. R. Ritvo, B. J. Freeman, E. M. Ornitz, & P. E. Tanguay (Eds.), *Autism: Diagnosis, current research and management.* New York: Spectrum.

Flanagan, J., & Lewis, G. (1969). Comparison of Negro and white lower class men on the General Aptitude Test Battery and the Minnesota Multiphasic Personality Inventory. *Journal of Social Psychology, 78*, 289–291.

Flanagan, R., & DiGiuseppe, R. (1999). Critical review of the TEMAS: A step within the development of thematic apperception instruments. *Psychology in the Schools, 36*, 21–30.

Fleege, P. O., Charlesworth, R., Burts, D. C., & Hart, C. H. (1992). Stress begins in kindergarten: A look at behavior during standardized testing. *Journal of Research in Childhood Education, 7*, 20–26.

Fleenor, J. W., & Taylor, S. (1994). Construct validity of three self-report measures of creativity. *Educational and Psychological Measurement, 54*, 464–470.

Fleishman, E. A. (1988). Some new frontiers in personnel selection research. *Personnel Psychology, 41*, 679–702.

Fleiss, J. L. (1971). Measuring nominal scale agreement among many raters. *Psychological Bulletin, 76*, 378–382.

Fleiss, J. L. (1975). Measuring agreement between two judges on the presence or absence of a trait. *Biometrics, 31*, 651–659.

Fleming, J., & Garcia, N. (1998). Are standardized tests fair to African Americans? *The Journal of Higher Education, 69*, 471–495.

Fleming, T. M., Perkins, D. V., & Lovejoy, M. C. (1991). Development of a brief self-report measure of quality in roommate relationships. *Behavioral Assessment, 13*, 125–135.

Fletcher, T. (1989). A comparison of the Mexican version of the Wechsler Intelligence Scale for Children-Revised and the Woodcock Psycho-Educational Battery in Spanish. *Journal of Psychoeducational Assessment, 7*, 56–65.

Fluckiger, F. A., Tripp, C. A., & Weinberg, G. H. (1961). A review of experimental research in graphology: 1933–1960. *Perceptual and Motor Skills, 12*, 67–90.

Folkins, C. H., & Sime, W. E. (1981). Physical fitness training and mental health. *American Psychologist, 36*, 373–389.

Folstein, M. D., Folstein, S. E., & McHugh, P. R. (1975). Mini-mental state: A practical method for grading the cognitive state of patients for the clinician. *Journal of Psychiatric Research, 12*, 189–198.

Forde, J. (1977). Data on the Peabody Picture Vocabulary Test. *American Annals of the Deaf, 122*, 38–43.

Fosberg, I. A. (1938). Rorschach reactions under varied instructions. *Rorschach Research Exchange, 3*, 12–30.

Fosberg, I. A. (1941). An experimental study of the reliability of the Rorschach psychodiagnostic technique. *Rorschach Research Exchange, 5*, 72–84.

Fosberg, I. A. (1943). How do subjects attempt to fake results on the Rorschach test? *Rorschach Research Exchange, 7*, 119–121.

Fowler, P. C. (1985). Factor structure of the Personality Research Form-E: A maximum likelihood analysis. *Journal of Clinical Psychology, 41*, 377–381.

Fowler, R. D. (1967). Computer interpretation of personality tests: The automated psychologist. *Comprehensive Psychiatry, 8*, 455–467.

Fowler, R. D. (1985). Landmarks in computer-assisted psychological assessment. *Journal of Counseling and Clinical Psychology, 53*, 748–759.

Fraboni, M., & Saltstone, R. (1992). The WAIS-R number-of-factors quandary: A cluster analytic approach to construct validation. *Educational and Psychological Measurement, 52*, 603–613.

Fraiberg, S. (1977). *Thoughts from the blind: Developmental studies of blind children.* New York: Basic Books.

Franco, J. N. (1983). An acculturation scale for Mexican-American children. *Journal of General Psychology, 108*, 175–181.

Frank, G. (1983). *The Wechsler enterprise.* Oxford: Pergamon Press.

Frank, G. H. (1970). The measurement of personality from the Wechsler tests. In B. A. Mahrer (Ed.), *Progress in experimental personality research.* New York: Academic Press.

Frank, J. (1968). The role of hope in psychotherapy. *International Journal of Psychiatry, 6*, 383–395.

Frankenburg, W. K., & Dodds, J. B. (1967). The Denver Developmental Screening Test. *The Journal of Pediatrics, 71*, 181–191.

Franzen, M. D. (1987). Luria-Nebraska Neuropsychological Battery. In D. J. Keyser & R. C. Sweetland (Eds.), *Test critiques compendium* (pp. 260–272). Kansas City, MO: Test Corporation of America.

Franzen, M. D. (1989). *Reliability and validity in neuropsychological assessment.* New York: Plenum Press.

Fraser, B. J. (1981). Using environmental assessments to make better classrooms. *Journal of Curriculum Studies, 13,* 131–144.

Frederick, R. I., Sarfaty, S. D., Johnston, D., & Powel, J. (1994). Validation of a detector of response bias on a forced-choice test of nonverbal ability. *Neuropsychology, 8,* 118–125.

Frederiksen, N. (1962). Factors in in-basket performance. *Psychological Monographs, 76* (22, whole No. 541).

Freedman, D. G., & Freedman, N. (1969). Behavioral differences between Chinese-American and European-American newborns. *Nature, 24,* 1227.

Freeman, B. J. (1976). Evaluating autistic children. *Journal of Pediatric Psychology, 1,* 18–21.

Freeman, B. J. (1985). Review of Child Behavior Checklist. In J. V. Mitchell, Jr. (Ed.), *The ninth mental measurements yearbook* (Vol. 1, pp. 300–301). Lincoln, NE: University of Nebraska Press.

Freeman, F. S. (1984). A note on E. B. Titchener and G. M. Whipple. *Journal of the History of the Behavioral Sciences, 20,* 177–179.

French, J. (1958). Validation of new item types against four-year academic criteria. *Journal of Educational Psychology, 49,* 67–76.

French, J. L. (1964). *Manual: Pictorial Test of Intelligence.* Boston, MA: Houghton, Mifflin.

Frenzel, R. R., & Lang, R. A. (1989). Identifying sexual preferences in intrafamilial and extrafamilial child sexual abusers. *Annals of Sex Research, 2,* 255–275.

Freund, K. (1965). Diagnosing heterosexual pedophilia by means of a test for sexual interest. *Behavioral Research and Therapy, 3,* 229–234.

Fricke, B. G. (1956). Response set as a suppressor variable in the OAIS and the MMPI. *Journal of Consulting Psychology, 20,* 161–169.

Friedman, M., & Rosenman, R. H. (1959). Association of specific overt behavior pattern with blood and cardiovascular findings. *Journal of the American Medical Association, 169,* 1286–1296.

Frisbie, D. A., & Becker, D. F. (1991). An analysis of textbook advice about true-false tests. *Applied Measurement in Education, 4,* 67–83.

Frostig, M., Lefever, W., & Whittlesey, J. R. B. (1966). *Administration and scoring manual for the Marianne Frostig Developmental Test of Visual Perception.* Palo Alto, CA: Consulting Psychologists Press.

Fruzzetti, A. E., & Jacobson, N. S. (1992). Assessment of couples. In J. C. Rosen, & P. McReynolds (Eds.), *Advances in Psychological Assessment* (Vol. 8, pp. 201–224). New York: Plenum Press.

Fullard, W., McDevitt, S. C., & Carey, W. B. (1984). Assessing temperament in one- to three-year-old children. *Journal of Pediatric Psychology, 9,* 205–217.

Funk, S. C., & Houston, B. K. (1987). A critical analysis of the hardiness scale's validity and utility. *Journal of Personality and Social Psychology, 53,* 572–578.

Furey, W., & Forehand, R. (1983). The Daily Child Behavior Checklist. *Journal of Behavioral Assessment, 5,* 83–95.

Furnham, A. (1986). Response bias, social desirability and dissimulation. *Personality and Individual Differences, 7,* 385–400.

Furnham, A. (1987). A content and correlational analysis of seven locus of control scales. *Current Psychological Research and Reviews, 6,* 244–255.

Furnham, A., & Henderson, M. (1982). The good, the bad and the mad: Response bias in self-report measures. *Personality and Individual Differences, 3,* 311–320.

Furnham, A., & Henry, J. (1980). Cross-cultural locus of control studies: Experiment and critique. *Psychological Reports, 47,* 23–29.

Gaddes, W. H. (1994). *Learning disabilities and brain function: A neuropsychological approach* (3rd ed.). New York: Springer-Verlag.

Gage, N. L. (1959). Review of the Study of Values. In O. K. Buros (Ed.), *The fifth mental measurements yearbook* (pp. 199–202). Highland Park, NJ: The Gryphon Press.

Gage, N. L., Leavitt, G. S., & Stone, G. C. (1957). The psychological meaning of acquiescence for authoritarianism. *Journal of Abnormal and Social Psychology, 55,* 98–103.

Gagnon, S. G., & Nagle, R. J. (2000). Comparison of the revised and original versions of the Bayley Scales of Infant Development. *School Psychology International, 21,* 293–305.

Galassi, J. P., & Galassi, M. D. (1974). Validity of a measure of assertiveness. *Journal of Counseling Psychology, 21,* 248–250.

Galen, R., & Gambino, S. (1975). *Beyond normality: The predictive value and efficiency of medical diagnoses.* New York: Wiley.

Gallagher, D., Thompson, L. W., & Levy, S. M. (1980). Clinical psychological assessment of older adults. In L. W. Poon (Ed.), *Aging in the 1980s* (pp. 19–40). Washington, DC: American Psychological Association.

Gallagher, J. J. (1966). *Research summary on gifted child education.* Springfield, IL: Office of the Superintendent of Public Instruction.

Gallagher, J. J. (1989). A new policy initiative: Infants and toddlers with handicapping conditions. *American Psychologist, 44,* 387–391.

Galton, F. (1884). Measurement of character. *Fortnightly Review, 36*, 179–185.

Galton, F. (1907). *Inquiries into human faculty and its development* (2nd ed.). New York: E. P. Dutton.

Ganster, D. C., Hennessey, H. W., & Luthans, F. (1983). Social desirability response effects: Three alternative models. *Academy of Management Journal, 26*, 321–331.

Garb, H. N. (1984). The incremental validity of information used in personality assessment. *Clinical Psychology Review, 4*, 641–655.

Garb, H. N., Florio, C. M., & Grove, W. M. (1998). The validity of the Rorschach and the Minnesota Multiphasic Personality Inventory: Results from meta-analyses. *Psychological Science, 9*, 402–404.

Garcia, M., & Lega, L. I. (1979). Development of a Cuban Ethnic Identity Questionnaire. *Hispanic Journal of Behavioral Sciences, 1*, 247–261.

Gardner, H. (1983). *Frames of mind: The theory of multiple intelligences.* New York: Basic.

Gardner, M. (1974). Mathematical games. *Scientific American, 231*, 98–103.

Garner, D. M. (1991). *The Eating Disorder Inventory-2 professional manual.* Odessa, FL: Psychological Assessment Resources.

Garner, D. M., & Olmsted, M. P. (1984). *The Eating Disorder Inventory Manual.* Odessa, FL: Psychological Assessment Resources.

Garry, R. (1953). Individual differences in ability to fake vocational interests. *Journal of Applied Psychology, 37*, 33–37.

Garth, T. R., Eson, T. H., & Morton, M. M. (1936). The administration of non-language intelligence tests to Mexicans. *Journal of Abnormal and Social Psychology, 31*, 53–58.

Gaugler, B. B., Rosenthal, D. B., Thornton, G. C. III, & Bentson, C. (1987). Meta-analysis of assessment center validity. *Journal of Applied Psychology, 72*, 493–511.

Gay, M. L., Hollandsworth, J. G., Jr., & Galassi, J. P. (1975). An assertiveness inventory for adults. *Journal of Counseling Psychology, 22*, 340–344.

Gear, G. H. (1976). Accuracy of teacher judgment in identifying intellectually gifted children: A review of the literature. *Gifted Child Quarterly, 20*, 478–490.

Geary, D. C., & Gilger, J. W. (1984). The Luria-Nebraska Neuropsychological Battery – Children's revision: Comparison of learning-disabled and normal children matched on full scale IQ. *Perceptual and Motor Skills, 58*, 115–118.

Geary, D. C., Jennings, S. M., Schultz, D. D., & Alper, T. G. (1984). The diagnostic accuracy of the Luria-Nebraska Neuropsychological Battery – Children's revision for 9-to 12-year-old learning-disabled children. *School Psychology Review, 13*, 375–380.

Geer, J. H. (1965). The development of a scale to measure fear. *Behaviour Research and Therapy, 3*, 45–53.

Geisinger, K. F. (1992). The metamorphosis of test validation. *Educational Psychologist, 27*, 197–222.

Geist, H. (1959). *Geist Picture Interest Inventory.* Los Angeles, CA: Western Psychological Services.

Geist, H. (1988). *The Geist Picture Interest Inventory. Revised.* Los Angeles, CA: Western Psychological Service.

Gelatt, H. B. (1967). Information and decision theories applied to college choice and planning. *In Preparing school counselors in educational guidance.* New York: College Entrance Examination Board.

Gelb, S. A. (1986). Henry H. Goddard and the immigrants, 1910–1917: The studies and their social context. *Journal of the History of the Behavioral Sciences, 22*, 324–332.

Genshaft, J., & Ward, M. E. (1982). A review of the Perkins-Binet tests of intelligence for the blind with suggestions for administration. *School Psychology Review, 11*, 338–341.

Gerardi, R., Keane, T. M., & Penk, W. (1989). Utility: Sensitivity and specificity in developing diagnostic tests of combat-related post-traumatic stress disorder (PTSD). *Journal of Clinical Psychology, 45*, 691–703.

Gerken, K. C. (1978). Performance of Mexican American children on intelligence tests. *Exceptional children, 44*, 438–443.

Gerken, K. C., & Hodapp, A. F. (1992). Assessment of preschoolers at-risk with the WPPSI-R and the Stanford-Binet L-M. *Psychological Reports, 71*, 659–664.

Gerst, M. S., Grant, I., Yager, J., & Sweetwood, H. (1978). The reliability of the social readjustment rating scale: Moderate and long-term stability. *Journal of Psychosmatic Research, 22*, 519–523.

Gesell, A., Halverson, H. M., & Amatruda, C. S. (1940). *The first five years of life.* New York: Harper.

Gesell, A., Ilg, F. L., & Ames, L. B. (1974). *Infant and child in the culture of today* (Rev. ed.). New York: Harper & Row.

Geschwind, N., & Levitsky, W. (1968). Human brain: Left-right asymmetrics in temporal speech regions. *Science, 161*, 186–187.

Getter, H., & Sundland, D. M. (1962). The Barron Ego Strength Scale and psychotherapy outcome. *Journal of Consulting Psychology, 26*, 195.

Ghiselli, E. E. (1966). *The validity of occupational aptitude tests.* New York: Wiley.

Ghiselli, E. E. (1973). The validity of aptitude tests in personnel selection. *Personnel Psychology, 26*, 461–477.

Ghiselli, E. E., & Haire, M. (1960). The validation of selection tests in the light of the dynamic character of criteria. *Personnel Psychology, 13,* 225–231.

Gibb, B. (1964). Testwiseness as secondary cue response (Doctoral dissertation, Stanford University, 1964). Ann Arbor, MI: University Microfilms (UMI No. 64-7643).

Gibbins. K. (1968). Response sets and the semantic differential. *British Journal of Social and Clinical Psychology, 7,* 253–263.

Gibbins, S. (1989). The provision of school psychological assessment services for the hearing impaired: A national survey. *The Volta Review, 91,* 95–103.

Gibson, J. J. (1966). *The senses considered as perceptual systems.* New York: Houghton Mifflin.

Gibson-Harman, K., & Austin, G. F. (1985). A revised form of the Tennessee Self-concept Scale for use with deaf and hard of hearing persons. *American Annals of the Deaf, 130,* 218–225.

Giedt, F. H., & Downing, L. (1961). An extraversion scale for the MMPI. *Journal of Clinical Psychology, 17,* 156–159.

Gierl, M. J., & Rogers, W. T. (1996). A confirmatory factor analysis of the Test Anxiety Inventory using Canadian high-school students. *Educational and Psychological Measurement, 56,* 315–324.

Gilberstadt, H., & Duker, J. (1965). *A handbook for clinical and actuarial MMPI interpretation.* Philadelphia, PA: W. B. Saunders.

Gilewski, M. J., & Zelinski, E. M. (1986). Questionnaire assessment of memory complaints. In L. W. Poon, T. Crook, K. L. Davis, C. Eisdorfer, B. J. Gurland, A. W. Kaszniak, & L. W. Thompson (Eds.), *Clinical memory assessment of older adults* (pp. 93–107). Washington, DC: American Psychological Association.

Gilewski, M. J., Zelinski, E. M., & Schaie, K. W. (1990). The Memory Functioning Questionnaire for assessment of memory complaints in adulthood and old age. *Psychology and Aging, 5,* 482–490.

Gill, D. L., & Deeter, T. E. (1988). Development of the Sports Orientation Questionnaire. *Research Quarterly for Exercise and Sport, 59,* 191–202.

Gillberg, I. C., & Gillberg, I. C. (1983). Three-year follow-up at age 10 of children with minor neurodevelopmental disorders. I. Behavioral problems. *Developmental Medicine and Child Neurology, 25,* 438–449.

Gillespie, B. L., Eisler, R. M. (1992). Development of the feminine gender role stress scale. *Behavior Modification, 16,* 426–438.

Ginzberg, E. (1951). *Occupational choice.* New York: Columbia University Press.

Glaser, R. (1963). Instructional technology and the measurement of learning outcomes. *American Psychologist, 18,* 519–521.

Glass, D. C. (1977). Stress, behavior patterns, and coronary disease. *American Scientist, 65,* 177–187.

Glass, G. V. (1976). Primary, secondary, and meta-analysis of research. *Educational Researcher, 5,* 3–8.

Glaub, V. E., & Kamphaus, R. W. (1991). Construction of a nonverbal adaptation of the Stanford-Binet fourth edition. *Educational and Psychological Measurement, 51,* 231–241.

Glennon, J. R., Albright, K. E., & Owens, W. A. (1966). *A catalog of life history items.* Greensboro, NC: Center for Creative Leadership.

Glow, R. A., Glow, P. A., & Rump, E. E. (1982). The stability of child behavior disorders: A one year test-retest study of Adelaide versions of the Conners Teacher and Parent Rating Scales. *Journal of Abnormal Child Psychology, 10,* 33–60.

Glueck, B. C., & Reznikoff, M. (1965). Comparison of computer-derived personality profile and projective psychological test findings. *American Journal of Psychiatry, 121,* 1156–1161.

Glutting, J. J., & McDermott, P. A. (1989). Using "teaching items" on ability tests: A nice idea but does it work? *Educational and Psychological Measurement, 49,* 257–268.

Goddard, H. H. (1913). The Binet tests in relation to immigration. *Journal of Psycho-Asthenics, 18,* 105–107.

Goddard, H. H. (1917). Mental tests and the immigrant. *Journal of Delinquency, 2,* 243–277.

Goebel, R. A. (1983). Detection of faking on the Halstead-Reitan Neuropsychological Test Battery. *Journal of Clinical Psychology, 39,* 731–742.

Goetzinger, C. P., Wills, R. C., & Dekker, L. C. (1967). Non-language I.Q. tests used with deaf pupils. *Volta Review, 69,* 500–506.

Goldband, S., Katkin, E. S., & Morell, M. A. (1979). Personality and cardiovascular disorder: Steps toward demystification. In I. G. Sarason & C. D. Spielberger (Eds.), *Stress and anxiety* (Vol. 6). New York: Wiley.

Goldberg, E. L., & Alliger, G. M. (1992). Assessing the validity of the GRE for students in Psychology: A validity generalization approach. *Educational and Psychological Measurement, 52,* 1019–1027.

Goldberg, L. R. (1959). The effectiveness of clinicians' judgments: The diagnosis of organic brain damage from the Bender-Gestalt test. *Journal of Consulting Psychology, 23,* 25–33.

Goldberg, L. R. (1968). Simple models or simple processes? Some research on clinical judgments. *American Psychologist, 23,* 483–496.

Goldberg, L. R. (1972). Review of the CPI. In O. K. Buros (Ed.), *The seventh mental measurements yearbook* (Vol. 1, pp. 94–96). Highland Park, NJ: Gryphon Press.

Goldberg, L. R. (1974). Objective personality tests and measures. *Annual Review of Psychology, 25,* 343–366.

Goldberg, L. R. (1981). Language and individual differences: The search for universals in personality lexicons. In L. Wheeler (Ed.), *Personality and social psychology review* (Vol. 2, pp. 141–165). Beverly Hills, CA: Sage.

Goldberg, L. R. (1990). An alternative "Description of Personality": The Big-Five Factor Structure. *Journal of Personality and Social Psychology, 59,* 1216–1229.

Goldberg, L. R., Grenier, J. R., Guion, R. M., Sechrest, L. B., & Wing, H. (1991). *Questionnaires used in the prediction of trustworthiness in pre-employment selection decisions: An A.P.A. Task Force Report.* Washington DC: American Psychological Association.

Goldberg, L. R., Rorer, L. G., & Greene, M. M. (1970). The usefulness of "stylistic" scales as potential suppressor or moderator variables in predictions from the CPI. *Oregon Research Institute Research Bulletin, 10,* No. 3.

Goldberg, P. (1965). A review of sentence completion methods in personality assessment. In B. I. Murstein (Ed.), *Handbook of projective techniques* (pp. 777–822). New York: Basic Books.

Golden, C. J. (1981). The Luria-Nebraska Children's Battery: Theory and formulation. In G. W. Hynd, & J. E. Obrzut (Eds.), *Neuropsychological assessment and the school-age child.* New York: Grune & Stratton.

Golden, C. J. (1989). The Nebraska Neuropsychological Children's Battery. In C. R. Reynolds & E. Fletcher-Janzen (Eds.), *Handbook of clinical child neuropsychology* (pp. 193–204). New York: Plenum.

Golden, C. J., Purisch, A. D., & Hammeke, T. A. (1985). *Luria-Nebraska Neuropsychological Battery: Forms I and II.* Los Angeles: Western Psychological Services.

Goldfried, M. R. (1964). A cross-validation of the Marlowe-Crowne Social Desirability Scale items. *Journal of Social Psychology, 64,* 137–145.

Goldfried, M. R., & Kent, R. N. (1972). Traditional vs. behavioral personality assessment: A comparison of methodological and theoretical assumptions. *Psychological Bulletin, 77,* 409–420.

Goldfried, M. R., & Zax, M. (1965). The stimulus value of the TAT. *Journal of Projective Techniques, 29,* 46–57.

Golding, S. L. (1978). Review of the Psychological Screening Inventory. In O. K. Buros (Ed.), *The eighth mental measurements yearbook* (Vol. 1, pp. 1019–1022). Highland Park, NJ: Gryphon Press.

Goldman, M. E., & Berry, C. A. (1981). Comparative predictive validity of the new MCAT using different admissions criteria. *Journal of Medical Education, 56,* 981–986.

Goldman, R. D., & Hewitt, B. N. (1976). Predicting the success of Black, Chicano, Oriental, and White college students. *Journal of Educational Measurement, 13,* 107–117.

Goldman, R. D., & Richards, R. (1974). The SAT prediction of grades for Mexican-American versus Anglo-American students at the University of California, Riverside, *Journal of Educational Measurement, 11,* 129–135.

Goldman, R. D., & Slaughter, R. E. (1976). Why college grade point average is difficult to predict. *Journal of Educational Psychology, 68,* 9–14.

Goldman, R. D., & Widawski, M. H. (1976). An analysis of types of errors in the selection of minority college students. *Journal of Educational Measurement, 13,* 185–200.

Goldman, R. L. (1992). The reliability of peer assessments of quality of care. *Journal of the American Medical Association, 267,* 958–960.

Goldman, R. L. (1994). The reliability of peer assessments. A metaanalysis. *Evaluation and the Health Professions, 17,* 3–21.

Goldschmidt, M. L., & Bentler, P. M. (1968). Manual: *Concept assessment kit: Conservation.* San Diego: Educational & Industrial Testing Service.

Goldsmith, D. B. (1922). The use of the personnel history blank as a salesmanship test. *Journal of Applied Psychology, 6,* 149–155.

Goldstein, G. (1984). Comprehensive neuropsychological assessment batteries. In G. Goldstein & M. Hersen (Eds.), *Handbook of psychological assessment* (pp. 181–210). Elmsford, NY: Pergamon Press.

Goldstein, G., & Shelly, C. H. (1975). Similarities and differences between psychological deficit in aging and brain damage. *Journal of Gerontology, 30,* 448–455.

Goldstein, I. L. (1971). The application blank: How honest are the responses? *Journal of Applied Psychology, 55,* 491–492.

Good, L. R., & Good, K. C. (1974). A preliminary measure of existential anxiety. *Psychological Reports, 34,* 72–74.

Good, R. H., III, Vollmer, M., Creek, R. J., Katz, L., & Chowdhri, S. (1993). Treatment utility of the Kaufman Assessment Battery for Children: Effects of matching instruction and student processing strength. *School Psychology Review, 22,* 8–26.

Goodenough, F. L. (1926). *Measurement of intelligence by drawings.* New York: Harcourt, Brace, & World.

Goodwin, F. K., & Jamison, K. R. (1990). *Manic-depressive illness.* New York: Oxford University Press.

Goodwin, W. L., & Driscoll, L. A. (1980). *Handbook for measurement and evaluation in early childhood education.* San Francisco, CA: Jossey-Bass.

Gordon, M. E., & Gross, R. H. (1978). A critique of methods for operationalizing the concept of fakeability. *Educational and Psychological Measurement, 38,* 771–782.

Gorenstein, C., Andrade, L., Filho, A., Tung, T., & Artes, R. (1999). Psychometric properties of the Portuguese version of the Beck Depression Inventory on Brazilian college students. *Journal of Clinical Psychology, 55,* 553–562.

Gorham, D. R. (1967). Validity and reliability studies of a computer-based scoring system for inkblot responses. *Journal of Consulting Psychology, 31,* 65–70.

Gorham, D. R., Moseley, E. C., & Holtzman, W. W. (1968). Norms for the computer-scored Holtzman Inkblot Technique. *Perceptual and Motor Skills, 26,* 1279–1305.

Gorman, B. (1968). Social desirability factors and the Eysenck Personality Inventory. *Journal of Psychology, 69,* 75–83.

Gorsuch, R. L. (1983). *Factor analysis* (2nd ed.). Hillsdale, NJ: Lawrence Erlbaum.

Gorsuch, R. L., & Key, M. K. (1974). Abnormalities of pregnancy as a function of anxiety and life stress. *Psychosomatic Medicine, 36,* 352–372.

Gotlib, I. H. (1984). Depression and general psychopathology in university students. *Journal of Abnormal Psychology, 93,* 19–30.

Gottesman, I. I., & Prescott, C. A. (1989). Abuses of the MacAndrew MMPI Alcoholism Scale: A critical review. *Clinical Psychology Review, 9,* 223–242.

Gottfredson, L. S., & Crouse, J. (1986). Validity versus utility of mental tests: Example of the SAT. *Journal of Vocational Behavior, 29,* 363–378.

Gottschalk, L. A. (1974). A Hope Scale applicable to verbal samples. *Archives of General Psychiatry, 30,* 779–785.

Gottschalk, L. (1985). Hope and other deterrents to illness. *American Journal of Psychotherapy, 39,* 515–524.

Gottschalk, L. A., & Gleser, G. C. (1969). *The measurement of psychological states through the content analysis of verbal behavior.* Los Angeles, CA: University of California Press.

Gough, H. G. (1947). Simulated patterns on the MMPI. *Journal of Abnormal and Social Psychology, 42,* 215–225.

Gough, H. G. (1950). The F minus K dissimulation index for the MMPI. *Journal of Consulting Psychology, 14,* 408–413.

Gough, H. G. (1954). Some common misconceptions about neuroticism. *Journal of Consulting Psychology, 18,* 287–292.

Gough, H. G. (1965). Conceptual analysis of psychological test scores and other diagnostic variables. *Journal of Abnormal Psychology, 70,* 294–302.

Gough, H. G. (1966). Appraisal of social maturity by means of the CPI. *Journal of Abnormal Psychology, 71,* 189–195.

Gough, H. G. (1968). An interpreter's syllabus for the California Psychological Inventory. In P. McReynolds (Ed.), *Advances in psychological assessment* (Vol. 1, pp. 55–79). Palo Alto, CA: Science and Behavior Books.

Gough, H. G. (1974). A 24-item version of the Miller-Fisk sexual knowledge questionnaire. *The Journal of Psychology 87,* 183–192.

Gough, H. G. (1984). A managerial potential scale for the California Psychological Inventory. *Journal of Applied Psychology, 69,* 233–240.

Gough, H. G. (1985). A Work Orientation scale for the California Psychological Inventory. *Journal of Applied Psychology, 70,* 505–513.

Gough, H. G. (1987). *CPI administrator's guide.* Palo Alto, CA: Consulting Psychologists Press.

Gough, H. G. (1989). The California Psychological Inventory. In C. S. Newmark (Ed.), *Major psychological assessment instruments* (Vol. 2, pp. 67–98). Boston, MA: Allyn & Bacon.

Gough, H. G. (1991). Some unfinished business. In W. M. Grove & D. Cicchetti (Eds.), *Thinking clearly about psychology* (Vol. 2, pp. 114–136) *Personality and psychopathology.* Minneapolis, MN: University of Minnesota Press.

Gough, H. G. (1992). Assessment of creative potential in psychology and the development of a Creative Temperament Scale for the CPI. In J. C. Rosen & P. McReynolds (Eds.), *Advances in psychological assessment* (Vol. 8, pp. 225–257). New York: Plenum.

Gough, H. G., & Bradley, P. (1992). Delinquent and criminal behavior as assessed by the revised California Psychological Inventory. *Journal of Clinical Psychology, 48,* 298–308.

Gough, H. G. , & Bradley, P. (1996). *CPI manual.* Palo Alto, CA: Consulting Psychologists Press.

Gough, H., & Domino, G. (1963). The D-48 test as a measure of general ability among grade-school children. *Journal of Consulting Psychology, 27,* 344–349.

Gough, H. G., & Heilbrun, A. L. (1965). *The Adjective Check List Manual.* Palo Alto, CA: Consulting Psychologists Press.

Gough, H. G., & Heilbrun, A. B., Jr. (1983). *The Adjective Check List manual-1983 edition.* Palo Alto, CA: Consulting Psychologists Press.

Gould, J. (1982). A psychometric investigation of the standard and long-form Beck Depression Inventory. *Psychological Reports, 51*, 1167–1170.

Gould. S. J. (1981). *The mismeasure of man.* New York: W. W. Norton.

Gowan, J. C., & Gowan, M. S. (1955). A teacher prognosis scale for the MMPI. *Journal of Educational Research, 49*, 1–12.

Gracely, R. H., McGrath, P., & Dubner, R. (1978). Ratio scales of sensory and affective verbal pain descriptions. *Pain, 5*, 5–18.

Graham, C., Bond, S. S., Gerkovich, M. M., & Cook, M. R. (1980). Use of the McGill Pain Questionnaire in the assessment of cancer pain: Replicability and consistency. *Pain, 8*, 377–387.

Graham, E. E., & Shapiro, E. (1963). Use of the Performance Scale of the WISC with the deaf child. *Journal of Consulting Psychology, 17*, 396–398.

Graham, J. R. (1987). The *MMPI: A practical guide* (2nd ed.). New York: Oxford University Press.

Graham, J. R. (1990). *MMPI-2: Assessing personality and psychopathology.* New York: Oxford University Press.

Graham, J. R. (1993). *MMPI-2: Assessing personality and psychopathology* (2nd ed.). New York: Oxford University Press.

Graham, J. R., Watts, D., & Timbrook, R. E. (1991). Detecting fake-good and fake-bad MMPI-2 profiles. *Journal of Personality Assessment, 57*, 264–277.

Grant, I., Sweetwood, H., Gerst, M. S., & Yager, J. (1978). Scaling procedures in life events research. *Journal of Psychosomatic Research, 22*, 525–530.

Grassi, J. R. (1973). *Grassi Basic Cognition Evaluation.* Miami, FL: University of Miami.

Greaud, V. A., & Green, B. F. (1986). Equivalence of conventional and computer presentation of speed tests. *Applied Psychological Measurement, 10*, 23–34.

Green, B. F. (1954). Attitude measurement. In G. Lindsey (Ed.), *Handbook of social psychology* (pp. 335–369) Cambridge, MA: Addison-Wesley.

Green, B. F. (1988). Critical problems in computer-based psychological measurement. *Applied Measurement in Education, 1*, 223–231.

Green, B. F. (1991). Guidelines for computer testing. In T. B. Gutkin & S. L. Wise (Eds.), *The computer and the decision-making process* (pp. 245–273). Hillsdale, NJ: Lawrence Erlbaum.

Green, C. J. (1982). The diagnostic accuracy and utility of MMPI and MCMI computer interpretive reports. *Journal of Personality Assessment, 46*, 359–365.

Green, R. F., & Goldfried, M. R. (1965). On the bipolarity of semantic space. *Psychological Monographs, 79*, 6 (Whole No. 599).

Greenbaum, P. E., Dedrick, R. F., & Lipien, L. (2004). The Child Behavior Checklist. In Hilsenroth, M. J., & Segal, D. L. (Eds.), Comprehensive handbook of Psychological assessment. Hoboken, NJ: Wiley & Sons.

Greene, A. C., Sapp, G. L., & Chissom, B. (1990). Validation of the Stanford-Binet Intelligence Scale: Fourth edition with exceptional black male students. *Psychology in the Schools, 27*, 35–41.

Greene, R. L. (1978). An empirically derived MMPI Carelessness Scale. *Journal of Clinical Psychology, 34*, 407–410.

Greene, R. L. (1980). *The MMPI: An interpretive manual.* New York: Grune & Stratton.

Greene, R. L. (1987). Ethnicity and MMPI performance: A review. *Journal of Consulting and Clinical Psychology, 55*, 497–512.

Greene, R. L. (1988). Assessment of malingering and defensiveness by objective personality inventories. In R. Rogers (Ed.), *Clinical assessment of malingering and deception* (pp. 123–158). New York: Guilford Press.

Greene, R. L. (1991). *The MMPI-2/MMPI: An interpretive manual.* Boston, MA: Allyn & Bacon.

Greenspoon, J., & Gersten, C. D. (1967). A new look at psychological testing: Psychological testing from the standpoint of a behaviorist. *American Psychologist, 22*, 848–853.

Greitzer, F. L., Hershman, R. L., & Kelly, R. T. (1981). The air defense game: A microcomputer program for research in human performance. *Behavior Research Methods and Instrumentation, 13*, 57–59.

Gresham, F. M., & Elliott, S. N. (1990). *Social Skills Rating System: Manual.* Circle Pines, MN: American Guidence Service.

Gridley, B. E. (1991). Confirmatory factor analysis of the Stanford-Binet: Fourth edition for a normal sample. *Journal of School Psychology, 29*, 237–248.

Gridley, B. E., & Treloar, J. H. (1984). The validity of the scales for rating the Behavioral Characteristics of Superior Students for the identification of gifted students. *Journal of Psychoeducational Assessment, 2*, 65–71.

Griffin, C. H. (1959). The development of processes for indirect or synthetic validity. 5. Application of motion and time analysis to dexterity tests. *Personnel Psychology, 12*, 418–420.

Griffiths, R. (1970). *The abilities of young children.* Chard, England: Young & Son.

Grigoriadis, S., & Fekken, G. C. (1992). Person reliability on the Minnesota Multiphasic Personality Inventory. *Personality and Individual Differences, 13*, 491–500.

Grisso, T. (1986). *Evaluating competencies: Forensic assessments and instruments.* New York: Plenum.

Gronlund, N. E. (1959). *Sociometry in the classroom.* New York: Harper & Brothers.

Gronlund, N. E. (1993). *How to make achievement tests and assessments* (5th ed.). Boston, MA: Allyn & Bacon.

Grønnerød, C. (1999). Rorschach interrater agreement estimates: An empirical evaluation. *Scandinavian Journal of Psychology, 40,* 115–120.

Gross, J., Rosen, J. C., Leitenberg, H., & Willmuth, M. E. (1986). Validity of the Eating Attitudes Test and the Eating Disorders Inventory in bulimia nervosa. *Journal of Consulting and Clinical Psychology, 54,* 875–876.

Grossman, F. M., & Johnson, K. M. (1983). Validity of the Slosson and Otis-Lennon in predicting achievement of gifted students. *Educational and Psychological Measurement, 43,* 617–622.

Grosze-Nipper, L. M. H., & Rebel, H. J. C. (1987). Dimensions of pacifism and militarism. In H. J. C. Rebel & L. Wecke (Eds.), *Friends, foes, values and fears.* (pp. 55–91). Amsterdam: Jan Mets.

Grotevant, H. D., Scarr, S., & Weinberg, R. A. (1977). Patterns of interest similarity in adoptive and biological families. *Journal of Personality and Social Psychology, 35,* 667–676.

Groth-Marnat, G. (1984). *Handbook of psychological assessment.* New York: Van Nostrand Reinhold Co.

Grove, W. M., Zald, D. H., Lebow, B. S., Snitz, B. E., & Nelson, C. (2000). Clinical versus mechanical prediction: A meta-analysis. *Psychological Assessment, 12,* 19–30.

Guastello, S. J., Guastello, D. D., & Craft, L. L. (1989). Assessment of the Barnum effect in computer-based test interpretations. *The Journal of Psychology, 123,* 477–484.

Guastello, S. J., & Rieke, M. L. (1990). The Barnum effect and validity of computer-based test interpretations: The human resource development report. *Psychological Assessment, 2,* 186–190.

Guertin, W. H., Ladd, C. E., Frank, G. H., Rabin, A. I., & Hiester, D. S. (1966). Research with the Wechsler intelligence scales for adults: 1960–1965. *Psychological Bulletin, 66,* 385–409.

Guilford, J. P. (1954). *Psychometric methods.* New York: McGraw-Hill.

Guilford, J. P. (1959a). Three faces of intellect. *American Psychologist, 14,* 469–479.

Guilford, J. P. (1959b). *Personality.* New York: McGraw-Hill.

Guilford, J. P. (1967a) Autobiography. In E. G. Boring & G. Lindzey (Eds.), *A history of psychology in autobiography* (Vol. 5, pp. 167–192). New York: Appleton-Century-Crofts.

Guilford, J. P. (1967b). *The nature of human intelligence.* New York: McGraw-Hill.

Guilford, J. P. (1988). Some changes in the Structure-of-Intellect Model. *Educational and Psychological Measurement, 48,* 1–4.

Guilford, J. P. & Fruchter, B. (1978). *Fundamental statistics in psychology and education.* New York: McGraw-Hill.

Guion, R. M. (1965a). *Personnel testing.* New York: McGraw-Hill.

Guion, R. M. (1965b). Synthetic validity in a small company: A demonstration. *Personnel Psychology, 18,* 49–63.

Guion, R. M. (1977). Content validity – the source of my discontent. *Applied Psychological Measurement, 1,* 1–10.

Guion, R. M. (1980). On trinitarian doctrines of validity. *Professional Psychology, 11,* 385–398.

Guion, R. M., & Gottier, R. F. (1965). Validity of personality measures in personnel selection. *Personnel Psychology, 18,* 135–164.

Gustafsson, J. E. (1984). A unifying model for the structure of intellectual abilities. *Intelligence, 8,* 179–203.

Gutkin, T. & Reynolds, C. R. (1980). Factorial similarity of the WISC-R for Anglos and Chicanos referred for psychological services. *Journal of School Psychology, 18,* 34–39.

Gutkin, T. B., & Reynolds, C. R. (1981). Factorial similarity of the WISC-R for white and black children from the standardization sample. *Journal of Educational Psychology, 73,* 227–231.

Gutterman, J. E. (1985). Correlations of scores of low vision children on the Perkins-Binet Tests of Intelligence for the Blind, the WISC-R and the WRAT. *Journal of Visual Impairment and Blindness, 79,* 55–58.

Guttman, L. (1944). A basis for scaling qualitative data. *American Sociological Review, 9,* 139–150.

Guttman, L. (1945). A basis for analysing test-retest reliability. *Psychometrika, 10,* 255–282.

Gynther, M. D. (1972). White norms and Black MMPI's: A prescription for discrimination. *Psychological Bulletin, 78,* 386–402.

Gynther, M. D. (1979). Aging and personality. In J. N. Butcher (Ed.), *New developments in the use of the MMPI* (pp. 39–68). Minneapolis: University of Minnesota Press.

Gynther, M. D., Fowler, R. D., & Erdberg, P. (1971). False positives galore: The application of standard MMPI criteria to a rural, isolated, Negro sample. *Journal of Clinical Psychology, 27,* 234–237.

Gynther, M. D., & Gynther, R. A. (1976). Personality inventories. In I. B. Weiner (Ed.), *Clinical methods in psychology.* New York: Wiley.

Hackman, J. R., Wiggins, N., & Bass, A. R. (1970). Prediction of long-term success in doctoral work in psychology. *Educational and Psychological Measurement, 30*, 365–374.

Haemmerlie, F. M., & Merz, C. J. (1991). Concurrent validity between the California Psychological Inventory-Revised and the Student Adaptation to College questionnaire. *Journal of Clinical Psychology, 47*, 664–668.

Hagen, E., Delaney, E., & Hopkins, T. (1987). *Stanford-Binet Intelligence Scale examiner's handbook: An expanded guide for fourth edition users.* Chicago, IL: Riverside.

Hainsworth, P. K., & Hainsworth, M. L. (1980). *Preschool Screening System.* Pawtucket, RI: Early Recognition Intervention Systems.

Hakstian, A. R., & Farrell, S. (2001). An openness scale for the California Psychological Inventory. *Journal of Personality Assessment, 76*, 107–134.

Haladyna, T. M., & Downing, S. M. (1989a). A taxonomy of multiple-choice item-writing rules. *Applied Measurement in Education, 2*, 37–50.

Haladyna, T. M., & Downing, S. M. (1989b). Validity of a taxonomy of multiple-choice item-writing rules. *Applied Measurement in Education, 2*, 51–78.

Haladyna, T., & Downing, S. (1994). How many options is enough for a multiple-choice test item? *Educational and Psychological Measurement, 53*, 999–1009.

Hale, R. L. (1978). The WISC-R as a predictor of WRAT performance. *Psychology in the Schools, 15*, 172–175.

Hale, R. L., & Landino, S. A. (1981). Utility of WISC-R subtest analysis in discriminating among groups of conduct problem, withdrawn, mixed, and non-problem boys. *Journal of Consulting and Clinical Psychology, 49*, 91–95.

Hall, C. S., & Lindzey, G. (1970). *Theories of personality.* New York: Wiley.

Hall, G., Bansal, A., & Lopez, I. (1999). Ethnicity and psychopathology: A meta-analytic review of 31 years of comparative MMPI/MMPI-2 research. *Psychological Assessment, 11*, 186–197.

Hall, H. V., & Pritchard, D. A. (1996). *Detecting malingering and deception.* Delray Beach, FL: St. Lucie Press.

Haller, N., & Exner, J. E. Jr. (1985). The reliability of Rorschach variables for inpatients presenting symptoms of depression and/or helplessness. *Journal of Personality Assessment, 49*, 516–521.

Halpin, G., Halpin, G., & Schaer, B. B. (1981). Relative effectiveness of the California Achievement Tests in comparison with the ACT Assessment, College Board Scholastic Aptitude Test, and High school grade point average in predicting college grade point average. *Educational and Psychological Measurement, 41*, 821–827.

Halverson, C. F. (1995). Measurement beyond the individual. In J. C. Conoley & E. B. Werth (Eds.), *Family assessment* (pp. 3–18). Lincoln, NB: Buros Institute of Mental Measurements.

Hambleton, R. K. (1984). Validating the test score. In R. A. Berk (Ed.), *A guide to criterion-referenced test construction* (pp. 199–230). Baltimore, MD: Johns Hopkins University Press.

Hambleton, R. K., & Murphy, E. (1992). A psychometric perspective on authentic measurement. *Applied Measurement in Education, 5*, 1–16.

Hambleton, R. K., & Swaminathan, H. (1985). *Item response theory: Principles and applications.* Boston, MA: Kluwer-Nijhoff.

Hamilton, S. (1960). A rating scale for depression. *Journal of Neurology, Neurosurgery and Psychiatry, 23*, 56–62.

Hammen, C. L. (1980). Depression in college students: Beyond the Beck Depression Inventory. *Journal of Consulting and Clinical Psychology, 48*, 126–128.

Hammer, E. F. (1978). *The clinical application of projective drawings.* Springfield, IL: Charles C Thomas.

Hampton, N. H. (1986). Luria-Nebraska Neuropsychological Battery (LNNB) Forms I and II microcomputer diskette. *Computers in Human Behavior, 2*, 92–93.

Haney, W. (1981). Validity, vaudeville, and values. *American Psychologist, 36* 1021–1034.

Haney, W., & Madaus, G. (1978). Making sense of the competency testing movement. *Harvard Educational Review, 48*, 462–484.

Haney, W. M., Madaus, G. F., & Lyons, R. (1993). *The fractured marketplace for standardized testing.* Boston, MA: Kluwer Academic Publishers.

Hanford, G. H. (1985). Yes, the SAT does help colleges. *Harvard Educational Review, 55*, 324–331.

Hannah, M. T., Domino, G., Figueredo, A. J., & Hendrickson, R. (1996). The prediction of ego integrity in older persons. *Educational and Psychological Measurement, 56*, 930–950.

Hansen, J. C. (1984). *User's guide for the SVIB-SCII.* Stanford, CA: Stanford University Press.

Hansen, J. C. (1986). Strong Vocational Interest Blank/Strong-Campbell Interest Inventory. In W. B. Walsh & S. H. Osipow (Eds.), *Advances in Vocational Psychology* (Vol. 1, pp. 1–29). Hillsdale, NJ: Lawrence Erlbaum Associates.

Hansen, J. C., & Campbell, D. P. (1985). *Manual for the SVIB-SCII* (4th ed.). Stanford, CA: Stanford University Press.

Hansen, R., Young, J., & Ulrey, G. (1982). Assessment considerations with the visually handicapped child. In G. Ulrey & S. Rogers (Eds.), *Psychological assessment of handicapped infants and young children.* (pp. 108–114). New York: Thieme-Stratton.

Hanson, S., Buckelew, S. P., Hewett, J., & O'Neal, G. (1993). The relationship between coping and adjustment after spinal cord injury: A 5-year follow-up study. *Rehabilitation Psychology, 38,* 41–52.

Hardy, J. B., Welcher, D. W., Mellits, E. D., & Kagan, J. (1976). Pitfalls in the measurement of intelligence: Are standard intelligence tests valid instruments for measuring the intellectual potential of urban children? *Journal of Psychology, 94,* 43–51.

Harkness, A. R., McNulty, J. L., & Ben-Porath, Y. S. (1995). The Personality Psychopathology Five (PSY-5): Constructs and MMPI-2 scales. *Psychological Assessment, 7,* 104–114.

Harmann, H. H. (1960). *Modern factor analysis.* Chicago, IL: University of Chicago Press.

Harmon, M. G., Morse, D. T., & Morse, L. W. (1996). Confirmatory factor analysis of the Gibb experimental test of testwiseness. *Educational and Psychological Measurement, 56,* 276–286.

Harnett, R. T., & Willingham, W. W. (1980). The criterion problem: What measure of success in graduate education? *Applied Psychological Measurement, 4,* 281–291.

Harrell, T. W. (1992). Some history of the Army General Classification Test. *Journal of Applied Psychology, 77,* 875–878.

Harrington, R. G., & Follett, G. M. (1984). The readability of child personality assessment instruments. *Journal of Psychoeducational Assessment, 2,* 37–48.

Harrington, R. G., & Jennings, V. (1986). Comparison of three short forms of the McCarthy Scales of Children's Abilities. *Contemporary Educational Psychology, 11,* 109–116.

Harris, D. B. (1963). *Children's drawings as measures of intellectual maturity.* New York: Harcourt, Brace & World.

Harris, M. M., & Schaubroeck, J. (1988). A metaanalysis of self-supervisor, self-peer, and peer-supervisor ratings. *Personnel Psychology, 41,* 43–62.

Harrower, M. R., & Herrmann, R. (1953). *Psychological factors in the care of patients with multiple scleroses: For use of physicians.* New York: National Multiple Sclerosis Society.

Hart, S. D., Roesch, R., Corrado, R. R., & Cox, D. N. (1993). The Referral Decision Scale. *Law and Human Behavior, 17,* 611–623.

Hartigan, J. A., & Wigdor, A. K. (1989). *Fairness in employment testing.* Washington, DC: National Academy Press.

Hartlage, L. C. (1987). Diagnostic assessment in rehabilitation. In B. Bolton (Ed.), *Handbook of measurement and evaluation in rehabilitation* (2nd ed., pp. 141–149). Baltimore, MD: Paul H. Brookes.

Hartlage, L. C., & Steele, C. T. (1977). WISC and WISC-R correlates of academic achievement. *Psychology in the Schools, 14,* 15–18.

Hartley, J., & Holt, J. (1971). A note on the validity of the Wilson-Patterson measure of conservatism. *British Journal of Social and Clinical Psychology, 10,* 81–83.

Hartman, A. A. (1970). A basic T.A.T. set. *Journal of Projective Techniques and Personality Assessment, 34,* 391–396.

Hartman, D. E. (1986). Artificial intelligence or artificial psychologist? Conceptual issues in clinical microcomputer use. *Professional Psychology, 17,* 528–534.

Hartmann, D. P. (1977). Considerations in the choice of interobserver reliability estimates. *Journal of Applied Behavior Analysis, 10,* 103–116.

Hartmann, D. P., Roper, B. L., & Bradford, D. C. (1979). Source relationships between behavioral and traditional assessment. *Journal of Behavioral Assessment, 1,* 3–21.

Hartmann, G. (1938). The differential validity of items in a Liberalism-Conservatism Test. *Journal of Social Psychology, 9,* 67–78.

Hartnett, R. T., & Willingham, W. W. (1980). The criterion problem: What measure of success in graduate education? *Applied Psychological Measurement, 4,* 281–291.

Hartshorne, H., & May, M. A. (1928). *Studies in deceit.* New York: Macmillan.

Hartshorne, T. S. (1993). Psychometric properties and confirmatory factor analysis of the UCLA Loneliness scale. *Journal of Personality Assessment, 61,* 182–195.

Hase, H. D., & Goldberg, L. R. (1967). Comparative validity of different strategies of constructing personality inventory scales. *Psychological Bulletin, 67,* 231–248.

Hathaway, S. R., & McKinley, J. C. (1943). *The Minnesota Multiphasic Personality Inventory.* Minneapolis, MN: University of Minnesota Press.

Hathaway, S. R., McKinley, J. C., Butcher, J. N., Dahlstrom, W. G., Graham, J. R., Tellegen, A., & Kaemmer, B. (1989). *MMPI-2: Manual for administration and scoring.* Minneapolis, MN: University of Minnesota Press.

Hathaway, S. R., & Meehl, P. E. (1951). *An atlas for the clinical use of the MMPI.* Minneapolis, MN: University of Minnesota Press.

Hawkins, N. C., Davies, R., & Holmes, T. H. (1957). Evidence of psychosocial factors in the development of pulmonary tuberculosis. *American Review of Tuberculosis and Pulmonary Disorders, 75,* 768–780.

Hayden, D. C., Furlong. M. J., & Linnemeyer, S. (1988). A comparison of the Kaufman Assessment

Battery for Children and the Stanford-Binet IV for the assessment of gifted children. *Psychology in the Schools, 25,* 239–243.

Hayes, F. B., & Martin, R. P. (1986). Effectiveness of the PPVT-R in the screening of young gifted children. *Journal of Psychoeducational Assessment, 4,* 27–33.

Hayes, S. C., Nelson, R. O., & Jarrett, R. B. (1986). Evaluating the quality of behavioral assessment. In R. O. Nelson & S. C. Hayes (Eds.), *Conceptual foundations of behavioral assessment* (pp. 463–503). New York: Guilford Press.

Hayes, S. N., Floyd, F. J., Lemsky, C., Rogers, E., Winemiller, D., Heilman, N., Werle, M., Murphy, T., & Cardone, L. (1992). The Marital Satisfaction Questionnaire for older persons. *Psychological Assessment, 4,* 473–482.

Hayes, S. N., Richard, D. C. S., & Kubany, E. S. (1995). Content validity in psychological assessment: A functional approach to concepts and methods. *Psychological Assessment, 7,* 238–247.

Hayes, S. P. (1929). The new revision of the Binet Intelligence Tests for the blind. *Teachers Forum, 2,* 2–4.

Haynes, J. P., & Bensch, M. (1981). The PV sign on the WISC-R and recidivism in delinquents. *Journal of Consulting and Clinical Psychology, 49,* 480–481.

Haynes, S. N., & Wilson, C. C. (1979). *Behavioral assessment.* San Francisco, CA: Jossey-Bass.

Hays, D. G., & Borgatta, E. P. (1954). An empirical comparison of restricted and general latent distance analysis. *Psychometrika, 19,* 271–279.

Hays, R. D., & DiMatteo, M. R. (1987). A short-form measure of loneliness. *Journal of Personality Assessment, 51,* 69–81.

Hayslip, B., Jr. (1984). Idiographic assessment of the self in the aged: A case for the use of the Q-sort. *International Journal of Aging and Human Development, 20,* 293–311.

Heath, R. L., & Fogel, D. S. (1978). Terminal and instrumental? An inquiry into Rokeach's Value Survey. *Psychological Reports, 42,* 1147–1154.

Heaton, R. K., Grant, I., Anthony, W. Z., & Lehman, R. A. W. (1981). A comparison of clinical and automated interpretation of the Halstead-Reitan battery. *Journal of Clinical Neuropsychology, 3,* 121–141.

Heaton, R. K., Smith, H. H., Jr., Lehman, R. A. W., & Vogt, A. J. (1978). Prospects for faking believable deficits on neuropsychological testing. *Journal of Consulting and Clinical Psychology, 46,* 892–900.

Heaton, R. R., Grant, I., & Matthews, C. G. (1991). *Comprehensive norms for an expanded Halstead-Reitan Battery.* Odessa, FL: Psychological Assessment Resources.

Heaton, S. M., Nelson, A. V., & Nester, M. A. (1980). *Guide for administering examinations to handicapped individuals for employment purposes* (PRR 80–16). Washington, DC: Personnel Research and Development Center.

Heckhausen, H. (1967). *The anatomy of achievement motivation.* New York: Academic Press.

Hedlund, J. L., & Vieweg, B. W. (1979). The Zung Self-Rating Depression Scale: A comprehensive review. *Journal of Operational Psychiatry, 10,* 51–64.

Heil, J., Barclay, A., & Endres, J. M. (1978). A factor analytic study of WPPSI scores of educationally deprived and normal children. *Psychological Reports, 42,* 727–730.

Heilbrun, A. B., Jr. (1972). Review of the EPPS. In O. K. Buros (Ed.), *The seventh mental measurements yearbook* (Vol. 1, pp. 148–149). Highland Park, NJ: Gryphon Press.

Heilbrun, A. B., & Goodstein, L. D. (1961). The relationships between individually defined and group defined social desirability and performance on the Edwards Personal Preference Schedule. *Journal of Consulting Psychology, 25,* 200–204.

Heilbrun (1992). The role of psychological testing in forensic assessment. *Law and Human Behavior, 16,* 257–272.

Heim, A. W. (1975). *Psychological testing.* London: Oxford University Press.

Helmes, E., & Reddon, J. R. (1993). A perspective on developments in assessing psychopathology: A critical review of the MMPI and MMPI-2. *Psychological Bulletin, 113,* 453–471.

Helms, J. E. (1992). Why is there no study of cultural equivalence in standardized cognitive ability testing? *American Psychologist, 47,* 1083–1101.

Hendershott, J. L., Searight, H. R., Hatfield, J. L., & Rogers, B. J. (1990). Correlations between the Stanford-Binet, fourth edition and the Kaufman Assessment Battery for Children for a preschool sample. *Perceptual and Motor Skills, 71,* 819–825.

Henderson, R. W., & Rankin, R. J. (1973). WPPSI reliability and predictive validity with disadvantaged Mexican-American children. *Journal of School Psychology, 11,* 16–20.

Henerson, M. E., Morris, L. L., & Fitz-Gibbon, C. T. (1987). *How to measure attitudes.* Newbury Park, CA: Sage.

Henry, P., Bryson, S., & Henry, C. A. (1990). Black student attitudes toward standardized tests: Does gender make a difference? *College Student Journal, 23,* 346–354.

Henry, W. E. (1956). *The analysis of fantasy: The thematic apperception technique in the study of personality.* New York: Wiley.

Herrmann, D. J. (1982). Know thy memory: The use of questionnaires to assess and study memory. *Psychological Bulletin, 92,* 434–452.

Hersen, M. (1973). Self-assessment of fear. *Behavior Therapy, 4,* 241–257.

Hersen, M., & Bellack, A. S. (1977). Assessment of social skills. In A. R. Ciminero, K. S. Calhoun, & H. E. Adams (Eds.), *Handbook of behavioral assessment* (pp. 509–554). New York: Wiley.

Hersen, M., & Bellack, A. S. (Eds.). (1981). *Behavioral assessment.* Elmsford, NY: Pergamon.

Hertzog, C., & Schear, J. M. (1989). Psychometric considerations in testing the older person. In T. Hunt & C. J. Lindley (Eds.), *Testing older adults* (pp. 24–50). Austin, TX: Pro-ed.

Herzog, A. R., & Rodgers, W. L. (1981). Age and satisfaction: Data from several large surveys. *Research on Aging, 3,* 142–165.

Hess, A. K. (1985). Review of Millon Clinical Multiaxial Inventory. In J. V. Mitchell, Jr. (Ed.), *The ninth mental measurements yearbook* (Vol. 1, pp. 984–986). Lincoln, NE: University of Nebraska Press.

Hess, D. W. (1969). Evaluation of the young deaf adult. *Journal of Rehabilitation of the Deaf, 3,* 6–21.

Hess, E. H. (1965). Attitude and pupil size. *Scientific American, 212,* 46–54.

Hess, E. H., & Polt, J. M. (1960). Pupil size as related to interest value of visual stimuli. *Science, 132,* 349–350.

Hetzler, S. A. (1954). Radicalism-Conservatism and social mobility. *Social Forces, 33,* 161–166.

Heveren, V. W. (1980). Recent validity studies of the Halstead-Reitan approach to clinical neuropsychological assessment. *Clinical Neuropsychology, 2,* 49–61.

Hevner, K. (1930). An empirical study of three psychophysical methods. *Journal of General Psychology, 4,* 191–212.

Hilgard, E. R. (1957). Lewis Madison Terman 1877–1956. *American Journal of Psychology, 70,* 472–479.

Hill, A. B., Kemp-Wheeler, S. M., & Jones, S. A. (1986). What does Beck Depression Inventory measure in students? *Personality and Individual Differences, 7,* 39–47.

Hill, K. T. (1972). Anxiety in the evaluative context. In W. Hartup (Ed.), *The young child* (Vol. 2). Washington, DC: National Association for the Education of Young Children.

Hill, K. T., & Sarason, S. B. (1966). The relation of test anxiety and defensiveness to test and school performance over the elementary school years: A further longitudinal study. *Monographs of the Society for Research in Child Development, 31* (No. 2).

Hiller, J. B., Rosenthall, R., Bornstein, R., Berry, D., & Brunell-Neuleib, S. (1999). A comparative meta-analysis of Rorschach and MMPI validity. *Psychological Assessment, 11,* 278–296.

Hilliard, A. G. (1975). The strengths and weaknesses of cognitive tests for young children. In J. D. Andrews (Ed.), *One child indivisible.* (pp. 17–33). Washington, DC: National Association for the Education of Young Children.

Hills, J. R., Bush, M., & Klock, J. A. (1964). Predicting grades beyond the freshman year. *College Board Review, 54,* 22–24.

Hilton, T. L., & Korn, J. H. (1964). Measured change in personal values. *Educational and Psychological Measurement, 24,* 609–622.

Himmelfarb, S. (1984). Age and sex differences in the mental health of older persons. *Journal of Consulting and Clinical Psychology, 52,* 844–856.

Hinckley, E. D. (1932). The influence of individual opinion on construction of an attitude scale. *Journal of Social Psychology, 3,* 283–296.

Hirshoren, A., Hurley, O. L., & Hunt, J. T. (1977). The WISC-R and the Hiskey-Nebraska Test with deaf children. *American Annals of the Deaf, 122,* 392–394.

Hirshoren, A., Hurley, O. L., & Kavale, K. (1979). Psychometric characteristics of the WISC-R Performance Scale with deaf children. *Journal of Speech and Hearing Disorders, 44,* 73–79.

Hiscock. M. (1978). Imagery assessment through self-report: What do imagery questionnaires measure? *Journal of Consulting and Clinical Psychology, 46,* 223–230.

Hiskey, M. S. (1966). *Hiskey-Nebraska Test of Learning Aptitude.* Lincoln, NE: Union College Press.

Hobbs, S. A., & Walle, D. L. (1985). Validation of the Children's Assertive Behavior Scale. *Journal of Psychopathology and Behavioral Assessment, 7,* 145–153.

Hocevar, D. (1979). A comparison of statistical infrequency and subjective judgment as criteria in the measurement of originality. *Journal of Personality Assessment, 43,* 297–299.

Hodges, W. F., & Spielberger, C. D. (1966). The effects of threat of shock on heart rate for subjects who differ in manifest anxiety and fear of shock. *Psychophysiology, 2,* 287–294.

Hoemann, H. W. (1972). Communication accuracy in a sign-language interpretation of a group test. *Journal of Rehabilitation of the Deaf, 5,* 40–43.

Hoffman, R. A., & Gellen, M. I. (1983). The Tennessee Self Concept Scale: A revisit. *Psychological Reports, 53,* 1199–1204.

Hogan, R. (1969). Development of an empathy scale. *Journal of Consulting and Clinical Psychology, 33,* 307–316.

Hogan R. (1989a). Review of the Personality Research Form (3rd ed.). In J. C. Conoley & J. J. Kramer (Eds.), *The tenth mental measurements yearbook* (pp. 632–633). Lincoln, NB: University of Nebraska Press.

Hogan, R. (1989b). Review of the NEO Personality Inventory. In J. C. Conoley & J. J. Kramer (Eds.), *The tenth mental measurements yearbook* (pp. 546–547). Lincoln, NE: University of Nebraska Press.

Hogan, R. (1990). What kinds of tests are useful in organizations? In J. Hogan & R. Hogan (Eds.), *Business and industry testing* (pp. 22–35). Austin, TX: Pro-Ed.

Hogan, R., DeSoto, C. B., & Solano, C. (1977). Traits, tests, and personality research. *American Psychologist, 32,* 255–264.

Hogan, R. T. (1983). A socioanalytic theory of personality. In M. Page (Ed.), 1982 *Nebraska Symposium on Motivation* (pp. 55–89). Lincoln, NB: University of Nebraska Press.

Hoge, D. R., & Bender, I. E. (1974). Factors influencing value change among college graduates in adult life. *Journal of Personality and Social Psychology, 29,* 572–585.

Hoge, S. K., Bonnie, R. J., Poythress, N., & Monahan, J. (1999). *The MacArthur Competence Assessment Tool – Criminal Adjudication.* Odessa, FL: Psychological Assessment Resources.

Hojat, M. (1982). Psychometric characteristics of the UCLA Loneliness Scale: A study with Iranian college students. *Educational and Psychological Measurement, 42,* 917–925.

Holaday, M., Smith, D. A., & Sherry, A. (2000). Sentence completion tests: A review of the literature and results of a survey of members of the Society for Personality Assessment. *Journal of Personality Assessment, 74,* 371–383.

Holahan, C. K., & Holahan, C. J. (1987). Life stress, hassles, and self-efficacy in aging: A replication and extension. *Journal of Applied Social Psychology, 17,* 574–592.

Holden, R. R., & Fekken, G. C. (1989). Three common social desirability scales: Friends, acquaintances, or strangers. *Journal of Research in Personality, 23,* 180–191.

Holland, J. L. (1966). *The psychology of vocational choice.* Waltham, MA: Blaisdell.

Holland, J. L. (1973). *Making vocational choices: A theory of careers.* Englewood Cliffs, NJ: Prentice-Hall.

Holland, J. L. (1985a). *Making vocational choices: A theory of vocational personalities and work environments* (2nd ed.). Englewood Cliffs, NJ: Prentice Hall.

Holland, J. L. (1985b). *Professional manual for the self-directed search.* Odessa, FL: Psychological Assessment Resources.

Holland, J. L., & Nichols, R. C. (1964). Prediction of academic and extracurricular achievement in college. *Journal of Educational Psychology, 55,* 55–65.

Hollandsworth, J. G., Galassi, J. P., & Gay, M. L. (1977). The Adult Self Expression Scale: Validation by the multitrait-multimethod procedure. *Journal of Clinical Psychology, 33,* 407–415.

Hollenbeck, G. P., & Kaufman, A. S. (1973). Factor analysis of the Wechsler Preschool and Primary Scale of Intelligence (WPPSI). *Journal of Clinical Psychology, 29,* 41–45.

Hollinger, R. D., & Clark, J. P. (1983). *Theft by employees.* Lexington, MA: Lexington Books.

Hollrah, J. L., Schlottmann, R. S., Scott, A. B., & Brunetti, D. G. (1995). Validity of the MMPI subtle items. *Journal of Personality Assessment, 65,* 278–299.

Holm, C. S. (1987). Testing for values with the deaf: The language/cultural effect. *Journal of Rehabilitation of the Deaf, 20,* 7–19.

Holmes, T. H., & Rahe, R. H. (1967). The Social Readjustment Rating Scale. *Journal of Psychosomatic Research, 11,* 213–218.

Holt, R. R. (1951). The Thematic Apperception Test. In H. H. Anderson & G. L. Anderson (Eds.), *An introduction to projective techniques.* Englewood Cliffs, NJ: Prentice Hall.

Holt, R. R. (1958). Clinical and statistical prediction: A reformulation and some new data. *Journal of Abnormal and Social Psychology, 56,* 1–12.

Holt, R. R. (1971). *Assessing personality.* New York: Harcourt Brace Jovanovich.

Holtzman, W. H. (1968). Cross-cultural studies in psychology. *International Journal of Psychology, 3,* 83–91.

Holtzman, W. H., Thorpe, J. S., Swartz, J. D., & Herron, E. W. (1961). *Inkblot perception and personality – Holtzman Inkblot Technique.* Austin, TX: University of Texas Press.

Honaker, L. M., Hector, V. S., & Harrell, T. H. (1986). Perceived validity of computer-vs. clinician-generated MMPI reports. *Computers in Human Behavior, 2,* 77–83.

Hong, K. E., & Holmes, T. H. (1973). Transient diabetes mellitus associated with culture change. *Archives of General Psychiatry, 29,* 683–687.

Hopkins, K. D., & McGuire, L. (1966). Mental measurement of the blind: The validity of the Wechsler Intelligence Scale for Children. *International Journal for the Education of the Blind, 15,* 65–73.

Hops, H., & Lewin, L. (1984). Peer sociometric forms. In T. H. Ollendick & M. Hersen (Eds.), *Child Behavioral Assessment* (pp. 124–147). New York: Pergamon.

Horiguchi, J., & Inami, Y. (1991). A survey of the living conditions and psychological states of elderly people admitted to nursing homes in Japan. *Acta Psychiatrica Scandinavica, 83,* 338–341.

Horn, J. (1986). Intellectual ability concepts. In R. J. Sternberg (Ed.), *Advances in the psychology of human intelligence* (Vol. 3). Hillsdale, NJ: Erlbaum.

Horn, J. L., Wanberg, K. W., & Foster, F. M. (1987). *Guide to the Alcohol Use Inventory*. Minneapolis, MN: National Computer Systems.

Hornick, C. W., James, L. R., & Jones, A. P. (1977). Empirical item keying vs. a rational approach to analyzing a psychological climate questionnaire. *Applied Psychological Measurement, 1*, 489–500.

Horowitz, M. D., Wilner, N., & Alvarez, W. (1979). Impact of event scale: A measure of subjective stress. *Psychosomatic Medicine, 41*, 209–218.

Hough, L. M. (1992). The "Big Five" personality variables – construct confusion: Description vs. prediction. *Human Performance, 5*, 139–155.

Hough, L. M., Eaton, N. K., Dunnette, M. D., Kamp, J. D., & McCloy, R. A. (1990). Criterion-related validities of personality constructs and the effect of response distortion on those validities. *Journal of Applied Psychology, 75*, 581–585.

House, A. E., House, B. J., & Campbell, M. B. (1981). Measures of interobserver agreement: Calculation formulas and distribution effects. *Journal of Behavioral Assessment, 3*, 37–57.

House, J. D., & Johnson, J. J. (1993a). Graduate Record Examination scores and academic background variables as predictors of graduate degree completion. *Educational and Psychological Measurement, 35*, 551–556.

House, J. D., & Johnson, J. J. (1993b). Predictive validity of the Graduate Record Examination Advanced Psychology Test for graduate grades. *Psychological Reports, 73*, 184–186.

House, J. D., Johnson, J. J., & Tolone, W. L. (1987). Predictive validity of the Graduate Record Examination for performance in selected graduate psychology courses. *Psychological Reports, 60*, 107–110.

Houston, L. N. (1980). Predicting academic achievement among specially admitted black female college students. *Educational and Psychological Measurement, 40*, 1189–1195.

Houtz, J. C., & Shaning, D. J. (1982). Contribution of teacher ratings of behavioral characteristics to the prediction of divergent thinking and problem solving. *Psychology in the Schools, 19*, 380–383.

Hoyt, D. R., & Creech, J. C. (1983). The Life Satisfaction Index: A methodological and theoretical critique. *Journal of Gerontology, 38*, 111–116.

Hu, S., & Oakland, T. (1991). Global and regional perspectives on testing children and youth: An empirical study. *International Journal of Psychology, 26*, 329–344.

Hubert, N. C., Wachs, T. D., Peters-Martin, P., & Gandour, M. J. (1982). The study of early temperament: Measurement and conceptual issues. *Child Development, 53*, 571–600.

Hudgens, R. W. (1974). Personal catastrophe and depression: A consideration of the subject with respect to medically ill adolescents, and a requiem for retrospective life-event studies. In B. S. Dohrenwend, & B. P. Dohrenwend (Eds.), *Stressful life events: Their nature and effects* (pp. 119–134). New York: Wiley.

Hui, C. H., & Triandis, H. C. (1985). Measurement in cross-cultural psychology. *Journal of Cross-Cultural Psychology, 16*, 131–152.

Hui, C. H., & Triandis, H. C. (1989). Effects of culture and response format on extreme response style. *Journal of Cross-Cultural Psychology, 20*, 296–309.

Huitema, B. E., & Stein, C. R. (1993). Validity of the GRE without restriction of range. *Psychological Reports, 72*, 123–127.

Hull, J. G., Van Treuren, R. R., & Virnelli, S. (1987). Hardiness and health: A critique and alternative approach. *Journal of Personality and Social Psychology, 53*, 518–530.

Humphreys, L. G. (1962). The organization of human abilities. *American Psychologist, 17*, 475–483.

Humphreys, L. G. (1985). Review of the System of Multicultural Pluralistic Assessment. In J. V. Mitchell (Ed.), *The ninth mental measurements yearbook* (pp. 1517–1519). Lincoln, NB: University of Nebraska Press.

Hunsley, J., Vito, D., Pinsent, C., James, S., & Lefebvre, M. (1996). Are self-report measures of dyadic relationships influenced by impression management biases? *Journal of Family Psychology, 10*, 322–330.

Hunter, J. E. (1986). Cognitive ability, cognitive aptitudes, job knowledge, and job performance. *Journal of Vocational Behavior, 29*, 340–362.

Hunter, J. E., & Hunter, R. F. (1984). Validity and utility of alternative predictors of job performance. *Psychological Bulletin, 96*, 72–99.

Hunter, J. E., Schmidt, F. L., & Hunter, R. F. (1979). Differential validity of employment tests by race: A comprehensive review and analysis. *Psychological Bulletin, 86*, 721–735.

Hunter, J. E., Schmidt, F. L., & Rauschenberger, J. M. (1977). Fairness of psychological tests: Implications of four definitions for selection utility and minority hiring. *Journal of Applied Psychology, 62*, 245–260.

Huntley, C. W. (1965). Changes in Study of Values scores during the four years of college. *Genetic Psychology Monographs, 71*, 349–383.

Hurtz, G. M., & Hertz, N. M. R. (1999). How many raters should be used for establishing cutoff scores with the Angoff method? A generalizability theory study. *Educational and Psychological Measurement, 59*, 885–897.

Hutt, M. (1977). *The Hutt adaptation of the Bender-Gestalt* (3rd ed.). New York: Grune & Stratton.

Hyde, J. S., Fennema, E., & Lamon, S. J. (1990). Gender differences in mathematics performance: A meta-analysis. *Psychological Bulletin, 107,* 139–155.

Hynd, G. W. (1988). *Neuropsychological assessment in clinical child psychology.* Newbury Park, CA: Sage.

Illerbrun, D., Haines, L., & Greenough, P. (1985). Language identification screening test for kindergarten: A comparison with four screening and three diagnostic language tests. *Language, Speech and Hearing Services in Schools, 16,* 280–292.

Inglehart, R. (1985). Aggregate stability and individual-level flux in mass belief systems: The level of analysis paradox. *American Political Science Review, 79,* 97–116.

Insko, C. A., & Schopler, J. (1967). Triadic consistency: A statement of affective-cognitive-conative consistency. *Psychological Review, 74,* 361–376.

Inwald, R., Knatz, H., & Shusman, E. (1983). *Inwald Personality Inventory manual.* New York: Hilson Research.

Ireton, H., & Thwing, E. (1979). *Minnesota Preschool Inventory.* Minneapolis, MN: Behavior Science Systems.

Ironson, G. H., & Davis, G. A. (1979). Faking high or low creativity scores on the Adjective Check List. *Journal of Creative Behavior, 13,* 139–145.

Irvine, S. H. (1969). Figural tests of reasoning in Africa. *International Journal of Psychology, 4,* 217–228.

Irwin, R. B. (1914). A Binet scale for the blind. *New Outlook for the Blind, 8,* 95–97.

Iwawaki, S., & Cowen, E. L. (1964). The social desirability of trait descriptive terms: Applications to a Japanese sample. *Journal of Social Psychology, 63,* 199–205.

Iwao, S., & Triandis, H. C. (1993). Validity of auto- and heterostereotypes among Japanese and American students. *Journal of Cross-Cultural Psychology, 24,* 428–444.

Jaccard, J. (1981). Attributes and behavior: Implications of attitudes towards behavioral alternatives. *Journal of Experimental Social Psychology, 17,* 286–307.

Jackson, D. N. (1967). *Personality research form manual.* Goshen, NY: Research Psychologists Press.

Jackson, D. N. (1970). A sequential system for personality scale development. In C. D. Spielberger (Ed.), *Current topics in clinical and community psychology* (Vol. 2, pp. 61–96). New York: Academic Press.

Jackson, D. N. (1977). *Manual for the Jackson Vocational Interest Survey.* Port Huron, MI: Research Psychologists Press.

Jackson, D. N. (1984). *Personality Research Form manual* (3rd ed.). Port Huron, MI: Research Psychologists Press.

Jackson, D. N., & Messick, S. (1958). Content and style in personality assessment. *Psychological Bulletin, 55,* 243–252.

Jackson, D. N., & Minton, H. (1963). A forced-choice adjective preference scale for personality assessment. *Psychological Reports, 12,* 515–520.

Jackson, J. L. (1999). Psychometric considerations in self-monitoring assessment. *Psychological Assessment, 11,* 439–447.

Jacob, S., & Brantley, J. C. (1987). Ethical-legal problems with computer use and suggestions for best practices: A national survey. *School Psychology Review, 16,* 69–77.

Jacobs, J. W., Bernhard, M. R., Delgado, A., & Strain. J. J. (1977). Screening for organic mental syndromes in the medically ill. *Annals of Internal Medicine, 86,* 40–46.

Jacobson, L. I., Kellogg, R. W., Cauce, A. M., & Slavin, R. S. (1977). A multidimensional social desirability inventory. *Bulletin of the Psychonomic Society, 9,* 109–110.

Jacobson, L. I., Prio, M. A., Ramirez, M. A., Fernandez, A. J., & Hevia, M. L. (1978). Construccion y validacion de una prueba de intelligencia para Cubanos. *Interamerican Journal of Psychology, 12,* 39–45.

Jaeger, R. M. (1985). Review of Graduate Record Examinations. In J. V. Mitchell, Jr. (Ed.), *The ninth mental measurements yearbook* (Vol. 1, pp. 624–626). Lincoln: University of Nebraska Press.

Jaeger, R. M., Linn, R. L., & Tesh, A. S. (1989). A synthesis of research on some psychometric properties of the GATB. In J. A. Hartigan & A. K. Wigdor (Eds.), *Fairness in employment testing* (pp. 303–324). Washington, DC: National Academy Press.

Janda, L., & Galbraith, G. (1973). Social desirability and adjustment in the Rotter Incomplete Sentences Blank. *Journal of Consulting and Clinical Psychology, 40,* 337.

Janis, I. (1980). Personality differences in decision making under stress. In K. Blandenstein, P. Pliner, & J. Polivy (Eds.), *Assessment and modification of emotional behavior* (pp. 165–189). New York: Plenum.

Janz, N. K., & Becker, M. H. (1984). The health belief model: A decade later. *Health Education Quarterly, 11,* 1–47.

Jastak, J. F., & Jastak, J. R. (1964). Short forms of the WAIS and WISC Vocabulary subtests. *Journal of Clinical Psychology, 20,* 167–199.

Jastak, J. F., & Jastak, S. R. (1972). *Manual for the Wide Range Interest Opinion Test.* Wilmington, DE: Guidance Associates of Delaware.

Jastak, J. F., & Jastak, S. (1979). *Wide Range Interest-Opinion Test*. Wilmington, DE: Jastak Associates.

Jastrow, J. (1930). Autobiography. In C. Murchison (Ed.), *A history of psychology in autobiography* (Vol. 1, pp. 135–162). Worcester, MA: Clark University Press.

Jencks, C. (1972). *Inequality: A reassessment of the effect of family and schooling in America*. New York: Harper & Row.

Jenkins, C. D., Rosenman, R. H., & Friedman, M. (1967). Development of an objective psychological test for the determination of the coronary-prone behavior pattern in employed men. *Journal of Chronic Diseases. 20*, 371–379.

Jenkins, C. D., Rosenman, R. H., & Zyzanski, S. J. (1974). Prediction of clinical coronary-prone behavior pattern. *New England Journal of Medicine, 290*, 1271–1275.

Jenkins, C. D., & Zyzanski, S. J. (1980). Behavioral risk factors and coronary heart disease. *Psychotherapy and Psychosomatics, 34*, 149–177.

Jensema. C. (1975a). A statistical investigation of the 16PF, Form E as applied to hearing-impaired college students. *Journal of Rehabilitation of the Deaf, 9*, 21–29.

Jensema, C. (1975b). Reliability of the 16 PF Form E for hearing-impaired college students. *Journal of Rehabilitation of the Deaf, 8*, 14–18.

Jensen, A. R. (1969). How much can we boost IQ and scholastic achievement? *Harvard Educational Review, 39*, 1–23.

Jensen, A. R. (1974). How biased are culture-loaded tests? *Genetic Psychology Monographs, 90*, 185–244.

Jensen, A. R. (1976). Test bias and construct validity. *Phi Delta Kappan, 58*, 340–346.

Jensen, A. R. (1980). *Bias in mental testing*. New York: Free Press.

Jensen, A. R. (1984). The black-white difference on the K-ABC: Implications for future tests. *The Journal of Special Education, 18*, 377–408.

Jensen, A. R. (1987). The g beyond factor analysis. In R. R. Ronning, J. C. Conoley, J. A. Glover, & J. C. Witt (Eds.), *The influence of cognitive psychology on testing* (pp. 87–142). Hillsdale, NJ: Erlbaum.

Jensen, A. R. (1998). The *g* factor. Westport, CT: Praeger.

Jensen, J. P., & Bergin, A. E. (1988). Mental health values of professional therapists: A national interdisciplinary survey. *Professional Psychology Research and Practice, 19*, 290–297.

Joe, V. C. (1971). Review of the internal-external control construct as a personality variable. *Psychological Reports, 28*, 619–640.

Joe, V. C. (1974). Personality correlates of conservatism. *Journal of Social Psychology, 93*, 309–310.

Joe, V. C., & Kostyla, S. (1975). Social attitudes and sexual behaviors of college students. *Journal of Consulting and Clinical Psychology, 43*, 430.

Johansson, C. B. (1975). *Manual for the Career Assessment Inventory*. Minneapolis, MN: National Computer Systems.

Johansson, C. B. (1986). *Manual for the Career Assessment Inventory-Enhanced Version*. Minneapolis, MN: National Computer Systems.

John, E., Cavanaugh, C., Krauss-Whitbourne, E. S. (Eds.). (1999). *Gerontology: An interdisciplinary perspective*. New York: Wiley.

Johnson, D. G., Lloyd, S. M. Jr., Jones, R. F., & Anderson, J. (1986). Predicting academic performance at a predominantly Black medical school. *Journal of Medical Education, 61*, 629–639.

Johnson, D. F., & White, C. B. (1980). Effects of training on computerized test performance in the elderly. *Journal of Applied Psychology, 65*, 357–358.

Johnson, D. L., & McGowan, R. J. (1984). Comparison of three intelligence tests as predictors of academic achievement and classroom behaviors of Mexican-American children. *Journal of Psychoeducational Assessment, 2*, 345–352.

Johnson, E. G. (1992). The design of the National Assessment of Educational Progress. *Journal of Educational Measurement, 29*, 95–110.

Johnson, J. H., & Overall, J. E. (1973). Factor analysis of the Psychological Screening Inventory. *Journal of Consulting and Clinical Psychology, 41*, 57–60.

Johnson, J. H., & Williams, T. A. (1980). Using online computer technology in a mental health admitting system. In J. B. Sidowski, J. H. Johnson, & T. A. Williams (Eds.), *Technology in mental health care delivery systems* (pp. 237–249). Norwood, NJ: Ablex.

Johnson, J. R., Null, C., Butcher, J. N., & Johnson, K. N. (1984). Replicated item level factor analysis of the full MMPI. *Journal of Personality and Social Psychology, 47*, 105–114.

Johnson, R. W. (1972). Contradictory scores on the Strong Vocational Interest Blank. *Journal of Counseling Psychology, 19*, 487–490.

Johnson, W. L., & Johnson, A. M. (1993). Validity of the quality of school life scale: A primary and second-order factor analysis. *Educational and Psychological Measurement, 53*, 145–153.

Johnson, W. R. (1981). Basic interviewing skills. In C. E. Walker (Ed.), *Clinical practice of psychology* (pp. 83–128). New York: Pergamon Press.

Joncich, G. (1966). Complex forces and neglected acknowledgments in the making of a young psychologist: Edward L. Thorndike and his teachers. *Journal of the History of the Behavioral Sciences, 2*, 43–50.

Jones, D. H., & Ragosta, M. (1982). *Predictive validity of the SAT on two handicapped groups: The deaf and the learning disabled (82–9)*. Princeton, NJ: Educational Testing Service.

Jones, E. E., & Sigall. H. (1971). The bogus pipeline: A new paradigm for measuring affect and attitude. *Psychological Bulletin. 76*, 349–364.

Jones, J. W. (Ed.). (1991). *Preemployment honesty testing*. New York: Quorum Books.

Jones, R. F. (1986). The effect of commercial coaching courses on performance on the MCAT. *Journal of Medical Education. 61*, 273–284.

Jones, R. F., & Adams, L. N. (1982). *An annotated bibliography of research on the Medical College Admission Test*. Washington, DC: Association of American Medical Colleges.

Jones, R. F., & Thomae-Forgues, M. (1984). Validity of the MCAT in predicting performance in the first two years of medical school. *Journal of Medical Education, 59*, 455–464.

Joynson, R. B. (1989). *The Burt affair*. London: Routledge.

Julian, J. Sotile, R. Henry, M. & Sotile, P. (1991) *The family Apperception Test: Manual*. New York: authors.

Jung, C. G. (1910). The association method. *American Journal of Psychology, 21*, 219–235.

Jurg, C. G. (1923). *Psychological types*. New York: Harcount, Brace, & Co.

Justen, J. E., & Brown, G. (1977). Definitions of severely handicapped: A survey of state departments of education. *AAESPH Review, 2*, 8–14.

Kabacoff, R. I., Miller, I. W., Bishop, D. S., Epstein, N. B., & Keitner, G. I. (1990). A psychometric study of the McMaster Family Assessment Device in psychiatric, medical, and nonclinical samples. *Journal of Family Psychology, 3*, 431–439.

Kahana, E., Fairchild, T., & Kahana, B. (1982). Adaptation. In D. J. Mangen & W. A. Peterson (Eds.), *Research instruments in social gerontology* (Vol. 1, pp. 145–193). Minneapolis, MN: University of Minnesota Press.

Kahle, L. (1984). *Attitudes and social adaptation*. Oxford, UK: Pergamon.

Kahn, M., Fox, H. M., & Rhode, R. (1988), Detecting faking on the Rorschach: Computer vs. expert clinical judgment. *Journal of Personality Assessment, 52*, 516–523.

Kahn, M. W., Fox, H., & Rhode, R. (1990). Detecting faking on the Rorschach: Computer versus expert clinical judgment. A reply to Cohen. *Journal of Personality Assessment, 54*, 63–66.

Kahn, R. L., Goldfarb, A. I., Pollack, M., & Peck, A. (1960). Brief objective measures for the determination of mental status in the aged. *American Journal of Psychiatry, 117*, 326–328.

Kalat, J. W., & Matlin, M. W. (2000). The GRE Psychology test: A useful but poorly understood test. *Teaching of Psychology, 27*, 24–27.

Kamphaus, R. W. (1993). *Clinical assessment of children's intelligence*. Boston, MA: Allyn & Bacon.

Kamphaus, R. W., & Lozano, R. (1984). Developing local norms for individually administered tests. *School Psychology Review, 13*, 491–498.

Kamphaus, R. W., & Pleiss, K. L. (1991). Draw-a-Person techniques: Tests in search of a construct. *Journal of School Psychology, 29*, 395–401.

Kamphaus, R. W., & Reynolds, C. R. (1987). *Clinical and research applications of the K-ABC*. Circle Pines, MN: American Guidance Service,

Kangas, J., & Bradway, K. (1971). Intelligence at middle-age: A thirty-eight year follow up. *Developmental Psychology, 5*, 333–337.

Kanner, A. D., Coyne, J. C., Schaefer, C., & Lazarus, R. S. (1981). Comparison of two modes of stress measurement: Daily hassles and uplifts vs. major life events. *Journal of Behavioral Medicine, 4*, 1–39.

Kanner, A. D., Feldman, S. S., Weinberger, D. A., & Ford, M. E. (1987). Uplifts, hassles, and adaptational outcomes in early adolescents. *Journal of Early Adolescence, 7*, 371–394.

Kantor, J. E., Walker, C. E., & Hays, L. (1976). A study of the usefulness of Lanyon's Psychological Screening Inventory with adolescents. *Journal of Consulting and Clinical Psychology, 44*, 313–316.

Kaplan, H. E., & Alatishe, M. (1976). Comparison of ratings by mothers and teachers on preschool children using the Vineland Social Maturity Scale. *Psychology in the Schools, 13*, 27–28.

Kaplan, R. (1977). Patterns of environmental preference. *Environment and Behavior, 9*, 195–216.

Kaplan, R. M. (1982). Nader's raid on the testing industry. *American Psychologist, 37*, 15–23.

Kardash, C. A., Amlund, J. T., & Stock, W. A. (1986). Structural analysis of Paivio's Individual Differences Questionnaire. *Journal of Experimental Education, 55*, 33–38.

Karnes, F. A., May, B., & Lee, L. A. (1982). Correlations between scores on Form A, Form B, and Form A+B of the Culture Fair Intelligence Test for economically disadvantaged students. *Psychological Reports, 51*, 417–418.

Karr, S. K., Carvajal, H., & Palmer, B. L. (1992). Comparison of Kaufman's short form of the McCarthy Scales of Children's Abilities and the Stanford-Binet Intelligence Scales – Fourth Edition. *Perceptual and Motor Skills, 74*, 1120–1122.

Kasmar, J. V. (1970). The development of a usable lexicon of environmental descriptors. *Environment and Behavior, 2,* 153–169.

Kassin, S. M., & Wrightsman, L. S. (1983). The construction and validation of a juror bias scale. *Journal of Research in Personality, 17,* 423–442.

Kaszniak, A. W. (1989). Psychological assessment of the aging individual. In J. E. Birren & K. W. Schaie (Eds.), *Handbook of the psychology of aging,* (3rd ed., pp. 427–445). New York: Academic Press.

Katz, E. (1955). Success on Stanford-Binet Intelligence Scale test items of children with cerebral palsy as compared with non-handicapped children. *Cerebral Palsy Review, 16,* 18–19.

Katz. J. N., Larson, M. G., Phillips, C. B., Fossel, A. H., & Liang, M. H. (1992). Comparative measurement sensitivity of short and longer health status instruments. *Medical Care, 30,* 917–925.

Katz, L., & Dalby, J. T. (1981). Computer and manual administration of the Eysenck Personality Inventory. *Journal of Clinical Psychology, 37,* 586–588.

Katz, S., Ford, A. B., Moskowitz, R. W., Jackson, B. A., & Jaffe, M. W. (1963). The index of ADL: A standardized measure of biological and psychosocial function. *Journal of the American Medical Association. 185,* 914–919.

Kauffman, J. M. (1989). *Characteristics of behavior disorders of children and youth* (4th ed.). Columbus, OH: Merrill.

Kaufman, A. S. (1972). A short form of the Wechsler Preschool and Primnary Scale of Intelligence. *Journal of Consulting and Clinical Psychology, 39,* 311–369.

Kaufman, A. S. (1973). The relationship of WPPSI IQs to SES and other background variables. *Journal of Clinical Psychology, 29,* 354–357.

Kaufman, A. S. (1975). Factor structure of the McCarthy Scales at five age levels between $2^1/_2$ and $8^1/_2$. *Educational and Psychological Measurement, 35,* 641–656.

Kaufman, A. S. (1977). A McCarthy short form for rapid screening of preschool, kindergarten, and first-grade children. *Contemporary Educational Psychology, 2,* 149–157.

Kaufman, A. S. (1979a). *Intelligent testing with the WISC-R.* New York: Wiley.

Kaufman, A. S. (1979b). WISC-R research: Implications for interpretation. *The School Psychology Digest, 8,* 5–27.

Kaufman, A. S. (1982). An integrated review of almost a decade of research on the McCarthy Scales. In T. R. Kratochwill (Ed.), *Advances in school psychology* (Vol. II, pp. 119–170). Hillsdale, NJ: Erlbaum.

Kaufman, A. S. (1983). Some questions and answers about the Kaufman Assessment Battery for Children (K-ABC). *Journal of Psychoeducational Assessment, 1,* 205–218.

Kaufman, A. S. (1990). *Assessing adolescent and adult intelligence.* Boston, MA: Allyn & Bacon.

Kaufman, A. S. (2000). Intelligence tests and school psychology: predicting the future by studying the past. *Psychology in the Schools, 37,* 7–16.

Kaufman, A. S., & Applegate, B. (1988). Short forms of the K-ABC Mental Processing and Achievement scales at ages 4 to $12^1/_2$ years for clinical and screening purposes. *Journal of Clinical Child Psychology, 17,* 359–369.

Kaufman, A. S., & Hollenbeck, G. P. (1974). Comparative structure of the WPPSI for blacks and whites. *Journal of Clinical Psychology, 30,* 316–319.

Kaufman, A. S., Ishikuma, T., & Kaufman-Packer, J. L. (1991). Amazingly short forms of the WAIS-R. *Journal of Psychoeducational Assessment, 9,* 4–15.

Kaufman, A. S., & Kaufman, N. L. (1975). Social class differences on the McCarthy Scales for black and white children. *Perceptual and Motor Skills, 41,* 205–206.

Kaufman, A. S., & Kaufman, N. L. (1977). *Clinical evaluation of young children with the McCarthy Scales.* New York: Grune & Stratton.

Kaufman, A. S., & Kaufman, N. L. (1983). *K-ABC interpretive manual.* Circle Pines, MN: American Guidance Service.

Kaufman, G. (1983). How good are imagery questionnaires? A rejoinder to David Marks. *Scandinavian Journal of Psychology, 24,* 247–249.

Kazdin, A. E. (1977). Assessing the clinical or applied importance of behavior change through social validation. *Behavior Modification, 1,* 427–452.

Kearns, N. P., Cruickshank. C., McGuigan, K., Riley, S., Shaw, S., & Snaith, R. (1982). A comparison of depression rating scales. *British Journal of Psychiatry, 141,* 45–49.

Keating, D. P., & MacLean, D. J. (1987). Cognitive processing, cognitive ability, and development: A reconsideration. In P. A. Vernon (Ed.), *Speed of information processing and intelligence.* New York: Ablex.

Keesling, J. W. (1985). Review of USES General Aptitude Test Battery. In J. V. Mitchell, Jr. (Ed.), *The ninth mental measurements yearbook* (Vol. 2, pp. 1645–1647). Lincoln, NE: University of Nebraska Press.

Keith, T. (1985). McCarthy Scales of Children's Abilities. In D. Keyser & R. Sweetland (Eds.), *Test critiques:* Vol. IV. Austin, TX: PRO-ED.

Keith, T. Z. (1990). Confirmatory and hierarchical confirmatory analysis of the Differential Ability Scales. *Journal of Psychoeducational Assessment, 8,* 391–405.

Keith, T. Z., Cool, V. A., Novak, C. G., White, L. J., & Pottebaum, S. M. (1988). Confirmatory factor analysis of the Stanford-Binet Fourth Edition: Testing the theory-test match. *Journal of School Psychology, 26*, 253–274.

Kelleher, D. (1958). The social desirability factor in Edwards' PPS. *Journal of Consulting Psychology, 22*, 100.

Keller, M. (1972). The oddities of alcoholics. *Quarterly Journal of Studies on Alcohol, 33*, 1147–1148.

Kelley, M. L. (1985). Review of Child Behavior Checklist. In J. V. Mitchell, Jr. (Ed.), *The ninth mental measurements yearbook* (Vol. 1, pp. 301–303). Lincoln, NE: University of Nebraska Press.

Kelley, P. L., Jacobs, R. R., & Farr, J. L. (1994). Effects of multiple administrations of the MMPI for employee screening. *Personnel Psychology, 47*, 575–591.

Kelley, T. L. (1927). *Interpretation of educational measurements.* New York: New World Book Company.

Kelley, T. L. (1928). *Crossroads in the mind of man: A study of differentiable mental abilities.* Stanford, CA: Stanford University Press.

Kelley, T. L. (1939). The selection of upper and lower groups for the validation of test items. *Journal of Educational Psychology, 30*, 17–24.

Kelly, T. A. (1990). The role of values in psychotherapy: A critical review of process and outcome effects. *Clinical Psychology Review, 10*, 171–186.

Kemp, D. E., & Stephens, J. H. (1971). Which AB scale? A comparative analysis of several versions. *The Journal of Nervous and Mental Disease, 152*, 23–30.

Keogh, B. K., & Smith, S. E. (1967). Visuo-Motor ability for school prediction: A seven-year study. *Perceptual and Motor Skills, 25*, 101–110.

Kerlinger, F. N. (1964). *Foundations of behavioural research.* New York: Holt.

Kerlinger, F. N. (1986). *Foundations of behavioral research* (3rd ed.). New York: Holt, Rinehart and Winston.

Kerlinger, F. N., & Pedhazur, E. J. (1973). *Multiple regression in behavioral research.* New York: Holt, Rinehart & Winston.

Kerr, W. A. (1952). Untangling the Liberalism-Conservatism continuum. *Journal of Social Psychology, 35*, 111–125.

Kessler, R. C., & Wethington, E. (1991). The reliability of life event reports in a community survey. *Psychological Medicine, 21*, 723–738.

Keston, J., & Jimenez, C. (1954). A study of the performance on English and Spanish editions of the Stanford-Binet Intelligence Test by Spanish-American children. *Journal of Genetic Psychology, 85*, 263–269.

Kidder, L. H., Judd, C. M., & Smith, E. R. (1986). *Research methods in social relations.* New York: Holt, Rinehart, & Winston.

Kiecolt-Glaser, J. K., & Glaser, R. (1986). Psychological influences on immunity. *Psychosomatics, 27*, 621–625.

Kiernan, R. J., Mueller, J., Langston, J. W., & Van Dyke, C. (1987). The Neurobehavioral Cognitive Status Examination: A brief but differentiated approach to cognitive assessment. *Annals of Internal Medicine, 107*, 481–485.

Kilpatrick, F. P., & Cantril, H. (1960). Self-anchoring scaling: A measure of individual's unique reality worlds. *Journal of Individual Psychology, 16*, 158–173.

Kilty, K. M., & Feld, A. (1976). Attitudes toward aging and toward the needs of older people. *Journal of Gerontology, 31*, 586–594.

King, J. D., & Smith, R. A. (1972). Abbreviated forms of the Wechsler Preschool and Primary Scale of Intelligence for a kindergarten population. *Psychological Reports, 30*, 539–542.

King, M., & King, J. (1971). Some correlates of university performance in a developing country: The case of Ethiopia. *Journal of Cross-Cultural Psychology, 2*, 293–300.

King, W. C., Jr., & Miles, E. W. (1995). A quasi-experimental assessment of the effect of computerizing noncognitive paper-and-pencil measurements: A test of measurement equivalence. *Journal of Applied Psychology, 80*, 643–651.

Kirk, S. A., McCarthy, J. J., & Kirk, W. D. (1968). *Illinois Test of Psycholinguistic Abilities.* Urbana, IL: University of Illinois Press.

Kirk Patrick, E. A. (1900) Individual tests of school children. *Psychological Review, 7*, 274–280.

Kirnan, J. P., & Geisinger, K. F. (1981). The prediction of graduate school success in psychology. *Educational and Psychological Measurement, 41*, 815–820.

Kirnan, J. P., & Geisinger, K. F. (1990). General Aptitude Test Battery. In J. Hogan & R. Hogan (Eds.), *Business and Industry Testing* (pp. 140–157). Austin, TX: Pro-ed.

Kivela, S. L., & Pahkala, K. (1986). Sex and age differences in the factor pattern and reliability of the Zung Self-Rating Depression Scale in a Finnish elderly population. *Psychological Reports, 59*, 587–597.

Klee, S. H., & Garfinkel, B. D. (1983). The computerized continuous performance task: A new measure of inattention. *Journal of Abnormal Child Psychology, 11*, 487–496.

Klein, M. H., Benjamin, L. S., Rosenfeld, R., Treece, C., Husted, J., & Greist, J. H. (1993). The Wisconsin

Personality Disorders Inventory: Development, reliability, and validity. *Journal of Personality Disorders, 7,* 285–303.

Klein, S. P., & Owens, W. A. (1965). Faking of a scored life history as a function of criterion objectivity. *Journal of Applied Psychology, 49,* 451–454.

Kleinmuntz, B. (1961). The College maladjustment scale (Mt): Norms and predictive validity. *Educational and Psychological Measurement, 21,* 1029–1033.

Kleinmuntz, B. (1967). *Personality measurement.* Homewood, IL: The Dorsey Press.

Kleinmuntz, B. (1969). Personality test interpretation by computer and clinician. In J. N. Butcher (Ed.), *MMPI: Research developments and clinical applications* (pp. 97–104). NY: McGraw-Hill.

Kleinmuntz, B. (1977). *Personality measurement.* New York: Krieger.

Kleinmuntz, B., & Szucko, J. J. (1984). Lie detection in ancient and modern times. *American Psychologist, 39,* 766–776.

Klieger, D. M., & Franklin, M. E. (1993). Validity of the Fear Survey Schedule in phobia research: A laboratory test. *Journal of Psychopathology and Behavioral Assessment, 15,* 207–217.

Klieger, D. M., & McCoy, M. L. (1994). Improving the concurrent validity of the Fear Survey Schedule-III. *Journal of Psychopathology and Behavioral Assessment, 16,* 201–220.

Klimoski, R., & Brickner, M. (1987). Why do assessment centers work? The puzzle of assessment center validity. *Personnel Psychology, 40,* 243–260.

Kline, P. (1986). *A handbook of test construction.* New York: Methuen.

Kline, R. B. (1989). Is the Fourth Edition Stanford-Binet a four factor test? Confirmatory factor analyses of alternative models for ages 2 through 23. *Journal of Psychoeducational Assessment, 7,* 4–13.

Kline, R. B., Snyder, J., Guilmette, S., & Castellanos, M. (1993). External validity of the profile variability index for the K-ABC, Stanford-Binet, and WISC-R: Another cul-de-sac. *Journal of Learning Disabilities, 26,* 557–567.

Klingler, D. E., Johnson, J. H., & Williams, T. A. (1976). Strategies in the evaluation of an on-line computer-assisted unit for intake assessment of mental health patients. *Behavior Research Methods and Instrumentation, 8,* 95–100.

Klingler, D. E., Miller, D. A., Johnson, J. H., & Williams, T. A. (1977). Process evaluation of an online computer-assisted unit for intake assessment of mental health patients. *Behavior Research Methods and Instrumentation, 9,* 110–116.

Klonoff, H., & Kennedy, M. (1965). Memory and perceptual functioning in octogenarians and nonagena-rians in the community. *Journal of Gerontology, 20,* 328–333.

Klonoff, H., & Kennedy, M. (1966). A comparative study of cognitive functioning in old age. *Journal of Gerontology, 21,* 239–243.

Klopfer, B., Ainsworth, M. D., Klopfer, W. G., & Holt, R. R. (1954). *Developments in the Rorschach Technique.* Yonkers-on-Hudson, NY: World Book Co.

Klopfer, W. G. (1973). The short history of projective techniques. *Journal of the History of the Behavioral Sciences, 9,* 60–65.

Kluger, A. N., Reilly, R. R., & Russell, C. J. (1991). Faking biodata tests: Are option-keyed instruments more resistant? *Journal of Applied Psychology, 76,* 889–896.

Knapp, R. H., & Garbutt, J. J. (1958). Time imagery and the achievement motive. *Journal of Personality, 26,* 426–434.

Knapp, R. R. (1960). The effects of time limits on the intelligence test performance of Mexican and American subjects. *Journal of Educational Psychology, 51,* 14–20.

Knapp, R. R. (1976). *Handbook for the Personal Orientation Inventory.* San Diego, CA: EdITS.

Knapp, R. R., Shostrom, E. L., & Knapp, L. (1978). Assessment of the actualizing person. In P. McReynolds (Ed.), *Advances in psychological assessment* (Vol. 4, pp. 103–140). San Francisco, CA: Jossey-Bass.

Knight, B. C., Baker, E. H., & Minder, C. C. (1990). Concurrent validity of the Stanford-Binet: Fourth edition and the Kaufman Assessment Battery for Children with learning disabled students. *Psychology in the Schools, 27,* 116–125.

Knight, H. V., Acosta, L. J., & Anderson, B. D. (1988). A comparison of textbook and microcomputer instruction in preparation for the ACT. *Journal of Computer Based Instruction, 15,* 83–87.

Knight, R. G., Chisholm, B. J., Marsh, N. V., & Godfrey, H. P. (1988). Some normative reliability, and factor analytic data for the Revised UCLA Loneliness Scale. *Journal of Clinical Psychology, 44,* 203–206.

Knobloch, H., & Pasamanick, B. (Eds.). (1974). Gesell and Amatruda's developmental diagnosis (3rd ed.). New York: Harper & Row.

Knobloch, H., Stevens, F., & Malone, A. F. (1980). Manual of developmental diagnosis. Hagerstown, MD: Harper & Row.

Knoff, H. M. (1989). Review of the Personality Inventory for Children. In J. C. Conoley & J. J. Kramer (Eds.), *The tenth mental measurements yearbook* (pp. 625–630). Lincoln, NE: University of Nebraska Press.

Kobasa, S. C. (1979). Stressful life events, personality and health: An inquiry into hardiness. *Journal of Personality and Social Psychology, 37*, 1–11.

Kobasa, S. C., Maddi, S. R., & Kahn, S. (1982). Hardiness and health: A prospective study. *Journal of Personality and Social Psychology, 42*, 168–177.

Koch, H. L. (1933). Popularity in preschool children: Some related factors and a technique for its measurement. *Child Development, 4*, 164–175.

Koelle, W. H., & Convey, J. J. (1982). The prediction of the achievement of deaf adolescents from self-concept and locus of control measures. *American Annals of the Deaf, 127*, 769–779.

Kogan, N., & Wallach. M. A. (1961). Age changes in values and attitudes. *Journal of Gerontology, 16*, 272–280.

Kohlberg, L. (1979). *The meaning and measurement of moral development.* Worcester, MA: Clark University Press.

Komaroff, A. L., Masuda, M., & Holmes, T. H. (1968). The social readjustment rating scale: A comparative study of Negro, Mexican and White Americans. *Journal of Psychosomatic Research, 12*, 121–128.

Komorita, S. S., & Graham, W. K. (1965). Number of scale points and the reliability of scales. *Educational and Psychological Measurement, 25*, 987–995.

Koppitz, E. M. (1964). *The Bender Gestalt Test for young children.* New York: Grune & Straton.

Koppitz, E. M. (1975). *The Bender Gestalt Test for young children: Vol. 2. Research and applications, 1963–1973.* New York: Grune & Stratton.

Korchin, S. J. (1976). *Modern Clinical Psychology.* New York: Basic Books.

Kornblith, S. J., Greenwald, D. P., Michelson, L., & Kazdin, A. E. (1984). Measuring the effects of demand characteristics on the Beck Depression Inventory responses of college students. *Journal of Behavioral Assessment, 6*, 45–49.

Koson, D., Kitchen, C., Kochen, M., & Stodolosky, D. (1970). Psychological testing by computer: Effect on response bias. *Educational and Psychological Measurement, 30*, 803–810.

Kosuth, T. F. (1984–1985). *The pictorial inventory of careers.* Jacksonville, FL: Talent Assessment.

Kramer, J., Shanks, K., Markely, R., & Ryabik, J. (1983). The seductive nature of WISC-R short forms: An analysis with gifted referrals. *Psychology in the Schools, 20*, 137–141.

Kranau, E. J., Green, V., & Valencia-Weber, G. (1982). Acculturation and the Hispanic woman: Attitudes toward women, sex-role attribution, sex-role behavior, and demographics. *Hispanic Journal of Behavioral Sciences, 4*, 21–40.

Kratochwill, T. R., Doll, E. J., & Dickson, W. P. (1985). Microcomputers in behavioral assessment: Recent advances and remaining issues. *Computers in Human Behavior, 1*, 277–291.

Krause, J. S., & Dawis, R. V. (1992). Prediction of life satisfaction after spinal cord injury: A four-year longitudinal approach. *Rehabilitation Psychology, 37*, 49–60.

Kravitz, D. A., Cutler, B. L., & Brock, P. (1993). Reliability and validity of the original and revised Legal Attitudes Questionnaire. *Law and Human Behavior, 17*, 661–677.

Krech, D., Crutchfield, R. S., & Ballachey, E. L. (1962). *Individual in society.* New York: McGraw-Hill.

Kremer, E. F., Atkinson, J. H., Jr., & Ignelzi, R. J. (1982). Pain measurement: The affective dimensional measure of the McGill Pain Questionnaire with a cancer pain population. *Pain, 12*, 153–163.

Krohn, E. J., & Lamp, R. E. (1989). Concurrent validity of the Stanford-Binet Fourth Edition and K-ABC for Head Start children. *Journal of School Psychology, 27*, 59–67.

Krout, M. H. (1954). An experimental attempt to produce unconscious manual symbolic movements. *Journal of General Psychology, 51*, 93–120.

Krug, S. E. (1987). *Psychware sourcebook* (2nd ed.). Kansas City, MO: Test Corporation of America.

Krumboltz, J. C., Mitchell, A., & Gelatt, H. G. (1975). Applications of social learning theory of career selection. *Focus on Guidance, 8*, 1–16.

Kübler-Ross, E. (1969). *On death and dying.* New York: Macmillan.

Kuder, G. F., & Diamond, E. E. (1979). *Occupational Interest Survey: General manual* (2nd ed.). Chicago, IL: Science Research Associates.

Kuder, G. F., & Richardson, M. W. (1937). The theory of estimation of test reliability. *Psychometrika, 2*, 151–160.

Kudoh, T., & Nishikawa, M. (1983). A study of the feeling of loneliness (I): the reliability and validity of the revised UCLA Loneliness Scale. *The Japanese Journal of Experimental Social Psychology, 22*, 99–108.

Kulberg, G. E., & Owens, W. A. (1960). Some life history antecedents of engineering interests. *Journal of Educational Psychology, 51*, 26–31.

Kulik, J. A., Bangert-Drowns, R. L., & Kulik, C. C. (1984). Effectiveness of coaching for aptitude tests. *Psychological Bulletin, 95*, 179–188.

Kumar, V. K., Rehill, K. B., Treadwell, T. W., & Lambert, P. (1986). The effects of disguising scale purpose on reliability and validity. *Measurement and Evaluation in Counseling and Development, 18*, 163–167.

Kunert, K. M. (1969). Psychological concomitants and determinants of vocational choice. *Journal of Applied Psychology, 53*, 152–158.

Kuo, W. H. (1984). Prevalence of depression among Asian-Americans. *Journal of Nervous and Mental Disorders, 172,* 449–457.

Kutner, B., Fanshel, D., Togo, A. M., & Langner, T. S. (1956). *Five hundred over sixty.* New York: Russell Sage Foundation.

Labeck. L. J., Johnson, J. H., & Harris, W. G. (1983). Validity of a computerized on-line MMPI interpretive system. *Journal of Clinical Psychology, 39,* 412–416.

Laboratory of Comparative Human Cognition (1982). Culture and intelligence. In R. J. Sternberg (Ed.), *Handbook of human intelligence* (pp. 642–719). Cambridge, UK: Cambridge University Press.

Lachar, D. (1974). *The MMPI: Clinical assessment and automated interpretation.* Los Angeles, CA: Western Psychological Services.

Lachar, D., & Gdowski, C. G. (1979). *Actuarial assessment of child and adolescent personality: An interpretive guide for the Personality Inventory for Children profile.* Los Angeles, CA: Western Psychological Services.

Lachar, D., & Wrobel, T. A. (1979). Validation of clinicians' hunches: Construction of a new MMPI critical item set. *Journal of Consulting and Clinical Psychology, 47,* 277–284.

LaGreca, A. M. (1981). Peer acceptance: The correspondence between children's sociometric scores and teachers' ratings of peer interactions. *Journal of Abnormal Child Psychology, 9,* 167–178.

Lah, M. I., & Rotter, J. B. (1981). Changing college student norms on the Rotter Incomplete Sentences Blank. *Journal of Consulting and Clinical Psychology, 49,* 985.

Lam, T. C. M. (1993). Testability: A critical issue in testing language minority students with standardized achievement tests. *Measurement and Evaluation in Counseling and Development, 26,* 179–191.

Lamb, R. R., & Prediger, D. J. (1981). *Technical report for the unisex edition of the ACT interest inventory* (UNIACT). Iowa City, IO: American College Testing Program.

Lambert, M. J., Hatch, D. R., Kingston, M. D., & Edwards, B. C. (1986). Zung, Beck, and Hamilton Rating scales as measures of treatment outcome: A metaanalytic comparison. *Journal of Consulting and Clinical Psychology, 54,* 54–59.

Lambert, N. M. (1991). The crisis in measurement literacy in psychology and education. *Educational Psychologist, 26,* 23–35.

Lambirth, T. T, Gibb, G. D., & Alcorn, J. D. (1986). Use of a behavior-based personality instrument in aviation selection. *Educational and Psychological Measurement, 46,* 973–978.

Lamp, R. E., & Krohn, E. J. (1990). Stability of the Stanford-Binet Fourth Edition and K-ABC for young Black and White children from low-income families. *Journal of Psychoeducational Assessment, 8,* 139–149.

Landis, C. (1936). Questionnaires and the study of personality. *Journal of Nervous and Mental Disease, 83,* 125–134.

Landis, C., Zubin, J., & Katz, S. E. (1935). Empirical evaluation of three personality adjustment inventories. *Journal of Educational Psychology, 26,* 321–330.

Landy, F. J., Rastegary, H., Thayer, J., & Colvin, C. (1991). Time urgency: The construct and its measurement. *Journal of Applied Psychology, 76,* 644–657.

Lane, B. (1964). Attitudes of youth toward the aged. *Journal of Marriage and the Family, 26,* 229–231.

Lane, S., Liv, M., Ankenmann, R. D., & Stone, C. A. (1996). Generalizability and validity of a mathematics performance assessment. *Journal of Educational Measurement, 33,* 71–92.

Lang, P. J., & Lazovik, A. P. (1963). Experimental desensitization of a phobia. *Journal of Abnormal and Social Psychology, 66,* 519–525.

Lankford, J. S., Bell, R. W., & Elias, J. W. (1994). Computerized vs. standard personality measures: Equivalency, computer anxiety, and gender differences. *Computers in Human Behavior, 10,* 497–510.

Lanning, K. (1989). Detection of invalid response patterns on the California Psychological Inventory. *Applied Psychological Measurement, 13,* 45–56.

Lansman, M., Donaldson, G., Hunt, E., & Yantis, S. (1982). Ability factors and cognitive processes. *Intelligence, 6,* 347–386.

Lanyon, R. I. (1967). Measurement of social competence in college males. *Journal of Consulting Psychology, 31,* 493–498.

Lanyon, R. I. (1968). *A Psychological Screening Inventory.* Paper presented to the Eastern Psychological Association, Washington, DC.

Lanyon, R. I. (1973). *Manual for the Psychological Screening Inventory.* Port Huron, MI: Research Psychologists Press.

Lanyon, R. I. (1978). *Psychological Screening Inventory: Manual* (2nd ed.). Port Huron, MI: Research Psychologists Press.

Lanyon, R. I. (1984). Personality assessment. *Annual Review of Psychology, 35,* 667–701.

Lanyon, R. I. (1993). Development of scales to assess specific deception strategies on the Psychological Screening Inventory. *Psychological Assessment, 5,* 324–329.

Lanyon, R. I. (1995). Review of the Imwald Personality Inventory. In J. C. Conoley & J. C. Impara (Eds.),

The twelfth mental measurements yearbook (pp. 503–504). Lincoln, NB: University of Nebraska Press.

Lanyon, R. I., Johnson, J. H., & Overall, J. E. (1974). Factor structure of the Psychological Screening Inventory items in a normal population. *Journal of Consulting and Clinical Psychology, 42,* 219–223.

Laosa, L. M. (1993). Family characteristics as predictors of individual differences in Chicano children's emergent school readiness. *ETS Research Report* 93–34. Princeton, NJ: Educational Testing Service.

Lasher, K. P., & Faulkender, P. J. (1993). Measurement of aging anxiety: Development of the Anxiety About Aging Scale. *International Journal of Aging and Human Development, 37,* 247–259.

Lau, S. (1988). The value orientations of Chinese University students in Hong Kong. *International Journal of Psychology, 23,* 583–596.

Laughton, J. (1988). Strategies for developing creative abilities of hearing-impaired children. *American Annals of the Deaf, 133,* 258–263.

Lautenschlager, G. J. (1986). Within-subject measures for the assessment of individual differences in faking. *Educational and Psychological Measurement, 46,* 309–316.

LaVoie, A. L. (1978). Review of the Survey of Interpersonal Values. In O. K. Buros (Ed.), *The eight mental measurements yearbook* (Vol. 1, pp. 1108–1110). Highland Park, NJ: Gryphon Press.

LaVoie, A. L., & Bentler, P. M. (1974). A short form measure of the expanded seven-dimensional semantic space. *Journal of Educational Measurement, 11,* 65–66.

Lavos, G. (1962). W.I.S.C. psychometric patterns among deaf children. *Volta Review, 64,* 547–552.

Lawler, E. E., III (1967). The multitrait-multirater approach to measuring managerial job performance. *Journal of Applied Psychology, 51,* 369–381.

Lawlis, G. F. (1971). Response styles of a patient population on the Fear Survey Schedule. *Behaviour Research and Therapy, 9,* 95–102.

Lawshe, C. H. (1952). What can industrial psychology do for small business? *Personnel Psychology, 5,* 31–34.

Lawshe, C. H. (1985). Inferences from personnel tests and their validity. *Journal of Applied Psychology, 70,* 237–238.

Lawshe, C. H., Kephart, N. C., & McCormick, E. J. (1949). The paired comparison technique for rating performance of industrial employees. *Journal of Applied Psychology, 33,* 69–77.

Lawshe, C. H., & Steinberg, M. D. (1955). Studies in synthetic validity. I. An exploratory investigation of clerical jobs. *Personnel Psychology, 8,* 291–301.

Lawson, J. S., & Inglis, J. (1985). Learning disabilities and intelligence test results: A model based on a principal components analysis of the WISCV-R. *British Journal of Psychology, 76,* 35–48.

Lawton, M. P. (1972). The dimensions of morale. In D. Kent, R. Kastenbaum, & S. Sherwood (Eds.), *Research planning and action for the elderly,* (pp. 144–165). New York: Behavioral Publications.

Lawton, M. P. (1975). The Philadelphia Geriatric Center Morale Scale: A revision. *Journal of Gerontology, 30,* 85–89.

Lazaridis, E. N., Rudberg, M. A., Furner, S. E., & Cassel, C, K. (1994). Do Activities of Daily Living have a hierarchical structure? An analysis using the longitudinal study of aging. *Journal of Gerontology, 49,* 47–51.

Lazarsfeld, P. F. (1950). The logic and mathematical foundation of latent structure analysis. In S. A. Stouffer, L. Guttman, E. A. Schuman, P. F. Lazarsfeld, S. A. Starr, & J. A. Clausen (Eds.), *Measurement and prediction,* (pp. 362–412). Princeton, NJ: Princeton University Press.

Lazarsfeld, P. F. (1954). A conceptual introduction to latent structure analysis. In P. F. Lazarsfeld (Ed.), *Mathematical thinking in the social sciences.* Glencoe, IL: Free Press.

Lazarsfeld, P. F. (1959). Latent structure analysis. In S. Koch (Ed.), *Psychology: A study of science* (Vol. 3, pp. 476–543). New York: McGraw-Hill.

Lazarus, R. S. (1966). *Psychological stress and the coping process.* New York: McGraw-Hill.

Lazarus, R. S. (1980). The stress and coping paradigm. In C. Eisdorfer, D. Cohen, & A. Kleinman (Eds.), *Conceptual models for psychopathology* (pp. 173–209). New York: Spectrum.

Leahy, J. M. (1992). Validity and reliability of the Beck Depression Inventory-Short Form in a group of adult bereaved females. *Journal of Clinical Psychology, 48,* 64–68.

Leckliter, I. N., Matarazzo, J. D., & Silverstein, A. B. (1986). A literature review of factor analytic studies of the WAIS-R. *Journal of Clinical Psychology, 42,* 332–342.

LecLercq, D. A., & Bruno, J. E. (1993). *Item banking: Interactive testing and self-assessment.* Berlin: Springer-Verlag.

Lee, H. B., & Oei, T. P. S. (1994). Factor structure, validity, and reliability of the Fear Questionnaire in a Hong Kong Chinese population. *Journal of Psychopathology and Behavioral Assessment, 16,* 189–199.

Lee, L. (1971). *Northwestern Syntax Screening Test.* Evanston, IL: Northwestern University Press.

Lees-Haley, P. R. (1992). Psychodiagnostic test usage by forensic psychologists. *American Journal of Forensic Psychology, 10,* 25–30.

Lefcourt, H. M. (1966). Internal vs. external control of reinforcement: A review. *Psychological Bulletin, 65,* 206–220.

Lefcourt, H. M. (1976). *Locus of control: Current trends in theory and research.* Hillsdale, NJ: Erlbaum.

Lei, H., & Skinner, H. A. (1980). A psychometric study of life events and social readjustment. *Journal of Psychosomatic Research, 24,* 57–66.

Leichsenring, F. (1999). Development and first results of the Borderline Personality Inventory: A self-report instrument for assessing borderline personality organization. *Journal of Personality Assessment, 73,* 45–63.

Leigh, I. W., Robins, C. J., Welkowitz, J., & Bond, R. N. (1989). Toward greater understanding of depression in deaf individuals. *American Annals of the Deaf, 134,* 249–254.

Leighton, A. H. (1959). Mental illness and acculturation. In I. Goldston (Ed.), *Medicine and anthropology* (pp. 108–128). New York: International University Press.

Leiter, R. G. (1952). *Leiter International Performance Scale.* Chicago, IL: Stoelting.

Lerner, B. (1981). The minimum competence testing movement: Social, scientific, and legal implications. *American Psychologist, 36,* 1057–1066.

Lerner, H., & Lerner, P. M. (1987). Rorschach Inkblot Test. In D. J. Keyser & R. C. Sweetland (Eds.), *Test critiques compendium* (pp. 372–401). Kansas City, MO: Test Corporation of America.

Lesser, G. (1959). Population differences in construct validity. *Journal of Consulting Psychology, 23,* 60–65.

Lettieri, D. J., Nelson, J. E., & Sayers, M. A. (1985). *Alcoholism treatment assessment research instruments.* Washington, DC.: Metrotec.

Levenson, H. (1973). Perceived parental antecedents of internal, powerful others, and chance locus of control orientations. *Developmental Psychology, 9,* 260–265.

Levenson, H. (1974). Activism and powerful others: Distinctions within the concept of internal-external control. *Journal of Personality Assessment, 38,* 377–383.

Leventhal, A. M. (1966). An anxiety scale for the CPI. *Journal of Clinical Psychology, 22,* 459–461.

Levine, E. S. (1971). Mental assessment of the deaf child. *The Volta Review, 73,* 80–105.

Levine, E. S. (1974). Psychological tests and practices with the deaf: A survey of the state of the art. *The Volta Review, 76,* 298–319.

Levine, M., & Wishner, J. (1977). The case records of the psychological clinic at the University of Pennsylvania (1896–1961). *Journal of the History of the Behavioral Sciences, 13,* 59–66.

Levonian, E. (1961). A statistical analysis of the 16 Personality Factor Questionnaire. *Educational and Psychological Measurement, 21,* 589–596.

Levonian, E., Comrey, A., Levy, W., & Procter, D. (1959). A statistical evaluation of Edwards Personal Preference Schedule. *Journal of Applied Psychology, 43,* 355–359.

Levy, S. (1982). Use of the Peabody Picture Vocabulary Test with low-functioning autistic children. *Psychology in the Schools, 19,* 24–27.

Lewandowski, D. G., & Saccuzzo, D. P. (1975). Possible differential WISC patterns for retarded delinquents. *Psychological Reports, 37,* 887–894.

Lewinsohn, P. M. (1976). Activity schedules in treatment of depression. In J. D. Krumboltz & C. E. Thoresen (Eds.), *Counseling methods* (pp. 74–83). New York: Holt, Rinehart and Winston.

Lewinsohn, P. M., & Graf, M. (1973). Pleasant activities and depression. *Journal of Consulting and Clinical Psychology, 41,* 261–268.

Lewinsohn, P. M., Mermelstein, R. M., Alexander, C., & MacPhillamy, D. J. (1985). The Unpleasant Events Schedule: A scale for the measurement of aversive events. *Journal of Clinical Psychology, 41,* 483–498.

Lezak, M. (1983). *Neuropsychological Assessment* (2nd ed.). New York: Oxford University Press.

Lezak, M. D. (1988). IQ: R.I.P. *Journal of Clinical and Experimental Neuropsychology, 10,* 351–361.

Libbrecht, K., & Quackelbeen, J. (1995). On the early history of male hysteria and psychic trauma. *Journal of the History of the Behavioral Sciences, 31,* 370–384.

Lichtenstein, E., & Bryan, J. H. (1965). Acquiescence and the MMPI: An item reversal approach. *Journal of Abnormal Psychology, 70,* 290–293.

Lichtenstein, R., & Ireton, H. (1984). *Preschool screening.* Orlando, FL: Grune & Stratton.

Liebert, R. M., & Morris, L. W. (1967). Cognitive and emotional components of test anxiety: A distinction and some initial data. *Psychological Reports, 20,* 975–978.

Lightfoot, S. L., & Oliver, J. M. (1985). The Beck Inventory: Psychometric properties in university students. *Journal of Personality Assessment, 49,* 434–436.

Likert, R. (1932). A technique for the measurement of attitudes. *Archives of Psychology,* No. 140, 1–55.

Linde, T., & Patterson, C. H. (1958). The MMPI in cerebral palsy. *Journal of Consulting Psychology, 22,* 210–212.

Lindzey, G. (1959). On the classification of projective techniques. *Psychological Bulletin, 56,* 158–168.

Linn, M. R. (1993). A brief history for counselors . . . college entrance examinations in the United States. *The Journal of College Admission, 140,* 6–16.

Linn, R. L. (1986). Educational testing and assessment. Research needs and policy issues. *American Psychologist, 41*, 1153–1160.

Linn, R. L., & Dunbar, S. B. (1992). Issues in the design and reporting of the National Assessment of Educational Progress. *Journal of Educational Measurement, 29*, 177–194.

Linn, R. L., Grave, M. E., & Sanders, N. M. (1990). Comparing state and district test results to national norms: The validity of the claims that "everyone is above average." *Educational Measurement: Issues and Practice, 9*, 5–14.

Linn, R. L., & Harnisch, D. L. (1981). Interactions between item content and group membership on achievement test items. *Journal of Educational Measurement, 18*, 109–118.

Linn, R. L., Harnisch, D. L., & Dunbar, S. B. (1981). Validity generalization and situational specificity: An analysis of the prediction of first-year grades in law school. *Applied Psychological Measurement, 5*, 281–289.

Lipsitt, L. P. (1958). A self-concept scale for children and its relationship to the children's form of the Manifest Anxiety Scale. *Child Development, 29*, 463–473.

Lissitz, R. W., & Willhoft, J. L. (1985). A methodological study of the Torrance Tests of Creativity. *Journal of Educational Measurement, 22*, 1–11.

Littell, W. M. (1960). The Wechsler Intelligence Scale for Children: Review of a decade of research. *Psychological Bulletin, 57*, 132–156.

Livneh, H., & Livneh, C. (1989). The five-factor model of personality: Is evidence of its cross-measure validity premature? *Personality and Individual Differences, 10*, 75–80.

Locke, H. J., & Wallace, K. M. (1959). Short marital adjustment and prediction tests: Their reliability and validity. *Marriage and Family Living, 21*, 251–255.

Loeb, R., & Sarigiani, P. (1986). The impact of hearing impairment on self perceptions of children. *The Volta Review, 88*, 89–101.

Loevinger, J. (1957). Objective tests as instruments of psychological theory. *Psychological Reports, 3*, 635–694.

Loevinger, J. (1972). Some limitations of objective personality tests. In J. N. Butcher (Ed.), *Objective personality assessment.* New York: Academic Press.

Loevinger, J. (1976). *Ego development.* San Francisco, CA: Jossey-Bass.

Loevinger, J. (1979). Construct validity of the sentence completion test of ego development. *Applied Psychological Measurement, 3*, 281–311.

Lohmann, N. (1977). Correlations of life satisfaction, morale, and adjustment measures. *Journal of Gerontology, 32*, 73–75.

Longstaff, H. P., & Jurgensen, C. E. (1953). Fakability of the Jurgensen Classification Inventory. *Journal of Applied Psychology, 37*, 86–89.

Lord, F. M. (1944). Reliability of multiple-choice tests as a function of number of choices per item. *Journal of Educational Psychology, 35*, 175–180.

Lord, F. M. (1952). The relation of the reliability of multiple-choice tests to the distribution of item difficulties. *Psychometrika, 17*, 181–194.

Lord, F. M. (1980). *Applications of item response theory to practical testing problems.* Hillsdale, NJ: Erlbaum.

Lord, F. M., & Novick, M. R. (Eds.). (1968). *Statistical theories of mental test scores.* New York: Addison-Wesley.

Lorr, M., Daston, P., & Smith, I. R. (1967). An analysis of mood states. *Educational and Psychological Measurement, 27*, 89–96.

Lovie, A. D., & Lovie. P. (1993). Charles Spearman, Cyril Burt, and the origins of factor analysis. *Journal of the History of the Behavioral Sciences, 29*, 308–321.

Lowe, N. K., & Ryan-Wenger, N. M. (1992). Beyond Campbell and Fiske: Assessment of convergent and discriminant validity. *Research in Nursing and Health, 15*, 67–75.

Loyd, B. H. (1988). Implications of item response theory for the measurement practitioner. *Applied Measurement in Education, 1*, 135–143.

Lubin, B. (1965). Adjective checklists for the measurement of depression. *Archives of General Psychology, 12*, 57–62.

Lubin, B. (1967). *Manual for the depression adjective check lists.* San Diego, CA: Education and Industrial Testing Service.

Lubin, B., Larsen, R. M., & Matarazzo, J. D. (1984). Patterns of psychological test usage in the United States: 1935–1982. *American Psychologist, 39*, 451–454.

Lubin, B., Wallis, R. R., & Paine, C. (1971). Patterns of psychological test usage in the United States: 1935–1969. *Professional Psychology, 2*, 70–74.

Lucas, R. W., Mullin, P. J., Luna, C. B. X., & McInroy, D. C. (1977). Psychiatrists and a computer as interrogators of patients with alcohol-related illnesses: A comparison. *British Journal of Psychiatry, 131*, 160–167.

Ludenia, K., & Donham, G. (1983). Dental outpatients: Health locus of control correlates. *Journal of Clinical Psychology, 39*, 854–858.

Lundy, A. (1988). Instructional set and Thematic Apperception Test validity. *Journal of Personality Assessment, 52*, 309–320.

Lunneborg, C. E., & Lunneborg, P. W. (1967). Pattern prediction of academic success. *Educational and Psychological Measurement, 27*, 945–952.

Lunneborg, P. W. (1979). The Vocational Interest Inventory: Development and validation. *Educational and Psychological Measurement, 39*, 445–451.

Luria, A. R. (1966). *Higher cortical functions in man.* New York: Basic Books.

Luria, A. R. (1973). *The working brain.* New York: Basic Books.

Lyman, H. B. (1978). *Test scores and what they mean* (3rd ed.). Englewood Cliffs, NJ: Prentice Hall.

Lynn, M. R. (1986). Determination and quantification of content validity. *Nursing Research, 35*, 382–385.

Lytton, H., Watts, D., & Dunn, B. E. (1986). Stability and predictability of cognitive and social characteristics from age 2 to age 9. *Genetic Psychology Monographs, 112*, 363–398.

MacAndrew, C. (1965). The differentiation of male alcoholic out-patients from nonalcoholic psychiatric patients by means of the MMPI. *Quarterly Journal of Studies on Alcohol, 26*, 238–246.

Maccoby, E. E., & Jacklin, C. N. (1974). *The psychology of sex differences.* Stanford, CA: United Press.

MacFarlane, J. W., & Tuddenham, R. D. (1951). Problems in the validation of projective techniques. In H. H. Anderson, & G. L. Anderson (Eds.), *An introduction to projective techniques* (pp. 26–54). Englewood Cliffs, NJ: Prentice-Hall.

Machover, K. (1949). *Personality projection in the drawing of the human figure: A method of personality investigation.* Springfield, IL: Charles C Thomas.

MacPhillamy, D. J., & Lewinsohn, P. M. (1976). *Manual for the pleasant events schedule.* Unpublished manuscript, University of Oregon.

Madianos, M. G., Gournas, G., & Stefanis, C. N. (1992). Depressive symptoms and depression among elderly people in Athens. *Acta Psychiatrica Scandinavica, 86*, 320–326.

Mael, F. A. (1991). A conceptual rationale for the domain and attributes of biodata items. *Personnel Psychology, 44*, 763–792.

Mahakian, C. (1939). Measuring the intelligence and reading capacity of Spanish-speaking children. *Elementary School Journal, 39*, 760–768.

Mahon, N. E., & Yarcheski, A. (1990). The dimensionality of the UCLA Loneliness Scale. *Research in Nursing and Health, 13*, 45–52.

Malgady, R. G., Costantino, G., & Rogler, L. H. (1984). Development of a Thematic Apperception Test for urban Hispanic children. *Journal of Consulting and Clinical Psychology, 52*, 986–996.

Mallory, E., & Miller, V. (1958). A possible basis for the association of voice characteristics and personality traits. *Speech Monographs, 25*, 255–260.

Maloney, M. P., & Ward, M. P. (1976). *Psychological assessment. A conceptual approach.* New York: Oxford University Press.

Mann, I. T., Phillips, J. L., & Thompson, E. G. (1979). An examination of methodological issues relevant to the use and interpretation of the Semantic Differential. *Applied Psychological Measurement, 3*, 213–229.

Mapou, A. (1955). Development of general working population norms for the USES General Aptitude Test Battery. *Journal of Applied Psychology, 39*, 130–133.

Mardell, C., & Goldenberg, D. (1975). *Developmental Indicators for the Assessment of Learning (DIAL).* Edison, NJ: Childcraft Education Corp.

Marin, G., Gamba, R. J., & Marin, B. V. (1992). Extreme response style and acquiescence among Hispanics. *Journal of Cross-cultural Psychology, 23*, 498–509.

Marin, G., Sabogal, F., Marin, B. V., Otero-Sabogal, R., & Perez-Stable, E. J. (1987). Development of a short acculturation scale for Hispanics. *Hispanic Journal of Behavioral Sciences, 9*, 183–205.

Maris, R. W. (1992). Overview of the study of suicide assessment and prediction. In R. W. Maris, A. L. Berman, J. T. Maltsberger, & R. I. Yufit (Eds.), *Assessment and prediction of suicide.* New York: Guilford Press.

Marks, D. F. (1973). Visual imagery differences in the recall of pictures. *British Journal of Psychology, 64*, 17–24.

Marks, I. M., & Mathews, A. M. (1979). Brief standard self-rating for phobic patients. *Behaviour Research and Therapy, 17*, 263–267.

Marks, P. A., & Seeman, W. (1963). *The actuarial description of personality: An atlas for use with the MMPI.* Baltimore, MD: Williams & Wilkins.

Marks, P. A., Seeman, W., & Haller, D. L. (1974). *The actuarial use of the MMPI with adolescents and adults.* Baltimore, MD: Williams & Wilkins.

Marland, S. (1972). *Education of the gifted and talented, I. Report to Congress of the United States by the Commissioner of Education.* Washington, DC: U.S. Office of Education.

Marquart, D. I., & Bailey, L. L. (1955). An evaluation of the culture-free test of intelligence. *Journal of Genetic Psychology, 86*, 353–358.

Marquart, J. M. (1989). A pattern matching approach to assess the construct validity of an evaluation instrument. *Evaluation and Program Planning, 12*, 37–43.

Marsh, H. W., & Richards, G. E. (1988). Tennessee Self-Concept Scale: Reliability, internal structure, and construct validity. *Journal of Personality and Social Psychology, 55*, 612–624.

Marshall, V. W. (1982). Death and dying. In D. J. Mangen & W. A. Peterson (Eds.), *Research instruments in social gerontology* (Vol. 1, pp. 303–381). Minneapolis, MN: University of Minnesota Press.

Marston, A. R. (1971). It is time to reconsider the Graduate Record Examination. *American Psychologist, 26*, 653–655.

Martin, D. (1986). *Is my child gifted?: A guide for caring parents.* Springfield, IL: Charles C Thomas.

Martin, R. P. (1986). Assessment of the social and emotional functioning of preschool children. *School Psychology Review, 15*, 216–232.

Martin, R. P. (1988). *Assessment of personality and behavior problems.* New York: Guilford Press.

Martinez, R., Norman, R. D., & Delaney, N. D. (1984). A Children's Hispanic Background Scale. *Hispanic Journal of Behavioral Sciences, 6*, 103–112.

Marx, M. B., Garrity, T. F., & Bowers, F. R. (1975). The influence of recent life experience on the health of college freshmen. *Journal of Psychosomatic Research, 19*, 87.

Maslach, C., Jackson, S. E. (1981). *Maslach Burnout Inventory.* Palo Alto, CA: Consulting Psychologists Press, Inc.

Masling, J. (1960). The influence of situational and interpersonal variables in projective testing. *Psychological Bulletin, 57*, 65–85.

Maslow, A. H. (1954). *Motivation and personality.* New York: Harper & Row.

Maslow, A. H. (1962). *Toward a psychology of being.* Princeton, NJ: D. VanNostrand.

Maslow, A. (1970). *Motivation and personality.* New York: Harper & Row.

Maslow, P., Frostig, M., Lefever, W., & Whittlesey, J. R. B. (1964). The Marianne Frostig Developmental Test of Visual perception, 1963 standardization. *Perceptual and Motor Skills, 19*, 463–499.

Mason, E. M. (1992). Percent of agreement among raters and rater reliability of the Copying subtest of the Stanford-Binet Intelligence Scale: Fourth edition. *Perceptual and Motor Skills, 74*, 347–353.

Masters, J. R. (1974). The relationship between number of response castegories and reliability of Likert-type questionnaires. *Journal of Educational Measurement, 11*, 49–53.

Masuda, M., & Holmes, T. H. (1967). The social readjustment rating scale: A cross cultural study of Japanese and Americans. *Journal of Psychosomatic Research, 11*, 227–237.

Matarazzo, J. D. (1972). *Wechsler's measurement and appraisal of adult intelligence* (5th ed.). Baltimore, MD: Williams & Wilkins.

Matarazzo, J. D. (1980). Behavioral health and behavioral medicine: Frontiers for a new health psychology. *American Psychologist, 35*, 807–817.

Matarazzo, J. D. (1983). Computerized psychological testing. *Science, 221*, 323.

Matarazzo, J. D. (1986). Computerized clinical psychological test interpretations. *American Psychologist, 41*, 14–24.

Matarazzo, J. D. (1992). Psychological testing and assessment in the 21st century. *American Psychologist, 47*, 1007–1018.

Matarazzo, J. D., & Wiens, A. N. (1977). Black Intelligence Test of Cultural Homogeneity and Wechsler Adult Intelligence Scale scores of black and white police applicants. *Journal of Applied Psychology, 62*, 57–63.

Matheny, A. P., Jr. (1980). Bayley's infant behavior record: Behavioral components and twin analyses. *Child Development, 51*, 1157–1167.

Mathis, H. (1968). Relating environmental factors to aptitude and race. *Journal of Counseling Psychology, 15*, 563–568.

Matluck, J. H., & Mace, B. J. (1973). Language characteristics of Mexican-American children: Implications for assessment. *Journal of School Psychology, 11*, 365–386.

Mattis, S. (1976). Mental status examination for organic mental syndrome in the elderly patient. In L. Bellak & T. B. Karasu (Eds.), *Geriatric psychiatry* (pp. 77–121). New York: Grune & Stratton.

Mauger, P. A., & Kolmodin, C. A. (1975). Long-term predictive validity of the Scholastic Aptitude Test. *Journal of Educational Psychology, 67*, 847–851.

May, K. M., & Loyd, B. H. (1994). Honesty tests in academia and business: A comparative study. *Research in Higher Education, 35*, 499–511.

May, R. (1966). Sex differences in fantasy patterns. *Journal of Projective Techniques and Personality Assessment, 30*, 576–586.

McAbee, T. A., & Cafferty, T. P. (1982). Degree of prescribed punishment as a function of subjects' authoritarianism and offenders' race and social status. *Psychological Reports, 50*, 651–654.

McAdams, D. P. (1992). The five-factor model in personality: A critical appraisal. *Journal of Personality, 60*, 329–361.

McAllister, L. W. (1986). *A practical guide to CPI interpretation.* Palo Alto, CA: Consulting Psychologists Press.

McAndrew, C. (1965). The differentiation of male alcoholic outpatients from nonalcoholic psychiatric outpatients by means of the MMPI. *Quarterly Journal of Studies on Alcohol, 26*, 238–246.

McArthur, D. S., & Roberts, G. E. (1982). *Roberts Apperception Test for Children: Manual.* Los Angeles, CA: Western Psychological Services.

McCabe, S. P. (1985). Career Assessment Inventory. In D. J. Keyser & R. C. Sweetland (Eds.), *Test critiques* (Vol. II, pp. 128–137). Kansas City, MO: Test Corporation of America.

McCallum, R. S., Karnes, F., & Crowell, M. (1988). Factor structure of the Stanford-Binet Intelligence Scale for gifted children (4th ed.). *Contemporary Educational Psychology, 13,* 331–338.

McCallum, R. S. (1990). Determining the factor structure of the Stanford-Binet – Fourth Edition: The right choice. *Journal of Psychoeducational Assessment, 8,* 436–442.

McCallum, R. S., Karnes, F. A., & Edwards, R. P. (1984). The test of choice for assessment of gifted children: A comparison of the K-ABC, WISC-R, and Stanford-Binet. *Journal of Psychoeducational Assessment, 2,* 57–63.

McCann, J. T. (1991). Convergent and discriminant validity of the MCMI-II and MMPI personality disorder scales. *Psychological Assessment, 3,* 9–18.

McCarney, S. B. (1989). *The Attention Deficit Disorders Evaluation Scale technical manual, school version.* Columbia, MO: Hawthorne Educational Services, Inc.

McCarthy, B. W., & Rafferty, J. E. (1971). Effect of social desirability and self-concept scores on the measurement of adjustment. *Journal of Personality Assessment, 35,* 576–583.

McCarthy, D. (1972). *Manual for the McCarthy Scales of Children's Abilities.* New York: Psychological Corporation.

McCarthy, D. (1978). *McCarthy Screening Test.* New York: Psychological Corporation.

McCaulley, M. H. (1981). Jung's theory of psychological types and the Myers-Briggs Type Indicator. In P. McReynolds (Ed.), *Advances in psychological assessment* (Vol. 5, pp. 294–352). San Francisco, CA: Jossey-Bass.

McClelland, D. C. (1951). *Personality.* New York: Sloane.

McClelland, D. C., Atkinson, J. W., Clark, R. A., & Lowell, E. L. (1953). *The achievement motive.* New York: Appleton-Century-Crofts.

McClelland, D. C., & Boyatzis, R. E. (1982). Leadership motive pattern and long-term success in management. *Journal of Applied Psychology, 67,* 737–743.

McClenaghan, B., & Gallahue, D. (1978). *Fundamental movement: A developmental and remedial approach.* Philadelphia, PA: Saunders.

McConaghy, N. (1967). Penile volume change to moving pictures of male and female nudes in heterosexual and homosexual males. *Behaviour Research and Therapy, 5,* 43–48.

McCormack, R. L. (1983). Bias in the validity of predicted college grades in four ethnic minority groups. *Educational and Psychological Measurement, 43,* 517–522.

McCrae, R. R. (1982). Consensual validation of personality traits: Evidence from self-reports and ratings. *Journal of Personality and Social Psychology, 43,* 293–303.

McCrae, R., & Costa, P. (1983a). Social desirability scales: More substance than style. *Journal of Consulting and Clinical Psychology, 51,* 882–888.

McCrae, R. R., & Costa, P. T., Jr. (1983b). Joint factors in self-reports and ratings: Neuroticism, extraversion, and openness to experience. *Personality and Individual Differences, 4,* 245–255.

McCrae, R. R., & Costa, P. T., Jr. (1985). Updating Norman's "Adequate Taxonomy": Intelligence and personality dimensions in natural language and in questionnaires. *Journal of Personality and Social Psychology, 49,* 710–721.

McCrae, R. R., & Costa, P. T., Jr. (1986). Clinical assessment can benefit from recent advances in personality psychology. *American Psychologist, 41,* 1001–1003.

McCrae, R. R., & Costa, P. T., Jr. (1987). Validation of the five-factor model of personality across instruments and observers. *Journal of Personality and Social Psychology, 52,* 81–90.

McCrae, R. R., & Costa, P. T., Jr. (1989a). Reinterpreting the Myers-Briggs Type Indicator from the perspective of the five-factor model of personality. *Journal of Personality, 57,* 17–40.

McCrae, R. R., & Costa, P. T., Jr. (1989b). More reasons to adopt the five-factor model. *American Psychologist, 44,* 451–452.

McCrae, R. R., Costa, P. T., Jr., & Busch, C. M. (1986). Evaluating comprehensiveness in personality systems: The California Q-set and the five factor model. *Journal of Personality, 54,* 430–446.

McCrone, W. P., & Chambers, J. F. (1977). A national pilot study of psychological evaluation services to deaf vocational rehabilitation clients. *Journal of Rehabilitation of the Deaf, 11,* 1–4.

McDermid, C. D. (1965). Some correlates of creativity in engineering personnel. *Journal of Applied Psychology, 49,* 14–19.

McDougall, W. (1932). Of the words character and personality. *Character Personality, 1,* 3–16.

McFall, R. M., & Lillesand, D. V. (1971). Behavior rehearsal with modeling and coaching in assertive training. *Journal of Abnormal Psychology, 77,* 313–323.

McFie, J. (1975). *Assessment of organic intellectual impairment.* London: Academic Press.

McGee, R. K. (1967). Response set in relation to personality: an orientation. In I. A. Berg (Ed.), *Response set in personality assessment* (pp. 1–31). Chicago, IL: Aldine.

McGill, J. C. (1980). MMPI score differences among Anglo, Black, and Mexican-American welfare recipients. *Journal of Clinical Psychology, 36,* 147–151.

McGreal, R., & Joseph, S. (1993). The Depression-Happiness Scale. *Psychological Reports, 73,* 1279–1282.

McGuire, F. L. (1980). The new MCAT and medical school performance. *Journal of Medical Education, 55,* 405–408.

McHenry, J. J., Hough, L. M., Toquam, J. L., Hanson, M. A., & Ashworth, S. (1990). Project A validity results: The relationship between predictor and criterion domains. *Personnel Psychology, 43,* 335–354.

McHorney, C. A., Ware, J. E., Jr., & Raczek, A. E. (1993). The MOS 36-item short-form Health Survey (SF-36) II: Psychometric and clinical tests of validity in measuring physical and mental health constructs. *Medical Care, 31,* 247–263.

McIntosh, D. E. (1999). Identifying at-risk preschoolers: The discriminant validity of the Differential Ability Scales. *Psychology in the Schools, 36,* 1–10.

McKee, M. G. (1972). Review of the EPPS. In O. K. Buros (Ed.), *The seventh mental measurements Yearbook* (Vol. 1, pp. 1459–151). Highland Park, NJ: Gryphon Press.

McKechnie, G. E. (1975). *Manual for the Leisure Activities Blank.* Palo Alto, CA: Consulting Psychologists Press.

McKinney, W. R. (1987). Public personnel selection: Issues and choice points. *Public Personnel Management Journal, 16,* 243–257.

McLain, D. L. (1993). The MSTAT-I: A new measure of an individual's tolerance for ambiguity. *Educational and Psychological Measurement, 53,* 183–189.

McMahon, R. J. (1984). Behavioral checklists and rating scales. In T. H. Ollendick & M. Hersen (Eds.), *Child behavioral assessment: Principles and procedures.* New York: Pergamon Press.

McNemar, Q. (1940). A critical examination of the University of Iowa studies of environmental influences upon the IQ. *Psychological Bulletin, 37,* 63–92.

McNemar, Q. (1950). On abbreviated Wechsler-Bellevue scales. *Journal of Consulting Psychology, 14,* 79–81.

McQuaid, M. F., & Alovisetti, M. (1981). School psychological services for hearing-impaired children in the New York and New England area. *American Annals of the Deaf, 126,* 37–42.

McQuitty, L. (1957). Elementary linkage analysis for isolating orthogonal and oblique types and typical relevancies. *Educational and Psychological Measurement, 17,* 207–229.

McReynolds, P. (1987). Lightner Witmer. *American Psychologist, 42,* 849–858.

McReynolds, P., & Ludwig, K. (1984). Christian Thomasius and the origin of psychological rating scales. *ISIS, 75,* 546–553.

McReynolds, P., & Ludwig, K. (1987). On the history of rating scales. *Personality and Individual Differences, 8,* 281–283.

McShane, D. A. (1980). A review of scores of American Indian children on the Wechsler Intelligence Scales. *White Cloud Journal, 1,* 3–10.

McShane, D. A., & Plas, J. M. (1982). Wechsler scale performance patterns of American Indian children. *Psychology in the Schools, 19,* 8–17.

McShane, S. L., & Karp, J. (1993). Employment following spinal cord injury: A covariance structure analysis. *Rehabilitation Psychology, 38,* 27–40.

Meador, D., Livesay, K. K., & Finn, M. H. (1983). Study Number 27. In A. S. Kaufman & N. L. Kaufman (Eds.), *Kaufman-Assessment Battery for Children: Interpretive manual.* Circle Pines, MN: American Guidance Service.

Meadow, K. P. (1983). An instrument for assessment of social-emotional adjustment in hearing-impaired preschoolers. *American Annals of the Deaf, 128,* 826–884.

Medley, M. L. (1980). Life satisfaction across four stages of adult life. *International Journal of Aging and Human Development, 11,* 192–220.

Meehl, P. E. (1954). *Clinical versus statistical prediction.* Minneapolis, MN: University of Minnesota Press.

Meehl, P. E. (1956). Wanted – A good cookbook. *American Psychologist, 11,* 263–272.

Meehl, P. E. (1957). When shall we use our heads instead of the formula? *Journal of Counseling Psychology, 4,* 268–273.

Meehl, P. E. (1978). Theoretical risks and tabular asterisks: Sir Karl, Sir Ronald, and the slow progress of soft psychology. *Journal of Consulting and Clinical Psychology, 46,* 806–834.

Meehl, P. E., & Hathaway, S. R. (1946). The K factor as a suppressor variable in the MMPI. *Journal of Applied Psychology, 30,* 525–564.

Meehl, P. E., Lykken, D. T., Schofield, W., & Tellegen, A. (1971). Recaptured-item technique (RIT): A method for reducing somewhat the subjective element in factor naming. *Journal of Experimental Research in Personality, 5,* 171–190.

Meehl, P. E., & Rosen, A. (1955). Antecedent probability and the efficiency of psychometric signs, patterns, or cutting scores. *Psychological Bulletin, 52,* 194–216.

Meeker, M. (1985). *A teacher's guide for the Structure of Intellect Learning Abilities Test.* Los Angeles, CA: Western Psychological Services.

Meeker, M., Meeker, R. J., & Roid, G. H. (1985). *Structure of intellect Learning Abilities Test (SOI-LA) manual.* Los Angeles, CA: Western Psychological Services.

Meer, B., & Baker, J. A. (1965). Reliability of measurements of intellectual functioning of geriatric patients. *Journal of Gerontology, 20,* 110–114.

Megargee, E. I. (1972). *The California psychological inventory handbook.* San Francisco, CA: Jossey-Bass.

Mehryar, A. H., Hekmat, H., & Khajavi, F. (1977). Some personality correlates of contemplated suicide. *Psychological Reports, 40,* 1291–1294.

Meier, S. T. (1993). Revitalizing the measurement curriculum. *American Psychologist, 48,* 886–891.

Meijer, R. R., & Nering, M. L. (1999). Computerized adaptive testing: Overview and introduction. *Applied Psychological Measurement, 23,* 187–194.

Melchior, L. A., Huba, G. J., Brown, V. B., & Reback, C. J. (1993). A short depression index for women. *Educational and Psychological Measurement, 53,* 1117–1125.

Melzack, R. (1975). The McGill Pain Questionnaire: Major properties and scoring methods. *Pain, 1,* 277–299.

Melzack, R. (1984). Measurement of the dimensions of pain. In B. Bromm (Ed.), *Pain measurement in man Neurophysiological correlates of pain.* New York: Elsevier.

Melzack, R. (1987). The short-form McGill Pain Questionnaire. *Pain, 30,* 191–197.

Melzack, R., & Torgerson, W. S. (1971). On the language of pain. *Anesthesiology, 34,* 50–59.

Melzack, R., & Wall, P. D. (1965). Pain mechanisms: A new theory. *Science, 150,* 971–979.

Mendoza, R. H. (1989). An empirical scale to measure type and degree of acculturation in Mexican-American adolescents and adults. *Journal of Cross-Cultural Psychology, 20,* 372–385.

Mercer, C. D., Algozzine, B., & Trifiletti, J. J. (1979). Early identification issues and considerations. *Exceptional Children, 46,* 52–54.

Mercer, J. (1973). *Labeling the mentally retarded.* Berkeley, CA: University of California Press.

Mercer, J. R. (1976). A system of multicultural pluralistic assessment (SOMPA) in *Proceedings: With bias toward none.* Lexington, KY: Coordinating Office for Regional Resource Centers, University of Kentucky.

Mercer, J., Gomez-Palacio, M., & Padilla, E. (1986). The development of practical intelligence in cross-cultural perspective. In R. J. Sternberg & R. K. Wag-

ner (Eds.), *Practical intelligence* (pp. 307–337). Cambridge, MA: Cambridge University Press.

Mercer, J., & Lewis, J. (1977). *System of multicultural pluralistic assessment.* New York: Psychological Corporation.

Merenda, P. F. (1958). Navy basic test battery validity for success in naval occupations. *Personnel Psychology, 11,* 567–577.

Merenda, P. F., & Reilly, R. (1971). Validation of selection criteria in determining success of graduate students in psychology. *Psychological Reports, 28,* 259–266.

Merrell, K. W. (1990). Teacher ratings of hyperactivity and self-control in learning disabled boys: A comparison with low achieving and average peers. *Psychology in the Schools, 27,* 289–296.

Merrell, K. W. (1994). *Assessment of behavioral, social, and emotional problems.* New York: Longman.

Mershon, B., & Gorsuch, R. L. (1988). Number of factors in the personality sphere: Does increase in factors increase predictability of real life criteria? *Journal of Personality and Social Psychology, 55,* 675–680.

Messick, S. (1960). Dimensions of social desirability. *Journal of Consulting Psychology, 24,* 279–287.

Messick, S. (1962). Response style and content measures from personality inventories. *Educational and Psychological Measurement, 22,* 41–56.

Messick, S. (1975). Meaning and values in measurement and evaluation. *American Psychologist, 35,* 1012–1027.

Messick, S. (1989). Validity. In R. L. Linn (Ed.), *Educational measurement* (3rd ed., pp. 13–103). New York: Macmillan.

Messick, S. (1995). Validity of psychological assessment. *American Psychologist, 50,* 741–749.

Messick, S., & Anderson, S. (1970). Educational testing, individual development, and social responsibility. *The Counseling Psychologist, 2,* 80–88.

Messick, S. J., & Jackson, D. N. (1958). The measurement of authoritarian attitudes. *Educational and Psychological Measurement, 18,* 241–253.

Messick, S. & Jungeblut, A. (1981). Time and method in coaching for the SAT. *Psychological Bulletin, 89,* 191–216.

Metcalfe, M., & Goldman, E. (1965). Validation of an inventory for measuring depression. *British Journal of Psychiatry, 111,* 240–242.

Metzger, A. M. (1979). A Q-methodological study of the Kübler-Ross stage theory. *Omega, 10,* 291–301.

Meyer, A. B., Fouad, N. A., & Klein, M. (1987). Vocational inventories. In B. Bolton (Ed.), *Handbook of measurement and evaluation in rehabilitation* (2nd ed., pp. 119–138). Baltimore, MD: Paul H. Brookes.

Meyer, G. J. (1997). Assessing reliability: Critical corrections for a critical examination of the Rorschach Comprehensive System. *Psychological Assessment, 9*, 480–489.

Meyer, G. J., Finn, S. E., & Eyde, L. D. (2001). Psychological testing and psychological assessment. *American Psychologist, 56*, 128–165.

Meyer, P., & Davis, S. (1992). *The California Psychological Inventory Applications Guide*. Palo Alto, CA: Consulting Psychologists Press.

Meyers, C. E., Nihira, K., & Zetlin, A. (1979). The measurement of adaptive behavior. In N. R. Ellis (Ed.), *Handbook of mental deficiency: Psychological theory and research* (2nd ed., pp. 215–253). Hillsdale, NJ: Erlbaum.

Michelson, L., & Wood, R. (1982). Development and psychometric properties of the Children's Assertive Behavior Scale. *Journal of Behavioral Assessment, 4*, 3–13.

Miethe, T. D. (1985). The validity and reliability of value measurements. *The Journal of Psychology, 119*, 441–453.

Millard. K. A. (1952). Is How Supervise? an intelligence test? *Journal of Applied Psychology, 36*, 221–224.

Miller, B. C., Rollins, B. C., & Thomas, D. L. (1982). On methods of studying marriages and families. *Journal of Marriage and the Family, 44*, 851–873.

Miller, D., Wertz, O., & Counts, S. (1961). Racial differences on the MMPI. *Journal of Clinical Psychology, 17*, 159–161.

Miller, J. F., & Powers, M. J. (1988). Development of an instrument to measure hope. *Nursing Research, 37*, 6–10.

Miller, K. M., & Biggs, J. B. (1958). Attitude change through undirected group discussion. *Journal of Educational Psychology, 49*, 224–228.

Miller, L. C., Murphy, R., & Buss, A. H. (1981). Consciousness of body: Private and public. *Journal of Personality and Social Psychology, 41*, 397–406.

Miller, M. D., & Linn, R. L. (2000). Validation of performance-based assessments. *Applied Psychological Measurement, 24*, 367–378.

Miller, W. R. (1976). Alcoholism scales and objective assessment methods: A review. *Psychological Bulletin, 83*, 649–674.

Millman, J., Bishop, C. H., & Ebel, R. (1965). An analysis of testwiseness. *Educational and Psychological Measurement, 25*, 707–726.

Millon, T. (1987). *Millon Clinical Multiaxial Inventory-II: MCMI-II* (2nd ed.). Minneapolis, MN: National Computer Systems.

Millon, T., & Green, C. (1989). Interpretive guide to the Millon Clinical Multiaxial Inventory (MCMI-II). In C. S. Newmark (Ed.), *Major psychological assessment instruments* (Vol. 2, pp. 5–43). Boston, MA: Allyn & Bacon.

Millon, T., Green, C. J., & Meagher, R. B. Jr. (1982a). *Millon Adolescent Personality Inventory Manual*. Minneapolis, MN: National Computer Systems.

Millon, T., Green, C. J., & Meagher, R. B. Jr. (1982b). *Millon Behavioral Health Inventory Manual* (3rd ed.). Minneapolis, MN: National Computer Systems.

Miner, J. (1964). *Scoring guide for the Miner Sentence Completion Scale*. New York: Springer-Verlag.

Minton, H. L. (1984). The Iowa Child Welfare Research Station and the 1940 debate of intelligence: Carrying on the legacy of a concerned mother. *Journal of the History of the Behavioral Sciences, 20*, 160–176.

Mischel, W. (1968). *Personality and assessment*. New York: Wiley.

Mischel, W. (1977). On the future of personality measurement. *American Psychologist, 32*, 246–254.

Mischel, W. (1981). *Introduction to personality* (3rd ed.). New York: Holt, Rinehart and Winston.

Mishra, S. P. (1971). Wechsler Adult Intelligence Scale: Examiner vs. machine administration. *Psychological Reports, 29*, 759–762.

Mishra, S. (1983). Evidence of item bias in the verbal subtests of the WISC-R for Mexican-American children. *Journal of Psychoeducational Assessment, 1*, 321–328.

Misiak, H., & Sexton, V. S. (1966). *History of Psychology*. New York: Grune & Stratton.

Mitchell, A. J. (1937). The effect of bilingualism on the measurement of intelligence. *Elementary School Journal, 38*, 29–37.

Mitchell, R. (1973). Defining medical terms. *Developmental Medicine and Child Neurology, 15*, 279.

Mitchell, T. W., & Klimoski, R. J. (1982). Is it rational to be empirical? A test of methods for scoring biographical data. *Journal of Applied Psychology, 67*, 411–418.

Mittenberg, W., Azrin, R., Millsaps, C., & Heilbronner, R. (1993). Identification of malingered head injury on the Wechsler Memory Scale-Revised. *Psychological Assessment, 5*, 34–40.

Mittenberg, W., Rotholc, A., Russell, E., & Heilbronner, R. (1996). Identification of malingered head injury on the Halstead-Reitan Battery. *Toxicology Letters, 11*, 271–281.

Mittenberg, W., Theroux-Fichera, S., Zielinski, R. E., & Heilbronner, R. L. (1995). Identification of malingered head injury on the Wechsler Adult Intelligence Scale-Revised. *Professional Psychology: Research and Practice, 26*, 491–498.

Mizes, J. S., & Crawford, J. (1986). Normative values on the Marks and Mathews Fear Questionnaire: A comparison as a function of age and sex. *Journal of*

Psychopathology and Behavioral Assessment, 8, 253–262.

Montgomery, G. T., & Orozco, S. (1984). Validation of a measure of acculturation for Mexican Americans. *Hispanic Journal of Behavioral Sciences, 6*, 53–63.

Moore, M. (1975). Rating vs. ranking in the Rokeach Value Survey: An Israeli comparison. *European Journal of Social Psychology, 5*, 405–408.

Moore, N. C., Summer, K. R., & Bloor, R. N. (1984). Do patients like psychometric testing by computer? *Journal of Clinical Psychology, 40*, 875–877.

Moos, R. H. (1968). The assessment of the social climates of correctional institutions. *Journal of Research in Crime and Delinquency, 5*, 174–188.

Moos, R. H. (1972). Assessment of the psychosocial environments of community-oriented psychiatric treatment programs. *Journal of Abnormal Psychology, 79*, 9–18.

Moos, R. H. (1979). *Evaluating educational environments*. San Francisco, CA: Jossey-Bass.

Moos, R. H., & Gerst, M. S. (1974). *University Residence Environmene Scale*. Palo Alto, CA: Consulting Psychologists Press.

Moos, R. H., & Houts, P. (1968). Assessment of the social atmosphere of psychiatric wards. *Journal of Abnormal Psychology, 73*, 595–604.

Moos, R. H., & Swindle, R. W., Jr. (1990). Stressful life circumstances: Concepts and measures. *Stress Medicine, 6* 171–178.

Moos, R. H., & Trickett, E. J. (1974). *Classroom Environment Scale manual*. Palo Alto, CA: Consulting Psychologists Press.

Moracco, J., & Zeidan, M. (1982). Assessment of sex knowledge and attitude of non-Western medical students. *Psychology, 19*, 13–21.

Moran, A. (1986). The reliability and validity of Raven's Standard Progressive Matrices for Irish apprentices. *International Review of Psychology, 35*, 533–538.

Moran, P. W., & Lambert, M. J. (1983). A review of current assessment tools for monitoring changes in depression. In M. S. Lambert, E. R. Christensen, & S. S. DeJulio (Eds.), *The assessment of psychotherapy outcome.* (pp. 263–303). New York: Wiley.

Moreland, K. L. (1987). Computerized psychological assessment: What's available. In J. N. Butcher (Ed.), *Computerized psychological assessment* (pp. 26–49). New York: Basic Books.

Moreland, K. L. (1991). Assessment of validity in computer-based test interpretations. In T. B. Gutkin & S. L. Wise (Eds.), *The computer and the decision-making process* (pp. 43–74). Hillsdale, NJ: Erlbaum.

Moreland, K. L., & Onstad, J. A. (1987). Validity of Millon's computerized interpretation system for the MCMI: A controlled study. *Journal of Consulting and Clinical Psychology, 55*, 113–114.

Morey, L. C., & LeVine, D. J. (1988). A multitrait-multimethod examination of Minnesota Multiphasic Personality Inventory (MMPI) and Millon Clinical Multiaxial Inventory (MCMI). *Journal of Psychopathology and Behavioral Assessment, 10*, 333–344.

Morgan, W. G. (1995). Origin and history of the Thematic Apperception Test images. *Journal of Personality Assessment, 65*, 237–254.

Morris, J. N., & Sherwood, S. (1975). A retesting and modification of the Philadelphia Geriatric Center Morale Scale. *Journal of Gerontology, 30*, 77–84.

Mosel, J. N. (1952). The validity of rational ratings on experience and training. *Personnel Psychology, 5*, 1–9.

Mosel, J. N., & Cozan, L. W. (1952). The accuracy of application blank work histories. *Journal of Applied Psychology, 36*, 365–369.

Mosher, D. L. (1965). Approval motive and acceptance of "fake" personality interpretations which differ in favorability. *Psychological Reports, 17*, 395–402.

Mosier, C. I. (1941). A short cut in the estimation of the split-halves coefficient. *Educational and Psychological Measurement, 1*, 407–408.

Mowrer, O. H. (1960). *The psychology of hope*. San Francisco, CA: Jossey-Bass.

Mowrer, O. H. (Ed.). (1967). *Morality and mental health*. Chicago, IL: Rand McNally & Co.

Mulaik, S. A. (1964). Are personality factors raters' conceptual factors? *Journal of Consulting Psychology, 28*, 506–511.

Mullis, I. V. S. (1992). Developing the NAEP content-area frameworks and innovative assessment methods in the 1992 assessments of mathematics, reading, and writing. *Journal of Educational Measurement, 29*, 111–131.

Mumford, M. D., & Owens, W. A. (1987). Methodology review: Principles, procedures, and findings in the application of background data measures. *Applied Psychological Measurement, 11*, 1–31.

Mumley, D., L., Tillbrook, C. E., & Grisso, T. (2003). Five year research update (1996–2000): Evaluations for Competence to Stand Trial (Adjudicative Competence). *Behavioral Sciences and the Law, 21*, 329–350.

Murphy, J. J. (1972). Current practices in the use of psychological testing by police agencies. *Journal of Criminal Law, Criminology, and Police Science, 63*, 570–576.

Murphy, K. R. (1994). Potential effects of banding as a function of test reliability. *Personnel Psychology, 47*, 477–495.

Murphy, K. R., & Constans, J. I. (1987). Behavioral anchors as a source of bias in rating. *Journal of Applied Psychology, 72*, 573–577.

Murphy, K. R., Jako, R. A., & Anhalt, R. L. (1993). Nature and consequences of halo error: A critical analysis. *Journal of Applied Psychology, 78*, 218–225.

Murray, H. A. (1938). *Explorations in personality*. New York: Oxford University Press.

Murray, H. A. (1943). *Thematic Apperception Test: Pictures and manual*. Cambridge, MA: Harvard University Press.

Murray, H. A. (1967). Autobiography. In E. G. Boring & G. Lindzey (Eds.), *A history of psychology in autobiography* (Vol. 5, pp. 283–310). New York: Appleton-Century-Crofts.

Murray, J. B. (1990). Review of research on the Myers-Briggs Type Indicator. *Perceptual and Motor Skills, 70*, 1187–1202.

Murstein, B. J. (1963). *Theory and research in projective techniques (emphasizing the TAT)*. New York: Wiley.

Myers, A. M., Holliday, P. J., Harvey, K. A., & Hutchinson, K. S. (1993). Functional performance measures: Are they superior to self-assessments? *Journal of Gerontology, 48*, 196–206.

Myers, I. B., & McCaulley, M. H. (1985). *Manual: A guide to the development and use of the Myers-Briggs Type Indicator*. Palo Alto, CA: Consulting Psychologists Press.

Myklebust, H. (1964). *The psychology of deafness*. New York: Grune & Stratton.

Nagle, R. J. (1979). The McCarthy Scales of Children's Abilities: Research implications for the assessment of young children. *School Psychology Digest, 8*, 319–326.

Nagle, R. J., & Bell, N. L. (1995). Validation of an item-reduction short form of the Stanford-Binet Intelligence Scale: Fourth edition with college students. *Journal of Clinical Psychology, 51*, 63–70.

Naglieri, J. A. (1981). Factor structure of the WISC-R for children identified as learning disabled. *Psychological Reports, 49*, 891–895.

Naglieri, J. A. (1988). *Draw A Person: A quantitative scoring system*. San Antonio, TX: Psychological Corporation.

Naglieri, J. A., & Kaufman, A. S. (1983). How many factors underlie the WAIS-R? *The Journal of Psychoeducational Assessment, 1*, 113–120.

Naglieri, J. A., & Welch, J. A. (1991). Use of Raven's and Naglieri's Noverbal Matrix Tests. *Journal of the American Deafness and Rehabilitation Association, 24*, 98–103.

Nairn, A. and associates (1980). *The reign of ETS*. Washington DC: Ralph Nader.

Narby, D. J., Cutler, B. L., & Moran, G. (1993). A meta-analysis of the association between authoritarianism and jurors' perceptions of defendant culpability. *Journal of Applied Psychology, 78*, 34–42.

Nathan, B. R., & Alexander, R. A. (1988). A comparison of criteria for test validation: A metaanalytic investigation. *Personnel Psychology, 41*, 517–535.

Nathan, B. R., & Tippins, N. (1990). The consequences of halo "error" in performance ratings: A field study of the moderating effect of halo on test validation results. *Journal of Applied Psychology, 75*, 290–296.

National Commission on Excellence in Education (1983). *A nation at risk: The imperative for educational reform*. Washington, DC: U.S. Government Printing Office.

National Society to Prevent Blindness (1974). *The Symbol Chart for Twenty Feet – Snellen Scale*. New York: Author.

Naughton, M. J., & Wiklund, I. (1993). A critical review of dimension-specific measures of health-related quality of life in cross-cultural research. *Quality of Life Research, 2*, 397–432.

Nedelsky, L. (1954). Absolute grading standards for objective tests. *Educational and Psychological Measurement, 14*, 3–19.

Needham, W. E., & Eldridge, L. S. (1990). Performance of blind vocational rehabilitation clients on the Minnesota Rate of Manipulation Tests. *Journal of Visual Impairment and Blindness, 84*, 182–185.

Neeper, R., & Lahey, B. B. (1984). Identification of two dimensions of cognitive deficits through the factor analysis of teacher ratings. *School Psychology Review, 13*, 485–490.

Neiner, A. G., & Owens, W. A. (1985). Using biodata to predict job choice among college graduates. *Journal of Applied Psychology, 70*, 127–136.

Neisser, U. (1976). General, academic, and artificial intelligence. In L. Resnick (Ed.), *The nature of intelligence* (pp. 135–144). Hillsdale, NJ: Erlbaum.

Neisser, U., Boodoo, G., Bouchard, T. J., Jr., & Boykin, A. W. (1996). Intelligence: Knowns and unknowns. *American Psychologist, 51*, 77–101.

Neisworth, J. T., & Bagnato, S. J. (1986). Curriculum-based developmental assessment: Congruence of testing and teaching. *School Psychology Review, 15*, 180–199.

Nelson, R. O. (1977). Methodological issues in assessment via self-monitoring. In J. D. Cone & R. P. Hawkins (Eds.), *Behavioral assessment: New directions in clinical psychology* (pp. 217–240). New York: Brunner/Mazel.

Nelson, R. O., & Hayes, S. C. (1979). Some current dimensions of behavioral assessment. *Behavioral Assessment, 1*, 1–16.

Nelson-Gray, R. O. (1991). DSM IV: Empirical guidelines for psychometrics. *Journal of Abnormal Psychology, 100*, 308–315.

Nester, M. A. (1984). Employment testing for handicapped persons. *Public Personnel Management Journal, 13,* 417–434.

Nester, M. A. (1993). Psychometric testing and reasonable accomodation for persons with disabilities. *Rehabilitation Psychology, 38,* 75–85.

Neugarten, B. (1974). Age groups in the young-old. *Annals of the American Academy of Political and Social Science, 415,* 187–198.

Neugarten, B. L., & Associates (Eds.). (1964). *Personality in middle and late life.* New York: Atherton.

Neugarten, B. L., Havighurst, R. J., & Tobin, S. S. (1961). The measurement of life satisfaction. *Journal of Gerontology, 16,* 134–143.

Nevo, B. (1985). Face validity revisited. *Journal of Educational Measurement, 22,* 287–293.

Newcomb, T. M. (1950). *Social psychology.* New York: Holt.

Newman, J. P. (1989). Aging and depression. *Psychology and aging, 4,* 150–165.

Ng, S. H., Akhtar Hossain, A. B. M., Ball, P., Bond, M. H., Hayashi, K., Lim, S. P., O'Driscoll, M. P., Sinha, D., & Yang, K. S. (1982). Human values in nine countries. In R. Rath, H. S. Asthana, D. Sinha, & J. B. P. Sinha (Eds.), *Diversity and unity in cross-cultural psychology.* Lissie, the Netherlands: Swets & Zeitlinger.

Nichols, R. C., & Schnell, R. R. (1963). Factor scales for the California Psychological Inventory. *Journal of Consulting Psychology, 27,* 228–235.

Nicholson, C. L. (1977). Correlations between the Quick Test and the Wechsler Scale for Children-Revised. *Psychological Reports, 40,* 523–526.

Nicholson, R. A., Briggs, S. R., & Robertson, H. C. (1988). Instruments for assessing competency to stand trial: How do they work? *Professional Psychology, 19,* 383–394.

Nietzel, M. T., Martorano, R. D., & Melnick, J. (1977). The effects of covert modeling with and without reply training on the development and generalization of assertive responses. *Behavior Therapy, 8,* 183–192.

Nihira, K., Foster, R., Shellhass, M., & Leland, H. (1974). *AAMD Adaptive Behavior Scale.* Washington, DC: American Association of Mental Deficiency.

Nolan, D. R., Hameke, T. A., & Barkley, R. A. (1983). A comparison of the patterns of the neuropsychological performance in two groups of learning-disabled children. *Journal of Clinical Child Psychology, 12,* 13–21.

Noonan, J. V., & Sarvela, P. D. (1991). Implementation decisions in designing computer-based instructional testing programs. In T. B. Gutkin & S. L. Wise (Eds.), *The computer and the decision-making process* (pp. 177–197). Hillsdale, NJ: Erlbaum.

Norman, R. D., & Daley, M. F. (1959). Senescent changes in intellectual ability among superior older women. *Journal of Gerontology, 14,* 457–464.

Norman, W. T. (1963). Toward an adequate taxonomy of personality attributes: Replicated factor structure in peer nomination personality ratings. *Journal of Abnormal and Social Psychology, 66,* 574–583.

Norring, C., & Sohlberg, S. (1988). Eating Disorder Inventory in Sweden: Description, cross-cultural comparison, and clinical utility. *Acta Psychiatrica Scandinavica, 78,* 567–575.

Norton, R. (1983). Measuring marital quality: A critical look at the dependent variable. *Journal of Marriage and the Family, 45,* 141–151.

Nowacek, G. A., Pullen, E., Short, J., & Blumner, H. N. (1987). Validity of MCAT scores as predictors of preclinical grades and NBME Part I examination scores. *Journal of Medical Education, 62,* 989–991.

Nowicki, S., & Duke, M. P. (1974). A locus of control scale for non-college as well as college adults. *Journal of Personality Assessment, 38,* 136–137.

Nowicki, S., & Strickland, B. R. (1973). A locus of control scale for children. *Journal of Consulting Psychology, 40,* 148–154.

Nunnally, J. (1962). The analysis of profile data. *Psychological Bulletin, 59,* 311–319.

Nunnally, J., & Husek, T. R. (1958). The phony language examination: An approach to the measurement of response bias. *Educational and Psychological Measurement, 2,* 275–282.

Nussbaum, K., Wittig, B. A., Hanlon, T. E., & Kurland, A. A. (1963). Intravenous mialamide in the treatment of depressed female patients. *Comprehensive Psychiatry, 4,* 105–116.

Nuttall, E. V., Romero, I., & Kalesnik, J. (Eds.). (1992). *Assessing and screening preschoolers.* Boston, MA: Allyn & Bacon.

Oakland, T. (1985a). Review of the Otis-Lennon School Ability Test. In J. V. Mitchell, Jr. (Ed.), *The ninth mental measurements yearbook* (Vol. 2, pp. 1111–1112). Lincoln, NE: University of Nebraska Press.

Oakland, T. (1985b). Review of the Slosson Intelligence Test. In J. V. Mitchell, Jr. (Ed.), *The ninth mental measurements yearbook* (Vol. 2, pp. 1401–1403). Lincoln, NE: University of Nebraska Press.

Oakland, T., & Matuszek, P. (1977). Using tests in nondiscriminatory assessment. In T. Oakland (Ed.), *Psychological and educational assessment in minority group children.* New York: Bruner/Mazel.

Obayuwana, A. O., Collins, J. L., Carter, A. L., Rao, M. S., Mathura, C. C., & Wilson, S. B. (1982). Hope Index Scale: An instrument for the objective assessment of hope. *Journal of the National Medical Association of New York, 74,* 761.

Oblowitz, N., Green, L., & Heyns, I. (1991). A self-concept scale for the hearing-impaired. *The Volta Review, 93,* 19–29.

O'Brien, N. P. (1988). *Test construction.* New York: Greenwood Press.

O'Dell, J. (1972). P. T. Bamum explores the computer. *Journal of Consulting and Clinical Psychology, 38,* 270–273.

O'Donnell, J. M. (1979). The clinical psychology of Lightner Witmer: A case study of institutional innovation and intellectual change. *Journal of the History of the Behavioral Sciences, 15,* 3–17.

O'Donohue, W., & Letourneau, E. (1992). The psychometric properties of the penile tumescence assessment of child molesters. *Journal of Psychopathology and Behavioral Assessment, 14,* 123–174.

Olbrisch, M. E. (1983). Development and validation of the Ostomy Adjustment Scale. *Rehabilitation Psychology, 28,* 3–12.

Olea, M. M., & Ree, M. J. (1994). Predicting pilot and navigator criteria: Not much more than g. *Journal of Applied Psychology, 79,* 845–851.

Oliver, J. M., & Burkham, R. (1979). Depression in university students: Duration, relation to calendar time, prevalence, and demographic correlates. *Journal of Abnormal Psychology, 88,* 667–670.

Oliveri. M. E., & Reiss, D. (1984). Family concepts and their measurement; Things are seldom what they seem. *Family Process, 23,* 33–48.

Ollendick, T. H. (1979). Discrepancies between Verbal and Performance IQs and subtest scatter on the WISC-R for juvenile delinquents. *Psychological Reports, 45,* 563–568.

Olmedo, E. L. (1979). Acculturation. A psychometric perspective. *American Psychologist, 34,* 1061–1070.

Olmedo, E. L. (1981). Testing linguistic minorities. *American Psychologist, 36,* 1078–1085.

Olmedo, E. L., Martinez, J. L., & Martinez, S. R. (1978). Measure of acculturation for Chicano adolescents. *Psychological Reports, 42,* 159–170.

Olmedo, E. L., & Padilla, A. M. (1978). Empirical and construct validation of a measure of acculturation, for Mexican-Americans. *Journal of Social Psychology, 105,* 179–187.

Olson, D. H., McCubbin, H. I, Barnes, H., Larsen, A., Muxen, M., & Wilson, M., & Wilson, M. (1985). *Family inventories.* St. Paul, MN: University of Minnesota.

Olson, D. H., & Rabunsky, C. (1972). Validity of four measures of family power. *Journal of Marriage and the Family, 34,* 224–234.

Oltman, P. K., & Hartnett, R. T. (1984). The role of GRE General and Subject Test scores in graduate program admission. *ETS Research Report,* 84–14.

Ones, D. S., Chockalingam, V., & Schmidt, F. L. (1995). Integrity tests: Overlooked facts, resolved issues, and remaining questions. *American Psychologist, 50,* 456–457.

Ones, D. S., Viswesvaran, C., & Schmidt, F. L. (1993). Comprehensive metaanalysis of integrity test validities: Findings and implications for personnel selection and theories of job performance. *Journal of Applied Psychology, 78,* 679–703.

Ong, J., & Marchbanks, R. L. (1973). Validity of selected academic and non-academic predictors of optometry grades. *American Journal of Optimetry, 50,* 583–588.

Oosterhof, A. C. (1976). Similarity of various item discrimination indices. *Journal of Educational Measurement, 13,* 145–150.

Oppenheim, A. N. (1992). *Questionnaire design, interviewing and attitude measurement.* London: Pinter.

Ortiz, V. Z., & Gonzalez, A. (1989). Validation of a short form of the WISC-R with accelerated and gifted Hispanic students. *Gifted Child Quarterly, 33,* 152–155.

Ortiz, V. Z., & Volkoff, W. (1987). Identification of gifted and accelerated Hispanic students. *Journal for the Education of the Gifted, 11,* 45–55.

Orvik, J. M. (1972). Social desirability for the individual, his group, and society. *Multivariate Behavioral Research, 7,* 3–32.

Osborne, R. T. (1994). The Burt collection. *Journal of the History of the Behavioral Sciences, 30,* 369–379.

Osgood, C., & Luria, Z. (1954). A blind analysis of a case of multiple personality using the Semantic Differential. *Journal of Abnormal and Social Psychology, 49,* 579–591.

Osgood, C., Suci, G., & Tannenbaum, P. (1957). *The measurement of meaning.* Urbana, IL: University of Illinois Press.

Osipov, V. P. (1944). Malingering: The simulation of psychosis. *Bulletin of the Meninger Clinic, 8,* 39–42.

Osipow, S. H. (1983). *Theories of career development* (3rd ed.). New York: Appleton-Century-Crofts.

Osipow, S. H. (Ed.). (1987). *Manual for the Career Decision Scale.* Odessa, FL: Psychological Assessment Resources.

Oskamp, S. (1991). *Attitudes and opinions* (2nd ed.). Englewood Cliffs, NJ: Prentice Hall.

OSS Assessment Staff (1948). *Assessment of men: Selection of personnel for the Office of Strategic Services.* New York: Rinehart.

Osterhouse, R. A. (1972). Desensitization and study-skills training as treatment for two types of test-anxious students. *Journal of Counseling Psychology, 19,* 301–307.

Osterlind, S. J. (1983). *Test item bias*. Newbury Park, CA: Sage.

Osterlind, S. J. (1989). *Constructing test items*. Boston, MA: Kluwer Academic.

Ostrom, T. M. (1969). The relationship between the affective, behavioral, and cognitive components of attitude. *Journal of Experimental Social Psychology, 5*, 12–30.

Ouellette, S. E. (1988). The use of projective drawing techniques in the personality assessment of prelingually deafened young adults: A pilot study. *American Annals of the Deaf, 133*, 212–218.

Overall, J. E. (1974). Validity of the Psychological Screening Inventory for psychiatric screening. *Journal of Consulting and Clinical Psychology, 42*, 717–719.

Overall, J. E., & Magee, K. N. (1992). Estimating individual rater reliabilities. *Applied Psychological Measurement, 16*, 77–85.

Owen, D. (1985). *None of the above*. Boston, MA: Houghton Mifflin.

Owen, S. V., & Baum, S. M. (1985). The validity of the measurement of originality. *Educational and Psychological Measurement, 45*, 939–944.

Owens, W. A. (1976). Background data. In M. D. Dunnette (Ed.), *Handbook of industrial psychology*. New York: Rand-McNally.

Owens, W. A., Glennon, J. R., & Albright, L. E. (1962). Retest consistency and the writing of life history items: A first step. *Journal of Applied Psychology, 46*, 329–332.

Ownby, R. L., & Carmin, C. N. (1988). Confirmatory factor analyses of the Stanford-Binet Intelligence Scale (4th ed.). *Journal of Psychoeducational Assessment, 6*, 331–340.

Pace, C. R., & Stern, G. G. (1958). An approach to the measurement of psychological characteristics of college environments. *Journal of Educational Psychology, 49*, 269–277.

Padilla, A. (1980). The role of cultural awareness and ethnic loyalty in acculturation. In A. Padilla (Ed.), *Acculturation: Theory, models, and some new findings*. Boulder, CO: Westview Press.

Padilla, E. R., Olmedo, E. L., & Loya, R. (1982). Acculturation and the MMPI performance of Chicano and Anglo college students. *Hispanic Journal of Behavioral Sciences, 4*, 451–466.

Paget, K. D., & Nagle, R. J. (1986). A conceptual model of preschool assessment. *School Psychology Review, 15*, 154–165.

Paivio, A. (1971). *Imagery and verbal processes*. New York: Holt, Rinehart and Winston.

Paivio, A. (1975). Imagery and synchronic thinking. *Canadian Psychological Review, 16*, 147–163.

Paivio, A., & Harshman, R. (1983). Factor analysis of a questionnaire on imagery and verbal habits and skills. *Casnadian Journal of Psychology, 37*, 461–483.

Pankratz, L., Fausti, S., & Peed, S. (1975). A forced-choice technique to evaluate deafness in the hysterical or malingering patient. *Journal of Consulting and Clinical Psychology, 43*, 421–422.

Panton, J. H. (1958). Predicting prison adjustment with the MMPI. *Journal of Clinical Psychology, 14*, 308–312.

Parker, K. (1983). A meta-analysis of the reliability and validity of the Rorschach. *Journal of Personality Assessment, 47*, 227–231.

Parrott, C. A. (1986). Validation report on the Verbalizer-Visualizer Questionnaire. *Journal of Mental Imagery, 10*, 39–42.

Pascal, G. R., & Suttell, B. J. (1951). *The Bender-Gestalt Test: Its quantification and validity for adults*. New York: Grune & Stratton.

Passow, H. (1985). Review of School and College Ability Tests, Series III. In J. V. Mitchell, Jr. (Ed.), *The ninth mental measurements yearbook* (Vol. 2, pp. 1317–1318). Lincoln, NE: University of Nebraska Press.

Pastore, N. (1978). The Army intelligence tests and Walter Lippmann. *Journal of the History of the Behavioral Sciences, 14*, 316–327.

Patterson, C. H. (1946). A comparison of various "short forms" of the Wechsler-Bellevue Scale. *Journal of Consulting Psychology, 10*, 260–267.

Paulhus, D. L. (1984). Two-component models of socially desirable responding. *Journal of Personality and Social Psychology, 46*, 598–609.

Paulhus, D. L. (1986). Self-deception and impression management in test responses. In A. Angleitner & J. S. Wiggins (Eds.), *Personality assessment via questionnaires* (pp. 143–165). Berlin: Springer-Verlag.

Paulhus, D. L. (1991). Measurement and control of response bias. In J. P. Robinson, P. R. Shaver, & L. S. Wrightsman (Eds.), *Measures of personality and social psychological attitudes* (pp. 17–59). New York: Academic Press.

Payne, S. L. (1951). *The art of asking questions*. Princeton, NJ: Princeton University Press.

Pearlman, K., Schmidt, F. L., & Hunter, J. E. (1980). Validity generalization results for tests used to predict job proficiency and training success in clerical occupations. *Journal of Applied Psychology, 65*, 373–406.

Pearson, B. Z. (1993). Predictive validity of the Scholastic Aptitude Test (SAT) for Hispanic bilingual students. *Hispanic Journal of Behavioral Sciences, 15*, 342–356.

Pederson, K. (1990). Candidate Profile Record. In J. Hogan & R. Hogan (Eds.), *Business and industry testing* (pp. 357–359). Austin, TX: Pro-ed.

Pedhazur, E. (1982). *Multiple regression in behavioral research: Explanation and prediction* (2nd ed.). New York: Holt, Rinehart and Winston.

Penner, L. A., Homant, R., & Rokeach, M. (1968). Comparison of rank-order and paired-comparison methods for measuring value systems. *Perceptual and Motor Skills, 27,* 417–418.

Pennock-Roman, M. (1990). *Test validity and language background: A study of Hispanic American students at six universities.* New York: College Entrance Examination Board.

Peplau, L. A., & Perlman, D. (Eds.). (1982). *Loneliness: A sourcebook of current theory, research and therapy.* New York: Wiley.

Perry, G. G., & Kinder, B. N. (1990). The susceptibility of the Rorschach to malingering: A critical review. *Journal of Personality Assessment, 54,* 47–57.

Petersen, N. S., & Novick, M. R. (1976). An evaluation of some models for culture-fair selection. *Journal of Educational Measurement, 13,* 3–29.

Peterson, J. (1926). *Early conceptions and tests of intelligence.* Yonkers, NY: World Book Company.

Petrie, B. M. (1969). Statistical analysis of attitude scale scores. *Research Quarterly, 40,* 434–437.

Pfeiffer, E. (1975). SPMSQ: Short Portable Mental Status Questionnaire. *Journal of the American Geriatric Society, 23,* 433–441.

Phares, E. J. (1976). *Locus of control in personality.* Morristown, NJ: General Learning Press.

Phelps, L. (1989). Comparison of scores for intellectually gifted students on the WISC-R and the fourth edition of the Stanford-Binet. *Psychology in the Schools, 26,* 125–129.

Phelps, L., & Bell, M. C. (1988). Correlations between the Stanford-Binet: Fourth Edition and the WISC-R with a learning disabled population. *Psychology in the Schools, 25,* 380–382.

Phelps, L., & Branyan, L. T. (1988). Correlations among the Hiskey, K-ABC Nonverbal Scale, Leiter, and WISC-R Performance Scale with public-school deaf children. *Journal of Psychoeducational Assessment, 6,* 354–358.

Phillips, B. L., Pasewark, R. A., & Tindall, R. C. (1978). Relationship among McCarthy Scales of Children's Abilities, WPPSI, and Columbia Mental Maturity Scale. *Psychology in the Schools, 15,* 352–356.

Phillips, S. (1980). Children's perceptions of health and disease. *Canadian Family Physician, 26,* 1171–1174.

Piaget, J. (1952). *The origins of intelligence in children.* New York: International Universities Press.

Piaget, J. (1967). *Six psychological studies.* New York: Random House.

Piedmont, R. L. (1998). *The revised NEO Personality Inventory: Clinical and research applications.* The Plenum series in social/clinical psychology. New York: Plenum.

Piers, E., & Harris, D. (1969). *Manual for the Piers-Harris Children's Self-concept Scale.* Nashville, TN: Counselor Recordings and Tests.

Piersma, H. L. (1987). Millon Clinical Multiaxial Inventory (MCMI) computer-generated diagnoses: How do they compare to clinician judgment? *Journal of Psychopathology and Behavioral Assessment, 9,* 305–312.

Pintner, R. (1924). Results obtained with the non-language group tests. *Journal of Educational Psychology, 15,* 473–483.

Pintner, R., & Paterson, D. G. (1915). The Binet Scale and the deaf child. *Journal of Educational Psychology, 6,* 201–210.

Piotrowski, C. (1983). Factor structure on the Semantic Differential as a function of method of analysis. *Educational and Psychological Measurement, 43,* 283–288.

Piotrowski, C. (1995). A review of the clinical and research use of the Bender-Gestalt Test. *Perceptual and Motor Skills, 81,* 1272–1274.

Piotrowski, C., & Keller, J. W. (1984). Psychodiagnostic testing in APA-approved clinical psychology programs. *Professional Psychology: Research and Practice, 15,* 450–456.

Piotrowski, Z. A. (1964). Digital-computer interpretation of inkblot test data. *Psychiatric Quarterly, 38,* 1–26.

Plag, J. A., & Goffman, J. M. (1967). The Armed Forces Qualification Test: Its validity in predicting military effectiveness for naval enlistees. *Personnel Psychology, 20,* 323–340.

Plake, B. S., Reynolds, C. R., & Gutkin, T. B. (1981). A technique for comparison of the profile variability between independent groups. *Journal of Clinical Psychology, 37,* 142–146.

Plemons, G. (1977). A comparison of MMPI scores of Anglo-and Mexican-American psychiatric patients. *Journal of Consulting and Clinical Psychology, 45,* 149–150.

Pollard, W. E., Bobbitt, R. A., Bergner, M., Martin, D. P., & Gilson, B. S. (1976). The Sickness Impact Profile: Reliability of a health status measure. *Medical Care, 14,* 146–155.

Ponterotto, J. G., Pace, T. M., & Kavan, M. G. (1989). A counselor's guide to the assessment of depression. *Journal of Counseling and Development, 67,* 301–309.

Pope, K. S. (1992). Responsibilities in providing psychological test feedback to clients. *Psychological Assessment, 4,* 268–271.

Popham, W. J. (1981). The case for minimum competency testing. *Phi Delta Kappan, 63,* 89–91.

Poresky, R. H., Hendrix, C., Mosier, J. E., & Samuelson, M. L. (1988). The Companion Animal Semantic Differential: Long and short form reliability and validity. *Educational and Psychological Measurement, 48*, 255–260.

Porter, T. M. (1986). *The rise of statistical thinking, 1820–1900.* Princeton, NJ: Princeton University Press.

Poteat, G. M., Wuensch, K. L., & Gregg, N. B. (1988). An investigation of differential prediction with the WISC-R. *Journal of School Psychology, 26*, 59–68.

Powers, D. E. (1993). Coaching for the SAT: A summary of the summaries and an update. *Educational Measurement: Issues and Practice, 12*, 24–39.

Powers, D. E., & Alderman, D. L. (1983). Effect of test familiarization on SAT performance. *Journal of Educational Measurement, 20*, 71–79.

Powers, S., & Barkan, J. H. (1986). Concurrent validity of the Standard Progressive Matrices for Hispanic and non-Hispanic seventh-grade students. *Psychology in the Schools, 23*, 333–336.

Pratkanis, A. R., & Greenwald, A. G. (1989). A sociocognitive model of attitude structure and function. In L. Berkowitz (Ed.), *Advances in experimental social psychology* (Vol. 22, pp. 245–285). San Diego, CA: Academic Press.

Praver, F., DiGiuseppe, R., Pelcovitz, D., Mandel, F. S., & Gaines, R. (2000). A preliminary study of a cartoon measure for children's reactions to chronic trauma. *Child Maltreatment, 5*, 273–285.

Preston, J. (1978). Abbreviated forms of the WISC-R. *Psychological Reports, 42*, 883–887.

Prieto, E. J., & Geisinger, K. F. (1983). Factor-analytic studies of the McGill Pain Questionnaire. In R. Melzack (Ed.), *Pain measurement and assessment* (pp. 85–93). New York: Raven Press.

Prigatano, G. P. (1978). Wechsler Memory Scale: A selective review of the literature. *Journal of Clinical Psychology, 34*, 816–832.

Prigatano, G. P., & Amin, K. (1993). Digit Memory Test: Unequivocal cerebral dysfunction and suspected malingering. *Journal of Clinical and Experimental Neuropsychology, 15*, 537–546.

Prigatano, G. P., & Redner, J. E. (1993). Uses and abuses of neuropsychological testing in behavioral neurology. *Neurologic Clinics, 11*, 219–231.

Pritchard, D. A., & Rosenblatt, A. (1980). Racial bias in the MMPI: A methodological review. *Journal of Consulting and Clinical Psychology, 48*, 263–267.

Prout, H. T., & Ferber, S. M. (1988). Analogue assessment: Traditional personality assessment measures in behavioral assessment. In E. S. Shapiro & T. R. Kratochwill (Eds.), *Behavioral assessment in schools: Conceptual foundations and practical applications* (pp. 322–350). New York: Guilford Press.

Prout, H. T., & Schwartz, J. F. (1984). Validity of the Peabody Picture Vocabulary Test-Revised with mentally retarded adults. *Journal of Clinical Psychology, 40*, 584–587.

Pulliam, G. P. (1975). Social desirability and the Psychological Screening Inventory. *Psychological Reports, 36*, 522.

Quay, H. C., & Peterson, D. R. (1967). *Manual for the Behavior Problem Checklist.* Champaign, IL: Children's Research Center, University of Illinois.

Quay, L. C. (1974). Language dialect, age, and intelligence-test performance in disadvantaged black children. *Child Development 45*, 463–468.

Quenk, N. L. (2000). *Essentials of Myers-Briggs Type Indicator Assessment.* New York: Wiley.

Rabideau, G. F. (1955). Differences in visual acuity measurements obtained with different types of targets. *Psychological Monographs, 69*, No. 10 (Whole No. 395).

Rabkin, J. G., & Struening, E. L. (1976). Life events, stress, and illness. *Science, 194*, 1013–1020.

Radloff, L. S. (1977). The CES-D Scale: A self-report depression scale for research in the general population. *Applied Psychological Measurement, 1*, 385–401.

Radloff, L. S., & Teri, L. (1986). Use of the Center for Epidemiological Studies-Depression Scale with older adults. *Clinical Gerontologist, 5*, 119–136.

Ragosta, M., & Nemceff, W. (1982). *A research and development program on testing handicapped people* (RM 82-2). Princeton, NJ: Educational Testing Service.

Rahe, R. H., & Lind, E. (1971). Psychosocial factors and sudden cardiac death: A pilot study. *Journal of Psychosomatic Research, 15*, 19–24.

Rahe, R. H., Lundberg, V., Bennett, L., & Theorell, T. (1971). The social readjustment rating scale: A comparative study of Swedes and Americans. *Journal of Psychosomatic Research, 15*, 241–249.

Rahe, R. H., Meyer, M., Smith, M., Kjaer, G., & Holmes, T. H. (1964). Social stress and illness onset. *Journal of Psychosomatic Research, 8*, 35–44.

Raine, A. (1991). The SPQ: A scale for the assessment of schizotypal personality based on DSM-III-R criteria. *Schizophrenia Bulletin, 17*, 555–564.

Rajecki. D. W. (1990). *Attitudes.* Sunderland, MA: Sinauer.

Ralston, D. A., Gustafson, D. J., Elsass, P. M., Cheung, F., & Terpstra, R. H. (1992). Eastern values: A comparison of managers in the United States, Hong Kong, and the People's Republic of China. *Journal of Applied Psychology, 77*, 664–671.

Ramanaiah, N. V., & Adams, M. L. (1979). Confirmatory factor analysis of the WAIS and the WPPSI. *Psychological Reports, 45*, 351–355.

Ramanaiah, N. V., & Martin, H. J. (1980). On the two-dimensional nature of the Marlowe-Crowne Social Desirability Scale. *Journal of Personality Assessment, 44*, 507–514.

Ramirez, M., Garza, R. T., & Cox, B. G. (1980). *Multicultural leader behaviors in ethnically mixed task groups* (Technical Report). Office of Naval Research: Organizational Effectiveness Research Program.

Randt, C. T., Brown, E. R., & Osborne, D. P., Jr. (1980). A memory test for longitudinal measurement of mild to moderate deficits. *Clinical Neuropsychology, 2*, 184–194.

Rankin, W. L., & Grobe, J. W. (1980). A comparison of ranking and rating procedures for value system measurement. *European Journal of Social Psychology, 10*, 233–246.

Raphael, E. G., Cloitre, M., & Dohrenwend, B. P. (1991). Problems of recall and misclassification with checklist methods of measuring stressful life events. *Health Psychology, 10*, 62–74.

Rasch, G. (1966). An item-analysis which takes individual differences into account. *British Journal of Mathematical and Statistical Psychology, 19*, 49–57.

Rathus, S. A. (1973). A 30-item schedule for assessing assertive behavior. *Behavior Therapy, 4*, 398–406.

Rathus, S. A., & Nevid, J. S. (1977). Concurrent validity of the 30-item Assertiveness Schedule with a psychiatric population. *Behavior therapy, 8*, 393–397.

Raven, J. C. (1938). *Standard Progressive Matrices.* London: H. K. Lewis.

Raven, J. C. (1947a). *Coloured Progressive Matrices.* London: H. K. Lewis.

Raven, J. C. (1947b). *Advanced Progressive Matrices.* London: H. K. Lewis.

Raven, J. C., Court, J. H., & Raven, J. (1977). *Coloured Progressive Matrices.* London: Lewis.

Raven, J., Raven, J. C., & Court, J. H. (1998). *Standard Progressive Matrices. 1998 edition.* Oxford: Oxford University Press.

Rawls, J. R., Rawls, D. J., & Harrison, C. W. (1969). An investigation of success predictors in graduate school in psychology. *Journal of Psychology, 72*, 125–129.

Ray, J. J. (1971). A new measure of conservatism: Its limitations. *British Journal of Social and Clinical Psychology, 10*, 79–80.

Ray, S., & Ulissi, S. M. (1982). *Adaptation of the Wechsler Preschool and Primary Scales of Intelligence for deaf children.* Natchitoches, LA: Steven Ray.

Razin, A. M. (1971). A-B variable in psychotherapy: A critical review. *Psychological Bulletin, 75*, 1–21.

Reading, A. E., & Newton, J. R. (1978). A card sort method of pain assessment. *Journal of Psychosomatic Research, 22*, 503–512.

Reardon, R. C., Hersen, M., Bellack, A. S., & Foley, J. M. (1979). Measuring social skill in grade school boys. *Journal of Behavioral Assessment, 1*, 87–105.

Ree, M. J., & Earles, J. A. (1991). Predictive training success: Not much more than g. *Personnel Psychology, 44*, 321–332.

Ree, M. J., Earles, J. A., & Teachout, M. (1994). Predicting job performance: Not much more than g. *Journal of Applied Psychology, 79*, 518–524.

Reed, M. (1970). Deaf and partially hearing children. In P. Mittler (Ed.), *The psychological assessment of mental and physical handicaps.* London: Tavistock.

Reed, P. F., Fitts, W. H., & Boehm, L. (1981). *Tenneseee Self-Concept Scale: Bibliography of research studies* (Rev. ed.). Los Angeles, CA: Western Psychological Services.

Rehfisch, J. M. (1958). A scale for personal rigidity. *Journal of Consulting Psychology, 22*, 11–15.

Rehfisch, J. M. (1959). Some scale and test correlates of a Personality Rigidity scale. *Journal of Consulting Psychology, 22*, 372–374.

Reich, J. H. (1987). Instruments measuring DSM-III and DSM-III-R personality disorders. *Journal of Personality Disorders, 1*, 220–240.

Reich, J. H. (1989). Update on instruments to measure DSM-III and DSM-III-R personality disorders. *Journal of Nervous and Mental Disease, 177*, 366–370.

Reich, T., Robins, L. E., Woodruff, R. A., Jr., Taibleson, M., Rich, C., & Cunningham, L. (1975). Computer-assisted derivation of a screening interview for alcoholism. *Archives of General Psychiatry, 32*, 847–852.

Reilly, R. R., & Chao, G. T. (1982). Validity and fairness of some alternative selection procedures. *Personnel Psychology, 35*, 1–62.

Reilly, R. R., Henry, S., & Smither, J. W. (1990). An examination of the effects of using behavior checklists on the construct validity of assessment center dimensions. *Personnel Psychology, 43*, 71–84.

Reilly, R. R., & Knight, G. E. (1970). MMPI scores of Mexican-American college students. *Journal of College Student Personnel, 11*, 419–422.

Reissland, N. (1983). Cognitive maturity and the experience of fear and pain in the hospital. *Social Science Medicine, 17*, 1389–1395.

Reitan, R. M. (1969). *Manual for administration of neuropsychological test batteries for adults and children.* Indianapolis, IN: Author.

Reitan, R. M., & Davison, L. A. (Eds.). (1974). *Clinical neuropsychology: Current status and applications.* Washington, DC: Winston.

Reitan, R. M., & Wolfson, D. (1985). *Halstead-Reitan Neuropsychological Test Battery: Theory and clinical interpretation.* Tucson, AZ: Neuropsychology Press.

Remmers, H. H., & Ewart, E. (1941). Reliability of multiple-choice measuring instruments as a function of the Spearman-Brown prophecy formula, III. *Journal of Educational Psychology, 32,* 61–66.

Rentoul, A. J., & Fraser, B. J. (1979). Conceptualization of enquiry-based or open classroom learning environments. *Journal of Curriculum Studies, 11,* 233–245.

Renzulli, J. S., Hartman, R. K., & Callahan, C. M. (1971). Teacher identification of superior students. *Exceptional Children, 38,* 211–214, 243–248.

Renzulli, J. S., Smith, L. H., White, A. J., Callahan, C. M., & Hartman, R. K. (1976). *Scales for rating the behavioral characteristics of superior students.* Wethersfield, CT: Creative Learning Press.

Reschly, D. J. (1978): WISC-R factor structures among Anglos, Blacks, Chicanos, and Native-American Papagos. *Journal of Consulting and Clinical Psychology, 46,* 417–422.

Reschly, D. J., & Reschly, J. E. (1979). Brief reports on the WISC-R: I. Validity of WISC-R factor scores in predicting achievement and attention for four socio-cultural groups. *Journal of School Psychology, 17,* 355–361.

Reschly, D. J., & Sabers, D. (1979). Analysis of test bias in four groups with the regression definition. *Journal of Educational Measurement, 16,* 1–9.

Resnick, D. (1982). History of educational testing. In A. K. Wigdor & W. R. Gamer (Eds.), *Ability testing: Uses, consequences, and controversies: Part II. Documentation section* (pp. 173–194). Washington, DC: National Academy Press.

Resnick, P. J. (1988). Malingering of post-traumatic disorders. In R. Rogers (Ed.), *Clinical assessment of malingering and deception* (pp. 84–103). New York: Guilford Press.

Reuter, J., Stancin, T., & Craig, P. (1981). *Kent scoring adaptation of the Bayley Scales of Infant Development.* Kent, OH: Kent Developmental Metrics.

Reynell, J. (1969). *Reynell Developmental Language Scales.* Windsor, England: NFER.

Reynolds, C. R. (1982). The problem of bias in psychological assessment. In C. R. Reynolds & T. B. Gutkin (Eds.), *The Handbook of School Psychology* (pp. 178–208). New York: Wiley.

Reynolds, C. R. (1985). Review of the System of Multicultural Pluralistic Assessment. In J. V. Mitchell (Ed.), *The ninth mental measurements yearbook* (pp. 1519–1521). Lincoln, NE: University of Nebraska Press.

Reynolds, C. R. (1989). Measurement and statistical problems in neuropsychological assessment of children. In C. R. Reynolds & E. Fletcher-Janzen (Eds.), *Handbook of clinical child neuropsychology* (pp. 147–166). New York: Plenum Press.

Reynolds, C. R., & Kamphaus, R. W. (1997). The Kaufman Assessment Battery for Children: Development, structure, and applications in neuropsychology. In A. M. Horton, D. Wedding, et al. (Eds.), *The neuropsychology handbook: Vol. 1. Foundations and assessment* (2nd ed., pp. 290–330). New York, NY: Springer-Verlag.

Reynolds, C. R., & Piersel, W. C. (1983). Multiple aspects of bias on the Boehm Test of Basic Concepts (Forms A and B) for white and for Mexican-American children. *Journal of Psychoeducational Assessment, 1,* 135–142.

Reynolds, C. R., Willson, V. L., & Chatman, S. R. (1984). Item bias on the 1981 revision of the Peabody Picture Vocabulary Test using a new method of detecting bias. *Journal of Psychoeducational Assessment, 2,* 219–224.

Reynolds, C. R., Willson, V. L., & Chatman, S. R. (1985). Regression analyses of bias on the Kaufman Assessment Battery for Children. *Journal of School Psychology, 23,* 195–204.

Reynolds, W. M. (1979). A caution against the use of the Slosson Intelligence Test in the diagnosis of mental retardation. *Psychology in the Schools, 16,* 77–79:

Reynolds, W. M. (1982). Development of reliable and valid short forms of the Marlowe-Crowne Social Desirability Scale. *Journal of Clinical Psychology, 38,* 119–125.

Reynolds, W. M. (1985). Review of the Slosson Intelligence Test. In J. V. Mitchell, Jr. (Ed.), *The ninth mental measurements yearbook* (Vol. 2, pp. 1403–1404). Lincoln, NE: University of Nebraska Press.

Rhodes, L., Bayley, N., & Yow, B. (1984). *Supplement to the manual for the Bayley Scales of Infant Development.* San Antonio, TX: The Psychological Corporation.

Rich, C. C., & Anderson, R. P. (1965). A tactual form of the Progressive Matrices for use with blind children. *Personnel and Guidance Journal, 43,* 912–919.

Rich, J. (1968). *Interviewing children and adolescents.* London: Macmillan.

Richards, J. T. (1970). Internal consistency of the WPPSI with the mentally retarded. *American Journal of Mental Deficiency, 74,* 581–582.

Richardson, A. (1977). Verbalizer-visualizer: A cognitive style dimension. *Journal of Mental Imagery, 1,* 109–126.

Richardson, A. (1978). Subject, task, and tester variables associated with initial eye movement responses. *Journal of Mental Imagery, 2,* 85–100.

Richardson, K. (1991). *Understanding intelligence.* Philadelphia, PA: Milton Keynes.

Richman, N., Stevenson, J., & Graham, P. J. (1982). *Preschool to school: A behavioural study.* New York: Academic Press.

Richmond, B. O., & Kicklighter, R. H. (1980). *Children's Adaptive Behavior Scale*. Atlanta, GA: Humanics.

Ridgway, J., MacCulloch, M. J., & Mills, H. E. (1982). Some experiences in administering a psychometric test with a light pen and microcomputer. *International Journal of Man-Machine Studies, 17,* 265–278.

Riethmiller, R. J., & Handler, L. (1997). The great figure drawing controversy: The integration of research and clinical practice. *Journal of Personality Assessment, 69,* 488–496.

Rigazio-DiGilio, S. A. (1993). The Family System Test (FAST): A spatial representation of family structure and flexibility. *The American Journal of Family Therapy, 21,* 369–375.

Ritzler, B. A., Sharkey, K. J., & Chudy, J. (1980). A comprehensive projective alternative to the TAT. *Journal of Personality Assessment, 44,* 358–362.

Roach, A. J., Frazier, L. P., & Bowden, S. R. (1981). The Marital Satisfaction Scale: Development of a measure for intervention research. *Journal of Marriage and the Family, 43,* 537–545.

Roberts, J. S., Laughlin, J. E., & Wedell, D. H. (1999). Validity issues in the Likert and Thurstone approaches to attitude measurement. *Educational and Psychological Measurement, 59,* 211–233.

Roberts, R. E., Vernon, S. W., & Rhoades, H. M. (1989). Effects of language and ethnic status on reliability and validity of the Center for Epidemiologic Studies – Depression Scale with psychiatric patients. *Journal of Nervous and Mental Disease, 177,* 581–592.

Robertson-Tchabo, E. A., & Arenberg, D. (1989). Assessment of memory in older adults. In T. Hunt & C. J. Lindley (Eds.), *Testing older adults* (pp. 200–231). Austin, TX: Pro-Ed.

Robertson, A., & Cochrane, R. (1973). The Wilson-Patterson Conservatism Scale: A reappraisal. *British Journal of Social and Clinical Psychology, 12,* 428–430.

Robinson, E. L., & Nagle, R. J. (1992). The comparability of the Test of Cognitive Skills with the Wechsler Intelligence Scale for Children – Revised and the Stanford-Binet: Fourth edition with gifted children. *Psychology in the Schools, 29,* 107–112.

Robinson, J. P., Athanasiou, R., & Head, K. B. (1969). *Measures of occupational attitudes and occupational characteristics*. Ann Arbor, MI: Institute for Social Research.

Robinson, J. P., Rusk, J. G., & Head, K. B. (1968). *Measures of political attitudes*. Ann Arbor, MI: Institute for Social Research.

Robinson, J. P., & Shaver, P. R. (1973). *Measures of social psychological attitudes*. Ann Arbor, MI: Institute for Social Research.

Robinson, J. P., Shaver, P. R., & Wrightsman, L. S. (1990). *Measures of personality and social psychological attitudes*. San Diego, CA: Academic Press.

Roe, A., & Klos, D. (1969). Occupational classification. *Counseling Psychologist, 1,* 84–92.

Roe, A., & Siegelman, M. (1964). *The origin of interest*. Washington, DC: American Personnel and Guidance Association.

Rogers, R. (1984). Towards an empirical model of malingering and deception. *Behavioral Sciences and the Law, 2,* 93–111.

Rogers, R., Bagby, M., & Gillis, R. (1992). Improvements in the M test as a screening measure for malingering. *Bulletin of the American Academy of Psychiatry and Law, 20,* 101–104.

Rogers, R., Harris, M., & Thatcher, A. A. (1983). Identification of random responders on the MMPI: An actuarial approach. *Psychological Reports, 53,* 1171–1174.

Rogers, R., Ustad, K. L., Sewell, K. W., & Reinhardt, V. (1996). Dimensions of incompetency: A factor analytic study of the Georgia Court Competency Test. *Behavioral Sciences and the Law, 14,* 323–330.

Roid, G. H. (1985). Computer-based test interpretation: The potential of quantitative methods of test interpretation. *Computers in Human Behavior, 1,* 207–219.

Rokeach, M. (1973). *The nature of human values*. New York: Free Press.

Rome, H. P., Swenson, W. M., Mataya, P., McCarthy, C. E., Pearson, J. S., & Keating, R. F. (1962). Symposium on automation techniques in personality assessment. *Proceedings of the Mayo Clinic, 37,* 61–82.

Romero, I. (1992). Individual assessment procedures with preschool children. In E. V. Nuttall, I. Romero, & J. Kalesnik (Eds.), *Assessing and screening preschoolers* (pp. 55–66). Boston: Allyn & Bacon.

Ronan, G. F., Colavito, V. A., & Hammontree, S. R. (1993). Personal problem-solving system for scoring TAT responses: Preliminary validity and reliability data. *Journal of Personality Assessment, 61,* 28–40.

Roper, B. L., Ben-Porath, Y., & Butcher, J. N. (1995). Comparability and validity of computerized adaptive testing with the MMPI-2. *Journal of Personality Assessment, 65,* 358–371.

Rorer, L. G. (1965). The great response-style myth. *Psychological Bulletin, 63,* 129–156.

Rosecranz, H. A., & McNevin, T. E. (1969). A factor analysis of attitudes toward the aged. *The Gerontologist, 9,* 55–59.

Rosen, A. (1967). Limitations of personality inventories for assessment of deaf children and adults as illustrated by research with the MMPI. *Journal of Rehabilitation of the Deaf, 1,* 47–52.

Rosen, E. (1956). Self-appraisal, personal desirability and perceived social desirability of personality traits. *Journal of Abnormal and Social Psychology, 52*, 151–158.

Rosen, R. C., & Beck, J. G. (1988). *Patterns of sexual arousal.* New York: Guilford Press.

Rosen, W. G., Motts, R. C., & Davis, K. L. (1984). A new rating scale for Alzheimer's disease. *American Journal of Psychiatry, 141*, 1356–1364.

Rosenbaum, C. P., & Beebe, J. E. (1975). *Psychiatric treatment: Crisis, clinic, consultation.* New York: McGraw-Hill.

Rosenberg, M. J., Hovland, C. I., McGuire, W. J., Abelson, R. P., & Brehm, J. W. (1960). *Attitude organization and change.* New Haven, CT: Yale University Press.

Rosenstock, I. M. (1974). Historical origins of the health belief model. *Health Education Monographs, 2*, 238–335.

Rosenthal, B. L., & Kamphaus, R. W. (1988). Interpretive tables for test scatter on die Stanford-Binet Intelligence Scale: Fourth edition. *Journal of Psychoeducational Assessment, 6*, 359–370.

Ross, C. E., & Minowsky, J. (1979). A comparison of life-event weighting scheles: Change, undesirability, and effect-proportional indices. *Journal of Health and Social Behavior, 20*, 166–177.

Ross, D. R. (1970). A technique of verbal assessment of deaf students. *Journal of Rehabilitation of the Deaf, 3*, 7–15.

Ross, L. M., & Pollio, H. R. (1991). Metaphors of death: A thematic analysis of personal meanings. *Omega, 23*, 291–307.

Rossi, P. H., Wright, J. D., & Anderson, A. B. (Eds.). (1983). *Handbook of survey research.* New York: Academic Press.

Rossini, E. D., & Kaspar, J. C. (1987). The validity of the Bender-Gestalt emotional indicators. *Journal of Personality Assessment, 51*, 254–261.

Rossman, J. (1931). *The psychology of the inventor.* Washington, DC: Inventors.

Rothbart, M. K. (1981). Measurement of temperament in infants. *Child Development, 52*, 569–578.

Rotter, J. B. (1946). The incomplete sentences test as a method of studying personality. *American Psychologist, 1*, 286.

Rotter, J. B. (1966). Generalized expectancies for internal vs. external control of reinforcement. *Psychological Monographs, 80*(Whole No. 609).

Rotter, J. B. (1967). A new scale for the measurement of interpersonal trust. *Journal of Personality, 35*, 651–665.

Rotter, J. B., & Rafferty, J. E. (1950). *Manual: The Rotter Incomplete Sentences Blanks.* New York: The Psychological Corporation.

Rounds, J. B. (1989). Review of the Career Assessment Inventory. In J. C. Conoley & J. J. Kramer (Eds.), *The tenth mental measurements yearbook* (pp. 139–141). Lincoln, NE: University of Nebraska Press.

Rourke, B. P., & Fuerst, D. R. (1991). *Learning disabilities and psychosocial functioning: A neuropsychological perspective.* New York: Guilford Press.

Rowe, D. C., & Plomin, R. (1977). Temperament in early childhood. *Journal of Personality Assessment, 41*, 150–156.

Rubenstein, C., & Shaver, P. (1982). *In search of intimacy.* New York: Delacorte Press.

Rubenzer, S. (1992). A comparison of traditional and computer-generated psychological reports in an adolescent inpatient setting. *Journal of Clinical Psychology, 48*, 817–826.

Ruebhausen, O. M., & Brim, O. G., Jr. (1966). Privacy and behavioral research. *American Psychologist, 21*, 423–437.

Ruebush, B. K. (1963). Anxiety. In H. W. Stevenson, J. Kagan, & C. Spiker (Eds.), *NSSE sixty-second yearbook, Part I: Child psychology.* Chicago, IL: University of Chicago Press.

Ruesch, J., Loeb, M. B., & Jacobson, A. (1948). Acculturation and disease. *Psychological Monographs: General and Applied, 292*, 1–40.

Rulon, P. J. (1939). A simplified procedure for determining the reliability of a test of split-halves. *Harvard Educational Review, 9*, 99–103.

Runco, M. A., & Mraz, W. (1992). Scoring divergent thinking tests using total ideational output and a creativity index. *Educational and Psychological Measurement, 52*, 213–221.

Ruschival, M. A., & Way, J. G. (1971). The WPPSI and the Stanford-Binet: A validity and reliability study using gifted preschool children. *Journal of Consulting and Clinical Psychology, 37*, 163.

Russell, D., Peplau, L. A., & Cutrona, C. E. (1980). The Revised UCLA Loneliness Scale: Concurrent and discriminant validity evidence. *Journal of Personality and Social Psychology, 39*, 472–480.

Russell, D., Peplau, L. A., & Ferguson, M. L. (1978). Developing a measure of loneliness. *Journal of Personality Assessment, 42*, 290–294.

Rust, J. O., & Lose, B. D. (1980). Screening for giftedness with the Slosson and the Scale for Rating the Behavioral Characteristics of Superior Students. *Psychology in the Schools, 17*, 446–451.

Rutter, M. (1973). The assessment and treatment of preschool autistic children. *Early Child Development and Care, 3*, 13–29.

Ryan, A. M., & Sackett, P. R. (1987a). A survey of individual assessment practices by I/O psychologists. *Personnel Psychology, 40*, 455–488.

Ryan, A. M., & Sackett, P. R. (1987b). Pre-employment honesty testing: Fakability, reactions of test takers, and company image. *Journal of Business and Psychology, 1*, 248–256.

Ryan, J. J. (1981). Clinical utility of a WISC-R short form. *Journal of Clinical Psychology, 37*, 389–391.

Ryan, R. M. (1987). Thematic Apperception Test. In D. J. Keyser & R. C. Sweetland (Eds.), *Test critiques compendium* (pp. 517–532). Kansas City, MO: Test Corporation of America.

Rybstein-Blinchik. E. (1979). Effects of different cognitive strategies on chronic pain experience. *Journal of Behavioral Medicine, 2*, 93–101.

Ryman, D. H., Naitoh, P., Englund, C., & Genser, S. G. (1988). Computer response time measurements of mood, fatigue, and symptom scale items: Implications for scale response time uses. *Computers in Human Behavior, 4*, 95–109.

Sabatelli, R. M. (1988). Measurement issues in marital research: A review and critique of contemporary survey instruments. *Journal of Marriage and the Family, 50*, 891–917.

Saccuzzo, D. P., Higgins, G., & Lewandowski, D. (1974). Program for psychological assessment of law enforcement officers: Initial evaluation. *Psychological Reports, 35*, 651–654.

Saccuzzo, D. P., & Lewandowski, D. G. (1976). The WISC as a diagnostic tool. *Journal of Clinical Psychology, 32*, 115–124.

Sachs, B., Trybus, R., Koch, H., & Falberg, R. (1974). Current developments in the psychological evaluation of deaf individuals. *Journal of Rehabilitation of the Deaf, 8*, 136–140.

Sackett, P. R. (1987). Assessment centers and content validity: Some neglected issues. *Personnel Psychology, 40*, 13–25.

Sackett, P. R., Burris, L. R., & Callahan, C. (1989). Integrity testing for personnel selection: An update. *Personnel Psychology, 42*, 491–529.

Sackett, P. R., & Dreher, G. F. (1982). Constructs and assessment center dimensions: Some troubling empirical findings. *Journal of Applied Psychology, 67*, 401–410.

Sackett, P. R., & Harris, M. M. (1984). Honesty testing for personnel selection: A review and critique. *Personnel Psychology, 37*, 221–245.

Sackheim, H. A., & Gur, R. C. (1979). Self-deception, other-deception, and self-reported psychopathology. *Journal of Consulting and Clinical Psychology, 47*, 213–215.

Saks, M. J. (1976). The limits of scientific jury selection: Ethical and empirical. *Jurimetrics Journal, 17*, 3–22.

Salive, M. E., Smith, G. S., & Brewer, T. F. (1989). Suicide mortality in the Maryland state prison system, 1979–1987. *Journal of the American Medical Association, 262*, 365–369.

Salthouse, T. A. (1986). Functional age: Examination of a concept. In J. E. Birren, P. K. Robinson, & J. E. Livingston (Eds.), *Age, health and employment* (pp. 78–92). Englewood Cliffs, NJ: Prentice Hall.

Saltzman, J., Strauss, E., Hunter, M., & Spellacy, F. (1998). Validity of the Wonderlic Personnel Test as a brief measure of intelligence in individuals referred for evaluation of head injury. *Archives of Clinical Neuropsychology, 13*, 611–616.

Samelson, F. (1977). World War I intelligence testing and the development of psychology. *Journal of the History of the Behavioral Sciences, 13*, 274–282.

Samuda, R. J. (1975). *Psychological testing of American minorities: Issues and consequences.* New York: Dodd, Mead, & Co.

Sanchez, G. I. (1932). Scores of Spanish-speaking children on repeated tests. *Journal of Genetic Psychology, 40*, 223–231.

Sanchez, G. I. (1934). Blingualism and mental measures. *Journal of Applied Psychology, 18*, 765–772.

Sanchez, R., & Atkinson, D. (1983). Mexican-American cultural commitment, preference for counselor ethnicity, and willingness to use counseling. *Journal of Counseling Psychology, 30*, 215–220.

Sandberg, S. T., Wieselberg, M., & Shaffer, D. (1980). Hyperkinetic and conduct problem children in a primary school population: Some epidemiological considerations. *Journal of Child Psychology and Psychiatry and Allied Disciplines, 21*, 293–311.

Sandler, I. S., & Guenther, R. T. (1985). Assessment of life stress events. In P. Karoly (Ed.), *Measurement strategies in health psychology* (pp. 555–600). New York: Wiley.

Sandoval, J. (1979). The WISC-R and internal evidence of test bias with minority groups. *Journal of Consulting and Clinical Psychology, 47*, 919–927.

Sandoval, J. (1981). Format effects in two Teacher Rating Scales of Hyperactivity. *Journal of Abnormal Child Psychology, 9*, 203–218.

Sandoval, J. (1985). Review of the System of Multicultural Pluralistic Assessment. In J. V. Mitchell (Ed.), *The ninth mental measurements yearbook* (pp. 1521–1525). Lincoln, NE: University of Nebraska Press.

Sanford, E. C. (1987). Biography of Granville Stanley Hall. *The American Journal of Psychology, 100*, 365–375.

Santor, D. A., & Coyne, J. C. (1997). Shortening the CES-D to improve its ability to detect cases of depression. *Psychological Assessment, 9*, 233–243.

Sapinkopf, R. C. (1978). A computer adaptive testing approach to the measurement of personality variables. *Dissertation Abstracts International, 38*, 1OB, 4993.

Sapp, S. G., & Harrod, W. J. (1993). Reliability and validity of a brief version of Levenson's Locus of Control Scale. *Psychological Reports, 72*, 539–550.

Sarason, I. G. (1958). Interrelationships among individual difference variables, behavior in psychotherapy, and verbal conditioning. *Journal of Abnormal and Social Psychology, 56*, 339–344.

Sarason, I. G. (1960). Empirical findings and theoretical problems in the use of anxiety scales. *Psychological Bulletin, 57*, 403–415.

Sarason, I. G. (1980) (Ed.). *Test anxiety*. Hillsdale, NJ: Erlbaum.

Sarason, I. G., Johnson, J. H., & Siegel, J. M. (1979). Assessing the impact of life changes. In I. G. Sarason & C. D. Spielberger (Eds.), *Stress and anxiety* (Vol. 6). New York: Wiley.

Sarason, S. B., Davidson, K. S., Lighthall, F. F., Waite, R. R., & Ruebush, B. K. (1960). *Anxiety in elementary school children*. New York: Wiley.

Sarason, S. B., & Mandler, G. (1952). Some correlates of test anxiety. *Journal of Abnormal and Social Psychology, 47*, 810–817.

Sarbin, T. R. (1943). A contribution to the study of actuarial and individual methods of prediction. *American Journal of Sociology, 48*, 593–602.

Sattler, J. M. (1974). *Assessment of children's intelligence*. Philadelphia, PA: W. B. Saunders.

Sattler, J. M. (1982). *Assessment of children's intelligence and special abilities* (2nd ed.). Boston, MA: Allen & Bacon.

Sattler, J. M. (1988). *Assessment of children* (3rd ed.). San Diego, CA: Author.

Sattler, J. M., & Gwynne, J. (1982).White examiners generally do not impede the intelligence test performance of black children: To debunk a myth. *Journal of Consulting and Clinical Psychology, 50*, 196–208.

Sattler, J. M., & Theye, F. (1967). Procedural, situational, and interpersonal variables in individual intelligence testing. *Psychological Bulletin, 68*, 347–360.

Sattler, J. M., & Tozier, L. L. (1970). A review of intelligence test modifications used with cerebral palsied and other handicapped groups. *The Journal of Special Education, 4*, 391–398.

Sauer, W. J., & Warland, R. (1982). Morale and life satisfaction. In D. J. Mangen & W. A. Peterson (Eds.), *Research instruments in social gerontology* (Vol. 1, pp. 195–240). Minneapolis, MN: University of Minnesota Press.

Sawicki, R. F., Leark, R., Golden. C. J., & Karras, D. (1984). The development of the pathognomonic, left sensorimotor and right sensorimotor scales for the Luria-Nebraska Neuropsychological Battery – Children's Revision. *Journal of Clinical Child Psychology, 13*, 165–169.

Sawyer, J. (1966). Measurement and prediction, clinical and statistical. *Psychological Bulletin, 66*, 178–200.

Saxe, S. J., & Reiser, M. (1976). A comparison of three police applicant groups using the MMPI. *Journal of Police Science and Administration, 4*, 419–425.

Saylor, C. F., Finch, A. J. Jr., Furey, W., Baskin, C. H., & Kelly, M. M. (1984). Construct validity for measures of childhood depression: Application of multi-trait-multimethod methodology. *Journal of Consulting and Clinical Psychology, 52*, 977–985.

Schaefer, C. E. (1967). *Biographical correlates of scientific and artistic creativity in adolescents*. Unpublished doctoral dissertation, Fordham University, New York.

Schaefer, C. E., & Anastasi, A. (1968). A biographical inventory for identifying creativity in adolescent boys. *Journal of Applied Psychology, 52*, 42–48.

Schakel, J. A. (1986). Cognitive assessment of preschool children. *School Psychology Review, 15*, 200–215.

Scherer, P. (1983). Psychoeducational evaluation of hearing-impaired preschool children. *American Annals of the Deaf, 128*, 118–124.

Schetz, K. (1985). Comparison of the Compton Speech and Language Screening Evaluation with the Fluharty Preschool Speech and Language Screening Test. *Journal of the American Speech-Language-Hearing Association, 16*, 16–24.

Schiff, M. (1977). Hazard adjustment, locus of control, and sensation seeking: Some null findings. *Environment and Behavior, 9*, 233–254.

Schippmann, J. S., Prien, E. P., & Katz, J. A. (1990). Reliability and validity of in-basket performance measures. *Personnel Psychology, 43*, 837–859.

Schirmer, B. R. (1993). Constructing meaning from narrative text. *American Annals of the Deaf, 138*, 397–403.

Schmid, K. D., Rosenthal, S. L., & Brown, E. D. (1988). A comparison of self-report measures of two family dimensions: Control and cohesion. *The American Journal of Family Therapy, 16*, 73–77.

Schmidt, F. L. (1991). Why all banding procedures in personnel selection are logically flawed. *Human Performance, 4*, 265–278.

Schmidt, F. L. (1985). Review of Wonderlic Personnel Test. In J. V. Mitchell, Jr. (Ed.), *The ninth mental measurements yearbook* (Vol. II, pp. 1755–1757). Lincoln, NE: University of Nebraska Press.

Schmidt, F. L., & Hunter, J. E. (1974). Racial and ethnic bias in psychological tests: Divergent implications of two definitions of test bias. *American Psychologist, 29*, 1–8.

Schmidt, F. L., & Hunter, J. E. (1977). Development of a general solution to the problem of validity generalization. *Journal of Applied Psychology, 62,* 529–540.

Schmidt, F. L., & Hunter, J. E. (1980). The future of criterion-related validity. *Personnel Psychology, 33,* 41–60.

Schmidt, F. L., & Hunter, J. E. (1981). Employment testing. Old theories and new research findings. *American Psychologist, 36,* 1128–1137.

Schmidt, F. L., Hunter, J. E., Pearlman, K., & Shane, G. S. (1979). Further tests of the Schmidt-Hunter Bayesian validity generalization procedure. *Personnel Psychology, 32,* 257–281.

Schmidt, F. L., Urry, V. W., & Gugel, J. F. (1978). Computer assisted tailored testing: Examinee reactions and evaluations. *Educational and Psychological Measurement, 38,* 265–273.

Schmidt, N., & Sermat, V. (1983). Measuring loneliness in different relationships. *Journal of Personality and Social Psychology, 44,* 1038–1047.

Schmit, M. J., & Ryan, A. M. (1993). The Big Five in personnel selection: Factor structure in applicant and nonapplicant populations. *Journal of Applied Psychology, 78,* 966–974.

Schmitt, F. A., & Ranseen, J. D. (1989). Neuropsychological assessment of older adults. In T. Hunt & C. J. Lindley (Eds.), *Testing older adults* (pp. 51–69). Austin, TX: Pro-Ed.

Schmitt, N., Gilliland, S. W., Landis, R. S., & Devine, D. (1993). Computer-based testing applied to selection of secretarial applicants. *Personnel Psychology, 46,* 149–165.

Schmitt, N., Gooding, R. Z., Noe, R. A., & Kirsch, M. (1984). Metaanalysis of validity studies published between 1964 and 1982 and the investigation of study characteristics. *Personnel Psychology, 37,* 407–422.

Schmitt, N., & Robertson, I. (1990). Personnel selection. *Annual Review of Psychology, 41,* 289–319.

Schneider, B. (1983). An interactionist perspective on organizational effectiveness. In K. S. Cameron & D. A. Whetten (Eds.), *Organizational effectiveness: A comparison of multiple models* (pp. 27–54). Orlando, FL: Academic Press.

Schneider, W. H. (1992). After Binet: French intelligence testing, 1900–1950. *Journal of the History of the Behavioral Sciences, 28,* 111–132.

Schneider, J. M., & Parsons, O. A. (1970). Categories on the locus of control scale and cross-cultural comparisons in Denmark and the United States. *Journal of Cross-Cultural Psychology, 1,* 131–138.

Schoenfeldt, L. F. (1985). Review of Wonderlic Personnel Test. In J. V. Mitchell, Jr. (Ed.), *The ninth mental measurements yearbook* (Vol. II, pp. 1757–1758). Lincoln, NE: University of Nebraska Press.

Schoenfeldt, L. F. (1989). Guidelines for computer-based psychological tests and interpretations. *Computers in Human Behavior, 5,* 13–21.

Scholl, G., & Schnur, R. (1976). *Measures of psychological, vocational, and educational functioning in the blind and visually handicapped.* New York: American Foundation for the Blind.

Schopler, E., & Reichler, R. J. (1979). *Individualized assessment and treatment for autistic and developmentally disabled children: Vol. I. Psychoeducational profile.* Baltimore, MD: University Park Press.

Schrader, A. D., & Osburn, H. G. (1977). Biodata faking: Effects of induced subtlety and position specificity. *Personnel Psychology, 30,* 395–404.

Schrader, W. B. (1971). The predictive validity of College Board admissions tests. In W. H. Angoff (Ed.), *The College Board admissions testing program* (pp. 117–145). New York: College Entrance Examination Board.

Schretlen, D. J. (1988). The use of psychological tests to identify malingered symptoms of mental disorder. *Clinical Psychology Review, 8,* 451–476.

Schretlen, D., & Arkowitz, H. (1990). A psychological test battery to detect prison inmates who fake insanity or mental retardation. *Behavioral Sciences and the Law, 8,* 75–84.

Schretlen, D., Wilkins, S. S., Van Gorp, W. G., & Bobholz, J. H. (1992). Cross-validation of a psychological test battery to detect faked insanity. *Psychological Assessment, 4,* 77–83.

Schriesheim, C. A. (1981). The effect of grouping or randomizing items on leniency response bias. *Educational and Psychological Measurement, 41,* 401–411.

Schriesheim, C. A., & DeNisi, A. A. (1980). Item presentation as an influence on questionnaire validity: A field experiment. *Educational and Psychological Measurement, 40,* 175–182.

Schriesheim, C. A., Eisenbach, R. J., & Hill, K. D. (1991). The effect of negation and polar opposite item reversals on questionnaire reliability and validity: An experimental investigation. *Educational and Psychological Measurement, 51,* 67–78.

Schriesheim, C. A., & Klich, N. R. (1991). Fiedler's Least Preferred Coworker (LPC) Instrument: An investigation of its true bipolarity. *Educational and Psychological Measurement, 51,* 305–315.

Schroeder, L. D., Sjoquist, D. L., & Stephan, P. E. (1986). *Understanding regression analysis.* Newbury Park, CA: Sage.

Schuessler, K. F. (1961). A note on statistical significance of scalogram. *Sociometry, 24,* 312–318.

Schuh, A. J. (1967). The predictability of employee tenure: A review of the literature. *Personnel Psychology, 20,* 133–152.

Schuldberg, D. (1988). The MMPI is less sensitive to the automated testing format than it is to repeated testing: Item and scale effects. *Computers in Human Behavior, 4*, 285–298.

Schuman, H., & Kalton, G. (1985). Survey methods. In G. Lindzey & E. Aronson (Eds.), *Handbook of social psychology* (Vol. 1, 3rd ed.). New York: Random House.

Schutte, N. S., & Malouff, J. M. (1995). *Sourcebook of adult assessment strategies.* New York: Plenum Press.

Schwab, D. P., & Oliver, R. L. (1974). Predicting tenure with biographical data: Exhuming buried evidence. *Personnel Psychology, 27*, 125–128.

Schwab, J. J., Bialow, M., Brown, J. M., & Holzer, C. E. (1967). Diagnosing depression in medical inpatients. *Annals of Internal Medicine, 67*, 695–707.

Scissons, E. H. (1976). Computer administration of the California Psychological Inventory. *Measurement and Evaluation in Guidance, 9*, 24–30.

Scogin, F., Schumacher, J., Gardner, J., & Chaplin, W. (1995). Predictive validity of psychological testing in law enforcement settings. *Professional Psychology, 26*, 68–71.

Scott, R. D., & Johnson, R. W. (1967). Use of the weighted application blank in selecting unskilled employees. *Journal of Applied Psychology, 51*, 393–395.

Scully, J. A., Tosi, H., & Banning, K. (2000). Life event checklists: Revisiting the Social Readjustment Rating Scale after 30 years. *Educational and Psychological Measurement, 60*, 864–876.

Seamons, D. T., Howell, R. J., Carlisle, A. L., & Roe, A. V. (1981). Rorschach simulation of mental illness and normality by psychotic and non-psychotic legal offenders. *Journal of Personality Assessment, 45*, 130–135.

Seashore, H. G., Wesman, A. G., & Doppelt, J. E. (1950). The standardization of the Wechsler Intelligence Scale for Children. *Journal of Consulting Psychology, 14*, 99–110.

Segal, D. L., Hersen, M., & Van Hasselt, V. B. (1994). Reliability of the Structured Clinical Interview for DSM-III-R: An evaluative review. *Comprehensive Psychiatry, 35*, 316–327.

Segal, D. L., Hersen, M., Van Hasselt, V. B., Kabacoff, R. I., & Roth, L. (1993). Reliability of diagnosis in older psychiatric patients using the Structured Clinical Interview for DSM-III-R. *Journal of Psychopathology and Behavioral Assessment, 15*, 347–356.

Seligman, M. (1975). *Helplessness.* New York: Freeman.

Selzer, M. L. (1971). The Michigan Alcoholism Screening Test: The quest for a new diagnostic instrument. *American Journal of Psychiatry, 127*, 1653–1658.

Serwer, B. J., Shapiro, B. J., & Shapiro, P. P. (1972). Achievement prediction of "high risk" children. *Perceptual and Motor Skills, 35*, 347–354.

Sewell, T. E. (1977). A comparison of WPPSI and Stanford-Binet Intelligence Scale (1972) among lower SES black children. *Psychology in the Schools, 14*, 158–161.

Shah, C. P., & Boyden, M. F. H. (1991). Assessment of auditory functioning. In B. A. Bracken (Ed.), *The psychoeducational assessment of preschool children* (2nd ed., pp. 341–378). Boston, MA: Allyn & Bacon.

Shapiro, E. S. (1987). *Behavioral assessment in school psychology.* Hillsdale, NJ: Erlbaum.

Sharp, S. E. (1898–1899). Individual psychology: A study in psychological method. *American Journal of Psychology, 10*, 329–391.

Shavelson, R. J., Webb, N. M., & Rowley, G. L. (1989). Generalizability theory. *American Psychologist, 44*, 922–932.

Shaycoft, M. F. (1979). *Handbook of criterion-referenced testing: Development, evaluation, and use.* New York: Garland STPM Press.

Sheehan, K. R., & Gray, M. R. (1991). Sex bias in the SAT and the DTMS. *The Journal of General Psychology, 119*, 5–14.

Shepard, L. (1980). Standard setting issues and methods. *Applied Psychological Measurement, 4*, 447–467.

Sherer, M., Parsons, O. A., Nixon, S., & Adams, R. L. (1991). Clinical validity of the Speech Sounds Perception Test and the Seashore Rhythm Test. *Journal of Clinical and Experimental Neuropsychology, 13*, 741–751.

Sherman, S. W., & Robinson, N. M. (Eds.). (1982). *Ability testing of handicapped people: Dilemma for government, science, and the public.* Washington, DC: National Academy Press.

Sherry, D. L., & Piotrowski, C. (1986). Consistency of factor structure on the Semantic Differential: An analysis of three adult samples. *Educational and Psychological Measurement, 46*, 263–268.

Shimberg, B. (1981). Testing for licensure and certification. *American Psychologist, 36*, 1138–1146.

Shneidman, E. S. (Ed.). (1951), *Thematic test analysis.* New York: Grune & Stratton.

Shore, T. H., Thornton, G. C., III, & Shore, L. M. (1990). Construct validity of two categories of assessment center dimension ratings. *Personnel Psychology, 43*, 101–116.

Shostrom, E. L. (1963). *Personal Orientation Inventory.* San Diego, CA: Education and Industrial Testing Service.

Shostrom, E. L. (1964). A test for the measurement of self-actualization. *Educational and Psychological Measurement, 24*, 207–218.

Shrauger, J. S., & Osberg, T. M. (1981). The relative accuracy of self-prediction and judgments by others in psychological assessment. *Psychological Bulletin, 90*, 322–351.

Shrout, P. E., Spitzer, R. L., & Fleiss, J. L. (1987). Quantification of agreement in psychiatric diagnosis revisited. *Archives of General Psychiatry, 44*, 172–177.

Shultz, K. S., & Chavez, D. V. (1994). The reliability and factor structure of a social desirability scale in English and in Spanish. *Educational and Psychological Measurement, 54*, 935–940.

Sibley, S. (1989). Review of the WISC-R iter 'Complete'. In J. C. Conoley & J. J. Kramer (Eds.), *The tenth mental measurements yearbook* (pp. 892–893). Lincoln, NE: University of Nebraska Press.

Sicoly, F. (1992). Estimating the accuracy of decisions based on cutting scores. *Journal of Psychoeducational Assessment, 10*, 26–36.

Sidick, J. T., Barrett, G. V., & Doverspike, D. (1994). Three-alternative multiple choice tests: An attractive option. *Personnel Psychology, 47*, 829–835.

Siebel, C. C., Faust, W. L., & Faust, M. S. (1971). Administration of design copying tests to large groups of children. *Perceptual and Motor Skills, 32*, 355–360.

Siegel, D. J., & Piotrowski, R. J. (1985). Reliability of K-ABC subtest composites. *Journal of Psychoeducational Assessment, 3*, 73–76.

Silverman, B. I., Bishop, G. F., & Jaffe, J. (1976). Psychology of the scientist: XXXV. Terminal and instrumental values of American graduate students in Psychology. *Psychological Reports, 39*, 1099–1108.

Silverstein, A. B. (1967). Validity of WISC short forms at three age levels. *California Mental Health Research Digest, 5*, 253–254.

Silverstein, A. B. (1968). Validity of a new approach to the design of WAIS, WISC, and WPPSI short forms. *Journal of Consulting and Clinical Psychology, 32*, 478–479.

Silverstein, A. B. (1970). Reappraisal of the validity of WAIS, WISC, and WPPSI short forms. *Journal of Consulting and Clinical Psychology, 34*, 12–14.

Silverstein, A. B. (1971). Deviation social quotients for the Vineland Social Maturity Scale. *American Journal of Mental Deficiency, 76*, 348–351.

Silverstein, A. B. (1973). Factor structure of the Wechsler Intelligence Scale for Children for three ethnic groups. *Journal of Educational Psychology, 65*, 408–410.

Silverstein, A. B. (1984). Pattern analysis: The question of abnormality. *Journal of Consulting and Clinical Psychology, 52*, 936–939.

Simeonsson, R. J., Bailey, D. B., Huntington, G. S., & Comfort, M. (1986). Testing the concept of goodness of fit in early intervention. *Infant Mental Health Journal, 7*, 81–94.

Simeonsson, R. J., Buckley, L., & Monson, L. (1979). Concepts of illness causality in hospitalized children. *Journal of Pediatric Psychology, 4*, 77–84.

Simeonsson, R. J., Huntington, G. S., & Parse, S. A. (1980). Expanding the developmental assessment of young handicapped children. *New Directions for Exceptional Children, 3*, 51–74.

Simola, S. K., & Holden, R. R. (1992). Equivalence of computerized and standard administration of the Piers-Harris Children's Self-Concept Scale. *Journal of Personality Assessment, 58*, 287–294.

Singer, E., & Presser, S. (1989). *Survey research methods.* Chicago, IL: University of Chicago Press.

Sipos, K., Sipos, M., & Spielberger, C. D. (1985). The development and validation of the Hungarian form of the Test Anxiety Inventory. In H. M. Van Der Ploeg, R. Schwarzer, & C. D. Spielberger (Eds.), *Advances in Test Anxiety Research* (Vol. 4, pp. 221–228). Lisse, the Netherlands: Swets & Zeitlinger.

Siu, A. L., Reuben, D. B., & Hayes, R. D. (1990). Hierarchical measures of physical function in ambulatory geriatrics. *Journal of the American Geriatric Society, 38*, 1113–1119.

Skinner, H. A., & Allen, B. A. (1983). Does the computer make a difference? Computerized vs. face-to-face vs. self-report assessment of alcohol, drug, and tobacco use. *Journal of Consulting and Clinical Psychology, 51*, 267–275.

Skinner, H. A., & Lei, H. (1980). Differential weights in life change research: Useful or irrelevant? *Psychosomatic Medicine, 42*, 367–370.

Slate, J. R., & Hunnicutt, L. C., Jr. (1988). Examiner errors on the Wechsler scales. *Journal of Psychoeducational Assessment, 6*, 280–288.

Slomka, G. T., & Tarter, R. E. (1984). Mental retardation. In R. E. Tarter & G. Goldstein (Eds.), *Advances in clinical neuropsychology* (Vol. 2, pp. 109–137). NY: Plenum Press.

Slosson, R. L. (1963). *Slosson Intelligence Test (SIT) for children and adults.* New York: Slosson Educational.

Slosson, R. L. (1991). *Slosson Intelligence Test (SIT-R).* East Aurora, NY: Slosson Educational.

Small, S. A., Zeldin, R. S., & Savin-Williams, R. C. (1983). In search of personality traits: A multimethod analysis of naturally occurring prosocial and dominance behavior. *Journal of Personality, 51*, 1–16.

Smith, A. L., Hays, J. R., & Solway, K. S. (1977). Comparison of the WISC-R and Culture Fair Intelligence Test in a juvenile delinquent population. *The Journal of Psychology, 97*, 179–182.

Smith, D. K., St. Martin, M. E., & Lyon, M. A. (1989). A validity study of the Stanford-Binet: Fourth edition with students with learning disabilities. *Journal of Learning Disabilities, 22*, 260–261.

Smith, J. D. (1985). *Minds made feeble: The myth and legacy of the Kallikaks*. Rockville, MD: Aspen Systems.

Smith, M. B. (1990). Henry A. Murray (1893-1988): Humanistic psychologist. *Journal of Humanistic Psychology, 30*, 6–13.

Smith, M. B., & Anderson, J. W. (1989). Obituary: Henry A. Murray (1893-1988). *American Psychologist 44*, 1153–1154.

Smith, P. C., & Kendall, L. M. (1963). Retranslation of expectations: An approach to the construction of unambiguous anchors for rating scales. *Journal of Applied Psychology, 47*, 149–155.

Smither, R. D., & Houston, J. M. (1992). The nature of competitiveness: the development and validation of the competitiveness index. *Educational and Psychological Measurement, 52*, 407–418.

Smyth, F. L. (1989). Commercial coaching and SAT scores. *Journal of College Admissions, 123*, 2–9.

Smyth, F. L. (1990). SAT coaching. *Journal of College Admissions, 129*, 7–17.

Snell, W. E., Jr. (1989). Development and validation of the Masculine Behavior Scale: A measure of behaviors stereotypically attributed to males vs. females. *Sex Roles, 21*, 749–767.

Snell, W. E., & Papini, D. R. (1989). The sexuality scale: An instrument to measure sexual-esteem, sexual-depression, and sexual-preoccupation. *The Journal of Sex Research, 26*, 256–263.

Snider, J. G., & Osgood, C. E. (Eds.). (1969). *Semantic Differential technique: A sourcebook*. Chicago, IL: Aldine.

Snow, J. H., & Hynd, G. W. (1985a). A multivariate investigation of the Luria-Nebraska Neuropsychological Battery – Children's Revision with learning-disabled children. *Journal of Psychoeducational Assessment, 3*, 101–109.

Snow, J. H., & Hynd, G. W. (1985b). Factor structure of the Luria-Nebraska Neuropsychological Battery – Children's Revision. *Journal of School Psychology, 23*, 271–276.

Snyder, C. R., Harris, C., Anderson, J. R., Holleran, S. A., Irving, L. M., Sigmon, S. T., Yoshinobu, L., Gibb, J., Langelle, C., & Harney, P. (1991). The Will and the Ways: Development and validation of an individual-differences measure of hope. *Journal of Personality and Social Psychology, 60*, 570–585.

Snyder, C. R., Shenkel, R. J., & Lowery, C. R. (1977). Acceptance of personality interpretations: The "Barnum effect" and beyond. *Journal of Consulting and Clinical Psychology, 45*, 104–114.

Snyder, D. K. (1979). Multidimensional assessment of marital satisfaction. *Journal of Marriage and the Family, 41*, 813–823.

Snyder, D. K. (1981). *Manual for the Marital Satisfaction Inventory*. Los Angeles, CA: Western Psychological Services.

Snyder, D. K., Lachar, D., & Wills, R. M. (1988). Computer-based interpretation of the Marital Satisfaction Inventory: Use in treatment planning. *Journal of Marital and Family Therapy, 14*, 397–409.

Snyder, D. K., Widiger, T. A., & Hoover, D. W. (1990). Methodological considerations in validating computer-based test interpretations: Controlling for response bias. *Psychological Assessment, 2*, 470–477.

Soares, A. T., & Soares, L. M. (1975). *Self-Perception Inventory Composite manual*. Bridgeport, CT: University of Bridgeport.

Sokal, M. M. (Ed.). (1987). *Psychological testing and American society 1890–1930*. New Brunswick, NJ: Rutgers University Press.

Sokal, M. M. (1990). G. Stanley Hall and the institutional character of psychology at Clark 1889–1920. *Journal of the History of the Behavioral Sciences, 26*, 114–124.

Sokal, M. M. (1991). Obituary: Psyche Cattell (1893–1989). *American Psychologist, 46*, 72.

Solomon, E., & Kopelman, R. E. (1984). Questionnaire format and scale reliability: An examination of three modes of item presentation. *Psychological Reports, 54*, 447–452.

Sonnenfeld, J. (1969). Personality and behavior in environment. *Proceedings of the Association of American Geographers, 1*, 136–140.

Space, L. G. (1981). The computer as a psychometrician. *Behavior Research Methods and Instrumentation, 13*, 596–606.

Spanier, G. B. (1976). Measuring dyadic adjustment: New scales for assessing the quality of marriage and similar dyads. *Journal of Marriage and the Family, 38*, 15–28.

Sparrow, S. S., Balla, D. A., & Cicchetti, D. V. (1984). *Vineland Adaptive Behavior Scales*. Circle Pines, MN: American Guidance Service.

Spearman, C. (1904). "General intelligence" objectively determined and measured. *American Journal of Psychology, 15*, 201–293.

Spearman, C. (1927). *The abilities of man*. London: Macmillan.

Spearman, C. (1930). Autobiography. In C. Murchison (Ed.), *A history of psychology in autobiography* (Vol. 1, pp. 299–334). Worcester, MA: Clark University Press.

Spector, P. (1982). Behavior in organizations as a function of employees' locus of control. *Psychological Bulletin, 91,* 482–497.

Spector, P. E. (1988). Development of the Work Locus of Control Scale. *Journal of Occupational Psychology, 61,* 335–340.

Spielberger, C. D. (1966) (Ed.), *Anxiety and behavior.* New York: Academic Press.

Spielberger, C. D. (1980). *Test Anxiety Inventory.* Palo Alto, CA: Consulting Psychologists Press.

Spielberger, C. D., Gorsuch, R. L., & Lushene, R. E. (1970). *STAI Manual.* Palo Alto, CA: Consulting Psychologists Press.

Spielberger, C. D., Gorsuch, R. L., Lushene, R., Vagg, P. R., & Jacobs, G. A. (1983). *Manual for the State-Trait Anxiety Inventory: A "self-evaluation questionnaire."* Palo Alto, CA: Consulting Psychologists Press.

Spitzer, R. L., & Endicott, J. (1977). *Schedule for Affective Disorders and Schizophrenia – Life-time version (SADS-L).* New York: New York State Psychiatric Institute.

Spitzer, R. L., & Williams, J. B. W. (1983). *Instruction manual for the Structured Clinical Interview for DSM-III (SCID).* New York: Biometrics Research Department, New York State Psychiatric Institute.

Spitzer, R. L., Williams, J. B. W., Gibbon, M., & First, M. B. (1992). The Structured Clinical Interview for DSM-III-R (SCID). *Archives of General Psychiatry, 49,* 624–629.

Spranger, E. (1928). *Types of men.* Translated from the 5th German edition of *Lebensformen* by P. J. W. Pigors. Halle: Max Niemeyer Verlag.

Spruill, J. (1988). Two types of tables for use with the Stanford-Binet Intelligence Scale: Fourth edition. *Journal of Psychoeducational Assessment, 6,* 78–86.

Spruill, J. (1991). A comparison of the Wechsler Adult Intelligence Scale – Revised with the Stanford-Binet Intelligence Scale (4th ed.) for mentally retarded adults. *Psychological Assessment, 3,* 133–135.

Staats, S. (1989). Hope: A comparison of two self-report measures for adults. *Journal of Personality Assessment, 53,* 366–375.

Staats, S. R., & Stassen, M. A. (1985). Hope: An affective cognition. *Social Indicators Research, 17,* 235–242.

Staff (1988). Validity service update. *GRE Board Newsletter,* p. 3.

Stanley, J. C., & Porter, A. C. (1967). Correlation of Scholastic Aptitude Test scores with college grades for Negroes vs. whites. *Journal of Educational Measurement, 4,* 199–218.

Stanton, J. M. (1956). Group personality profiles related to aspects of antisocial behavior. *Journal of Criminal Law, Criminology and Police Science, 47,* 340–349.

Steer, R. A., Beck, A. T., & Garrison, B. (1986). Applications of the Beck Depression Inventory. In N. Sartorius & T. A. Ban (Eds.), *Assessment of depression* (pp. 123–142). New York: Springer-Verlag.

Steer, R. A., Rissmiller, D. J., Ranieri, W. F., & Beck, A. T. (1994). Use of the computer-administered Beck Depression Inventory and Hopelessness Scale with psychiatric inpatients. *Computers in Human Behavior, 10,* 223–229.

Stein, K. B. (1968). The TSC scales: The outcome of a cluster analysis of the 550 MMPI items. In P. McReynolds (Ed.), *Advances in psychological assessment* (Vol. 1, pp. 80–104). Palo Alto, CA: Science and Behavior Books.

Stein, L. A. R., & Graham, J. R. (1999). Detecting fake-good MMPI-A profiles in a correctional facility. *Psychological Assessment, 11,* 386–395.

Stein, M. I. (1981). *Thematic Apperception Test* (2nd ed.). Springfield, IL: Charles C Thomas.

Stein, S. P., & Charles, P. (1971). Emotional factors in juvenile diabetes mellitus: A study of early life experience of adolescent diabetics. *American Journal of Psychiatry, 128,* 56–60.

Stephens, T. E., & Lattimore, J. (1983). Prescriptive checklist for positioning multihandicapped residential clients: A clinical report. *Physical Therapy, 63,* 1113–1115.

Stephenson, W. (1953). *The study of behavior.* Chicago, IL: University of Chicago Press.

Stern, W. (1930). Autobiography. In C. Murchison (Ed.), *A history of psychology in autobiography* (Vol. 1, pp. 335–388). Worcester, MA: Clark University Press.

Sternberg, R. J. (1984). The Kaufman Assessment Battery for Children: An information processing analysis and critique. *The Journal of Special Education, 18,* 269–279.

Sternberg, R. J. (1985). *Beyond IQ: A triarchic theory of human intelligence.* Cambridge, MA: Cambridge University Press.

Sternberg, R. J. (Ed.). (1988a). *Advances in the psychology of human intelligence* (Vols. 1–4). Hillsdale, NJ: Erlbaum.

Sternberg, R. J. (1988b). *The triarchic mind.* New York: Viking.

Sternberg, R. J. (1990). *Metaphors of mind: Conceptions of the nature of intelligence.* Cambridge, MA: Cambridge University Press.

Sternberg, R. J., & Davidson, J. E. (1986). *Conceptions of giftedness.* New York: Cambridge University.

Sternberg, R. J., & Detterman, D. K. (1986). *What is intelligence?* Norwood, NJ: Ablex.

Sternberg, R. J., & Grigorenko, E. L. (1997). Are cognitive styles still in style? *American Psychologist, 52,* 700–712.

Sternberg, R. J., Wagner, R. K., Williams, W. M., & Horvath, J. A. (1995). Testing common sense. *American Psychologist, 50*, 912–927.

Sternberg, R. J., & Williams, W. M. (1997). Does the Graduate Record Examination predict meaningful success in the graduate training of psychologists? *American Psychologist, 52*, 630–641.

Stewart, A. J., & Chester, N. L. (1982). Sex differences in human social motives: Achievement, affiliation, and power. In A. Stewart (Ed.), *Motivation and society* (pp. 172–218). San Francisco, CA: Jossey-Bass.

Stewart, A. L., Hays, R. D., & Ware, J. E. (1988). The MOS short-form General Health Survey: Reliability and validity in a patient population. *Medical Care, 26*, 724–735.

Stokols, D. (1992). Establishing and maintaining healthy environments. *American Psychologist, 47*, 6–22.

Stone, G. C., Cohen, F., & Adler, N. E. (Eds.). (1979). *Health psychology: A handbook.* Washington, DC: Jossey-Bass.

Stotland, E. (1969). *The psychology of hope.* San Francisco, CA: Jossey-Bass.

Stotland, E., & Blumenthal, A. L. (1964). The reduction of anxiety as a result of the expectation of making a choice. *Canadian Journal of Psychology, 18*, 139–145.

Strahan. R., & Gerbasi, K. C. (1972). Short, homogeneous versions of the Marlowe-Crowne Social Desirability Scale. *Journal of Clinical Psychology, 28*, 191–193.

Street, W. R. (1994). *A chronology of noteworthy events in American psychology.* Washington, DC: American Psychological Association.

Streiner, D. L. (1985). Psychological Screening Inventory. In D. J. Keyser & R. C. Sweetland (Eds.), *Test critiques* (Vol. IV, pp. 509–515). Kansas City, MO: Test Corporation of America.

Streiner, D. L., & Miller, H. R. (1986). Can a good short form of the MMPI ever be developed? *Journal of Clinical Psychology, 42*, 109–113.

Strenio, A. J. (1981). *The testing trap.* New York: Rawson, Wade.

Stricker, L. J., & Ross, J. (1964a). Some correlates of a Jungian personality inventory. *Psychological Reports, 14*, 623–643.

Stricker, L. J., & Ross, J. (1964b). An assessment of some structural properties of the Jungian personality typology. *Journal of Abnormal and Social Psychology, 68*, 62–71.

Strickland, B. R. (1989). Internal-external control expectancies: From contingency to creativity. *American Psychologist, 44*, 1–12.

Strickland, B. R., & Crowne, D. P. (1963). Need for approval and the premature termination of psychotherapy. *Journal of Consulting Psychology, 27*, 95–101.

Strong, E. K., Jr. (1935). Predictive value of the Vocational Interest Test. *Journal of Educational Psychology, 26*, 331–349.

Strong, E. K., Jr. (1955). *Vocational interests 18 years after college.* Minneapolis, MN: University of Minnesota Press.

Sue, D. W., & Sue, D. (1990). *Counseling the culturally different.* New York: Wiley.

Suinn, R. M., Ahuna, C., & Khoo, G. (1992). The Suinn-Lew Asian Self-Identity Acculturation Scale: Concurrent and factorial validation. *Educational and Psychological Measurement, 52*, 1041–1046.

Suinn, R., Dauterman, W., & Shapiro, B. (1967). The WAIS as a predictor of educational and occupational achievement in the adult blind. *New Outlook for the Blind, 61*, 41–43.

Suinn, R., Rikard-Figueroa, K., Lew, S., & Vigil, P. (1987). The Suinn-Lew Asian Self-Identity Acculturation Scale: An initial report. *Educational and Psychological Measurement, 47*, 401–407.

Sullivan, P. M. (1982). Administration modifications on the WISC-R Performance Scale with different categories of deaf children. *American Annals of the Deaf, 127*, 780–788.

Sullivan, P. M., & Vernon, M. (1979). Psychological assessment of hearing-impaired children. *School Psychology Digest, 8*, 271–290.

Sutter, E. G., & Battin, R. R. (1984). Using traditional psychological tests to obtain neuropsychological information on children. *International Journal of Clinical Neuropsychology, 6*, 115–119.

Swallow, R. (1981). Fifty assessment instruments commonly used with blind and partially seeing individuals. *Journal of Visual Impairment and Blindness, 75*, 65–72.

Swanson, H. L., & Watson, B. L. (1989). *Educational and psychological assessment of exceptional children* (2nd ed.). Columbus, OH: Merrill.

Swenson, W. M. (1985). An aging psychologist assesses the impact of age on MMPI profiles. *Psychiatric Annals, 15*, 554–557.

Swerdlik, M. E. (1977). The question of the comparability of the WISC and WISC-R: Review of the research and implications for school psychologists. *Psychology in the Schools, 14*, 260–270.

Szapocznik, J., Kurtines, W. M., & Fernandez, T. (1980). Bicultural involvement and adjustment in Hispanic-American youths. *International Journal of Intercultural Relations, 4*, 353–365.

Szapocznik, J., Scopetta, M. A., Aranalde, M., & Kurtines, W. (1978). Cuban value structure: Treatment implications. *Journal of Consulting and Clinical Psychology, 46*, 961–970.

Tamkin, A. S., & Klett, C. J. (1957). Barron's Ego Strength Scale: A replication of an evaluation of its construct validity. *Journal of Consulting Psychology, 21*, 412.

Tashakkori, A., Barefoot, J., & Mehryar, A. H. (1989). What does the Beck Depression Inventory measure in college students? Evidence from a non-western culture. *Journal of Clinical Psychology, 45*, 595–602.

Tasto, D. L. (1977). Self-report schedules and inventories. In A. R. Ciminero, K. S. Calhoun, & H. E. Adams (Eds.), *Handbook of behavioral assessment* (pp. 153–193). New York: Wiley.

Tasto, D. L., & Hickson, R. (1970). Standardization, item analysis, and scaling of the 122-item Fear Survey Schedule. *Behavior Therapy, 1*, 473–484.

Tasto, D. L., Hickson, R., & Rubin, S. E. (1971). Scaled profile analysis of fear survey schedule factors. *Behavior Therapy, 2*, 543–549.

Tate, D. G., Forchheiner, M., Maynard, F., Davidoff, G., & Dijkers, M. (1993). Comparing two measures of depression in spinal cord injury. *Rehabilitation Psychology, 38*, 53–61.

Tatsuoka, M. (1970). *Discriminant analysis: The study of group differences.* Champaign, IL: Institute for Personality and Ability Testing.

Taylor, H. C., & Russell, J. T. (1939). The relationship of validity coefficients to the practical effectiveness of tests in selection. Discussion and tables. *Journal of Applied Psychology, 23*, 565–578.

Taylor, J. A. (1953). A personality scale of manifest anxiety. *Journal of Abnormal and Social Psychology, 48*, 285–290.

Taylor, J. B. (1959). Social desirability and MMPI performance: The individual case. *Journal of Consulting Psychology, 23*, 514–517.

Taylor, R. L., Kauffman, D., & Partenio, I. (1984). The Koppitz developmental scoring system for the Bender-Gestalt: Is it developmental? *Psychology in the Schools, 21*, 425–428.

Taylor, R. L., Slocumb, P. R., & O'Neill, J. (1979). A short form of the McCarthy Scales of Children's Abilities: Methodological and clinical applications. *Psychology in the Schools, 16*, 347–350.

Taylor, S. E. (1990). Health psychology. *American Psychologist, 45*, 40–50.

Templer, D. I. (1970). The construction and validation of a Death Anxiety Scale. *The Journal of General Psychology, 82*, 165–177.

Tenopyr, M. L. (1977). Content-construct confusion. *Personnel Psychology, 30*, 47–54.

Tenopyr, M. L., & Oeltjen, P. D. (1982). Personnel selection and classification. *Annual Review of Psychology, 33*, 581–618.

Teplin, L. (1991). The criminalization hypothesis: Myth, misnomer, or management strategy. In S. A.

Shah & B. D. Sales (Eds.), *Law and mental health: Major developments and research needs* (pp. 149–183). Rockville, MD: U.S. Department of Health and Human Services.

Teplin, L., & Swartz, J. (1989). Screening for severe mental disorder in jails: The development of the Referral Decision Scale. *Law and Human Behavior, 13*, 1–18.

terKuile, M. M., Linssen, A. C. G., & Spinhoven, P. (1993). The development of the Multidimensional Locus of Pain Control Questionnaire (MLPC): Factor structure, reliability, and validity. *Journal of Psychopathology and Behavioral Assessment, 15*, 387–404.

Terman, L. M. (1916). *The measurement of intelligence.* Boston, MA: Houghton-Mifflin.

Terman, L. M. (1932). Autobiography. In C. Murchison (Ed.), *A history of psychology in autobiography* (Vol. 2, pp. 297–332). Worcester, MA: Clark University Press.

Terman, L. M., & Childs, H. G. (1912). A tentative revision and extension of the Binet-Simon measuring scale of intelligence. *Journal of Educational Psychology, 3*, 61–74; 133–143; 198–208; 277–289.

Terman, L. M., & Merrill, M. A. (1937). *Measuring intelligence.* Boston, MA: Houghton-Mifflin.

Tett, R. P., Jackson, D. N., & Rothstein, M. (1991). Personality measures as predictors of job performance: A metaanalytic review. *Personnel Psychology, 44*, 703–742.

Thayer, P. W. (1977). Somethings old, somethings new. *Personnel Psychology, 30*, 513–524.

Thistlethwaite, D. L. (1960). College press and changes in study plans of talented students. *Journal of Educational Psychology, 51*, 222–234.

Thomas, A., & Chess, S. (1977). *Temperament and development.* New York: Brunner/Mazel.

Thomas, K. R., Wiesner, S. L., & Davis, R. M. (1982). Semantic differential ratings as indices of disability acceptance. *Rehabilitation Psychology, 27*, 245–247.

Thomas, P. J. (1980). A longitudinal comparison of the WISC and WISC-R with special education students. *Psychology in the Schools, 17*, 437–441.

Thompson, B., & Daniel, L. G. (1996). Factor analytic evidence for the construct validity of scores: A historical overview and some guidelines. *Educational and Psychological Measurement, 56*, 197–208.

Thompson, B., & Vacha-Haase, T. (2000). Psychometrics is datametrics: The test is not reliable. *Educational and Psychological Measurement, 60*, 174–195.

Thompson, R. J. (1977). Consequences of using the 1972 Stanford Binet intelligence scale norms. *Psychology in the Schools, 14*, 445–448.

Thompson, R. J. (1980). The diagnostic utility of WISC-R measures with children referred to a developmental evaluation center. *Journal of Consulting and Clinical Psychology, 48*, 440–447.

Thorndike, E. L. (1926). *Measurement of intelligence.* New York: Teacher's College, Columbia University.

Thorndike, R. L. (1940). "Constancy" of the IQ. *Psychological Bulletin, 37*, 167–186.

Thorndike, R. L. (1949). *Personnel selection.* New York: Wiley.

Thorndike, R. L. (1971). Concepts of culture-fairness. *Journal of Educational Measurement, 8*, 63–70.

Thorndike, R. L. (1977). Causation of Binet IQ decrements. *Journal of Educational Measurement, 14*, 197–202.

Thorndike, R. L., & Hagen, E. P. (1977). *Measurement and evaluation in Psychology and Education* (4th ed.). New York: Wiley.

Thorndike, R. L., Hagen, E. P., & Sattler, J. M. (1986a). *The Stanford-Binet Intelligence Scale: Fourth edition, guide for administering and scoring.* Chicago, IL: Riverside.

Thorndike, R. L., Hagen, E. P., & Sattler, J. M. (1986b). *The Stanford-Binet Intelligence Scale: Technical manual* (4th ed.). Chicago, IL: Riverside.

Thorndike, R. M. (1990). Origins of intelligence and its measurement. *Journal of Psychoeducational Assessment, 8*, 223–230.

Thorne, A., & Gough, H. G. (1991). *Portraits of type: An MBTI research compendium.* Palo Alto, CA: Consulting Psychologists Press.

Thorne, F. C. (1966). The sex inventory. *Journal of Clinical Psychology, 22*, 367–374.

Thornton, G. C., III, & Byham, W. C. (1982). *Assessment centers and managerial performance.* New York: Academic Press.

Throop, W. F., & MacDonald, A. P. (1971). Internal-external locus of control: A bibliography. *Psychological Reports, 28*, 175–190.

Thurstone, L. L. (1934). The vectors of mind. *Psychological Review, 41*, 1–32.

Thurstone, L. L. (1938). Primary mental abilities. *Psychometric Monographs* (No. 1).

Thurstone, L. L. (1946). Comment. *American Journal of Sociology, 52*, 39–50.

Thurstone, L. L. (1952). Autobiography. In E. G. Boring et al. (Eds.), *A history of psychology in autobiography* (Vol. 4, pp. 295–322). Worcester, MA: Clark University Press.

Thurstone, L. L., & Chave, E. J. (1929). *The measurement of attitudes.* Chicago, IL: University of Chicago Press.

Tiedeman, D. V., & O'Hara, R. P. (1963). *Career development: Choice and adjustment.* Princeton, NJ: College Entrance Examination Board.

Tillman, H. M. (1973). Intelligence scales for the blind: A review with implications for research. *Journal of School Psychology, 11*, 80–87.

Tilton, J. W. (1937). The measurement of overlapping. *Journal of Educational Psychology, 28*, 656–662.

Timbrook, R. E., & Graham, J. R. (1994). Ethnic differences on the MMPI-2. *Psychological Assessment, 6*, 212–217.

Timbrook, R. E., Graham, J. R., Keiller, S. W., & Watts, D. (1993). Comparison of the Winener-Harmon subtle-obvious scales and the standard validity scales in detecting valid and invalid MMPI-2 profiles. *Psychological Assessment, 5*, 53–61.

Timmons, L. A., Lanyon, R. I., Almer, E. R., & Curran, P. J. (1993). Development and validation of sentence completion test indices of malingering during examination for disability. *American Journal of Forensic Psychology, 11*, 23–38.

Tolor, A. L., & Brannigan, G. G. (1980). *Research and clinical applications of the Bender-Gestalt Test.* Springfield, II: Charles C Thomas.

Torrance, E. P. (1966). *Torrance tests of creative thinking. Norms – technical manual.* Princeton, NJ: Personnel Press.

Torrance, E. P. (1981). Empirical validation of criterion-referenced indicators of creative ability through a longitudinal study. *Creative Child and Adult Quarterly, 6*, 136–140.

Treffinger, D. J. (1985). Review of the Torrance Tests of Creative Thinking. In J. V. Mitchell, Jr. (Ed.), *The ninth mental measurements yearbook* (pp. 1632–1634). Lincoln, NE: University of Nebraska.

Triandis, H. C. (1980). Values, attitudes, and interpersonal behavior. In M. M. Page (Ed.), *Nebraska Symposium on Motivation 1979* (pp. 195–259). Lincoln, NE: University of Nebraska Press.

Triandis, H. C., Kashima, Y., Hui, C. H., Lisansky, J., & Marin, G. (1982). Acculturation and biculturalism indices among relatively acculturated Hispanic young adults. *Interamerican Journal of Psychology, 16*, 140–149.

Trickett, E. J., & Moos, R. H. (1970). Generality and specificity of student reactions in high school classrooms. *Adolescence, 5*, 373–390.

Trickett, E. J., & Moos, R. H. (1973). Social environment of junior high and high school classrooms. *Journal of Educational Psychology, 65*, 93–102.

Trieschmann, R. B. (1988). *Spinal cord injuries: Psychological, social, and vocational rehabilitation* (2nd ed.). New York: Pergamon Press.

Trochim, W. M. K. (1985). Pattern matching, validity, and conceptualization in program evaluation. *Evaluation Review, 9*, 575–604.

Truch, S. (1989). *WISC-R Companion.* Seattle, WA: Special Child Publications.

Trull, T. J., & Hillerbrand, E. (1990). Psychometric properties and factor structure of the Fear Questionnaire Phobia Subscale items in two normative samples. *Journal of Psychopathology and Behavioral Assessment, 12,* 285–297.

Trull, T. J., Neitzel, M. T., & Main, A. (1988). The use of meta-analysis to assess the clinical significance of behavior therapy for agoraphobia. *Behavior Therapy, 19,* 527–538.

Trybus, R. (1973). personality assessment of entering hearing-impaired college students using the 16PF, Form B. *Journal of Rehabilitation of the Deaf, 6,* 34–40.

Trybus, R., & Karchmer, M. A. (1977). School achievement scores of hearing impaired children: National data on achievement status and growth patterns. *American Annals of the Deaf, 122,* 62–69.

Tryon, G. S. (1980). The measurement and treatment of test anxiety. *Review of Educational Research, 50,* 343–372.

Tryon, W. W. (1991). *Activity measurement in psychology and medicine.* New York: Plenum Press.

Tsushima, W. T. (1994). Short form of the WPPSI and WPSSI-R. *Journal of Clinical Psychology, 50,* 877–880.

Tucker, M. F., Cline, V. B., & Schmitt, J. R. (1967). Prediction of creativity and other performance measures from biographical information among pharmaceutical scientists. *Journal of Applied Psychology, 57,* 131–138.

Tucker, W. H. (1994). Fact and fiction in the discovery of Sir Cyril Burt's flaws. *Journal of the History of the Behavioral Sciences, 30,* 335–347.

Tucker, W. H. (1997). Re-considering Burt: Beyond a reasonable doubt. *Journal of the History of the Behavioral Sciences, 33,* 145–162.

Tuckman, J., & Lorge, I. (1952). The attitudes of the aged toward the older worker for institutionalized and non-institutionalized adults. *Journal of Gerontology, 7,* 559–564.

Tuckman, J., & Lorge, I. (1953). Attitudes toward old people. *Journal of Social Psychology, 37,* 249–260.

Tuckman, J., & Lorge, I. (1958). Attitude toward aging of individuals with experiences with the aged. *Journal of Genetic Psychology, 92,* 199–204.

Tuddenham, R. D., Davis, L., Davison, L., & Schindler, R. (1958). An experimental group version for school children of the Progressive Matrices. *Journal of Consulting Psychology, 22,* 30.

Tupes, E. C., & Christal, R. E. (1961). *Recurrent personality factors based on trait ratings.* (USAF ASD Technical Report No. 61-97). Lackland Air Force Base, TX: U.S. Air Force (cited in McCrae & Costa, 1986).

Turk, D. C., Rudy, T. E., & Salovey, P. (1985). The McGill Pain Questionnaire reconsidered: Confirming the factor structure and examining appropriate uses. *Pain, 21,* 385–397.

Turner, R. G. (1978). Individual differences in ability to image nouns. *Perceptual and Motor Skills, 47,* 423–434.

Turner, R. J., & Wheaton, B. (1995). Checklist measurement of stressful life events. In S. Cohen, R. C. Kessler, & L. U. Gordon (Eds.), *Measuring stress* (pp. 29–58). New York: Oxford University Press.

Tursky, B. (1976). The development of a pain perception profile: A psychophysical approach. In M. Weisenberg & B. Tursky (Eds.), *Pain: New perspectives in therapy and research.* New York: Plenum.

Tuttle, F. B., & Becker, L. A. (1980). *Characteristics and identification of gifted and talented students.* Washington, DC: National Educational Association.

Tyler, F. B., Dhawan, N., & Sinha, Y. (1989). Cultural contributions to constructing locus-of-control attributions. *Genetic, Social, and General Psychology Monographs, 115,* 205–220.

Tyler, S., & Elliott, C. D. (1988). Cognitive profiles of groups of poor readers and dyslexic children on the British Ability Scales. *British Journal of Psychology, 79,* 493–508.

Tzeng, O. C. S., Maxey, W. A., Fortier, R., & Landis, D. (1985). Construct evaluation of the Tennessee Self Concept Scale. *Educational and Psychological Measurement, 45,* 63–78.

Tzeng, O. C. S., Ware, R., & Bharadwaj, N. (1991). Comparison between continuous bipolar and unipolar ratings of the Myers-Briggs Type Indicator. *Educational and Psychological Measurement, 51,* 681–690.

Ulissi, S. M., Brice, P. J., & Gibbins, S. (1989). Use of the Kaufman-Assessment Battery for Children with the hearing impaired. *American Annals of the Deaf, 134,* 283–287.

Ullman, L. P., & Krasner, L. (1975). *A psychological approach to abnormal behavior* (2nd ed.). Englewood Cliffs, NJ: Prentice Hall.

Ullman, R. K., Sleator, E. K., & Sprague, R. L. (1991). ADDH *Comprehensive Teacher's Rating Scale* (ACTeRS). Champaign, IL: Metritech, Inc.

Urban, W. J. (1989). The Black scholar and intelligence testing: The case of Horace Mann Bond. *Journal of the History of the Behavioral Sciences, 25,* 323–334.

U.S. Department of Labor (1970). *Manual for the USES General Aptitude Test Battery.* Washington, DC: Manpower Administration, U.S. Department of Labor.

Valencia, R. R. (1979). Comparison of intellectual performance of Chicano and Anglo third-grade boys on the Raven's Coloured Progressive Matrices. *Psychology in the Schools, 16*, 448–453.

Van den Brink, J., & Schoonman, W. (1988). First steps in computerized testing at the Dutch Railways. In F. J. Maarse, L. J. M. Mulder, W. P. B. Sjouw, & A. E. Akkerman (Eds.), *Computers in psychology: Methods, instrumentation and psychodiagnostica* (pp. 184–188). Amsterdam: Swets & Zeitlinger.

Vander Kolk, C. J. (1982). A comparison of intelligence test score patterns between visually impaired subgroups and the sighted. *Rehabilitation Psychology, 27*, 115–120.

Vandeveer, B., & Schweid, E. (1974). Infant assessment: Stability of mental functioning in young retarded children. *American Journal of Mental Deficiency, 79*, 1–4.

Van de Vijver. F. J. R., & Harsveld, M. (1994). The incomplete equivalence of the paper-and-pencil and computerized versions of the General Aptitude Test Battery. *Journal of Applied Psychology, 79*, 852–859.

Van Gorp, W., & Meyer, R. (1986). The detection of faking on the Millon Clinical Multiaxial Inventory (MCMI). *Journal of Clinical Psychology, 42*, 742–747.

Van Hagan, J., & Kaufman, A. S. (1975). Factor analysis of the WISC-R for a group of mentally retarded children and adolescents. *Journal of Consulting and Clinical Psychology, 43*, 661–667.

Vansickle, T. R., & Kapes, J. T. (1993). Comparing paper-pencil and computer-based versions of the Strong-Campbell Interest Inventory. *Computers in Human Behavior, 9*, 441–449.

Varble, D. L. (1971). Current status of the Thematic Apperception Test. In P. McReynolds (Ed.), *Advances in psychological assessment* (Vol. 2, pp. 216–235). Palo Alto, CA: Science and Behavior Books, Inc.

Veldman, D. J. (1967). Computer-based sentence completion interviews. *Journal of Counseling Psychology, 14*, 153–157.

Vernon, M. (1968). Fifty years of research on the intelligence of the deaf and hard-of-hearing: A survey of the literature and discussion of implications. *Journal of Rehabilitation of the Deaf, 1*, 1–12.

Vernon, M. (1970). Psychological evaluation and interviewing of the hearing impaired. *Rehabilitation Research and Practice Review, 1*, 45–52.

Vernon, M., & Brown, D. W. (1964). A guide to psychological tests and testing procedures in the evaluation of deaf and hard-of-hearing children. *Journal of Speech and Hearing Disorders, 29*, 414–423.

Vernon, M. C., & Andrews, J. F. (1990). The psychology of deafness. New York: Longman.

Vernon, P. E. (1960). *The structure of human abilities* (Rev. ed.). London: Methuen.

Vernon, P. E., & Allport, G. W. (1931). A test for personal value. *Journal of Abnormal and Social Psychology, 26*, 231–248.

Vescovi, G. M. (1979). The emerging private psychologist practitioner as contributer to vocational rehabilitation process for deaf clients. *Journal of Rehabilitation of the Deaf, 13*, 9–19.

Vieweg, B. W., & Hedlund, J. L. (1984). Psychological Screening Inventory: A comprehensive review. *Journal of Clinical Psychology, 40*, 1382–1393.

Vincent, K. R., & Cox, J. A. (1974). A re-evaluation of Raven's Standard Progressive Matrices. *The Journal of Psychology, 88*, 299–303.

Vinson, D. E., Munson, J. M., & Nakanishi, M. (1977). An investigation of the Rokeach Value Survey for consumer research applications. In W. D. Perreault (Ed.), *Advances in consumer research* (pp. 247–252). Provo, UT: Association for Consumer Research.

Vodanovich, S. J., & Kass, S. J. (1990). A factor analytic study of the boredom proneness scale. *Journal of Personality Assessment, 55*, 115–123.

Volicer, L., Hurley, A. C., Lathi, D. C., & Kowall, N. W. (1994). Measurement of severity in advanced Alzheimer's disease. *Journal of Gerontology, 49*, 223–226.

Volicer, L., Seltzer, B., Rheaume, Y., & Fabiszewski, K. (1987). Progression of Alzheimer-type dementia in institutionalized patients: A cross-sectional study. *Journal of Applied Gerontology, 6*, 83–94.

Volker, M. A., Guarnaccia, V., & Scardapane, J. R. (1999). Sort forms of the Stanford-Binet Intelligence Scale: Fourth edition for screening potentially gifted preschoolers. *Journal of Psychoeducational Assessment, 17*, 226–235.

Von Mayrhauser, R. T. (1989). Making intelligence functional: Walter Dill Scott and applied psychological testing in World War I. *Journal of the History of the Behavioral Sciences, 25*, 60–72.

Vredenburg, K., Krames, L., Flett, G. L. (1985). Reexamining the Beck Depression Inventory: The long and short of it. *Psychological Reports, 57*, 767–778.

Vulpe, S. G. (1982). *Vulpe Assessment Battery.* Toronto: National Institute on Mental Retardation.

Vygotsky, L. S. (1978). *Mind in society: The development of higher psychological processes.* Cambridge, MA: Harvard University Press.

Waddell, D. D. (1980). The Stanford-Binet: An evaluation of the technical data available since the 1972 restandardization. *Journal of School Psychology, 18*, 203–209.

Wagner, R. K., & Sternberg, R. J. (1986). Tacit knowledge and intelligence in the everyday world. In R. J. Sternberg & R. K. Wagner (Eds.), *Practical intelligence* (pp. 51–83). Cambridge, MA: Cambridge University Press.

Wahler, R. G., House, A. E., & Stanbaugh, E. E., II (1976). *Ecological assessment of child problem behavior: A clinical package for home, school, and institutional settings.* New York: Pergamon.

Wainer, H. (1987). The first four millenia of mental testing: From Ancient China to the computer age. *Educational Testing Service Research Report*, No. 87–34.

Wainer, H. (1993). Measurement problems. *Journal of Educational Measurement, 30*, 1–21.

Walczyk, J. J. (1993). A computer program for constructing language comprehension tests. *Computers in Human Behavior, 9*, 113–116.

Walk, R. D. (1956). Self ratings of fear in a fear-invoking situation. *Journal of Abnormal and Social Psychology, 22*, 171–178.

Walker, D. K. (1973). *Socioemotional measures for preschool and kindergarten children.* San Francisco, CA: Jossey-Bass.

Walker, N. W., & Myrick, C. C. (1985). Ethical considerations in the use of computers in psychological testing and assessment. *Journal of School Psychology, 23*, 51–57.

Wallace, W. L. (1950). The relationship of certain variables to discrepancy between expressed and inventoried vocational interest. *American Psychologist, 5*, 354 (abstract).

Wallas, G. (1926). *The art of thought.* London: Watts.

Wallbrown, F. H., & Jones, J. A. (1992). Reevaluating the factor structure of the Revised California Psychological Inventory. *Educational and Psychological Measurement, 52*, 379–386.

Walls, R. T., Werner, T. J., Bacon, A., & Zane, T. (1977). Behavior Checklists. In J. D. Cone & R. P. Hawkins (Eds.), *Behavioral Assessment* (pp. 77–146). New York: Brunner/Mazel.

Wallston, B. S., Wallston, K. A., Kaplan, G. D., & Maides, S. A. (1976). Development and validation of the Health Locus of Control Scale. *Journal of Consulting and Clinical Psychology, 44*, 580–585.

Wallston, K. A., Wallston, B. S., & DeVellis, R. (1978). Development of the Multidimensional Health Locus of Control (MHLC) Scales. *Health Education Monographs, 6*, 160–169.

Walsh, J. A. (1972). Review of the CPI. In O. K. Buros (Ed.), *The Seventh mental measurements yearbook* (Vol. 1, pp. 96–97). Highland Park, NJ: Gryphon Press.

Walters, G. D. (1988). Schizophrenia. In R. L. Greene (Ed.), *The MMPI: Use with specific populations* (pp. 50–73). Philadelphia, PA: Grune & Stratton.

Walters, G. D., White, T. W., & Greene, R. L. (1988). Use of the MMPI to identify malingering and exaggeration of psychiatric symptomatology in male prison inmates. *Journal of Consulting and Clinical Psychology, 56*, 111–117.

Wampler, K. S., & Halverson, C. F. (1990). The Georgia Marriage Q-sort: An observational measure of marital functioning. *American Journal of Family Therapy, 18*, 169–178.

Wang, K. A. (1932). Suggested criteria for writing attitude statements. *Journal of Social Psychology, 3*, 367–373.

Wang, M. W., & Stanley, J. C. (1970). Differential weighting: A review of methods and empirical studies. *Review of Educational Research, 40*, 663–705.

Wapner, S. (1990). Introduction. *Journal of the History of the Behavioral Sciences, 26*, 107–113.

Ward, C. H., Beck, A. T., Mendelson, M., Mock, J. E., & Erbaugh, J. K. (1962). The psychiatric nomenclature. Reasons for diagnostic disagreement. *Archives of General Psychiatry, 7*, 198–205.

Wardrop, J. L. (1989). Review of the California Achievement Tests. In J. C. Conoley & J. J. Kramer (Eds.), *The tenth mental measurements yearbook* (pp. 128–133). Lincoln, NE: University of Nebraska Press.

Ware, J. E., & Sherbourne, C. D. (1992). The MOS 36–item short-form Health Survey (SF-36). I. Conceptual framework and item selection. *Medical Care, 30*, 473–483.

Ware, J. E., Snow, K. K., & Kosinski, M. (1993). *SF-36 Health Survey: Manual and interpretation guide.* Boston, MA: The Health Institute, New England Medical Center Hospitals.

Waring, D., Farthing, C., & Kidder-Ashley, P. (1999). Impulsive response style affects computer-administered multiple choice test performance. *Journal of Instructional Psychology, 26*, 121–128.

Waters, L. K. (1965). A note on the "fakability" of forced-choice scales. *Personnel Psychology, 18*, 187–191.

Watkins, C. E., Jr. (1986). Validity and usefulness of WAIS-R, WISC-R, and WPPSI short forms: A critical review. *Professional Psychology, 17*, 36–43.

Watkins, E. O. (1976). *The Watkins Bender-Gestalt scoring system.* Novato, CA: Academic Therapy.

Watson, B. U. (1983). Test-retest stability of the Hiskey-Nebraska Test of Learning Aptitude in a sample of hearing-impaired children and adolescents. *Journal of Speech and Hearing Disorders, 48*, 145–149.

Watson, B. U., & Goldgar, D. E. (1985). A note on the use of the Hiskey-Nebraska Test of Learning Aptitude with deaf children. *Language, Speech, and Hearing Services in Schools, 16*, 53–57.

Watson, D. (1979). Guidelines for the psychological and vocational assessment of deaf rehabilitation clients. *Journal of Rehabilitation of the Deaf, 13*, 27–57.

Watson, D. (1989). Strangers' ratings of the five robust personality factors: Evidence of a surprising convergence with self-report. *Journal of Personality and Social Psychology, 57,* 120–128.

Watson, R. I. (1966). The role and use of history in the Psychology curriculum. *Journal of the History of the Behavioral Sciences, 2,* 64–69.

Watts, K., Baddeley, A., & Williams, M. (1982). Automated tailored testing using Raven's matrices and the Mill Hill vocabulary test: A comparison with manual administration. *International Journal of Man-Machine Studies, 17,* 331–344.

Webb, J. T., Miller, M. L., & Fowler, R. D. Jr. (1970). Extending professional time: A computerized MMPI interpretation service. *Journal of Clinical Psychology, 26,* 210–214.

Webb, S. C. (1955). Scaling of attitudes by the method of equal-appearing intervals: A review. *Journal of Social Psychology, 42,* 215–239.

Wechsler, D. (1939). *The measurement of adult intelligence.* Baltimore, MD: Williams & Wilkins.

Wechsler, D. (1941). *The measurement of adult intelligence* (2nd ed.). Baltimore, MD: Williams & Wilkins.

Wechsler, D. (1958). *The measurement and appraisal of adult intelligence.* Baltimore, MD: Williams & Wilkins.

Wechsler, D. (1967). *Manual for the Wechsler Preschool and Primary Scale of intelligence.* New York: Psychological Corporation.

Wechsler, D. (1974). *Manual for the Wechsler Intelligence Scale for Children – Revised.* New York: Psychological Corporation.

Wechsler, D. (1975). Intelligence defined and undefined: A relativistic approach. *American Psychologist, 30,* 135–139.

Wechsler, D. (1981). *Wechsler Adult Intelligence Scale – Revised.* New York: Psychological Corporation.

Wechsler, D. (1984). *WISC-RM escala de inteligencia para nivel scolar Wechsler.* Mexico, DF: El Manual Moderno.

Wechsler, D. (1987). *Wechsler Memory Scale – Revised manual.* New York: The Psychological Corporation.

Wechsler, D. (1989). *Wechsler Preschool and Primary Scale of Intelligence – Revised (WPPSI-R).* San Antonio, TX: Psychological Corporation.

Wechsler, D. (1991). *Wechsler Intelligence Scale for Children-Third Edition: Manual.* New York: The Psychological Corporation.

Weckowicz, T. E., Muir, W., & Cropley, A. J. (1967). A factor analysis of the Beck Inventory of Depression. *Journal of Consulting Psychology, 31,* 23–28.

Weinberger, M., Hiner, S. L., & Tierney, W. M. (1987). In support of hassles as a measure of stress in predicting health outcomes. *Journal of Behavioral Medicine, 10,* 19–31.

Weiner, B. (1980). *Human motivation.* New York: Holt, Rinehart and Winston.

Weiner, I. (1977). Approaches to Rorschach validation. In M. A. Rickers-Ovsiankina (Ed.), *Rorschach psychology.* Huntington, NY: Robert E. Krieger.

Weiner, I. B. (1994). The Rorschach Inkblot Method (RIM) is not a test: Implications for theory and practice. *Journal of Personality Assessment, 62,* 498–504.

Weiss, D. J. (1985). Adaptive testing by computer. *Journal of Consulting and Clinical Psychology, 53,* 774–789.

Weiss, D. J., & Davison, M. L. (1981). Test theory and methods. *Annual Review of Psychology, 32,* 629–658.

Weiss, D. J., & Dawis, R. V. (1960). An objective validation of factual interview data. *Journal of Applied Psychology, 44,* 381–385.

Weiss, R. L., & Margolin, G. (1977). Marital conflict and accord. In A. R. Ciminero, K. S. Calhoun, & H. E. Adams (Eds.), *Handbook for behavioral assessment.* New York: Wiley.

Weiss, R. S. (1973). *Loneliness: The experience of emotional and social isolation.* Cambridge, MA: MIT Press.

Weissman, M. M., Sholomskas, D., Pottenger, M., Prusoff, B. A., & Locke, B. Z. (1977). Assessing depressive symptoms in five psychiatric populations: A validation study. *American Journal of Epidemiology, 106,* 203–214.

Weitz, J. (1950). Verbal and pictorial questionnaires in market research. *Journal of Applied Psychology, 34,* 363–366.

Weitz, J., & Nuckols, R. C. (1953). A validation study of "How Supervise?" *Journal of Applied Psychology, 37,* 7–8.

Welch, G., Hall, A., & Norring, C. (1990). The factor structure of the Eating Disorder Inventory in a patient setting. *International Journal of Eating Disorders, 9,* 79–85.

Welch, G., Hall, A., & Walkey, F. (1988). The factor structure of the Eating Disorders Inventory. *Journal of Clinical Psychology, 44,* 51–56.

Welch, G., Hall, A., & Walkey, F. (1990). The replicable dimensions of the Beck Depression Inventory. *Journal of Clinical Psychology, 46,* 817–827.

Wellman, B. L., Skeels, H. M., & Skodak, M. (1940). Review of McNemar's critical examination of Iowa studies. *Psychological Bulletin, 37,* 93–111.

Welsh, G. S. (1948). An extension of Hathaway's MMPI profile coding system. *Journal of Consulting Psychology, 12,* 343–344.

Welsh, G. S. (1956). Factor dimensions A & R. In G. S. Welsh & W. G. Dahlstrom (Eds.), *Basic readings on the MMPI in psychology and medicine* (pp. 264–281). Minneapolis, MN: University of Minnesota Press.

Welsh, G. S. (1966). Comparison of the D-48, Terman CMT, and Art Scale scores of gifted adolescents. *Journal of Consulting Psychology, 30*, 88.

Werner, E. E., Bierman, J. M., & French, F. E. (1971). *The children of Kavai: A longitudinal study from the prenatal period.* Honolulu, HI: University of Hawaii Press.

Werner, P. D. (1993). A Q-sort measure of beliefs about abortion in college students. *Educational and Psychological Measurement, 53*, 513–521.

Werner, S. H., Jones, J. W., & Steffy, B. D. (1989). The relationship between intelligence, honesty, and theft admissions. *Educational and Psychological Measurement, 49*, 921–927.

Wertheimer, M. (1958). Principles of perceptual organization. In D. C. Beardsless & M. Wertheimer (Eds.), *Readings in perception.* New York: Van Nostrand.

Wesman, A. G. (1968). Intelligent testing. *American Psychologist, 23*, 267–274.

Wesman, A. G. (1971). Writing the test item. In R. L. Thorndike (Ed.), *Educational Measurement* (2nd ed.). Washington, DC: American Council on Education.

Westman, J. C. (1990). *Handbook of learning disabilities: A multisystem approach.* Boston, MA: Allyn & Bacon.

Wetzler, S. (1989a). Parameters of psychological assessment. In S. Wetzler & M. M. Katz (Eds.), *Contemporary approaches to psychological assessment* (pp. 3–15). New York: Brunner/Mazel.

Wetzler, S. (1989b). Self-report tests: The patient's vantage. In S. Wetzler & M. M. Katz (Eds.), *Contemporary approaches to psychological assessment* (pp. 98–117). New York: Brunner/Mazel.

Wetzler, S., Kahn, R., Strauman, T. J., & Dubro, A. (1989). Diagnosis of major depression by self-report. *Journal of Personality Assessment, 53*, 22–30.

Wetzler, S., & Marlowe, D. B. (1993). The diagnosis and assessment of depression, mania, and psychosis by self-report. *Journal of Personality Assessment, 60*, 1–31.

Wharton, Y. L. (1977). *List of hypotheses advanced to explain the SAT score decline.* New York: College Entrance Examination Board.

Whipple, G. M. (1910). *Manual of mental and physical tests.* Baltimore, MD: Warwick and York.

White, D. M., Clements, C. B., & Fowler, R. D. (1986). A comparison of computer administration with standard administration of the MMPI. *Computers in Human Behavior, 1*, 153–162.

White, D. R., & Jacobs, E. (1979). The prediction of first-grade reading achievement from WPPSI scores of preschool children. *Psychology in the Schools, 16*, 189–192.

White, K., Sheehan, P. W., & Ashton, R. (1977). Imagery assessment: A survey of self-report measures. *Journal of Mental Imagery, 1*, 145–170.

White, K. O. (1978). *Testing the handicapped for employment purposes: adaptations for persons with motor handicaps* (PS 78–4). Washington, DC: Personnel Research and Development Center, U.S. Civil Service Commission.

Whitehorn, J. C., & Betz, B. J. (1960). Further studies of the doctor as a crucial variable in the outcome of treatment with schizophrenics. *American Journal of Psychiatry, 117*, 215–223.

Whitney, D. R., Malizio, A. G., & Patience, W. M. (1986). Reliability and validity of the GED tests. *Educational and Psychological Measurement, 46*, 689–698.

Whitworth, R. H. (1984). Bender Visual Motor Gestalt Test. In D. J. Keyser & R. C. Sweetland (Eds.), *Test critiques* (Vol. I., pp 90–98). Kansas City, MO: Test Corporation of America.

Whitworth, R. H. (1987). The Halstead-Reitan Neuropsychological battery and allied procedures. In D. J. Keyser & R. C. Sweetland (Eds.), *Test critiques compendium* (pp. 196–205). Kansas City, MO: Test Corporation of America.

Whitworth, R. H., & Barrientos, G. A. (1990). Comparison of Hispanic and Anglo Graduate Record Examination scores and academic performance. *Journal of Psychoeducational Assessment, 8*, 128–132.

Wicker, A. W. (1969). Attitudes versus actions: The relationship of verbal and overt behavioral responses to attitude objects. *Journal of Social Issues, 25*, 41–78.

Wider A. (1948). *The Cornell Medical Index.* New York: Psychological Corporation.

Widiger, T. A., & Frances, A. (1987). Interviews and inventories for the measurement of personality disorders. *Clinical Psychology Review, 7*, 49–75.

Widiger, T. A., & Kelso, K. (1983). Psychodiagnosis of Axis II. *Clinical Psychology Review, 3*, 491–510.

Widiger, T. A., & Sanderson, C. (1987). The convergent and discriminant validity of the MCMI as a measure of the DSM-III personality disorders. *Journal of Personality Assessment, 51*, 228–242.

Widiger, T. A., Williams, J. B., Spitzer, R. L., & Frances, A. (1985). The MCMI as a measure of DSM-III. *Journal of Personality Assessment, 49*, 366–378.

Widiger, T. A., Williams, J. B., Spitzer, R. L., & Frances, A. (1986). The MCMI and DSM-III: A brief rejoinder to Millon (1985). *Journal of Personality Assessment, 50*, 198–204.

Wiederman, M. W., & Allgeier, E. R. (1993). The measurement of sexual-esteem: Investigation of Snell and Papini's (1989) Sexuality Scale. *Journal of Research in Personality, 27*, 88–102.

Wiechmann, G. H., & Wiechmann, L. A. (1973). Multiple factor analysis: An approach to attitude validation. *Journal of Experimental Education, 41,* 74–84.

Wiener, D. N. (1948). Subtle and obvious keys for the Minnesota Multiphasic Personality Inventory. *Journal of Consulting Psychology, 12,* 164–170.

Wierzbicki, M., & Daleiden, E. L. (1993). The differential responding of college students to subtle and obvious MCMI subscales. *Journal of Clinical Psychology, 49,* 204–208.

Wiggins, G. (1990). The case for authentic assessment. *ERIC clearinghouse on tests, measurement, and evaluation.* Washington, DC: American Institutes for Research.

Wiggins, J. S. (1968). Personality structure. *Annual Review of Psychology, 19,* 293–350.

Wiggins, J. S. (1973). *Personality and Prediction: Principles of personality assessment.* Reading, MA: Addison-Wesley.

Wiggins, J. S. (1982). Circumplex models of interpersonal behavior in clinical psychology. In P. C. Kendall & J. N. Butcher (Eds.), *Handbook of research methods in clinical psychology* (pp. 183–221). New York: Wiley.

Wiggins, J. S. (1989). Review of the Personality Research Form (3rd ed.). In J. C. Conoley & J. J. Kramer (Eds.), *The tenth mental measurements yearbook* (pp. 633–634). Lincoln, NE: University of Nebraska Press.

Wiggins, J. S., & Pincus, A. L. (1992). Personality: Structure and assessment. In M. R. Rosenzweig & L. W. Porter (Eds.), *Annual review of psychology* (Vol. 43, pp. 473–504). Palo Alto, CA: Annual Reviews.

Wikoff, R. L. (1979). The WISC-R as a predictor of achievement. *Psychology in the Schools, 16,* 364–366.

Wilkening, G. N., Golden, C. J., MacInnes, W. D., Plaisted, J. R., & Hermann, B. P. (1981, August). *The Luria-Nebraska Neuropsychological Battery – Children's revision: A preliminary report.* Paper presented at the meeting of the American Psychological Association, Los Angeles, CA.

Williams, J. B. W., Gibbon, M., First, M. B., Spitzer, R. L., Davies, M., Borus, J., Howes, M. J., Kane, J., Pope, H. G., Rounsaville, B., & Wittchen, H. (1992). The Structured Clinical Interview for DSM-III-R (SCID): Multiple test-retest reliability. *Archives of General Psychiatry, 42,* 630–636.

Williams, R. L. (1970). Black pride, academic relevance, and individual achievement. *The Counseling Psychologist, 2,* 18–22.

Williams, R. L. (1971). Abuses and misuses in testing black children. *The Counseling Psychologist, 2,* 62–73.

Williams, R. L. (1972). Abuses and misuses in testing black children. In R. L. Jones (Ed.), *Black psychology.* New York: Harper & Row.

Williams, R. L. (1974). Scientific racism and IQ: The silent mugging of the black community. *Psychology Today, 7,* 32ff.

Williams, R. L. (1975). The BITCH-100: A culture-specific test. *Journal of Afro-American Issues, 3,* 103–116.

Willingham, W. W. (1989). Standard testing conditions and standard score meaning for handicapped examinees. *Applied Measurement in Education, 2,* 97–103.

Willingham, W. W., Ragosta, M., Bennett, R. E., Braun, H., Rock, D. A., & Powers, D. E. (1988). *Testing handicapped people.* Boston, MA: Allyn & Bacon.

Wilson, E. L. (1980). The use of psychological tests in diagnosing the vocational potential of visually handicapped persons who enter supportive and unskilled occupations. In B. Bolton & D. W. Cook (Eds.), *Rehabilitation client assessment* (pp. 65–77). Baltimore, MD: University Park Press.

Wilson, F. R., Genco, K. T., & Yager, G. G. (1985). Assessing the equivalence of paper-and-pencil vs. computerized tests: Demonstration of a promising methodology. *Computers in Human Behavior, 1,* 265–275.

Wilson, G. D. (1973). *The psychology of conservatism.* New York: Academic Press, 1973.

Wilson, G. D., & Patterson, J. R. (1968). A new measure of conservatism. *British Journal of Social and Clinical Psychology, 7,* 264–269.

Wilson, K. M. (1974). The contribution of measures of aptitude (SAT) and achievement (CEEB Achievement Average), respectively in forecasting college grades in several liberal arts colleges. *ETS Research Bulletin,* No. 74–36.

Wilson, R. C., Christensen, P. R., Merrifield, P. R., & Guilford, J. P. (1960). *Alternate uses. Manual of administration, scoring, and interpretation.* Beverly Hills, CA: Sheridan Supply Co.

Wilson, R. S. (1975). Twins: Patterns of cognitive development as measured on the Wechsler Preschool and Primary Scale of Intelligence. *Developmental Psychology, 11,* 126–134.

Wilson, S. L. (1991). Microcomputer-based psychological assessment – an advance in helping severely physically disabled people. In P. L. Dann, S. H. Irvine, & J. M. Collis (Eds.), *Advances in computer-based human assessment* (pp. 171–187). Durdrecht, The Netherlands: Kluwer Academic Publishers.

Wilson, S. L., Thompson, J. A., & Wylie, G. (1982). Automated psychological testing for the severely physically handicapped. *International Journal of Man-Machine Studies, 17,* 291–296.

Wing, J. K. (Ed.). (1966). *Early childhood autism.* Oxford: Pergamon Press.

Winter, W. D., Ferreira, A. J., & Olson, J. L. (1966). Hostility themes in the family TAT. *Journal of Projective Techniques and Personality Assessment, 30,* 270–274.

Winterling, D., Crook, T., Salama, M., & Gabert, J. (1986). A self-rating scale for assessing memory loss. In A. Bes, J. Cahn, S. Hoyer, J. P. Marc-Vergnes, & H. M. Wisniewski (Eds.), *Senile dementias: Early detection* (pp. 482–486). London: John Libbey Eurotext.

Winters, K. C., & Henley, G. A. (1989). *Personal experience inventory (PEI) test and manual.* Los Angeles, CA: Western Psychological Services.

Wirt, D. D., Lachar, D., Klinedinst, J. K., & Seat, P. D. (1984). *Multidimensional description of child personality: A manual for the Personality Inventory for Children (Revised 1984 by D. Lachar).* Los Angeles, CA: Western Psychological Services.

Wirt, R. D., Lachar, D., Klinedinst, J. K., & Seat, P. D. (1990). *Personality Inventory for Children – 1990 edition.* Los Angeles, CA: Western Psychological Services.

Wirtz, W., & Howe, W. (1977). *On further examination: Report of the advisory panel on the Scholastic Aptitude Test score decline.* New York: College Entrance Examination Board.

Wise, S. L., & Wise, L. A. (1987). Comparison of computer-administered and paper-administered achievement tests with elementary school children. *Computers in Human Behavior, 3, 15–20.*

Wisniewski, J. J., & Naglieri, J. A. (1989). Validity of the Draw A Person: A quantitative scoring system with the WISC-R. *Journal of Psychoeducational Assessment, 7,* 346–351.

Witt, J. C., Heffer, R. W., & Pfeiffer, J. (1990). Structured rating scales: A review of self-report and informant rating processes, procedures, and issues. In C. R. Reynolds & R. W. Kamphaus (Eds.), *Handbook of psychological and educational assessment of children* (pp. 364–394). New York: Guilford Press.

Wodrich, D. L., & Kush, S. A. (1990). *Children's psychological testing* (2nd ed.). Baltimore, MD: Paul H. Brookes.

Wolf, T. H. (1969a). The emergence of Binet's conception and measurement of intelligence: A case history of the creative process. *Journal of the History of the Behavioral Sciences, 5,* 113–134.

Wolf, T. H. (1969b). The emergence of Binet's conception and measurement of intelligence: A case history of the creative process. Part II. *Journal of the History of the Behavioral Sciences, 5,* 207–237.

Wolf, T. H. (1973). *Alfred Binet.* Chicago, IL: University of Chicago Press.

Wolf, T. M., Elston, R. C., & Kissling, G. E. (1989). Relationship of hassles, uplifts, and life events to psychological well-being of freshman medical students. *Behavioral Medicine, 15,* 37–45.

Wolk, R. L. (1972). Refined projective techniques with the aged. In D. P. Kent, R. Kastenbaum, & S. Sherwood (Eds.), *Research planning and action for the elderly* (pp. 218–244). New York: Behavioral Publications.

Wolk, R. L., & Wolk, R. B. (1971). *Manual: Gerontological Apperception Test,* New York: Human Sciences Press.

Wolk, S., & Zieziula, F. R. (1985). Reliability of the 1973 Edition of the SAT-HI over time: Implications for assessing minority students. *American Annals of the Deaf, 130,* 285–290.

Wollersheim, J. P. (1970). Effectiveness of group therapy based upon learning principles in the treatment of overweight women. *Journal of Abnormal Psychology, 76,* 462–474.

Wolman, B. B. (Ed.). (1985). *Handbook of intelligence.* New York: Wiley.

Wolpe, J. (1973). *The practice of behavior therapy* (2nd ed.). New York: Pergamon.

Wolpe, J., & Lang, P. J. (1964). A fear survey schedule for use in behavior therapy. *Behavior Research and Therapy, 2,* 27–30.

Wolpe, J., & Lang, P. J. (1977). *Manual for the Fear Survey Schedule* (Rev.). San Diego, CA: Educational and Industrial Testing Service.

Wong, Y. I. (2000). Measurement properties of the Center for Epidemiologic Studies – Depression Scale in a homeless population. *Psychological Assessment, 12,* 69–76.

Wood, J. M., Nezworski, M. T., & Stejskal, W. J. (1996). The comprehensive system for the Rorschach: A critical examination. *Psychological Science, 7,* 3–10.

Wood, J. M., Nezworski, M. T., & Stejskal, W. J. (1997). The reliability of the Comprehensive System for the Rorschach: A comment on Meyer (1997). *Psychological Assessment, 9,* 490–494.

Woodworth, R. S. (1920). *Personal Data Sheet.* Chicago, IL: Stoelting.

Woon, T., Masuda, M., Wagner, N. N., & Holmes, T. H. (1971). The Social Readjustment Rating Scale: a cross-cultural study of Malaysians and Americans. *Journal of Cross-Cultural Psychology, 2,* 373–386.

Worchel, F. F., Aaron, L. L., & Yates, D. F. (1990). Gender bias on the Thematic Apperception Test. *Journal of Personality Assessment, 55,* 593–602.

Worthen, B. R., Borg, W. R., & White, K. R. (1993). *Measurement and evaluation in the schools: A practical guide.* White Plains, NY: Longman.

Wright, B. D., & Stone, M. H. (1985). Review of the British Ability Scales. In J. V. Mitchell, Jr. (Ed.),

The ninth mental measurements yearbook (Vol. 1, pp. 232–235). Lincoln, NE: University of Nebraska Press.

Wright, D., & DeMers, S. T. (1982). Comparison of the relationship between two measures of visual-motor coordination and academic achievement. *Psychology in the Schools, 19*, 473–477.

Wright, J. H., & Hicks, J. M. (1966). Construction and validation of a Thurstone scale of Liberalism-Conservatism. *Journal of Applied Psychology, 50*, 9–12.

Wylie, R. C. (1974). *The self-concept: A review of methodological considerations and measuring instruments* (Rev. ed., Vol. 1). Lincoln, NE: University of Nebraska Press.

Wytek, R., Opgenoorth, E., & Presslich, O. (1984). Development of a new shortened version of Raven's Matrices Test for application and rough assessment of present intellectual capacity within psychopathological investigation. *Psychopathology, 17*, 49–58.

Yachnick, M. (1986). Self-esteem in deaf adolescents. *American Annals of the Deaf, 131*, 305–310.

Yank, J., McCrae, R. R., Costa, P. T. Jr., Dai, X., Yao, S., Cai, T., & Gao, B. (1999). Cross-cultural personality assessment in psychiatric populations: The NEO-PI-R in the People's Republic of China. *Psychological Assessment, 11*, 359–368.

Yerkes. R. M., & Foster, J. C. (1923). *A point scale for measuring mental ability*. Baltimore, MD: Warwick and York.

Yin, P., & Fan, X. (2000). Assessing the realibility of Beck Depression Inventory scores: realibility generalization across studies. *Educational and Psychological Measurement, 60*, 201–223.

Ying, Y. (1988). Depressive symptomatology among Chinese-Americans as measured by the CES-D. *Journal of Clinical Psychology, 44*, 739–746.

Yudin, L. W. (1966). An abbreviated form of the WISC for use with emotionally disturbed children. *Journal of Consulting Psychology, 30*, 272–275.

Zajonc, R. B., & Bargh, J. (1980). Birth order, family size, and decline of SAT scores. *American Psychologist, 35*, 662–668.

Zakahi, W. R., & Duran, R. L. (1982). All the lonely people: The relationship among loneliness, communicative competence, and communication anxiety. *Communication Quarterly, 30*, 203–209.

Zanna, M. P., Olson, J. M., & Fazio, R. H. (1980). Attitude-behavior consistency: An individual difference perspective. *Journal of Personality and Social Psychology, 38*, 432–440.

Zanna, M. P., & Rempel, J. K. (1988). Attitudes: A new look at an old concept. In D. Bartal & A. W. Kruglanski (Eds.), *The social psychology of knowl-edge* (pp. 315–334). New York: Cambridge University Press.

Zapf, P. A., & Viljoen, J. L. (2003). Issues and considerations regarding the use of assessment instruments in the evaluation of competency to stand trial. *Behavioral Sciences and the Law, 21*, 351–367.

Zautra, A. J., & Reich, J. W. (1983). Life events and perceptions of life quality: Developments in a two-factor approach. *Journal of Community Psychology, 1*, 121–132.

Zea, M. C., & Tyler, F. B. (1994). Illusions of control – A factor-analytic study of locus of control in Colombian students. *Genetic, Social and General Psychology Monographs, 120*, 201–224.

Zebb, B. J., & Meyers, L. S. (1993). Reliability and validity of the Revised California Psychological Inventory's Vector 1 scale. *Educational and Psycological Measurement, 53*, 271–280.

Zehrbach, R. R. (1975). *Comprehensive Identification Process*. Bensenville, IL: Scholastic Testing Service.

Zeiss, A. M. (1980). Aversiveness vs. change in the assessment of life stress. *Journal of Psychosomatic Research, 24*, 15–19.

Zeleznik, C., Hojat, M., & Veloski, J. J. (1987). Predictive validity of the MCAT as a function of undergraduate institution. *Journal of Medical Education, 62*, 163–169.

Zelinski, E. M., Gilewski, M. J., & Thompson, L. W. (1980). Do laboratory tests relate to self-assessment of memory ability in the young and old? In L. W. Poon, J. L. Fozard, L. S. Cermak, D. Arenberg, & L. W. Thompson (Eds.), *New directions in memory and aging* (pp. 519–544). Hillsdale, NJ: Erlbaum.

Zenderland, L. (1997). The Bell Curve and the shape of history. *Journal of the History of the Behavioral Sciences, 33*, 135–139.

Zerbe, W. J., & Paulhus, D. L. (1987). Socially desirable, responding in organizational behavior: A reconception. *Academy of Management Review, 12*, 250–264.

Zielinski, J. J. (1993). A comparison of the Wechsler Memory Scale – Revised and the Memory Assessment Scales: Administrative, clinical, and interpretive issues. *Professional Psychology, 24*, 353–359.

Zieziula, F. R. (Ed.). (1982). *Assessment of hearing-impaired people*. Washington, DC: Gallaudet College.

Zigler, E., Balla, D., & Hodapp, R. (1984). On the definition and classification of mental retardation. *American Journal of Mental Deficiency, 89*, 215–230.

Zigler, E., & Muenchow, S. (1992). *Head Start: The inside story of America's most successful educational experiment*. New York: Basic Books.

Zilboorg, G. (1941). *A history of medical psychology*. New York: Norton.

Zimiles, H. (1996). Rethinking the validity of psychological assessment. *American Psychologist 51*, 980–981.

Zimmerman, I. L., & Woo-Sam, J. (1972). Research with the Wechsler Scale for Children: 1960–1970 (Special Monograph Supplement). *Psychology in the Schools, 9*, 232–271.

Zimmerman, I. L., Woo-Sam, J., & Glasser, A. J. (1973). *The clinical interpretation of the Wechsler Adult Intelligence Scale*. Orlando, FL: Grune & Stratton.

Zimmerman, M. (1983). Methodological issues in the assessment of life events: A review of issues and research. *Clinical Psychology Review, 3*, 339–370.

Zimmerman, M. (1983). Weighted versus unweighted life event scores: Is there a difference? *Journal of Human Stress, 9*, 30–35.

Zimmerman, M. (1986). The stability of the revised Beck Depression Inventory in college students: Relationship with Life Events. *Cognitive Therapy and Research, 10*, 37–43.

Zingale, S. A., & Smith, M. D. (1978). WISC-R patterns for learning disabled children at three SES levels. *Psychology in the Schools, 15*, 199–204.

Ziskin, J., & Faust, D. (1988). *Coping with psychiatric and psychological testimony* (Vols. 1–3, 4th ed.). Marina Del Rey, CA: Law and Psychology Press.

Zuckerman, M. (1985). Review of Sixteen Personality Factor Questionnaire. In J. V. Mitchell, Jr. (Ed.), *The ninth mental measurements yearbook* (Vol. II, pp. 1392–1394). Lincoln, NE: University of Nebraska Press.

Zuckerman, M., & Lubin, B. (1965). *Manual for the Multiple Affect Adjective Check List*. San Diego, CA: Educational & Industrial Testing Service.

Zung, W. W. K. (1965). A Self-rating Depression Scale. *Archives of General Psychiatry, 12*, 63–70.

Zung, W. W. K. (1969). A cross-cultural survey of symptoms in depression. *American Journal of Psychiatry, 126*, 116–121.

Zwiebel, A., & Mertens, D. M. (1985). A comparison of intellectual structure in deaf and hearing children. *American Annals of the Deaf, 130*, 27–31.

Zytowski, D. G. (1981). *Counseling with the Kuder Occupational Interest Survey*. Chicago, IL: Science Research Associates.

Zytowski, D. G. (1985). *Kuder DP manual supplement*. Chicago, IL: Science Research Associates.

Zytowski, D. G., & Kuder, F. (1986). Advances in the Kuder Occupational Interest Survey. In W. B. Walsh & S. H. Osipow (Eds.), *Advances in vocational psychology* (Vol. 1, pp. 31–53). Hillsdale, NJ: Erlbaum.

Zytowski, D. G., & Laing, J. (1978). Validity of other-gender-normed scales on the Kuder Occupational Interest Survey. *Journal of Counseling Psychology, 3*, 205–209.

Zytowski, D. G., & Warman, R. E. (1982). The changing use of tests in counseling. *Measurement and Evaluation in Guidance, 15*, 147–152.

Test Index

Index of Acronyms

Subject Index